Marc W

Microsoft
Dynamics®
CRM 2016

UNLEASHED

 800 East 96th Street, Indianapolis, Indiana 46240 USA

Microsoft Dynamics® CRM 2016 Unleashed

ISBN-13: 978-0-672-33760-4
ISBN-10: 0-672-33760-6

Library of Congress Cataloging-in-Publication Data: 2016912594

Printed in the United States of America

1   16

Trademarks

Warning and Disclaimer

Special Sales

For information about buying this title in bulk quantities, or for special sales opportunities (which may include electronic versions; custom cover designs; and content particular to your business, training goals, marketing focus, or branding interests), please contact our corporate sales department at corpsales@pearsoned.com or (800) 382-3419.

For government sales inquiries, please contact governmentsales@pearsoned.com.

For questions about sales outside the U.S., please contact intlcs@pearson.com.

Editor-in-Chief
Greg Wiegand

Senior Acquisitions Editor
Trina MacDonald

Development Editor
Mark Renfrow

Managing Editor
Sandra Schroeder

Project Editor
Mandie Frank

Copy Editor
Kitty Wilson

Indexer
Tim Wright

Proofreader
Uma Kumar

Cover Designer
Chuti Prasertsith

Compositor
codeMantra

Contents at a Glance

Table of Contents

About the Author

Marc Wolenik has been involved with customer relationship management systems for more than 20 years and Microsoft Dynamics CRM since version 3.0. His experience led to the creation of Webfortis (recently merged with Avtex), one of the largest Microsoft Dynamics CRM partner firms in North America.

Dedication

This book is dedicated to the readers and to their infinite patience and understanding of how difficult it is writing a book about a product that evolves quicker than an author can physically write. (Even as this book neared completion, Microsoft released the newest version!)

Acknowledgments

Several people helped with the completion of this book, and I'm in indebted to them for their help. Deepak (Deeps) Mehta provided research and content on several topics and was invaluable in providing necessary feedback. Damian Sinay, the technical editor, worked late nights and early mornings to provide code review and additional research.

We Want to Hear from You!

As the reader of this book, *you* are our most important critic and commentator. We value your opinion and want to know what we're doing right, what we could do better, what areas you'd like to see us publish in, and any other words of wisdom you're willing to pass our way.

We welcome your comments. You can email or write to let us know what you did or didn't like about this book—as well as what we can do to make our books better.

Please note that we cannot help you with technical problems related to the topic of this book.

When you write, please be sure to include this book's title and author as well as your name and email address. We will carefully review your comments and share them with the author and editors who worked on the book.

Email: feedback@samspublishing.com

Mail: Sams Publishing
ATTN: Reader Feedback
800 East 96th Street
Indianapolis, IN 46240 USA

Reader Services

Register your copy of *Microsoft Dynamics CRM 2016 Unleashed* at informit.com for convenient access to downloads, updates, and corrections as they become available. To start the registration process, go to informit.com/register and log in or create an account*. Enter the product ISBN, 9780672337604, and click Submit. Once the process is complete, you will find any available bonus content under Registered Products.

*Be sure to check the box that you would like to hear from us in order to receive exclusive discounts on future editions of this product.

Introduction

With the release of Microsoft Dynamics CRM 2016, Microsoft has turned its attention to a long-neglected feature of Dynamics CRM: customer engagement. To this end, Microsoft has added features such as ADX, FieldOne, Parature, and Voice of the Customer that allow users of Microsoft Dynamics CRM to directly engage with customers in ways that previously were difficult or required third party add-ons.

To be clear, Microsoft has added most of this functionality through the acquisition of various components and companies. There are too many to name, and the roadmap for them is a fully integrated suite, but at this writing, many of these features are separate add-ins. However, Microsoft's release cadence has increased, and it is expected that by the time you pick up this book, a more consolidated and streamlined Microsoft Dynamics CRM may exist.

This book shows you how to work with and configure Microsoft Dynamics CRM 2016, and it also includes information on complementary technologies, such as the following:

- ▶ SharePoint
- ▶ Azure
- ▶ SQL Server Reporting Services (SSRS)
- ▶ SQL Server
- ▶ Online versus On-Premises options
- ▶ Visual Studio and the .NET Framework

By reading and applying what you learn in this book, you'll be able to get the most from your CRM system. This book delves into how Microsoft Dynamics CRM works, explains why you should set up certain features, and explores advanced configuration and customization options.

This book provides an excellent overview of 99% of the application; however, with the other 1%, your mileage may vary, depending on your requirements. That 1% is often the hardest, most complex, and even the most imaginative part of using Dynamics CRM. I've worked exclusively with Microsoft Dynamics CRM for more than 12 years, and I still often see organizations with situations and requirements that I never could have imagined. In addition, the application becomes more powerful all the time, delivering options that previously existed only with extensive programming and workarounds.

> **NOTE**
>
> If you believe that this book has omitted anything or if you would like to share the 1% that your requirements might fall into, please write to me using the contact information in the beginning of the book! Perhaps your story and feedback will be featured in my next book on CRM.

You can use Microsoft Dynamics CRM 2016 to manage almost anything within your organization (or household, or farm, or retail store, etc....!). This book shows you how.

> **NOTE**
>
> The majority of this book was researched and written using the prereleased version of the Dynamics CRM 2016 software, including the related technologies, such as ADX, FieldOne, and Parature. Every attempt was made to update the contents based on the final version of the software that was released to customers. However, some areas may not perform as shown here because of differences in beta and final software releases.

CHAPTER 1

How This Book Is Arranged

With this version of Microsoft Dynamics CRM, Microsoft has not only combined a suite of new products but is bringing to play all its combined investments in Office, Windows, and mobility.

Microsoft Dynamics CRM 2016 is a major release that combines all the cumulative updates into a major release for Microsoft. It is provided to customers as both Online and On-Premises versions.

> **NOTE**
>
> A majority of this book was written using preview versions of the Microsoft Dynamics CRM 2016 software, and while every attempt was made to update the material to the current release at the time of publication, some things may be different by the time you use the product.

Before releasing Microsoft Dynamics CRM 2016, Microsoft released a series of updates to earlier versions of software, such as the Microsoft Dynamics CRM Online Fall '13 release and the Microsoft Dynamics CRM Online 2015 Update 1.

> **TIP**
>
> For access to the updates and/or to see previews of the software that Microsoft is staging for release, as well as for some in-depth training videos, visit www.microsoft .com/en-us/dynamics/crm-customer-center/get-ready -for-the-next-release.aspx.

Chapter 2, "New Features of Microsoft Dynamics CRM 2016," explains what has changed since the previous version of the product and the book *Dynamics CRM 2013 Unleashed* were released. The product has many major enhancements (enough for a whole book!), and it includes a rapidly growing suite of products that fall under the Microsoft Dynamics CRM umbrella. At this writing, the Dynamics CRM suite consists of the following products:

▶ Dynamics CRM 2016

▶ xRM (version 2016)

▶ Parature

▶ Yammer

▶ Social Engagement

▶ Microsoft Dynamics Marketing

▶ FieldOne

▶ FantasySalesTeam

▶ ADX Studios

▶ Voice of the Customer

These products are mentioned in Chapter 2 and discussed in greater depth throughout the book.

If you have Microsoft Dynamics CRM installed or have started with the Online version and are ready to go and you're wondering where to click to get started, skip ahead to Chapter 5, "Navigation," which provides a great starting point for people who are familiar with earlier versions of Microsoft Dynamics CRM. If you're new to Microsoft Dynamics CRM, it's probably best to start with this chapter and make your way to Chapter 5 (but there's nothing to stop you from skipping ahead to get a sneak peek).

When you log on to Microsoft Dynamics CRM 2016, you see the Explore CRM page (see Figure 1.1).

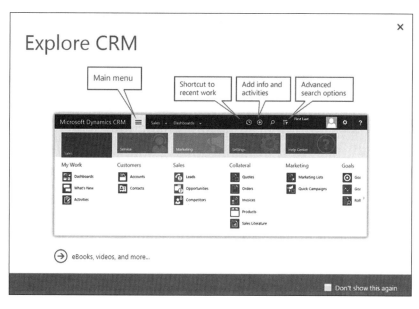

FIGURE 1.1   Microsoft Dynamics CRM 2016 welcome splash screen.

This book provides the information you need to not only explore your CRM system but make the most out of it.

Online Versus On-Premises

This books is written from the "Online-first" perspective. This does *not* mean that the book ignores the On-Premises aspects of Microsoft Dynamics CRM 2016, but the chapters have been shifted to prioritize the information on the Online option since the majority of users take advantage of that option.

> **NOTE**
>
> There is a huge amount of overlap and consistency between the On-Premises and Online versions of Microsoft Dynamics CRM 2016 (including application configuration). As a result, where appropriate, this book highlights differences between the two, and if you're using the Online version, you can largely ignore the chapters specific to the On-Premise version.

If you're still in the decision-making process about which version is the best choice for you, consider these great features in the Online option:

▶ Additional production instances

▶ A development/sandbox instance for development isolation, trusts, and statistics

▶ Scaled data storage options (based on users)

▶ New pricing to address various usage requirements

> **TIP**
>
> At this writing, Microsoft has indicated that all the pricing for On-Premises licenses will increase by 25%. If this takes effect as planned, then the lower TCO and ROI for the Online option provide much more of an argument—especially when you consider the investments Microsoft has made in its data centers.

Table 1.1 highlights some of the specific options to consider when looking at the Online versus On-Premises versions.

TABLE 1.1   Microsoft Dynamics CRM 2016 Online or On-Premises

	Online	On-Premises
Price		
Prefer to pay a single price and own the software (usually categorized as a capital expense)		X
Comfortable with a regular pay-as-you-go model (usually categorized as an operational expense)	X	
Infrastructure		
Existing hardware (servers and so on) and related software (SQL Server, Windows Server, and so on)		X
Heavy storage requirements		X
Existing/dedicated IT staff		X
Existing backup strategy		X
Comfortable with having data stored and maintained by Microsoft	X	
Don't want to have to worry about availability/backup	X	
Want to integrate with SharePoint or OneDrive	X	X
Updates/Customizations		
Heavy customization that requires validation prior to installation of any upgrades, updates, or rollups to the application		X
Comfortable with regular updates delivered automatically	X	
Want/need direct back-end database access (typically used for advanced reporting or integration)		X
Want to control all aspects of delivery and consumption of data (bandwidth, authentication methods, and so on)		X

Table 1.1 seems to indicate that On-Premises has more recommendations and while more and more organizations are becoming comfortable about moving to the cloud, careful consideration should be given to both options. If you break down the pros and cons at a very high level, the one constant is this: "Do you want to own/control your data and application?" If you do, then you face the responsibility for providing access and maintenance.

> **NOTE**
>
> A breakeven point typically occurs on the pay-as-you-go Online model versus On-Premises at about 24 to 28 months. (But note that this number will be different if the price adjustments noted previously come to pass.) However, a number of variables affect this rule of thumb, such as updates, downward infrastructure and hosting pricing, and so forth. In addition, when you factor in things such as extensive data storage requirements, integration requirements, and mandatory updates or uptime, the model can change significantly.

The section is meant to provide a high-level analysis of the two options—Online and On-Premises—and is by no means declarative. If you are a new customer or a customer considering switching from one platform to another, you should analyze a host of questions and considerations before committing.

Updates/Release Cadence

The question about updating Microsoft Dynamics CRM is usually not one of *if* there is an update, but *when*. Microsoft has committed to regular updates of Microsoft Dynamics CRM every 8 to 12 weeks. These updates are installed automatically for Online and are available from Microsoft for On-Premises.

> **NOTE**
>
> Microsoft updates are in the form *a.b.c.d*, where *a* is the version of CRM (7 = 2015, 8 = 2016), *b* is whether it is a release update (1 or 0), *c* is whether it is a rollup update, and *d* is the version number.
>
> The previous major version to Microsoft Dynamics CRM 2016 was Microsoft Dynamics CRM 2015 Update 1 (aka Carina). The major version prior to that was called Vega.

On-Premises Updates

Many organizations deploy Microsoft Dynamics CRM in an On-Premises mode so that they can carefully control deployments and the stability of the application.

> **NOTE**
>
> Yes, as hard as it is to believe, Microsoft does occasionally release updates that break the application. Although Microsoft does its best to regression test all the code, the fact that the application can be so extended dynamically results in variations that the company hasn't even considered. Therefore, many organizations deploy multiple environments to test and then release both custom code and Microsoft updates.
>
> Chapter 29, "On-Premises Deployments," describes a typical large-scale multiple-environment scenario in detail.

Online Updates

With Dynamics CRM Online, Microsoft pushes down updates to customers. Updates come in two forms: minor and major. Microsoft does two major updates a year, and customers must take at least one update a year; or in other words, customers can be only one version behind.

Customers can select when they want to go through the process of updating and can even go so far as to schedule (or reschedule) the date on which an update will happen. This gives customers adequate time to test their builds against updates and fix anything that might be necessary before the upgrade occurs.

Figure 1.2 shows the CRM Online Administration Center and the options available to users.

> **NOTE**
>
> To see pending updates, be sure to select UPDATES at the upper left of the CRM Online Administration Center.

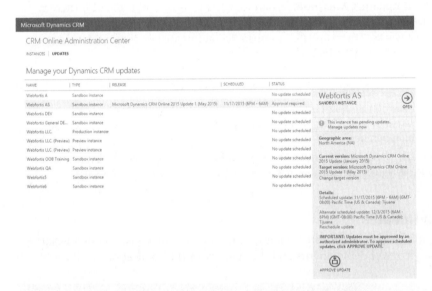

FIGURE 1.2   Microsoft Dynamics CRM 2016 Online Administration Center.

Of particular note in Figure 1.2 is the second row, which shows a pending update to Microsoft Dynamics CRM 2015 Update 1. When you select that row, as shown in the figure, you get more the information on the far right, which includes the following:

▶ The instance name and type. In this case, it is the Webfortis AS instance, which is a sandbox instance

▶ The ability to open or navigate to the instance (which opens in a separate window)

▶ The geographic area of the instance and the current and target versions, with an option to change the target version, if available

> **NOTE**
>
> The geographic instance of CRM correlates to the URL, which is
> https://Unleased.*crm-geo*.dynamics.com, where *crm-geo* can be any of the following:
>
> CRM = North America
>
> CRM2 = South America
>
> CRM4 = EMEA (Europe)
>
> CRM5 = APAC (Asia/Pacific)
>
> CRM6 = OCE (Australia)
>
> CRM7 = JPN (Japan)
>
> CRM9 = GCC (Reserved for Government/Public Sector)

▶ The specific details related to the update and the ability to reschedule the update

▶ The ability to approve the update, which is required to proceed with the update

▶ For more information about managing updates to your Microsoft Dynamics CRM Online instance, **SEE CHAPTER 4**, "CRM 2016 Online."

Summary

With this book now in your hands, you should be getting excited about starting the journey of working with Microsoft Dynamics CRM 2016.

This chapter's primary goal is to provide you with a primer on some of the author and editing decisions made when writing this book and to stress Microsoft's approach to maximizing both its investment in and the customer benefits related to the Online version.

CHAPTER 2

New Features of Microsoft Dynamics CRM 2016

As indicated in Chapter 1, "How This Book Is Arranged," Dynamics CRM has undergone significant change since the publication of *Microsoft Dynamics CRM 2013 Unleashed*. This book covers a majority of the features in Microsoft Dynamics CRM 2016, and this particular chapter showcases the *newest* features introduced with Dynamics CRM 2016.

It is important to understand the cadence at which Microsoft rolls out changes and updates and why CRM 2016 is unique. Typically, Microsoft rolls out updates to the Online version of CRM first and then to the On-Premises version. Dynamics CRM 2016 is considered a "major" release, however, and it is being released jointly to Online and On-Premises customers as either an upgrade or a new application.

> **NOTE**
>
> Throughout this book, we talk about features that are available for both Online and On-Premises or only Online or only On-Premises.

Many people wonder what exactly Dynamics CRM 2016 is. Microsoft has made several acquisitions over the past few years and has rolled these products under the Dynamics

CRM umbrella. As a result, when we talk about Dynamics CRM, we include (and possibly differentiate between) the following:

▶ Dynamics CRM 2016

▶ xRM (version 2016)

▶ Parature

▶ Yammer

▶ Social Engagement

▶ Microsoft Dynamics Marketing

▶ FieldOne

▶ FantasySalesTeam

▶ Voice of the Customer

▶ ADX Studios

All these are considered part of the suite of Dynamics CRM solutions, and the list continues to grow as Microsoft expands its service offerings.

> **NOTE**
>
> Several of the products mentioned in this section are standalone products, which means they can be purchased separately from Dynamics CRM.

Major investments by Microsoft in the underlying platform have resulted in increased performance and scalability for users. This chapter outlines a majority of these changes.

> **TIP**
>
> The term *platform* is used throughout this book to refer to CRM/xRM as the base from which the suite of products and/or custom extensions are derived.

Forms and the Interface

Microsoft has continued to invest in an application interface that can be used easily across both regular computers and touchscreen and tablet interfaces. The following sections discuss the navigation updates to Microsoft Dynamics CRM.

Enhanced Navigation

The navigation bar in earlier versions of Microsoft Dynamics CRM forced users to scroll to the right to find what they needed. In Microsoft Dynamics CRM 2016, the navigation bar has been modified to include a larger number of icons, which makes it easier to work with. Figure 2.1 shows the new navigation bar.

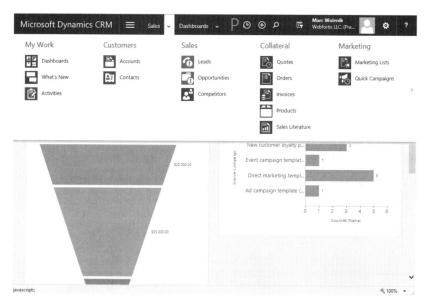

FIGURE 2.1   New navigation bar options in Microsoft Dynamics CRM 2016.

In addition, you can now quickly navigate to form sections by selecting the drop-down near the entity topic. Figure 2.2 shows this option selected.

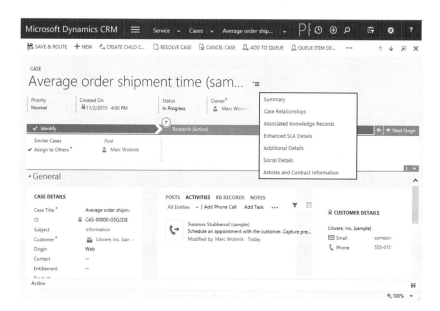

FIGURE 2.2   Microsoft Dynamics CRM tab navigation.

Themes

Perhaps one of the most compelling features is the ability for system administrators to customize the look and feel of the application by using themes to brand Microsoft Dynamics CRM.

Figure 2.3 shows a theme applied to Microsoft Dynamics CRM, including the option for a custom logo in the top left.

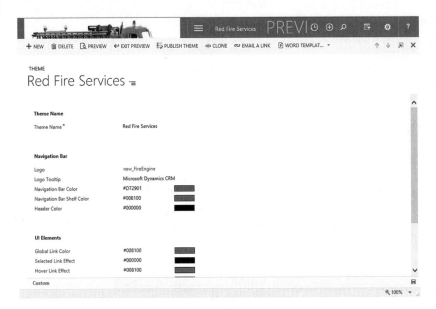

FIGURE 2.3   Custom theme applied to Microsoft Dynamics CRM.

▶ For more information about how to customize the themes and configure the system, **SEE CHAPTER 22,** "Customizing the System."

New Forms Rendering Engine

With the release of Microsoft Dynamics CRM 2015 Update 1, Microsoft significantly increased the loading time for its forms. This version, previously known as Turbo Forms, loads forms faster and more efficiently, with little no impact to end users.

NOTE

While the forms were designed to be compatible, a new dialog was added that displays script errors for unsupported customizations.

The new rendering engine parallelized many of the loading operations, and the cache was increased, changing the load time of a form from a linear process to an optimized one.

Some conditions cause the new forms to break. Administrators can run the CRM 2015 custom code validator to confirm support for new forms. In the event of failure, the system still supports legacy forms; to use them, just navigate to System Settings and select Use Legacy Form Rending at the bottom of the General tab.

Quick Search

Microsoft Dynamics CRM now includes global search capabilities. To take advantage of Quick Search, select the magnifying glass and type in your search (which can include wildcards, such as *). Figure 2.4 shows the search results for the letter a, across entities. You can drill down into the results directly from the Quick Search results.

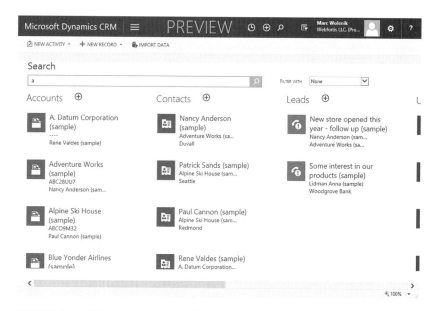

FIGURE 2.4   Using Quick Search for the letter a across the application.

System administrators can configure Quick Search for up to 10 entities, including customizing the entities searched and the order in which results are presented.

Quick Search does not eliminate or replace Advanced Find, which allows users to develop and use intricate search parameters.

Enhanced Templates

You can upload document templates, or preconfigured reports, using either Excel or Word into Dynamics CRM.

▶ For more information about working with templates, **SEE CHAPTER 21**, "Office Integration."

NOTE

Templates were previously available only for Word documents.

Figure 2.5 shows the new template options in Dynamics CRM. You can easily either create templates from scratch or upload your own custom templates.

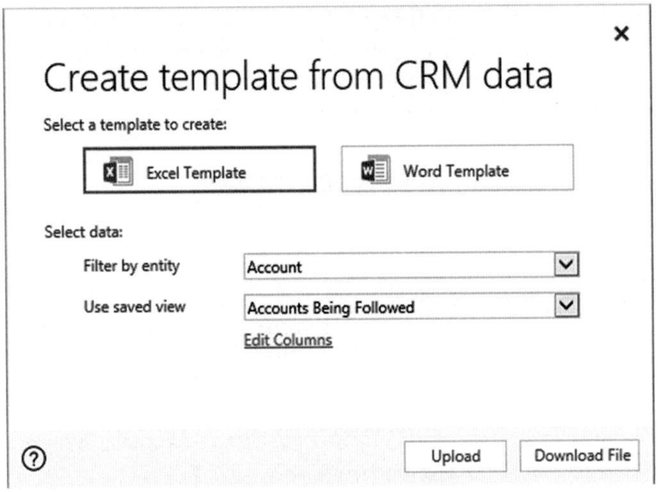

FIGURE 2.5   Creating Word and Excel templates in CRM.

Hierarchy Visualization

Microsoft has added a new way to look at relationships between records for accounts, campaigns, cases, contacts, opportunities, orders, products, quotes, teams, and user entities. Figure 2.6 shows an example of the hierarchy relationship visualizations.

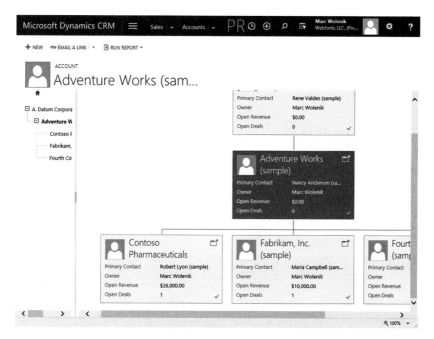

FIGURE 2.6   Microsoft Dynamics Hierarchy.

A hierarchy relationship visualization allows users to easily see relationships and navigate through the system by drilling down on the selected record. This functionality is even available on mobile devices.

TIP

Microsoft added new language options in Advanced Find for the hierarchies. The option Under and Not Under allows users to query relationships expressed as hierarchies.

NOTE

Microsoft enhanced the security model for working with hierarchies by including the Management Chain and Position Hierarchy options. These new options provide additional security for users at hierarchical positions.

▶ For more information about hierarchies, **SEE CHAPTER 22**.

Entity/Field Enhancements

Whereas field-level security was previously available only for custom fields, it has been extended to every field in Microsoft Dynamics CRM 2016.

▶ For more information about field-level security, **SEE CHAPTER 22**.

Business Flow Branching

For business process flows, users can add branching (introduced in CRM 2013), based on criteria defined for the process flow.

While only one active process per record is possible, the business process flow can span up to 5 entities and have as many as 30 stages per process.

Product Catalog Configuration

With new product catalog configuration options, system administrators can configure the product catalog to contain fewer SKUs, create product and service bundles, and define up-selling and cross-selling of products.

In addition, as shown in Figure 2.7, product line items on an opportunity can have suggestion opportunities that allow for easy up-selling and cross-selling.

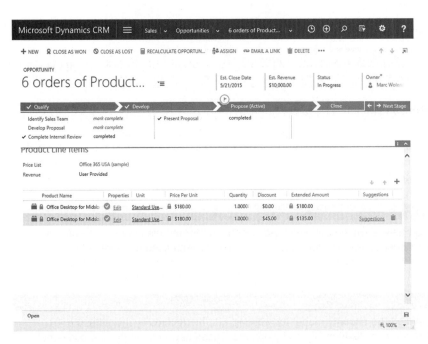

FIGURE 2.7   Microsoft Dynamics opportunity suggestions.

▶ For more information about how to configure the product catalog, **SEE CHAPTER 17,** "Settings."

Calculated and Rollup Fields

Microsoft Dynamics CRM supports the ability for the system to calculate across entities automatically and return, in read-only form, the values specified. For example, you might want to do this on an account record that shows the total number of cases that a customer has opened. Using a calculated field, you might want to calculate the total number of all the closed orders.

▶ For more information about calculated and rollup fields, **SEE CHAPTER 7**, "Working with Sales."

Service Improvements

Microsoft has put significant effort into the concept of customer service with this release of Dynamics CRM. Integrated tools, knowledge management, and interactive dashboards provide a new level of service intelligence for users of Dynamics CRM 2016.

The Interactive Service Hub

New to this version of Dynamics CRM is the concept of dedicated dashboards for customer service scenarios. Designed as a centralized one-stop spot for configured information, these dashboards allow agents and managers to easily navigate from the displayed data.

These new dashboards, referred to as *interactive experience dashboards*, are configured in the dashboard customization area of Dynamics CRM. You can configure them using a variety of options, and they are solution aware and have the same security options as regular dashboards.

NOTE

The experience dashboards in the interactive service hub are configured through Dynamics CRM in the regular customization area, but to access these special dashboards, you need to navigate to the interactive service hub, using a different URL than your regular CRM instance. The URL for Online is:

https://<ORG NAME>.crm.dynamics.com/engagementhub.aspx

The URL for an On-Premises deployment is:

https://<CRM SERVER>/engagementhub.aspx

When accessing the interactive service hub, users have two options for interacting with data, depending on the type of data stream they want to work with:

▶ **Multi-stream**—Just as it sounds, multi-stream provides data over multiple data options, such as different entities or views.

▶ **Single-stream**—Single-stream provides data from a single source, such as one entity.

Microsoft has further positioned the streaming concept in terms of customer service tiers, aligning multi-stream with tier 1 service/support and single-stream with tier 2 service/support. While either type of streaming can be configured and used in either tier, tier 2 agents have a much more focused need on their relevant data (which is the reason for the single stream), whereas tier 1 agents have a requirement for multiple data sources.

When you first navigate to the interactive service hub (using the URL previously noted), you see the screen shown in Figure 2.8.

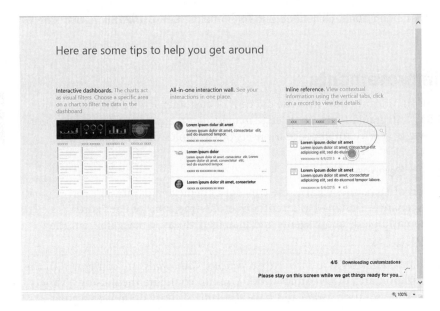

FIGURE 2.8   Microsoft Dynamics interactive service hub screen.

Once the interactive service hub is configured, customer service agents can use the interactive dashboards to manage cases by drilling down and creating cases in real time, as shown in Figure 2.9.

FIGURE 2.9   Microsoft Dynamics interactive dashboard.

▶ **SEE CHAPTER 10**, "Working with Service," and **CHAPTER 11**, "The Interactive Service Hub," for more information.

Surveys: Voice of the Customer

Thanks to the purchase of Mojo Survey in early 2015, Microsoft Dynamics CRM 2016 now includes the ability to send surveys. This feature, called Voice of the Customer, is found in the MDM part of Dynamics CRM and includes easy-to-configure and easy-to-manage survey tools with aggregated data available to the organization for reporting and analytics.

▶ **SEE CHAPTER 34**, "Voice of the Customer," for more information on working with this feature.

Parature

Parature provides organizations the ability to more effectively manage the customer engagement experience, including the following:

▶ Real-time chat capabilities

▶ Knowledge management

▶ Interactive support options (ticket tracking, etc.)

All this is done via a portal delivered by Parature and integrated with Microsoft Dynamics CRM.

A number of features have been added to Microsoft Dynamics CRM since CRM 2013, including the following:

▶ e-commerce integration, including integrated billing and purchasing within Dynamics CRM

▶ Expanded social networking support, including Facebook, Twitter, YouTube, and Instagram

▶ Information on what the customer searched for, for more proactive customer management

▶ Integrated knowledge

▶ Case management via mobile

▶ Enhanced portal options

▶ Multilingual support for more than 40 languages, including the following options:

  ▶ Right-to-left display options in the portal

  ▶ Custom translation

  ▶ Ability to link translations to articles or files

▶ Multilingual search

▶ Live chat with real-time machine translation

▶ Ticket routing based on the customer's preferred language

▶ Search enhancements

▶ Reporting enhancements

▶ For more information about Parature, **SEE CHAPTER 12**, "Parature for Microsoft."

Unified Service Desk (USD)

Unified Service Desk (USD) has been updated and provides an extension of the service features available for Microsoft Dynamics CRM that are commonly used in call center and agent help organizations.

USD is a separate application that is installed on a client's workstation and connects to a Dynamics CRM instance. It is a rich application that allows agents to manage service issues and open, in a single window, records related to the caller.

> **NOTE**
>
> USD actually shipped as part of the Spring 2014 release of Dynamics CRM 2013, but it was too late to be included in *Microsoft Dynamics CRM 2013 Unleashed* so is included here.
>
> USD is a free application from Microsoft that you can download by searching Microsoft for "Unified Service Desk Dynamics CRM" or by navigating to www.microsoft.com/en-us/download/details.aspx?id=50355.

USD includes the following features:

▶ Enhanced installation, administration, and user experience

▶ Integrated knowledge management with Parature

▶ New security roles specific for USD

▶ Advanced settings for configuration, including support for OAuth and enhanced integration options

▶ For more information about USD, **SEE CHAPTER 13**, "Unified Service Desk (USD)."

Social Engagement

Previously named Social Listening (prior to CRM 2015 Update 1), Social Engagement is a tool for social management, providing expanded opportunities for connecting and engaging with customers. Figure 2.10 shows the redesigned interface for Social Engagement.

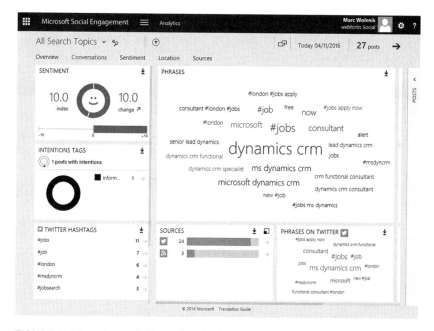

FIGURE 2.10   Microsoft Dynamics Social Engagement.

> **NOTE**
>
> Social Engagement is a standalone product, purchased separately from Dynamics CRM.

Four major revisions have been made to Social Engagement:

▶ The user interface has been simplified now provides centralized information.

▶ New social analytics and dashboards can be displayed.

▶ Configurable monitoring streams allow for customer engagement by channel.

▶ Facebook or Twitter can be used for customer engagement.

▶ For more information on Social Engagement, **SEE CHAPTER 14**, "Microsoft Dynamics Social Engagement."

Integrated Knowledge

Users of Dynamics CRM can now enjoy the knowledge options from Parature, including the following:

▶ Automatic suggestions based on search results

▶ Filtering options

▶ Article use action options

▶ The ability to add the knowledge search to any entity, including custom entities

Enhanced Case SLA

Introduced with Dynamics CRM 2015 is the concept of Enhanced service-level agreements (SLAs).

> **NOTE**
>
> SLAs prior to CRM 2015 are now referred to as *standard SLAs* and can still be created when necessary.

Enhanced SLAs provide the ability to pause an SLA so that time isn't considered in the calculations, add success actions to an SLA, and track SLA status directly on the case form and through the SLA KPI record type.

Also new to the case form, is the ability to add a native timer control that can manage the case time. Figure 2.11 shows the timer control options on a form.

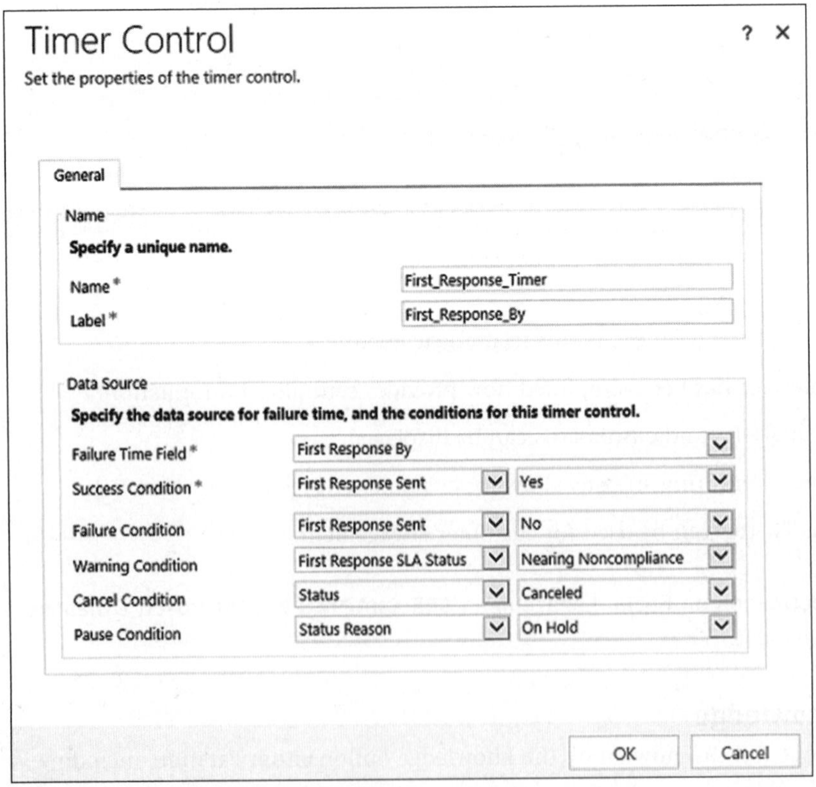

Timer Control   ? ✕

Set the properties of the timer control.

General

Name

Specify a unique name.

Name *	First_Response_Timer
Label *	First_Response_By

Data Source

Specify the data source for failure time, and the conditions for this timer control.

Failure Time Field *	First Response By	
Success Condition *	First Response Sent	Yes
Failure Condition	First Response Sent	No
Warning Condition	First Response SLA Status	Nearing Noncompliance
Cancel Condition	Status	Canceled
Pause Condition	Status Reason	On Hold

OK   Cancel

FIGURE 2.11   Timer control properties.

▶ For more information about the changes to the case entity, **SEE CHAPTER 10.**

Office 365 and Outlook Enhancements

With tighter integration with Office 365 via the Online Administration Center, office products such as Excel, Outlook, Delve, OneNote, OneDrive for Business, and SharePoint, Dynamics CRM 2016 offers a truly immersive Office 365 experience.

The following sections explains some of the enhancements and new features.

Excel Integration

Excel has been integrated directly into Dynamics CRM. This eliminates the need to open a separate application to work with data, as Dynamics CRM maintains the state and context of the data. Figure 2.12 shows account data in Dynamics CRM (notice the Export to Excel option selected in the navigation menu), and Figure 2.13 shows the same data loaded into the inline Excel format for editing.

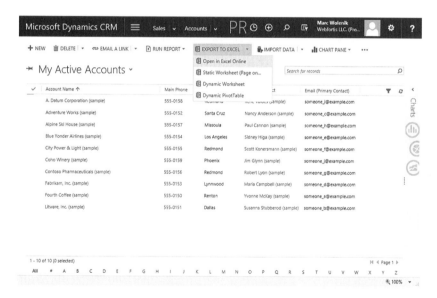

FIGURE 2.12   Microsoft Dynamics account data.

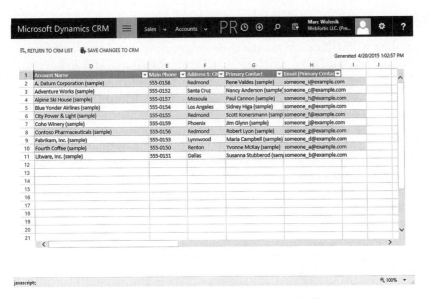

FIGURE 2.13   Microsoft Dynamics account data loaded in Excel.

▶ For more information about working with Excel and Dynamics CRM, **SEE CHAPTER 21.**

Microsoft Dynamics CRM App for Outlook

There is now a dedicated application that works directly within your Office 365 or Outlook Web Access environment to allow you to work with Dynamics CRM data. This app is not as feature rich as the complete Outlook client, but it provides essential functionality not previously available.

Figure 2.14 shows the Microsoft Dynamics CRM app for Outlook. This application extends Microsoft Dynamics CRM tracking capabilities directly within the Office 365 Outlook experience—a feature that was previously reserved for the full version of Outlook only.

FIGURE 2.14   Microsoft Dynamics CRM app for Outlook.

> **NOTE**
>
> The Microsoft Dynamics CRM app for Outlook can be downloaded from the Office Store and must be enabled by the system administrator.

As discussed shortly, users can set up specific folders within Exchange and then place email messages in those folders to have them automatically tracked. This is especially ideal for users who are on their mobile devices.

▶ For more information about email options, **SEE CHAPTER 20**, "Email Configuration."

Server-Side Synchronization Enhancements

Before Dynamics CRM 2016, users were limited in their deployment and configuration options to Exchange. The limitation was that CRM Online did not have an integration to Exchange On-Premises.

With Dynamics CRM 2016, users can perform the following server-side synchronizations:

▶ CRM Online to Exchange Online

▶ CRM Online to Exchange On-Premises

▶ CRM On-Premises to Exchange On-Premises

> **NOTE**
>
> CRM On-Premises to Exchange Online is not currently supported.

In addition, there is a new dashboard available for monitoring the health of the mailboxes, as shown in Figure 2.15.

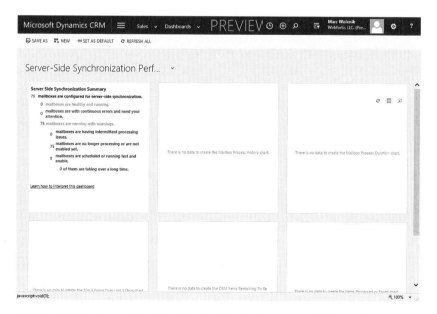

FIGURE 2.15   Server-Side Synchronization Performance dashboard.

Exchange Synchronization Folders

As mentioned earlier, users can now set up folders that automatically track the emails they contain. This is extremely helpful for mobile users, as they can simply move a message into a folder on their device to have it tracked. It is also helpful for Outlook Web Access and Outlook for Mac users, who don't have a rich client plug-in that gives them the capability to track emails.

Outlook

Arguably one of the best features of Microsoft Dynamics CRM is the tightly coupled integration with Outlook. It is this feature that allows Microsoft to continue to deliver a consolidated application for its users.

▶ For more information about email options, **SEE CHAPTER 19**, "Outlook Configuration."

Two important enhancements have been made related to Outlook:

▶ **Configuration**—The Outlook configuration wizard has been redesigned, and new functionality gives users new synchronization options. In addition, system administrators can control synchronization.

▶ **OAuth**—Available for both CRM Online and On-Premises, multifactor authentication (MFA) through the OAuth 2.0 framework now enables users to authenticate with access tokens instead of credentials.

NOTE

MFA can be used only with Office Outlook 2016.

OneNote, OneDrive for Business, Delve, and Office 365 Integration

OneNote is now embedded inside Microsoft Dynamics CRM, allowing users to work directly within Dynamics CRM on OneNote. OneNote allows users to capture much more than notes; it can also be used for voice, photos, and freehand drawings. Figure 2.16 shows OneNote within Dynamics CRM.

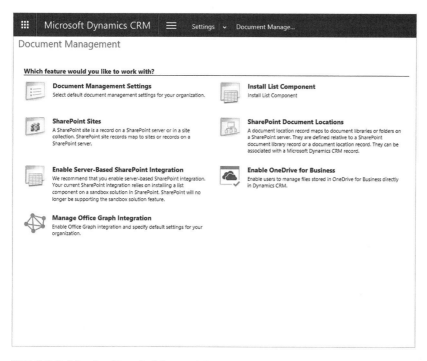

FIGURE 2.16   OneNote in Microsoft Dynamics CRM.

Along with this integration, Microsoft Dynamics CRM allows for group collaboration across the Office products, and users don't need to have access to Microsoft Dynamics CRM to share details related to accounts or opportunities.

> **NOTE**
>
> In order to use integrated OneNote, users must have a subscription to Office 365.

OneDrive for Business

For deeper collaboration options, OneDrive for Business, which is part of SharePoint Online, provides another option for document storage and sharing/collaboration.

Office Delve

Office Delve allows Dynamics CRM users to search across multiple organizational silos and offers both relevant and trending documents directly to users.

▶ For more information about OneNote, Delve, OneDrive for Business, and Office 365 integration, **SEE CHAPTER 21**.

SharePoint Enhancements

SharePoint now supports the following scenarios:

▶ CRM Online to SharePoint Online

▶ CRM Online to SharePoint On-Premises

▶ CRM On-Premises to SharePoint Online

▶ CRM On-Premises to SharePoint On-Premises

When setting up and configuring SharePoint to work with CRM, system administrators need to enable server-based SharePoint integration.

TIP

When possible, Microsoft recommends using the server-based SharePoint integration option because it provides the following benefits:

▶ Single sign-on to both CRM and the SharePoint instance

▶ Richer CRM experience, with SharePoint actions available from CRM and SharePoint documents displayed in CRM lists

In addition—and most importantly—the List Component (a Microsoft supported mechanism for enabling communication between SharePoint and CRM) will likely not be continued for future environments, as it has been deprecated by Microsoft.

NOTE

It is possible to switch between the List Component and server-based integration by setting up and configuring the server-based integration and then deactivating and deleting the List Component from the SharePoint site collection.

Platform and Architecture Changes

A host of improvements to the Dynamics CRM platform have been added since the 2013 release. These improvements allow users to scale broadly across the globe and control the environment in which they're developing.

Development and Test Instances

Sandbox support including resetting and copying is available to preview instances. In addition, system administrators can perform the following:

▶ Delete sandbox instances

▶ Restore instances from backups

▶ Make backups

▶ Download backups to Azure storage subscriptions

▶ Manage storage limits across instances

▶ Switch instance types between production and sandbox instances

These features allow development organizations to safely make changes to their environments and at the same time safeguard against data loss.

Multi-geo Instance Support

Organizations can take advantage of the fact that Microsoft has multiple data centers around the world and that Microsoft Dynamics CRM allows for instance provisioning in foreign data centers to support users in that geo. Organizations that support multiple geo regions can provision instances of CRM in specific geos, within a single tenant.

NOTE

This feature was announced as part of the 2015 Update 1 release but was not available to test at the time of release.

TIP

The upside to this is that the administration of the users via the tenant is much easier than in a tenant-by-tenant model. However, the downside is that data replication might be necessary between instances, so be sure to consider the ramifications when considering this type of deployment.

API Enhancements

The following are the major API enhancements since CRM 2013:

▶ **Alternate keys**—You can allow integrations to work within Microsoft Dynamics CRM by creating key columns that external data sources use instead of the GUID.

▶ **Transaction batching**—You can have batch transactions occur or roll back gracefully.

▶ **Upsert**—Upsert allows records to be created or updated at the same time, using only one API method call.

▶ **Optimistic concurrency**—Record updates can occur at the same time as a check to ensure that no previous update to the same record will cause an error.

▶ **Change tracking**—Server-to-server one-way data synchronization is possible, with change tracking for only those records that have had changes made.

▶ **OData V4 endpoints**—OData V4 endpoints (available in preview at the time of this writing) are available for system integrators to begin development and testing against. This feature is also referred to as the Web API and offers better performance than previous OData endpoints, returning JSON instead of XML.

▶ **API preview**—Now system configurators and developers can experiment against future releases (and provide feedback) by testing code against v.NEXT versions of the code. To use this feature, you must turn it on in System Settings (as shown in Figure 2.17).

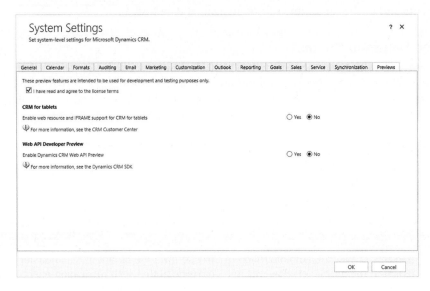

FIGURE 2.17   API preview option in System Settings.

▶ For more information about software development kit (SDK), **SEE CHAPTER 26**, "Process Development."

Solution Enhancements

New to Microsoft Dynamics CRM 2016, solutions can be exported with only selected entity components. Previous versions, in contrast, required all components for solution exports, via solution segmentation.

▶ For more information about working with solution segmentation, **SEE CHAPTER 26**, "Process Development."

External Party Access

Microsoft understands that external users will interact with the data contained in Dynamics CRM. Typically this is done through self-service and/or portal access, with customers accessing, modifying, or closing cases that pertain to them directly.

As an API enhancement, the CRM SDK now allows tighter and more controlled data access, via a channel concept. You can set the availability of external channels at the entity level, and you can configure and manage them in the External Party Access tab of System Settings, as shown in Figure 2.18.

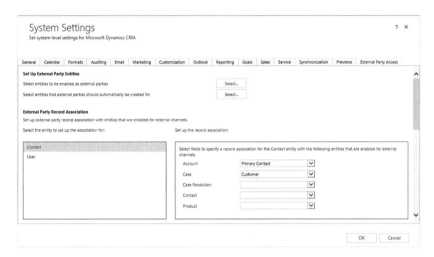

FIGURE 2.18   System Settings for external party data access.

When this is configured, you can manage the following permissions:

▶ **None Selected**—No external access is granted.

▶ **External Party**—External access is granted but only to those records that are defined in System Settings (see Figure 2.19).

▶ **Parent: Child External Party**—External access is granted to not just the entities that have permission but the child records as well.

▶ **Full**—Full external party access is allowed.

Figure 2.19 shows the profile for channel access.

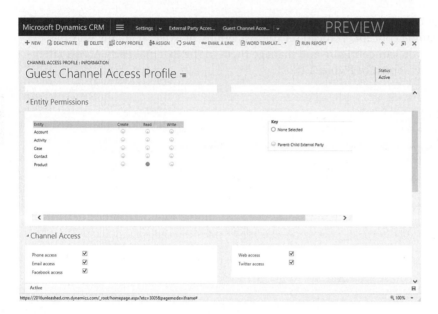

FIGURE 2.19   External channel access profile management.

Supported Configurations

Microsoft On-Premises (only) is designed for Windows Server 2012 and SQL Server 2012 or 2014 (64-bit versions only), and the following have been deprecated from the support matrix:

- ▶ Operating systems

- ▶ Windows 2012 Foundation and Essentials

- ▶ Windows Server 2000

- ▶ Windows Server 2008 r2

- ▶ Windows Small Business Server (all versions)

- ▶ SQL Server versions

  - ▶ Microsoft SQL Server 2008

  - ▶ Microsoft SQL Server 2008 R2

- ▶ Microsoft Dynamics CRM for Outlook

  - ▶ Windows Vista

  - ▶ Windows Server 2008 Remote Desktop Services

  - ▶ Microsoft Office 2007

In addition, the following SDK API calls have been removed since Dynamics CRM 2013:

▶ `GetServerUrl()`

▶ `IsOutLookClient()`

▶ `IsOutlookOnline()`

If an implementation uses any of these API commands, the code will break when you upgrade to Dynamics CRM 2016 and so needs to be refactored appropriately.

▶ For more information about architecture options, **SEE CHAPTER 29**, "On-Premises Deployments."

New Support and Pricing Options

In addition to continuing to refine the options available to users with regard to how they can use the system, Microsoft continues to enhance and bundle Dynamics CRM with the other Office 365 offerings.

> **TIP**
>
> Pricing is subject to change, but at the time of publication, Microsoft was offering Microsoft Dynamics CRM Online Professional, Office 365 Enterprise E3, and Power BI for Office 365 all for $65 per user/per month.

Be sure to check the pricing page for Microsoft Dynamics CRM for current offerings and bundles: www.microsoft.com/en-us/dynamics/crm-purchase-online.aspx.

▶ For more information about pricing and licensing options, **SEE CHAPTER 4**, "CRM 2016 Online."

Support

Microsoft has increased the support options available to users, providing direct vendor support when required. The new options supplement the existing support model of unlimited break/fix incidents directly from Microsoft, known as Subscription, but now include Enhanced at $5 a user per month for higher response and escalation rates.

If your organization has more than 100 users, you qualify for Professional Direct and/or Premier at higher pricing.

▶ For more information about support, **SEE CHAPTER 30**, "How to Get Support for Your System."

Pricing

Dual licensing now exists for On-Premises to Online at no additional cost. This means that if you have purchased a subscription license for Dynamics CRM Online, you have the ability (at no additional cost) to use the On-Premises version—provided that it matches the licensing you're paying for (and are current on) with the Online version.

Mobile

Microsoft remains committed to the mobile environment. Dynamics CRM has continued to receive updates that allow for easy access even for users with fat fingers (via the tile layout). However, Microsoft intends to deliver seamless user experiences across all mobile devices in a "configure once, deploy everywhere" model.

Mobile Client

The Dynamics CRM mobile client is tailored specifically for phones and tablets, and it includes the ability for offline access.

Dashboards have been enabled for mobile use, and Microsoft has included new mobile app SDK samples to complement its applications.

> **TIP**
>
> The new mobile app SDK samples, which include templates, are available at http://blogs.msdn.com/b/crm/archive/2014/12/19/new-mobile-app-samples.aspx.
>
> In addition, mobile development helper code for Dynamics CRM is available at https://code.msdn.microsoft.com/Mobile-Development-Helper-3213e2e6.

Figure 2.20 shows the mobile client fully extended.

FIGURE 2.20   Microsoft Dynamics CRM mobile client.

Mobile Forms

In addition to providing a new set of visual controls, Microsoft Dynamics CRM makes it easier than ever before to design rich interfaces for the mobile application of your choice. You can now use the inline visual interface immediately previewing your changes. Figure 2.21 shows the mobile preview for a phone.

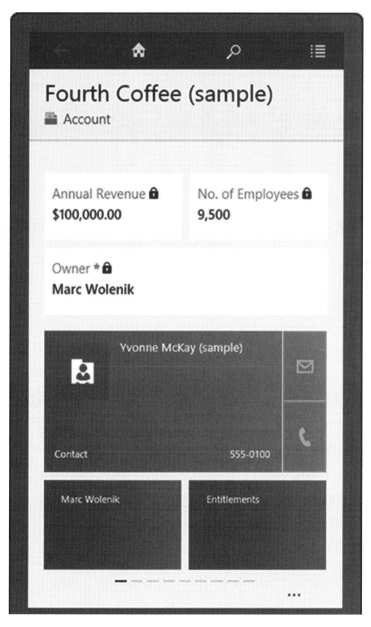

FIGURE 2.21   Microsoft Dynamics CRM mobile form editor preview.

In addition, the following new visual controls have been added to allow customizers to build rich apps:

▶ Linear slider

▶ Option set

▶ Flip switch

▶ Star rating

▶ Radial knob

▶ Multimedia controls

▶ Pen controls

▶ Website preview

▶ Number input

▶ Auto-complete

▶ Input mask

▶ Linear gauge

▶ Bullet graph

▶ Arc knob

▶ Phone calendar control

▶ Table calendar control

When configuring mobile options, customizers can include offline options and also leverage InTune to encrypt and manage devices.

NOTE

There are two different options for offline access: the new offline experience and offline cache mode and drafts. The new offline experience requires 30 or more Enterprise or Professional licenses and is configured via profile filtering rule by entity and assigned to mobile users.

TIP

Offline capability for phones and tablets is available only with Dynamics CRM 2016 Online.

Finally, mobile applications now support iFrame and HTML web resources to allow for a fully integrated and immersive mobile environment.

Integration with Cortana

Using Windows 8.1+ phones, users can speak to Microsoft Dynamics CRM by using phone commands.

Secured Data with Good

An option that can be used either with or instead of Microsoft InTune, is Microsoft Dynamics CRM for Good, which allows system administrators to remotely wipe data in the event of a theft or loss. This additional layer of protection allows organizations to rest assured that their data is secure while on a mobile device.

> **NOTE**
>
> Microsoft Dynamics CRM for Good is available only for the iPad (with iOS 7.0 or later) at this writing.

Microsoft Dynamics Marketing (MDM)

Microsoft continues to expand capabilities with its marketing capabilities via Microsoft Dynamics Marketing (MDM). MDM enables marketing agencies to use Dynamics CRM to plan and execute on marketing campaigns, including specific information such as A/B testing, email marketing management, and campaign ROI.

> **NOTE**
>
> MDM is a separate application that requires its own paid subscription. To learn more about MDM, refer here:
>
> https://www.microsoft.com/en-us/dynamics/crm-marketing.aspx

Email Marketing

Enhancements to the email marketing options for MDM include the following:

▶ Enhanced options for opting in or out of campaigns

▶ Duplication options

▶ Tracking blocked emails due to duplication

Enhanced Campaign and Lead Management

MDM now supports customizable fields that synchronize with corresponding task events in Dynamics CRM. It also allows multiple-keyword searches for digital asset management (DAM).

▶ For more information about MDM, **SEE CHAPTER 9**, "Microsoft Dynamics Marketing."

Summary

We're excited that you have this book in your hands and that you're starting the journey of working with Microsoft Dynamics CRM 2016. This is the eighth iteration of Microsoft Dynamics CRM, and adoption continues at levels never anticipated. The innovation in Dynamics CRM 2016 continues at breakneck speed, and we have attempted to highlight most of the new features available with Dynamics CRM 2016. However, a few features either didn't make it into the chapter because of space considerations or were added to the product too late to be included. Be sure to check the latest *Implementation Guide* from Microsoft for the current list.

CHAPTER 3

Customizing and Designing Applications Within Dynamics CRM 2016 (xRM)

Since the earliest days of Microsoft CRM, the term *xRM* has been used constantly. The basic idea behind xRM is that the *x* can stand for anything, and it can be applied to Dynamics CRM as a relationship management tool. Consider this list for a second: cows, vendors, candy, ice cream, money, people, automobiles, semiconductors, airplane seats. Is there anything in this list that couldn't be managed in an xRM deployment? My answer is always and steadfastly no, and in fact, I've seen and built xRM deployments for all of these and many more. If you have been handed a project to build a system for management of something (the *x*), this chapter is the right place to start!

NOTE

While I make every effort to consider xRM design concepts and principles, this topic is very large and broad and could fill and entire book. That being said, this book would be lacking without this chapter, which provides the essential basics to give you an understanding of the how and why for xRM.

TIP

Microsoft has moved away from the term xRM in recent years in its marketing materials, instead preferring the term *extended CRM*.

xRM Explained

In December 2005, Microsoft introduced the third version of Microsoft Dynamics CRM, 3.0 (previous versions were 1.0 and 1.2; 2.0 was skipped altogether). With the introduction of 3.0, Microsoft moved away from the old name Microsoft Business Solutions Customer Relationship Management (aka MBS) to Dynamics CRM. At the same time, it joined the family together with the other Dynamics products—Solomon (SL), Axapta (AX), Great Plains (GP), and Navision (NAV). In addition, the concept of xRM was introduced for the first time.

Explained at the time as the ability to manage anything, xRM provided the building blocks for many organizations to put together applications on top of CRM. One way to think about this is that you use Dynamics CRM as a platform and leverage all the things you need out of it as a sort of "quick start" to get your application done.

> **TIP**
>
> Many organizations have adopted RAD (rapid application design) principles, and Dynamics CRM is an excellent platform for this.

xRM Considerations

When considering an xRM deployment, it is critical to consider the following points:

- ▶ The end application
- ▶ The user experience
- ▶ What comes with Dynamics CRM out of the box
- ▶ Where you're going to have to build/extend
- ▶ The licensing model

The following sections look at each of these in turn.

The End Application

To determine whether Dynamics CRM is a good fit for your situation, you need to consider the end application, or what you're going to be building. Sometimes it's a great fit for building out prototypes or proofs of concepts, but the full-scale application might require a different approach. In addition, when you consider application development and a Microsoft environment, you typically consider the following as the base platforms:

- ▶ Microsoft Dynamics CRM
- ▶ Microsoft SharePoint
- ▶ Custom (typically a .NET application built from the ground up)

The first two options, CRM and SharePoint, provide customizers with a platform on which to build their applications. While the last option (.NET) doesn't, it has much greater flexibility for overall design as there are things that you can't do using CRM or SharePoint.

> **TIP**
>
> A common way of determining whether an application should be built in CRM or in SharePoint is to consider the following uses:
>
> ▶ **CRM**—Better with structured data, such as appointments and emails
>
> ▶ **SharePoint**—Better with unstructured data, such as pictures and documents
>
> This does not mean that you can't use either application for what you need, but you need to be aware of the limitations of each. For example, while both have strong workflow engines, CRM does not include native versioning for documents (whereas SharePoint does), and SharePoint does not have the ability to easily cross-reference (that is, relate) dependent objects (whereas CRM does).

The User Experience

How your users interact with your application might determine your platform choice:

▶ Does everybody have strong dependencies on Microsoft Office?

▶ Is the organization standardized on Microsoft Outlook?

▶ Is there a strong demand for a native mobile application?

▶ Does the IT department currently support a large number of Microsoft applications?

▶ Are there any other Dynamics CRM deployments already in place?

If the answers to any of these questions are yes, an xRM deployment will help in designing the deployment and enable users to quickly and easily consume the new application.

What Comes with Dynamics CRM Out of the Box

Leveraging what comes with Dynamics CRM out of the box will help with your planned deployment immeasurably. The best features of Dynamics CRM are often undersold and underutilized, but understanding what they are can help get you to a working application much more quickly than having to design it from scratch.

Some of the highest-value features, discussed in other chapters in this book, include the following:

▶ Native integration with Outlook

▶ Native integration with Microsoft Excel and Word

▶ Strong reporting workflow and reporting engine (SQL Server Reporting Services)

▶ COLAC (explained later in this chapter)

▶ Ability to form dependencies between objects in many relationship types

▶ A user-friendly user interface for configuration

▶ A framework that can be customized easily (with or without code)

For these reasons, organizations continue to use and adopt Dynamics CRM as a base platform both for RAD and for prototyping new applications.

TIP

I often hear that Dynamics CRM comes with **too much** out of the box. However, you can easily remove all the unneeded objects via two methods:

▶ If you remove (or not grant) permissions to most/all users, the user interface doesn't display the restricted items, making the application more streamlined.

▶ You can remove objects by customizing the back end of the system and actually removing the unnecessary relationships and objects.

Of these two options, the first is recommended, and Dynamics CRM has been designed with this in mind.

Where You're Going to Have to Build/Extend

Knowing where you're going to have to build and extend the application will help with you determine the level of effort before you start. Customizers become more and more comfortable with estimating the level of effort as they get experience working with xRM deployments and learn to understand where the limitations might be.

NOTE

I'm a huge believer in the notion that Microsoft Dynamics CRM can do anything other than walk your dog, and you'll see that bias in this book. However, in some cases, the time and money required to make CRM work are too much, and it in those situations, it makes sense to consider alternatives.

For example, there is no core entity for the purpose of cow management, so customizers would have to build this entity to get the development process started. An option to creating an entity for cow management would be to rename an existing entity for this purpose (for example, change the Account entity to the Cow entity). This option works in a lot of cases, but when you use this method, you subject the organization to a potential increase (or step up) in base licensing as you have now used one of the core entities and have disqualified the organization from the lowest and cheapest licensing cost option (that is, Essential).

The Licensing Model

The licensing model of Dynamics CRM provides huge elasticity with regard to what and how an application can be designed. This point can't be understated.

▶ The section "Licensing Explained," later in this chapter, provides more information on licensing.

xRM Design Principles

By now you can see that there are some interdependencies when working with Dynamics CRM as an xRM application. When working with xRM, and important question is how to design the application, leveraging the considerations explained earlier in this chapter.

The principles discussed in this section have been tried and true in the real world. That being said, your mileage may vary, and requirements are never exactly the same from one project to another. Sometimes a very small requirement may change the design greatly. The following sections discuss some important considerations: COLAC and licensing.

COLAC

The base entities in Dynamics CRM, which add up to the acronym COLAC, are as follows:

▶ Contacts

▶ Opportunities

▶ Leads

▶ Accounts

▶ Cases

Virtually every standard deployment of Dynamics CRM that is not an xRM deployment uses at least one of these entities. Knowing when and how to use them (as well as the other native entities) is critical in a successful xRM deployment.

> **TIP**
>
> In the 500+ deployments of Dynamics CRM that I've personally seen, fewer than a dozen have *not* had at least one custom entity added to the system. By definition, including a custom entity makes the deployment an xRM deployment.
>
> The dozen deployments that haven't had custom entities were used strictly for out-of-the-box functions such as lead management or salesforce automation.

Best practices typically dictate one of the following design methods:

▶ Leverage as many out-of-the-box features, functions, and entities as possible and use the fewest possible customizations to make the application meet the requirements.

▶ Build the application around the requirements with an xRM mindset but leverage as much out-of-the-box functionality as possible by renaming and reusing core/ native components.

▶ Ignore all out-of-the-box objects and create everything from scratch.

Prior to designing an application and deciding which principle you should follow, it is important to understand how licensing can affect the modeling.

Figure 3.1 shows the effect of using the COLAC, as the entities that are shown (i.e. Opportunity, Lead, and Case) have native integration with Outlook, and there is no way to add new entities to this option in Outlook. As a result, if you wish to extend this type of functionality to Outlook, you need to consider using them.

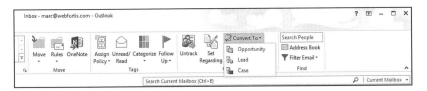

FIGURE 3.1   Converting an email to a CRM record in Outlook.

Licensing Explained

Microsoft has changed the licensing model several times during the life of Dynamics CRM.

In the original iteration of CRM (prior to 3.0), organizations had to pay per module, which means that if an organization wanted to access the Service are or the Marketing area of CRM, it had to pay for it. This was extremely burdensome and difficult for both Microsoft and customers to manage.

The licensing model that Microsoft currently uses is a role-based model that allows users to access certain functions within the system, depending on the license type, or client access license (CAL), they have purchased.

TIP

The concepts related to the license types discussed in this section have been in place for several versions. However, there is no enforcement in the application for any of them. This means you could purchase an Essential CAL and use all the Professional features if you wanted; the system won't know or care.

That being said, Microsoft has repeatedly indicated that in-app licensing enforcement is coming (it's actually relatively easy to validate and check with a role report), and there are severe penalties for any organization that is not in compliance with Microsoft licensing.

While the risk to save a few bucks to go with an invalid licensing model might be tempting, most compliance calls to Microsoft licensing are from previous and disgruntled employees, so it's your call on whether it's worth it (and you'll likely have to purchase up once the in-app validation is rolled out).

Figure 3.2 shows the licensing model as it applies to Microsoft Dynamics CRM and any xRM deployment.

● Full access rights ○ READ only / Limited access rights ⊘ No access rights

Entities and functionality	Professional $65 / u./mo.	Basic $30 / u./mo.	Essential $15 / u./mo.
Create workflows, bulk data import and customizations across any entity	●	⊘	⊘
Run workflows*	●	○	○
Opportunities, goals, contracts, quotes, orders, invoices, competitors	●	○	⊘
Marketing campaigns, quick campaigns, marketing lists, price lists, product lists	●	○	⊘
Services, resources, work hours, facility, equipment, articles	●	○	⊘
System reports, system charts, system dashboards, CRM application data	●	○	⊘
User reports, dashboards and charts	●	●	⊘
Accounts, contacts, cases and leads	●	●	⊘
Custom entities	●	● **	● **
Activities, notes	●	●	●

FIGURE 3.2 Microsoft Dynamics CRM Online license model.

TIP

On-Premises licensing varies substantially but still follows the same principles with regard to license type.

As shown, there are three different licensing options available:

- Professional
- Basic
- Essential

NOTE

In addition, two other licensing options are not shown:

- Sales Productivity
- Enterprise

These options are not included in this section because they have all the features available under the Professional option and include additional components and applications, such as Parature, Power BI, and so on, depending on the option.

Considering the information shown in Figure 3.2, you can build an application using Microsoft Dynamics CRM, and if you *only* use custom entities, activities, and notes, you can have a per-user cost of only $15 per user per month.

NOTE

For more information about pricing and options, see www.microsoft.com/en-us/dynamics/crm-purchase-online.aspx.

A Pure xRM Deployment

A deployment created under the Essential option is considered a pure xRM deployment. A pure xRM deployment leverages almost all custom entities (for example, a custom entity for the purpose of cow management) and doesn't use anything else in the system. Only a small percentage of deployments can be handled this way, but when they do work, they get all the features mentioned previously—native Outlook, Excel and Word integration, relationship dependencies, and so on.

CAUTION

Only the most experienced of developers/architects should consider designing an application using the Essential licensing type as it is very easy to neglect some of the dependencies (such as no dashboards or accidently using opportunities or invoices). If you end up using some features you shouldn't, you will need to step up to a more expensive license or refactor the system completely.

A Hybrid xRM Deployment

The Professional and Basic licensing options yield hybrid xRM deployments. While the Basic CAL meets a lot of requirements, the majority of deployments are a mix of both Professional and Basic licensing. A typical deployment of 100 users might involve 30 Professional and 70 Basic users, but sometimes the numbers can be a lot different, depending on the requirements.

NOTE

The licensing model shown in Figure 3.2 is subject to change. Be sure to check with Microsoft for any updates prior to estimating actual cost. Microsoft online pricing can be found here: https://www.microsoft.com/en-us/dynamics/purchase-crm-online.

The Effect of Licensing on Design

As the previous sections show, considering licensing when designing an xRM deployment can put severe limitations on the cost of the final application when approved for production. As a result, organizations have to decide if they wish to sacrifice functionality and potentially limit increased usage or desired usage of future functionality for cost today or pay more and having unlimited options. There is no right answer. The best answer is typically a measured approach to design, where the right mix of licenses match with the desired functionality.

The scenario explained earlier—with a 100-user deployment having 30 Professional users and 70 Basic users—is very common, and if the application is architected correctly, the

70 Basic users won't even be aware of any system limitations. If, however, they someday want to use one of the restricted objects (workflows or opportunities being the most common), they will have to upgrade their CAL.

> **NOTE**
>
> Microsoft is very aware the organizational needs change, and in fact counts on changes to CALs. If you have an On-Premises deployment and your needs increase, you only have to purchase a step-up CAL to Professional, which is the price difference between the Basic and Professional licenses.
>
> CRM Online customers simply change the pricing selection for the number of users licensed for Professional.

Summary

Considering an xRM deployment of Dynamics CRM is as much art as it is science. The science piece relates to the following:

▶ When, where, and how to use native/OOB functionality versus custom

▶ Whether the considerations for functionality outweigh the implications of cost

The art piece relates to the following:

▶ Which of the half dozen or so different ways the system is designed

▶ Whether the system is as elegant as possible, taking cost and functionality into account

Sometimes the requirements today are not the requirements tomorrow, and prospective owners of an xRM system should consider the future when designing a system, as the hassle of upgrading custom code and entities will cost the customer significantly more than just paying for the additional CALs today.

The take-away from all of this is that there is no right answer, no one size fits all. Yes, you can consider the design requirements, the costs, and the other factors, but if you had the best, clearest, and most detailed requirements in the world, as well as a dozen of the smartest and most experienced CRM designers, you would likely end up with a dozen different final designs. This isn't a failure but a design feature.

CRM 2016 Online

Microsoft has made substantial investments in Microsoft Dynamics CRM Online to provide a cost-effective and full-featured experience for users. The integration with Microsoft Office 365 Online has streamlined the process and provides an opportunity for organizations to consolidate their Office 365 and Microsoft Dynamics CRM Online experiences.

> **NOTE**
>
> To be clear, Microsoft Office 365 is *not* Dynamics CRM. Instead, Office 365 is a suite of applications, including SharePoint, Outlook, Excel, PowerPoint, Word, and Dynamics CRM.
>
> It is possible to buy Dynamics CRM or Office 365 without each other. So if you have an existing Office 365 subscription and you're looking for CRM but can't find it, it might be because you haven't selected it as a purchased option.

This chapter is devoted to the Online version of Microsoft Dynamics CRM 2016. In some places, this chapter explicitly notes differences between On-Premises and Online, but where it doesn't, you can assume that the text is about CRM Online.

▶ For more information about On-Premises installations of CRM, **SEE CHAPTER 29**, "On-Premises Deployments."

Overview of Microsoft Dynamics CRM 2016 Online

Microsoft Dynamics CRM is available in three basic installation options: On-Premises, CRM Online, and partner hosted. This chapter covers CRM Online, including licensing, benefits and limitations, an operational overview of the services provided by Microsoft, and a guide on how to sign up and manage a CRM Online instance.

Microsoft Dynamics CRM Online is a Microsoft-hosted service that offers tight integration with the Office 365 platform. Microsoft started offering CRM Online during the CRM 4.0 days, with close feature parity with what you would receive using an On-Premises or partner hosted implementation. With the release of CRM 2011, the Online offering was also updated, and the differences between the options narrowed, but limitations imposed because of a shared hosting environment kept some organizations from using this service offering. In 2012, Microsoft rolled out updates that further narrowed the differences and improved security, allowing CRM Online to be a true first-class citizen in the Microsoft CRM world.

Why Use Microsoft Dynamics CRM 2016 Online?

Microsoft Dynamics CRM Online is a quick gateway to the Microsoft CRM universe and an easy way to "dip your toe in the CRM waters" without diving in head first. A traditional On-Premises deployment of Microsoft CRM requires a substantial investment in both money and time, as well an experienced administrator to keep the platform running smoothly. Microsoft CRM Online removes the barriers, providing fast entry and low initial investment to get started. In less than 20 minutes, you can have a full CRM implementation up and running and ready for data and users. Figure 4.1 shows five key reasons to use CRM Online:

Key Advantages of CRM Online

FIGURE 4.1   Key advantages of CRM Online.

▶ **Fast deployment**—Microsoft Dynamics CRM Online provides all the hosting hardware, software, and infrastructure support as part of the monthly costs. As you will see later in this chapter, you can "spin up" a new organization in as little as 20 minutes. There is no need to install and configure servers and the CRM server software.

▶ **Lower initial investment**—For many organizations, this is the key to selecting CRM Online. There are no upfront infrastructure costs or licensing costs; instead, all costs are included in the monthly licensing fee. Even a small On-Premises implementation of just 20 users could run $20,000 to $25,000 for servers and license costs.

▶ **No IT infrastructure necessary for setup and maintenance**—Because Microsoft provides all the hardware and software, there is no need for additional hardware, software, or dedicated IT resources. This means there are no ongoing IT costs related to maintenance, backups, and management of additional servers.

▶ **Immediate external access**—Microsoft Dynamics CRM Online is a hosted solution. Therefore, on day one it is available to any user who has an Internet connection, from a variety of devices, including iPads and mobile phones. On-Premises installations require additional steps and complexity to expose the CRM services outside a company's network.

▶ **High level of redundancy**—As you will see in this chapter, Microsoft provides a high level of redundancy with its Online offering. This level of redundancy would greatly increase the initial costs, maintenance expenses, and complexity of an On-Premises installation.

The Microsoft Dynamics CRM 2016 Online Experience

The average user of CRM Online would be hard pressed to know the difference between a CRM Online and CRM On-Premises installation; after all, the feature parity is very close, however in most cases, new features are available earlier with CRM Online than with CRM On-Premises.

> **NOTE**
>
> Regardless of whether you use Microsoft Dynamics CRM Online or On-Premises, you have the same ability to use Outlook, the web browser, and the mobile client at no additional cost.

Update Schedule

Microsoft provides two basic types of updates to the CRM platform: feature releases and update rollups (URs). Early in the development of CRM Online, the team at Microsoft targeted the release of a UR every eight weeks and a major release (what could be called a major feature release) twice per year. The early URs were arguably very stable and were automatically deployed to the CRM Online environment. Then, as the releases became increasingly complex and negative impacts grew, Microsoft rethought its schedule and began to put out releases for CRM Online and CRM On-Premises concurrently.

Late in the 2011 life cycle and based on feedback from On-Premises customers, Microsoft moved away from the concurrent release schedule. Going forward, Microsoft would still target UR releases every eight weeks, but now it would only include fixes and not new features. For CRM Online customers, there would be twice-per-year new feature releases, which were automatically deployed to the customer environment and, depending on the size, could include an optional opt-in to help with deployment timing. On-Premises gets new feature releases once per year, putting the CRM Online users in a position to receive new features twice as often.

This new approach has greatly improved the stability of releases and given organizations a chance to evaluate and decide which features to adopt. The different release schedules impact an organization's ability to move between Online and On-Premises environments, and timing and other considerations are important. Figure 4.2 visually lays out the planned release cycle for URs.

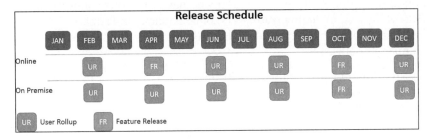

FIGURE 4.2   Microsoft CRM release schedule.

Microsoft Data Centers

Microsoft has made a serious investment in its online and cloud services, such as CRM, Office 365, and Windows Azure, as well as top websites such as Microsoft.com, MSN.com, and Bing.com. CRM Online leverages the infrastructure Microsoft has in place for these services and benefits from the investments and attention in the Microsoft organization. Microsoft depends on a centralized team called Global Foundation Services (GFS) to operate its data centers worldwide.

Global Data Centers

Microsoft offers a global data center footprint with facilities located throughout the world that are managed and operated directly by Microsoft (see Figure 4.3).

FIGURE 4.3   Microsoft global data centers worldwide.

NOTE

For an updated map and more information on Microsoft's global data centers, see http://o365datacentermap.azurewebsites.net.

Regional Data Redundancy

Within a region, Microsoft replicates customer data in real time between at least two data centers. This provides for failover on planned (for example, maintenance) and unplanned bases. This redundant architecture eliminates a single point of failure. Figure 4.4 shows an example of data replication.

FIGURE 4.4   Example of U.S. data replication.

In addition to the real-time replication of data, Microsoft also performs near-real-time replication at the data center at the other side of the region for resiliency and disaster recovery.

NOTE

Each customer database is also backed up onto encrypted media for near-line backup and recovery.

Data Center Redundancy

The Microsoft Dynamics CRM Online data centers are built using "scale group" infrastructure to provide a high level of redundancy and scalability. The data center is built around the concept of pods, which are groupings of multiple server racks. Each scale group is a logical grouping of servers that share responsibility for workflow, sandbox, and other asynchronous activities. Each scale group consists of six database servers—three local and three remote. Each customer's database (instance) is stored independent of other customers. Each customer can have one or more instances (for example, production and development instances), and each is referred to as a *tenant*.

Using this architecture, each scale group can support a large number of instances. If one instance starts consuming a large number of resources, it is automatically moved to another scale group that has more capacity. Figure 4.5 shows the scale group architecture.

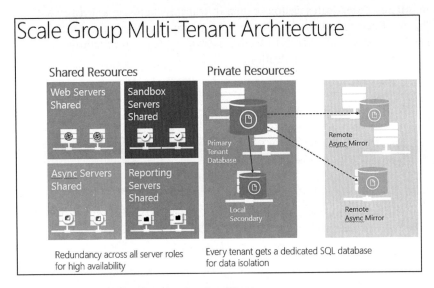

FIGURE 4.5   Example of scale group architecture.

Privacy and Certifications

Microsoft has placed a high priority on developing detailed and specific guidelines with regard to privacy and certifications, as explained in the following sections.

Privacy

Figure 4.6 highlights the three aspects of privacy that Microsoft espouses:

Privacy

No Advertising	No Mingling	Data Portability

FIGURE 4.6   Three aspects of privacy.

▶ **No advertising**—A customer's data is considered confidential, and Microsoft does not scan the contents of the database or documents to analytic, data-mining, or advertising products.

▶ **No mingling**—Microsoft uses independent databases to separate one customer's data from other customers' data. Each database is provisioned for one customer to maximize data security and ensure integrity.

▶ **Data portability**—The isolation of the Microsoft Dynamics CRM Online customer simplifies moving data between Online and On-Premises environments. The customer's data belongs to the customer and can be removed whenever the customer desires.

Certifications

Microsoft Dynamics CRM Online is certified to multiple world-class industry standards, providing a secure and tested platform. Current certifications include SSAE 16 SOC 1 (SAS 70 Type I), ISO 27001, EU Safe Harbor, EU Model Clauses, and HIPAA–HITECH, as shown in Figure 4.7.

> **NOTE**
>
> New certifications are being added all the time. For a complete and current list, see www.microsoft.com/en-us/trustcenter/CloudServices/Dynamics.

Certifications and Compliance

FIGURE 4.7   Certifications and industry standards.

Just a few of these certifications include:

▶ **Independently verified**—Microsoft uses independent third parties to verify compliance.

▶ **Certified for ISO 27001**—ISO 27001 is one of the best security benchmarks available in the world.

▶ **EU model clauses/EU safe harbor**—At the request of a customer, Microsoft will sign the standard agreements for "EU model clauses," which address international transfer of data.

▶ **HIPAA-business associate agreement**—The U.S. Health Insurance Portability and Accountability Act (HIPAA) governs the use, disclosure, and safeguarding of protected health information.

> **NOTE**
>
> Microsoft does not permit direct customer audits; instead, it uses independent third-party verifications of Microsoft security, privacy, and continuity controls.

Understanding the Microsoft Dynamics CRM 2016 Licensing Options

With the release of Microsoft Dynamics CRM 2016, Microsoft has expanded its license offerings to better suit the needs of its diverse customer base.

License Options Explained

As detailed in Figure 4.8, Microsoft now offers four levels of subscriber licenses for Online:

▶ **Enterprise**—This top-end license for CRM Online includes all features as well as most of the rest of the items that fall under the Dynamics CRM umbrella, such as Parature and Social Engagement.

▶ **Professional**—This license includes access to the core functionality, the ability to customize and access all modules delivered by Microsoft, and xRM solutions developed in house or by external vendors.

▶ **Basic**—This mid-tier license provides basic access to several core entities, such as Contact, Account, Case, and Lead (in addition to xRM solutions). This is a good option for organizations that do not use the Sales Force Automation, Customer Service, or Marketing components that are delivered with CRM.

▶ **Essential**—The entry point for CRM Online is the Essential license. With this level of license, the user cannot access any of the core components or core entities. A good example is a pure xRM solution, as described in Chapter 3, "Customizing and Designing Applications Within Dynamics CRM 2016 (xRM)."

The availability and licensing options by user vary, and as new products are added, they continue to evolve. Figure 4.8 provides a sample breakout of the features available at each license level, but be sure to check out the licensing and purchasing options available at the time of purchase for changes to this list.

Use Right	Professional & Enterprise	Basic	Essential
View Announcements	✓	✓	✓
Manage saved views	✓	✓	✓
Use relationships between records	✓	✓*	✓*
Create personal views	✓	✓	✓*
Advanced Find search	✓	✓	✓*
Search	✓	✓	✓*
Use a queue item	✓	✓*	✓*
Export data to Microsoft Excel	✓	✓	✓
Perform Mail Merge	✓	✓	✓
Start dialog	✓	✓*	✓*
Run as an On-demand process	✓	✓*	✓*
Run an automated workflow	✓	✓*	✓*
Read articles	✓	✓	✓
Notes	✓	✓	✓
Activity management	✓	✓	✓
Yammer collaboration**	✓	✓	✓
Post activity feeds	✓	✓	✓
Follow activity feeds	✓	✓	✓
Shared calendar	✓	✓	✓
Write custom entity records	✓	✓***	✓***
Read custom application data	✓	✓	✓
Microsoft Dynamics CRM Mobile Express	✓	✓	✓
Microsoft Dynamics CRM for iPad & Windows 8	✓	✓	✓
Microsoft Dynamics CRM for Outlook	✓	✓	✓
Microsoft Dynamics CRM Web application	✓	✓	✓
Manage user reports, user charts, and user dashboards	✓	✓	
Run reports	✓	✓	
Create, update, and customize Reports	✓	✓	
Create and update announcements	✓	✓	
Read Dynamics CRM application data	✓	✓	
User dashboards	✓	✓	
User charts	✓	✓	
User Interface Integration for Microsoft Dynamics CRM	✓	✓	
Convert an activity to a case	✓	✓	
Case management	✓	✓	
SLAs	✓	✓	
Add or remove a customer relationship for a contact	✓	✓	
Associate an opportunity with a contact	✓	✓	

FIGURE 4.8   User capabilities by license level for CRM Online.

In addition to the access and functional rights provided with each license, as the number of licensed users within an organization grows, additional free capacity enhancements are included. A quirk that existed before Dynamics CRM 2016 was that regardless of the number of users, every organization received 5GB of storage. This meant that organizations with only one or two users had 5GB, and organizations with thousands of users also had 5GB. Luckily, Microsoft has recognized this deficiency and added scaled storage, as described in the next section.

TIP

With the exceptions mentioned previously related to usage and access rights, there is no concept of limited or administrative access with Online deployments as there is with On-Premises deployments.

For On-Premises deployments, the following options now exist:

▶ Server

▶ Enterprise users

▶ Professional user or Device client access license (CAL)

▶ Basic user or device CAL

▶ Essential CAL

Although this new licensing is significantly simplified over previous licensing, it still requires some conversation with regard to the actual pricing because Microsoft licensing is as diverse as its many offerings.

> **NOTE**
>
> The much maligned and rarely understood Internet Connector license required for external access to CRM data has been eliminated and is no longer a requirement for this type of programmatic access.

Online Add-on Features

Microsoft recognizes that the number of users is not always a clear indicator of the needs of an organization and that the additional storage and non-production instance scale-up outlined previously may not meet an organization's needs. To address this, Microsoft allows an organization to, on a monthly basis, purchase additional capacity:

▶ **Additional production instance**—An organization may purchase an additional production instance as an add-on license. Each user licensed in the main production instance has access to this new production instance. The projected cost for this is $549 per month per additional production instance. For example, a service organization may decide to use the additional production instance to segregate a client's data.

▶ **Additional non-production instance**—An organization may elect to purchase additional non-production instances for activities such as development, testing, or demonstrations. The cost for a non-production instance is $150 per month for each additional non-production instance. This comes as a great relief for organizations that require additional instances but do not want to purchase full production instances.

▶ **Additional storage**—For each additional 20 licensed users, an organization is granted 2.5GB, up to a maximum of 995GB total, at no charge. However, if the organization wants to purchase more storage than allocated, it can do so at $9.99 per gigabyte.

TIP

If an organization has 25 or more Professional user subscription licenses (USLs), it is entitled to 1 free non-production instance.

Figure 4.9 shows the options available.

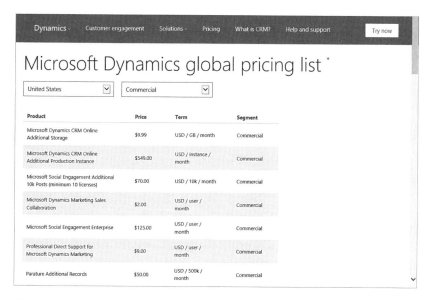

FIGURE 4.9   Optional add-on features for CRM Online.

NOTE

For a complete and current list of options available, see www.microsoft.com/en-us/dynamics/pricing-list.aspx.

New License Paradigm

The new license levels and features are part of a shift in licensing for Microsoft:

- ▶ **Multitier model**—Organizations have flexibility to license the right level of functionality for every user; it is no longer one-size-fits-all.

- ▶ **Parity between offerings**—Now there are consistent multitier license offerings for Online CRM and On-Premises CRM.

- ▶ **Mobile access**—Mobile access for Windows, Android, and iOS devices is included with each license at no additional charge.

- ▶ **Non-production instances**—Non-production instances provide better support for organizations with non-production needs.

▶ **Updated EA (Enterprise Agreement) availability**—Microsoft offers favorable terms for license transitions from On-Premises to Online.

▶ **Flexible premium support offerings**—Microsoft offers several different levels of premium support for each Online client.

Signing Up for CRM 2016 Online

Microsoft has made the signup process for Microsoft Dynamics CRM Online fast and almost effortless. The signup process only requires a small amount of information, which is covered in this section. In only a few minutes, an organization is provisioned and ready to start using Dynamics CRM Online. Getting started involves four basic steps:

1. Provision an Office 365 account.

2. Configure additional users.

3. Grant security roles to users.

4. Manage your CRM Online subscription.

CRM Online Provisioning Process

Provisioning an Office 365 account means setting up the portal used for Microsoft's Office 365 and CRM Online administration. This section covers the step-by-step process to provision a new CRM trial account using Office 365, add users, perform initial CRM configuration, and grant security roles:

1. Go to www.microsoft.com/en-us/dynamics/crm-free-trial-overview.aspx, where you see a web page similar to is the one shown in Figure 4.10.

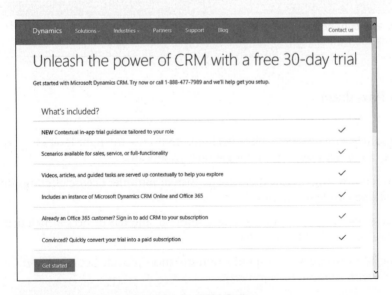

FIGURE 4.10   30-day free trial for CRM Online.

2. Click the Get Started button.

3. On the signup page, fill out the requested information, as shown in Figure 4.11. Be sure to set the organization size to greater than 5, or the trial won't be created. Key points include the following:

▶ **Business Email Address**—Use a real email account. A helpful link will be sent to this address, allowing you to log in again in the future.

▶ **Company Name**—This will be your default subdomain used to directly access your site. You might want to aim for the short version of your company name (for example, http://mycompanyname.crm.dyanamics.com).

▶ **User ID**—This will be the default administrator for the new organization, as shown in Figure 4.12. It will set you up with an @companyname.onmicrosoft .com address. The recommendation here is to use administrator or admin.

FIGURE 4.11   30-day free trial signup for CRM Online.

FIGURE 4.12   Creating a new user for CRM Online.

4. Next you are prompted to select Text Me or Call Me and enter a phone number, as shown in Figure 4.13.

FIGURE 4.13   Alternate access methods for CRM Online.

▶ At this point, a screen displays, much like the one in Figure 4.14. The provisioning process takes between 5 and 15 minutes. When the provisioning process is complete, you are ready to perform some initial setup.

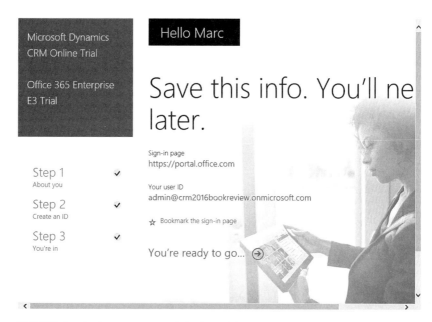

FIGURE 4.14   In-process provisioning of CRM Online.

5. At the top of the screen, as shown in Figure 4.15, click the CRM link.

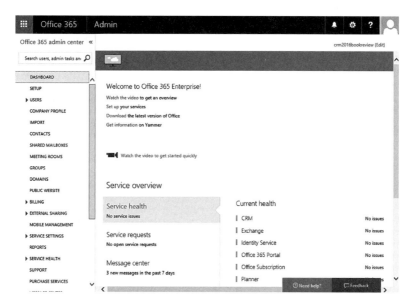

FIGURE 4.15   Office 365 Admin Portal in CRM Online.

TIP

After you do this initial setup, clicking the CRM link takes you directly into CRM.

6. As shown in Figure 4.16, set the purpose (Sales, Customer Service, or Both) of your new CRM Online site, the currency, and the base language. The default is based on the country you selected when you signed up. When you are done with these selections, click Finish to start the last step in the setup process.

CAUTION

Once the base currency is set, it can't be changed. However, Microsoft Dynamics CRM supports multiple currencies, so you can install other currencies later. See Chapter 22, "Customizing Entities," for more information on how to install currencies.

7. In the provisioning page that appears (see Figure 4.17), watch the video introduction to CRM if you are relatively new to CRM and this is your first organization. When the setup is complete, you see a button allowing you to launch CRM. When you launch CRM, make sure that you add a link for your CRM site to your favorites.

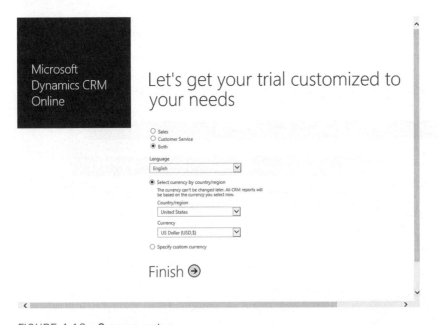

FIGURE 4.16   Currency setup.

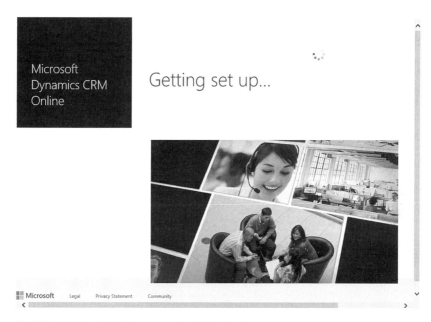

FIGURE 4.17   Finalizing setup for CRM Online.

Congratulations, you have provisioned your CRM organization! Clicking Launch CRM Online takes you to the default screen for CRM, as shown in Figure 4.18.

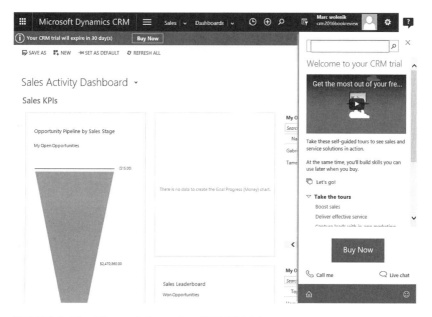

FIGURE 4.18   Microsoft Dynamics CRM 2016 home page.

Adding and Setting Up Additional Users

Adding new users to CRM Online differs a little from adding users to CRM On-Premises. From the Office 365 Admin Portal you can add users individually or in bulk. Follow these steps to add them individually:

1. If the Office 365 Admin Portal (or starting at http://portal.microsoftonline.com), go to Users > Active Users and then click + to get to the screen shown in Figure 4.19. You must be a global administrator or user management administrator to access this function.

2. When the Office 365 Admin Portal asks for basic information about the new user, fill out the Display Name and User Name fields, which are required, as well as the other fields (see Figure 4.20).

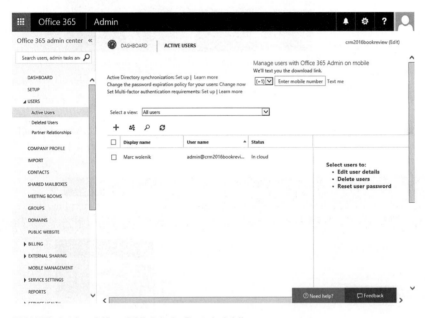

FIGURE 4.19   Office 365 Admin Portal: Adding new users.

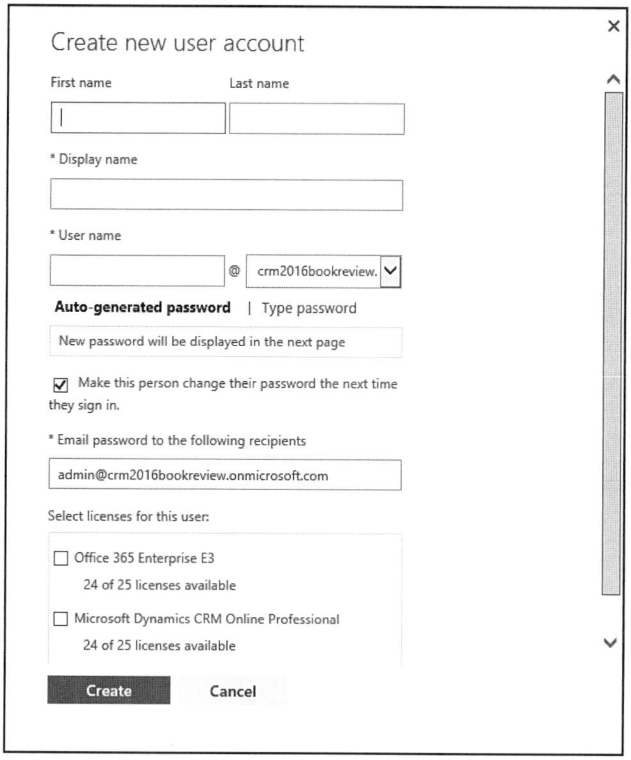

FIGURE 4.20   Adding new user details.

NOTE

The administrator right in Office 365 or Active Directory is not the same as the CRM System Administrator role.

3. Select the check box Make This Person Change Their Password the Next Time They Sign In and fill in the person's email address so that an email with the new temporary password will be sent to the user.

4. Assign a license or licenses to this user, as shown in Figure 4.21. A count of the licenses is displayed for each option.

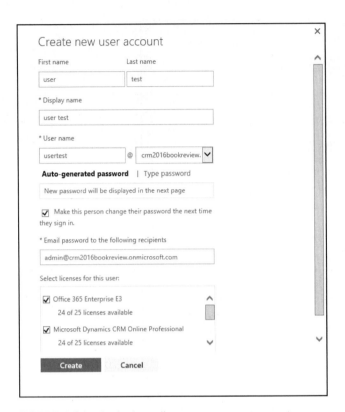

FIGURE 4.21   Assigning a license.

5. Click Create to create the user. When the process is complete, the username and a temporary password are will be displayed, as shown in Figure 4.22. The user will be able to access CRM after one or more security roles are assigned to this user.

▶ For details on how to add security roles to users, **SEE CHAPTER 22**.

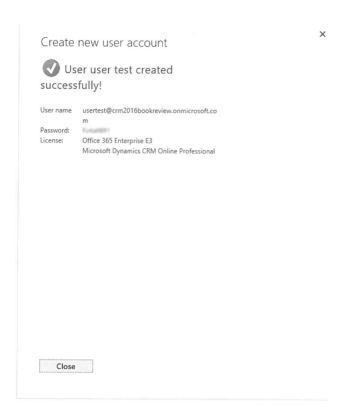

FIGURE 4.22   New user setup confirmation.

Managing Users

After you as a global administrator or user management administrator create users, you can edit existing users. From the Office 365 Admin Portal, click the Admin link in the upper-right of the screen (right next to the link for CRM). A list of Active Users appears, as shown in Figure 4.23.

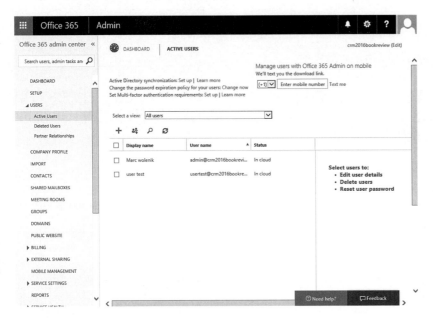

FIGURE 4.23   List of active users.

In the active users list in the Office 365 Admin Portal, you can manage the user population in CRM. The four options above the grid are as follows:

▶ **Add User**—This option repeats the process outlined earlier to add additional users on a case-by-case basis and is the most commonly used of the four options.

▶ **Bulk Add**—This option allows you to add multiple new users via an upload.

▶ **Filter**—This option applies a filter to display only a subset of the users listed.

▶ **Search**—This option allows you to search for a specific user account.

Editing an Individual User

When you click the blue text of the display name for the user you want to edit, you see a small link to the right, with three possible options. The first icon, the pencil, allows you to edit information about this user. Next to it is a trash can icon for deleting the user. The Reset Passwords link allows you to quickly reset the user's password. Figure 4.24 shows how to edit a user.

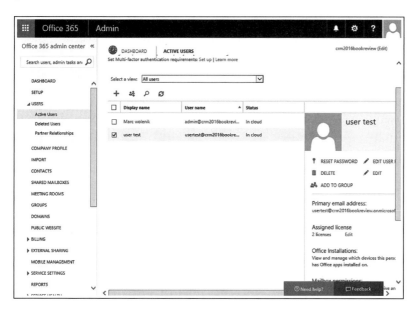

FIGURE 4.24   Editing a user in the Office 365 Admin Portal.

Bulk Adding Users

Microsoft Dynamics CRM Online allows you to add users in bulk by using a file upload. On the Users and Group page in the Office 365 Admin Portal, you can click the Bulk Add Users icon to get to the web page shown in Figure 4.25. CRM provides sample files to illustrate the correct file format to use.

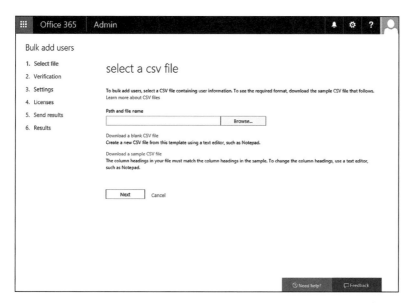

FIGURE 4.25   Office 365 Admin Portal bulk load users.

In a federated environment, the users from an organization's active directory can be synchronized automatically, which allows for local changes to be synchronized with the cloud service.

Managing Your Subscription

Few differences exist between CRM Online and CRM On-Premises in terms of managing your subscription. However, two areas specific to CRM Online are important:

▶ Subscription management

▶ Resources in use

Both features are available in the administration page in CRM. To get to the administration page, follow these steps:

1. Click Microsoft Dynamics CRM at the top of the page.

2. Select Settings > Administration.

Figure 4.26 shows the standard administration functions you see at this point.

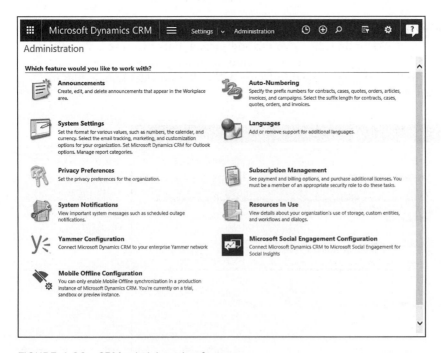

FIGURE 4.26   CRM administration features.

If you click the Subscription Management icon shown in Figure 4.27, you end up at the Office 365 Admin Portal. As shown in Figure 4.28, you can select Billing > Subscriptions on this page.

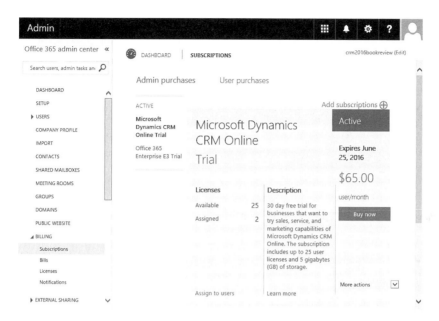

FIGURE 4.27   Office 365 Admin Portal subscription and license management.

You can then purchase a license, add users to an existing subscription, purchase additional storage, and view billing history. Here you can also access additional privacy and security supplements.

Many users may not have to view the resources in use under normal circumstances, as this is typically reserved for administration and billing purposes.

It is a good practice to regularly (perhaps monthly) check storage growth in your CRM organization because Microsoft does not automatically allocate additional storage when you run out. Figure 4.29 shows the resources in use for a sample organization. If you exceed the limit, you will not able to change or update your existing data until you make space or purchase additional storage. Microsoft sends a warning at 80% full, but you should not depend on that email; the space can fill quickly under certain circumstances.

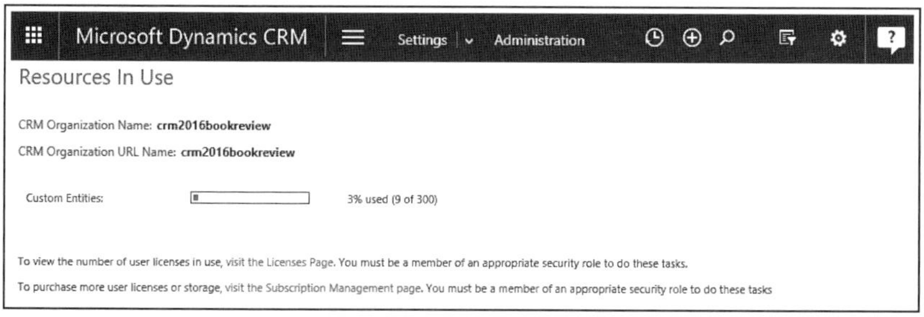

Microsoft Dynamics CRM	≡	Settings ∨	Administration						

Resources In Use

CRM Organization Name: **crm2016bookreview**
CRM Organization URL Name: **crm2016bookreview**

Custom Entities:	▇▁▁▁▁▁	3% used (9 of 300)

To view the number of user licenses in use, visit the Licenses Page. You must be a member of an appropriate security role to do these tasks.
To purchase more user licenses or storage, visit the Subscription Management page. You must be a member of an appropriate security role to do these tasks

FIGURE 4.28   CRM resources in use.

Checking System Health Status

Within the Office 365 Admin Portal, you can log in and check the health of your organization and the Microsoft services. As shown in Figure 4.29, the Service Health page provides a quick overview of the organization and the service offerings from Microsoft.

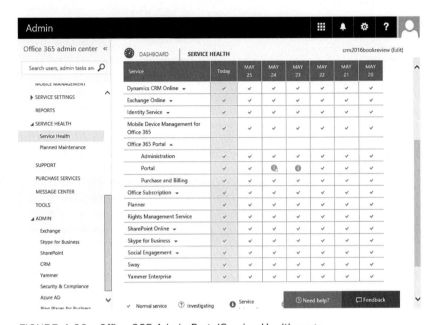

FIGURE 4.29   Office 365 Admin PortalService Health page.

Adding a Production or Development Instance

Microsoft now includes the option for users to add additional development or production instances to the Online environment. By default, users are provided with the following with every Online subscription:

▶ One production instance

▶ One non-production instance (if there are at least 25 users)

▶ 5GB of storage

Additional instances and storage can be purchased directly from Microsoft. Prices are typically quoted on a per-month basis.

> **NOTE**
>
> The prices are subject to change. To see the current pricing, visit http://crm.dynamics.com.

To add additional instances to your Dynamics CRM Online instance, follow these steps:

1. Navigate to http://portal.office.com.

2. Enter your username and password to go to the Office 365 Admin Portal interface (see Figure 4.30).

3. Select Purchase Services from the left-side navigation area.

4. Navigate down to your Microsoft CRM Online instance and select Buy Now. If you are still within the initial 30 days, you see Microsoft Dynamics CRM Online Trial (see Figure 4.31), and if you are not on trial anymore, you see Microsoft Dynamics CRM Online.

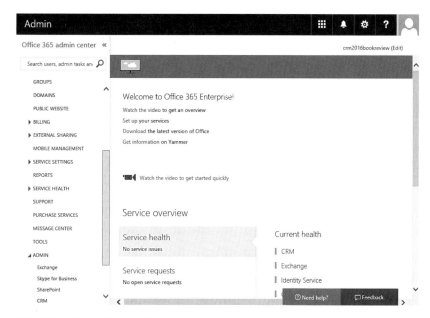

FIGURE 4.30   Office 365 Admin Portal interface.

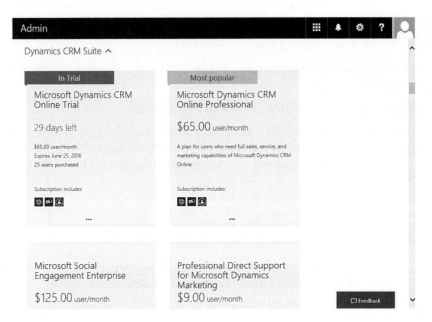

FIGURE 4.31   Purchasing more services.

▶ The purchase options appear, as shown in Figure 4.32. You have the option to purchase one or more of the following, at the prices shown at the website:

▶ User licenses

▶ Non-production instances

▶ Production instances

▶ Additional storage

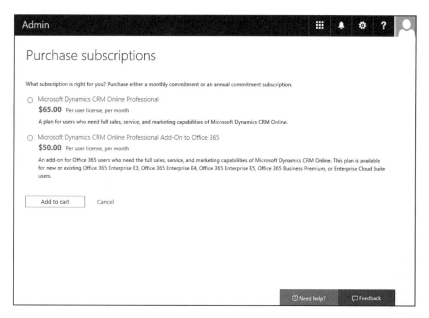

FIGURE 4.32   Office 365 order interface for additional Dynamics CRM products.

5. Select the purchase option you want, and navigate to the checkout to complete for the purchase for your new services. The new services are immediately available for use and can be modified through this interface.

Summary

This chapter covers the CRM Online environment, the infrastructure and security provided by Microsoft, licensing, and how to sign up and administer CRM Online. The administration of CRM through the Office 365 interface includes managing and installing updates as well as installing preferred solutions. In addition, you provision and manage the instance environments.

The free 30-day trial and low barrier to entry provide an ideal way for your organization to get started with Microsoft Dynamics CRM 2016. In addition, the rapid tempo of updates provided by Microsoft for CRM Online eases the burden on your IT team and keeps you focused on your business.

CHAPTER 5

Navigation

The interface of Microsoft Dynamics CRM 2016 has been modified to be much cleaner, and it is easier than ever before to locate sections and find information.

The interface still lets users navigate from left to right, and the intuitive design includes large buttons for each of the various sections. However, after selecting a major group like Sales or Service, you now see a more "sticky" menu with expanded menu items. In addition, the options across the top now include a clock icon for accessing recently opened pages, a + icon for quickly adding information, a magnifying glass icon for systemwide quick searches, and the Advanced Find button.

NOTE

The flow navigation of Microsoft Dynamics CRM has been a key differentiator from other CRM systems. This modern design allows users to easily navigate across mobile devices with its large and easy-to-click buttons.

Figure 5.1 shows the options that are presented to users when they first navigate to the application.

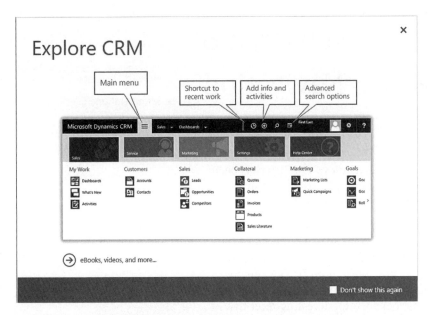

FIGURE 5.1   Microsoft Dynamics CRM welcome screen.

TIP

You can force the welcome screen to always appear, or you can globally turn it off by selecting Settings > Administration > System Settings and then, in the General tab, checking or unchecking the Set Whether Users See Welcome Screen check box. In addition, you choose to always display the welcome screen by selecting See Welcome Screen from the gear icon in the navigation bar.

How to Navigate

In earlier versions of Microsoft Dynamics CRM and in some other similar office products (Microsoft Outlook, for example), the navigation bar was located on the left side of the screen. Figure 5.2 shows what the navigation screen looked like for Microsoft Dynamics CRM 2011.

FIGURE 5.2   Microsoft Dynamics CRM 2011 main navigation.

The navigation bar in Microsoft Dynamics CRM 2016 is located across the top of the screen, and it contains five main areas:

▶ Sales

▶ Service

▶ Marketing

▶ Settings

▶ Help Center

You can access these options by selecting the hamburger icon near the top of the page (see Figure 5.3).

FIGURE 5.3   Microsoft Dynamics CRM 2016 navigation bar.

Figure 5.4 shows this icon selected.

FIGURE 5.4   Opening the Microsoft Dynamics CRM 2016 navigation bar.

If you select any of the five areas from the navigation bar, corresponding options appear just below, fully expanded. (In previous versions of Dynamics CRM, you had to either manually scroll or, with a mobile or touchscreen display, sweep across your screen to see the subareas available). In addition, the navigation bar changes to reflect the new focus that you have selected.

In previous versions of Microsoft Dynamics CRM, when you selected a major group (such as Sales or Service), you were automatically taken to the dashboards for that area. Now you can select which subgroup you wish to navigate to after selecting the major group.

> **TIP**
>
> It might seem as if several options are repeated (for example, with whatever main area you select, you always see Accounts), but some actions can only be found by navigating to their parent areas. As an example, the only way to navigate to Quick Campaigns is to select Marketing first. Similarly, if you want to navigate to the Service Calendar, you must select Service.

The drop-down arrow in the navigation bar is the Recently Viewed option. When you select this arrow, you see any records that have recently been accessed. In Figure 5.5, for example, the drop-down shows three case records that have recently been viewed, and you can select one to easily navigate to it from here.

FIGURE 5.5 Microsoft Dynamics CRM 2016 Recently Viewed drop-down.

In addition to accessing recently viewed files through the drop-down arrow, there is still a global recently accessed pages, which you find by clicking the clock icon in the navigation bar. Figure 5.6 shows what happens when you select that icon. Notice that this option lists many more entities to choose from than the drop-down arrow's list of recently viewed files.

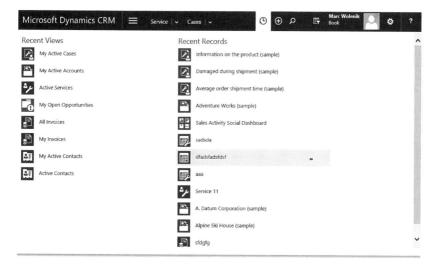

FIGURE 5.6 Microsoft Dynamics CRM 2016 Global Recently Viewed icon.

If you click the + icon, the ribbon bar expands to show you what can be created, as shown in Figure 5.7.

FIGURE 5.7   Microsoft Dynamics CRM 2016 + icon.

This option is handy because it allows you to create a new record of your selected type and supply the user with a quick create form, as shown in Figure 5.8.

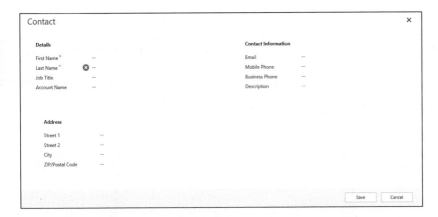

FIGURE 5.8   Microsoft Dynamics CRM 2016 quick create form for a Contact entity.

You can customize the quick create form based on your business needs.

▶ For more information on customizing quick create forms, **SEE CHAPTER 22,** "Customizing Entities."

To the right of the + icon is the quick search option, which looks like a magnifying glass. Here you can enter any criteria for systemwide searching. Finally, the Advanced Find icon, which allows you to do more complicated searched.

At the end of the navigation bar you see your name (which you can click to sign out) and an avatar where you can add your picture easily by simply clicking once on the avatar and uploading an image. Next is a Settings icon (the gear), followed by the question mark icon, which takes you to Help. The Settings icon allows you to navigate to the following:

▶ Options

▶ Apps for Dynamics CRM

▶ See welcome screen

▶ About

▶ Privacy Statement

Finally, when you are actually working with a record, a new option appears that shows the record and related information for that record. Figure 5.9 shows the common records associated with a selected case. In this situation, the case record Average Order Shipment Time is selected. Notice that the top navigation has that title (truncated somewhat) next to the drop-down arrow for cases. This shows that a case record is selected and provides the name of that record.

FIGURE 5.9   Microsoft Dynamics CRM 2016 related records.

> **NOTE**
>
> Unlike in Microsoft Dynamics CRM 2013, there is no navigation tour in CRM 2016. However, there is a link at the bottom of the welcome screen that says eBooks, Videos and More. Navigating from that link takes you to a navigation tour option available from Microsoft.

Saving Your Data

When working with Microsoft Dynamics CRM 2016, you'll notice that there is no save menu option. Instead, the form you're working on now auto saves by default.

> **NOTE**
>
> You can turn off auto save for the entire system at Settings > Administration > System Settings. At the top of the General tab is an option to enable auto save for all forms.

Auto save occurs as follows:

▶ Every 30 seconds

▶ When you navigate off the record

Although there is no administrative way to selectively turn off auto save (for example, on the account form but not on the contacts form), it is possible to use a script to disable the auto save on all forms. Simply load this script to the OnSave event of the form to turn off auto save:

```
function preventAutoSave(econtext) {
var eventArgs = econtext.getEventArgs();
if (eventArgs.getSaveMode() == 70) {
eventArgs.preventDefault();
}
}
```

TIP

In the event that you add data and then click the Back button, getSaveMode might need to be checked for both 2 and 70 instead of just 70. Be sure to test a number of scenarios with your system to verify expected functionality.

NOTE

With auto save, if another user is working on the same form at the same time, any new data is be presented to the other user automatically when the next auto save occurs.

If you want to manually execute a save on a record (without waiting the 30 seconds or navigating to a new form to trigger an auto save), just click the small disk icon at the bottom right of the page (see Figure 5.10).

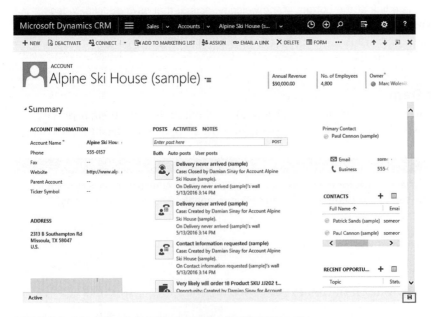

FIGURE 5.10   Microsoft Dynamics CRM 2016 save option.

Unlike in previous versions of Dynamics CRM, new records now have a save icon. (Previous versions required that users manually save new records before the save button would appear.)

It is important to note the following conditions with auto save:

▶ Auditing captures every save as a separate transaction. This differs significantly from previous behavior, in which auditing captured all the changes on a form at once.

▶ Any programmatic logic that runs when a record is saved (plug-ins, workflows, or integration logic) fires upon auto save. This results in significantly increased overhead if the logic is not designed to run with auto save. So give serious consideration to the design of such logic before implementing the default auto save feature.

The previous point about auto save firing resulting in new overhead cannot be overstated. A classic example is an integration of CRM and ERP (Enterprise Resource Planning) that results in traffic to and from the ERP via middleware. Prior to the introduction of auto save with Dynamics CRM 2013, updates would happen when users saved and closed a record. Now updates can happen every 30 seconds (or sooner), which is much faster than a typical user would work with a form. As a result, integration jobs now have more traffic, which can result in delayed or missed communication.

Menu Options

When users navigate to a record, they are presented with a variety of menu options at the top of the page. These options are dynamic and varied, depending on what the record allows or what it has been customized to include. Figure 5.11 shows the menu options for a new case, and Figure 5.12 shows the menu options for an existing contact.

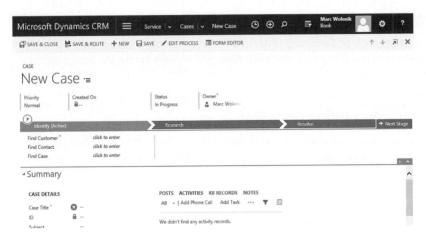

FIGURE 5.11   Microsoft Dynamics CRM 2016 menu options for a new case.

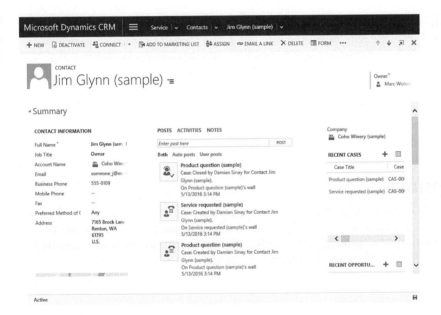

FIGURE 5.12   Microsoft Dynamics CRM 2016 menu options for an existing contact.

Notice that the menu options shown in these two figures are different.

As previously stated, the available options are varied and depend on the following conditions:

▶ Record type

▶ Customizations

▶ Permissions

In the case of the last option, it is possible for some users to see the option Form (as shown in Figure 5.12), while other users (those who do not have the ability to customize the system) do not see that option in the menu.

The available menu options continue to the end of the page, and unlike in previous versions where only the first five menu options were shown, they now continue to the width of the screen. If there are more options than can be shown, you get an ellipsis (...) that acts as a drop-down option (see Figure 5.13).

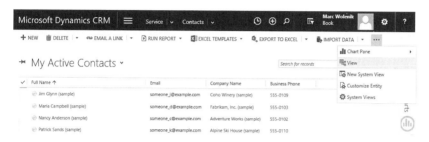

FIGURE 5.13   Microsoft Dynamics CRM 2016 ... menu options.

Figure 5.13 shows that the ellipsis is dynamic, depending on the entity you are working with as well as the permissions of the user. (For example, this menu shows an option for customizing if the user has customization permissions.)

▶ For more information about customizing forms, **SEE CHAPTER 22**.

Common Functions

The following are the most common options on the dynamic submenu when you're working on main (grouped) entities (such as Account or Contact):

▶ New

▶ Delete

▶ Email a link

▶ Run Report

▶ Excel Templates

▶ Export to Excel

▶ Import Data

▶ Chart Pane

▶ View

▶ New System Views

When you drill down into an existing account or contact record, the menu changes and allows you to perform additional functions, using these menu choices:

▶ New

▶ Deactivate

▶ Connect

▶ Add to Marketing List

▶ Assign

▶ Email a Link

▶ Delete

▶ Form

▶ Add to Queue (cases only)

▶ Queue Item Details (cases only)

▶ Share

▶ Share Secured Fields (might not be present on all entities)

▶ Follow

▶ Run Workflow

▶ Start Dialog

▶ Switch Process

▶ Word Templates

▶ Run Report

NOTE

Remember that the options listed here do not necessarily reflect what users will see or, more importantly, what they *should* see. This book shows what you see if you have full system administrator access, and if you don't have that kind of access, you will not see all the same options. For example, only those who have permissions to customize forms will see the Form button.

Ribbons in Outlook

The usage of Microsoft Dynamics CRM 2016 in Microsoft Outlook has not changed substantially. Figure 5.14 shows the Outlook interface for CRM, with its familiar look and feel.

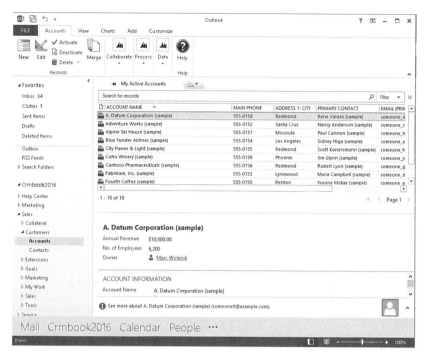

FIGURE 5.14   Microsoft Dynamics Outlook with Microsoft Dynamics CRM 2016 data.

Note that when you're working with a record that you've opened from Outlook, as shown in Figure 5.15, there is no ability to "go up" to the main application (though you can always navigate to related records by drilling down) because the drop-down arrow is missing from the top ribbon bar.

TIP

To get full navigation functionality, press Ctrl+N, and the record you're currently working in opens in a new window.

When you're working with records launched from Outlook, there is no Home tab (typically located in the upper left of the ribbon menu). Instead, the experience is designed specifically to keep you on the record that you selected.

▶ For more information about working with Dynamics CRM in Outlook, **SEE CHAPTER 19,** "Outlook Configuration."

TIP

You can click the small icon in the top-right corner of a record launched from Outlook to open the record in a new window.

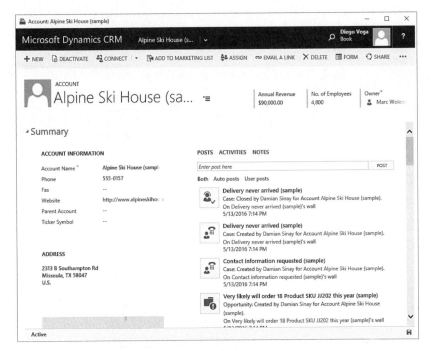

FIGURE 5.15   Microsoft Dynamics Record view, as launched from Outlook.

Summary

This chapter shows how to use Microsoft Dynamics CRM 2016 and where to find specific features.

Remember that the dynamic submenu has different options, depending on whether you're on one of the main areas (such as accounts) or on a single record (such as a contact). Also keep in mind that when you use Outlook with CRM, you have persistent navigation. Finally, when making customizations to the ribbon menu, you are performing edits to the sitemap. There are several tools available to do this; the most popular one is available at http://xrmtoolbox.codeplex.com. This concept is explained further in Chapter 22.

Working with Customers

Customers are defined in several different ways. When working in a conventional environment, customers are individuals or organizations that you have conducted business with. When considering an xRM deployment of Microsoft Dynamics CRM, your customers are usually whatever the x designation is. Examples might include the following:

▶ Vendors

▶ Employees

▶ Recruits

▶ Grantee

▶ Patients

▶ Suppliers

> **NOTE**
>
> An xRM deployment requires a thorough understanding of the base entities in Microsoft Dynamics CRM. We recommend that you thoroughly read this book in its entirety to gain the required level of understanding before attempting a buildout of an xRM deployment. Knowing when, where, and why to use native entities versus custom ones can help you create a deployment that's significantly easier to support and maintain in the long term.

▶ For more information about xRM deployment, review Chapter 3, "Customizing and Designing Applications Within Dynamics CRM 2016 (xRM)."

When working with customers in Microsoft Dynamics CRM, you become familiar with two entities: Account and

Contact. Both of these entities can contain records that organizations may consider customers. In fact, when associating parent/child records with customers—as on a contact form under Company Name (previously Parent Customer)—you select either an Account entity or a Contact entity. Therefore, you can consider customers in Microsoft Dynamics CRM to be equal to either of these entities.

TIP

It may be helpful to rename the Account entity Company and the Contact entity Customer. You can easily do this by editing the display name of each under Settings and Customization.

▶ For more information about settings and customization, **SEE CHAPTER 22**, "Customizing the System."

We often hear customers ask whether leads can be considered customers in Microsoft Dynamics CRM. It is important to remember that leads are *potential* customers—not actual customers. Although we have in rare cases seen the Lead entity used for customers, it is not common.

NOTE

Microsoft Dynamics CRM 2016 does *not* require a reference to an existing customer (that is, an account or a contact) when working with opportunities. You can create "orphan" opportunities and associate them with customers at a future date if required.

▶ **SEE CHAPTER 7**, "Working with Sales," for more details on working with opportunities and leads.

Working with Accounts

In general, users should consider accounts as businesses or organizations. Some accounts have many contacts associated with them (such as a normal customer that has two dozen employees with whom you have contact on some level). Other accounts have no contacts associated with them (the U.S. government, for example).

You can use the Account entity not only for businesses you sell to but also for vendors you purchase from, to track contacts that work for the vendor.

Finally, although not generally common, another use for the Account entity is to track competitors. This situation arises if you have a lot of information about competitors (such as individual employee data) or if the existing Competitor entity (found in the Sales area) in Microsoft Dynamics CRM is not sufficient for your needs.

The most common types for the Account entity can be found in the Relationship Type drop-down list (see Figure 6.1):

▶ Competitor

▶ Consultant

▶ Customer

▶ Investor

▶ Partner

▶ Influencer

▶ Press

▶ Prospect

▶ Reseller

▶ Supplier

▶ Vendor

▶ Other

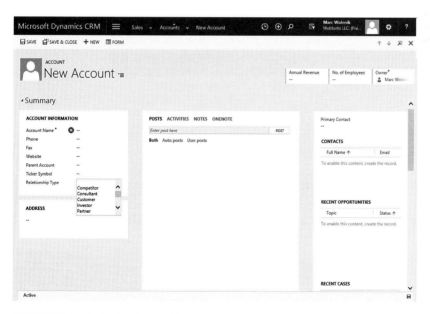

FIGURE 6.1   Default relationship types shown on the Account form.

NOTE

The Relationship Type field is not on the Account form by default in Dynamics CRM 2016; it has been added here to show the types available out of the box. (But keep in mind that you can easily update/manage the relationship types.) For more information about adding fields to forms, see Chapter 22.

TIP

We don't usually recommend using the Account entity to track competitors. Instead, we recommend augmenting the out-of-the-box Competitor entity found in the Sales area with customizations, as necessary, and using it. When you close opportunities in Microsoft Dynamics CRM, you have the option to tie lost opportunities to only the Competitor entity (and not Account or Contact). Therefore, you effectively lose visibility into competitors' win/loss metrics related to your opportunities when you don't use the Competitor entity.

Required Fields for Accounts

When working with accounts, only two fields are required by default: Account Name and Owner. (However, you can easily customize the form to make other fields required.) Because Account Name is the first field shown on the default account list view (see Figure 6.2), it is important to be descriptive here. The Owner field is prefilled with the user who created the record, so even though it is required, it has a value by default. You can change this by selecting another user in the system, if desired.

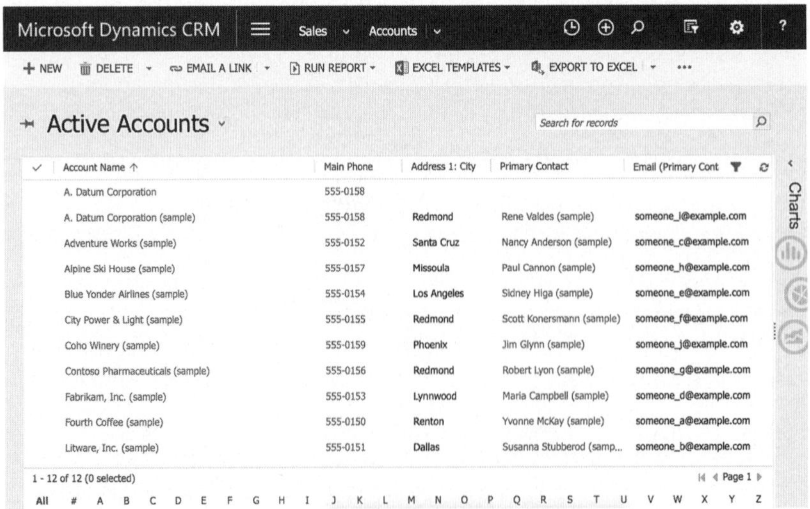

FIGURE 6.2   Active accounts, listed by Account Name.

NOTE

As with the previous version of Dynamics CRM, you can assign record ownership to not just users but also teams. This has a significant impact in that multiple users' rights to records can be set or shared by using the Owner field.

TIP

Be sure that the user has permission to view a record. If not, you receive a security warning prompt indicating that the user doesn't have the necessary security permissions to access the record, in which case you cannot assign it to him or her.

To add a new Account entity, navigate to Sales, select Accounts, and then click the + (for new) on the command bar. The new account form opens.

Besides the two required fields previously indicated, the following are a few of the recommended fields to consider when building Account entity records:

▶ **Account Number (must be added to the form)**—This free-form entry field can be used to enter any number or alphanumeric combination. This field can be tied to existing enterprise resource planning (ERP), accounting, or other systems for quick-and-easy reference. In that case, we recommend setting the value to read-only or similarly controlling it so that it can be modified only through an approved business process.

CAUTION

As noted earlier for the Account Name field, duplicate entries are not checked on the Account Number field by default. Therefore, unless you have a duplicate detection rule running here, it is possible for a user to enter the same account number multiple times.

▶ **Parent Account**—The Parent Account field is used when the account rolls up to another account. An example of this is a customer that has several different business units that report to a corporate entity.

▶ **Primary Contact**—The Primary Contact field ties to the Contact record. This is not a required association, but the primary contact is shown on the Account quick view by default and can make identifying and working with similar accounts easier.

▶ **Currency**—The Currency field enables users to select the primary currency that the entity deals with. You must select a currency option here in order to work with other attributes of the form (such as the Annual Revenue field on the Details tab).

> **NOTE**
>
> The currency options shown are only those that the system administrator has set within the system. Note that the Currency field automatically populates with the default currency specified when CRM was first installed. However, you can change it as required on an account-by-account basis.

▶ For more information about currency, **SEE CHAPTER 17**, "Settings."

▶ **Phone and Fax**—These free-form entry fields accept any alphanumeric value. Because any value is accepted here, you might want to enforce entry standards by using business rules or scripting.

▶ For more information about adding custom data validation, **SEE CHAPTER 25**, "Plug-ins."

▶ **Website**—The Website field accepts any value and automatically formats it as a URL by prepending the entered value with http://. Users can click the entered value to go directly to the website, which opens in a new window, or a new tab, depending on the browser settings.

> **TIP**
>
> When you are working with the Website field, if the entered value already has http://, Dynamics CRM does not add it again.

▶ **Credit Hold and Payment Terms**—Users can select these fields when setting up the account, and you can change them during the account's life.

> **NOTE**
>
> When integrating CRM into an existing ERP or other accounting system, the fields in the Billing Information section typically receive special attention. For example, field-level security is important for viewing or modifying data.

▶ **Credit Limit**—As with to the Annual Revenue field, you must select a currency value before you can enter a number in the Credit Limit field.

▶ **Contact Methods**—When you select this field, the system defaults all values to Allow. This field is extremely helpful when you're doing bulk activities such as email campaigns because you can exclude accounts that do not want to be contacted by specified methods.

When working with the Contact Methods field, if you have selected Do Not Allow for email, you get the error message shown in Figure 6.3 when you try to send the account an email from CRM.

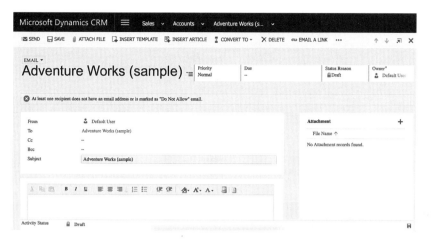

FIGURE 6.3   Email with the Do Not Allow error shown.

> **NOTE**
>
> Although the system prevents you from sending an email from CRM to an account that has Do Not Allow set for email in CRM, nothing prevents users from sending email to that account directly from Outlook (provided that the email is not tracked).

In addition, the system recommends the following fields in the header section, located near the Owner field:

▶ **Annual Revenue**—The Annual Revenue field is a free-form field that requires you to enter the base currency for the account. If you leave it blank, it auto-populates with the default base currency. If you have selected a currency and entered a value here and then try to change the currency, you get an error message saying that you must remove the entered value before setting the currency again.

▶ **No. of Employees**—This field is used for metrics related to the potential size of the account.

Top Menu Options for Accounts

After you save a record, you are presented with new navigation bar options, as shown in Figure 6.4, which you access using the drop-down arrow near the newly saved account name in the navigation bar. Here is where you go to work with related records and view record particulars such as audit history.

FIGURE 6.4   Navigation bar options for the Account entity.

By default, the navigation bar provides the following options:

► **Activities**—Adding new activities to the account

► **Social Profiles**—Capturing social identities for Twitter, Facebook, etc.

► **Contacts**—Associating additional contacts

► **Documents**—Integrating OneNote and SharePoint for document management

► **Connections**—Creating associations to other objects within CRM

► **Audit History**—Showing the audit history of a record

► **Entitlements**—Showing whether the customer has this service option

► **Opportunities**—Showing associated opportunities

► **Cases**—Showing related cases

► **Marketing Lists**—Showing marketing lists related to the account

Contacts Associated with Accounts

The Contact area shows the contacts that are associated with the selected account. This is different from the regular Contact area, which has all contacts, regardless of whether they are associated with an account.

By default, no contacts are associated with a new account, and you have to add either a new contact or an existing contact. To do so, click the + (for adding a new record) on the command bar, and the quick create form is load (see Figure 6.5). On this form, you can perform the functions required to add or edit contacts associated with the account.

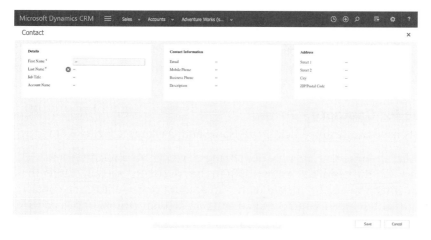

FIGURE 6.5   Adding a new contact to an account.

Working with Contacts

Contacts are usually individuals that are either customers or in some way related to an account. Although they aren't required to have a relationship with an account, they often do. An example of a contact without a relationship to an account might be a mail carrier, who you want to keep in the system so that all the employees can get information about him (such as his name or birth date; everyone should wish the mail carrier happy birthday!), but there might not be a reason to have the U.S. Postal Service as an account just for the mail carrier.

When creating/adding new contacts to the system, there are several easy methods:

▶ Navigate to Contacts in the navigation bar (in the Sales, Marketing, or Service sections) and click +. This method enables you to select the account name (if applicable).

▶ In the Accounts form (as explained earlier in this chapter), select Contacts > New Contact. This method prepopulates the account name information for you. (The address information and currency information are populated from the account that spawned the new contact form, and therefore this method is the recommended method.)

▶ In the navigation bar, click + and then select Contact.

TIP

Keep in mind that creating a new contact in the quick create form does not prepopulate the Account Name field (for the parent customer).

Required Fields for Contacts

By default, contacts have two required fields: Full Name and Owner (see Figure 6.6).

Account Name is also an important field: By populating it, you create a relationship between the contact and the customer. As discussed in the "Accounts" section, earlier in this chapter, if you enter a value in this field (either an account or a contact), the contact you're working with shows up as a contact (if you enter an account customer) related to that entry. In addition, this relationship facilitates the rollup of all information (activities, opportunities, quotes, orders, and so on) from the contact to the account, so you can get a consolidated view of all activities related to the account and associated contacts.

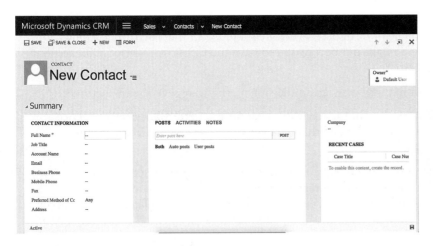

FIGURE 6.6   New contact interface.

As mentioned previously, in addition to setting Account Name, you should populate the other fields on this form as necessary because they all correlate to a contact in Microsoft Outlook.

> **TIP**
>
> Do not confuse the Phone field with Business Phone, Home Phone, or Mobile Phone—all of which are transferred to the Outlook contact form and vice versa. Phone does not appear in the Outlook contact form, so you can use this field as an extra field for a phone number or not use it at all. This is important because when you synchronize these contacts with Outlook contacts on a mobile device, you will not have the Phone field available—only Business Phone, Home Phone, and Mobile Phone.

The Currency field here has the same purpose as Currency for the Account entity, and it is explained earlier in this chapter.

Additional Fields for Contact Records

Some additional fields for contacts are invaluable when you're trying to develop a personal relationship. For example, the Personal information fields are of great benefit when you need to know salient details about a contact. The Personal section has fields for general information relevant to the contact that isn't likely to change (see Figure 6.7).

> **NOTE**
>
> Using the Birthday field gives you a great excuse for customer contact. Who wouldn't like to receive a call, an email, or a small gift from a vendor on his or her birthday?

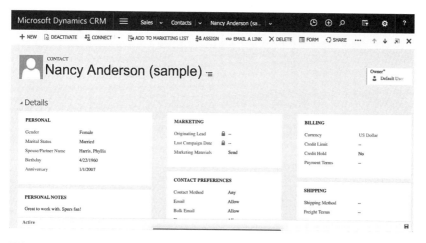

FIGURE 6.7   Contact Details tab.

General Information for Either Accounts or Contacts

The information discussed in this section applies to both the Account and Contact entity forms. With many of the entities in the system, some options are available only after the record is saved. The following options are available for the Account and Contact entities prior to saving (and completing the required fields):

▶ New (Lead, Opportunity, Account, and so on from the navigation bar)

▶ Save (on new records only; otherwise, there is a small disk icon in the lower right of the form that functions as a manual save option—though auto save is enabled by default)

▶ Save & Close (on new records only)

▶ Form

CAUTION

The Form option is the option to open the form in design view. We usually recommend that you avoid allowing this permission to most users; if you do, this option is removed from the interface.

You receive a warning prompt if you attempt to close a record after you have already started to enter data but not filled in required fields (for the Account entity, Account Name and Owner, and for the Contact entity, Last Name and Owner), as shown in Figure 6.8.

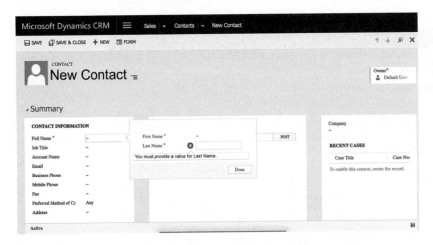

FIGURE 6.8   Error on trying to save when required fields are blank.

The options listed here are available after saving and are found in either the navigation bar or under the ellipsis, as shown in Figure 6.9:

▶ All options listed previously (but the save button has moved to the bottom-right corner)

▶ Delete

▶ Deactivate

▶ Assign

▶ Share

▶ Add to Marketing List

▶ Connect

▶ Run Report

▶ Run Workflow

▶ Start Dialog

▶ Relationship

▶ Follow

▶ Email a Link

▶ Form

▶ Word Templates

▶ All the options on the associated top navigation bar

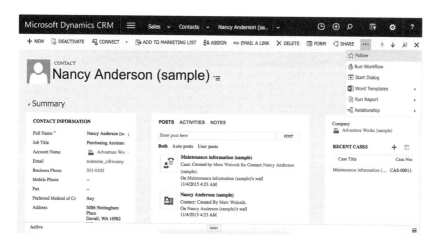

FIGURE 6.9   Contact options after saving.

If there doesn't appear to be any way to send an email or upload a document to an account or a Contact, check to make sure you've saved the record.

Account and Contact Reports

By default, the Account entity has the following reports associated with it:

▶ Account Overview

▶ Account Summary

▶ Products by Account

The Contact entity has just one report:

▶ Products by Contact

When you select any of these reports, it opens, displaying the account or contact you're working by default.

> ▶ **SEE CHAPTER 16**, "Reporting and Dashboards," for more information about reports.

More Addresses

More Addresses is a feature previously available in Dynamics CRM by default, but it has been removed from the base build of Microsoft Dynamics CRM 2016 and you need to configure the system to add it back. It is generally used when an account or a contact has multiple locations, such as different departments within an organization, different shipping addresses, or different primary addresses. The Address Name field (not the Address Type field) should differentiate them because it is displayed on the list view.

To add the more addresses back to the form, follow these steps:

1. Open an account record and select Form from the top command bar, as shown in Figure 6.10. The form opens in design mode, as shown in Figure 6.11.

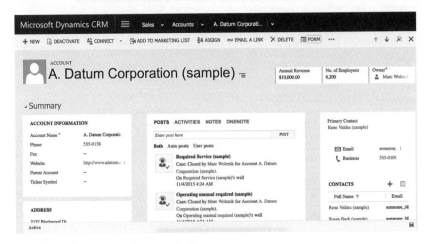

FIGURE 6.10   The Form option in the navigation bar.

FIGURE 6.11   The form in design view.

2. Select Navigation from the top menu bar. Notice that the right-side Field Explorer changes to Relationship Explorer, as shown in Figure 6.12.

FIGURE 6.12   Relationship Explorer view.

3. Select Addresses from the list and drag it over to the leftmost column under Common, as shown in Figure 6.13.

4. Click Save then Publish.

When you refresh the form and select the top navigation option for the account, you now see Addresses as part of the related records (see Figure 6.14).

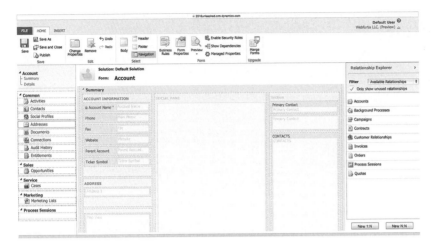

FIGURE 6.13   Addresses added to left-hand navigation area.

FIGURE 6.14   Addresses available in the top navigation bar.

> **NOTE**
>
> You can move over the other relationships in the Relationship Explorer (Quotes, Orders, Invoices, and so on) to have them displayed. Conversely, you can remove relationships by dragging them out of the Relationship Explorer.

Activities

You can select Activities in the top navigation bar to see all future events. Figure 6.15 shows the activities for a selected Account entity with the default view shown (in this case, Closed Activities).

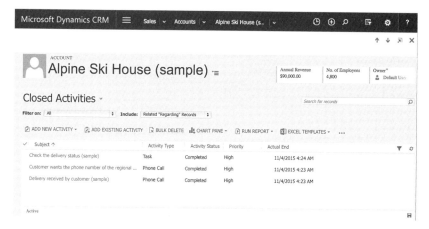

FIGURE 6.15   Account activities.

When a new Activity entity is created (either in CRM or in Outlook, provided that it is tracked to CRM), it is shown here until it is marked as closed.

> **CAUTION**
>
> Even if you set the date for something as being previous to today's date, the activity will remain open until it is marked as closed. One way to address this is to create a workflow that automatically closes all activities that have prior dates; however, by doing this, you risk closing items that should remain pending.

Common Closed Activities

After activities are marked as completed, they are shown under Closed Activities (refer to Figure 6.15). Closed Activities have limited properties and offer limited editing options because they become read-only after being marked as completed.

Connections

You can establish connections directly to an account or a contact record from the Connection section, and you can allow users to connect the record to any other entity type that doesn't have a relationship created. Figure 6.16 shows an example of creating a connection.

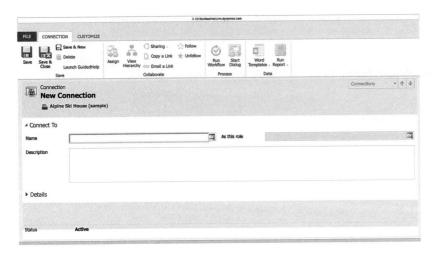

FIGURE 6.16   Creating a connection.

Documents

With the inclusion of OneDrive and SharePoint native integration in Microsoft Dynamics CRM 2013, document libraries are now easily referenced and directly accessible from the Account or Contact entities.

Although document libraries can be created from any entity in CRM, they are created by default on Account, Article, Lead, Opportunity, Product, Quote, and Sales Literature entities.

▶ SEE CHAPTER 27, "SharePoint," for instructions on setting up SharePoint servers for document library usage.

Audit History

If auditing is enabled and applied to an entity, the audit history for the attributes of that entity will be visible in the Audit History section.

Auditing is extremely useful for determining the old and new values of a particular field as well as the timestamp for a change and the user who made the change. The data stored in timestamps can be a great reference tool for managing changes to a field.

Processes, Workflows, and Dialog Sessions

Any processes (previously referred to as workflows) that have been run or are currently running that affect the account you're working with are displayed in the Process Sessions area. You can bulk delete, enable/disable filters, cancel, resume, postpone, or pause any process from More Actions, located at the top of the list view.

Summary

In this chapter, we have discussed when a customer is an Account entity or a Contact entity when working with Microsoft Dynamics CRM, as well as how to use these entities.

Understanding how the Account and Contact entities function and relate is important when you're working with customers, and these two entities usually serve as the cornerstone of Microsoft Dynamics CRM 2016.

▶ Refer to **CHAPTER 2**, "New Features of Microsoft Dynamics CRM 2016," for additional new features.

CHAPTER 7

Working with Sales

The Sales area in Microsoft Dynamics CRM is where you work with current and prospective customers, where you manage leads and opportunities, and where you work with business process flows (BPFs).

The new navigation bar breaks out the areas as follows:

- ▶ **My Work**
  - ▶ Dashboards
  - ▶ What's New
  - ▶ Activities
- ▶ **Customers**
  - ▶ Accounts
  - ▶ Customers
- ▶ **Sales**
  - ▶ Leads
  - ▶ Opportunities
  - ▶ Competitors
- ▶ **Collateral**
  - ▶ Quotes
  - ▶ Orders
  - ▶ Invoices
  - ▶ Products
  - ▶ Sales Literature
- ▶ **Marketing**
  - ▶ Marketing Lists
  - ▶ Quick Campaigns

- ▶ **Goals**

  - ▶ Goals

  - ▶ Goal Metrics

  - ▶ Rollup Queries

- ▶ **Tools**

  - ▶ Reports

  - ▶ Alerts

  - ▶ Calendar

Figure 7.1 shows the Sales navigation bar with the categories My Work, Customers, Sales, Collateral, and Marketing, as well as their subcategories.

FIGURE 7.1   Sales categories in the navigation bar.

> **NOTE**
>
> Notice the right-pointing arrow at the right, near Quick Campaigns. Clicking this (or simply mouse wheeling down while hovering over this area) opens this menu to the right, revealing more options.

- ▶ Accounts and contacts are explained in **CHAPTER 6**, "Working with Customers." Marketing lists, sales literature, and quick campaigns are included in **CHAPTER 8**, "Working with Marketing."

Flow Interface for Sales

The flow interface of Dynamics CRM 2016 brings all the entities into a single flowing interface that allows users to easily manage their sales processes (or, in the case of an xRM deployment, whatever process leverages leads, accounts, customers, opportunities, quotes, orders, and invoices).

Unlike in previous versions of Dynamics CRM, where independent forms related to each other based on originating lead (for example), a single unified interface now allows for uninterrupted usage.

Figure 7.2 shows a flow process in a step diagram, and the following section describes how to take these steps in the CRM interface.

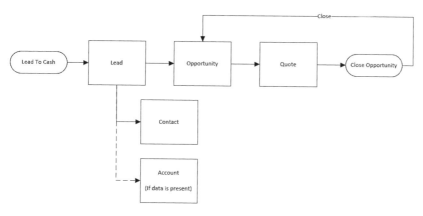

FIGURE 7.2   Lead-to-opportunity sales flow.

Lead to Opportunity Flow Example

The lead-to-opportunity sales process shown in Figure 7.2 is provided by default with the system. Here are the steps for this sales process:

1. Create a new lead, enter the topic and the name, and then select Save in the navigation bar. The lead starts a sales process, which is displayed across the screen. To understand what process this is, navigate to the information icon (i) located below the words Next Stage and click it (see Figure 7.3). In this example, you're going to be using the default lead-to-opportunity sales process.

2. If your sales default process is not the lead-to-opportunity process, select ... > Switch Process, as shown in Figure 7.4, and then select Lead to Cash, as shown in Figure 7.5.

TIP

To add additional system business processes, navigate to Settings > Data Management and click Add Ready-to-Use Business Processes.

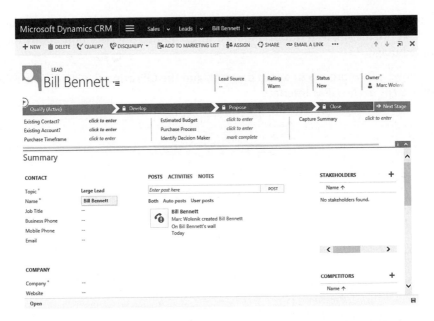

FIGURE 7.3   New lead with the lead-to-opportunity sales process selected.

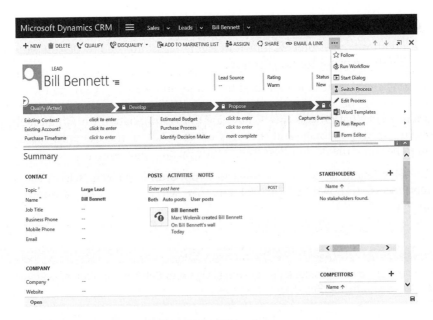

FIGURE 7.4   Switching processes from the ... menu.

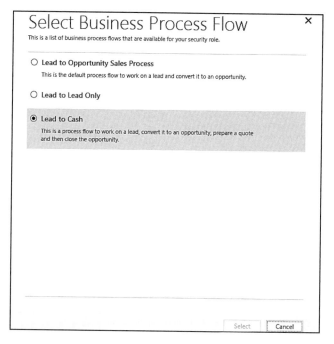

FIGURE 7.5   Selecting the new process.

The lead has a new process ribbon in the center, and you can easily see that there are new steps, as well as a new process name, by navigating to the information icon. Once you've selected the right process, you can perform the required actions to complete the process.

TIP

If the process steps aren't shown, they are likely collapsed. To expand the process steps, select the flag on the active process step. To collapse them, select the up arrow near the information icon.

NOTE

You can navigate from one stage to the next by selecting the stages that are shown. However, if you have a closed lock icon on a stage, you cannot edit it. This is useful in that it shows what needs to be done in the next stages.

3. To move from one stage to the next, complete at least the required fields (indicated with small red asterisks). In this example, you can see a red asterisk next to the custom field Identify Decision Maker, which means it's required. If you try to move to the next stage by selecting Next Stage, you are prompted with the warning shown in Figure 7.6. Complete the required field by mousing over it and clicking it as complete. A checkmark appears by it.

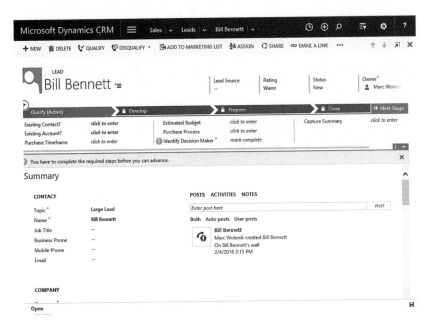

FIGURE 7.6   Error from incomplete data.

4. Click Next Stage, and you are asked to select the opportunity for the record. Because you haven't qualified this lead yet, you have no records yet, and you need to first select Qualify from the navigation bar (see Figure 7.7). Once qualified, the record moves to the next stage and goes from being a lead to being an opportunity.

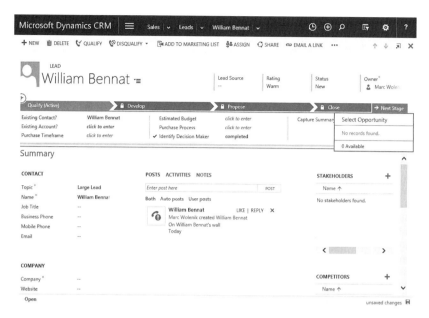

FIGURE 7.7   Selecting an opportunity.

5. Select the (now locked) stage Qualify, and the record moves back to the lead form, and it shows in highlight at the bottom that it was qualified (see Figure 7.8). In addition, the lead record is now read-only, and nothing on that stage can be modified unless the lead is reactivated.

6. Navigate back to the Develop stage (and thus the opportunity record), and we can see that there are no required fields for this stage. You can advance the sales process by selecting Next Stage after you optionally enter the suggested information.

TIP

Selecting the stages only navigates you to the stage and doesn't actually promote the process to the next stage. The way to promote the process to the next stage is by selecting either the left- or right-pointing arrow by Next Stage on the far right. If Next Stage is not highlighted, no action is available.

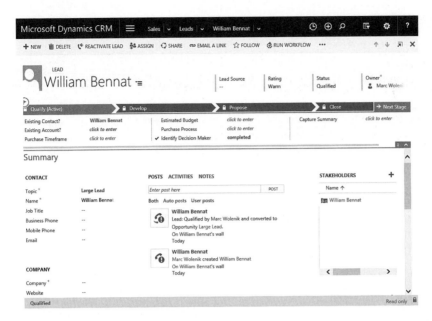

FIGURE 7.8   Qualified lead record.

7. Complete the present proposal in the Propose stage on the opportunity record. When you're finished, mark the present proposal as complete and click Next Stage. You now move back to the opportunity and the final process, which is Close, as shown in Figure 7.9.

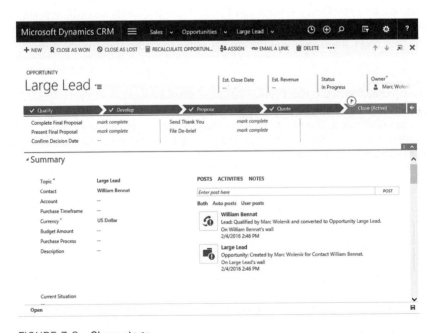

FIGURE 7.9   Close stage.

In this example, you completed the sales process and worked with three different record types, all on one form. In the process, you've seen that the navigation and system usage are very easy.

> **NOTE**
>
> You can navigate back to this record and go up and down the stages to see the various individual records, or you can navigate directly to an entity (Lead, Opportunity, or Quote) and see the records that were created as part of this process.

Stage Gating

The concept of stage gating involves providing required fields that must be populated before the user can continue. In the flow example in the preceding section, a number of stages have both required and nonrequired fields, and as noted earlier, a balance in terms of data input should determine what is required.

The Business Process

It is easy to determine what the required fields are and what the stages look like by selecting ... > Edit Process. When you do this, you open up the business process and see the included entities at the top and what fields are necessary for navigation to the next stage (see Figure 7.10).

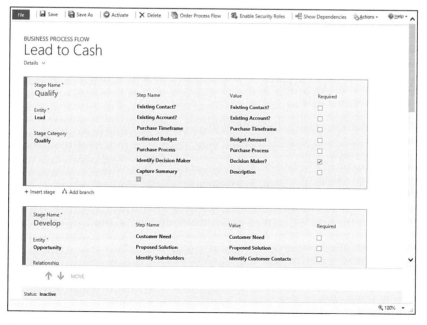

FIGURE 7.10   Business process for the lead-to-opportunity process.

▶ For more information about developing and designing business processes,
SEE CHAPTER 26, "Process Development."

Leads

Leads are not customers but rather potential customers. This is an important distinction because it provides a needed level of separation when working with your customer base. As explained later in this chapter, leads are converted to customers when they become qualified. If they are disqualified, they remain as inactive leads.

Using leads properly can provide rich insight into your organization on several levels. Because leads are not yet qualified (again, they are potential customers who haven't yet met internal criteria to be converted to customers), they should be considered the customer entry point into the CRM system.

Although it is certainly possible that you will be adding accounts and contacts directly to Microsoft Dynamics CRM, entering leads enables you to manage the following:

▶ What new customers might be interested in your products

▶ How your salespeople are cultivating their new customer base

▶ What kind of criteria are being used to convert leads to customers

NOTE

When working with leads, you should not include potential sales information anywhere other than in the Notes and Description fields. This is because leads are considered potential customers, not potential sales. This is an important distinction: Potential sales information should be captured with an opportunity, not with a lead.

As mentioned earlier, leads are also used for specific marketing efforts. Growing businesses usually aim to add new customers, and creating marketing tailored to interested customers is much more efficient than preparing marketing for everyone.

When creating a lead, you must specify the following:

▶ **Topic**—What the lead pertains to, such as the specific product or service specific to the lead

▶ **Name**—The first and last name (required) of the lead (see Figure 7.11)

These fields are used when the lead is qualified and converted to an account, a contact, or an opportunity.

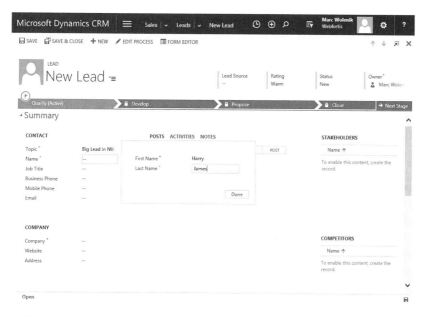

FIGURE 7.11   New lead.

Working with New Leads

When working with new leads, the default business process starts automatically and attaches itself to the lead (as shown in Figure 7.11). If you have a business need to work only with leads (or any other entity) and don't want to have a business process associated with them, you have the following options:

▶ Remove the Lead entity from any business process.

▶ Remove or deactivate any lead business processes.

▶ Create a new business process flow that only references the Lead entity.

To create a new lead, navigate to Sales > Leads and select New.

> **NOTE**
>
> There is no lookup for or association with any existing data in the CRM system other than Currency, which is in the Details section of the form. This is because the lead is a new record and is not related to any existing record. If you're creating a lead and want to associate it with an existing customer, you probably want to work with opportunities, as explained in the next section.

Although the remaining fields on the form are not required, it is helpful to populate them; the information entered and saved automatically carries over to the converted account, contact, and opportunity records when they have been qualified.

Most of the information on the various sections is self-explanatory, with the exception of Rating, in the Header section. This is a self-assessment of the lead itself and can be set to Cold, Warm, or Hot. When used properly, this setting can drive workflow events, such as a callback by the sales manager within one day if the lead is hot or within five days if the lead is cold.

The Lead Source drop-down list, shown in Figure 7.12, offers a great way of running reverse metrics on a trade show or seminar. You can easily add to this drop-down list by customizing the `leadsourcecode` attribute, adding specific events that your company might sponsor or attend.

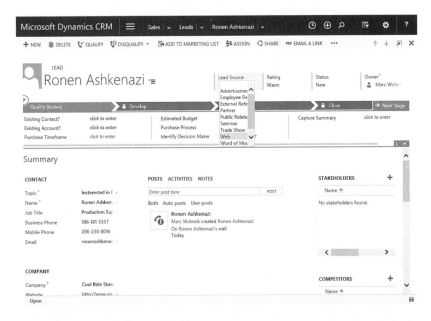

FIGURE 7.12   Lead Source options.

Figure 7.13 shows the customization options for the Lead Source field (refer to Figure 7.12). To customize this field, navigate to Settings > Customizations > Customize the System > Customize Lead Entity. Then select Fields and the Lead Source field.

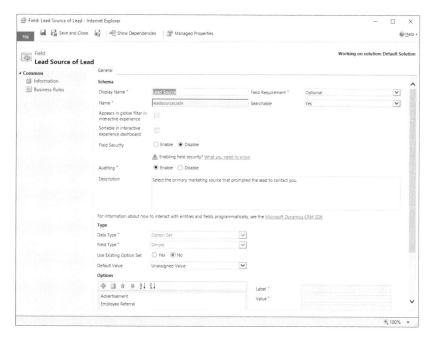

FIGURE 7.13   Adding a new value to the Lead Source field.

After you make this customization, you can easily determine who was contacted and at which event by querying on this field.

▶ **SEE CHAPTER 22**, "Customizing Entities," for more information on fully customizing Microsoft Dynamics CRM entities.

The Header section of the lead form enables you to set the owner, which, by default, is populated with the user who created the record, as well as the status reason, lead source, and rating. The bottom left of the form shows the status reason. When you're working with unqualified or new leads, the status reason enables you to select whether the lead is new or contacted. When a lead is converted, the status reason changes to Qualified if the lead was converted to a customer, or it changes to the reason it was disqualified (as selected during the conversion process).

The contact methods and marketing information for leads are the same as those on the account and contact forms (see Figure 7.14).

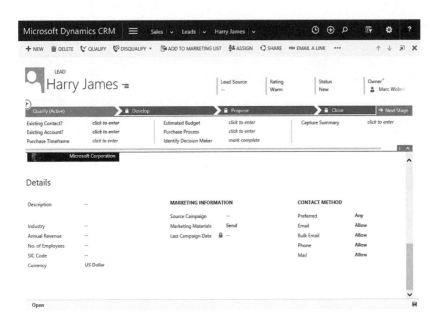

FIGURE 7.14   New Lead, Marketing Information, and Contact Method sections.

Converting Leads

Leads are converted to customers when they have met internal qualifications and become customers. Internal qualifications can be anything from a lead indicating that he is ready to buy to a background/credit check and line-of-credit approval prepared by your accounting department. In addition, leads are converted to disqualified customers (and removed as active leads) through the conversion processes for a variety of reasons, such as lead disinterest or inability to contact the lead.

To convert a lead, select the Qualify or Disqualify option from the navigation bar. When you select Qualify, the Duplicate Warning dialog may open if triggered by your business process flow, as shown in Figure 7.15, and the lead is converted to an opportunity. If you select Disqualify from the navigation bar, you must select a reason, as shown in Figure 7.16.

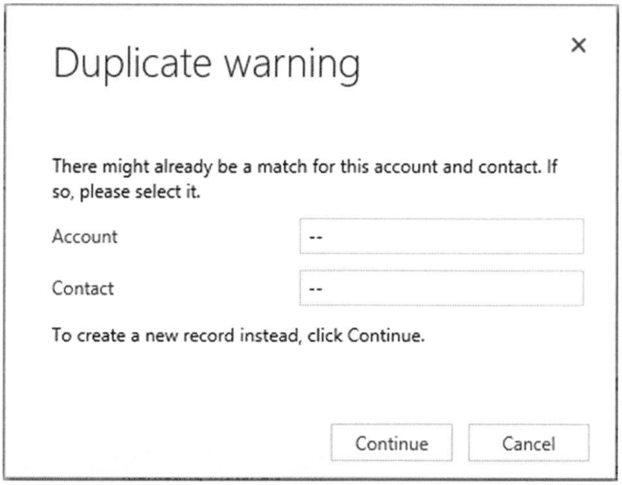

Duplicate warning   ✕

There might already be a match for this account and contact. If
so, please select it.

Account | -- |

Contact | -- |

To create a new record instead, click Continue.

Continue   Cancel

FIGURE 7.15   Duplicate Warning dialog.

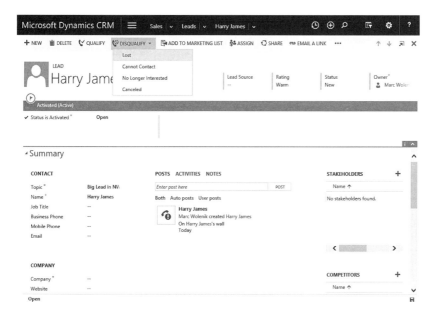

FIGURE 7.16   Disqualifying a lead.

Lead conversion in Microsoft Dynamics CRM enables you to quickly create the necessary
customer records in Microsoft Dynamics CRM by automatically creating an account, a
contact, or an opportunity from the existing information on the lead.

> **TIP**
>
> Lead fields are automatically mapped to your contact fields and can be customized. To customize lead fields or to view existing mappings, navigate to the Lead entity in Customizations and click 1:N Relationships. There you find the mappings (by opening `contact_orginating_lead` and clicking Mappings) that exist, and you can modify them as necessary.

When a lead is converted (either qualified or disqualified), the original lead record status is changed to indicate the new status of the lead, and the lead is closed. When a lead is closed, no further edits can be made to it unless it is reactivated.

Reactivating and Viewing Closed Leads

You can reactivate any closed lead by opening the closed lead and selecting Reactivate Lead from the navigation bar. Any activities remain with the lead, regardless of whether it is active or deactivated.

> **CAUTION**
>
> When a lead is reactivated for any reason, qualified records that were generated (such as accounts, contacts, or opportunities) continue to exist. You can end up creating duplicate records if you frequently reactivate closed leads.

> **TIP**
>
> Lead notes do not transfer to the opportunity record. Keep in mind, however, that you can still check the original lead notes by opening the lead and checking the notes there.

The next section further explains opportunities, which are the next step in the sales process. If you select only to create either an account or a contact from the lead, the customer will exist in the Microsoft Dynamics CRM customer base, but you will have to manually create opportunities if you choose to use them.

> **CAUTION**
>
> Depending on your security permissions, you might not be able to qualify leads that you do not own. In addition, the user of the originating lead owns all newly created records created from the conversion process.

You can view closed leads and their conversion status from the leads interface by selecting Closed Leads (see Figure 7.17). You can reactivate any lead by opening it and selecting Reactivate Lead from the navigation menu, as explained earlier.

Closed leads can be an important auditing tool for an organization because they can be analyzed to get a look at the effectiveness of your sales team and to determine which campaigns created how many leads.

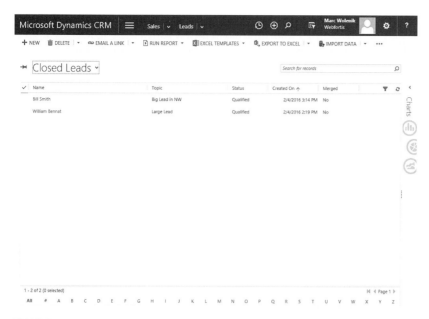

FIGURE 7.17   Viewing closed leads.

Microsoft Dynamics CRM includes these tools for querying on the status of leads:

▶ Two reports, the Lead Source Effectiveness report and the Neglected Leads report, found in the Report menu, in the Tools section

▶ The lead view, which allows you to view closed leads

▶ More complex queries using Advanced Find to determine conversion dates, as well as opportunities and customer records or associations with existing customer records

Converting Multiple Leads at Once

You can also convert multiple leads at once, if required, instead of doing so one by one. To convert multiple leads, you can either add them to a marketing list as marketing list members and then select Convert Lead from the navigation menu, or you can simply select multiple records from the lead view and then click Qualify in the navigation bar.

▶ For information about working with marketing lists, **SEE CHAPTER 8**.

Opportunities

Just as a lead can ultimately lead to a customer, an opportunity is considered a potential sale. For this reason, opportunity records should associate with existing customer records. Also, although they are not a required part of a sales process, opportunities provide insight into potential upcoming sales and, when used in conjunction with the Sales Pipeline report, can be used to forecast revenue by date, probability, and potential revenue.

Opportunities tie closely to quotes, orders, and invoices because they use the base information found on the originating opportunity when they are being created. In addition, opportunities are commonly created from leads and contain the base information from the originating lead.

Opportunities are created when "an opportunity" to make a sale is found for an existing customer. Although opportunities do *not* require the existence of a customer record, you can easily create a new account or contact record to associate with an opportunity if the customer is new. By doing this, however, you skip the step of creating leads and then converting them to customers and opportunities. This might be how your business works. Perhaps your sales cycle is very quick, and leads are not something that you cultivate. However, if you generally have potential customers, consider using leads to qualify them and then using opportunities to build potential sales around them.

The following section shows how to create a new opportunity. However, remember that you can easily work with an opportunity that was created as part of the conversion process from a lead, as shown earlier in this chapter.

Creating a New Opportunity

To create a new opportunity, navigate to Sales > Opportunities > New. The required fields for an opportunity are Topic and Currency (see Figure 7.18).

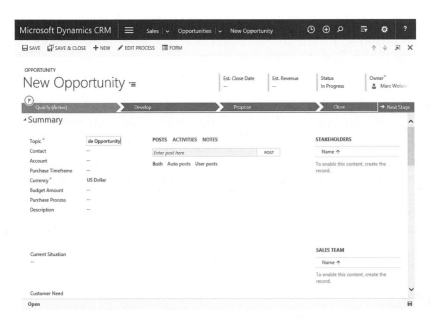

FIGURE 7.18   New opportunity form.

Although the Price List field is not required, you cannot add any products to the opportunity until you have selected a price list; otherwise, you receive an error, as shown in Figure 7.19.

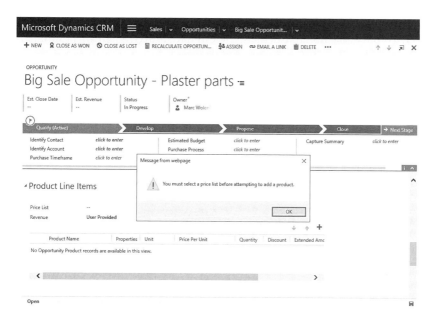

FIGURE 7.19   Price list error when trying to add products.

The following items make up the header section of an opportunity:

▶ **Est. Close Date**—Indicates the date that the opportunity might be converted to a sale, which is necessary for forecasting when considering sales. Failure to enter the estimated close date prevents the opportunity from appearing on the Sales Pipeline report.

▶ **Est. Revenue**—Defaults to System Calculated and, when first created, has a total value of $0. When products are added to the opportunity, the estimate revenue adjusts accordingly. Alternatively, you can select User Provided and enter any value into the Estimated Revenue text box. If User Provided is selected, however, adding products and clicking Recalculate has no effect on the estimated revenue.

▶ **Status**—Shows the status of the opportunity as it moves through the qualification stages.

▶ **Owner**—Shows the current owner of the opportunity. As with most other records in the system, the default is the owner who created it.

The options in the navigation bar for an opportunity (after it is saved) include Close (as either Won or Lost) and Recalculate the Opportunity.

Adding Products to an Opportunity

To create a complete opportunity, including adding products, follow these steps:

1. Select Sales > Opportunity > New.

2. Complete the Topic and Currency fields.

3. Select whether the opportunity estimated revenue should be calculated by the system or user. To have the system calculate the estimated revenue for this example, change User Provided to Revenue as System Calculated.

TIP

You can only edit Est. Revenue directly in the header if User Provided is selected in the Product Line Items section. Otherwise, the Est. Revenue field is locked because it is set to System Calculated, as shown in Figure 7.20, and it updates when product line items are added or when Recalculate Opportunity is selected.

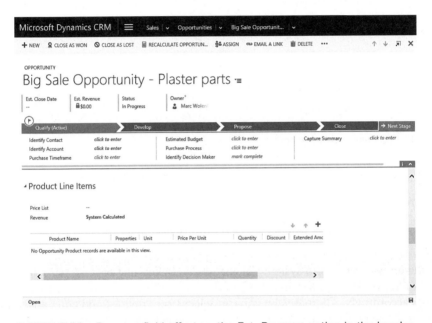

FIGURE 7.20   Revenue field effect on the Est. Revenue option in the header.

4. Enter a value for the Est. Close Date field (recommended), and then, before you can add products, also select an option from the Price List drop-down (see Figure 7.21). The record is saved.

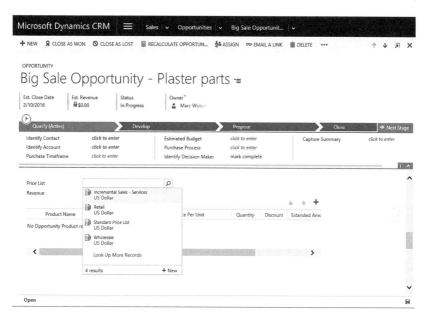

FIGURE 7.21   Price List field selection.

▶ For information on constructing price lists, **SEE CHAPTER 17**, "Settings."

5. Click the + option and then select either Existing Product or Write-in Product (see Figure 7.22).

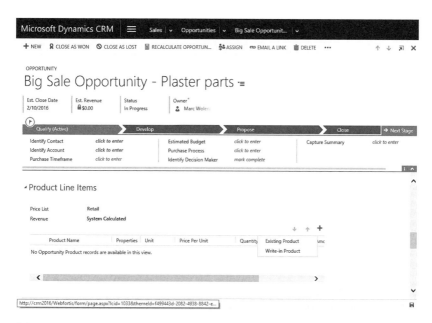

FIGURE 7.22   Adding new products to an opportunity.

6. Select an existing product (as shown in Figure 7.23) or a write-in product (as shown in Figure 7.24). Or select a mix of existing products and write-in products, as shown in Figure 7.25. Once the product is added to the form, perform edits appropriately on Price per Unit, Quantity, and Discount.

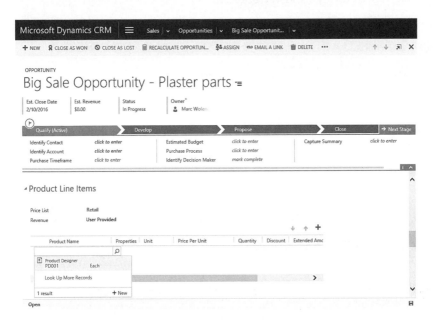

FIGURE 7.23   Adding an existing product to an opportunity.

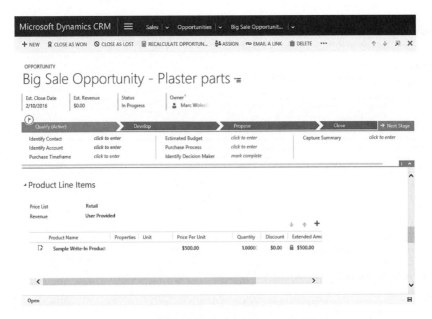

FIGURE 7.24   Adding a new write-in product to an opportunity.

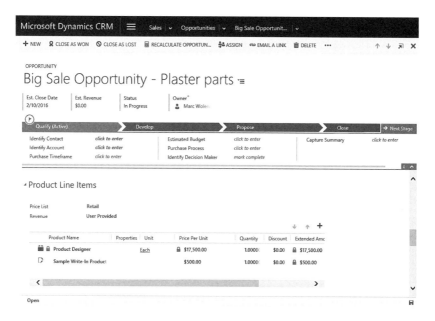

FIGURE 7.25   Adding new write-in and existing products to an opportunity.

If you right-click any of the product line items, you can open that product line item directly (or in a new window) and edit it, if necessary, as shown in Figure 7.26.

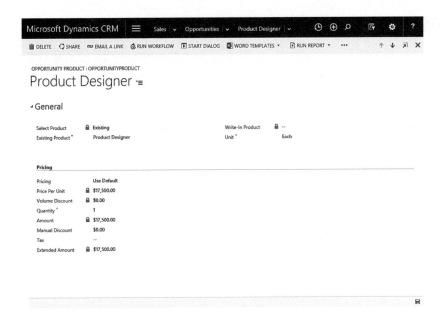

FIGURE 7.26   Opening a product line item directly.

> **TIP**
>
> If you have Revenue set to User Provided, clicking Recalculate Opportunity has no effect on the Est. Revenue field.

You can add products that are in your product catalog or write-in products. Write-in products are covered in the "Quotes, Orders, and Invoices" section, later in this chapter.

The handy Recalculate Opportunity option enables you to easily recalculate the estimated revenue when performing edits on the product line items. You might use this, for example, when you are building an opportunity and want to change the underlying price list for it, or when you are adding products and need to be sure you have the underlying calculations correct.

Closing Opportunities

Before you close an opportunity, you can associate quotes, orders, and invoices with it. When an opportunity has been realized (by either winning or losing the business), you must close it. Closing opportunities helps you effectively manage forecasted sales.

When you close an opportunity, you are prompted for information about why you are doing so. To close an opportunity, select Close as Won or Close as Lost from the navigation bar.

When an opportunity is closed, it is either won or lost. Selecting the status Won when closing an opportunity indicates that the revenue associated with the opportunity has been realized and that the business has been closed (or will be closed on the date indicated). When you select Lost, you indicate that the opportunity is no longer viable; either it has been lost to a competitor or the customer is no longer interested (see Figure 7.27).

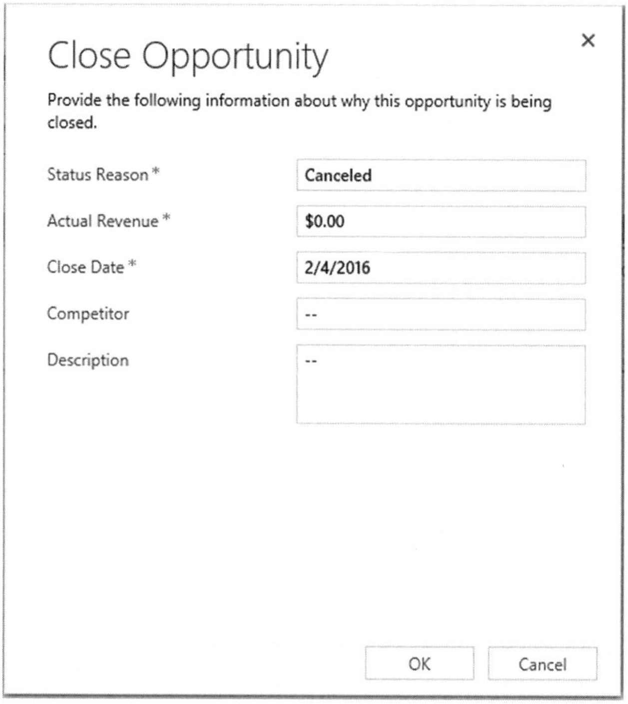

Close Opportunity ✕

Provide the following information about why this opportunity is being closed.

Status Reason *	Canceled
Actual Revenue *	$0.00
Close Date *	2/4/2016
Competitor	--
Description	--

[OK]   [Cancel]

FIGURE 7.27   Close Opportunity dialog box.

TIP

You cannot close an opportunity (as either won or lost) if active or draft quotes are associated with it. To close such an opportunity, you must first close the active or draft quotes.

After you close an opportunity, it can no longer have new quotes, orders, and invoices associated with it unless it is reopened. You can easily reopen an opportunity by selecting Reopen Opportunity from the navigation bar (see Figure 7.28).

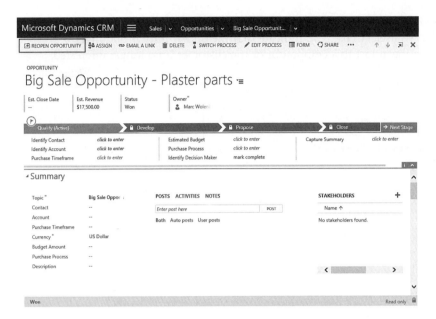

FIGURE 7.28   Reopen Opportunity option.

CAUTION

If you are working with probability ratings (a field not on the form by default but commonly used to manage the probability of the opportunity), closing the opportunity does not affect the probability rating of the opportunity. Depending on your situation, this might be fine, but you might end up closing opportunities with a 0 probability rating as won. Based on your business needs, you might want to consider adding a custom workflow that updates the probability rating to 0 if you close the opportunity as lost and to 100 if you close the opportunity as won.

Competitors

Managing your competitors is just as important as managing your customers. The more you know about your competition, the better you'll be able to compete.

Microsoft Dynamics CRM can track competitors associated with your opportunities and sales literature, which provides rich information to your salesforce when working with either of these records. In addition, as previously explained in the "Opportunities" section of this chapter, closed opportunities that are lost can be associated with competitors. When you make this association, you provide the underlying data for the default Competitor Win Loss report.

A competitor record is a high-level overview of the competitor's company, related analysis, and associated products (see Figure 7.29).

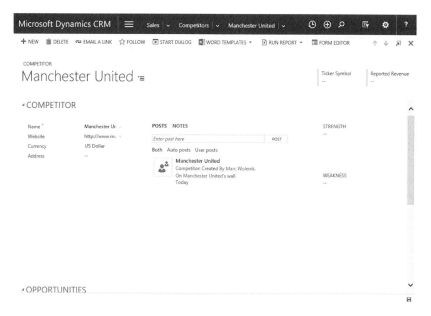

FIGURE 7.29   Competitor form.

When working with competitor records, you can easily add key information about the competitor and include overview information as well as strengths and weaknesses. Any opportunities associated with a competitor will be listed on the form as well.

You can easily manage and track what competitive products might exist by adding that information to the Products section for a competitor (as shown in Figure 7.30). Be aware that the list of competitive products is limited to product lines that you maintain in your product catalog.

NOTE

If you want to show information related to other product lines or similar ones, consider including that information in the Notes section or creating a new entity to track that information.

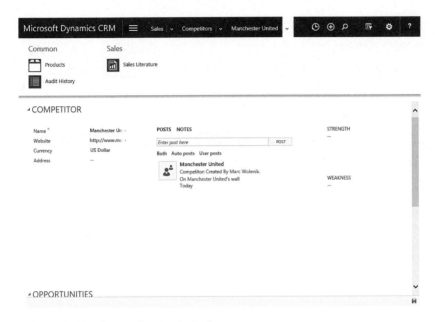

FIGURE 7.30   Competitor products form.

Products

Products in the Sales area show the products available to sell. You can create new products directly from this interface, provided that you have the necessary security permissions to do so. You can also add products by selecting Settings > Product Catalog.

▶ **SEE CHAPTER** 17 for more information about working with products.

You can now create product families and product bundles to group products. You can also use dynamic properties to let the user select the values when they are creating quotes, orders, or invoices.

Quotes, Orders, and Invoices

Microsoft Dynamics CRM includes functionality for working with the following:

▶ **Quote**—A quote is a proposed offer for products or services for an existing customer. A quote can include specific payment terms, a discount, and delivery terms.

▶ **Order**—An order is an accepted quote.

▶ **Invoice**—An invoice is a billed order.

Additional features apply to these entities:

▶ Multiple pricing lists/models

▶ Line-item discounting based on volume, customer type, or manual overrides

▶ Quote-level discounting

NOTE

It is important to understand how quotes, orders, and invoices work with Microsoft Dynamics products, particularly product inventory. Although Microsoft Dynamics CRM enables you to create orders, quotes, and invoices, it is not designed to be a stock-control application. If you want to affect inventory levels (quantity on hand, for instance), you must do this either with custom workflows or by integrating an accounting/ERP system. That system should also be used to handle additional calculations, such as sales tax and value-added tax (VAT).

Working with Quotes

As the name implies, a *quote* in Microsoft Dynamics CRM is an offer to sell your product(s) or service(s) for a certain price. When working with a quote from an associated opportunity, you can generate the quote using some, all, or none of the product items on the opportunity. This means you have the flexibility to create quotes based on a number of criteria, such as mixed product-delivery dates, other optional products (referred to as write-in products), and discounts.

Several common scenarios and statuses arise when you're working with quotes and existing opportunities. For example, say that you have an opportunity that might be realized within the next three months for $25,000. During this time period, you might prepare a quote and submit it to the customer for review. The customer might decide to move forward with the quote and agree to the sale. You would complete the sales process and close the opportunity as won.

Another scenario might be a 12-month opportunity with multiple sales activities associated with it. In this example, it could be product sales every 30 days. Instead of creating 12 opportunities, you could create one opportunity for the total amount and then create 12 associated quotes (and orders and invoices). This is a little tricky from a forecasting perspective, however, because your realized/earned dollars will be represented on the invoices, and your estimated revenue will be consistent with a single close date.

Working with Quotes with Associated Opportunities

A quotes does not need to have an associated opportunity. However, some advantages apply to working with quotes that have associated opportunities:

▶ Quotes can easily get product information from the opportunity.

▶ When a quote is spawned from an opportunity directly (by selecting Quote from the opportunity record rather than selecting Quote from the Sales area), the quote information is autopopulated with the underlying customer and product information.

▶ Although it might not apply to your organization, business rules can be enforced if you require a quote to have an active/open opportunity.

As with the previous version of Dynamics CRM, the ability to reflect both negative quantity and sales amounts exists.

You can create a quote by selecting Sales > Quotes > New (see Figure 7.31).

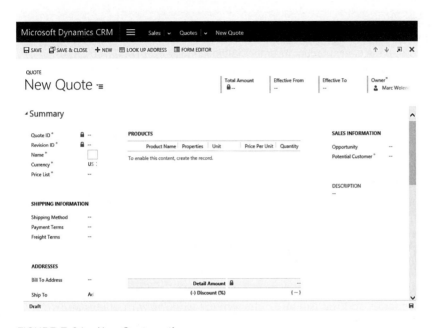

FIGURE 7.31   New Quote option.

When working with quotes, it is important to understand their status options:

▶ Draft

▶ Active

▶ Won

▶ Closed

Figure 7.32 illustrates how a quote correlates to an existing customer, products/price lists (required), and opportunities (optional), and also shows the status options.

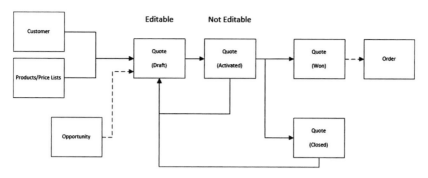

FIGURE 7.32   Quote life cycle.

Draft Status

A quote is likely to be revised many times, and Microsoft Dynamics CRM has built-in functionality for this via the draft status and active status.

When a quote is in draft status, it has been created but is generally not ready to be submitted to customers. This is the only time quotes can be completely modified with products added or removed and discounts applied as well as deleted (see Figure 7.33).

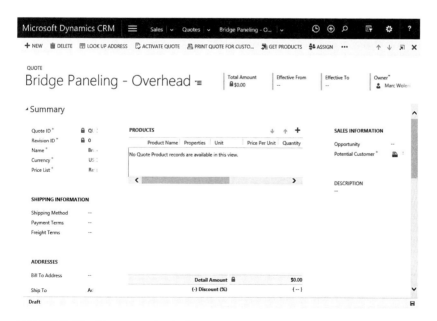

FIGURE 7.33   New quote in draft status.

Revising Quotes

After a quote is created, CRM automatically sets the Quote ID field by using the auto-numbering set up by the system administrator. You can change this by configuring Auto-Numbering in the Settings area. The Revision ID field is automatically established and set as 0 when first created. If the quote is revised, it goes from active to draft status, and the Revision ID setting automatically increases. You can modify the Name field, but it is the same as the name of the opportunity that spawned it and blank if it is not associated with an opportunity. The Potential Customer, Currency, and Price List fields must be selected and are also the same as for the opportunity that spawned the quote; with the exception of the Currency field (which defaults to the base currency), these fields are blank if there is no associated opportunity.

▶ Refer to **CHAPTER 17** for more information about working with the auto-numbering option.

Quote Details

The quote form includes the following sections:

▶ **Shipping Information section**—The Shipping section has the Shipping Method, Payment, and Freight Terms fields (see Figure 7.34)

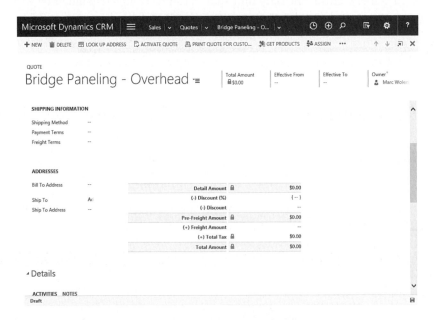

FIGURE 7.34   New Quote shipping information.

▶ **Addresses section**—The Summary tab includes address information that enables you to easily set the billing and shipping information for the quote. By default, this information is blank, regardless of whether the customer has this information on file.

You can either manually enter it here or select Look Up Address on the navigation bar. If you select Look Up Address, the dialog box shown in Figure 7.35 appears.

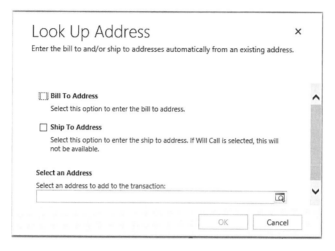

FIGURE 7.35   Look Up Address dialog.

From this dialog, you can select to autopopulate either the Bill to Address or the Ship to Address information with address information from customer records. When you select the lookup option, you can see the addresses that you have on file, listed by address name.

TIP

When CRM autopopulates, it pulls only from the More Addresses section of the selected customer.

This example has only one address on file for the customer, but you select it as the address for both the Bill To and Ship To addresses. After you select it, click OK. The address information is then populated in the Addresses section.

TIP

The Look Up Address option overwrites any existing address information entered. If you want to edit or add information related to the addresses, be sure to perform the lookup first and then edit it.

▶ **Options in the draft status**—When in draft status, a quote has a large amount of flexibility. Options exist to add products (both existing and write-in) and perform a number of actions from the navigation menu. These options include the following:

   ▶ Add Existing Products

   ▶ Add Write-in Products

- ▶ Delete the Quote

- ▶ Look Up Address

- ▶ Get Products

- ▶ Activate Quote

- ▶ Print Quote for Customer

- ▶ Run the Quote Report

▶ **Add Existing Products**—You can add products to a quote in several ways:

- ▶ If the quote is spawned from an opportunity, the products are automatically listed on the Existing Products tab.

- ▶ You can add an existing product to the quote, regardless of whether the product is on the underlying opportunity, by selecting the + in the Products section and then selecting Existing Product (see Figure 7.36).

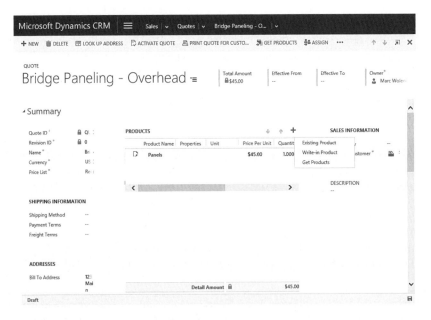

FIGURE 7.36   Products added by selecting +.

▶ You can select + in the Products section and then select Get Products. This option automatically adds the product list from any existing opportunity (see Figure 7.37).

FIGURE 7.37   Products added by selecting Get Products.

▶ **Add Write-in Products**—If your product catalog doesn't have the product, you can manually create it on-the-fly by selecting Write-in Products > New Quote Product. From this screen, you can add virtually anything and complete the necessary fields. The quote reflects the new total, including this information.

▶ **Delete the Quote**—To delete a quote, select Delete from the navigation bar.

▶ **Activate Quote**—When the quote has been completed and you are ready to send it to the customer, you must activate it. This changes the status of the quote to active and prevents further modifications. To activate a quote, select Activate Quote from the navigation bar. When a quote is active, it must be revised before it can be modified. Revising a quote is explained further in the bullet "Active Status" below.

▶ **Print Quote for Customer**—You can print a quote for a customer at any point in time by selecting the Print Quote for Customer option from the navigation bar. When the Print Quote option is selected, a mail merge is started that enables you to merge data fields from the Quote into a Microsoft Word document (see Figure 7.38). With the mail merge you can select a template language and merge to either a blank document or an organizational or personal template, and you can also select the data fields. By default, Microsoft Dynamics CRM comes with an organizational template for quotes called Quote for Customer.

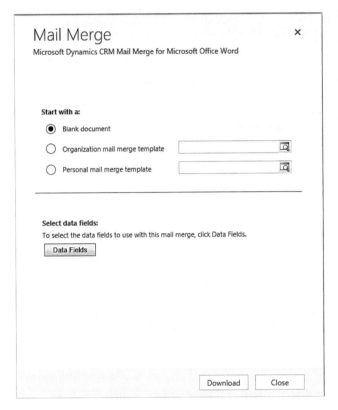

FIGURE 7.38   Printing a quote for a customer.

TIP

If you select the Print Quote option, be sure you have customized it for your organizational layout requirements by modifying the quote template report.

▶ **Active Status**—When a quote moves to active status, it has been or will shortly be submitted to the customer and therefore can't be edited. Figure 7.39 shows an active status quote that indicates that it is read-only mode (at the lower-right corner).

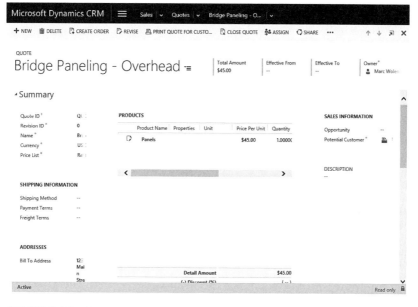

FIGURE 7.39   An active quote that it is read-only and cannot be edited.

If modifications are necessary, you can revise the quote by selecting Revise from the navigation bar. Revising a quote closes the existing quote, opens a new quote with a status of draft, and assigns a new revision ID. The quote ID remains the same, however.

▶ **Revise, Close, or Convert the Quote to an Order**—A quote can be revised, closed, or won (converted to an order). To convert a quote to an order, select Create Order from the navigation bar. Selecting Create Order opens the Create Order dialog (see Figure 7.40).

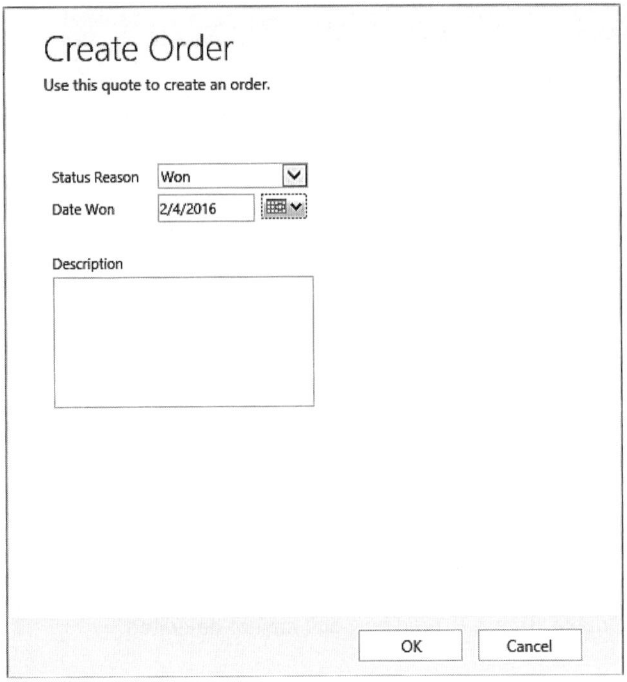

FIGURE 7.40   Converting a quote to an order—updating the status.

The Create Order dialog enables you to select the date the order was won and to calculate the revenue or enter it manually; you can also close the related opportunity. After you click OK, the status of the quote changes to Won, and the corresponding order opens.

A quote that is in won status generally has an order associated with it, but you can select Create Order and create another order, if necessary. Quotes that are in closed status can be revised and reactivated for approval or made active.

Working with Orders

An order is created when a customer is ready to make a purchase. The customer either has accepted the quote or is ready to make a purchase, regardless of a quote.

TIP

Keep in mind that a quote is not required to create an order. While an order can be spawned from a quote, orders are separate entities and many have no quote correlation.

Figure 7.41 illustrates how an order correlates to an existing customer (required), products/price lists (required), opportunities (optional), and quotes (optional).

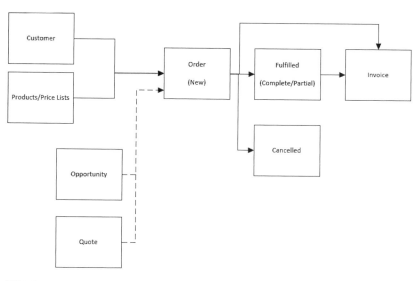

FIGURE 7.41   Order life cycle.

When working with orders, it is important to understand their different status options:

▶ Active

▶ Fulfilled

▶ Canceled

An active order can be deleted, canceled, and edited (see Figure 7.42). Editing an active order includes updating products associated with the order, as well as discount, shipping, and address information.

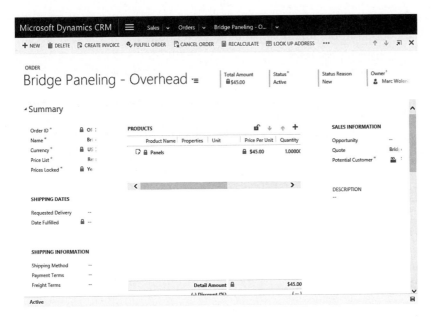

FIGURE 7.42   Active order.

An order that has been fulfilled has had its products shipped or delivered. To fulfill an order, select Fulfill Order from the navigation bar. The Fulfill Order dialog appears (see Figure 7.43). This dialog enables you to indicate that the order has been shipped.

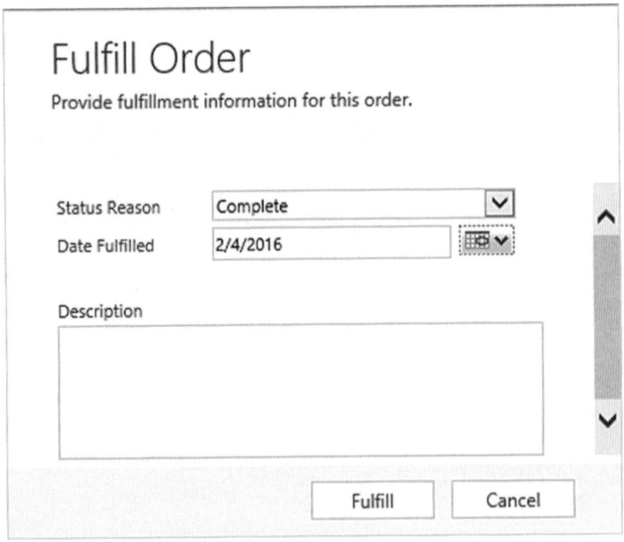

Fulfill Order

Provide fulfillment information for this order.

Status Reason	Complete
Date Fulfilled	2/4/2016

Description

[Fulfill]   [Cancel]

FIGURE 7.43   Fulfill Order dialog.

CAUTION

When selecting how to fulfill an order, remember that you cannot edit the order after you select any option, including Partial Fulfillment.

You can select whether an order should use current pricing or whether to lock the pricing. This is a helpful option when there are price fluctuations and the order might remain unfulfilled for a period of time. By default, the prices are locked if an order is created from a quote, but you can change that by selecting Use Current Pricing from the navigation bar.

Finally, you can create an invoice from an order by selecting Create Invoice from the navigation bar. When you create an Invoice from an order, the order remains in active status until it is fulfilled.

Working with Invoices

When the terms of a sale have been completed, the sale is recorded in the system using an invoice. When working with invoices, it is important that you understand their different status options:

▶ Active

▶ Closed

Figure 7.44 illustrates how an invoice correlates to an existing customer (required), products/price lists (required), opportunities (optional), and quotes (optional).

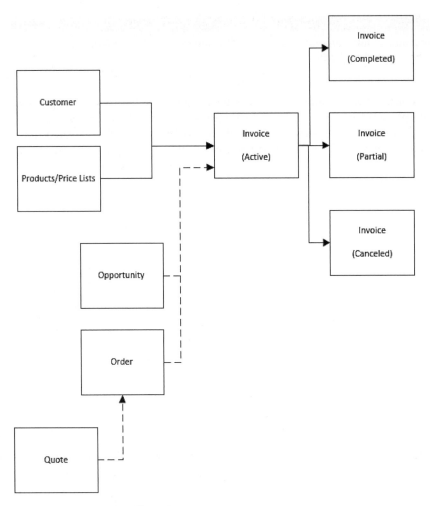

FIGURE 7.44   Invoice life cycle.

An invoice is very similar to an order, in that you can perform the following actions:

▶ You can add new products from your product catalog.

▶ You can perform various functions on the invoice, including selecting whether to use current or locked pricing and recalculate accordingly.

Figure 7.45 illustrates an active invoice. The tab options for Shipping, Addresses, Administration, and Notes are similar to those defined in quotes.

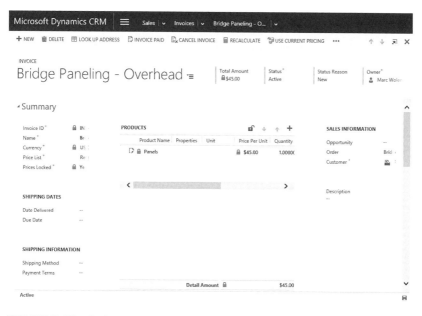

FIGURE 7.45   Active invoice.

As with order fulfillment, if you mark an invoice as paid, you have the option to select Partial or Complete (see Figure 7.46). After you mark an invoice as Paid or Partial, you cannot edit it.

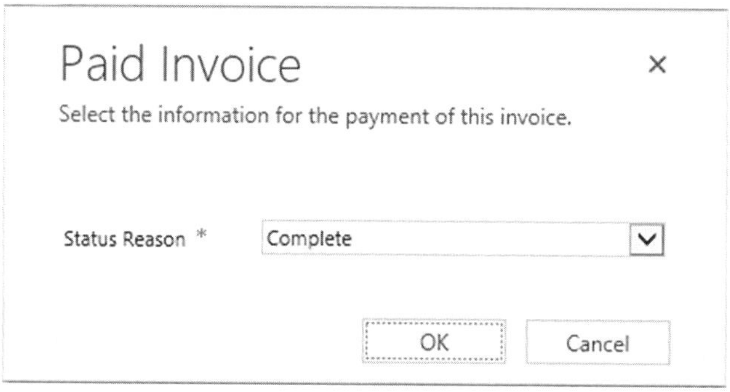

FIGURE 7.46   Marking an invoice as paid.

NOTE

When working with a back-end accounting or ERP system, you might often create and manage orders in Microsoft Dynamics CRM and have them posted (when approved) in the back-end/ERP system. Doing so can enforce more complex business rules (such as VAT calculations), and the back-end/ERP posting process should be responsible for creating an invoice record in Microsoft Dynamics CRM so that sales staff can see the process status without having to navigate to the ERP system.

> **NOTE**
>
> Extending functionally of sales quotes, orders, and invoices to specific back-end/ERP systems is beyond the scope of this book. You can learn more about extending functionality in *Microsoft Dynamics CRM 4.0 Integration Unleashed*.

Goals, Goal Metrics, and Rollup Queries

Goals allow an organization to capture and track achievements. A nice aspect of goals is that they are not singularly revenue based (that is, the total sum of something sold for a given period) but rather can be aggregate based (such as the total number of cases closed). As such, they provide a robust format for capturing performance metrics.

To create goals, you first need to create goal metrics and rollup queries. Goal metrics are used to determine which metric you want to use to measure your goal (count or amount), and rollup queries are the specific field you want to pull the data from.

By default, you can find at least three goal metrics included with the system (see Figure 7.47):

▶ No. of Cases

▶ No. of Product Units

▶ Revenue

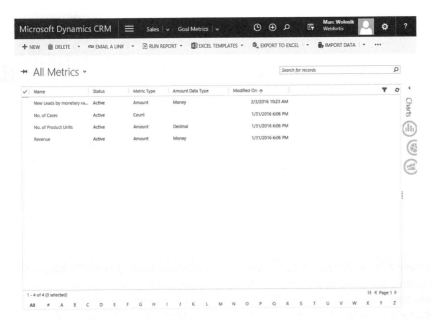

FIGURE 7.47   Default goal metrics.

Defining Goal Metrics

To create a new goal metric, select New and then follow the steps on the Goal Metric interface (see Figure 7.48):

1. Define the metric by completing the Name and the Metric Type fields. The Metric Type field can be either Count or Amount. For this example, you want to track the dollar amounts of new leads created.

> **NOTE**
>
> The Metric Type field can't be changed once the record is created.

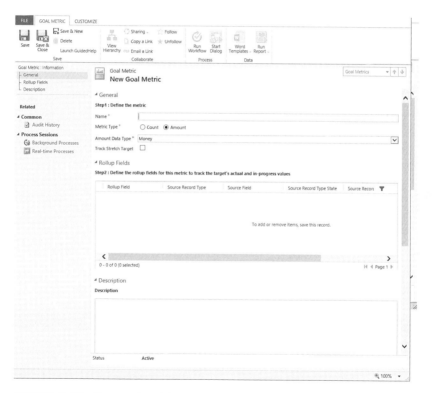

FIGURE 7.48   New goal metric.

If you select the Track Stretch Target check box, you have the option of using this metric to have a stretch target field, which means the main goal has two target values: a regular (target) value and a stretch target value. If you leave this unchecked, you're assuming a single target for the salesperson, and there isn't an option for stretch on the salesperson's fixed goal.

NOTE

Think of stretch targets as "overachiever" goals for salespeople. Organizations typically use stretch targets as extra incentives. I've worked with organizations that have set up stretch goals, and if they're hit by all the salespeople, then everybody gets a prize such as a new Microsoft Surface.

2. Create a new Rollup field that tracks the metric data by selecting File > Add New Rollup Field (see Figure 7.49).

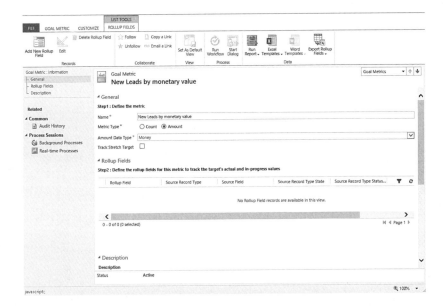

FIGURE 7.49   Rollup fields on a goal metric.

TIP

You cannot create a new rollup metric or add a new one until the form is saved and you are presented with the List Tools ribbon menu, as shown in Figure 7.49.

3. Set the field for Rollup Field to Actual (Money).

4. Complete the source data fields.

5. Complete the date field for the rollup. Figure 7.50 shows an example of a created rollup field.

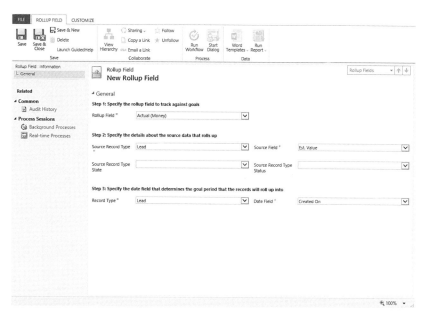

FIGURE 7.50   Rollup field.

6. Click Save to finish creating the goal metric and the rollup query associated with it.

Creating a New Goal

You can create a goal by completing the following steps:

1. Select Goal > New from the navigation bar. The New Goal interface opens (see Figure 7.51).

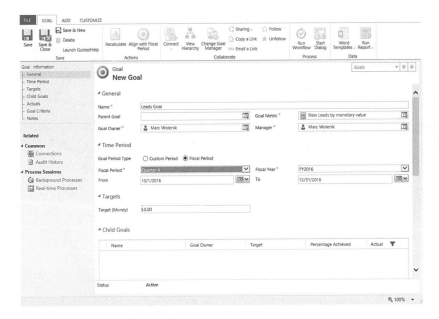

FIGURE 7.51   Creating a goal.

2. Complete the following fields on the form:

▶ **Name**—The name of the goal.

▶ **Parent Goal**—Whether this is a child goal.

▶ **Goal Metric**—Reference to the previously created goal metric.

▶ **Goal Owner**—Who owns this goal.

▶ **Manager**—The user's manager for a team goal.

▶ **Goal Period Type**—By default, Fiscal Period, but you can select any custom period you define (by selecting Custom Period).

▶ **Fiscal Period**—The period for which the goal should be applicable.

▶ **Fiscal Year**—Either current or future years. (This is set in Settings > Business.)

Targets are not shown on the goal form unless the Track Target Stretch Goal option is selected on the goal metric. If it is selected, populate the target with the goal's target value and stretch target with the appropriate value for the stretch goal.

You can add additional child goals to the goal. Because goals can have a parent/child relationship, the child goal shares its data with the parent goal when it is rolled up to the parent level.

> **CAUTION**
>
> The parent and child goals must have the same goal metric and time period.

Results of the goals are shown in the Actual section on the form.

> **TIP**
>
> Actuals data is run once every 24 hours (as found on the Goals tab in System Settings); however, you can click the Recalculate button at the top of the form to refresh the data.

Setting Goal Criteria

You can set goal criteria that are used for rolling up actuals data against the goal:

▶ **Roll Up Only from Child Goals**—Sets the goal as a summary of only child goals or as a summation of both child and parent goals.

▶ **Record Set for Rollup**—Limits the rollup to include only the owner or all records and has an effect on the underlying data, depending on desired results.

▶ **Rollup Query**—Selects the query used for rollup: Actual, In-Progress, or Custom Rollup Field.

The usual scenario with parent/child goals is a manager who has multiple salespeople comprising the manager's total/overall goal, and the salespeople's goals are usually child goals summarized into the manager's goal.

Summary

This chapter shows how to work with the Sales area of Microsoft Dynamics CRM. The most important aspects to remember from this chapter are that leads are separated from the regular customer base and that you can convert them to accounts, contacts, or opportunities by using the included sales force automation.

In addition, this chapter explains how to manage and use opportunities, and it thoroughly examines the quotes, orders, and invoice functionality. Because Microsoft Dynamics CRM is not designed to be a stock control, accounting, or invoicing system, you should consider integrating with other applications (ERP/accounting systems) if necessary.

The chapter concludes with a review of the features provided with goals and goal management. It is important to remember that a number of sales charts available by default on the dashboards use goal data for performance indicators.

CHAPTER 8

Working with Marketing

A powerful feature that sets Microsoft Dynamics CRM ahead of its competitors is its ability to build, manage, track, and report on the effectiveness of marketing efforts. When thinking about marketing, consider how you currently market. Do you want to send the same sales literature to potential customers that you would send to existing customers? Probably not. When you're creating a marketing campaign, you need to consider your audience.

The marketing functionality of Dynamics CRM 2016 has not been improved and enhanced since Dynamics CRM 2013. If you are familiar with the marketing functionality in previous versions of CRM, you won't find any new features here, but you will find an updated user interface and other enhancements. If you are a new user of Dynamics CRM 2016, this chapter will help you understand the basic marketing features.

> **NOTE**
>
> Microsoft Dynamics CRM refers to any kind of targeted marketing effort as a *campaign*, and it differentiates between a quick campaigns and campaigns, as explained later in this chapter.

Marketing efforts designed to appeal to existing customers usually include incentives to buy more, reestablish buying after a lapse, or purchase in other ways. Marketing efforts designed to appeal to potential customers are usually very different and tend to focus on asking them to start purchasing.

Many books and companies specialize in marketing to potential and existing customers. We're by no means attempting to explain the best way for your organization to handle its marketing. Instead, this chapter explains in depth the marketing features Microsoft Dynamics CRM provides so that when you want to market your organization, products, or personnel, you have a solid understanding of how Microsoft Dynamics CRM can do help.

This chapter reviews the items specific to marketing found in the Marketing section, such as marketing lists, campaigns, sales literature, and quick campaigns, in addition to other areas in the application that touch on marketing.

▶ For information about the other aspects of the Marketing tab, such as Lead or Product entities, **SEE CHAPTER 7**, "Working with Sales." For information about Account and Contact entities, **SEE CHAPTER 6**, "Working with Customers."

NOTE

This chapter does not cover Microsoft Dynamics Marketing (MDM) or its related integration components. Instead, consider this chapter a standalone option on marketing. For more information about Dynamics Marketing, refer to Chapter 9, "Microsoft Dynamics Marketing."

Marketing Lists

Marketing lists are great tools for managing marketing efforts. You can use a marketing list to create a list of members—either existing customers (Account or Contact entities) or potential customers (Lead entities)—who will receive the marketing material. There is no way to prepare a single marketing list for both existing and potential customers; instead, you should consider creating two or more marketing lists.

After you've creating marketing lists, you can directly market to their members via a mail merge, a quick campaign, or a campaign.

TIP

After you have created a marketing list, you cannot change its base entity assignment (for example, from an Account entity marketing list to a Lead entity marketing list). Instead, you must create a new marketing list if you need to use a different base entity.

To create a new marketing list, navigate to the Marketing tab and then select Marketing Lists > New.

You can create a new marketing list by completing the Name and Member Type (Targeted At field), as shown in Figure 8.1, and saving the list. (Note that the only member types allowed are Account, Contact, and Lead.)

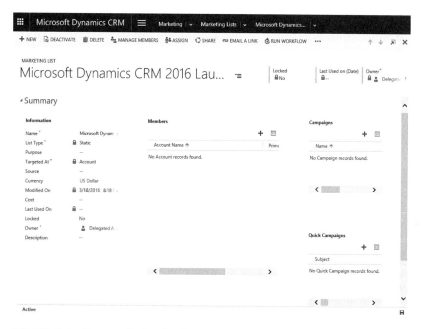

FIGURE 8.1   New marketing list for an Account entity.

Other fields for the marketing list include Source, which can be any free-form value, Currency, Cost, and Locked, which allows you to specify whether new members can be added to the list. In addition, notice in the lower-left corner the status of the marketing list. By default, new marketing lists are Active, but you can easily deactivate them when necessary by selecting Deactivate from the More Actions drop-down menu.

> **TIP**
>
> Be sure not to lock a marketing list by selecting the Locked option, as shown in Figure 8.1, before you've added members to it. You will be unable to perform any additions or subtractions to the membership if it is locked. (Of course, you can always unlock a marketing list if you need to by opening the marketing list and changing the Locked option.)

Dynamic marketing lists are great because they are updated as new members meet the defined criteria, and they are available by setting the List Type field to either Static or Dynamic. By default, List Type is set to Static, which means that after the list is created, the members are not updated. If Dynamic is selected, the marketing list members are updated whenever the list is used.

> **NOTE**
>
> You cannot convert dynamic lists to static lists, but you can copy them to static lists. (This option is on the navigation menu of any dynamic list and can be set only when the list is initially created.)

To add members to a marketing list, select Manage Members from the command bar. As with many of the other forms in Microsoft Dynamics CRM, a marketing list must first be saved before you can add members.

When adding members, you have the options shown on Figure 8.2:

▶ **Add Using Lookup**—Use Lookup to add members.

▶ **Add Using Advanced Find**—Use Advanced Find to add members.

▶ **Remove Using Advanced Find**—Use Advanced Find to remove members.

▶ **Evaluate Using Advanced Find**—Use Advanced Find to evaluate members.

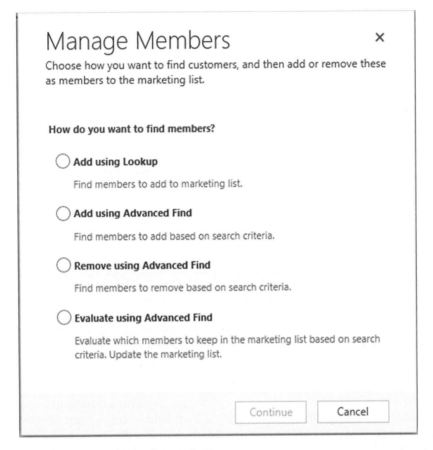

FIGURE 8.2   Manage Members dialog.

You can select any one of these options and then change it any time if the list has not been locked. This is helpful when you have specific criteria to query on because you can add, remove, or evaluate members before or after they've been added to the marketing list to ensure that you are marketing to the correct members.

> **NOTE**
>
> You can't add members to a marketing list multiple times. This is a nice limitation because sometimes you need to use the previous options more than once. For example, you might use Advanced Find to find all members located in a certain geographic area, and then use Lookup to add more members that might or might not be in the geographic area you previously selected. If the new members are already on the marketing list, they will appear only once, ensuring that they don't receive duplicate marketing material.

Using Lookup to Add Members

When you select Add Using Lookup in the Manage Members dialog, you get the Look Up Records dialog box for the target marketing list entity selected (in this case, Account), as shown in Figure 8.3. You can use this dialog to search and add quickly and easily by selecting active records and adding them to the members list.

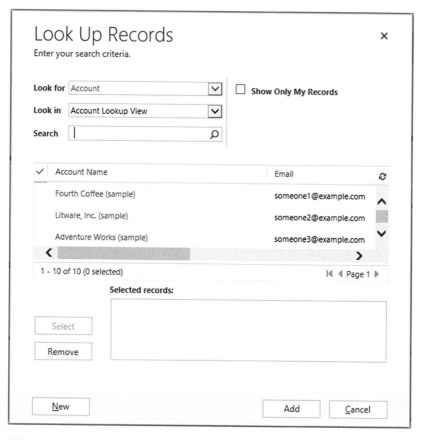

FIGURE 8.3   Look Up Records dialog box.

Using Advanced Find to Add Members

When you select Add Using Advanced Find in the Manage Members dialog, you can add complex (or previously saved via an Advanced Find) criteria to ensure that you find only the specific members to whom you want to market.

Figure 8.4 shows how to create a query using Advanced Find to add only Account entities that you own of and that have an address with State equal to California. Note that Advanced Find will have no criteria until you create your query.

You can easily use the Advanced Find features to adjust this query to include contacts that have not placed an order with you in x number of months, have x number of sales with you over the past x number of months, or meet any similar criteria.

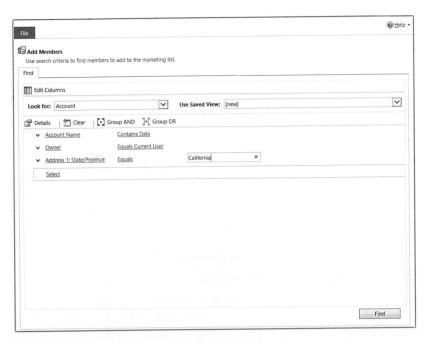

FIGURE 8.4   Advanced Find dialog box.

When you've prepared your query, click the Find button to view members that match your query logic. In the Advanced Find results (see Figure 8.5), you can select individual members from the results or simply add all members returned by the search to the marketing list by selecting the appropriate radio button on the lower-left side and clicking Add to Marketing List. (The Add to Marketing List button is Remove from Marketing List if you're using Advanced Find to remove members.)

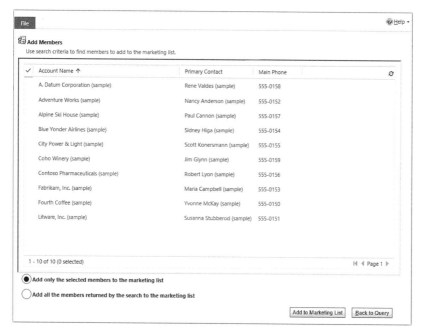

FIGURE 8.5   Advanced Find results.

Using Advanced Find to Remove Members

Much like using Advanced Find to add members, you can use Advanced Find to remove members. You can create complex query logic via Advanced Find to remove any previously added members that match your entered criteria.

Using Advanced Find to Evaluate Members

Also much like using Advanced Find to add members (as explained previously), you can use Advanced Find to evaluate members. You can use the existing membership list to evaluate and update the existing members with any additional logic regarding whether to keep existing members after you've applied the new logic.

> **NOTE**
>
> When a marketing list has the desired members in it, you can lock it to prevent any further modifications to the membership.

Other Marketing List Features

You can perform several functions on the marketing lists you create. You can use marketing lists on multiple campaigns or quick campaigns. You can merge them provided that the target entity for each is the same (for example, both lists are Account entities, Contact entities, or Lead entities). To do this, you select More Actions > Copy To.

You can easily see where and which campaigns or quick campaigns have been used by opening any marketing list and selecting Campaign or Quick Campaign from the navigation bar.

Campaigns

Campaigns are structured events that enable you to create and manage targeted marketing efforts. Campaigns differ from quick campaigns in several ways:

▶ Campaigns can work with multiple marketing lists, whereas quick campaigns can only work with single marketing lists.

▶ Campaigns can have complex activity distribution, whereas a quick campaign can only have a single activity type.

▶ Campaigns can have complex planning and management information, whereas quick campaigns don't have this capability.

However, both campaigns and quick campaigns can receive campaign responses. A marketing effort can be almost anything—a new product announcement, company exposure at a popular event, or even an effort to convince previous customers to buy products again.

Campaigns allow for the structured creation of tasks related to planning the campaign, activities specific to the campaign, and metrics related to the responses received from a campaign.

This section shows an example of a campaign that involves some simple tasks and activities to illustrate how a campaign might work. Obviously, when creating a campaign for your organization, you want to consider your specific needs related to tasks and activities, but using the example provided here can give you a solid foundation for working with campaigns.

> **TIP**
>
> Campaigns in Microsoft Dynamics CRM are designed to define, create, task, and track marketing efforts from beginning to end. They can have multiple tasks and activities associated with them, and they allow for a large amount of structure. Consider using a quick campaign (explained later in this chapter) if your organization won't benefit from the structure that campaigns provide.

Working with New Campaigns and Campaign Templates

When working with new campaigns, you have two options: Use a new campaign or use a new campaign template. You should use a campaign template when you anticipate needing to use the same campaign and its related tasks and activities again.

When working with campaigns and campaign templates, you can easily manage which one to work with by navigating to Marketing, campaigns and viewing the All Campaigns and Campaign Templates list (see Figure 8.6).

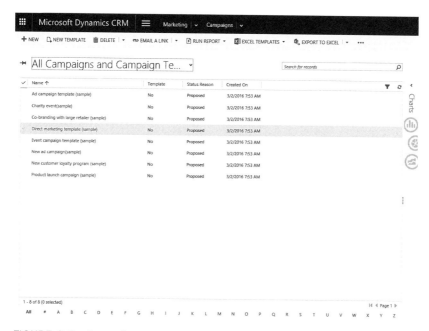

FIGURE 8.6   Campaigns template quick view.

A campaign template differs from a campaign in that it is the framework on which campaigns can be created (typically multiple times) and then used to record campaign responses.

You can copy a campaign templates as a campaign or as a template from the Navigation menu. A campaign template generally doesn't include any scheduling data because it a reusable template, and that information is generally populated only when an actual campaign is planned.

To create a new campaign, follow these steps:

1. In the Marketing tab, navigate to Campaigns and select New. For this example, create a campaign without using a template and start in the General section. With most entities in CRM, you should manually save the record after you enter the initial data, and then you can work with additional menu options in the navigation bar, as shown in Figure 8.7.

2. Enter a descriptive name for the campaign and select the status detail for the campaign from the header. In this case, because you're creating a new campaign, leave it at the default, Proposed. You can enter a code in the Campaign Code field or have the system assign an automatic campaign code to your campaign by leaving it

blank; however, after the campaign has been saved, you cannot edit this field. Select an option for the Campaign Type field to tell others the type of campaign it is.

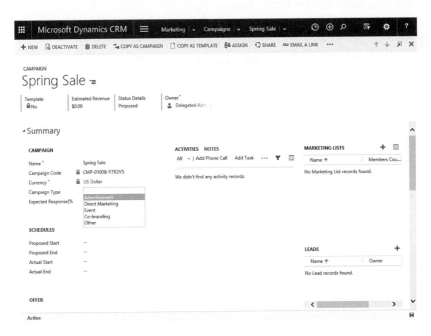

FIGURE 8.7   Creating a new campaign.

TIP

Although it is not required, entering price information such as estimated revenue, allocated budget, and so on enables you to compare the cost versus revenue generated from the campaign. Use the Offer fields to explain the details of the campaign.

---

3. Enter the schedule information and description, if desired.

4. Select the Financials section and enter the budget allocated, miscellaneous costs, and estimated revenue (located on the header) for the campaign (see Figure 8.8). The Total Cost field calculates automatically and, if you have no activities yet, equals the miscellaneous costs only. When you add costs to the campaign by adding campaign Activities, costs will automatically be shown here.

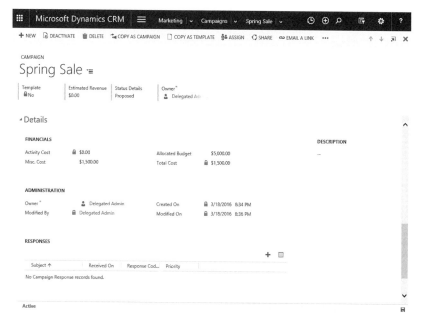

FIGURE 8.8 Making selections in the Financials section for a new campaign.

TIP

The cost should autocalculate during the automatic save. If it doesn't, you can manually refresh the form to see the correct calculated total cost.

---

5. If desired, add or edit information in the Administration and Notes sections. When you have created this basic framework for the campaign, save the campaign.

6. Add any planning tasks you want to associate with the campaign. Planning activities are simply activities with the Regarding field set to the campaign. Select Planning Activities from the navigation bar and then select Add New Activity to create a planning activity (see Figure 8.9).

TIP

Be sure to save the campaign before adding any planning tasks to it.

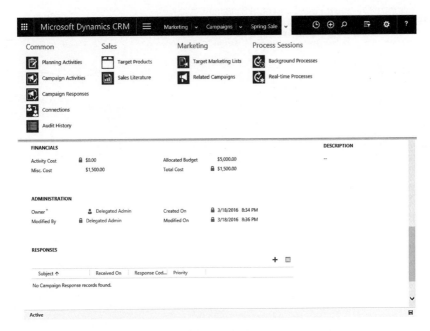

FIGURE 8.9 Creating planning activities for a new campaign.

TIP

As with any other activity, after you have created a planning activity, you can assign it to another user or queue. It will appear as an activity in the assigned user's My Work and will have associated follow-up tasks or activities assigned to the user, if there are any.

For this campaign, you'll have only one activity. Normally, however, a campaign has several planning activities. If the campaign will be reused, the planning activities likely will be common to the campaign. In that case, it might make sense to copy your campaign to a campaign template from the More Actions drop-down menu when you finish adding the necessary planning tasks.

Adding Campaign Activities

Campaign activities differ from common activities and are specific to a campaign. The following steps show how to add campaign activities to a campaign and manage them:

1. From the navigation menu, select Campaign Activities and then select Add New Campaign Activity. You see a new campaign activity, as shown in Figure 8.10.

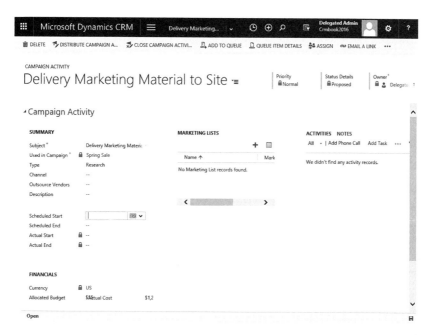

FIGURE 8.10   Creating a campaign activity in a new campaign.

2. Make selections in the Channel and Type fields. These are some of the selections to make on this page:

   a. The Channel field directly correlates to the distribution of the activity, as explained shortly.

   b. The Owner field, by default, is set to the user creating the campaign activity. However, you can change it by clicking the Assign option in the command bar and assigning the campaign activity to another user.

   c. To assign an activity to a queue, create it and then select Add to Queue from the command bar.

   d. Select any outsource vendors that might be used with this particular task and enter the scheduled start and end dates and any budget allocated.

   e. The Anti-Spam field excludes a member from receiving any marketing material by preventing the activity from being distributed to the member for the number of days entered.

NOTE

You must assign campaign activities to marketing list members by distributing them to the members of the associated marketing lists. *Distribution* simply means assigning the specified activity to the owner of the member in the marketing list. Before distributing campaign activities, you must set which marketing lists to use as part of the campaign.

3. To add marketing lists, navigate to the Marketing Lists section on the Campaign form and click the + icon. In the Look Up Records dialog that appears (see Figure 8.11), click Add.

FIGURE 8.11   The Look Up Records dialog.

NOTE

The view shown in the Look Up marketing lists is an associative view and only pulls from marketing lists that are added to the campaign.

4. After you select a marketing list by selecting 'Select' and then clicking 'Add', you have the option to distribute the campaign activities. For this example, the channel for this campaign activity is set to Email, so you see the New Emails dialog (see Figure 8.12).

NOTE

If you select a different channel, you get a different dialog for distributing the campaign activities.

FIGURE 8.12   New Emails dialog.

5. Either create the email or use a preexisting template, as shown in Figure 8.13.

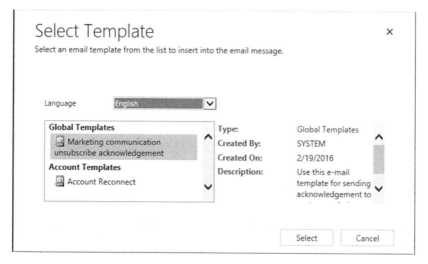

FIGURE 8.13   The Select Template dialog for a campaign activity.

6. Once you've created the campaign activity and associated a marketing list, assign the campaign activities by selecting Distribute, as shown in Figure 8.14. The activities are then assigned to the designated owners and appear as open activities for each member in the marketing list.

FIGURE 8.14   Distribute Email Messages.

7. Complete the actual cost amount of the campaign activity so the correct information rolls up to the total campaign cost on the Campaign Financials tab.

NOTE

When you're working with mail merge campaign activities, be sure that the selected marketing lists are all the same base entity (Contact, Account, or Lead); otherwise, the merge will fail. If you want to create a mail merge campaign for mixed entities, you must create a separate campaign activity for each entity.

Campaign Responses

As the name indicates, *campaign responses* are responses that an organization receives in response to a campaign. They are very useful in determining the effectiveness of a campaign and can indicate many things, such as geographic trending, responsiveness to campaign particulars such as discounts and other incentives, and how well the target audience is receiving the campaign.

It is important to note that campaign responses are responses received from potential customers in response to a campaign; they are not automated responses sent to your customers as part of your campaign. You can automatically convert campaign activities to campaign responses, or you can manually create them.

You create campaign responses by selecting Campaign Responses from the navigation bar or by navigating to Activities and selecting New Campaign Response. Figure 8.15 shows a newly added and saved campaign response.

> **TIP**
>
> You can also import records into the system as campaign responses by using the Import Data Wizard. This method is useful when you're working with a large number of records offline because you can easily manipulate them and then tie them to the campaign as responses when uploaded.

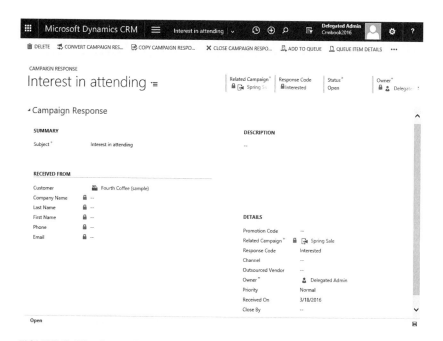

FIGURE 8.15   Campaign response.

Another way to create a campaign response is via email responses if email tracking has been enabled in System Settings. When an email is sent in response to a campaign, the incoming email can be automatically created as a campaign response.

Convert Campaign Responses

When a campaign response has been entered and saved, you can select Convert Campaign Response from the command bar. The Convert Response dialog appears, as shown in Figure 8.16. This dialog allows you to close the response and select one of the following options:

▶ Create a Lead

▶ Convert to an Existing Lead

▶ Create a Quote, Order, or Opportunity for an Account or Contact

▶ Close Response

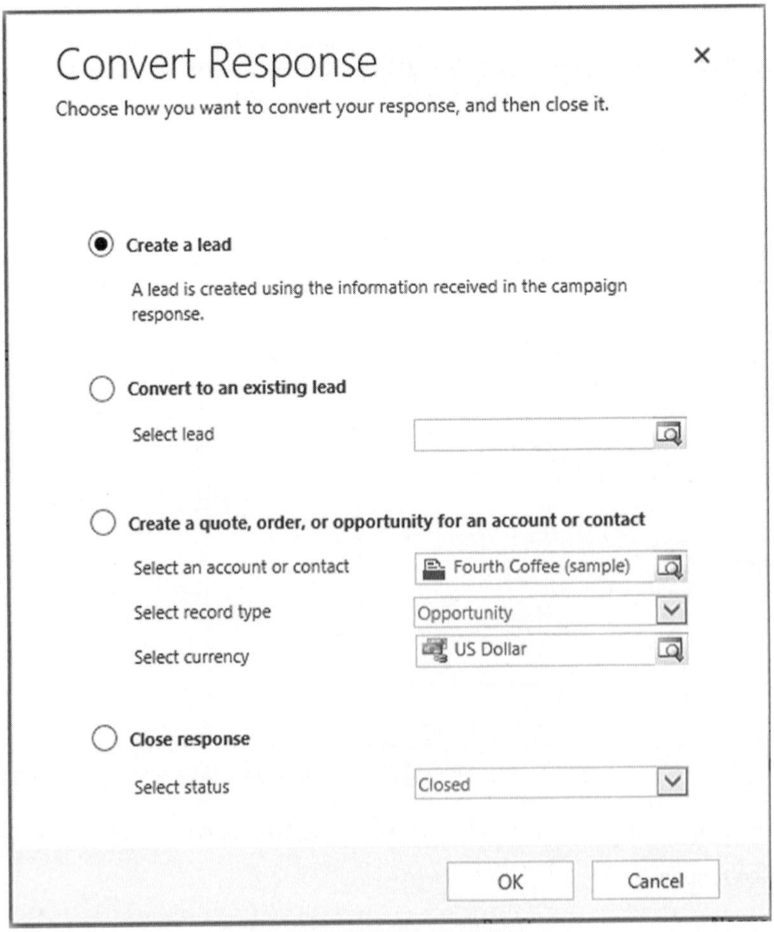

FIGURE 8.16   Converting a campaign response.

Although the campaign response functionality described here is applicable to campaigns and quick campaigns, the three campaign reports available in the Reports area (Campaign Activity Status, Campaign Comparison, and Campaign Performance) are applicable only to campaigns by default. These reports are powerful and display campaign information in a manner that is easy to understand and useful for determining metrics on campaigns. We recommend reviewing all of them often when building campaigns and when viewing the status of executed campaigns.

Sales Literature

Found in the Marketing area, sales literature is documentation about products that is meant to be used by your salesforce to gain deeper knowledge about your products; it can also be given to customers to drive sales. In addition, sales literature can provide specific instructions on how to use a given product or services and can identify competitors.

To create a new piece of sales literature, select New and then, as shown in Figure 8.17, enter the title of the literature in the Title field and the subject in the Subject field.

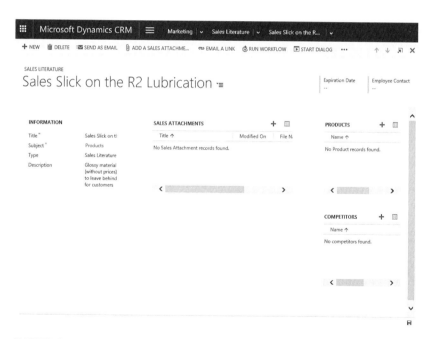

FIGURE 8.17   Sales literature.

▶ For more information about working with subjects, **SEE CHAPTER 17**, "Settings."

Additional optional fields you can set for sales literature include Employee Contact, Type, Expiration Date, and Description.

NOTE

Although the Expiration Date field has no functionality other than to tell the salesperson when the literature expires, it would be easy to add another custom view to the sales literature interface that shows only current or nonexpired sales literature.

Sales attachments can have as many pieces of documentation as desired. To create a new sales attachment document, select Add a Sales Attachment from the command bar and then click the + icon. Figure 8.18 shows the new Sales Attachment form that appears.

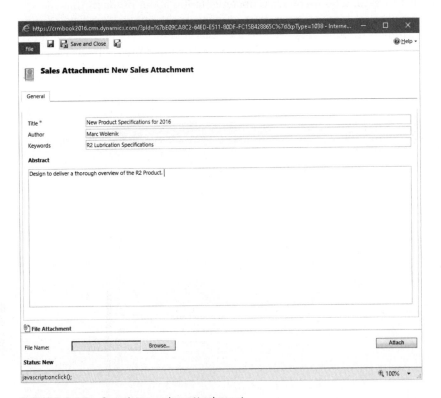

FIGURE 8.18   Creating a sales attachment.

When working with sales literature, you can add products and identify competitors, which helps to provide context around the literature.

Sales literature can be sent directly from CRM. To make this happen, navigate to Sales Literature, select the sales attachments you want to send, and then click the envelope (Send as Email) icon in the command bar. A new CRM email opens, with the sales literature attached, and you can enter the contact information and then send the material.

Quick Campaigns

A quick campaign is a simplified version of a campaign. Unlike a campaign, which can contain many activities, a quick campaign has one activity type. It is easy to create a quick campaign by using a wizard that you can launch from Advanced Find or directly from the Account, Contact, or Lead forms.

The following sections discuss how to create and see the status of quick campaigns.

Creating a Quick Campaign

Creating quick campaigns is as easy as the name implies. To create a quick campaign, follow these steps:

1. Open Advanced Find and select Contact as the base entity. Then to do a targeted quick campaign for all your contacts in the state of California, choose the settings shown in Figure 8.19 and click Results.

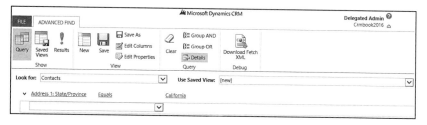

FIGURE 8.19   Creating a quick campaign for contacts in California.

2. From the results screen, select one or more records and then select Quick Campaign > For All Records on All Pages (see Figure 8.20). On the Create a Quick Campaign welcome screen that appears, click Next.

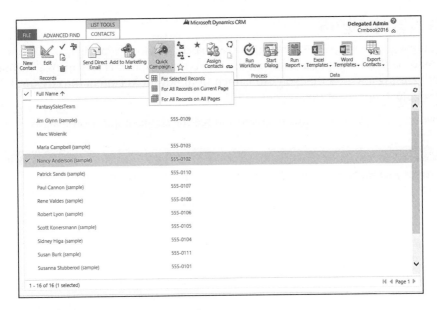

FIGURE 8.20   Advanced Find results.

3. Enter the name of the campaign and click Next to continue. On the next screen, shown in Figure 8.21, select the activity type of the quick campaign and who will own the activities. If the Activity Type selection is Email (as shown here), the system can automatically send the emails and close the activities, if selected. Otherwise, the activities will belong to the selected owners as pending and will require action by the owners to be closed out.

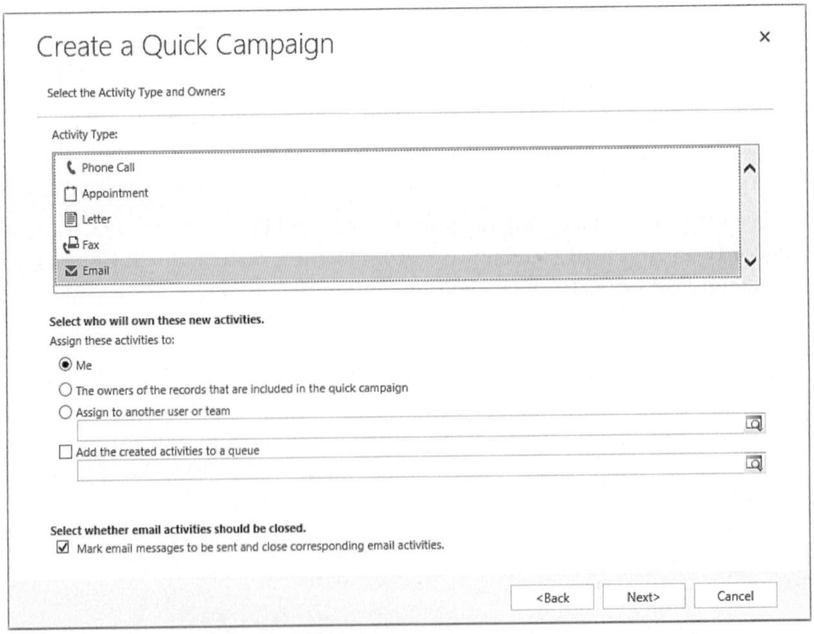

Create a Quick Campaign   ✕

Select the Activity Type and Owners

Activity Type:

- 📞 Phone Call
- 📋 Appointment
- 📄 Letter
- 🖨 Fax
- ✉ Email

Select who will own these new activities.
Assign these activities to:

- ⦿ Me
- ◯ The owners of the records that are included in the quick campaign
- ◯ Assign to another user or team

☐ Add the created activities to a queue

Select whether email activities should be closed.
☑ Mark email messages to be sent and close corresponding email activities.

<Back   Next>   Cancel

FIGURE 8.21   Selecting the activity type.

After you select Email, you're prompted to enter the email information shown in Figure 8.22. If you had selected another activity, you would be prompted to complete the appropriate fields for that activity. This example shows a simple email, which has the downside of limited customization. If you were to use the Channel option of Letter via Mail Merge, you could personalize the letter fully and include additional data fields.

4. Click Next to continue and then click Create to create the quick campaign.

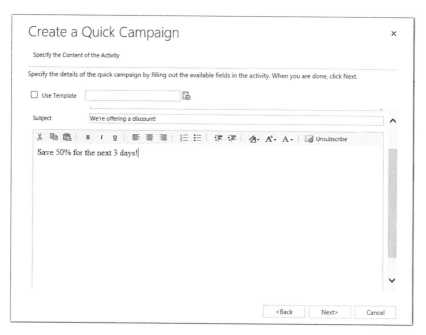

FIGURE 8.22   Selecting the Email activity type.

NOTE

To use the Unsubscribe option, select some text in the body of the Email by highlighting it and then click the Unsubscribe button (refer to Figure 8.22). (For example, add and select the following text: To stop receiving our emails, click here.) The selected text is then formatted as a link that users can click to set their preferences to not allow marketing materials.

The wizard completes, and the activity or activities (if you have more than one contact) are created. The activities then wait for the person to complete them unless it was an email (in which case the email goes out directly).

Finding the Status of a Quick Campaign

Although you can't launch quick campaigns directly by selecting Quick Campaigns from the navigation bar, you can monitor the status of quick campaigns by doing so. Figure 8.23 shows the My Quick Campaigns form, which appears when you make this selection. Inside this form, you can open a quick campaign by double-clicking it to bring up information about its success and failure by looking at the members excluded (and why).

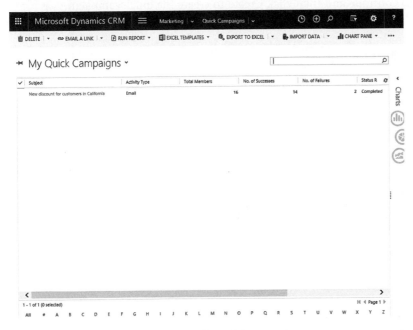

FIGURE 8.23   Checking the status of a quick campaigns.

In the My Quick Campaigns form, you can easily see what the quick campaign was for and who received email messages by selecting Email Messages Created from the form. In addition, you can track any responses to the quick campaign, just as you would for a regular campaign. Finally, you can easily see which contacts received the email and which were excluded and why by examining the details found in each node. (For example, perhaps a contact didn't have a valid email address.)

Summary

In this chapter, you have seen that Microsoft Dynamics CRM offers a full set of marketing options and capabilities. From its powerful campaign-management features to its quick-and-easy quick campaigns, you can easily market to existing and potential clients, report on results, and determine which marketing efforts worked.

Remember that this chapter does not cover Microsoft Dynamics Marketing (MDM) or its related integration components. Instead, consider this chapter as a standalone option on the native marketing functions found within Dynamics CRM.

▶ For more information about Dynamics Marketing, **SEE CHAPTER 9**.

Microsoft Dynamics Marketing

While Dynamics CRM has basic marketing capabilities that include the ability to segment and send emails (and even track responses), the ability to execute on complex campaigns requires a more sophisticated tool for marketing. This tool is Microsoft Dynamics Marketing (MDM), which is a product specifically oriented toward marketing departments.

> **NOTE**
>
> MDM is a separate product from Microsoft Dynamics CRM that fully integrates with Dynamics CRM. Users can purchase it through an Office 365 subscription.

> **TIP**
>
> MDM is available only with CRM Online, and there are no plans for it to be available for On-Premises installations. However, you can integrate the MDM Online service with your On-Premises deployment of Dynamics CRM.

> **NOTE**
>
> This chapter covers only the most common usage scenarios related to MDM, as an entire book could be written about MDM.

The current version of MDM (Dynamics Marketing 2016, Update 0.3) is the third generation since Microsoft acquired Marketing Pilot in 2012.

Key Features of MDM

MDM is a robust marketing solution for marketing operations, planning, execution, and analytics across different channels, such as email, social media, SMS, and various other digital options (blogs, Twitter, and so on).

> **NOTE**
>
> You can get a free one-month trial of the Enterprise version of MDM for 25 users by going to www.microsoft.com/en-us/dynamics/marketing-test-drive.aspx.

While the MDM user interface (UI) shares the same look and feel as the Dynamics CRM application, these are actually two different systems and applications, using different databases and entity models behind the scenes.

These are the key features of MDM:

▶ Marketing resource management

▶ Multichannel campaigns

▶ Lead management and scoring

▶ Sales and marketing collaboration

▶ Social marketing

▶ Marketing intelligence

All these features present a mature and enterprise-class system for marketing, and the typical deployment of MDM is to a marketing department, not to a casual user who wants to send occasional emails announcing sales (not that you couldn't do that).

MDM Setup

After navigating to the Office 365 portal and selecting MDM to add to your subscription (or getting a free trial, as mentioned earlier in this chapter), you need to perform an initial setup and configuration. As part of this initial setup, you need to select a default currency, which will later be used to manage the marketing budgets, and the language (as shown in Figure 9.1). Note that you can change the configurations later, if necessary, by going to Settings > Site Settings, as explained later in this chapter.

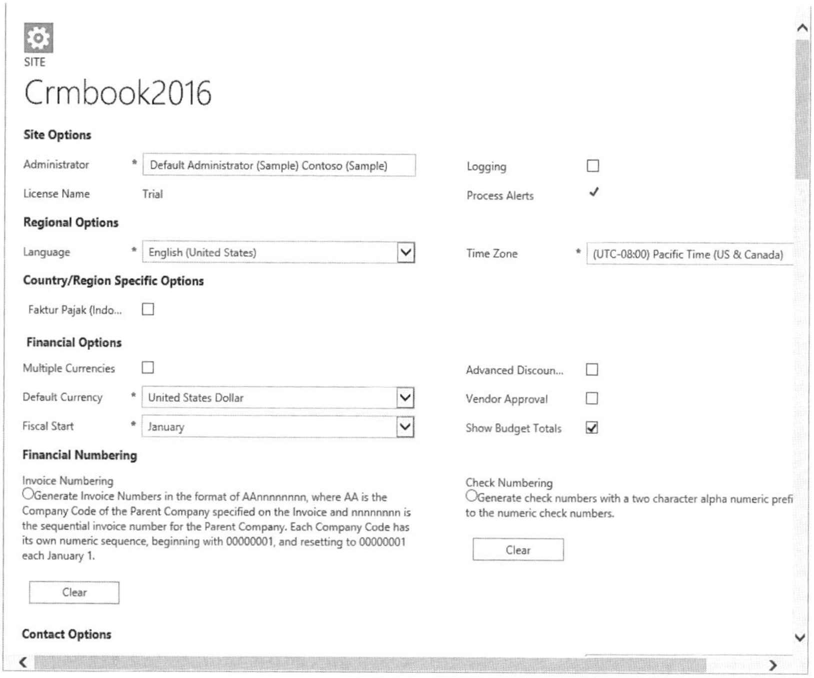

FIGURE 9.1   MDM first-time configurations.

You must also agree to the terms of the applicable MDM license or subscription and click the Submit button to start using the application, as shown in Figure 9.2.

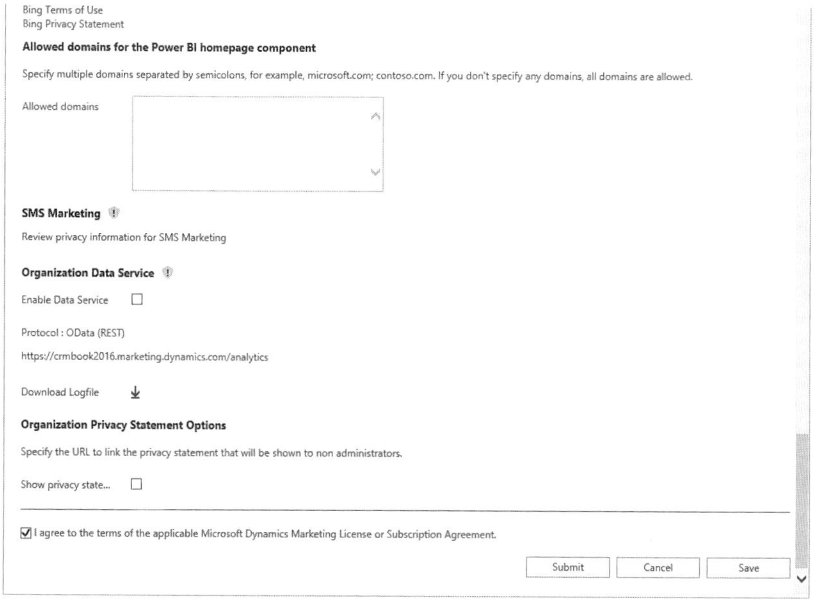

FIGURE 9.2   Agreeing to the terms of the MDM agreement.

The welcome screen, which appears next, presents a drop-down list with the following options to help you select your role:

▶ Marketing Manager

▶ Creative

▶ Media Buyer

▶ All

After you select a role selection, a video presentation shows how to initially use and navigate the system, and you can opt to not see this welcome screen again in the future by selecting Don't Show Me This Again. After you view the video or click Skip Intro, you see the home page.

> **NOTE**
>
> To navigate back to the welcome page, select the gear in the top-right corner of the window and choose Welcome Dialog.

The first time you log in to MDM, you get a series of warnings across the top of the screen:

▶ Turn On Full-Text Search

▶ Double Opt-in for Emails

▶ SMS Marketing Information

▶ Standardized KPIs for SMS

The following sections describe how to deal with these messages.

Turn On Full-Text

To turn on the full-text search, click Go to Site Settings in the yellow warning bar. Alternatively, you can navigate to Home > Settings > Site Settings. Figure 9.3 shows where to turn on/off full-text search, in the Contact Options section.

FIGURE 9.3   Use Full-Text Search option.

Check this option and then click Submit at the bottom of the page.

> **NOTE**
>
> Notice that under Settings > Site Settings you can find all the configurations that were made the first time MDM was configured, and you can change them here as well.

Double Opt-in for Emails

This warning suggests using double verification before setting a contact to receive marketing materials. The reason for this is that usually a contact is created in the system after completing a form on a web page, and in most cases that automatically sets the contact to allow receipt of marketing emails. However, it is recommended that you ask the contact if he or she really wants to receive these emails by sending them another email with a link so they can opt in.

To get rid of the double opt-in emails warning, navigate to Settings > Company Settings to go to the My Company Page, as shown in Figure 9.4.

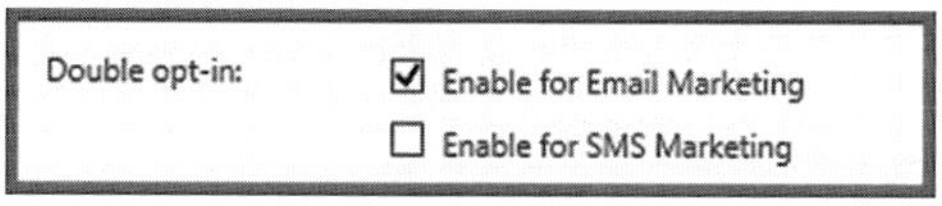

| Double opt-in: | ☑ Enable for Email Marketing |
| | ☐ Enable for SMS Marketing |

FIGURE 9.4   My Company page.

Check the Enable for Email Marketing check box next to Double Opt-in and click Submit at the bottom of the page to save your changes. Then click OK on the confirmation alert.

> **NOTE**
>
> The Double Opt-in setting is a global setting, which means that it will apply to all emails.

SMS Marketing Information

The SMS Marketing Information warning suggests that you review user permissions and privacy information about SMS marketing and relevant contact duplicate detection options. To do so, click the link that appears in this warning's yellow bar (or navigate to Settings > Site Settings).

As shown in Figure 9.5, when you navigate from the SMS Marketing subtitle, you can click the Review Privacy Information for SMS Marketing link to see instructions on how to configure SMS.

SMS Marketing ⚠

Review privacy information for SMS Marketing

FIGURE 9.5   SMS Marketing section.

> **NOTE**
>
> SMS requires you to set up a short code for each region and then purchase SMS message credits before you can use SMS Marketing features.

Standardized KPIs for SMS

For the Standardized KPIs for SMS warning, navigate to Settings > Marketing Automation and select whether to view standardized or legacy KPIs, as shown in Figure 9.6.

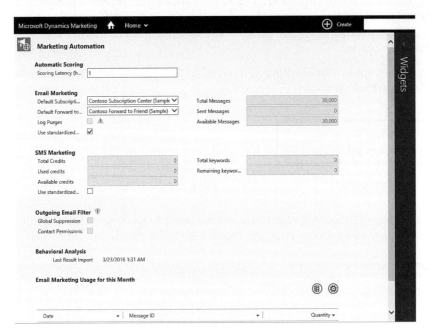

FIGURE 9.6   Marketing automation settings.

MDM Navigation

From the navigation bar you can access the main functionalities of the MDM application. Selecting Microsoft Dynamics Marketing always takes you home.

Home

Select the Home icon to go to your home page, where you can customize the application by adding widgets.

If you click Add Widgets, you get icons for the following options (see Figure 9.7):

- ▶ Add Charts
- ▶ Add Budget Usage
- ▶ Add Power BI
- ▶ Add Widgets

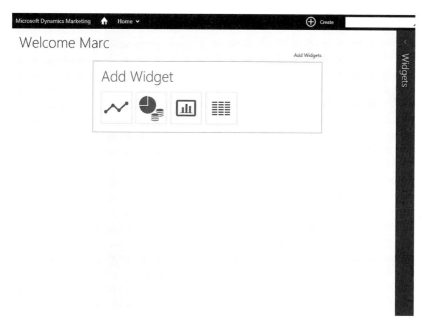

FIGURE 9.7   Adding widgets.

Adding Charts

Figure 9.8 shows the options available after you select the chart icon on the Add Widget page. When you add a chart, you need to select a data source, which can be any of the following:

- ▶ Expense Item
- ▶ Lead Performance
- ▶ File Usage
- ▶ Email Deliverability
- ▶ Budget Usage
- ▶ Campaign Effectiveness

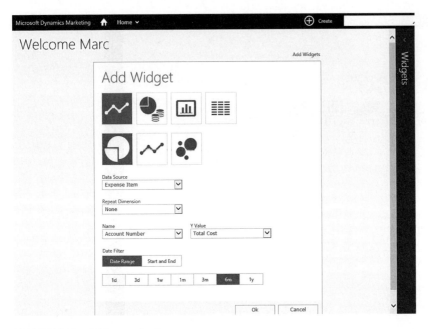

FIGURE 9.8 Adding a chart.

You can select one of the following type of charts:

▶ Pie chart

▶ Area chart

▶ Bubble chart

Adding Widgets

Selecting the last icon on the Add Widget page allows you to add the following widgets:

▶ Approvals

▶ Favorite Files

▶ My Jobs

▶ Job Status

▶ My Tasks

▶ My Time Slips

▶ My opportunities

▶ Account Balances

▶ My Leads

▶ Lead Performance

▶ My Scheduled Emails

▶ Email Marketing

Figure 9.9 shows the Approvals and Favorite Files widgets added to the home page.

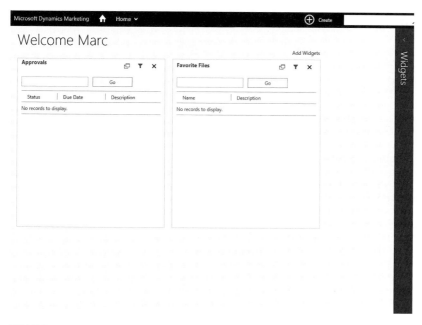

FIGURE 9.9   Approvals and Favorite Files widgets.

NOTE

From the Add Widget page you can also add Budget Usage and Power BI components to the application to provide analytics and reporting.

Main Areas of the MDM Application

The MDM application is divided in the following areas, which are dependent on the user roles and privileges you are configured to be able see (see the "Settings" section, later in this chapter):

▶ Projects

▶ Marketing Execution

▶ Assets & Media

▶ Budgeting

▶ Performance

▶ Settings

Figure 9.10 shows these main navigation options in the navigation bar, and the following sections provide details.

FIGURE 9.10   Main navigation options.

Projects

As shown in Figure 9.10, the Projects area is divided in the following sections and items:

▶ Jobs Management

　　▶ Jobs

　　▶ Jobs Request Templates

　　▶ Jobs Request Menu

▶ Approvals

　　▶ Approvals

　　▶ Templates

▶ Tasks

　　▶ Tasks

▶ Notes

　　▶ Notes

▶ Emails

　　▶ Emails

　　▶ Templates

▶ Reports

　　▶ Approval Workload

　　▶ Tasks Workload

▶ Tasks Gantt

▶ Jobs % on Time

▶ Jobs Actual vs. Est Time

▶ Jobs Performance

▶ Estimated Time

▶ Time Utilization/Realization

▶ Time Workload

▶ Invoices Time

Jobs   Jobs track overall projects and are necessary for tasks to be assigned, distributed, and completed. Figure 9.11 shows the new job form.

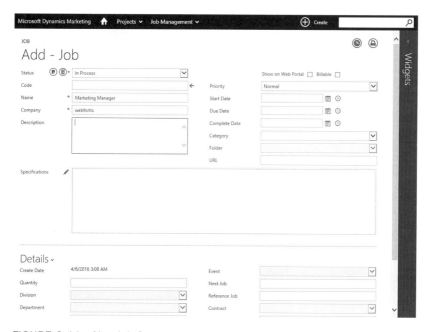

FIGURE 9.11   New job form.

In addition to using jobs to manage and track projects, you can complete the specifications and related note fields to provide context related to the jobs. In addition, if you add time slips to the job form, you can later aggregate effort on any given project by clicking the clock icon in the top-right corner of the new job form. Figure 9.12 shows the time slip addition form.

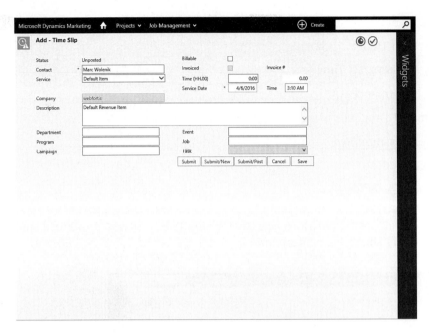

FIGURE 9.12   Adding time slips.

Project Templates   You can use project templates when you find that a job is used more than once. After you create a project template, it must be used to create requests.

In essence, project templates create the layout and necessary questions that the requestor then completes in order to make a request.

To create a project template, navigate to Projects > Project Request > Templates and click the + button.

Enter at least the name of the template and save the form. After you save the new template, you can add new requirements by clicking the + button near the requirements.

Complete the required information and click Save to save the requirement.

After you add all the requirements you need, you can click Submit to activate them. Figure 9.13 shows the project template with several requirements. Notice the order that was selected/entered when creating the task; you can adjust this manually if necessary by selecting tasks with the mouse and moving them in the preferred order. (MDM automatically reorders the sequence.)

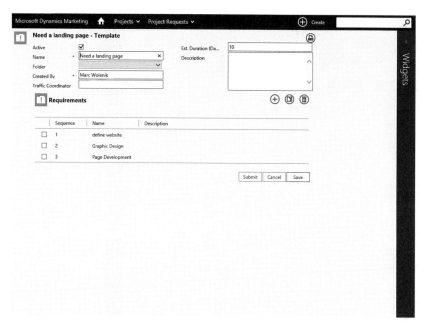

FIGURE 9.13   Project templates with requirements.

Click Submit to finish your project template configurations.

Project Requests   Not to be confused with job requests, project requests develop projects, and they typically require approval, queuing of permissions, resources, and so on before the requests can become jobs. (Job requests, on the other hand, skip the approval step and create a job immediately.)

When creating a new project request, you are required to enter the name of the request and a type. From the Type drop-down you can select from a list of the active project templates you have in the system, so be sure you have at least one project template created before trying to create a new project request.

When you create a new request, the estimated completion date is automatically calculated based on the estimated duration in days you entered and the project template you selected from the Type drop-down list.

Click Save to create the new project request, and the list of requirements that were predefined in the project template is shown (see Figure 9.14).

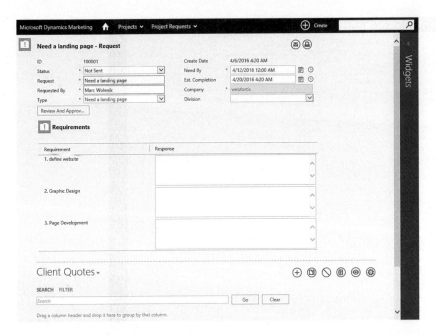

FIGURE 9.14   New request requirements.

> **NOTE**
>
> If you want to select a division, you must create a divisions first by going to the Settings area, as explained later in this chapter. Once the division is selected and saved, this value can't be changed.

Approvals   There are two types of approval requests: approval and review. An approval request requires the user to approve or reject an item, whereas a review request is only a request for feedback and doesn't include or involve any workflow. Figure 9.15 shows the new approval request form.

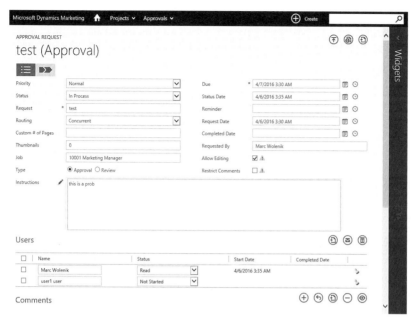

FIGURE 9.15   New approval request form.

If you have a complex approval process, you can customize the basic workflow by clicking the Workflow button after you have completed the required fields and clicking Save. You then see the screen shown in Figure 9.16.

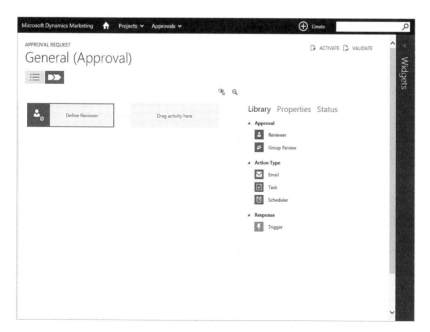

FIGURE 9.16   Approval request workflow designer.

You can add a reviewer by dragging and dropping the Reviewer component from the right list to the workflow designer area, and then you can switch to the Properties tab to specify the user who will act as a reviewer for this workflow. After you select the user, click Select.

You can use the following library components:

▶ Approval

    ▶ Reviewer

    ▶ Group Review

▶ Action Type

    ▶ Email

    ▶ Task

    ▶ Scheduler

▶ Response

    ▶ Trigger

After configuring the workflow, you must validate it by clicking the Validate button. After it is validated, the workflow can be activated.

> **NOTE**
>
> All approvers or reviewers must be users of MDM.

> **TIP**
>
> An extensive audit log is created during the approval and review process that allows the requestor to view all comments made during the process.

Marketing Execution

The Marketing Execution area is divided in the following sections and items:

▶ Campaign Management

    ▶ Campaigns

    ▶ Campaign Templates

    ▶ Programs

    ▶ Marketing Calendar

    ▶ Offers

▶ A/B Testing

    ▶ A/B Testing

- ▶ Marketing Database
  - ▶ Marketing Companies
  - ▶ Marketing Contacts
- ▶ Vendors
  - ▶ Vendor Companies
  - ▶ Vendor Contacts
- ▶ Clients
  - ▶ Client Contacts
  - ▶ Client Companies
  - ▶ Contracts
- ▶ Marketing Lists
  - ▶ Marketing Lists
- ▶ Lead Management
  - ▶ Landing Pages
  - ▶ Leads
  - ▶ Opportunity Metrics
  - ▶ Opportunity Forecast
- ▶ Marketing Plans
  - ▶ Marketing Plans
- ▶ Internet Marketing
  - ▶ Online Visitors
  - ▶ Redirecting URLs
  - ▶ Websites
- ▶ Event Management
  - ▶ Events
  - ▶ Lodging
  - ▶ Attendance
  - ▶ Registrations
  - ▶ Sponsorships
  - ▶ Staffing
  - ▶ Templates

- ▶ Equipment Requests

- ▶ Equipment Availability

- ▶ Equipment Inventory

- ▶ Venues

- ▶ Venue Facilities

- ▶ Travel

▶ Social Media

- ▶ Social Media

▶ Email Marketing

- ▶ Email Marketing Messages

- ▶ Templates

- ▶ External Content

▶ SMS Marketing

- ▶ SMS Marketing Messages

▶ Calendar

- ▶ Activities

- ▶ Calendar

▶ Results

- ▶ Results

Figure 9.17 shows the Marketing Execution navigation options from the navigation bar.

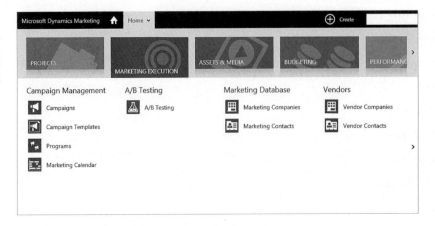

FIGURE 9.17   Marketing Execution area.

Campaigns   When considering marketing, one of the most important features is campaigns. MDM allows you to see the campaigns you have already created that are running.

To create a new campaign, navigate to the Campaign Templates option. Once there, start a campaign by using one of the existing templates or by creating a new campaign template (see Figure 9.18).

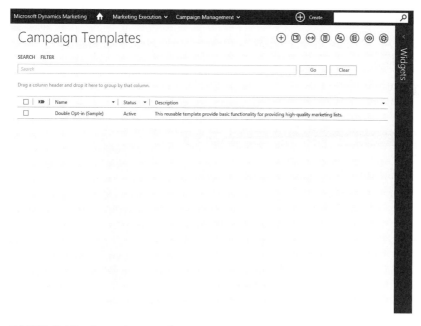

FIGURE 9.18   Campaign templates.

To create a new campaign template, click on the + icon in the command bar.

Each campaign has three navigation options, represented by icons right under the word Create:

▶ Summary

▶ Automation

▶ Dashboard

To complete the summary information, enter a name for your campaign, and the company name is populated with your personal company name; you can change this later, if needed, in the Settings area. Click Save to create your campaign.

NOTE

To be able to start editing the automation of your campaign, be sure to set start and end dates for the campaign.

Automation   You can add automation in order to preconfigure the follow-up related to actions that have occurred. For example, a user might request information from a webpage, and from that you would want to send the user the information and then follow up with additional emails and assign the lead to a sales agent (via a task).

By using the process of automation, marketers can scale their outreach, leveraging the power of technology.

Figure 9.19 shows the automation page for a campaign. Microsoft refers to this area as the Campaign Canvas.

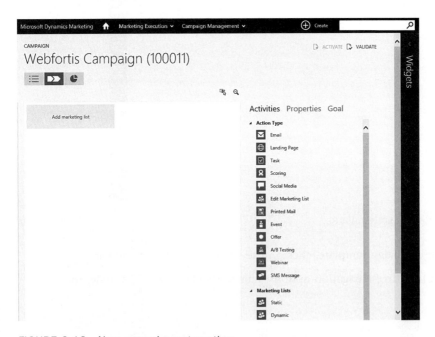

FIGURE 9.19   New campaign automation.

With the automation editor, You can drag and drop tiles to specify what events should happen and when. You drag the activities from the right and drop them on the design area on the left. You can then select an activity you dropped and switch to the Properties tab to configure the activity for the automation, as shown in Figure 9.20.

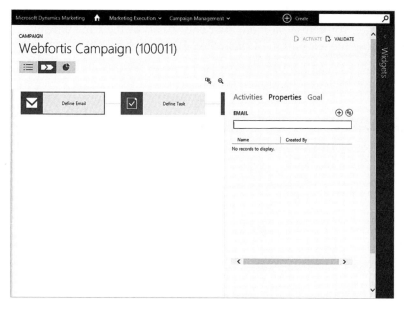

FIGURE 9.20   Email activity properties.

To delete an activity, just right-click it and select Delete. You can also copy and paste from this context menu.

Dragging an activity and dropping just below an existing activity allows you to add activities in parallel. Figure 9.21 shows campaign automation with parallel activities added.

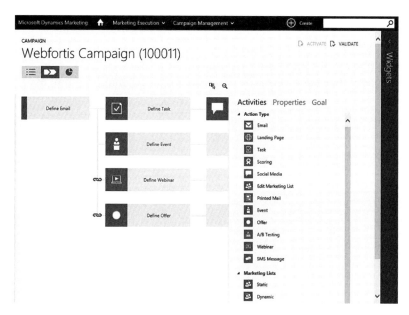

FIGURE 9.21   Campaign with activities in parallel.

By clicking the multi-selector icon (which looks like a mouse pointer and is at the top of the automation designer), you can select more than one activity at the same time by drawing a square by holding the left button of the mouse as you click activities.

If you have lot of activities, you can use the zoom mode that is near the multi-selection icon to zoom in and out of the canvas, as shown in Figure 9.22.

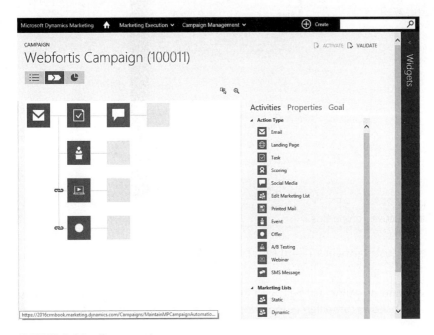

FIGURE 9.22   Zoom mode.

When you are done configuring campaign automation, you must validate it prior to activating it. You can do this by clicking the Validation button in the top-right corner (see Figure 9.22). Any activity that has errors is shown with a red exclamation point, as shown in Figure 9.23.

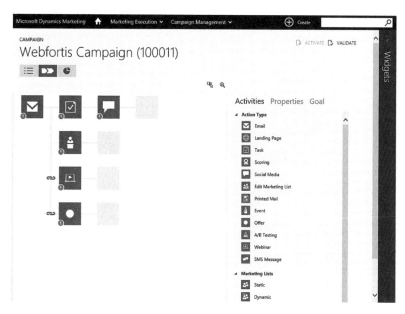

FIGURE 9.23   Campaign validation.

To correct these errors, you need to enter data in their required fields. To do that, double-click the tile to see the properties displayed in the right panel. Each activity type has its own specific set of properties.

The Goal tab is where you can set the leads, unit costs, average score, and grade for the campaign (see Figure 9.24).

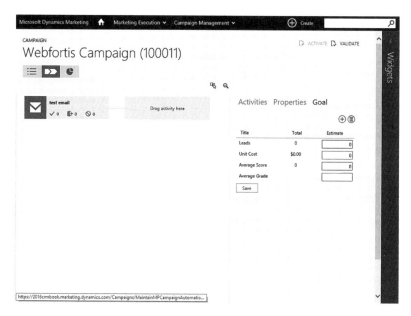

FIGURE 9.24   Campaign goals.

You can add more goals if necessary by clicking the + button and selecting one of the result types listed and clicking OK. Figure 9.25 shows the result type options available.

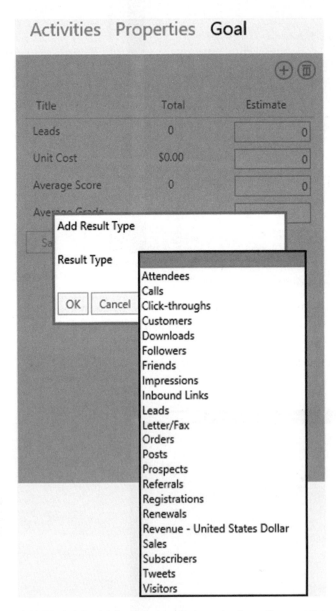

FIGURE 9.25   Adding more goals by selecting other result types.

You can create your own custom result types by going to Settings > Result Types.

Campaign Dashboard   When all issues are fixed and a campaign is validated, you can switch to the dashboard (see Figure 9.26) to see detailed information about the campaign performance.

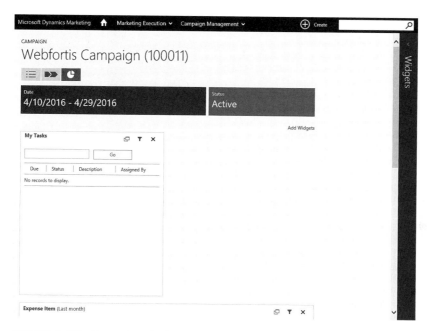

FIGURE 9.26   Campaign dashboard.

As with the home page, you can add widgets on the campaign dashboard to take advantage of additional management features.

Email Marketing   You can use email marketing to send emails using templates. Navigate to Marketing Execution and then select the Email Marketing Messages option. Here you see the email messages that were executed as well as important information about the reaming messages quota limit you can use for the day and the month, as shown in Figure 9.27.

▶ To learn how to enable the sample email templates, **SEE** the "Templates" section, later in this chapter.

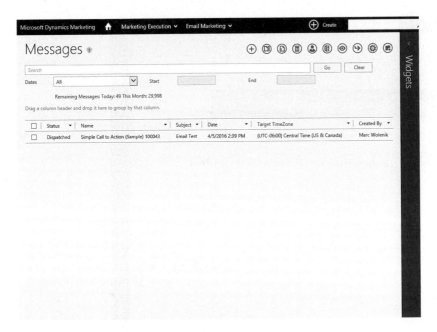

FIGURE 9.27   Email marketing messages.

You can create a new email message by clicking the + button, selecting an email template, and entering your company name, as shown in Figure 9.28. Click Submit and then enter a name for your email and select a subscription center.

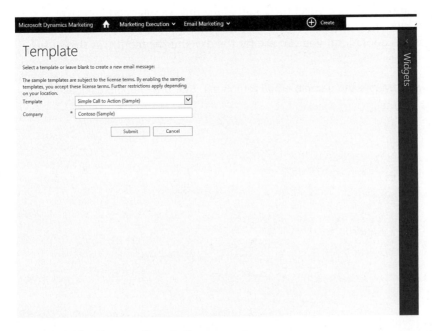

FIGURE 9.28   New email marketing message.

The subscription center is a mandatory plug-in that ensures that all emails are CAN-SPAM compliant. See the "Settings" section of this chapter for more details.

Either create a new subscription center in the Settings area or use the sample subscription center, as shown in Figure 9.29.

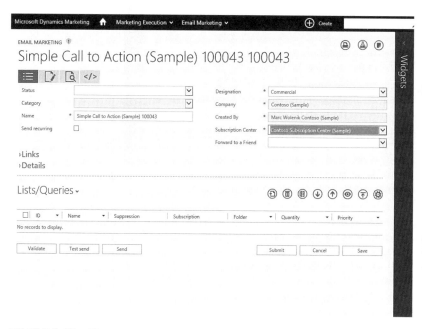

FIGURE 9.29   New email marketing message with a subscription center.

Select the Edit Content icon just above the Status field to enter the design mode, which is shown in Figure 9.30.

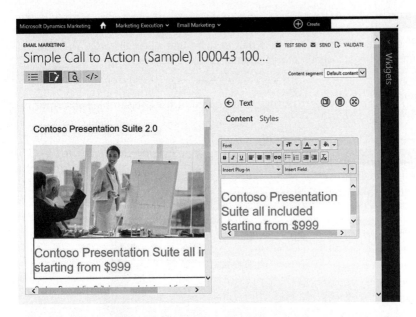

FIGURE 9.30   New email marketing message design mode rich text editor.

Depending on the control you select on the design palate, you will see different properties that can be applied in the right panel.

By clicking Validate in the command bar you can see what must be completed to ensure that the email is valid and can be sent. Figure 9.31 shows the result with a poorly formed email.

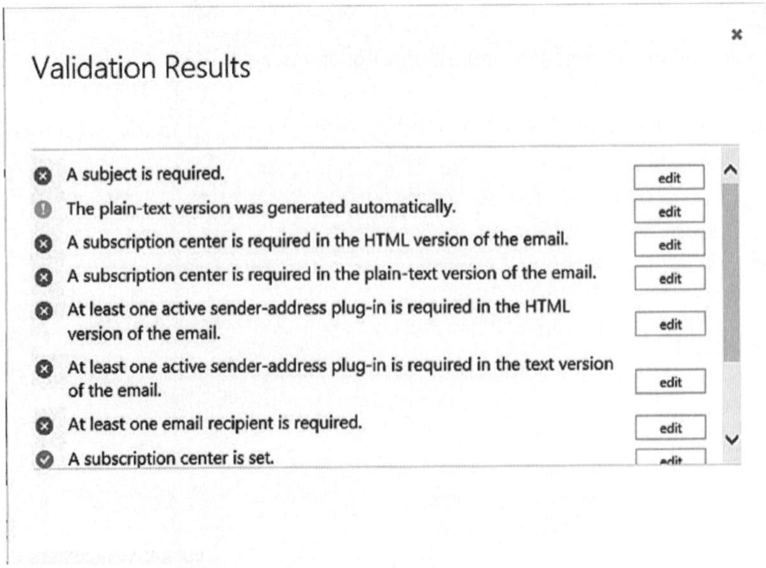

Validation Results

❌ A subject is required.	edit
ⓘ The plain-text version was generated automatically.	edit
❌ A subscription center is required in the HTML version of the email.	edit
❌ A subscription center is required in the plain-text version of the email.	edit
❌ At least one active sender-address plug-in is required in the HTML version of the email.	edit
❌ At least one active sender-address plug-in is required in the text version of the email.	edit
❌ At least one email recipient is required.	edit
✅ A subscription center is set.	edit

FIGURE 9.31   Email marketing message validation results.

> **NOTE**
>
> For every error or warning displayed on the Validation Results page, you can click the Edit button to go to the place on the form where you need to fix the problem.

For example, a common error is not selecting the recipients of the email. Figure 9.32 shows the options for selecting recipients from one of the existing lists.

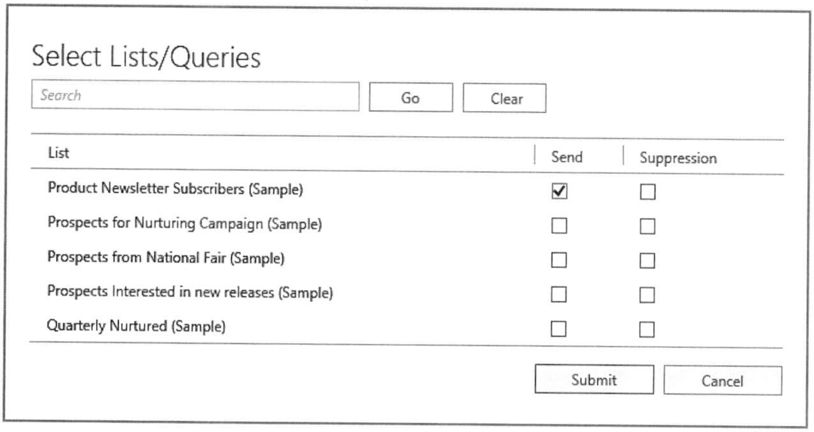

Select Lists/Queries

List	Send	Suppression
Product Newsletter Subscribers (Sample)	☑	☐
Prospects for Nurturing Campaign (Sample)	☐	☐
Prospects from National Fair (Sample)	☐	☐
Prospects Interested in new releases (Sample)	☐	☐
Quarterly Nurtured (Sample)	☐	☐

Submit   Cancel

FIGURE 9.32   Email marketing message recipients.

You can also preview the email message in multiple devices and change the orientation to make sure mobile users can read your messages on any device, as shown in Figure 9.33.

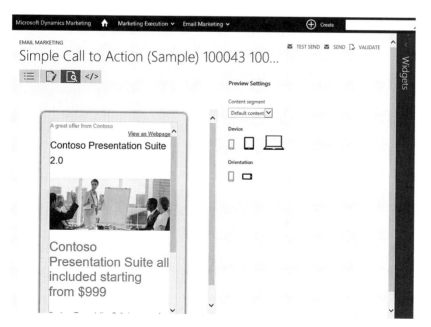

FIGURE 9.33   Email marketing message preview.

If you want to take a look at the generated HTML code of the email, you can click the View HTML button. You then see a read-only view of the generated HTML code, as shown in Figure 9.34.

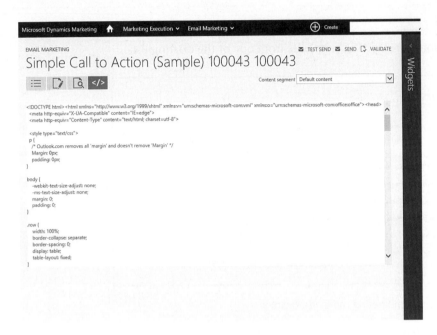

FIGURE 9.34   Email marketing message HTML view.

When you are done fixing all validation issues, it is recommended that you send a Test Send email to make sure the email looks good before you sent it to the selected recipients. Figure 9.35 shows the Test Send dialog, where you can enter a custom email address manually.

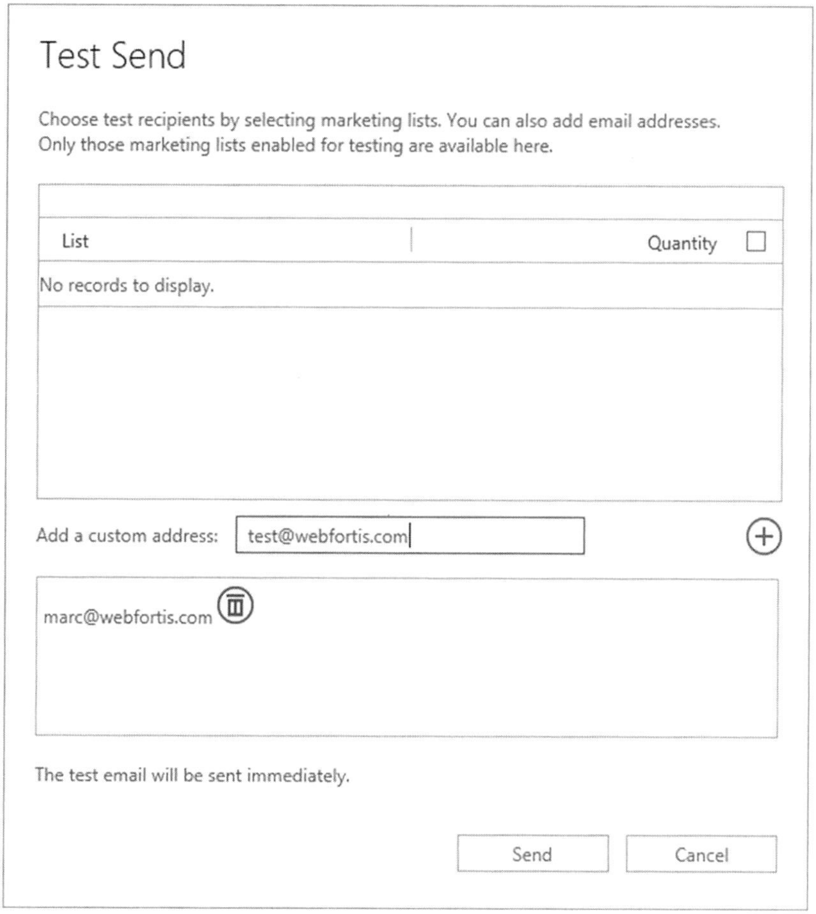

Test Send

Choose test recipients by selecting marketing lists. You can also add email addresses. Only those marketing lists enabled for testing are available here.

List		Quantity ☐
No records to display.		

Add a custom address: test@webfortis.com   ⊕

marc@webfortis.com 🗑

The test email will be sent immediately.

| Send | Cancel |

FIGURE 9.35   Email marketing message Test Send dialog.

After you enter an email address in the Test Send dialog, click the + button to add it to the list and then click the Send button.

Examine the email on your devices for form, function, and portability. When you're satisfied with the results, click the Send button to rerun the validation. When you see the confirmation dialog, click Send again to send the message to all the selected recipients.

After you send emails, you can switch to the summary view to see the result of the email messages (see Figure 9.36). To see the performance charts, you need to expand the details section, which is collapsed by default.

9

FIGURE 9.36   Email marketing message summary view.

Landing Pages   With MDM you can easily create landing pages without having to use an external website. You go to Marketing Execution > Landing Pages and click the + icon to create a new landing page, as shown in Figure 9.37.

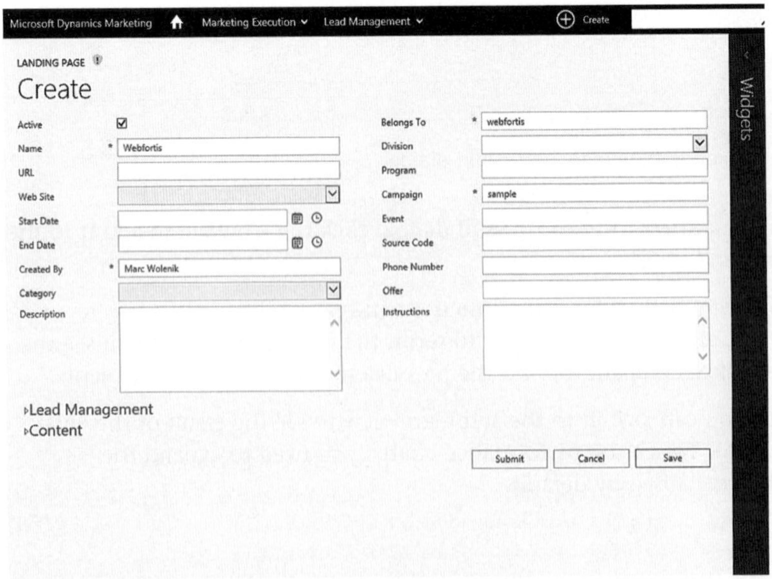

FIGURE 9.37   Creating a new landing page.

Assets & Media

The Assets & Media area is divided in the following sections and items:

- ▶ Components
    - ▶ Components
    - ▶ Component Adjustments
    - ▶ Component Packs
    - ▶ Component Requests
    - ▶ Main
    - ▶ Sub Folder
- ▶ Advertisements
    - ▶ Advertisements
- ▶ Files
    - ▶ Files
    - ▶ File Libraries
    - ▶ File Usage
- ▶ Media Planning
    - ▶ Media Outlets
    - ▶ Rate Cards
- ▶ Media Buying
    - ▶ Ad Scheduler

Components   Components are physical marketing items such as brochures and business cards. Figure 9.38 shows the form for adding a component; you can use this form to create and catalog your assets.

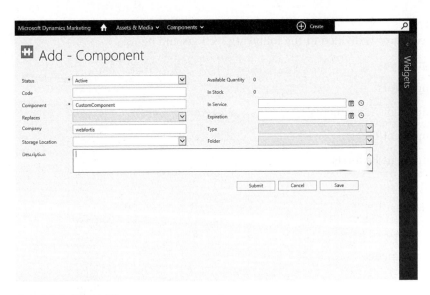

FIGURE 9.38   Adding a new component.

The Type drop-down shows a list of component types that you can manage by going to Settings > Categories, as explained later in this chapter.

You can create folders by selecting Settings > Categories > Component Folder Category. You can also create them from the Assets & Media Components list, but instead of creating a new component, you can click the new folder icon as follows:

1. Click the Make Folder icon, as shown in Figure 9.39.

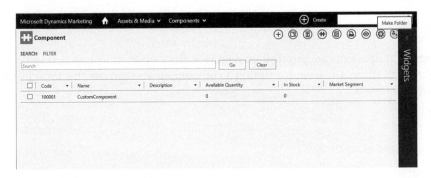

FIGURE 9.39   Make Folder icon.

2. Enter the name of the folder and click Save and then Submit (see Figure 9.40).

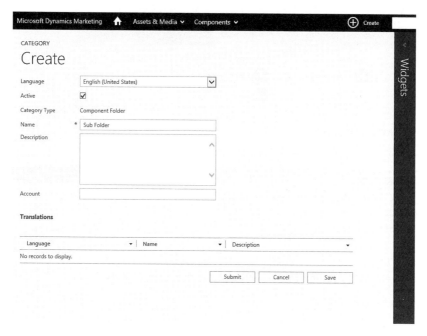

FIGURE 9.40   New component folder.

3. Enter the information required to build and host the component folder.

Budgeting

The Budgeting area is divided into the following sections and items:

- ▶ Payments
  - ▶ Expenses
  - ▶ Purchase Orders
- ▶ Settings
  - ▶ Budget Workbooks
- ▶ Reconciliation
  - ▶ Expense Reconciliation
  - ▶ Closing

Figure 9.41 shows the navigation options for the Budgeting area.

FIGURE 9.41   Budgeting area.

NOTE

The Budgeting area is beyond the scope of this chapter. However, you can check the online help for MDM for further information.

Performance

The Performance area is divided in the following sections and items:

▶ Campaign Management

    ▶ Campaign Performance

    ▶ Marketing Results

    ▶ Online Visitors

▶ Projects

    ▶ Jobs % on Time

    ▶ Jobs Actual vs. Est Time

    ▶ Jobs Performance

    ▶ Request Metrics

    ▶ Approval Workload

    ▶ Tasks Workload

    ▶ Tasks Gantt

▶ Marketing Database

    ▶ Opportunity Metrics

    ▶ Opportunity Forecast

▶ Other Reports

    ▶ Other Reports

Figure 9.42 shows the options in the Performance area.

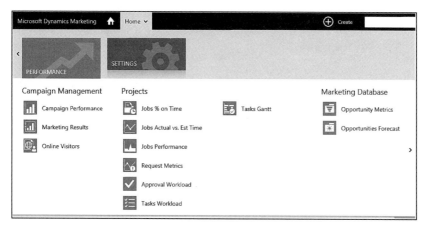

FIGURE 9.42   Performance area.

In the Other Reports section (the last option in the Performance area), there are a variety of reports you can run, email, print, and export to Microsoft Excel or PDF. The following are some of them (see Figure 9.43):

▶ Administration

▶ Banking

▶ Campaigns

▶ Clients and Receivables

▶ Company and Budgeting

▶ Email

▶ Estimates

▶ Events

▶ Jobs

▶ Media

▶ Programs

▶ Results

▶ Sales

▶ Tasks

▶ Time Slips

▶ Vendor and Payables

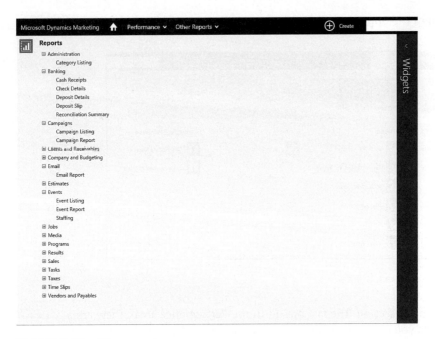

FIGURE 9.43   Other reports.

Settings

The Settings area is divided into the following sections and items:

▶ Administration

    ▶ Site Settings

    ▶ Users

    ▶ Roles

    ▶ File Options

    ▶ Reports

    ▶ Languages

    ▶ Import Monitor

    ▶ Shipping

    ▶ Integration Options

    ▶ Social Engagement Option

    ▶ Alert Settings

    ▶ Update Options

▶ Business Administration

    ▶ Categories

    ▶ Dashboards

    ▶ Marketing Automation

    ▶ Media Buying

    ▶ Budgeting

    ▶ Jobs & Components

    ▶ External Entities

▶ My Company

    ▶ Company Settings

    ▶ Channels

    ▶ Departments

    ▶ Divisions

    ▶ Locations

    ▶ Regions

    ▶ Virtual Teams

    ▶ Staff

▶ Campaign Management

    ▶ Campaign Templates

    ▶ Email Marketing Plug-ins

    ▶ Marketing Automation

▶ Rules and Models

    ▶ Lead Scoring Models

    ▶ Lead Assignment Rules

    ▶ Approval Templates

    ▶ Approvals

    ▶ Cross-Campaign Rules

▶ Templates

    ▶ Campaign Templates

    ▶ Email Marketing Templates

    ▶ Event Templates

6

▶ Job Request Templates

▶ Approval Templates

▶ Email Templates

Figure 9.44 shows the navigation options for the Settings area.

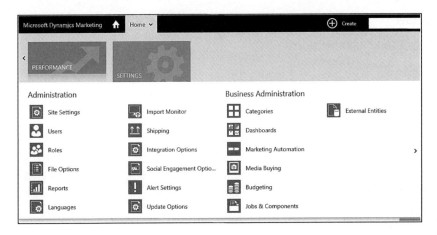

FIGURE 9.44   Settings area.

While there are a number of settings here (all of which are important), the following sections familiarize you with only the most commonly used settings in this area.

NOTE

As previously mentioned, an entire book could be devoted to the MDM application, and the coverage here is limited to only the most commonly used features and functions.

Users   The Users page shows a list of all users who have an MDM license assigned (see Figure 9.45).

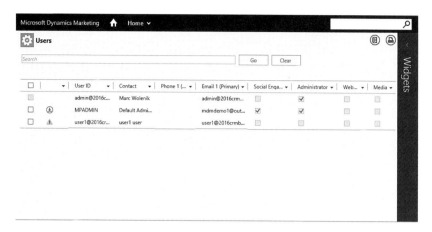

FIGURE 9.45   Users.

An exclamation point next to a user who doesn't have any role assigned means that a role needs to be assigned; to assign a role, click the name in the User ID column, and the user details screen, shown in Figure 9.46, appears.

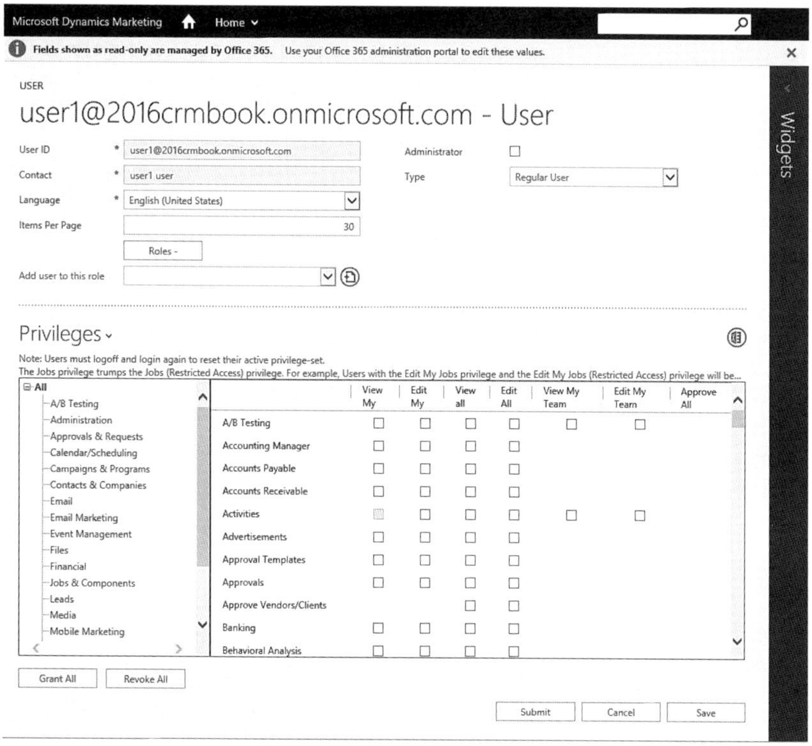

FIGURE 9.46   Editing user privileges.

In the user details screen, you can either assign privileges manually or select a predefined role and assign it to the user to configure the user to have the privileges specified for the assigned role.

You can select one of the following predefined roles:

▶ Accounting Professional

▶ Administrator

▶ Agency Marketing Professional

▶ Designer

▶ Marketing Manager/VP

▶ Marketing Professional

▶ Media Buyer

▶ Salesperson

▶ Seller Portal User

There are four types of users:

▶ Media Buyer

▶ Regular User

▶ Web Portal User

▶ Public User

NOTE

Media Buyer and Regular User require both Office 365 and MDM licenses, while Web Portal User requires only an Office 365 license. Public User, which doesn't require a license, is an external user of the system.

Clicking your name in the top-right corner takes you to your site contact details, as shown in Figure 9.47.

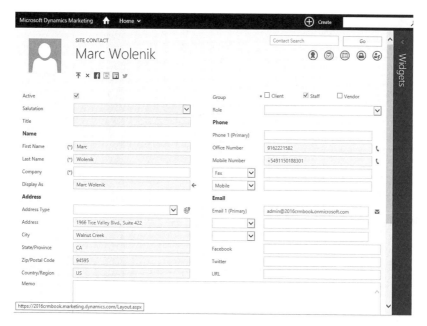

FIGURE 9.47   Site contact details.

On this page you can change the company.

Templates   MDM trials come with some sample email templates that you can enable by going to Settings > Templates > Email Marketing Templates. However, you don't see any emails initially.

To view the sample email templates, click the user icon to view all user templates and then click the eye icon to see inactive templates (see Figure 9.48).

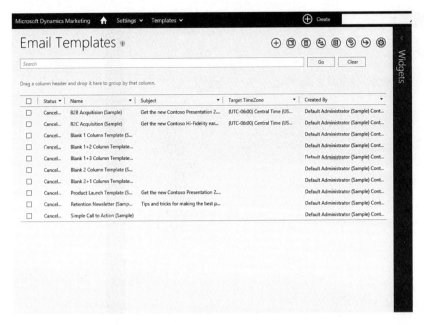

FIGURE 9.48   All users' inactive sample email marketing templates.

To enable any of these templates, select the template you want to enable and open it. Once it is open, change the status to blank and then click the Save button, as shown in Figure 9.49.

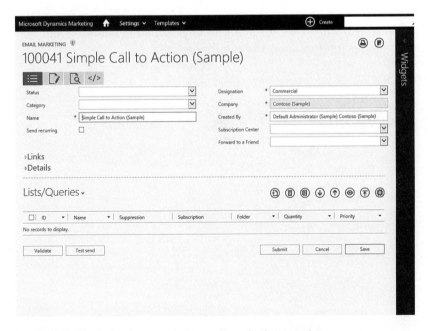

FIGURE 9.49   Activating a sample email marketing template.

Subscription Center To be able to send marketing email messages, you must select a subscription center. To create a new subscription center, navigate to Settings > Campaign Management > Email Marketing Plug-ins, and the dialog shown in Figure 9.50 appears.

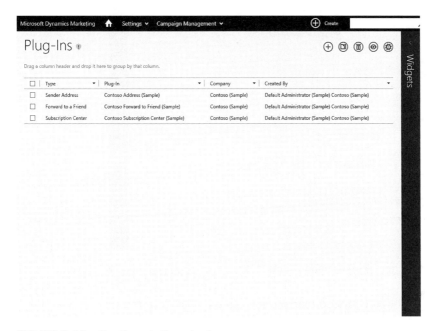

FIGURE 9.50   Email marketing plug-ins.

Click the + icon to create a new plug-in and select Subscription Center from the Type drop-down list. Then click OK to go to the subscription center page, as shown in Figure 9.51.

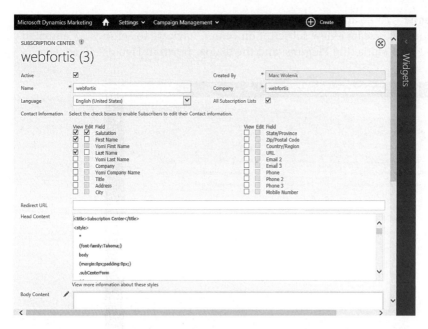

FIGURE 9.51   Adding a new subscription center.

Sender Address   To be able to send marketing email messages, you must use a valid and active sender address. To create a new sender address, navigate to Settings > Campaign Management > Email Marketing Plug-ins.

Then click the + icon to create a new plug-in and select Sender Address from the Type drop-down list.

Enter a name for your new sender address and complete the required fields, as shown in Figure 9.52. Then click Save and then Submit.

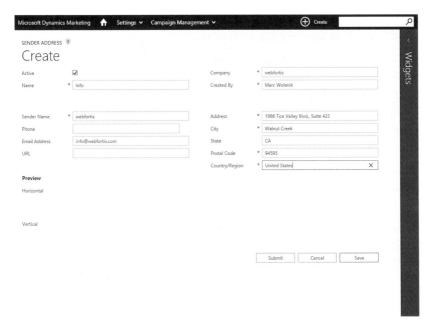

FIGURE 9.52   New sender address.

You can then use the new sender address when editing an email message by using the Info/Horizontal or Info/Vertical options, as shown in Figure 9.53.

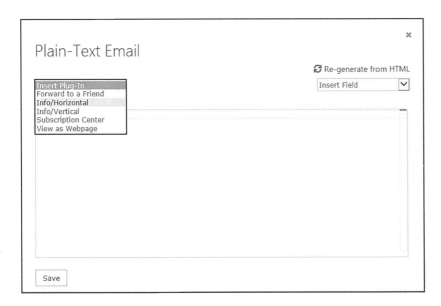

FIGURE 9.53   Using the sender address on an email message.

Result Types   You can go to Settings > Result Types to see the complete list of result types, which you use in the Goal tab of the campaign template.

There are predefined result types. In addition, you can create your own result types by clicking the + button and entering the name of the result type you want to create.

Divisions   Divisions are different from companies; a company can have an unlimited number of divisions. While not required (information can associate to companies directly), divisions are useful for accurately reflecting the structure of your organization.

If you go to Settings > Divisions > My Company, you can see the complete list of divisions. There are no sample divisions records created out of the box, so you need to create your own. You add a new division by entering the name and then clicking Save and then Submit.

Categories   You can go to Settings > Categories > Business Administration to see the complete list of categories. Categories in MDM are divided by language and category type, and they serve as the source of many of the drop-downs used by MDM in the different areas. For example, when you create a component, you see a drop-down option from which you can select the type of the component that is returned by the Component Type Category type. Figure 9.54 shows the categories for the 1099 Vendor category type.

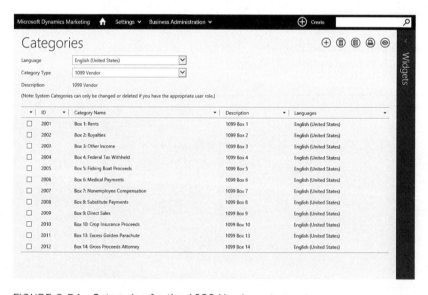

FIGURE 9.54   Categories for the 1099 Vendor category type.

To create a new category, select the category type, wait for the list to be updated, and then click the + icon. The dialog shown in Figure 9.55 appears. After filling in the required field, click Save and then click Submit.

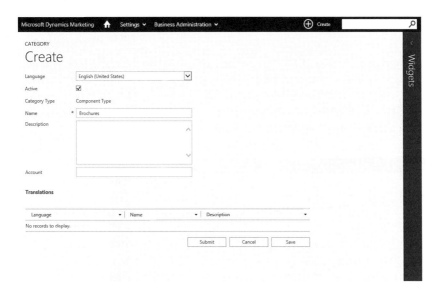

FIGURE 9.55   New categories for a component type.

Languages   By default, MDM comes in English, but there are 11 other available languages you can install. To install another language, you can download Microsoft Dynamics Marketing 19.2.5056-Language Pack.msi from www.microsoft.com/en-us/download/details.aspx?id=43108.

After downloading and executing this language pack, you can find the languages in the C:\Program Files (x86)\Microsoft Dynamics Marketing\LanguagePack folder.

The following languages are available for installation:

▶ **Danish (Denmark)**—Found in the da-DK folder

▶ **German (Germany)**—Found in the de-DE folder

▶ **English (United States)**—Found in the en-US folder

▶ **Spanish (Spain)**—Found in the es-ES folder

▶ **Finnish (Finland)**—Found in the fi-FI folder

▶ **French (France)**—Found in the fr-FR folder

▶ **Italian (Italy)**—Found in the it-IT folder

▶ **Japanese (Japan)**—Found in the ja-JP folder

▶ **Dutch (Netherlands)**—Found in the nl-NL folder

▶ **Portuguese (Brazil)**—Found in the pt-BR folder

▶ **Russian (Russia)**—Found in the ru-RU folder

▶ **Swedish (Sweden)**—Found in the sv-SE folder

To make another language available in MDM, navigate to the MDM web interface and go to Settings > Languages > Administration Group. Then click the Browse button and locate the file for language you want (for example, C:\Program Files (x86)\Microsoft Dynamics Marketing\LanguagePack\es-ES\Base.xml for Spanish). Then click the Import button, and you see the new language installed, as shown in Figure 9.56.

FIGURE 9.56   Installing a new language.

Dynamics Marketing/CRM Integration

You can integrate Dynamics Marketing with any version of Dynamics CRM (Online and On-Premises). To do this, you need to install and run an integration component called the Microsoft Dynamics Marketing Connector. You can download this component from the Microsoft Download Center or by going to www.microsoft.com/en-us/download/details.aspx?id=43108.

There are different versions of the connector, and you need to download and install the one that matches the Dynamics Marketing version you are running. To find your version, you can go to the Dynamics Marketing user interface, click the gear icon, and select About. The About page that appears lists the version number, as shown in Figure 9.57.

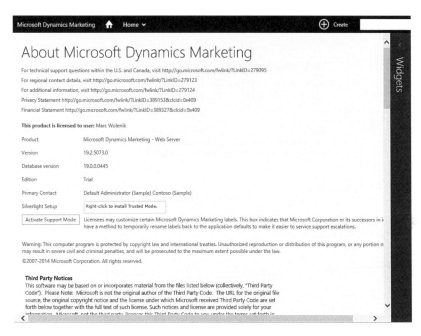

FIGURE 9.57   About Microsoft Dynamics Marketing.

Connector Requirements

The Microsoft Dynamics Marketing Connector supports the following operating systems:

▶ Windows 7

▶ Windows 8

▶ Windows 8.1

▶ Windows Server 2008

▶ Windows Server 2012 and 2012 R2

It supports the following Microsoft Dynamics CRM versions:

▶ CRM Online

▶ CRM On-Premises (at least CRM 2011 with Rollup Update 12)

Connector Setup

To set up the Microsoft Dynamics Marketing Connector, follow these steps:

1. Navigate to the downloaded Microsoft Dynamics Marketing 19.2.5056-CRM Connector.msi file and double-click it. The setup wizard begins, as shown in Figure 9.58. Click Next.

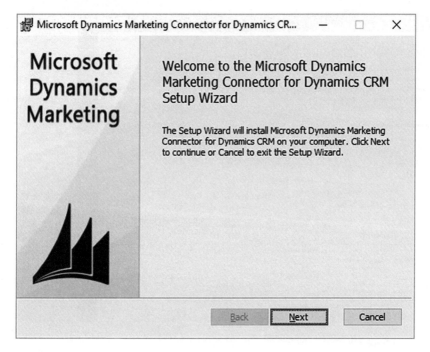

FIGURE 9.58   Welcome to the Microsoft Dynamics Marketing Connector for Dynamics CRM.

2. To and accept the terms, click Next.

3. Select the location and components you want to set up and click Next.

4. Click Install to complete the setup wizard. The setup takes a few minutes to complete. When it finishes, you have the option to configure the CRM Connector.

5. Go to the Dynamics CRM web interface and import the CRM2015-CRM2016 -ConnectorSolution.zip solution file that is located in the C:\Program Files (x86)\ Microsoft Dynamics Marketing\Solutions\CRMConnector folder.

▶ To learn more about how to import solutions in Dynamics CRM, **SEE CHAPTER 22**, "Customizing Entities."

CRM Online Configurations

To configure the CRM Connector for CRM Online, you must go to the MDM web application and select Settings > Integration Options > Administrator and then click Enable CRM Connector Services, as shown in Figure 9.59.

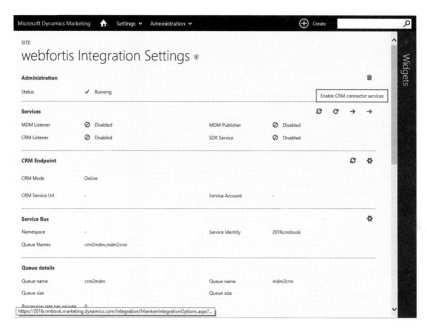

FIGURE 9.59   MDM integration options.

After you have enabled the CRM Connector services, a confirmation window prompts you to start the services (see Figure 9.60). Click OK to do so.

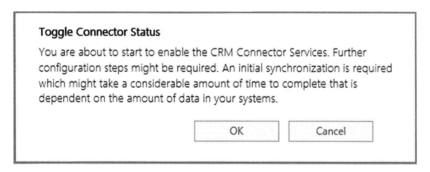

FIGURE 9.60   MDM CRM integration confirmation dialog.

The integration is then enabled but it is not running. Navigate to the CRM Endpoint section and click the gear icon to configure the CRM endpoint. Figure 9.61 shows the interface preconfiguration (notice the Not Configured messages).

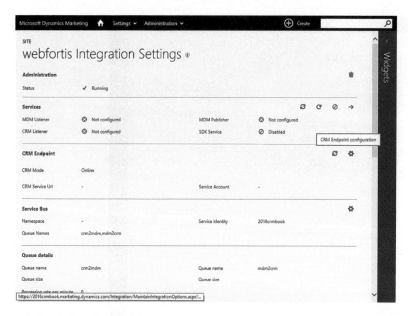

FIGURE 9.61   MDM CRM Online integration for the CRM endpoint.

Enter the CRM Online URL and the CRM Online credentials with system administrator rights. Then click the Verify button (see Figure 9.62).

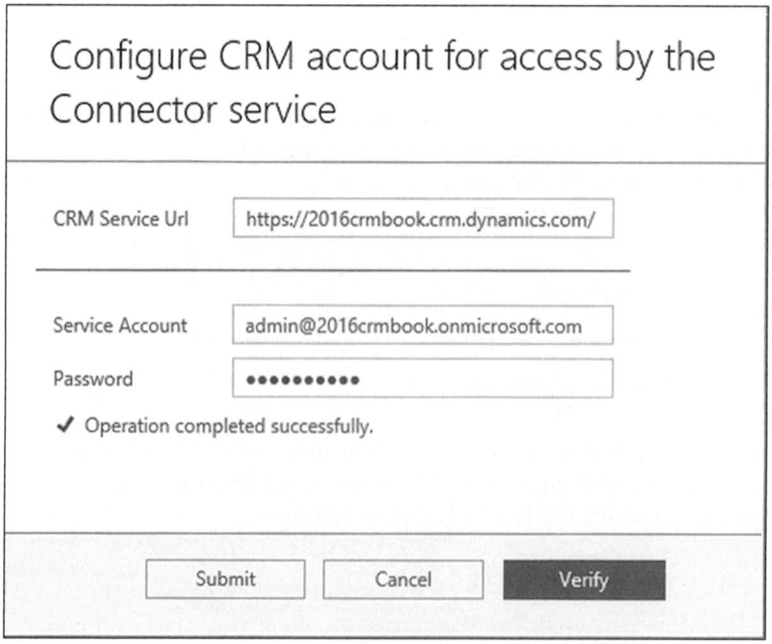

Configure CRM account for access by the Connector service

CRM Service Url	https://2016crmbook.crm.dynamics.com/

Service Account	admin@2016crmbook.onmicrosoft.com
Password	●●●●●●●●●●

✓ Operation completed successfully.

Submit   Cancel   Verify

FIGURE 9.62   MDM CRM Online integration CRM endpoint configuration.

When the verification is complete, click Submit, and when you are back to the integration configuration page, click Save and then Submit.

Configuring the Azure Service Bus Message Queues
The next thing you need to do is configure the Azure Service Bus message queues. To do this, go to the MDM web interface and select Settings > Administration > Integration Options.

Find the Service Bus section and click on the gear icon in the top-right corner. Figure 9.63 shows the dialog that appears.

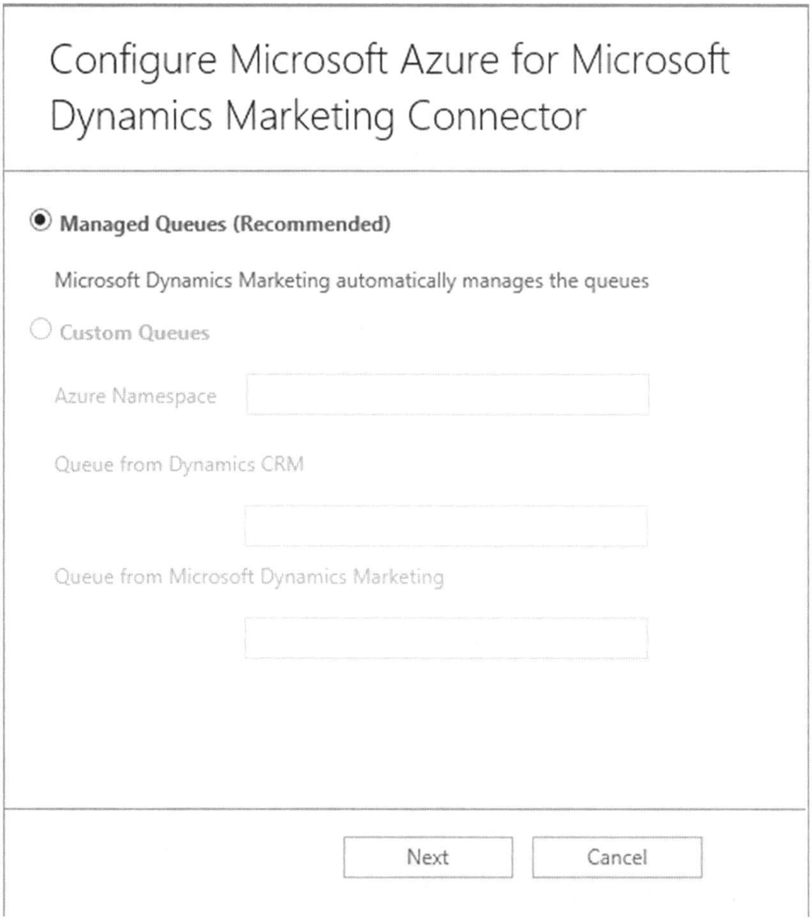

FIGURE 9.63   Configuring Azure for the MDM Connector.

Select Managed Queues (Recommended) and click Next. You now need to enter the Dynamics CRM certificate issuer name and upload the certificate, as shown in Figure 9.64.

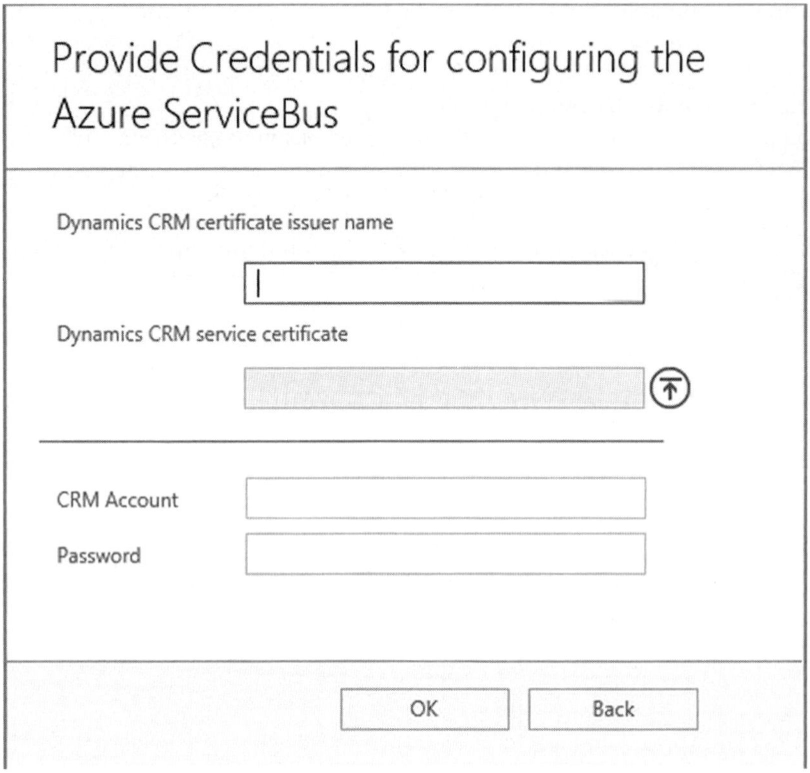

Provide Credentials for configuring the Azure ServiceBus

Dynamics CRM certificate issuer name

Dynamics CRM service certificate

CRM Account

Password

OK   Back

FIGURE 9.64   Providing credentials for Azure for MDM Connector.

To find the certificate file and issuer name, navigate to Dynamics CRM and go to Settings > Customizations > Developer Resources. As shown in Figure 9.65, you need to look in the Connect This Instance to Dynamics CRM to Azure Service Bus section near the bottom of the page.

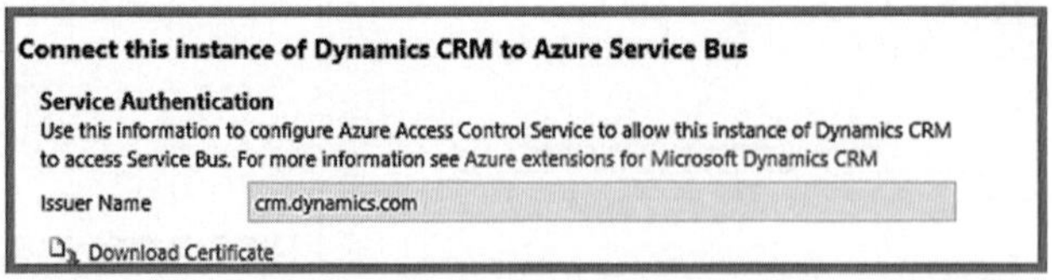

Connect this instance of Dynamics CRM to Azure Service Bus

Service Authentication
Use this information to configure Azure Access Control Service to allow this instance of Dynamics CRM to access Service Bus. For more information see Azure extensions for Microsoft Dynamics CRM

Issuer Name   crm.dynamics.com

Download Certificate

FIGURE 9.65   Dynamics CRM Online to Azure Service Bus.

Get the issuer name, which should be similar to crm.dynamics.com, and click the Download Certificate link to download the certificate to your local computer.

Go back to the MDM user interface and enter the certificate issuer name, upload the certificate, and enter the CRM credentials of a user with the System Administrator role in CRM Online, and click OK.

The configuration starts. When it is successful, you see the Service Bus section.

Manually start the initial synchronization by clicking the right-pointing arrow in the Initial Synchronization section. When the confirmation dialog appears, click Yes, as shown in Figure 9.66.

Do you really want to start an initial synchronization process?
In an ongoing initial synchronization it is advised to not use Microsoft Dynamics Marketing for any transactional processing in order to assure a clean starting point for later synchronized operations.

YES   NO

FIGURE 9.66   Initial synchronization confirmation dialog.

The status changes to In Progress, as shown in Figure 9.67.

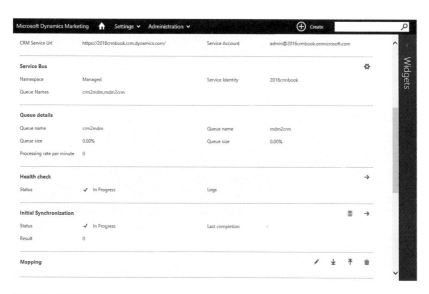

FIGURE 9.67   In-progress synchronization.

How long the synchronization takes depends on the number of records you have in the CRM Online organization.

> **NOTE**
>
> For more information about how to configure the Azure Service Bus to manage queues, see www.microsoft.com/en-us/dynamics/marketing-customer-center/configure -synchronization-for-dynamics-crm-online.aspx.

CRM On-Premises Configurations

If you want to integrate Dynamics Marketing with CRM On-Premises, you need to run the configuration manually. To do so, you start the .msi file you downloaded and manually run the configuration wizard located at C:\Program Files (x86)\Microsoft Dynamics Marketing\CRMConnectorService\DataIntegrationConfigurationWizard\Microsoft .Dynamics.Marketing.DataIntegration.ConfigurationWizard.exe.

You see the wizard shown in Figure 9.68.

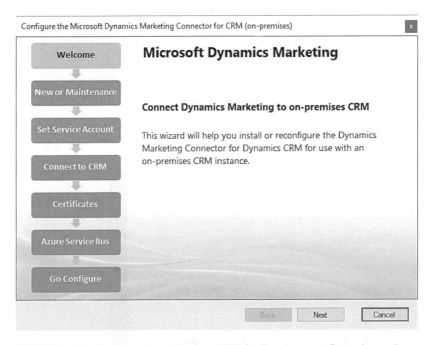

FIGURE 9.68   Dynamics Marketing to CRM On-Premises configuration welcome screen.

Click Next and in the next screen, select Add a New Connector and enter name for the new instance, as shown in Figure 9.69.

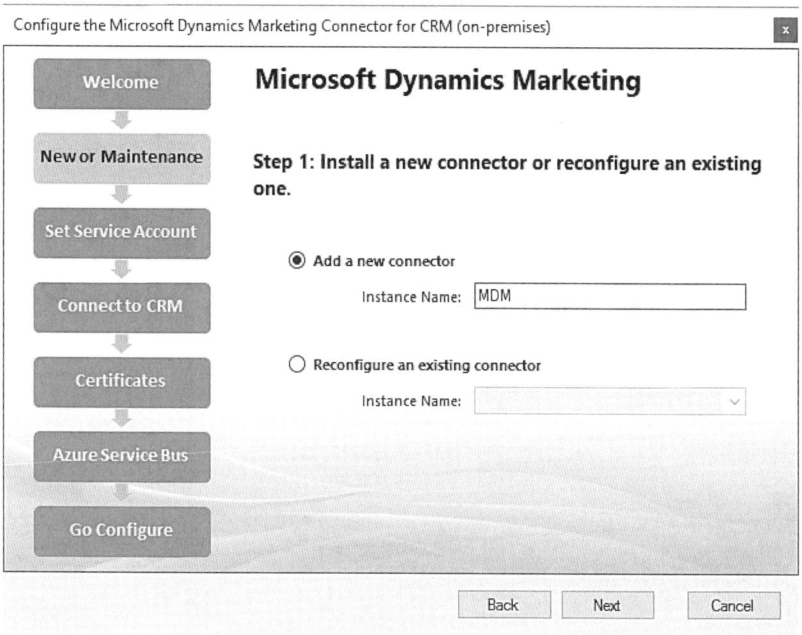

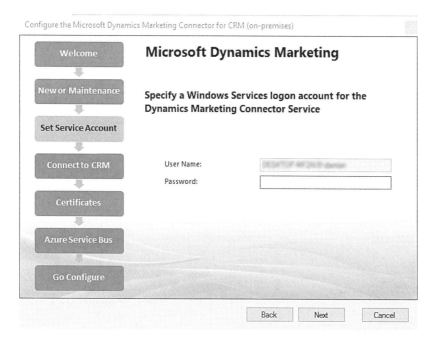

FIGURE 9.69   MDM to CRM new instance.

Click Next and enter your password, as shown in Figure 9.70. Notice that you cannot change the username here, so you must be logged in as a user that belongs to your domain.

FIGURE 9.70   MDM to CRM Set Service Account page.

Click Next to continue, and the tool attempts to validate your credentials.

Enter you CRM organization URL (for example, http://crm2016dev/book/) and CRM system administrator credentials, as shown in Figure 9.71.

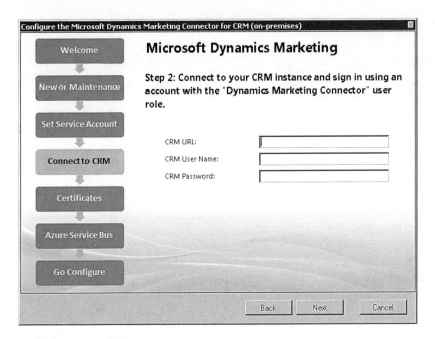

FIGURE 9.71   MDM to CRM Connect to CRM page.

Click Next, and the tool validates the CRM connection. If there are errors, you cannot continue until you fix them.

Enter the certificate location of the Azure Service Bus (as explained for the Online version earlier in this chapter), as shown in Figure 9.72.

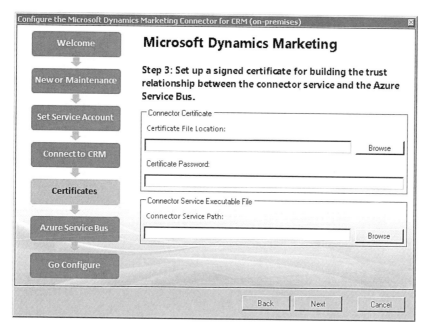

FIGURE 9.72   MDM to CRM Certificates page.

Summary

While Dynamics CRM has some basic marketing features, Microsoft Dynamics Marketing (MDM) is a more robust enterprise solution for marketing purposes. MDM, which is licensed separately from Dynamics CRM, is a full solution for marketing professionals who want to run complex campaigns, involving managing budget, tracking expenses, and more.

> **NOTE**
>
> Due to the specific nature and complexities inherent with marketing (for example, ROI, A/B testing results), MDM is becoming widely used by marketing agencies, and it is recommended for organizations that have these requirements.

This chapter describes how MDM can be integrated with both Online and On-Premises Dynamics CRM, using the CRM Connector.

Working with Service

The Service interface for Microsoft Dynamics CRM 2016 is where organizations manage the following:

▶ Support cases

▶ Shared calendar and resources

▶ The knowledge base (referred to as Articles)

▶ Contracts (usually used in support of inbound support cases)

The Service area is most commonly used by call centers and for customer support issues.

NOTE

▶ For information on the interactive service hub, **SEE CHAPTER 11**, "The Interactive Service Hub." For information on Parature, **SEE CHAPTER 12**, "Parature."

From the Service area you can create new support incidents and associate them with the master record (account, contact, and so on) in Dynamics CRM 2016. In fact, by default, you are required to select a customer when you create a case record.

NOTE

Microsoft typically defines a customer record as either an account or a contact record.

Understanding Service and Service Activities

Using the Service section is the best way to manage resources such as time and materials in the organization. Resources can consist of users, resource groups, or teams; and materials are defined as facilities or equipment.

A service is basically anything that involves resource time and materials. It differs from a product, for which you have to manage stock and quantities. With a service, the critical considerations are the time allocated to the necessary resources and the stock of materials. For example, suppose that an IT company has two technicians who can repair computers. When one goes to a client to repair a computer, that technician might take an hour or more to perform the work and, depending on the service required, might need to use materials such as a new CD-ROM or computer part. You can schedule such tasks in Microsoft Dynamics CRM via service activities. Although you can also schedule such services as appointments, the difference between them is that a service activity has an associated service. You use appointments for meetings with clients that do not involve performing any service.

When service activities are scheduled, they appear on the user's CRM calendar (found in the Calendar section); in the Outlook client, they appear as appointments on the Outlook calendar.

> **NOTE**
>
> When working with the Outlook client, you have full-featured functionality with services unless you are offline. When you're offline, the service calendar is unavailable, but you can still view appointments on the Outlook calendar.

The Service area of Microsoft CRM has the following options, by default:

▶ My Work

    ▶ Dashboards

    ▶ Activities

▶ Customers

    ▶ Accounts

    ▶ Contacts

    ▶ Social Profiles

- ▶ Service
    - ▶ Cases
    - ▶ Service Calendar
    - ▶ Queues
- ▶ Collateral
    - ▶ Articles
    - ▶ Contracts
    - ▶ Products
    - ▶ Services
- ▶ Goals
    - ▶ Goals
    - ▶ Goal Metrics
    - ▶ Rollup Queries
- ▶ Tools
    - ▶ Reports
    - ▶ Alerts
    - ▶ Calendar

▶ You can customize these entries from the Site Map entity, as explained in **CHAPTER 22**, "Customizing Entities."

▶ The Accounts and Contacts options are covered in **CHAPTER 6**, "Working with Customers," and Products is covered in **CHAPTER 7**, "Working with Sales."

Services

You use Services under the Service section to define and configure how time and resources will be managed when a user schedules a service activity.

10

For example, consider an IT company that has a service called Network Installation, which might take three hours to complete and which requires one of the three technicians to go to the customer's office. To set up this service example, follow these steps:

1. Go to the Service area and click Services. Then click the + New button on the navigation bar. The New Service form appears (see Figure 10.1). By default, each service has the following required fields:

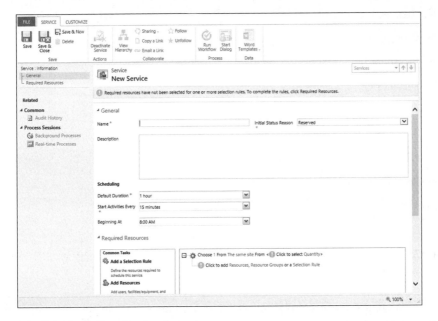

FIGURE 10.1   New Service form.

▶ Name

▶ Initial Status Reason

▶ Default Duration

▶ Start Activities Every

To configure the resources needed to accomplish the service, navigate to the Required Resources tab or scroll down (see Figure 10.2).

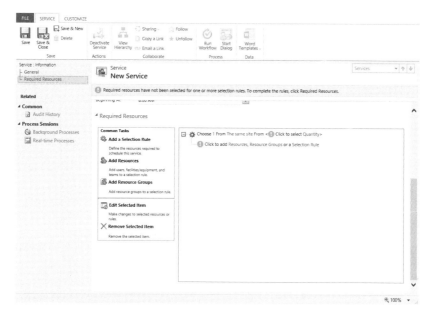

FIGURE 10.2   Configuring required resources.

2. Double-click the first option from the tree displayed on the right, Choose 1 from the Same Site from <(!) Click to Select Quantity>, to display the window shown in Figure 10.3.

TIP

If you don't see the Scheduling Details field, click the arrow at the right of that title to expand the section.

10

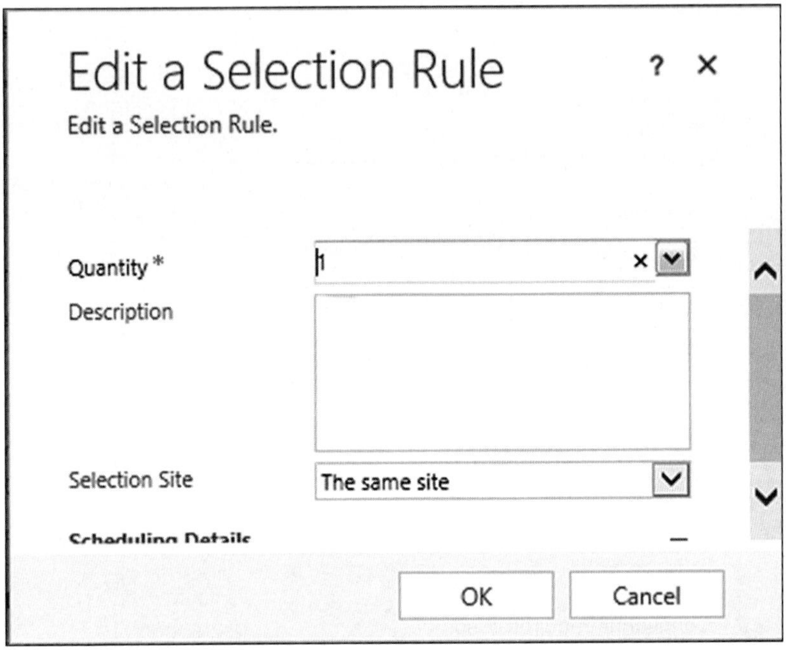

FIGURE 10.3   Editing a selection rule.

This example requires only one technician to perform the service, so you can close the Edit a Selection Rule dialog by clicking OK. (If you needed more than one technician, you would change the value here to the number needed.) When you close the window, the selected rule is updated to display Choose 1 from the Same Site From, assuming that you left the defaults unchanged, as shown in Figure 10.3.

3. Select the child option that says Click to Add Resources, Resource Groups, or a Selection Rule. The window shown in Figure 10.4 displays the available resources that you want to assign.

FIGURE 10.4   Adding resources to a selection rule.

Click the Search for Records button (the one with the magnifying glass icon) to display all available records on the left.

4. Select the users you want to include from the left list box and click the Select button to move them to the Selected Records list. When you're finished with this, click Add to close this dialog.

If you add more than one user, you are asked whether you want to create a new resource group (see Figure 10.5). You should do this if you want to reuse the same group of users on other services instead of selecting the users one by one.

To further work with services, you might need to create Facility/Equipment and Resource Groups, if you haven't done so yet. You can do this by going to Settings > Service Management.

10

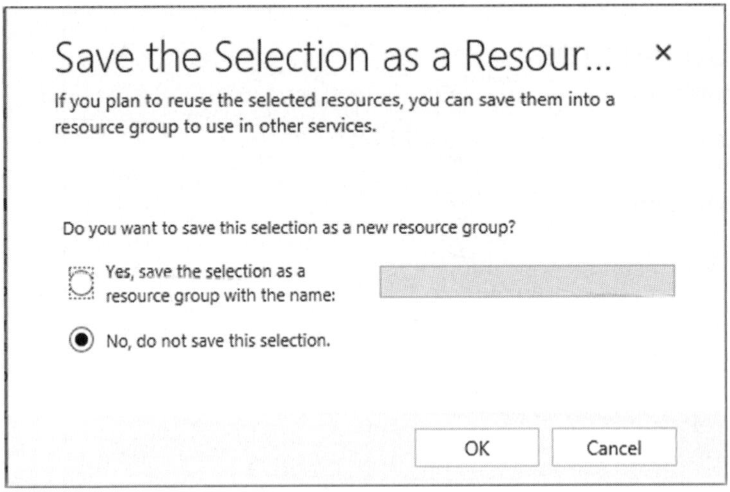

Save the Selection as a Resour...   ✕

If you plan to reuse the selected resources, you can save them into a resource group to use in other services.

Do you want to save this selection as a new resource group?

⬚ Yes, save the selection as a resource group with the name:

◉ No, do not save this selection.

OK   Cancel

FIGURE 10.5   Saving the selection as a resource group.

Facility/Equipment refers to the ability to manage either locations or, as the name implies, equipment, as part of the service-scheduling activity. Resource Groups is just a basic grouping that can be reused.

▶ **SEE CHAPTER 17**, "Settings," for detailed information about how to add and manage these kinds of entities.

After you select the required resources, they display as shown in Figure 10.6. (This example shows a resource group created from the selected users shown in Figure 10.5, and that resource group is shown in Figure 10.6.)

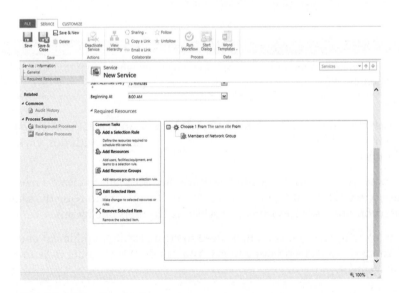

FIGURE 10.6   Required resources.

These resources are the ones the user must choose when scheduling a service activity.

You also can perform some common tasks related to managing the required resources:

- ▶ Add a Selection Rule
- ▶ Add Resources
- ▶ Add Resource Groups
- ▶ Edit Selected Item
- ▶ Remove Selected Item

5. Click the Save & Close button to complete the new service creation.

You have now finished creating a service and allocated one or more resources for the service activity. If you allocated users (or teams and resource groups), the saved service activity appears on their calendars when it is assigned/used.

Service Calendar

The service calendar checks resource availability and schedules appointments for resources. Figure 10.7 shows the service calendar interface. When a customer calls to request a service, you can easily manage a general agenda and reserve or request a time for a resource or equipment, based on the requested service. In addition, you can manage the existing schedules and make changes, if necessary.

By default, the service calendar shows the time and usage allocation for facility/equipment and the tasks scheduled for the users.

10

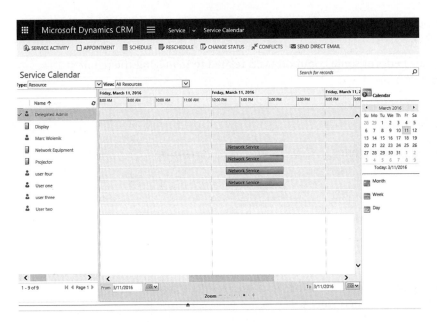

FIGURE 10.7   Main service calendar interface.

> **NOTE**
>
> The service calendar is available only to users assigned the System Administrator role or one of the Scheduler roles. Users who do not have these roles see the time allocated on their personal calendars as appointments, which they can access by going to Service > Service Calendar.

Each activity state has a different color so that you can easily recognize its status (see Figure 10.8).

Color	Status
■	Requested
■	Tentative
■	Pending
■	Reserved
■	Arrived
■	Canceled
■	Completed
■	No Show
■	Busy
■	Out of Office
□	Not Working or Business Closure
■	Canceled
■	Completed

FIGURE 10.8   Color table for a service activity's status.

10

TIP

You can change the status colors by customizing the ISV Config, as explained in Chapter 22.

You can display the service calendar by month, week, or day, and you can also display it within a custom date range.

To view it by month, week, or day, select the View option in the lower right of the interface. For a custom date range, navigate to the bottom of the calendar view and enter the date range.

If you have many resources and a lot of equipment, you can easily locate a resource by using the search box at the top by typing the first few letters of the resource name.

The service calendar shows the two types of activities you can create from this interface: service activity and appointment activities.

Service Activity

A service activity helps you schedule appointments for resources associated with a service. Before creating service activities, you must define and create your business services, as discussed earlier in this chapter.

To create a new service activity from the service calendar interface, click the Service Activity button on the command bar. The New Service Activity window appears (see Figure 10.9).

FIGURE 10.9   New Service Activity window.

When creating a new service activity, you are required to enter a subject, a service, and the time (start and end dates) for the activity. Depending on the service selected, you might also be required to select one or more resources or equipment. If so, after selecting the service or equipment, click the Schedule button on the command bar.

A new window opens for scheduling a service. In this example (see Figure 10.10), the form assistant displays the resources available for completion in the Resources field when you click the resource lookup field. When the Resources field has the focus, you see service rule options in the form assistant that must be selected. In this example, one of the displayed resources must be selected (see Figure 10.11).

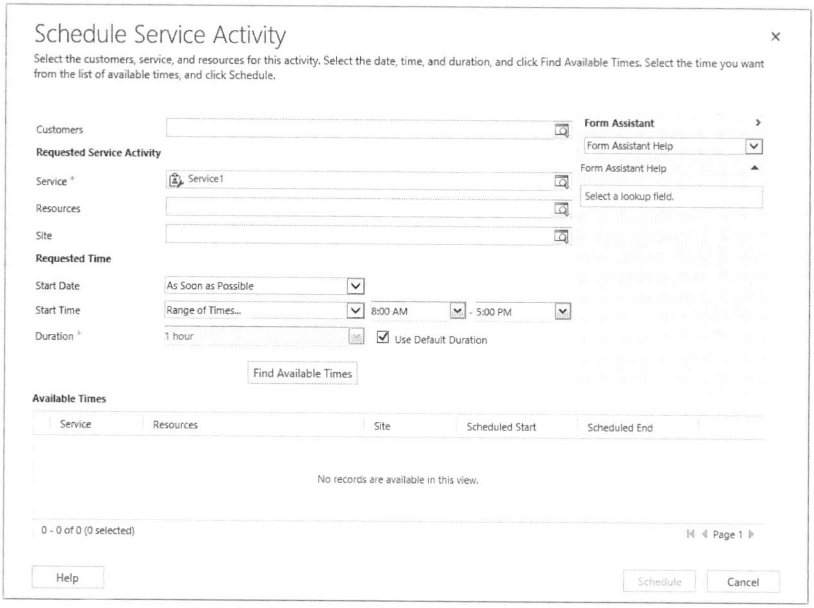

FIGURE 10.10   Scheduling a service activity.

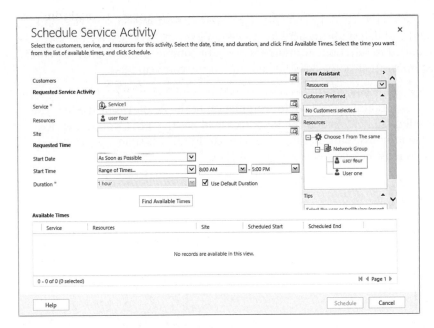

FIGURE 10.11   Selecting resources.

You can select one of the resources from the form assistant or click the Find Available Times button to list all the available resources and times (see Figure 10.12).

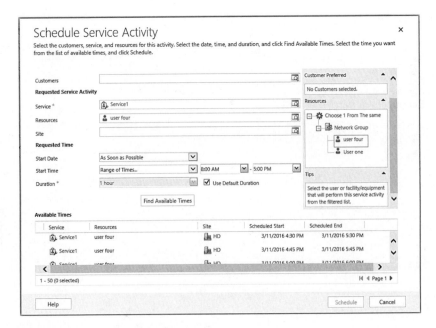

FIGURE 10.12   Available Resource Times.

> **NOTE**
>
> If you see errors after you click the Find Available Times button, it might be because the resources did not have a site specified. Be sure that the facilities and users have one site set to prevent this type of error.

Select the resource that matches your desired time availability and click the Schedule button. Notice that you might have to select more than one resource, depending on how the service was initially defined.

Finally, click Save and Close to finish creating the service activity. You now see the scheduled activity on the service calendar, and each affected user sees the service activity on his or her calendar (see Figure 10.13).

> **TIP**
>
> By default, users are not notified via email when you schedule a service activity for them. However, you can easily create a custom workflow for the service activity that sends a user an email when he or she is scheduled for something. See Chapter 26, "Process Development," for details about how to create custom workflows and processes.

You can easily reschedule service activities, if necessary. For example, suppose that a customer has to reschedule an appointment. A customer service representative could easily handle that by clicking the Reschedule button and then checking the next available time to verify availability of the resources for the service to be rescheduled.

A hidden pane at the bottom of the window shows resources and facility details. If you click the black arrow located in the middle bottom of the main service calendar window, the selected resource details appear, as shown in Figure 10.13.

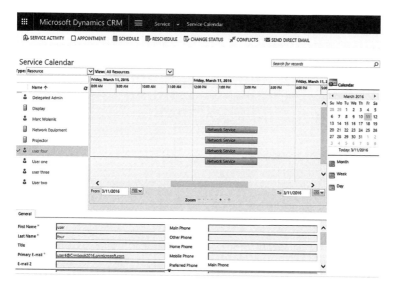

FIGURE 10.13   Resource details panel expanded.

Managing Users' Working Time

You can change the working hours for a user from the service calendar. To do so, you open the user's details by selecting and opening the user and then selecting Work Hours from the navigation bar (see Figure 10.14). Figure 10.15 shows the monthly view of work hours that appears.

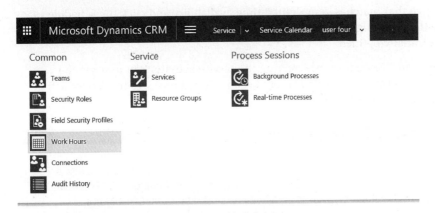

FIGURE 10.14   Work Hours menu.

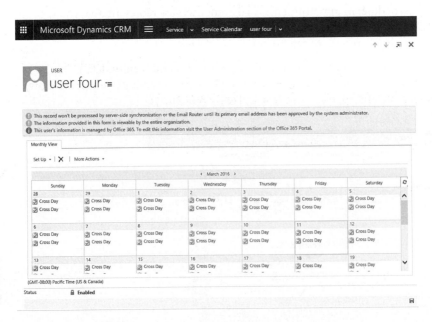

FIGURE 10.15   Work hours for a user.

Suppose that the user Bill is going on vacation for a few days. You can easily set up these days as time off to prevent other users from scheduling appointments or service activities with him. From the Set Up menu inside the Monthly View tab, click Time Off to configure the vacation time on the dialog shown in Figure 10.16.

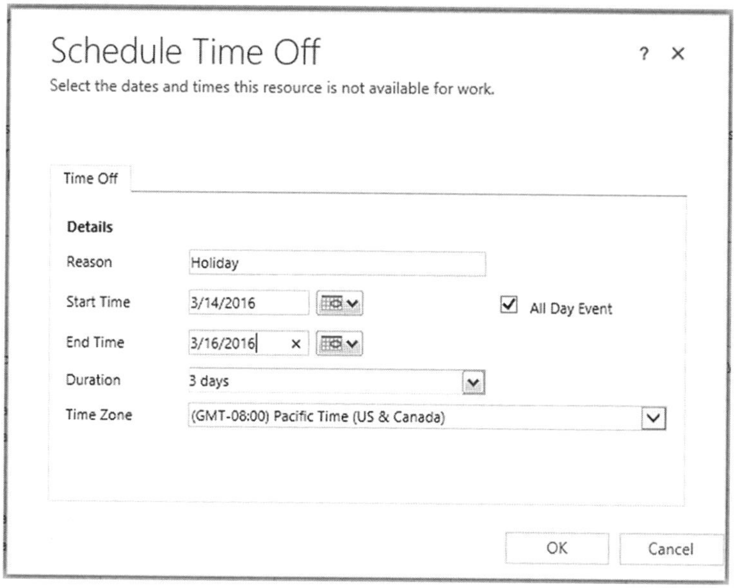

FIGURE 10.16   Scheduling time off.

Figure 10.17 shows how the work hours are displayed after you schedule the time off.

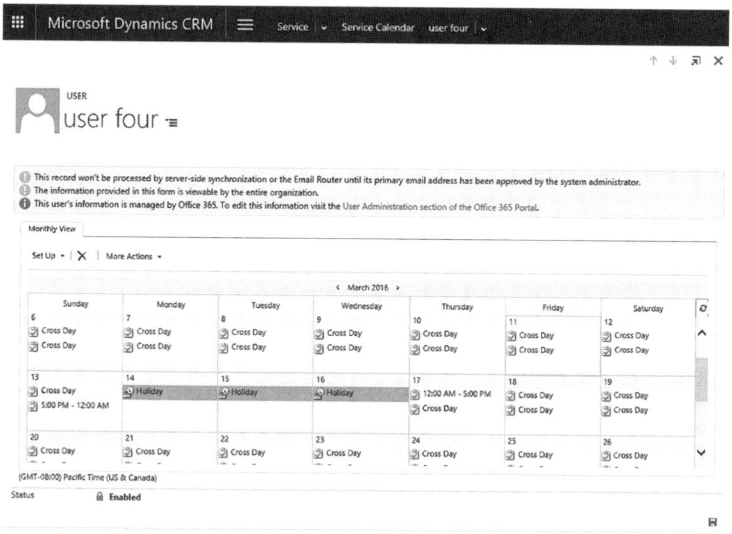

FIGURE 10.17   Work hours with holiday (vacation) time off.

You can also use this process to configure sick days, personal errands, and similar situations.

For general holidays when the business will be closed, use the business closures calendar under Settings > Service Management, as shown in Figure 10.18.

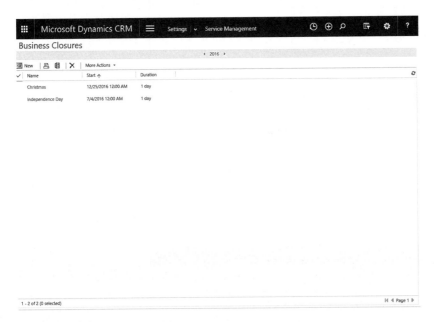

FIGURE 10.18   Business closures interface.

Appointments

Appointments differ from service activities in that they don't need to have a service associated with them. To create a new appointment, select Service > Service Calendar and then click Appointment. Figure 10.19 shows the Appointment window.

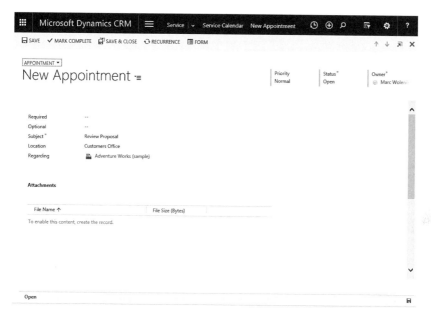

FIGURE 10.19   Creating a new appointment.

The required fields for the appointment are the Subject field and the Start Time and End Time fields. If you want, you can specify the required resources or materials necessary for the appointment and the optional resources.

After the appointment is created, you can save the activity as completed, or you can convert the activity to an opportunity or a case.

CAUTION

If you choose to save an activity as completed, you can neither change any of the properties for that activity nor change the status back to its previous status. Unlike service activities, appointments cannot be rescheduled.

When you create a service activity, you can set its initial status to Open (and then either Requested or Tentative) or Scheduled (and then Pending, Reserved, In Progress, or Arrived). To change the status of a service activity, select the activity and then click the Change Status button (see Figure 10.20).

10

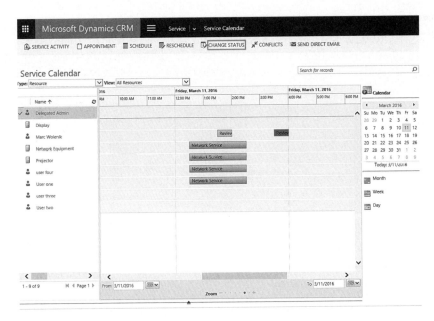

FIGURE 10.20   Changing a service activity's status.

After you click the Change Status button, the dialog displayed in Figure 10.21 appears, giving you the option to change the service activity's status. You can also close the activity and complete it.

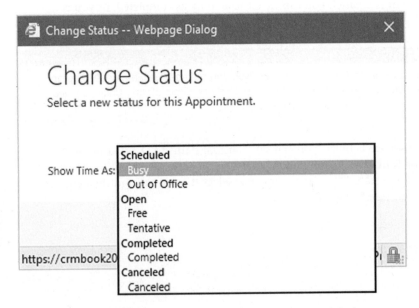

FIGURE 10.21   Changing a service activity's status to completed.

Users can create a recurring appointment (or edit an uncompleted one). For example, if you have to meet a client once a week for two months, you can configure this by clicking the Recurrence option on the navigation bar. Figure 10.22 shows the options you can use to set the recurrence; they are the same options you are familiar with from Microsoft Outlook.

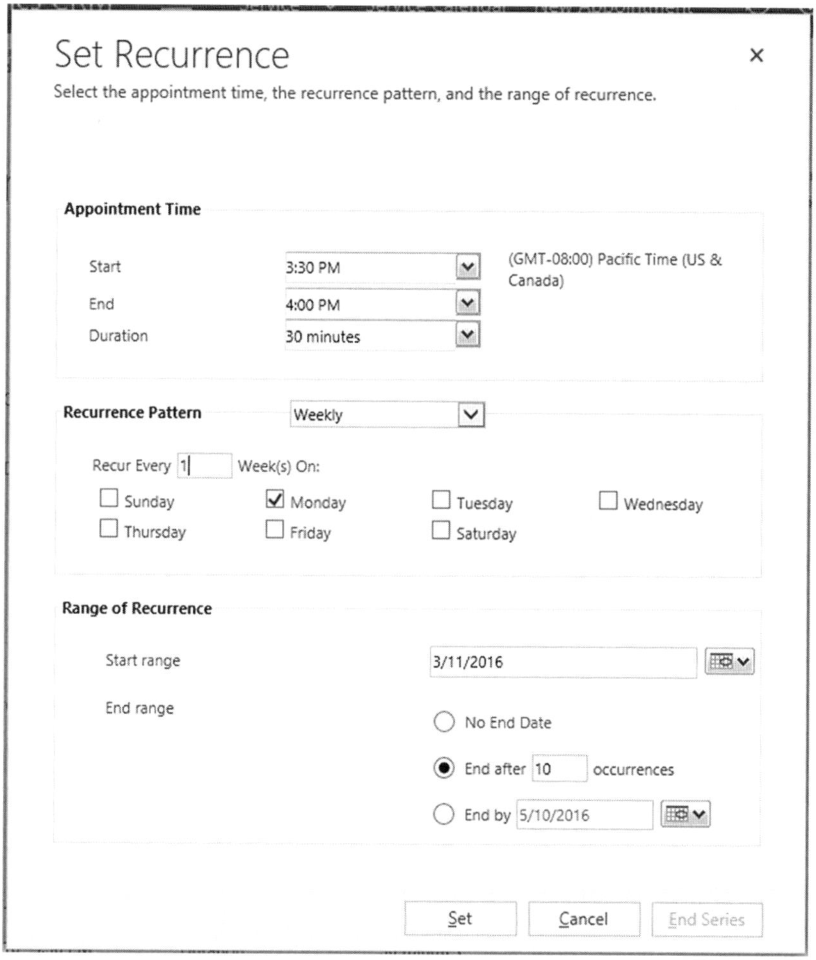

Set Recurrence ×

Select the appointment time, the recurrence pattern, and the range of recurrence.

Appointment Time

Start	3:30 PM	(GMT-08:00) Pacific Time (US & Canada)
End	4:00 PM	
Duration	30 minutes	

Recurrence Pattern   Weekly

Recur Every 1   Week(s) On:

☐ Sunday   ☑ Monday   ☐ Tuesday   ☐ Wednesday
☐ Thursday ☐ Friday   ☐ Saturday

Range of Recurrence

Start range   3/11/2016

End range

○ No End Date

● End after 10   occurrences

○ End by 5/10/2016

Set   Cancel   End Series

FIGURE 10.22   Appointment recurrence.

Cases

Cases are normally used to track customer problems, questions, and issues. To work with them, you select Service > Cases. Figure 10.23 shows the My Active Cases interface that appears.

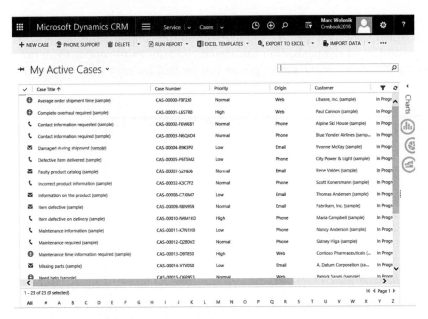

FIGURE 10.23   My Active Cases interface.

Each case is assigned a unique identifier with the prefix CAS by default. You can customize this by selecting Settings > Administration > Auto-Numbering.

The case number numbering scheme can be unfriendly in some cases. People often ask if there is any flexibility around this naming, so that instead of using CAS-01002-T8N2C3, they can use something more like CAS-5401. The answer is no. However, there is no reason you cannot create your own plug-in to auto-number and create a case number for you. Microsoft Dynamics CRM On-Premises is the reason for the complexity of the case numbers in Microsoft Dynamics CRM. Because it is not necessarily connected to the server, the On-Premises client needs a complex algorithm to ensure uniqueness—even when offline.

Before you start to work with cases, it is a good idea to prepare and define the subject tree as explained later in this chapter. To create a new case, click New. Even though this is not required by default, you can enter the subject in the Subject field, as shown in Figure 10.24.

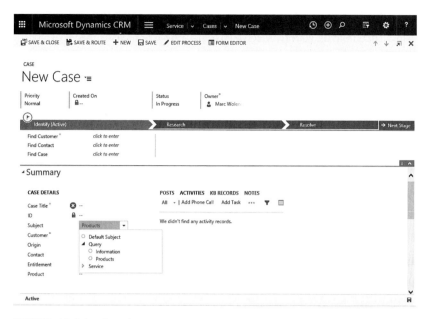

FIGURE 10.24   Creating a new case.

After selecting the subject and entering a title and customer, you can move to the Contract and Product Information section and look up the Knowledge base (KB) articles associated with the selected subject. You can do this by selecting the magnifying glass next to the Knowledge Base Article field to open the Add Article dialog (see Figure 10.25).

FIGURE 10.25   Associating a KB article to a case.

After entering the required values, click Save & Close to create the new case.

TIP

You can also create a case from an activity by converting the activity to a case. This is useful when you need to open a case that originated from an email or a phone conversation.

In addition, in Microsoft Dynamics 2016, there are now icons to the left of the list of cases, indicating the activity type that originated each case.

After you create a case, you can perform these actions, as described in the following sections:

▶ Add Related Activities

▶ Delete Case

▶ Resolve Case

▶ Cancel Case

Add Related Activities

By clicking a case title (for example, Case Sample), you can easily create an activity that will be associated with the case by selecting Activities from the navigation bar (see Figure 10.26). You can do this, for example, to add a reminder to call a customer about the resolution of a case at a specific date and time.

TIP

You can also easily create an activity by using the Activities tab near the notes in the form to create and mark activities as completed.

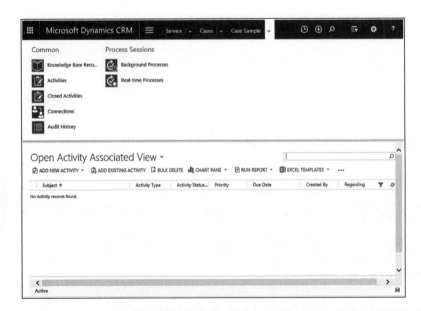

FIGURE 10.26   Adding a related activity.

In addition, by looking at the process flow at the top of the screen, you can easily see the recommended process to follow for case closeout. (The example in this chapter is Phone to Case, which you can easily access by clicking the Phone Support button instead of clicking + New.)

Delete Case

The Delete Case option deletes the case and its associated records and activities. You must confirm this operation, and there is no way to roll it back.

Resolve Case

You can resolve a case by opening the case and clicking Resolve Case on the command bar. The Resolve Case dialog appears (see Figure 10.27), and in it you can enter the resolution description and billable time.

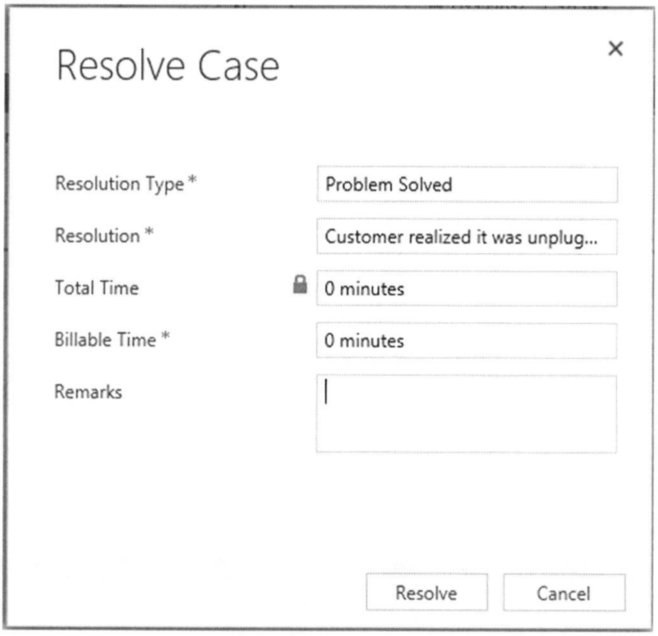

FIGURE 10.27   Resolve Case dialog.

> **CAUTION**
>
> After a case is resolved, you cannot edit its properties. If you want to change a resolved case, you must reactivate it by selecting Actions > Reactivate. You can then make changes and resolve the case again.

Cancel Case

The Cancel Case option changes the case status to Canceled. You can reactivate the case later, if necessary. After you select this option, a confirmation dialog appears, allowing you to select the status reason for the cancelation, which can be Merged or Canceled.

> **CAUTION**
>
> To cancel a case, you cannot have an open activity associated with the case.

Reports

Some predefined reports are available for cases that you can run for a selected record or for all records. To see these reports from the Cases interface, click the Run Report option on the command bar, as shown in Figure 10.28.

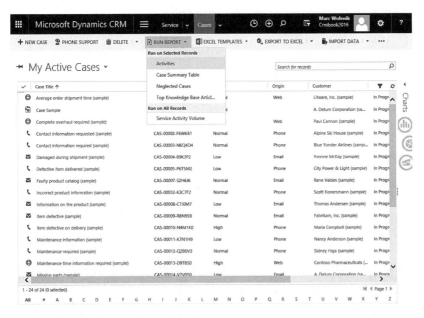

FIGURE 10.28   Case-related reports.

These are the available reports:

▶ Activities

▶ Case Summary Table

▶ Neglected Cases

▶ Top Knowledge Base Articles

▶ Service Activity Volume

Figure 10.29 shows the Case Summary Table report.

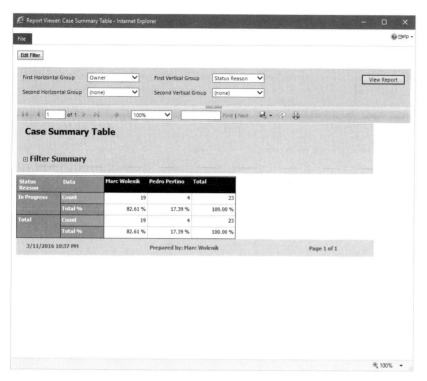

FIGURE 10.29   Case Summary Table report.

TIP

If the predefined reports don't meet your needs, you can easily create custom reports by using the Report Wizard.

▶ For more information about working with reports, **SEE CHAPTER 16**, "Reporting and Dashboards." To learn more about accounts and contacts, refer to **CHAPTER 6**.

Articles

Articles used to be called the knowledge base in earlier versions of CRM. This is a common repository where users can share their experience and solutions for common issues and customer questions.

TIP

Microsoft Dynamics CRM 2016 provides a new experience for working with articles, using the interactive service hub. For more information about this experience, see Chapter 11.

An article has a small predefined workflow:

1. Anyone who has the right permissions can create articles.

2. Articles are submitted for review.

3. A higher-level-permissions user reviews articles and then approves or rejects them.

4. When approved, articles are published.

Figure 10.30 shows the steps in this workflow.

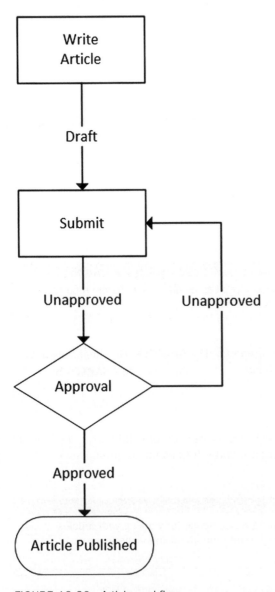

FIGURE 10.30   Article workflow.

Before you start writing articles, consider the following:

▶ Be sure to prepare the right article templates so that you have a consistent knowledge base of articles. You can manage templates under Settings > Templates > Articles Templates (see Figure 10.31).

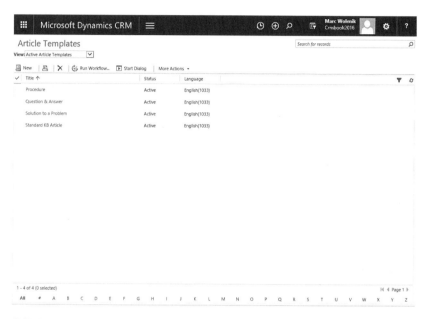

FIGURE 10.31   Managing article templates.

▶ Be sure to set up the topics where you want people to submit their articles so that users can search for them more easily after they are published. You can do this under Settings > Service Management > Subjects (see Figure 10.32).

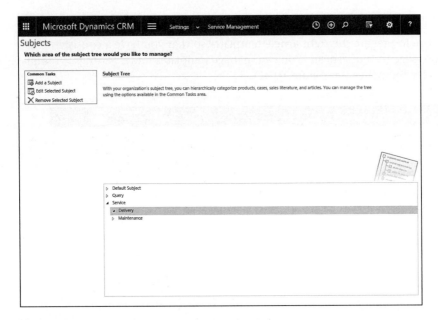

FIGURE 10.32   Configuring the subject tree.

▶ Be sure to set up the right permissions for the users who can write and submit articles, the users who can approve or reject the articles, and the users who can publish the articles.

TIP

By default, users with a CSR (Customer Service Representative) role can only write and submit articles; those with the CSR Manager role can approve, reject, and publish articles.

Figure 10.33 shows the default interface when you access the articles interface as the Administrator role. This interface is divided into the following views:

▶ All Articles

▶ Draft Articles

▶ Published Articles

▶ Unapproved Articles

▶ Unpublished Articles

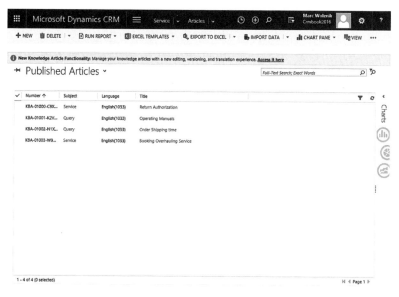

FIGURE 10.33   Articles interface.

No matter which view you are using, you can always create a new article. To create a new article, follow these steps:

1. Click the +New button on the command bar. The window shown in Figure 10.34 opens.

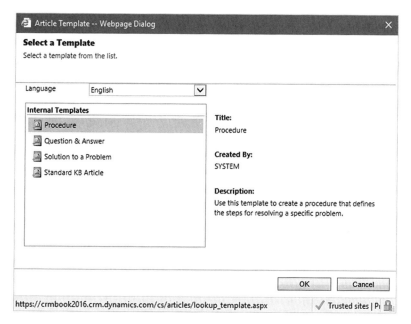

FIGURE 10.34   Selecting a template.

> **NOTE**
>
> Microsoft Dynamics CRM 2016 also enables you to create Articles for different languages, depending on the language packs you have installed. In addition to creating articles for a specific language, you can create an article for all languages if you want to have the article available for everybody. "For more information on language packs, see Chapter 17."

2. Select the language and select a template from the list. Notice that the internal templates vary depending on the language selected. Click OK to continue. Figure 10.35 shows the New Article interface.

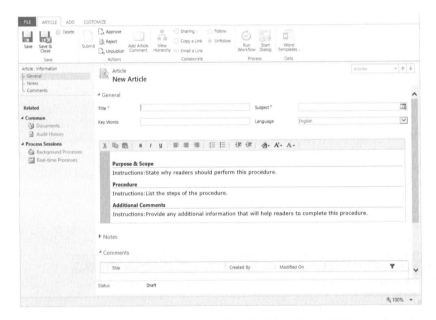

FIGURE 10.35   Writing an article based on the Procedure Article template.

3. Enter the title and subject. The body format of the article depends on the selected template. You should enter keywords for a faster search and lookup of the articles.

4. Click Save & Close.

Subjects

To create new subjects, you must be logged in as a user assigned the System Administrator role. As shown previously, Subjects are added to Cases which allow for reporting segmentation. Under Settings > Business Management > Subjects, click any existing subject in the subject tree and then click the Add a Subject link from the Common Tasks list box. The dialog shown in Figure 10.36 appears.

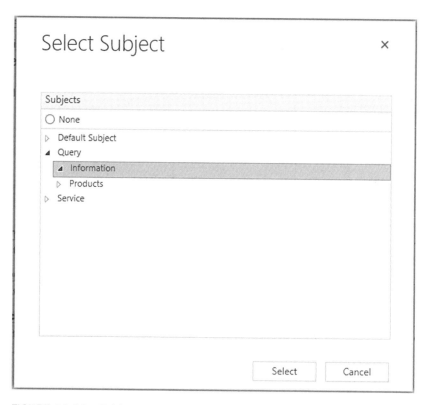

FIGURE 10.36   Subject tree options.

Submitting an Article

Every article goes directly to the Draft folder when created, which means it isn't available to users until it is published.

An article must be submitted before it can be approved or rejected. To submit an article, you must move to the Draft Articles view, select the article you want to submit, and click the Submit button on the command bar. You then receive a dialog alert to confirm the operation, as shown in Figure 10.37.

FIGURE 10.37   Article submission.

Click OK to submit the article, and the article is moved to the Unapproved Articles view.

Approving an Article

To approve an article, move to the Unapproved Articles view and select the article you want to approve. Then click the Approve button on the command bar. The confirmation dialog show in Figure 10.38 appears.

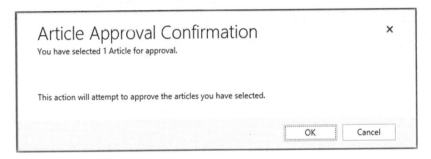

FIGURE 10.38   Article approval.

Approved articles move to the Published Articles view, where they are ready and available for other users.

Rejecting an Article

To reject an article, open the article in the Unapproved Articles view and click the Reject button on the command bar. The Provide a Reason dialog appears (see Figure 10.39).

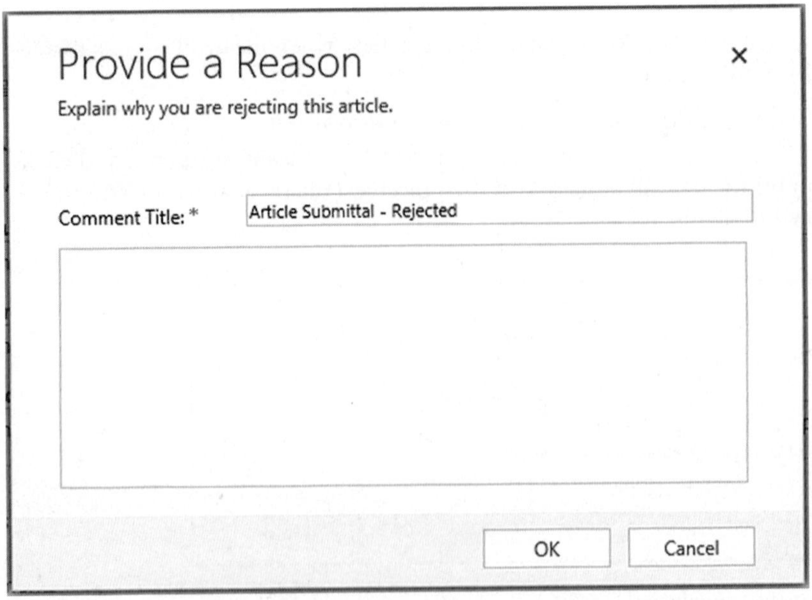

FIGURE 10.39   Reason for rejecting an article.

After you click OK, the article moves back to the Draft Articles view. If the user who wrote the article wants to see the comments and reason for the rejection, he or she must move to the Draft queue, double-click the article to open it, and then look at the Comments tab to see the rejection reasons (see Figure 10.40).

FIGURE 10.40   Article rejection reasons.

TIP

The default workflow for articles doesn't send alerts when a user submits, approves, or rejects an article, so it is a good practice to create a custom workflow for Article and Article Comment entities so that users can be notified via email when an article is submitted, approved, or rejected.

▶ **SEE CHAPTER 26** for more information about how to create custom workflows.

Reports

Top Knowledge Base Articles is a predefined report built for the knowledge base that shows the top articles associated and used on cases (see Figure 10.41).

CAUTION

The Top Knowledge Base Articles report is empty if you do not have at least one case record associated with the knowledge base articles.

FIGURE 10.41   Top Knowledge Base Articles report.

Articles Security

By default, the knowledge base is not available to all the roles. For example, the Salesperson role doesn't have access to create new articles, whereas the Customer Representative role does. Of course, you can customize and change this configuration as necessary.

Contracts

You can create a contracts from a template that is defined by a language. A contract is a group of services and products that you sell to a client during a period of time. On a contract, you define when you start providing services to the customer and when you finish; both dates are required for creating a contract. Each contract also has billing information associated with it, such as which client you will bill, to what address you will send invoices, and billing frequency (monthly, quarterly, annually, and so on). The products you sell are defined in contract lines, where you can enter product details such as the quantity, the time you will include for support cases, and the total price and discounts.

To create new contracts, follow these steps:

1. Navigate to Service > Contracts and click New.

2. Select a template (see Figure 10.42) and click Select.

> **NOTE**
>
> To create a new template, under Settings > Templates, select the Contract Templates option.

▶ **SEE CHAPTER 17** for more information on how to manage and create new templates.

FIGURE 10.42   Selecting a contract template for a new contract.

3. Fill in the required fields: Contract Name, Customer, Contract Start Date, Contract End Date, and Customer (see Figure 10.43). Click Save.

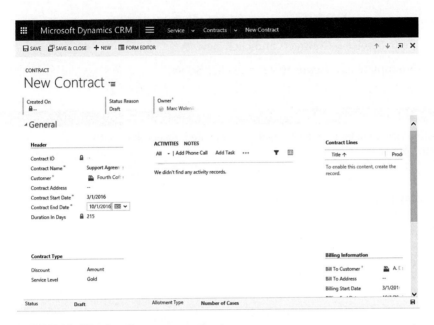

FIGURE 10.43   Creating a new contract.

4. Go to the Contract Lines section on the form and click the + icon.

5. Fill in the required fields (see Figure 10.44).

6. Click Save & Close to complete the contract line.

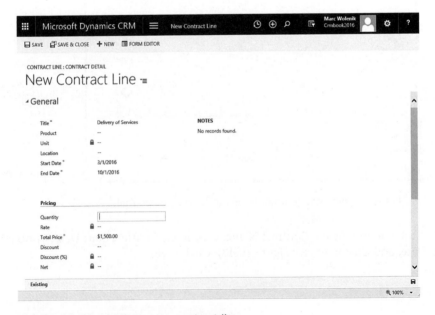

FIGURE 10.44   Adding a new contract line.

Each contract line has a specific calendar associated with it. You can access it by clicking the Set Calendar button on the command bar of the contract line form. This is useful when a customer service representative needs to know whether the client should be supported 24 × 7 or only at regular business times such as 9 to 5. You can easily convert the calendar to 24 × 7 support by clicking the check box shown at the bottom of Figure 10.45.

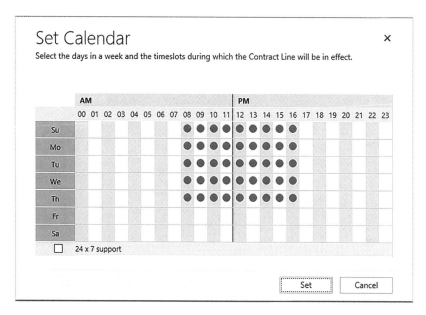

FIGURE 10.45   Contract line calendar.

After the contract is created, its status is draft. To make a contract active, you must open the contract record and click the Invoice Contract button on the command bar.

NOTE

The contract will be active between the contract start date and the contract end date. Before the contract start date, the contract will have the status Invoiced.

▶ Refer to **CHAPTER 7** for information related to goals, goal metrics, and rollup queries.

Service Management

Under Settings you can find the Service Management area, which is now the main centralized location for managing and configuring the service-related entities.

The Service Management area is divided in five sections, as shown in Figure 10.46 and described in the following sections:

▶ Case Settings with Record Creation and Update Rules

▶ Service Terms

▶ Knowledge Base Management

▶ Templates

▶ Service Scheduling

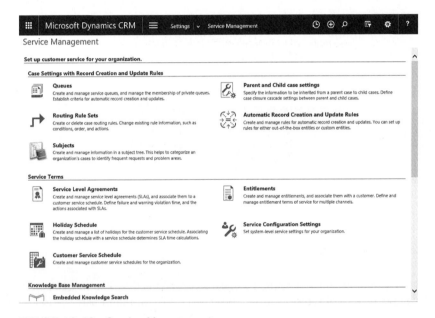

FIGURE 10.46   Service Management area.

Case Settings with Record Creation and Update Rules

In the Case Settings with Record Creation and Update Rules section you can manage the following features:

▶ Queues

▶ Parent and Child Case Settings

▶ Routing Rule Sets

▶ Automatic Record Creation and Update Rules

▶ Subjects

Queues

You use queues to assign or route case or activities records. If you click Queues in the Service Management area, you end up at the same page as if you clicked Queues in the Business Management area. The creation of queues is explained in Chapter 17.

Because by default every user and team has a default queue created by the system (prefaced with < and suffixed with >), you probably don't need to create new queues to start working with them. You often use queues when you are working with activities. To access them, go to Service > Activities.

To add items to a queue, you select an activity and click … > Add to Queue (see Figure 10.47).

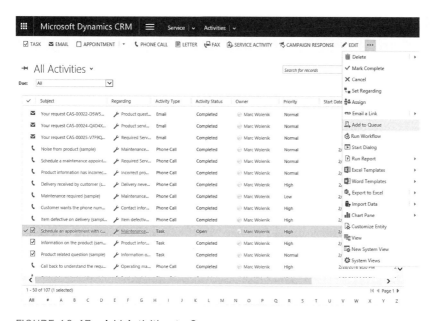

FIGURE 10.47   Add Activities to Queue.

The dialog shown in Figure 10.48 asks you to enter the name of the queue.

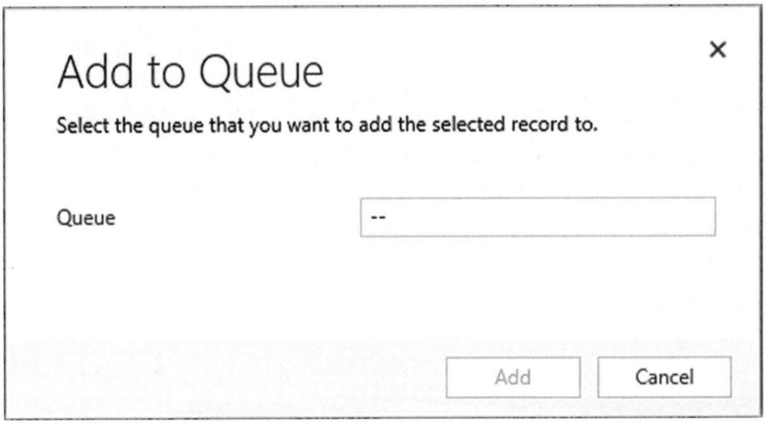

Add to Queue

×

Select the queue that you want to add the selected record to.

Queue   --

Add   Cancel

FIGURE 10.48   Add to Queue dialog.

TIP

You can select more than one record from the activities view to add more than one activity at a time to each queue. You can also create a workflow to automate the queue assignment every time a new activity is created. To learn more about working with workflows, see Chapter 26.

To view the items that are assigned to each queue, go to the Service area select Service > Queues. Change the view to All Items. (The first time you enter into this section, the default view shows the Items I Am Working On view, which is empty.) Select the queue to which you added items to view the items so you can work with them (see Figure 10.49).

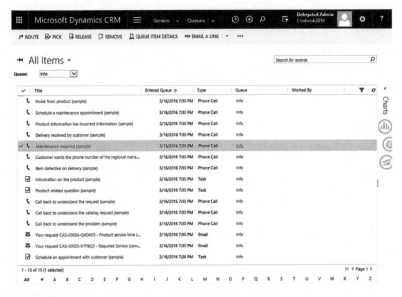

FIGURE 10.49   All queue items for the Info queue.

When you select one or more items, you can select any of the following actions for the queue items:

▶ **Route**—Use this option to move the queue item to another queue.

▶ **Pick**—Use this option to have a queue item displayed in the Items I am Working On view.

▶ **Release**—Use this option to release a queue item so it will be removed from the Items I am Working On view.

▶ **Remove**—Use this option to remove the queue item from the queue.

Queues help users assign records to themselves without taking the ownership of the record. For example, user A can be the owner of a record, and user B can be working on that record. Only one person can work on a queue item at a time, preventing other users from picking records that someone else is working on.

Not all the entity types are queue enabled by default. If you create a custom entity or have one of the existing system entities, like Account or Contact, and want users to add their records to queues, you need to select the Queues check box on the General tab, as shown in Figure 10.50. (After you select this option and save the change, you cannot uncheck it.) If the entity you created has the ownership set to user or team, you also have the option to automatically move the records to the owners' default queue when a record is created or assigned.

FIGURE 10.50   Queue customization settings.

Parent and Child Case Settings

If you select Parent and Child Case Settings, the Case Settings dialog appears (see Figure 10.51). In it you can configure the attributes you want a child case to inherit from a parent case when the child case is created. (By default only the case title and customer are inherited.)

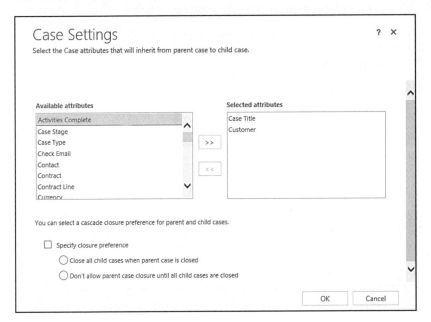

FIGURE 10.51   Case Settings dialog.

You can also set whether the case can be closed if there are child cases open and whether to close all child cases when the parent case is closed.

The ability to work with child cases was new in Dynamics CRM 2015 and is also available in CRM 2016. You can split a case into child cases that are hierarchy related. To create a child case, you must be working with a case record. You go to Service > Cases and open any case record, and then click the Create Child Case button in the command bar (see Figure 10.52).

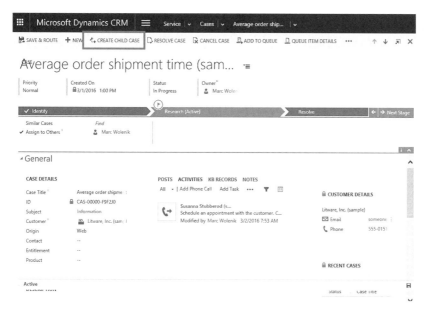

FIGURE 10.52   Create Child Case button.

When you click this button, a quick create form appears, with the prepopulated fields you defined in Case Settings (see Figure 10.53).

FIGURE 10.53   The quick create form for a child case, with prepopulated fields from Case Settings.

Routing Rule Sets

Routing Rule Sets allows you to configure routing with some defined criteria so that a customer service representative doesn't need to think, decide, or known how to route the cases to the right user, team, or queue. Figure 10.54 shows the Routing Rule Sets area where we can manage them.

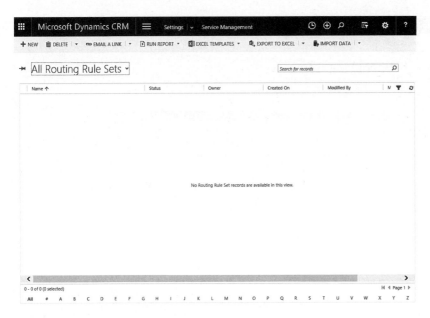

FIGURE 10.54   Routing rule sets.

By default, there are no routing rules created. You can create a new Routing Rule by clicking + New in the command bar. The form shown in Figure 10.55 appears.

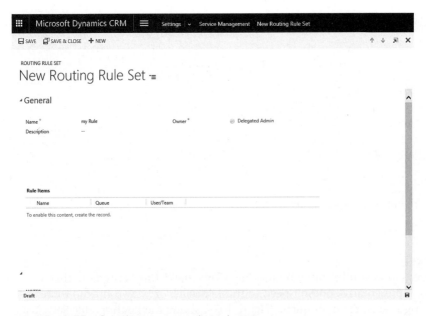

FIGURE 10.55   Creating a new routing rule set.

Enter a name and then click Save in the command bar to create rule items. After it has been saved, then click the + icon that is on the Rule Item subgrid.

Enter the name for your new rule item and then enter the criteria. Figure 10.56 shows the creation of a simple rule to route the cases with the origin equal to Email to the info queue. Click Save & Close when you are done. You must now activate your new routing rule set by clicking Activate in the command bar.

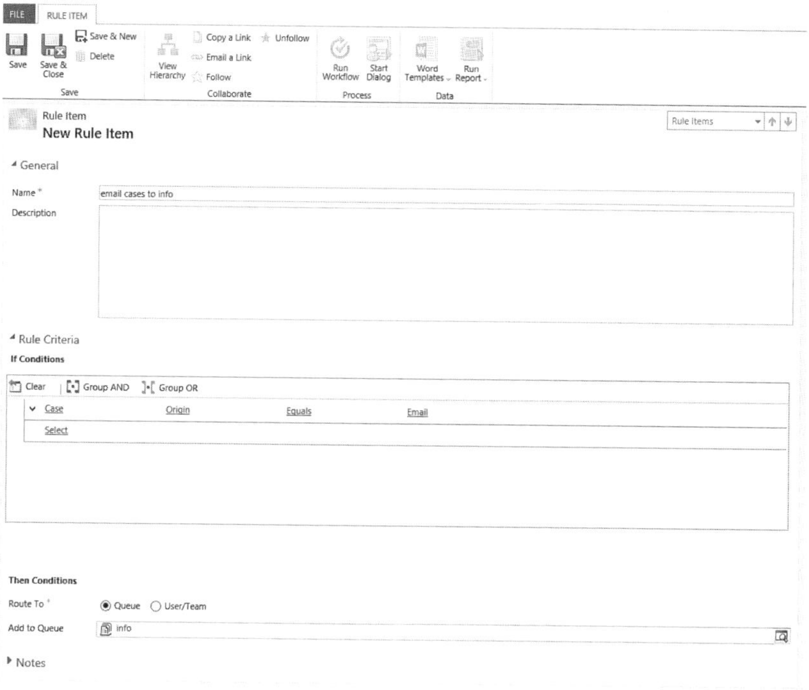

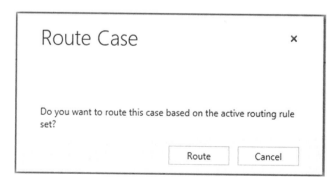

FIGURE 10.56   Creating a new rule item.

You can now use the new routing rules. When you work with a case record, you now see a Save & Route button. If you click it, you see the confirmation dialog shown in Figure 10.57. If you click Route, the rules are applied.

Route Case   ✕

Do you want to route this case based on the active routing rule set?

Route   Cancel

FIGURE 10.57   Saving and routing a case.

10

If you want to apply these rules to more than one record, you can do so by going to Cases and selecting the records from any view. You then see the button Apply Routing Rule. Click it and then confirm your choice in the dialog that appears.

Automatic Record Creation and Update Rules

Automatic Record Creation and Update Rules allows you to configure the automatic creation of records and updates in a few easy steps, without having to create custom workflows. By default, there are no rules of this type created, as shown in Figure 10.58.

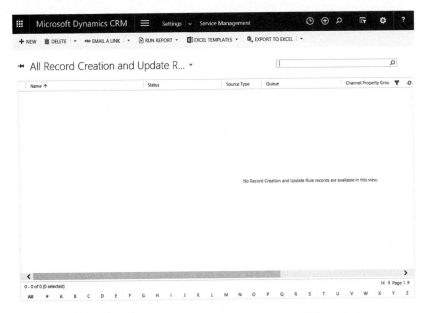

FIGURE 10.58   Automatic Record Creation and Update Rules window.

To create a new rule, click + New, enter a name for the rule, and specify the conditions for record creation, including the source type, which can be any activity entity, such as Email, Phone, or a custom activity (see Figure 10.59).

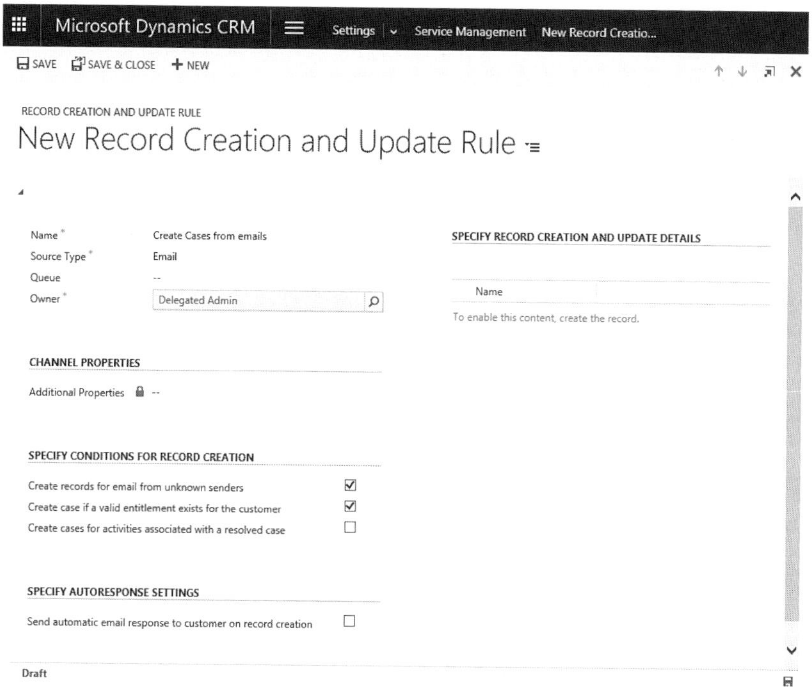

FIGURE 10.59   New Automatic Record Creation and Update Rule window.

After you save the rule, you can add conditions to perform other operations, such as creating records, updating records, sending emails, or starting a child workflow (see Figure 10.60).

FIGURE 10.60   Creating a new update rule.

Subjects

If you click Subjects on the Service Management page, you end up at the same page as if you clicked Subjects on the Business Management page. The creation of subjects is explained in Chapter 17.

Service Terms

The Service Terms group contains the following configurations, as described in the following sections:

▶ Service Level Agreement

▶ Entitlements

▶ Holiday Schedule

▶ Service Configuration Settings

▶ Customer Service Schedule

Service Level Agreement

Service Pack 1 of Dynamics CRM 2013 introduced service level agreement (SLAs). In that version, you needed to take the optional step of enabling SLAs. Now with the 2016 version, SLAs are enabled out of the box if you start from a fresh organization.

When you create a new SLA, you must enter a name for it and enter a value in the Applicable From field, which can be any of the following:

▶ Created On

▶ Modified On

▶ Follow Up By

▶ Record Created On

▶ Resolved By

▶ First Response By

▶ Escalated On

▶ Last On Hold Time

You must also select the SLA type, which can be either standard or enhanced. For more information about the enhanced SLA type, see the section "Enhanced Case SLAs," later in this chapter. Finally, you must specify whether you want to allow pause and resume or not (see Figure 10.61).

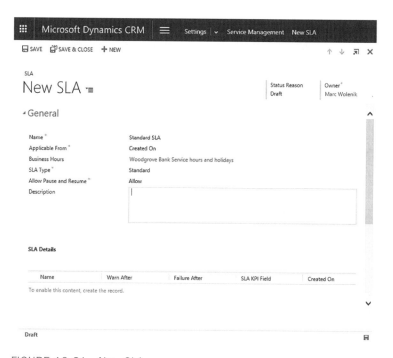

FIGURE 10.61   New SLA.

> **NOTE**
>
> The Allow Pause and Resume option is valid only for enhanced SLA types; you cannot set this field for standard SLAs.

Optionally, you can set the Business Hours field by going to the Customer Service Schedule option, as described in the following sections.

> **NOTE**
>
> After you save a new SLA record, you cannot change the Applicable From, SLA Type, and Allow Pause and Resume fields. If you need to change these values, you must create a new SLA record.

After you saved the new SLA, you can start entering its details. As shown in Figure 10.62, you can configure criteria where you want the SLA to be applicable.

FIGURE 10.62   New SLA detail record.

You can specify the time after which you can consider the SLA item to be a failure and the time after which you want to receive a warning. After you save the record, you can add actions as steps for the failure or success events.

You can perform the following actions in the SLA details for success and/or failure events (see Figure 10.63):

▶ Send Email

▶ Create Record

▶ Update Record

▶ Assign Record

▶ Change Status

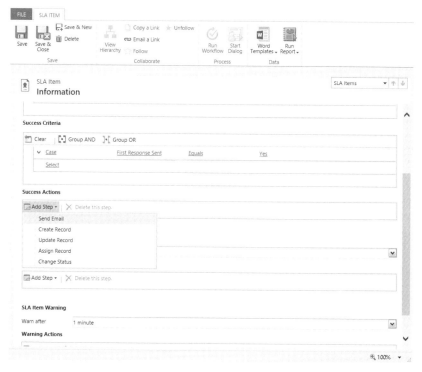

FIGURE 10.63   SLA detail actions.

Entitlements

Entitlements are used to configure service licenses that can optionally be associated with an SLA record. You are required to enter a primary customer that can be either a contact or an account, start and end dates, and a name for the entitlement (see Figure 10.64).

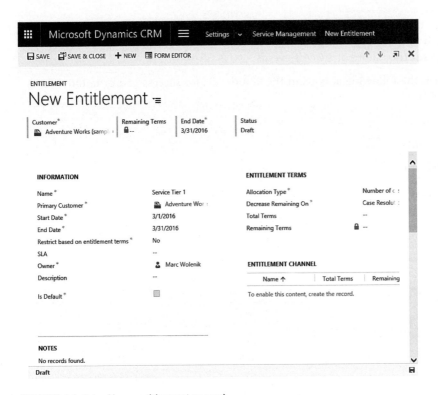

FIGURE 10.64 New entitlement record.

The Allocation Type field can be set to either Number of Cases or Number of Hours. Depending which allocation type you enter, the Total Terms field counts either cases or hours. The value you enter for Total Terms is decreased depending on the case resolution or case creation if you configure the allocation type to count the number of cases; otherwise this decrease field is locked.

After you save a new entitlement, you can add entitlement channels, which can be any of the following:

▶ Email

▶ Phone

▶ Web

▶ Facebook

▶ Twitter

For each channel line you can set a specific value for Total Terms, and you see the value in Remaining Terms when it is in use (see Figure 10.65).

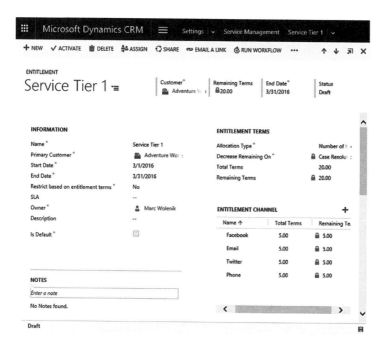

FIGURE 10.65   Entitlement channels.

You can also set products and contacts for where you want the entitlement to be applied, as shown in Figure 10.66.

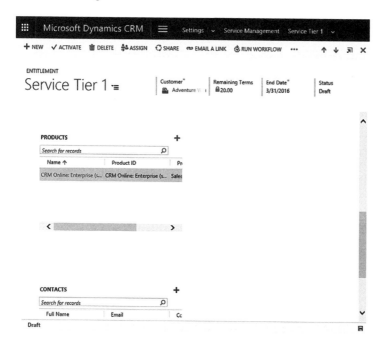

FIGURE 10.66   Entitlement products and contacts.

Holiday Schedule

The holiday schedule calendar differs from the business closure calendar as the holiday schedule calendar applies to the SLA module only.

When you create a new holiday schedule, you must supply a name and a description, as shown in Figure 10.67.

FIGURE 10.67   New holiday schedule.

After you click Create, you can open the created holiday schedule to define the days, as shown in Figure 10.68.

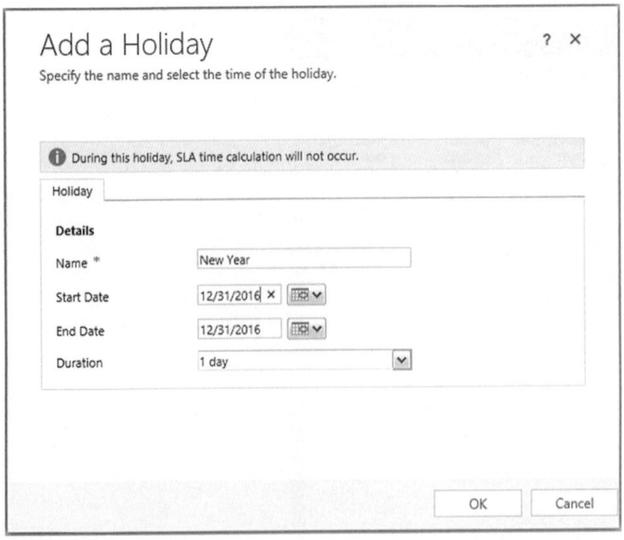

Add a Holiday
Specify the name and select the time of the holiday.

? ×

ⓘ During this holiday, SLA time calculation will not occur.

Holiday

Details

Name *	New Year
Start Date	12/31/2016 ×
End Date	12/31/2016
Duration	1 day

OK   Cancel

FIGURE 10.68   New holiday.

NOTE

During these holidays, the SLA time calculation does not occur.

Service Configuration Settings

The Service Configuration Settings option opens the Service tab of the System Settings dialog (see Figure 10.69). You can also access this tab dialog by going to Setting > Administration > System Settings > Service.

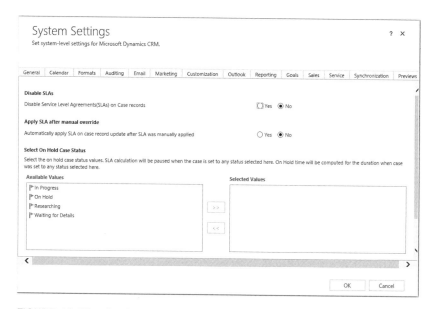

FIGURE 10.69   Service configuration settings.

On this tab, you can disable the SLAs on case records, apply an SLA after a manual override, and select the on hold case status.

Customer Service Schedule

As with the holiday schedule calendar, discussed previously, you can create specific customer service schedules. This is useful if you have customers outside the United States who observe different holidays.

When you click + New to create a new customer service schedule, you get the dialog shown in Figure 10.70, where you must enter the name and click Create.

10

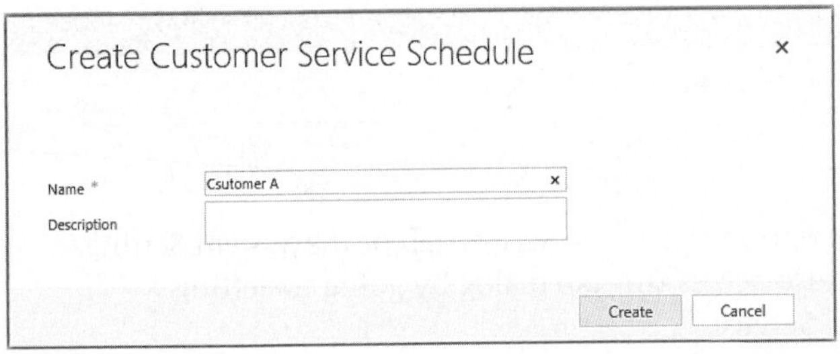

FIGURE 10.70   Creating a new customer service schedule.

After you create the record, you can configure the recurring weekly schedule. There are the main options you have (see Figure 10.71):

▶ Work Hours Are the Same Each Day

▶ Work Hours Vary by Day

▶ 24 × 7 support

FIGURE 10.71   Configuring a weekly schedule.

If you selected the work hours to be the same each day, you can click on Set Work Hours link to configure the hours (as shown in Figure 10.72).

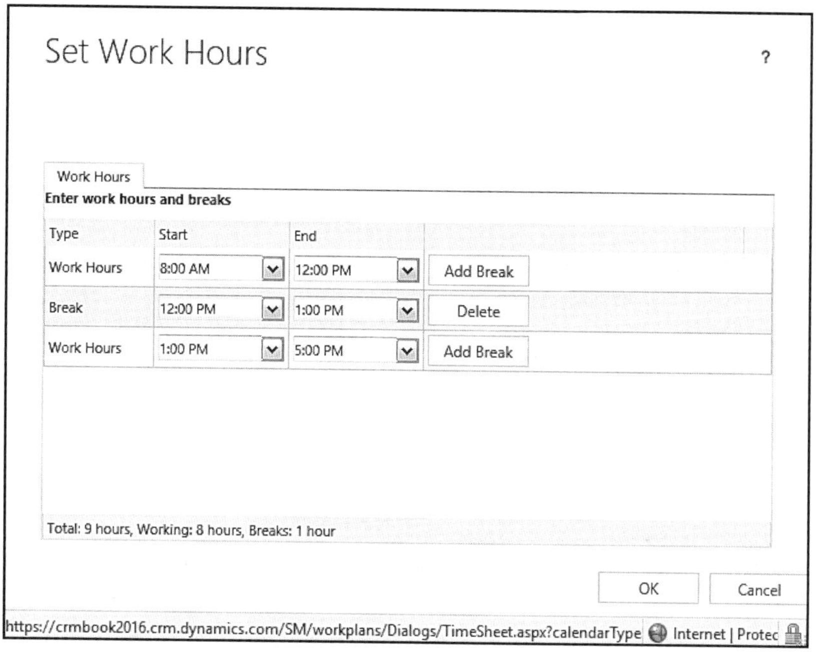

FIGURE 10.72   Work Hours.

If you select Work Hours Vary by Day, then you must configure the work hours for each day, as shown in Figure 10.73.

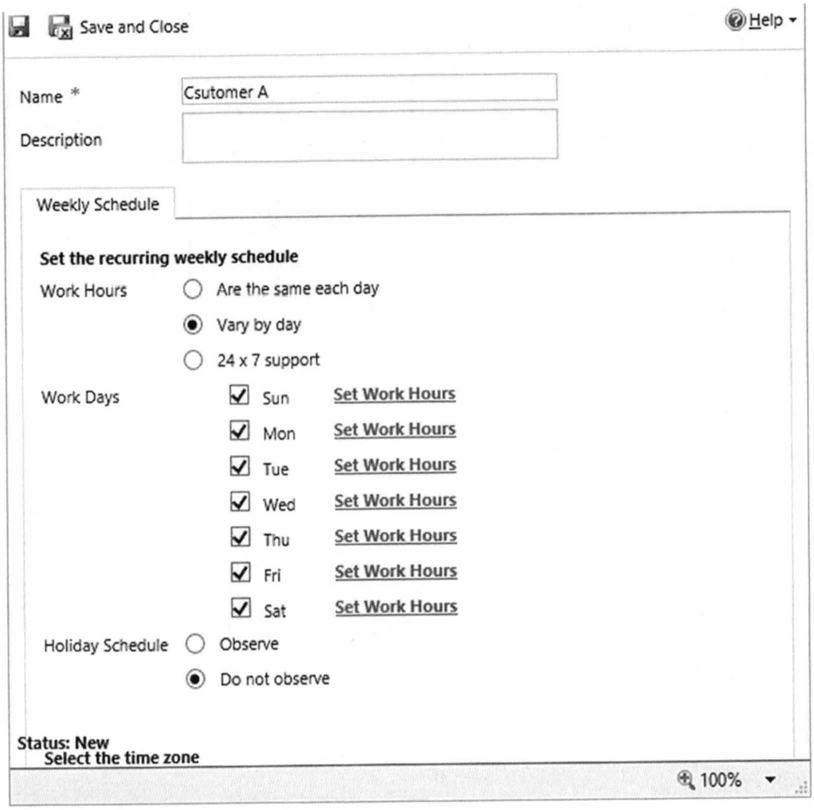

FIGURE 10.73 Configuring the work hours for each day.

You can then use the customer service schedules you have created in your SLAs.

Knowledge Base Management

In the Knowledge Base Management section you can configure the entities where you want the knowledge base search to be turned on (see Figure 10.74). By default this is enabled only for the Case entity but you can enable it for Account, Contact, or any custom entity if you want.

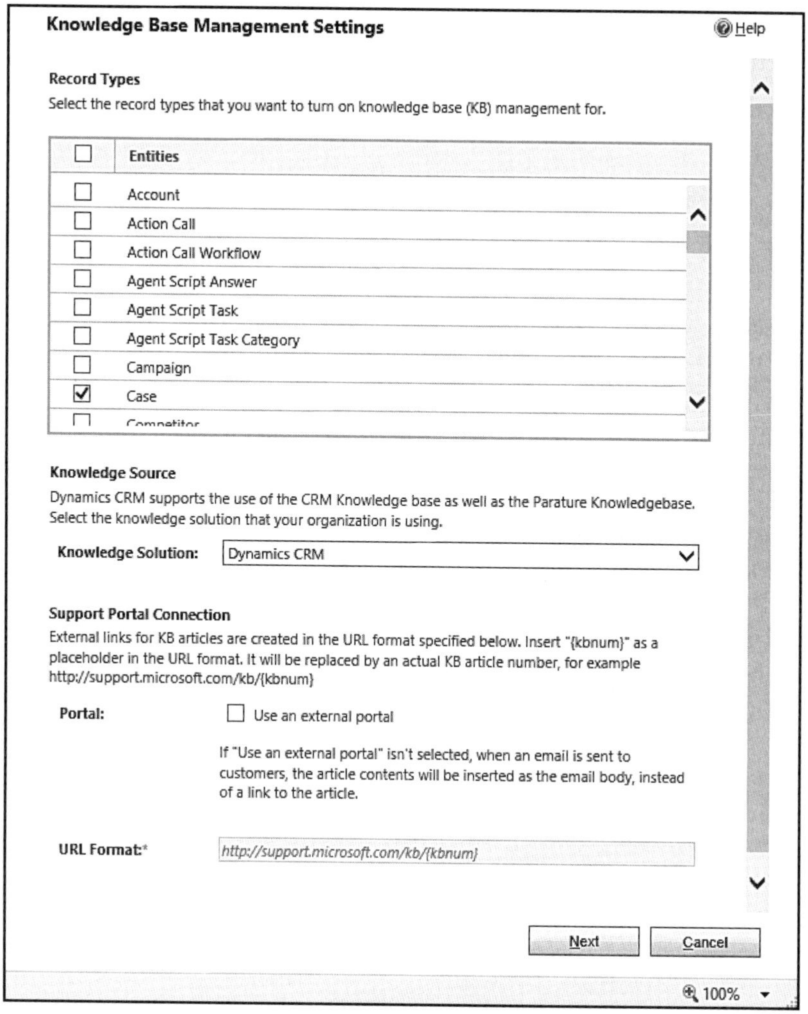

FIGURE 10.74   Knowledge base management settings.

You can also configure the Knowledge Solution field to either of the following:

▶ Dynamics CRM

▶ Parature

If you have an external knowledge base solution, you can check the Use an External Portal option and then enter the URL of your custom/external knowledge base application.

Templates

In the Templates section you can configure the following template types:

▶ Entitlement templates

▶ Email templates

▶ Article templates

▶ Contract templates

You can also access email, article, and contract templates by going to Settings > Templates. However, the Templates section is the only place to get the entitlement templates.

Creating a new entitlement template is very similar to creating an entitlement, except that you don't need to enter the customer and the contacts, and you are not required to set the start and end dates (see Figure 10.75).

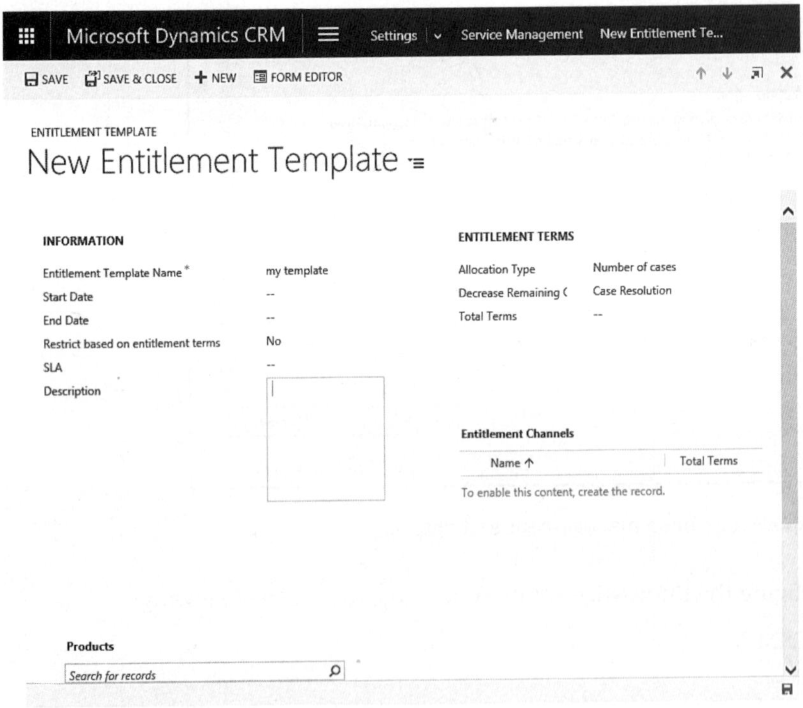

FIGURE 10.75   New entitlement template.

When you have templates set, you can go to the Entitlement option and click New to see the option to create a new entitlement from a template. Here you are asked to select one of the entitlement templates you created (see Figure 10.76).

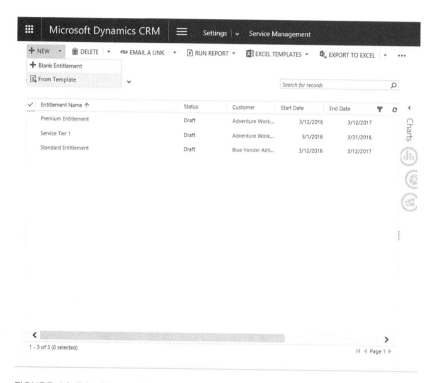

FIGURE 10.76   New entitlement from a template.

Service Scheduling

In the Service Scheduling section, you can configure the following:

▶ Business Closure

▶ Services

▶ Facilities/Equipment

▶ Resource Groups

▶ Sites

These options are described earlier in this chapter, in the section "Services."

Enhanced Case SLAs

Enhanced SLAs are different from standard SLAs. They support the following:

▶ Case on hold support

▶ Auto pause and resume of time calculation

▶ Support for success actions

▶ Creation of dashboards and reports based on the SLA KPI instance entity

You can put a case on hold for an unlimited period of time, until a reply from a customer is received. This stops the timer and calculations that might apply to the SLA.

To see how enhanced SLA works, create an SLA with two SLA details, one for each KPI type, as shown in Figure 10.77.

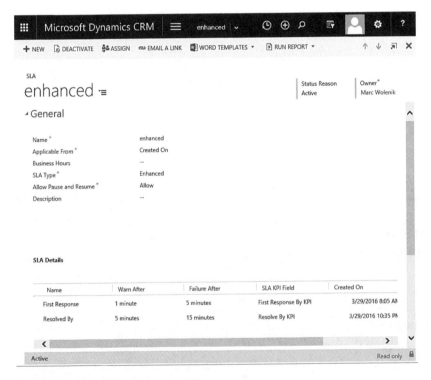

FIGURE 10.77   SLA with two details.

Save the SLA and make sure you activate it. Also make it the default SLA by clicking the Set as Default button on the command bar.

To test the SLA, create a new case, save it, and go to the Enhanced SLA Details tab, as shown in Figure 10.78.

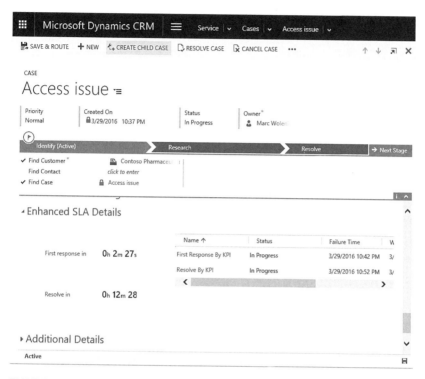

FIGURE 10.78   Enhanced SLA Details tab on a case record.

You can pause the case by changing the status to On Hold. You can resume the case by changing the status back to In Progress.

After the amount of time specified in the Warn After field elapses, you see a warning like the one shown in Figure 10.79.

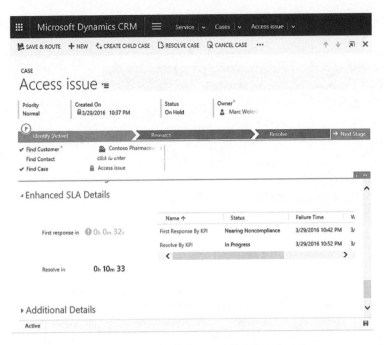

FIGURE 10.79   Warning in the Enhanced SLA Details tab on a case record.

After the time amount of time specified in the Failure After elapses, you see a warning like the one shown in Figure 10.80.

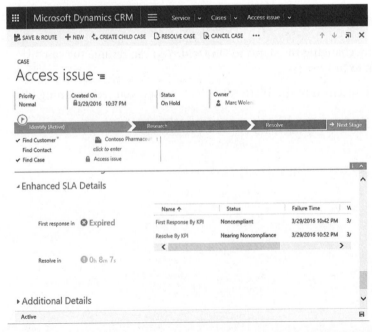

FIGURE 10.80   Expired a case record on the Enhanced SLA Details tab.

Dynamics CRM 2016 comes with some out-of-the-box dashboards that make use of the SLA and entitlement entities:

▶ Customer Service Manager Dashboard

▶ Customer Service Performance Dashboard

▶ Customer Service Representative Social Dashboard

Summary

The Service area is a valuable and important part of Microsoft Dynamics CRM. It provides a centralized view of calendars and schedules and allows you to easily perform scheduling tasks.

When working with cases, keep in mind that the summary of the activities that make up the case (and therefore the case resolution) are the resultant work effort—something neither expressed nor available on the main Case entity by default. Organizations often request the ability to see case resolution times and the ability to quickly/easily track times directly against the Case entity. (An example of this might be a spinning/countdown clock when a form is opened/being worked on.) Microsoft Dynamics CRM does *not* support this requirement without custom development. However, the work required to put this in place is actually quite minimal. The majority of effort in putting something like this together is in defining the business process and deciding how best to implement it. (For example, does the clock start automatically on open, or does the user click a button to start it? What happens on form load? Does the clock stop, or does it stay open until it is proactively stopped?)

In this chapter you have learned how to work with services in Microsoft Dynamics CRM 2016 by using the service calendar, working with cases to track customer issues, working with contracts, and managing articles to share typical business procedures.

This chapter shows that case configurations are now grouped on a dedicated page under Settings > Case Management.

Finally, this chapter explains how to use SLAs and entitlements, and it provides an example of how to work with enhanced SLAs to manage cases and support in a more controlled way.

Two features in the Service area are not discussed in this chapter: integrated service hub (see Chapter 11) and FieldOne (see Chapter 33, "FieldOne").

The Interactive Service Hub

Using the Interactive Service Hub

The interactive service hub is a new web user interface designed to be used by service support teams. It is divided into two types of usage:

▶ **Tier 1**—Tier 1 users see data with real-time multi-stream dashboards, and the data is based on entity views or queues. Multi-stream dashboards show data based on the same entity and are ideal for service support teams that support many cases at the same time.

▶ **Tier 2**—Tier 2 users see real-time single-stream dashboards. This is typically useful for managers who need to monitor less data, but they need to see sophisticated data (either escalated or complex, for example).

Both types of dashboards (multi-stream and single-stream) are real time and are interactive in nature, allowing users to drill down on the data.

The interactive service hub architecture is similar to that of the Dynamics CRM mobile clients, in that the customization and business rules are cached in a local store. Every time you make a customization or change in the entities associated to the interactive service hub, you are asked to download the customizations, and that takes some time to complete, much like what happens with mobile clients.

> **TIP**
>
> You can improve the download wait time by using a new features introduced with Update 0.1 to prepare client customization. Refer to Chapter 22 "Customizing the System," for detailed information.

The first time you access the standard CRM web interface, the system prompt you to try the interactive service hub, as shown in Figure 11.1 (found in the information bar across the top).

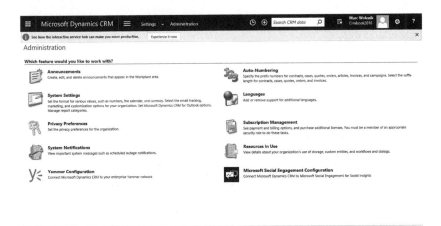

FIGURE 11.1   Interactive service hub suggestion.

If you click the Experience It Now button, you are directed to the new interactive service hub user interface on a new tab or browser window (see Figure 11.2).

FIGURE 11.2   Preparing the interactive service hub.

TIP

The direct links to the interactive service hub are as follows (where orgname is your organizations name):

For Online: https://orgname.crm.dynamics.com/engagementhub.aspx

For On-Premises: http://crmserver/orgname/engagementhub.aspx

Once the interface downloads the metadata, you can start using this new interface, as shown in Figure 11.3.

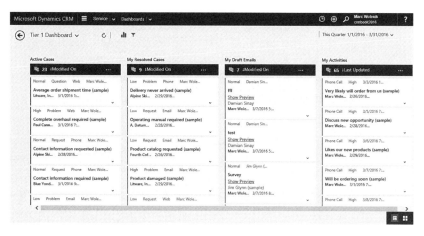

FIGURE 11.3   The interactive service hub.

The interactive service hub comes with four predefined dashboards out of the box:

▶ Tier 1 Dashboard

▶ Tier 2 Dashboard

▶ Knowledge Manager

▶ My Knowledge Dashboard

You can create custom (interactive service hub) dashboards but only at the system level in Dynamics CRM 2016. Note that this is different from the standard CRM user interface, where users can create their own personal dashboards.

▶ **SEE** the "Configurations and Customizations" section, later in this chapter, to learn how to create custom dashboards.

You can use these dashboards to see some nice graphical interfaces of the data by clicking the chart icon next to the dashboard name (see Figure 11.4).

FIGURE 11.4   Interactive service hub dashboard with visual filters.

The charts shown in Figure 11.4 are also called visual filters because they allow you to filter the data by clicking on the chart components directly.

Clicking the icon buttons in the lower-right corner of the screen allows you to change the dashboard view to tiles (see Figure 11.5).

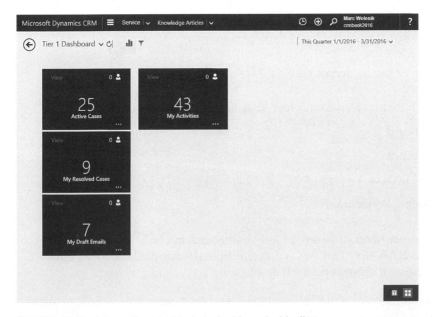

FIGURE 11.5   Interactive service hub dashboard with tiles.

You can click each tile to display the list of records to easily navigate to them.

When you look at the stream view (shown in the columns on the form), there are some hidden (or not easy to catch) controls in the stream records. You can click the check boxes of any records inside the stream to display a list of actions on the top. For example, if you select a case, you see actions like Resolve, Cancel, and Do Not Decrement Entitlement Terms at the top of the column, as shown in Figure 11.6.

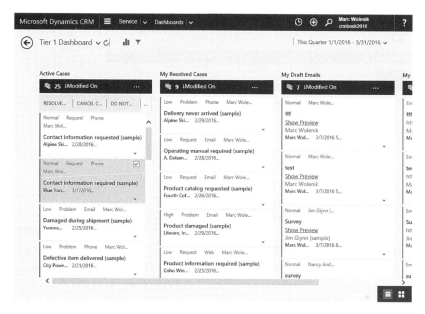

FIGURE 11.6   Interactive service hub stream record actions.

If you click the ellipsis (...), you see more actions you can take for the selected record(s), like Delete, Apply Routing Rule, Assign, and Add to Queue (see Figure 11.7).

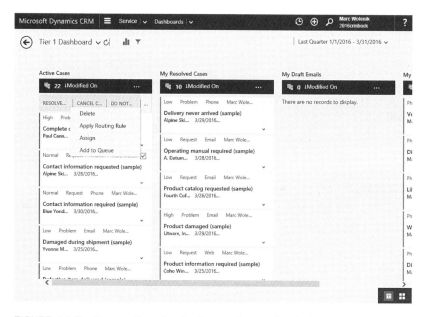

FIGURE 11.7   More actions for the interactive service hub stream records.

Navigation

You may notice that the navigation bar in the interactive service hub is very similar to the standard Dynamics CRM user interface. However, when expanded it, you find only Service and a few entities there (see Figure 11.8).

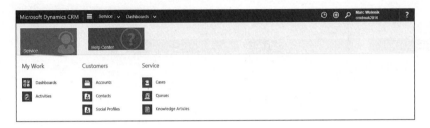

FIGURE 11.8   Interactive service hub navigation.

You can add more entities here or add custom entities, but this navigation area is designed to be streamlined for the Tier 1 and 2 agents. You can make configurations here, though, as described in the "Configurations and Customizations" section, later in this chapter.

Filters

Dashboards in the interactive service hub have two types of filters: time frame and field. The time frame filters allow you to quickly filter by the following time frames:

- ▶ Today
- ▶ Yesterday
- ▶ This Week
- ▶ Last Week
- ▶ This Month
- ▶ Last Month
- ▶ Month Till Date
- ▶ This Quarter
- ▶ Last Quarter
- ▶ Custom Time Frame

Figure 11.9 shows the interactive service hub time filters.

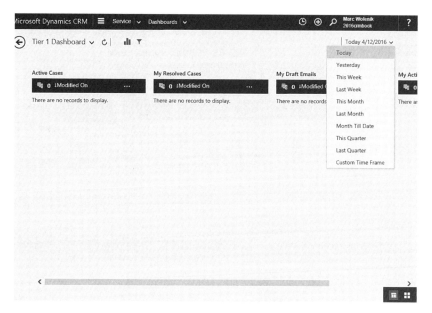

FIGURE 11.9   ISH time frame filters.

If you select the Custom Time Frame option, you see the Start-Date and End-Date calendars.

Apart from the time frame filters, each entity may have other fields configured to be used as filters. If you click the filter icon, you see the filters, as shown in Figure 11.10.

▶ **SEE** the "Configurations and Customizations" section, later in this chapter for information on how to configure filter fields.

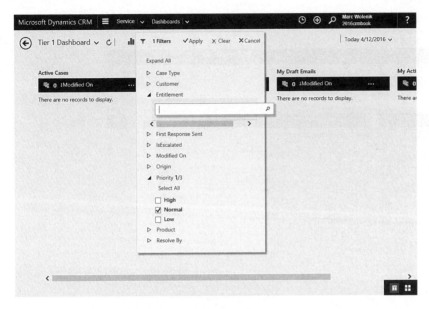

FIGURE 11.10   Interactive service hub field filters.

Recent Views and Records

You can click the clock icon in the navigation bar to access the recent views and records in the interactive service hub, as shown in Figure 11.11.

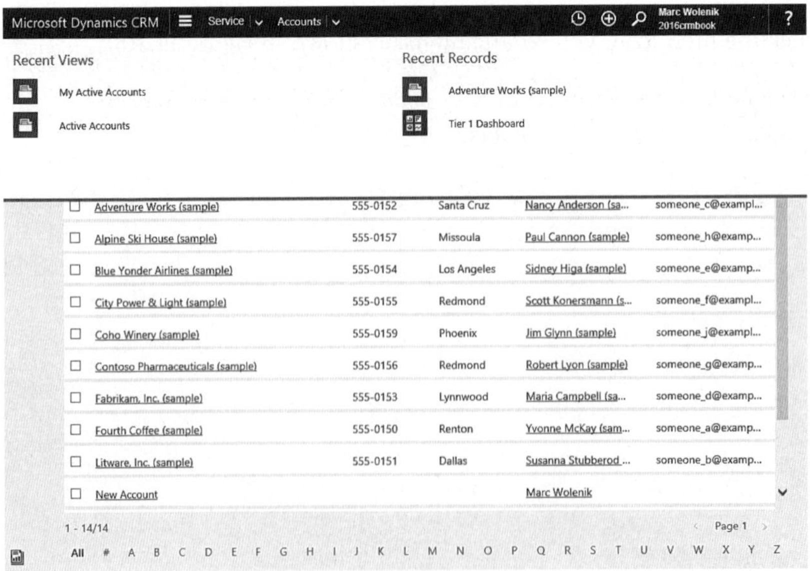

FIGURE 11.11   Recent views and records.

The recent record list also shows you the dashboard records you recently viewed.

Quick Search

By clicking the find icon in the navigation bar, you can access to the Quick Search tool, as shown in Figure 11.12.

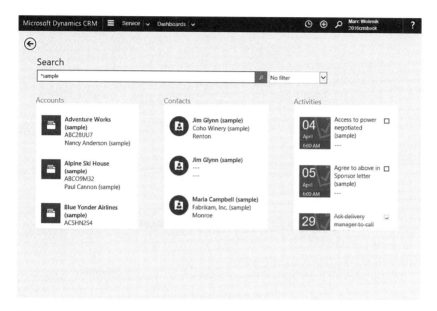

FIGURE 11.12   Quick Search.

The entities configured out of the box are Account, Contact, Activity, and Case. To add custom entities to this list, you can go to the CRM standard web interface and click Settings > Administration > System Settings. Then, on the General tab, you can set the Set Up Search options (see Figure 11.13).

FIGURE 11.13   Set Up Search options in System Settings.

Click Select to add entities, as shown in Figure 11.14. Be aware that the entities must be enabled for interactive experience.

▶ **SEE** the "Configurations and Customizations" section, later in this chapter.

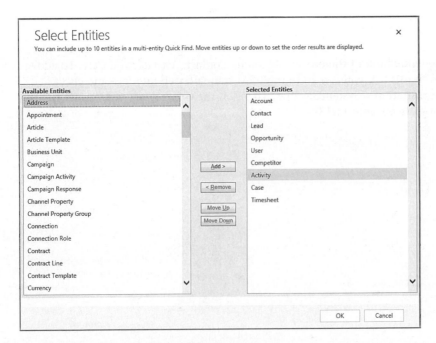

FIGURE 11.14   Selecting entities for Quick Search.

You see more entities here than in the interactive service hub because the interactive service hub shows only the entities that are configured to be displayed in the Service area. So if you add a new entity here, make sure the entity is configured to be displayed in the Service area so you can use it in the interactive service hub.

Quick Create

You can quickly create new entity records by clicking on the + icon in the navigation bar. You can then see the list of entities you can create, as shown in Figure 11.15

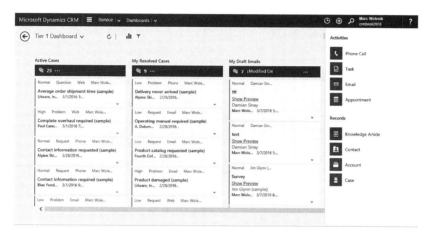

FIGURE 11.15   Interactive service hub Quick Create.

By default, you can only create entities of types Activity, which can be Phone Call, Task, Email, or Appointment. (Note that you cannot create Service activity records, nor can you enable them to work with this interface.) By default you can also create other records of the types Knowledge Article, Contact, Account, and Case.

Streams

Streams are basically views in the interactive service hub dashboards, and you can edit the properties in them by clicking the ... to the right of a stream title. In this way, you can change the sorting of the stream. Clicking the stream title changes the sort direction from ascending to descending and vice versa, as shown in Figure 11.16.

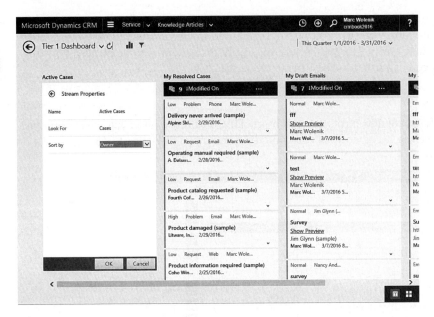

FIGURE 11.16   Stream properties.

Customers

Customers in the interactive service hub are divided in accounts and contacts. To see the accounts, go to Service and then click Accounts in the navigation bar. The view shown in Figure 11.17 appears.

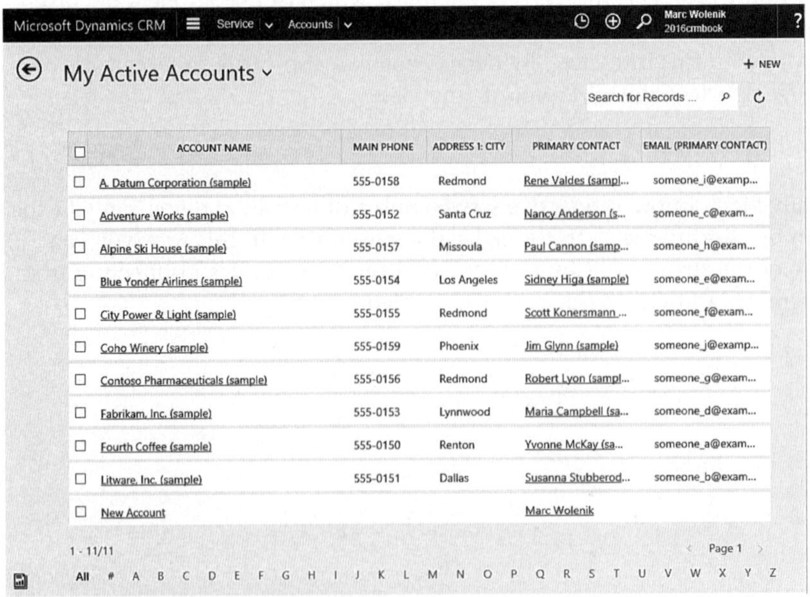

	ACCOUNT NAME	MAIN PHONE	ADDRESS 1: CITY	PRIMARY CONTACT	EMAIL (PRIMARY CONTACT)
☐	A. Datum Corporation (sample)	555-0158	Redmond	Rene Valdes (sampl...	someone_i@examp...
☐	Adventure Works (sample)	555-0152	Santa Cruz	Nancy Anderson (s...	someone_c@exam...
☐	Alpine Ski House (sample)	555-0157	Missoula	Paul Cannon (samp...	someone_h@exam...
☐	Blue Yonder Airlines (sample)	555-0154	Los Angeles	Sidney Higa (sample)	someone_e@exam...
☐	City Power & Light (sample)	555-0155	Redmond	Scott Konersmann ...	someone_f@exam...
☐	Coho Winery (sample)	555-0159	Phoenix	Jim Glynn (sample)	someone_j@examp...
☐	Contoso Pharmaceuticals (sample)	555-0156	Redmond	Robert Lyon (sampl...	someone_g@exam...
☐	Fabrikam, Inc. (sample)	555-0153	Lynnwood	Maria Campbell (sa...	someone_d@exam...
☐	Fourth Coffee (sample)	555-0150	Renton	Yvonne McKay (sa...	someone_a@exam...
☐	Litware, Inc. (sample)	555-0151	Dallas	Susanna Stubberod...	someone_b@exam...
☐	New Account			Marc Wolenik	

1 - 11/11

All # A B C D E F G H I J K L M N O P Q R S T U V W X Y Z

FIGURE 11.17   My Active Accounts.

This view shows a list of accounts. Notice that the view is not very different from the views in the standard CRM web user interface. However, there is a new icon in this interface, down in the lower-left corner. When you click this icon, you go to an entity-specific dashboard (in this case, a dashboard that works only for Account entities) that is not available from the Service > Dashboard menu option (see Figure 11.18).

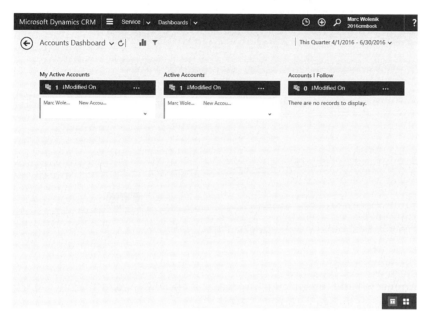

FIGURE 11.18   Accounts Dashboard view.

If you click the chart icon, you see the visual filters, as shown in Figure 11.19.

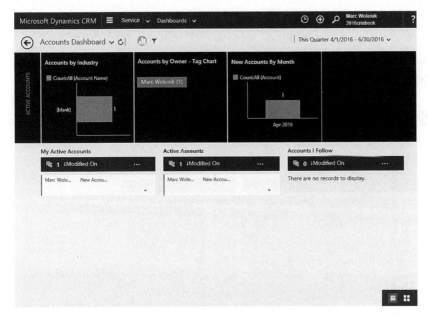

FIGURE 11.19   Accounts Dashboard view with visual filters.

Social Profiles

If you have CRM connected and integrated with Microsoft Social Engagement, you can see the social profiles, as shown in Figure 11.20.

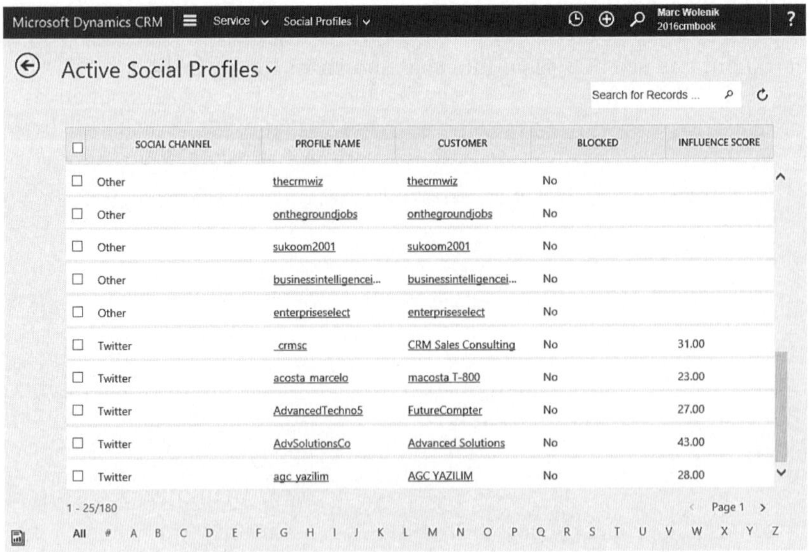

FIGURE 11.20   Active Social Profiles view.

► For more information about Microsoft Social Engagement and how to connect it with Dynamics CRM, **SEE CHAPTER 14**, "Microsoft Dynamics Social Engagement."

Cases

To work with cases, click on Service > Cases in the navigation bar. On the My Active Cases page that appears, you see a list of cases in a view that is similar to the views in the standard CRM web user interface (see Figure 11.21).

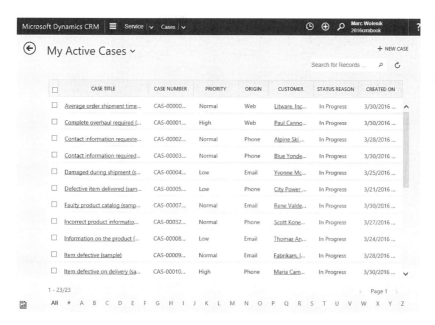

FIGURE 11.21   My Active Cases view from the interactive service hub.

This interface also has the entity-specific dashboard icon in the lower left, and you can click it to go to the dashboard.

If you click the chart icon, you will see the visual filters, as shown in Figure 11.22.

FIGURE 11.22   Cases Dashboard view with visual filters.

To open a case, click a title record. Cases in the interactive service hub are displayed by default with a modern user interface, as shown in Figure 11.23.

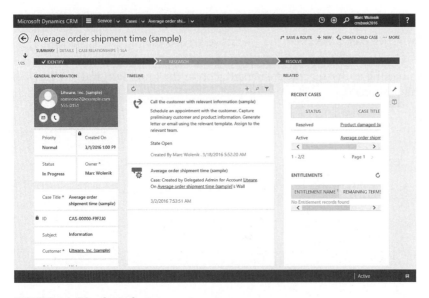

FIGURE 11.23   Case form.

You can click the phone icon to make a quick phone call to the customer, and when you do, an alert confirmation is displayed, as shown in Figure 11.24.

> **NOTE**
>
> The example shown in Figure 11.24 assumes that you have Skype installed on your computer. If you don't, you do not see this confirmation.

FIGURE 11.24   Alert for a Skype phone call.

At the same time a quick form for a new phone call record opens on the right side of the screen, as shown in Figure 11.25.

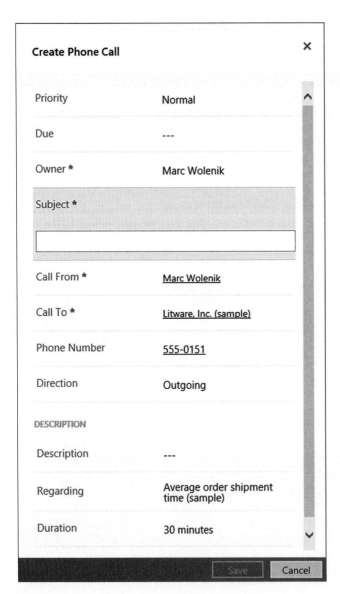

FIGURE 11.25   Phone call record.

There are some differences in the process flow between the interactive service hub interface and Dynamics CRM. For example, click the stage you want to work with, and you see the Make Active link on the bottom of the box displayed for the stage, as shown in Figure 11.26.

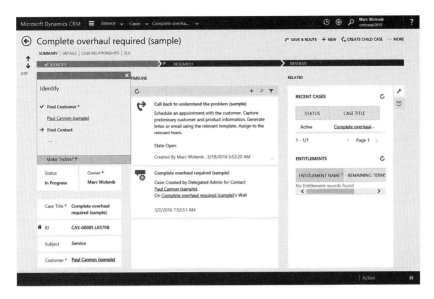

FIGURE 11.26   The make active process flow.

Making the stage active allows you to move to the next stage. When you do, you can click the Next Stage link to move the process flow to the next stage.

Knowledge Articles

The knowledge articles in the interactive service hub have an improved interface compared with the one that comes with the standard CRM user interface. Remember that the standard interface forces you to start an article by selecting a template. However, this is not required for new articles created with the interactive service hub interface. Figure 11.27 shows the My Active Articles interface.

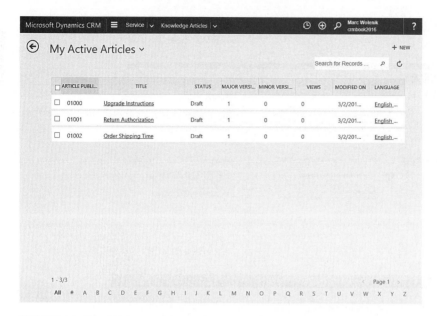

FIGURE 11.27   My Active Articles view.

When you choose to create a new knowledge base article, you see a process flow not shown in the standard CRM user interface (see Figure 11.28).

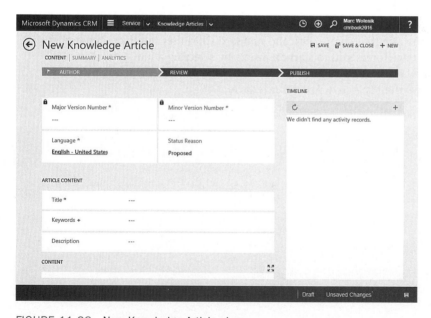

FIGURE 11.28   New Knowledge Article view.

The interactive service hub user interface has a rich text editor for entering article content that allows you to easily add images and links, as shown in Figure 11.29.

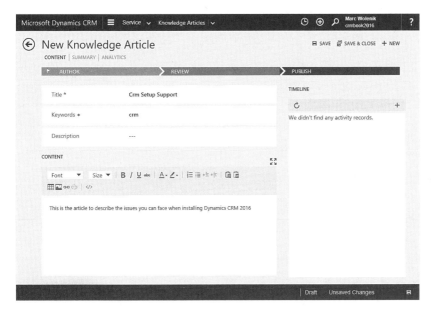

FIGURE 11.29   New Knowledge Article view.

You add an image by entering the URL of an image file you have stored on any external website, and you can easily see a preview of the image before adding it to the content of the article (see Figure 11.30).

FIGURE 11.30   Adding images to the New Knowledge Article view.

Configurations and Customizations

You can customize the interactive service hub in several different ways. If you want to add a custom entity or any system entity that doesn't come with the interactive service hub by default, you can add it by going to Settings > Customizations and opening the default solution. There you see the Enable for Interactive Experience check box (see Figure 11.31).

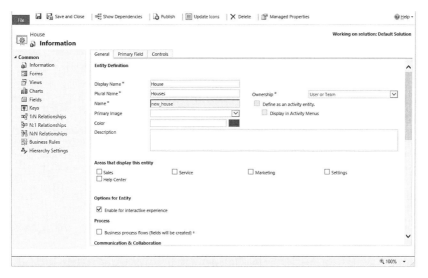

FIGURE 11.31   Enable for Interactive Experience option.

Enabling this check box alone is not enough to have your custom entity appear in the interactive service hub interface, however; you also need to add your entity to the Service area by checking the Service check box under Areas That Display This Entity (which basically adds the entity to the sitemap for the Service area).

> **NOTE**
>
> In the interactive service hub there is no way to customize the sitemap to add other links to web resources or custom pages as you can do with the standard CRM web interface. The interactive service hub shows only the entities that are enabled for interactive experience in the Service area.

When you check Enable for Interactive Experience for an entity, two new type of forms are created:

▶ Main—Interactive Experience

▶ Card

These new forms are explained in the next section.

Main—Interactive Experience Form

Interactive experience will not work without at least one Main—Interactive Experience form. When you check Enable for Interactive Experience for an entity, one form of this type is created. You can, however, create more forms of this type by clicking Forms > New > Main Form—Interactive Experience. You might need to create new forms of this type, for example, to assign to different CRM roles.

> **NOTE**
>
> Even though the interactive service hub application interface is based on the new mobile client application, it does not support the new interactive controls available for mobile clients. For more information about these controls, see Chapter 18, "Mobility."

The interactive service hub interface doesn't allow you to change the form if you have more than one form created with permissions. Only the first one is displayed, and you might need to change the order by clicking the Form Order option and then selecting Main Form Set—Interactive Experience, as shown in Figure 11.32.

FIGURE 11.32   Form order for Main Form Set—Interactive Experience.

Choose the form you want to use and move it to the top and click OK.

Card Form

The other new form type introduced with the interactive service hub is the Card form. The Card form is used to display data in dashboards under streams. To create a new form of this type, Forms > New > Card Form. Figure 11.33 shows the card form).

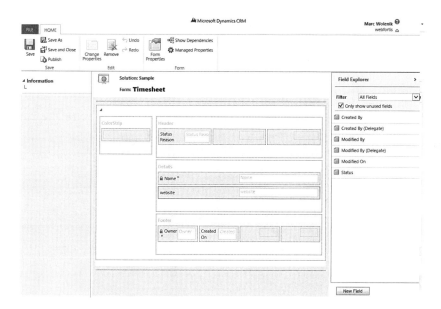

FIGURE 11.33   Card form editor.

Card forms are limited forms for which you cannot edit field attributes to configure events that occur on changes or loading or saving events. In addition, the sections are limited to only four fields (see Figure 11.34).

FIGURE 11.34   Card form properties.

For example, if you add a new field called Website, it appears in the dashboard as shown in Figure 11.35.

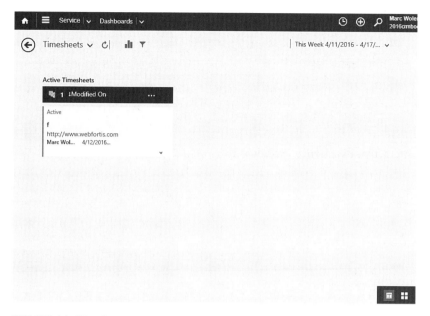

FIGURE 11.35   Card form used in the dashboard.

A Card form has a special section called Color Strip, and you can add only one field to this section, and it can be of type Boolean Picklist or status Reason. You can configure the color in the field property page by selecting the option and then clicking the Edit button for the selected option. Figure 11.36 shows a color setting.

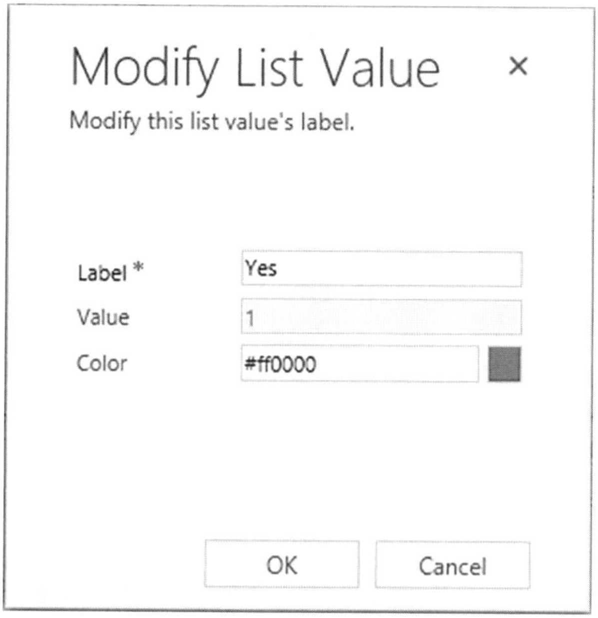

Modify List Value   ×

Modify this list value's label.

Label *   Yes

Value   1

Color   #ff0000

OK   Cancel

FIGURE 11.36   Editing the color for a Card form.

The colors you select are displayed to the left of the stream record as a vertical colored line.

Fields

Field properties have two new specific interactive service hub—related attributes (see Figure 11.37):

► Appears in Global Filter in Interactive Experience

► Sortable in Interactive Experience Dashboard

FIGURE 11.37   Field interactive service hub–related attributes.

Appears in Global Filter in Interactive Experience

You can use the Appears in Global Filter in Interactive Experience option with the following field data types:

► Option Set (picklist)

► Two options (Booleans)

► Whole Number (integers)

► Floating Point Number

▶ Decimal Number

▶ Currency

▶ Date and Time

▶ Lookup

When you set this flag on a field, you can use it in the global filter in the Entity interactive dashboards. Figure 11.38 shows a Billable field of type Boolean for the Timesheet entity.

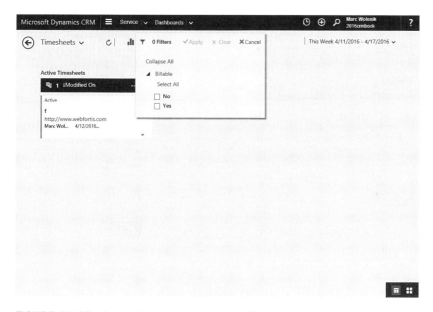

FIGURE 11.38   Interactive service hub field filters.

Select the value you want to filter on and click Apply. You can then remove all filters by clicking on the last X (Cancel) button. To remove only a particular filter field, you can hover on the field and click the X button that appears.

Sortable in Interactive Experience Dashboard

You can use the Sortable in Interactive Experience Dashboard option with any field type. Setting this option allows you to use the field in dashboard streams to change the sort field. You can do this when you go to an entity dashboard and click the ... under the stream title and then select Edit Properties. You then see the field available in the Sort By drop-down, as shown in Figure 11.39.

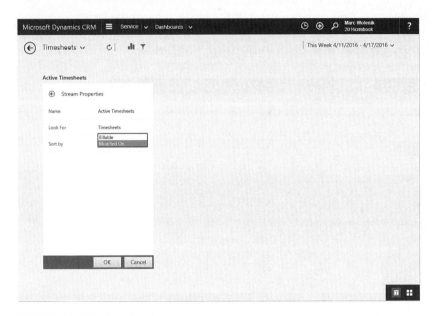

FIGURE 11.39   Sort By drop-down.

When you select the field and click OK, you then see the field in the stream title, so you can click there to change the direction from ascending to descending or vice versa.

Dashboards

As mentioned earlier in this chapter, you can create new system dashboards. To do that, you select Settings > Customizations > Customize the System. Then you select Dashboards > New > Interactive Experience Dashboard, as shown in Figure 11.40.

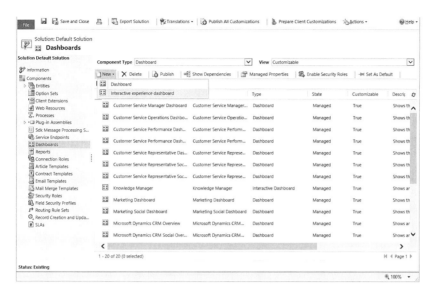

FIGURE 11.40   Creating a new interactive experience dashboard.

You are then asked to choose a layout, and you can select one of the following options:

▶ Multi-Stream:

    ▶ 4-Column Overview

    ▶ 3-Column Overview

    ▶ 2-Column Overview

    ▶ 3-Column Overview II

▶ Single-Stream:'

    ▶ 5-Column Overview

    ▶ 3-Column Overview

    ▶ 5-Column Overview II

    ▶ 2-Column Overview

The Multi-Stream and Single-Stream types differs in terms of where the visual filters and tiles will be displayed. The Multi-Stream option shows the visual filters on the top, while the Single-Stream option shows the visual filters and tiles to the right, as shown in Figure 11.41.

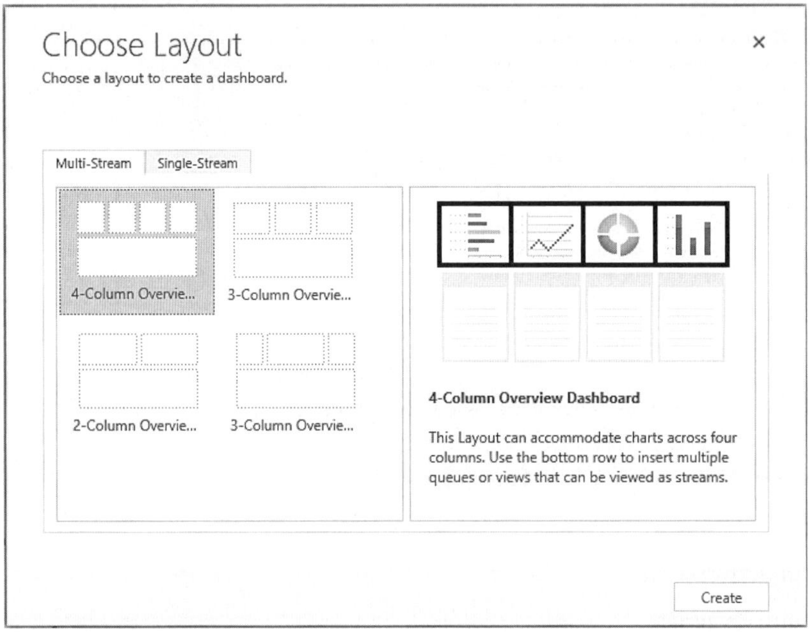

FIGURE 11.41   Choosing a layout.

Say that you select the Multi-Stream 4 Columns Overview option (which is the default) and click the Create button. The new dashboard editor window opens, an in it, you enter a name for the dashboard. Also, unlike with standard dashboards, you must select a filter entity and the view for the selected entity (see Figure 11.42).

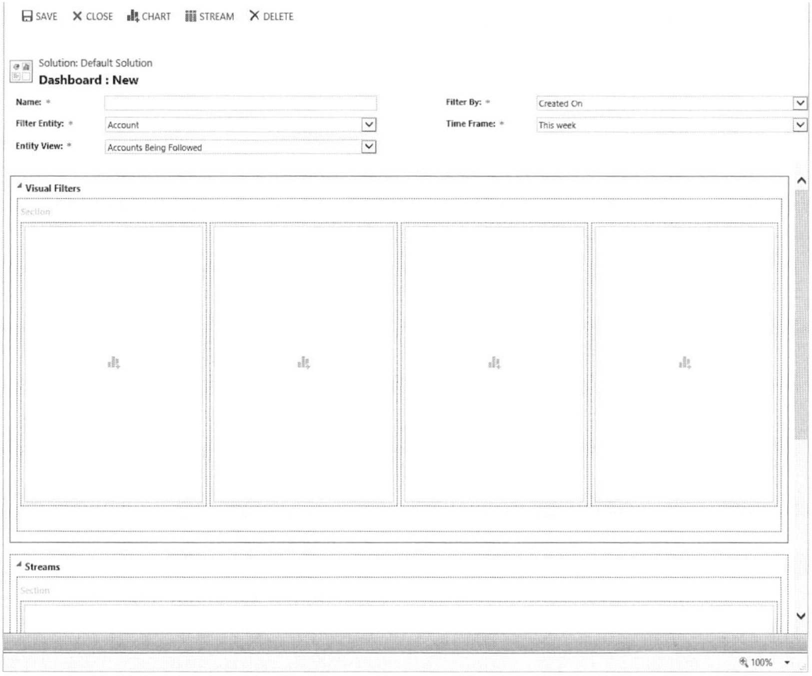

🖫 SAVE   ✕ CLOSE   📊 CHART   ☰ STREAM   ✕ DELETE

Solution: Default Solution
Dashboard : New

Name: *		Filter By: *	Created On ▾
Filter Entity: *	Account ▾	Time Frame: *	This week ▾
Entity View: *	Accounts Being Followed ▾		

▲ **Visual Filters**

Section

| 📊 | 📊 | 📊 | 📊 |

▲ **Streams**

Section

🔍 100% ▾

FIGURE 11.42   Dashboard editor.

With the selected layout, you can add charts only on the top layer of the Visual Filters section for the entity type you selected for the dashboard (see Figure 11.43).

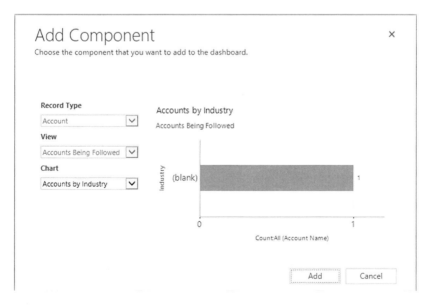

FIGURE 11.43   Add Component dialog for visual filters.

You can then add streams to the bottom layer of the dashboard. Here you can select any of the interactive service hub—enabled entities, and you can indicate whether you want to display a queue or an entity view (see Figure 11.44).

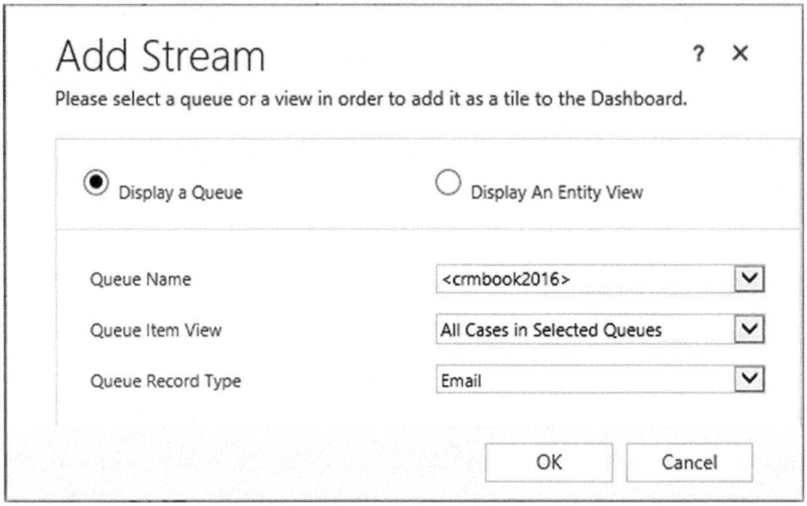

Add Stream   ? ✕

Please select a queue or a view in order to add it as a tile to the Dashboard.

- ● Display a Queue   ○ Display An Entity View

Queue Name	\<crmbook2016\> ▼
Queue Item View	All Cases in Selected Queues ▼
Queue Record Type	Email ▼

OK   Cancel

FIGURE 11.44   Add Stream dialog.

When you finished adding the visual filters and streams, click Save and then on Close in the command bar. Make sure to publish all the customizations before you try to load the new dashboard in the interactive service hub interface.

Entity Dashboards

New to the interactive service hub interface is the ability to create entity-specific dashboards that, as discussed earlier in this chapter, are available when you click the dashboard icon in the lower-left corner of the entity views. If you enabled a custom entity, you have to create a dashboard manually as there is not one created by default when you enable the interactive experience. To do that, expand the entity and click Dashboards > New > Interactive Experience Dashboard. This option only allows you to create a multi-stream dashboard using one of the four layouts, as described earlier in this chapter.

Summary

This chapter looks at the interactive service hub, a new user experience interface for the service support team. You have seen how to use it and how to configure and customize it by creating interactive forms and dashboards. The interactive service hub will likely be improved in the future to look more like the mobile client applications.

CHAPTER 12

Parature

Parature is a cloud-based solution that helps organizations provide customers great service experience, accessible 24/7, through knowledge base management, self-service, and multi-channel engagement. Parature can be used by organizations internally for employee self-service, where employees get quick access to consistent and organized information. The Parature self-service portal increases customer satisfaction through the availability of knowledge base articles accessible 24/7 and consistent engagement across multiple channels. Microsoft acquired Parature in 2014 to boost its Service module capabilities for the Dynamics CRM platform; it is a standalone application that is designed to integrate with Microsoft Dynamics CRM.

> **NOTE**
>
> This chapter was written before the roadmap and final integration for Parature and CRM were complete. As a result, this chapter may serve as a reference point for existing (legacy) integrations of Parature, and users should look for updated content on the Pearson website for this book for more up-to-date information on Parature.

To obtain a trial Parature account, go to www.parature.com/request-a-trial/.

Overview of Parature

The Parature product has two main components: Service Desk and Support Center.

Service Desk

An organization's support team can use Service Desk to configure and customize Support Center. The support team can create knowledge base articles, upload files for download from Support Center, maintain SLAs, handle contact management, and work with other settings. The support team handles ticket routing rules and chat routing rules from Service Desk. Customer support representatives are added through Service Desk and assigned proper privileges to perform their work.

A customer support representative (CSR) who logs on to Parature Service Desk typically sees a system overview, as shown in Figure 12.1.

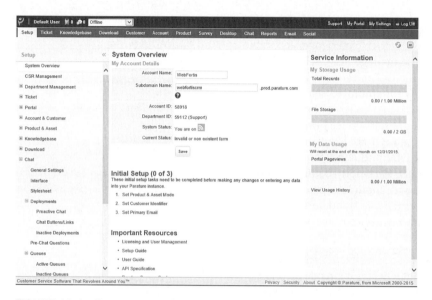

FIGURE 12.1   Parature system overview.

The page is broken out as follows:

▶ **Personal resource toolbar**—The first black bar at top where you see your name (Default User in Figure 12.1) is the personal resource toolbar. The number after the purple icon shows number of open tickets assigned to you. On the far right of this toolbar, Support opens http://support.parature.com and lets you access the Parature knowledge base and submit tickets. My Portal opens your customer-facing Support Center. My Settings takes you to the page where you can see the privileges assigned to you. You can see your calendar, events, team calendar, team events, login history, and recent tickets. Log Off ends the Service Desk session and takes you back to the logon page.

▶ **Module tabs**—The gray bar just under the personal resource tool bar displays the modules available in Service Desk. The module links are displayed based on the privileges assigned to the CSR. When you click a specific module, you get access to specific information and tools related to the selected module.

▶ **Menu row**—The menu row shows different action buttons, depending on the module you are viewing. These action buttons let you perform various functions within the module. There are two buttons in the far-right corner, Refresh and Fast Forward, for all modules.

▶ **Filters/nav frame**—The left navigation pane contains links to filter the data within a specific module. When you click one of the filter links, the information is displayed in the main content frame. For example, in Figure 12.2 you can see that in the Customer module, the Registered Customers filter has been applied.

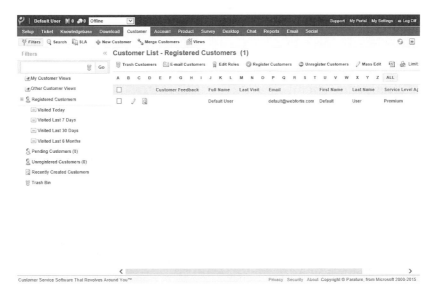

FIGURE 12.2   Registered Customers filter.

▶ **Main content frame**—This is the workspace in Service Desk. When you click module tabs, menu row button, or filters, the corresponding information is displayed in the main content frame. You can view, create, and edit records in this frame. As you can see in Figure 12.2, registered customers' record are displayed in the main content frame.

Support Center

Customers access Support Center to interact with self-service channels such as the knowledge base, to download files, to access assisted support channels such as chat with CSRs, and to create/view the status of support tickets. By default Support Panel has these three tabs (see Figure 12.3), but you can create your own tabs also:

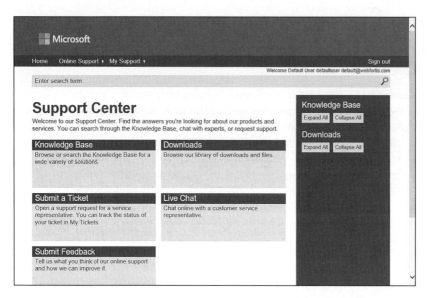

FIGURE 12.3   Parature Support Center.

▶ **Home**—The home page is the first page end users see when they visit the Support Center. Users can quickly click several links to go to self-service content or submit a ticket.

▶ **Online Support**—This tab lists all the self-service options Parature offers, such as Knowledge Base, Downloads, Glossary, Submit a Ticket, Submit an Email, and Live Chat.

▶ **My Support**—This tab provides one-click access to personal support service for end users. Users can keep track of all communications here. My Support contains a user's entire support history, including tickets, products, profile, and chats.

Contact Management

In Parature, you store information about your customer or contact in the Customer and Accounts modules. A customer is an individual end user who accesses Support Center, views the knowledge base, downloads files, and submits tickets, whereas an account is a group of customers or large organizations.

Parature provides different configuration options to suit business scenarios in which every customer needs to be associated with an account, some customers need to be associated with an account, or no customers are associated with an account.

The Account module is mostly used for companies and organizations. It is similar to Account entity in Microsoft Dynamics CRM. You can create new accounts in the Account module in Parature and associate them with your customers. To create a new account, follow these steps:

1. In Parature Service Desk, click the Account tab and then click the New Account button (see Figure 12.4).

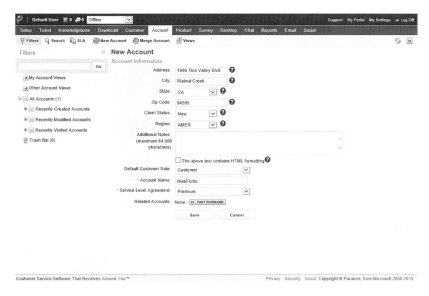

FIGURE 12.4   Creating a new account in Parature.

2. Fill in the address fields and then select Customer from the Default Customer Role drop-down menu.

3. Provide a name in the Account Name field. This field is the unique identifier for the account.

4. Select Premium from the Service Level Agreement drop-down. The selected SLA is then applied to all the customers associated with this account. Customers associated with an account cannot have a different SLA than their parent account.

5. Click the Fast Forward button to select a parent account for the current record.

6. Click the Save button.

The Account module is designed to help group your customers together and keep their profiles organized. You can create a new account and then associate new customers with it directly from the Account module. Follow these steps to create a new customer and associate it with an account (see Figure 12.5):

1. On the Account tab, click the Account Name field of the account where you want to create and associate a new customer.

2. Click the Customers button.

3. Click the Associate New Customer button.

4. Enter the email address of the customer in Email field.

5. Provide the customer's first name and last name in the appropriate fields.

6. If you want to associate the customer to an account other than the default specified in the Find Account field, click Remove and user Fast Forward to select another account.

NOTE

The Service Level Agreement field is disabled because the customer inherits the selected account's SLA.

7. Select the customer's status from the Status drop-down.

8. Provide a username for the customer in the Username field.

9. If desired, change the language, date format, and time format for the customer in the Default Locale Settings section.

10. Select the Notify Customer That Their Account Has Been created check box to have Parature send a notification email to the customer's email address.

11. Click Save.

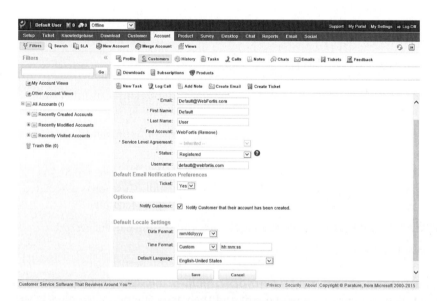

FIGURE 12.5   Creating a new account in Parature.

You can use the Associate Existing Customer button to associate the existing customer records with the account and the Dis-Associate Customers button to dis-associate customers from the account.

NOTE

You can associate as many customers with account as you want, but each customer can be associated with only one account. If you do not want to create any account records and you want to directly create customer records only, you can click the Customers tab and create records there in a similar way.

Service Level Agreements (SLAs)

A service level agreement (SLA) is an agreement between a customer and an organization providing support to that organization. In business-to-consumer scenarios, customers can be individual users, and in that case, an SLA is associated with individual customer records. In business-to-business scenarios, an SLA is associated with account records, and customer records inherit the SLA from their parent account.

SLAs are used to manage customer entitlements. Parature has four default SLAs: Guest, Basic, Premium, and Escalated (see Figure 12.6). You can edit these existing SLAs, and you can also create new SLAs. SLAs help you define the features of Support Center that your customers will have access to once they are associated with the SLA. For example, if you want to give chat feature to Premium customers, you need to remove the permission for this from other SLAs.

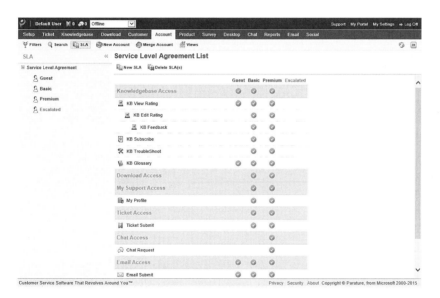

FIGURE 12.6   SLA list.

SLAs are helpful in maintaining standards for support. Parature reporting can be used to evaluate CSR performance based on the number of tickets or chat requests handled. SLA timers set goals for a CSR to work toward and give customer-realistic expectations for response and resolution on chat or tickets.

Follow these steps to create a new SLA (see Figure 12.7):

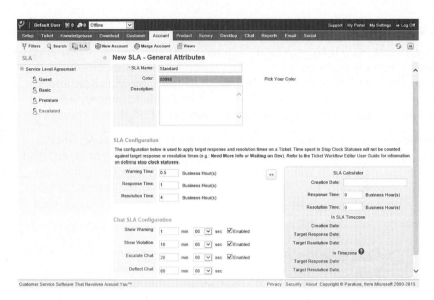

FIGURE 12.7   Creating a new SLA.

1. Go to either the Account or Customer tab and click the SLA button.

2. Click the New SLA button.

3. Provide a name for the SLA, keeping in mind that this name will be displayed to your customers.

4. Click Pick Your Color to select and associate a color with the SLA.

5. Configure SLA timers for tickets submitted under this SLA:

   ▶ **Warning Time**—Provide the number of business hours that should remain before an SLA resolution or response warning is displayed on the ticket.

   ▶ **Response Time**—Provide the maximum number of business hours that can pass before a CSR responds to a ticket submitted under this SLA. If there is no response from a CSR in the specified time, a response time violation will be noted.

   ▶ **Resolution Time**—Provide the maximum number of business hours that can pass before a CSR resolves a ticket submitted under this SLA. If the ticket is not resolved with the specified number of business hours, a resolution time violation is noted.

6. In the Chat SLA Configuration section, set SLA timers for chat requests submitted by customers associated with this SLA:

   ▶ **Show Warning**—Select the Enabled check box to enable this feature. It shows a warning to a CSR who has grabbed or been assigned to a chat that is idle for the amount of specified time.

▶ **Show Violation**—You can alert CSRs that an SLA violation has occurred if a chat they have grabbed or are assigned to has been idle for a certain number of minutes. A chat response violation is noted for the chat. You can enable/disable this feature by selecting the check box.

▶ **Escalate Chat**—If a chat request is idle for specified number of minutes, it is escalated.

▶ **Deflect Chat**—If a chat request is idle for specified number of minutes, chat deflection rules run automatically.

7. Click the Next button to define the following SLA permissions (see Figure 12.8):

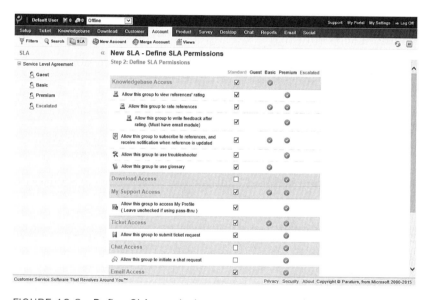

FIGURE 12.8   Define SLA permissions.

▶ **Knowledgebase Access**—This permission gives customers access to the Support Center knowledge base.

▶ **Allow This Group to View a Reference's Rating**—This permission allows customers to view the average rating of knowledge base content.

▶ **Allow This Group to Rate References**—This permission allows customers to rate knowledge base content.

▶ **Allow This Group to Write Feedback After Rating**—This permission allows customers to write feedback after rating knowledge base content.

▶ **Allow This Group to Subscribe to References and Receive Notification When Reference Is Updated**—This permission allows customers to receive notifications when references are updated.

▶ **Allow This Group to Use the Troubleshooter**—The Service Center Troubleshooter helps customers find answers in the knowledge base before they submit tickets or emails. You can configure which channels (email, ticket) should display Troubleshooter in Service Center.

▶ **Allow This Group to Use the Glossary**—This permission allows the customers to use the Glossary in Service Center.

▶ **Download Access**—This permission allows customers to download files uploaded via the Download module in Service Desk.

▶ **My Support Access**—This permission allows customers to access the My Support page in Service Center if they have created their profile.

▶ **Ticket Access**—This permission allows customers to access the ticketing features of Support Center.

▶ **Allow This Group to Submit Ticket Request**—This permission allows customers to submit tickets using Service Center.

▶ **Chat Access**—This permission grants customers access to the Parature live chat feature of Support Center.

▶ **Allow This Group to Initiate a Chat Request**—This permission allows customers to start a live chat session with available CSRs.

▶ **Allow This Group to Submit Email Request**—This permission allows users to send email to the support team, using Support Center.

NOTE

The SLA in this example does not allow access to download and chat functionality.

Knowledge Base Management

Knowledge base articles help organizations address a number of issues that customers face while using their products or services. Knowledge base articles provide answers to frequently asked questions, documentation of product features, solutions to common problems related to a product, and so on. Knowledge base articles help organizations reduce the cost for support of their products by cutting down phone calls from customers to their support center. Customers get answers to common problems from knowledge base articles published from Service Desk to Support Center. By default, there is one Glossary folder for publishing knowledge base articles. You can create new folders to categorize your articles. To create a new folder, follow these steps (see Figure 12.9):

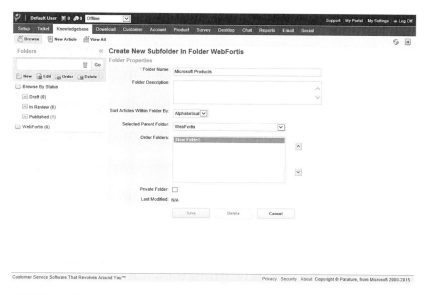

FIGURE 12.9   Creating a new folder.

1. In the Knowledgebase tab, select the parent folder (called Webfortis in this case) from the left navigation pane and click the New button in this pane.

2. In the right content frame, provide the folder name and folder description.

3. Change the parent folder by using the Selected Parent Folder drop-down.

4. Keep the Private Folder check box unchecked if you want articles listed under this folder to be published to Support Center. If this check box is checked, articles are not published to Support Center.

5. Click the Save button at bottom to create a new folder.

Follow these steps to publish a knowledge base article:

1. In Service Desk, click the Knowledgebase tab and then click the New Article button.

2. In the Questions field, type the issue or problem you want to address.

3. In the Answer field, use the rich text editor to format the answer to your question.

4. Enter appropriate keywords, separated by spaces or commas, to help customers find knowledge base articles easily (see Figure 12.10).

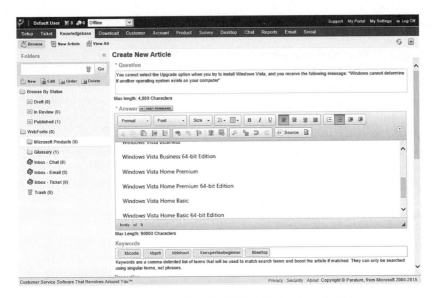

FIGURE 12.10   Keywords associated with knowledge base articles.

5. In the Properties section, select the folder(s) in which you want your article to be listed. You can select more than one folder by holding down the Ctrl key as you click the folders you want.

6. In Permission, select the check boxed in front of SLA names where you want your article to be accessible.

7. Click the Fast Forward button to select and associate article with a product.

8. Select the check box Exclude Article from Portal Search if you want the article to be excluded from search results in Support Center.

9. In the Advance Options section, select the check box to reset the view count of the article. This option is used when articles are already published.

10. Provide an expiration date for the article so that the article will not be unpublished on or after the provided expiration date. It will then be displayed in the Expired References list in the Knowledgebase module.

11. Select the Notify Subscribers check box so that when article is published, customers can subscribe to the article. If you select this check box, all the customers who have subscribed to the article will receive an email notification when any change is made to the article.

12. Set the External URL to Reference if you want to link the article outside Support Center.

13. Click the Save button at the bottom to save the article in draft status.

14. Go to Drafts folder in left navigation pane, select the article, and click Send for Review at the bottom. The article is now moved to the Review folder.

15. Open the same article in the Review folder from the left navigation pane and click the Publish Article button at the bottom to publish the article. You must have the Administrator role for the knowledge base to publish the article.

For a knowledge base article to be available to customers on Support Center, make sure it is in the public folder, the status is Published, and the proper SLA is set.

When you edit an article, there are several options available on the navigation bar:

▶ **Alternate Questions**—This option allows you to provide answers to similar questions with a single knowledge base article. Creating alternate questions helps you identify the different ways customers might ask the same question while avoiding and also helps you avoid the need to create duplicate articles. When you edit an article, you see the Alternate Questions button at the top.

▶ **Attachments**—You can attach files to an article for customers to download from Support Center. You need to upload a file first in the Download module and then associate the same file with the article by using Attachments button.

▶ **Subscribers**—You can view current subscribers, subscribe more customers, and unsubscribe customers to an article by using the Subscribers button. You can also send email to subscribers from here when there is any update to the knowledge base article.

▶ **Feedback**—Click the Feedback button to see feedback received from customers on the knowledge base article. You can delete the feedback and also reply to customers from here by using the Email Customer(s) button.

Download

The Download module helps you easily manage and upload electronic files via Service Desk that can be made available to customers to download from the Support Center. You can manage your electronic files by using a folder hierarchy that is just like the hierarchy in the Knowledgebase module.

The Download module lets you to do batch uploads your files. Follow these steps to do a batch upload of your files:

1. Click the Download module tab and then click Batch Uploads.

2. Click the Browse button to open file upload control (see Figure 12.11).

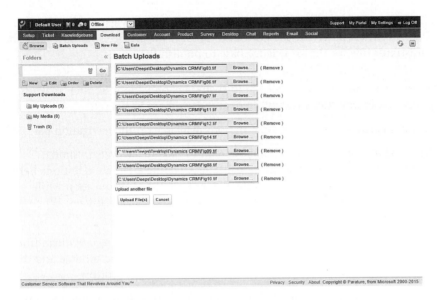

FIGURE 12.11   File uploads.

3. Click the Upload Another File link to show another Browse button.

4. You can select maximum of.

5. With up to 10 files selected for the batch upload, click the Upload File(s) button.

EULA (End User License Agreement)

The EULA is a document that shows rights and responsibilities that end users must agree to in exchange for the use of downloadable content. Parature enables you to create a EULA and attach it to files that you allow your customers to download from Support Center. To use this option, click the Download module and then click the EULA button. You need to provide a short title, a title, and a description to create the new EULA. The Short Title field has a maximum length of 128 character, Title is limited to 512 characters, and Description is limited to 30,000 characters.

Parature Video

You can embed Parature video files directly into knowledge base articles to allow customers to view related videos without having to navigate away from the knowledge base article. Customers can then play videos directly from Service Desk or Support Center, using the hosted Parature video player. When you are uploading a video file, select the Parature Video check box, and the upload process converts the file into a Parature video file (see Figure 12.12).

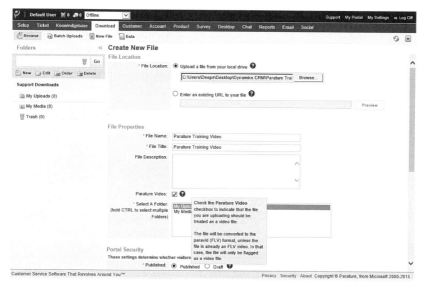

FIGURE 12.12   Parature video options.

Product

The Product module helps you maintain the products owned by your customers and accounts. It consists of catalog, products, and unique assets. CSRs have access to all production information by customer or account. CSRs can create new products and associate them with customers and accounts.

Follow these steps to create a product (see Figure 12.13):

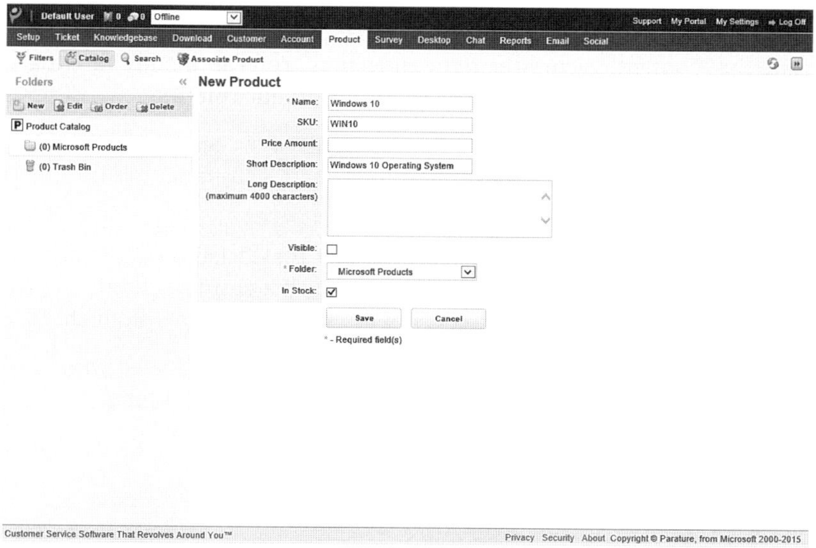

FIGURE 12.13   New product form.

1. In the Product module tab, then click Catalog.

2. Select the product catalog folder where you want to create products. If there is no folder for the product catalog, create one.

3. Click the New button in the left navigation pane and enter the required fields on the right.

4. From the Folder drop-down, select the folder where you want to create the product.

5. Click the Save button at the bottom.

Catalog Folders

You can manage your product inventory by creating a folder hierarchy in the product catalog. The product catalog folder structure can be created, ordered, edited, and deleted just like Knowledgebase module and Download module folder structures. The product catalog folder is for Service Desk use only; it is not published on Service Center.

Follow these steps to create a new product catalog folder:

1. On the Product module tab, then click Catalog.

2. In the left navigation pane, click the New button.

3. Provide the folder name and description.

4. Use the up and down arrows in the Order Folder field to order the folders.

5. Set Folder Privacy drop-down to Private or Public.

6. Click the Save button.

Product Association

You can filter the content delivered to your customers based on product associations. This helps you ensure that content reaches the right customers. You can modify filtering behavior by using configurations. There are four methods for product filtering:

▶ If a customer has associated products, show content that is associated with matching products and content that is associated with no products; if a customer has no associated products, show all content.

▶ If a customer has associated products, show content that is associated with matching products and content that is associated with no products; if a customer has no associated products, show only content that is not associated with any product.

▶ If a customer has associated products, show only content that is associated with matching products; if a customer has no associated products, show nothing.

▶ Do not filter any content by product at all.

Associate Products with Customer or Account

Creating relationships between accounts, customers, and their products allows you to provide more personalized customer service. Customers can view articles and downloads related to their specific product. CSRs can also provide better support to customers if they know in advance what products customers use.

Follow these steps to associate a customer with a product (see Figure 12.14):

FIGURE 12.14   Associating a product with a customer.

1. Go to the Customers module tab and select a customer record.

2. Click the Products button in the customer record to see a list of all the existing products associated with the customer.

3. Click the Associate Product button.

4. Click the Fast Forward button and then select the product you want to associate.

5. Provide the other product details and click the Save button.

NOTE

You can also associate products by using the Fast Forward button next to Related Products for knowledge base articles and Download module content files.

Chat

The Chat module helps you manage chat deployments, queues, and routing rules; customize chat settings; and manage CSR chat with customers. Customers do not always need to visit Support Center to initiate a chat request with a CSR. Parature chat deployment provides the option to use chat buttons and chat links to give customers access to live chat from anywhere on the web. Follow these steps to create chat buttons and links:

1. In the Setup module, click Chat > Deployments > Chat Buttons/Links.

2. Click the New Deployment button.

3. Enter the name of the chat deployment in the Name text field.

4. In the Deployment Settings step, click the Edit button. You have two options: Select either existing default images or user custom images. If you select the Use Custom Images option, you need to provide two images—one for when agents are available and one for when agents are offline. Provide alternate text for both images in the appropriate text fields.

5. Click the Save Images button to save your images.

6. In the Set Offline Message field, enter the text you want to display to customers when there is no CSR available for chat.

7. Click the Generate Deployment Code button to generate code for your chat button and chat link (see Figure 12.15).

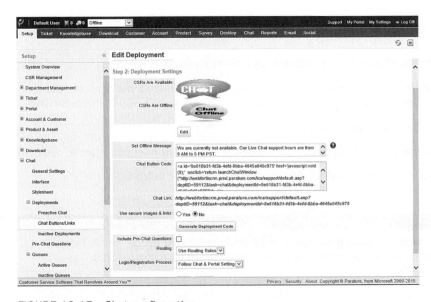

FIGURE 12.15   Chat configuration.

8. Select the check box Include Pre-Chat Questions to ask questions of customers who request a chat session before they are linked to a CSR.

9. Use the Routing drop-down to select the routing behavior for chat requests from chat buttons and links. It can be either of the following:

▶ **Use Routing Rules**—All chat requests follow the routing rules that have been configured in Service Desk.

▶ **Direct to Queue**—All chat requests are routed directly to specific chat queues. Use the Queue drop-down (which appear when the Direct to Queue option is selected) to select the queue these requests will be routed to.

10. Click the Save button.

Chat Queues

Pairing chat queues with routing rules and pre-chat questions helps ensure that customers are helped as soon as possible by CSRs. In some cases, CSRs may be subject matter experts for a specific product. If a customer's pre-chat information indicates a need for a subject matter expert, he or she can be linked to an appropriate CSR.

Follow these steps to create a chat queue:

1. Go to the Setup module and select Chat > Queues > Active Queues.

2. Click the New Queue button.

3. Provide a name for the chat queue in Name field.

4. In the Permissions section, select the check box for the role(s) that will have permission to take action on chats routed to this queue. These are the options:

▶ **All Chat Techs**—All CSRs with the Chat Technician Role or higher will be able to see this chat queue and take action on chats routed to it.

▶ **All Chat Techs View All**—All CSRs with the Chat Technician View All Role or higher will be able to see this chat queue and take action on chats routed to it.

▶ **All Chat Supervisors**—All CSRs with the Chat Supervisor Role will be able to see this chat queue and take action on chats routed to it.

5. Optionally, select individual CSRs who will have access to this queue by moving the desired CSRs from the Available CSRs list to the Permitted CSRs list.

6. Click the Save button.

Chat Routing Rules

Chat routing rules route new chat requests to the appropriate CSR or queue based on the business logic mentioned in rules. You can create three types of chat rules:

▶ **New chat rules**—These rules determine where new chat requests are routed. These rules run in order from first to last as soon as a new chat request is submitted by a customer. For example, if you want to have a dedicated queue for premium customers, you can create a chat rule to assign all chats where customer SLA is Premium to the premium chat queue (see Figure 12.16).

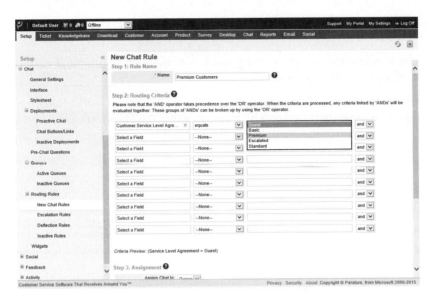

FIGURE 12.16   Chat routing rule criteria.

▶ **Escalation rules**—These are special routing rules that apply to chat requests after they have been idle for a certain period of time.

▶ **Deflection rules**—These rules display custom message to customers when no chat representatives are available or when a chat has been idle for a certain period of time. Select the Auto Create Ticket for Chat Request check box to automatically create a ticket using the customer's responses to pre-chat questions. Tickets will not be created for customers who are not logged on to Support Center.

Ticket

CSRs can view a tickets summary, create new tickets, attach files to tickets, assign tickets to CSRs, create ticket routing rules, and customize ticket queues from the Ticket module. CSRs can create tickets directly from customer or account record page.

When a ticket is submitted to a ticket queue, only the CSRs assigned to that ticket queue can take action on that ticket. CSRs with the Trouble Ticket (TT) Admin role can only delete a ticket. You can archive resolved tickets to keep ticket queues clean. When you close out a ticket, it is moved from its original queue to the Archived Tickets folder.

E2T (Email to Ticket Conversion)

As Microsoft Dynamics CRM has the email-to-case feature, Parature Service Desk has similar capabilities. E2T allows you to convert emails sent to your main support email address to Parature tickets and submit them to ticket queues. Follow these steps to configure E2T conversion (see Figure 12.17):

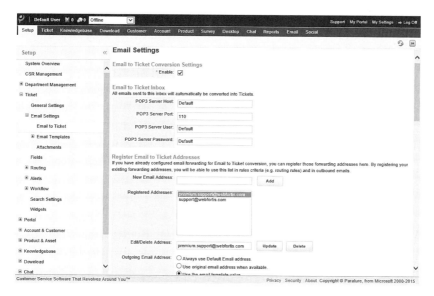

FIGURE 12.17   E2T configuration.

1. In the Setup tab, go to Ticket > Email Settings > Email to Ticket.

2. Under Email to Ticket Conversion Settings, select the Enable check box to display your settings.

3. Under Email to Ticket Inbox, provide the POP3 server details for the mailbox for which you want received emails to be converted into Parature tickets.

4. Under Register Email to Ticket Addresses, if you have multiple support email addresses and you want to specify that every email sent to any of these addresses should convert into a Parature ticket, add all those email addresses here.

5. Under Ticket Replies from Email, if you set Ticket Reply to No, you disable customer ticket replies, and all email replies will be converted to new tickets. Select Yes to enable ticket replies from customers and then set the following:

   ▶ **Reopen Ticket by Email Reply**—You have four options here: You can select to allow reopen tickets of type Only Solved, Only Closed, Both Closed and Solved, or None when a customer sends a reply.

   ▶ **Rejection Email Subject and Rejection Email Body**—If you opted not to reopen a ticket by email reply, you can edit the rejection email subject and body that will be sent to customers.

   ▶ **Email Reply Options**—You can configure how to handle email replies from customers:

      ▶ If you select the option Display up to 4000 Characters in History, Attach Message if Necessary, then if email content is over this limit, the first 4,000 characters are added to the ticket comments, and the email message is attached to the ticket.

▶ If you select the option Only Attach the Message to the History, the email will be attached to the ticket, and no comments will be added.

▶ If you select the option Truncate Reply at _____ Characters and Attach the Message, the email will be attached to the ticket, and the specified number of characters will be truncated from the email message and added to the comments in the ticket.

▶ **Unknown Sender**—You can specify how you can process a reply—as a CSR or a customer—if Parature cannot identify the sender of the reply.

6. Under Ticket Create, set the following:

▶ **Max Email**—How many emails from a single customer should be processed in one day. Specify -1 if you do not want any limit.

▶ **Max Duplicate Emails**—How many emails from the customer that look identical to emails sent by same customer should be processed in one day. Specify -1 to remove any limit.

▶ **Convert Customer Registration Emails to Tickets**—Select this check box if you want to convert customer emails received for registration at Support Center into tickets.

▶ **Convert Customer Feedback to Tickets**—Select this check box if you want to have this option.

▶ **Original Email Transcript Processing**—You can select to attach the email to ticket always or when it is more than 4,000 characters.

7. Under Remove CC Email Addresses, add the email addresses that you want to remove from CC list during the E2T conversion process.

8. Under Blocked Email Addresses, add the email addresses from which you do not want emails to be converted into tickets.

9. Click the Save button.

Figure 12.18 shows the E2T configuration screen for the Remove CC and Blocked Email Addresses option.

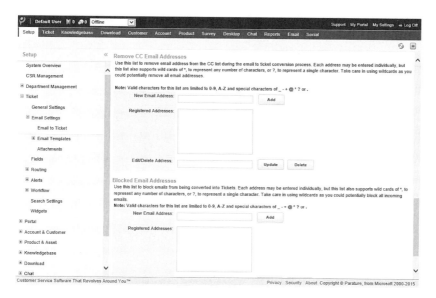

FIGURE 12.18 Email to ticket configuration the for Remove and Blocked Email Addresses option.

Survey

Parature enables you to capture feedback from customers by using surveys. You can create and preview surveys and then distribute them.

> **NOTE**
>
> The feature Voice of the Customer that also provides surveys to customers in Dynamics CRM 2016. See Chapter 34, "Voice of the Customer," for more information related to this feature.

Follow these steps to create a new survey (see Figure 12.19):

1. Click the Survey module tab and then click the New Survey button.

2. Provide a name and description for the survey in the Survey Details section.

3. In the Design Wizards section, either select an existing design for the survey or create your own design by using Design Builder.

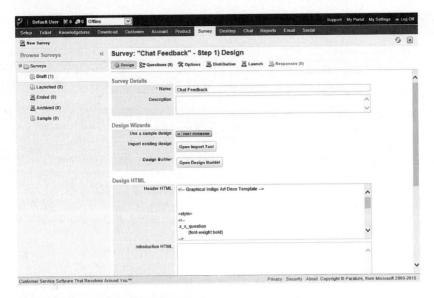

FIGURE 12.19   Creating a survey.

4. To copy an existing survey, click the Open Import Tool button and select an existing survey by clicking the Fast Forward button. You have the option to import only the design of the selected survey or append questions of the selected survey to an existing survey or import distributions or all.

5. Click the Preview button to see a preview of the survey in a pop-up window.

6. Click the Continue to Step 2 button to add questions for the survey.

7. Click the New Question button to create new questions and select the types of questions.

8. To change the order of questions, click the Update Order button, and to import existing questions, click the Import Question button.

9. Click the Continue to Step 3 button to configuration the following:

   ▶ Create a response message to be displayed when a survey is submitted.

   ▶ Prevent re-submissions from the same browser.

   ▶ End the survey after a specified date and number of responses.

   Figure 12.20 shows the response options available.

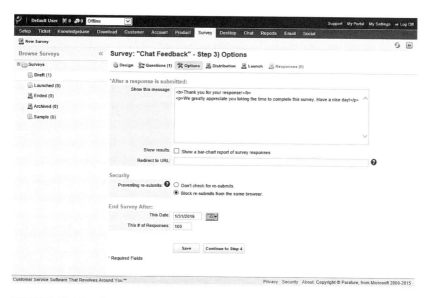

FIGURE 12.20   Survey response feedback options.

10. Click the Continue to Step 4 button to start distribution of the survey. You can distribute the survey by using one of these methods: email, web, or phone.

11. For the email distribution method, select the email template and recipients and then launch the survey.

12. Click the Fast Forward button to select the image button template to use for the survey link, pop-up, or image button you use for a chat buttons or chat link.

13. Click the Continue to Step 5 button to go through the survey summary before launch.

14. Click the Preview Survey check box to complete the pre-launch checklist. Click the Launch Survey button to launch the survey. The survey is visible to customers, and you can see responses by clicking the Responses button.

You can edit, delete, or end the launched survey at any point in time. You can edit questions or the design of a launched survey, too. And you can disable survey responses any time and enter your own response. In a business case scenario, you can set up a chat rule which says that when a chat with a customer ends, the system should send an email to the customer with a link to a survey to get feedback on the chat.

Summary

Parature, as described in this chapter, is designed to provide rich customer interactions, leveraging a strong feature set. Parature has several important features that are beyond the scope of this book, including the following:

▶ Para-connect (the integration component for Dynamics CRM)

▶ Portal

▶ Advanced customization

Because Parature's features are being included directly in Dynamics CRM, they will be eliminated from Parature in the near future.

Be sure to check the Pearson website for this book for updated information on Parature as it becomes available.

CHAPTER 13

The Unified Service Desk (USD)

The Unified Service Desk (USD) is a separate installed application, designed for desktop users (that is, there is no online interface), typically customer service agents.

The USD delivers a rich experience to agents, allowing them open multiple windows within a single container—the USD application. In addition, it is an extensible application that can have increased capabilities and features added to it with simple configurations, some of which are shown in this chapter.

> **NOTE**
>
> You can make more complex customizations to USD involving the CRM software development kit (SDK). However, such customizations are beyond the scope of this book.

The first version of the USD (version 1.0.0) was released in May 2014, and it was designed to be used with Dynamics CRM 2013, Service Pack 1. With the release of Dynamics CRM 2016, a new version (version 2.0) has been released; this is the version covered in this chapter.

The USD application requires a few solutions to be installed on the CRM server, and it works with either CRM Online or CRM On-Premises.

You can download the USD from the Microsoft website by searching for "Dynamics CRM USD download" or by going to https://www.microsoft.com/en-us/download/details.aspx?id=50355. The download page offers three files: a package deployer and two versions of the USD client app—one for i386 machines (which run a Windows 32-bit versions) and another for amd64 machines (which run Windows 64-bit versions). You should download the package deployer as well as the appropriate client version.

The following section explains how to set up the different components in the client and the Dynamics CRM server.

Requirements

The setup of USD involves installing some solutions with the USD package deployer and installing a client application on the agent desktop computers. The following sections cover both the server setup and the client setup.

Server Setup

To install the USD package deployer, follow these steps:

1. Run the CRM2016-8.0.1-USD-PackageDeployer.exe file you downloaded from the Microsoft website. The screen shown in Figure 13.1 appears.

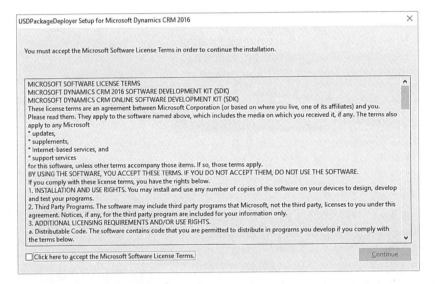

FIGURE 13.1   USDPackageDeployer Setup screen.

2. Check the check box to accept the Microsoft software license terms and then click Continue.

3. Select a folder where you want the files to be extracted and click OK. Once the files are extracted, you see the welcome screen shown in Figure 13.2.

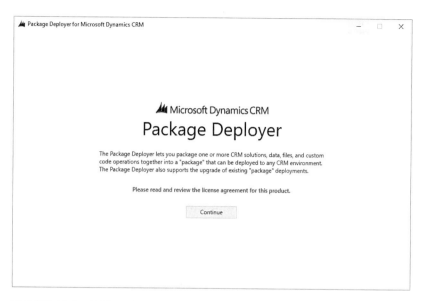

FIGURE 13.2   USD package deployer welcome screen.

4. Click Continue, and you are asked to enter the connection information for connecting to your Microsoft Dynamics CRM server (see Figure 13.3).

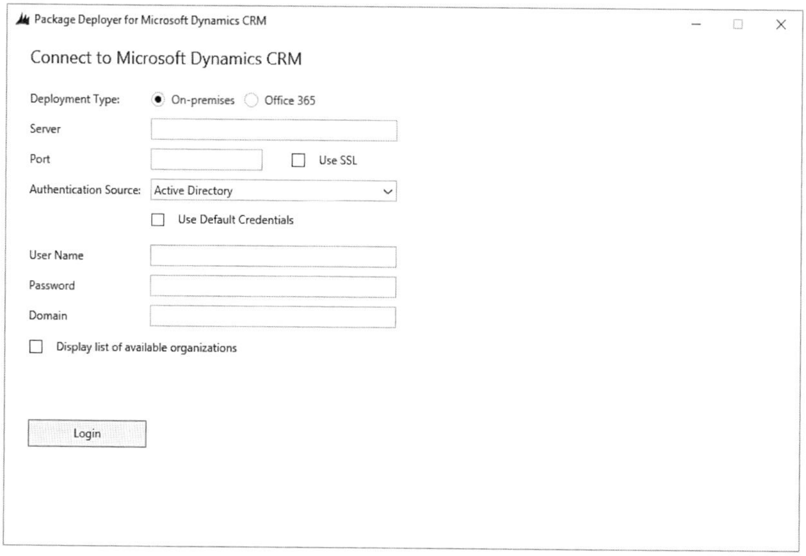

FIGURE 13.3   USD package deployer Connect to Microsoft Dynamics CRM screen.

5. If you want to connect to CRM Online, select the Office 365 option and enter the online region information if you know it (see Figure 13.4).

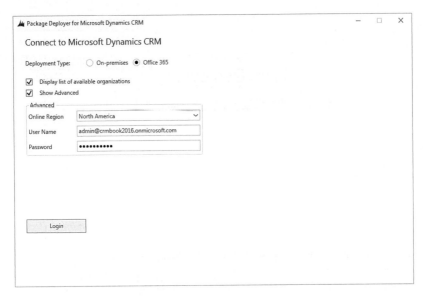

FIGURE 13.4   USD package deployer screen for connecting to CRM Online.

When you are connected, you are presented with a list of available import packages (see Figure 13.5).

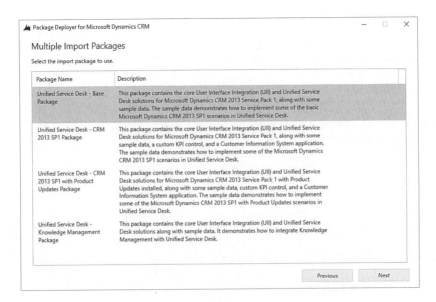

FIGURE 13.5   USD Multiple Import Packages screen.

6. Select the Unified Service Desk—Base Package option and click Next. You now see a guideline and a description of the base setup tool (see Figure 13.6).

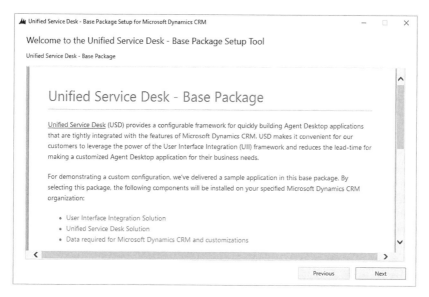

FIGURE 13.6   USD Base Package Setup tool.

7. Click Next to continue, and you are now ready to install the base package, as shown in Figure 13.7.

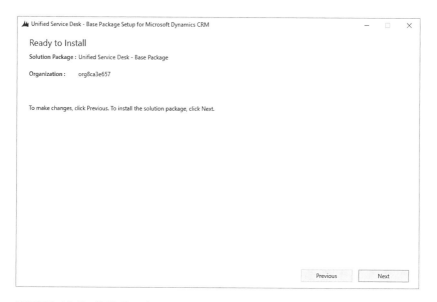

FIGURE 13.7   USD Ready to Install page.

8. Click Next to continue, and a verification process starts. If everything is okay, you see green checkmarks for each status, as shown in Figure 13.8.

FIGURE 13.8   USD validations.

9. Click Next to continue. The package deployer now installs the solution in Dynamics CRM, and it loads and imports the records necessary for the solution to work (see Figure 13.9). This process takes several minutes to complete.

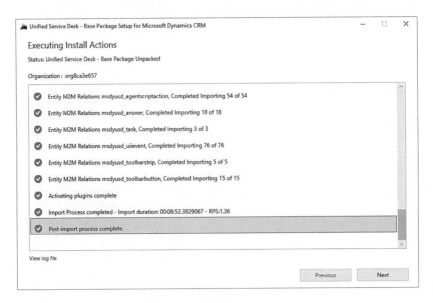

FIGURE 13.9   USD Executing Install Actions screen.

10. When the installation is complete (see Figure 13.10), click Finish.

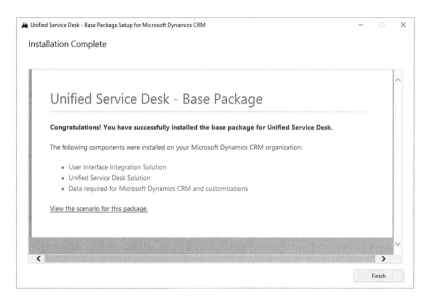

FIGURE 13.10   USD Installation Complete screen.

11. Navigate to Dynamics CRM > Settings > Solutions, and you now see the solutions installed, as shown in Figure 13.11.

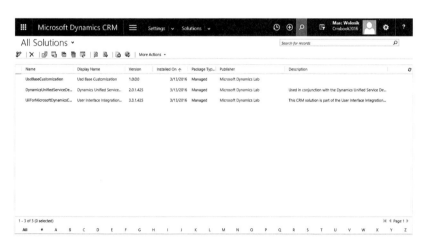

FIGURE 13.11   Solutions installed by the USD package deployer.

Client Setup and Configuration

To set up the USD client, follow these steps:

1. Run the CRM2016-USD-2.0.2-amd64.exe file you downloaded from the Microsoft website. You see the welcome screen shown in Figure 13.12.

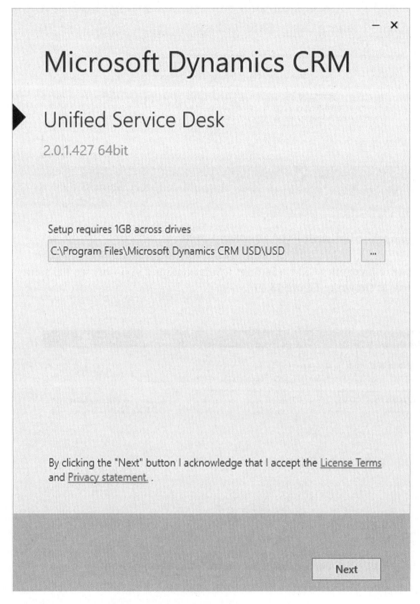

FIGURE 13.12   USD setup welcome screen.

2. Click on Next to continue to the prerequisites screen (see Figure 13.13).

FIGURE 13.13   USD setup prerequisites screen.

3. Leave the recommended pre-requisites selected as shown, and click Install to begin the setup. When the setup completes, you see the success screen shown in Figure 13.14. The client is now set up and needs to be configured to work properly.

FIGURE 13.14   USD setup success screen.

4. Click Launch to start the configuration. The first time you run the USD, you are asked to enter the CRM connection details, as shown in Figure 13.15.

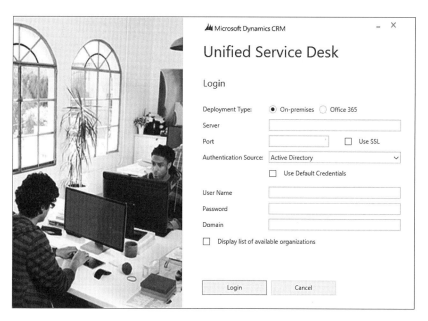

FIGURE 13.15   USD CRM Login screen.

5. If you need to connect with CRM Online, select the Office 365 option for Deployment Type and then check the Display List of Available Organizations check box (which will help you chose whether you want to connect to your production or sandbox environments, if you have any). Click Login. The screen shown in Figure 13.16 appears.

6. Check the Show Advanced check box and then enter your credentials. If you set your Online Region (found within your CRM URL), you will get a faster connection login.

FIGURE 13.16   USD CRM Online login.

7. If you get the error shown in Figure 13.17 (which shows what happens if the USD package was not deployed to the CRM server yet), close the interface, run the server deployment, and return to the client configuration.

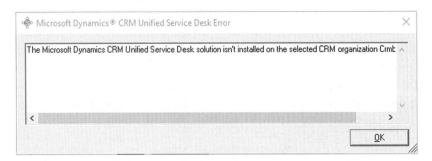

FIGURE 13.17   No USD solution installed in CRM error.

When your connection is successful, you see the application load, as shown in Figure 13.18.

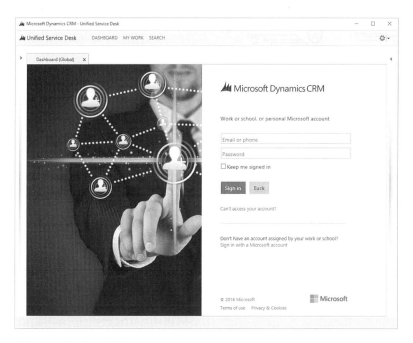

FIGURE 13.18   USD login screen.

8. Enter your user credentials and authentication, and you are logged into USD and see the dashboard, as shown in Figure 13.19. The top menu here shows three options: Dashboard, My Work, and Search.

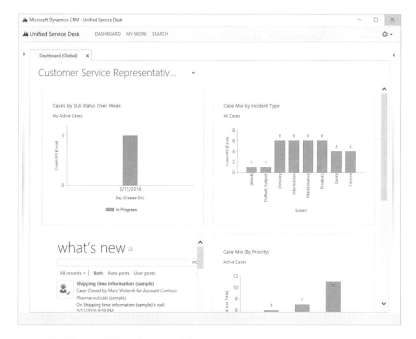

FIGURE 13.19   USD client dashboard.

9. Click My Work to see the active cases in a second tab. You can quickly switch between the My Work tab and the Dashboard tab (see Figure 13.20).

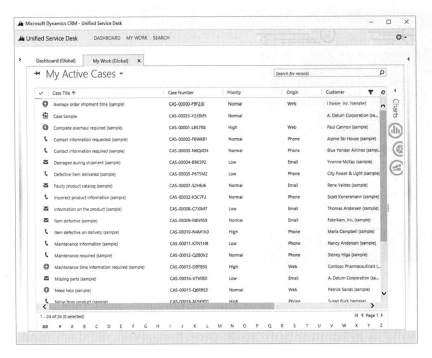

FIGURE 13.20   USD client My Work tab.

10. Click Search to open a tab that shows your active accounts by default (see Figure 13.21). You can quickly switch to see your active contacts from here as well as search for accounts or open an existing account or contact.

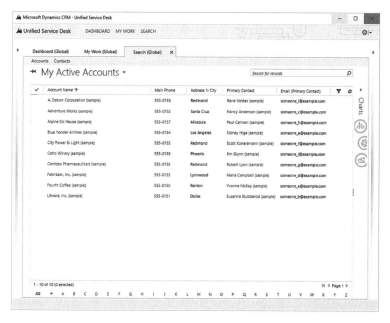

FIGURE 13.21   USD client Search tab.

11. Open one account or contact record to start a new session where the time spent on the record is recorded. You see the account form loaded, and in the bottom-left corner of the screen is a session timer (see Figure 13.22). This is useful for managing time spent on a particular customer and helps with escalation protocol.

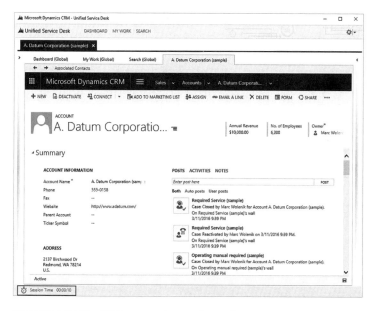

FIGURE 13.22   USD account record session.

12. Expand the left panel to see more information related to the record. If you like, you can use this page to run call scripts (see Figure 13.23).

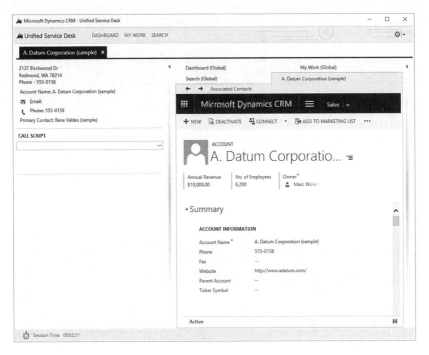

FIGURE 13.23 Expanded left panel of the USD.

13. Click back to search on the top navigation and open another account record in a secondary session, via the tab across the screen (see Figure 13.24).

> **NOTE**
>
> When you have a secondary session open, the timer will keep running for each session.

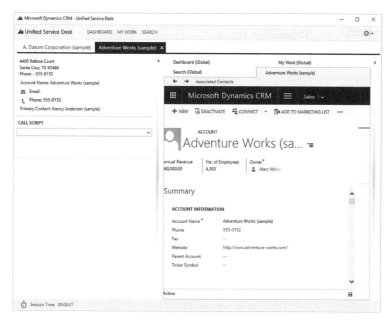

FIGURE 13.24   Two account records open in the USD.

14. Open a case from the My Work tab and expand the left navigation panel, and you see a sample script as well as a section where you can add notes, as shown in Figure 13.25.

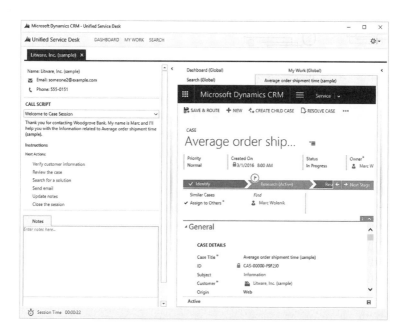

FIGURE 13.25   Expanded left panel of the USD for a case.

15. Click the Verify Customer Information action to open the account form on a separate tab in the same session (see Figure 13.26). Click Review the Case to go back to the case form tab.

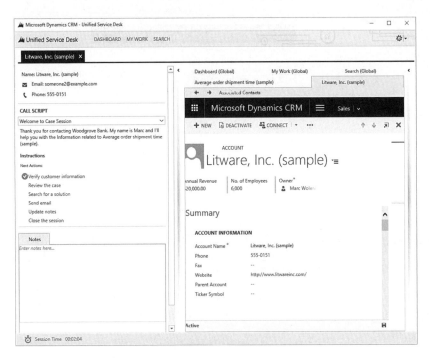

FIGURE 13.26   USD Verify Customer Information action from script.

16. Click Search for a Solution to open another two tabs. The first tab has a web browser embedded, with Bing search open, so you can find a solution online without leaving the USD application (see Figure 13.27).

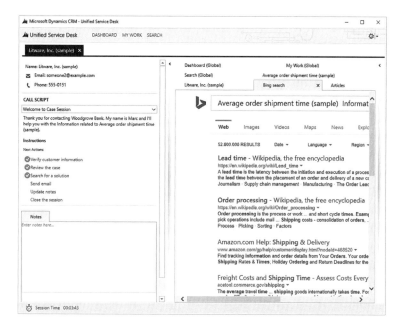

FIGURE 13.27   USD Bing Search tab.

The second tab shows the published articles so you can find the solution by using one of your organization's internal knowledge base articles (see Figure 13.28).

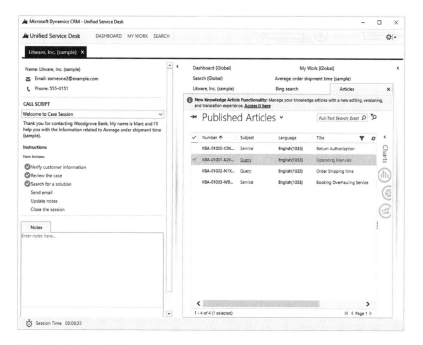

FIGURE 13.28   USD Articles tab.

17. Click Send Email to start composing an email to the customer that will be automatically associated with the case (see Figure 13.29).

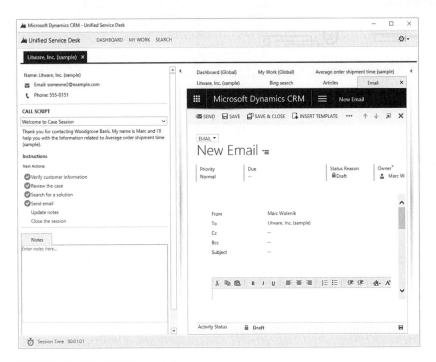

FIGURE 13.29   USD Email tab.

18. Click Update Notes, enter notes in the box below, and then click Close the Session to close all the open tabs related to the case you were working on and also finish the session and stop the timer.

Configurations and Customizations

In the Dynamics CRM web interface, navigate to Settings > Unified Service Desk, and you see the configuration page with all the components you can configure, as shown in Figure 13.30.

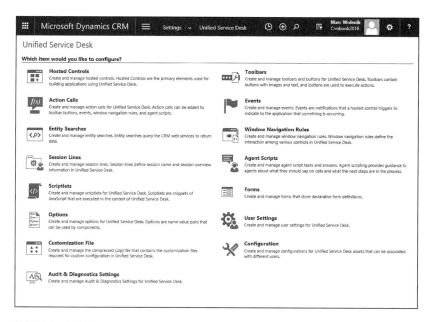

FIGURE 13.30   USD configuration page.

From this page you can configure the following components:

▶ Hosted Controls

▶ Toolbars

▶ Action Calls

▶ Events

▶ Entity Searches

▶ Window Navigation Rules

▶ Session Lines

▶ Agent Scripts

▶ Scriptlets

▶ Forms

▶ Options

▶ User Settings

▶ Customization File

▶ Configuration

▶ Audit & Diagnostics Settings

The following sections describe these components.

Hosted Controls

Hosted controls are the main controls displayed in the different areas of the USD client. For example, the account form, contact form, Bing search, and so on are all hosted controls. If you go to the Hosted Controls option on the configuration page, you see a view of the active hosted controls that are installed by the USD base solution (see Figure 13.31).

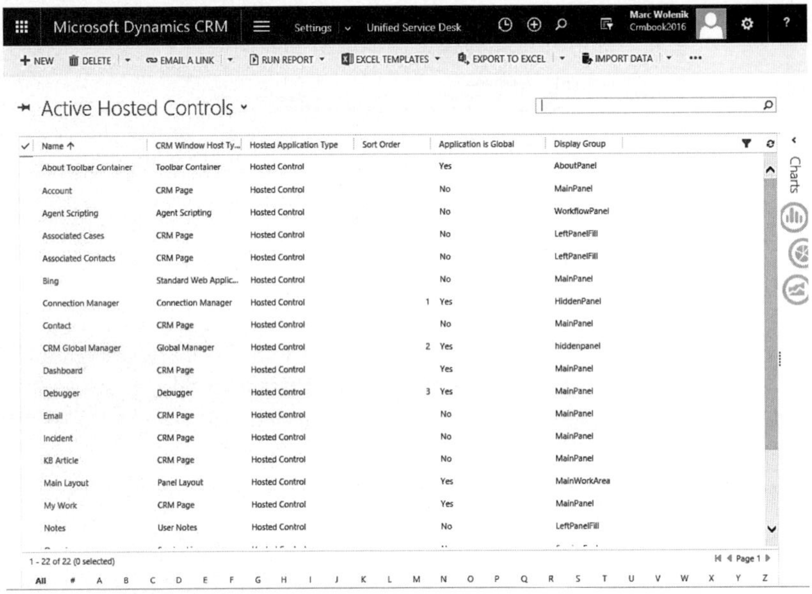

FIGURE 13.31   Active Hosted Controls screen.

An example of a simple configuration would be to swap out Google to do searches instead of Bing. To do this, you would create a new hosted control for that as follows:

1. Click New.

2. In the form that appears (see Figure 13.32), enter Google for Name and Display Name and select Standard Web Application for USD Component Type. Select Internal WPF for Hosting Type and check the Application Is Global check box. Make sure you also enter MainPanel in the Display Group field to present the control in the main panel.

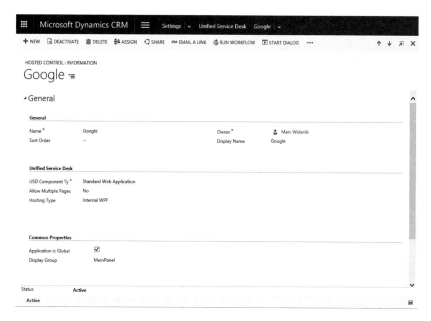

FIGURE 13.32   Creating a new hosted control.

3. Click Save to create the new hosted control. You then see that some predefined UII actions are also created (and you find them by clicking the drop-down arrow next to the name of the hosted control you just created, as shown in Figure 13.33).

FIGURE 13.33   UII actions menu option.

4. Click UII Actions to see a list of predefined actions that you can use or customize (see Figure 13.34).

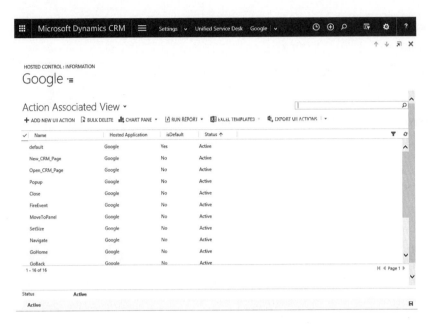

FIGURE 13.34   UII actions.

5. Open the default UII action and configure its properties, as shown in Figure 13.35. Then click Save.

NOTE

Don't confuse the URL field in Figure 13.35 with the field where you set the Google URL. You set the default action's URL field later, with the action calls, which are different from these UII actions.

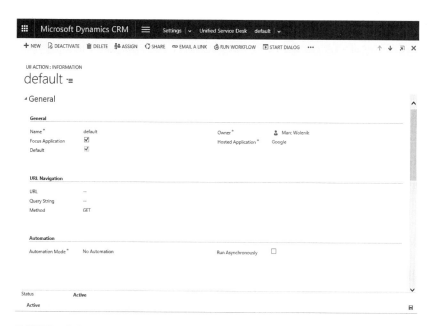

FIGURE 13.35   The default UII action.

The following predefined UII actions are created for this hosted control type:

- ▶ **Close**—Closes the hosted control.
- ▶ **Default**—Specifies the default action of the hosted control.
- ▶ **FireEvent**—Fires a user-defined event.
- ▶ **GoBack**—Responds to the back button in a browser instance.
- ▶ **GoForward**—Responds to the forward button in a browser instance.
- ▶ **GoHome**—Goes to the initial URL in a browser instance.
- ▶ **MoveToPanel**—Moves the hosted control between panels at runtime.
- ▶ **Navigate**—Navigates to a URL.
- ▶ **New_CRM_Page**—Creates a new CRM record.
- ▶ **Open_CRM_Page**—Opens an existing CRM record.
- ▶ **Popup**—Opens a pop-up window.
- ▶ **RealignWindow**—Specifies the location on a monitor in case you have more than one display.
- ▶ **RunScript**—Injects JavaScript into the hosted control browser.
- ▶ **SetSize**—Sets the width and height of the hosted control.

▶ **SetUserCanClose**—Validates whether the user can close the hosted control.

▶ **WaitForComplete**—Blocks the processing until the page content has finished loading.

You can use several types of USD hosted controls The fields you see depend on what hosted control type you select. Here is the complete list:

▶ **Agent Scripting**—This control provides a call script where you can add instructions for the agents to guide them during a call with the customer (see Figure 13.36).

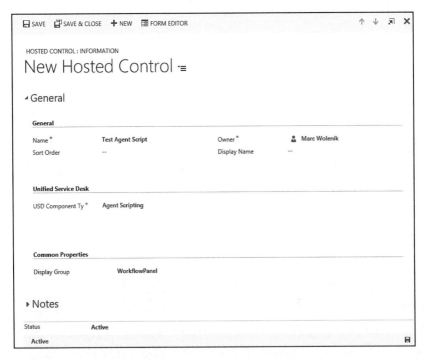

FIGURE 13.36   Agent Scripting hosted control.

▶ **CCA Hosted Application**—CCA stands for Customer Care Accelerator, and this control connects to a host, web, external, or remote hosted application—for example, the ones used for computer telephony integration (CTI). Usually you use this control with UII application adapters that are created with Visual Studio. Figure 13.37 shows the CCA Hosted Application control.

▶ **SEE** "Advanced Customizations," later in this chapter, for information on CCA
Hosted Application control configuration.

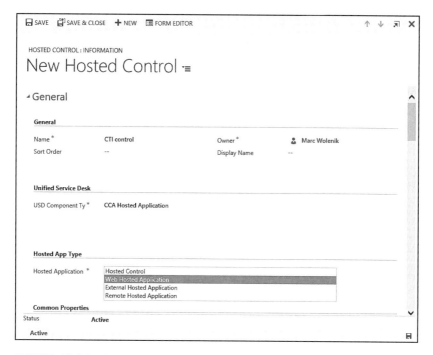

FIGURE 13.37   CCA Hosted Application control.

▶ **Connection Manager**—This control manages the connection to the CRM
server, and there should be only one of these control types running in the agent
application. This control doesn't expose any UII actions or events. The base solution
has a control of this type already created, named Connection Manager, so if you
create a new instance of this control type, the agent clients get the error shown in
Figure 13.38.

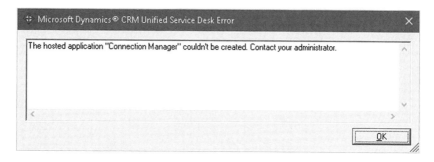

FIGURE 13.38   Connection Manager error message.

▶ **CRM Dialog**—This control works with CRM dialogs, calling the StartDialog UII action, which starts a CRM dialog in the USD agent app (see Figure 13.39).

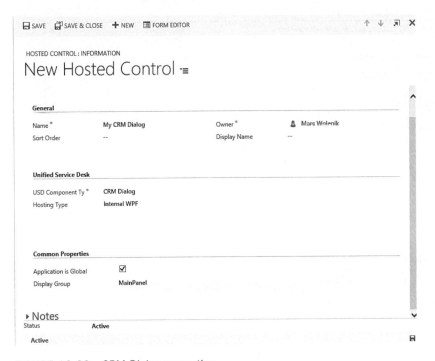

FIGURE 13.39   CRM Dialog properties.

▶ **CRM Page**—This control works with CRM pages such as forms, views, or dashboards (see Figure 13.40).

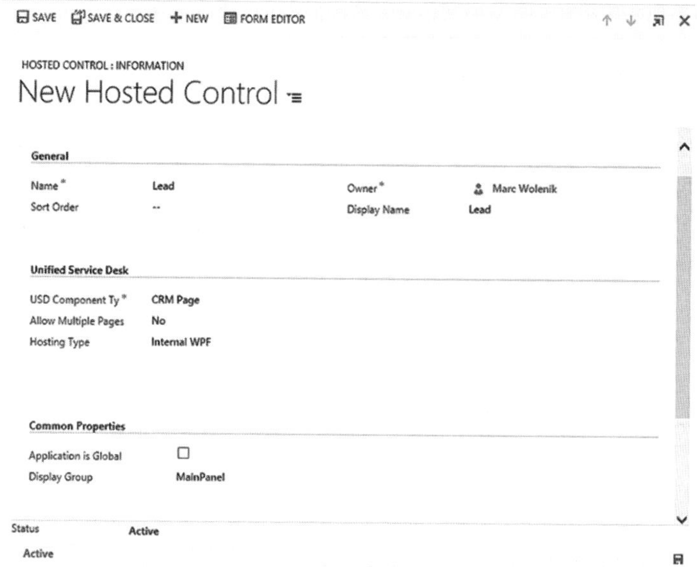

FIGURE 13.40   CRM Page properties.

▶ **CTI Desktop Manager**—This control manages the CTI adapter connections to control screen pop-ups, call routing, and other CTI features. The CTI adapters are usually created in C# with Visual Studio. By default, these hosted controls are put in the hidden panel (as shown in Figure 13.41).

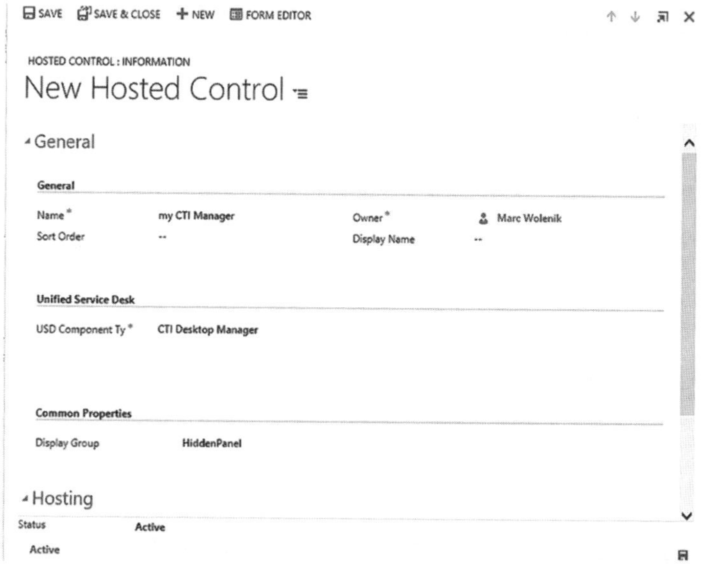

FIGURE 13.41   CTI Desktop Manager properties.

▶ **Debugger**—This control helps in showing debugging information. The base solution and the other samples you can install with the USD package deployer come with predefined controls of this type (see Figure 13.42). See the "Troubleshooting" section, later in this chapter, for information on debugging configurations and customizations.

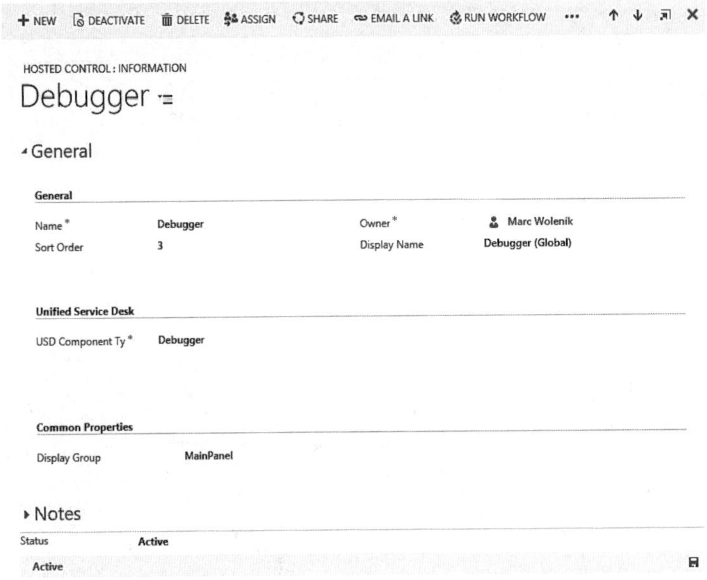

FIGURE 13.42 Debugger properties.

▶ **Global Manager**—This control is the core of the USD client application, and only one instance of this control can exist. The base solution comes with a control of this type, named CRM Global Manager, and it is vital for the USD agent client to run (see Figure 13.43). In this control type, you also find the configuration files for the multilanguage support that the USD agent application supports.

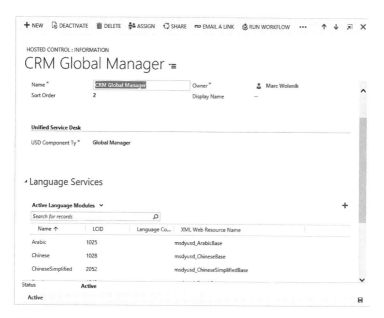

FIGURE 13.43   Global Manager properties.

▶ **KM Control**—This control displays knowledge base articles that can be stored in Parature or Dynamics CRM. With this control, agents can search, share, or email knowledge base articles without leaving the USD application.

▶ **Listener Hosted Control**—This control traces and debugs diagnostics logs to audit the USD application behavior.

▶ **Panel Layout**—You use this hosted control type to create custom layout panels that you can build using Visual Studio, for example. You will find a good example of this hosted control later on this chapter, in the "Advanced Customizations" section.

▶ **Ribbon Hosted Control**—This control is necessary to host the ribbon, and it is for internal use only.

▶ **Session Lines**—This control manages the session lines you configure in the Settings > Unified Service Desk > Session Lines section that are of the type Session Overview. SeesionExplorerPanel is the common display group for this type of control (see Figure 13.44).

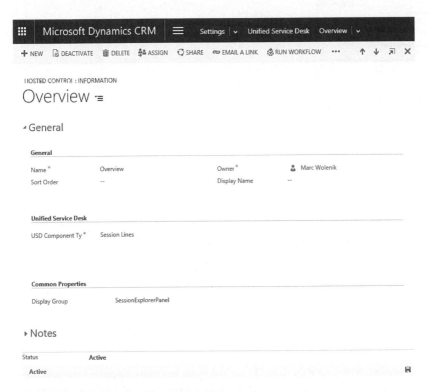

FIGURE 13.44   Session Lines properties.

▶ **Session Tabs**—Much like the Session Lines hosted control, this control manages sessions like the ones you configure in the Settings > Unified Service Desk > Session Lines section that are of the type Session Name.

▶ **Standard Web Application**—As you saw earlier, in the Google example, this control hosts a web browser that is used to present a configured page or URL.

▶ **Todo List**—This control provides a section for follow-up actions.

▶ **Toolbar Container**—This control creates toolbars that can contain buttons. The base solution comes with two of these type of controls created: one for the main toolbar and another for the About controls.

▶ **USD Hosted Control**—You can create this type of control with Visual Studio to extend the USD application. A USD Hosted Control called Timer that comes with the base solution is controls the time elapsed for each session.

▶ **User Notes**—This control provides an interactive notepad the agent can use to enter notes during the session. A User Notes control called Notes comes with the base solution.

Toolbars

Clicking Tollbars on the configuration page takes you to a page that shows the five predefined toolbars (see Figure 13.45). You can also add your own custom buttons to toolbars. To see how toolbar configuration works, follow these steps:

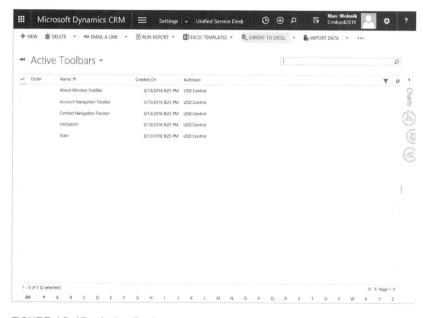

FIGURE 13.45   Active Toolbars page.

1. On the Active Toolbars page, click the Main toolbar record. A page showing the Main toolbar buttons appears, as shown in Figure 13.46.

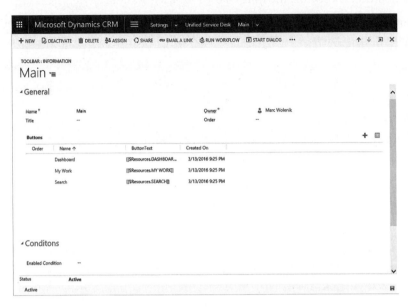

FIGURE 13.46   Main toolbar buttons.

2. Click + at the top of the Buttons subgrid to create a new button for this toolbar. Figure 13.47 shows the page that appears.

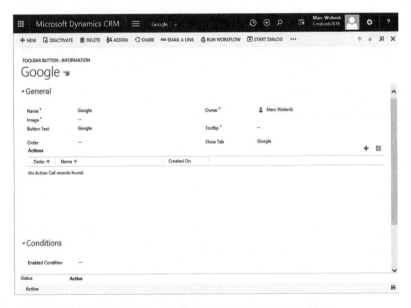

FIGURE 13.47   Creating a new button for the Main toolbar.

3. To create a new toolbar button for Google, enter Google in the Name and Button Text fields, in the Show Tab field find the hosted control Google that you created earlier, and click Save.

4. To add a new action, click the + icon at the top of the Actions subgrid and then click New in the actions lookup.

5. Enter Google in the Name field and select the Google hosted control you created earlier. Then select Navigate in the Action field and enter the url=http://www .google.com in the Data field (see Figure 13.48).

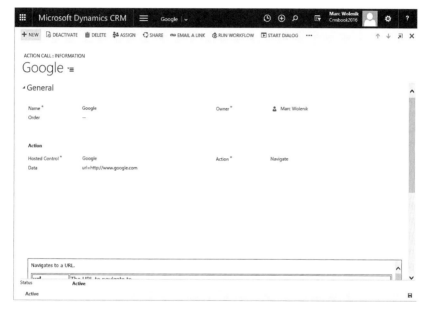

FIGURE 13.48   Creating a new action call.

6. Click Save and then Close.

To test this new control, restart the USD client application, and you see the new Google button added to the top toolbar. When you click this button, you see a new tab open, with the browser window pointing to the Google URL, as shown in Figure 13.49.

FIGURE 13.49   Testing the Google button in the USD client.

Action Calls

Clicking Action Calls on the configuration page allows you to manage all the action calls, including creating custom actions and modifying existing ones. Figure 13.50 shows the Active Actions page.

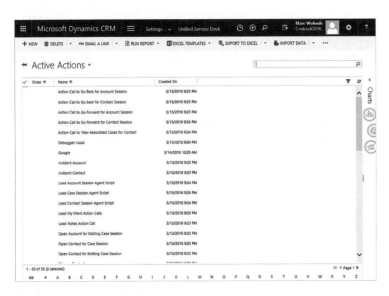

FIGURE 13.50   Active Actions page.

The base solution installs 54 action calls by default. You can easily modify them. The sample action calls are helpful because they display information related to how the USD reads data. Notice the case title in the search URL and the context used there.

For example, instead of creating a new Google button (as shown in the previous example), you could simply change the Bing URL to the URL of some other search engine. As a result, the Bing action call would still be there, but the URL would be for whatever search engine you entered. Figure 13.51 shows the details of the Initiate Bing Search action call, including how you can pass parameters to the URL—in this case, the case title and the subject name for the search.

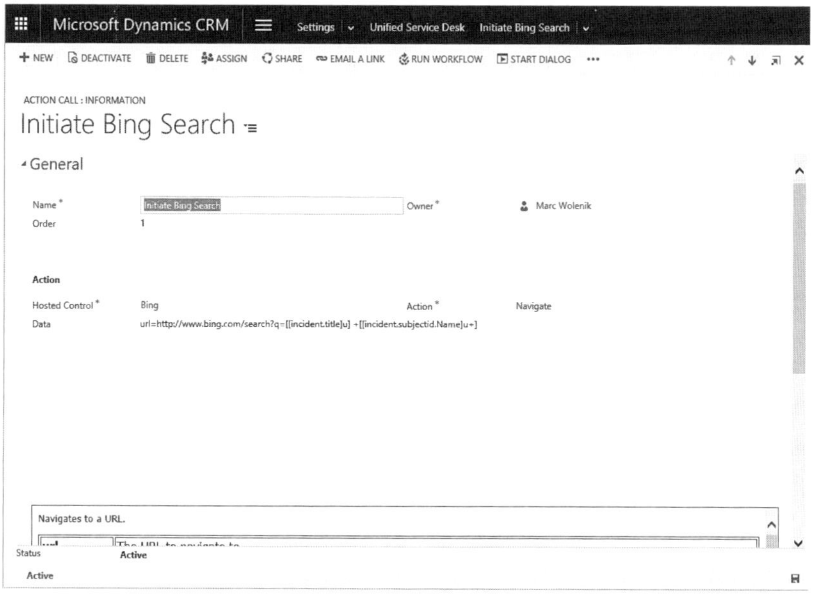

FIGURE 13.51   Initiate Bing Search action call.

Events

Events are related to hosted controls; every time you create a new hosted control, events are created that depend on the USD component type you selected. Figure 13.52 shows the Active Events page.

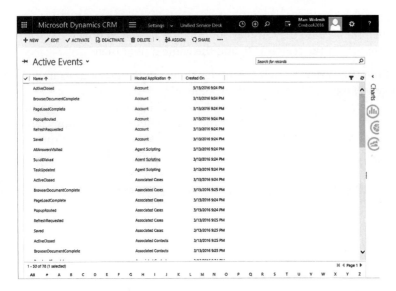

FIGURE 13.52   Active Events page.

For example, a standard web application has two events: `BrowserDocumentComplete` and `PopupRouted`.

Entity Searches

Entity searches show the entities you can use in the search button that appears in the top toolbar (see Figure 13.53). By default, the base solution adds records for Contact and Account entities.

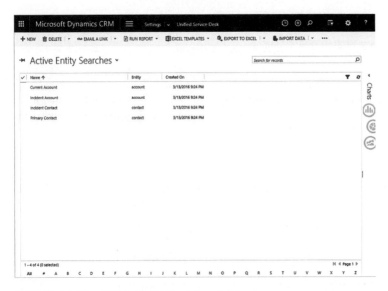

FIGURE 13.53   Active Entity Searches page.

If you want to add another entity in a search, you can do so by clicking New. For example, suppose you want to allow the user to search for leads. To do this, you need to add the Lead entity, which is not by default shown as an option (see Figure 13.54).

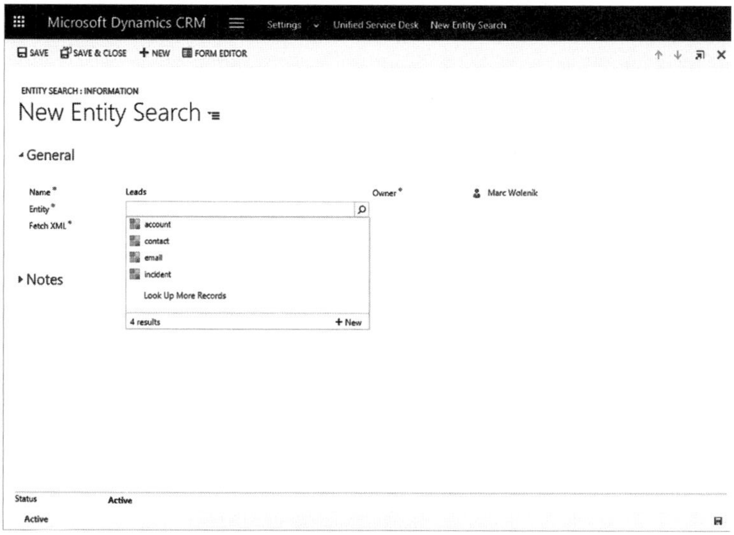

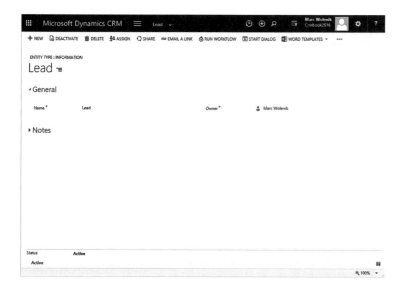

FIGURE 13.54   New Entity Search page.

To add the Lead entity, on the New Entity Search page click +New to create a new entity type. Enter Lead in the Name field, as shown in Figure 13.55, and click Save.

FIGURE 13.55   A new entity type for Lead.

Now you need to complete the Fetch XML field on the New Entity Search page. The easiest way to do this is to use the Advanced Find tool and click the Download FetchXML button to get the Fetch XML code, which is as follows:

```
<fetch version="1.0" output-format="xml-platform" mapping="logical" distinct="false">
  <entity name="lead">
    <attribute name="fullname" />
    <attribute name="createdon" />
    <attribute name="statuscode" />
    <attribute name="subject" />
    <attribute name="leadid" />
    <order attribute="createdon" descending="true" />
    <filter type="and">
      <condition attribute="statecode" operator="eq" value="0" />
    </filter>
  </entity>
</fetch>
```

Figure 13.56 shows the embedded Fetch XML code for the Lead entity search.

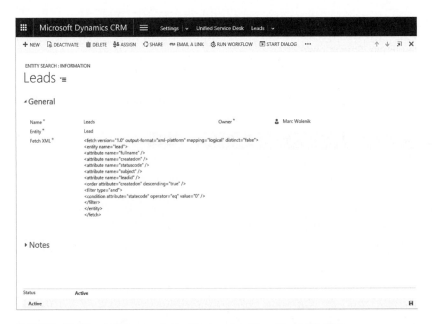

FIGURE 13.56   Entity search for the Lead entity with Fetch XML.

Because you modified the button for the Google search earlier in this chapter, you now need to edit the search toolbar so the agents can search for leads. Therefore, on the configuration page, select Toolbars and edit the HA:Search toolbar; create a new button there with the name Lead and create a new action call for the lead search, as shown in Figure 13.57 and Figure 13.58.

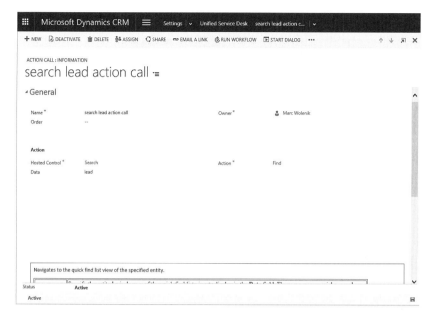

FIGURE 13.57   Search lead action call.

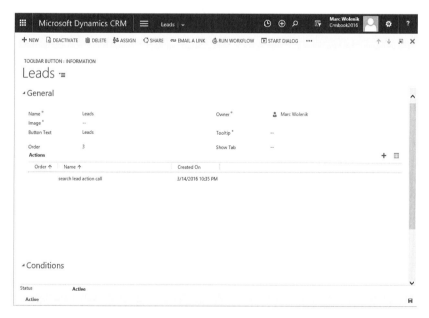

FIGURE 13.58   Lead button.

Figure 13.59 shows the HA:Search buttons with Leads added to it.

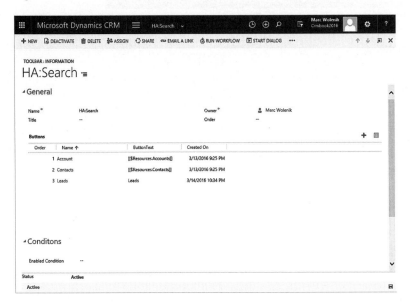

FIGURE 13.59   HA:Search with the Leads button.

If you now restart the USD client, the application will allow agents to search on leads. Figure 13.60 shows the result of such a search. Note that the navigation bar shows the Leads button for quick navigation.

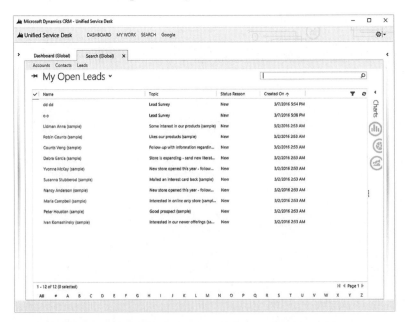

FIGURE 13.60   USD client with the lead search feature added.

Window Navigation Rules

The window navigation rules help in routing—for example, routing a search to one entity type to another (see Figure 13.61).

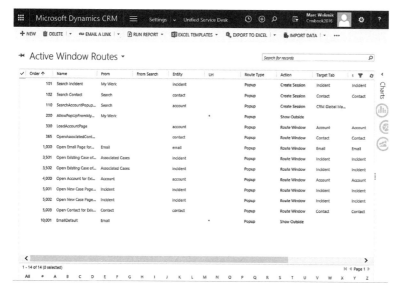

FIGURE 13.61   Window navigation routes.

To create a new navigation rule, click +New to open the window shown in Figure 13.62 and complete the required fields and routing logic.

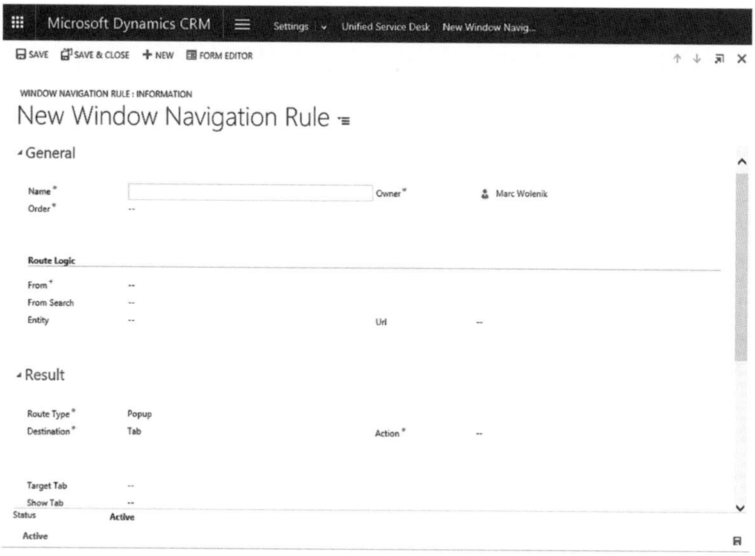

FIGURE 13.62   Creating a new window navigation rule.

Session Lines

USD allows users to open, maintain, and work on different calls, and session lines allow the system to control the calls to the application.

Session lines can be either of two types:

▶ **Session Name**—The Session Name type displays a single field like this: [[*account. name*]].

▶ **Session Overview**—The Session Overview type displays a grid with all the session lines, as shown in Figure 13.63.

When you create a new session line, you must specify the type, which you can't change it after you save the session line.

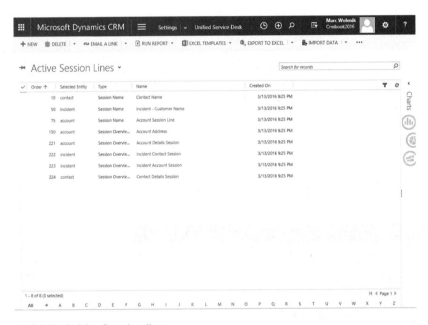

FIGURE 13.63   Session lines.

To create a new session line, click +New and then fill out the screen that appears (see Figure 13.64).

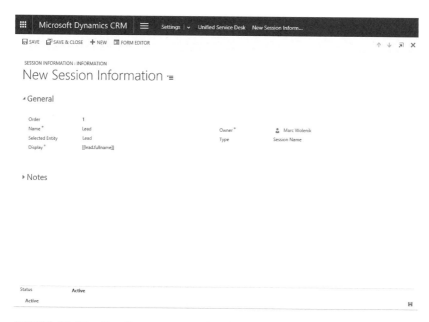

FIGURE 13.64   Creating a new session line for Lead.

The account details session display is configured with the following code in the base solution:

```xml
<Grid Margin="0"
      xmlns:x="http://schemas.microsoft.com/winfx/2006/xaml"
      xmlns:CCA="clr-namespace:Microsoft.Crm.UnifiedServiceDesk.
      Dynamics;assembly=Microsoft.Crm.UnifiedServiceDesk.Dynamics">
<Grid.Resources>
 <CCA:CRMImageConverter x:Key="CRMImageLoader" />
<Style x:Key="ImageLogo" TargetType="{x:Type Image}">
<Setter Property="Width" Value="16" />
<Setter Property="Height" Value="16" />
<Setter Property="Margin" Value="5" />
</Style>
    </Grid.Resources>
    <Grid.RowDefinitions>
        <RowDefinition Height="auto" />
        <RowDefinition Height="auto" />
        <RowDefinition Height="auto" />
        <RowDefinition Height="auto" />
        <RowDefinition Height="auto" />
        <RowDefinition Height="auto" />
    </Grid.RowDefinitions>
```

```
<TextBlock Margin="5,6,0,0" Grid.Row="0" TextWrapping="Wrap" Padding="5,0,0,5"
FontFamily="Tahoma" FontSize="12" Text="Account Name: [[account.name]x]"
Foreground="#262626"/>
<StackPanel  Orientation="Horizontal"  Grid.Row="1"  Margin="5,0,0,0">
<Image Style="{DynamicResource ImageLogo}" Source="{Binding Source=msdyusd_Email16,
Converter={StaticResource CRMImageLoader}}" />
<TextBlock  TextWrapping="Wrap" Padding="5,0,0,5" Text="Email: [[account.
emailaddress1]+x]" Foreground="#262626"  VerticalAlignment="Center"/>
</StackPanel>
<StackPanel Orientation="Horizontal"  Grid.Row="2" Margin="5,0,0,0">
<Image Style="{DynamicResource ImageLogo}" Source="{Binding Source=msdyusd_Phone16,
Converter={StaticResource CRMImageLoader}}" />
<TextBlock  TextWrapping="Wrap" Padding="5,0,0,5" Text="Phone: [[account.telephone1]
x]" />
</StackPanel>
<TextBlock Margin="5,0,0,0" Grid.Row="3" TextWrapping="Wrap" Padding="5,0,0,5"
FontFamily="Tahoma" FontSize="12" Style="{DynamicResource AutoCollapse}"
Text="Primary Contact: [[account.primarycontactid.name]x]" Foreground="#262626"
VerticalAlignment="Center"/>
</Grid>
```

This code then is rendered in the panel of an account record that you open with the USD client, as shown in Figure 13.65.

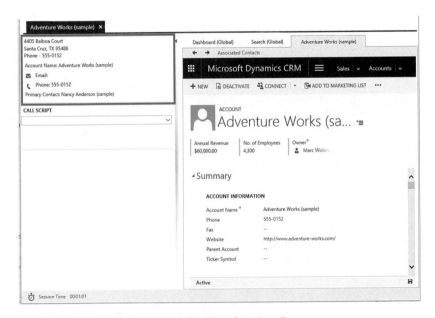

FIGURE 13.65 Account details Session Overview line.

> **NOTE**
>
> The code used here is XAML and is the same code used in WPF applications. If you make any update here, you must restart the USD client to see the changes.

Agent Scripts

Agent scripts help an agent follow the necessary steps to perform the work as expected (that is, process-driving guidance). Figure 13.66 shows the default agent scripts.

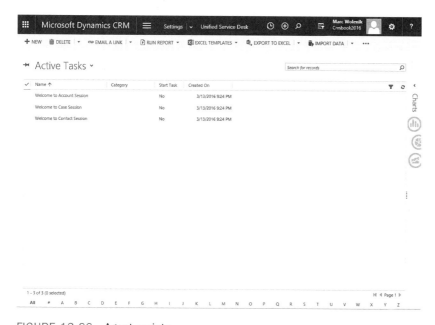

FIGURE 13.66   Agent scripts.

To create a new agent script, click the +New and then fill out the New Agent Script Task page that appears (see Figure 13.67).

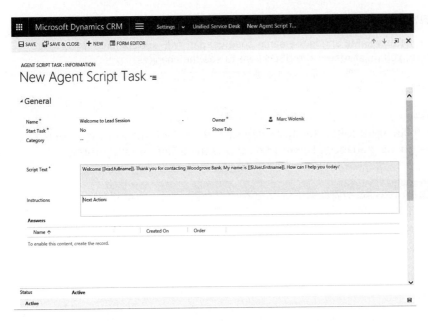

FIGURE 13.67   New Agent Script Task page for a Lead entity.

Save the new agent script so you can optionally create answers and click +at the top of the Answers subgrid to open the New Agent Script Answer page, shown in Figure 13.68.

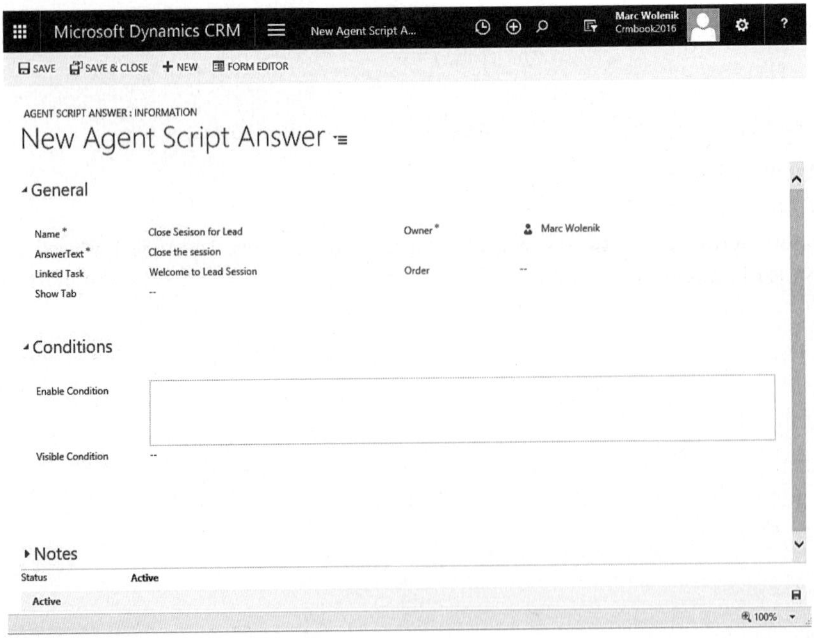

FIGURE 13.68   New Agent Script Answer page.

NOTE

While you can add agent scripts, complex routing and if/then statements require complex customizations. A good solution is to use TKDialogs for this, as it is a robust and supportable tool for just this need. Find it at www.teamknowledge.co.uk.

Scriptlets

Sciptlets are JavaScript code snippets that you can use to replace parameters. The base solution comes with a scriptlet to resolve the case name by the case title (see Figure 13.69).

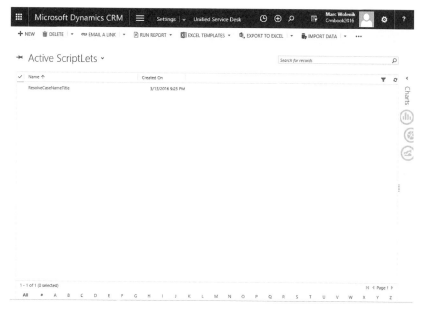

FIGURE 13.69   Scriptlets.

To create a new scriptlet click +New and complete the required fields in the page that appears (see Figure 13.70).

FIGURE 13.70   New scriptlet to convert a lead.

Forms

Forms are used to store declarative form definitions, and the base solution doesn't come with any forms created by default. Figure 13.71 shows the Active Forms page (which is empty).

FIGURE 13.71   Active Forms page.

To create a new form, click +New and complete the required fields in the page that appears (see Figure 13.72).

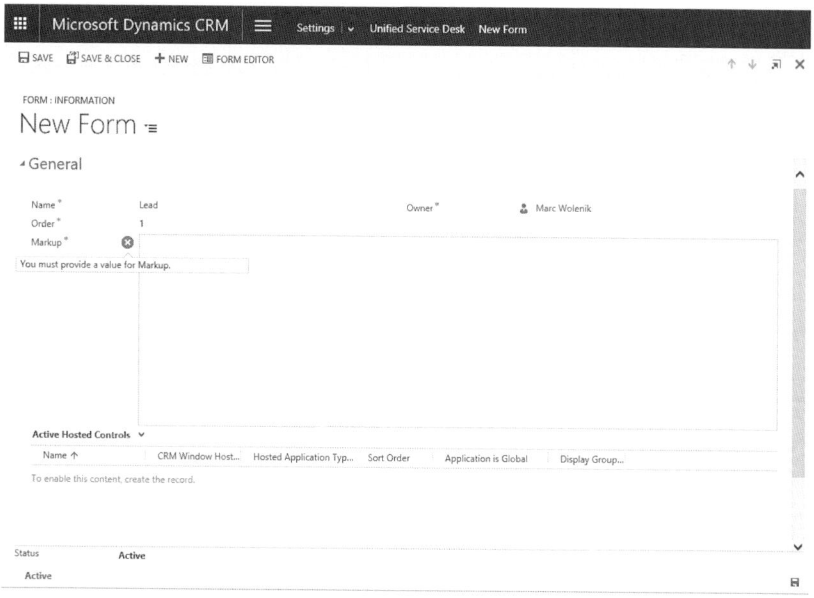

FIGURE 13.72   New form for a lead.

After you have completed and saved a form, it can be referenced in the USD interface for agent interaction.

Options

Options are used to create name/value pairs that can be used by other components. Some of the options you can configure are enabling and disable auditing flags. Figure 13.73 shows the Active UII Options page.

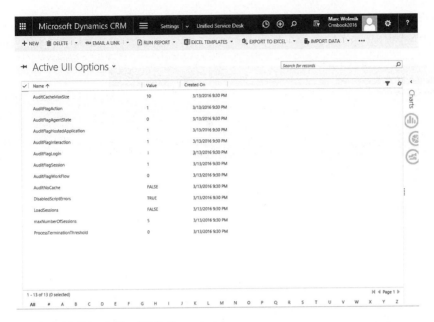

FIGURE 13.73   Active UII Options page.

To create a new option, click +New and complete the required information, as shown in Figure 13.74.

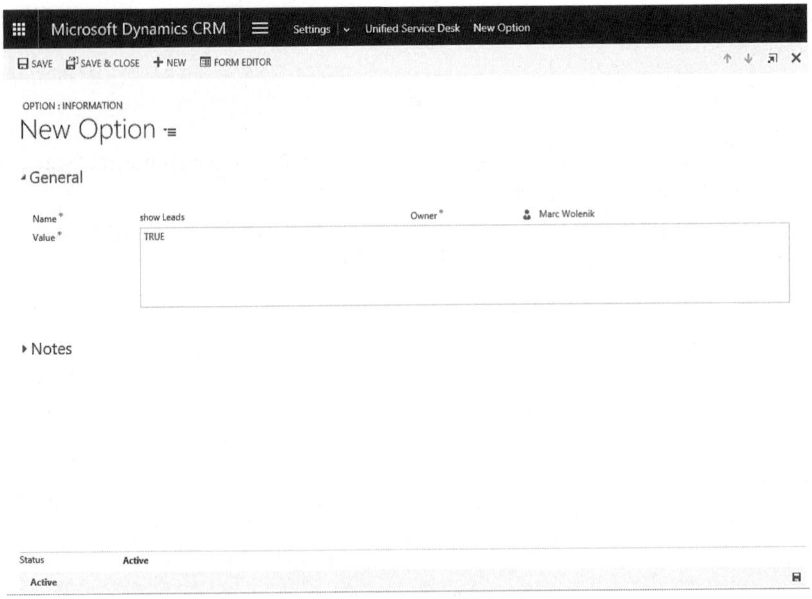

FIGURE 13.74   New Option page.

User Settings

User settings are used to configure personal settings via programmatic manipulation of the values stored in the settings configuration. They allow users to have different experiences within the USD interface.

To create a new user setting, select User Settings on the configuration page and then, on the page shown in Figure 13.75, click +New to create a new setting.

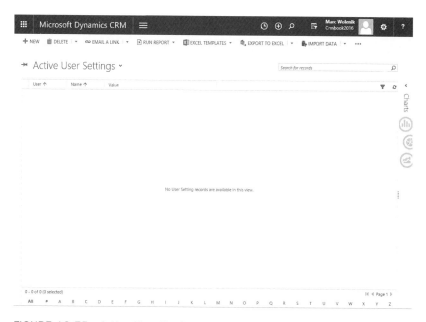

FIGURE 13.75   Active User Settings page.

Figure 13.76 shows the default values for user settings.

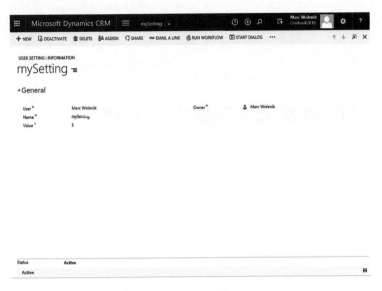

FIGURE 13.76   Creating a new user setting.

Customization File

The customization file contains the generic customization file for the USD. Figure 13.77 shows the Active USD Customization Files page.

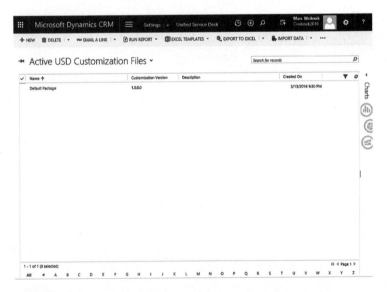

FIGURE 13.77   Active USD Customization Files page.

The Default Package customization, shown in Figure 13.78, can be modified or copied for enhanced configuration.

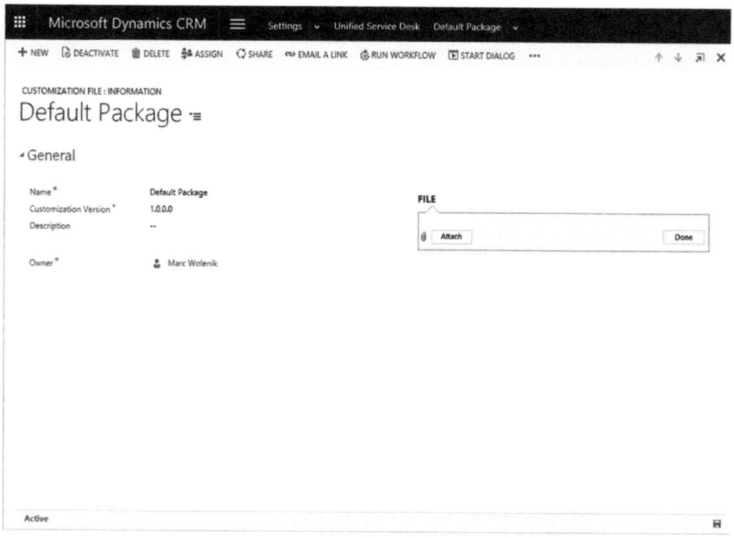

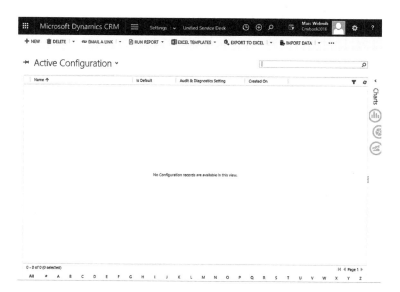

FIGURE 13.78   Default Package customization file record.

Configuration

You can use a configuration to associate the Audit & Diagnostic setting records with users and hosted controls. In addition, you can manage security by setting which user can use each hosted control. Figure 13.79 shows the Active Configuration page.

FIGURE 13.79   Active Configuration page.

It is necessary to have at least one record here for the standard audit to work. Then you can add the users who will use this configuration. Each user can have one only configuration set, and the USD solution adds a lookup in the System User entity, and you can also select the configuration to be used by that user. Figure 13.80 shows a new configuration record.

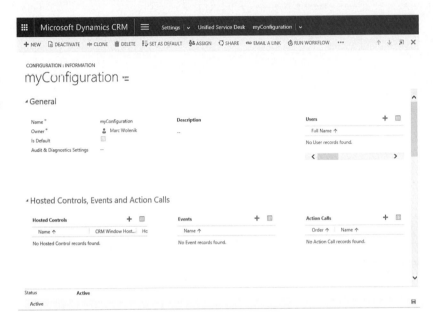

FIGURE 13.80   New configuration record.

Audit & Diagnostics Settings

You use Audit & Diagnostics Settings to troubleshoot the USD client. This section is especially useful when you're developing complex customizations. Figure 13.81 shows the default settings.

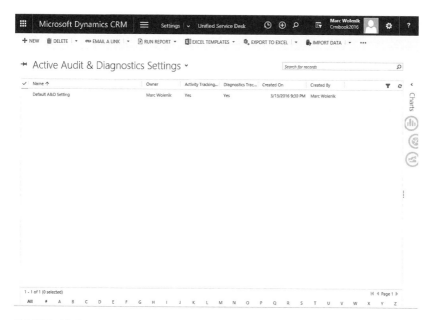

FIGURE 13.81   Active Audit & Diagnostics Settings page.

You can enable or disable the following auditing options (see Figure 13.82):

▶ Activity Tracking

▶ Activity Tracking for Customer Session

▶ Activity Tracking for Hosted Controls

▶ Activity Tracking for Events

▶ Activity Tracking for Agents Scripts

▶ Activity Tracking for Agent Login

▶ Activity Tracking for UII Calls

▶ Activity Tracking for Action Calls

▶ Activity Tracking for Sub Action Calls

▶ Activity Tracking for Windows Navigation Rules

▶ Caching

▶ Cache Size

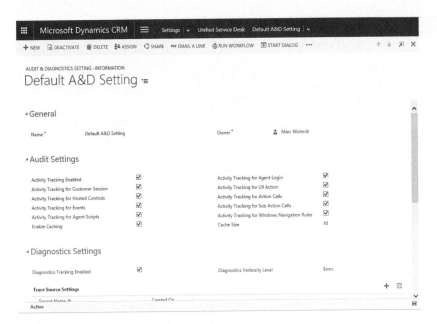

FIGURE 13.82   Default A&D Setting page.

Regardless of these settings, you need to configure both what you want to audit or log and what is then routed to the listener hosted controls that will be responsible for storing this information in files, Windows event log, and so on.

There are two main ways to see the audit information generated by the USD. One way is to create a listener hosted control, as explained in the USD Developer Guide in the UII SDK. Another way, which doesn't require development of a listener assembly (and is therefore a little easier), is to add the audit flag in the options settings; you can do this by navigating to Settings > Unified Service Desk > Options. These are the options you can then use for auditing:

- ► AuditFlagAction

- ► AuditCacheMaxSize

- ► AuditFlagAgentState

- ► AuditFlagHostedApplication

- ► AuditFlagInteraction

- ► LoadSessions

- ► MaxNumberOfSessions

- ► ProcessTerminationThreshold

- ► ShowScriptsError

▶ `AuditFlagLogin`

▶ `AuditFlagSession`

▶ `AuditFlagWorkflow`

Setting any of the preceding option to 1 enables that audit option. Setting it to 0 disables that audit. One other option related to auditing, `AuditNoCache`, must be set to either `True` or `False`.

NOTE

To start auditing, you must create a configuration record and associate the Audit & Diagnostic Setting record to it.

Troubleshooting

When adding and changing configurations and applying custom configurations and customizations, sometimes the application doesn't behave as expected. In such cases, you need to debug the application. To do so, click the gear in the top-right corner and select Debug (see Figure 13.83).

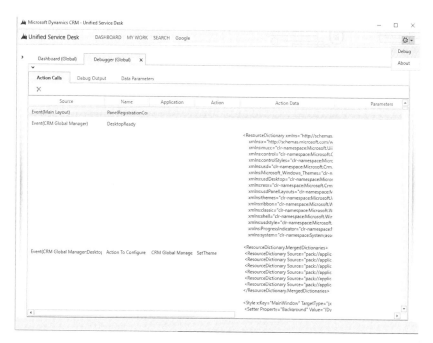

FIGURE 13.83   Opening the Debugger tab.

Advanced Customizations

To extend the USD, you need to download and install the UII (User Interface Integration) SDK package. You can find it at the same place you download the MicrosoftDynamicsCRM2016UII.exe: https://www.microsoft.com/en-us/download/details.aspx?id=50032. You install the UII SDK on your development by executing the MicrosoftDynamicsCRM2016UII.exe file and then completing the installation steps.

With the UII you can extend USD with the following components:

▶ UII Application Adapter

▶ UII web application Adapter

▶ UII Windows Forms Customer Search Control

▶ UII Windows Forms Hosted Control

▶ UII WPF Customer Search Control

▶ UII WPF Hosted Control

▶ USD CTI Connector

▶ USD Custom Hosted Control

▶ USD Custom Panel Layout

You need to use Visual Studio (version 2012, 2013, or 2015) to build and create these components.

> **NOTE**
>
> For more information on advanced customizations, see the Unified Service Desk 2.0 Developer Guide, which is available at https://msdn.microsoft.com/library/dn864923.aspx.

To start developing these types of controls with Visual Studio, you can download and install the Dynamics CRM SDK and then install the CRMSDKTemplates.vsix that is in the SDK\Templates folder. An alternative method is to follow these steps:

1. From Visual Studio, select Tools > Extensions and Updates. Then, in the Online node on the left, search for the Microsoft Dynamics CRM SDK (see Figure 13.84).

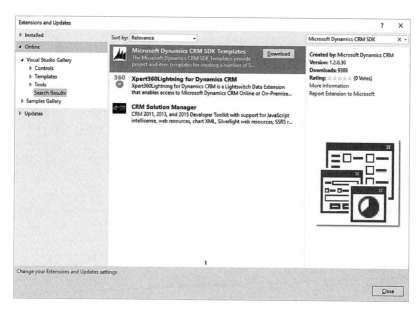

FIGURE 13.84   Microsoft Dynamics CRM SDK Templates download.

2. Select Microsoft Dynamics CRM SDK Templates and click the Download button. The window shown in Figure 13.85 appears.

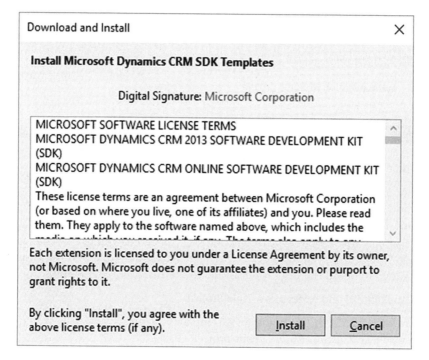

FIGURE 13.85   Install Microsoft Dynamics CRM SDK Templates dialog.

3. Click the Install button.

4. When the installation finishes, click Close.

This CRM SDK installs the necessary Visual Studio templates you need to build the different controls. When they are installed, you can create new UII application adapter projects, under the Templates > Visual C# > CRM SDK Templates > Unified Service Desk, as shown in Figure 13.86.

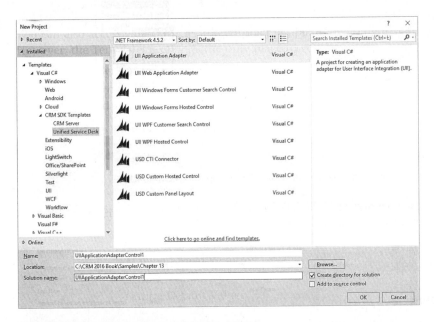

FIGURE 13.86   UII Application Adapter project.

NOTE

Refer to the UII SDK for examples that also show you how to pass data between USD client and external applications.

USD Custom Panel Layout

With a USD Custom Panel Layout type of component, you can do things like change the default logo that is displayed in the USD interface. This is helpful if you want to use your company logo to brand the USD application. To do this, follow these steps:

1. Open Visual Studio and select File > New Project.

2. Go to Templates > Visual C# > CRM SDK Templates > Unified Service Desk and create a new USD Custom Panel Layout project

3. Double-click the CustomLayout.xaml file to open it from the Solution Explorer window and find this code line:

```
<Image Grid.Column="0" Source="{Binding Source=msdyusd_Logo,
Converter={StaticResource CRMImageLoader}}"  Style="{DynamicResource
ImageLogo}"   />
```

and replace it with the following:

```
<Image Grid.Column="0" Source="C:\CRM 2016 Book\Samples\Chapter 13\
USDCustomPanelLayout1\USDCustomPanelLayout1\Webfortis New Logo.png"  />
```

4. Build the solution, copy the generated assembly (USDCustomPanelLayout1.dll) that is found in the bin\debug folder of your project to the USD application directory (usually C:\Program Files\Microsoft Dynamics CRM USD\USD if you installed in the default directory), and register the assembly. (You will need to do this on every machine of every agent that has the USD installed.) You also need to copy the image file of the logo to the exact location you used on the target client machines.

If you want to avoid having to copy the image file of the logo, you can create a web resource in Dynamics CRM and use the following code to reference the source of the image in the same code line you modified in step 3 above:

```
<Image Grid.Column="0" Source="{Binding Source=new_WebfortisLogo,
Converter={StaticResource CRMImageLoader}}" Style="{DynamicResource ImageLogo}" />
```

To register the component, follow these steps

1. Go to Dynamics CRM and navigate to Settings > Unified Service Desk.

2. Click the Hosted Controls option.

3. Create a new hosted control and enter a name for it. Select Panel Layout in the USD Component Type field. In the PanelType field select User Defined. Check the Application Is Global check box and leave Display Group set to MainWorkArea. Figure 13.87 shows the new USD custom Panel Layout hosted control.

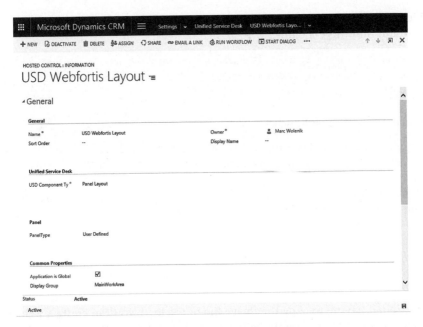

FIGURE 13.87   New USD custom Panel Layout hosted control.

4. Scroll down and set Application Is Dynamic to No and make sure the User Can Close check box is not checked. Set Assembly URI with the Visual Studio project namespace and set Assembly Type to the Visual Studio project namespace with the class name shown in Figure 13.88.

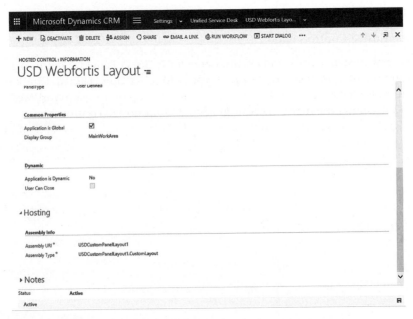

FIGURE 13.88   USD custom Panel Layout namespace and assembly type.

5. Click Save.

6. Deactivate any existing hosted control with the type Panel Layout.

7. Start the USD client to see the logo and the new Panel Layout hosted control. Figure 13.89 shows the new logo.

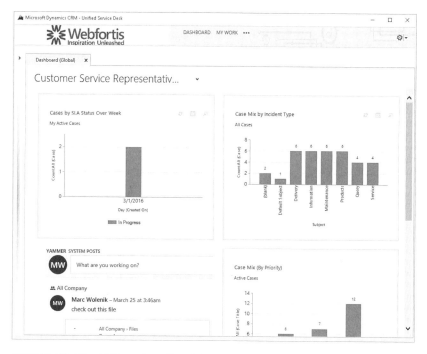

FIGURE 13.89   USD custom Panel Layout with a company logo.

Summary

This chapter looks at the Unified Service Desk solution and how to customize and configure it. You've learned how to install the USD for both the server and client, and you've learned different ways to configure the USD application client by adding records in the different entity types and hosted controls in the USD solution. This chapter also covers adding and configuring auditing and troubleshooting, as well as what is necessary if you are planning to extend the USD client by creating custom hosted controls using the USD SDK and the UII SDK. You have also learned how to brand the USD client by adding a company logo to the USD client application.

Microsoft Dynamics Social Engagement

Previously known as Social Listening, Microsoft Dynamics Social Engagement brings together Microsoft Dynamics CRM and social channels (Facebook, Twitter, and so on) in a combined package.

Microsoft Dynamics Social Engagement helps your company monitor various social media channels to find what users and customers are saying and feeling about your products and services. You can use Dynamics Social Engagement to analyze these channels to quickly see if users are happy or unhappy with the services and products provided by your company.

> **NOTE**
>
> Microsoft Dynamics Social Engagement is part of Office 365 and requires an Office 365 subscription for it specifically in addition to Dynamics CRM.

> **TIP**
>
> For a free 30-minute trial of Social Engagement, visit https://listening-trial.microsoft.com/trial-bridge/. Note that this is not a fully functional trial version, but it has enough of the features that it's worth trying out.

Using Microsoft Dynamics Social Engagement

The Dynamics Social Engagement interface is similar in look and feel to Dynamics CRM. However, it is a completely separate application and uses a separate database. Figure 14.1 shows the user interface for Dynamics Social Engagement.

FIGURE 14.1   Dynamics Social Engagement user interface.

The Dynamics Social Engagement navigation bar is divided into the following main areas (see Figure 14.2):

▶ Search Setup

▶ Analytics

▶ Social Center

▶ Activity Maps

▶ Message Center

▶ Settings

▶ Help

FIGURE 14.2   Dynamics Social Engagement navigation bar.

Pricing

Social Engagement, which is licensed through Office 365, is available as the following types of subscriptions:

▶ Social Engagement Enterprise at $125 per user per month

▶ Social Engagement Professional at $75 per user per month

The pricing used is current at the time of publication but may be subject to change. Check here for the most current pricing: https://www.microsoft.com/en-us/dynamics/crm -social-purchase.aspx

The primary difference between the two options is the number of posts per month: Professional has 10,000 per month, versus Enterprise with 20,000. However, both versions have step-up options that allow you to purchase additional posts if necessary. In addition, the Enterprise version includes the Social Engagement option and also includes Parature and Microsoft Dynamics Marketing. If you're just looking for Social Engagement, the Professional license may be sufficient.

▶ For more information on Parature, **SEE CHAPTER 12**, "Parature." For more information about Microsoft Dynamics Marketing, **SEE CHAPTER 9**, "Microsoft Dynamics Marketing."

There are a variety of licensing options and limitations with regard to Social Engagement, including a minimum number of CRM Professional users. For current details, see www.microsoft.com/en-us/dynamics/crm-social-purchase.aspx.

The following sections discuss how to set up, configured, customize, and use Dynamics Social Engagement.

Configuration

When you access Social Engagement for the first time, you see an empty dashboard with a few recommendations for initial setup, as shown in Figure 14.3.

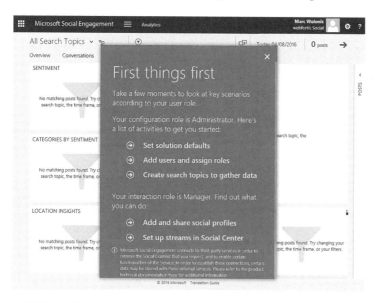

FIGURE 14.3   First Things First page.

As discussed in the following sections, you need to complete three activities:

▶ Set solution defaults.

▶ Add users and assign roles.

▶ Create search topics to gather data.

Setting Solution Defaults

To set solution defaults you need to go to Settings, where you see the Personal Settings by default. Select Personal Settings > Global Settings (see Figure 14.4).

NOTE

Depending on your screen size and resolution, you may initially be able to see the whole Settings menu and not need to first select Personal Settings.

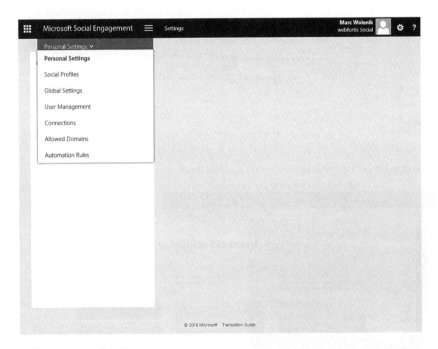

FIGURE 14.4   Settings.

Under Global Settings you can configure the following:

▶ Default Preferences

▶ Search Languages

▶ Search Setup Defaults

▶ Sentiment

▶ Labels

▶ Location Groups

▶ Privacy

Default Preferences

When you are in the Global Settings area, click Default Preferences, and on this page you can change the name, default language, time, and number formats, as shown in Figure 14.5.

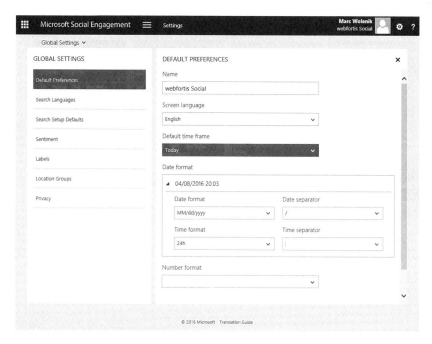

FIGURE 14.5   Default Preferences page.

You can set more than a dozen screen languages. At publication time, Social Engagement was available in 15 languages:

▶ Danish

▶ Dutch

▶ English

▶ Finish

▶ French

▶ German

▶ Greek

▶ Italian

▶ Norwegian

▶ Polish

▶ Portuguese

▶ Russian

▶ Spanish

▶ Swedish

▶ Turkish

On the Default Preferences page, you can set the following time frame options:

▶ Today

▶ Last Week

▶ Last Month

Search Languages

On the Search Languages page you can select the languages you want the Social Engagement solution to look for.

At publication time, there were 20 search languages available:

▶ Arabic

▶ Chinese

▶ Danish

▶ Dutch

▶ English

▶ Finish

▶ French

▶ German

▶ Greek

▶ Hebrew

▶ Italian

▶ Japanese

▶ Norwegian

▶ Polish

▶ Portuguese

▶ Russian

▶ Spanish

▶ Swedish

▶ Thai

▶ Turkish

NOTE

Unselecting a language here removes any search rule associated with that language. As a result, to ensure accurate results, you should check as many options as you think might contain your listening keywords.

Search Setup Defaults

On the Search Setup Defaults page you can select the sources and languages you want the new searches to use, as shown in Figure 14.6.

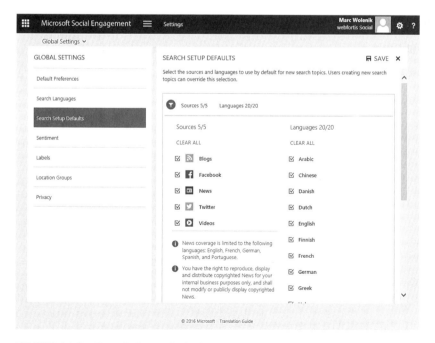

FIGURE 14.6   Search Setup Defaults page.

These are the different sources you can select:

▶ Blogs

▶ Forums

▶ Facebook

▶ News

▶ Twitter

▶ Videos

▶ Custom sources

The News source option is limited to English, French, German, Spanish, and Portuguese.

Sentiment

On the Sentiment page you can select whether you want to use adaptive learning. Adaptive learning helps the system learn based on the user's selection and is a valuable tool in sentiment analysis. You can reset it by clicking the Reset button, which lets the adaptive learning module start learning again from scratch.

Labels

You can use the Labels page to classify posts using different colors. The list of colors is limited to 10:

▶ Blue

▶ Cyan

▶ Green

▶ Lime

▶ Magenta

▶ Orange

▶ Purple

▶ Red

▶ Teal

▶ Yellow

You can reuse the colors on more than one label.

Location Groups

The Location Groups page helps you organize data in different locations. The system is predefined to use continents as the main location groups, which obviously contain countries inside of them. However, you can edit and configure your own locations for more discreet searching.

By default, the system comes with eight location groups:

▶ Africa

▶ Antarctica

▶ Asia

▶ Australia/Pacific

▶ Europe

▶ Middle East

▶ North America/Central

▶ South America

NOTE

While you can edit and create your own location groups, you cannot add new countries other than the predefined locations listed.

Privacy

The Privacy page lets you configure a privacy link to show to the users to let them know the Social Engagement solution needs to share some private data with the third-party services it connects to.

Adding Users and Assigning Roles

To add a user to Dynamics Social Engagement, you must first create the user in the Office 365 portal and assign a Social Engagement license to that user. After that, you can go to the Social Engagement web interface and navigate to Settings > User Management. There you select the user and assign a role from the right panel, as shown in Figure 14.7.

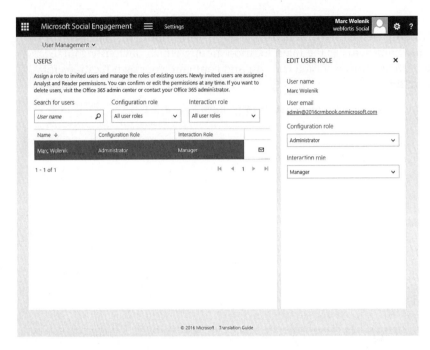

FIGURE 14.7   User Management page.

There are two different type of roles:

▶ Configuration roles

▶ Interaction roles

The configuration roles be any of the following:

▶ Analyst

▶ Power Analyst

▶ Administrator

The interaction roles be any of the following:

▶ Manager

▶ Responder

▶ Reader

Table 14.1 shows the effects of the different configuration roles on the Social Engagement system.

TABLE 14.1   Configuration Roles

Permission	Analyst	Power Analyst	Administrator
View all analysis	✕	✕	✕
Edit sentiment value for posts	✕	✕	✕
Delete posts		✕	✕
Exclude/delete authors		✕	✕
Create and edit search topics		Can only edit own search topics	✕
Create and manage categories		Can only edit own categories	✕
Manage custom sources			✕
Create and edit location groups		Can only edit own location groups	✕
Manage user roles			✕
Exclude sources and terms			✕
Set up connections to Dynamics CRM			✕
Create and manage alerts	✕	✕	✕
Define global settings			✕
Create and edit activity maps	✕	✕	✕
Manage automation rules			✕

Table 14.2 shows the effects of the different interaction roles in the system.

TABLE 14.2   Interaction Roles

Permission	Reader	Responder	Manager
View streams	✕	✕	✕
Manage social profiles		✕	✕
Edit labels on posts		✕	✕
Edit post assignments		✕	✕
Manage streams			✕
React on a post		✕	✕
Publish a new post		✕	✕
Create a CRM record from a social post		✕	✕
Unlink a post from a CRM record			✕
View record details	✕	✕	✕
Manage automation rules			✕
View automation rules	✕	✕	✕

14

Creating Search Topics to Gather Data

You can set up searches to start listening to social media conversations about topics and keywords that are interesting or topical for your business.

The first thing you need to do is to go to the Search Setup option in the navigation bar. Then click in the + icon in the Search Topics section. Next, you can enter a name for your new search topic and select a category, as shown in Figure 14.8.

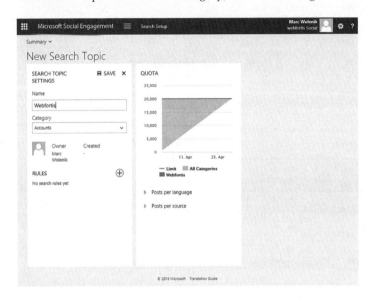

FIGURE 14.8   Selecting a new search topic.

Click on the + icon near Rules to create a new rule, as shown in Figure 14.9.

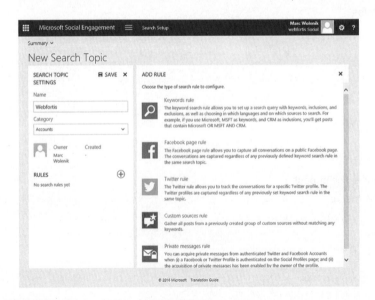

FIGURE 14.9   Adding a new rule.

You can create several different types of rules:

▶ Keywords rules

▶ Facebook page rules

▶ Twitter rules

▶ Custom sources rules

▶ Private messages rules

> **NOTE**
>
> In order to create a search topic, you must have at least one search rule created.

The following sections explain the rule types.

Keyword Rules

For each keyword rule, you can select the sources and languages you want the search topic to run. Then you enter the keywords, inclusions, and exclusions.

Clicking Continue takes you to the quota check page, as shown in Figure 14.10. After a successfully quota check you can save the search topic.

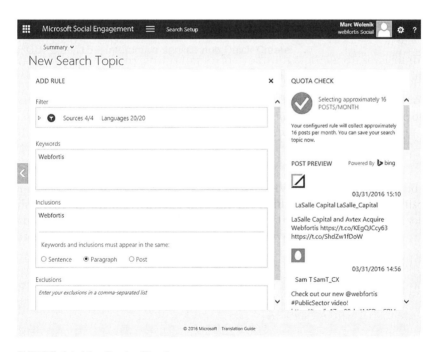

FIGURE 14.10   Quota Check page.

> **TIP**
>
> Since Dynamics Social Engagement is restricted by posts, it is helpful to analyze the results of the quota check. A large result set here could easily put you over your limit and force you to pay more to continue listening. If this happens or threatens to happen, try more restrictive keywords or try adding additional restrictors. For example, instead of just using "CRM," try "Microsoft Dynamics CRM 2016."

Facebook Page Rules

By setting Facebook rules you can search Facebook pages. Figure 14.11 shows the initial configuration page for Facebook page searching.

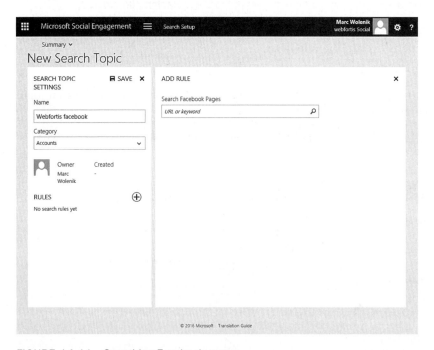

FIGURE 14.11   Searching Facebook pages.

You can enter search criteria and click the search icon (the magnifying glass) to see results (see Figure 14.12).

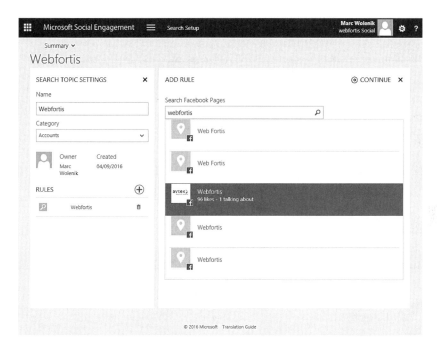

FIGURE 14.12   Facebook pages search results.

Select the page you want and then click Continue to see the Quota Check page. From here, be sure to save the search topic and add additional rules as necessary.

Twitter Rules

When you set Twitter rules, you can select from the following Twitter actions:

▶ Tweets

▶ Replies

▶ Retweets

▶ Mentions

In order to use Twitter rules, you must sign in to Twitter, and to do that you click the Twitter link at the bottom of the Add Rule window. The authorization screen shown in Figure 14.13 appears.

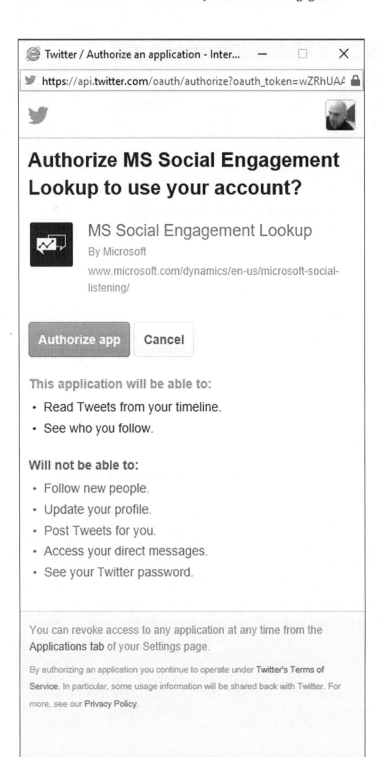

FIGURE 14.13   Authorizing Twitter.

Click the Authorize App button. When you are successfully authorized, you see a text box for searching Twitter (see Figure 14.14). Enter the keyword(s) you want to search for and click the search icon to see the results.

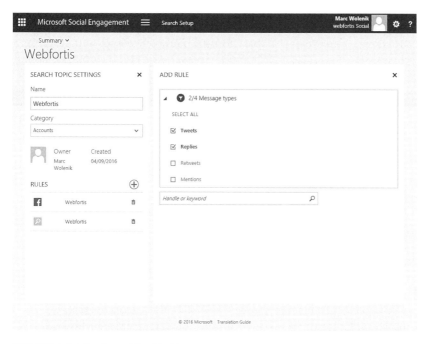

FIGURE 14.14   Searching Twitter.

Select one of the results and click Continue to see the Quota Check page. After a successful quota check, make sure to save the search topic.

Custom Sources Rules

Custom sources rules allow you to select any other rule that is not by default available in the system. Figure 14.15 shows the configuration page for a custom sources rule.

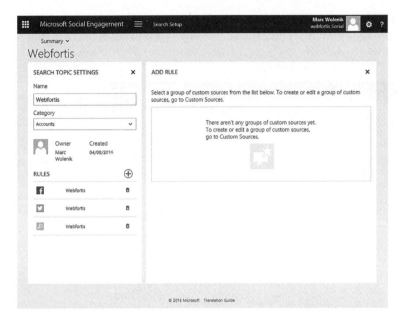

FIGURE 14.15   Creating a custom sources rule.

The first time you go to this page, there are no custom rules available. You need to click the Custom Sources link to create a custom source. Then click the + icon to create a new custom source, as shown in Figure 14.16. As an example, you can create a custom sources rule for the MSDN forums.

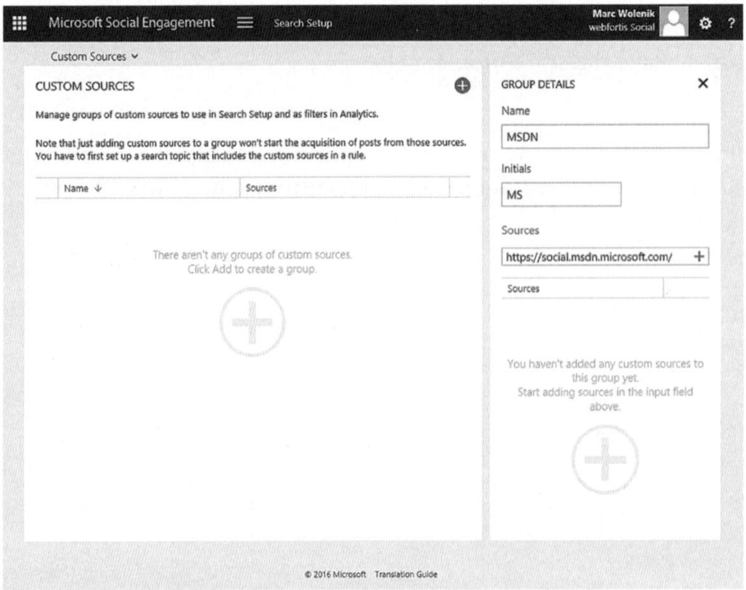

FIGURE 14.16   New custom sources rule.

Enter MSDN in the Name field (refer to Figure 14.16). In the URL field, enter the URL for the MSDN forum at the Dynamics CRM forums, which is https://social.msdn.microsoft .com/Forums/en-S/crm/threads?outputAs=rss. Then click the + icon. Next to the Group Details title, click Save.

Now you can go back to the search setup and add a custom sources rule (see Figure 14.17). Select the custom MSDN source you created and then click Continue. Be sure to save the search topic after the quota check is successful by clicking save.

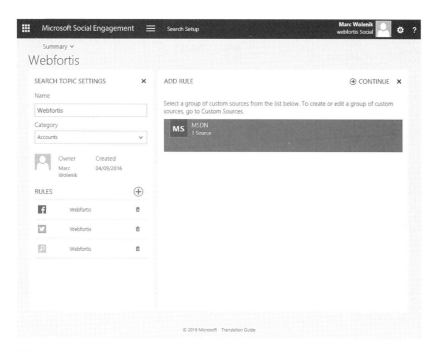

FIGURE 14.17   New custom sources rule.

Private Messages Rules

To configure private messages rules, you must also configure a Twitter or Facebook account because you need a valid Twitter or Facebook user to get private messages from these social media channels.

To create a social profile, go to Settings > Social Profiles. Click the + button to add a new profile, as shown in Figure 14.18.

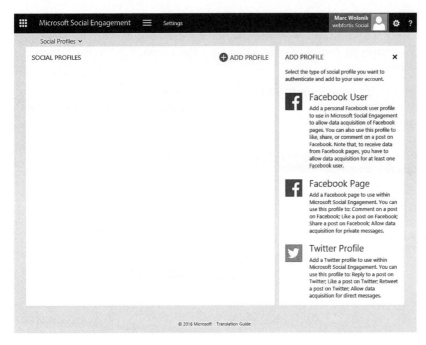

FIGURE 14.18   Adding a new social profile.

Select whether you want to create a Facebook user, Facebook page, or Twitter profile.

NOTE

A private message rule, while sent privately within the social channel, will become available to all the Social Engagement users in the organization.

Provide your Twitter username and password and click the Authorize App button. Then activate the acquisition of private messages (see Figure 14.19).

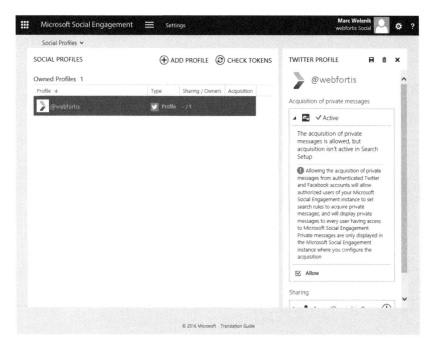

FIGURE 14.19   Twitter Acquisition of Private Massages page.

Now you can go back to the Search Setup page and create a new rule for private messages. Click Continue and complete the configuration. Be sure to save the rule after the quota check.

Customizations

You can connect other external custom applications with Microsoft Social engagement to use the API endpoint. In doing so, you must add your custom solution domain to the list of allowed domains. To do that, go to Settings > Connection > Allowed Domains, as shown in Figure 14.20.

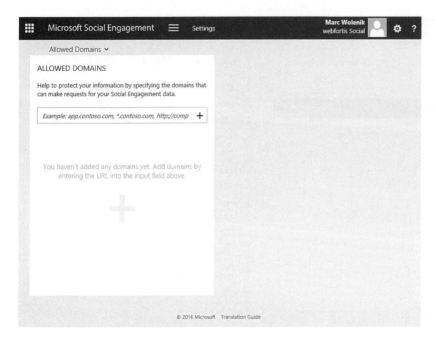

FIGURE 14.20   Allowed domains.

Enter the URL of your application that will connect to Microsoft Social Engagement and then click the + button. You can then use the solution URL from your custom application to include it within the Social Engagement platform.

> **TIP**
>
> At publication time, there is no Social Engagement software development kit (SDK) or application programming interface (API) reference document available.

Connections

The Connections page allows you to connect your Social Engagement solution with Dynamics CRM so you can create CRM records from Social Engagement. This is necessary to create and configure the automation rules you will see in the next section.

To configure the connections, navigate to Settings > Connections and click the + icon to add a new connection.

When you see the Add Connection disclaimer note, click OK.

Select the connection type, which can be CRM Online or CRM On-Premises (with Internet-Facing Deployment).

Enter the URL of your Dynamics CRM organization as well as a name, as shown in Figure 14.21.

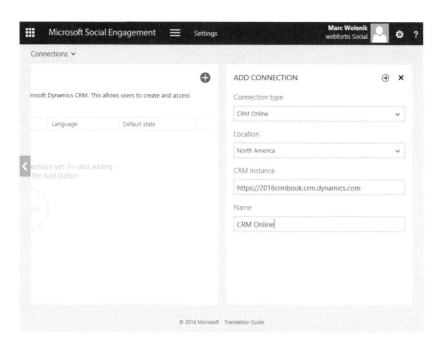

FIGURE 14.21   Adding a connection.

Click right-pointing arrow icon. You might be prompted to log in on your CRM organization if you were not logged in before.

> **NOTE**
>
> Make sure your browser doesn't have the pop-up blocker enabled when you are trying to add a new connection.

When the Authentication Required warning appears in a yellow bar at the top of the page, click on the Sign In button. Upon a successful connection, you see the page shown on Figure 14.22. On this page you can enabled, disable, or configure this as the default instance. Click the Save button to continue.

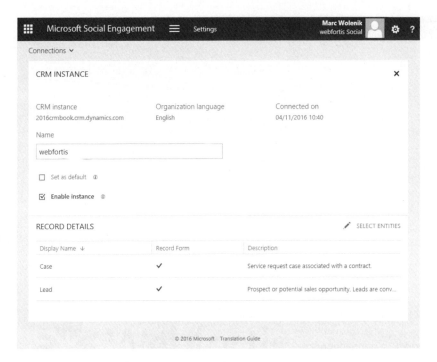

FIGURE 14.22   Configuring the connection.

By default, only the lead and case entities are selected, but you can click Select Entities to select other entities if you want. After you select an entity, click the X in the top-right corner to close the selection window and then select the entity you just added.

Click Add More to add the entity and then click the X in the top-right corner and then Save to complete the configuration.

Automation Rules

You can use automation rules to automate a process for identifying post messages, such as those that create contacts, accounts, cases, or leads.

To configure automation rules, you must go to Settings > Automation Rules. By default, the system doesn't come with any automation rules created. To create a new automation rule, click the + icon. The window shown in Figure 14.23 appears.

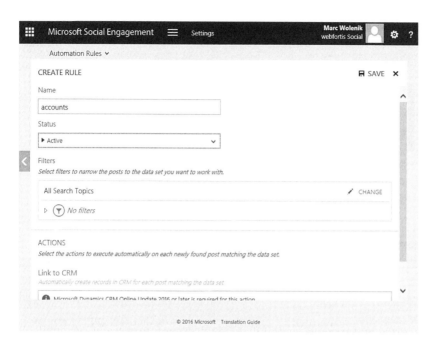

FIGURE 14.23   Creating a new automation rule.

You must have a CRM connection created (as explained earlier in this chapter, in the section "Connections") in order to be able to create an automation rule.

Enter a name for your rule and then select the search topic you want to filter.

The automation rules work only with Microsoft Dynamics CRM Online 2016 or later.

Scroll down so you can see the Link to CRM options (see Figure 14.24) and select the instance of your CRM online and the entity (for example, Account).

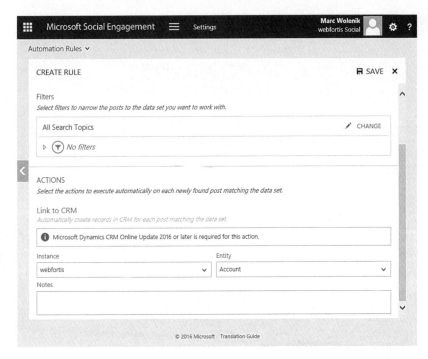

FIGURE 14.24   Link to CRM options.

Click Save. After the automation rule is created, you can click View in Analytics to use the rule.

Analytics

The Analytics area helps you analyze the search topics you created previously in the configuration. This means users can perform analysis to determine how to react to feedback. They might, for example, react by changing a marketing campaign (if the response is negative) or increasing spending or coverage of a campaign (if it is favorable). The information gathered might also help the organization learn early on about something important that the public is talking about.

The first time you click Analytics, you see an empty dashboard. In order to see data, you might need to change the time frame or configure search topics, as described earlier in this chapter. These are the time frame options you can select:

▶ Today

▶ Last Week

▶ Last Month

▶ Custom Time Frame

If you select Custom Time Frame, you see a calendar control you can use to choose dates, as shown in Figure 14.25.

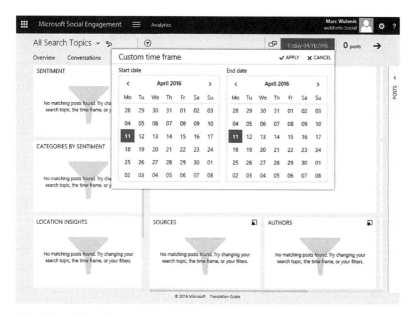

FIGURE 14.25   Setting a custom time frame.

As shown in Figure 14.26, selecting a previous month gives you data that can be analyzed.

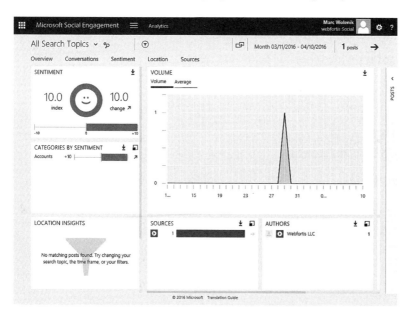

FIGURE 14.26   Dashboard for the previous month.

You can select filters to get a more discrete result set. In addition, you can change the search topic, as shown in Figure 14.27.

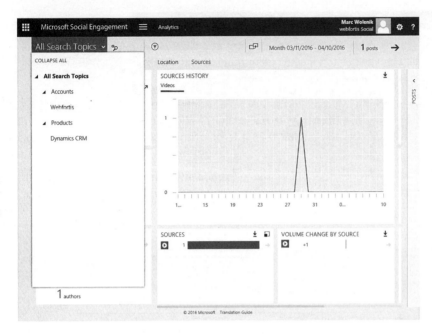

FIGURE 14.27   Selecting a search topic.

With most of the dashboard components, you can export the data to Excel by clicking the down-arrow icon in the top-right corner of the component.

The analytics dashboard is divided into the following tabs:

▶ Overview

▶ Conversations (see Figure 14.28)

▶ Sentiment (see Figure 14.29)

▶ Location (see Figure 14.30)

▶ Sources (see Figure 14.31)

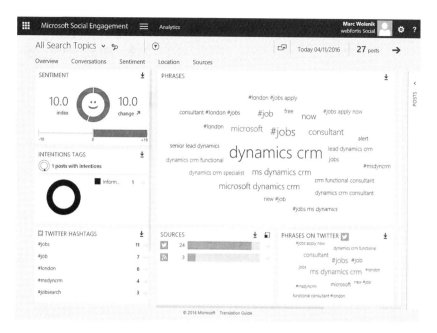

FIGURE 14.28   Conversations tab.

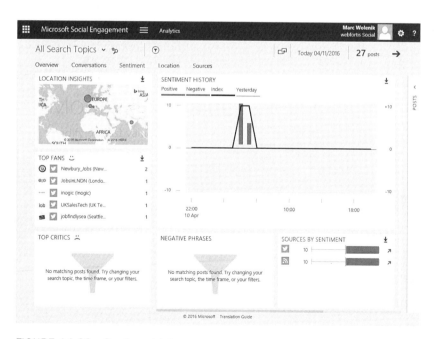

FIGURE 14.29   Sentiment tab.

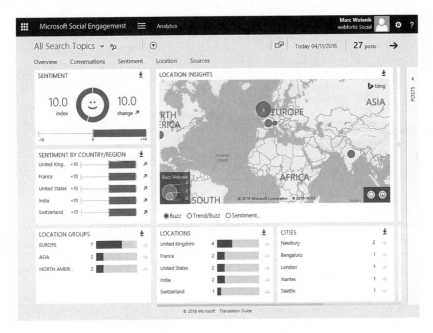

FIGURE 14.30   Location tab.

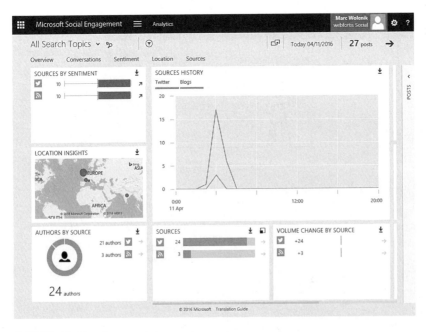

FIGURE 14.31   Sources tab.

All these dashboards allow you to refine and drill down on the data, providing a rich interface from which to mine social data. In addition, on each tab there is a Posts panel on the right that you can open to see the individual posts.

Social Center

The Social Center section allows you to configure streams so you can see information in different ways than you can see it using the analytics previously shown.

The first time you access the Social Center section, no streams are created. To add one, you click the Add Stream button. The window shown in Figure 14.32 appears.

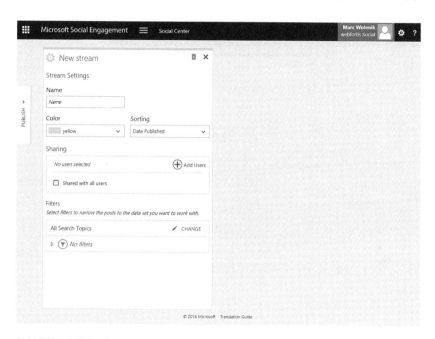

FIGURE 14.32   Creating a new stream.

Enter a name for the stream and select a color, which can be any of the following:

▶ Blue

▶ Cyan

▶ Green

▶ Lime

▶ Magenta

▶ Orange

▶ Purple

▶ Red

▶ Teal

▶ Yellow

You can select all the search topics or select a particular one or ones. Also, you can apply filters.

You can change the sentiment presented by clicking the sentiment icon (which looks like a face). You then have the option to select the value to positive, neutral, or negative for the selected post. When you manually change the sentiment this way, the sentiment icon for the messages appears with a star icon in it, as shown at the top of Figure 14.33.

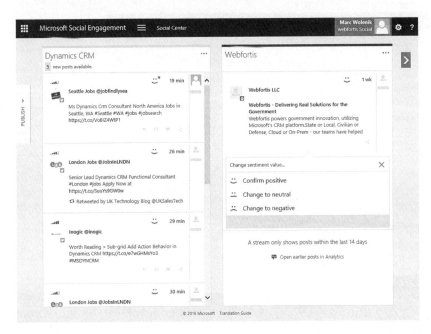

FIGURE 14.33   Manually changed sentiment value.

Clicking the user icon on the right of the post allows you to assign the message to a user so another user can take care of replying or setting the sentiment value.

Clicking the line bellow the user icon allows you to set a label for the message.

NOTE

Labels are explained earlier in this chapter, in the "Labels" section.

Publish Pane

On the left side of the Social Center page, you can see the Publish pane collapsed. You can select it to expand it, and depending on the social profiles configured in the Settings area, you may get the option to select a post type.

Select the post type, and you can compose a post message to either Twitter or Facebook from here. Click Send to post the message to the social type selected.

Activity Maps

The Activity Maps section shows posts geographically and allows you to view them graphically on a map. To create an activity map, navigate to the Activity Maps section and click the + icon.

You can create two main activity map types:

▶ **Buzz map**—A map that displays post volume

▶ **Sentiment map**—A map that displays sentiment values based on location

These are the default time span options you can select:

▶ Past 30 Minutes

▶ Past Hour

▶ Past 12 Hours

▶ Past 24 Hours

After you choose the options you want and click Save, you see an Open button that you can click to see the activity map. Figure 14.34 shows an example of an activity map.

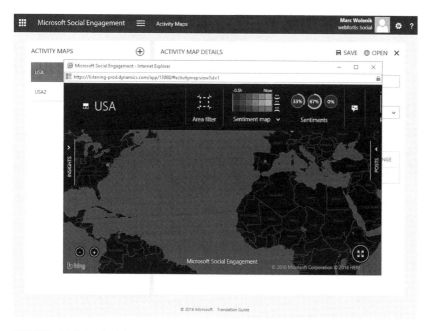

FIGURE 14.34   Activity map.

You can use the Area Filter control to filter by area or by country (see Figure 14.35).

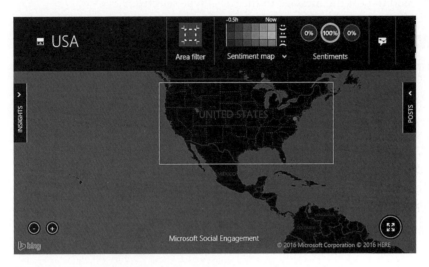

FIGURE 14.35   Filtering by area.

You can expand the Insights pane on the left and/or the Posts pane on the right to see more detailed information about the phrases and post messages analyzed (see Figure 14.36).

FIGURE 14.36   Posts and insights.

Message Center

The Message Center section shows you and your users alerts.

To create a new alert click the + button. You can create two main types of alerts:

▶ **Post alert**—With a post alert, you get an alert when a post message matches the filters you specify. You also have the option to send an email to the recipient email addresses you configure for each alert, as shown in Figure 14.37.

▶ **Trend alert**—You can use a trend alert to send an alert when the volume of the post messages exceeds the statistical number expected (see Figure 14.38).

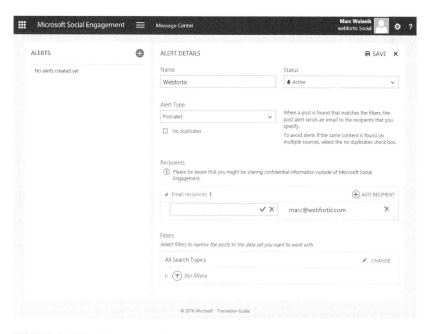

FIGURE 14.37   New post alert.

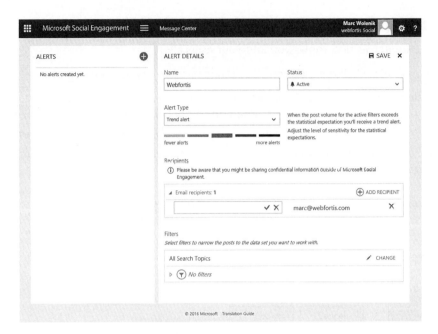

FIGURE 14.38   New trend alert.

Post and trend alerts are extremely important when you're configuring brand awareness. A good example of when to use a trend alert is to monitor one (or more) of your brands; if the volume (or trend) exceeds normal volume, this might be an indicator that something is up. In the event of a new product release, that can be a good thing. You can measure the reception of the product by comparing the trend data gathered with this release to data gathered for previous releases.

Connecting with Dynamics CRM

To connect Microsoft Dynamics Social Engagement with Dynamics CRM, in the Dynamics CRM web interface, select Settings > Administration and click Microsoft Social Engagement Configuration. You then see the Microsoft Social Engagement Disclaimer page. Click the Continue button on this page and then select the Microsoft Social Engagement Solution, as shown in Figure 14.39, and click Select.

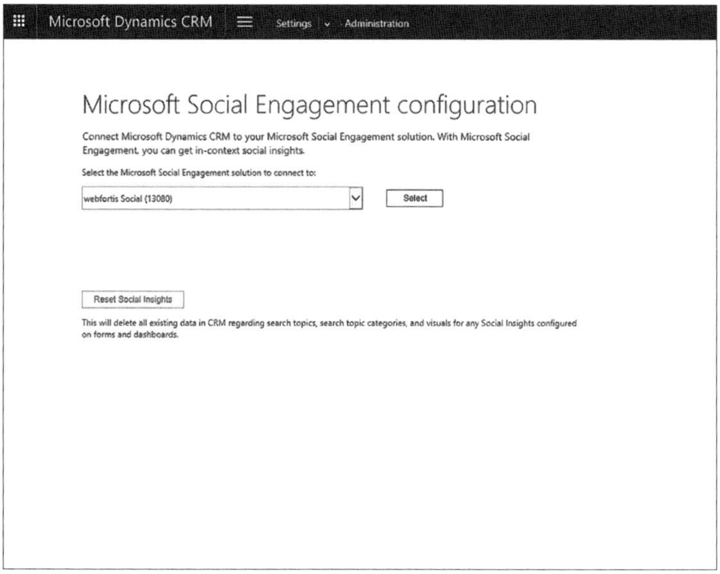

FIGURE 14.39   Microsoft Social Engagement Configuration page.

If you have previously configured social engagement, you can optionally reset the data. Click Confirm, and you see a message asking you to confirm removal of previous data. Click Confirm.

After you establish the connection between Dynamics CRM and Dynamics Social Engagement, you can enable or disable this connection by going to Settings > Administration > System Settings. You can find the option to disable social engagement on the General tab (see Figure 14.40).

FIGURE 14.40   Disable Social Engagement option.

After the connection is completed, you can configuration the integration. The following sections explain in detail how to do this.

Social Insights Controls for CRM Entity Forms

Once Social Engagement is successfully connected with Dynamics CRM, you can add the Social component to any entity form. This section shows an example of adding it to the Account entity.

Navigate to Settings > Customizations > Customize the System. Then select > Entities > Account and Forms > Main.

Open the account main form and move to the Insert tab, where you can see the Social Insights button (see Figure 14.41).

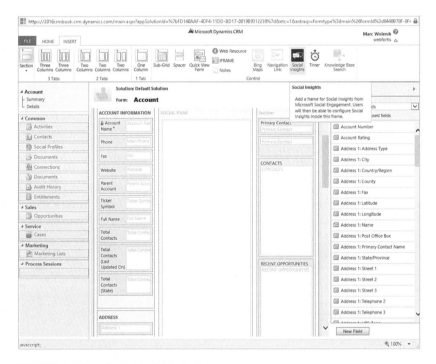

FIGURE 14.41   Social Insights button.

Click the Social Insights button and enter the label text that you want to be displayed (see Figure 14.42).

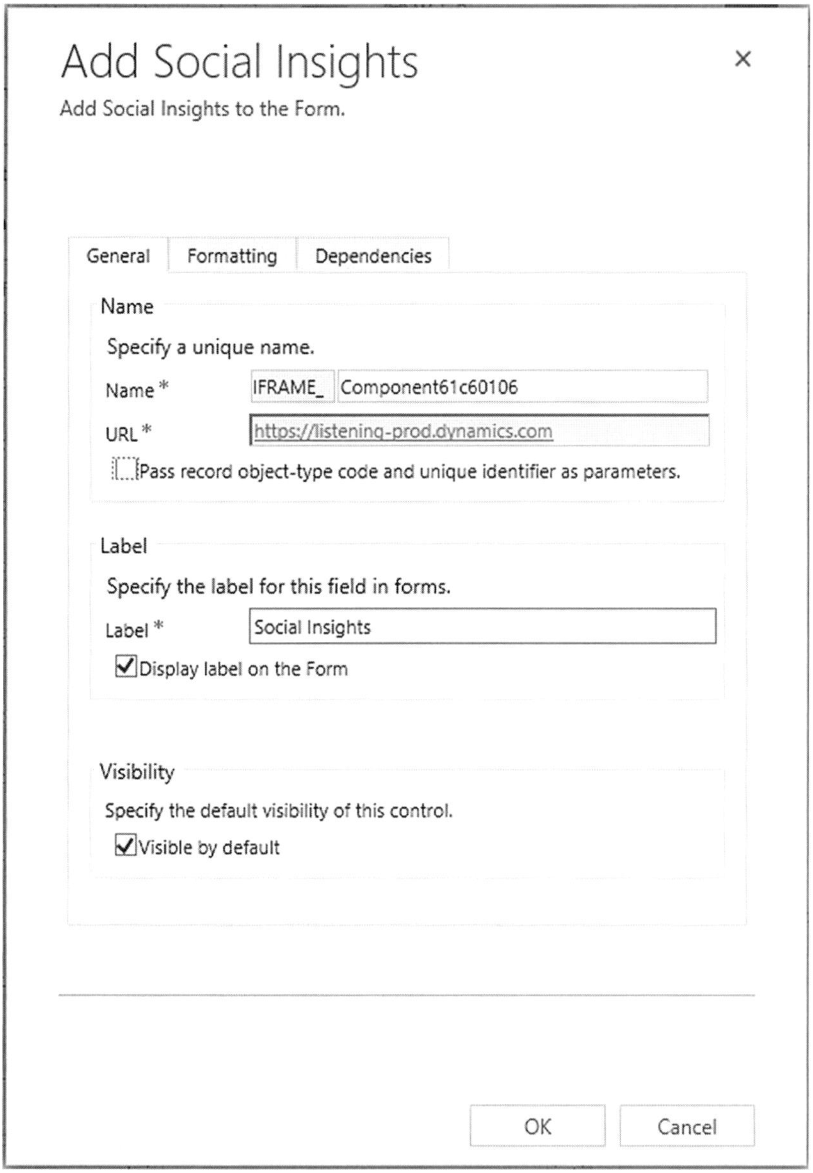

Add Social Insights ✕

Add Social Insights to the Form.

General | Formatting | Dependencies

Name

Specify a unique name.

Name *   IFRAME_ | Component61c60106

URL *   https://listening-prod.dynamics.com

☐ Pass record object-type code and unique identifier as parameters.

Label

Specify the label for this field in forms.

Label *   Social Insights

☑ Display label on the Form

Visibility

Specify the default visibility of this control.

☑ Visible by default

OK | Cancel

FIGURE 14.42   Add Social Insights page.

Click OK to add the Social Insights control and then move to the Home tab and click Save and then click Publish.

Now if you go to any existing account record, you see the Configure Social Insights link. In Figure 14.43, this link appears in the lower-left part of the screen.

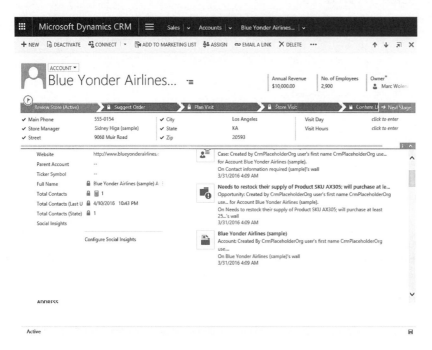

FIGURE 14.43   Configure Social Insights link.

Clicking the Configure Social Insights link starts the setup wizard. On the first screen of the wizard, you can select whether to search a topic or a topic category. For this example, click Search Topic and click Next. A connection with the Social Engagement solution start, and you see the wait screen. After a few seconds you are presented with two options (see Figure 14.44):

▶ Pick a Search Topic (if you already created search topics)

▶ Create a New Search Topic

FIGURE 14.44   Picking a search topic.

If you select Create a New Search Topic, you next see the screen shown in Figure 14.45.

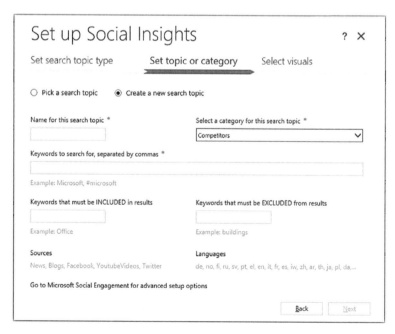

FIGURE 14.45   Creating a new search topic.

For this example, choose a search topic you have already created and click Next. You can now select the Visuals associated with the topic (see Figure 14.46).

FIGURE 14.46   Selecting visuals.

You can select from 16 different visuals:

▶ Analytics Summary

▶ Buzz

▶ Languages

▶ Languages Share of Voice

▶ Locations

▶ Most Active Authors

▶ Recent Posts

▶ Sentiment History

▶ Sentiment Share of Voice

▶ Sentiment Summary by Sources

▶ Sentiment Volume

▶ Source History

▶ Sources Share by Voice

▶ Sources Summary

▶ Trend

▶ Volume History

You can add more than one visual here (see Figure 14.47). When you are done selecting the visuals, click the Finish button.

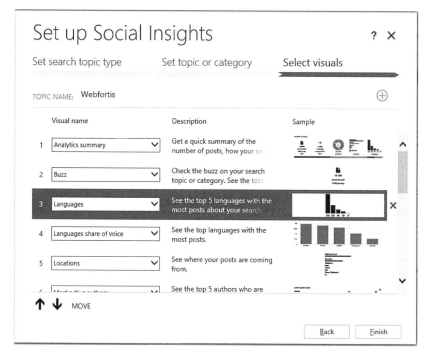

FIGURE 14.47   Selecting multiple visuals selected.

Figure 14.48 shows the Social visual displayed on the form. If you hover your mouse over this control, you see three small icons in the top-right corner.

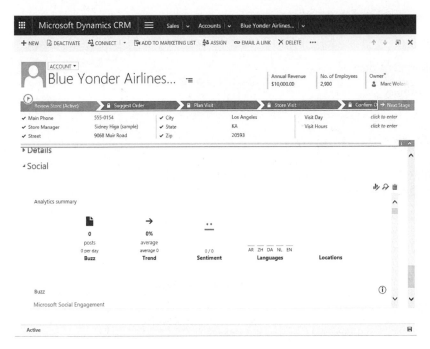

FIGURE 14.48   Analytics Summary view of an account record.

The first icon, which looks like a pencil on top of a bar graph, allows you to change the visuals. The second icon, which shows a pencil over a magnifying glass, start the setup wizard again, allowing you to change the search topic or create a new search topic. The last icon, the trash can, removes the Social Insights control from the form. If you click the trash can icon, you need to confirm the removal, as shown in Figure 14.49.

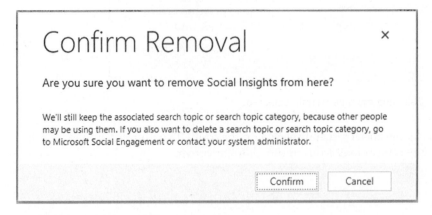

FIGURE 14.49   Removal confirmation dialog.

If you click the Confirm button, the configurations are removed from the entity record.

▶ To learn more about entity form customization, refer to Chapter 22, "Customizing Entities."

Social Insights Controls for a CRM Dashboards

In the previous section, you added a Social Insights control to an entity form, but you can also add one or many of these controls to any system or personal CRM dashboard. When you create or edit a dashboard, you see a Social Insights button on the command bar (see Figure 14.50).

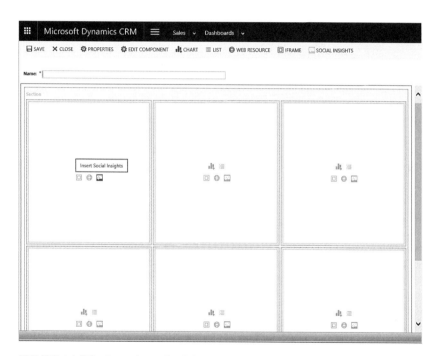

FIGURE 14.50   Inserting a Social Insights control on a dashboard.

Clicking this button starts the same setup wizard you use to add a Social Insights control to an entity form.

Complete the wizard by selecting or creating a new search topic and adding the visuals you want to be displayed. Then save and close the Dashboard Designer. Figure 14.51 shows an example of a new dashboard.

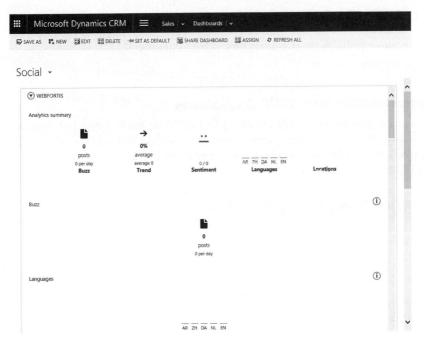

FIGURE 14.51   Social Insights dashboard.

Summary

This chapter looks at the Microsoft Dynamics Social Engagement solution that Microsoft offers through Office 365 subscriptions. It reviews the configuration of the search topics and global settings, and it looks at the Analytics, Social Center, Activity Maps, and Message Center areas. Finally, this chapter shows how to add Social Insights visuals in Dynamics CRM entity forms and dashboards and how you can connect Microsoft Dynamics Social Engagement with Microsoft Dynamics CRM.

Microsoft acquired Yammer in 2012 and initially integrated it with Dynamics CRM 2013. Since then Yammer has continued to grow, with broader functionality and many enhancements. With the release of Microsoft Dynamics CRM 2016, integrated Yammer represents a significant and powerful tool for collaboration.

Often described as *enterprise social software*, Yammer has controlled access (via email address) to certain networks, and it allows individuals within an organization to communicate privately. Yammer offers its collaborative interface with both Dynamics CRM 2016 and SharePoint.

It is important to realize that because Yammer is a dedicated social communication platform, and because this book focuses on Dynamics CRM 2016, this discussion covers only the core functionality of Yammer as it relates to Dynamics CRM 2016, not Yammer's full functionality and range of options.

> **NOTE**
>
> Full coverage of the Yammer product is beyond the scope of this book. In fact, each component and its integrated usage with Microsoft Dynamics CRM 2016 could fill an entire book on its own. This chapter provides a high-level overview of Yammer.

Yammer Basics

Microsoft acquired Yammer about a year before the launch of Microsoft Dynamics CRM 2013. Yammer is a dedicated (that is, separate) service that many people compare to Facebook because of to the way it allows "conversations" between users in the same organization.

Despite it being a standalone produce (see www.yammer.com), you can acquire/purchase Yammer through an Office 365 subscription.

Users log in to their Yammer accounts at Yammer.com. Yammer has a dedicated desktop and mobile client set that includes Android, iPhone, iPad, BlackBerry, and Windows Phone. Figure 15.1 shows the Yammer home page.

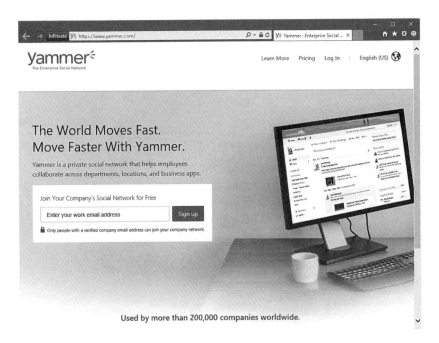

FIGURE 15.1   Yammer.com.

Once logged in, users have access to their network (see Figure 15.2). They can then interact with their groups, networks, and feeds by creating, commenting, or taking other actions in relation to posts.

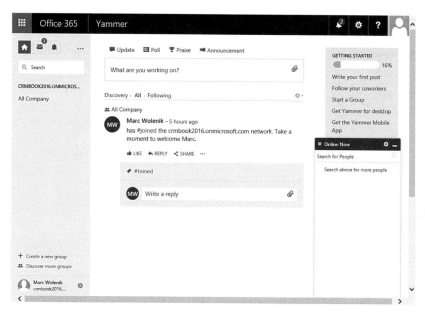

FIGURE 15.2   Logged in to Yammer.

With Yammer integrated with Dynamics CRM 2016, users will likely spend a significant amount of time on Yammer.com because the feeds display directly there and then are also displayed in Dynamics CRM 2016.

In addition to the web version shown, users have the option of running a desktop app, which is available for download from the Yammer site and can also be obtained by clicking the Get Yammer for Desktop link inside the yellow box shown in Figure 15.2. The desktop app creates real-time notifications that are displayed to users while they're working at their computer, so users don't have to remember to log back in and check or read emails. Typical notifications are for new posts being created from a conversations you are following and for a new post being created.

The installation for the desktop version uses ClickOnce technology to ensure that the latest version of the app is installed and updated, as shown in Figure 15.3.

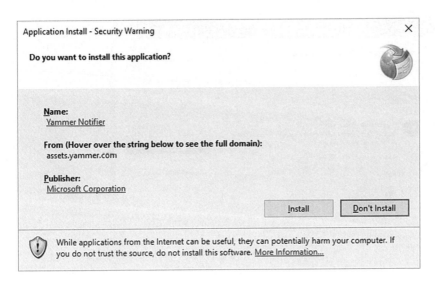

FIGURE 15.3   Yammer App installation with ClickOnce technology.

Once Yammer is installed, a new icon appears your service tray, and you can click it to see a notification window related to your feeds (see Figure 15.4). Selecting one of the options from the icon takes you directly to your page at the Yammer site.

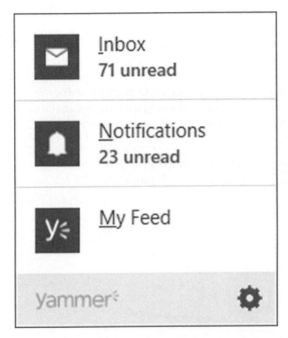

FIGURE 15.4   Yammer app notification window.

Yammer, like many other Microsoft products, is an extensible platform that allows you to extend its capabilities by either creating custom applications or consuming Yammer data from other custom applications.

Yammer provides a RESTful API endpoint that allows you to query Yammer data such as users, groups, or messages. By using a standard protocol like REST, you can also authenticate with Yammer from an external application by using OAuth 2.0, the standard and popular authentication protocol that is used by applications such as Facebook and Twitter.

The software development kit (SDK) for Yammer is available for JavaScript, Ruby, Python, iOS, .NET, and Windows Phone 8.

NOTE

There is another API available specifically for the export of data (such as messages), called Yammer Data Export API, that allows users to export Yammer data. To use this API, navigate to the Office 365 administrative portal and select Yammer > Admin Settings. Then select Content and Security > Export Data.

To learn more about the Yammer API, go to https://developer.yammer.com.

Yammer and Dynamics CRM 2016

When Microsoft Dynamics CRM 2016 is integrated with Yammer, data feeds are available to users of Yammer either natively in Yammer.com or via Dynamics CRM 2016 directly. If you plan to use Yammer with Microsoft Dynamics CRM 2016, keep the following in mind:

▶ The free edition of Yammer does not work with Dynamics CRM 2016.

▶ Activity feeds and Yammer are incompatible. Once you install Yammer, activity feeds (and their data) are available only programmatically.

▶ User conversations are stored in Yammer, not in Microsoft Dynamics CRM.

▶ System posts are stored in Microsoft Dynamics CRM.

▶ Because Yammer information lives in the Yammer system, the Microsoft Dynamics CRM security model does not exist for Yammer information on Yammer.com. In addition, depending on what you're trying to do, searching and reporting on Yammer data can be challenging.

If you are uncertain about installing Yammer (or if you want to test its functionality), Microsoft suggests that you create a test organization (that is, a free 30-day trial of Dynamics CRM Online) and preview the functionality. Table 15.1 shows the default configuration when you initially install Yammer.

TABLE 15.1   Yammer Default Configuration

Entity	Name	Enabled to Post Automatically
Case	New Case for an Account	Yes
Case	New Case for a Contact	Yes
Case	Case Closed for an Account	
Case	Case Closed for a Contact	
Case	Case Assigned to User/Team	
Case	Case Routed to Queue	
Lead	New Lead Created	
Lead	A Lead Has Been Qualified	
Case	Case Merged	
Case	Case Reactivated for an Account	
Case	Parent Associated for a Case	
Opportunity	New Opportunity for an Account	Yes
Opportunity	New Opportunity for a Contact	Yes
Opportunity	Probability for an Opportunity Updated for an Account	
Opportunity	Probability for an Opportunity Updated for a Contact	
Opportunity	Opportunity Won for an Account	Yes
Opportunity	Opportunity Won for a Contact	Yes
Opportunity	Opportunity Lost for an Account	
Opportunity	Opportunity Lost for a Contact	
Opportunity	New Competitor for an Opportunity for an Account	
Opportunity	New Competitor for an Opportunity for a Contact	
Account	New Account Created	Yes
Contact	New Contact Created	
Competitor	New Competitor Created	Yes

Integrating Yammer with Dynamics CRM

While you can integrate Yammer with either Dynamics CRM Online or Dynamics CRM On-Premises, it is recommend that you have an Internet Facing Deployment (IFD) deployment configured. If you're not using HTTPS and/or IFD, you need to run the following PowerShell commands in the CRM server before you enable the integration:

```
Add-PSSnapin Microsoft.Crm.PowerShell

$itemSetting = new-object 'System.Collections.Generic.KeyValuePair[String,Object]'
("AllowCredentialsEntryViaInsecureChannels",1)
$configEntity = New-Object "Microsoft.Xrm.Sdk.Deployment.ConfigurationEntity"
$configEntity.LogicalName="Deployment"
$configEntity.Attributes = New-Object "Microsoft.Xrm.Sdk.Deployment.
AttributeCollection"
$configEntity.Attributes.Add($itemSetting)
Set-CrmAdvancedSetting -Entity $configEntity
```

▶ For more information about IFD, **SEE CHAPTER 28**, "Forms Authentication."

To integrate Yammer with Dynamics CRM, follow these steps:

1. Navigate to Settings > Administration and select Yammer Configuration
(see Figure 15.5).

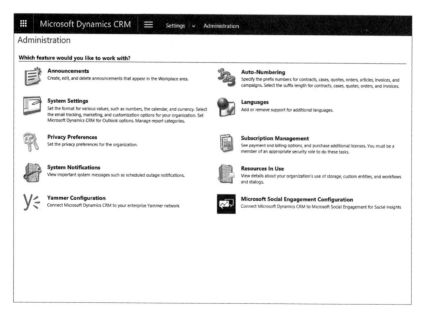

FIGURE 15.5   The Microsoft Dynamics CRM Administration interface.

2. When the Yammer disclaimer appears (see Figure 15.6), click Continue.

FIGURE 15.6   Yammer disclaimer.

3. When the Yammer configuration options appear, click Authorize Microsoft Dynamics CRM Online to Connect to Yammer (see Figure 15.7).

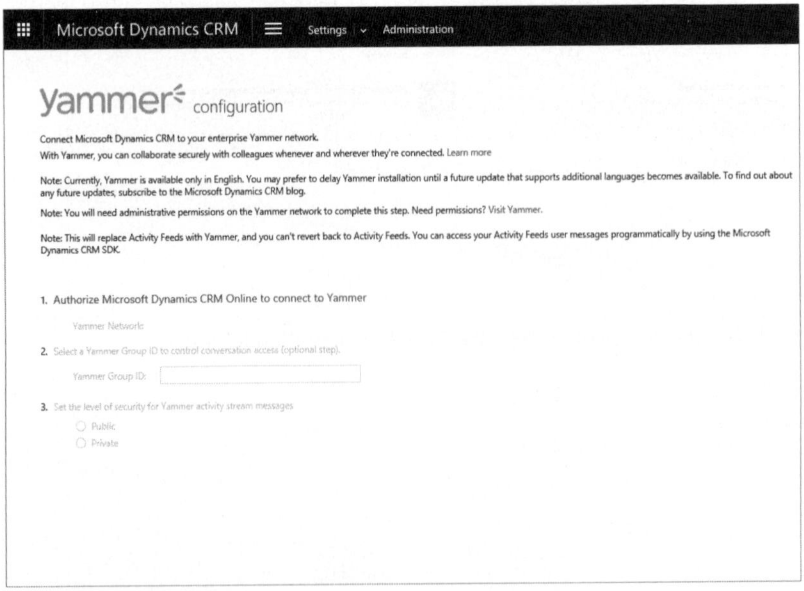

FIGURE 15.7   Connecting Dynamics CRM to Yammer.

4. When Yammer asks you to log in to its website, to make the connection between your instance of Dynamics CRM and Yammer (see Figure 15.8), complete the requested information and click Log In. Alternatively, if you are already logged in to Yammer, you see an authorization dialog you can use to allow the integration (see Figure 15.9).

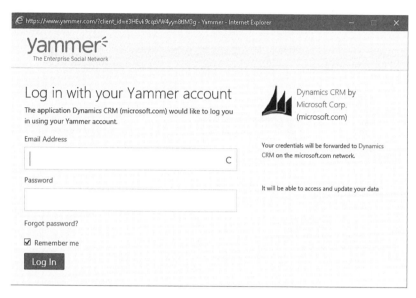

FIGURE 15.8   Logging in to Yammer.com.

NOTE

You must have administrative rights within Yammer to perform the integration.

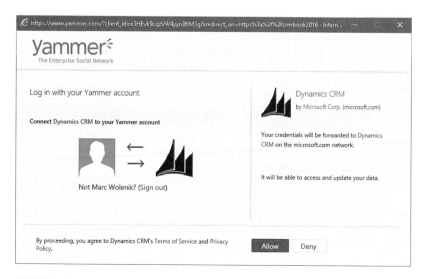

FIGURE 15.9   Authorizing Yammer.

5. Once the login or authorization is complete, in Dynamics CRM, set the group ID and select the security for messages (see Figure 15.10). By default, the security is set to Private, which means that users must select to follow a record to see posts about that record. If you change it to Public, all posts show up for everyone. For this example, leave it set to Private. The configuration is now complete, and Yammer is connected to Dynamics CRM.

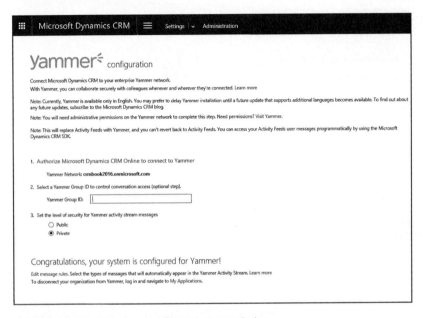

FIGURE 15.10   Yammer configuration completion.

You can also specify the default group that will be used by users when posting to Yammer because Yammer now allows you to select which users' or groups' posts you want to see created from CRM. If you leave this group configuration empty, all Yammer users will be able to see the posts, but it might be a good idea to specify the name of a group with a limited number of users in it, such as just the Sales Team or others who work with CRM.

> **NOTE**
>
> Notice that the Yammer connection page says Connect to Dynamics CRM Online, however in our test (and, in fact, for this example), we connected just fine to Microsoft Dynamics CRM On-Premises by using this method.

You must consider a few things when you upgrade Dynamics CRM after the Yammer integration is enabled. Yammer stores the Dynamics CRM URL to link the posts with the CRM records, so you need to make sure you use the same Dynamics CRM URL after upgrading the organization from one version to another if you want to keep seeing the previous posts in CRM.

Removing Yammer

To remove the Yammer integration from Microsoft Dynamics CRM 2016, follow these steps:

1. Navigate to Settings > Administration > Yammer Configuration. The same screen shown in Figure 15.10 appears. At the bottom of this screen, click My Applications. Yammer opens, and a list of devices connected/authorized to use the Yammer group appears.

2. To remove the access, select the Revoke Access link shown in Figure 15.11. Yammer displays a message that the access has been revoked (see Figure 15.12).

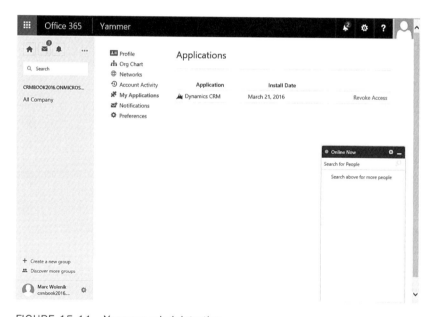

FIGURE 15.11   Yammer administration.

FIGURE 15.12   Yammer access revoked.

Optimizing Yammer Integration with Dynamics CRM 2016

Once you've established a connection between Yammer and Dynamics CRM, you can configure Yammer for entities. Figure 15.13 shows the default configurations and the various configuration options for each. To reach this page, choose Settings > Activity Feeds Rules and change the view to All Yammer Rules.

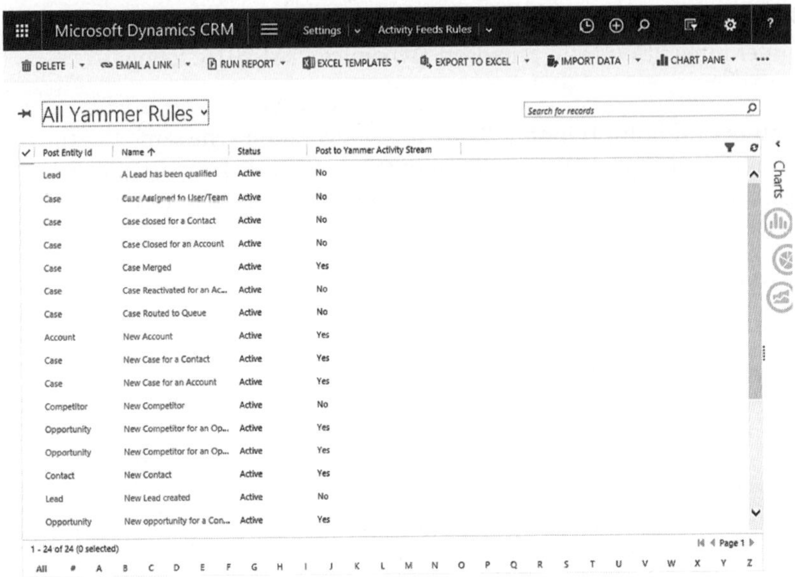

✓	Post Entity Id	Name ↑	Status	Post to Yammer Activity Stream
	Lead	A Lead has been qualified	Active	No
	Case	Case Assigned to User/Team	Active	No
	Case	Case closed for a Contact	Active	No
	Case	Case Closed for an Account	Active	No
	Case	Case Merged	Active	Yes
	Case	Case Reactivated for an Ac...	Active	No
	Case	Case Routed to Queue	Active	No
	Account	New Account	Active	Yes
	Case	New Case for a Contact	Active	Yes
	Case	New Case for an Account	Active	Yes
	Competitor	New Competitor	Active	No
	Opportunity	New Competitor for an Op...	Active	Yes
	Opportunity	New Competitor for an Op...	Active	Yes
	Contact	New Contact	Active	Yes
	Lead	New Lead created	Active	No
	Opportunity	New opportunity for a Con...	Active	Yes

FIGURE 15.13   Yammer configuration for entities.

If you want to enable another system entity that is not listed here, you must go to Settings > Activity Feeds Configurations, as shown in Figure 15.14.

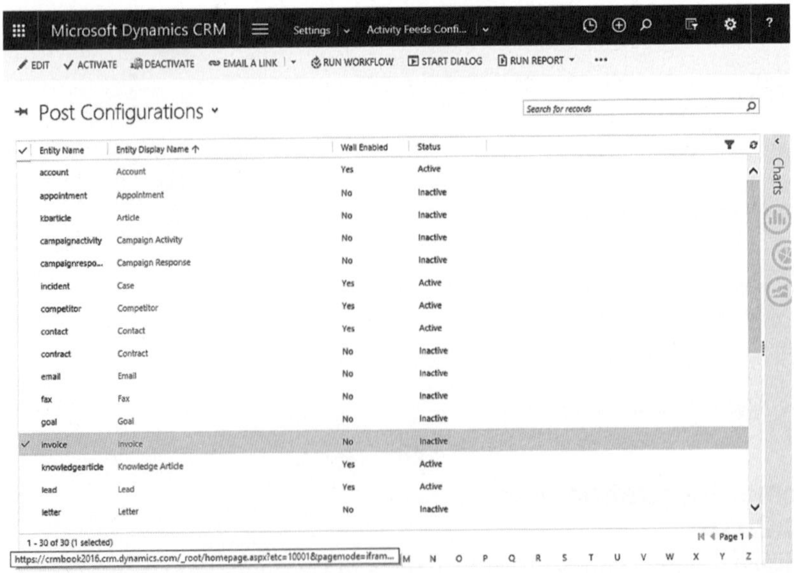

✓	Entity Name	Entity Display Name ↑	Wall Enabled	Status
	account	Account	Yes	Active
	appointment	Appointment	No	Inactive
	kbarticle	Article	No	Inactive
	campaignactivity	Campaign Activity	No	Inactive
	campaignrespo...	Campaign Response	No	Inactive
	incident	Case	Yes	Active
	competitor	Competitor	Yes	Active
	contact	Contact	Yes	Active
	contract	Contract	No	Inactive
	email	Email	No	Inactive
	fax	Fax	No	Inactive
	goal	Goal	No	Inactive
✓	invoice	Invoice	No	Inactive
	knowledgearticle	Knowledge Article	Yes	Active
	lead	Lead	Yes	Active
	letter	Letter	No	Inactive

FIGURE 15.14   Post Configurations page.

Select the entity you want to enable (for example, invoice) and click Activate. On the page that appears next (see Figure 15.15), make sure the Enable walls for this is checked.

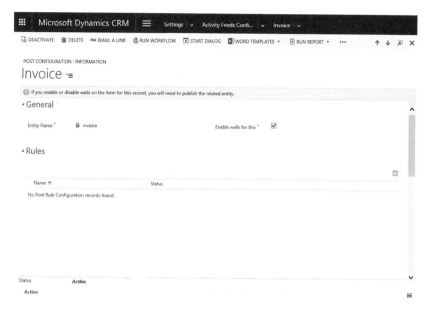

FIGURE 15.15   Post configuration for the Invoice entity.

Working with Yammer in Dynamics CRM 2016

Once you have connected, installed, and configured Yammer, you're ready to work with it in Dynamics CRM.

The following example shows collaboration (both in Dynamics CRM and externally) with another user on an opportunity:

1. Navigate to Opportunity and select an opportunity to open. Notice that the activity feed part of the screen is replaced with Yammer (see Figure 15.16).

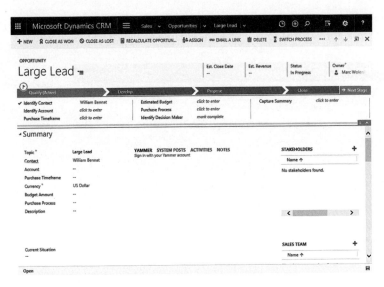

FIGURE 15.16   Opening an opportunity with Yammer.

2. Click the Sign In with Your Yammer Account link and, when prompted, enter
your Yammer credentials. If you have an email address in Microsoft Dynamics CRM
that differs from what you're using for Yammer, the error shown in Figure 15.17
appears. To correct this error, update your email address in either Yammer or
Microsoft Dynamics CRM so that they match.

NOTE

To avoid having to repeat step 2 next time you log in, check the Remember Me box.

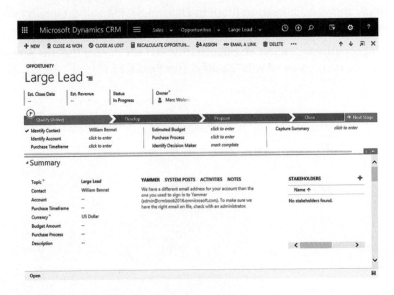

FIGURE 15.17   Yammer error.

3. When you see the warning shown in Figure 15.18 (because you've set the conversation option to Private, and you won't see any posts about this record unless you follow it), click the ... and select Follow (see Figure 15.19).

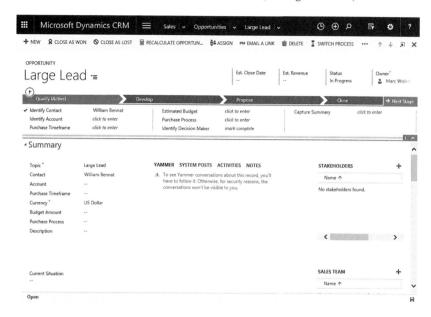

FIGURE 15.18   Yammer warning.

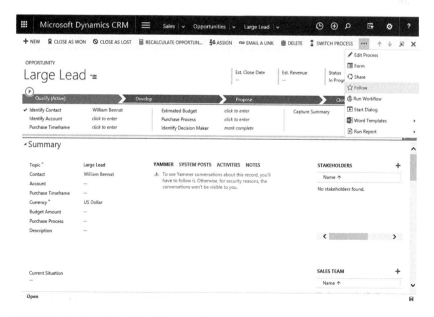

FIGURE 15.19   Following the record.

4. Now we can post in Yammer, so enter some information to create a post, as shown in Figure 15.20 and then select where you want to post it and click Post. The post shows up on the feed in the record.

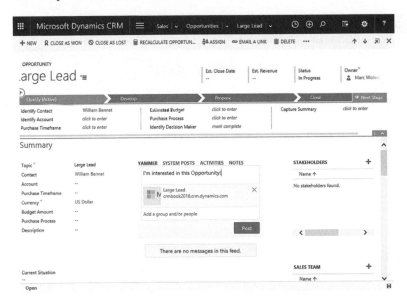

FIGURE 15.20   Posting to Yammer within Microsoft Dynamics CRM.

5. Go to Yammer.com, and you can see that the post is also available there, shown at the top of the feed (see Figure 15.21).

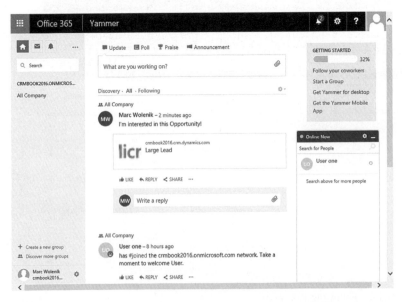

FIGURE 15.21   A post created in Dynamics CRM, shown in Yammer.com.

6. To see how you can also perform additional updates at Yammer.com that go back to Dynamics CRM, at Yammer.com add a new comment below the original comment, as shown in see Figure 15.22.

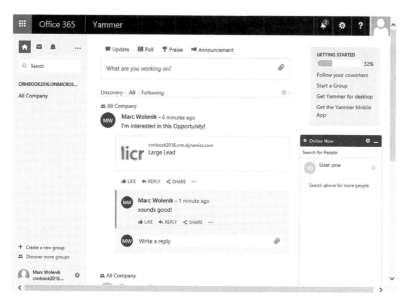

FIGURE 15.22   A new Yammer conversation.

7. Navigate back to Microsoft Dynamics CRM, and you can see the complete thread, with the external data added from Yammer.com on the record after the page is refreshed (see Figure 15.23).

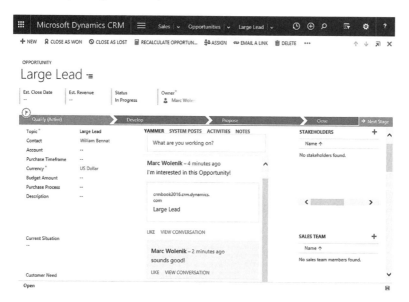

FIGURE 15.23   Yammer conversation thread in Microsoft Dynamics CRM 2016.

One of the enhancements of this new version of Dynamics CRM and Yammer integration is the ability to select the groups or people for which you want a post to be displayed.

You can select the groups or people before clicking the Post button inside a CRM record, as shown in Figure 15.24.

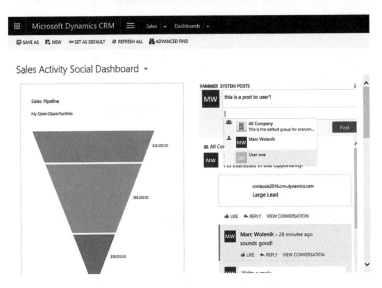

FIGURE 15.24   Posting to a specific user in Yammer.

Notice that the Post button changes to have a lock icon in it after you have selected the users or groups you want to see the post. This adds more security that was not available in the initial release of the Yammer and CRM integration (see Figure 15.25).

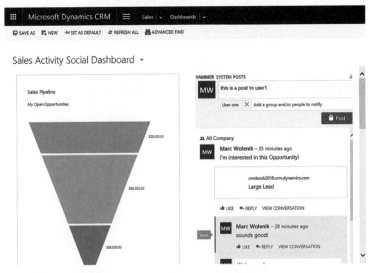

FIGURE 15.25   Post button containing a lock icon.

Yammer Features

Yammer comes with some cool features that you can use to improve collaboration with your team members; it doesn't limit you to just writing and/or posting messages. Here are some of the other features available in Yammer:

▶ Poll

▶ Praise

▶ Announcement

▶ Post Actions

▶ Chat

Common to all these features is the ability to add file attachments to the posts. You can add attachments from the Yammer interface if desired, and the attached files can then be downloaded from the Dynamics CRM interface, as shown in Figure 15.26.

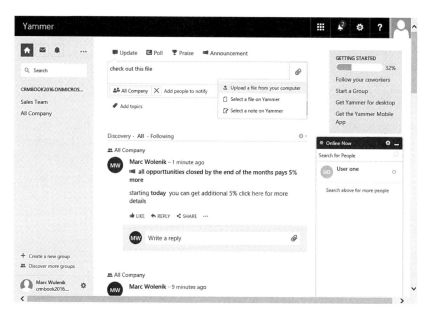

FIGURE 15.26   File Attachment.

You can add attachments from the following:

▶ Your local computer

▶ A file stored in Yammer

▶ A note in Yammer

Users can then download or see your file attachment by hovering the mouse on the file-name to see the download link (see Figure 15.27).

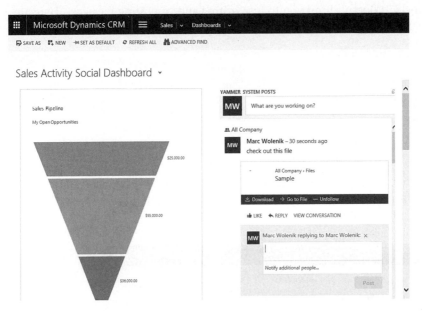

FIGURE 15.27   File attachment options in Dynamics CRM.

The Go to File link lets you see the file in a web browser. For example, if the file attached is a Microsoft Word document, you can see it with Word Online, which can be helpful if you are on a machine or device that doesn't have Microsoft Word installed.

Polls

Polls that are created in the Yammer user interface are open to participation of CRM users in the Dynamics CRM web application.

You can create a poll in Yammer by clicking the Poll link that is to the right of Update (the default option for writing a post message), as shown in Figure 15.28

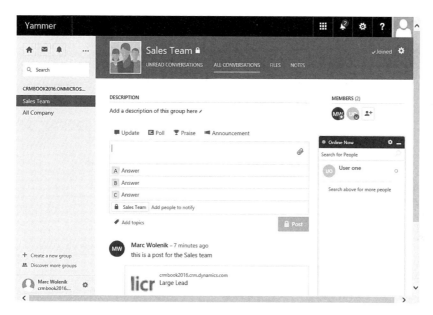

FIGURE 15.28   Creating a poll.

Even though you by default get three spaces for answers, another answer box appears as soon as you fill in what was previously the last answer box, as shown in Figure 15.29.

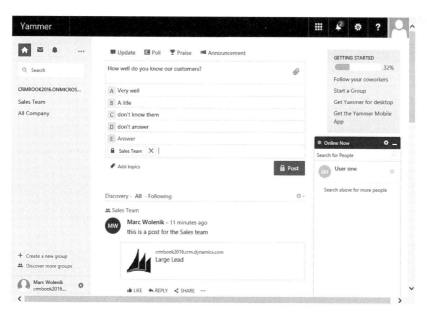

FIGURE 15.29   Creating a poll with more than three answers.

Users can then participate in the poll from Dynamics CRM (see Figure 15.30).

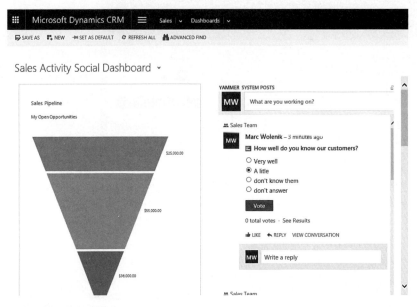

FIGURE 15.30   Voting in a Yammer poll.

After a user clicks the Vote button, poll results appear. It is also possible to check the results before voting by clicking the See Results link (see Figure 15.31).

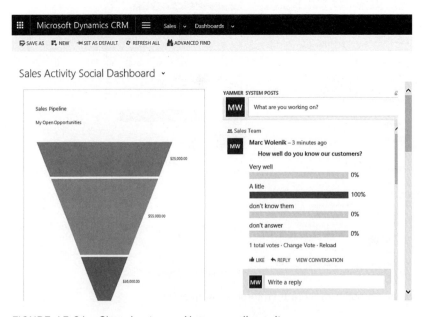

FIGURE 15.31   Choosing to see Yammer poll results.

Praise

You can create praises from the Yammer web interface by clicking the Praise button to the right of Poll (see Figure 15.32).

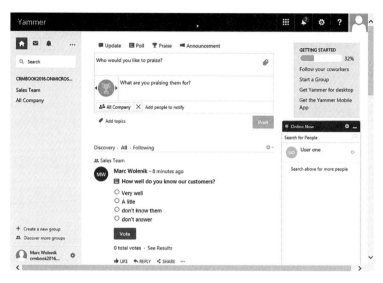

FIGURE 15.32   Yammer praise.

You can then choose the praise icon from a gallery of icons available with Yammer.

Praises are also visible from the Dynamics CRM interface in the Yammer section, as shown in Figure 15.33.

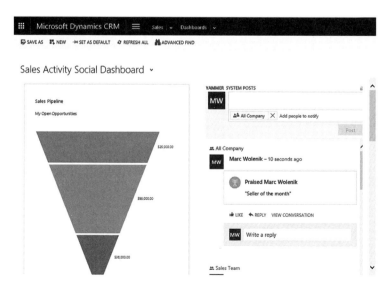

FIGURE 15.33   Yammer praise created at Yammer.com and shown in Dynamics CRM.

Announcements

When you create announcements in the Yammer user interface, they can be then seen by Dynamics CRM users. An announcement differs from a standard post in that you can use some rich text functionality in the announcement description. Figure 15.34 shows this functionality.

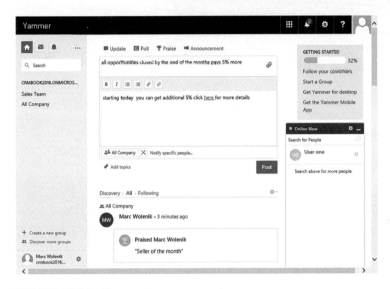

FIGURE 15.34   Yammer announcement.

After you create an announcement, CRM users can see it in Dynamics CRM but with a different icon on the left (see Figure 15.35).

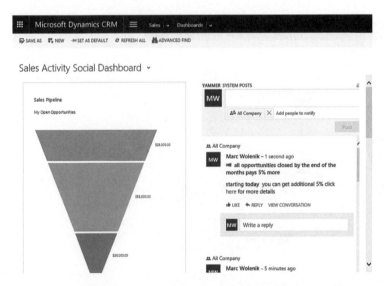

FIGURE 15.35   Yammer announcement created at Yammer.com and shown in Dynamics CRM.

Post Actions

Users can perform some actions on Yammer posts. The first three actions already described (polls, praise, and announcements) are available in both Yammer and Dynamics CRM, but the rest of the actions are available only via the Yammer web interface (see Figure 15.36):

▶ Like

▶ Reply

▶ Share

▶ Stop Following

▶ View Conversation

▶ Add Topics

▶ Bookmark

▶ Email Me

▶ Delete

▶ Hide Conversation

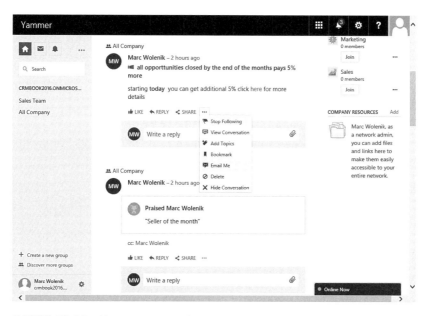

FIGURE 15.36   Yammer post actions.

Chat

Chat is a feature you can use only with the Yammer web interface; it is not available in the integration with Dynamics CRM. The chat feature is similar to the one in Facebook, and you can use it to send instant messages to other Yammer users (see Figure 15.37).

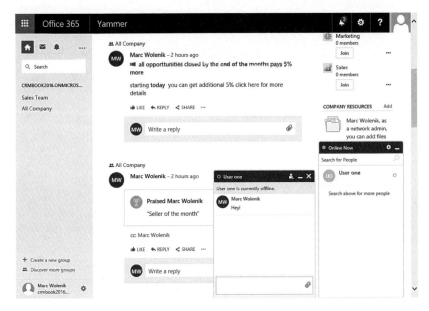

FIGURE 15.37 Yammer chat.

Yammer Settings

To access the Yammer settings, navigate to the gear icon that is located in the bottom-left corner of the screen, near your username, as shown in Figure 15.38. Navigating to Settings gives the available settings:

- ▶ Profile
- ▶ Org Chart
- ▶ Networks
- ▶ Account Activity
- ▶ My Applications
- ▶ Notifications
- ▶ Preferences

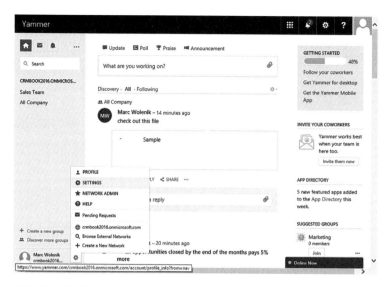

FIGURE 15.38   Yammer settings.

Profile

In the profile settings, you can configure your name and image, as well as other personal fields (see Figure 15.39). Notice that the image you configure here is independent of the one you configure in Dynamics CRM or the one in your Office 365 profile.

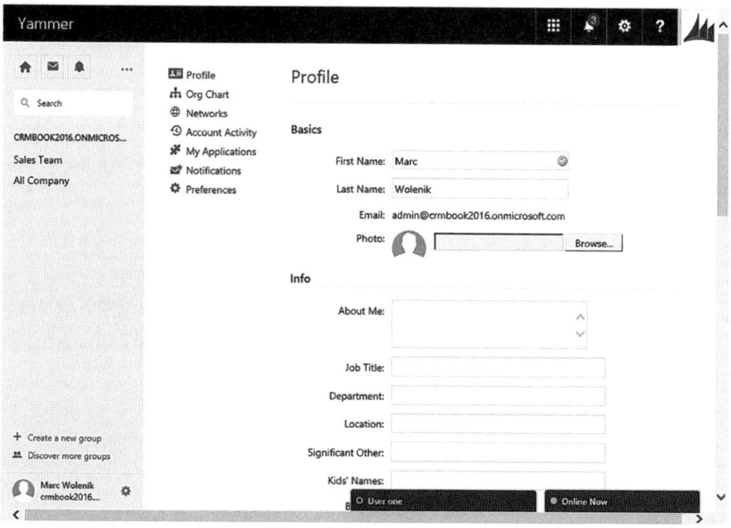

FIGURE 15.39   Yammer profile.

Some of the fields you can configure are profiles for other social networks, such as Skype, Facebook, LinkedIn, and Twitter.

Org Chart

As shown in Figure 15.40, users can create a dynamic organization chart.

> **NOTE**
>
> Unfortunately, the Yammer org chart is not yet integrated with the Dynamics CRM charts.

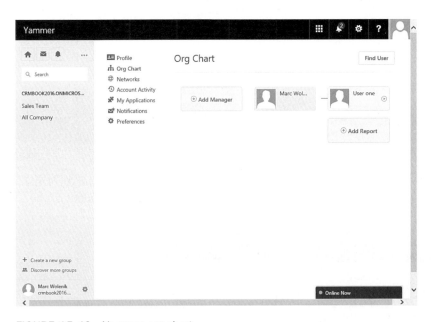

FIGURE 15.40   Yammer org chart.

Networks

You can choose the Networks option to see the other networks where Yammer is integrated. If you have it integrated with Dynamics CRM, you see the Dynamics CRM URL here. You can also join other external networks or create other internal networks to use with your individual Yammer account (see Figure 15.41).

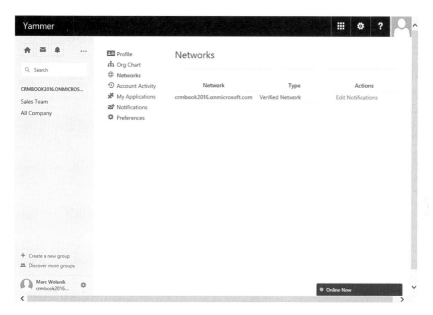

FIGURE 15.41   Yammer Networks option.

You can click Edit Notifications to configure the email notifications that can be fired from the application selected, in this case Dynamics CRM (see Figure 15.42).

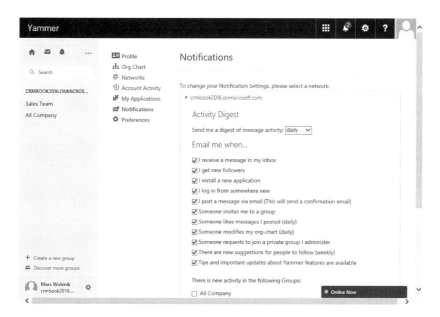

FIGURE 15.42   Yammer email notifications.

These are the email notifications you can configure here:

▶ I receive a message in my inbox.

▶ I get new followers.

▶ I install a new application.

▶ I log in from somewhere new.

▶ I post a message via email.

▶ Someone likes the messages I posted (daily).

▶ Someone invites me to a group

▶ Someone modified my org-chart (daily).

▶ Someone request to join a private group I administer.

▶ There are new suggestions for people to follow (weekly).

▶ Tips and important updates about Yammer features are available.

▶ There is a new activity in the following groups (*you can select the groups from the list of the available groups you have in your Yammer subscription*).

Account Activity

You can click the Account Activity option to see the different applications, when they last authorized, and from what IP addresses the apps accessed (see Figure 15.43). If you see an application you don't know, you can click Logout to disconnect that application.

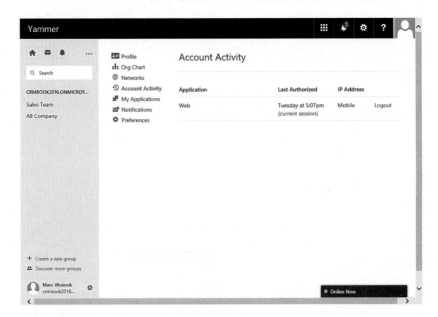

FIGURE 15.43   Yammer account activity.

My Applications

You can click My Applications to see all the related applications you installed to use Yammer outside the web user interface (see Figure 15.44).

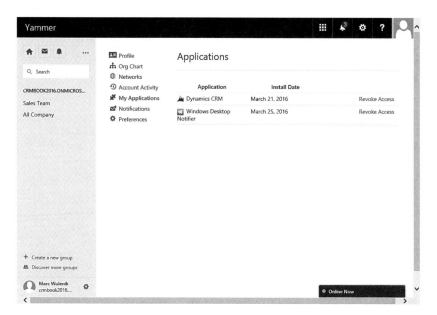

FIGURE 15.44   Yammer applications.

Notifications

Notifications allow you to see and configure email notifications. Refer to Figure 15.42 to see the notifications options.

Preferences

The preferences setting, as shown in Figure 15.45, allow you to change the time zone. When you make this change, it affects the times of the posts you see in Yammer or Dynamics CRM, and, unfortunately this time zone option is not synchronized with your personal settings in Dynamics CRM.

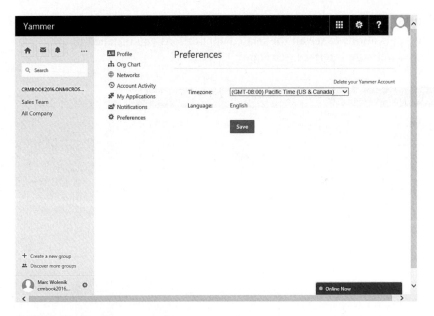

FIGURE 15.45   Yammer preferences.

You can also change the language in this section, and you can delete your Yammer account here as well. Be careful about using the Delete Your Yammer Account link, though, because this action is permanent and irreversible across all your Yammer networks.

Summary

This chapter covers Yammer, the private social network solution available in Microsoft Office 365.

> **NOTE**
>
> Remember that Yammer requires an additional purchase; it is not included in the base of Dynamics CRM product.

Yammer can be used extensively in both development and production environments. It is a powerful tool, and this chapter barely begins to explore its full potential. Some of the following functionality is also available:

- ▶ Portal integration so that external users or customers can monitor record conversations in real time

- ▶ Integration with the portal or email so that, based on escalation evaluation, alerts can automatically be posted to users or the organization

- ▶ Tests for staleness of records or records that have velocity based on things such as number of posts or number of likes

Reporting and Dashboards

Microsoft Dynamics CRM continues to improve the reporting and dashboard capabilities. Reports are more dynamic and flexible, and the Reporting Wizard that is included enables users to create basic reports on-the-fly and share them with the organization.

In addition, reporting options are extremely flexible with CRM Online. As with the previous version of Dynamics CRM, the ability to upload reports remains, but Microsoft has increased the flexibility of FetchXML (a requirement for online reports) from previous versions of Dynamics CRM to include left outer joins. What this means is that you can now define criteria that will find matches of nonexistence, which was nearly impossible before. For example, you might query the system to find all contacts that don't have any opportunities associated with them.

> ▶ For more information about these capabilities, **SEE** the "Fetch-Based Reports" and "Left Outer Joins" sections, later in this chapter.

> **NOTE**
>
> Some limitations still apply with CRM Online. See the "Report Wizard" section, later in this chapter, to learn about SQL versus Fetch limitations and how to address and overcome them.

When discussing reporting, we often dig a little deeper to understand exactly what is being asked because the most common answer might not be the right one. This means that although there exists an enterprise reporting service within Dynamics CRM (SQL Server Reporting Services [SSRS]), when most people ask about reports, they are usually looking for ways to view their data; this can be more (or less) than full enterprise reports. Therefore, we usually discuss reporting falling into one of these categories:

▶ SSRS (full reporting services)

▶ Charts and dashboards

▶ Advanced Find functionality

▶ Custom/personalized views

▶ Exporting to Excel

All these categories can deliver aggregate data to end users and, hence, "report" on what customers want to see. Therefore, it is important to understand what is being asked when discussing reporting. This chapter explains the first two options: SSRS and charts and dashboards.

▶ **SEE CHAPTER 22** "Customizing the System," to learn more about the other options listed.

Reporting

Whether you're using Online or On-Premises, Microsoft Dynamics CRM uses SSRS as the engine for creating and rendering reports. SSRS is a separate application that you can install on a different server than SQL Server or even the Microsoft Dynamics CRM server, if desired. Microsoft Dynamics CRM then connects to SSRS by using the reporting services URL, as specified during an On-Premises installation. There are two differences between online and on-premise usage of SSRS:

▶ **Online usage**—Reporting usage through CRM Online does not require configuration. It simply works out of the box, and the following sections are specific only for On-Premises installations, where configurations are required between the reporting service and the Dynamics CRM service.

▶ **On-Premises usage**—The CRM Reporting Extensions are required during installation. The Reporting Extensions are twofold:

▶ SQL elements for scheduling reports

▶ Fetch elements required for creating, running, and scheduling Fetch reports

▶ To install the CRM Reporting Extensions for SSRS, follow the steps outlined in **CHAPTER 29**, "On-Premises Deployments."

After the Reporting Extensions are installed, you can access reports in Microsoft Dynamics CRM from the top navigation menu for all major areas (Sales, Service, or Marketing; under the Tools group, see Figure 16.1) or directly from various entities in the system (Account, Contact, and so on). The Available Reports page is shown when the Reports option is selected (see Figure 16.2).

FIGURE 16.1   Reports in the Sales area.

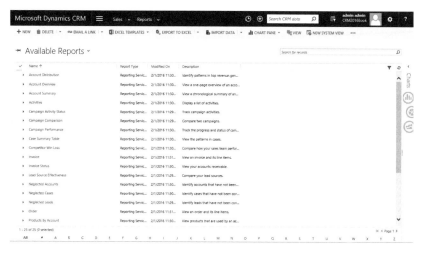

FIGURE 16.2   All available reports.

CAUTION

When viewing reports in the system, you can see all available reports; however, you might or might not be able to display the underlying data, depending on your permissions.

When working with entity records, such as the Contact records shown in Figure 16.3, you can run specific entity reports without needing to access the main Reports area.

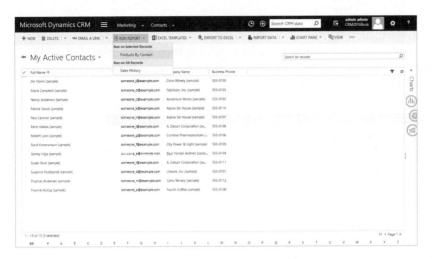

FIGURE 16.3   Running reports from the Contact entity.

Although some reports are already configured to run directly from the entity, you can easily configure a report so that it is available as part of the entity if you desire, as shown in Figure 16.3. To do so, follow these steps:

1. Select (by clicking) a report from the main Reports interface located on the navigation bar (as shown in Figure 16.1) and then select Edit.

2. When the report definition window opens, select Related Record Types from the Categorization section and then click the ellipsis (…) button. Add something from the Available Values selection box to the Selected Values box so that you will be able to run that report directly from the selected entity (see Figure 16.4).

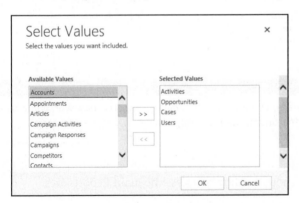

FIGURE 16.4   Related record types for reports.

3. Use the Display In option to configure where you want to have the reports available. You can set the following values for this property:

▶ Forms for Related Record Types

▶ Lists for Related Record Types

▶ Reports Area

▶ You can choose any of these values to display the report.

Report Filters

All reports in CRM have a special feature that enables you to prefilter the underlying data when you run a report. You can configure this feature on the first screen when you double-click a report (see Figure 16.5).

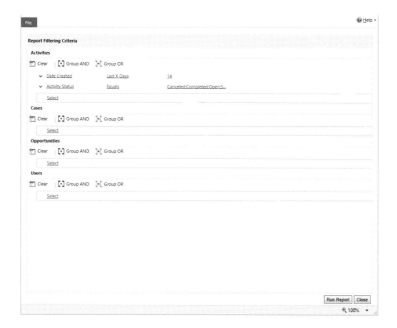

FIGURE 16.5   Report filtering criteria.

Here you see the report criteria that were defined as part of the report definition during initial report creation. Although you can manually change these values and properties every time you run a report, you can also change the default filtering criteria by editing the report definition. To do so, go to the main Reports option located on the navigation bar under Sales, Service, or Marketing; click the report you want to modify; and then select Edit Default Filter from the ribbon (see Figure 16.6).

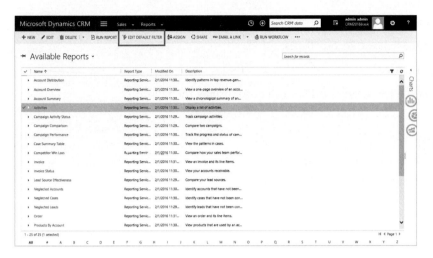

FIGURE 16.6   Modifying the default report filtering criteria.

Make any necessary changes and then click Save Default Filter to save your changes.

Categories

Reports are divided into categories so that they can be easily grouped. This is especially useful when an organization is working with many custom reports.

By default, only the following four categories are created in the system, but you can easily create more as necessary:

► Administrative reports

► Marketing reports

► Sales reports

► Service reports

Each category has a predefined view to filter and is easily accessible, as shown in Figure 16.7.

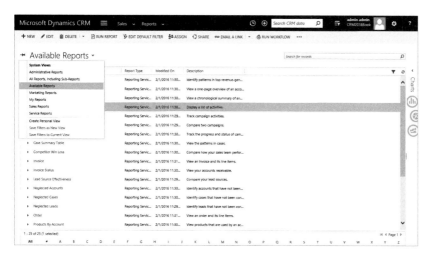

FIGURE 16.7   Report categories.

To set a category on a report, select the report from the Reports interface and then click Edit on the ribbon. Click the ... button under the last section, Categorization (next to the field Categories), and then select the required categories for the report and click the >> button (see Figure 16.8).

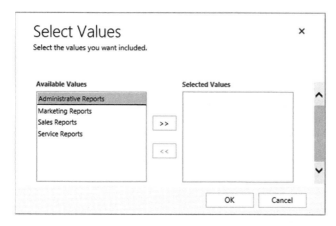

FIGURE 16.8   Associating report categories.

To create new report categories, navigate to Settings > System > Administration and click System Settings. Select the Reporting tab to edit the categories, as shown in Figure 16.9.

16

FIGURE 16.9   Managing reporting categories.

Click the Add button to create a new category, enter a label for the new category, and then click OK twice to close the dialogs.

NOTE

Creating a new category doesn't mean that a view is also created.

TIP

To use the new category in the shortcut list (refer to Figure 16.8) as part of the report, you must create the view with the new category manually.

▶ For details about how to create custom views, **SEE CHAPTER 22.**

You can use the shortcut menu that becomes available when you select the drop-down arrow next to Reports on the navigation bar to access recently used reports, as shown in Figure 16.10.

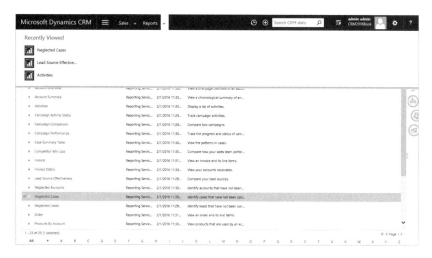

FIGURE 16.10   Recently run reports.

Administration

When editing a report (by selecting it and then selecting Edit from the ribbon), you see two tabs: General and Administration. The Administration option is used to configure the administrative options for the report. By using the options on the tab, you can set the owner of the report and whether the report should be viewed by the user or by the entire organization (see Figure 16.11).

16

> **TIP**
>
> You can also change the report owner by selecting Assign from the Actions drop-down.

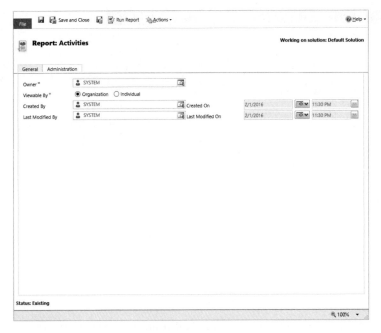

FIGURE 16.11   Report administration.

Report Wizard

The Report Wizard provides an easy-to-use interface that enables users to build basic reports without development knowledge. With Microsoft Dynamics CRM 2016, reports are generated using native Fetch-based queries through the data source (called MSCRM_FetchDataSource) found in the Report Manager and available to support Fetch queries.

In addition, the final reports are actually Microsoft SSRS reports, or .rdl files, which you can manipulate by using more advanced editing tools such as Visual Studio, provided that you have Report Authoring Extension installed.

> **NOTE**
>
> As with earlier versions of Dynamics CRM, reports built with the Report Wizard can be edited using Visual Studio. This is usually done to increase performance, layout, and report complexity. To do so, you need to download and install a Visual Studio 2010 or 2012 plug-in called Microsoft Dynamics CRM 2016 Report Authoring Extension (CRM2016-Bids-ENU-i386.exe). (You can find this Visual Studio plug-in by searching for "CRM 2016 Report Authoring Extension" at Microsoft.com or by going directly to www.microsoft.com/en-us/download/details.aspx?id=50375.) Once this is installed, you can use the required Fetch data source type to parse the Fetch queries in the report's data source generated by the Report Wizard. You will learn how to install this component later in this chapter.

When working with reports, remember that although you can continue to have the Data Source Type set to SQL (typically to query older reporting versions), for security reasons, CRM Online does not support SQL queries, and the Fetch extension must be used instead.

If you are unfamiliar with the FetchXML query schema, you can create any query with the Advanced Find tool and easily download or view the FetchXML generated by this tool for reuse on custom reports.

An example of a FetchXML query is as follows:

```
<fetch>
  <entity name="account" enableprefiltering="1" >
  <attribute name="name" />
</entity>
</fetch>
```

This code would be equivalent to the following SQL query:

```
select name from FilteredAccount
```

Notice that the `enableprefiltering` attribute in the entity node allows the user to query prefilters.

▶ Be sure to review the "Fetch-Based Reports" section, later in this chapter, for more information about Fetch.

If you are new to Advanced Find, refer to the section "Fetch-Based Reports," later in this chapter. FetchXML is an advanced topic.

To use the Report Wizard, follow these steps:

1. Navigate to Reports from the Sales, Service, or Marketing navigation bar. Select New to open the dialog shown in Figure 16.12. The Report Type option defaults to Report Wizard Report, which is the one used in this example. If you had created an external report, such as one using Visual Studio, you would select Existing File and upload the file directly. Link to a Web Page enables you to link to a web page that contains a report on a custom web page, such as what you could do for a custom report in HTML5.

2. Click the Report Wizard button to start the wizard. After it starts, you have two options for creating a new report (see Figure 16.13):

   ▶ Start a New Report

   ▶ Start from an Existing Report

16

FIGURE 16.12   New Report dialog.

FIGURE 16.13   Report Wizard.

The second option only enables you to create a new report from a report that was previously generated through this wizard and to make edits to an existing report through the wizard. For this example, create a new report by selecting the first option and clicking Next to continue.

3. In the Report Properties dialog that appears, enter a name for the report and select an option from the Primary Record Type drop-down. The primary record type must be one of the entities available in the system, such as Account, Contact, and so on (see Figure 16.14). Click Next to continue.

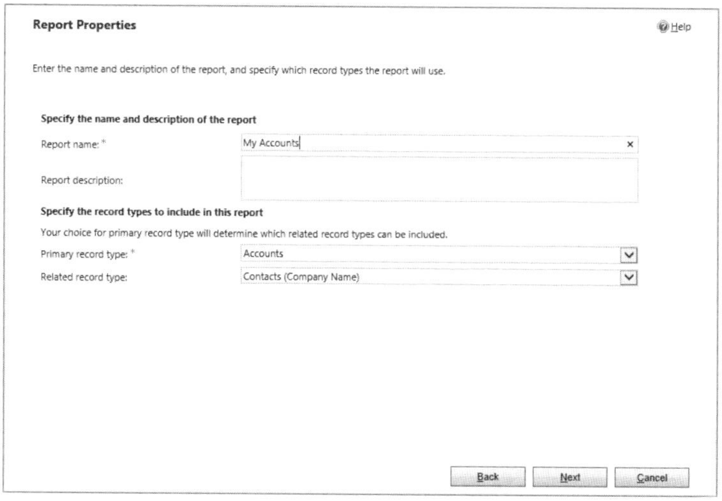

FIGURE 16.14   Report Properties dialog.

> **NOTE**
>
> The Related Record Type option values depend on the entity you select for Primary Record Type. Related Record Type shows all the entities related to the primary entity selected. For example, you can select Contacts for Related Record Type so that you can create a report of the contacts by account.

4. Select the default report filters for the primary or related record types selected in step 3 (see Figure 16.15). You can use a previously used view or create a new one. To add a new filter, click the Select link and select the property you want to use. For this example, select the property Owner with the criteria Equals Current User. Click Next to continue.

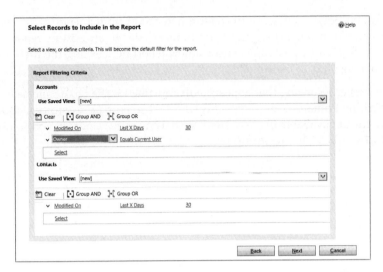

FIGURE 16.15   Report Wizard report filtering criteria.

5. In the Lay Out Fields dialog that appears, define the properties you want to have displayed on the report (see Figure 16.16).

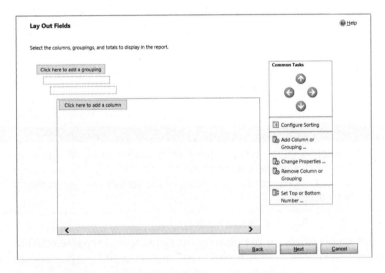

FIGURE 16.16   Lay Out Fields dialog.

6. Select Click Here to Add a Column to add the fields you want to see in the report. You can choose the record type, which is limited to the entities you selected for Primary Record Type and Related Record Type in earlier steps.

7. After selecting the record type, select the column, which will be any of the properties of the record type you previously selected. The data type and name are displayed only for informational purposes, and you can't change them from this interface. The only thing you can change is the column width, in pixels.

The last option in the Add Column dialog, Summary Type, is available for only some data types, such as money and numeric data types. Figure 16.17 shows the available options that you can select for Summary Type. (They are similar to SQL aggregate functions.)

FIGURE 16.17   Summary Type options.

8. If any of the Summary Type options were used, configure the grouping by selecting Click Here to Add a Grouping (refer to Figure 16.16). Figure 16.18 shows the grouping options.

Add Grouping ✕

Define how to group data in the report.

Record type: *	Accounts
Column: *	Account Name
Time interval:	Month
Data type:	Single Line of Text
Name:	name
Sort order:	Ascending
Column width: *	100 pixels
Summary type:	None

OK   Cancel

FIGURE 16.18   Add Grouping dialog.

The columns that you can select in the Add Grouping dialog are based on any of the entities previously selected. You can create up to three different groupings that will be nested among themselves. Click Next to continue.

> **NOTE**
>
> The Time Interval option is available only for fields that have datetime as their data type. This option enables grouping by day, week, month, year, fiscal period, and fiscal year.

9. Now that you have defined which columns to display and how they should be grouped, specify their format. You can select the basic format of the report, which includes charting. In this case, select Table Only because you're building a basic report for this example. Click Next to continue.

10. In the last step of the wizard, which provides the report summary, click Next to continue. The report is generated, and the results are displayed. Note that a delay might occur while the report is being generated.

11. Click Finish to close the wizard. If necessary, you can now select and edit the properties of the report. Notice that the wizard has automatically populated the name of the report and the categorization fields.

12. To test the new report, select the report from the Reports interface and either select Run Report from the top menu or double-click the report name. The report runs, as shown in the example in Figure 16.19.

FIGURE 16.19   Running the report.

Modifying a Report

If you want to modify the report you just created, you can easily run the Report Wizard again. For example, suppose that you want to change the selected format from a table to a graphical chart representation. Follow these steps:

1. Click the Report Wizard button, and the wizard starts with the starting point selected for this report, with the option to overwrite it (see Figure 16.20).

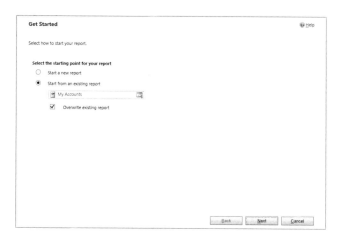

FIGURE 16.20   Modifying the report.

2. Continue through the Report Wizard steps, changing the format from Table to Chart and Table and selecting the Chart Type (see Figure 16.21).

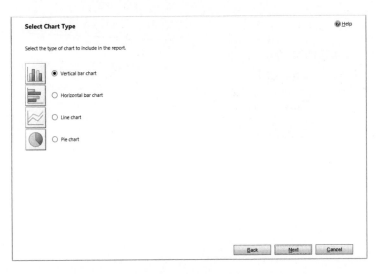

FIGURE 16.21 Select Chart Type dialog.

TIP

The pie chart type might be disabled if you didn't select the Sum or Percent of Total option in the Summary columns.

3. Click Next to customize the chart format. You can select the labels of the x-axis and y-axis, as well as the fields for them, as shown in Figure 16.22.

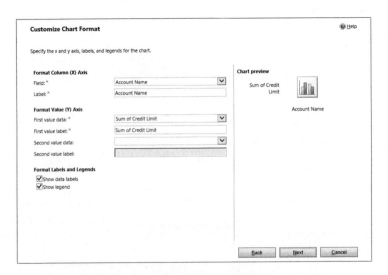

FIGURE 16.22 Customize Chart Format dialog.

4. Click Next to go to the summary screen for review and then click Next to modify the report.

Now if you run the report, it will look as shown in Figure 16.23.

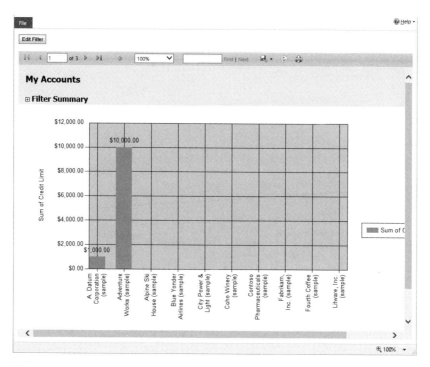

FIGURE 16.23   Running the report with the chart format.

Scheduling Reports

SSRS has many advanced features that are closely integrated in this version of Microsoft Dynamics CRM. For example, you can schedule report execution to receive a copy of a report automatically.

> **TIP**
>
> This option is limited to On-Premises users of Microsoft Dynamics CRM only.

This is a great feature that many organizations use to proactively receive data. For example, a CFO usually wants to see all orders entered into the system for the week; SSRS can generate a report for this automatically every Friday morning and then email the report to the CFO, with no user intervention, so that when the CFO arrives in the office in the morning, there is an email from CRM with the report attached.

To access this feature, select Reports > Schedule Report (see Figure 16.24). The Report Scheduling Wizard starts and presents two options, discussed in the following sections:

▶ On Demand

▶ On a Schedule

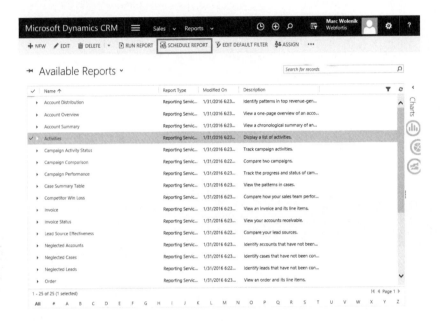

FIGURE 16.24   Scheduling a report.

By default, only administrators can schedule reports. To give this feature to a lower-privileged role, an administrator must grant permission in the Add Reporting Services Reports security option, under Miscellaneous Privileges in the Core Records tab of the security role configuration interface. If you are an administrator, you can access this area from the Administration section of the Settings area. You then click Security Roles and then double-click the role you want to customize. Figure 16.25 shows this permission added to the Customer Service Representative role.

Miscellaneous Privileges

Add Reporting Services Reports	●	Bulk Delete	○
Delete Audit Partitions	○	Manage Data Encryption key - Activate	○
Manage Data Encryption key - Change	○	Manage Data Encryption key - Read	○
Manage User Synchronization Filters	○	Publish Duplicate Detection Rules	○
Publish Email Templates	○	Publish Mail Merge Templates to Organization	○
Publish Reports	○	Run SharePoint Integration Wizard	○
View Audit History	○	View Audit Partitions	○
View Audit Summary	○		

FIGURE 16.25   Setting permissions for scheduling reports.

Running a Report on Demand

An on-demand report generates a snapshot as soon as you finish the wizard. In this example, you're going to work with the Activities report.

Depending on the report selected, you must specify values for the report parameters. You can also edit the default filters by clicking the Edit Filter button.

After you click Next, you can choose whether to generate the report snapshot right away or just save the report snapshot definition for later use (see Figure 16.26). If you choose the first option and then click Save, the new snapshot is generated, and the overview is detailed.

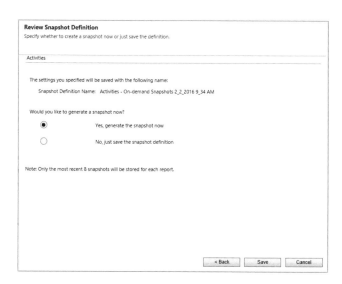

FIGURE 16.26   Review Snapshot Definition dialog.

The Completing the Report Scheduling Wizard dialog that appears next contains all the necessary instructions to access and view the snapshot report that was just created. Click Finish to close the wizard. You then see the snapshot shown in Figure 16.27.

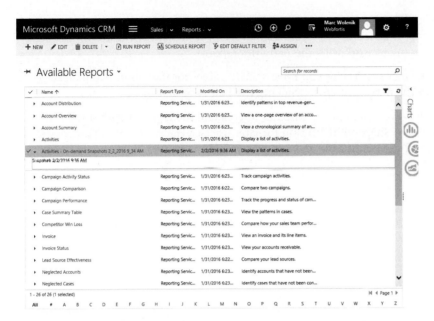

FIGURE 16.27   Snapshot report.

Running a Report on a Schedule

Selecting On a Schedule in the Report Scheduling Wizard enables you to select the
frequency of the report execution, as well as the time when you want the report to execute
(see Figure 16.28). The available options for the frequency are as follows:

▶ Once

▶ Hourly

▶ Daily

▶ Weekly

▶ Monthly

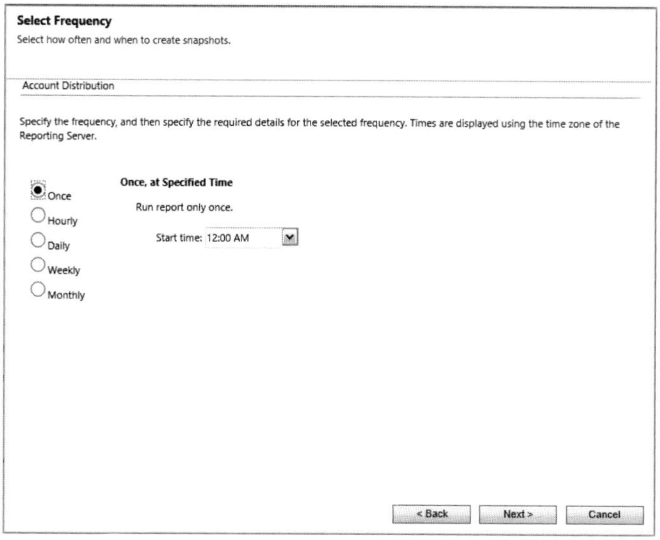

FIGURE 16.28   Select the frequency option Once.

The options that appear here depend on the frequency selected. For example, if you select Once, you can select only the start time. But if you select Hourly, you can select the number of hours and minutes you want the report to be run. Similarly, the options change for Daily, Weekly, and Monthly. With Once selected, click Next, then on the next dialog, set the start date and the end date for the report.

TIP

If you want the report to be generated forever, do not specify an end date.

After you set the starting and ending dates, you can define the report parameters and edit the default filters for the report. These interfaces are similar to the ones for the On Demand option, explained previously. When you have defined the parameters, click Next. An overview is presented so that you can review the scheduled report settings.

If errors occur when you're trying to schedule a report, the SSRS server most likely is not configured properly. To check or change your configuration, start the Reporting Services Configuration Manager application that is inside the Microsoft SQL Server programs group and inside the configuration tools (see Figure 16.29).

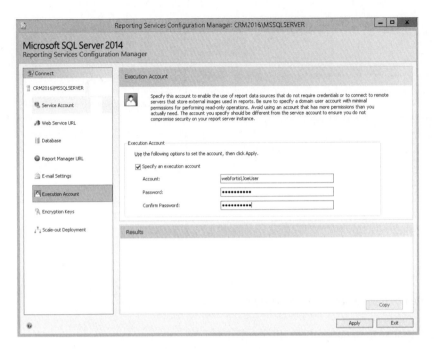

FIGURE 16.29   Execution account configuration.

Exporting Reports

You can export all Microsoft Dynamics CRM reports and report data in the following formats:

- ▶ XML file with report data
- ▶ CSV (comma delimited)
- ▶ Acrobat (PDF) file
- ▶ MHTML (web archive)
- ▶ Excel
- ▶ TIFF file
- ▶ Word

You find these options for a report by clicking the Save icon in the navigation bar (see Figure 16.30). Microsoft Dynamics CRM reports are be completely portable, and the various export options enable you to easily manipulate the data.

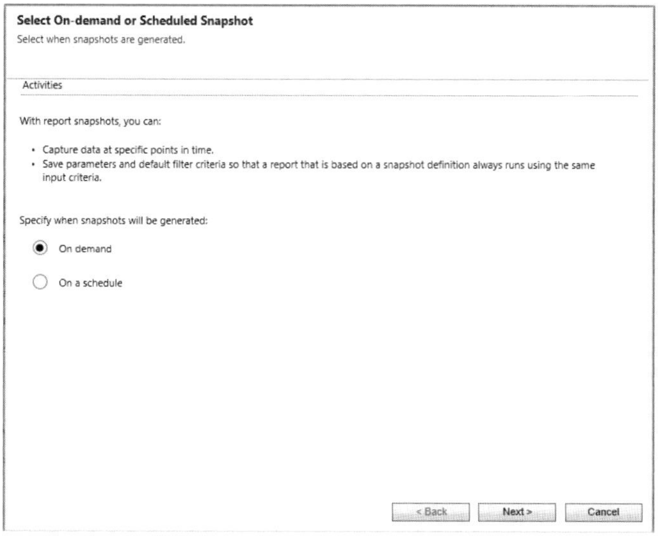

FIGURE 16.30   Exporting the report created earlier in this chapter.

To export the report definition (not just the report format or data), select the report you want to export from the Reports interface and select Report > Edit from the command bar. When the report properties window appears, select Actions > Download Report, as shown in Figure 16.31.

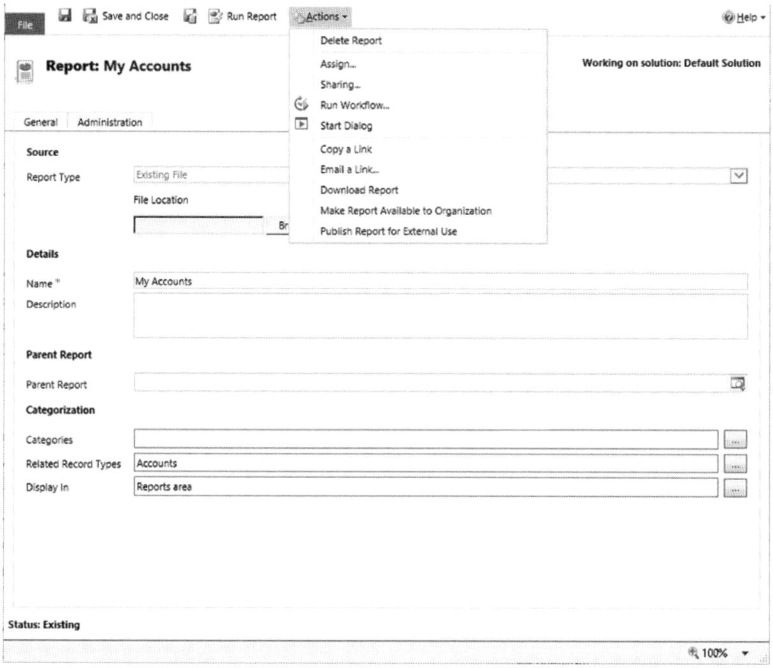

FIGURE 16.31   Downloading a report.

You can download the report in its Report Definition Language (RDL) format. This is the standard SSRS extension, based on XML, that you can edit using an editor such as Visual Studio, as mentioned earlier in this chapter.

▶ **SEE** the section "Building Custom Reports with SSRS," later in this chapter, for information on advanced report customization.

TIP

Reports can also belong to a solution, and you can easily move a solution from one deployment to another. For more information about solutions and solution management, see Chapter 22.

Advanced Features

In addition to running, creating, editing, or downloading reports, you can perform other actions when working with reports, as detailed next.

Sharing Reports

Any reports that you create are available to you. If you want to share a custom report with a user who has a lower-privilege role, select the report from the main Reports interface and then select ... > Share (see Figure 16.32). From the interface that appears, you can give the following permissions to users:

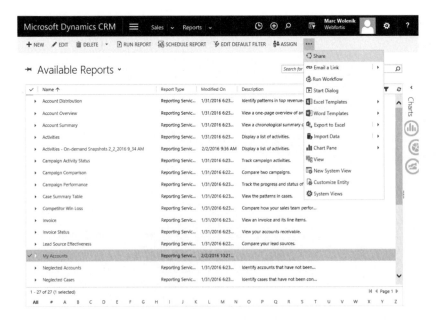

FIGURE 16.32   Sharing reports.

▶ **Read**—Enables the user to run the report.

▶ **Write**—Enables the user to modify the report definition and to change the properties and default filters.

▶ **Delete**—Enables the user to delete the report.

▶ **Append**—Not applicable.

▶ **Assign**—Enables the user to change the owner of the report. This setting also gives write permission to the user for the report.

▶ **Share**—Enables the user to share the report with other users.

Note that if you add only read permissions for a user, that user can share the report with other users even though you didn't select the Share option. This is because the default permissions are set to allow sharing between users. Of course, the user can give only read permissions to the other users, but you should carefully consider the implications of each permission before you set them. Figure 16.33 illustrates the sharing options available with reports.

FIGURE 16.33   Report sharing permissions.

Exposing Reports to SSRS

As with earlier versions of Microsoft CRM, Dynamics CRM 2016 doesn't expose every report in the SSRS Report Manager application. If you want to use a report from another application, it must be published in Microsoft CRM. For example, if you go to the Report Manager application of SSRS (by navigating to http://<<srs server name>>/reports), you see a folder created for the organization; however, it is empty (see Figure 16.34).

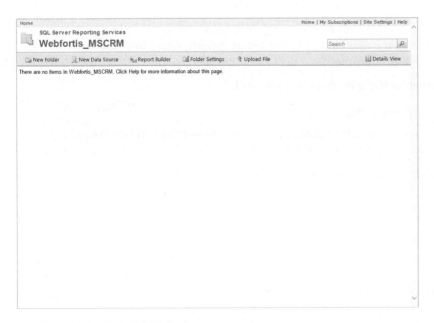

FIGURE 16.34   Report Manager.

All the predefined reports are now on a different common folder for all the organizations in the system; this folder is called SharedReports/8.0.xxx. This folder contains all the out-of-the-box reports created (see Figure 16.35).

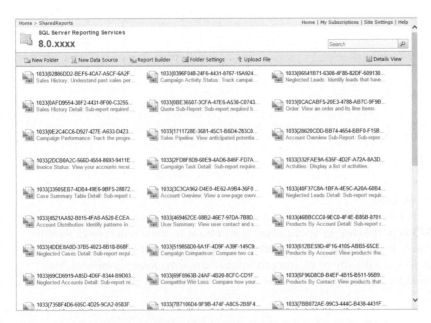

FIGURE 16.35   CRM 2016 SharedReports in Report Manager.

> **NOTE**
>
> Every custom report you create using the Report Wizard and every report snapshot
> is placed in SharedReports/8.0.xxx folder. (Dynamics CRM 2015 used the folder
> SharedReports/7.0.xxx, and 2013 used SharedReports/6.0.xxx.)

If you need to use any of these reports or expose them to another application, go
to the CRM interface, select the report you want to expose, and select Edit Report >
Actions > Publish Report for External Use. After you select this option, no confirmation
or message states that the operation is complete. In fact, the only way to verify that
it was published is to go to the Report Manager web application and navigate to your
SharedReports/8.0.xxx folder, where you should see the report available.

Fetch-based Reports

Microsoft Dynamics CRM uses a proprietary type of query language known as FetchXML
(which is Fetch based). It supports similar query capabilities to query expressions and
is based on a schema that describes the capabilities of the language. You can find the
schema in the SDK\Schemas\fetch.xsd file in the SDK package.

To create a query using Fetch, you must build an XML query string. Then you can execute
the query string.

Consider the following when constructing the query string:

- ▶ It must conform to the schema definition for the FetchXML language.

- ▶ The resultant records are only those that the querying user has permission to read.

- ▶ Be cautious to limit the attributes requested in a query, as requesting a lot of
  attributes may result in long-running queries.

- ▶ There is a limitation of 50,000 records per page.

The following is an example of a FetchXML query that retrieves all contacts:

```
<fetch mapping="logical">
    <entity name="contact">
        <attribute name="fullname">
    </entity>
</fetch>
```

FetchXML allows complex querying and filtering. The following is an example of a
FetchXML query that retrieves all contacts that were created in the past 30 days, are
active, and are owned by the current user:

```
<fetch distinct="false" mapping="logical">
    <entity name="contact">
        <attribute name="fullname">
        <filter type="and">
```

16

```
                       <condition attribute="ownerid" operator="eq-userid"/>
                       <condition attribute="statecode" operator="eq" value="0"/>
                         <condition attribute="createdon" operator="last-x-days"
value="30"/>
                       </filter>
         </entity>
</fetch>
```

This code would get translated into C# using the FetchExpression and using the EntityCollection holder.

TIP

An easy way to learn Fetch is to consult the software development kit (SDK), as noted previously, and at the same time run some Advanced Finds in Dynamics CRM and then view the FetchXML directly from the Advanced Find.

Figure 16.36 shows the preceding query, and when you click the Download Fetch XML button, the query is displayed as shown in Figure 16.37.

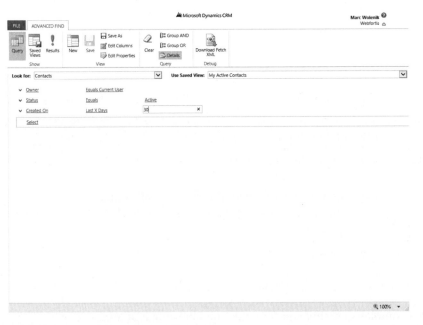

FIGURE 16.36   Advanced Find for contacts.

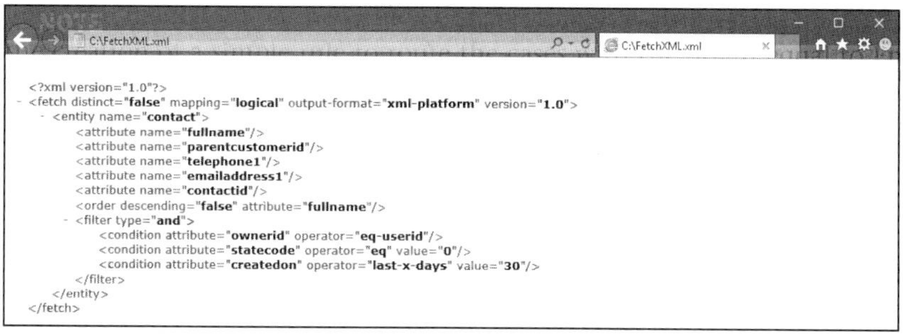

FIGURE 16.37   FetchXML downloaded from the Advanced Find.

Requirements

When you work with Fetch-based reports, the following components are required:

▶ Microsoft Visual Studio 2010 or 2012

▶ Business Intelligence Development Studio or SQL Server Data Tools

▶ Microsoft Dynamics CRM 2016 Reporting Authoring Extension

These components are explained earlier in this chapter, as well has how to configure and install them.

Left Outer Joins

With the addition of left outer joins, users can perform queries on data and show where a negative condition might exist. For example, to show all contacts without any opportunities, you can easily write a FetchXML statement that has the following new properties:

▶ Link type

▶ Operator

Here is an example of this query for contacts without any opportunities:

```
<fetch mapping="logical">
   <entity name="contact">
      <attribute name="fullname">
      <link-entity name="opportunity" from="opportunityid" to="contactid"
link-type="outer"/>
         <filter operator="and">
            <condition entityname="opportunity" attribute="opportunityid"
operator="null"/>
         </filter>
   </entity>
</fetch>
```

Charts and Dashboards

The first part of this section covers general charts, which play a significant part in dashboards. Therefore, the discussion now turns to dashboards.

Charts allow you to show data graphically as the following types:

▶ Column

▶ Bar

▶ Line

▶ Pie

▶ Funnel

The core entities come with predefined charts that you can display by clicking the entity from the sidebar list (for example, Account or Contact) and then clicking the collapsed pane labeled Charts on the right side of the grid, as shown in Figure 16.38.

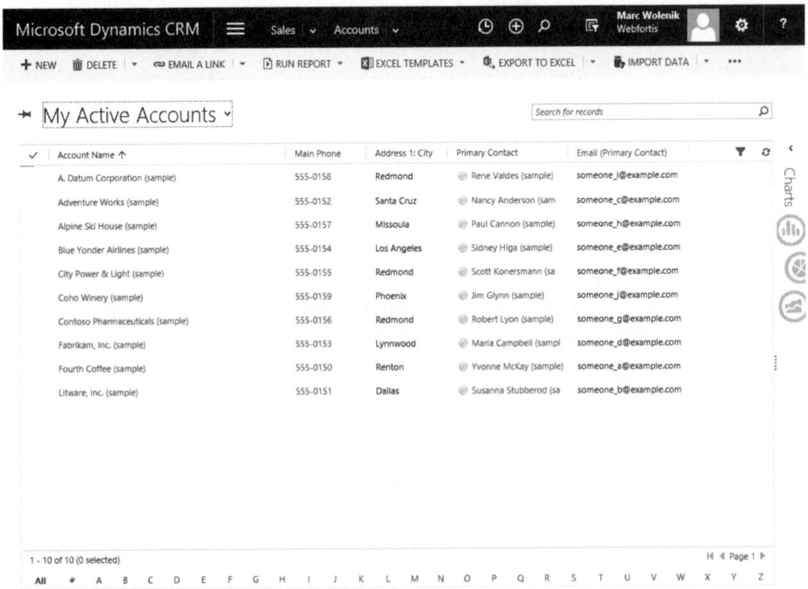

FIGURE 16.38   The collapsed Charts pane.

The charts are displayed on the right side of the grid view. For example, Figure 16.39 shows a bar chart of active accounts by owner.

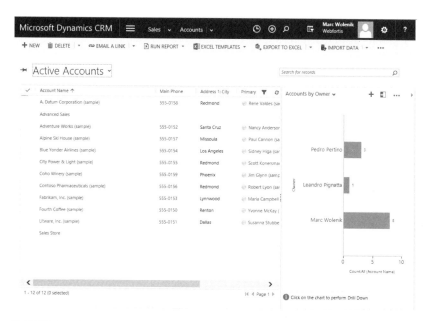

FIGURE 16.39   Accounts by Owner chart.

Any system or custom view is also tied to charts and affects the results displayed not only on the grid but also on the chart. So, if you change the view to see the inactive accounts, you also update the selected chart result. To change the view, you can click the current view name and select a different view from the drop-down list. For this example, select Active Accounts, as shown in Figure 16.40.

16

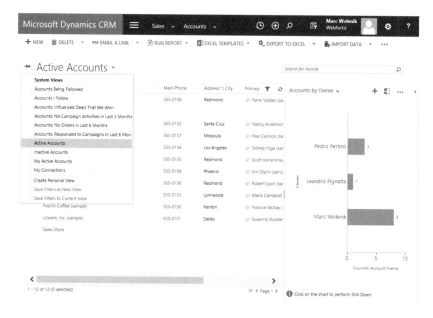

FIGURE 16.40   Changing views.

In addition, you can drill down in the chart bars. When you click any bar, the underlying data of the grid changes to display the new data represented by the chart.

Because the chart results are tied to the results displayed on the grid, you can also use the Filter feature to modify the chart results. Because it is easy to use with the predefined views, this helpful new feature in some cases replaces Advanced Find. To use the Filter feature, find the small filter icon next to the chart and click it. You now have filter controls added to each of the column headers of the grid so that you can add specific or custom filters (see Figure 16.41).

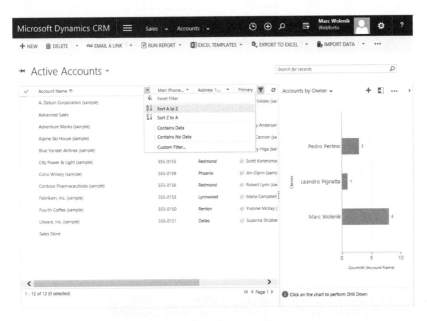

FIGURE 16.41   Working with the Filter feature.

After you apply a filter, a Refresh Chart button appears in the middle of the chart. You can click it to refresh the chart (see Figure 16.42).

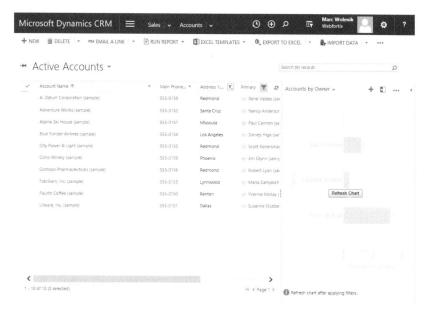

FIGURE 16.42   The Refresh Chart button.

Working with Charts

There are two main types of charts: system charts and personal charts. System charts can be created with customizations and are available to all users. Personal charts are created by users (as explained in this chapter) and are visible only to the user who created them.

▶ To learn more about system charts, **SEE CHAPTER 22**.

NOTE

Check the CRM 2016 SDK for types of charts other than the ones available to the user though the CRM 2016 web user interface. You can also include web resources as charts, as explained later in this chapter; that is also documented in the CRM 2016 SDK.

Chart Tools

To create a new personal chart, click the + at the top of the chart, as shown in Figure 16.43. The Chart Designer is displayed, and you can start creating your new chart.

When creating a new chart, you must specify a name for the chart and choose a legend, an aggregate function, and a category. Optionally, you can add a description to the chart.

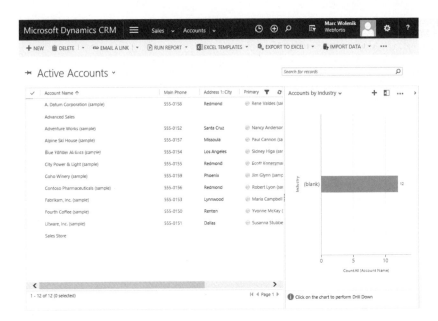

FIGURE 16.43   New chart.

If you are working with the core entities, it is important to review the current charts before creating a new one; after all, a chart that fits your needs might already exist.

> **TIP**
>
> When creating a new chart, you can skip the Name field, which is autocompleted with the concatenation of the fields selected—for example, "*Legend* by *Category*" when you select the Legend and Category fields. For example, if you select the legend Credit Limit and the category Owner, the name is autocompleted as Credit Limit by Owner.

The Aggregate option changes depending on the type of field you selected for the legend. If the type of this field is numeric, you can use Sum, Average, Count: All, Count: Non-empty, Max, and Min for the aggregation type.

Figure 16.44 shows a custom chart that shows the Credit Limit by Owner of the Account entity.

Each chart also has some advanced options. To access them, you just click the grid icon at the far right of the series row (known as *Top/Bottom rules*), and you can then limit the X or Y items that will be displayed if the chart is hard to read because it contains a large number of series (see Figure 16.59).

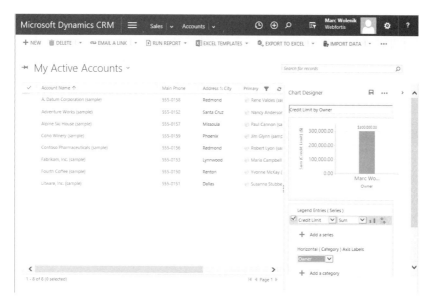

FIGURE 16.44   Custom personal chart.

NOTE

The advanced option allowing the top *X* and bottom *Y* options (as shown in Figure 16.45) is a great feature that allows you to represent data quickly and accurately.

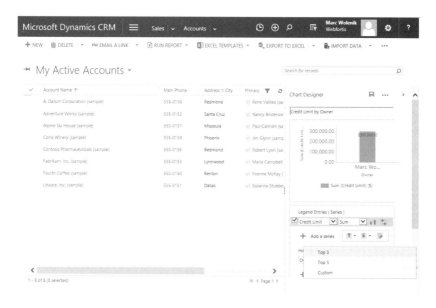

FIGURE 16.45   Advanced options.

Click the save icon at the top of the Chart Designer to save your chart.

Personal charts, which users create from entity views, can be shared with other users in different ways. If the user you want to share a chart with belongs to the same organization, you must close the Chart Designer by selecting the right-pointing arrow (>) and then selecting the ... and the Share option, as shown in Figure 16.46.

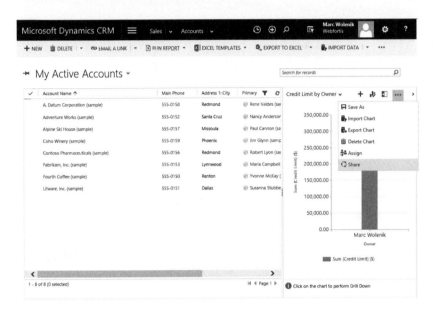

FIGURE 16.46   Sharing a chart.

The sharing options for a chart are the same as the sharing options for a report, described earlier in this chapter (refer to Figure 16.33).

You can change the chart layout by selecting Chart Pane, which changes the position of the chart (see Figure 16.47). Selecting Off completely removes the chart from the main view, leaving the grid option only. To go back to the original layout, click ... > Chart Pane and select the preferred option.

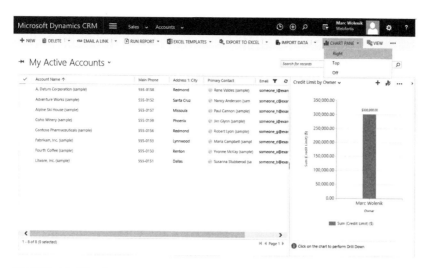

FIGURE 16.47   Changing the chart layout.

Exporting Charts

If the user you want to share a chart with is in another organization, you can export the chart to an XML file by selecting ... > Export Chart.

The exported XML file can then be easily imported by another organization, as long as the other organization contains the same entities and fields used by the organization where the chart was created.

The following is an example of the XML generated for a chart after it is exported and opened:

```
<visualization>
    <visualizationid>{EC32AA46-6155-E311-BFC9-00155D002B01}</visualizationid>
    <name>Credit Limit by Owner</name>
    <primaryentitytypecode>account</primaryentitytypecode>
    ...
    </Chart>
    </presentationdescription>
    <isdefault>false</isdefault>
</visualization>
```

TIP

You can edit the XML by using any editing tool of your choice (such as Visual Studio 2015) and then easily import it back by using the Import Chart option.

16

With only a little knowledge of XML, you can change the font type of the chart fonts and colors by changing the Font attribute of the AxisY node. The following syntax makes the axis text bigger (see Figure 16.48):

```
<AxisY LabelAutoFitMinFontSize="8" TitleForeColor="255, 0, 0"
TitleFont="{0}, 64px" IntervalAutoMode="VariableCount">
```

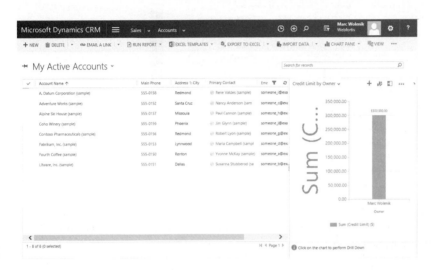

FIGURE 16.48   Chart with a different title font.

You can edit the XML file with any editor, such as Notepad, and then import the modified XML file to CRM. When importing the XML file, you are asked whether you want to replace the existing chart (if one exists) or create a new copy.

Visualizations

The CRM SDK refers to charts as *visualizations*. The reason for this is that there is a tricky way to add other kinds of charts by writing a little code. You can have charts that are actually web resources that can be displayed side-by-side with the grid. For example, you could show a Bing Map control in the visualization area instead of a chart. To do this, you need to create a simple XML file to which you assign a name and a description, identify the name of the web resource you want to use and the primary entity where you want the visualization to be displayed, and specify whether it will be the default visualization for the entity. Here is an example of the XML file you would need to create for this:

```
<visualization>
  <name>BingMaps</name>
  <description>Bing Map</description>
  <webresourcename>webforti_map.htm</webresourcename>
  <primaryentitytypecode>account</primaryentitytypecode>
  <isdefault>true</isdefault>
</visualization>
```

Then you save this file with the .xml extension (for example, Customchart.xml), and you can import it just as you would any other chart, as explained earlier in this chapter. The result, however, is what you have put on the web resource, which can be an image, an HTML file, and so forth.

Dashboards

Dashboards enable the user to see more than one chart from different entities on a single page. In addition to adding charts (as discussed earlier in this chapter), you can add grids, IFRAMEs, and web resources to a dashboard.

Grids are representations of underlying CRM data (for example, activities that relate to an account or leads that relate to a region), IFRAMEs are pass-through connections to other web pages (either externally or internally, or even self-referencing), and web resources are files that can be images, Silverlight applications, HTML pages, or script files.

The CRM system comes with 16 predefined system dashboards you can use as models:

- ▶ Customer Service Manager Dashboard

- ▶ Customer Service Operations Dashboard

- ▶ Customer Service Performance Dashboard

- ▶ Customer Service Performance Dashboard (original version)

- ▶ Customer Service Representative Dashboard

- ▶ Customer Service Representative Social Dashboard

- ▶ Customer Service Representative Social Dashboard (original version)

- ▶ Marketing Dashboard

- ▶ Marketing Social Dashboard

- ▶ Microsoft Dynamics CRM Overview

- ▶ Microsoft Dynamics CRM Social Overview

- ▶ Sales Activity Dashboard

- ▶ Sales Activity Social Dashboard

- ▶ Sales Dashboard

- ▶ Sales Performance Dashboard

- ▶ Server-Side Synchronization Performance

As with charts, you can use two main types of dashboards: the system dashboards that are available to all users in the organization and the personal dashboards that a user can create. In addition, dashboards can be assigned by roles, if desired.

Figure 16.49 shows an example of the Microsoft Dynamics CRM Overview Dashboard.

16

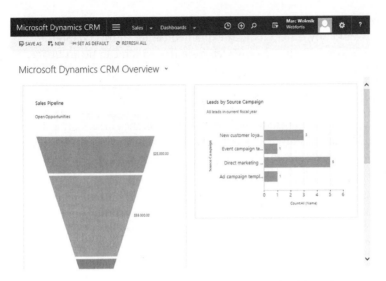

FIGURE 16.49   Microsoft Dynamics CRM Overview Dashboard.

Creating a New Dashboard

To create a new personal dashboard, follow these steps:

1. Go to the Dashboard area from within the Sales, Service, or Marketing navigation bar and then click Dashboards.

2. Click the New button, and the Choose Layout dialog appears.

3. Select a layout from the predefined layouts on the left side of the Choose Layout dialog. Sample charts on the right show you how the layouts will look.

4. Click the Create button. The Dashboard Editor window appears (see Figure 16.50).

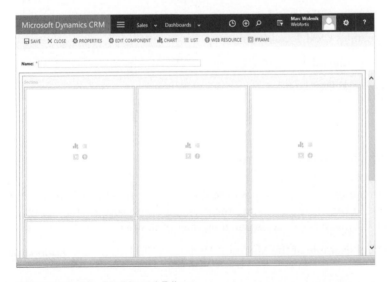

FIGURE 16.50   Dashboard Editor.

5. To add a chart, click the chart icon that is inside of the first component. Select the entity record type (for example, Account), the view (for example, My Active Accounts), and the chart you want to display (for example, Accounts by Industry).

6. Click Add to add the chart, and the chart is added to the dashboard.

7. Move to the next component and click the list icon. Select the entity and view you want to display.

8. Click Add to add the list component, and the list component is added to the dashboard.

9. Move to the next component and click the IFRAME icon. In the Add an IFRAME dialog that appears (see Figure 16.51), enter a name and the URL of the page you want to display. In this case, you don't want to pass parameters to the URL, so you need to confirm that the Pass Record Object-Type Code and Unique Identifier as Parameters check box is unchecked. (You would check this box, however, if you entered a URL of a custom application you created that needs to know the record type and ID of who is calling it, for example.) Also notice that a new addition to Dynamics CRM 2016 allows the selection of whether you want the IFRAME to be visible in the client for tablets such as iPads.

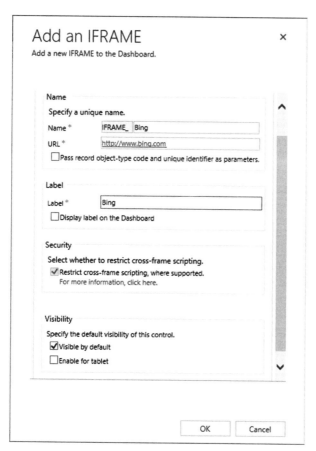

FIGURE 16.51   Adding an IFRAME to a component.

10. Click OK to add the IFRAME, and the IFRAME is added to the dashboard. Note, however, that the URL is not rendered in the design view (see Figure 16.52).

11. Move to the next component and click the web resource icon. Select a web resource (such as a PNG image that displays your company logo).

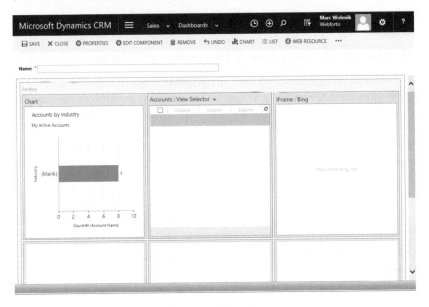

FIGURE 16.52   IFRAME added to a dashboard.

12. Click OK to add the web resource. You see only the name of the web resource added to the dashboard, and the image is not rendered in the design mode (see Figure 16.53).

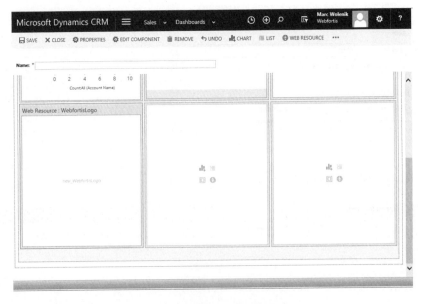

FIGURE 16.53   Web resource added to a dashboard.

13. Drag and drop the components around as necessary and then finish this dashboard by entering the dashboard name and clicking Save.

14. To clean the empty space, select the component where you added the image and click ... > Increase Width.

15. Click Save to save the work and then click Close. The dashboard opens in a new window, showing the rendered content (see Figure 16.54).

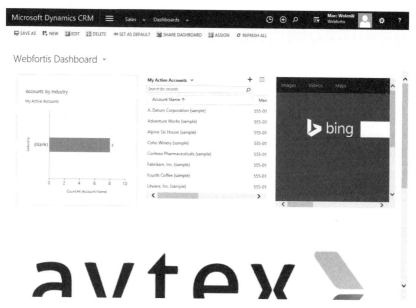

FIGURE 16.54   Completed dashboard.

Dashboard Features

Unfortunately, there is no intuitive way to add new components to a dashboard. If you start from one of the predefined templates, you can add from four to six components, depending on the layout selected. However, if you want to have a dashboard with more components, you need to click the section first and then click any of the Chart, List, IFRAME, or Web Resource buttons on the command bar (under ...). By clicking any of those buttons you can add a new component to a dashboard, but if you have an empty component selected first (instead of the entire section), by clicking a button you replace the empty component space with the selected component.

TIP

You cannot change the component type once you select it; for example, you cannot change from Chart to IFRAME. To change the type you must remove the component and create a new one.

You can share dashboards with other users within the same organization, and you can also assign them to other users. However, unlike charts, they cannot be easily exported or imported. If you want to export a dashboard to be used in a different organization, you must create a solution and include the dashboard inside that solution. (However, personal dashboards cannot be added to solutions for export.)

▶ To learn more about solutions, **SEE CHAPTER 22**.

When working with the charts on a dashboard, you can use some cool features. When you drag your mouse over to a chart, three icons appear at the top-right corner of the component.

The first icon refreshes the chart because the underlying data might have been changed; you have to manually click this icon to get an updated version of the chart. If you have more than one chart on the dashboard, you can click the Refresh All button on the command bar to update all charts and components used in the dashboard.

The second icon, the grid, enables you to see the list of records used by the chart. You can see the details of the view used to generate the chart, as shown in Figure 16.55.

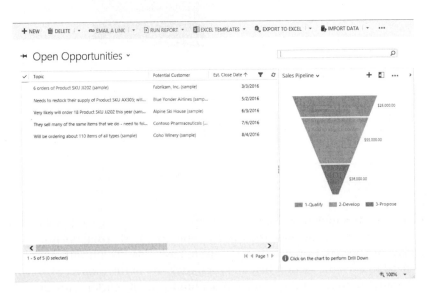

FIGURE 16.55   Viewing the record details of the chart.

The last icon is an enlargement image you can click to enlarge the chart to occupy the entire dashboard.

NOTE

You cannot print charts except by taking a screenshot. If you want printable charts, you should use SSRS reports, as described in the next section.

Introduction to SSRS

Microsoft SQL Server Reporting Services (SSRS) is a client/server reporting platform installed within Microsoft SQL Server. It is based on a service-oriented architecture (SOA), so it can be used as a service. SSRS was first introduced within Microsoft Dynamics CRM 3.0, using Microsoft SQL Server 2000 (before that, CRM used Crystal Reporting), and it has progressed with every version of CRM and SQL since then.

SSRS consists of the following components:

▶ **Report Manager**—This web application acts as a user interface application for managing and deploying the reports in the platform, as well as managing the security access for each report. You can usually find it from the server that has SSRS loaded, via http://localhost/reports.

▶ **Report Server**—This web service provides a common interface and entry point for all applications (including Report Manager and Microsoft Dynamics CRM) to interact with Report Server. You can usually find it from the server that has SSRS loaded, via http://localhost/reportsserver.

▶ **Report database**—SSRS uses two databases stored in SQL Server as the repository of the deployed reports, usually named ReportServer and ReportServerTempDB.

▶ **SRSS (using the Microsoft SQL Server instance name)**—This Windows service is responsible for processing related functions, such as report scheduling.

▶ **Other components**—The other components include configuration tools, Visual Studio project templates for report authoring, .NET controls to render and display reports in Windows, and custom web applications and API documentation for extensibility and development.

In addition to these components, SSRS has the following features:

▶ Support for report snapshot creation

▶ Support for scheduling of automated snapshot reports

▶ Alerts so you can be notified via email when a report is created

▶ Capability for all reports to be exported in the following formats:

  ▶ Microsoft Excel

  ▶ Acrobat PDF

  ▶ MSHTML (web archive)

  ▶ TIFF images

  ▶ Microsoft Word

  ▶ XML file with report data

  ▶ CSV (comma delimited)

16

▶ Capability to build reports with the open standard Report Definition Language (RDL), which is based on the XML standard (Reports can then be built not only with Visual Studio but also with other third-party tools.)

▶ Capability for each report to manage different data sources (This means that it is not necessarily tied to Microsoft SQL Server data. Reports can show data from any .NET-compatible data provider or from any OLEDB data provider.)

▶ Capability to display data in either tabular, matrix, or graphical forms, as well as to use expressions to format the data properly

Microsoft Dynamics CRM handles all the reports through SSRS, so you have access to all its benefits.

TIP

Unlike in previous versions of SSRS, SSRS with SQL Server 2012 or 2014 now includes the ability to add HTML into a report. This was a limitation that resulted in challenges with report rendering but has now been resolved.

NOTE

SSRS is a complex platform and providing complete details about it is beyond the scope of this book. For more information about SSRS, see Microsoft SQL Server books online or similar topics by Sams Publishing. To understand this chapter, you need only a basic understanding of SSRS and SQL.

Custom Reports

Custom reports are reports written with an external tool such as Visual Studio. As explained earlier in this chapter, you can easily build new basic custom reports with the Report Wizard in Microsoft Dynamics CRM; however, reports created using the wizard are not so flexible. In some cases, you need to write more complex reports and have a more flexible page layout and design. In those cases, you need to use a tool such as Visual Studio to create and build your custom reports.

When Are Custom Reports Recommended?

You may need custom reports for a variety of reasons, including the following:

▶ You might want special or custom designs such as those with complex layouts that can't be done with the Report Wizard.

▶ You might need to have a report with mixed data from data sources other than Microsoft CRM. For example, say that you control the inventory counts of your products on a separate system that uses an Oracle database, and you want to have one report that shows the CRM orders with their product details from Oracle and their inventory counts.

You can build custom reports with SSRS or with any other report application, such as Crystal Reports, or even with a custom application built in ASP.NET. The range of applications that you can use to build custom reports is beyond the scope of this book.

Installing CRM 2016 Report Authoring Extension

If you want to modify the reports generated by the Report Wizard or if you want to use Fetch queries in a report, you must install the CRM 2016 Report Authoring Extension, which you do by following these steps:

1. Download the Microsoft Dynamics CRM 2016 Report Authoring Extension from http://download.microsoft.com.

2. Run the file CRM2016-Bids-ENU-i386.exe, and a welcome screen appears.

3. Click Next to have the Setup Wizard check for updates and then click Next to continue to the next step and accept the licensing agreement. Check the I Accept the License Agreement check box and click I Accept to continue.

4. Install any necessary components, as required, and then click Next.

5. Setup checks the software components necessary to run this setup again. If everything is okay with your system, click Next and then install CRM Report Authoring Extension by clicking Install (see Figure 16.56).

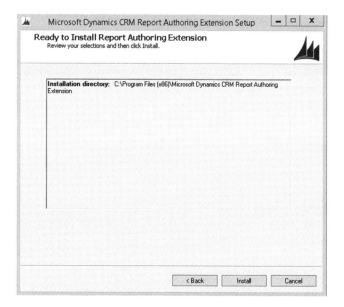

FIGURE 16.56   Final installation confirmation dialog.

6. When Setup finishes, click Finish.

After installing the CRM 2016 Report Authoring Extension, you can work with any report generated by the Report Wizard by opening it with Visual Studio. You can see that the data source connection type is Microsoft Dynamics CRM Fetch, and the connection string points to the CRM 2016 organization URL. Figure 16.57 shows the Data Source Properties dialog with the report opened in Visual Studio 2012.

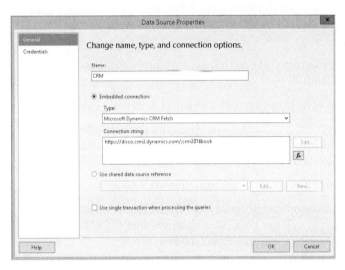

FIGURE 16.57   Microsoft Dynamics CRM Fetch data source type.

TIP

It is very important that the connection string have the URL and the organization name separated with a semicolon (as shown in Figure 16.57).

As shown in the Dataset Properties dialog, the query is written in Fetch (as shown in Figure 16.58).

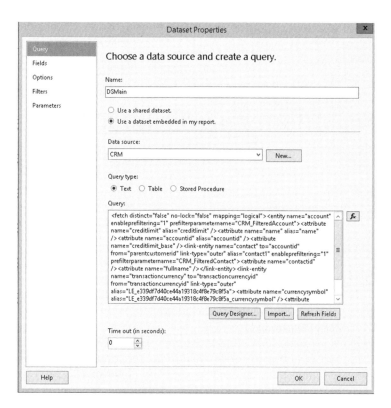

FIGURE 16.58   Fetch query.

> **NOTE**
>
> The Fetch query shown in Figure 16.86 might seem daunting the first time you work with it. As mentioned earlier in this chapter, learning the syntax and language of (and how to write) Fetch queries can take some time. If you are unfamiliar with the Fetch language, we recommend working with the CRM 2016 Advanced Find tool and then downloading via the Download Fetch XML button. Doing so will help you better understand the Fetch language.

Building Custom Reports with SSRS

When you install Microsoft SQL Server Data Tools, you automatically also install Visual Studio and project templates that you can use to build SSRS reports. You can find these project templates under the Business Intelligence group (see Figure 16.59).

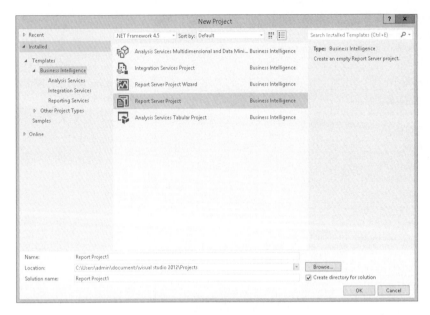

FIGURE 16.59   Business Intelligence group in Visual Studio.

> **NOTE**
>
> If you do not have Visual Studio installed, SQL Server Setup installs a limited version of Visual Studio (called SQL Server Data Tools, using the 2012 version), which only allows you to build reports and use the Business Intelligence projects. You cannot create Windows Forms applications or custom websites with this version.

The Microsoft Dynamics CRM SDK comes with detailed documentation about custom reports development. Refer to the Developers Guide to Reports for Microsoft Dynamics CRM in the SDK.

Even though you can create a new report in Visual Studio from scratch, we recommend using one of the existing preinstalled reports as a template. (For Dynamics CRM Online, you should start with the Report Wizard.) Follow these steps to use a preinstalled report as a template:

1. Go to Reports in the navigation bar, under Sales, Service, or Marketing.

2. Select the report you want to use as a template. Generally, you want to select a report that is similar to the one you want to create. For example, if you want to create a custom sales report, select one of the existing sales reports. Then click the Edit button on the navigation bar.

3. Select Actions > Download Report and then select the report (in this case, use the Account Distribution report).

4. Save the report on your local machine.

5. Rename the file with the new name of the report you want to build. In this example, rename the report to **Contacts Report.rdl**.

6. Start Visual Studio and select New > Project.

7. Click Business Intelligence in the Project Templates area and select the Report Server Project template.

8. In the Solution Explorer, right-click the Reports folder and click Add > Existing Item.

9. Navigate to the folder where you stored the Contacts Report.rdl report in step 4 and click the Add button.

When you open the report in Visual Studio, it should look similar to the one in Figure 16.60.

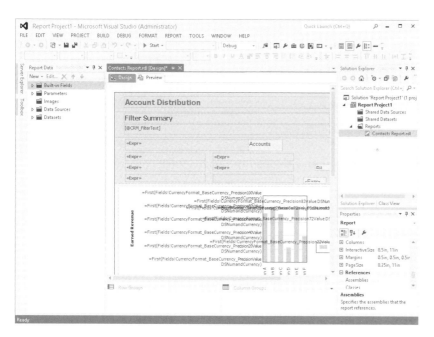

FIGURE 16.60   Account Distribution report opened in Visual Studio.

Developing and Testing Reports in Visual Studio

After you create a report project and add the report in Visual Studio, as explained earlier, you are ready to start modifying the report. To test a report quickly, you must fix the dataset's connection strings to point to your CRM server database. To do this, follow these steps:

1. Open the report you want to edit, go to the Report Data Explorer, and expand the Data Sources node, where you should see a data source named CRM, as shown in Figure 16.61.

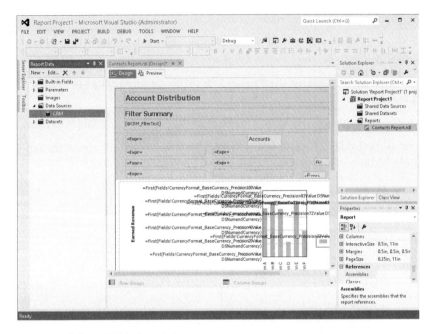

FIGURE 16.61   CRM shared data source.

2. Double-click the CRM data source to open the Data Source Properties dialog, as shown in Figure 16.62.

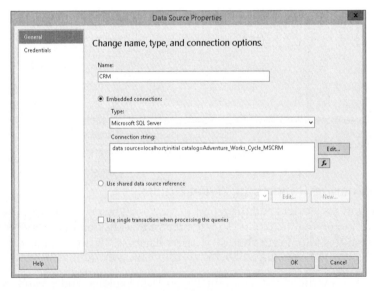

FIGURE 16.62   Data Source Properties dialog.

3. Select the server name in the Server Name field and locate the CRM database and change its name to <<*Your Organization Name*>>_MSCRM (see Figure 16.63).

FIGURE 16.63   Configuring the connection.

4. Click the Test Connection button to ensure that it connects successfully.

5. Click OK three times to close the dialogs.

CAUTION

The reports running on the SSRS server use a shared data source, so you should not deploy this data source.

As shown in Figure 16.64, Microsoft Dynamics CRM has three different types of custom reports:

▶ **Report Wizard Report**—This option is explained earlier in this chapter.

▶ **Existing File**—This option is described later in this chapter.

▶ **Link to Webpage**—This option is used only to link to an existing web page. It is explained later in this chapter.

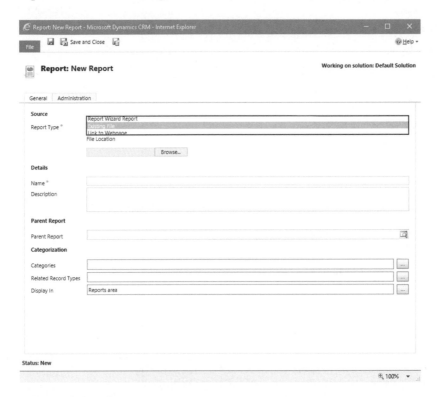

FIGURE 16.64   Report types.

To take advantage of the benefits of the CRM prefiltering feature, you need to keep some important considerations in mind when writing custom reports in Visual Studio, as described in the following section.

Filtered Views

Although you can build SQL queries by using the tables directly from the CRM SQL Server dataset, doing so is not recommended. The CRM SQL Server tables are shown in Figure 16.65.

Instead of using these tables directly for SQL queries, you can use predefined views and thus make life a lot easier because you don't have to spend time trying to understand the complexity of the tables by studying an entity-relationship diagram (ERD).

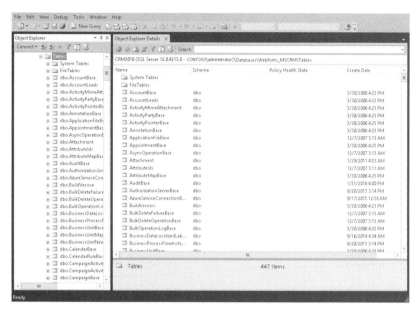

FIGURE 16.65   CRM SQL database tables.

A lot of views have names similar to the CRM entity names. The views you should use with your reports are the ones with the Filtered prefix. If you want to create a report that shows all the contact names, your underlying query will look similar to this:

```
select fullname from FilteredContact
```

One advantage of using these views is that they are updated automatically every time you add a custom attribute to an entity from the CRM customization interface. In addition, when a custom entity is created in CRM, it automatically creates a filtered view for the new custom entity. In the preceding example, the database view name would be dbo.FilteredContact.

Most importantly, filtered views provide security based on the user record permissions, so they show only the data that the user who is running the report has permission to see as well as the fields the user has permission to see if field-level security configurations are deployed.

NOTE

The custom properties and entities also have the prefix shown in the schema name. By default, this prefix is New_. However, you can change it in the Publisher setting of each solution. If you create a custom entity with the name Event, for example, the filtered view created is dbo.FilteredNew_event by default.

▶ To learn more about customizing solution settings, refer to **CHAPTER 22**.

Deployment

To deploy a report in SSRS, you normally use the Report Manager web application. However, you should not use this option when working with custom CRM reports because you won't be able to see the report in CRM if you do.

You can deploy reports from either the web or Outlook client interfaces. To deploy a report for CRM, you must use the CRM web client interface and follow these steps:

1. Go to the Reports area from the navigation bar, under either Sales, Service, or Marketing.

2. Click the New button.

3. Select Existing File in the Report Type dropdown (see Figure 16.66).

4. Under File Location, enter the full path of the report you built.

5. Optionally, change the name of the report, which by default is autopopulated with the name of the report file, and the two don't need to be the same.

6. Optionally, select the categories, related record types, and display in the options.

7. Click Save and Close.

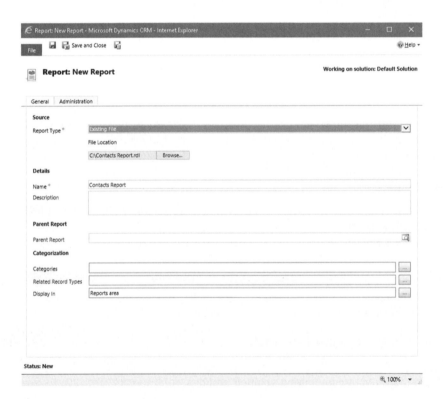

FIGURE 16.66   Deploying a new report.

Report Parameters

To see the predefined report parameters from Visual Studio, open the report you are authoring and expand the Parameters node on the Report Data window (see Figure 16.67).

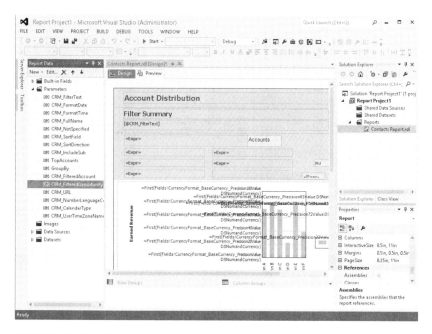

FIGURE 16.67   Report parameters.

The parameters include the following:

▶ **CRM_FilterText**—This parameter is used to display the Filter Summary text box (located in the report header), which displays the prefilters selected by the user.

▶ **CRM_URL**—This parameter provides drill-through capabilities on the CRM reports. You can use this to supply quick links to edit the instances of entities that you display on your report, for example.

▶ **CRM_FilteredEntity**—This parameter is used to set up the default prefilters on reports. You can add as many parameters as you like on the same report; you might have parameters such as CRM_FilteredContact and CRM_FilteredAccount, for example. When you deploy and run the report, you see the prefilters.

CAUTION

If you don't have any of these parameters defined, the report runs automatically without having the user select the prefilters. Also, users can't add prefilters by modifying the default report filters from the CRM reports area through the web or Outlook client interfaces.

16

▶ **CRM_NumberLanguageCode**—This parameter determines the language of the
user running the report. It is useful for multilanguage report implementations. This
parameter must have a default value from a query using the `fn_GetFormatStrings()`
function and using NumberLanguageCode for the Value field, as shown in
Figure 16.68. For example, this function returns a value of en-US for English
language in the United States.

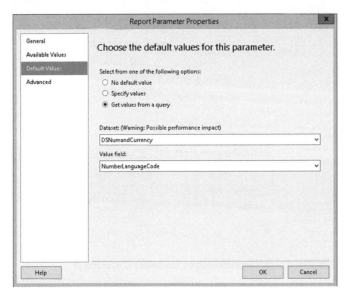

FIGURE 16.68   CRM_NumberLanguageCode parameter.

NOTE

When adding these parameters, be sure to set them as internal and set a default value of
distinct or null. This default value can be a nonqueried value or might come from a query.

After you add a query to the dataset, click the Refresh button so that you can start using
the fields on your report; otherwise, you get errors when you try to test and deploy it.

NOTE

It is always recommended to use the filtered views. With these types of reports, if you use
Windows authentication in your application, the security will be in place.

Building Custom Reports with ASP.NET

In addition to basing a new report on an existing one, another way to create a custom
report is to create an ASP.NET web application and then use the Link to Web Page option
to deploy it, as explained earlier. When you use this method, you don't get all the benefits

inherent to SSRS (including the capability to pass parameters to the reports and also use prefiltering), but you can extend a report with other features that are not possible with SSRS but easy to do with a custom ASP.NET application. Just keep in mind that if you need to create a report using this method, you must handle the filtering options in your application manually.

This following steps walk you through an example of a custom report built in ASP.NET 4.6 that takes advantage of LINQ and Visual Studio 2015 (although it would also work with Visual Studio 2013):

1. Open Visual Studio 2015 and create a new project by going to File > New Website.

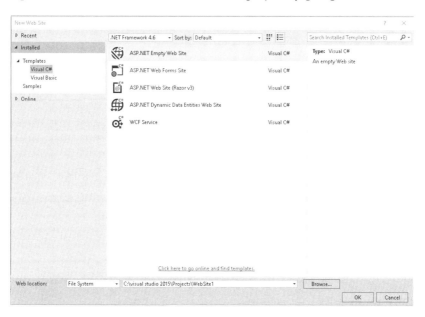

FIGURE 16.69   Creating a New Website project.

2. In the New Website window that appears (see Figure 16.69), select ASP.NET Empty Website and enter the location address for your website. For the language in this example, use C# and the 4.6 Framework. Then click OK to create the website.

3. In the Solution Explorer, right-click your website URL and select Add > Add New Item.

4. In the window that appears, select LINQ to SQL Classes, as shown in Figure 16.70, and click Add.

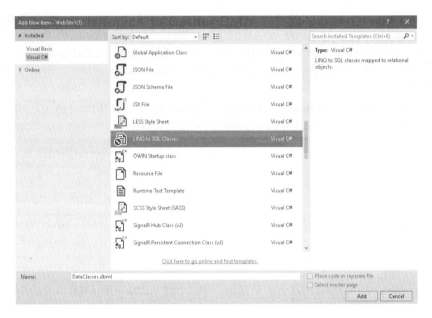

FIGURE 16.70   Adding LINQ to SQL Classes.

5. If you get a warning telling you to place the file in the app_code folder, click Yes.

6. In the Server Explorer on the left, right-click Data Connections and select the Add Connection option to add a new connection, as shown in Figure 16.71.

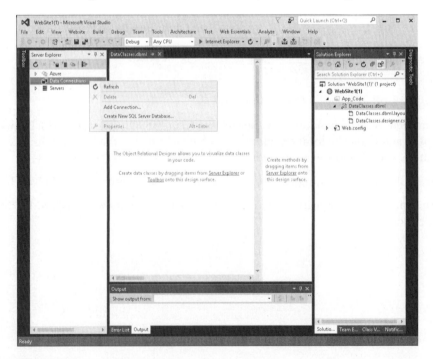

FIGURE 16.71   Adding the database connection.

7. In the Add Connection dialog that appears, select your data source type and provider and then select Microsoft SQL Server followed by your CRM database server and then your organization database name (which ends in _MSCRM), as shown in Figure 16.72. Click Test Connection to ensure that you have access, and then click OK.

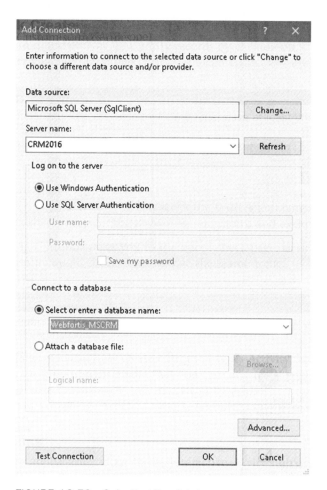

FIGURE 16.72   Selecting the database.

8. Expand the data connection you just created in the Server Explorer and expand the Views folder.

9. Locate the FilteredContact view and drag and drop it into the Object Relational Designer, as shown in Figure 16.73.

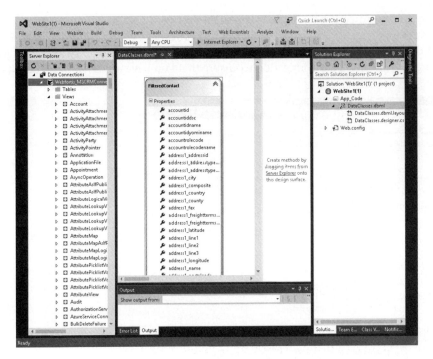

FIGURE 16.73   Adding FilteredContact to the Object Relational Designer.

10. Build your solution within Visual Studio and check and correct any errors you might have.

11. Go to the Solution Explorer, right-click your website URL, and select Add > Add New Item > Web Form and enter **Default.aspx** for the name. Click Add and drag and drop a GridView control, as shown in Figure 16.74.

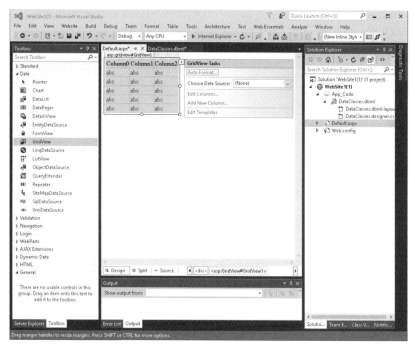

FIGURE 16.74   Adding a GridView control.

12. Under GridView Tasks, choose a data source and select New Data Source.

13. Select LINQ and click OK, as shown in Figure 16.75.

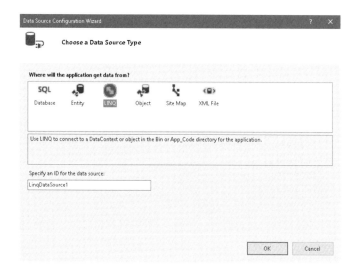

FIGURE 16.75   Adding a data source.

14. Leave the option that is displayed as the context object, as shown in Figure 16.76, and click Next.

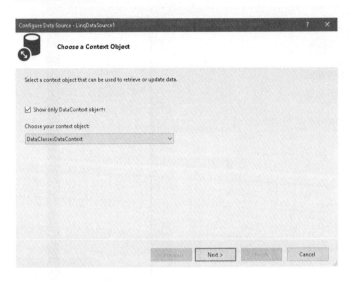

FIGURE 16.76   Choosing a context object.

15. Select the fields you want to display in the GridView control. Figure 16.77 shows fullname and jobtitle selected. Click Finish.

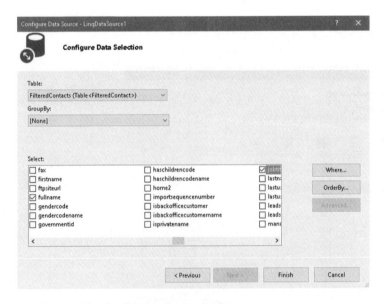

FIGURE 16.77   Configuring data selection.

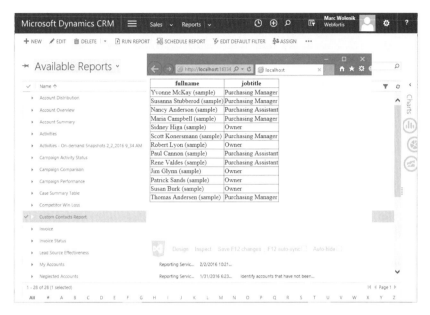

FIGURE 16.80   Testing the custom report in CRM.

Summary

This chapter describes how Microsoft Dynamics CRM addresses the concept of reporting. Keep in mind that reports include all of the following:

- ▶ SSRS reports

- ▶ Charts/visualizations/dashboards

- ▶ Custom reports

This chapter covers how to quickly and easily create new reports either by using the Report Wizard or via custom development. It also reviews the report scheduling feature and how to export reports for backups or redeployment.

In addition, this chapter discusses how to work with charts and their associated components, as well as how to work with dashboards. It also looks at different options for building custom reports with SSRS using Visual Studio and the Business Intelligence projects or by using Visual Studio for custom web application development.

16

Proper setup and configuration of Microsoft Dynamics CRM are critical to a successful implementation.

As you have seen in previous chapters, and as this chapter makes clear, the Settings area drives most of the core functionality in Microsoft Dynamics CRM. From user setup to template management to language options and customizations and processes, the Settings area is the place to go for proper configuration and tuning of your business.

> **NOTE**
>
> The Settings area should be a carefully controlled access point. If you want to remove access (aside from role membership, as discussed later in this chapter), you can modify the Site Map entity so that it does not appear. See Chapter 22, "Customizing Entities," for more information about working with the Site Map entity.

Components of a Good Implementation

A good Microsoft Dynamics CRM implementation consists of at least two main processes:

▶ **Physical setup**—For On-Premises solutions, this includes everything from loading the application on the server to ensuring that a proper backup strategy is in place. For hosted solutions, this includes proper setup and configuration of client access.

▶ **Configuration and customization of the application**—Configuration and customization in this case refer to how the application works compared to how you need it to work. For example, Microsoft

Dynamics CRM has several business processes when it is first loaded. Your business might never need to use them, but most businesses that use Microsoft Dynamics CRM can really benefit from them when they're configured to work like their business.

> ▶ Refer to the workflow information in **CHAPTER 26**, "Process Development," when considering building any workflow.

Additional considerations related to configuration include the processes mentioned earlier: setting up users, choosing which languages to deploy, selecting the currency types, and so on.

This chapter focuses on the options in the Settings section, which is divided in the following groups:

- ▶ Business
- ▶ Customization
- ▶ System
- ▶ Process Center

This chapter covers the Business and System groups.

> ▶ The Customization group is covered in **CHAPTER 22**, and the Process Center group is covered in **CHAPTER 26**.

Business Management

The Business Management group gives you the following options (see Figure 17.1):

- ▶ Fiscal Year Settings
- ▶ Goal Metrics
- ▶ Business Closures
- ▶ Facilities/Equipment
- ▶ Queues
- ▶ Resource Groups
- ▶ Sales Territories
- ▶ Services
- ▶ Sites
- ▶ Subjects
- ▶ Currencies
- ▶ Connection Roles

▶ Relationship Roles

▶ Automatic Record Creation and Update Rules

The following sections describe all these options except for the last one, as they are covered in Chapter 10, "Working with Service".

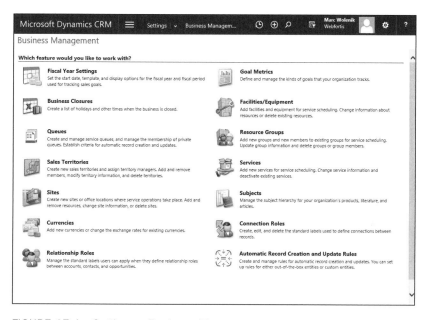

FIGURE 17.1   Settings > Business Management.

Fiscal Year Settings

The Fiscal Year settings determine how your calendar year and fiscal year are divided and are commonly used for managing goals.

> **CAUTION**
>
> Be careful with the fiscal period; you should not change this setting unless absolutely necessary because doing so will affect reporting.

The following fields are available in the Fiscal Year Settings dialog (see Figure 17.2):

▶ **Start Date**—The date the fiscal year starts.

▶ **Fiscal Period Template**—A description of how the fiscal year is divided. Typically, this is set to Quarterly, but it can be any of the options in the drop-down: Annually, Semiannually, Quarterly, Monthly, or 4-Week Period.

▶ **Fiscal Year**—The fiscal year display options.

▶ **Named Based On**—Whether the displayed name is based on the start or end of the fiscal year.

▶ **Fiscal Period**—The fiscal period abbreviation.

▶ **Display As**—How the fiscal year is displayed.

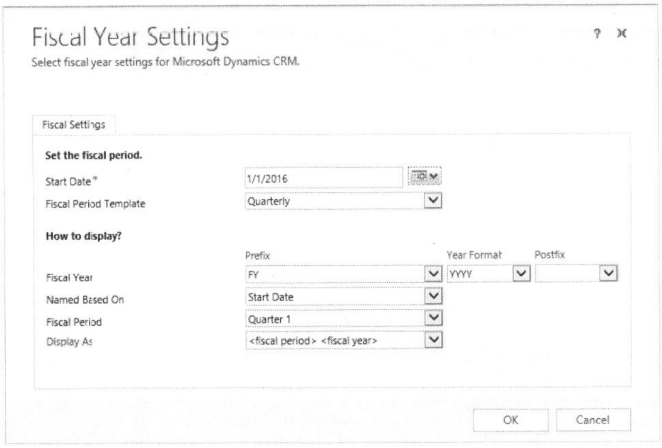

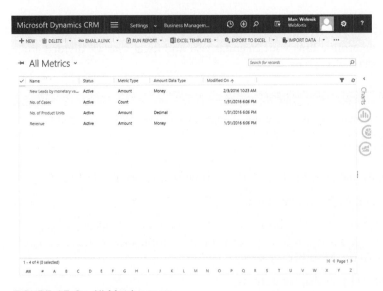

FIGURE 17.2   Fiscal Year Settings dialog.

Goal Metrics

Dynamics CRM 2016 offers an easy-to-use and easy-to-manage option for goals. Selecting Goal Metrics from the Business Management interface brings you to the All Metrics page in the Settings section (see Figure 17.3).

FIGURE 17.3   All Metrics page.

▶ For more information about goals, refer to **CHAPTER 7**, "Working with Sales."

Business Closures

The Business Closures option is useful for managing service activities. A user cannot schedule activities during a time when a business closure is designated unless the Do Not Observe option is selected. (The Do Not Observe option is selected when working with resources and setting up work hour schedules.)

When creating a business closure, you have the option to create it as a full-day, multiple-day, or part-of-the-day event (see Figure 17.4).

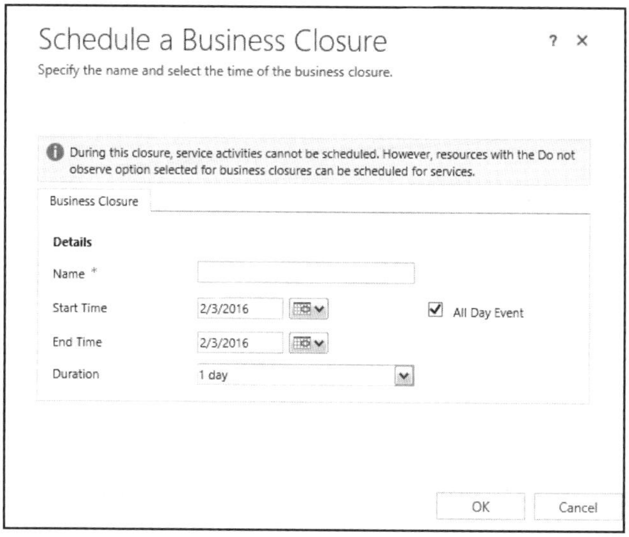

FIGURE 17.4   Adding designated business closures.

You can create business closures for any time period, and when you create one, you prevent service activities from being scheduled (unless the Do Not Observe option is selected for the resource).

▶ To learn more about service functionality, refer to **CHAPTER 10** "Working with Service."

Facilities/Equipment

Services use the Facilities/Equipment option when scheduling resources (see Figure 17.5). You use the Facilities/Equipment area when performing service scheduling because it works with the resources component. It differs from a business location because it involves the necessary services to complete a service task. If a business location is needed, you need to add a site, as explained later in this chapter.

▶ For more information on service scheduling, refer to **CHAPTER 10**.

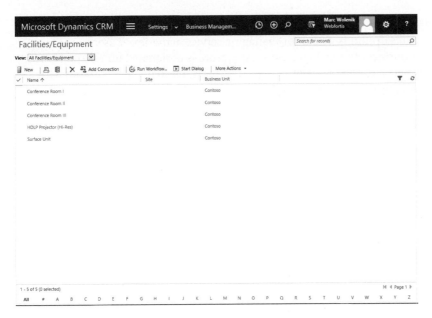

FIGURE 17.5   Facilities/Equipment.

Queues

Queues serve as general access areas that are used to store items. You can set up custom queues to automatically process incoming email and convert them to activities (awaiting assignment in a queue).

There is a default queue set up for every user and team in Microsoft Dynamics CRM 2016, and these queues are available for everyone to use. If you click View on the command bar, you see all the queues, as shown in Figure 17.6.

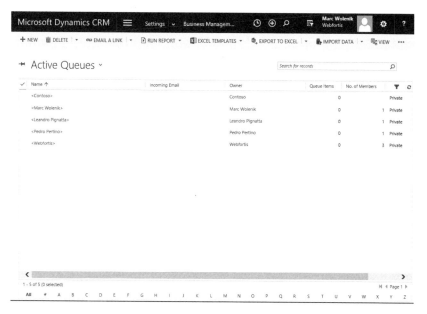

FIGURE 17.6   All Queues.

> **NOTE**
>
> Notice that the users' queues (refer to Figure 17.6) are surrounded by < and >. These symbols indicate default queues, which are provided so that items can be routed automatically when an item is created (or is assigned via a change of ownership). The < and > symbols are the default format, but on the user setup page you can specify a different symbol for the default queue assignment.

To create a queue, follow these steps:

1. Navigate to Settings > Business Management > Queues. Select New to create a new queue. The form shown in Figure 17.7 appears.

2. Enter the queue name and owner.

3. Optionally enter the email address that the queue will use to gather incoming emails and automatically convert them to activities.

FIGURE 17.7 Queue setup.

4. In the Email Settings section, select how Microsoft CRM should work with emails received by the email address entered for the queue. By default, the system processes all incoming email messages and converts them to activities. However, you can select to process only incoming emails that are in response to other emails previously sent from CRM; or only emails received that resolve to existing CRM leads, contacts, or accounts; or only emails that resolves to exiting CRM email-enabled entities.

5. Click Save. The mailbox for the email configuration is created for this queue as soon as the queue is created.

▶ For more information about configuring email access, **SEE CHAPTER 20**, "Email Configuration."

Queues can be activated, deactivated, or deleted. If a queue is deactivated, all items are removed from it, and if it is reactivated, it remains empty until it is used again. Before you can delete a queue, you need to move all of its items to another queue.

You can set security on queues by using roles (as explained later in this chapter). In addition, one of the most significant features is the concept of Working On; the owner of a record maintains ownership, but another person can be a Working On user. (This option is found on the Queue Item record, via the Queue view navigation.)

> **NOTE**
>
> New features have been added to queues since Dynamics CRM 2013 to help in configuring the automation of email activity to case or from social activity to case, for example. See Chapter 10.

Resource Groups

A resource group consists of users, teams, facility/equipment, or other resources grouped for the purposes of service scheduling.

To create a resource group, in the Resource Groups area, select New and enter the name of the resource group (see Figure 17.8).

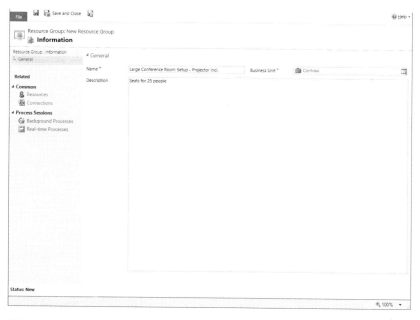

FIGURE 17.8   Creating a new resource group.

After you save the resource group, you can add resources to it (see Figure 17.9).

▶ For more information on service scheduling, refer to **CHAPTER 10**.

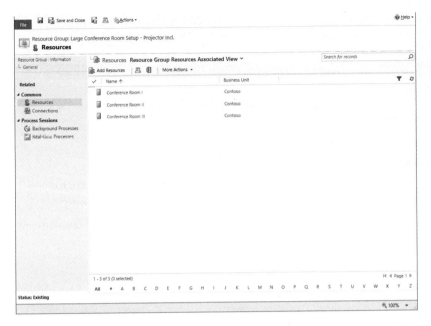

FIGURE 17.9   Resources added to a resource group.

Sales Territories

A sales territory groups users into one territory, with a common manager specific to the territory (see Figure 17.10).

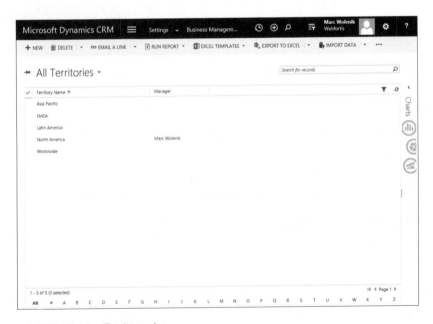

FIGURE 17.10   Territory view.

> **NOTE**
>
> The territory manager is not necessarily the user's manager. Because users can be assigned to only one territory, if you want to assign a user to more than one of your existing territories, you must create a new territory that covers the existing ones and assign the user to that new territory.

To create a new territory, in the Sales Territory area, select New and enter the territory name and, if applicable, the territory manager. Users in territories are either users or a manager. The territory manager is used for reporting/workflow purposes.

Click Members in the left navigation pane and then select users to add to the territory. Because a user can be assigned to only a single territory, each one is removed from any previously assigned territories when assigned to a new one.

Territories are very useful for summarizing data in sales reports, as well as obtaining various metrics data on activities by territory.

Services

Services are activities performed by one or multiple resources that are scheduled using the Service Scheduling module.

▶ For more information about working with services, refer to **CHAPTER 10**.

Sites

Sites are the physical locations where work is done. They are assigned in using the Service Scheduling module. When you create a site, the only required information are the location name and the time zone (see Figure 17.11).

FIGURE 17.11   Creating a site.

After a site has been created, you can assign resources consisting of either users or facility/ equipment to it by selecting Resources from the left navigation pane (see Figure 17.12).

▶ For more information on service scheduling, refer to **CHAPTER 10**.

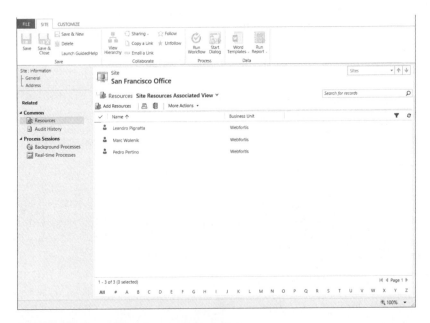

FIGURE 17.12   Adding resources to a site.

Subjects

Subjects are the individual topics that make up your organization. They provide context and are required relations when you're working with and creating the following entities:

- ▶ Case
- ▶ Sales Literature
- ▶ Knowledge Article
- ▶ Product

Generally, subjects include information related to these entities and are hierarchal in nature (see Figure 17.13).

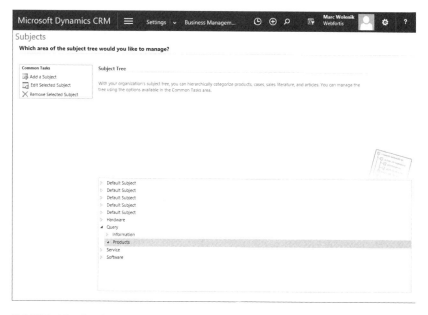

FIGURE 17.13   Subject hierarchy example.

To create a new subjects, select the node of the subject tree under which you want to add a new subject and then click Add a Subject. By default, the parent subject populates with the subject you selected (see Figure 17.14). Enter a value in the Title field, as well as any corresponding description. Then click Add to add the entered subject to the subject tree, where it is then available for selection when working with the previous entities.

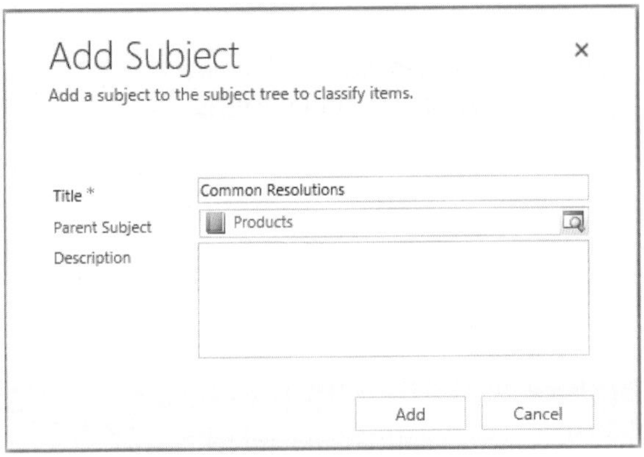

Add Subject   ×

Add a subject to the subject tree to classify items.

Title *   Common Resolutions

Parent Subject   Products

Description

                                    Add   Cancel

FIGURE 17.14   Adding a new subject.

NOTE

Carefully consider setting up the subject tree for your products. Although an association is not required, subjects let you effectively categorize products for searching and reporting. When you are setting up the subject tree for products, the subjects are usually at a more general level than the actual product. For example, a subject might be Computers, and actual products associated might be Laptop, Desktop, and Handheld.

Currencies

When you add and activate currencies, they are available to the user. When a currency other than the base currency is used, the values associated with the record are converted (based on the conversion rate entered for that currency) to the base currency.

Although you cannot delete a currency if it has been associated with a record, you can disable it, which prevents it from being used on any new records.

To add a new currency option, select New. In the form that appears (see Figure 17.15), select the code from the Currency Code field lookup (or select Custom for Currency Type to enter a new custom currency). The Currency Name and Currency Symbol fields populate automatically, but you can change this information, if necessary. Finally, enter the currency conversion rate, which is the rate at which the selected currency converts to the base currency rate.

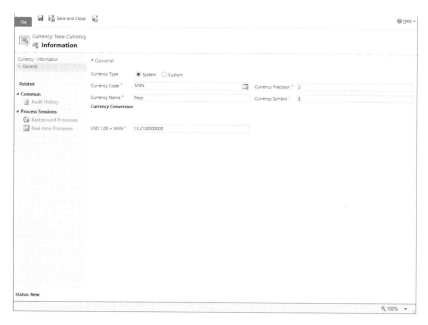

FIGURE 17.15   Creating a new currency.

NOTE

The conversion rate entered for a currency remains in effect until a system administrator updates it. Inaccurate data can potentially be reported if the conversion rate is not updated relatively frequently, based on the selected currency conversion fluctuations. You might want to extend the functionality of Microsoft Dynamics CRM by calling a web service to automatically calculate conversion monthly, weekly, daily, or even hourly.

▶ For more information on extending Microsoft Dynamics CRM, **SEE CHAPTER 22**.

After new currencies are created, different currencies can be assigned to transactions such as quotes, orders, invoices, and price lists. When this happens, Microsoft Dynamics CRM converts the money fields to the base currency, using the exchange rate entered for the selected currency.

It is important to understand when this conversion might happen because the exchange rate may change between the time of a transaction and the time of its conversion. For example, if a quote is created but waits for approval for three months, during that time, the exchange rate could adjust several times.

Exchange rates are updated when quotes, orders, invoices, or price lists are created and when any field that relates to currency is updated. In addition, if the state of the entity changes, exchange rates are recalculated.

> **NOTE**
>
> Changing a currency rate has no effect on any entity that is using that currency unless one of the conditions previously mentioned (update or state change) is met. Therefore, you could view a transaction that has an old exchange rate unless you explicitly update it by changing the values or changing the entity state.

Connection Roles

Meant to replace relationship roles, connection roles are a more flexible variant of establishing a relationship (or connection) to other records. Figure 17.16 shows the default connection roles available.

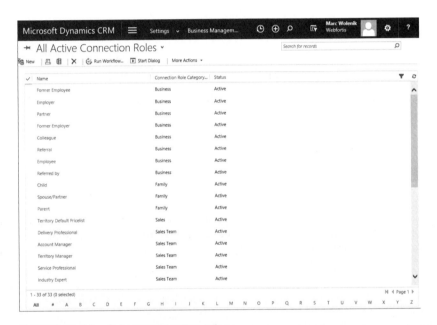

FIGURE 17.16   Default connection roles.

To create a new connection role, in the Connection Roles option, select New and fill out the form shown in Figure 17.17. After you establish connection roles, they are available on the entity level (as selected in step 2 in the form shown in Figure 17.17) for reporting/management.

FIGURE 17.17   Creating a new connection role.

Relationship Roles

Relationship roles are available only for accounts, contacts, and opportunities. They are designed to enable users to configure relationship types that might exist between records of these entities in the system. Relationship roles can be used for any kind of relationship (such as business, family, and social).

To create a new relationship role, in the Relationship Roles option, select New and enter the role name (see Figure 17.18). Account, Contact, and Opportunity settings are not required; however, if you do not make selections for them, the relationship role will be active but not available to use on any entity.

FIGURE 17.18   Creating a relationship role.

When creating a relationship, you can set the type of relationship based on the relationship roles that have been created. For this example, select the Vendor relationship role you created earlier but select it only for the sample contact not for the sample account shown (refer to Figure 17.18).

Select ... > Relationships > Customer Relationships for the sample contact record, and you can see the roles in the drop-downs after you select the Party 2 field. Figure 17.19 shows the Relationship dialog with the various options.

After you do this setup, users can easily query on any roles; however, the results are not displayed in any kind of graphical format without a third party add-on.

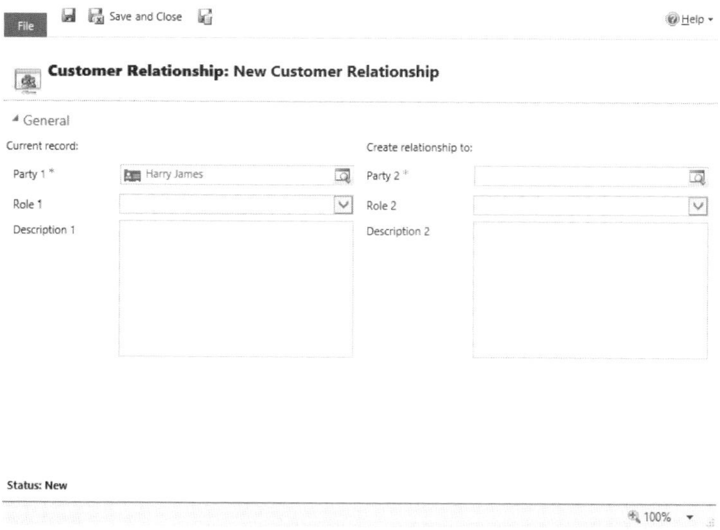

File   Save and Close   Help ▾

Customer Relationship: New Customer Relationship

▲ General

Current record: Create relationship to:

Party 1 *   Harry James   Party 2 *

Role 1   Role 2

Description 1   Description 2

Status: New

100% ▾

FIGURE 17.19   Relationship role example.

Templates

Templates facilitate the management of predefined articles, contracts, emails, and both Word and Excel mail merges. You can build email templates to dynamically include context-sensitive information such as senders and receivers.

A Templates tile is available in the navigation bar, as shown in Figure 17.20.

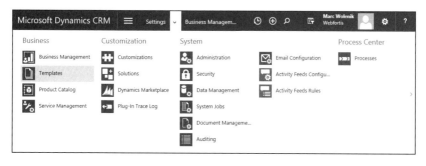

FIGURE 17.20   Templates tile.

If you click the Templates tile, you see five template categories:

▶ Article Templates

▶ Contract Templates

▶ Email Templates

▶ Mail Merge Templates

▶ Document Templates

The last option, Document Templates, is a new addition to Dynamics CRM 2016 that better integrates Microsoft Word and Excel with Dynamics CRM.

Templates can be active or inactive, and they can be in any language that the system administrator makes available.

> **NOTE**
>
> You can find templates for data import under Settings > Data Management, not here. You can also find the entitlements templates under Settings > Service Management, not here.

Article Templates

You use article templates when working with the built-in knowledge base (found in the Service section of Microsoft Dynamics CRM). They can include formatted titles, sections, and section titles.

Contract Templates

You use contract templates to manage contracts. They include information such as billing frequency and service allotment.

▶ For more information about templates, refer to **CHAPTER 10**.

Email Templates

Email templates are the richest templates because they allow for customizations specific to the sender and receiver. Email templates have several core properties that affect how they work:

▶ Template Type

▶ Viewable By

▶ Language

Template Type   You select an option from the Template Type drop-down when you first create a template (see Figure 17.21).

FIGURE 17.21   Template Type field.

The template type determines what data fields are available to work with on the template. Table 17.1 describes which entities' data fields are available with the various template types.

TABLE 17.1   Entity Data Fields Available for Various Template Types

Template Type	Entity Data Fields Available
Global	User
Lead	User, Lead
Opportunity	User, Account, Contact, Opportunity
Account	User, Account, Contact
Contact	User, Account, Contact
Quote	User, Account, Contact, Quote
Order	User, Account, Contact, Order
Invoice	User, Account, Contact, Invoice
Case	User, Account, Contact, Case
Contract	User, Account, Contact, Contract
Service Activity	User, Account, Contact, Service Activity, Site, Service
System Job	User, System Job

Viewable By   The Viewable By property identifies where the email template is available. The entire organization can view and use templates created in the Settings area (assuming that everyone has adequate permission from their security roles).

Users can create their own email templates from their personal options, and, by default, the permissions on their personal templates are set at Individual. You can promote these templates to Organizational and use them across the organization by selecting Make Template Available to Organization from the Actions drop-down menu.

17

> **TIP**
>
> A user who owns a personal template or an administrator can promote it by navigating to All Email Templates and setting Viewable By to Individual.

Language   The Language property specifies the language of the template. By default, templates are displayed in the view as All Email Templates, and only the base language templates appear there. If a new template is created and another language is selected, it does not appear in All Email Templates; you must select All Language Email Templates to see the templates that exist outside the base template.

As with the rest of the system, the only language options are those that the system administrator has loaded and made available in Settings > Languages.

To create a template, follow these steps:

1. Select New > Template Type.

2. Select the language, the title, and (optionally) the description. These are specific to the template properties, and the recipient will not see them. The recipient will see the subject and the body, and these are available for dynamic content.

3. To enter dynamic content, place the cursor in either the subject or the body and click the Insert/Update button at the top of the form. (If the cursor is in the title or the description, the dynamic fields will be placed in the body by default.) The Data Field Values dialog then opens, enabling you to add data fields. Click Add to add a data field (see Figure 17.22).

FIGURE 17.22   Data Field Values dialog.

TIP

The Default Text field enables you to enter alternative text that appears when the selected data field is blank.

---

4. Select the record type to work with. By default, the user record information will always be available, along with content-specific information related to the template type. (See the previous discussion about template type.)

5. Select the attribute from Record Type and add it to Data Field Values dialog. Selecting more than one value causes Microsoft Dynamics CRM to add only one value from the list—whichever one it finds first. In addition, each data field must be added uniquely. (For example, for the name of the contact, if you select First Name and then Last Name as part of the same data field, Microsoft Dynamics CRM uses the first name (if available), not the last name. If the first name is not available, CRM uses the last name. If neither is available, CRM uses the default text entered. If there is no default text, CRM leaves this field blank.) Format the text/dynamic areas as desired (see Figure 17.23).

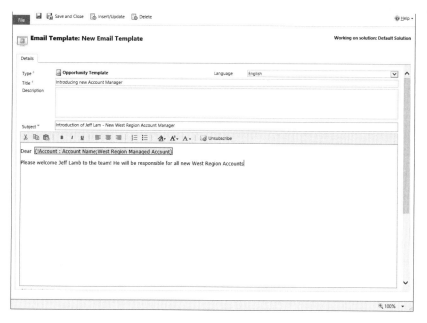

FIGURE 17.23   Selecting data field values.

Templates can have attachments. To add an attachment to a template, scroll down to the bottom of the template and add an attachment.

You can include an image in a template as an attachment, or you can copy and paste the image from any public website. To do this, navigate to the website and then copy and paste the image directly into the body of the template.

Another use for templates is in the creation of an email signature. You can create a template with Template Type set to Global and add the desired signature values. Then, when you create an email, select the Insert Template option and insert the signature template.

TIP

You can add multiple templates to a single email.

Mail Merge Templates

Mail merge templates are powerful because they allow for the creation of formatted Word documents with data from Microsoft Dynamics CRM.

To create a new mail merge template, navigate to the templates and select New and complete the required fields. The Categorization field enables you to select the associated entity: Quote, Opportunity, Lead, Account, Case, Profile Album, Contact, or any custom entity that is mail merge enabled. The ownership defaults to Individual, but you can change that to Organizational later. Template language is limited to the language options installed and made active by the system administrator.

In the File Attachment area, you specify the merge document that is associated with the mail merge template.

NOTE

The only acceptable file type for mail merge templates is Microsoft Office Word documents saved in Office XML format.

Figure 17.24 shows a mail merge template associated with the Contact entity.

FIGURE 17.24   Mail merge template.

Document Templates

Document templates, as mentioned earlier, are a new addition to Dynamics CRM 2016 that better integrate Microsoft Word and Excel with Dynamics CRM.

▶ Refer to **CHAPTER 21**, "Office Integration," for information about working with document templates.

Product Catalog

Information about the products being sold is managed in the Product Catalog section, where you can provide information in four areas:

▶ Families & Products

▶ Price Lists

▶ Discount Lists

▶ Unit Groups

TIP

Although they're not listed here, products associated with currencies are classified by subject. If you're setting up a large product list, it might make sense to build the subject categories and add whatever currencies you want to work with before you start working with products. If you need to make changes after the products have been created, you can select the Reclassify option from the command bar.

Figure 17.25 shows the Product Catalog section and its four areas.

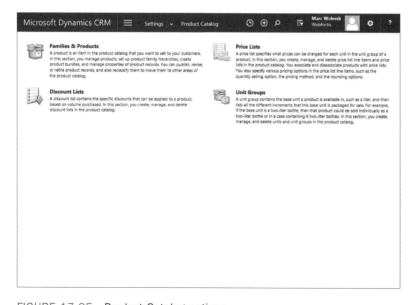

FIGURE 17.25   Product Catalog options.

NOTE

Many Microsoft Dynamics CRM users will undoubtedly be interested in having their product catalog managed by another application, typically their accounting or ERP system. This is a best practice and highly recommended. This management is usually handled programmatically and can be configured for almost any type of ERP/accounting system using integration software such as Scribe (www.scribesoft.com).

Families & Products

There have been some enhancements made in the Families & Products area: You can now create families, products, and bundles. Products can now have dynamic properties defined, and they can be hierarchically related. You can also manage drafts of products that need to be published in order for users to be able to use the products in quotes, orders, and invoices.

Families   A product family doesn't require you to set a unit group, a default unit, or the decimals supported. You use a product family to set Dynamics CRM properties that can be inherited by other products that belong to the product family. This extends the use of the product catalog in a flexible way.

▶ Refer to **CHAPTER 7**, "Working with Sales," for information about working with products.

Products   You can set up and maintain the products you sell, using the following options:

▶ Product Details

▶ Substitutes

▶ Price List Items

▶ Kit Products

NOTE

It is possible for users to create products as write-in products. Write-in products are products that are not set up in the product catalog.

TIP

Be sure to monitor the use of write-in products by your users. Salespeople often use write-in products to manipulate the system to sell products that are in the product catalog but create product discounts or solve other limitations that aren't normally available.

In the Product Designer, you use the Summary tab to set required information such as product ID, product name, unit group, default unit, and decimals supported (see Figure 17.26).

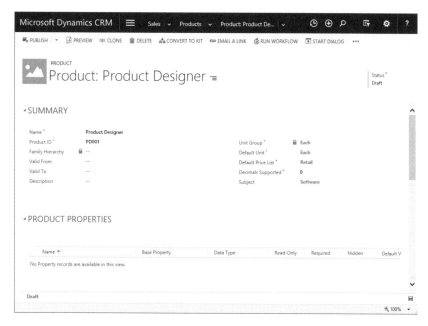

FIGURE 17.26   Product Designer.

You can also enter vendor information. This is helpful for automation and shipping routines that might be incorporated into the system related to e-commerce situations.

In the Substitutes section, you can specify products from the product catalog that can be substituted for the product being created or edited. Substitutions are not the same as write-in products, which can consist of any item; rather, they are predefined substitutions for the product being edited.

In the Price List Items section, you specify the product groupings applicable to the product, as well as their associations to the actual product and units.

Another important option is Quantity Selling Option, which enables you to sell in any fashion. This is good, for example, if you have selected hours as your product, and you want to invoice in only 15-minute increments, or 1/4 quantity.

In the Kit Products section, you can specify a number of products bundled as a kit for purposes of selling as a group. A kit product has a single price for all the items in the kit. To create a kit product, select the product and select … > Convert to Kit. (Similarly, if you want to demote a kit product to a regular product, select … > Convert to Product.) An example of a kit product might be a 1-hour service call on a computer that includes a new mouse and a new computer (see Figure 17.27).

FIGURE 17.27   Converting to a kit product.

Bundles   A product bundle allows you to group different products in a bundle so sales-people can sell products together in a combo, possibly at a special price.

▶ Refer to **CHAPTER 7**" for information about working with products and product bundles.

Price Lists

Price lists are groupings of products with associated pricing. If you don't have varied pricing for some reason, you could easily set up a single price list (called Standard Price List, Default Price List, or something similar) with all your products and their pricing on it. In addition, you might have only a small number of price lists, such as Retail and Wholesale. However, no limit governs the number of available price lists; you can create multiple price lists by customer, region, time of year, or based on some other consideration.

> **TIP**
>
> Having too many price lists can create confusion when your salespeople are attempting to build quotes, orders, or invoices. If you use many price lists, be sure to use a comprehensive naming strategy to ensure that the right list is used.

Although you need to create price lists next in the hierarchy, they aren't completed until you add products to each list. Fortunately, you can do this in the final step when the products are built, and, if necessary, you can return to the price list items for each price list to edit the items.

A price list consists of the name, currency, and start/end dates that the price list is applicable for, as well as price list items (see Figure 17.28).

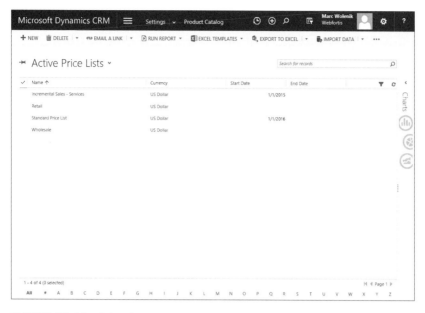

FIGURE 17.28   Price lists.

> **NOTE**
>
> Although you can configure the start and end dates for a price list, these dates are not enforced, and users can continue to use a price list after the end date has passed. You must manually deactivate or delete a price list after the date has passed to prevent it from being used.

> **TIP**
>
> You can easily set up price lists in conjunction with discount lists for promotional and seasonal pricing for specific products. To do this, create a new discount list with the discount and quantity of discount (see the next section). (For this scenario, in which the promotional pricing would apply to every item, regardless of quantity, the beginning quantity would be 1, and the ending quantity would be whatever maximum level you wanted to set.) Then create a new price list and add existing products and units, as well as the discount list you previously set up. Be sure to name both the price list and the discount list appropriately so that you'll know what they are for.

A price list is active by default when you create a new one unless you explicitly deactivate it.

Discount Lists

Commonly referred to as *discount schedules,* discount lists allow discounts to be given based on quantity. Discounts can be based on either percentage or amount or quantity ordered within a specified range (see Figure 17.29).

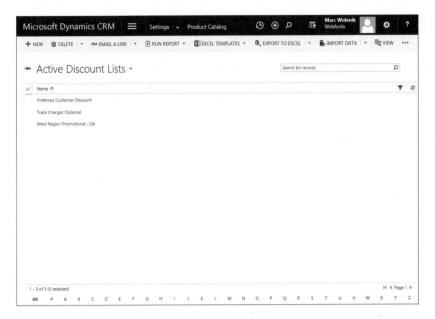

FIGURE 17.29   Discount list configured for varied quantities.

When you're thinking about setting up a discount list, consider how you want the discount to be applied. The following example shows how a discount list might work using percentages:

Beginning Quantity	Ending Quantity	Percentage Discount
1,000	5,000	3.50
5,001	25,000	5.00
25,001	100,000+	7.50

If you wanted to set up a discount list with amounts, you could do it as follows:

Beginning Quantity	Ending Quantity	Amount Discount
1,000	5,000	$50.00
5,001	25,000	$150.00
25,001	100,000+	$500.00

In both cases, no discount is applied if the quantity ordered is less than 1,000.

You can create as many discount lists as necessary and, although not required, you can associate them with different price lists and price list items. (See the "Price Lists" section, earlier in this chapter.)

Unit Groups

Unit groups determine groupings for selling products. A good example of unit groups is for cans of soda. The quantity (or unit group) is determined by how the soda is purchased because it is possible to purchase a single can, a six-pack, a case consisting of 12 cans, or a case of 24 cans. Unit groups could also consist of minutes, hours, and days for services offered. These are just a couple examples. Unit groups can comprise any level of quantities for whatever products or services your company sells.

Each of the quantities for a unit group consists of a primary unit, which is the lowest level of unit available and, in the case of services, could be at any level. The example shown in Figure 17.30 illustrates a services company that sells its services by the second. (Granted, this is a somewhat far-fetched scenario, but it clearly illustrates how to set up quantities.)

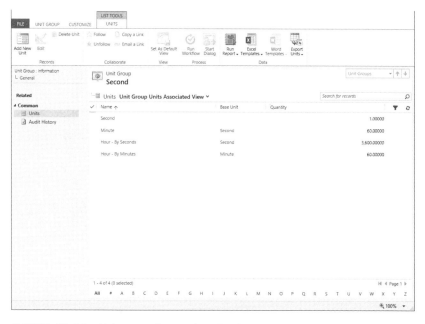

FIGURE 17.30   Unit group for services by the second.

> **NOTE**
>
> In this example, note that you can charge for an hour of time in a couple different ways, but the base units differ depending on whether you're using minutes or seconds. Unit groups are associated with products and the default units for the products.

Service Management

Service Management is a new area in Dynamics CRM where you find all the necessary configurable components in a single page. This area has the following groups (see Figure 17.31):

▶ Case Settings with Record Creation and Update Rules

▶ Service Terms

▶ Knowledge Base Management

▶ Templates

▶ Service Scheduling

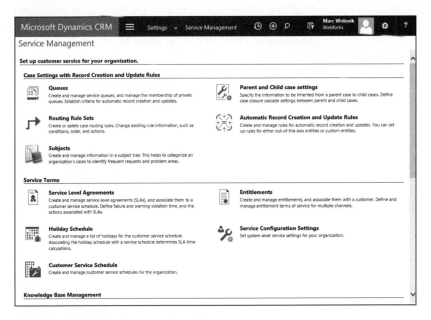

FIGURE 17.31   Service Management area.

▶ Refer to **CHAPTER 10** for information about working with services.

Customization

The Customization area allows you to modify Microsoft Dynamics CRM extensively. In this area you get the following options:

▶ Customizations

▶ Solutions

▶ Dynamics Marketplace

▶ Plug-in Trace Log

▶ **SEE CHAPTER 22** for information about working with customizations.

System Administration

The System features are features that should be carefully controlled and be given limited access, as the changes to these features can have severe effects, including revoking permissions for intended users. Organizations typically limit access to the System features to only one or two system administrators.

There are two main System categories: Administration and Security.

Administration

Administration is where a majority of the system setup, configuration, and maintenance is performed. The Administration page has the following options:

▶ Announcements

▶ Auto-Numbering

▶ System Settings

▶ Languages

▶ Privacy Preferences

▶ Subscription Management (CRM Online only)

▶ System Notifications (CRM Online only)

▶ Resources in Use (CRM Online only)

▶ Product Updates (partner hosted or On-Premises only)

▶ Yammer Configuration

▶ Microsoft Social Engagement Configuration

> **NOTE**
>
> When working with CRM Online, the options on the Administration screen may be slightly different, depending on whether your organization is using an upgraded version or not. For example, you may or may not see the Subscription Management, System Notifications, and Resources in Use options.

Figure 17.32 shows the Administration screen from the Settings area with the On-Premises options visible. The following sections describe all the possible options on the Administration screen.

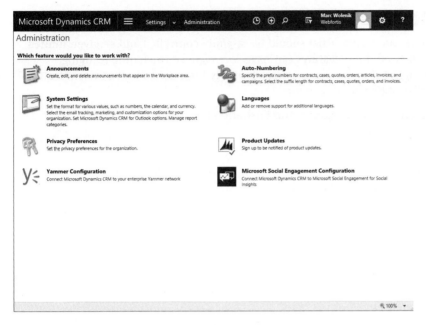

FIGURE 17.32   Settings > Administration screen.

Announcements

Announcements previously enabled you to communicate with CRM users by creating messages that could be displayed to users in the system. With this version of Microsoft Dynamics CRM, the announcements home page has been removed and is not available to end users unless you either customize the interface (by adding back the /home/homepage/home_news.aspx URL in a SubArea to a SiteMap entity) or implement it programmatically inside a web resource or an IFRAME inside a dashboard.

Announcements are listed by creation date, with the most recent at the top. When creating announcements, select New and complete the required information (see Figure 17.33). Announcements have four properties:

- ▶ **Title**—This field is required.

- ▶ **Body**—This field is required.

- ▶ **More Information URL**—This field is optional. However, when entered, it displays on the main announcements page, allowing users to navigate directly to the entered URL.

- ▶ **Expiration Date**—This field is an optional value that automatically hides the announcement after the date has expired. After the announcement has expired, you can reactivate it by changing the expiration date to a future date.

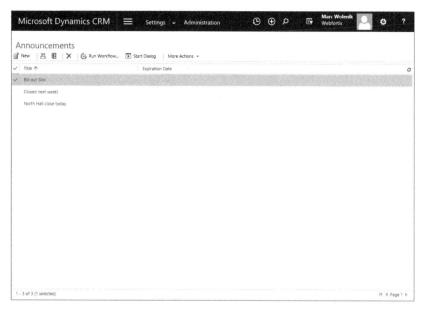

FIGURE 17.33   Announcements.

NOTE

Announcements do not support either rich formatting or having documents attached. If you need to refer to external documents, consider placing them in a common web directory and inserting the More Information URL into the announcement record.

Auto-Numbering

By default, Microsoft Dynamics CRM auto-numbers the following entities incrementally:

▶ Contract

▶ Case

▶ Article

▶ Quote

▶ Order

▶ Invoice

▶ Campaign

▶ Knowledge Article

With the exception of Article and Knowledge Article entities, you can adjust the Suffix Length setting to 4, 5, or 6.

NOTE

Changing a prefix number to a new value applies to newly created records; it does not change existing records.

System Settings

Located on the main Administration page after you select Settings -> Administration, the System Settings interface is similar to (and often confused with) the User Options interface. Here, unlike with the User Options interface, you make systemwide settings that affect all users.

The System Settings interface is divided into 13 tabbed sections in On-Premises and 14 tabbed sections in CRM Online (see Figure 17.34):

▶ General

▶ Calendar

▶ Formats

▶ Auditing

▶ Email

▶ Marketing

▶ Customization

▶ Outlook

▶ Reporting

▶ Goals

▶ Sales

▶ Service

▶ Synchronization

▶ Previews (CRM Online only)

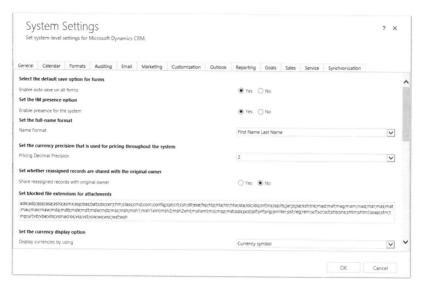

FIGURE 17.34   System Settings in CRM On-Premises.

General   In the General section, you can set and change the following options:

▶ **Default Save Option for Forms**—You can set this to enable or disable auto save on the forms. This setting affects all entities.

▶ **IM Presence Option**—You can set whether instant messaging will display the current presence status for users, contacts, opportunities, or leads for either Lync or Skype. If you are sure you don't want to use Lync or Skype, you should disable this option to increase the web application performance.

▶ **Full-Name Format**—This is the default way the user and customer names are displayed when using Microsoft Dynamics CRM. You can set whether you want the first name or the last name displayed first and also whether to show the middle name.

17

NOTE

If you select to change the Full-Name Format setting, your change affects the format only for new records added to the system. All existing records continue to display in the original format. Although it can take some effort (and is not recommended because you lose any related record associations), one way of correcting this for existing records is to export all of them, delete or deactivate them, and then reimport them. They will take on the new format during reimport. Be sure to carefully consider this prior to attempting it, though, because it might be more trouble than it's worth.

▶ **Currency Precision**—When working with currency fields throughout Microsoft Dynamics CRM, you can set the level of precision (from 0 to 4) for the decimal.

▶ **Reassigned Records Are Shared**—This option enables you to specify whether an entity is shared with the original owner by default when it is reassigned or whether the new owner assumes complete ownership of the entity. By default, this is set to No.

▶ **Blocked File Extensions for Attachments**—By default, the listed file extensions are blocked and prevented from being uploaded. Attempting to upload a document with one of the blocked file extensions listed results in an error (see Figure 17.35). These are the recommended and default extensions designed to keep your system safe and prevent malicious files from being uploaded. However, you can edit this list as you see fit.

FIGURE 17.35   File upload error.

▶ **Currency Display Options**—You can choose to display either the currency symbol (in the case of U.S. dollars and euros, this would be $ and €, respectively) or the currency code (again, in the case of U.S. dollars and euros, this would be USD and EUR, respectively).

▶ **Set Up Search**—Enabling Quick Search record limits sets a performance throttle of 10,000 records and alerts users to try a different search. The search on CRM for tablets allows users to select which entities are searched on tablets. Because tablets and now also the full web client application allow multi-entity search, this is an extremely helpful feature, but users need to be sensitive to the performance impact of selecting too many fields (see Figure 17.36). There is a still limitation of 10 entities for a multi-entity Quick Search. The Dynamics CRM On-Premises has an option to allow the use of full-text search for Quick Search. Using this feature, introduced in CRM 2015 Update 0.1, drastically improves Quick Search performance. For example, a search using wildcards that might take 74 seconds with this feature set to No would take 0.067 seconds with this setting set to Yes. By default, this setting is set to No, so you must enable it manually here if you want to use it.

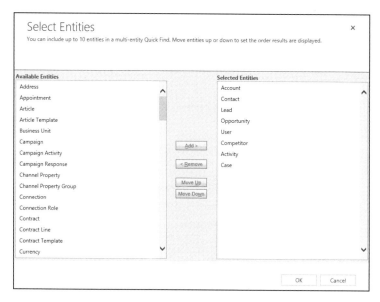

FIGURE 17.36   Multi-entity quick find entity selection.

▶ **Enable Bing Maps**—You can show Bing Maps natively on the records that have Bing Maps enabled (see Figure 17.37). The key is set by default for online users, but On-Premises users need to manually procure a key to enable this functionality.

NOTE

To obtain a Bing Maps On-Premises key, navigate to www.bingmapsportal.com, register your instance, and select the Create Key option from the left navigation pane. Set Create Key to the key value you obtained from the web page.

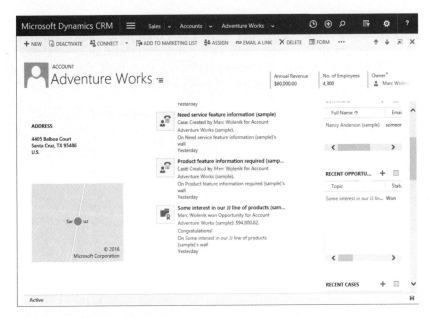

FIGURE 17.37   Bing Maps on the account record.

▶ **Default Country/Region Code**—You use this for dialing purposes. Microsoft Dynamics CRM attempts to prefix the number with the country/region code.

▶ **Telephony Provider**—You can set whether the clicked telephone number dials either Skype or Skype for Business/Lync by default.

NOTE

This setting has no effect on mobile devices.

▶ **Whether Users See CRM for Tablets Message**—If this is enabled, users who access CRM on a tablet are prompted to download the tablet client.

▶ **SEE CHAPTER 18**, "Mobility," for more information related to the tablet options.

▶ **Custom Help**—These settings allow you to point to a custom web application that will be responsible for providing help for custom and customizable entities. Make sure you include the protocol in the URL (for example, https:// or http://). Setting the Append parameters to URL will help you identify in your custom web app for what entity and what language the user is trying to get help. This URL will be fired when users go to a custom entity and click the ? sign in the top-right corner of the application.

▶ **Disable Social Engagement**—Social Engagement is enabled by default, but you can disable it with this system setting.

▶ Refer to **CHAPTER 14**, "Microsoft Dynamics Social Engagement," for more information related to this feature.

▶ **Welcome Screen**—Every time a new user accesses the CRM web application interface, a welcome screen is displayed, with some links to find additional help that is useful for starters. However, if you also remove the cookies every day, you will find this welcome screen annoying. As a system administrator, you can turn off this feature by setting this value to No.

▶ **Use Legacy Form Rendering**—Dynamics CRM 2016 has new redesigned forms called turbo-forms that might not work properly on upgraded organizations with custom code. While you can take the time to fix problems on the customization, you can set this option to Yes to be able to use the forms but reduce the form load performance.

Calendar   You can use the Calendar section to set the scheduling options with regard to the maximum durations of an appointment in days.

If you try to schedule an appointment and it exceeds the amount of time set here, you get the error message shown in Figure 17.38. You have the option to ignore the error, save, and continue.

FIGURE 17.38   Appointment duration is exceeded.

Formats   The Formats section enables you to customize how Microsoft Dynamics CRM formats data such as dates, times, and numbers.

Selecting a value from the drop-down menu populates the default values for the selected region in the Format Preview, showing you how the information will be formatted. If you need to further edit the values for regional settings, custom formats, or other settings, select Customize and make the necessary advanced configurations.

Auditing   To enable auditing, you can use the Auditing options shown in Figure 17.39. Regardless of your individual entity or attribute settings, auditing will not start until this is enabled. See "Auditing," later in this chapter, for more information about working with this feature.

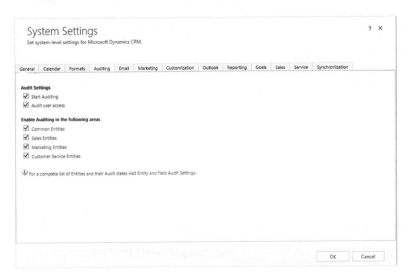

FIGURE 17.39   Auditing settings.

Email   The Email options involve configuration changes to how Microsoft Dynamics CRM works with email (see Figure 17.40):

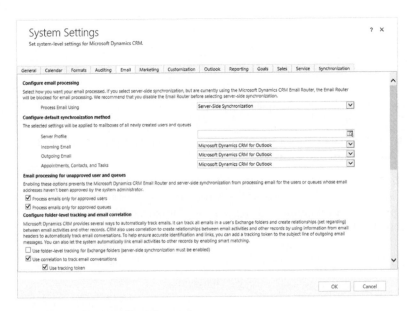

FIGURE 17.40   Email setting options.

▶ **Configure Email Processing**—This option helps the email router by processing only emails that have met the selected criteria.

▶ **SEE CHAPTER 20** for more information about working with email options.

▶ **Folder-Level Tracking**—This new feature in CRM 2016 allows a folder to automatically track emails that are moved to it. This requires the server-side sync option to be enabled, and it works with Exchange servers.

▶ **Email Correlation**—As with previous versions of Microsoft Dynamics CRM, you are not required to use a tracking token to track emails. Instead, CRM uses smart matching to automatically track emails using the From, To, and Subject information to match the email. For a variety of reasons, this correlation might not be 100% accurate. (Common reasons you might lose correlation are someone changing the Subject line or the email being forwarded to another individual.) If you require 100% correlation, use the tracking token, which automatically appends itself to the subject of all outbound emails in whatever form you select in this section.

NOTE

The prefix of the tracking token cannot be blank, it can contain spaces, and it allows a maximum value of 20 characters.

Figure 17.41 shows how the tracking token is structured, as well as options available to tune the smart matching feature:

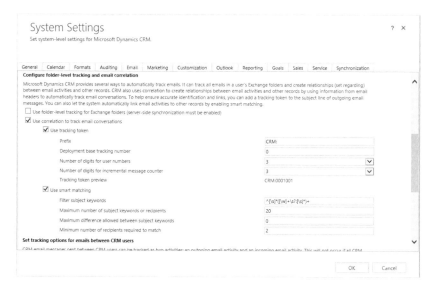

FIGURE 17.41   Email correlation options.

▶ **CRM User Tracking Options**—By default, when a user sends a CRM email to another CRM user and the second user replies, both emails are recorded as an activity for the selected record (one activity of type email outgoing and one activity of type email incoming).

▶ **Email Form Options**—You can select whether to restrict email message content via secure frames and whether to allow messages with unresolved email recipients. Secure frames are used to prevent malicious code execution that might exist when opening emails in CRM. Unresolved email recipients are recipients that are not found in the Account, Contact, Lead, or User Email Address fields.

▶ **File Size Limitations**—You can enter the file size allowed for uploading attachments to emails. The default is 5,120Kb (5MB), and the maximum value is 131,072Kb (128MB), which has been increased since the previous versions of Dynamics CRM.

TIP

The File Size Limitations setting also affects attachments added to notes.

▶ **Configure Alerts**—You can turn off or on the alerts related to system errors, warnings, or information to CRM users. This global setting applies to all the options/users.

Marketing   The Marketing options allow for powerful and easy management related to marketing when using Microsoft Dynamics CRM (see Figure 17.42):

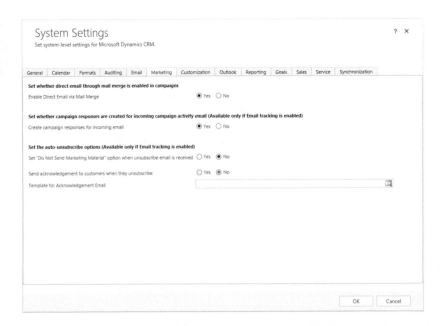

FIGURE 17.42   Marketing settings.

▶ **Enable Direct Email via Mail Merge**—By default, users can send email as campaign activities by using mail merge. If you want to prevent this functionality, change the value here.

▶ **Create Campaign Responses for Incoming Email**—If email tracking is enabled, you can configure Microsoft Dynamics CRM to automatically create a campaign response for incoming email. This is enabled by default.

▶ **Auto-Unsubscribe**—If email tracking is enabled, you can configure Microsoft Dynamics CRM to change the value on the customer record of Do Not Send Marketing Material to True if an unsubscribe email is received. Furthermore, you can configure whether the customer will receive an acknowledgment of the unsubscribe request and select a template for this acknowledgment.

The Unsubscribe option is available when you're preparing marketing: You can insert an option that allows users to click a link to unsubscribe from future marketing campaigns.

▶ **SEE CHAPTER 8**, "Working with Marketing," for more information about working with the Unsubscribe feature.

Customization   You can set whether Microsoft Dynamics CRM opens in Application mode (full browser screen for CRM usage only), as shown in Figure 17.43.

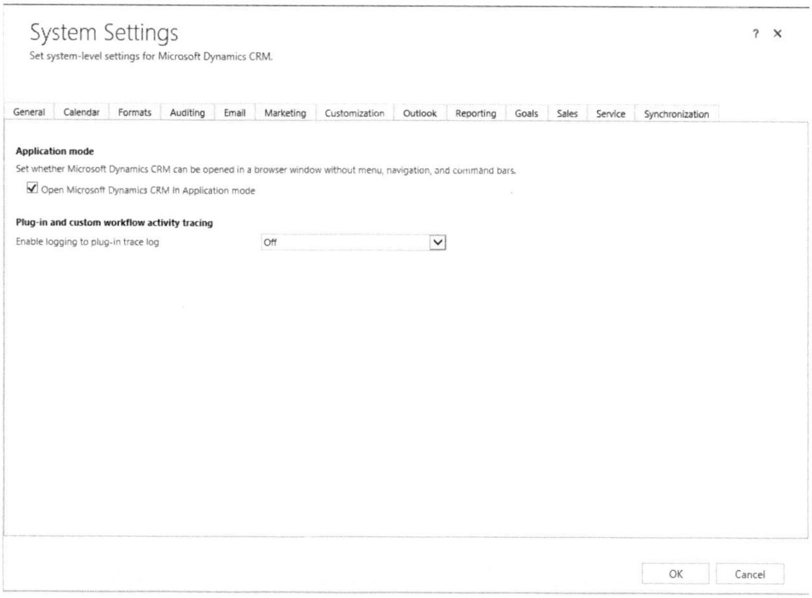

FIGURE 17.43   Customization options.

TIP

When working in Application mode, you can press Ctrl+N to open a new window.
The application opens and has Application mode off for as long as that new browser is open.

A new setting has been added here for plug-in and custom workflow activity tracing. This option is disabled by default but is useful for developers who want to debug plug-in and custom workflow activities so that they can be seen in the Settings > Customization > Plug-in Trace Log.

▶ For more information about plug-ins, **SEE CHAPTER 25**, "Plug-ins."

Outlook   Distinctly separate from the Email options, the Outlook options are specifically designed to optimize the Outlook Client (see Figure 17.44):

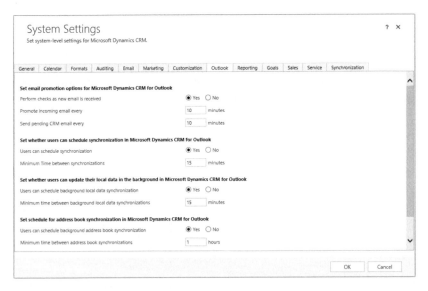

FIGURE 17.44   Outlook options.

▶ **Email Promotion Options**—Incoming email is automatically promoted to CRM based on the user settings configured. The options here set whether the email is eligible for promotion as it arrives, performs the actual promotion at specified intervals, and sends pending CRM-specific email at the specified interval.

▶ **User Schedule Synchronization**—You can set whether users can manually schedule synchronization from Outlook and at what interval synchronizations should occur. For optimal performance, set this to no less than the recommended default of 15 minutes.

▶ **Local Data Synchronization**—You can set whether and how often users can update the data that is stored on their computers for use offline.

▶ **Address Book Synchronization**—Like the User Schedule Synchronization option, this option enables users to schedule background address book synchronization and set the time interval between synchronizations.

▶ **Get the Outlook Client**—Sets whether users see the option to download the client (if not already downloaded).

▶ For more information about configuring the application to work with Outlook, **SEE CHAPTER 19**, "Outlook Configuration."

Reporting   The Reporting options enable you to create and manage the categories in to which reports are grouped (see Figure 17.45).

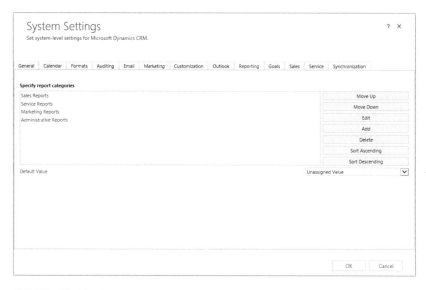

FIGURE 17.45   Reporting options.

Reports can belong to none, one, or multiple categories, and you can easily group together different kinds. When you edit an existing report or create a new report, you assign the categories listed here.

> **NOTE**
>
> If you add a new category here, you can assign it to new or existing reports; however, it is not an available option in the report views until you create a view for the new category.

Goals   The Goals options enable you to set the expiration time and rollup recurrence frequency (see Figure 17.46).

FIGURE 17.46   Goals options.

Languages

Microsoft Dynamics CRM is incredibly multilingual. It can serve as many languages as it has available, and users can select the language they want to work with. Table 17.2 shows the languages available at press time.

TABLE 17.2   Languages

Language	Language Code	Language	Language Code
Arabic	1025	Japanese	1041
Basque	1069	Kazakh	1087
Bulgarian	1026	Korean	1042
Catalan	1027	Latvian	1062
Chinese (Hong Kong SAR)	3076	Lithuanian	1063
Chinese (Simplified)	2052	Malay (Malaysia)	1086
Chinese (Traditional)	1028	Norwegian (Bokmål)	1044
Croatian	1050	Polish	1045
Czech	1029	Portuguese (Brazil)	1046
Danish	1030	Portuguese (Portugal)	2070
Dutch	1043	Romanian	1048
English	1033	Russian	1049
Estonian	1061	Serbian (Cyrillic)	3098
Finnish	1035	Serbian (Latin)	2074
French	1036	Slovak	1051
Galician	1110	Slovenian	1060
German	1031	Spanish	3082
Greek	1032	Swedish	1053
Hebrew	1037	Thai	1054
Hindi	1081	Turkish	1055
Hungarian	1038	Ukrainian	1058
Indonesian	1057	Vietnamese	1066
Italian	1040		

17

When you select a language, Microsoft Dynamics CRM translates most of the labels within CRM to the selected language. In rare cases when the language is unavailable for translation, Microsoft Dynamics CRM falls back to the installed base language. Note that setting a different language does not translate the data contained within Microsoft Dynamics CRM.

NOTE

Although customizations must be done in the base language, they can be translated so that they are viewed in a different language.

To allow a different language, select Languages and select the language you would like to have deployed on the system. Click Apply and then click OK (see Figure 17.47).

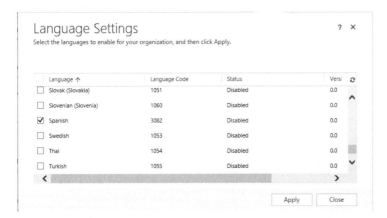

FIGURE 17.47   Languages available to deploy in CRM Online.

TIP

Unlike with CRM Online, where all the languages are available for deployment, On-Premises versions of CRM require that a languages be downloaded and installed on the server first. You can download languages from Microsoft by searching for "CRM 2016 Language Pack" or by going directly to www.microsoft.com/en-us/download/details .aspx?id= 50371.

The system provisions the language and makes it available to users. This process might take several minutes and may disrupt users' ability to use the system, so you should consider adding the languages after hours or when nobody else is using the system.

TIP

By default, any installed languages are disabled and must be enabled.

Users can now select which language they want to work with by navigating to the gear icon in the top-right corner and selecting Options and then selecting the Languages tab (see Figure 17.48). Only the languages that have been enabled are available for selection in this dialog.

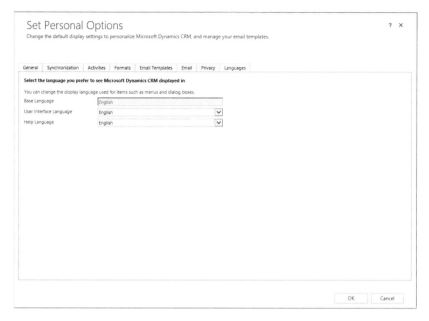

FIGURE 17.48   Installed languages available to users.

NOTE

There is a special setting in the business management role under Miscellaneous Privileges called Language Settings. It allows the enabling and disabling of languages. If you're unable to perform language configuration changes, be sure to check your role settings for this permission.

TIP

Check the mail merge templates after the language packs have been installed. Several different ones are loaded with each language installed.

Privacy Preferences

Privacy preferences are different depending on whether you are in CRM Online or On-Premises. In CRM Online, you can specify both whether you will see an error message and whether that error message will be sent to Microsoft. You also have the option to specify an external URL with you own privacy statement; if you do, users can then access it by going to the gear icon and selecting Privacy Statement.

With Dynamics CRM On-Premises, you have the option to select whether you want to participate in the Customer Experience Improvement Program. The default for this is established when Microsoft Dynamics CRM is installed. It is a good idea to participate because doing so will help Microsoft improve future releases and products.

Subscription Management (CRM Online Only)

In CRM Online, the Settings > Administration area has a Subscription Management option that allows CRM Online administrators to set payment and billing options. When you select the Subscription Management option, a new window takes you to the Subscription Management interface for your CRM Online account (the Office 365 Admin Portal). From this interface, you can add subscriptions, view your payment details, and see what licenses you are using.

System Notifications (CRM Online Only)

The System Notifications options are found only with CRM Online in Settings > Administration. The System Notifications status screen shows information related to your CRM Online account.

Resources in Use (CRM Online Only)

The Resource in Use options is found only with CRM Online in Settings > Administration. This option shows you the usage of the resources, such as the storage, which by default is 5 GB, and the number of custom entities. The limitation in CRM Online is 300 custom entities (see Figure 17.49).

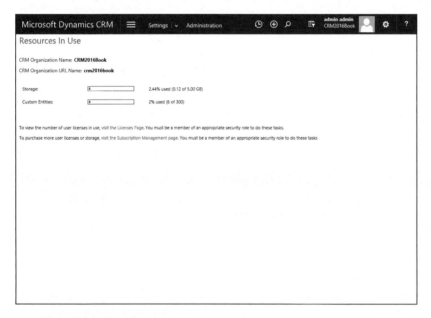

FIGURE 17.49   CRM Resources in Use options.

Product Updates (Partner Hosted or On-Premises Only)

The Product Updates options enable you to sign up for the Microsoft Dynamics CRM Product Update newsletter so you can receive email notifications when a CRM update is released.

A Windows Live ID is required to complete the registration. When you are subscribed, you can receive communications from Microsoft related to Microsoft Dynamics CRM product updates.

> **NOTE**
>
> A Windows Live ID is an account that is set up, verified, and administrated by Microsoft. With Windows Live, you can verify your identity with any system using the Live/Passport network.

Keep in mind that Microsoft Dynamics CRM product updates are now delivered through the update service automatically. The signup described here is simply for a newsletter informing you of information related to the updates (not the actual updates themselves).

Yammer Configuration

You can use the Yammer Configuration section to configure the integration between Yammer and Dynamics CRM.

▶ Refer to **CHAPTER 15**, "Yammer," for details related to Yammer configuration and usage.

Microsoft Social Engagement Configuration

You can use the Microsoft Social Engagement Configuration section to configure integration between Social Engagement and Dynamics CRM.

▶ Refer to **CHAPTER 14** for details related to Social Engagement configuration and usage.

Security

You use the Security section to set up and configure users, roles, and permissions. It has the following options (see Figure 17.50):

▶ Users

▶ Teams

▶ Security Roles

▶ Business Units

▶ Field Security Profiles

▶ Hierarchy Security

▶ Positions

▶ Access Team Templates

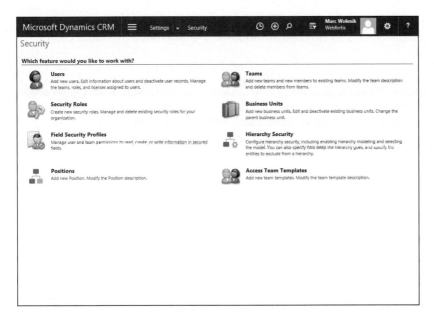

FIGURE 17.50   Settings > Security screen.

Users

You can go to Settings > Security > Users to create and manage Microsoft Dynamics users (see Figure 17.51).

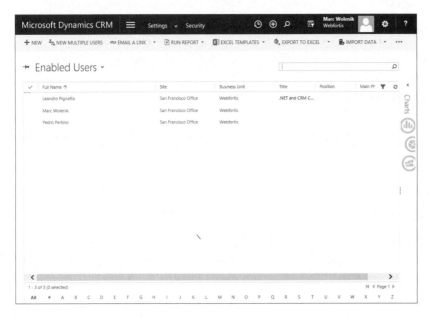

FIGURE 17.51   Users section.

When working with the Users section, you can perform several operations:

▶ Add a new user(s)

▶ Enable or disable users

▶ Manage roles

▶ Reassign records

▶ Change business units

▶ Change managers

▶ Change position

▶ Open mailbox

▶ Approve/reject emails

▶ View users

Adding a New User   To add a new user, select + New > User and follow the steps outlined next for your implementation of Dynamics CRM (Online or On-Premises) to complete the user addition.

> **NOTE**
>
> If you do not have a + New option here, you might not have sufficient rights or privileges to create new users.

> **NOTE**
>
> After you add users to the CRM system, you can only deactivate them; you cannot delete them. Therefore, you can add a user as new only once. If you have already added a user and you don't see him or her, be sure to check the Disabled Users view to see whether that user has already been added.

> **TIP**
>
> If your organization is not using another tool for user management, such as a human resource management tool, you might want to consider using the Dynamics CRM User Management for your user management. You can customize it to include other fields, and you can easily report on it using Advanced Find.

Adding users for CRM Online is slightly different from adding them for On-Premises because the Online implementation uses the email address as the primary key rather than doing a lookup into Active Directory (as shown later in the chapter), and the users must be configured in the Office 365 Admin Portal.

17

Adding New Users: CRM Online   To add new users in CRM Online, follow these steps:

1. Select New.

2. When you are prompted to navigate to the Office 365 Admin Portal (see Figure 17.52), click Add and License Users.

FIGURE 17.52   Prompt to navigate to the Office 365 Office 365 Admin Portal.

3. Once in the Office 365 Admin Portal (as shown in Figure 17.53), manage your users.

NOTE

After you set up a user in the Office 365 Admin Portal, you still have to navigate back to CRM to set up the user's security permissions.

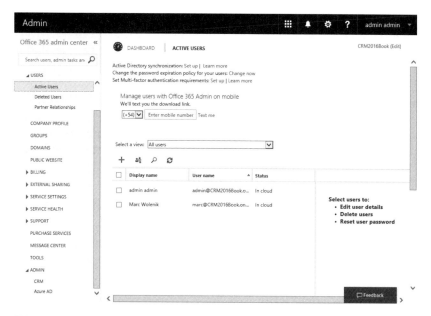

FIGURE 17.53   Office 365 Admin Portal.

▶ Working with the Office 365 Office 365 Admin Portal is explained more fully in
CHAPTER 4, "CRM 2016 Online."

Users receive an email, asking them to join the organization, and can start using
the system immediately after they've accepted the terms and conditions.

Adding New Users: On-Premises   To add a single user in Dynamics CRM On-Premises,
follow these steps:

1. Click +New on the navigation bar. A blank new user form opens.

NOTE

Selecting New Multiple Users opens the Add New Multiple Users Wizard, which is
explained later in this chapter, in the "Adding Multiple Users (CRM On-Premises Only)"
section.

---

2. Enter a value for the User Name field. When you move to the next field, CRM
   attempts automatic resolution on the entered value and populates other fields.
   If autopopulation does not occur, be sure to enter the exact first name and last name
   as well as the email address for the user that exists in Active Directory (for example,
   domain\username, where *domain* is the domain for your organization, and *username*
   is the domain username).

3. For richer reporting, fill out the remaining fields in the User Information section. You should complete at least the Primary Email field so the user can receive emails. If no email is entered, events (such as workflows and system alerts) that need to send emails to users will fail.

Organizational Information   The default master parent unit automatically populates business units, but you can change this to any available business unit before you click Save. After you save a record, you can also click Change Business Unit on the navigation bar to change the business unit. Remember that changing the business unit to a user removes all the roles that were assigned to the user, so you must reassign a role after you change the business unit.

As with business units, you can set the manager before you click Save. After you save the record, you can select Change Manager on the navigation bar to change or set the manager.

Similarly, you can set the position before you click Save. After you save the record, you can select Change the Position on the navigation bar to change or set the position.

Territory and Site are optional lookup fields. If you have not created any territories or sites in the system, you can leave these blank.

Although not required, you can set service activities to use sites.

▶ For more information about configuring service activities, refer to **CHAPTER 10**.

In the Administration section, with regard to the client access license (CAL) information, you can set the access mode for users to the following:

▶ **Read-Write**—Allows full access to the system, provided that users have the security permissions needed.

▶ **Administrative**—Grants permission only to limited administrative areas of the system.

▶ **Read**—Allows full access in a read-only capacity to the system.

License type can be set for the following:

▶ Professional

▶ Administrative

▶ Basic

▶ Device Professional

▶ Device Basic

▶ Essential

▶ Device Essential

▶ **SEE CHAPTER 29**, "On-Premises Deployments," and **CHAPTER 4** for more information about the licensing models.

Once a user is created and when you are in the user form, you can see more options by clicking the down-pointing arrow that appears to the right of the username in the navigation bar (see Figure 17.54).

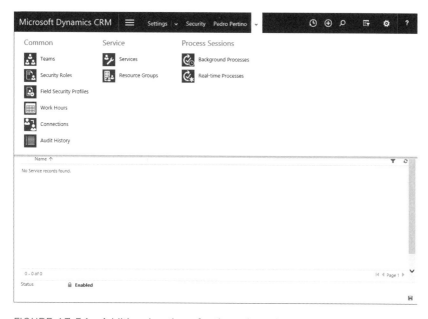

FIGURE 17.54   Additional options for the selected user.

These options are divided in three main groups, Common, Service, and Process Sessions:

▶ Common

  ▶ Teams

  ▶ Security Roles

  ▶ Field Security Profiles

  ▶ Work Hours

  ▶ Connections

  ▶ Audit History

▶ Service

  ▶ Services

  ▶ Resource Groups

▶ Process Sessions

  ▶ Background Processes

  ▶ Real-Time Processes

The following sections explain the additional options that are not found in their own dedicated chapters (such as Service, found in Chapter 10, "Working with Service" and Processes, found in Chapter 26, "Process Development).

Teams Users can belong to one or many teams. If they belong to a team, they benefit from team record sharing and permissions.

After you have successfully created and saved a user, you can have that user join an existing team by selecting Teams. By default, a user belongs to a team with the name of the CRM organization, and the user cannot be removed from that group. To join another team, click the + in the Teams subgrid and click the lookup icon to view all the available teams.

▶ For more information about teams, **SEE** the "Teams" section, later in this chapter.

Security Roles For users to be able to do anything in Microsoft Dynamics CRM, they must be assigned security roles. However, after a user has been created, or if a user has had the business unit changed, that user has no security roles and must be assigned a role before he or she can use the system.

To grant the user access to a role, select Manage Roles and then select the roles you want the user to belong to (see Figure 17.55).

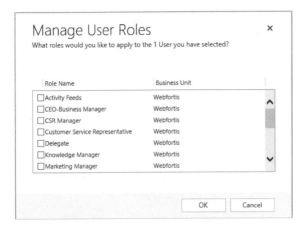

Manage User Roles ✕

What roles would you like to apply to the 1 User you have selected?

Role Name	Business Unit
☐ Activity Feeds	Webfortis
☐ CEO-Business Manager	Webfortis
☐ CSR Manager	Webfortis
☐ Customer Service Representative	Webfortis
☐ Delegate	Webfortis
☐ Knowledge Manager	Webfortis
☐ Marketing Manager	Webfortis

OK   Cancel

FIGURE 17.55 Manage User Roles dialog.

NOTE

A user must belong to at least one role, and the user's permissions are based on the highest role selected. If the user has both the restrictive Customer Service Representative role as well as the System Administrator role (the highest role possible), that user will have System Administrator rights throughout the system.

Field Security Profiles   As explained later in this chapter, you can establish field security profiles per user by selecting Field Security Profiles from the top navigation bar.

Work Hours   The Work Hours section enables you to control user schedules and schedule activities.

> ▶ **CHAPTER 10** discusses how the service calendar and scheduling engine work with work hours.

Services   When you are viewing an existing user record, any service records associated with the user are available by selecting Services from the navigation bar (refer to Figure 17.54). A service is any work performed for a customer by a user and resources. By default, a new user has no services associated with it.

> ▶ For more information about creating and working with services, refer to **CHAPTER 10**.

Resource Groups   You can add users to existing resource groups by selecting Resource Groups from the navigation bar. A resource group is a collection of users, facilities, or equipment. The advantage to having them is that they can be scheduled interchangeably. For example, a resource group of everyone who works for you who is qualified to service a particular line of cars can be grouped. Then, when you need to schedule that service, you can pick from that group instead of among individual employees.

> ▶ For more information about resource groups, refer to the "Resource Groups" section, earlier in this chapter.

Process Sessions (Background Processes and Real-Time Processes)   In the Background Processes and Real-Time Processes sections, you can see any completed workflows or dialog sessions that were run on the User entity. For a new user, you don't see any completed workflows or dialog sessions here unless you have a workflow built for the `Create` event of the User entity from initial setup of your system (such as a welcome email).

> ▶ For more information about process development, **SEE CHAPTER 26**, "Process Development."

Adding Multiple Users (CRM On-Premises Only)   You can easily add multiple users at one time. To do so, select New Multiple Users. The adding users wizard opens. To complete the wizard, follow these steps:

1. Select the business unit and click Next (see Figure 17.56).

17

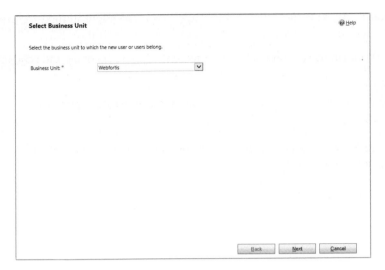

FIGURE 17.56 Adding users wizard.

2. Select which security roles the users should belong to (see Figure 17.57). As with individual users, all users must have at least one security role to be able to use the system. When setting the roles for multiple users, all users who will be added will have the same security roles selected. Click Next.

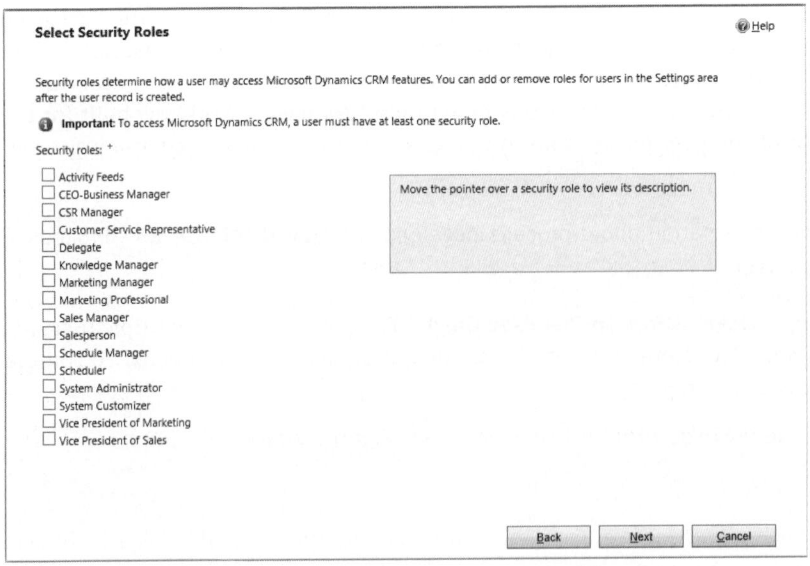

FIGURE 17.57 Selecting security roles.

NOTE

If you don't select security roles, the users will still be created, but you will receive an alert after they have been added, saying that you must assign at least one security role to the new users. When you are adding many users, this can be time-consuming, so consider adding the role here.

3. Select the licensing for the users (see Figure 17.58). The access type, the license type, and the email access configuration selected will apply to all users to be added. Click Next to continue.

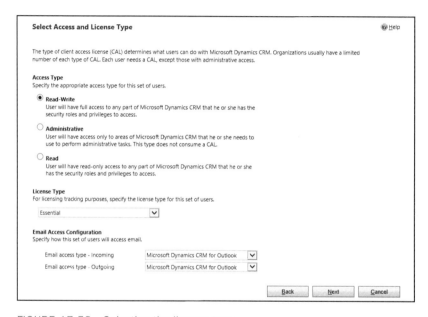

FIGURE 17.58   Selecting the license type.

4. Select the domain or group from Activity Domain to which the users belong. If you select Select Users from All Trusted Domains and Groups, all available users on the current trusted domain/groups are presented on the next screen. If you select Select Users from the Following Domain or Group, the option to select the specific group is presented. Be sure the group node you select contains your users; if a node is selected that does not have the users, it does not show up on the next screen; you have to navigate back to this screen to select an alternative node containing the users. Click Next.

5. Select the users you want to add by either typing their names, separated by semicolons, or searching for them by selecting the lookup icon. When the lookup dialog box opens, either enter your users' search criteria or leave it blank to return all users available to be added to CRM. After you have confirmed the users to be added, they are added to the text box, and you can selectively remove individuals, if necessary.

17

TIP

Only users who have not been already added to Microsoft Dynamics CRM are available to be added.

---

6. Click Add > Create New Users. The users are added to Microsoft Dynamics CRM. This step might take several minutes. When this is finished, you see the Finish screen. Any alerts or problems with the addition process display here. Select either Add More Users to add more users or Close to complete the wizard.

Enabling or Disabling Users   You can use the navigation bar to enable and disable selected users. By disabling a user, you remove the license from that user, and you can add a new user to use that license if you want.

NOTE

Disabling users might cause any existing workflows or system jobs that the user has created or owns to fail. It can be a good idea to reassign the records of the disabled user to another user; you do this by going to the disabled user record and clicking the Reassign Records button on the navigation bar.

Managing Roles   From the navigation bar, you can manage selected users' roles. Microsoft Dynamics CRM is role based, which provides a powerful mechanism to manage users. Because users must belong to at least one role but are allowed to belong to more than one, it is important to remember that a user will have the permissions of the higher role (refer to Figure 17.55).

NOTE

When you're managing roles, you can select multiple users at the same time by selecting one or more on the left check box option. So if you select a single user, only the existing roles display. If you select multiple users, no roles are selected, by default.

Changing Business Units   By clicking the ... on the navigation bar, you can select Change Business Unit to open the Change Business Unit dialog, where you can change selected users' business units (see Figure 17.59).

FIGURE 17.59   Changing a business unit.

▶ For more information about business units and the effects of changing users' assigned business units, refer to the "Business Units" section, later in this chapter.

Changing Managers   By clicking the ... on the navigation bar, you can select Change Managers to change the selected user manager. You can set another user as the manager, provided that the selected user is not one previously selected as the change manager.

Changing Position   By clicking the ... on the navigation bar, you can select Change Position to change the selected user position (see Figure 17.60).

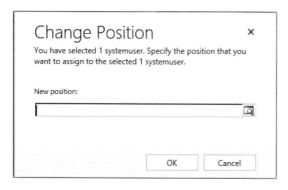

FIGURE 17.60   Changing position.

Viewing Users   When working with the main Users interface, built-in views allow you to select subcategories of users. These are helpful when users need to work with a small group of users, such as only the enabled users.

Teams

The concept of teams in Microsoft Dynamics CRM is designed around the idea that members of a team can share records that those members wouldn't ordinarily have access to. An example of this is users in different business units belonging to the same team and being able to view records across the business units by sharing them. Figure 17.61 shows the teams form found in Settings > Security.

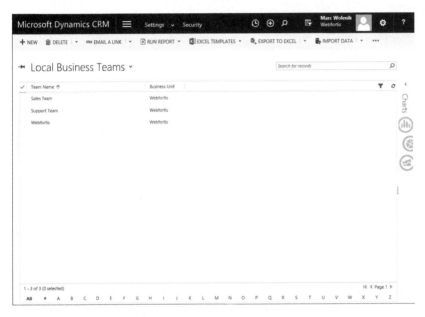

FIGURE 17.61   Teams in Microsoft Dynamics CRM.

A default team is established when an organization is deployed. The default team is the same as the root business unit, and a new team is created for each business unit created. The only way to delete a created team is to first delete the correlating business unit.

> **NOTE**
>
> If your organization is upgraded, a new team is automatically created for each business unit in the organization.

The process of creating and managing teams in Microsoft Dynamics CRM is very straightforward. To create a new team, follow these steps:

1. Navigate to Settings > Security > Teams (refer to Figure 17.61). Select New.

2. Enter the team name and select the business unit and the administrator. (The administrator is the owner of the team.) By default, the root business unit is selected.

3. Click Save to enable the options.

4. Select the users from the system who will be part of the team by clicking Add Members. Click Add and then click OK.

5. Because teams can have record ownership in this version of Microsoft Dynamics CRM, they need to have security roles set for them. Just as with new members, they are created without security roles and need to have at least one set. In addition, you can set up the field security profiles for the team at this point.

Because Microsoft Dynamics CRM 2016 offers users the ability to assign records to teams (unlike earlier versions, which only allowed sharing), it is important to outline the differences between sharing and assignment.

Sharing a record has the following effects:

▶ You retain ownership of the record.

▶ You give permission for the record to be read, edited, or deleted.

Assigning a record has the following effects:

▶ You lose ownership of the record (and the new owner has permission to do whatever his or her security context allows).

So be sure to assign or share appropriately.

Once you have created a team, sharing records with the team is simple. Follow these steps:

1. Navigate to a lead record and select ... > Share.

2. In the Sharing interface that appears, select Add User/Team.

3. Select to share the record with either a user or a team.

4. Select from the available teams and add them. Click OK to continue. The selected team is now available on the Sharing interface, and you can give it access for Read, Write, Delete, Append, Assign, or Share.

5. Select a record to assign to the team and click Assign in the navigation bar.

6. Navigate to and select the team to assign the record to and click OK. The record is now assigned to that team.

If you have not yet assigned a security role to a team, you see the Team Error message shown in Figure 17.62. To correct this, navigate to the team and assign the appropriate security role.

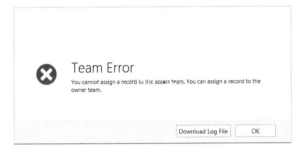

FIGURE 17.62   Record assignment error.

Access Teams   Microsoft Dynamics CRM 2016 has a new type of team, known as an access team. Access teams don't have security roles or records directly assigned to them. Instead, they have record access via sharing (explained earlier in this chapter).

You might want to use access teams in the following situations:

▶ When it is not known in advance (that is, during initial design/implementation of Microsoft Dynamic CRM) what the required team composition might look like

▶ When the members of the team need different access privileges for the shared records

To assign a team as an access team, on the teams form, set the Team Type field to Access (rather than Owner).

CAUTION

You can change an owner team to an access team by selecting the Convert to Access Team option on the navigation bar. However, you cannot convert access teams into owner teams.

Security Roles
Microsoft Dynamics CRM controls user permissions with security roles by business units.

NOTE

Although Microsoft Dynamics CRM integrates tightly with Active Directory (AD) to determine its user base, permissions established in AD have no correlation with users in Microsoft Dynamics CRM. Therefore, it is quite possible to have an AD membership of enterprise administrator but be in read-only user mode or have a minimal role setting in Microsoft Dynamics CRM and vice versa.

By default, the following security roles are included with Microsoft Dynamics CRM 2016:

▶ Activity Feeds

▶ CEO-Business Manager

▶ CSR Manager

▶ Customer Service Representative

▶ Delegate

▶ Knowledge Manager

▶ Marketing Manager

▶ Marketing Professional

▶ Sales Manager

▶ Salesperson

▶ Schedule Manager

▶ Scheduler

▶ System Administrator

▶ System Customizer

▶ Vice President of Marketing

▶ Vice President of Sales

With Microsoft Dynamics CRM, security roles are flexible, they are easily created and maintained, and they extend to new entities added by users. By default, new security roles are created on the organizational level and inherited by child business units, regardless of which business unit is selected from the Security Roles Administration screen. In addition, consider the following with regard to how security roles are inherited:

▶ New security roles are automatically created on the selected business unit (which is the master by default) and inherited to all child business units.

▶ Copied security roles are created on the selected business unit, are available only on the selected business unit, and are inherited by all child business units of the selected business unit (not any parent business units).

▶ Inherited security roles cannot be modified or deleted. To make changes to inherited security roles, you must select the business unit that the security role is assigned to and then make changes there. All changes are inherited by the child business units. Another option is to copy the security role to another name and make your changes on the copied version.

17

If a specific security role is required on a child business unit, you can now create a new security role for that specific business unit. The security role also will apply to any child business unit where it was created.

To view the specific access granted by any role, double-click the desired role to bring up the role settings screen (see Figure 17.63).

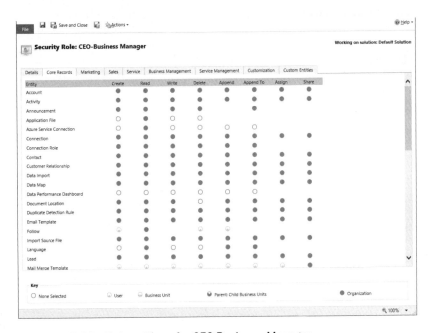

FIGURE 17.63   Role settings for CEO-Business Manager.

The tabs across the top of the role settings screen break out the major access points within Microsoft Dynamics CRM 2016 (see Figure 17.64):

- ▶ Details
- ▶ Core Records
- ▶ Marketing
- ▶ Sales
- ▶ Service
- ▶ Business Management
- ▶ Service Management
- ▶ Customization
- ▶ Custom Entities

FIGURE 17.64   Security role key.

Before looking at each of the sections, it is important to review the key at the bottom of each form: It applies to all tabs except the Details tab. The symbols here indicate how permissions are granted on the records for the selected security role. Records in Microsoft Dynamics CRM 2016 have either organizational permissions or user permissions. When applying permissions, you select the entity (for example, Account, Contact, or Lead) and then associate the action with the record (Create, Read, Write, and so on) and, finally, the level of access (as indicated in the key).

The levels of access are as follows:

▶ **None Selected**—The user cannot perform the selected action.

▶ **User**—The user can perform the selected action only on the records that he or she owns.

▶ **Business Unit**—The user can perform the selected action on records owned by anyone in the business unit that this user belongs to but cannot perform the selected action in records owned by those in child or parent business units.

▶ **Parent: Child Business Units**—The user can perform the selected action on records within his or her business unit and perform the selected action on any child business units of his or her business unit (but not the parent business unit).

▶ **Organization**—The user can perform the selected action on any record within the organization.

NOTE

Some entities either can't have permission levels set on them or have only limited options. In the first case, where there is no ability to set a permission level, this is usually because that functionality doesn't exist, so there is no reason to set permissions on it. An example of this is on the Business Management tab, for the entity User and the action Delete. Because users can't be deleted (they can only be deactivated), there is no capability to set a permission level on it.

Carefully consider how you want to set permissions and select the level of access for each role; users might have trouble accessing records if they don't have the correct permissions.

TIP

If you want to share only some records between users, consider using teams. Team membership is often used to allow access to records that users normally don't have access to. For more information about teams, see the "Teams" section, earlier in this chapter.

You can set security levels across all entities horizontally by clicking Actions at the top of the screen or by clicking the entity name to apply security levels vertically.

Details   The Details tab displays the security role name and the business unit that the role applies to. If the security role is an inherited role (as previously described), you cannot change the role name.

Core Records   As its name implies, Core Records is where you set permissions for general or core access to the system. Access from everything to accounts to contacts to leads and so on is controlled on this screen.

The permission options are presented across the top of the Core Records tab, whereas the entities affected are listed in rows. The permissions (or privileges) are as follows:

▶ **Create**—The ability to create a new record

▶ **Read**—The ability to open and read an existing record

▶ **Write**—The ability to make and save changes to an existing record, including deleting data from the record (however, not to delete the entire record)

▶ **Delete**—The ability to delete an existing record

▶ **Append**—The ability to append the current record to another record

▶ **Append To**—The ability to append a different record to the current record

▶ **Assign**—The ability to assign the record to another user or team

▶ **Share**—The ability to share the record with another user or team

---

NOTE

The difference between Append and Append To is that Append enables you to append the current record to another record, whereas Append To gives enables you to append another record to this record.

An additional option is Miscellaneous Privileges, located at the bottom of the form, which includes options such as the capability to publish various objects and add reports.

Marketing   The Marketing tab has the same permission options listed in the Core Records tab. The Marketing Miscellaneous privilege allows management of the Create Quick Campaign option. Quick campaigns differ from campaigns; the only permission for a quick campaign is the ability to create one.

▶ Refer to **CHAPTER 8**, "Working with Marketing," to review the differences between campaigns and quick campaigns.

Sales   The Sales tab has the same permission options listed on the Core Records tab. The miscellaneous privileges give a user with this role the ability to override pricing on a quote, an invoice, or an order.

▶ Refer to **CHAPTER 7** for more information about sales.

Service   The Service tab has the same permission options listed in the Core Records tab. The ability to publish articles and the ability to approve and/or publish the articles are the only other miscellaneous privileges available on the Service tab.

▶ Refer to **CHAPTER 10** for more information about services.

Business Management   The Business Management tab has two groups of additional settings:

▶ The privacy-related privileges associated with business management include several settings that can affect usage of CRM, including important features such as CRM for mobile, Go Offline, and Export to Excel.

17

▶ The miscellaneous privileges associated with business management include settings like allow the user to change the language, send email as another user, and more.

Service Management   The Service Management tab has the same permission options listed in the Core Records tab. The miscellaneous privileges for service management enable the user to search and browse as well as manage the user's calendar.

▶ Refer to **CHAPTER 10** for more information about services.

Customization   The Customization tab has the same permission options listed in the Core Records tab. Miscellaneous privileges include the capability to work with ISV extensions; execute processes; and export, import, and publish customizations.

▶ **SEE CHAPTER 22** for more information about customization.

Custom Entities   The Custom Entities tab gives options to set permissions only if a custom entity exists (as shown in Figure 17.65). When an entity is created, permissions need to be established across the security roles, and they are the same as those listed in the Core Records tab.

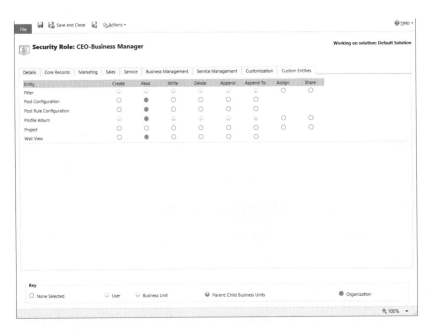

FIGURE 17.65   Security role for custom entities.

Business Units

You control access to information across the organization by using business units, teams, and territories. With Microsoft Dynamics CRM, you can create multiple child business units and assign users that have access to only the information within their business unit, not their parent business unit.

When Microsoft Dynamics CRM is first installed, you specify the root business unit as the organization name during the installation. This is the default business unit that will derive any child business units. If your organization is relatively small or has no separate business units (other than the organization itself), there is little reason to make any changes to the business units because you would end up with one business unit with the same name as your organization. However, if you have multiple business units, you should configure them here.

You may have multiple child business units (see Figure 17.66), but you cannot disable the parent business unit (which is created during setup). In addition, you can change the parent business unit (to correct a spelling error or because the wrong business unit was assigned as the parent, and so on).

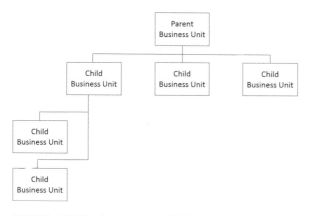

FIGURE 17.66   Parent and child business units.

Because of the way the security roles work, it is important to consider setting up both business units and security roles. In addition, because users must be assigned business units for their setup, when you disable a business unit, all users assigned to that business unit (and any child business units) are deactivated and cannot log in to the system until they are reassigned to an active business unit.

▶ For more information about security roles, **SEE** the "Security Roles" section, earlier in this chapter.

> **NOTE**
>
> Users are not deactivated or deleted if their business unit is deactivated. They remain valid/active users in the system, but they cannot log in because their business unit is disabled. This is an important distinction because they continue to consume a client access license (CAL), even though they have no access to the system. A user can be moved to a different business unit after the original business unit is deactivated, if necessary; however, the roles for that user are removed and need to be reassigned.

▶ For more information about working with users, **SEE** the "Users" section, earlier in this chapter.

By default, when you view the business units on the Security screen, the active business units appear with their parent business unit. By selecting More Actions on this screen, you can enable a deactivated business unit, disable an active business unit, and change the parent business unit of a child business unit. To create a new business unit, select New on the main Business Units screen.

The New Business Unit screen has two required fields that must be populated: Name (of the business unit) and Parent Business Unit. By default, the Parent Business Unit field is populated with the organization business unit (or master business unit), but you can change this to a child business unit if you want. As mentioned previously, you must have a parent business unit for any new business units that are created.

> **NOTE**
>
> You can disable business units after creating them, but you cannot delete them until they are disabled.

After you enter a name and select the parent business unit, enter specific address information related to the business unit, as well as other details specific to the business unit (see Figure 17.67).

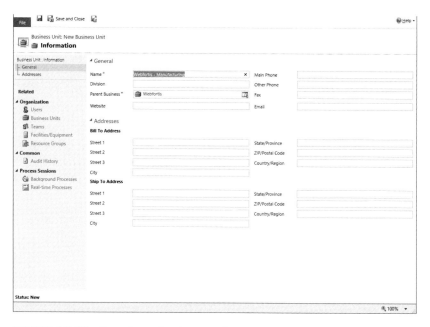

FIGURE 17.67   Saved new business unit.

TIP

Although the parent business unit appears to be locked, you can easily change it by selecting Actions > Change Parent Business.

Security roles are specific to business units, with certain limitations. The Business Units options are as follows:

▶ Users

▶ Business Units

▶ Teams

▶ Facilities/Equipment

▶ Resource Groups

Users   Selecting Users shows you who is assigned to the selected business unit.

▶ User assignment to business units is explained in greater detail earlier in this chapter, in the "Users" section.

When adding users, be aware of the following:

▶ Only users who have not been added to CRM can be added to newly created business units from the New Business Unit screen. If you want to assign to a newly created business unit users who are already in the system, you must first navigate to the user (Settings > Security > Users) and select Change Business Unit from the navigation bar.

▶ You cannot move the current user (that is, the user who is logged in) to a business unit. Instead, you must delegate access to another user and either request that the other user make the changes or log in as the other user and make the changes. (Be sure to grant the necessary security role System Administrator to the other user before you attempt to make this change.)

▶ Only users who are assigned to the business unit you're working with appear on the Users screen. To see users of child business units, you must select the child business units separately.

▶ When users are moved from an existing business unit to a new business unit, all role information is removed, and it must be manually reassigned.

Business Units Business Units displays the child business units of the selected business unit (see Figure 17.68). From here, you can easily create a new child business unit by selecting New Business Unit. You can also enable and disable any existing business units displayed.

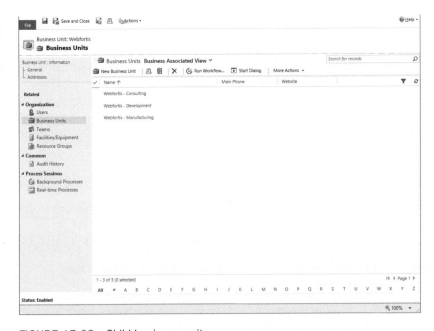

FIGURE 17.68 Child business units.

Only the direct child business units display on the Business Units screen. To view child business units that might exist, you must select the child business unit and navigate to the Business Units section of the child business unit.

Teams   Because teams are specific to business units, selecting Teams shows you which teams are assigned to the selected business unit. This example of teams is specific to business units.

▶ The concept of teams is explained in greater detail earlier in this chapter, in the "Teams" section.

Facilities/Equipment   Like teams, facilities/equipment is specific to business units. Selecting Facilities/Equipment shows you what facilities/equipment are assigned to the selected business unit.

▶ Facilities/Equipment is explained in greater detail earlier in this chapter, in the section "Facilities/Equipment."

Resource Groups   As with both teams and facilities/equipment, resource groups are specific to business units. Selecting Resource Groups shows you what resource groups are assigned to the selected business unit.

▶ Resource groups are explained in greater detail earlier in this chapter, in the section "Resource Groups."

Every time a business unit is created, a new team is created with the new business unit name.

Field Security Profiles

Field-level security (FLS) allows users to set up security on specific fields. When working with FLS, you have to create field security profiles and then apply them to either teams or users.

The profiles created are completely separate from the security roles created.

Field level security was previously available for only custom fields/attributes. With Dynamics 2016, Field level security is an option for almost every field. To dig deeper into which fields can be secured, users need to check whether the setting for field level security is allowed in either the customization area for that attribute, or browse the metadata browser solution found in the SDK called EntityMetadata.xlsx.

> **NOTE**
>
> If you create field security profiles and then select Field Permissions but don't see any records, it is because you haven't set the field security value to allowed for any of your attributes.

Figure 17.69 shows what the various profiles look like from the Administration page.

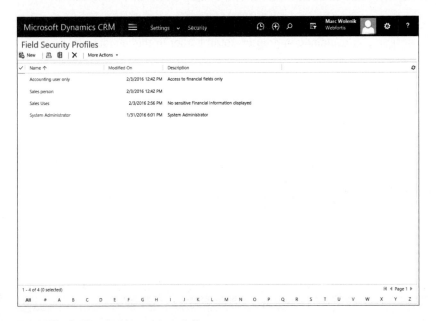

FIGURE 17.69   Field security profiles.

Figure 17.70 shows an example with a field called Drivers License Number added to the case form and with Field Security set to Enable.

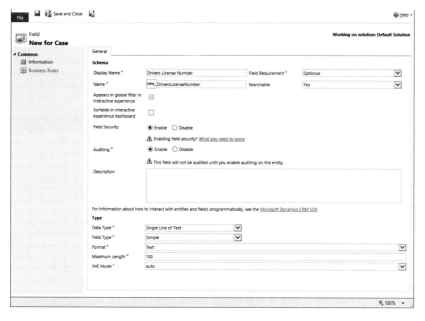

FIGURE 17.70   New field called Drivers License Number with the Field Security setting shown.

Once the field is added to the form (as shown in Figure 17.71), it is shown with a key icon to indicate that it has some level of security applied to it.

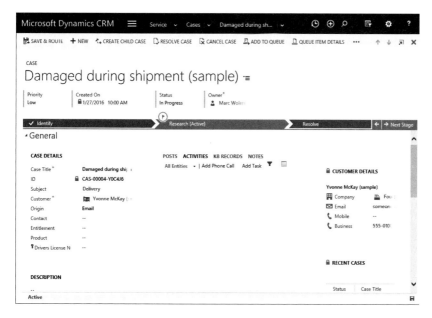

FIGURE 17.71   Case form with a secured field on it.

To enforce the security, select one of the profiles and select Field Permissions and the field whose security you want to edit. Clicking Edit opens the field security settings specific to that field and gives you the ability to set the permissions in a variety of ways.

When you have multiple profiles, the same field can be reflected differently depending on which profile is assigned. This results in a very dynamic and flexible approach to security.

> **NOTE**
>
> As with security roles, users can receive multiple FLS profiles, and the least restrictive one wins.

Hierarchy Security

The Hierarchy Security option lets you configure hierarchy modeling, and then you can enable it to select the model, which can be Manager Hierarchy or Custom Position Hierarchy. You can also exclude some entities to use this new model. This adds another level for controlling the security of the records in addition to the business units and security roles. This model is useful for simplifying the security configuration when you have a large number of business units. This feature was introduced with CRM 2015. Figure 17.72 illustrates the hierarchy.

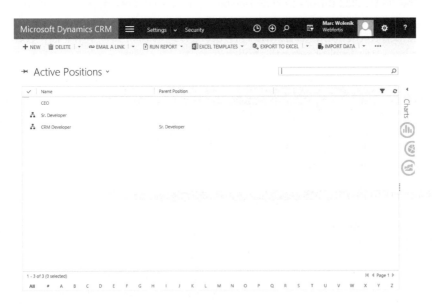

FIGURE 17.72   Hierarchy Security settings.

Positions

The Positions option lets you configure the positions that will help you configure security if you want to use hierarchy modeling. Creating new positions only requires that you enter a name; you can also select a parent position if you like and assign users to each position.

Access Team Templates

The Access Team Templates option lets you configure access team templates. By default the system comes with one predefined access team template, called Opportunity Sales Team Template.

You can only create access team templates for the entities that have the access teams feature enabled. These templates are used only by access teams. All the changes you make in an access team template are applied only to new access teams and not to existing ones.

Other Settings Navigation Options

Other options available under Settings include the following:

- ▶ Data Management
- ▶ System Jobs
- ▶ Document Management
- ▶ Auditing
- ▶ Email Configuration
- ▶ Activity Feeds Configuration
- ▶ Activity Feeds Rules
- ▶ CRM App for Outlook (only available for CRM Online)

Most of these options are discussed briefly in the following sections, while the other sections have dedicated chapters for them.

Data Management

The Data Management section is designed to easily manage the following:

- ▶ Duplicate Detection Settings
- ▶ Duplicate Detection Rules
- ▶ Duplicate Detection Jobs
- ▶ Bulk Record Deletion
- ▶ Data Maps
- ▶ Imports
- ▶ Templates for Data Import
- ▶ Sample Data
- ▶ Add Ready-to-Use Business Processes
- ▶ Data Encryption
- ▶ Export Field Translations
- ▶ Import Field Translations

System Jobs

Just as every entity in Microsoft Dynamics CRM has a workflow entity association with it that displays any workflow used by that entity, the system itself has a workflow. This workflow is referred to as a system job, and it generally runs in the background. The System Jobs interface provides the capability to view the status of system jobs and cancel, postpone, pause, or resume them. Some examples of system jobs are the calculation of rollup fields that is executed every hour and the mass calculation of rollup fields that is executed every 12 hours.

By default, the interface displays the system jobs and their status. You can open any of the displayed jobs by double-clicking them, and any errors are displayed here.

Document Management

Document Management is where you can manage your SharePoint settings. There are six options here:

▶ Document Management Settings

▶ Install List Component

▶ SharePoint Sites

▶ SharePoint Document Locations

▶ Enabled Server-Based SharePoint Integration

▶ Enable OneDrive for Business

▶ Document management is covered in **CHAPTER 27**, "SharePoint."

Auditing

Auditing enables you to record changes made by any record update, creation, or deletion—on either the attribute or entity level. The four options are as follows:

▶ Global Auditing Settings

▶ Entity and Field Audit Settings

▶ Audit Summary View

▶ Audit Log Management

Global Auditing Settings   You can select Global Auditing Settings to open the System Settings interface (as explained earlier in this chapter), where you can turn the global setting Start Auditing on or off (see Figure 17.73). By default, it is not selected; however, it must be on for auditing of any type to be active.

FIGURE 17.73   Auditing system settings.

Audit User Access allows you to audit when a user logs in to CRM. This is very useful for seeing who is using the system as most of the time they might only do read operations, which are not tracked by the auditing.

The System Settings page also provides check boxes to enable entities in the following categories:

▶ **Common Entities**—Enabling this option automatically enables auditing in the following entities: User, Contact, Goal, Goal Metric, Lead, Marketing List, Product, Quick Campaign, Report, Rollup Query, Sales Literature, Security Roles, and User.

▶ **Sales Entities**—Enabling this option automatically enables the auditing in the following entities: Competitor, Invoice, Opportunity, Order, Quote, and any other entity configured to be displayed in the Sales area.

▶ **Marketing Entities**—Enabling this option automatically enables the auditing in the Campaign entity and any other entity configured to be displayed in the Marketing area.

▶ **Customer Service Entities**—Enabling this option automatically enables the auditing in the following entities: Article, Case, Contract, Queue Item, Service, Social Profile, and any other entity configured to be displayed in the Service area.

NOTE

If you see any of the check boxes just described disabled, they might be disabled because one of the entities under that area is be configured differently than the other entities in the same area.

Entity and Field Audit Settings   When you select Entity and Field Audit Settings, the Default Solution for Edit opens, allowing you to set auditing for any entity or field. This is critical because even though you can enable auditing on the attribute level, if you have not enabled auditing on the entity level, auditing will not occur.

To enable auditing on the attribute level, expand the entity you want to work with and select Fields. Select a field on which you want to enable (or disable) auditing and double-click to open the details. Change the value on the attribute to Auditing and select Save and Close. Auditing now occurs on that field.

Audit Summary View   Audit Summary View provides a summary view of both the audits that have occurred in the system and any audit changes (such as enabling or disabling auditing).

If you double-click a record's row, you can see the details related to the record change (as shown in Figure 17.74). If you have selected System Access Auditing, you can see when users access the system (see Figure 17.75).

FIGURE 17.74   Attribute auditing changes.

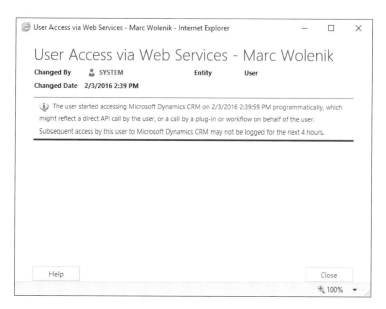

FIGURE 17.75   User access audit details.

Audit Log Management   Audit Log Management allows users to delete audit logs. When you delete a log, however, you lose the audit history.

Process Center

The Process Center is where you can access the processes to manage actions, business process flows, dialogs, and workflows.

▶ Refer to **CHAPTER 26** for information about working with processes.

Summary

This chapter reviews the areas that make up the Settings area for CRM and discusses how they are important and relevant to setting up, maintaining, and managing your business. In addition, this chapter details how to configure the security of CRM through the use of roles, teams, and business units.

You will visit many aspects of the Settings area only occasionally, but others (such as adding and removing users and permissions, activating and deactivating product lists, and creating customizations for the system) you will use often.

This chapter illustrates the importance of becoming familiar with the different Settings areas, and it can be a frequently accessed resource area for system administrators.

CHAPTER 18

Mobility

Microsoft started supporting multiple browsers with the release of CRM 2011 Update Release (UR) 12 in December 2012. With the release of Dynamics CRM 2016, however, Microsoft launched new Dynamics CRM mobile apps that work in tablets and phones and that offer a consistent interface and multiple-device support.

The Microsoft Dynamics CRM 2016 mobile apps are available for iPhone, Windows, and Android phones. Mobile app access is available with all Essential, Basic, and Professional licenses, at no additional cost.

New Features

CRM mobile existed for CRM 2015, but the new version has a lot of new features and enhancements in this area. Here is an overview of the new features introduced in CRM 2016:

▶ **Document integration**—You can now access the SharePoint/OneDrive documents in mobile apps. You must have SharePoint or OneDrive integration enabled in System Settings for this new feature to work.

▶ For more information about SharePoint integration, **SEE CHAPTER 27**, "SharePoint."

▶ **Exporting data to Excel**—You can now export data to Excel on mobile devices.

▶ **Emailing links to pages**—You can send links to records by email to share with other CRM users. These links can open the CRM records either directly in the mobile interface or the browser interface.

▶ **New mobile OS support**—This includes support for Windows 10 and iOS 9.

▶ **Support for web resources and IFRAMEs**—You can now use web resources like HTML and JavaScript as well as IFRAMEs in your mobile forms and dashboards. You cannot use Silverlight web resources as that technology has been deprecated and replaced by HTML5/CSS3. Make sure the web resource has the Enabled for Tablets check box checked in the web resource as well as in the web resource properties window that is in the form where you insert it. Even though the check box says Enabled for Tablets, it works for phones as well as tablets.

▶ **New visual controls**—A set of very cool visual controls has been designed to be used specially in mobile devices. You'll learn about them later in this chapter, in the section "Visual Controls."

▶ **Knowledge base**—You can now search the knowledge base and view the articles in mobile devices.

Tablets

The Dynamics CRM for Tablets app can connect to both Microsoft Dynamics CRM Online and On-Premises deployments. On-Premises deployments require the deployment to be configured as an Internet-facing deployment (IFD) for users to access their data using tablets.

▶ For more information about IFD, **SEE CHAPTER 28** "Forms Authentication."

NOTE

You can download the iPad version of the Dynamics CRM for Tablets app from https://itunes.apple.com/us/app/microsoft-dynamics-crm/id678800460?mt=8 or by searching for "Dynamics CRM" in iTunes.

You can download the Windows 10 version of the Dynamics CRM for Tablets app from https://www.microsoft.com/store/apps/9wzdncrfjbcm.

Windows 10 Installation

To install the Dynamics CRM for Tablets app on a Windows 10 tablet, follow these steps:

1. Go to www.microsoft.com/store/apps/9wzdncrfjbcm, or search for "Dynamics CRM" in the Windows Store. Figure 18.1 shows the Dynamics CRM for Tablets app in the Windows Store.

FIGURE 18.1   Dynamics CRM app in the Windows Store.

2. Install the App from the Store.

3. When the app is installed, launch it from your list of apps by clicking it or by typing **Dynamics CRM**.

4. Click the app tile (see Figure 18.2), and a window opens, asking for your company CRM web address (see Figure 18.3). Enter it and then click the big right-pointing arrow.

FIGURE 18.2   Dynamics CRM app tile on a Windows tablet.

18

FIGURE 18.3   Dynamics CRM web address screen.

5. On the Connecting to a Service screen that appears, provide your credentials to connect to the CRM organization (see Figure 18.4).

FIGURE 18.4   Sign-in screen.

After successful authentication (which may take a few minutes), you see some tips on how to use the app (see Figure 18.5).

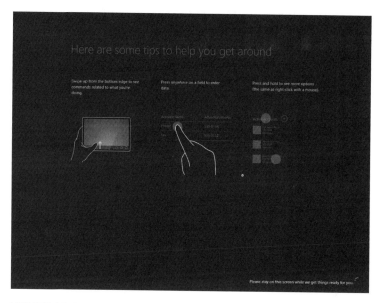

FIGURE 18.5 Tips for using the Dynamics CRM for Tablets app.

After you close the tips screen, the next screen shown is the Sales Dashboard (see Figure 18.6).

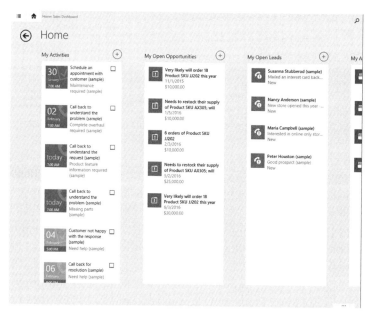

FIGURE 18.6 Sales Dashboard.

Additional Installation Options

A special privilege has been added to Dynamics CRM 2016: CRM for Mobile. This privilege, which appears is in the Business Management tab under the Privacy Related Privileges group, grants users access to Dynamics CRM from tablets and phones, and it is available to the following security roles by default:

▶ CEO-Business Manager

▶ Sales Manager

▶ Salesperson

▶ System Administrator

▶ System Customizer

▶ Vice President of Sales

You can also add or remove this privilege from security roles as necessary. You can do so under the Privacy Related Privileges section on the Business Management tab for any security role (see Figure 18.7).

FIGURE 18.7   CRM for Mobile privilege.

NOTE

Field-level security is enforced on the Dynamics CRM for Tablets app, just as it is on the main application.

Customizing Options and Features

The CRM for Mobile privilege takes the main form of an entity and shows it in optimized manner for tablets. The form is displayed in panorama layout, and users can swipe the screen to look for elements.

The following items are always available (see Figure 18.8):

▶ **Navigation bar**—This is the first button in the top-left corner of the screen. It displays the navigation links to all the entities that are have CRM for Mobile and are available on the site map of the CRM web application.

▶ **Home**—This button, which is next to the navigation bar, takes you to the Sales Dashboard of the tablet. This new version now supports more than one dashboard that you can access by clicking the navigation bar then the Dashboards option.

▶ **Search**—This button, in the top-right corner of the screen, takes you to the multi-entity search.

TIP

Multi-entity search is a feature that is now available on the web client as well.

▶ **Process bar**—If enabled for the entity, the process bar is located just to the left of the search icon.

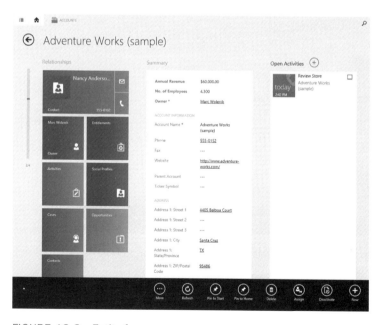

FIGURE 18.8   Entity form.

▶ **Command bar**—The command bar is available at the bottom of the screen. If you swipe up from the bottom (or, when working on a desktop computer with a mouse, right-click), the command bar appears. Some of the commands that are available when using the full web or Outlook client are not available on the tablet. Also, the command bar is context sensitive, which means it displays commands based on what is currently viewed or selected.

The Dynamics CRM for Tablets app uses the main form definition for each entity, so the same fields are configured in the web application and in the app. However, you cannot switch between forms on a tablet.

If you add or remove a field from a form, the Dynamics CRM for Tablets app reflects the changes. If you have multiple main forms for an entity, the Dynamics CRM for Tablets app form displays on the basis of the form order set and security roles assigned to the form.

Form Fields

Lookup fields behave slightly differently in the web application than in the full version. You need to type a few characters in the lookup field, and the Dynamics CRM for Tablets app shows you matching records in the command bar at the bottom of the screen.

The example shown in Figure 18.9 shows the first few letters of a name typed (in this case, **Re**). As a result, the New option appears in the lower-right corner, so you can create a new record (see Figure 18.9).

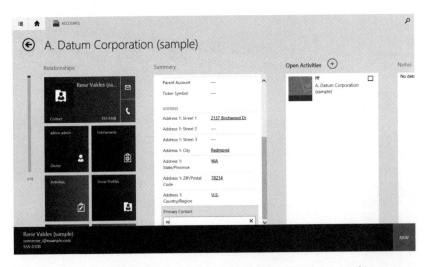

FIGURE 18.9   Lookup field on the Dynamics CRM for Tablets app form.

Phone number and email fields are clickable in the Dynamics CRM for Tablets app, and you can start a Skype call and send an email using your default email application on the tablet directly.

Communication Card

A special kind of tile called the communication card exists in the Dynamics CRM for Tablets app. This tile appears on the top of the list of tiles in the Relationship section of the form (as shown in Figure 18.10), and it appears on the Contact and User entity form by default and for other entities if the quick view card is embedded on the main form.

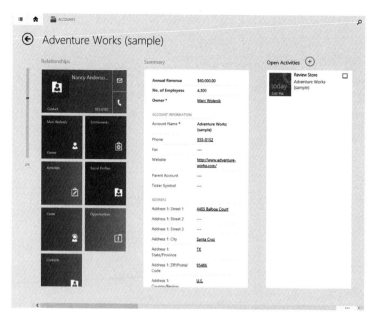

FIGURE 18.10   First three panels of the form.

When you tap the main section of the communication card, the corresponding record form opens, and you can quickly send an email or make a call with Skype.

Navigating Records
When you open a record from a list, you see a slider bar on the record. You can use this slider bar to navigate to another record from the list. You need to tap and hold the slider bar and move it up or down to navigate to other records.

Form Elements
The first panel of the form displays contact information for relationships that exist in the record. The first item on the panel is the communication card which display information for the Contact and User entities. The tiles are displayed based on the associated view with the entity.

The second panel shows the name of the first tab on the main form. It has header fields in bold and then other fields from the first tab.

The next panel displays the current business process stage fields, if enabled for the entity, as shown in Figure 18.11.

The rest of the panels display any subgrids on the form and other content available (see Figures 18.11 and 18.12).

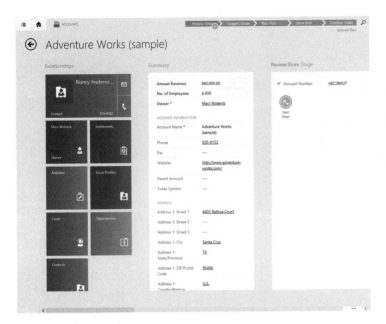

FIGURE 18.11   First three form panels.

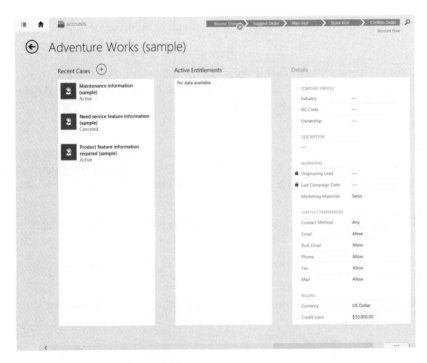

FIGURE 18.12   The rightmost form panels.

The Dynamics CRM for Tablets app can show up to 5 tabs, 75 fields (including hidden fields), and 10 subgrids. Except for some of the methods, JavaScript web resources are supported in the Dynamics CRM for Tablets app. (They do not throw any errors but also do not return any values.)

You can use the following conditional code to separate code that will not work with tablets:

```
if (Xrm.Page.context.client.getClient() != "Mobile")
{
    //Code that should not run in Dynamics CRM for Tablets app can be included here
}
```

Limitations of the Dynamics CRM for Tablets App

The following form features are not available in the Dynamics CRM for Tablets app:

▶ Yammer

▶ Activity feeds

▶ Bing Maps integration

▶ SQL Server reports

Entities Enabled for the Dynamics CRM for Tablets App

The following system entities are available for read-write operations in the Dynamics CRM for Tablets app:

▶ Account

▶ Activity

▶ Appointment

▶ Case

▶ Competitor

▶ Connection

▶ Contact

▶ Lead

▶ Note

▶ Opportunity

▶ Opportunity Product

▶ Phone Call

18

▶ Queue Item

▶ Social Activity

▶ Social Profile

▶ Task

The following entities are available for read-only operations in the Dynamics CRM for Tablets app:

▶ Attachment

▶ Email

▶ Entitlement

▶ Knowledge Base Record

▶ Product

▶ Queue

▶ SLA KPI Instance

▶ Team

▶ User

▶ Web Resource

The entities that are not enabled out of the box cannot be enabled for the Dynamics CRM for Tablets app, but you can enable custom entities to be available and used for the Dynamics CRM for Tablets app by setting the Enable for Mobile privilege, as shown in Figure 18.13. If you want the entity to be read-only, check the Read-Only in Mobile check box.

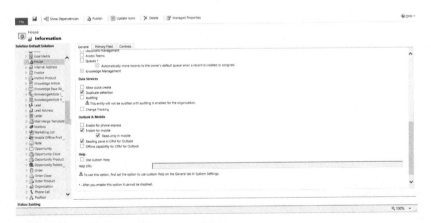

FIGURE 18.13   Enabling an entity for the Dynamics CRM for Tablets app.

> **NOTE**
>
> Entities for which the Dynamics CRM for Tablets app is not enabled have the same options, but those options are disabled and not clickable.

Sales Dashboard

The home page in the Dynamics CRM for Tablets app is the Sales Dashboard, which is a combination of views and charts (see Figure 18.14). You can have more than one dashboard for the Dynamics CRM for Tablets app, and users can switch between dashboards in tablets by right-clicking the bottom command options and selecting Dashboard. You can customize this dashboard in the web application, and changes are then reflected in the Dynamics CRM for Tablets app. A dashboard can have a maximum of six components, and the same dashboard is shown to all users.

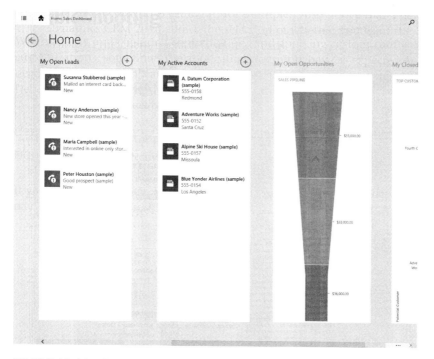

FIGURE 18.14   Sales Dashboard.

Navigation Bar

The navigation bar displayed in tablets uses the same site map as the web application. All entities that are enabled for the Dynamics CRM for Tablets app and are visible in the navigation bar of the web application appear on the navigation bar in the Dynamics CRM for Tablets app. It is shown as a flat list in the order based on the site map from the web application, without any duplicates. Figure 18.15 shows the navigation bar.

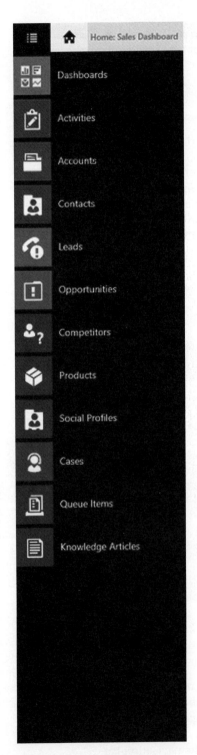

FIGURE 18.15   Navigation bar.

Command Bar

Just as with the web application, there is a command bar for the Dynamics CRM for Tablets app. It displays context-sensitive commands based on what you are viewing or the record currently selected. It uses the same RibbonDiffXML that is used by the web application to control which command buttons are displayed on the command bar, and you can also use RibbonDiffXML to decide whether to show a button only in the web application, the Dynamics CRM for Tablets app, or both. Figure 18.16 shows the command bar at the bottom of the screen.

FIGURE 18.16   Command bar.

To view the command bar on a Windows 10 device, you swipe up from the bottom of the tablet. (There is a bottom tab in the iPad for the command bar.) You can toggle what the command bar shows. To do this on a regular computer, select the ... in the bottom-right corner and hold the mouse key on a selected record. To do this on a tablet, press your finger on a record for 2 seconds.

Quick Create

In a dashboard, you can see a + (quick create) icon at the far-left corner of the command bar (see Figure 18.17). When you click it, you have the option to create a record for entities that have the CRM for Mobile privilege enabled.

FIGURE 18.17   Quick create.

18

Refresh

The Refresh command is available on the command bar on all pages in a tablet. Click it to refresh data for the page. You can find this command in the lower-right corner of the command bar on the dashboard, as shown in Figure 18.17.

Metadata Sync

When you configure the Dynamics CRM for Tablets app, metadata is retrieved. If you made any customization changes, you need to download the latest customizations either immediately or later (see Figure 18.18). The app checks for changes in the metadata each time it is opened or when the app is inactive in the background and the last check was made 24 hours or more previously.

FIGURE 18.18   Metadata sync alert.

Simple Lists

Simple lists are special lists that are rendered on a dashboard and within a form (see Figure 18.19). A simple list shows 10 records by default, and you can scroll down the list to retrieve more records if they exist. The primary field is always shown at the top, and the rest of the fields are taken from the selected view.

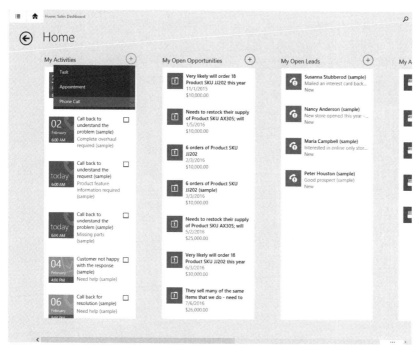

FIGURE 18.19   Create Record menu from a simple list on a dashboard.

You can perform a few actions on simple lists:

▶ Tap the header of a list to open the full list for the current view.

▶ Tap and hold a record in the list to display the command bar.

▶ Tap on the record in the list to open that record.

▶ Tap the + button at the top of a list to create a new record. This button is available for entities that are enabled for tablets. It opens a quick create form if quick create forms are enabled (and otherwise it opens the main entity form).

Activities Simple List

Figure 18.20 shows the Activities simple list, which has some extra functionality compared to other simple lists.

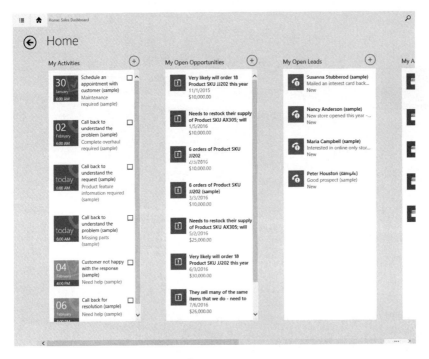

FIGURE 18.20   Activities simple list.

You can check a check box next to an activity to mark it as completed. In the My Activities list, activities that are due today (and that are past due) appear in a darker color, and activities that are not yet due appear in a lighter color. An activity for which a due date and time are set displays the date and time in the icon.

You can create new activities by clicking the + at the top of the Activities simple list.

Stakeholders and Sales Team Lists

The Stakeholders and Sales Team lists appear on the Opportunity entity form, and they display the primary field and role for the listed contacts/users. With these lists you can create and edit directly from the Dynamics CRM for Tablets app by tapping on the + button at the top of a list (see Figure 18.21). When creating a new record, you have two options: User Name (Contact lookup) and Role. Similarly, for Sales Team, the first field lookup is for the User entity, instead of the Contact entity.

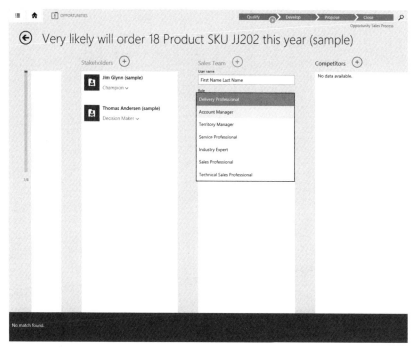

FIGURE 18.21   The Stakeholders and Sales Team lists.

Views

In the Dynamics CRM for Tablets app, views display columns in a similar way to what you see in the web application (see Figure 18.22). If a view has more columns than can fit onscreen, you can swipe from left to right. A view shows 25 records by default, and you can scroll down to see additional records. You can change a view by selecting the Select View command from the command bar. Tap this button to see all the views for that entity.

> **NOTE**
>
> Unlike in the web/Outlook application, in the Dynamics CRM for Tablets app, the personal views are shown before system views.

You can resize the width of columns in a view by selecting Resize Columns from the command bar: Just tap it and then drag the column to resize it as necessary. You can also sort the records by tapping on a column header in this view.

FIGURE 18.22   Select View command.

Business Process Flows

Business process flows (BPFs) are available in the Dynamics CRM for Tablets app just as in the web application. There are two components on a form:

▶ The stage chart (shown in the upper right)

▶ The stage requirements

> **NOTE**
>
> If a BPF spans multiple entities and if any of those entities are not available in the Dynamics CRM for Tablets app, you cannot go to that record type.

Charts

Charts appear on tablets if they are included in dashboards.

> **NOTE**
>
> There is no other way to show charts in tablets other than by having them included in dashboards.

Just as with the web/Outlook application, with the Dynamics CRM for Tablets app, you can tap a section of a chart to drill through and see the records that represent that portion of the chart. When you do this, you see a border along the section that you tapped on the chart (see Figure 18.23).

FIGURE 18.23   Charts drill-down.

You can change the current view by selecting Select View from the command bar. You can then see all the personal and system views for the selected entity.

If you change the view, the chart refreshes to show the selected view. You can change the chart by using the Select Chart command on the command bar, as shown in Figure 18.23.

NOTE

If you export a chart's XML and modify it and then import it back into Dynamics CRM, it might not render properly in the Dynamics CRM for Tablets app. To use charts in the Dynamics CRM for Tablets app, you should modify the charts by using the Chart Designer in the Dynamics CRM web application.

18

Multi-Entity Quick Find/Search

By using the search functionality in the Dynamics CRM for Tablets app, you can execute a quick find query against 10 entities at a time, and the results are grouped by entity and sorted by the order specified in the quick search view of that entity (see Figure 18.24).

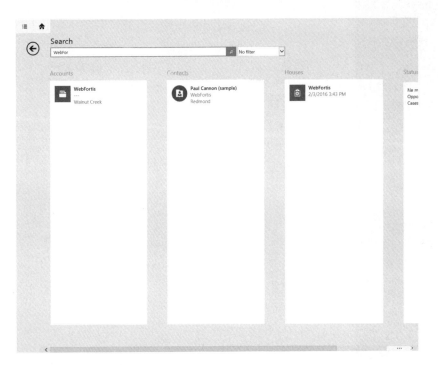

FIGURE 18.24   Multi-entity search results.

Multi-entity search uses quick search views of entities as the underlying search criteria, which means it searches in columns that are specified in the quick find columns of the entities.

In addition, you can always select the entity you want to search by selecting the Filter option located next to the search when you start a Quick Search from the dashboard. Change that filter to select the entity from the drop-down (see Figure 18.25). If you do a search from a list or a form, the Filter With condition has that entity selected by default.

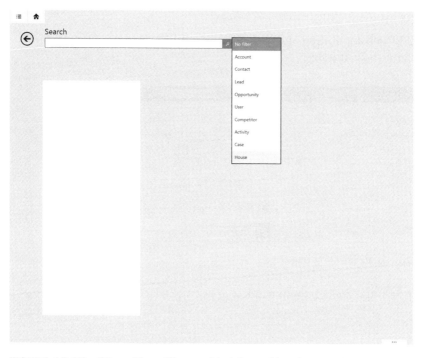

FIGURE 18.25   Filter with entities enabled for multi-entity search.

The following entities are enabled by default for multi-entity quick find:

▶ Account

▶ Case

▶ Contact

▶ Lead

▶ Opportunity

▶ User

▶ Competitor

▶ Activities

However, you can configure the search across other entities easily enough, as explained in the next section.

Configuring Multi-Entity Quick Search

You can configure which entities multi-entity search should work against and the order in which entities should display in the results.

Follow these steps to configure the search:

1. Go to the CRM web application and click Settings > Administration. The window shown in Figure 18.26 appears.

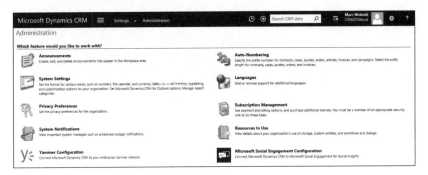

FIGURE 18.26   Administration page.

2. Click System Settings, and a pop-up window appears (see Figure 18.27).

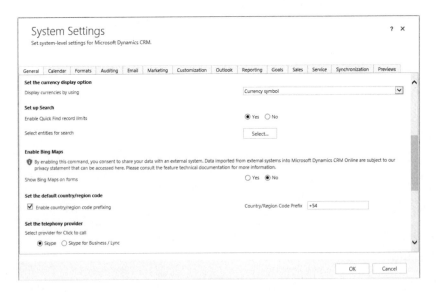

FIGURE 18.27   System Settings window.

3. On the General tab, in the Set Up Search section, click the Select button to the right of Select Entities for Search. A pop-up window opens, showing a list of entities that are enabled for search on the Dynamics CRM for Tablets app (see Figure 18.28).

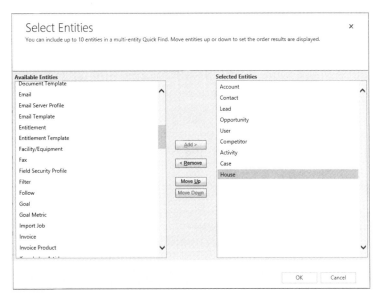

FIGURE 18.28   Configuring a multi-entity search.

4. Add or remove up to 10 entities by using the Add and Remove buttons. When you're finished with this, click OK.

5. Click OK in the next window and then close and restart the Dynamics CRM for Tablets app.

Offline Access/Usage

The Dynamics CRM for Tablets app caches data when you access records. The next time you open a record, the app tries to show you cached data; a background process gets updated data from the server if there are any changes and renders updated data (and also updates the cache). This means you can access cached data when you are disconnected from the Dynamics CRM server; however, the data you view while you're offline is cached, so you can only read that data and not update or create records.

> **NOTE**
>
> Unlike when working with the Microsoft Outlook client, where you can define filters to control data for synchronization and schedule synchronization intervals for the offline client, you cannot schedule or control what to cache.

When you're working with the app and you connect to the server, you do not automatically reconnect. Instead, you get an alert, and you have to click Reconnect to connect to the server again (see Figure 18.29).

18

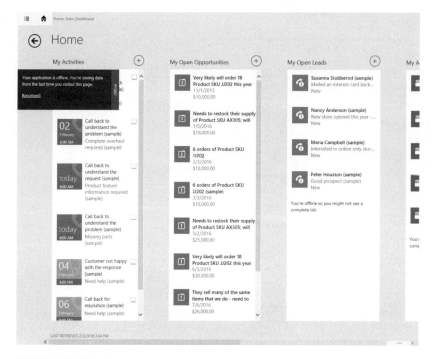

FIGURE 18.29   Reconnect alert.

You also see a timestamp on the bottom left of the screen, showing when the data was last retrieved.

When you're offline, you cannot use the search feature, and if you try to use it, you get an error (see Figure 18.30).

FIGURE 18.30   Error on a search in offline mode.

In addition, when you open in offline mode a record that was cached, the Dynamics CRM for Tablets app shows a lock sign at the bottom, and all fields are noneditable because this is a read-only record (see Figure 18.31).

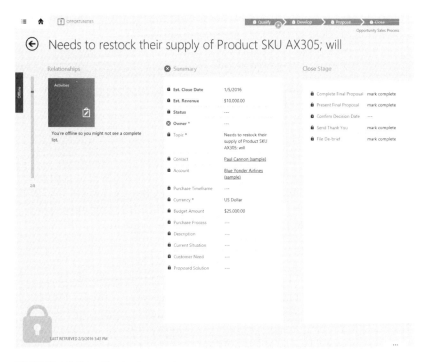

FIGURE 18.31   Cached record.

If you open a record that was not cached, the app shows you an error message
(see Figure 18.32).

FIGURE 18.32   Error on a record that was not cached.

Cache Priority

When you work offline, the data is cached in the following order of priority:

1. **Dashboard lists and data for tiles**—The records displayed on lists in the dashboard and any records pinned to Sales Dashboard are prioritized for caching.

2. **Entity pages**—The records that are opened from lists and the dashboard get second priority. The records that are cached are based on what you accessed in the Dynamics CRM for Tablets app previously, not what you accessed in the web application.

Attachments and charts are not available in offline mode, and images like contact photos are cached in browser mode, so they might not be available when you are offline.

> **NOTE**
>
> Data is cached in the HTML5 local store, which is different for each operating system; it is Index DB for Windows 10, and Web SQL for iOS 9.

Auto-Save

Auto-Save is a feature in CRM 2016 that can be disabled in System Settings. If it is disabled in the CRM web application, it is also disabled in the Dynamics CRM for Tablets app. If it is enabled the CRM web application, the record is saved automatically if you move away from the form. If it is disabled, the user has to open the command bar and tap the Save command.

Images

A new feature in CRM 2016 is that you can upload images for records. In the Dynamics CRM for Tablets app, you can view images, but you cannot change or upload images through a tablet. You have to upload images through the web application, and then you can view them in the Dynamics CRM for Tablets app.

> **NOTE**
>
> This is counterintuitive, in our opinion, as nearly every tablet has a built-in camera application, and it would seem like an easy extension to provide this functionality within the Dynamics CRM for Tablets app.

Server-Side Extensibility

Any create, read, update, and delete (CRUD) requests from a tablet trigger plug-ins and workflows, much as when you're working with the web application. However, you need to be sure to thoroughly test these custom processes because the Dynamics CRM for Tablets app is still in initial release and may produce unexpected results.

Mobile Phones

Specific mobile phone apps for Dynamics CRM help users connect and be productive while working with their phones. Users can access Customer info; update opportunities, notes, and tasks; and get prepared for meetings while on the go. As with the Dynamics CRM for Tablets app, there are no additional license fees to access these mobile apps. Users can access Dynamics CRM 2016 or Dynamics CRM Online in the following ways:

- ▶ Dynamics CRM for Phones app
- ▶ Dynamics CRM Mobile Express app
- ▶ Dynamics CRM on a phone's web browser

> **NOTE**
>
> Mobile Express, the default "light" application for Dynamics CRM, is a supported interface for access to Dynamics CRM. However, because of its low usage and limited customization options, we have excluded it from this book.

Dynamics CRM for Phones Apps

Table 18.1 lists the phones and the operating systems supported for the Dynamics CRM for Phones app.

TABLE 18.1   Phones and Operating Systems Supported by Dynamics CRM

Phone	OS Version
iPhone	iOS7 and later
Android	Android 4.4 and later
Windows	Windows 8.0, 8.1, and 10

> **NOTE**
>
> You can download the Dynamics CRM for Phones app for the supported phones as follows:
>
> ▶ For iPhone, visit https://itunes.apple.com/us/app/dynamics-crm-for-phones/id1003997947?mt=8.
>
> ▶ For Android, visit https://play.google.com/store/apps/details?id=com.microsoft.crm.crmphone.
>
> ▶ For Windows phone, visit www.microsoft.com/en-us/store/apps/microsoft-dynamics-crm/9wzdncrfjbcm.

> **NOTE**
>
> Microsoft has not released an app for BlackBerry devices, and it is unlikely that it will do so in the future. You can access Dynamics CRM on BlackBerry devices using the BlackBerry mobile browser and Dynamics CRM Mobile Express.

Dynamics CRM on a Phone's Web Browser

Users who do not have the Dynamics CRM for Phones app installed can access Dynamics CRM data by using the mobile phone browser. Table 18.2 lists the mobile browser and phone operating system versions supported for accessing Dynamics CRM 2016 on a phone.

TABLE 18.2   Supported Phone Operating Systems

Browser	OS Version
Windows phone—Internet Explorer Mobile	Windows 8.1 and 10
Safari (iPhone)	iOS 7.x, 8.x, and 9.x
Android	Android 4.4 and 5.0

Required Privileges

To use Dynamics CRM from a mobile phone, you need to enable the CRM for Mobile privilege (called CRM for Phones in Dynamics CRM 2015). Figure 18.33 shows this security privilege on the Business Management tab in the Privacy Related Privileges section. This privilege is available in all new installations of Dynamics CRM 2016 On-Premises and Online, and you can configure it as necessary.

FIGURE 18.33   CRM for Mobile privilege.

Enabling Entities for the Dynamics CRM for Phones App

You need to enable entities for the Dynamics CRM for Phones app just as you do for tablets. You have to customize an entity and enable the Enable for Mobile option under the Outlook & Mobile section, as shown in Figure 18.34.

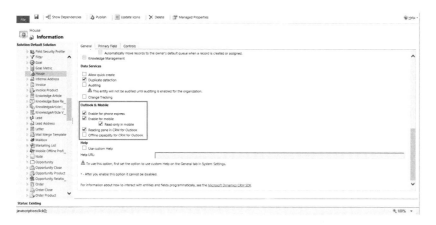

FIGURE 18.34   Enabling CRM for Mobile for an entity.

Customization and Features

As with the web application, you can have multiple web forms for the Dynamics CRM for Phones app, but you cannot switch between forms on the Dynamics CRM for Phones app. You need to set the form order and assign security roles to the forms. Users then see a form based on the form order set and the security role assigned.

The following steps guide you through creating a new form and customizing it:

1. Log in to the CRM web application and go to Settings > Customizations > Customize the System. The default solution opens. Expand the Entities node and select the Account entity or another entity for which you want to create a mobile form (see Figure 18.35).

FIGURE 18.35   Selecting the Account entity in the default solution.

2. Click Forms and then open the existing mobile form. From the menu, click Save As and provide a new name and description for the form, and then click OK.

3. Add or remove existing fields on the form by using the Add or Remove buttons (see Figure 18.36). All required fields are included in the form by default and cannot be removed.

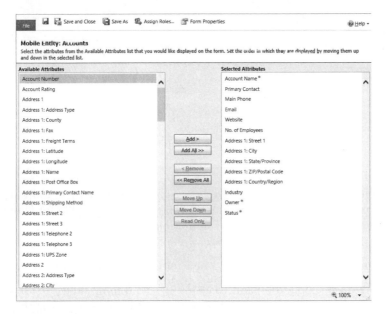

FIGURE 18.36   Mobile Express form customizations.

4. Select a field and then click or tap the Read Only button to make that field read-only. In Figure 18.36, No. of Employees is a read-only field.

5. Click Enable Security Roles and then, in the Assign Security Roles dialog, select the security roles for which you want this form to be available (see Figure 18.37). Then click OK.

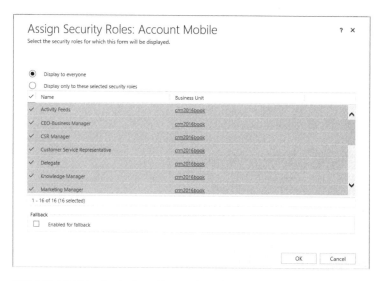

FIGURE 18.37   Assigning all security roles to the new mobile form.

6. Click Save and Close to close the Form Designer for the new Mobile Express form. Click Form Order and select Mobile Express Form Set, and you see two mobile forms with green arrow buttons. Select the new form and then use the arrow buttons to move the new form to the top.

7. Publish the customizations when you are done, and the new form is the one shown when users access the Mobile Express app.

Installing and Using the Dynamics CRM for Phones App

Follow these steps to install the Dynamics CRM for Phones app on an iPhone:

1. Go to the App Store and search for "Microsoft Dynamics CRM." Select and download the Dynamics CRM for Phones app (see Figure 18.38).

FIGURE 18.38   Dynamics CRM for Phones app in the App Store.

2. Once the app is installed on your phone, tap the app icon to open it, provide your company's CRM web address, and then click the right-arrow button.

3. Provide your login credentials to log in to CRM (see Figure 18.39). After authentication, the application takes some time to download the customizations, which might be seconds or minutes, depending on the number of customizations and business rules on your CRM organization.

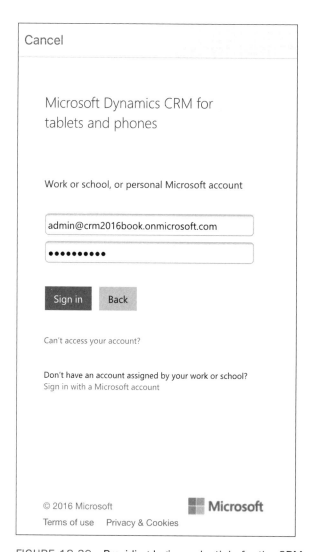

FIGURE 18.39   Providing login credentials for the CRM organization.

4. When the update process finishes, swipe to the right, and you see the Sales Dashboard. You should see four buttons on the top bar. The left-arrow button takes you back to the previous screen. The home button takes you to the home page, the third button is for search functionality, and the last button shows the icons available for sitemap navigation.

5. Click the last icon, and you are presented with a list of icons including Accounts, Contacts, Opportunities, and so on (see Figure 18.40).

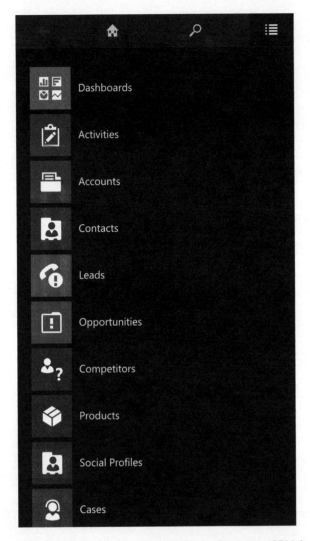

FIGURE 18.40   Icons available in the Dynamics CRM for Phones app.

6. Click an icon, such as Accounts, to see a list of records for that entity type (see Figure 18.41).

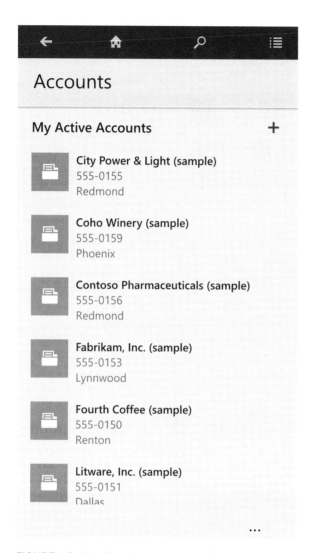

FIGURE 18.41   List of account records.

7. To search for a specific account, click the third icon at the top of the screen and enter some text to search, as shown in Figure 18.42. Then tap the search icon on the mobile form to see the results (see Figure 18.43). If you didn't select a filter, you might have more results than you can see on one screen, in which case you can simply swipe from right to left.

18

FIGURE 18.42   Enter some text and tap the search icon on the mobile form.

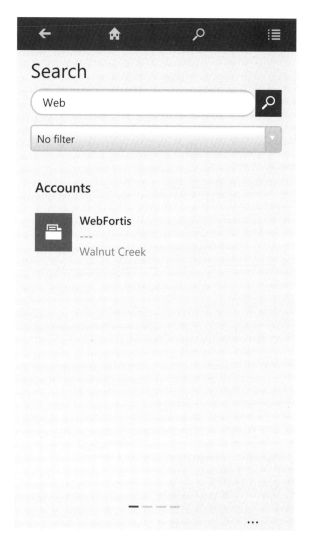

FIGURE 18.43   Search results.

8. Tap the + icon near the view name (which is also available when you tap the ... at the bottom-right corner of the screen) to create records for the selected entity type. A new mobile form for the entity appears (see Figure 18.44). Complete the form and click the Save icon at the bottom to save the record or tap the Cancel icon to cancel and close the form.

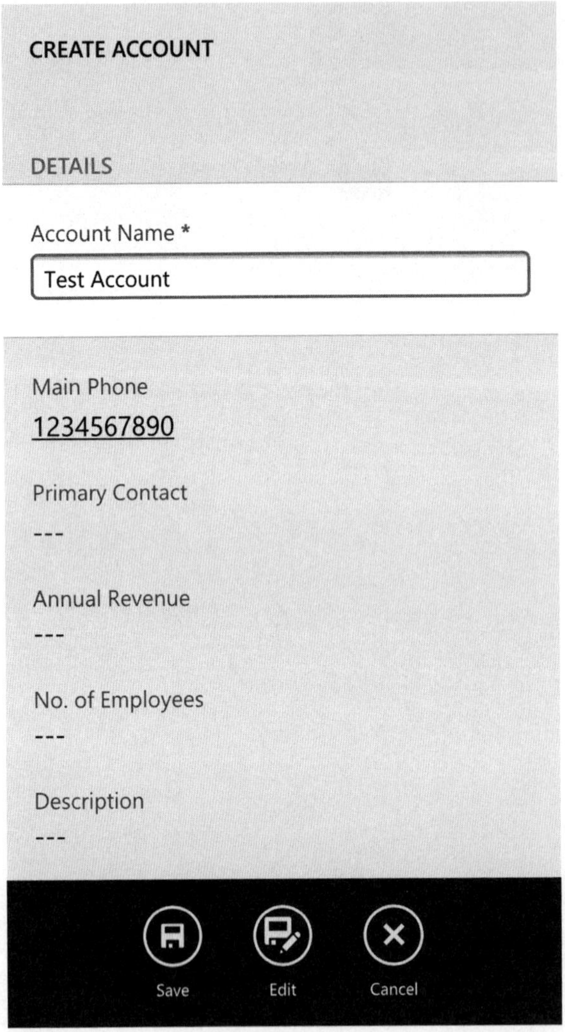

CREATE ACCOUNT

DETAILS

Account Name *

Test Account

Main Phone
1234567890

Primary Contact

Annual Revenue

No. of Employees

Description

Save   Edit   Cancel

FIGURE 18.44   New account entity mobile form.

9. To add values in a lookup field, select the field, and you see a list of records (see Figure 18.45).

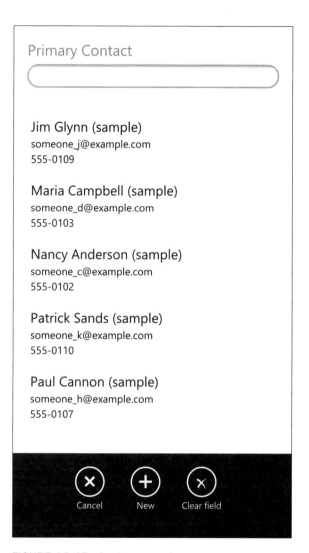

FIGURE 18.45   Lookup records.

Enter a few characters and tap Done, then Find at the bottom (see Figure 18.46).

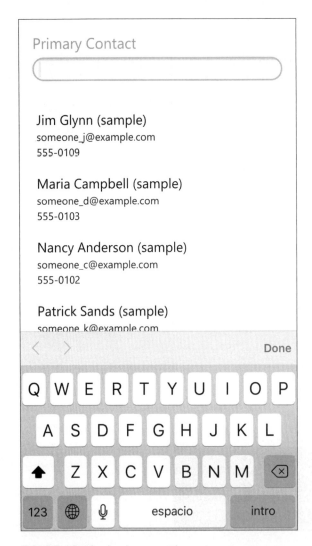

FIGURE 18.46 Lookup search.

Select the record from the displayed results and tap the Done button (see Figure 18.47).

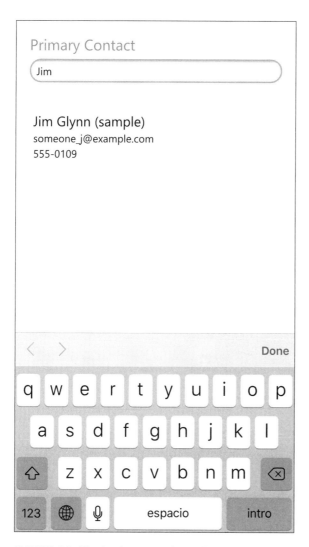

FIGURE 18.47   Lookup search results.

10. When you open a record, you see only the fields that contain data. You also see links to related entities under the list of fields on the form on iPhone or Android phones, as shown in Figure 18.48. On Windows phones, you have to swipe to view related entities.

18

FIGURE 18.48   Related entities of a record.

You see more actions when you are viewing a record if you click the ... in the bottom-right corner of the screen (see Figure 18.49):

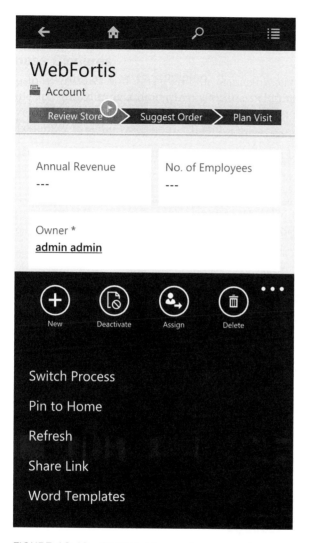

FIGURE 18.49   Contextual menu for a record.

▶ **New**—This takes you to the new record form.

▶ **Deactivate**—Tap this icon to deactivate the record.

▶ **Assign**—Tap this icon to assign this record to another user or team.

▶ **Delete**—Tap this icon to delete the record.

▶ **Switch Process**—Tap this option to change the process flow of this record.

▶ **SEE CHAPTER 26**, "Process Development," to learn more about the process flow usage.

▶ **Pin to Home**—Tap this option to add a shortcut to this record on the home screen, where the Sales Dashboard will be displayed, along with the records you pinned.

▶ **Share Link**—This opens a new email containing a URL that links to the selected record so you can share with a user who has access to CRM.

▶ **Word Templates**—Tap this option to create a Word document using the Word templates available in the system.

▶ **SEE CHAPTER 21**, "Office Integration," to learn more about Word templates.

You can tap a phone number in the application to start a call and tap an email address to send an email message. In addition, you can mark activities as completed from your Dynamics CRM for Phones app. Open any Activity record and then tap the Mark Complete icon to mark it as complete, as shown in Figure 18.50.

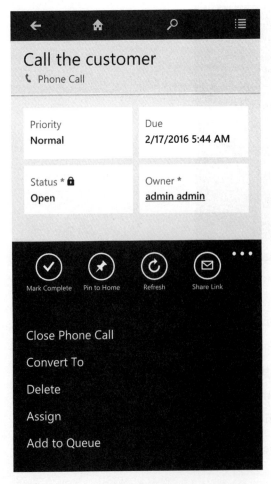

FIGURE 18.50   Marking an activity complete.

What's Extra in the Dynamics CRM for Phones App

In addition to the features already described, the following features are also available:

▶ **Activity feeds**—If activity feeds are enabled in your Dynamics CRM organization, you can view user or auto posts in CRM by using the Dynamics CRM for Phones app.

▶ **Offline access**—You can view recently accessed records while you are disconnected from the network. However, you cannot update or create new records while you're offline.

▶ **Local cache clearing**—If you have modified some organizational settings or customizations, you can force those changes to appear on your phone by clearing the cache. Tap the gear icon on the home page and then tap Clear Local Cache.

Visual Controls

Dynamics CRM has the following new visual controls. Some of them are available only for specific field types; some of them are interactive, allowing you to modify the values; and others are read-only, as described here. There are controls designed to be used specifically in phones, tablets, or both but not in web or Outlook client applications.

For whole numbers, decimals, and currency fields, you can use the following visual controls:

▶ **Arc Knob**—This control has Edit and Read modes, and the property values you must set are Min, Max, and Step.

▶ **Bullet Graph**—This control has Read-Only mode, and the property values you must set are Min, Max, Good, Bad, and Target.

▶ **Linear Gauge**—This control has Edit and Read modes, and the property values you must set are Min, Max, and Step.

▶ **Linear Slider**—This control has Edit and Read modes, and the property values you must set are Min, Max, and Step.

▶ **Number Input**—This control has Edit and Read modes, and the property value you must set is Step.

▶ **Radio Knob**—This control has Edit and Read modes, and the property values you must set are Min, Max, and Step.

For single-line strings fields, you can use the following visual controls:

▶ **Input Mask**—This control has Edit and Read modes, and the property value you must set is the Mask.

▶ **Auto-Complete**—This control has Edit mode, and the property value you must set is Source, which can be either View or Option Set. This control is useful for letting the user start typing a state name, for example, and presenting a list of the predefined states from which the use can choose that can be stored in either a custom entity or option set.

18

For single-line strings fields with URL formats, you can also use the following visual controls:

▶ **Multimedia Control**—This control has Read-Only mode, and it doesn't have any additional property. It is useful for showing URLs such as YouTube-embedded controls so the user can play a video without leaving the record.

▶ **Website Preview**—This control has Read-Only mode, and it doesn't have any additional property. It is useful for showing a preview of a URL without leaving the record.

For option set fields, you can use the following visual control:

▶ **Option Set**—This control has Edit and Read modes, and it doesn't have any additional property.

For two options fields, you can use the following visual control:

▶ **Flip–Switch**—This control has Edit and Read modes, and it doesn't have any additional property.

For text fields with multiple lines, you can use the following visual control:

▶ **Pen Control**—This control has Edit and Read modes, and it doesn't have any additional property. This control is useful for capturing signatures, for example.

For subgrids, you can use the following visual control:

▶ **Calendar Control**—This control has Edit and Read modes, and the property values you must set are Start Date and Description; optionally you can also set End Date and Duration.

Summary

This chapter covers the different types of mobility options for Microsoft Dynamics CRM 2016, including the installation, customization, use, and features of the Dynamics CRM mobile apps.

Note that, as previously mentioned, the data caching option is really handy for users who are not connected to network, but it is limited with regard to usage (for example, it requires users to be connected to perform updates).

> **NOTE**
>
> One of the darlings of mobility for Dynamics CRM, CWR Mobility, has merged with Resco, and they continue to provide a third-party alternative for mobility. For more information visit www.resco.net.

CHAPTER 19

Outlook Configuration

Microsoft Dynamics CRM has always offered users the ability to work within Outlook seamlessly. The Outlook integration provided by Microsoft Dynamics CRM tightly delivers CRM data in and through Outlook so that users can truly work in one place without having to navigate to separate applications.

Features provided with the Microsoft Dynamics CRM 2016 for Microsoft Office Outlook (known as the Outlook client) include the following:

▶ Full MAPI integration

▶ Customizable views of CRM data in Outlook

▶ Ribbon enhancements

▶ Data filters

▶ Email enhancements

When accessing Microsoft Dynamics CRM via a client (and not programmatically, such as through a custom interface or a portal), users have two options for accessing the application:

▶ Browser/web client

▶ Outlook client (Microsoft Dynamics CRM for Outlook)

In addition, users can access the application directly by using the mobile client or custom solutions; however, the full client experience is limited to these options.

> **NOTE**
>
> Outlook for Mac is not supported using the full client, but be sure to check the section "CRM App for Outlook," later in this chapter, for this functionality.

▶ **SEE CHAPTER 18**, "Mobility," for more information about the mobile client.

Although this chapter covers both client options for Microsoft Dynamics CRM 2016, with the exception of the next section, the focus of this chapter is on the Outlook client.

Browser/Web Client

As shown in Figure 19.1, Microsoft Dynamics CRM offers full-featured functionality using only a browser interface.

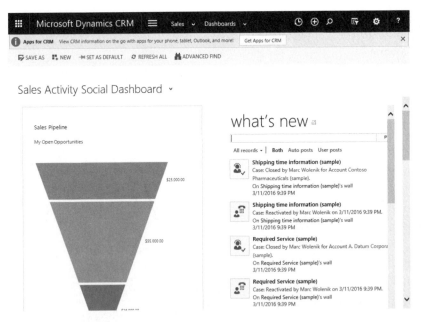

FIGURE 19.1   Browser interface for Dynamics CRM 2016.

The following operating systems are supported for the Microsoft Dynamics CRM web client:

▶ Windows 10 (Internet Explorer 11 and Edge)

▶ Windows 8.1 (Internet Explorer 11 only)

▶ Windows 8 (Internet Explorer 10 only)

▶ Windows 7 (Internet Explorer 10 and 11 only)

▶ The following non-Internet Explorer browsers:

    ▶ Mozilla Firefox (latest publicly released version)

    ▶ Google Chrome (latest publicly released version)

    ▶ Apple Safari (latest publicly released version)

All versions listed here must be running on Windows 7 or later, and Apple Safari must be on Mac OS 10.8 or higher.

To use several of the Office features available within the web client, such as exporting to Excel, the following minimum components must also be installed on the client computer:

▶ Microsoft Office 365

▶ Microsoft Office 2016

▶ Microsoft Office 2013

▶ Microsoft Office 2010

When considering using the browser for Microsoft Dynamics CRM, there are a few pros and cons:

Pros:

▶ Microsoft Dynamics CRM is lightweight and almost always available (for example, on guest computers).

▶ Little or no configuration is required to use it.

Cons:

▶ The ability to correlate (or track) emails to CRM does not exist without using Outlook.

▶ You must u use another application (instead of just using Outlook).

▶ There is no offline availability/access; using a browser requires an Internet connection.

19

If you click the Get Apps for CRM button at the top of the browser interface, you are directed to the Apps for Dynamics CRM page, where you can download the CRM for Outlook client and other CRM applications for phones and tablets, as shown in Figure 19.2.

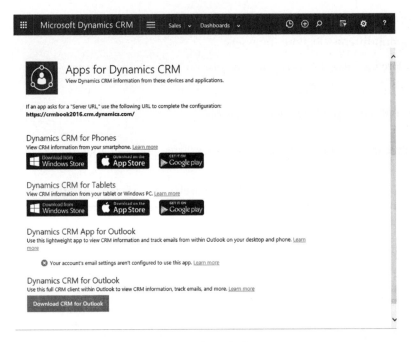

FIGURE 19.2   Apps for Dynamics CRM 2016.

> **TIP**
>
> If you don't see the Get Apps for CRM button, you can get to the same place by clicking the gear icon in the top-right corner and selecting Apps for Dynamics CRM.

Click the Download CRM for Outlook button, and you see a dialog box that lists the steps necessary to download and configure the Outlook client, as shown in Figure 19.3.

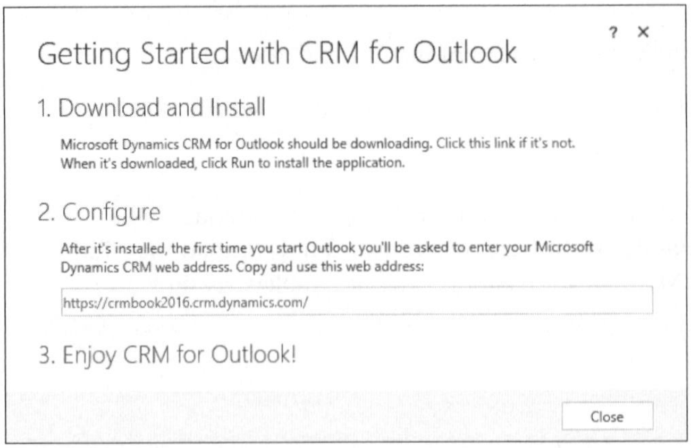

Getting Started with CRM for Outlook   ? ✕

1. Download and Install

Microsoft Dynamics CRM for Outlook should be downloading. Click this link if it's not. When it's downloaded, click Run to install the application.

2. Configure

After it's installed, the first time you start Outlook you'll be asked to enter your Microsoft Dynamics CRM web address. Copy and use this web address:

https://crmbook2016.crm.dynamics.com/

3. Enjoy CRM for Outlook!

Close

FIGURE 19.3   Getting Started with CRM for Outlook dialog.

You can turn off the Get Apps for CRM message by clicking the X on the far right. In addition, you can set the system to not display this message in System Settings > Outlook, as shown in Figure 19.4. This is helpful for organizations such as help desk operations that have no need for the Outlook client.

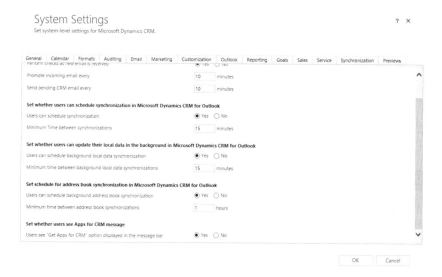

FIGURE 19.4   System settings for displaying the message for Get Apps for CRM.

Microsoft Dynamics CRM 2016 for Outlook

The integration with Microsoft Dynamics CRM and Outlook is known officially as *Microsoft Dynamics CRM 2016 for Outlook*. However, it is commonly referred to as the *Outlook Client*, and it brings Microsoft Dynamics CRM 2016 into Outlook for a unified user experience.

Unlike other applications (or competitors), users can use Microsoft Dynamics CRM within Microsoft Outlook. Additional benefits include the following:

▶ Integrated email tracking options are available.

▶ You can quickly convert emails to cases, leads, or opportunities.

▶ You can add connections.

▶ It is possible to visualize data quickly and easily.

Figure 19.5 shows Microsoft Outlook with the Microsoft Dynamics CRM 2016 for Outlook client installed.

19

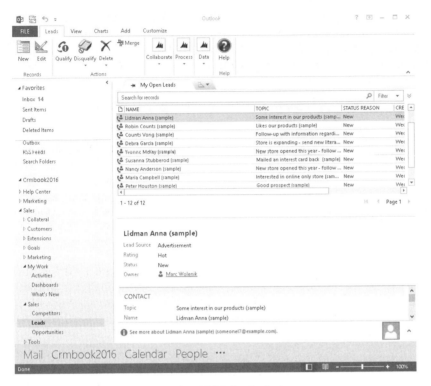

FIGURE 19.5   Microsoft Dynamics 2016 for Outlook.

Requirements

These are the minimum hardware requirements for running Microsoft Dynamics CRM 2016 for Outlook:

▶ **Processor**—2.9GHz or faster (3.3GHz or faster for offline enabled)

▶ **Memory**—2GB or more (4GB or more for offline enabled)

▶ **Hard disk**—1.5GB or more (2GB or more for offline enabled)

▶ **Display**—1024 × 768 resolution

In addition to the hardware requirements, the following software requirements apply:

▶ Windows 10 (64-bit and 32-bit versions)

▶ Windows 8.1 or Windows 8 (64-bit and 32-bit versions)

▶ Windows 7 Service Pack 1 (64-bit and 32-bit versions)

▶ Windows Server 2012 (when running as a Remote Desktop Services [RDS] application)

In addition, one of the supported web browsers must be installed and running:

▶ Internet Explorer 10 or later

▶ Mozilla Firefox (latest publicly released version) running on Windows 10, Windows 8.1, Windows 8, or Windows 7

▶ Google Chrome (latest publicly released version) running on Windows 10, Windows 8.1, Windows 8, Windows 7, or Android 10 tablet

▶ Apple Safari (latest publicly released version) running on Mac OS X 10.8 (Mountain Lion) or Apple iPad

---

NOTE

Internet Explorer 9 or earlier is not supported for use with Dynamics CRM 2016.

Because Microsoft Dynamics CRM for Outlook is supported in both 64- and 32-bit versions, you can install either one on your computer if you are running Windows 64-bit. However, you must have a 64-bit version of Microsoft Office 2013/2016 in order to install the 64-bit version of the client. (Otherwise, you will see a compatibility error.)

Client Setup

Much as with previous versions of Microsoft Dynamics CRM, the Outlook client configuration in Microsoft Dynamics CRM 2016 is broken down into two separate processes:

▶ Client installation

▶ Client configuration

The following sections describe these processes.

Client Installation

To install Microsoft Dynamics CRM for Outlook, follow these steps:

1. Ensure that Outlook has been run at least once on the client computer. Running Outlook once creates an Outlook profile for the user, and Microsoft Dynamics CRM for Outlook uses that profile for installation.

2. Download the client installation file and double-click it to start the installation. The executable is CRM2016-ClientOnlineInstaller-ENU.exe, and you can find it by searching Microsoft.com for "Dynamics CRM Outlook Client" or by clicking the yellow notification on the web client, as shown at the top of the screen in Figure 19.1, to download the files to your computer.

▶ The installation process checks for and installs missing components. If Offline Access is selected, Microsoft SQL Server 2012 SP2 Express Edition is installed as well.

3. Accept the license agreement shown in Figure 19.6 and click Next to continue.

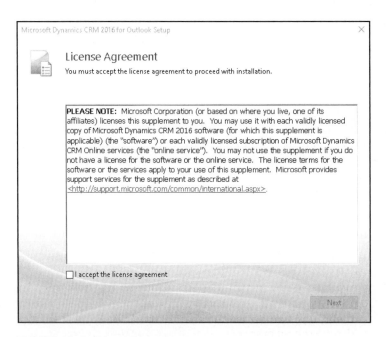

FIGURE 19.6   License agreement.

4. Click Install Now to install the client (as shown in Figure 19.7) or click Options to change whether to install the offline capabilities and the installation location, as shown in Figure 19.8.

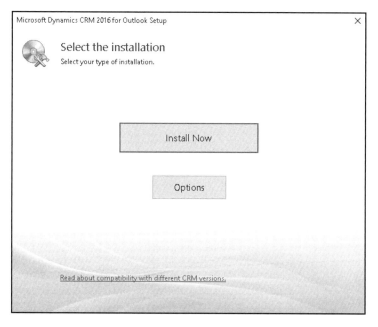

FIGURE 19.7   Select the installation.

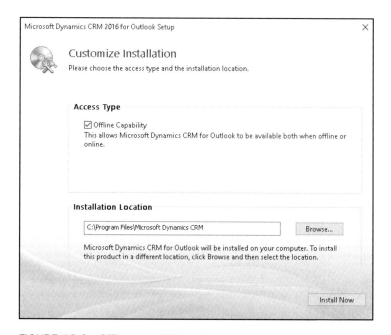

FIGURE 19.8   Offline capability options.

5. When the install is completed, click Close and restart Outlook (see Figure 19.9).

TIP

If your Internet connection is less than 300Kbps, installation of the Outlook client might fail. Ensure that your network connection is reliable and available at speeds above 300Kbps to avoid installation problems.

Microsoft Dynamics CRM for Outlook is now successfully installed on the client computer and is ready to be configured.

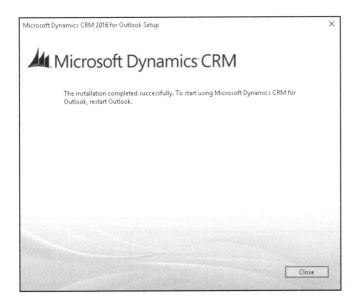

FIGURE 19.9   Successful installation of the client component.

Client Configuration

With the client successfully installed, you now need to configure it to work with the CRM organization.

NOTE

You should use the same email address in Outlook that you use in CRM in order to track emails.

To configure the client, either open Outlook after installation or make sure you have the Outlook application closed and select Start and type CRM in the search box, open the Configuration Wizard, and follow these steps:

1. Configure the organization by entering the server URL in the first drop-down box (see Figure 19.10) and then clicking Connect. (With CRM Online, you log in, and the organization tries to self-configure based on the login.)

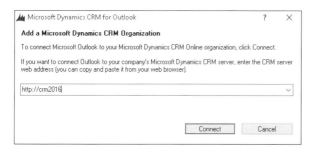

FIGURE 19.10   Client configuration.

TIP

If you have an On-Premises deployment, the URL you use in step 1 should be in the following format:

http(s)://<<servername>>:<<Port>>

Figure 19.11 shows a properly configured On-Premises configuration

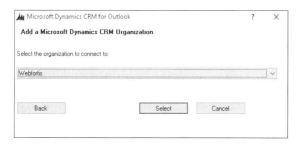

FIGURE 19.11   On-Premises client configuration.

TIP

Notice that because the CRM server is installed on the default port 80 in this example, it is not necessary to enter the port information. When you select the organization and then click Test Connection, the Configuration Wizard uses your current Active Directory (AD) information for verification/authorization.

2. If you have an Online deployment (that is, you are connecting to Microsoft Dynamics Online), select CRM Online from the Server drop-down shown in Figure 19.12) and then click Connect. When you click Connect, you are presented with an authorization option that stores and caches your connection information for your CRM Online provision (see Figure 19.13).

FIGURE 19.12   CRM Online client configuration.

FIGURE 19.13   Entering online credentials.

3. Enter your Office 365 online credentials information and click Sign In to continue. Figure 19.14 shows the proper configuration for a CRM Online instance.

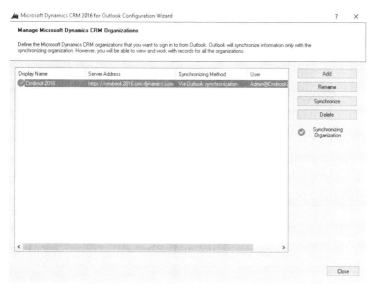

FIGURE 19.14   CRM Online client configuration.

4. Select the organization from the drop-down shown in Figure 19.15. If you only have one organization, this option is automatically skipped, as shown in Figure 19.14. If you have multiple organizations (or in the case of CRM Online, where you have multiple associations with the same Online credentials), you need to select the organization with which you want to integrate.

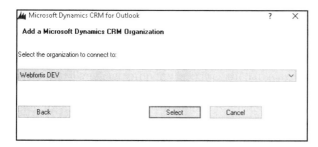

FIGURE 19.15   CRM Online client configuration with multiple organizations.

5. Optionally change the display name, by clicking the Rename button, and set whether to synchronize with the organization. You should set the synchronization option if you have multiple organizations attached to a single Outlook instance.

19

Although you can have multiple organizations attached to Outlook, you can have only one synchronizing organization. This is especially important considering the fact that when you track an item in CRM from Outlook, it tracks to the synchronizing organization, regardless of how many different CRM organizations you have in Outlook.

> **NOTE**
>
> Having multiple organizations in one instance of Outlook would happen only when there is a business need for multiple or completely different organizations to be accessed through a single Outlook interface as there is no data interchange between the organizations.

Now the Microsoft Dynamics CRM client is loaded and configured for use with Microsoft Outlook and CRM navigation, and you can access records via the navigation area on the left.

Client Troubleshooting

The CRM Outlook client also installs an application called Microsoft Dynamics CRM Diagnostics. You can find it by clicking the Windows Start button and searching for the word "diagnostics." You will recognize it easily by the CRM icon. Figure 19.16 shows the Diagnostics dialog.

FIGURE 19.16   Microsoft Dynamics CRM Diagnostics.

This tool is helpful if you ever face problems connecting the Outlook client. There are a variety of reasons you might not be able to connect the Outlook client to Dynamics CRM, depending whether you are trying to connect to CRM Online or Dynamics

CRM On-Premises. The challenges are greater when connecting to On-Premises as some requirements and configurations might not be in place there, whereas they are automatically configured in CRM Online deployments.

Some of the common issues are not having Internet-Facing Deployment (IFD) configured properly for On-Premises deployments.

▶ **SEE CHAPTER 28**, "Forms Authentication," for more information about IFD.

Another factor might be that the user doesn't have the necessary roles and rights to use the Outlook client.

▶ **SEE CHAPTER 17**, "Settings," to learn more about how to configure the roles and rights in Dynamics CRM.

Whatever the issue you are facing, CRM Diagnostics will help you. To use it, you start by enabling tracing; to do this, go to the Advanced Troubleshooting tab (see Figure 19.17), click Delete to delete temporary files that the Outlook client may have installed to start from a fresh configuration, and enable or disable the Outlook add-in. (You do not have to remove it by uninstalling the application from the Windows operating system.)

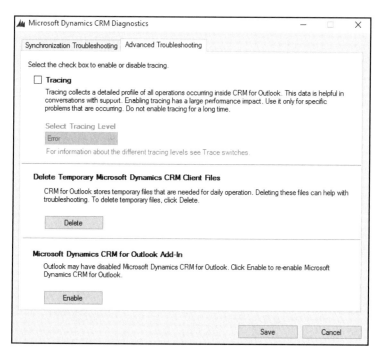

FIGURE 19.17   Advanced Troubleshooting tab.

Advanced Configuration

With the Microsoft Dynamics CRM for Outlook client installed, you can configure some additional options. To find these options in Microsoft Outlook 2016, navigate to File > CRM (as shown in Figure 19.18):

FIGURE 19.18   Microsoft Outlook 2016 CRM configuration options.

▶ **Set Personal Options**—You can set personal and local data options.

▶ **Synchronize**—You can perform a manual synchronization (instead of waiting the default 15 minutes) for data between CRM and Outlook. In addition, you can use this option to set the data filters, as shown in Figure 19.19.

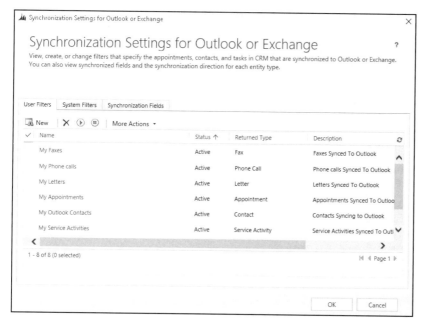

FIGURE 19.19   User data filters.

NOTE

The options for synchronization are available only for one computer that you have configured as the synchronizing computer.

▶ **Go Offline**—You can take the data offline and set the filters for doing so.

▶ **Import Contacts**—This option allows you to import data as contacts.

▶ **Manage Records**—You can perform duplicate detection or perform bulk updates.

▶ **Sign Out**—You can sign out of your CRM session.

CAUTION

Be sure to notice the option to select either Outlook Synchronization Filters or Offline Synchronization Filters. These options present different values in the user and system filters.

TIP

Although you can upgrade the Outlook client, it must match the base architecture. Therefore, if you want to upgrade the 32-bit client for CRM 2015 to the 64-bit client for CRM 2016, you must uninstall and reinstall the Outlook client because the one you have is not supported.

NOTE

Another option for tracking is folder-level tracking. You accomplish this by configuring Dynamics CRM on the client level by setting Configure Folder Tracking Rules and specifying a particular folder to be a tracking folder. As a result, all emails that end up in this folder (either based on rules or because they are manually dragged/dropped) will automatically be tracked to a specific Regarding record.

Using the CRM Outlook Client

The main operations you can do in the CRM Outlook client are the ones you find in the Outlook ribbon, in the CRM group:

▶ Track/Untrack

▶ Set Regarding

▶ Convert To

▶ Add Connection

▶ View in CRM

The following sections describe how to use these operations.

Tracking Emails

Tracking emails is likely to be the feature you will use most. When you receive an email you want to track in CRM, you can do it by clicking either the Track button or the Set Regarding button on the Outlook ribbon. Figure 19.20 shows what happens when you click the Track button.

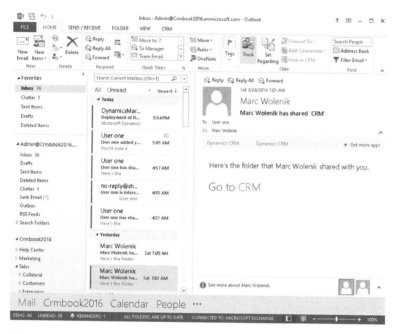

FIGURE 19.20   Tracking emails.

After you click Track to track an email, you can set a Regarding record, as shown in Figure 19.21, by clicking Set Regarding.

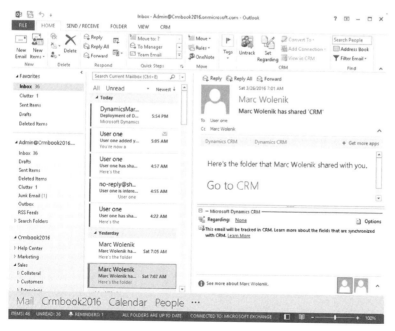

FIGURE 19.21   Email tracked, with a Regarding record set.

The changes made in Dynamics CRM 2016 to improve the performance experience when using the Outlook client may mean that it takes a little while to see the email created in CRM. After a few seconds, you should see the email in CRM, with a special icon in the email list of Outlook which notes that the email is tracked (see Figure 19.22). When the email is actually in CRM, you also see the Convert To, Add Connection, and View in CRM buttons enabled (also shown in Figure 19.22).

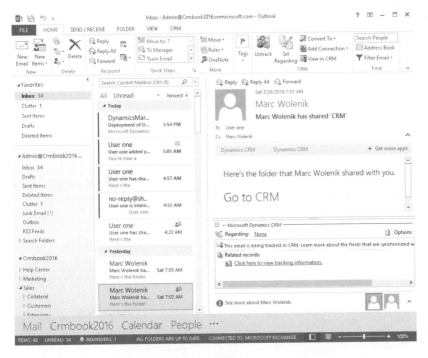

FIGURE 19.22   Email tracked and in CRM.

Once an email is tracked you can set a Regarding record to associate the email to a CRM record by either clicking the None link next to Regarding in the bottom panel of the email or by clicking the Set Regarding button in the ribbon, as described in the next section.

CAUTION

After you have tracked an email, the Track button changes to Untrack. Clicking the Untrack button completely removes the email record from Dynamics CRM and it will no longer be tracked.

Set Regarding

You can click the Set Regarding button in the ribbon to associate an email with a CRM record, such as a contact or an account. If you don't have an existing contact or account for the email sender, you can click the Convert To button instead. Notice that you do not have to track an email first before clicking Set Regarding. If you simply click Set Regarding, the email is automatically tracked as well, so you can use this button as a shortcut if you want to set a Regarding record for every email you track.

When you click this button, you are asked to select a CRM record, as shown in Figure 19.23. In the Look For field, you can specify any entity that is email enabled, such as Account, Contact, or Lead.

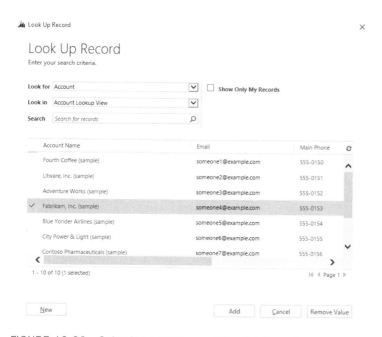

FIGURE 19.23   Selecting a CRM record for Set Regarding.

Figure 19.24 shows a tracked email in Outlook, with the Regarding record highlighted.

19

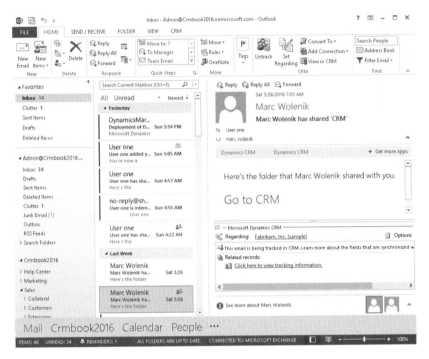

FIGURE 19.24   Email tracked with a Regarding record set to an Account entity.

Convert To

The Convert To button is enabled only for tracked emails. You can click this button to convert a tracked email to any of the following entities:

▶ Opportunity

▶ Lead

▶ Case

Converting to an Opportunity entity requires that you enter the customer record, which can be either an account or a contact in Dynamics CRM, and you can optionally enter a campaign, as shown in Figure 19.25.

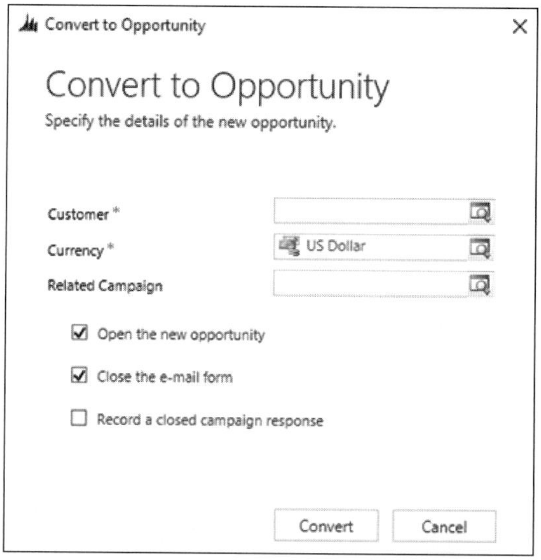

FIGURE 19.25   Converting to an Opportunity entity.

The Set Regarding field automatically changes to the new opportunity created from the conversion process.

If you choose to convert to a Lead entity, you need to enter first name, last name, company, and email address, as shown in Figure 19.26. Doing this creates a new lead record in Dynamics CRM and automatically changes the Regarding field to the new lead created from the conversion process.

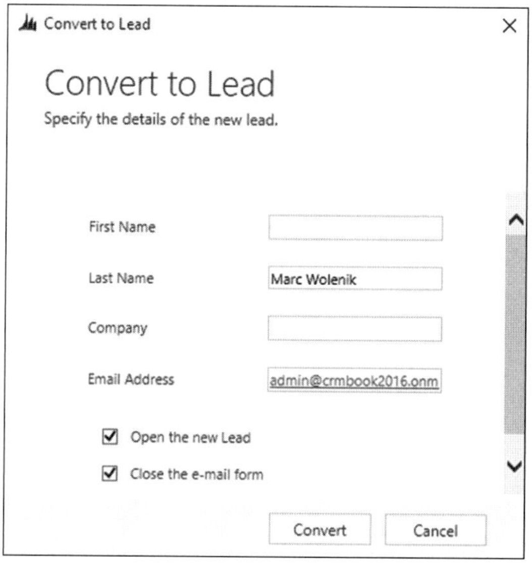

FIGURE 19.26   Converting to a Lead entity.

If you choose to convert to a Case entity, you need to enter the customer record, which can be either an account or a contact in Dynamics CRM, and you can optionally enter a subject for the case, as shown in Figure 19.27. Doing this creates a new Case record in Dynamics CRM and automatically changes the Regarding field to the new case created from the conversion process.

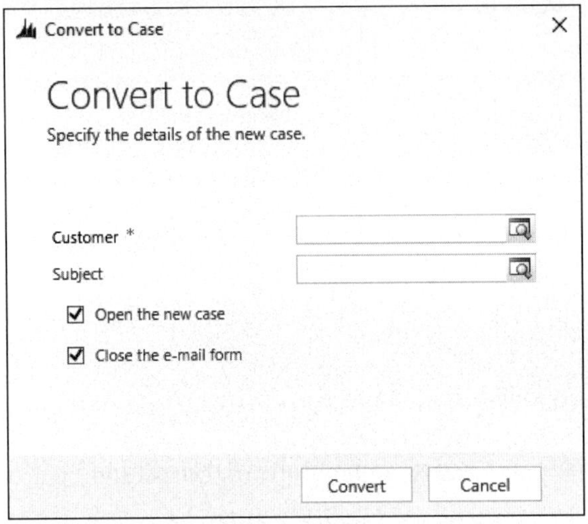

FIGURE 19.27   Converting to a Case entity.

Add Connection

Because you can set the Regarding field only to one record, if you want to relate an email to more than one record, adding connections is the way to go. When you click the Add Connection button, you see two options:

▶ Add to Another

▶ Add to Me

If you click Add to Another, a new dialog appears, where you can select the record you want to connect with the connection role, as shown in Figure 19.28.

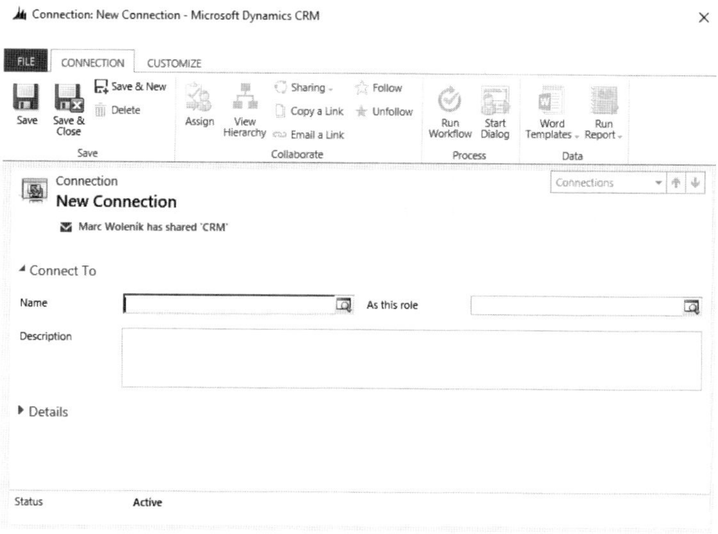

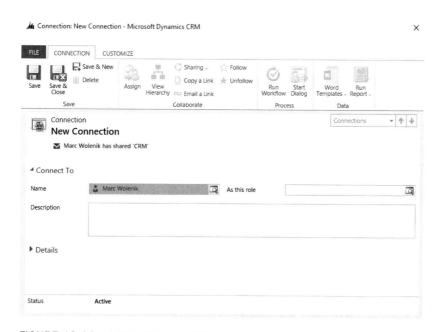

FIGURE 19.28   Add to Another connection.

If you click Add to Me, the same dialog appears as with Add to Another, only this time the name is prepopulated with your system user record, as shown in Figure 19.29.

FIGURE 19.29   Add to Me connection.

View in CRM

Clicking the View in CRM button opens the email record that exists in Dynamics CRM. This allows you to do other CRM operations, such as share and assign that you cannot do directly from the Outlook client (see Figure 19.30).

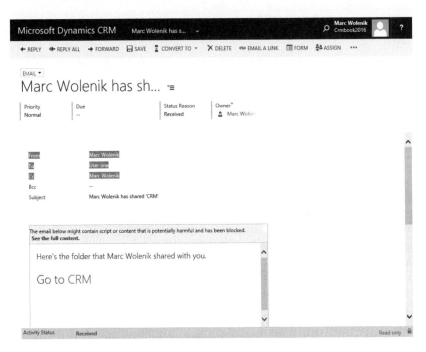

FIGURE 19.30 View in CRM.

Outlook CRM Views

The entity views are displayed differently in the Outlook client than the Dynamics CRM web client. You can navigate to the entities by using the left panel in Outlook, where you see a node with the name of your CRM organization that you can expand to see the entities that are configured in the sitemap for Outlook.

You can see all your account records without leaving the Outlook client by navigating to Sales > Customers > Accounts, as shown in Figure 19.31.

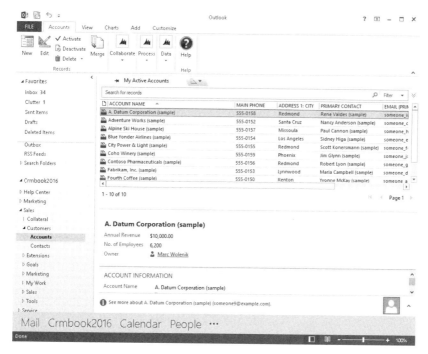

FIGURE 19.31   Viewing account records in the Outlook client.

Notice that the panel is divided into two areas—a list of records at the top and the selected record form at the bottom—so you can quickly see the selected record fields that are not displayed in the view. Notice that this is a read-only view of the selected record. To make edits or updates, you must open the record manually by double-clicking the selected record in the view.

Changing the view is different in the Outlook client than in Dynamics CRM. Instead of switching the view, you can open another view on a new tab when you select it by clicking the last tiny tab on the right. Figure 19.32 shows the views you can select for the Account entity.

19

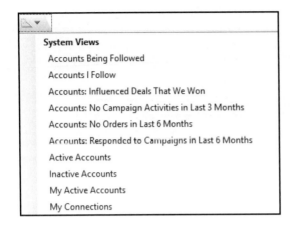

FIGURE 19.32   Selecting another view for the Account entity.

You can see multiple views for the same entity in different tabs, and you can pin them (by clicking the pin to the left of the tab name). Pinning a view tells Outlook to open that view by default the next time you go to this entity. For example, Figure 19.33 shows three pinned views.

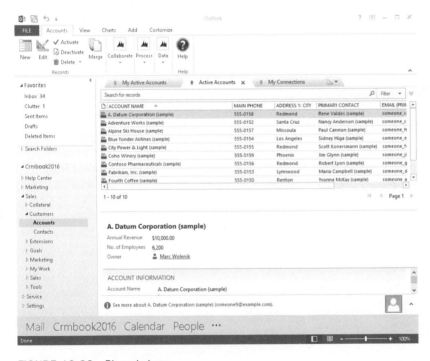

FIGURE 19.33   Pinned views.

Views in the Outlook client are more powerful than the ones in the web client. For example, you can set rules to use conditional formatting on rows, such as if you want to show the highlight the account records that are from Redmond. You could use a bigger font with bold letters and a different color to make sure these accounts stand out from the others. To do this, follow these steps:

1. Right-click the Address 1: City column header and select View Settings (see Figure 19.34).

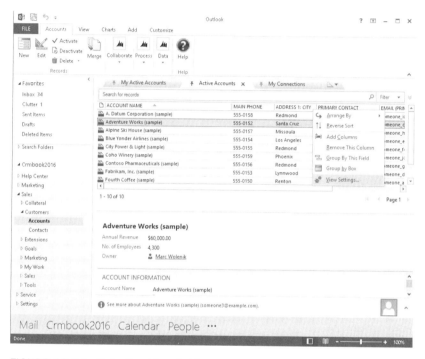

FIGURE 19.34   Selecting View Settings.

You now see the Advanced View Settings dialog for the view you selected (see Figure 19.35).

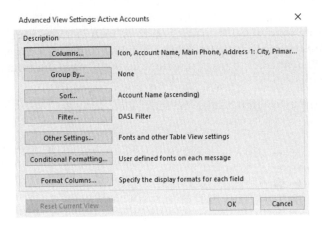

FIGURE 19.35   Advanced View Settings dialog.

2. Click the Conditional Formatting button, and the Conditional Formatting dialog appears, as shown in Figure 19.36.

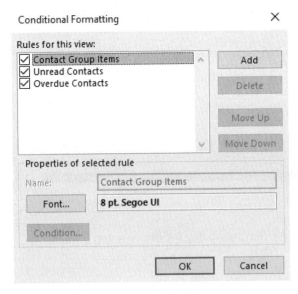

FIGURE 19.36   Conditional Formatting dialog.

3. Click the Add button to create a new rule and enter a name like Accounts in Redmond, as shown in Figure 19.37. Then click the Condition button.

FIGURE 19.37   Creating a new rule.

4. In the Filter dialog that appears, select the Advanced tab, as shown in Figure 19.38.

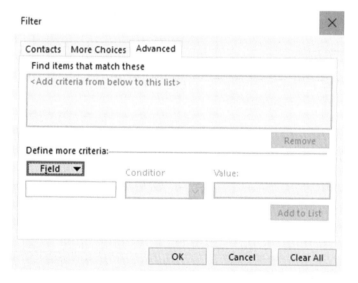

FIGURE 19.38   Filter dialog.

5. Click the Field drop-down and select User-Defined Fields in Folder > Address 1: City, as shown in Figure 19.39.

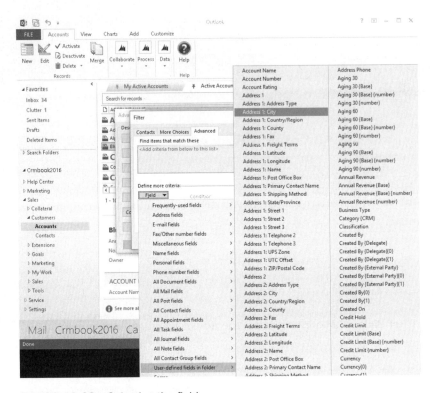

FIGURE 19.39   Selecting the field.

6. Change Conditior (that is, the condition) to Is (Exactly) and enter Redmond in the Value field, as shown in Figure 19.40.

FIGURE 19.40   Defining criteria.

7. Click the Add to List button and then click OK to close the Filter dialog.

8. Back to the Conditional Formatting dialog, click the Font button. The Font dialog appears, as shown Figure 19.41.

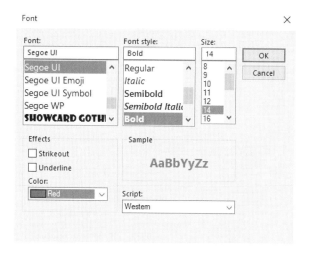

FIGURE 19.41   Font dialog.

9. Change the font color to Red, make it 14 points, and make it bold. Click OK to close the Font dialog. Your conditional formatting should now look as shown in Figure 19.42.

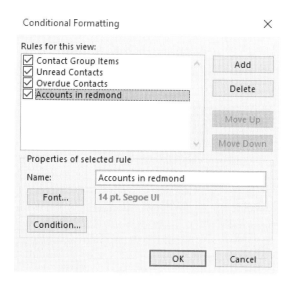

FIGURE 19.42   Conditional formatting completed.

10. Click OK to close the Conditional Formatting dialog then click OK to close the Advanced View Settings dialog.

The view should refresh and display apply the conditional formatting to the records that have Redmond in the Address 1: City field. They should appear in the font size and color you selected earlier, as shown in Figure 19.43.

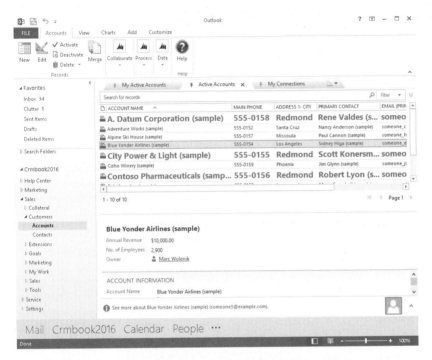

FIGURE 19.43   Account view with conditional formatting applied.

Previous Version Compatibility

As more and more enterprise organizations use Microsoft Dynamics CRM, Microsoft anticipates increasingly complex upgrade scenarios. The latest version of the Outlook client may or may not work with an earlier version of Dynamics CRM (depending on the UR version as well), so be sure to check the configuration options in this scenario. If the client is compatible, users must still configure the client to point to the new instance if the upgrade is to a new server, as discussed in the "Client Configuration" section, earlier in this chapter. However, system administrators can make an appropriate DNS entry that automatically redirects users to the new server.

> **TIP**
>
> Although the CRM 2015 Outlook client can be used with Microsoft Dynamics CRM 2016, offline access works only if the client and server versions match.

> **NOTE**
>
> For a complete guide to upgrading, as well as system compatibility options, download the installation guide from Microsoft at http://msdn.microsoft.com.

CRM App for Outlook

The CRM app for Outlook is an app that integrates Dynamics CRM with the Outlook Web Access (OWA) application. This is an excellent option for Mac users since the Outlook client doesn't work with Office for Mac.

If you go to Settings > CRM App for Outlook, you see the configuration page shown in Figure 19.44.

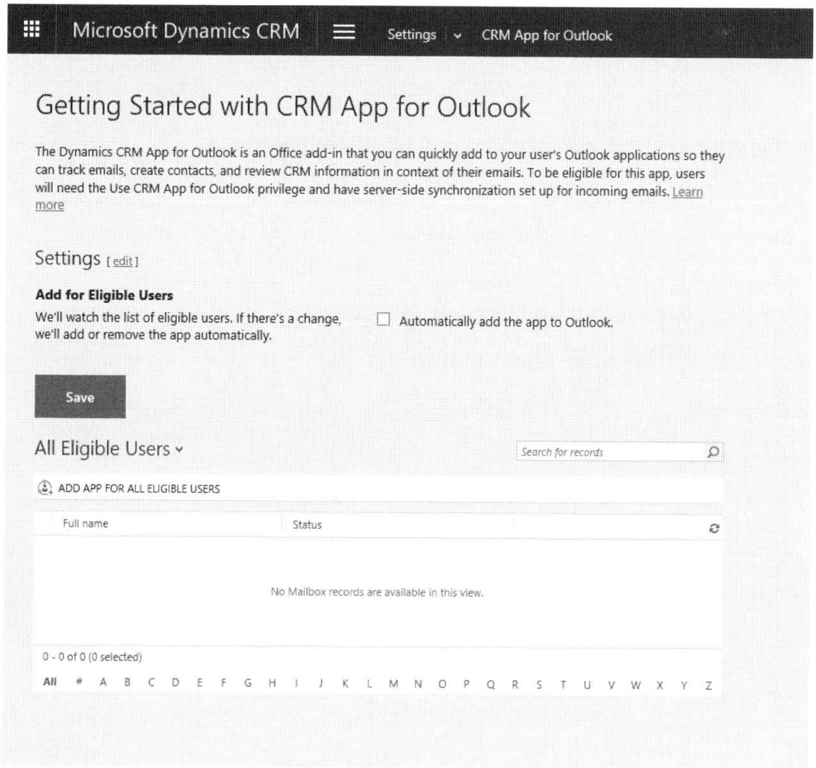

FIGURE 19.44   CRM app for Outlook settings.

You may not see any eligible user. To have eligible users, you must go to the mailbox configurations for the user and ensure that they are configured to use server-side synchronization (see Figure 19.45).

FIGURE 19.45   Mailbox configurations.

▶ To learn more about the server-side synchronization and email router,
SEE CHAPTER 20 "Email Configuration."

The administrator must also install the CRM app for Outlook in Exchange. To do this, follow these steps:

1. Go to the Office 365 portal and then to the Exchange online administration site.

2. Click Organization and then select the Add-ins tab.

3. Click the + button and then click Add from the Office Store (see Figure 19.46).

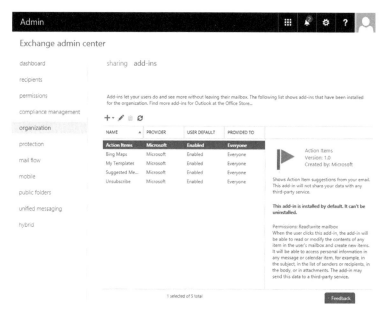

FIGURE 19.46   Add from the Office Store in the Exchange Admin Center.

4. Search for CRM in the Office Store and click the first application that says Microsoft Dynamics CRM (at this writing, this application is in Preview mode, as you can see in Figure 19.47).

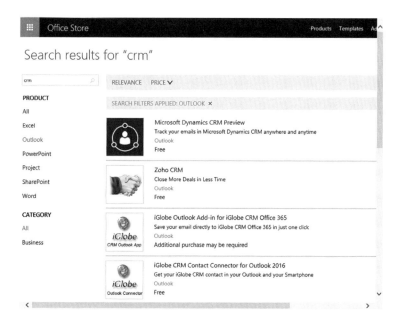

FIGURE 19.47   Finding the Microsoft Dynamics CRM app for Outlook.

5. In the Microsoft Dynamics CRM page that appears (see Figure 19.48), install the application, which will add it to all users in Exchange.

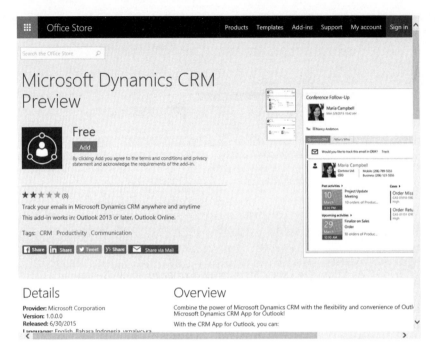

FIGURE 19.48   Adding the Microsoft Dynamics CRM app for Outlook.

6. Click on Yes in the Add-In Installation dialog (see Figure 19.49).

FIGURE 19.49   Add-In Installation dialog.

7. Once the app is installed, the user must go to OWA, click the gear icon, and select Manage Add-ins, as shown in Figure 19.50.

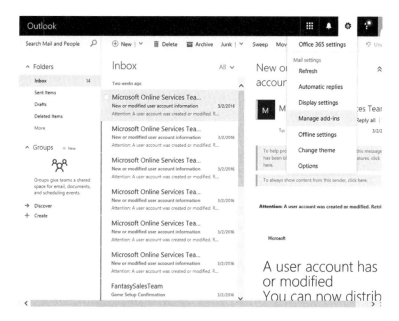

FIGURE 19.50   Selecting Manage Add-Ins.

8. Ensure that the Dynamics CRM check box is selected (see Figure 19.51).

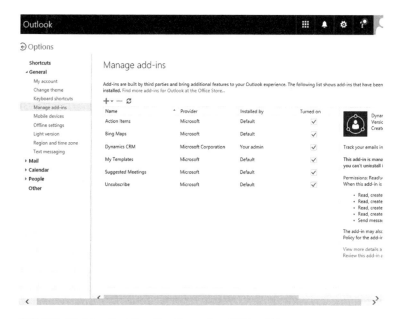

FIGURE 19.51   Enabling the Dynamics CRM add-in.

19

9. Go back to the CRM web application and into Settings and then to CRM App for Outlook. You can now see the eligible users pending setup (see Figure 19.52).

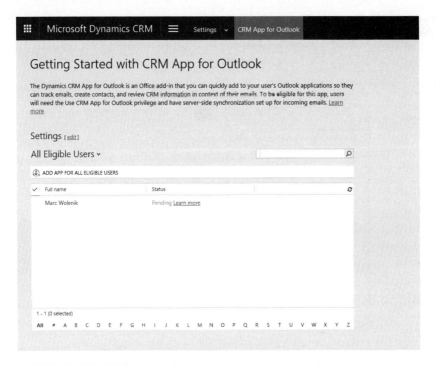

FIGURE 19.52   Eligible users pending setup.

10. Click the Add App for All Eligible Users button. This process might take a few minutes to complete. When it finishes, you should see the application added for the user, as shown in Figure 19.53.

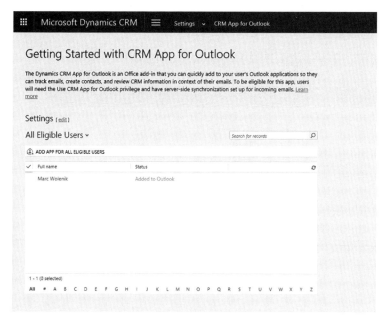

FIGURE 19.53   Added to Outlook confirmation.

11. Go to OWA, and you will see the Dynamics CRM link in each email message. When you clicks the message the first time, it takes some time to connect to Dynamics CRM. If the contact or account is not matched, you see a Create New Contact button, as shown in Figure 19.54.

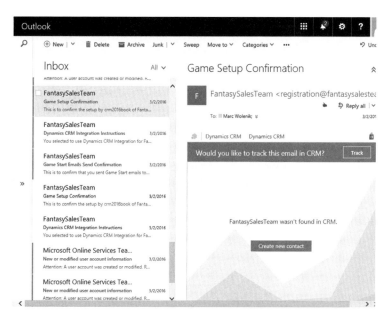

FIGURE 19.54   Dynamics CRM app for Outlook installed.

12. Click the Create New Contact button, and you see a form inside OWA that helps you quickly create an account in Dynamics CRM.

13. Click Save button on the right-hand side, as shown in Figure 19.55.

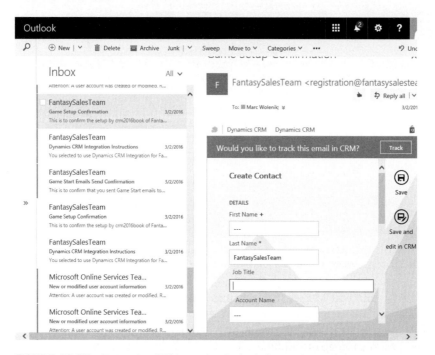

FIGURE 19.55   Dynamics CRM app for Outlook for a new contact.

14. Click the Track button (see Figure 19.56) to push this email to Dynamics CRM. Clicking Track helps you set the Regarding field.

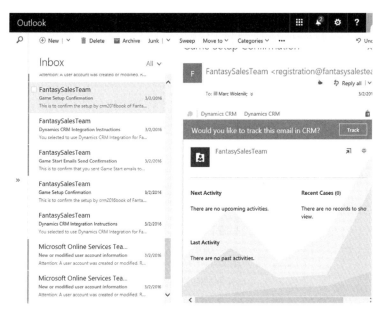

FIGURE 19.56   Tracking email with the Dynamics CRM app for Outlook.

15. Make a choice under Track This Email in CRM Regarding record (see Figure 19.57), and you see that the email is pending being tracked.

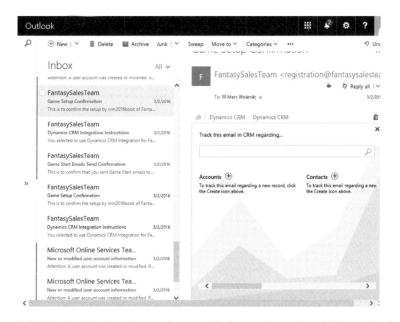

FIGURE 19.57   Pending tracked email with the Dynamics CRM app for Outlook.

16. After a few minutes, when the email is being tracked, either change or untrack the email if you like, as shown in Figure 19.58.

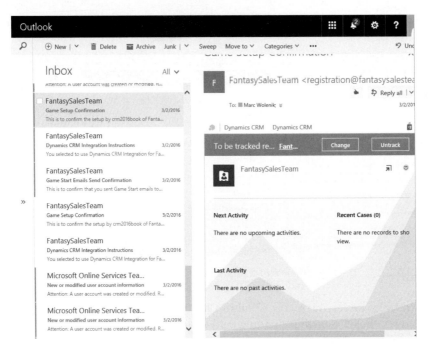

FIGURE 19.58   Tracked email with the Dynamics CRM app for Outlook.

Summary

The Outlook client provides a best-in-class experience for users by delivering CRM functionality from within Outlook. In addition, the Outlook client is easy to install, set up, and maintain.

Although the application can be accessed via either Outlook or a web browser (even after the client is installed), a supported browser is still required in both cases.

This chapter discusses how to install, use, and troubleshoot the Outlook client, as well as the CRM app for Outlook, which you can use in a browser, using Outlook Web Access.

CHAPTER 20

Email Configuration

The introduction of server-side synchronization with Microsoft Dynamics CRM 2013 meant that organizations could leverage the power of Dynamics CRM for email tracking without requiring Outlook or the email router to synchronize emails. Microsoft Dynamics CRM 2016 improves and enhances the server-side synchronization even further, and the system is now more stable and usable than ever before.

This chapter explains when and how to use server-side synchronization and the email router and the limitations of both scenarios.

> **NOTE**
>
> During server installation, email is not configured by default. Users can set up their preferred settings afterward.

Microsoft Dynamics CRM provides the following email processing options:

▶ Server-side synchronization integrates Microsoft Dynamics CRM with Exchange (or POP3/SMTP services).

▶ Microsoft Dynamics CRM for Microsoft Office Outlook and Microsoft Dynamics CRM for Outlook with Offline Access are both options for users.

▶ The email router manages both incoming and outgoing messages.

▶ The email router supports POP3 email systems for incoming messages and SMTP email systems for outgoing messages.

▶ Microsoft Dynamics CRM email messages are sent asynchronously via the email router.

In addition to this chapter explaining server-side synchronization, this chapter covers the email configuration options required for proper usage by explaining all the available components and their options.

Server-Side Synchronization

Earlier versions of Microsoft Dynamics CRM required Outlook to manage and track emails to and from Outlook and also required installation and configuration of the email router. Server-side synchronization eliminates both of these needs.

Microsoft Dynamics CRM integrates with Outlook using the Microsoft Dynamics CRM for Outlook client (the Outlook plug-in), but earlier versions of Microsoft Dynamics CRM usually required both an installed and configured email router (typically on a separate machine) and Outlook to be running (for it to send and receive emails). Use of server-side synchronization eliminates the need for the email router. In addition, server-side synchronization now provides a level of integration with Exchange directly to allow for this functionality. An example of this is as follows:

1. A user creates a new email and selects the Track in CRM option.

2. The user clicks Send on the email, and it is sent it to Exchange for routing (sending).

3. Exchange communicates with Microsoft Dynamics CRM, which creates a corresponding record in CRM, which in turn updates Exchange.

> **NOTE**
>
> The Outlook client is still necessary to promote (i.e. track in CRM) emails from Outlook to CRM.

Dynamics CRM 2016 now supports new scenarios for server-side synchronization:

▶ Microsoft Dynamics CRM On-Premises using either Exchange Online or Exchange Server 2010/2013 or 2016

▶ Gmail, MSN, Outlook.com, Windows Live Mail, or Yahoo! Mail using POP3/SMTP

> **NOTE**
>
> Only Exchange supports both email and appointment, contacts, and tasks synchronization. A POP3/SMTP email server provides email synchronization, but it does *not* synchronize appointments, contacts, and tasks.

The following scenarios are now supported for server-side synchronization:

▶ Microsoft Dynamics CRM Online with Exchange On-Premises 2010/2013 or 2016

▶ Microsoft Dynamics CRM On-Premises with Exchange Online

Any version of Exchange prior to 2010 is *not* supported for server-side synchronization.

In addition, the server-side synchronization requires a mailbox record for every user and queue in the organization that wants to leverage server-side synchronization, and this can create some administrative overhead.

TIP

If your organization has many mailboxes, it might make sense to use the Forward mailbox, which creates a single mailbox that forwards the email to the user's mailbox.

Configuring Server-Side Synchronization

To configure server-side synchronization, follow these steps:

1. Navigate to Settings > Email Configuration. Select Email Server Profiles to create a profile (see Figure 20.1).

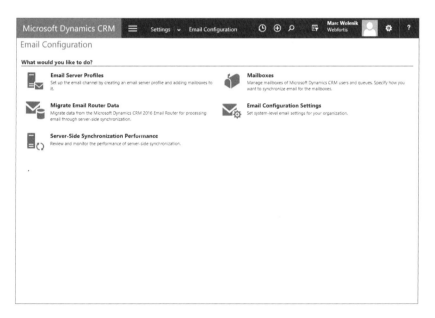

FIGURE 20.1   Email configuration settings.

2. Click +New to create a new profile and select Exchange (see Figure 20.2). (You might need to choose POP3-SMTP Profile, depending on your email server.) Data encryption must be active. If it's not, you see the warning shown in Figure 20.3.

20

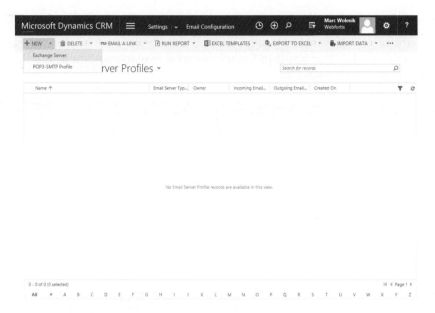

FIGURE 20.2   Selecting a new configuration.

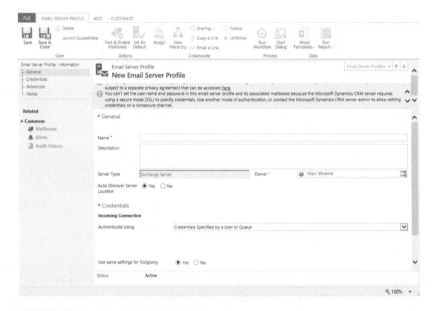

FIGURE 20.3   Data encryption requirement error.

3. To activate data encryption, navigate to Settings > Data Management and select the Data Encryption option (see Figure 20.4).

FIGURE 20.4   Disabled data encryption.

4. Click Activate to enable data encryption (see Figure 20.5). The new email server profile page opens (see Figure 20.6), allowing you to enter the information for the Exchange server.

20

FIGURE 20.5   Activated data encryption.

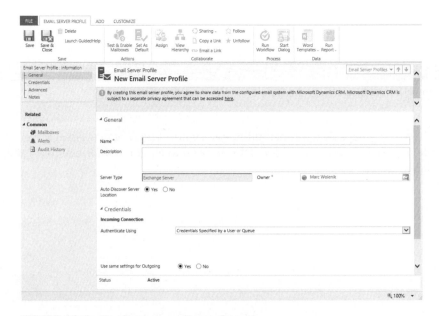

FIGURE 20.6   Email server profile configuration.

If you are accessing Dynamics CRM without Secure Sockets Layer (SSL), you get the error message shown in Figure 20.7, which prevents you from setting the username and password for the profile. To enable the username and password, you must adjust the `AllowCredentialsEntryViaNonSecureChannels` value in the configuration database. Alternatively, you can change the authentication to use Integrated Windows Authentication.

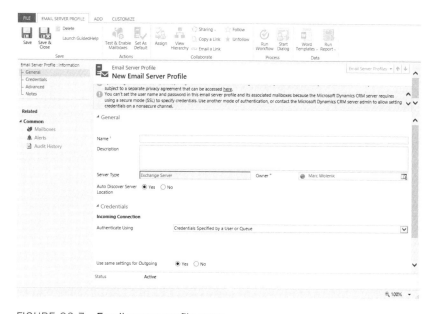

FIGURE 20.7   Email server profile error.

5. Enter a value in the Name field and click Save. The ribbon menu now gives you a Test & Enable Mailboxes option (see Figure 20.8), and it sets the profile as the default.

20

FIGURE 20.8   Enabled profile.

At this point, you can also specify the credentials used by Exchange server (for On-Premises deployments) by choosing one of the following from the Authenticate Using drop-down:

▶ **Credentials Specified by a User or Queue**—Use this option when you want to use credentials specified in the mailbox record of the user or queue.

▶ **Credentials Specified in Email Server Profile**—Use this option when you want to use a single credential for all the mailboxes. The credential must have impersonation rights on Exchange.

▶ **Integrated Windows Authentication**—This option leverages the same credentials that the CRM asynchronous service is configured with. (It is only applicable to Exchange and SMTP servers.)

▶ **Without Credentials (Anonymous)**—This is not a valid selection when working with Exchange.

In this case, select Credentials Specified by a User or Queue. Because you're only going to set up one profile, you need to set this profile as the default profile by clicking Set as Default from the ribbon menu.

6. To set up your mailboxes, close this window and navigate to Mailboxes > Active Mailboxes. By default, you see a mailbox for all created users in the CRM system (see Figure 20.9).

7. Select the mailbox you want to update and open it. By default, the Incoming Email, Outgoing Email, and Appointments, Contacts, and Tasks fields are set to Microsoft Dynamics CRM for Outlook (see Figure 20.10).

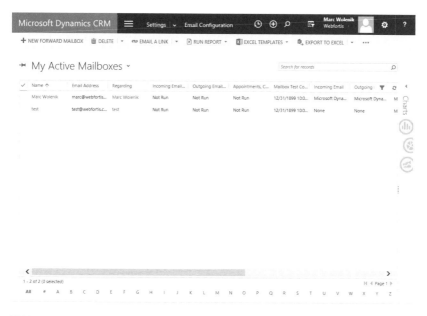

FIGURE 20.9   Active mailboxes.

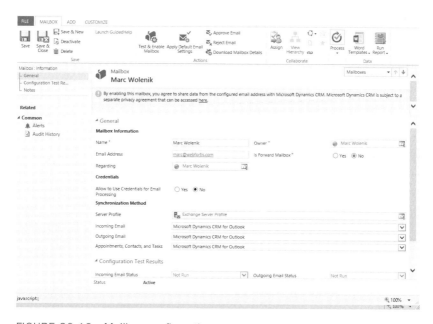

FIGURE 20.10   Mailbox configuration.

8. Change the settings for the Incoming Email, Outgoing Email, and Appointments, Contacts, and Tasks fields to Server-Side Synchronization or Email Router, as shown in Figure 20.11. Notice also that the Server Profile value is the newly created server profile that you created in step 4. Click Save. Because you selected Server-Side

Synchronization, you are prompted to specify credentials. (If you select CRM for Outlook or Integrated Windows Authentication, no credentials are necessary.)

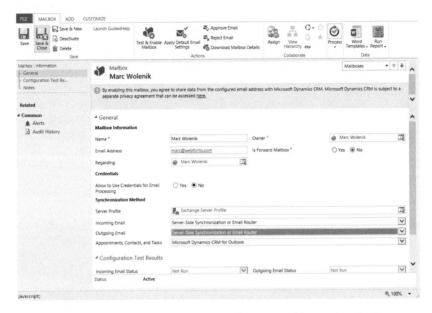

FIGURE 20.11   Mailbox configuration set for server-side synchronization.

9. Enter the credentials, as shown in Figure 20.12 and click Save. Notice that the alert still indicates that the mailbox is disabled for incoming email processing. This is because the mailbox has not been tested/enabled.

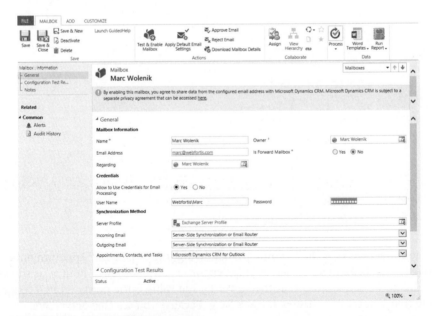

FIGURE 20.12   Entering credentials.

10. Click Test & Enable Mailbox in the ribbon menu. The dialog shown in Figure 20.13 appears.

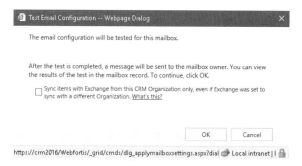

FIGURE 20.13   Testing and enabling the mailbox.

11. In the Test Email Configuration dialog, confirm the dialog by clicking OK. If the test is successful, you receive an email showing the test message (see Figure 20.14).

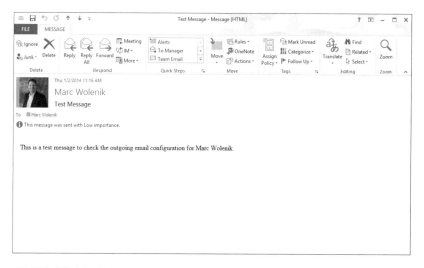

FIGURE 20.14   Test message.

TIP

You may also need to approve the email address by clicking the Approve Email button to verify the test (see Figure 20.12).

If you review the record in Dynamics CRM, you see that the results show Success for the test (see Figure 20.15). The server-side synchronization is now set up and configured to work. You can perform the same configurations on a Forward mailbox.

FIGURE 20.15   Successful test results.

If you have failures during the setup and configuration, you can navigate to the Alerts section (see Figure 20.16) and review and correct any specific problems shown.

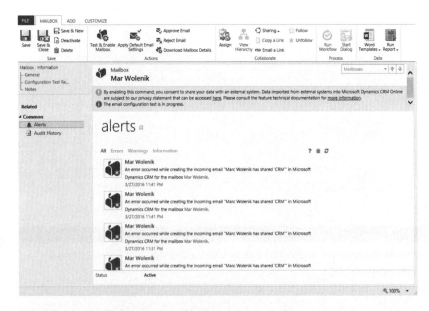

FIGURE 20.16   Alerts section showing errors.

Dynamics CRM 2016 has a new dashboard called the Server-Side Synchronization Performance Dashboard (see Figure 20.17), which you can find by going to Sales > Dashboards.

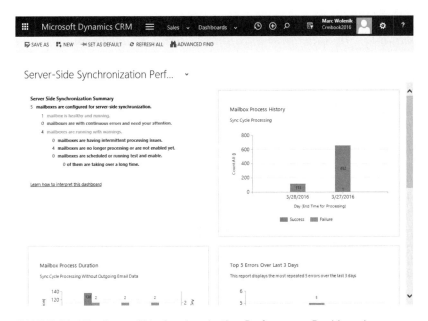

FIGURE 20.17   Server-Side Synchronization Performance Dashboard.

This dashboard shows useful information about the status of the server-side synchronization health.

> **NOTE**
>
> For more information about how to troubleshoot and understand this dashboard, go to https://technet.microsoft.com/library/dn850386.aspx.

Migrating Email Router Data

With the new server-side synchronization configuration, there is no need for an email router. If you upgraded Dynamics CRM from a previous version that was using the email router, you can use the migration tool described next to migrate the data and eliminate the email router.

20

To perform the migration, follow these steps:

1. From Settings > Email Configuration, select Migrate Email Router Data (see Figure 20.18).

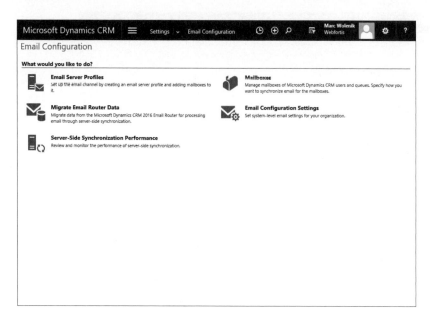

FIGURE 20.18   Email configuration.

2. The Email Router Data Migration tool opens and prompts you for three files that are required for the migration process (see Figure 20.19):

   ▶ EncryptionKey.xml

   ▶ Microsoft.Crm.Tools.EmailAgent.SystemState.xml

   ▶ Microsoft.Crm.Tools.EmailAgent.xml

      ▶ On the server with the email router installed, you can usually find these files in C:\Program Files\Microsoft CRM Email\Service (as shown in Figure 20.20).

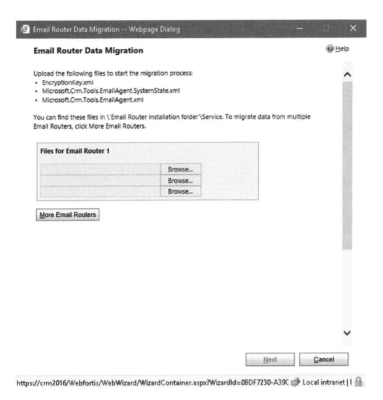

FIGURE 20.19   Email Router Data Migration tool.

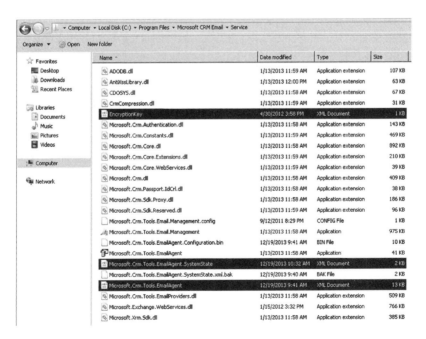

FIGURE 20.20   Required email router files.

> **TIP**
>
> The maximum size for all the files cannot exceed 32MB.

3. After uploading the files, click Next.

4. Confirm the details displayed on the Select Email Server Profile to Migrate pane and click Next and Start to complete the migration.

Microsoft Dynamics CRM for Outlook

You can use Microsoft Dynamics CRM for Outlook to perform the following tasks:

▶ Deliver received email messages to Microsoft Dynamics CRM

▶ Send email messages generated from Microsoft Dynamics CRM

As explained earlier in this chapter, server-side synchronization eliminates the need for the CRM Outlook client and the email router. The rest of this chapter is devoted to users who don't meet the minimum requirements for server-side synchronization or who want to deploy Microsoft Dynamics CRM without server-side synchronization.

> **CAUTION**
>
> Microsoft Dynamics CRM for Outlook does not require the email router to process Microsoft Dynamics CRM email messages. However, when it is not used, and when server-side synchronization is not set up, the only time CRM can process emails into the CRM system is when Outlook and the Dynamics CRM client are running. Therefore, situations can arise in which important emails might be sent and received by the organization but are not acted upon by CRM because the individual's Outlook is not running and has not processed the email yet.

▶ For more information about using and configuring the Outlook client, refer to **CHAPTER 19**, "Outlook Configuration."

Email Router

The CRM email router is a piece of software that receives messages from a service and forwards the messages to another service. For example, the messages are received from the CRM server, and they are forwarded to Microsoft Exchange or to the configured email server or vice versa.

The email router performs the following tasks:

▶ Routes incoming email messages to Microsoft Dynamics CRM

▶ Sends email messages generated from Microsoft Dynamics CRM

The CRM email router comes as a separate installation and must be installed after the CRM server installation. You can install the CRM email router on a separate server; it doesn't need to be the same machine where you have Microsoft Exchange Server installed or the same machine where you have the CRM server installed. You can even install it on a separate server or computer running Windows 7, Windows 8, Windows 8.1, Windows 10, or Windows Vista Business or Enterprise, because those are the versions that can be joined to a domain.

The computer on which you install the email router must have a connection to the Exchange server, to a POP3/SMTP email server, or to the Internet if you are connecting to Exchange Online. Also, the server is not required to be a member of the same domain as the CRM server.

> **NOTE**
>
> You might also be required to install the Microsoft Exchange Server MAPI client and Collaboration Data Object component before installing the CRM email router. The component can be downloaded from www.microsoft.com/en-us/download/details .aspx?id=1004. For more information on how to install this component, navigate to http://support.microsoft.com/kb/951401.

The email router contains the following components:

▶ Email router service and program files

▶ Email Router Configuration Manager

▶ Rule Deployment Wizard (This wizard lets you deploy rules that are used to route email messages to a Forward mailbox.)

> **CAUTION**
>
> The Rule Deployment Wizard does not work with POP3/SMTP email servers.

Configuring the Email Services

By default, users must use the Microsoft Outlook client to be able to send and track incoming emails in Microsoft Dynamics CRM via the Send button, as shown in Figure 20.21.

20

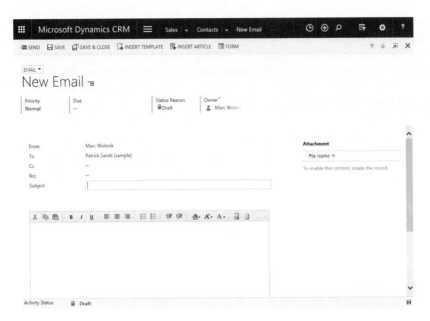

FIGURE 20.21   Sending direct email to a contact from Microsoft Dynamics CRM.

CAUTION

If you do not install the Outlook client and you send a direct email to a contact using the CRM web interface, the email will not be sent unless you configure server-side synchronization or without using a CRM router. In this case, the email is still created with a Pending Send status. If you configure the email router after this time or if you configure server-side synchronization, all the emails will be sent that have this status so be sure to run an Advanced Find to make sure you don't have any unwanted emails pending, as they will all go out upon successful completion of the email router configuration.

However, after you compose the email and click the Send button, the email might not go out as expected. When you view the Closed Activity for that contact, you can see that the email is there. However, when you open the email you just sent, you might see the yellow warning bar, alerting you that the message has not been delivered, with a message such as "This message has not yet been submitted for delivery. For more information, see help" (see Figure 20.22). Notice also in Figure 20.22 the Pending Send status.

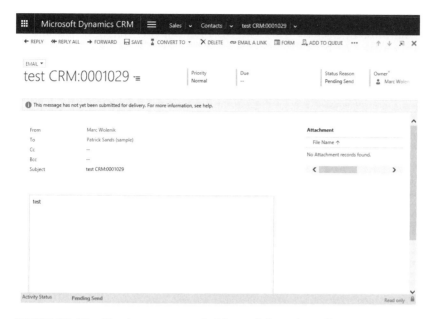

FIGURE 20.22   Warning message alert for undelivered email.

When the user setting for Outgoing is set to Microsoft Dynamics CRM for Outlook, the user must have the Microsoft Dynamics CRM for Outlook client installed and running. An alternative option is to use an email router or configure server-side synchronization, as explained earlier in this chapter; these options do not require Outlook to be running (see Figure 20.23).

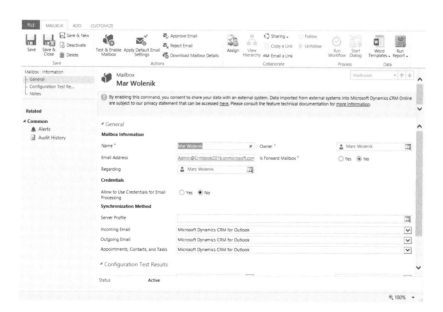

FIGURE 20.23   Outlook client email options.

You need to consider a few factors when using the Outlook client to send emails. First, the emails actually go out through Outlook. This happens when the user starts Outlook and Outlook synchronizes with the CRM server.

CAUTION

If the user prepares several emails through the web application, they will not be sent until the user opens Outlook. If the user does not open the Outlook application for a long time (for example, a month), this can be a real problem.

Using Outlook as the email gateway is the default configuration, and you must consider whether this configuration will work well with your business.

NOTE

If you want to have the emails composed through the web application sent out directly (not through Outlook), you can install and configure the CRM email router as described later in this chapter.

You also need to configure each user's preferences to use server-side synchronization or email router, as shown in Figure 20.24. This has to be configured for every user because you might want to have some users use the Outlook client only.

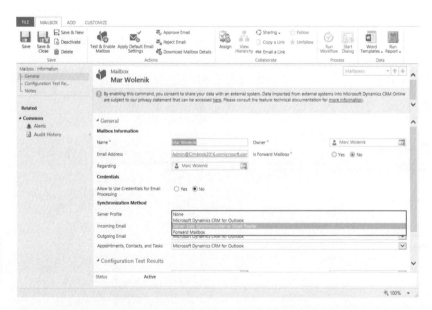

FIGURE 20.24   Configuring outgoing email access type to use server-side synchronization or the email router.

To properly configure the email router for outbound emails, go to Settings > Email Configuration > Mailboxes (see Figure 20.25), open the mailbox of the user for whom you want to configure the email router, and change the Synchronization Method drop-down for Incoming or Outgoing to the Server-Side Synchronization or Email Router option.

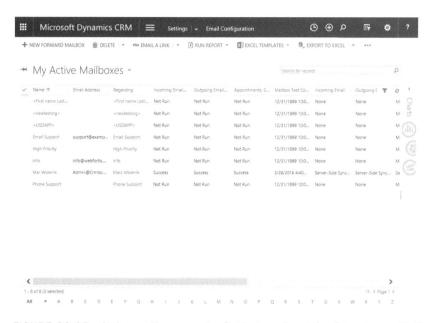

FIGURE 20.25   Active mailboxes under Settings -> Email Configuration -> Mailboxes.

TIP

Remember that you must first install and configure the CRM email router before the Synchronization Method selection Email Router will work correctly.

Installing the Email Router and the Rule Deployment Wizard

You install the email router and the Rule Deployment Wizard by running the Microsoft Dynamics CRM Email Router Setup. To install the email router and the Rule Deployment Wizard, follow the instructions in this section.

NOTE

Download the Microsoft Dynamics CRM 2016 email router (either 32- or 64-bit) from Microsoft.com by searching for "Dynamics CRM 2016 email router" or by going directly to www.microsoft.com/en-us/download/details.aspx?id=50373.

The following operating systems support installing the email router:

▶ Windows Vista

▶ Windows 7

▶ Windows 8

▶ Windows 8.1

▶ Windows 10

▶ Windows Server 2012 and 2012 R2

To install and configure the email router on a server, follow these steps:

1. Log on to the computer you have designated for use with the email router (which can be either a server or a regular computer) as a Domain User with Local Administrator permissions if you are planning to use the Email Router in On-Premises deployment.

2. Locate the installation files. If the setup doesn't start automatically after the files are extracted, navigate to the folder where you extracted the downloaded solution and double-click SetupEmailRouter.exe.

3. On the Welcome page, select whether you want to get updates. It is recommended to download the latest updates from the web (see Figure 20.26). To do this, select Get Updates for Microsoft Dynamics CRM (recommended) and click Next. Wait until the update process is complete and then click Next. If you are asked to install required components, click Install. The missing required components are automatically downloaded and installed. Once the required components are installed, click Next.

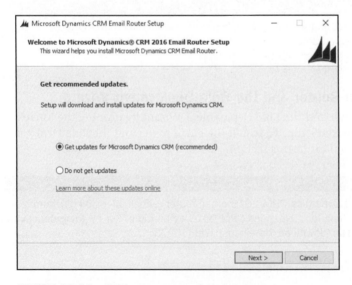

FIGURE 20.26   Getting recommended updates.

4. Accept the license agreement.

5. On the Select Router Components page (see Figure 20.27), select either or both of these options:

> ▶ **Microsoft Dynamics CRM Email Router Service**—This option installs the email router service and Email Router Configuration Manager.

> ▶ **Rule Deployment Wizard**—This option installs the Rule Deployment Wizard, which is used to deploy rules for Forward mailbox users. Optionally, you can install this wizard on another computer that has access to the Exchange servers in the organization.

>> ▶ Click Next.

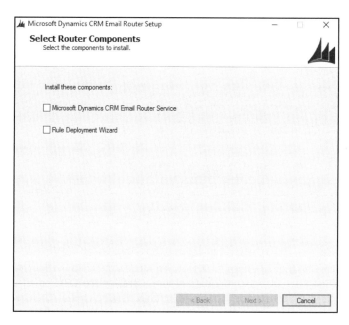

FIGURE 20.27   Selecting components.

6. On the Select Install Location page, either accept the default file installation directory or browse for a different location and then click Next. The System Checks page appears, showing a summary of all system requirements for a successful email router installation (see Figure 20.28).

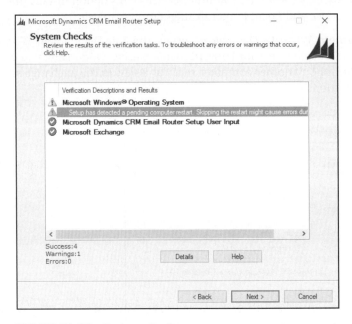

FIGURE 20.28   System checks.

7. When all tests are successful, click Next.

8. On the Ready to Install the Application page that appears, click Install.

9. When the Email Router Setup is finished installing files, click Finish.

NOTE

By default, Microsoft Dynamics CRM users are set up with both the incoming email server type and the outgoing email server type Microsoft Dynamics CRM for Outlook. For web application users, you must change the incoming type to Email Router or Forward Mailbox and the outgoing type to Server-Side Synchronization or Email Router for each user.

Installing the Email Router on Multiple Computers

Should you wish, you can deploy and run the Microsoft Dynamics CRM email router on multiple computers in a Microsoft cluster to provide high availability and failover functionality. With Windows Server, this is known as *failover clustering*. Either of these server clustering technologies are supported with the email router.

CAUTION

The email router supports only an active/passive cluster deployment; it does not support an active/active cluster deployment.

You install the email router to the active primary node in the cluster as follows:

1. Run Email Router Setup on the active primary node in the cluster.

TIP

You do not have to install the email router on a computer that is running Microsoft Exchange Server. It is recommended to install the email router as the only application on a cluster.

2. Open the Email Router Configuration Manager on the first node and configure the email router. Verify that the email router is routing messages correctly to and from the Microsoft Dynamics CRM and email systems.

3. Copy all email router application files to the common storage or shared hard disk. By default, the files are located at Drive:\Program Files\Microsoft CRM Email.

4. Ensure that the following files are located on the common storage or shared disk so that they can be moved to the secondary node in the event of a failover. You can find these files in the Drive:\Program Files\Microsoft CRM Email\Service folder:

> ▶ Microsoft.Crm.Tools.EmailAgent.Configuration.bin

> ▶ Microsoft.Crm.Tools.EmailAgent.SystemState.xml

> ▶ Microsoft.Crm.Tools.EmailAgent.xml

> ▶ Microsoft.Crm.Tools.Email.Management.config

> ▶ EncryptionKey.xml (if encryption is enabled)

20

5. Update the following Windows Registry setting to allow the email router to use the shared disks:

`HKEY_LOCAL_MACHINE\SYSTEM\CurrentControlSet\Services\MSCRMEmail`

Change the `ImagePath` value to point to the shared disk drive that houses the email router files.

6. Restart the Microsoft CRM email router service for these changes to take effect.

CAUTION

The email router files should be manually secured on the common storage or shared disk. You should grant full control only to the service account running the email router service (Microsoft CRM Email Router) and to administrators who might have to update configuration files manually.

Install the email router to the passive node in the cluster, as follows:

1. Run Email Router Setup on the second node in the cluster.

2. Update the following Windows Registry setting to allow the email router to use the shared disks:

`HKEY_LOCAL_MACHINE\SYSTEM\CurrentControlSet\Services\MSCRMEmail`

Change the `ImagePath` value to point to the shared disk drive that houses the email router files.

3. Restart the Microsoft CRM Email Router Service for these changes to take effect.

TIP

Do not run the Email Router Configuration Manager and do not copy the files to the shared hard disks. Because the configuration files are placed on the shared disks, they are automatically available on the passive server.

Follow these steps to create the generic resource service to manage the Microsoft CRM email router service on the cluster:

1. On each node in the cluster, set the Microsoft CRM email router service to manually start on Windows start.

2. Ensure that each of the nodes is a member of PrivUserGroup {GUID} in Active Directory.

3. In the Failover Cluster Management pane, create a generic resource service with the following parameters:

▶ **Name**—Create a descriptive name for the generic resource service, such as MSCRM Email Router.

▶ **Resource Type**—Set this to the generic service.

▶ **Group**—Set this to the cluster group.

▶ **Possible Owners**—Add all nodes in the cluster.

▶ **Dependencies**—If you are using Exchange Server and you have installed the email router on the Exchange server (which is not recommended), add Microsoft Exchange Information Store. Otherwise, just enter the network name registration in DNS.

▶ **Service Name**—Set this to Microsoft CRM Email Router.

▶ **Start Parameters**—Leave this blank.

▶ **Use Network Name for Computer Name**—Leave this unchecked.

▶ Do not checkpoint any Registry keys.

4. Bring the resource online. If necessary, configure the resource properties, such as the failover policies.

TIP

To verify and monitor the cluster, open Cluster Management and force a failover. Ensure that you see the services stop on node 1 and fail over to node 2.

Email Router Configuration Manager and Configuration Profiles

The Email Router Configuration Manager tool enables you to configure the email router. This tool is usually installed on the server running the email router. All configurations are saved in the file Microsoft.Crm.Tools.EmailAgent.xml.

You must configure at least one incoming email profile and one outgoing email profile to enable the email router to route email to and from your Microsoft Dynamics CRM organization. Depending on the complexity of your organization's email system, you might have to create multiple incoming and outgoing configuration profiles. For example, if your organization requires incoming email router services for multiple email servers, you have to create one incoming configuration profile for each email server.

Authentication Types

Authentication for the email router is required for the connections to the email system and the user's mailbox for each incoming and outgoing email profile.

Exchange Server supports only Windows authentication for the incoming profiles. Exchange Online supports clear-text authentication. For POP3-compliant servers, incoming profiles can use NTLM or clear-text authentication.

20

Clear-text authentication transmits unencrypted usernames and passwords. If you use clear-text authentication, you should do so only with Secure Sockets Layer (SSL). The Use SSL option should be selected, and the Network Port field (on the Advanced tab) must be set to a value appropriate for your environment. Verify your POP3 server requirements with your email administrator.

Outgoing (SMTP) profiles support Windows authentication, clear-text, and anonymous authentication types. The Exchange Online type supports only clear-text authentication.

> **TIP**
>
> Anonymous SMTP is valid only for internal, non-Internet-facing SMTP servers. Many SMTP servers do not support anonymous authentication. To ensure uninterrupted email flow from the email router, verify your SMTP server requirements with your email administrator.

Access Credentials

Depending on how you set the other configuration profile options, the options described in this section are available for specifying the username and password that the email router will use to access each mailbox the profile serves.

> **CAUTION**
>
> If you use access credentials that are valid for the email server but not for a particular mailbox, a 401 Access Denied error is generated when you test access.

Incoming profiles support the following access credentials:

- ▶ **Local System Account**—This option requires a machine trust between the computer where the email router is running and the computer where the Exchange server is running. The email router must be included in the PrivUserGroup security group. For incoming profiles, this option is available only for Exchange Server (not for other POP3-compliant email servers).

- ▶ **User Specified**—This option requires that each user enter his or her username and password in the Set Personal Options dialog box (available via File > Options in the Microsoft Dynamics CRM web client). This enables the email router to monitor mailboxes by using each user's access credentials. When users change their domain password (for example, when it expires), they must update their password in Microsoft Dynamics CRM so that the email router can continue to monitor their mailbox. This option is available only in the On-Premises version of Microsoft Dynamics CRM.

- ▶ **Other Specified**—This option enables the administrator to configure the email router to connect to user mailboxes as a specified user. The specified user must have full access to all the mailboxes that the incoming profile will serve, and it impersonates and "send as" permissions on the mailboxes configured for the profile.

Outgoing profiles support the following access credentials:

▶ **User Specified**—This option requires a machine trust between the computer where the email router is running and the computer where Exchange server is running. The email router must be included in PrivUserGroup. For outgoing profiles, this is the only option available if you select the anonymous authentication type.

▶ **Other Specified**—This option enables you to configure the email router to send email messages on each user's behalf by using the access credentials of a specified user account that has full access to all the mailboxes that the outgoing profile will serve.

NOTE

For more information on the email router, see the Microsoft Dynamics CRM Implementation Guide, which you can download from www.microsoft.com/en-us/download/details.aspx?id=50039.

Configuring Email Routing for Multiple Configurations and Deployments

You can add or edit an email router configuration that contains a single incoming and outgoing method that routes email to the email server. In this configuration, you must specify the following components:

▶ A name for display and reference

▶ Whether the configuration is incoming or outgoing

▶ The email transport type, such as Exchange or Exchange Online or POP3 for incoming and SMTP for outgoing

In addition, you can add or edit email router deployments. An email router deployment contains a URL to a Microsoft Dynamics CRM server computer, one incoming configuration, and one outgoing configuration. In an email router deployment object, you specify the following components:

▶ A name for display and reference (required)

▶ A URL to the Microsoft Dynamics CRM server computer (required)

▶ A default incoming configuration (optional)

▶ A default outgoing configuration (optional)

If you are using your local SMTP server, configure the Relay Restrictions property and have the reverse DNS records set for the server IP address. Also, to avoid being blacklisted for spam, be sure the domain is configured properly.

20

Configuring the CRM Email Router

The email router, like the Outlook client, requires both installation and configuration. The following sections describe how to properly configure the email router after it is installed.

Creating the Incoming Profile

To create a profile for the incoming email, open the Email Router configuration manager and click the New button on the right side of the screen. Figure 20.29 shows a new profile using Microsoft Exchange Server 2007.

You also have the option to use the POP3 protocol for incoming emails if you don't use Microsoft Exchange Server.

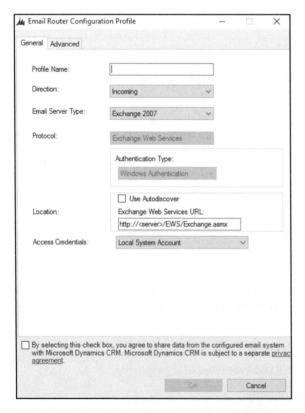

FIGURE 20.29   Configuring the incoming profile for Exchange.

NOTE

If you want to use the POP3 protocol with Microsoft Exchange, be aware that this service is disabled by default on Microsoft Exchange. To enable it, go to Control Panel > Administrative Tools > Services and double-click the service named Microsoft Exchange POP3 to open the settings. Change the startup type to Automatic, click the Apply button, and then click Start.

CAUTION

Because Exchange does not allow you to use POP3 for the domain administrator account, you need to create a separate account for using the POP3 accounts for the domain admin user only.

The Server field in the Location area must be a valid URL with http:// or https:// for the Microsoft Exchange option or a valid address without the protocol for the POP3 option.

The authentication type supported for Exchange can only be Windows authentication. The authentication types supported for POP3 are NTLM and clear-text authentication. If you are going to use the latter, it is recommended that you use SSL to secure the user's credentials over the network. For the credentials, you can have the user specify a credential (discussed in the next section, "Deployments"), or you can enter a fixed username and password when creating the incoming profile.

To test the POP3 or Exchange information, you need to create an incoming profile. You can use the Microsoft Outlook application and create an account manually to be sure that you have the right connection and credential information.

Deployments

Next the profiles need to be configured for deployment to the appropriate protocol and email server type.

To configure the profiles for the email transport options, follow these steps:

1. Open the Email Router Configuration Manager.

2. Click New on the Configuration Profiles tab.

3. Create a profile for Incoming with the following values (see Figure 20.30):

    ▶ **Profile Name**—Select Incoming.

    ▶ **Email Server Type**—Select Exchange 2010 or 2013.

    ▶ **Location**—Check Use Autodiscover.

    ▶ **Access Credentials**—Select Local System Account.

FIGURE 20.30   Incoming profile.

4. Check the check box at the bottom of the dialog to agree to share data and click OK.

5. Click New on the Configuration Profiles tab and create a profile for Outgoing with the following values (see Figure 20.31):

  ▶ **Profile Name**—Select Outgoing.

  ▶ **Email Server Type**—Select SMTP.

  ▶ **Authentication Type**—Select Windows Authentication.

  ▶ **Location**—Enter your email server here (for example mail.webfortis.com).

  ▶ **Access Credentials**—Select Local System Account.

6. Check the check box at the bottom of the dialog to agree to share data and click OK.

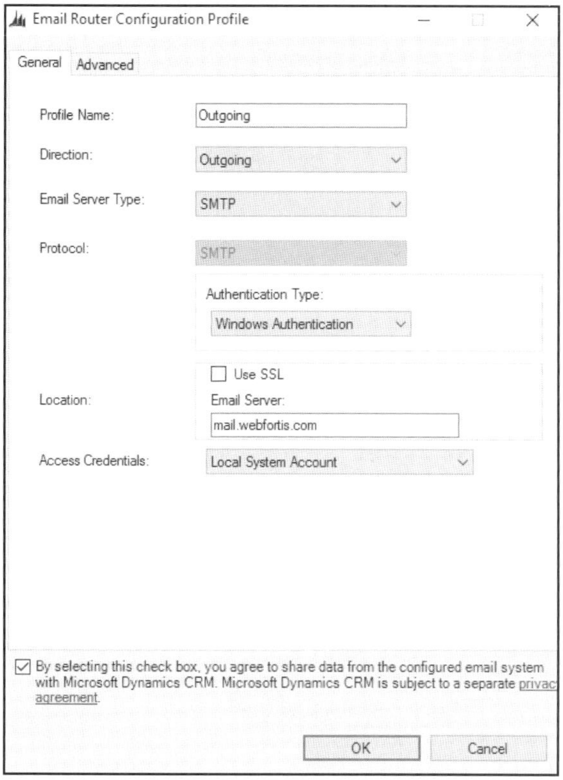

FIGURE 20.31   Outgoing profile.

After configuring the profiles, you need to create and set up the deployment where you want to use and apply the profiles. You will be able to set the profiles for each user after configuring the deployment in the next section, "Users, Queues, and Forward Mailboxes."

You can configure the following types of deployments:

▶ **My Company**—You use this option with On-Premises deployments (see Figure 20.32).

▶ **An Online Service Provider**—You use this option when Internet-Facing Deployment (IFD) is enabled.

▶ **Microsoft Dynamics CRM Online**—You use this option with Dynamics CRM Online deployments.

20

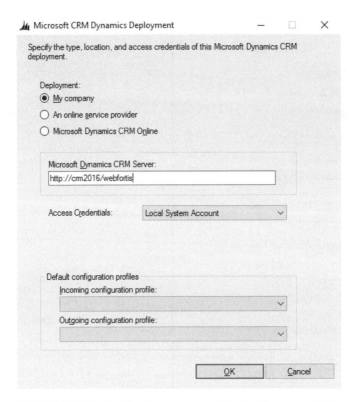

FIGURE 20.32   Configuring deployment for On-Premises CRM organizations.

▶ For more information about IFD, **SEE CHAPTER 28**, "Forms Authentication."

Enter the appropriate values for the Microsoft Dynamics CRM server: http://
servername/organization for the My Company option or https://dev.crm.dynamics.com/
OrganizationName or https://disco.crm.dynamics.com/*OrganizationName* for Dynamics
CRM Online option. Enter the access credentials and select Default Configuration Profiles.
In this case, select your newly created Incoming and Outgoing profiles. The profiles
selected here will be the default options for the users and queues, but you can change
these values for each user, as described in the following section, if desired.

User, Queues, and Forward Mailboxes

If you select the Users, Queues, and Forward Mailboxes tab, you see the screen shown in Figure 20.33.

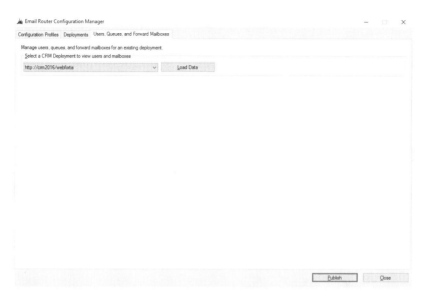

FIGURE 20.33   Users, Queues, and Forward Mailboxes tab.

Click Load Data, and the tab changes as shown in Figure 20.34.

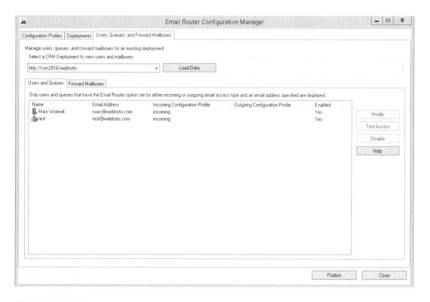

FIGURE 20.34   Users and queues.

> **NOTE**
>
> Only the users and queues configured to use server-side synchronization or the email router are shown here. These mailboxes must have the email address approved as well in order to appear in this list.

On the Users, Queues, and Forward Mailboxes tab, you can configure specific incoming and outgoing profiles for each user if you want. Only the users and queues that have the mailbox configured for server-side synchronization or the email router will be displayed here. To configure a specific user or queue, select the user or queue and click Modify. The dialog shown in Figure 20.35 appears.

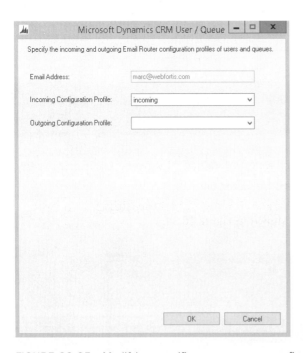

FIGURE 20.35   Modifying specific user or queue configuration profiles.

You can change the incoming or outgoing profile for the selected user if you don't want it to use the default configured profiles.

You can also test and verify that each profile functions correctly by click the Test Access button. This option performs a test that displays the results, with any errors in red or a successful message in green (see Figure 20.36).

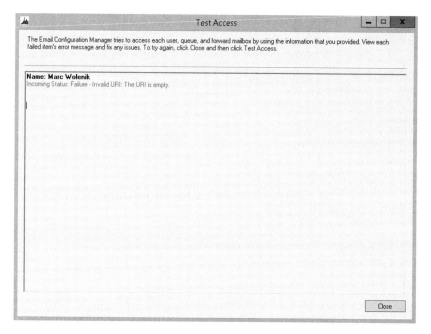

FIGURE 20.36   Testing access.

> **TIP**
>
> You can test the access for more than one mailbox at the time. To do so, make sure you select the mailboxes first by holding the Ctrl key while clicking the Test Access button to check multiple mailboxes.

You can also disable the mailboxes for the user or queue from this tab. By clicking the Disable button, you disable the mailbox and change the button name to Enable so you can re-enable the mailbox if it is disabled.

When you are done with the changes, you must click the Publish button to save the changes and apply them to the email router service. You don't need to restart the service because the updates are automatically updated when you click Publish (see Figure 20.37).

FIGURE 20.37   Publishing configurations.

Forward Mailboxes

You can use Forward mailboxes to process incoming emails. This type of mailbox requires a dedicated mailbox to receive and forward emails. There are a couple reasons you might want to use Forward mailboxes. Primarily, you can use a single set of credentials for a single mailbox; however, you benefit from polling (only one mailbox is polled) and get to take advantage of Exchange forwarding rules.

Forward mailboxes can process incoming emails without using Microsoft Outlook. This option works only with Microsoft Exchange Server (both Online and On-Premises), and it requires a dedicated mailbox to process the incoming emails. The users or queues that want to use this option must have some rules deployed that you can create using the Rule Deployment Wizard, described later in this chapter. The email is first received by the user's mailbox and then is forwarded to the router's mailbox.

> **NOTE**
>
> Many users can forward their emails to a single router mailbox.

The CRM email router service polls the router mailbox, looking for incoming messages. When it finds an email, it inserts that email into CRM as a new email activity for the user or queue that forwarded the email. The email is then deleted from the router mailbox, depending on the configurations.

Microsoft recommends this technique if you are using Microsoft Exchange Server as your primary email server. However, you don't actually need to set up a Forward mailbox to receive emails. The incoming profile configured to use Exchange suffices in most cases.

The outgoing emails are processed asynchronously, and the default polling is scheduled for every 60 seconds (about 1 minute), so you must wait that amount of time before the emails are actually sent. (This polling is set to 1,000 seconds [about 15 minutes] for email router processing.)

> **TIP**
>
> To increase the speed at which outgoing emails are sent, you can edit the configuration file Microsoft.Crm.Tools.EmailAgent.xml (which you can find at C:\Program Files\Microsoft CRM Email\Service)—specifically the `SchedulingPeriod` element. It is a good idea to change its default value to 10 seconds.

On the Forward Mailboxes tab (see Figure 20.38), you can also test access as you did for the user and queues, and you can disable or re-enable the Forward mailboxes.

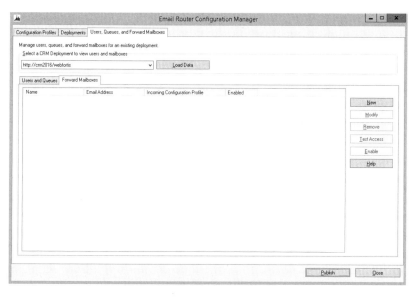

FIGURE 20.38   Forward Mailboxes tab.

You must create a Forward mailbox using this tab in order to see it. The Forward mailboxes configured in Dynamics CRM won't show up here automatically. To create a new Forward mailbox, click New, and the dialog shown in Figure 20.39 appears. Here you must enter a name, the email address, and the incoming configuration profile.

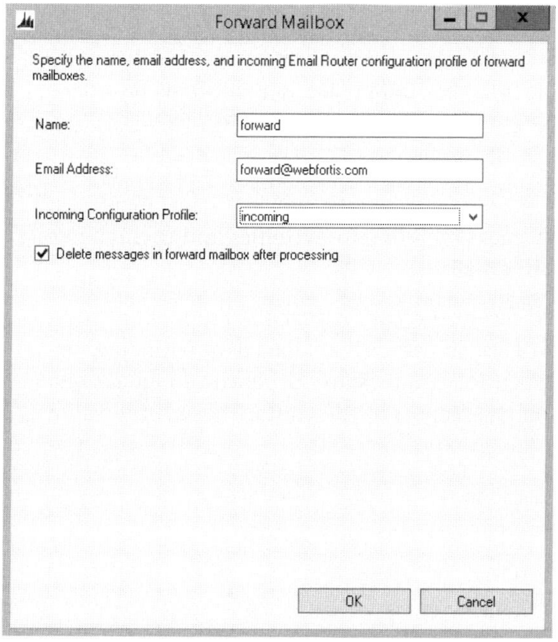

FIGURE 20.39   Forward Mailbox dialog.

Tracking Incoming Emails

You can track incoming emails in two ways:

▶ **By using the CRM tracking token**—The token works by appending a code in the subject of the email with a form similar to CRM:0001006.

▶ **Through message filtering and correlation**—Filtering and correlation to track incoming emails involves a method that doesn't require appending data on the email's subject line. Instead, it uses an intelligent way to figure out the thread of the email using the email's sender, the email's recipient, the email subject, and any CC. This method is not 100% effective, but you can use it if you don't want CRM tracking tokens to alter emails.

▶ To learn more about how to configure incoming email tracking, **SEE CHAPTER 17**, "Settings."

TIP

By default, only incoming emails that are received in response to emails sent from Dynamics CRM are tracked. If you want CRM to track all incoming emails, you must change your personal settings.

You can select to track all emails, the emails that are responses to CRM emails, email messages from CRM records that are email enabled, or the email messages from CRM leads, contacts, and accounts.

NOTE

The option that says Allow other Microsoft Dynamics CRM Users to Send Email on Your Behalf is available only if your user is configured to receive or send emails through the CRM email router.

You can see all the incoming emails CRM tracks by going to Activities and then changing the view selection from My Activities to All Emails.

One of the most common issues related to received emails is that the From email address sometimes cannot be mapped properly. This is shown with an alert icon with an X in it, as shown in Figure 20.40. This can happen for two reasons: Either the email address doesn't exist (that is, no value for email on the record) or the contact has set the value as Do Not Allow for email.

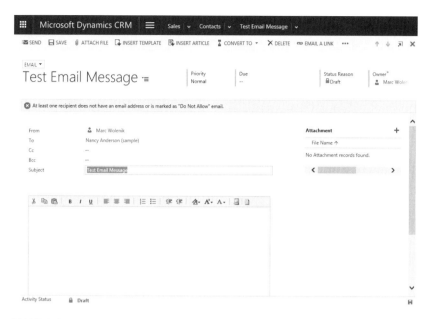

FIGURE 20.40   Email with an error message.

Queues

Queues are primarily used for general incoming emails that are not related to a specific user. A common example for using a queue is to receive emails sent to your organization for queries related to general information, support, or customer support. In these cases, you could create queues with related email addresses similar to info@*yourdomain*.com, support@*yourdomain*.com, and customerservice@*yourdomain*.com, for example.

To track emails using these addresses, you must first create a queue by going to Settings > Business Management > Queues. Then you need to click New to create a new queue and then set the email options accordingly (see Figure 20.41).

20

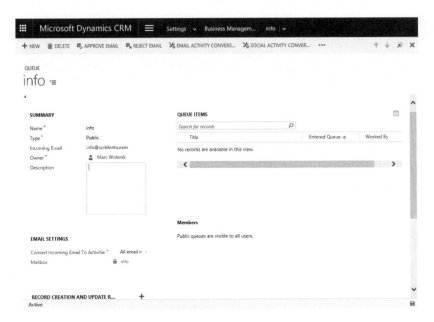

FIGURE 20.41   Creating a new Info queue.

> **TIP**
>
> The good thing about using queues to receive and track emails is that a queue doesn't consume a license in CRM, so if you have a generic mailbox for info or support, you don't need to create a user for it and consume a CRM license for it.

Rule Deployment Wizard

Users or queues configured as Forward mailboxes need server rules installed on Microsoft Exchange to forward emails to the router mailbox. These rules send a copy of each message received by a Microsoft Dynamics CRM user to the Microsoft Dynamics CRM system mailbox. From the Microsoft Dynamics CRM system mailbox, the email router retrieves the messages and creates an email activity in Microsoft Dynamics CRM.

To deploy the Microsoft Dynamics CRM user inbox rules, you can use the Rule Deployment Wizard. You can run it any time to add or change the inbox rules for your Microsoft Dynamics CRM users.

> **CAUTION**
>
> The Rule Deployment Wizard can only deploy rules to Exchange Server mailboxes. You cannot deploy rules by using the Rule Deployment Wizard with POP3 email servers or Exchange Online. To use the wizard, you also need owner access on the users' mailboxes.

You can access this wizard by following these steps:

1. On the computer where you have installed the email router, run the Rule Deployment Wizard. The first time you run the Rule Deployment Wizard, you will see a welcome page, as shown in Figure 20.42.

FIGURE 20.42   Welcome to the Rule Deployment Wizard.

NOTE

The Rule Deployment Wizard does not have to be run on a computer with an instance of Exchange Server. To run the Rule Deployment Wizard, the following must be true:

- ▶ You must be logged on as a Microsoft Dynamics CRM user with a security role. (The user can be in restricted access mode.)
- ▶ You must be a local administrator on the computer where the wizard is running.
- ▶ You must have Exchange administrative permissions.

To deploy rules to the mailbox of a Microsoft Dynamics CRM user, the person running the Rule Deployment Wizard must have Exchange administrative permissions for the mailbox. Use the Exchange System Manager and the Exchange Delegation Wizard to designate Exchange administrators or make sure that the person running the Rule Deployment Wizard has full permissions on the Exchange mailbox store or storage group where the users' mailboxes are located.

---

2. Click Next on the welcome page.

20

3. Enter the CRM deployment type and CRM server address as well as the credentials to be used (see Figure 20.43). Click Next.

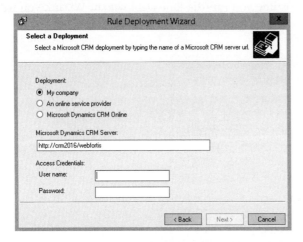

FIGURE 20.43   Selecting the deployment for the Rule Deployment Wizard.

4. Enter the forward email address and the email server type, which can be Exchange 2007 or Earlier or Exchange 2010 or 2013 (see Figure 20.44). Click Next.
The wizard tries to locate the mailboxes you have configured as Forward mailbox in the Dynamics CRM deployment you selected before (see Figure 20.45).

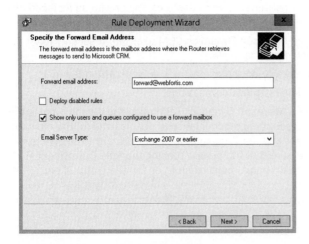

FIGURE 20.44   Specifying the forward email address.

FIGURE 20.45   Selecting users and queues.

5. Select the user or queue for which you want to deploy the rules and click Next.

Creating a Rule Manually

For POP3 email servers that support email system rules where an email message can be forwarded as an attachment, you can create a rule manually, as follows:

1. Open Outlook.

2. If you are working with Outlook 2007, choose Tools > Rules and Alerts. If you are working with Outlook 2010, 2013, or 2016, click Rules on the ribbon.

3. On the Email Rules tab, click New Rule; or click Create Rule if you are in Outlook 2016.

4. Select the Start from a Blank Rule option, make sure Check Messages When They Arrive is selected, and then click Next. Or select Advanced options if you are in Outlook 2016.

5. Select Where My Name Is in the To or Cc Box (see Figure 20.46) and then click Next.

20

FIGURE 20.46   Outlook Rules Wizard.

6. Select Forward It to People or Public Group as an Attachment and then edit the rule description by clicking People or Public Group (see Figure 20.47).

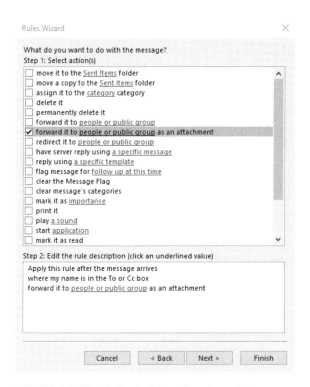

FIGURE 20.47   Outlook Rules Wizard conditions.

7. Select the name of your email router Forward mailbox, click the To button, and click OK.

8. Click Next two times.

9. Make sure the Turn on This Rule option is selected and then click Finish.

10. Make sure the rule is at the top of the list and then click Apply.

> **NOTE**
>
> For Exchange Online, you can create the rule manually (as described here) or by using Outlook Web Access.

20

Summary

This chapter describes how Microsoft CRM processes incoming and outgoing emails and covers the available options for sending and receiving emails that will be tracked as activities in Dynamics CRM. It also describes the different system configuration options to track the incoming emails: server-side synchronization, the email router service, the Microsoft Outlook client, and Forward mailboxes.

Office Integration

Microsoft Dynamics CRM 2016 has improved and enhanced integration with Microsoft Office, especially with Microsoft Word, Excel, OneNote, and OneDrive for Business. In addition, these integrations extend from the desktop to the web client and also to the mobile client, making the usability and experience more interesting than ever before.

Microsoft Word Integration

One of the great new features added to Dynamics CRM 2016 is the new Microsoft Word integration that is available for most of the entities. Before this feature existed, the only way to create something similar was by using a custom report, usually created in Visual Studio, which required development knowledge. Now any user can easily create a Word document by using the Word templates only, without needing to know any development techniques.

▶ For more information about creating custom reports, refer to **CHAPTER 16**, "Reporting and Dashboards."

Creating a Word Document Template

In the command bar of almost every entity in the system when you open a record, you can find the Word Templates option under the ... menu. Figure 21.1 shows this option for a contact record. (If you don't see this option, be sure to select a contact record first before clicking the ... button.)

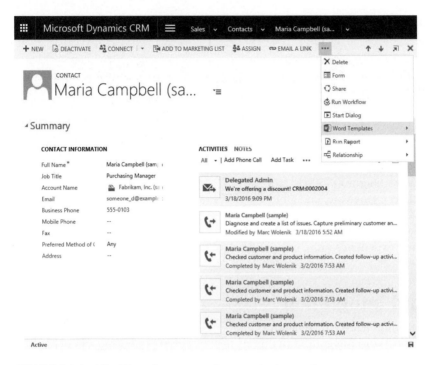

FIGURE 21.1   Word Templates menu for a contact record.

Because there are no out-of-the-box Word templates for contacts, the first option you see is Create Word Template. Clicking this option starts a wizard to help you create a Word template (see Figure 21.2).

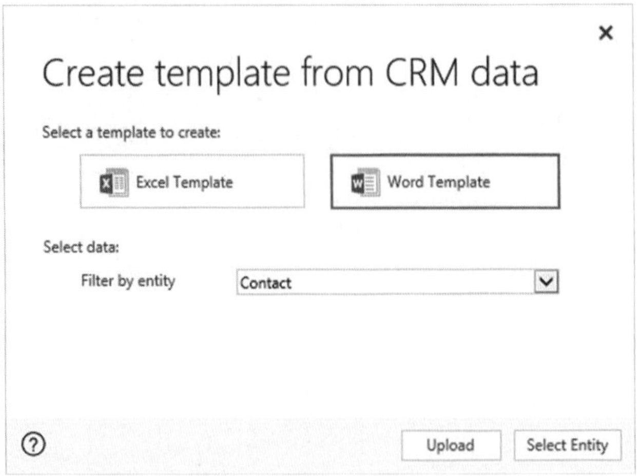

FIGURE 21.2   Create Template from CRM Data dialog.

Using this wizard, you can create either Word or Excel templates. This section focuses on Microsoft Word templates; the following section focuses on Excel templates.

Because you fired this wizard from a contact record, you see the Word Template button selected and the Filter by Entity drop-down set to Contact by default. All you need to do is click the Select Entity button to open the Select Entity dialog, shown in Figure 21.3.

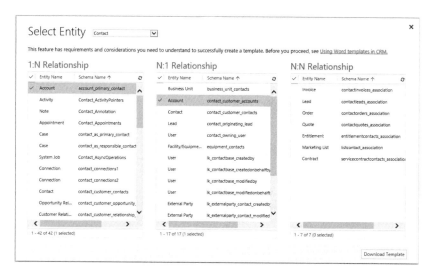

FIGURE 21.3   Select Entity dialog.

In the Select Entity dialog, you must explicitly select the relationships you want to have included in the template. All fields are included by default, with the exception of the lookup fields in the N:1 relationships section. Select the N:1 relationships and click the Download Template button.

When you are asked to download the Word document file to your local computer, as shown in Figure 21.4, click Open. You now see an empty Word document in which you can start writing your correspondence.

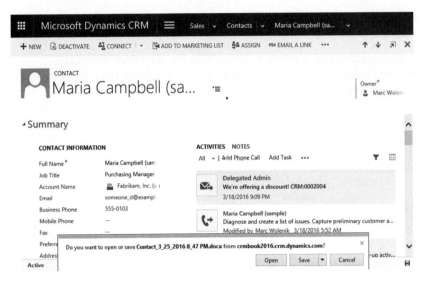

FIGURE 21.4   Word document download dialog.

To make sure you have the Developer tab visible in Microsoft Word, click File > Options, as shown in Figure 21.5.

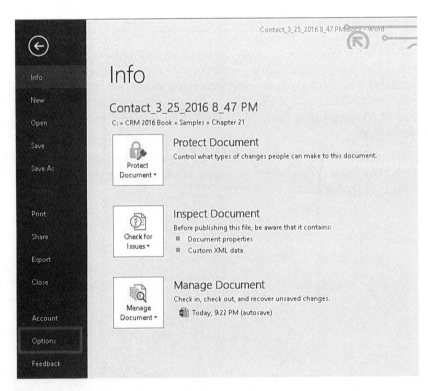

FIGURE 21.5   Options menu.

In the Word Options dialog that appears, click Customize Ribbon on the left and then make sure the check box for Developer is checked on the right (see Figure 21.6). Click OK to close the Word Options dialog.

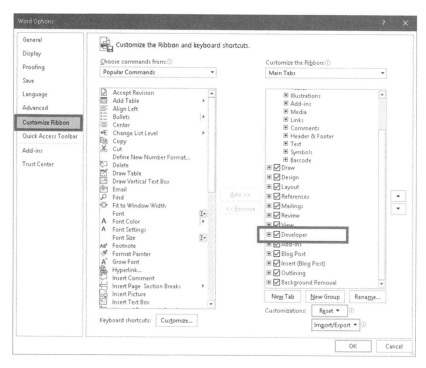

FIGURE 21.6   Enabling the Developer tab.

Click the Developer tab that now appears on the ribbon and click XML Mapping Pane. The XML Mapping pane opens to the right, and in it you need to select urn:Microsoft-crm from the Custom XML Part drop-down (see Figure 21.7).

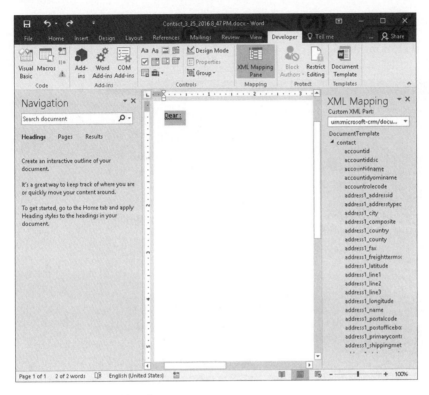

FIGURE 21.7   XML Mapping pane.

You now see the entity you selected for the template—in this case Contact—with the all the fields and relationships you selected before.

You choose fields here that you want to insert into the document where you want the CRM data to be replaced. To do this, right-click the field you want to insert and select Insert Content Control > Plain Text (see Figure 21.8).

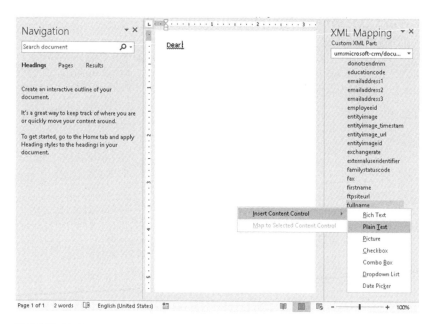

FIGURE 21.8   Inserting a CRM field.

When you click the text field control, you see the field inserted in the Word document with a square around (see Figure 21.9).

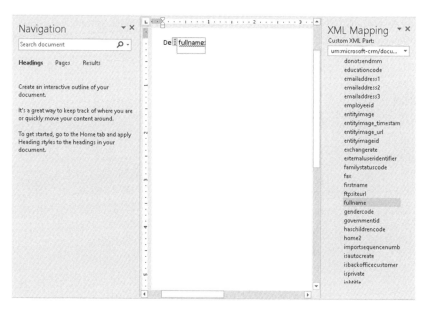

FIGURE 21.9   CRM field inserted.

Uploading the Word Document Template

When you finish editing the document and adding the fields, you can save the document and upload it back to Dynamics CRM by going to ... > Word Templates > Create Word Template as you did before, except that this time you will click the Upload Button instead of the Select Entity button in the Create Template from CRM Data dialog (see Figure 21.10).

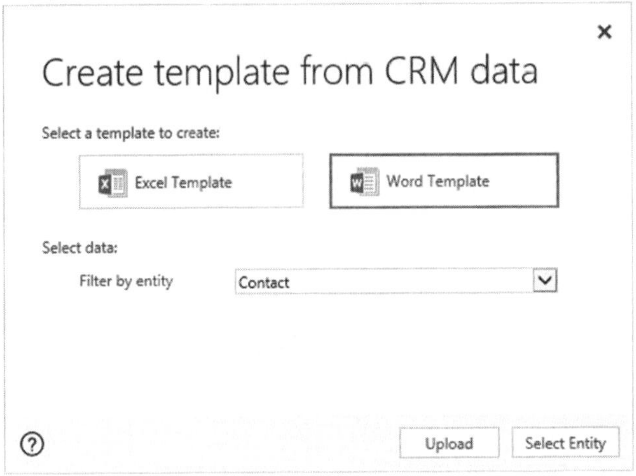

FIGURE 21.10   Uploading the Word template.

Drag and drop the file you edited before from Windows Explorer to the Upload Template dialog or use the Browse link to select the file (see Figure 21.11).

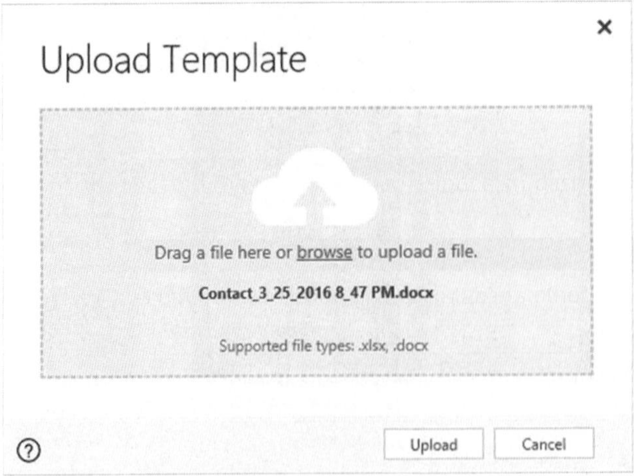

FIGURE 21.11   Upload Template dialog.

After you click the Upload button, you see information for the document you just uploaded. You can change the name of the document to something more descriptive name, and you can select the language. All the other fields are read-only, so you cannot change their values (see Figure 21.12).

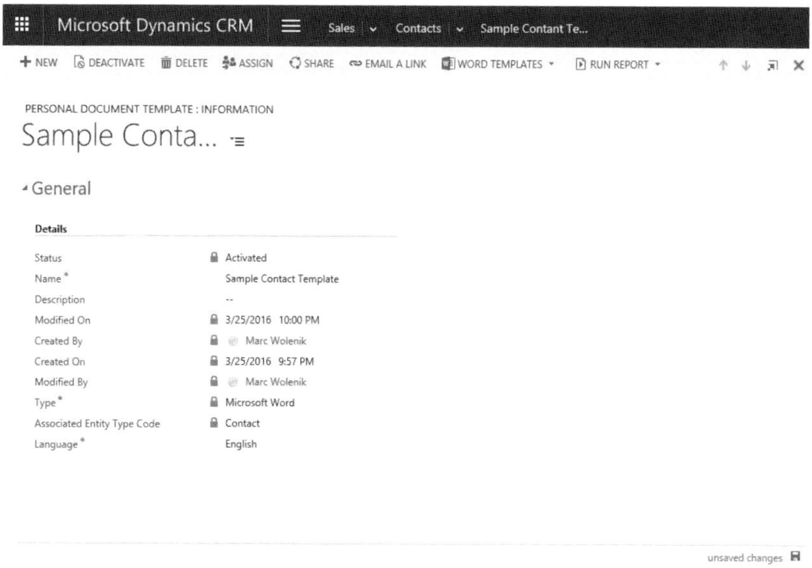

FIGURE 21.12   Document template information.

NOTE

You can only select the languages that match the installed languages of your system. If you are using CRM On-Premises, you must install the language pack on the server first and then enable the language. If you are using CRM Online, you just need to enable the language by going to Settings > Administration and clicking the Languages option. For more detailed information about installing languages, refer to the Chapter 17, "Settings."

Using the Word Document Template

Now you are ready to use the Word document template you created and uploaded earlier. To use the document template, you need to go to the Contacts view (which doesn't work the same as going to the Contact form) and select the record from the list. (You can select only one record for Word templates.) Then you select ... > Word Templates. Here you see the template you uploaded in the Personal Word Templates group, as shown in Figure 21.13.

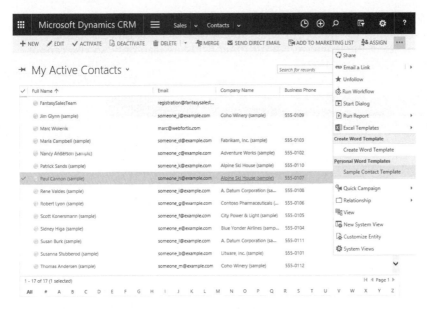

FIGURE 21.13 Selecting a Word document template.

The Exporting to Word dialog tells you your template is being generated. This process might take some time, depending on the field and relationships you have on the document (see Figure 21.14). When it is done, you are asked to download the new Word document.

FIGURE 21.14 Generating a Word document template.

When you open the new Word document. you see it populated with the CRM data of the record you selected, as shown in Figure 21.15.

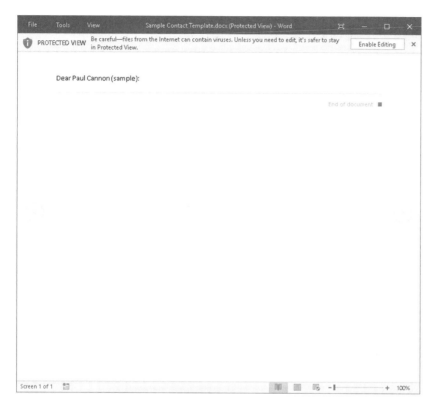

FIGURE 21.15   Word document template output.

Advanced Word Templates

Creating a very basic Word template with a single field is easy. Adding other fields is very similar, but what if you want to show a list of related entities for the 1:N relationships? Suppose you want to create a template for the Account entity, and you want to display a table of the related contacts.

To do this, you need to go to the Account entity, select a record, and then click Word Templates to create a Word template as described earlier in this chapter. When selecting entities, make sure you also select Contact from the 1:N Relationship section, as shown in Figure 21.16.

FIGURE 21.16   Selecting Contact from the 1:N Relationship section.

Now you need to insert a table to show the contacts. To do that, go to the Insert tab and add a table with two rows as many columns as you have fields you want to display. In this example, you can add three columns to display the first name, the last name and the email address (see Figure 21.17).

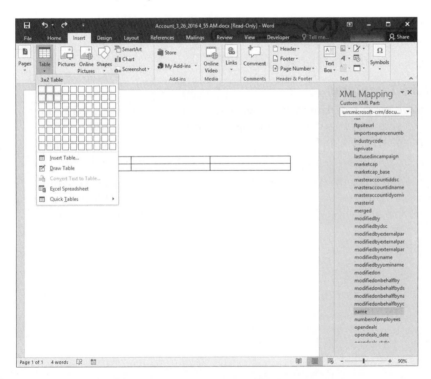

FIGURE 21.17   Adding a table to show the contacts.

Now enter the column headers for the table. Then select the second row of the table completely and right-click contact_customer_accounts in the XML Mapping pane and select Insert Content Control > Repeating (see Figure 21.18).

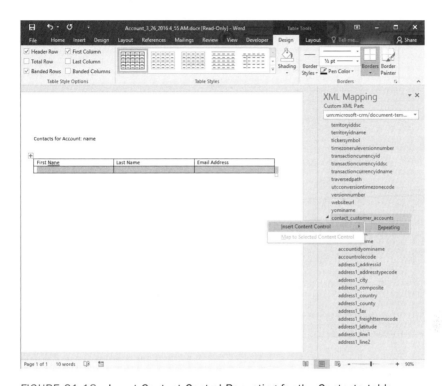

FIGURE 21.18   Insert Content Control Repeating for the Contacts table.

Map the first name, last name, and email address from the child nodes under contact_customer_accounts similarly to the way you did it before for the account fields, but make sure you're adding them inside the row of the table you added (see Figure 21.19).

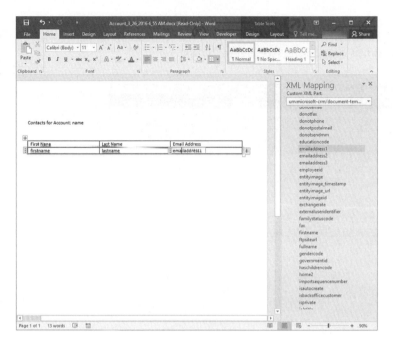

FIGURE 21.19   Contact table with fields mapped.

To test the solution, save the Word document and upload it as explained earlier in this chapter. Then run it to see the results. You should see something similar to what's shown in Figure 21.20.

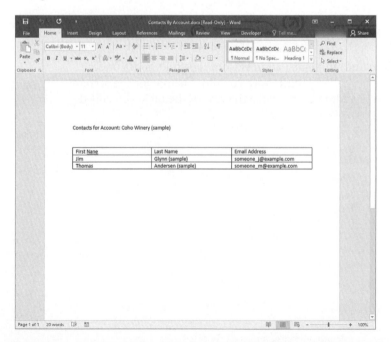

FIGURE 21.20   Testing the Word document template with the contact table.

Using Word templates allows you to easily incorporate advanced graphics and designs. To find design templates online, open Word and search for "invoice," as shown in Figure 21.21. You get results that include some well-designed documents. You can use them to copy content and paste it to the Word document you downloaded from Dynamics CRM.

FIGURE 21.21   Searching for online templates in Microsoft Word.

Personal and System Templates

There are two types of Word templates: system templates and personal templates.

Personal templates are templates you create, and they are not shared with other users. If you want to have other users use your templates, you must create them as system templates. To do this, you select Settings > Document Templates (see Figure 21.22).

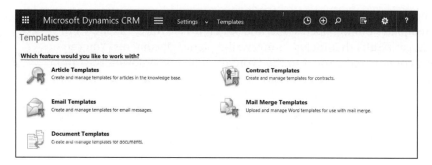

FIGURE 21.22 Creating system templates.

CRM comes with the following out-of-the-box Microsoft Office document templates, ready for you to use and modify as a quick start (see Figure 21.23):

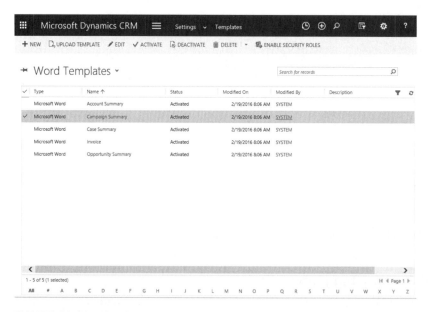

FIGURE 21.23 Word system templates.

- ▶ **Account Summary**—You can find this template in the Account entity.
- ▶ **Campaign Summary**—You can find this template in the Campaign entity.
- ▶ **Case Summary**—You can find this template in the Case entity.
- ▶ **Invoice**—You can find this template in the Invoice entity.
- ▶ **Opportunity Summary**—You can find this template in the Opportunity entity.

For the system templates, you can select the roles you want to make the template available to by selecting the template from the list and clicking Enable Security Roles in the command bar. You then select the roles as shown in Figure 21.24. By default, the system document templates are available to all roles.

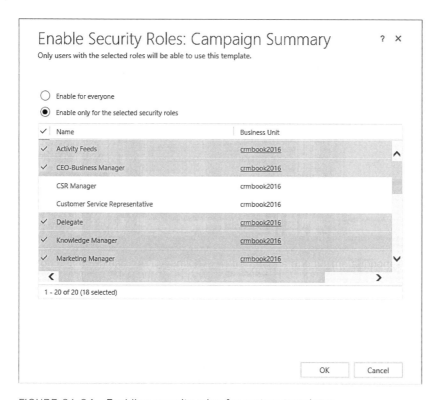

FIGURE 21.24   Enabling security roles for system templates.

Microsoft Excel Integration

Previous versions of Dynamic CRM had an Export to Excel function that addressed a variety of issues related to working with Dynamics CRM and Excel. While this functionality is still available, there is now a deeper native integration with Excel that provides more functionality than Export to Excel could provide.

Creating an Excel Document Template

Navigating to the command bar for almost any entity in the system shows the Excel template option. Figure 21.25 shows this option for the Opportunity entity.

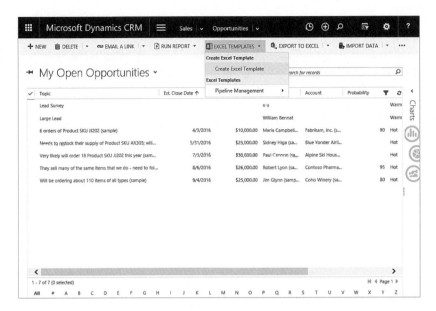

FIGURE 21.25   Excel Templates menu for the Opportunity entity.

You can see that there is already an Excel template for the Opportunity entity. However, in this case, you should select Create Excel Template (see Figure 21.26) to start a wizard to help you create a Word template.

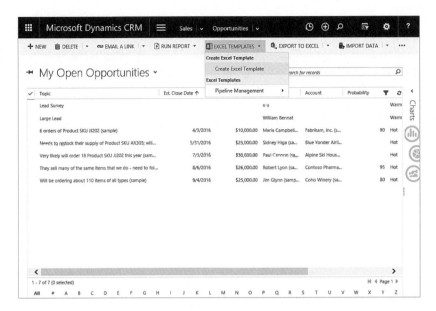

FIGURE 21.26   Create Template from CRM Data dialog.

From the Create Template from CRM Data dialog, you can either create a Word or Excel template, as you saw earlier in this chapter. At this point, of course, we are focusing on Microsoft Excel templates.

Because you fired this wizard from the Opportunity entity, you see Excel Template selected by default, and you see Filter by Entity set to Opportunity. Unlike for a Word template, for an Excel template, you also need to select the view you want to use. Click Download File to download the template, as shown in Figure 21.27.

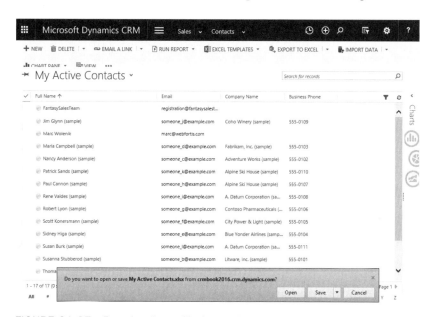

FIGURE 21.27   Downloading a file for an Excel template.

Unlike with Word templates, with Excel templates you are not asked to select the relationships because the fields that are included in the template are the ones that are part of the CRM view you selected. However, you can click the Edit Columns link to modify the fields in the Edit Columns dialog (see Figure 21.28).

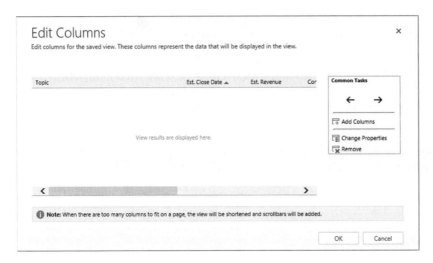

FIGURE 21.28   Edit Columns dialog.

When the Excel document you downloaded is opened, you see a document with the list of the CRM records that belong to the view criteria you selected (see Figure 21.29).

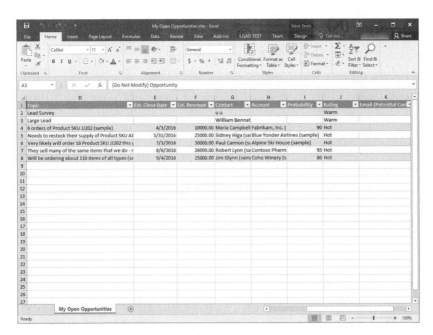

FIGURE 21.29   Excel document.

One of the cool things you can do now with Excel is add a chart that will become resident to the Excel document even after you upload it; this chart will show updated data the next time it's used. To do this, select an empty cell and then select Insert > 3-D Column, as shown in Figure 21.30.

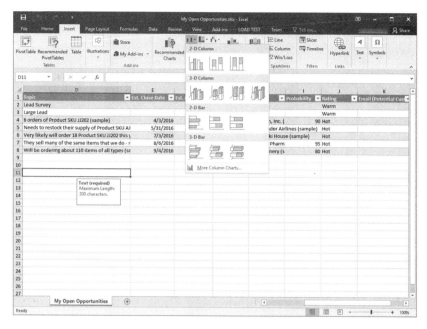

FIGURE 21.30   Adding a 3-D chart to the Excel template.

After you insert the chart, right-click the empty space inside the chart and click Select Data, as shown in Figure 21.31.

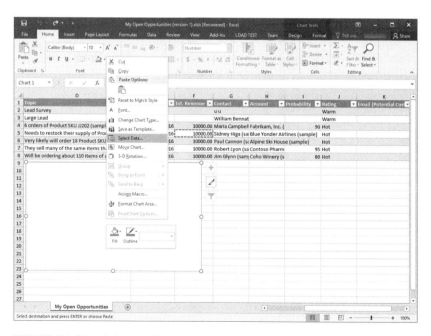

FIGURE 21.31   Selecting Data.

Now select the values in the Est. Revenue column in the chart data range (see Figure 21.32).

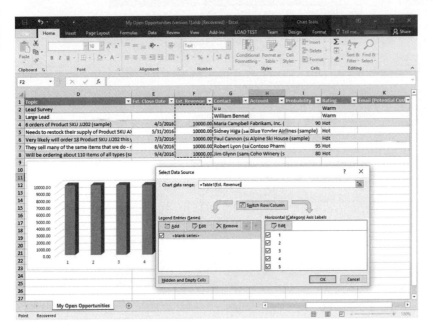

FIGURE 21.32   Adding the Est. Revenue column to the chart data range.

Uploading the Excel Document Template

When you finished editing the Excel file and adding the charts or formulas, you can save the spreadsheet and upload it back to Dynamics CRM by selecting Excel Templates > Create Excel Template to once again open the Create Template from CRM Data dialog (see Figure 21.33). This time, click Upload to upload the document.

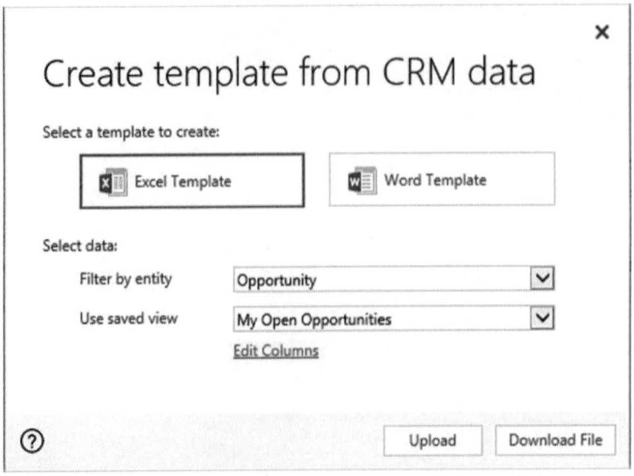

FIGURE 21.33   Uploading the Excel template.

Drag and drop the file you edited before from Windows Explorer to the Upload Template dialog or use the Browse link to select the file (see Figure 21.34).

21

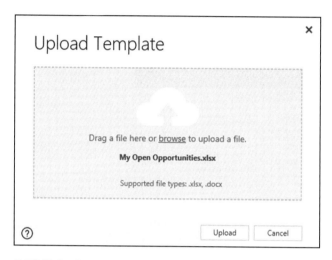

Upload Template   ✕

Drag a file here or <u>browse</u> to upload a file.

My Open Opportunities.xlsx

Supported file types: .xlsx, .docx

⑦ | Upload | | Cancel |

FIGURE 21.34   Upload Template dialog.

After you click the Upload button, you see information for the document you just uploaded. You can change the name of the document to something more descriptive name, and you can select the language. All the other fields are read-only, so you cannot change their values (see Figure 21.35).

⠿ Microsoft Dynamics CRM   ☰   Sales ⌄   Opportunities ⌄   My Open Opportun...

➕ NEW   ⟲ DEACTIVATE   🗑 DELETE   👥 ASSIGN   ↻ SHARE   ⟳ EMAIL A LINK   📄 WORD TEMPLATES ▾   ▷ RUN REPORT ▾   ↑ ↓ ⋊ ✕

PERSONAL DOCUMENT TEMPLATE : INFORMATION
My Open Op...   ▾≡

⌄ General

Details

Status	🔒 Activated
Name*	My Open Opportunities
Description	--
Modified On	🔒 3/26/2016 3:22 AM
Created By	🔒 👤 Marc Wolenik
Created On	🔒 3/26/2016 3:22 AM
Modified By	🔒 👤 Marc Wolenik
Type*	🔒 Microsoft Excel
Associated Entity Type Code	🔒 Opportunity
Language*	English

FIGURE 21.35   Document template information.

Using the Excel Document Templates

Now you are ready to use the Excel template you created and uploaded earlier. To use the document template, you need to go to the Opportunities list (which doesn't work the same as if you go to the Opportunity form) and select Excel Templates. There you see the template you uploaded, under Personal Excel Templates (see Figure 21.36).

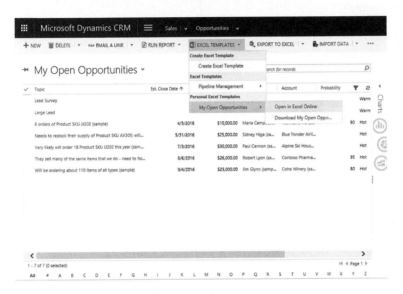

FIGURE 21.36   Selecting Excel templates.

You have two options here: First, you can open the Excel template in Excel Online, which doesn't require you to have the Microsoft Excel application installed on the computer or device you are using. The second option requires you to have the Microsoft Excel application installed on your computer or device. Figure 21.37 shows the interface when you select Excel Online.

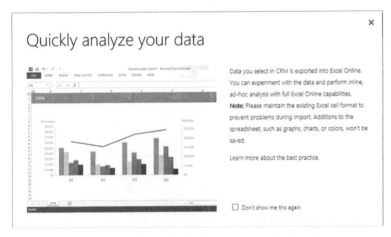

FIGURE 21.37   Opening the Excel template with Excel Online.

You can work with your Excel document in Excel Online. If you make changes to the Est. Revenue column, the chart changes when you do updates (see Figure 21.38).

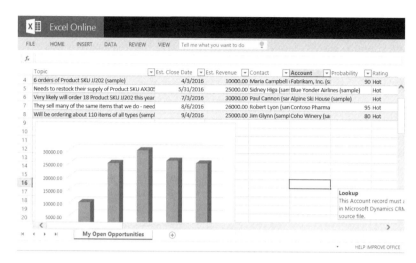

FIGURE 21.38   Analyzing data with Excel Online.

When you are done and want to go back to the CRM list of opportunities, you just click the Return to CRM List button on the command bar, and the system alerts you that any changes will be lost, as shown in Figure 21.39. Select your appropriate action, as the data will not be saved otherwise.

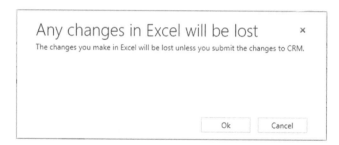

FIGURE 21.39   Returning to the CRM list.

System Templates

As with Word, there are two types of Excel templates: personal and system.

Personal templates are the ones you create that only you can see. You created a personal Excel template earlier in this chapter. If you want to have all users use the templates you create, you must create them as system templates. To do this, you must select Settings > Templates.

CRM comes with the following out-of-the-box templates, ready for you to use and modify as a quick start (see Figure 21.40):

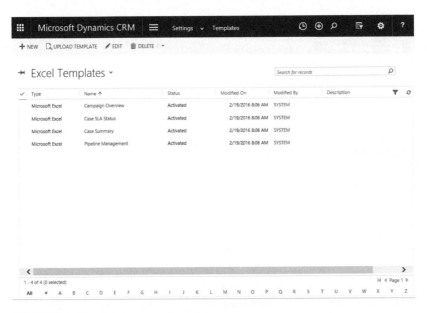

FIGURE 21.40   Excel system templates.

▶ **Campaign Overview**—You can find this template it in the Campaign entity.

▶ **Case SLA Status**—You can find this template in the Case entity.

▶ **Case Summary**—You can find this template in the Case entity.

▶ **Pipeline Management**—You can find this template.

Microsoft OneNote Integration

OneNote is a tool that allows users to take notes easily, without having to deal with the constraints and limitations of Microsoft Word or Excel. More users are getting accustomed to using this tool, which can help you easily use screen scraping and embedded notes, audio, videos, and graphics.

Enabling OneNote Integration

To enable CRM integration with Microsoft OneNote, you must go to the Dynamics CRM web interface and select Settings > Document Management, as shown in Figure 21.41.

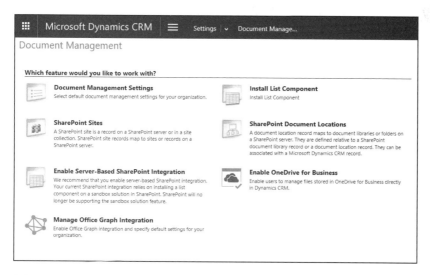

FIGURE 21.41   Document Management page.

Then you need to enable SharePoint integration by clicking Enable Server-Based SharePoint Integration, which starts the configuration wizard shown in Figure 21.42.

▶ To learn more about SharePoint integration, **SEE CHAPTER 27**, "SharePoint."

FIGURE 21.42 Enable Server-Based SharePoint Integration dialog.

Click Next to continue and then select where you want to have the SharePoint server located (see Figure 21.43). For Dynamics CRM Online, you need to have an Online subscription. This example shows how to integrate with SharePoint Online, but the integration with On-Premises is very similar.

FIGURE 21.43   SharePoint location.

Click Next and then enter the SharePoint site URL in the dialog shown in Figure 21.44. You must use a site with HTTPS if you are working with CRM Online. Also make sure you add a / character at the end of the URL.

FIGURE 21.44   Specifying the SharePoint site URL.

Click Next to start a validation process, If everything is okay, you see the word Valid in green (see Figure 21.45).

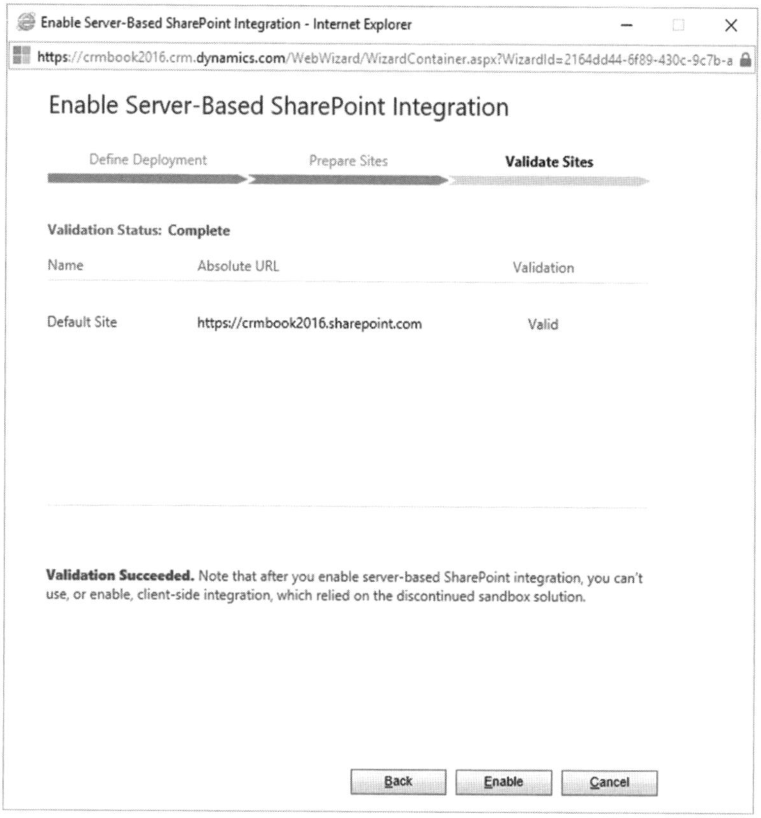

FIGURE 21.45   SharePoint site validation.

Click the Enable button, and when the configuration finishes, you see a congratulations message. Click Finish to close this dialog. When the SharePoint integration is successfully configures, you see the OneNote Integration option in the Settings > Document Management page, as shown in Figure 21.46.

FIGURE 21.46   OneNote Integration option in Document Management.

Click Document Management Settings to complete the SharePoint configuration on the page that appears (see Figure 21.47).

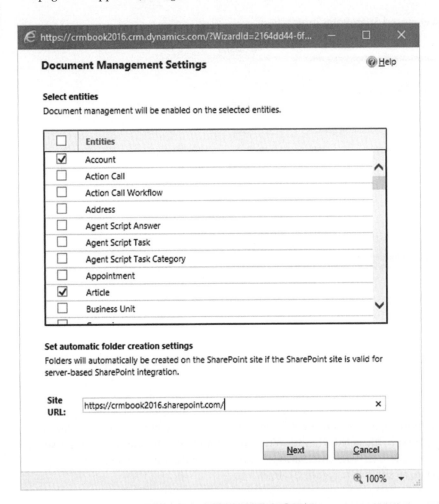

FIGURE 21.47   Selecting Document Management Settings.

Select the entities you want to configure, enter the SharePoint Site URL, and click Next. For this example, you can leave the default entities selected.

Under Select Folder Structure, select Base on Entity and leave it set to Account (see Figure 21.48).

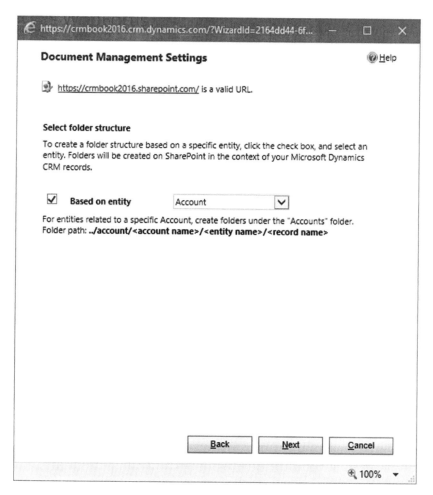

FIGURE 21.48   Folder structure.

After you click Next, if a confirmation dialog appears, alerting you that a document library will be created in the site you entered, click OK. When the process finishes, you see the status, as shown in Figure 21.49. Click Finish to close the dialog.

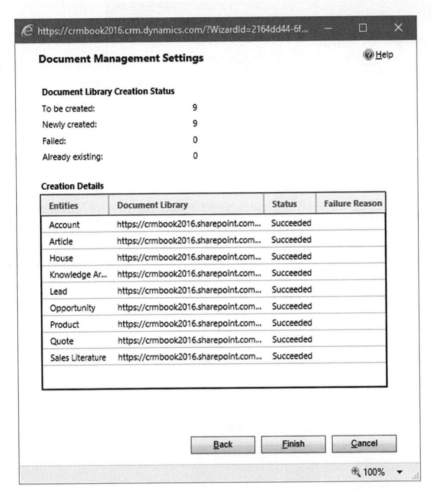

FIGURE 21.49   Document Management Settings completed.

Now you can click OneNote Integration to start the OneNote integration process. You see a list of the entities that are document enabled, as shown in Figure 21.50.

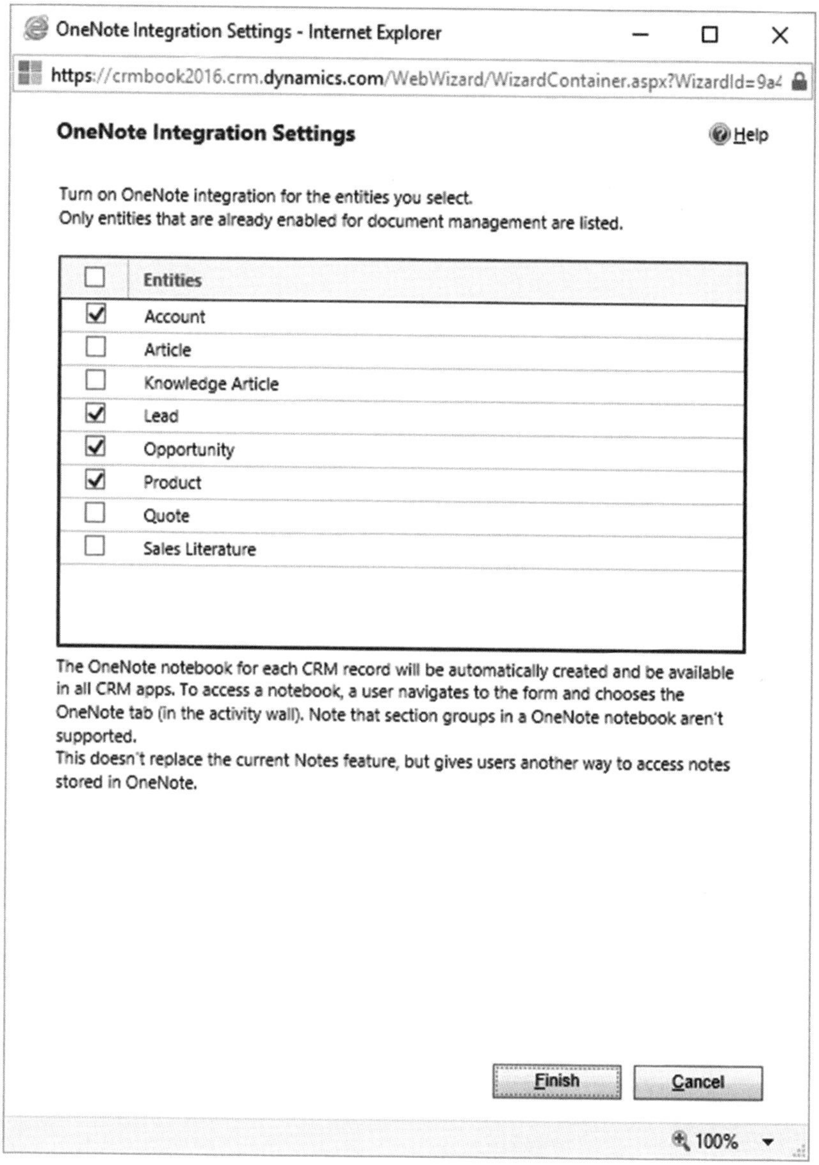

FIGURE 21.50   OneNote Integration Settings dialog.

Select the entities for which you want to have OneNote integration and click Finish. For this example, leave the default entities—Account, Lead, Opportunity, and Product—selected.

To verify that everything is working fine, go to any account record, and you see the OneNote link near the notes (see Figure 21.51).

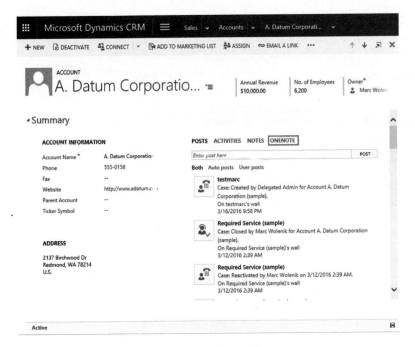

FIGURE 21.51   OneNote in an account record.

If you have a custom entity or if you want one of the existing system entities not listed in the OneNote configuration list, you can go to Settings > Customizations > Customize the System. Then you can click the entity for which you want to enable OneNote integration and make sure you check the Document Management check box and OneNote Integration check box, as shown in Figure 21.52.

FIGURE 21.52   Enabling a custom entity for OneNote integration.

Using OneNote with Dynamics CRM

When you have the OneNote integration enabled, you can go to any record of the configured entities and click the OneNote link just to the right of Notes. A new Untitled OneNote document is generated when you do this the first time (see Figure 21.53).

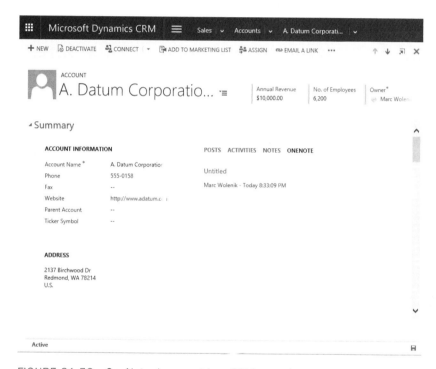

FIGURE 21.53   OneNote document in a CRM record.

Clicking the Untitled link opens OneNote in the web browser, and you can now work with this document, which will be associated with the CRM record (see Figure 21.54).

FIGURE 21.54   Editing a OneNote document.

Microsoft OneDrive Integration

OneDrive is a great online repository for files, and it is exclusively designed to store files. In addition to SharePoint, it is another storage option in Dynamics CRM.

There is a free version of OneDrive, and there is a paid version called OneDrive for Business. Dynamics CRM integrates with the paid version, which can be obtained through an Office 365 subscription or as a standalone product. (It is included with the enterprise plans.)

It's a good idea to use an external repository to store CRM data–related documents for a couple reasons:

▶ CRM storage is usually more expensive than external storage such as SharePoint or OneDrive.

▶ CRM has a file size limitation (which can be uploaded into the notes section) that is usually lower than the SharePoint and OneDrive limits.

Enabling OneDrive Integration

To enable OneDrive integration, you select Settings > Document Management, as shown in Figure 21.55.

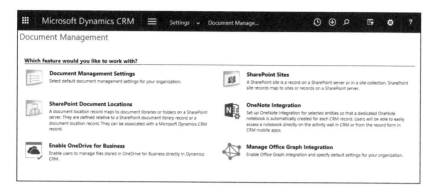

FIGURE 21.55   Document Management page.

▶ Click the Enable OneDrive for Business option (see Figure 21.56).

FIGURE 21.56   Enabling OneDrive for Business.

To complete the integration, check the Enable OneDrive for Business check box and click OK.

You now see a new option in the Document Management page: OneDrive for Business Folder Settings (see Figure 21.57).

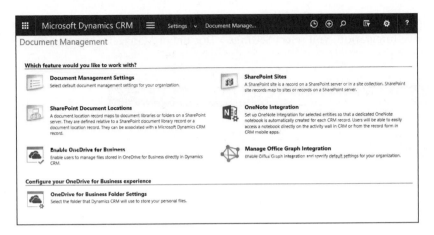

FIGURE 21.57   OneDrive for Business Folder Settings.

If you click this option, you can specify the CRM folder where the documents will be stored, as shown in Figure 21.58.

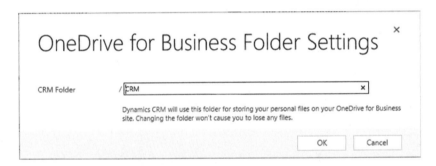

FIGURE 21.58   OneDrive for Business Folder Settings dialog.

Make sure to configure the entities for which you want to use OneDrive for Business by clicking Document Management Settings in the Document Management page, selecting the entities as shown in Figure 21.59, and clicking Next.

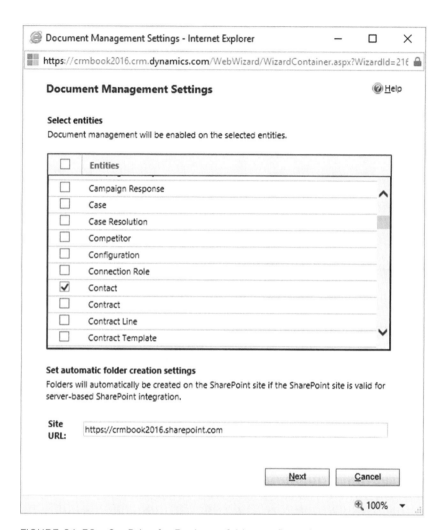

FIGURE 21.59   OneDrive for Business folder configuration.

Using OneDrive with Dynamics CRM

To use OneDrive for Business, you can go any Dynamics CRM record that is document enabled. In the navigation bar, click the Documents option, as shown in Figure 21.60.

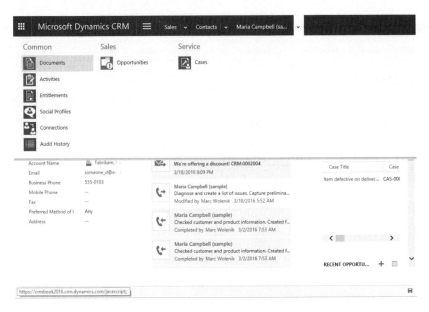

FIGURE 21.60   Documents option for a contact record.

When you are in the document associated view, you can upload a document, and when you click the Upload button, you can select the CRM folder location, which now has the option to select OneDrive, as shown in Figure 21.61.

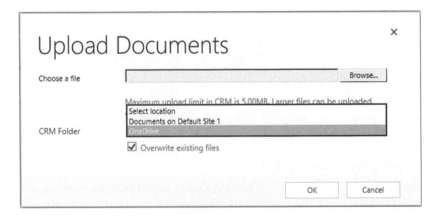

FIGURE 21.61   OneDrive document location for uploads.

The first time you try to upload a document, you see a dialog asking you to change the folder location if you don't want to use the default one, CRM (see Figure 21.62).

FIGURE 21.62   OneDrive for Business first-time upload message.

After you click Continue (or change the location), the file is uploaded to your OneDrive folder, as shown in Figure 21.63.

NOTE

You must go to OneDrive and manually share the document with other people if you want to allow them to access it.

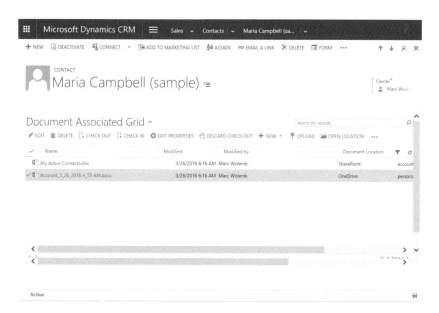

FIGURE 21.63   Document associated view, showing the document location.

TIP

With Microsoft Dynamics CRM 2016, documents can easily be opened from any device or computer in Word Online or Excel Online.

Microsoft Delve Integration

Delve is a Microsoft online tool that helps you find documents easily and quickly. It comes with Office 365 enterprise subscriptions.

Enabling Delve Integration

To enable Office Delve, select Settings > Document Management, > Manage Office Graph Integration. The dialog shown in Figure 21.64 appears.

FIGURE 21.64   Enable Office Graph Integration dialog.

Check the Enable Office Graph Integration check box and click Next. When the process is complete, you see the success message shown in Figure 21.65. Click Finish to close the dialog.

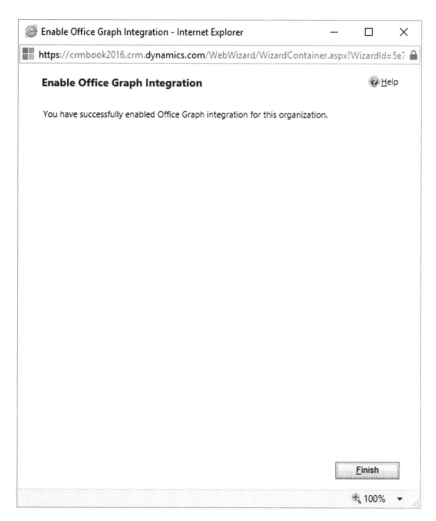

21

FIGURE 21.65   Office Graph integration successfully enabled.

Configuring Delve with Dynamics CRM

Once the Office Graph integration is enabled, there are some extra steps you need to take to configure Delve in Dynamics CRM.

You have to manually create a dashboard by going to the system dashboards (or your personal dashboards, if you want this only for yourself).

When you create a new dashboard, you can select any layout, and then you see the Delve button in the command bar. You can either click that or click the new icon that appears with the tooltip Insert Trending Documents (see Figure 21.66).

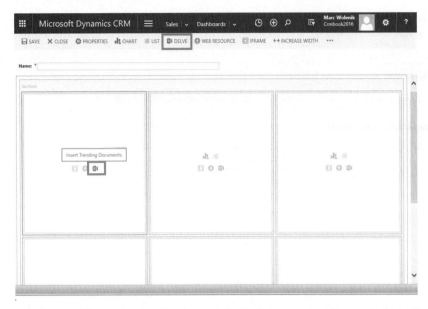

FIGURE 21.66   Insert trending documents (Delve) component on a dashboard.

Insert the trending documents component and increase the width and height to fill the complete area of the dashboard, as shown in Figure 21.67. Enter a name for the dashboard and click Save.

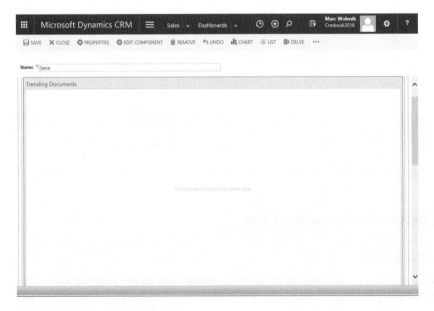

FIGURE 21.67   Delve dashboard.

Using Delve with Dynamics CRM

After you have configured the dashboard, you can open it to see Delve in action. If you have never used Delve before, you might see an empty page.

To work with Delve, you need to create a folder in OneDrive and share it with some people. Then you can upload documents that can be shared; they might take a while to appear in Delve. If you manually open Delve and try the search feature, you see lots of results similar to what's shown in Figure 21.68.

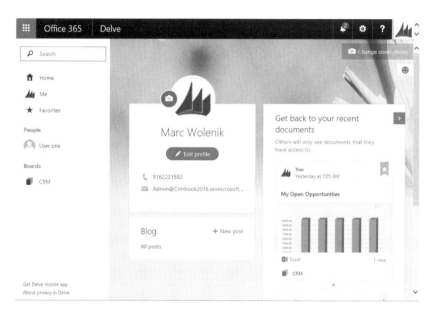

FIGURE 21.68   Office Delve Interface.

Summary

This chapter looks at enhancements related to Microsoft Office integrations, starting with Microsoft Word integrations, which now allow you to produce more professional documents with data integrated with Dynamics CRM. This chapter also examines the new Excel templates, which go beyond the Export to Excel functionality that existed before to helping you analyze data more efficiently. This chapter also discusses integrations with Microsoft OneNote, OneDrive for Business, and the new Office Delve to help you find the documents that are relevant to the work you are doing.

Customizing Entities

One of the most powerful features of Microsoft Dynamics CRM is that you can customize (or configure) almost all entities, such as Account, Contact, and Opportunity entities, as well as add new custom entities to suit your needs.

Navigate to the main entity customization screen by going to Settings > Customizations, and you see that you can customize entities in several ways (see Figure 22.1).

FIGURE 22.1   Customization interface.

The customization screen presents the following options, which are all covered in this chapter:

▶ Customize the System

▶ Publishers

▶ Solutions

▶ Developer Resources

▶ Themes

You can customize existing entities or create new entities. In CRM 2016, you can customize an entity without going to the Settings area; instead, you can just go to any entity and click … > Customize Entity, as shown in Figure 22.2.

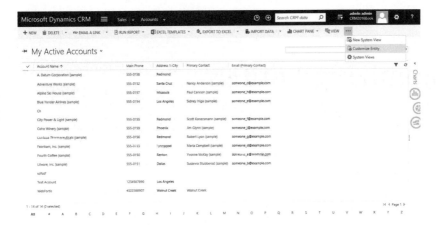

FIGURE 22.2   Customizing an entity.

Alternatively, you can open a form for an entity and click ... > Form, as shown in Figure 22.3, to start making changes.

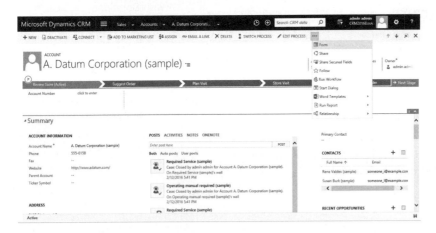

FIGURE 22.3   Customizing a form.

Customization Principles

The most basic principle with regard to customization is that Microsoft Dynamics CRM is built according to an n-tier model, with the user interface layers (web client, Outlook client, phone client, and tablet client) on top, the application layer in the middle, and the database layer (SQL Server) on the bottom. To avoid layer conflict and have a properly managed n-tier application model, you should always make the customizations following the principles described in this chapter.

▶ Refer to the section "Solution Concepts," later in this chapter, to review some basic principles related to customizations.

> **NOTE**
>
> If you are an expert SQL database administrator or developer, you might be tempted to create database triggers or stored procedures or change the database schema. However, I strongly recommend that you not touch the database directly in any situation. Doing so is considered an unsupported customization and might cause the application to break or fail.

Customization can be characterized in two ways in Microsoft Dynamics CRM: supported and unsupported. This chapter covers only supported customizations that follow Microsoft best practices and that generally do not fail when the product is upgraded. Unsupported customizations might perform any function, but they fall outside the range of Microsoft's testing when considering upgrades, database schema changes, and support rollups. The following results can occur with unsupported customizations:

▶ Service packs might fail, break, or not install.

▶ Upgrades to the product might cause unexpected results or fail.

▶ The application or database might become unstable and fail to work.

The Dynamics CRM Entity Model

Much as in an XML document, all objects in Microsoft Dynamics CRM are treated as entities or attributes. Account, Contact, Activity, and so on are entities in the CRM system, and every entity has related attributes and relationships, which are also called fields. For example, Figure 22.4 shows the fields (such as Account Name) for the Account entity.

FIGURE 22.4   Fields for the Account entity.

NOTE

You can rename the existing system entities if the default names don't work for your business. For example, lot of companies rename the Account entity Company or Organization. If you do this, keep in mind that only the name of the entity that is displayed is renamed; the logical name (in this example Account) remains the same.

Fields

Fields can be of the following data types:

▶ **Single line of text (nvarchar type)**—This type is used for small texts or strings. It can have a maximum of 4,000 characters.

▶ **Option set (picklist type)**—This type is used for drop-downs or combo boxes, with a limited set of fixed options. Option sets were called picklists in earlier versions of Dynamics CRM.

NOTE

Because an option set can display only simple, nondynamic options, you might want to use a new custom entity if you need something that is more dynamic or complex than the options provided, and use a lookup control type instead.

TIP

You can reuse an option set on more than one entity by using global option sets.

▶ **Two options (bit type)**— This type is used for Boolean values such as yes or no.

▶ **Image (image type)**—This type is used to store an image (maximum 5120KB size). You can have a maximum of one image type field per entity, and you cannot add a field of this type to system entities.

▶ **Whole number (int type)**—This type is used for numbers that can be any of these formats:

   ▶ **None**—Sets the min and maximum values.

   ▶ **Duration**—Presents a drop-down list so the user can select X Minutes, X Hours, or X Days. Hours and days can also be entered using decimals—for example, x.x hours or x.x days.

   ▶ **Time Zone**—Shows a drop-down list with the different time zones the user can select, such as (GMT -08:00) Pacific time.

▶ **Language**—Shows a drop-down with the different languages installed by the system. The data will be stored using the language code; for example, English in United States is1033. For a complete table of language codes, visit https://msdn.microsoft.com/en-us/library/ms912047(WinEmbedded.10).aspx.

▶ **Floating-point number (float type)**—This type is used for floating-point decimal numbers.

▶ **Decimal number (decimal type)**—This type is used for numbers with decimals.

▶ **Currency (money type)**—This type is used for amounts.

▶ **Multiple lines of text (ntext type)**—This type is used for large texts or strings with a maximum length of 1,048,576.

▶ **Date and time (datetime type)**—This type is used for dates and times, which can have the following behaviors:

    ▶ **User Local**—This option, used by all the previous version of Dynamics CRM, shows the value of the date and time in the user's local time zone.

    ▶ **Date Only**—This option, which is new to Dynamics CRM 2016, shows only the date, regardless of the user time zone configuration.

    ▶ **Time Zone Independent**—This option, which is new to Dynamics CRM 2016, shows the date and time field without doing any time zone conversion, so if the original user entered a date with the time 7:00 AM any user, regardless of location or configured time zone, will see 7:00 AM. This is a great new addition. You can use it, for example, for an entity called Course when you want to enter the value for the course start time in New York; then if you have a customer rep in California, he will be able to see that date and time in New York time and not converted to the California time zone, as used to happen in older versions of Dynamics CRM.

▶ **Lookup (lookup type)**—This type is used to look up other entities' relationships.

Entities are associated with other entities via a customization referred to as a *relationship*.

Calculated Fields

A new addition to CRM is calculated fields, which you can use to perform automated calculations that you used to have to do using JavaScript or other code. The following data types supports calculated fields:

▶ Single line of text

▶ Option set

▶ Single

▶ Two options

- ▶ Whole number
- ▶ Decimal number
- ▶ Currency
- ▶ Date and time

When you select Calculated from the Field Type drop-down, a new Edit button appears, as shown in Figure 22.5.

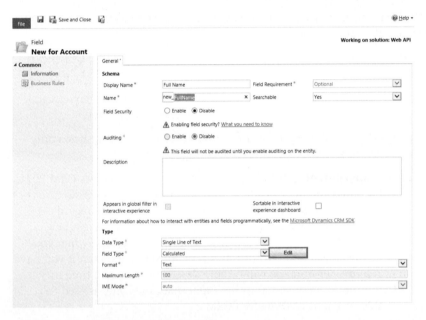

FIGURE 22.5   Adding a calculated field.

NOTE

Before clicking the Edit button, you must enter the display name and name of the field because clicking the Edit button creates the field as if clicked Save.

When the field is created, you see the calculated field editor (see Figure 22.6), in which you can configure conditions and actions.

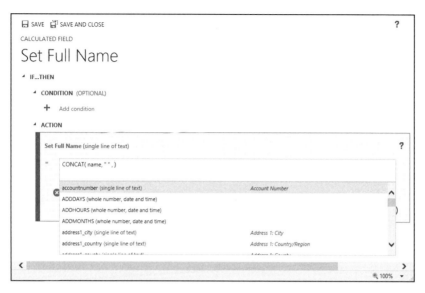

FIGURE 22.6   Calculated field editor.

The calculated field editor has IntelliSense, so it is very easy to find the fields.
For example, for a single line of text you can use the CONCAT function to concatenate fields with fixed text.

You can then use your calculated fields in forms and views. When you use calculated fields on forms, they are always displayed as read only, and the calculation happens as soon as you save the record.

These are the functions you can use in the calculated field editor:

▶ ADDHOURS

▶ ADDDAYS

▶ ADDWEEKS

▶ ADDMONTHS

▶ ADDYEARS

▶ SUBTRACTHOURS

▶ SUBTRACTDAYS

▶ SUBTRACTWEEKS

▶ SUBTRACTMONTHS

▶ SUBTRACTYEARS

▶ DIFFINDAYS

▶ DIFFINHOURS

▶ DIFFINMINUTES

▶ DIFFINMONTHS

▶ DIFFINWEEKS

▶ DIFFINYEARS

▶ CONCAT

▶ TRIMLEFT

▶ TRIMRIGHT

Rollup Fields

Rollup fields allow you to perform automated calculations based on the related entity records. To do this in previous versions of Dynamics CRM, you had to use JavaScript or other code. The following data types support rollup fields:

▶ Whole number

▶ Decimal number

▶ Currency

▶ Date and time

With a rollup field, you could, for example, show the count of contacts related to an account, using a whole number field.

When you select Rollup from the Field Type drop-down, a new Edit button appears, as shown in Figure 22.7.

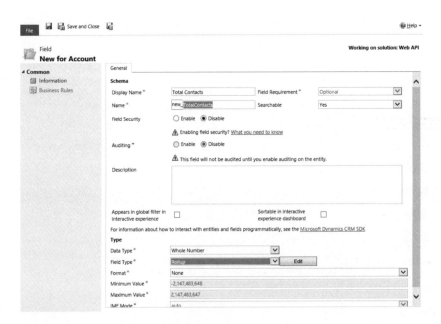

FIGURE 22.7   Adding a rollup field.

22

NOTE

Before clicking the Edit button, you must enter the display name and name of the field because clicking the Edit button creates the field as if clicked Save.

When the field is created, you see the rollup field editor (see Figure 22.8), which you can use to configure the source entity, the related entity, the filters with conditions, and the aggregation method, which can be any of the following:

▶ SUM

▶ MAX

▶ MIN

▶ COUNT

▶ AVG

FIGURE 22.8   Rollup field editor.

NOTE

For each rollup field, two system jobs are created. One of them will run every 5 minutes, and the other will be a massive update that runs every 12 hours to update the values of all the records that use the rollup field.

For each rollup field you create, three fields are created in CRM: one with the calculated value, another with the date of the last update, and another to see the state of the field (see Figure 22.9).

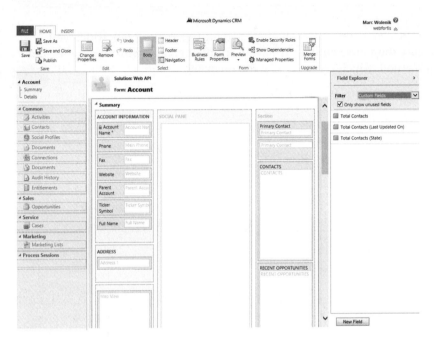

FIGURE 22.9   Rollup field available for use.

Like calculated fields, rollup fields are displayed as read-only in forms, so users can't change the calculated value. However, a rollup field has a calculator icon the user can use to force the calculation if the system job didn't execute yet.

By clicking the refresh button inside a rollup field, you can force the evaluation of the data. Then, after you save the record, you see the other two related fields updated.

Keys

You can define your own alternate keys on entities. When creating a new alternate key, you can define one or more fields. For example, you can create a key for the Account Number field of the Account entity. By creating a key like, you can prevent users from creating accounts with duplicate account numbers. Figure 22.10 shows the custom key options.

FIGURE 22.10   Custom key options.

Depending on how much data you have, a custom key you create might take some time to become active.

You can then use the alternate keys you create in the update and upsert operations. Alternate keys are used for integration jobs, providing a key reference that allows for updates to occur. See the Dynamics CRM software development kit (SDK) for more information about how to work with alternate keys.

Relationships

Not to be confused with relationships/connections at the interface level, relationships at the schema level are programmatic. Even so, relationships are very user friendly; you don't need to be a database system administration expert to use and configure relationships between entities.

Microsoft Dynamics CRM supports the following relationships:

▶ 1:N relationships (one to many)

▶ N:1 relationships (many to one)

▶ N:N relationships (many to many)

You can add as many relationships as you want, and you can also add more than one relationship to the same entity. For example, you can have a custom entity called Customer and add two fields called Primary Contact and Secondary Contact, both related to the entity Contact.

Finally, another feature to relationships is the ability to relate an entity to itself, which is referred as *self-referential*. Using this type of relationship, you can use any type of relationship (1:N, N:1, or N:N) to relate an entity to itself.

1:N Relationships

Figure 22.11 shows the window where you can create a new 1:N relationship. With this type of relationship, the primary entity is the one you are customizing. For example, if you are working with the Account entity, you could use a 1:N relationship to specify the primary account for another entity, such as Contact, for which the custom field defined by this relationship will contain only one account.

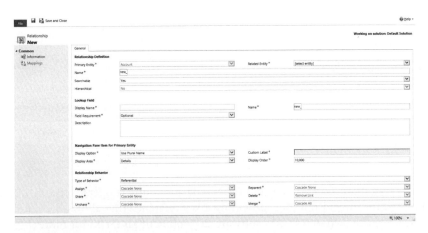

FIGURE 22.11   Creating a new 1:N relationship.

N:1 Relationships

With an N:1 relationship, the primary entity is the one you select. Therefore, the entity you are customizing is the related entity. For example, if you want a Contact entity to have multiple Account entities associated with it, you apply an N:1 relationship to the Account entity.

N:N Relationships

With an N:N relationship, there is not one primary entity and another secondary or related entity; rather, they both act as both types. For example, you might want to have one Contact entity related to many Account entities or one Account related to many Contact entities. You might, for instance, have a Contact with a new person who works for two companies, and each company might have many Contact entities apart from this one.

Relationship Behavior

For N:1 and 1:N relationships, there are settings for the relationship behavior, called *cascading rules*, that apply to the following operations:

▶ Assign

▶ Share

▶ Unshare

▶ Reparent

▶ Delete

▶ Merge

The Type of Behavior drop-down in the relationship cascading rules contains four options:

▶ Parental

▶ Referential

▶ Referential, Restrict Delete

▶ Configurable Cascading

The first three options are templates, and the last option, Configurable Cascading, allows you to configure the cascading manually for each operation.

The first four operations—Assign, Share, Unshare, and Reparent—all have the same cascading types:

▶ **Cascade All**—This option affects the current entity record and its related entity records. So the operation is performed on both entities.

▶ **Cascade Active**—This option affects the current entity record and its related entity records that have a status of Active.

▶ **Cascade User-Owned**—This option affects the current entity record and its related entity records that are owned by the user who is performing the operation only.

▶ **Cascade None**—This option affects only the current entity and not the related entity records.

The Delete operation has different cascading options, as follows:

▶ **Cascade All**—This option is the same as explained above except that if you have a 1:N relationship between Account and Contact and you have 1 account record with 10 contacts related, when you delete the account, all 10 contacts are also deleted.

▶ **Remove Link**—With this option, you can remove a link. Using the preceding example, if you delete the account record, the contacts aren't deleted, but the link between the contacts and the account are removed.

▶ **Restrict**—With this option, only when the account doesn't have any related records can it be deleted. Using the earlier example, you won't be able to delete the account until you delete all the related contacts manually first.

The Merge operation changes between Cascade None and Cascade All, depending on the primary entity selected, and you can't modified it.

Messages

Messages display information to the user based on a variety of actions. Users can customize these messages to display richer or different information, if desired.

> **NOTE**
>
> Remember to manually update the messages if you have renamed a system entity because the messages aren't updated automatically.

Basic Customizations

Basic customizations are customizations to Microsoft Dynamics CRM that don't require any knowledge of programming or database design and configuration. Basic customizations include showing and hiding controls on a form and hiding or showing columns in a view.

> **NOTE**
>
> For conditional showing and hiding of controls, you can use business rules, which are explained later in this chapter, in the section "Business Rules."

To make this type of customization, go to the entity you want to customize and go to the Forms or Views node in the left navigation area, as shown in Figure 22.12. The following sections describe the particular form customizations and view customizations that are possible.

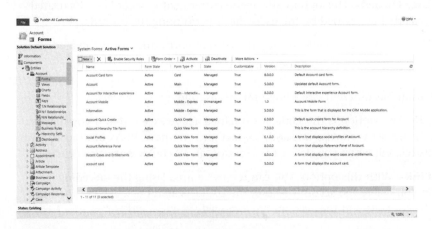

FIGURE 22.12   Form and view customizations.

Form Customizations

Microsoft Dynamics CRM 2016 supports more than one type of form. A form can be any of the following types:

- ▶ Main
- ▶ Mobile - Express
- ▶ Quick View
- ▶ Quick Create
- ▶ Card
- ▶ Main-interactive Experience

You can create new form designs and layouts, as well as Quick Create and Quick View forms. Quick Create forms allow you to create records quickly and with fewer fields on the form—without leaving the entity with which you're working. Quick View forms show the data of the parent record on a child record form but in read-only mode.

Main Forms

The following sections explain how you can customize the Main forms, using features in Microsoft Dynamics CRM 2016.

Adding, Removing, or Moving Tabs   The tabs in CRM 2016 behave differently than in earlier versions. You can now navigate to the tabs by using the tab navigator (see Figure 22.13), and the navigation bar has links pointing to bookmarks in the form. You can add tabs with one, two, or three columns, and each column can have one or more sections. Figure 22.14 shows a form with multiple tabs and different column options.

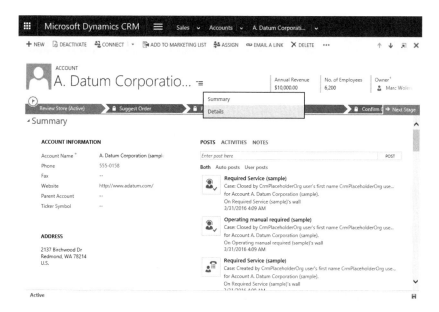

FIGURE 22.13   New tab navigator for the Account entity Main form.

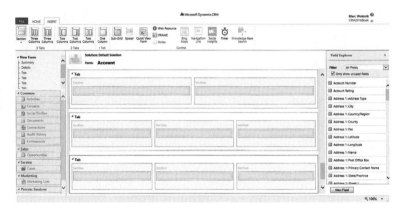

FIGURE 22.14   New custom tabs named Tab.

Every time you add a new tab, you also get at least one new section inside the new tab.

Adding, Removing, or Moving Sections   Sections are used to group controls for related fields. The sections must be within a tab. To add a new section, click the buttons on the Insert tab under the Section group. When you double-click the new added section, the Section Properties dialog appears (see Figure 22.15).

FIGURE 22.15   Section Properties dialog.

You can choose whether a label displays the section name, and you can also specify the width of the field area (refer to Figure 22.15). You also have some layout options such as the number of columns to display data as shown in Figure 22.16.

FIGURE 22.16   Formatting section properties.

TIP

To move a section from one tab to another, just drag and drop the section.

NOTE

If the predefined layouts don't match your requirements, consider adding a web resource (type HTML) or developing a custom page in ASP.NET and adding an IFRAME to display your custom page inside the form, as detailed in the "Adding, Removing, or Moving IFRAMEs" section, later in this chapter.

Adding, Removing, or Moving Fields   Fields are used to display the entity fields with input controls. If you have created a custom field, as described earlier in this chapter, you need to add an input control for that field to allow users to enter the values. To add a field to the form, just select the field from the Field Explorer list and drag and drop it to the section or tab where you want it.

NOTE

To avoid adding duplicate fields, the Field Explorer by default shows only the available fields that have not already been added to any tab or section in the form. If you uncheck the Only Show Unused Fields check box, you always see all fields, and you can add the same field more than once on the same form—but only in different sections.

You can also select the section where you want to place a field and then go to the Field Explorer and double-click the field you want; it is then added to the selected section.

TIP

You can drag and drop to move a field to any place inside a section. You can also add fields to the header or footer of a form, which are always shown, regardless of the tab the user has selected. Be sure to click the Header button that is on the Home tab of the ribbon if you want to be able to add fields on the header. You can customize the navigation links when you click the Navigation button on the ribbon.

Adding, Removing, or Moving IFRAMEs   You can use IFRAMEs to display custom applications or pages inside a form. Doing so is extremely helpful when you want to show content from external applications or when you need to use advanced input/output controls that are not included in the CRM controls toolset. Examples include a complex grid, a picture control, or a movie control. When you click the IFRAME button, you get the Add an IFRAME dialog, shown in Figure 22.17, which requires the name for the IFRAME as well as the URL of your application.

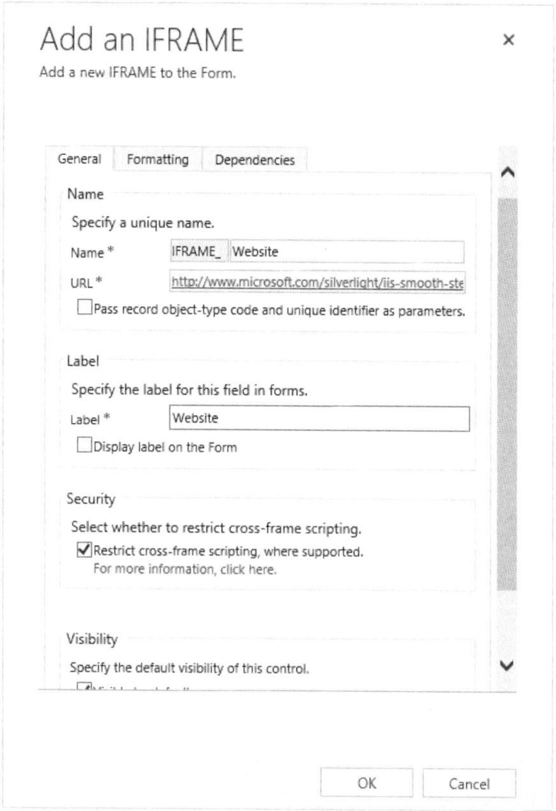

FIGURE 22.17   Adding an IFRAME.

For example, say that you want to enter Website in the Name field and www.microsoft.
com/silverlight/iis-smooth-streaming/demo/ in the URL field. When adding the
IFRAME with these settings and the default values, you then see the IFRAME inserted in
the form.

Most of the time, you want an IFRAME to expand vertically to fill the entire form. To make
that happen, select the IFRAME, click Change Properties, and then, on the Formatting
tab, in the Row Layout section, check the Automatically Expand to Use Available
Space check box.

In the Scrolling section, you can choose whether you want to have the IFRAME show the
scrollbars (vertical and horizontal) as necessary (which is the default value), always, or
never. Finally, you can specify whether you want to show a border around the IFRAME by
clicking the Display Border property in the Border section.

Click the OK button when you're ready to accept your changes. You do not see the
IFRAME expand on the form in design mode, but you will see it expanded when you run
the application.

In the URL used in this example, there are Silverlight controls in the page contents to be displayed in an IFRAME, and you won't see the page render properly inside the IFRAME.

Changing Default IFRAME Properties   When you first set an IFRAME URL, you may get a Page Can't Be Loaded error message or a message about unexpected results (for example, No Silverlight Content Displayed). This behavior is normal. It is the default behavior because of the protection that is set by default on the IFRAME properties to prevent the external pages from executing JavaScript codes or ActiveX controls that might perform unintended operations on the CRM application, such as closing the form unexpectedly without allowing CRM to control the window and save the data properly. However, you can change this security setting to have a page load correctly if you're sure there will not be a problem. To do so, select the IFRAME and click Change Properties. In the Security section of the dialog, uncheck the Restrict Cross-Frame Scripting, Where Supported check box (see Figure 22.18).

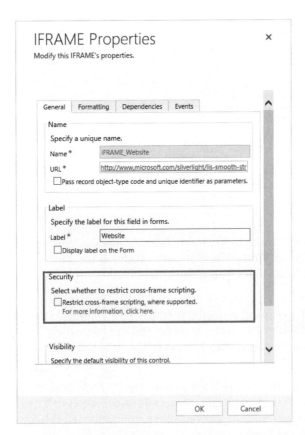

FIGURE 22.18   Removing the cross-frame scripting protection.

Click OK to close the dialog and test it by opening an Account record form. You now see the page load properly, without any warnings (see Figure 22.19).

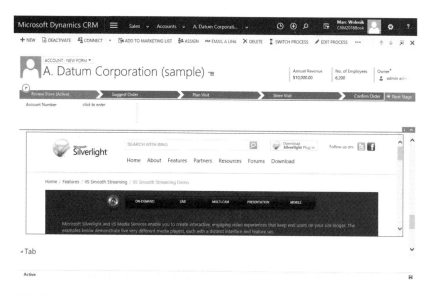

FIGURE 22.19   IFRAME test with active content displayed.

This example uses a web page URL that shows the same content regardless of when and where in CRM it is shown. Most of the time, however, you will want to use an IFRAME to show different content depending on the entity and record instance being displayed. For instance, you might want to show the company web page in an IFRAME when working with accounts and then show an individual's picture in the IFRAME when working with contacts. In that case, you need to create either a web resource (type HTML) or a custom ASP.NET application and read the globally unique identifier (GUID) of the record that will be passed to the web application. This is accomplished by checking the Pass Record Object-Type Code and Unique Identifier as Parameters check box.

Changing Properties of a Tab, Section, Field, or IFRAME   Here you can access the properties of the section you are positioning. For example, if you select a tab, you have access to the tab properties. If you select a field, the properties are related to the field selected.

Adding a Bing Map to Multiple Forms   In CRM 2016, you can add a Bing map control to system entities that have a composite address field. The following entities can display Bing maps on forms:

▶ Account

▶ Contact

▶ Lead

▶ User

▶ Quote

▶ Order

▶ Invoice

▶ Competitor

You need to sign in to the Bing Maps portal and create an API key to use for On-Premises deployment, but you do not need to do any additional configuration to use it in Microsoft Dynamics CRM Online. When you put a Bing Maps component on a form, select the address that will be displayed.

You can create multiple forms for an entity in CRM 2016. To do so, you can open an existing form and click Save As to create a copy or you can click New and select the type of form you want to create. You can assign security roles to a form to control access to it; to do so, click the Enable Security Roles button at the top of the command bar.

> **NOTE**
>
> You can only have one Bing Maps control on each form. If you need to show more than one map, consider using a web resource or an IFRAME.

Quick View Forms

Quick View forms are embedded in child forms to show data of parent records. This type of form includes one tab that has one column, which can have more than one section. Sections can have fields, subgrids, or spacers. Information that is shown in a Quick View form is read-only.

You can use a Quick View form to view parent account details or primary contact details on the Main form. If you select Insert > Quick View Form, you can select for which lookup field you want to see the Quick View form and then select the Quick View form (see Figure 22.20).

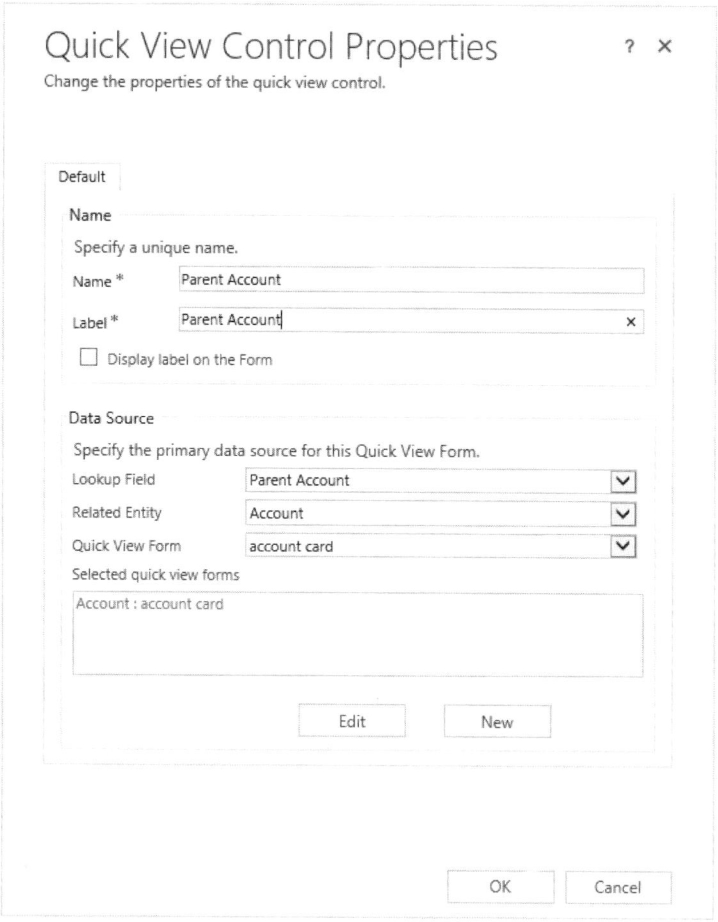

FIGURE 22.20   Embedding a Quick View form.

There is a special Quick View form in the system that you can customize, the Hierarchy Tile form. This form is available for the following entities:

▶ Account

▶ Position

▶ Product

▶ User

You can use the Hierarchy Tile form to customize the tiles shown in the hierarchy view of these entities.

Quick Create Forms

A Quick Create form is a shortened version of a form that includes important fields for creating a record. A Quick Create form does not have any subgrids or other components. It has one tab with three columns, and each column has a single-column section.

When you click + on the top navigation bar, you see a list of entities. If you select the Account entity, you are then presented with a Quick Create form, as shown in Figure 22.21.

FIGURE 22.21   Quick Create form for an account.

TIP

You can have multiple Quick Create forms; however, only one will be displayed to the user. If you create a new Quick Create form for an entity that is not listed here, make sure the entity has the Allow Quick Create option set in the entity properties.

Card Form

The Card form is a new type of form in Dynamics CRM 2016. This type of form is used in the interactive service hub.

▶ For more information about the interactive service hub, refer to **CHAPTER 11**, "The Interactive Service Hub".

Main-interactive Experience

The Main-interactive Experience form is a new type of form in Dynamics CRM 2016. This type of form is used in the interactive service hub. The following sections describe the customizations you can make to these forms.

Editing the Form Navigation   You can easily modify the form navigation links without having to touch the Site Map directly. By clicking the Navigation button, you can remove or add links to the form navigation bar.

Changing Form Properties   Here you have access to the general form properties. These properties are not visible to the user; they include such events as form assistance integration and nonevent dependencies fields.

Previewing Form Customizations   Dynamics CRM 2016 has enhanced the Preview form features, which allow a user to preview form changes in the mobile client without having to go to a mobile device and then preview the changes in the desktop computer.

After you complete your customizations to a form, you can easily preview them by clicking the Preview button and choosing either Desktop Client or Mobile Client and then selecting a form mode option.

For the desktop client you can select Create Form, Update Form, or Read-Only Form.

For the mobile client you can select Tablet or Phone, as shown in Figure 22.22.

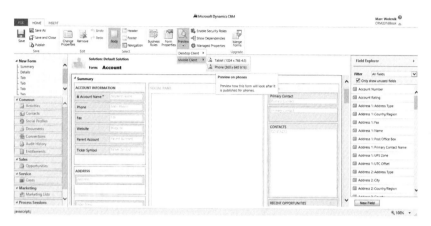

FIGURE 22.22   Preview menu items for the mobile client.

Selecting one of the mobile options takes you to the mobile preview screen, which first downloads the metadata changes. Once the metadata is loaded, which might take a few minutes, you get an emulator screen, as shown in Figure 22.23.

FIGURE 22.23   Preview for the mobile client.

You can easily switch from Phone to Table without leaving the emulator screen by using the icons next to Platform in the top-right corner of the emulator. Notice that this is not a full phone or tablet emulator where you can run other apps; this emulator has limited interaction, and its only purpose is to help you preview the forms in mobile devices.

▶ Refer to **CHAPTER 18**, "Mobility," for more information about mobile client features and visual controls.

When you are done with the customizations, you can click Save and Close to save your work.

> **NOTE**
>
> Customizations to the forms will not be visible and usable by users until they are published. See the "Publishing Customizations" section on the next page for how to do this.

View Customizations

A view is a read-only representation of an entity's records. It shows just a few of the entity's fields. You can see views in the Advanced Find results and in the Look Up Records results.

Several different types of views are created by default for each entity, and you can easily create new views. For each view, you can customize the fields to be displayed by adding, removing, or changing the display position of the columns. You can also set the desired width, in pixels, for each column. By default, the columns have a fixed width of 100 pixels, and the options available for column width are fixed at 25px, 50px, 75px, 100px, 125px, 150px, 200px, and 300px.

Publishing Customizations

When you have completed your desired changes to an entity, you must publish the customizations so that users can see and use them. To publish, select the entity you want to publish and then click either Publish on the entity/form you're working with or the Publish All Customizations button.

> **NOTE**
>
> If you delete an entity or a field, you don't need to publish the customizations. The deleted entity or field will be unavailable to users as soon as you delete it.
>
> After you make a customization to either a form or a view, you must publish it in order for users to see the change.

Preparing Client Customizations

Update 0.1 of Dynamics CRM 2016 introduced a new option for deployments which is used to improve the performance experience for mobile clients and with the interactive service hub. Users must wait for all the metadata updates after you publish the customizations, but clicking this option makes that wait time shorter.

Menu and Command Bar Customizations

Ribbons in CRM 2011 were replaced by a command bar in CRM 2013, and CRM 2016 still uses the command bar.

> **NOTE**
>
> The ribbon is still present in nonrefreshed entity forms such as Connection and in the list view in Microsoft Outlook.

The command bar still uses the RibbonDiffXML structure, but it is rendered differently in the user interface.

You can customize the navigation bar and controls in three ways:

- ▶ Site Map
- ▶ ISV Config
- ▶ Command bars

All three of these methods require a little knowledge about managing XML files. When working with XML files, remember the following rules:

- ▶ XML files are case sensitive, so be sure to respect the case of each node name to avoid problems. For example, the node name <root> is not the same as <ROOT>.
- ▶ Each node needs to be closed. For example, if you open a node with <root>, you need to later close it with </root>. If the node doesn't contain child nodes, you can open and close it in the same line (for example, <root />).

> **NOTE**
>
> For more information about working with XML files and their specifications, visit www.w3.org.

> **TIP**
>
> Although XML files can be edited with any text editor, such as Notepad, I recommend using a richer text editor, such as Visual Studio. From there, you can see the nodes colored, and you can also expand and collapse the nodes. In addition, you can take advantage of IntelliSense by assigning the schema files included in the CRM SDK, in the SDK\Schemas folder, and using the CustomizationsSolution.xsd file.

Site Map

The Site Map is the file that describes the items that will be shown in each area. For example, when you are in the Sales area, you can select any of these options: Dashboard,

Activities, Calendar, Imports, and so on. These options are quick links to the entity's administration that you can customize when you want to have another frequently used entity.

The Site Map is an XML file that needs to be exported first to be edited, and then it needs to be reimported to be updated. It is recommended that you create a new custom solution with only the Site Map extension to update the Site Map quickly. Go to Settings > Solutions > New, enter the display name for your solution, press Tab to quickly populate the Name field, select the publisher and enter the Version number, and click Save. Then select the view Client Extensions, as shown in Figure 22.24.

FIGURE 22.24   Locating the Site Map customization by using the Client Extensions view.

NOTE

To make changes to the Site Map without having to touch the XML directly, I recommend the CRM Sitemap Editor tool that you can download for free from www.crmsolutionmanager. com/Download.aspx.

▶ For more information about exporting the Site Map, **SEE** the "Exporting and Importing Entity Customizations" section, later in this chapter.

The following code illustrates the Site Map node structure:

```
<Site Map>
        <Site Map>
            <Area>
                <Group>
                    <SubArea>
```

Site Map Node

Site Map is the main and root entry-level node. Inside this node is another node with the same name, Site Map, which contains all the Area nodes as children.

Area Node

Each Area node provides the main navigation buttons displayed on the main interface. By default, the Site Map is configured with five main areas:

▶ Sales

▶ Service

▶ Marketing

▶ Settings

▶ Help Center

The following code illustrates the Area node with its default attributes for the Sales area:

```
<Area Id="SFA" ResourceId="Area_Sales" DescriptionResourceId="Sales_Description"
Icon="/_imgs/sales_24x24.gif" ShowGroups="true" IntroducedVersion="7.0.0.0">
```

These are the attributes of the Sales area node:

▶ **Id**—This is the unique identifier for each area.

▶ **ResourceId**—This is the resource identifier.

▶ **ShowGroups**—This attribute is necessary only if the area has more than one group child node.

▶ **Icon**—This is the URL for the icon to be displayed near the area title.

▶ **DescriptionResourceId**—This is for internal use only.

▶ **IntroducedVersion**—This gives the version where this area was introduced; 7.0.0.0 means CRM 2015, and 8.0.0.0 means CRM 2016.

Group Node

The Group node contains a group of SubArea nodes. Each group is displayed in the navigation bar. Types of groups include My Work and Customers, which are included by default in the Sales area.

SubArea Node

A SubArea node is used to provide a link to a page or website (configured by its URL) inside a Group section.

Suppose, for example, that you want to add a new area to the Site Map called Webfortis to be used as a collection of links related to the organization and external application. You could edit the Site Map by adding the code in Listing 22.1 to the Site Map file right after the last `</Area>` node and before the `</SiteMap>`.

LISTING 22.1   Adding a New Area to a Site Map

```
<Area Id="WebfortisArea" Title="Webfortis" ShowGroups="true"
Icon="/_imgs/resourcecenter_24x24.gif" >
        <Group Id="Group1" Title="External">
                <SubArea Id="nav_SubArea1" Title="Website"
Icon="/_imgs/ico_18_129.gif" Url="http://www.webfortis.com" />
                <SubArea Id="nav_SubArea2"  Title="Microsoft"
Icon="/_imgs/ico_16_sales.gif" Url="http://www.microsoft.com"
AvailableOffline="false" />
        </Group>
        <Group Id="Group2" Title="Internal">
                <SubArea Id="nav_SubArea11" Title="Intranet"
Icon="/_imgs/ico_18_129.gif" Url="http://www.webfortis.com/Internal"
AvailableOffline="false" />
                <SubArea Id="nav_SubArea12" Title="Cost Control"
Icon="/_imgs/ico_16_sales.gif" Url="http://www.webfortis.com/CC"
AvailableOffline="false" />
        </Group>
</Area>
```

Next, you save the changes and import the solution that contains the Site Map. To import the Site Map customizations, go to Settings > Solutions > Import. Then upload the customizations you edited and click the Import Selected Customizations button.

▶ For detailed instructions on how to import Site Map customizations, **SEE** the "Exporting and Importing Entity Customizations" section, later in this chapter.

NOTE

Important considerations when adding a new Area, Group, or SubArea are to be sure to use unique names for the Id attributes and to not use the ResourceId and DescriptionResourceId attributes in your custom elements (because they are for internal use only). Instead, use the Titles and Title elements to display the text for the different languages.

ISV Config

ISV Config is an XML structure that is part of the customizations.xml file included in every solution. The only functionality of ISV Config is to provide the appearance and behavior of the Service Calendar.

To be able to work with the ISV Config XML, you need to explicitly specify it when importing the solution by selecting the ISV Config option, as shown in Figure 22.25.

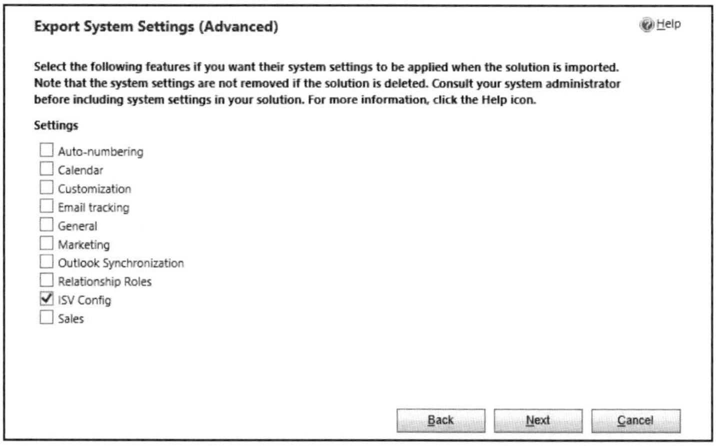

Export System Settings (Advanced)   ⊘ Help

Select the following features if you want their system settings to be applied when the solution is imported.
Note that the system settings are not removed if the solution is deleted. Consult your system administrator
before including system settings in your solution. For more information, click the Help icon.

Settings

☐ Auto-numbering
☐ Calendar
☐ Customization
☐ Email tracking
☐ General
☐ Marketing
☐ Outlook Synchronization
☐ Relationship Roles
☑ ISV Config
☐ Sales

  [Back] [Next] [Cancel]

FIGURE 22.25   Export System Settings dialog, choosing ISV Config.

Notice that because ISV Config is considered a system setting, any customization made here is not removed when you remove the solution. Listing 22.2 illustrates the main node structure in the ISV Config XML.

LISTING 22.2   Main Node Structure for the ISV Config XML

```
<IsvConfig>
    <configuration version="3.0.0000.0">
      <Root />
      <ServiceManagement>
        <AppointmentBook>
           <SmoothScrollLimit>2000</SmoothScrollLimit>
           <TimeBlocks>
             <TimeBlock EntityType="4214" StatusCode="1"
CssClass="ganttBlockServiceActivityStatus1" />
             <TimeBlock EntityType="4214" StatusCode="2"
CssClass="ganttBlockServiceActivityStatus2" />
             <TimeBlock EntityType="4214" StatusCode="3"
CssClass="ganttBlockServiceActivityStatus3" />
             <TimeBlock EntityType="4214" StatusCode="4"
CssClass="ganttBlockServiceActivityStatus4" />
             <TimeBlock EntityType="4214" StatusCode="6"
CssClass="ganttBlockServiceActivityStatus6" />
             <TimeBlock EntityType="4214" StatusCode="7"
CssClass="ganttBlockServiceActivityStatus7" />
             <TimeBlock EntityType="4214" StatusCode="8"
CssClass="ganttBlockServiceActivityStatus8" />
             <TimeBlock EntityType="4214" StatusCode="9"
CssClass="ganttBlockServiceActivityStatus9" />
             <TimeBlock EntityType="4214" StatusCode="10"
```

```
CssClass="ganttBlockServiceActivityStatus10" />
            <TimeBlock EntityType="4201" StatusCode="1"
CssClass="ganttBlockAppointmentStatus1" />
            <TimeBlock EntityType="4201" StatusCode="2"
CssClass="ganttBlockAppointmentStatus2" />
            <TimeBlock EntityType="4201" StatusCode="3"
CssClass="ganttBlockAppointmentStatus3" />
            <TimeBlock EntityType="4201" StatusCode="4"
CssClass="ganttBlockAppointmentStatus4" />
            <TimeBlock EntityType="4201" StatusCode="5"
CssClass="ganttBlockAppointmentStatus5" />
            <TimeBlock EntityType="4201" StatusCode="6"
CssClass="ganttBlockAppointmentStatus6" />
          </TimeBlocks>
        </AppointmentBook>
      </ServiceManagement>
    </configuration>
  </IsvConfig>
```

ServiceManagement Node

The ServiceManagement node customizes the service calendar. The ServiceManagement node contains only a child node with the name AppointmentBook.

The AppointmentBook node can have one of these nodes:

▶ **SmoothScrollLimit**—This option sets the maximum number of blocks to be displayed by a service activity before autoscrolling the appointment when it is selected or displayed.

▶ **ValidationChunkSize**—This option is used to configure the number of activities to be validated simultaneously by the server. The validation occurs in cases where more than one activity requires the same resources or materials.

▶ **TimeBlocks**—This is the reserved time during which a service can start.

▶ Refer to **CHAPTER 10**, "Working with Service," for more information about the `ServiceManagement` node.

With each TimeBlock element, you can apply a different style to each status code of a service activity. Consider this example:

```
<ServiceManagement>
  <AppointmentBook>
    <SmoothScrollLimit>2000</SmoothScrollLimit>
    <TimeBlocks>
      <!-- All CSS Class mapping for Service activities -->
```

```
    <TimeBlock EntityType="4214" StatusCode="1"
[ccc]CssClass="ganttBlockServiceActivityStatus1" />
    </TimeBlocks>
  </AppointmentBook>
</ServiceManagement>
```

The EntityType attribute can be one of the following values:

▶ **4214**—Service activity

▶ **4201**—Appointment

The Command Bar

As mentioned earlier in this chapter, CRM 2016 uses a command bar rather than a ribbon. You can customize the Dynamics CRM command bar by adding custom buttons. The command bar provides a new way of displaying buttons and provides better performance. Command bars are located three main places:

▶ **Grid (Mscrm.HomepageGrid)**—HomepageGrid is located in the home page of any entity where the main grid is located.

▶ **Subgrid (Mscrm.SubGrid)**—The command bar for subgrids located on forms.

▶ **Form (Mscrm.Form)**—The entity record shows the command bar located on the top of the form.

Adding a simple button to a command bar involves editing the customization file to include nodes in the RibbonDiffXml node, adding web resources for the images to be displayed in the button, and adding a web resource for the JavaScript method to be used when clicking the button.

> **NOTE**
>
> Much like editing the Site Map, as was discussed earlier in this chapter, I recommend using a visual ribbon editor for easier modifications. The Ribbon Workbench is one such tool, and it's available at www.develop1.net/public/Download%20Ribbon%20Workbench%202013.aspx.

Command Bar Buttons

The command bar can show a maximum of nine buttons at any time, with the rest moving to the overflow (ellipsis) section. This is a welcome enhancement to previous versions, which showed a maximum of five or seven. The command bar does not display a button if it is disabled, and because the command buttons are smart and can change while the user is using the application, there are some rules that need to be configured for this case so that you can make a button visible or enabled, depending on the following conditions:

▶ **Based on form state**—The Create, Existing, Read Only, Disabled, and Bulk Edit buttons are enabled or disabled based on form state.

▶ **Configure custom rules**—You can write custom rules by using JavaScript functions with the following parameters:

   ▶ **CrmClientTypeRule**—Detects whether running in the Outlook client or web client.

   ▶ **CommandClientTypeRule**—Detects whether running in the Outlook client, the CRM for tablets client, or the web client.

   ▶ **CrmOfflineAccessStateRule**—Detects whether Outlook is running in offline or online mode.

   ▶ **CrmOutlookClientTypeRule**—Types CrmForOutlook or CrmForOutlookOfflineAccess.

   ▶ **OrRule**—Contains a collection of rules so that this rule evaluates as true if any of the rules in the collection evaluates as true.

   ▶ **OutlookItemTrackingRule**—Detects whether the item is enabled for items tracked in Microsoft Dynamics CRM to enable a ribbon element.

   ▶ **OutlookVersionRule**—Detects the version of the Microsoft Office Outlook client.

   ▶ **PageRule**—Evaluates the address of the current page.

   ▶ **RecordPrivilegeRule**—Detects a user's privileges for a specific record in order to enable a ribbon element.

   ▶ **SkuRule**—Detects the Microsoft Dynamics CRM edition.

   ▶ **ValueRule**—Detects the value of a specific field.

   ▶ **ReferencingAttributeRequiredRule**—Detects whether the referencing attribute for an entity is required.

   ▶ **RelationshipTypeRule**—Detects whether a specific type of formal entity relationship exists between two entities.

   ▶ **EntityPrivilegeRule**—Detects the current user's privileges for a specific entity.

   ▶ **EntityPropertyRule**—Detects specific Boolean entity properties.

   ▶ **FormEntityContextRule**—Detects whether a form ribbon is displayed in the context of a specific entity.

   ▶ **HideForTabletExperienceRule**—Specifies when the web application is viewed in a mobile browser on a tablet device.

   ▶ **MiscellaneousPrivilegeRule**—Detects whether the user possesses a specific Microsoft Dynamics CRM privilege.

   ▶ **OrganizationSettingRule**—Detects two specific organization settings within a DisplayRule: IsSharepointEnabled and IsSOPIntegrationEnabled.

▶ **OutlookRenderTypeRule**—Detects whether a form or list item is rendered as a web page or natively in Outlook in order to determine whether a ribbon element should be displayed.

▶ **SelectionCountRule**—Detects how many items in a grid are selected.

The display rule named `CommandClientTypeRule` shows buttons on the command bar if they do not have any `CommandClientTypeRule` associated with them, and if associated, they should have `Type="Refresh"`. The `Type` property can have the following values:

▶ `Modern`—The button is visible in tablets.

▶ `Refresh`—The button is presented using an updated interface (that is, the command bar).

▶ `Legacy`—The button is visible on nonrefreshed entities such as Connection and in the list view of Microsoft Outlook.

The SDK comes with samples that help you easily add custom buttons to an existing group for all entities or add custom buttons to an existing group for specific entities. In addition, you can add custom groups to an existing tab for a specific entity, add a custom tab to a specific entity, add custom groups to the Developer tab for all entities in a form, and hide ribbon elements. The SDK includes all the XML files for the system entity ribbons, in the SDK\Resources\ExportedRibbonXml folder.

NOTE

There is also a good source code sample called ExportRibbonXml in the SDK, in the SDK\SampleCode\CS\Client\Ribbon folder. It exports all the entities' XML ribbon data so that you can use it to easily locate each ribbon tab, group, or button.

RibbonDiffXml

The RibbonDiffXml node defines the tabs, groups, and buttons, and it contains the following child nodes:

```
<RibbonDiffXml>
        <CustomActions />
        <Templates>
          <RibbonTemplates Id="Mscrm.Templates"></RibbonTemplates>
        </Templates>
        <CommandDefinitions />
        <RuleDefinitions>
          <TabDisplayRules />
          <DisplayRules />
          <EnableRules />
        </RuleDefinitions>
        <LocLabels />
</RibbonDiffXml>
```

The CustomActions node defines the tabs, groups, and buttons and contains the following child nodes:

```
<CustomActions>
  <CustomAction >
    <CommandUIDefinition>
        <Controls>
          <Button />
        </Controls>
    </CommandUIDefinition>
  </CustomAction>
</CustomActions>
```

The Button node contains the following attributes:

▶ **Id**—The unique identifier for the button.

▶ **Command**—The ID of the command that will be defined in the CommandDefinitions node of the RibbonDiffXml root node. Each command definition is defined as follows:

```
<CommandDefinitions>
  <CommandDefinition Id="Solution.all.HomepageGrid.MyGroup.Help.Command">
    <EnableRules />
    <DisplayRules />
    <Actions>
      <JavaScriptFunction FunctionName="ShowHelp"
Library="$webresource:webforti_Script.js" />
    </Actions>
  </CommandDefinition>
</CommandDefinitions>
```

Inside the command definitions, you can include the rules for enabling or disabling the buttons (inside the EnableRules node), and you can show or hide the buttons (in the DisplayRules node) and the actions to be performed when the button is clicked:

▶ **Sequence**—The integer number of the sequence to define the position of the button related to the other buttons in the same group.

▶ **LabelText**—The ID of the localized label that is defined inside the LocLabels node. Here is an example:

```
<RibbonDiffXml>
    ..................
    <LocLabels>
      <LocLabel Id="Solution.all.HomepageGrid.MyGroup.Help.ToolTip">
        <Titles>
          <Title languagecode="1033" description="Help" />
        </Titles>
```

```
      </LocLabel>
    </LocLabels>
  </RibbonDiffXml>
```

Inside the Titles node, you can enter as many Titles node languages as you want. In this example, `languagecode="1033"` refers to the English language.

22

> **NOTE**
>
> For a complete list of language codes, see http://msdn.microsoft.com/en-us/library/0h88fahh.aspx.

- ▶ `ToolTipTitle`—The ID of the localized label that is defined inside the LocLabels node, similar to the LabelText node.

- ▶ `ToolTipDescription`—The ID of the localized label that is defined inside the LocLabels node, similar to the LabelText node.

- ▶ `TemplateAlias`—The alias of the template to be used; this affects the way the button will be displayed; `o1` displays the button big, and `o2` displays the button small.

- ▶ `Image16by16`—The ID of the web resource used for the 16-by-16-pixel image. This is the image used for small buttons. If you use a web resource, you need to enter a value as follows: `$webresource:name of the web resource.png`.

- ▶ `Image32by32`—The ID of the web resource used for the 32-by-32-pixel image. This is the image used for big buttons. If you use a web resource, you need to enter a value as follows: `$webresource:name of the web resource.png`.

> **NOTE**
>
> You might wonder whether you need to use either the `Image16by16` or `Image32by32` attributes; however, it is recommended that you set both because some templates use one or the other, depending on the window's size.

JavaScript Events

JavaScript events are related to forms and the controls inside the forms only. Each form has `OnLoad` and `OnSave` events, which can accept JavaScript. Each field also has the `OnChange` event, which can also accept JavaScript. You can also add events for the `Tab` control to track the `TabStateChange` event and to IFRAMEs to track the `OnReadyState Complete` event (see Figure 22.26). Dynamics CRM 2011 supported the `crmForm.all` object collection, but CRM 2016 does not; instead, the Xrm.Page object collection is used for CRM 2016 JavaScript customizations.

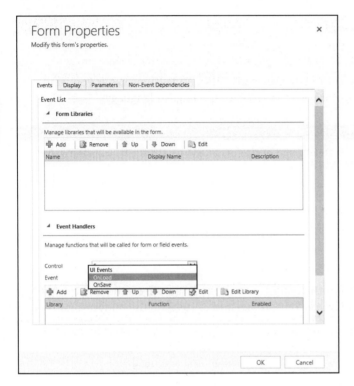

FIGURE 22.26   Form events that you can customize with JavaScript.

The list of JavaScript events is as follows:

▶ **OnLoad event**—Occurs every time the window of an entity is open, either when you edit an existing record or when you create a new one.

▶ **OnSave event**—Occurs every time the save icon or the Save and Close button is pressed.

▶ **OnChange event**—Fires every time the value of the field is changed and after it loses the focus.

▶ **TabStateChange event**—Occurs every time the user switches from one tab to the other.

▶ **OnReadyStateComplete event**—Fires when the content of the IFRAME has been loaded.

To start adding script to this event, you need to create a web resource of type JavaScript that you can use as a library where you can have a common repository for the event scripts you will handle. This allows you to reuse the JavaScript function on different forms and entities.

> **NOTE**
>
> Microsoft released a tool named the Custom Code Validation Tool. This tool lets you know which scripts don't work in CRM 2015/2016 (CRM 4.0 or 2013 code, some common DOM manipulations, and so on). You can download this tool from www.microsoft.com/en-us/download/details.aspx?id=45535. Notice while the tool says it is for CRM 2015, it works for CRM 2016.

22

Event-Handling Tips and Tricks

CRM releases since CRM 2011 Rollup 12 provide support for multiple browsers. You can run Dynamics CRM in any browser, including Internet Explorer, Firefox, Chrome, and Safari.

It used to be possible to easily access the DOM in JavaScript. This is not recommended now, though, because these scripts might work on one browser and not on another. As a result, you should not try to access DOM objects in your scripts. Instead, you can attach functions to the onChange event or field through form customization, or you can simply do the same thing by using the addOnChange method. Suppose that you have a custom entity called House to which you have added the following custom fields: Width, Height, and Area. In this case, you want to have the field area automatically change based on the width and height of the fields displayed. You could add the Listing 22.3 code in the OnLoad event to attach an onChange event to the field control.

LISTING 22.3   Attaching the onChange Event to a Field Control

```
function setupEvents()
{
 Xrm.Page.getAttribute("webforti_height").addOnChange(doCalc);
 Xrm.Page.getAttribute("webforti_width").addOnChange(doCalc);
}
function doCalc()
{
var area= Xrm.Page.getAttribute("webforti_height").getValue() * Xrm.Page.
getAttribute("webforti_width").getValue();
 Xrm.Page.getAttribute("webforti_area").setValue(area);
}
```

To see this example at work, follow these steps:

1. Go to Settings > Customizations > Solutions.

2. Create a new solution and go to Entities.

3. Click New to create a new entity.

4. Enter House in the Display Name field and Houses in the Plural Name field.

5. Click the Save button but do not close the window.

6. Click Fields from the Common section in left-side navigation.

7. Click the New button to add the custom field.

8. Enter Height in Display Name and select Whole Number in the Type field.

9. Click Save and Close to save the field.

10. Repeat steps 7 through 9, but this time enter Width as the Display Name.

11. Repeat steps 7 through 9, but this time enter Area as the Display Name.

12. Click Fields from the Common section in left-side navigation.

13. Double-click the Information Main type form record to edit it.

14. Drag and drop the new attributes you created: Height, Width, and Area.

TIP

Click the General section and double-click the fields to easily add them to the section.

---

15. Click Form Properties on the Home tab of the ribbon. The Form Properties dialog appears (see Figure 22.27).

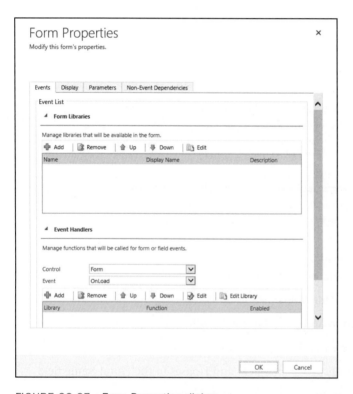

FIGURE 22.27   Form Properties dialog.

16. Click Add in the Form Libraries section. The Look Up Record dialog appears (see Figure 22.28).

FIGURE 22.28   Web resources lookup.

17. Click New to create a new JavaScript file.

18. Enter mainlib.js in the Name and Display Name fields and select the Script (JScript) type, as shown in Figure 22.29.

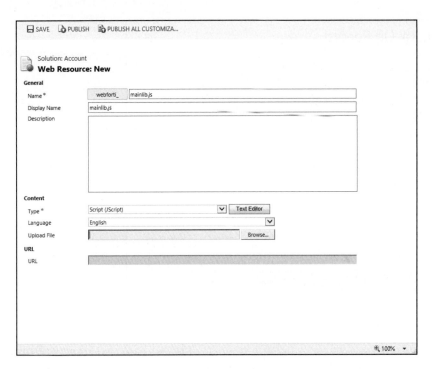

FIGURE 22.29   Creating a new JavaScript web resource.

19. Click Text Editor and enter the code in Listing 22.4, as shown in Figure 22.30.

LISTING 22.4   Code for the JavaScript Web Resource Event

```
function setupEvents()
{
 Xrm.Page.getAttribute("webforti_height").addOnChange(doCalc);
 Xrm.Page.getAttribute("webforti_width").addOnChange(doCalc);
}
function doCalc()
{
var area= Xrm.Page.getAttribute("webforti_height").getValue() * Xrm.Page.
getAttribute("webforti_width").getValue();
 Xrm.Page.getAttribute("webforti_area").setValue(area);
}
```

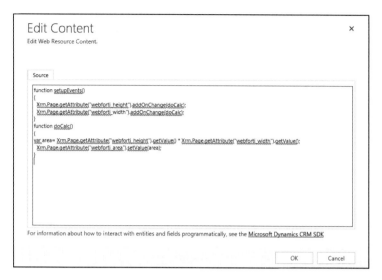

FIGURE 22.30   Adding code to the JavaScript web resource event.

20. Click the OK button to close the text editor.

21. Click Save, click Publish, and then close the Web Resource dialog.

22. Select the new web resource you created and click Add.

23. In the form library you added, go to the event handlers and set Control to Form and Event to OnLoad. Click Add.

24. Type setupEvents in the Function field (see Figure 22.31).

FIGURE 22.31   Handler Properties dialog box.

25. Click OK to close the Handler Properties dialog. Click OK to close the Form Properties dialog.

26. To test the code, select Preview > Create Form. Alternatively, you can publish all the customization and view the entity directly.

27. Enter a value on the Height field (for example, 10) and enter a value to the Width field (for example, 10). The Area field is set automatically with the calculated result, 100.

NOTE

Notice that the field names might vary depending on the solution prefix, which is set on the Publisher record that is associated to the solution (and is limited to eight characters). This example uses webforti_, but you might use new_ or some other prefix.

When working with JavaScript code, it is important to publish the JavaScript web resource every time you make a change to it so that you can preview your changes.

Tips and Tricks When Working with Events

When you work with JavaScript code, you encounter some disadvantages of using the regular web interface:

▶ The interface lacks IntelliSense.

▶ The JavaScript code is not colored for better understanding and manipulation.

▶ It is tedious to debug and correct errors in some situations when you can't use the preview feature to simulate your changes. Instead, you need to manipulate the code, save the changes, publish the updates, and then see whether it works as expected.

To avoid all these disadvantages, you can use a richer JavaScript editor, such as Visual Studio. When working with JavaScript in Visual Studio, having the script located in a separate web resource enables you to easily copy and paste the script from CRM to Visual Studio. That way you can get access to IntelliSense and colored code. A good technique for debugging scripts is to enable the Internet Explorer debugger. You can do this by going to Tools > Internet Options and selecting the Advanced tab. Be sure that you have unchecked the Disable Script Debugging (Internet Explorer) and Disable Script Debugging (Other) options.

When you have script debugging enabled, you can put the sentence debugger on your code to start the debugger. Here's an example:

```
function setupEvents()
{
debugger;
 Xrm.Page.getAttribute("webforti_height").addOnChange(doCalc);
 Xrm.Page.getAttribute("webforti_width").addOnChange(doCalc);
}
```

When you run this code on the `OnLoad` event, the dialog shown in Figure 22.32 opens, enabling you to select the debugger you want—in case you have Visual Studio installed on your machine.

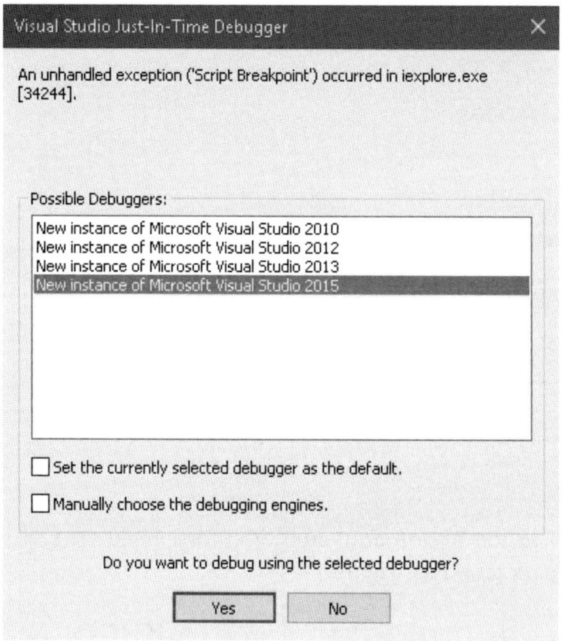

FIGURE 22.32   Launching a debugger from JavaScript code.

This is a good technique for debugging JavaScript code because normal users will have the script debugger disabled by default and won't get rich error messages that tell them exactly what broke.

TIP

A good utility for working with JavaScript customizations is the Internet Explorer Developer Tools, available inside Internet Explorer. Just press the F12 key while in Internet Explorer.

Calculated Fields

This section shows the same example from the preceding sections but this time using calculated fields. The new calculated field feature allows you to get the solution shown before but without doing any JavaScript development.

Go to Fields and create a new calculated field with the name Calculated Area, with the Data Type field set to Whole Number, as shown in Figure 22.33.

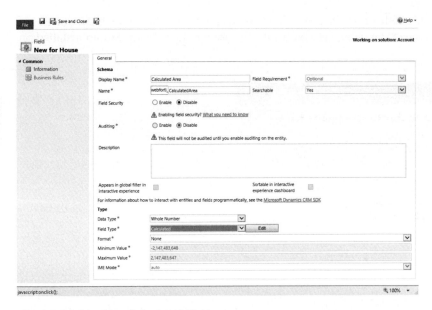

FIGURE 22.33   New Calculated Field.

Click Edit button, then under Action, Click Add Action and enter "webforti_height * webforti_width" and click on the checkmark icon (see Figure 22.34).

Click Save and Close.

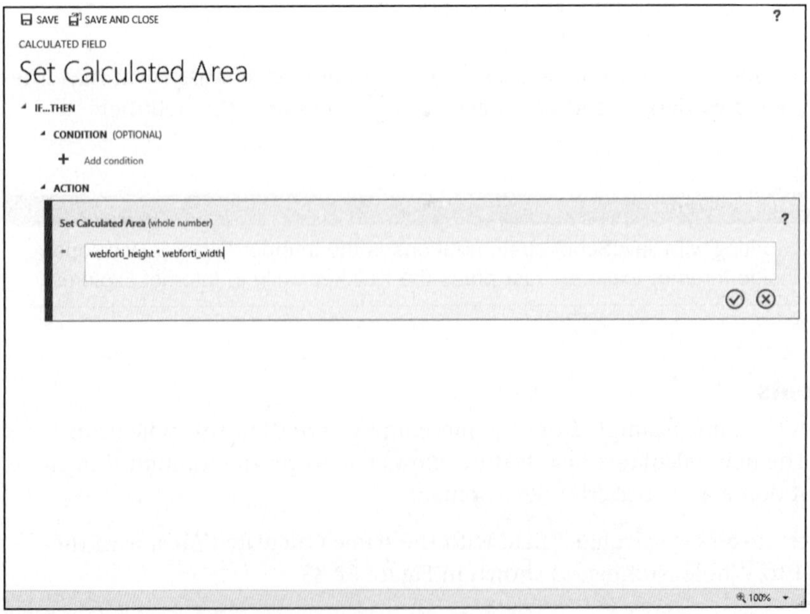

FIGURE 22.34   Calculated formula.

Add the new field to the form and try it. You see the calculated Area field updated as soon as you save the record. The field is read-only, preventing other users from manually entering values there.

Business Rules

Business rules give non-developer users the ability to add logic to fields without adding JavaScript code. Before business rules, simple logic required some knowledge of JavaScript. Even if you have good knowledge of JavaScript already, it's worth getting a good understanding of the business rules because they can save a lot of time. Business rules can be run in the server scope, doing work that custom plug-ins used to be required to do.

You can access to the business rules in different ways. One way is to open a solution and expand Entities and then a specific entity, as shown in Figure 22.35.

FIGURE 22.35   Business rules from a solution.

Another way to access the business rules is to open a form and click the Business Rules button on the Home tab of the ribbon.

If you click the New Business Rule button in the bottom-right corner of a form, you can create a business rule for that form. Later, you can change the scope, which can be any of the following.

▶ Entity (server and client)

▶ All forms (client only)

▶ Specific form (client only)

A business rule must have a name, and it must be activated in order to be used by users. When you create a new business rule, it starts in a draft state, where you can add conditions and actions. Activating the business rule makes the business rule read-only so no changes can be made while the rule is active. Remember to publish all customizations after activating a business rule.

The conditions used by business rules are similar to the conditions you find in the Advanced Find tool with the exception that you can compare fields with other field values.

You can use business rules to do the following actions:

▶ Show error messages.

▶ Set a field value.

▶ Set a rule as required.

▶ Set visibility. You can show or hide a field based on a condition.

▶ Set default values. You can set a default value based on a condition.

▶ Lock or unlock a field.

Showing Error Messages

You can use a business rule to show an error message based on a condition or validation. Figure 22.36 shows how to design a business rule using this action.

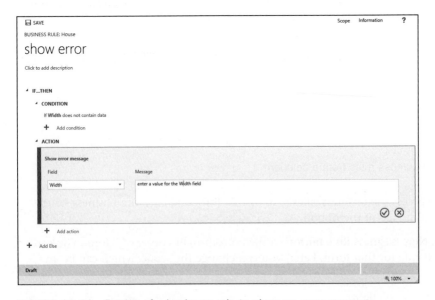

FIGURE 22.36   Design of a business rule to show an error message.

Once the business rule is activated, the user sees the error shown in Figure 22.37.

FIGURE 22.37   Business rule showing an error message in action.

The error and logic validation are shown before and/or after the form is saved, preventing invalid data from being inserted or updated to the CRM system.

NOTE

Notice that if you create this error message business rule and have the scope set to Entity, any application that tries to create or update an entity with a business rule triggers the error message.

Setting a Field Value

You can use a business rule to set a value for a field, based on a condition. You can set a fixed value or a constant, you can set the value of another field, and depending of the type of the field, you can use formulas or can clear the value to make the field blank.

Using the same example used earlier for JavaScript and the calculated field, you can now calculate the area of a house by using a business rule, as shown in Figure 22.38.

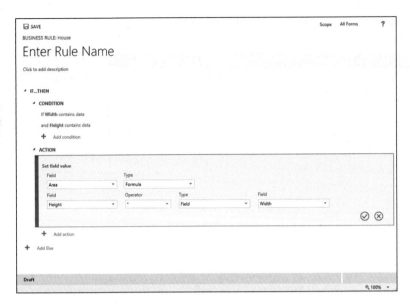

FIGURE 22.38   Set Field Value action.

Making a Field Required

You can use a business rule to makes a field required or not required, based on a condition. This action can be useful if you want a field to be required in one form and not in other forms. Or you can make a field required only if another field has a value, based on a condition (see Figure 22.39).

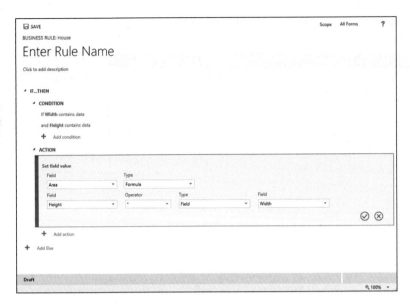

FIGURE 22.39   Set Business Required action.

Setting Visibility

You can use a business rule to show or hide fields based on conditions. The Set Visibility action has no effect on the server side when you set the Entity scope as it is applied only when a form is loaded in the web client or the mobile client (see Figure 22.40).

FIGURE 22.40   Set Visibility action.

Setting Default Values

You can use a business rule to set a default value for a field, based on a condition. You can set a fixed value or a constant, you can set the value of another field, and depending of the type of the field, you can use formulas or can clear the value to make the field blank.

You may wonder why there are two similar actions—Set Field Value and Set Default Value—and when to use each one. The answer is simple: You use Set Default Value to initialize fields that then can be replaced by values entered by the user; using Set Field Value may overwrite users' entries when evaluating the business logic every time a record is loaded on a form. This was a common issue users faced in older versions of Dynamics CRM, such as CRM 2013, which don't include the Set Default Value action.

Locking or Unlocking a Field

You can use a business rule to set a field as read-only, based on a condition. In this case, you must select a field and a status, which can be either Lock or Unlock.

Exporting and Importing Entity Customizations

You can export all customizations made on any entity out of the CRM system to be used on other CRM implementations or for backup purposes. You can achieve this by using solutions.

▶ Refer to the section "Solution Concepts," later in this chapter, for more details about how to work with solutions, as well as how to export and import customizations as part of solutions.

> **NOTE**
>
> An important consideration when importing customizations is that they can only add or append new attributes to existing entities and don't delete any missing attribute or data. So there is no risk of losing the data you or any other user added if you had previously added a new attribute and then you import an older version that does not include that attribute. However, any new fields you added to the form or the views are removed in this case.
>
> Another important consideration is that if you delete a managed solution, the new entities and data that belong to that solution are deleted. However, the data and entity are not deleted if you remove an unmanaged solution. To restore any custom entity you created with the data inside a custom solution, you must also manually delete the entity in the default solution.

When importing customizations for the Site Map, you might accidentally delete the Settings area or import an error file that breaks the web application. If that happens, you can use the following link to directly access the Import Customization interface to restore a backup and take the application to a good state, as shown in Figure 22.41: http://*servername:port/organizationname*/tools/systemcustomization/systemcustomization.aspx.

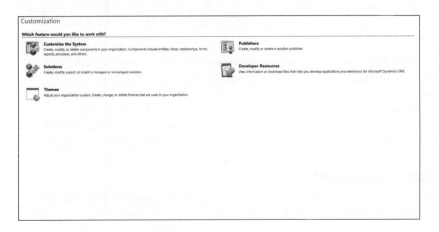

FIGURE 22.41   Customizations interface for recovering a broken application.

For example, the link for an On-Premises deployment might be as follows: http://crm2016/webfortis/tools/systemcustomization/systemcustomization.aspx. And the link for an Online deployment might be the following: https://webfortis2016.crm .dynamics.com/tools/systemcustomization/systemCustomization.aspx.

Solution Concepts

When making changes to a system, organizations typically need to modify entities' views or forms or modify and add new attributes to the entities (or even add new entities). These changes can be as small as adding or removing a desired field to completely changing how the system works with custom workflows and code. When making a change to the system, these changes are captured in a *solution*, which is a package that contains the changes. A system may have no custom solutions, or it may have many solutions. In addition, solutions can be used to interact with components from one another, and they may even be dependent on each other.

Many of the solutions that currently exist in CRM and xRM environments involve other pieces of software, such as plug-ins, reports, custom static/dynamic pages, images, scripts, Silverlight applications, templates, and web services, just to name a few.

Solutions help you in the deployment, support, upgrade, sale, and distribution of all the customizations you can think of. Each solution is compiled into a single zip file that contains the following components:

- ▶ Entities
- ▶ Option sets
- ▶ Client extensions
- ▶ Web resources
- ▶ Processes
- ▶ Plug-in assemblies
- ▶ SDK message processing steps
- ▶ Service endpoints
- ▶ Dashboards
- ▶ Reports
- ▶ Connection roles
- ▶ Article templates
- ▶ Contract templates
- ▶ Email templates
- ▶ Mail merge templates
- ▶ Security roles

▶ Field security profiles

▶ Routing rule sets

▶ Record creation and update rules

▶ SLAs

By default, each CRM organization has a base solution, known as the default solution, which cannot be deleted. To work with the default solution, go to Settings > Customizations and then click Customize the System, as shown in Figure 22.42.

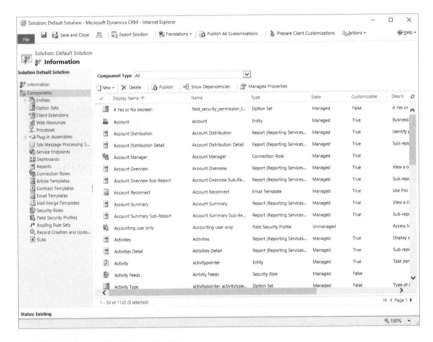

FIGURE 22.42   Default solution.

NOTE

Even though you can customize the default solution, it is strongly recommended that you not do this but instead create a custom solution and work with any customizations there. The reason for this is that a custom solution can easily be rolled back to its original state when needed, such as when it's imported as managed to another organization. Customizations in unmanaged solutions cannot be rolled back after the solution is removed.

Working with Custom Solutions

To work with custom solutions, go to Settings > Customization > Solutions, as shown in Figure 22.43.

FIGURE 22.43   Solutions.

To create a new solution, following these steps:

1. Click New. You see a screen similar to the one shown in Figure 22.44.

FIGURE 22.44   A new solution.

2. To create a new publisher, select Look Up More Records, select New, and complete the information on the form. (If this is the first time you have created a solution, you need to create a publisher for it or use the default publisher for the organization. For this example, I've created a new publisher, CRMPMG, but I still have the default one as an option.)

> **NOTE**
>
> Publishers are helpful in that they provide a mechanism for updating and managing solutions. Because you can control the prefix and option value, you can manage when and who creates a solution via the publisher, which is especially important when you're working with managed solutions.

> **NOTE**
>
> Even though the description is not required to create a publisher in CRM, it is required if you want to publish the solution to the Dynamics Marketplace, as you will see later in this chapter, so it is recommended that you enter a company description and fill in all the fields in the Contact Details tab (for phone number, email, website, address, state, city, and country).

> **TIP**
>
> To see the list of publishers, go to Settings > Customizations and then click Publishers.

3. In the Look Up Record dialog, because the new publisher you created in the previous step is selected by default, click OK.

4. Enter a display name, a name, and a version for your solution. Note that you can press the Tab key after entering the display name to autopopulate the Name field, but you can change this if desired.

> **TIP**
>
> The version number is not autopopulated, so you should expect to enter a value here.

5. Click Save to enable all the items in the left-side navigation area.

Each solution can contain a configuration page, which is a web resource that can be used to provide general settings as well as license keys configured for independent software vendor (ISV) providers. Those license keys can be managed and verified using custom plug-ins.

As with the Publisher description, the Solution description is not required for creating
a solution in CRM. However, it is required if you want to publish the solution to
the Dynamics Marketplace.

To create a configuration page, create an HTML file and add it as a web resource to the
solution. To do this, click Web Resources > New, enter a name and a display name for the
configuration page, select Webpage (HTML) as the type in the Content area, and then
select the language and upload the HTML file you created (see Figure 22.45).

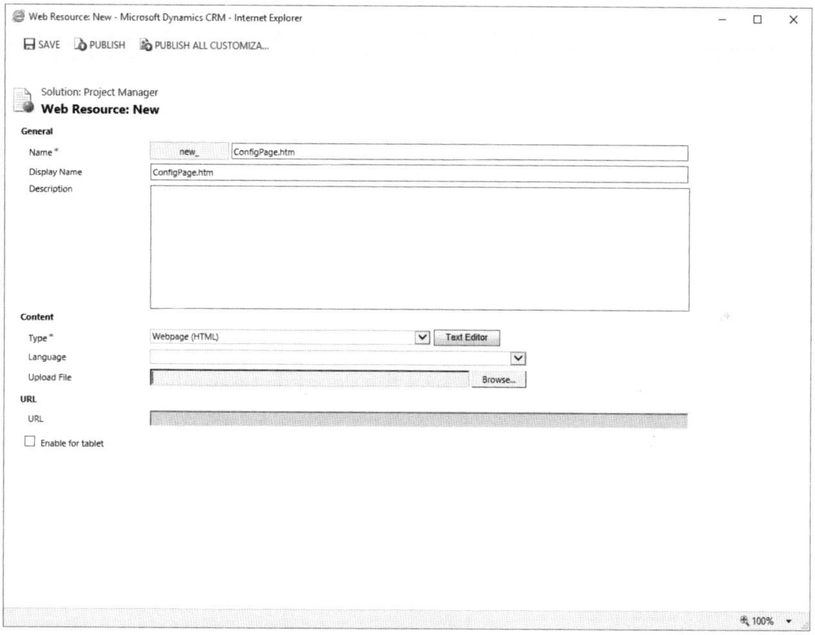

FIGURE 22.45   Creating a configuration page.

Then click Save and Close, and you can click the Information link to assign the
configuration page to your solution.

You must publish the new HTML web resource before assigning the configuration page, or
you will get an error when you try to work with the resource.

Click Save, and you see that the configuration page can now be accessed from a new link
that appears in left-side navigation area, with the name Configuration.

Solution components share some functions, and some others depend on the component
type. The functions shared by all components are discussed in the following subsections.

Adding Required Components

The Add Required Components function is available on all component types and requires you to select a component from the list before you can use it. It is useful, for example, when you create a dashboard that contains a chart on the Account entity or any other system or managed entity. Clicking the Add Required Components button adds the Account entity to the entity's components so that you can be sure it will be part of the solution.

The same happens with reports and processes. If you have a workflow that needs to create a record of any of the system entities, the Add Required Components feature adds that entity to the entity's component.

> **NOTE**
>
> Note that the Add Required Components function does not work for custom code, where you can add web resources with JavaScript or by calling the CRM web services from an event of a form or field.

Showing Dependencies

New in Dynamics CRM 2016 is the addition of the Show Dependencies button, which quickly shows you the decencies for the selected component so you can evaluate them before clicking Add Required Components. This function is useful when you want to delete a custom component because the CRM system won't let you do it if you have dependencies on that component. Figure 22.46 shows the dependencies for the custom House entity.

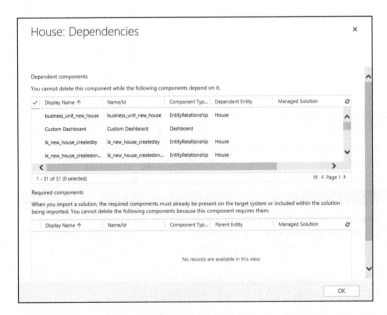

FIGURE 22.46   Showing dependencies for the custom House entity.

This option is also available when you are in the form editor. If you click the Show Dependencies button there, you see any web resource you may have referenced that the forms depends on.

Managed Properties

There are two types of solutions: managed and unmanaged. Unmanaged solutions are used for development, whereas managed solutions are used for distribution. These are explained further later in this chapter, in the section "Best Practices When Working with Solutions."

Each component on an unmanaged solution has some properties, called managed properties, that depend on the component type selected. These properties enable you to specify the ability you want to give to the end users when the solution is exported as managed and then imported to another organization.

Figure 22.47 shows the managed properties you can set on a custom entity when the Managed Properties button is clicked.

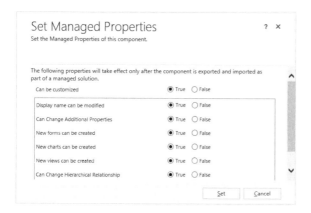

FIGURE 22.47   Managed properties.

If you set the first option, Can Be Customized, to False, all the other options are disabled. Notice that by default any customization you make will have this option set to True, which means any person who implements your solution can make further customization, so it is a good idea to change these values if you want to protect your customization.

For each solution component, you can perform some functions that depend on the component type. For example, you can create new entities from the solution form, new option sets, new security roles, new processes, new reports, new templates, new dashboards, new web resources, new connection roles, and new field security profiles. But you cannot create new client extensions, plug-ins, SDK message processing steps, or service endpoints.

Plug-ins

If you want to include a plug-in in a solution, you must create the plug-in first in Visual Studio and then register it with the Plug-in Registration Tool.

▶ Refer to **CHAPTER 25**, "Plug-ins," for details on working with plug-ins.

After you successfully register a plug-in, you can go to the solution form, click the Plug-in Assemblies node, and click the Add Existing button to include the plug-in on your solution (see Figure 22.48).

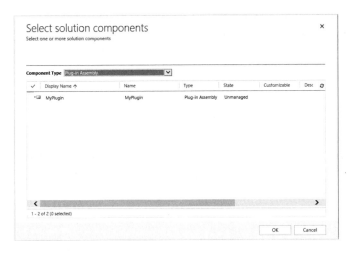

FIGURE 22.48   Adding plug-ins to a solution.

> **TIP**
>
> On the Plug-in Assembly tab, you see the button How to Register Assemblies. It takes you to the MSDN website, to a detailed walkthrough about how to register plug-ins.

Keep in mind that plug-ins don't support managed properties, and with managed properties, the Add Required Components button doesn't work. If a plug-in refers to any entity that is missing from the solution, you have to add it manually.

When you add a plug-in to a solution, you don't necessarily add all the steps you registered. If you only add the plug-in, export the solution, and implement your package on another CRM 2016 organization, the plug-in won't work as expected because there wasn't a step registered for the plug-in. This means you have to also include the steps you want to include on your solution right after adding the plug-in to the solution. To add the steps, you need to go to the solution form, click the Sdk Message Processing Step node, and then click the Add Existing button. Then select the steps you want to register, as shown in Figure 22.49.

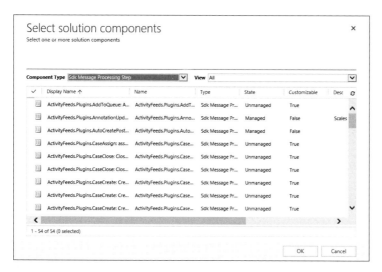

FIGURE 22.49   Adding SDK message processing steps to a solution.

When adding the steps, you are also asked to include the required components associated with the steps. For example, if you have a step created for the Create event of the Account entity, you should include the Account entity in your solution.

Best Practices When Working with Solutions

Although every Dynamics CRM organization has a default solution from which to start making customizations, I recommend making a backup of this solution by exporting it before you start making any customizations. Then you can customize a fresh CRM deployment. Keep in mind that any customization you make inside a custom solution will also be included on the default solution, as will any change you make on existing system entities.

> **NOTE**
>
> It is a good practice to start making any customizations in a new custom solution so that they can be easily managed in the future. If you want to customize a system entity such as Account, you can do it by adding the entity to a custom solution.

To customize a system, follow these steps:

1. Open your custom solution and ensure that the Components node is selected in the left navigation area (see Figure 22.50).

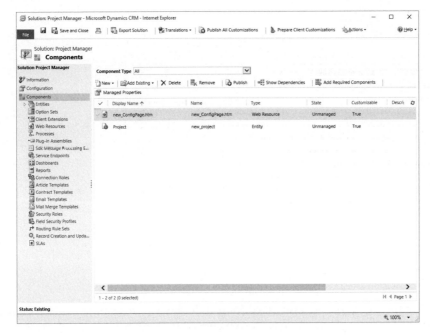

FIGURE 22.50   A solution with Components selected.

2. Click the Add Existing button and select Entity (see Figure 22.51).

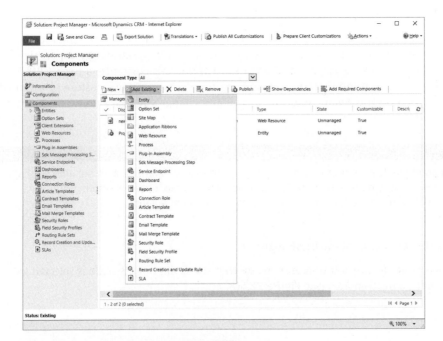

FIGURE 22.51   Adding an existing entity.

3. Select the entity you want to add—in this case, Account (see Figure 22.52).

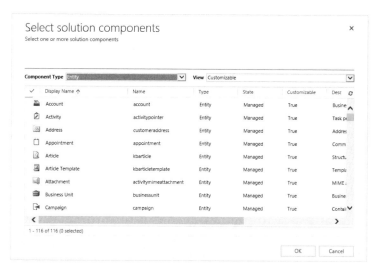

FIGURE 22.52   Selecting the existing Account entity.

4. Click OK to add the entity assets (see Figure 22.53).

▶ For more information on the entity assets, **SEE** the section of "Solution Enhancements," later in this chapter.

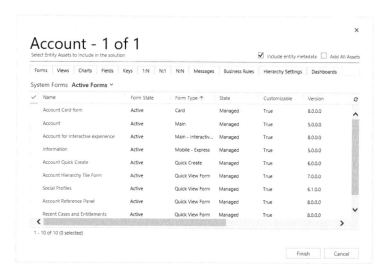

FIGURE 22.53   Selecting entity assets to include in a solution for the Account entity.

5. Check the Add All Assets check box and click Finish to add the entity. If prompted, and add any required/missing components. You see the entity with all the assets added to the solution.

You can now customize the Account entity by working with it directly from this solution. When you install this solution in another instance of Microsoft Dynamics CRM 2016, the customizations made will be affected on the new instance.

Solution Enhancements

Solutions have been really improved in Dynamics CRM 2016. Prior this version, every system entity you included on a solution included all the related subcomponents (also called *entity assets*), which made it difficult to manage and prevent overriding when importing solutions on the target organization.

With Dynamics CRM 2016, you can now select what entity assets you want to include in a solution. You can select from the following asset types:

▶ Forms

▶ Views

▶ Charts

▶ Fields

▶ Keys

▶ 1:N relationships

▶ N:1 relationships

▶ N:N relationships

▶ Messages

▶ Business rules

▶ Hierarchy settings

▶ Dashboards

So when you add an existing system entity to a solution, you are asked to select the entity assets you want to include on your solution, as shown in Figure 22.54 for the Lead entity.

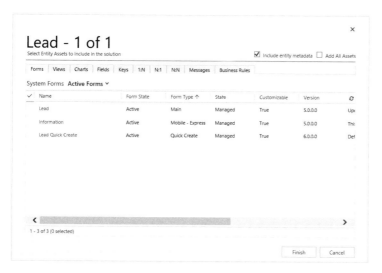

FIGURE 22.54   Selecting entity assets to include in a solution.

With this solution enhancement, you can now include a custom form you created on the Lead entity without having to add all the other relationships, forms, fields, or any other asset detailed before. This produces smaller solutions, which is especially important when you export them. (You will see how to export solutions in the next section.) It also prevents errors when you import a solution along with third-party solutions that might involve the same system entities.

If you include a system entity on a solution and include only a few assets, and then later you need to add another asset, you can do so without having to remove the system entity. You can do this by selecting the entity and clicking the Add Subcomponents button.

Exporting Solutions

You can export solutions in two different package types:

▶ **Unmanaged**—The unmanaged option enables developers to maintain backups of the customizations; it is possible to modify unmanaged packages when applying them to another environment. Note that when you remove unmanaged solutions, the new customizations are not removed; to remove customizations, you must remove them manually by going to the default solution.

▶ **Managed**—If you would like to distribute a solution, you should export the solution as managed so that people can't make any customizations to the package. This gives you to control over your customizations, which is important for troubleshooting as well as control of intellectual property (IP).

> **CAUTION**
>
> Before exporting a solution, be sure to include the Site Map on the solution because it isn't added automatically by the entities you added or created. You can add the Site Map by going to the Client Extensions node and clicking Add Existing > Site Map.

Follow these steps to export your solution:

1. Open the solution you want to export and click the Export Solution button. The Export Solution Wizard opens, suggesting that you publish all customizations before continuing (see Figure 22.55).

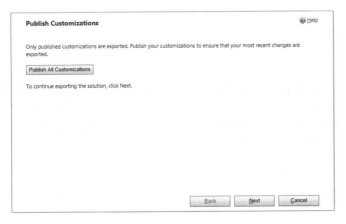

FIGURE 22.55   Export Solution Wizard.

2. Click the Publish All Customizations button if necessary and then click Next. If prompted, include any missing required components that your solution might require and then click Next.

3. In the next screen, select the settings you want to export. The available settings are Auto-numbering, Calendar, Customization, Email Tracking, General, Marketing, Outlook Synchronization, Relationship Roles, ISV Config, and Sales (see Figure 22.56). Click Next when you're finished making selections.

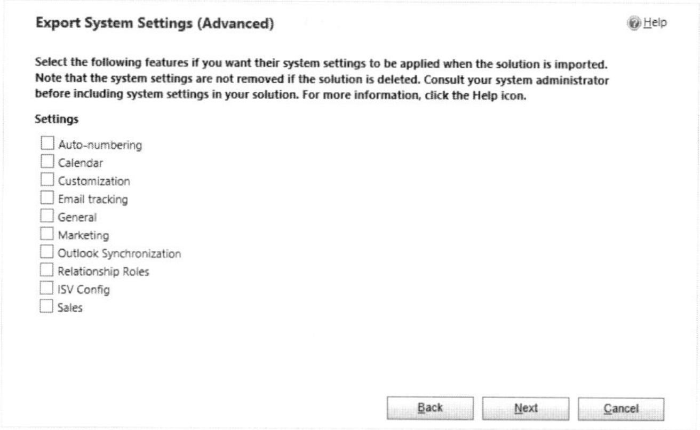

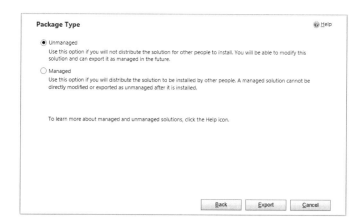

Export System Settings (Advanced)   Help

Select the following features if you want their system settings to be applied when the solution is imported. Note that the system settings are not removed if the solution is deleted. Consult your system administrator before including system settings in your solution. For more information, click the Help icon.

Settings

☐ Auto-numbering
☐ Calendar
☐ Customization
☐ Email tracking
☐ General
☐ Marketing
☐ Outlook Synchronization
☐ Relationship Roles
☐ ISV Config
☐ Sales

[Back]   [Next]   [Cancel]

FIGURE 22.56   Export settings.

CAUTION

Notice that when you remove the solution, these settings won't be removed from the organization where you implemented this solution, even if you export the solution as managed.

---

4. Set the package type to either Unmanaged or Managed (see Figure 22.57). Click Export button, and you are asked to download the exported solution. Notice that by default the name includes the solution name, the version, and the suffix managed, if you selected a managed package type.

Package Type   Help

◉ Unmanaged
   Use this option if you will not distribute the solution for other people to install. You will be able to modify this solution and can export it as managed in the future.

○ Managed
   Use this option if you will distribute the solution to be installed by other people. A managed solution cannot be directly modified or exported as unmanaged after it is installed.

   To learn more about managed and unmanaged solutions, click the Help icon.

[Back]   [Export]   [Cancel]

FIGURE 22.57   Selecting the package type.

> **NOTE**
>
> Using a managed solution is a good way to distribute packages for ISV and also for Microsoft partners to avoid allowing customers to mess with any customization whose functionality can be broken (as happened in previous versions of Dynamics CRM) and also to protect the copyright of the solution. For example, users can't export or customize a managed solution they have installed.

If you expand the compressed file you downloaded, after the import you see that it contains the following files and folders (see Figure 22.58), assuming you have exported a solution that has all these components:

▶ WebResources folder

▶ Workflows folder

▶ Reports

▶ PluginAssemblies

▶ [Content_Types] XML file

▶ Customizations XML file

▶ Solution XML file

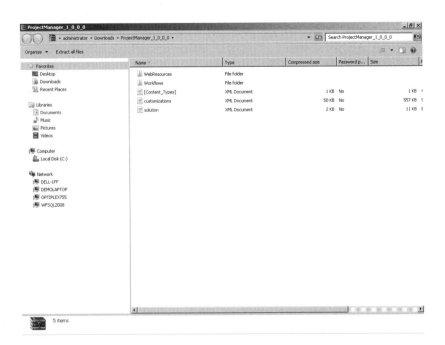

FIGURE 22.58   Expanded solution file.

The number of folders depends on the type of components you added to the solution. If you added reports, you see them inside the Reports folder. If your solution doesn't include any reports, however, this folder doesn't exist.

It is important to maintain the solution version properly because this number is not automatically incremented every time you export the solution. You are responsible for incrementing this number on each export before publishing a new version to the public.

One consideration regarding versioning is that versions have four numbers, separated by dots, in the format *A.B.C.D*:

▶ *A*—Major version number

▶ *B*—Minor version number

▶ *C*—Build number

▶ *D*—Revision number

Use the first two numbers when you add new features to a solution and the last two numbers when you fix bugs or make improvements on existing features.

Importing Solutions

To import a solution to another organization, complete the following steps:

1. Go to Settings > Customization > Solutions.

2. Click Import. You see the dialog shown in Figure 22.59.

FIGURE 22.59   Importing a solution.

3. Click Browse, locate the package zip file on your local hard drive, and then click Next. You now see the screen shown in Figure 22.60.

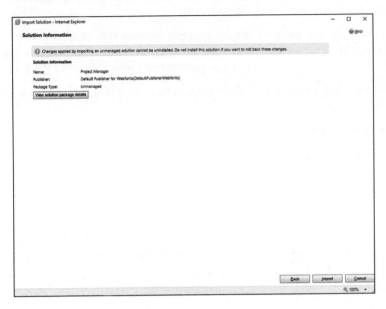

FIGURE 22.60　Solution information.

4. Optionally, you can check the solution package details by clicking the View Solution Package Details button. You can then see the detailed contents of the package, as shown in Figure 22.61.

FIGURE 22.61　Solution package details.

5. Click Close to close the Solution Details dialog and then click Import. You see the import options from which you can activate the processes and plug-in SDK messages (see Figure 22.62).

FIGURE 22.62   Import options.

NOTE

The option to activate the processes and plug-in SDK messages, as shown in Figure 22.62, is shown only if the solution contains plug-ins or processes.

TIP

If your solution includes plug-ins and SDK message processing steps, it is important that you check the Activate Any Processes check box and then enable any SDK message processing steps included in the solution when prompted during import so that the plug-in steps will be registered successfully.

---

6. Click Import to import the solution. This process might take some time, depending on the customizations and assemblies included in the package. When the import finishes, you are presented with a screen showing the details (see Figure 22.63).

FIGURE 22.63   Import solution details.

7. Publish the solution by clicking Publish All Customizations.

TIP

The Publish All Customizations option appears only if you are importing an unmanaged solution. If you import a managed solution, you don't see this button, as managed solutions are published automatically.

CAUTION

If you don't have sufficient permissions and the solution you are importing contains plug-ins that are not configured with sandbox isolation (as required for CRM Online), you get an error.

After importing the solution, you can download the log file, which is an XML file that can be viewed easily in Microsoft Excel. In case of any error, a user should send this file to the solution provider.

If you imported a solution that contains plug-ins and SDK message processing steps and you didn't check the Activate Any Processes check box and the Enable Any SDK Message Processing Steps Included in the Solution check box, you can activate them later, but you will have to do that in the solution, so activate them at this point in time. When you open the solution and go to the Sdk Message Processing Step node, you can then activate or deactivate any step you want to register on the plug-in assemblies installed by the managed solutions (see Figure 22.64).

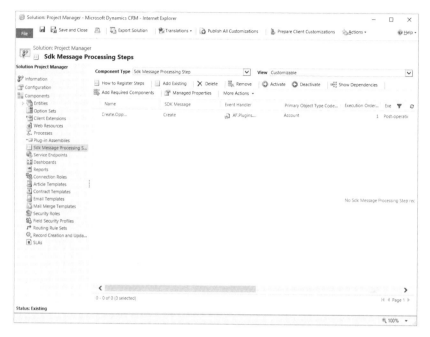

FIGURE 22.64   Activating or deactivating SDK message processing steps.

All the functions that are on the solution's user interface (UI) are also available on the API and the SDK, so you can automate the creation of solutions dynamically as well as manage the solutions from an external application. This can be useful, for example, for automating the deployment of testing environments.

> **NOTE**
>
> Microsoft does not recommend using solutions such as ASP.NET, Silverlight, or a Windows Forms application to package custom application deployments that run outside the CRM environment because they only consume the CRM resources through the Windows Communication Foundation (WCF) web services. For those applications, you should use the old way of packaging and create custom installers; you can generate these installers by using tools such as InstallShield or Package Deployer, as discussed later in this chapter.

It is a good practice to add jQuery scripts as a web resource on a solution if you are going to use jQuery on your form events. To add jQuery on your solution, download the most current version from http://jquery.com/download, go to Web Resources, and click New. Then enter the name and display name, select the type to script (JScript), and locate the jQuery file you downloaded (see Figure 22.65).

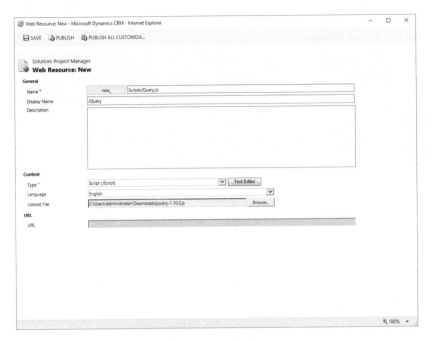

FIGURE 22.65   Creating a web resource for jQuery.

You can add the backslash character (/) in the Name field to simulate virtual directories. For example, Figure 22.66 shows the Scripts folder being used.

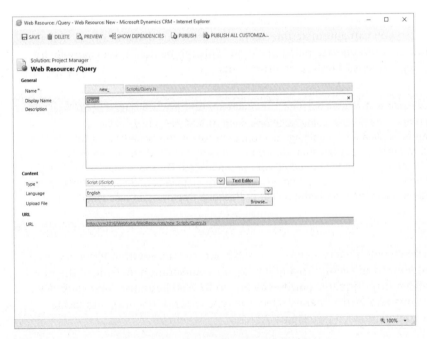

FIGURE 22.66   Adding jQuery with a custom virtual path.

Once you create this web resource, you can use jQuery on any form event.

> **CAUTION**
>
> You cannot import a managed solution into an organization that has a solution with the same name but in an unmanaged state. If you try to do that, you will see an error. If you want to test the managed package in this case, you need to import it into another organization.

Removing Solutions

After you import a custom managed solution to an organization that contains custom entities and you create records for those custom entities, CRM deletes all the records and SQL tables when you delete the managed solution. You are asked to confirm this before proceeding with the deletion operation, as shown in Figure 22.67.

FIGURE 22.67   Confirming the deletion.

It is always recommended that you make a backup of the SQL Server database (if you're working with an On-Premises version of CRM) or export the custom entities' records to an Excel file before deleting a solution. Deleting the solution cleans the CRM database by removing all the tables and views that were created by the managed solution entities. It is important to understand this, especially if you are going to try a third-party solution on a production environment because after playing with it you may want to remove it from the CRM system.

However, if you remove a custom unmanaged solution, the SQL tables and data of the custom entities are not removed from the database.

> **TIP**
>
> Remember the following when removing solutions:
>
> ▶ **Managed solutions**—All customizations applied are removed, as is all data.
>
> ▶ **Unmanaged solutions**—The solution record is removed; however, tables, views, and data remain in the default solution.

Cloning a Patch

New to Dynamics CRM 2016 is the ability to clone a patch. This is helpful when you don't want to distribute the entire solution if you only need to provide a patch to the customer for a single component. For example, if you have a big solution that includes a lot of components, when the customer finds a bug or an issue that must be fixed, you can distribute a patch to the customer that contains only the components you altered to fix that problem.

When you click the Clone to Patch button, you are asked to change the build and/or revision numbers of the version of the solution (see Figure 22.68).

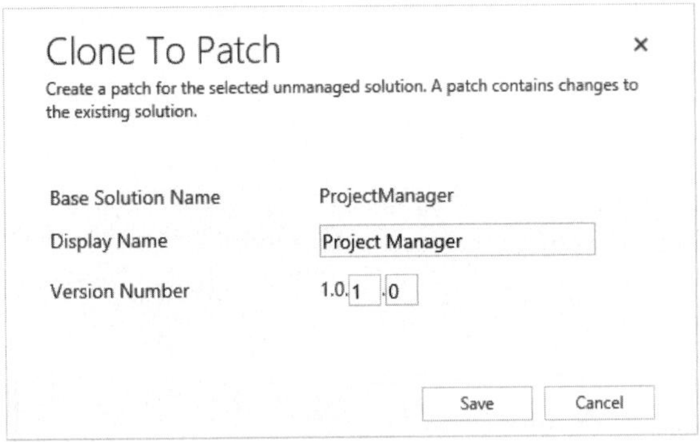

Clone To Patch	✕

Create a patch for the selected unmanaged solution. A patch contains changes to the existing solution.

Base Solution Name	ProjectManager
Display Name	Project Manager
Version Number	1.0.1 .0

Save   Cancel

FIGURE 22.68   Cloning a patch.

This dialog automatically suggests the next recommended version number, so if your solution is version number 1.0.0.0, the dialog suggests that you use the version number 1.0.1.0. If this is what you want to do, just click Save.

A new clean solution is created for the patch, and you can add the updated components there. You can then export the patch and import it to the target organization, as shown in Figure 22.69.

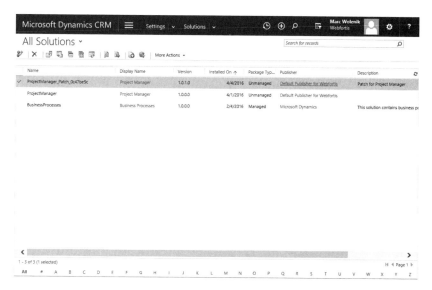

FIGURE 22.69   Solution patch.

After you have cloned a patch for a solution, you can no longer export the original solution as long as solution patches exist. If you try to export the original solution, you get the warning message shown in Figure 22.70.

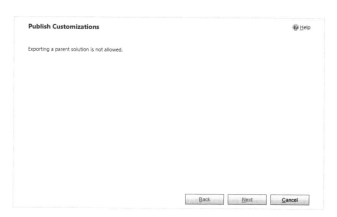

FIGURE 22.70   Exporting a parent solution is not allowed after you clone a patch.

Cloning Solutions

New to Dynamics CRM 2016 is the ability to clone a solution. You can only clone unmanaged solutions. When you click the Clone to Solution button on the command bar, you are asked to change the major and/or minor number of the version of the solution (see Figure 22.71).

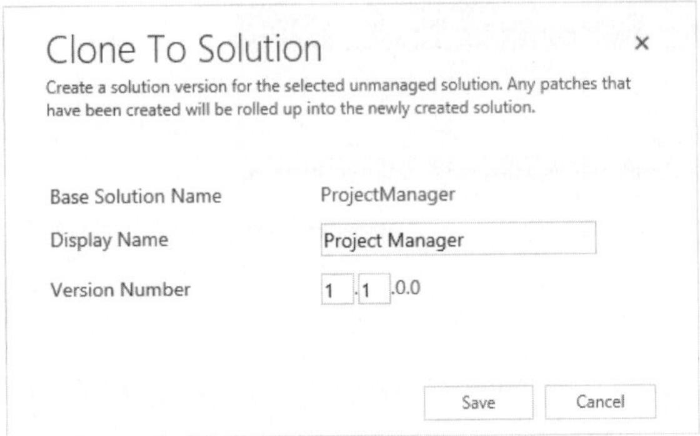

Clone To Solution   ✕

Create a solution version for the selected unmanaged solution. Any patches that
have been created will be rolled up into the newly created solution.

Base Solution Name	ProjectManager
Display Name	Project Manager
Version Number	1 . 1 .0.0

Save   Cancel

FIGURE 22.71   Cloning a Solution.

This dialog automatically suggests the next recommended version number, so if your
solution is version number 1.0.0.0, the dialog suggests that you use the version number
1.1.0.0. If this is what you want to do, just click Save. This action merges the patches with
the original solution, producing a new single release of your solution.

CAUTION

Clone to Solution removes any patch solution you have created. Therefore, before you use
this option, make sure to export the patches and have a backup of the exported patch
solution files.

Patching Solutions

New to Dynamics CRM 2016 is the ability to patch a solution. By clicking the Apply
Solution Upgrade button on the command bar, you can import a patch for a solution.
This is possible only when you import a solution that was previously cloned and it is
a major or minor version upgrade.

After you import the new solution, you are asked to apply the solution upgrades in the
last step of the Import Solution Wizard, as shown in Figure 22.72.

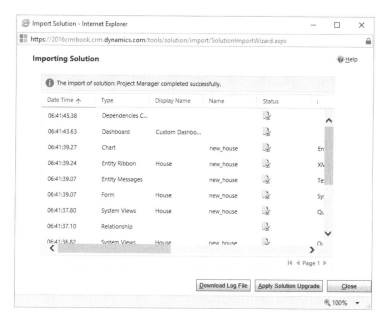

FIGURE 22.72   Applying solution upgrades.

All the existing previous solutions and patches are combined on the new installed/ imported solution, and you end up with a single reference to the latest version of the solution in the target organization.

Working with Multiple Solutions

CRM implementations are likely to contain multiple custom solutions. In addition to having multiple solutions containing custom modifications in their CRM systems, organizations typically have multiple vendor (ISV) solutions as well.

When importing solutions, you should consider some things related to the predefined system entities. If you import a solution that includes a customized form of any system entity—for example, the Contact entity—this solution could be applied (or "layered") by removing some fields and tabs on the existing Contact entity. These customizations will take precedence over any other solution that includes the same Contact entity without any customization. So, if you need to include the system Contact entity in a solution, you need to make at least one customization to the form so that you can be sure all the needed fields will not be overwritten by another solution.

> **TIP**
>
> When working on a custom solution that will require a system entity, it is a good idea to consider adding new custom roles and creating new forms associated with these new security roles. Doing so helps you avoid having other solutions overlap with your solution customizations. If you do this, users need to use your custom roles to have a better experience with your solution.

Entity Forms Security

One important consideration when working with solutions that contain custom entities is the security configuration for the necessary roles. By default, when you create a custom entity, only the System Administrator and System Customizer roles are granted permission to use the custom entity. You are responsible for giving the right permissions to any other role (such as the Customer Representative role) so that users who have that role can work with the custom entity you included in the solution.

To configure security roles, open a solution and complete the following steps:

1. Navigate to Components > Entities > your custom entity > Forms and select the form (see Figure 22.73).

FIGURE 22.73   Customization of a form.

2. Click Enable Security Roles from the command bar, and the Assign Security Roles dialog appears (see Figure 22.74).

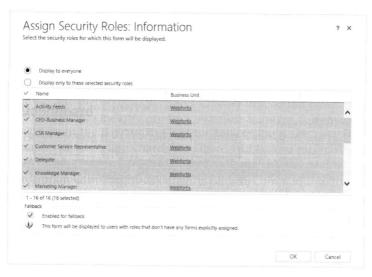

FIGURE 22.74   Assigning security role information.

3. Click the role you want to configure (in this example, the Customer Service Representative role) to open the Security Role editor page.

4. Go to the Custom Entities tab. You will see that all the solution custom entities are there, with no permissions set, as shown for the Project row in Figure 22.75.

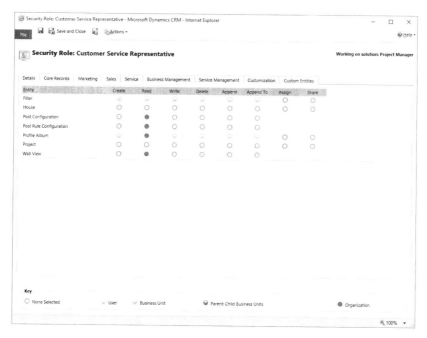

FIGURE 22.75   The Custom Entities tab.

5. Grant the permissions to the operations you want to have them by clicking the circles. Notice that if you click the entity name, you configure all the operations in the entire row at the same time (see Figure 22.76).

FIGURE 22.76   The Custom Entities tab with permissions set.

Because CRM 2016 allows you to have different forms for each security role, you can create new forms with different fields and assign them to different roles. For example, you might have sensitive fields on an entity that you would like to hide to a lower role, such as the Customer Service Representative role. You can easily do this by creating a new form and designing it to show only the fields this user role should see.

Figure 22.77 shows an entity with more than one main form created to be used by different roles.

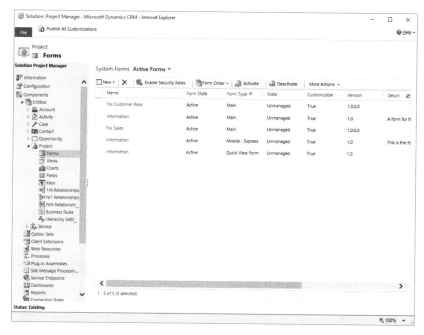

FIGURE 22.77   Entity with multiple main forms.

If you have a user who has more than one role assigned and there is one form created for each role, you need to be sure to set the order in which these forms are displayed for such cases (see Figure 22.78). You can do this by selecting Form Order > Main Form Set.

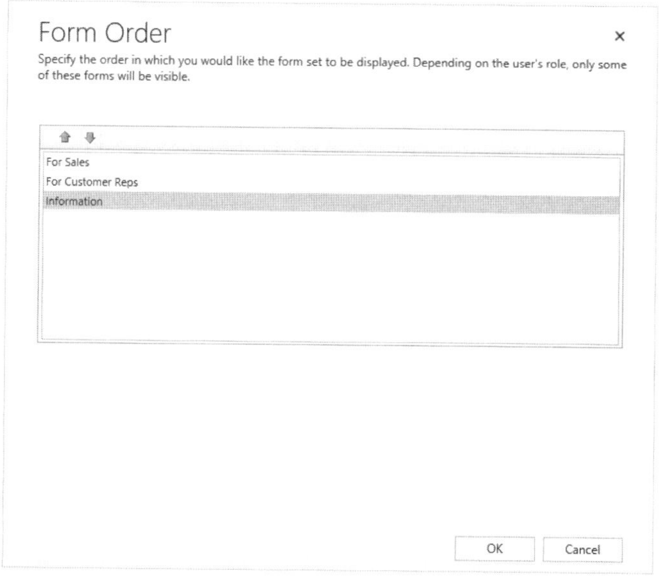

FIGURE 22.78   Setting the form order.

Because the first form on this list is displayed on the first role match, you might consider reordering the forms so that the more detailed form is displayed first.

> **TIP**
>
> If you include a customized role as part of your solution that is derived from one of the standard roles (such as Customer Service Representative), you may accidently override the end user role configurations already set for that role. This is why creating a custom role is always recommended.

Migrating Customizations from Previous Versions

Because some custom code will not work when you upgrade from Dynamics CRM 2013/2015, it is recommended that you run the Custom Code Validation Tool that Microsoft supplies.

> **NOTE**
>
> You can find the Custom Code Validation Tool by searching Microsoft.com for "Custom Code Validation Tool" or by going directly to www.microsoft.com/en-us/download/details.aspx?id=30151.

The tool focuses primarily on custom JavaScript, and it gives output that allows you to address scripts that don't work in CRM 2016 prior to running an upgrade.

Third-Party and Marketplace Solutions

The Microsoft Dynamics Marketplace is a website where Microsoft partners and ISVs publish their solutions so that users of CRM can easily find and install them in their environments.

For ISVs

The Microsoft Dynamics Marketplace is located at http://dynamics-crm.pinpoint.microsoft.com (see Figure 22.79), and the AppSource is located at: https://appsource.microsoft.com.

The AppSource is brand new and will replace the Dynamics Marketplace by the end of 2016, however its functionality and purpose are the same.

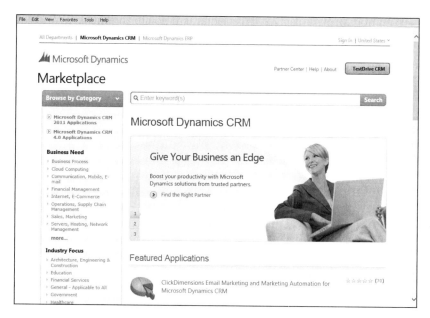

FIGURE 22.79   Microsoft Dynamics Marketplace.

If you are an ISV and want to have your solution in the Microsoft Dynamics Marketplace, you first have to be listed in Microsoft Pinpoint. To do that, your company needs to be a Microsoft partner. Microsoft partners can list software solutions using the Solution Profiler tool and can also be listed in the Microsoft Pinpoint website.

There are two types of product registrations: For Microsoft CRM applications, go to the Microsoft Platform Ready website and test the application using free tools, and for Microsoft ERP applications, get the solution tested and certified with the CfMD (Certified for Microsoft Dynamics) certification.

The Microsoft Dynamics Marketplace helps you find the right customers by exposing your application to Microsoft Dynamics users from around the world, who will be able to download your application from this site and also connect with your company.

For Customers

If you are a customer, the Microsoft Dynamics Marketplace will help you discover and try custom solutions developed by third-party vendors that are be of interest and that might prevent you from having to develop a new custom solution from scratch. Because the solutions that are available in the Marketplace are verified and certified, you can feel confident installing them and not worry about system stability.

Developer Resources

You can access the developer resources by going to the CRM web interface and navigating to Settings > Customizations (see Figure 22.80).

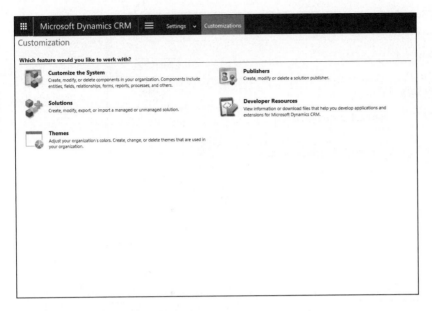

FIGURE 22.80   Customizations page.

If you click the Developer Resources link, you are directed to a page that contains all the information necessary for development with Dynamics CRM 2016, as shown in Figure 22.81.

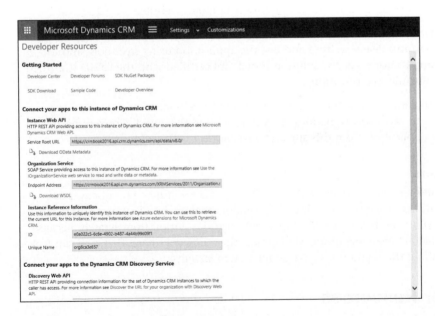

FIGURE 22.81   Developer Resources page.

The Getting Started Section provides several links:

▶ **Developer Center**—This takes you to https://msdn.microsoft.com/dynamics/crm/crmdevelopercenter.aspx.

▶ **Developer Forums**—This takes you to https://community.dynamics.com/crm/f/117?pi51520=0&category=Development%20%2F%20Customization%20%2F%20SDK.

▶ **SDK NuGet Packages**—This takes you to www.nuget.org/profiles/crmsdk.

▶ **SDK Download**—This takes you to www.microsoft.com/en-us/download/details.aspx?id=50032.

▶ **Sample Code**—This takes you to https://msdn.microsoft.com/dynamics/crm/samplecode.

▶ **Developer Overview**—This takes you to https://msdn.microsoft.com/library/gg334635.aspx (for Dynamics CRM On-Premises, the link takes you to https://msdn.microsoft.com/en-us/library/gg309589.aspx).

Configuration Migration

CRM Configuration Migration is a tool you can find in the SDK in the SDK\Tools\ConfigurationMigration folder. This tool helps ensure that the import and export of entity records necessary for your solution run properly.

When you run this tool by executing the DataMigrationUtility.exe file, you see Figure 22.82.

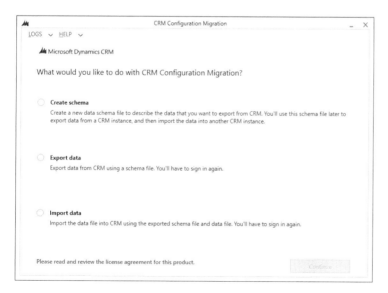

FIGURE 22.82   CRM Configuration Migration Start screen.

With this tool you can choose any of these options:

- ▶ Create Schema

- ▶ Export Data

- ▶ Import Data

The following sections explain these operations in detail.

Create Schema

Before you can try to export data, you need to create a schema that defines the entities and fields you want your exported data to have. To do this, click the Create Schema option button and then click Continue. You need to provide your CRM connection information. Once you enter the CRM connection information and click the Login button, you see a page where you can select the solution file, as shown in Figure 22.83.

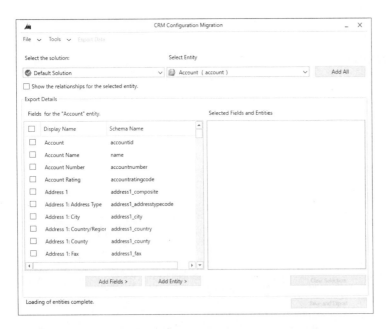

FIGURE 22.83   CRM Configuration Migration export details.

When you select a solution and an entity, the tool filters only the entities included in the selected solution.

Select the fields of the entity selected and click the Add Fields button to include them in your schema. You can then change the entity and select fields for that entity. You can repeat this as many times as needed. For this example, select the account name and account number of the Account entity and first and last names and Account ID of the Contact entity, as shown in see Figure 22.84.

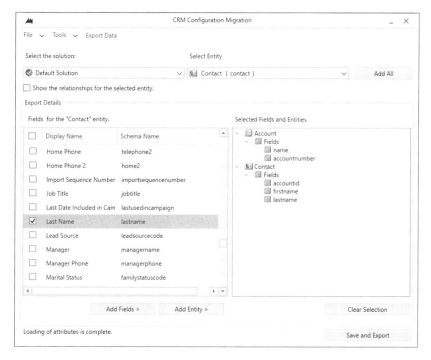

FIGURE 22.84   CRM Configuration Migration selected schema fields.

When you are done adding fields, click the Save and Export button. Select the file location where you want to store the schema and click OK. After the schema is saved, you are prompted about exporting the data (see Figure 22.85).

FIGURE 22.85   Export confirmation.

If you click Yes, you are directed to the Export Data Wizard.

Export Data

To export data, you can click the Export Data option button on the main start screen of the Configuration Migration tool and then click Continue. Enter the CRM connection information and click Login. Then provide the input schema file that you created earlier and the output zip data file that will contains the records (see Figure 22.86).

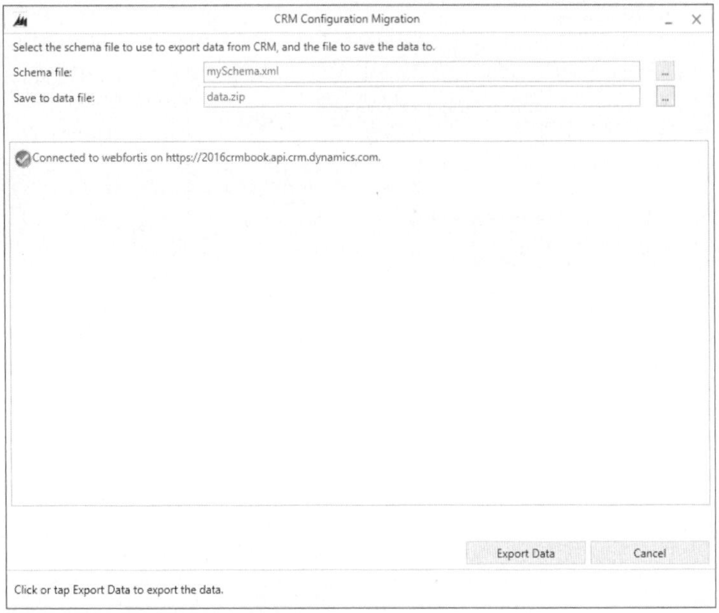

FIGURE 22.86   Exporting Data.

Click the Export Data button to continue. When the export data process is completed, you see the results in the lower part of the screen, as shown in Figure 22.87.

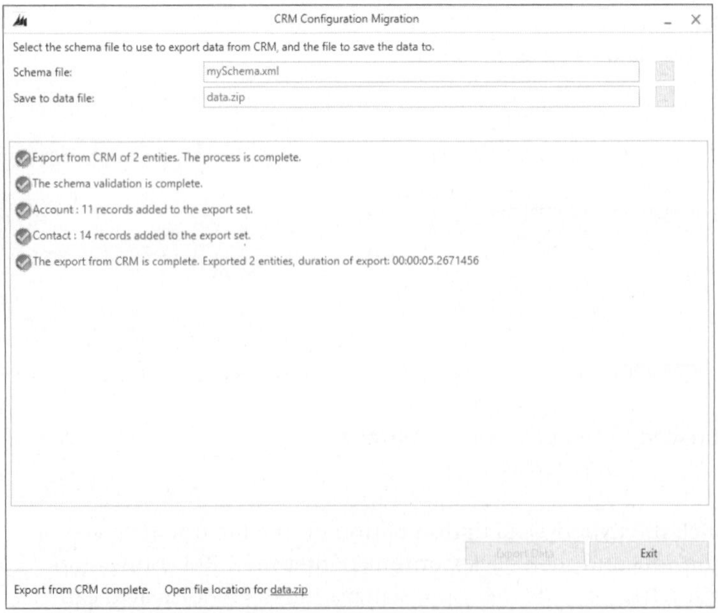

FIGURE 22.87   Data export completed.

Click Exit to go back to the main startup screen.

Import Data

To import the data you exported before, you can click the Import Data option button on the main start screen of the Configuration Migration tool and click Continue. Enter the CRM connection information and click Login. Then provide the input zip data file that will contains the records (the one you created using the Export Data function), as shown in Figure 22.88.

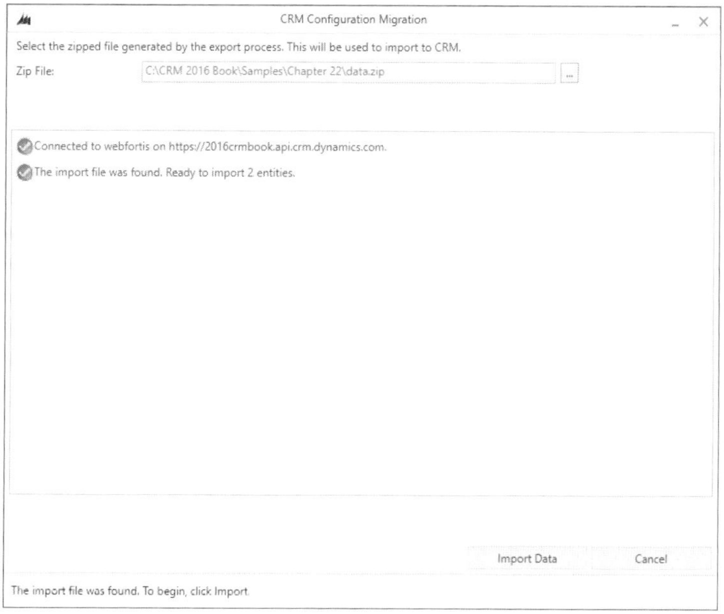

FIGURE 22.88   Importing data.

Click Import Data to continue. When the import data process is complete, you will see the results in the lower part of the screen.

Click Exit to go back to the main startup screen.

Package Deployer

Package Deployer is a tool you can find in the SDK, in the SDK\Tools\PackageDeployer folder. This tool helps in the deployment of solutions as well as the creation of the records your solution needs to run properly.

Sometimes installing a solution by importing it is not enough. For your product to work properly, you need to create some records that the solution relies on. This is where you use the Package Deployer tool.

You run this tool by executing the PackageDeployer.exe file. When you click Continue on the welcome screen, if you don't have any package created, you see the error shown in Figure 22.89, and the tool exits.

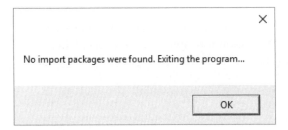

FIGURE 22.89   "No import packages found" error.

> **NOTE**
>
> The Unified Service Desk (USD) uses the Package Deployer to install the USD solutions. For more information about this, refer to Chapter 13, "The Unified Service Desk (USD)".

Create Package

To create a package, you need to use Visual Studio 2013 or 2015, and use the .NET Framework 4.5.2. In this example, you will use Visual Studio 2015, and you will create a new CRM package project type (see Figure 22.90).

> **NOTE**
>
> To create this project type, you must first install CRMSDKTemplates.vsix, which you find in the SDK\Templates folder.

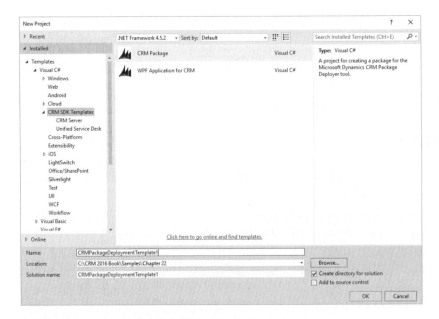

FIGURE 22.90   CRM Package Visual Studio project.

Each CRM package contains the following components:

- ▶ CRM solution files, which you export from the CRM web interface, as explained earlier in this chapter

- ▶ Compressed data files, which you can create using the Configuration Migration tool, as explained earlier in this chapter

- ▶ Custom code you can write to be fired on events during the package installation process

- ▶ HTML content you can display when the package is deployed

Edit the ImportConfig.xml file to include the CRM solutions you want to be imported by the package and include the data files you want to be imported.

Here is an example of the ImportConfig.xml file:

```
<?xml version="1.0" encoding="utf-16"?>
<configdatastorage xmlns:xsi="http://www.w3.org/2001/XMLSchema-instance"
xmlns:xsd="http://www.w3.org/2001/XMLSchema"
                    installsampledata="true"
                    waitforsampledatatoinstall="true"
                    agentdesktopzipfile=""
                            agentdesktopexename=""
                    crmmigdataimportfile="data.zip">
  <solutions>
    <configsolutionfile solutionpackagefilename="solutionFile_1_0_0_0.zip" />
  </solutions>
</configdatastorage>
```

Put the data.zip file and solutionFile_1_0_0_0.zip in the PkgFolder. Change Build Action to Content and set Copy to Output Directory to Copy Always (see Figure 22.91).

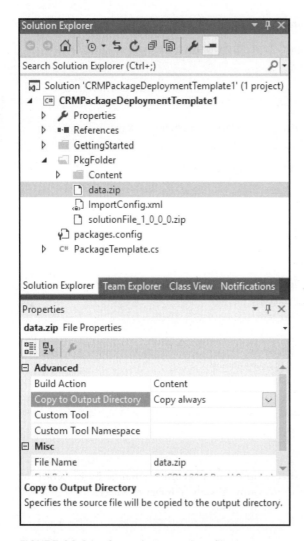

FIGURE 22.91   Copy always content files.

Build the solution and copy all the files generated by the output under the bin debug folder to the folder where you have the Package Deployer (SDK\Tools\PackageDeployer). Do not replace any existing file; just copy the new ones.

Package Deployment

After you created a package with Visual Studio and copy the files to the SDK\Tools\PackageDeployer folder, you can start the PackageDeployer.exe application again.

When the start page appears, click Continue, enter your CRM connection details, and click Login. You see the first custom welcome screen (the one that you can customize in your package that is located in the PkgFolder\Content\en-us\WelcomeHtml\HTML\Default.htm folder), as shown in Figure 22.92.

FIGURE 22.92   Custom welcome screen.

Click Next, and the next screen asks you to confirm details before starting the deployment (see Figure 22.93).

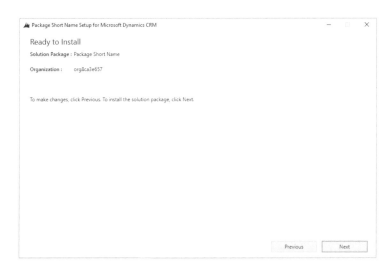

FIGURE 22.93   Ready to Install screen.

Click Next to continue, and a first initial validation occurs before the deployment starts (see Figure 22.94).

FIGURE 22.94   Validation screen.

Click Next, and the deployment process starts. It might take some time, depending on the solutions and data you included in the package.

If any error occurs during the deployment process, you can click the View Log link to open the log file, where you can see more details about the error.

Click Next again, and you see the custom installation complete screen (which you can customize by editing the \PkgFolder\Content\en-us\EndHtml\HTML\Default.htm file).

Click Finish to close the Package Deployer tool.

Themes

New to Dynamics CRM 2016 is the ability to brand the Dynamics CRM user interface with your company logo and also change some basic styles, such as using the colors of your company. You do this type of branding by using themes.

To access the themes configuration, select Settings > Customizations. There, when you click the Themes option, you will see the list of available themes.

To create a new theme, click New. As shown in Figure 22.95, enter a name for the new theme.

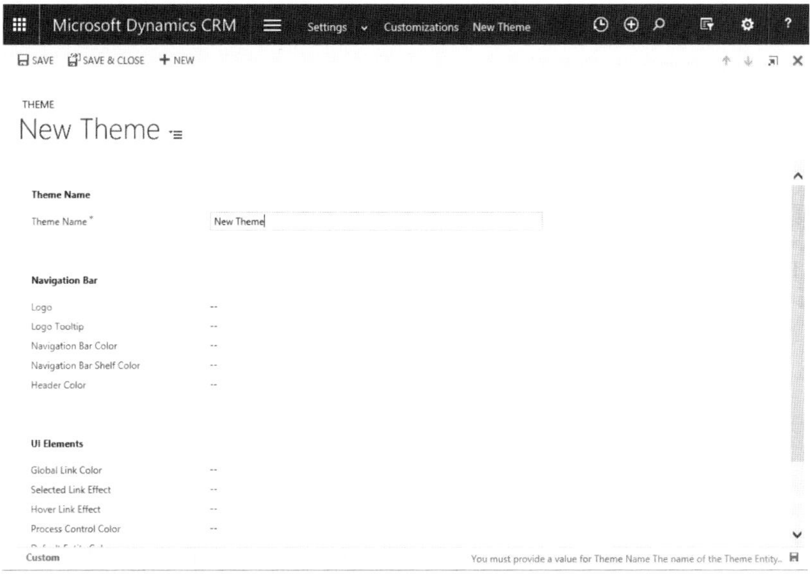

FIGURE 22.95   New theme.

It is recommended that you copy the default theme before creating a new theme and not modify the default theme. This way, you can make the changes more quickly, and you can restore the default theme easily if you need it in the future.

As you can see, there are a lot of empty fields here. This is why it's better to copy the default theme than to try to create a theme from scratch. To do that, go back to the list of themes, select the default theme, and click the Clone button.

Open the copy of the theme you cloned and make your edits. These are the styles you can change:

▶ Logo

▶ Logo Tooltip

▶ Navigation Bar Color

▶ Navigation Bar Shelf Color

▶ Header Color

▶ Global Link Color

▶ Selected Link Effect

▶ Hover Link Effect

- ▶ Process Control Color

- ▶ Default Entity Color

- ▶ Default Custom Entity Color

- ▶ Control Shade

- ▶ Control Border

The logo size must be 400px (width) by 50px (height).

To add a logo for your company, you must create a web resource, so you click the lookup icon at the end of the Logo field and click +New, as shown in Figure 22.96.

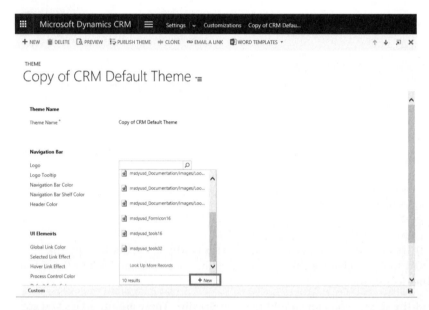

FIGURE 22.96   Editing a logo.

You now see a Web Resource window. In it, enter the name for your web resource and a display name and select PNG, GIF, or JPG from the Type drop-down. Then browse to a logo file on your local computer, as shown in Figure 22.97.

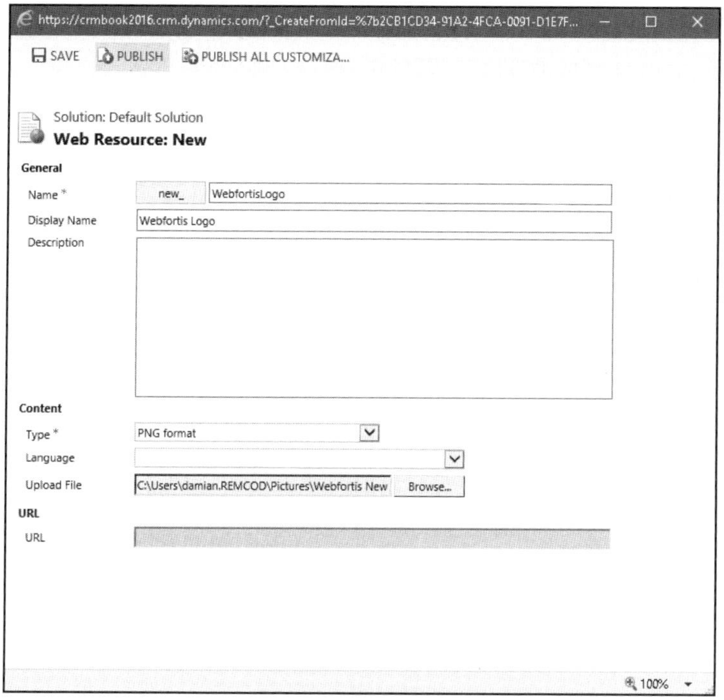

FIGURE 22.97 Selecting a logo web resource.

Click Save and then click Publish. Close the Web Resource dialog and find the logo you just created. Click the Preview button to preview your changes before publishing the logo to the rest of the users.

If you like how it looks, then go back to Settings > Customizations > Themes, select the theme, and click Publish Theme in the top command bar. If you don't like how it looks, click the Exit Preview button and make any additional changes prior to publishing.

NOTE

You can have only one theme active for the entire organization. Dynamics CRM 2016 still doesn't support custom theming to different OUs or roles.

Working with the SDK

The SDK includes help files, documentation, binary tools, and code samples that give developers the capability to extend and understand advanced Microsoft Dynamics CRM customizations. By *advanced customizations*, I refer to all customizations that can't be done through the standard CRM user interfaces, such as the ones you saw earlier in this chapter. To develop these advanced customizations, you need a tool such as Visual Studio 2015, along with solid knowledge and understanding of .NET development and programming in languages such as C# or Visual Basic .NET and JavaScript.

> **NOTE**
>
> The SDK does not usually come with the Dynamics CRM media, so you must download it from Microsoft. You can find it by searching for "CRM 2016 SDK" at Microsoft.com or by navigating to http://msdn.microsoft.com/dynamics/crm.

Advanced customizations can include the following:

▶ Server programming

▶ Advanced workflow development

▶ For details about workflow development, **SEE CHAPTER 26**, "Process Development."

▶ Plug-in development

▶ Client programming

▶ Report development

▶ Advanced report development with SQL Server Reporting Services (SSRS)

▶ For details about report development, **SEE CHAPTER 16**, "Reporting and Dashboards."

> **TIP**
>
> The main SDK help file, CrmSdk2016.chm, contains detailed documentation about all these topics.

Summary

This chapter looks at the CRM entity model, the attribute types you can use to add new fields to the entity forms, the alternate keys you can create, and the relationships between the entities (1:N, N:1, or N:N). In this chapter you have learned how to make some basic customizations, such as adding tabs, sections, and controls to forms. You have used and reviewed the IFRAME control and also added menus and controls to the toolbar by using the Site Map, command bars, and ISV Config files. You have learned how to use JavaScript events exposed by the form controls, such as OnLoad and OnSave, to extend the forms and the OnChange event for fields. In this chapter you have also seen how to easily debug scripts and how to import and export customizations.

This chapter describes how to customize Microsoft Dynamics CRM for deployment, support, and distribution by using solution packages. It reviews the differences between managed and unmanaged solutions and looks at the Microsoft Dynamics Marketplace, where ISVs can promote their solutions and customers can find solutions.

This chapter also reviews some of the SDK tools you can use, such as the Configuration Migration to manage import data and the Package Deployer tool to create packages you can distribute. The chapter wraps up by quickly covering the SDK and its uses.

22

Web Services

Microsoft Dynamics CRM allows developers to take advantage of web services at no additional cost. These web services allow for programmatic implementation of the system (usually via custom logic or of a custom interface), while controlling back-end business processes, security, and auditing.

> **NOTE**
>
> While Microsoft doesn't charge for use of the web services included with Microsoft Dynamics CRM, there may be licensing charges depending on how your users interact with the data. Be sure to check the latest licensing guide for the current status.

Web Services Fundamentals

Microsoft Dynamics CRM 2016 uses the common service-oriented architecture (SOA) concept for extensibility, which involves implementing a series of web services to provide extensibility support. By using these web services, you can integrate other applications and systems with Microsoft CRM and extend its capabilities.

Web services are based on Simple Object Access Protocol (SOAP) messages. This protocol uses Extensible Markup Language (XML), which provides usability through Hypertext Transfer Protocol (HTTP) communication transports. In simple terms, this gives applications and systems an easy way to communicate using standard protocols to interoperate and share functionalities.

Web services are language and platform independent, so they can be consumed by an application written in

Java, Visual Basic, or C#. They also can be used on a Microsoft Windows–based operating system (OS) and on UNIX, Linux, and Macintosh platforms.

NOTE

The examples included in this chapter are written using C# with Visual Studio 2015. However, as shown in the "Examples of Web Services" section, later in this chapter, you can consume web services using JavaScript if desired.

CRM 2016 does not support web services endpoints from Microsoft Dynamics CRM (version 4.0 and lower); however, it does support CRM 2011, 2013, and 2015 endpoints.

The following sections describe the components and standards available in Microsoft Dynamics CRM 2016.

Windows Communication Foundation

Windows Communication Foundation (WCF) is the next generation of web services. WCF is independent of the protocol to be used, so it is not tied to HTTP as the old web services were. WCF can be implemented and can use other protocols, such as TCP, HTTP, or peer-to-peer protocols that are configured on a configuration.

Representational State Transfer

Representational state transfer (REST) is a modern and easy way to consume a web service without using the SOAP or Web Services Description Language (WSDL) protocols. By just using the query string for retrieve operations using the GET method of the HTTP protocol and the POST method for adding, the DELETE method for deleting, and the PUT method for updating operations, you can quickly get the data you want in XML format without having to create any special proxy client, as you would need to do with SOAP.

JavaScript Object Notation

JavaScript Object Notation (JSON) is a simplified way to send and receive messages that improves the number of bytes being sent or received by a service comparing it with XML.

For example, an XML message like this:

```
<customers>
        <customer>John</customer>
        <customer>Lucas</customer>
</customers>
```

is formed like this in JSON:

```
"Customers" : { "customer" : "John" , "Lucas" }
```

As you can see, the JSON involves fewer characters than the corresponding XML message, but the result is the same.

> **NOTE**
>
> For more information about JSON, visit www.json.org.

Open Data Services

Open Data Services (OData) is a standard way of communicating via the REST protocol that allows filtering, sorting, choosing the columns returned, and more.

> **NOTE**
>
> Microsoft CRM 2016 supports OData 2.0 for now, but it is being deprecated. Therefore, it is recommended that you start changing any OData code to use the new Web API explained later in this chapter.

To easily see the web services definitions and get the URL addresses of the WSDL documents from within Microsoft CRM 2016, follow these steps:

1. Go to Settings > Customizations (see Figure 23.1).

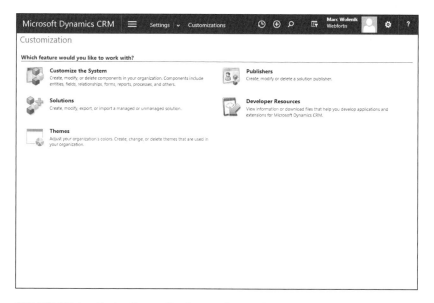

FIGURE 23.1   Navigating to Settings > Customizations.

2. Select Developer Resources option, and the page shown in Figure 23.2 appears.

FIGURE 23.2   Downloading web services description files.

As you can see in Figure 23.2, you can download the WSDL definitions for two web services: The Discovery and Organization services.

To understand how to use these services, you need to create a new console application in C# to follow the examples in this chapter. To do so, open Visual Studio 2015 and choose File > New > Project. From the project templates, go to Visual C#/Windows and select Console Application from the installed templates (see Figure 23.3).

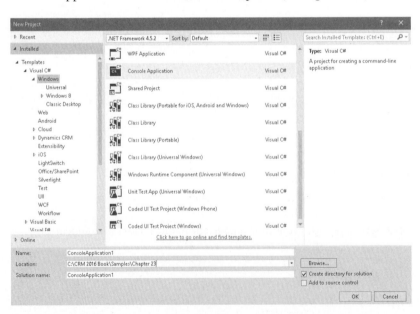

FIGURE 23.3   Creating a console application in Visual Studio 2015.

The next section explains the web services definition files.

Discovery Web Service

Microsoft CRM 2016 has multi-tenancy capability, which means it supports more than one organization on the same server. You therefore need to query a general web service called XRMDiscoveryService, which will give you the right web service for the organization you want to work with. You can find this by navigating to http://*servername:portnumber*/XRMServices/2011/Discovery.svc?wsdl (for example, http://crm2016/XRMServices/2011/Discovery.svc?wsdl for CRM On-Premises).

> **NOTE**
>
> The port number can be omitted for the default port 80 of HTTP in this example.

To add a web reference for this service, go to Visual Studio 2015 and use the new console application project you created. Right-click the project name in the Solution Explorer and choose Add Service Reference from the menu, enter the URL of the Discovery Service, click Go, and then enter XrmSdk.Discovery in the Namespace field (see Figure 23.4). Click OK to add the WCF service reference to your project.

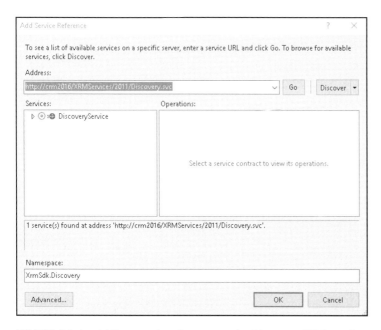

FIGURE 23.4   Adding a web reference to the Discovery WCF service.

By querying this service, you can retrieve all the organizations that a specific user belongs to and get the right service location. Listing 23.1 shows how this is done for CRM On-Premises (non-IFD).

LISTING 23.1   Querying a Service Namespace

```
ConsoleApplication1
{
        static void Main(string[] args)
        {
            Console.WriteLine(GetCrmServiceForOrganization("Webfortis"));
            Console.ReadKey();
        }

        private static string GetCrmServiceForOrganization(string organizationName)
        {
            using (XrmSdk.Discovery.DiscoveryServiceClient myCrm =
            new XrmSdk.Discovery.DiscoveryServiceClient())
            {
                myCrm.ClientCredentials.Windows.ClientCredential =
            System.Net.CredentialCache.DefaultNetworkCredentials;

                XrmSdk.Discovery.RetrieveOrganizationsRequest myRequest =
            new XrmSdk.Discovery.RetrieveOrganizationsRequest();

                XrmSdk.Discovery.RetrieveOrganizationsResponse myResponse =



                (XrmSdk.Discovery.RetrieveOrganizationsResponse)myCrm.
Execute(myRequest);
                foreach (XrmSdk.Discovery.OrganizationDetail detail in myResponse.
Details)
                {
                    Console.WriteLine("Organization = " + detail.UniqueName);
                    if (detail.UniqueName == organizationName)
                    {
                        return detail.Endpoints[1].Value;
                    }
                }
            }
            return "";
        }
}
```

NOTE

In all the examples in this chapter, replace Webfortis with your organization name.

Organization Service

This section shows how to get the correct Organization service endpoint address to use for the organization you want to work with. For a custom application you need the Organization service, which is structured like this:

```
http://servername:portnumber/XRMServices/2011/Organization.svc?wsdl
```

Here is an example:

```
http://crm2016/XRMServices/2011/Organization.svc?wsdl
```

Adding a Service Reference

To add a service reference for the Organization service, go to Visual Studio 2015. Then, using the new console application project you created, right-click the project name in the Solution Explorer and choose Add Service Reference from the menu. Enter the URL of the Organization service, click Go, and then enter XrmSdk in the Namespace field (see Figure 23.5). Click OK to add the service reference to your project.

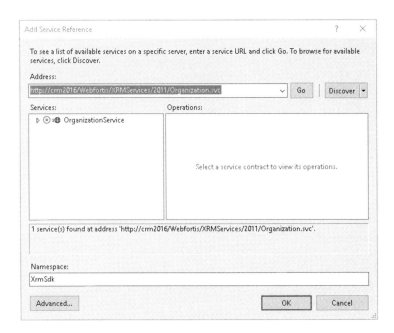

FIGURE 23.5   Adding a service reference for the Organization service.

The Organization service has the following methods:

▶ Create

▶ Retrieve

▶ RetrieveMultiple

▶ Delete

▶ Associate

▶ Disassociate

▶ Execute

▶ Update

Create **Method**

The Create method is used to create new instances of an existing entity, such as a new Account or Contact entity.

This method has only one implementation: It returns a globally unique identifier (GUID), which is the unique identifier of the new entity to be created; it accepts one parameter of type Entity.

Listing 23.2 shows how to create a new account programmatically in Visual Studio 2015 with C#:

LISTING 23.2   Creating a New Account

```csharp
private static string CreateAccount(string organizationName, string accountName)
{
    using (XrmSdk.OrganizationServiceClient myCrm =
                        new XrmSdk.OrganizationServiceClient())
    {
        try
        {
            myCrm.Endpoint.Address =
            new System.ServiceModel.EndpointAddress(GetCrmServiceForOrganization
(organizationName));
            myCrm.ClientCredentials.Windows.ClientCredential =
            System.Net.CredentialCache.DefaultNetworkCredentials;
            XrmSdk.Entity newAccount = new XrmSdk.Entity();
            newAccount.LogicalName = "account";
            XrmSdk.AttributeCollection myAttributes = new XrmSdk.
AttributeCollection();
            myAttributes.Add(new KeyValuePair<string, object>("name", accountName));
            newAccount.Attributes = myAttributes;
            Guid newAccountId = myCrm.Create(newAccount);
            return newAccountId.ToString();
        }
        catch (Exception ex)
        {
            Console.WriteLine("General exception: " + ex.ToString());
            return "General exception: " + ex.ToString();
        }
    }
}
```

Testing the `Create` **Method**

To test the `Create` method, you need to pass the organization name and the name of the new account you want to create to the method parameters as follows:

```
Console.WriteLine("New Account GUID = " + CreateAccount("Webfortis", "New Account"));
```

You can put the line above inside the `Main` function of your program to test it, so the `Main` function should look like this:

```
static void Main(string[] args)
{
    Console.WriteLine("New Account GUID = " + CreateAccount("Webfortis", "New
Account"));
    Console.ReadKey(); //added for debugging purposes only
}
```

You can run this code by either pressing F5 or by going to the Debug menu and choosing the Start Debugging option. In either case, similar output appears, as shown in Figure 23.6.

FIGURE 23.6   Creating an account through the Main Data web service.

Now if you go to the CRM web client application, you can see the new account (see Figure 23.7).

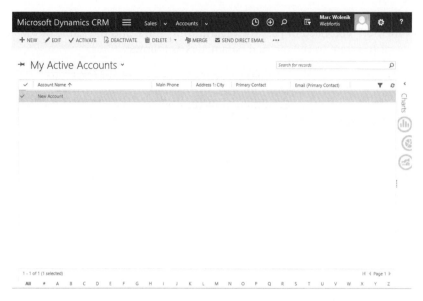

FIGURE 23.7   Reviewing the new account created through the Main Data web service.

Be sure to assign a value for each required field for the entity. Even if you are creating those fields programmatically, you need to enter values for them in CRM as they won't raise any exception if you avoid them, and you might end up creating records without required data.

Retrieve **Method**

The `Retrieve` method gets an instance of an entity object. To get more than one instance of an entity, use the `RetrieveMultiple` method (explained in the next section).

The `Retrieve` method returns a class type of `Entity`. The input parameters are the string of the entity name, the GUID of the instance of the entity, and a set of columns or fields you want to retrieve.

> **TIP**
>
> It is important to define the columns you want to retrieve in the last parameter; otherwise, you get null values even though the instance in the CRM system has values.

Listing 23.3 provides an example of the `Retrieve` method.

LISTING 23.3   Using the `Retrieve` Method

```
private static XrmSdk.Entity RetrieveAccount(string organizationName, Guid
accountId)
        {
            using (XrmSdk.OrganizationServiceClient myCrm = new XrmSdk.
            OrganizationServiceClient())
```

```
        {
            try
            {
                myCrm.Endpoint.Address =
new   System.ServiceModel.EndpointAddress(GetCrmServiceForOrganization
(organizationName));
                myCrm.ClientCredentials.Windows.ClientCredential =
System.Net.CredentialCache.DefaultNetworkCredentials;
                XrmSdk.ColumnSet columns = new XrmSdk.ColumnSet();
                // add more attributes if you want separated by comma below
                columns.Columns = new string[] { "name", "accountid" };
                Guid myAccountId = accountId;
                XrmSdk.Entity myAccount = myCrm.Retrieve("account", myAccountId,
                columns);
                return myAccount;
            }
            catch (Exception ex)
            {
                Console.WriteLine("General exception: " + ex.ToString());
                return null;
            }
        }
    }
}
```

Testing the `Retrieve` **Method**

As you can see from the example in Listing 23.3, you need to know the GUID of the account record (or the entity you want to retrieve) in order to use this method. You can use the `CreateAccount` method you created in the previous section to test this as follows:

```
static void Main(string[] args)
{
    string newAccountId = CreateAccount("Webfortis", "Test Account");
    Console.WriteLine("New Account GUID = " + newAccountId);
    Console.WriteLine("Checking new account created = " +
        RetrieveAccount("Webfortis", new Guid(newAccountId)
        ).Attributes[0].Value);
    Console.ReadKey(); //added for debugging purposes only
}
```

After running this test, you see output similar to that shown in Figure 23.8.

FIGURE 23.8   Testing the `Retrieve` method of the Main Data web service.

You must know the GUID in order to use this code, so this method might not be practical if you know only the name and not the GUID. In such a case, you have to use the `RetriveMultiple` method, as explained in the next section.

RetrieveMultiple **Method**

The `RetrieveMultiple` method gets one or more instances of an entity. For example, you can use this method as shown in Listing 23.4 to retrieve all the accounts for an organization.

LISTING 23.4   Retrieving an Organization's Accounts

```
private static void GetAllAccounts(string organizationName)
       {
           using (XrmSdk.OrganizationServiceClient myCrm =  new XrmSdk.
           OrganizationServiceClient())
           {
              try
              {
                  myCrm.Endpoint.Address =
              new System.ServiceModel.EndpointAddress
              (GetCrmServiceForOrganization(organizationName));
                  myCrm.ClientCredentials.Windows.ClientCredential =
                  System.Net.CredentialCache.DefaultNetworkCredentials;
                  // Creates a column set holding the names of the
                  // columns to be retrieved
                  XrmSdk.ColumnSet colsPrincipal = new XrmSdk.ColumnSet();
                  // Sets the Column Set's Properties
                  colsPrincipal.Columns = new string[] { "accountid", "name" };
                  // Create the Query Expression

                  XrmSdk.QueryExpression queryPrincipal =
                  new XrmSdk.QueryExpression();
```

```
                    // Set the QueryExpression's Properties
                    queryPrincipal.EntityName = "account";
                    queryPrincipal.ColumnSet = colsPrincipal;
                    /// Retrieve the accounts.
                    XrmSdk.EntityCollection myAccounts =
                    myCrm.RetrieveMultiple(queryPrincipal);
                    Console.WriteLine("\nGetAllAccounts found {0} accounts\n",
                    myAccounts.Entities.Length);
                    foreach (XrmSdk.Entity myEntity in myAccounts.Entities)
                    {
                        Console.WriteLine(myEntity.Attributes[1].Value);
                    }
                }
                catch (Exception ex)
                {
                    Console.WriteLine("General exception: " + ex.ToString());
                }
            }
        }
```

Testing the `RetrieveMultiple` **Method**

To test the method in Listing 23.4, you need to pass the organization name to the method parameter. The `Main` function should be as follows:

```
static void Main(string[] args)
{
    GetAllAccounts("Webfortis");
    Console.ReadKey(); //added for debugging purposes only
}
```

You can run this code either by pressing F5 or by going to the Debug menu and choosing the Start Debugging option. In either case, similar output appears, as shown in Figure 23.9.

FIGURE 23.9 `RetrieveMultiple` **example.**

You can apply filters on the data you want, as well as retrieve only the fields or properties you want to get. For example, to retrieve all the accounts whose names match or start with the first few letters of each other, use the code in Listing 23.5.

LISTING 23.5   Retrieving Matching Accounts

```
private static List<XrmSdk.Entity> GetAllAccountsByName(string organizationName,
  string accountName, XrmSdk.ConditionOperator conditionalOperator)
        {
          List<XrmSdk.Entity> accounts - null;
          using (XrmSdk.OrganizationServiceClient myCrm =
          new XrmSdk.OrganizationServiceClient())
          {
            try
            {
                myCrm.Endpoint.Address =
                new System.ServiceModel.EndpointAddress
                (GetCrmServiceForOrganization(organizationName));
                myCrm.ClientCredentials.Windows.ClientCredential =
                System.Net.CredentialCache.DefaultNetworkCredentials;
                // Creates a column set holding the names of the
                // columns to be retrieved
                XrmSdk.ColumnSet colsPrincipal = new XrmSdk.ColumnSet();
                // Sets the Column Set's Properties
                colsPrincipal.Columns = new string[] { "accountid", "name" };
                // Create a ConditionExpression
                XrmSdk.ConditionExpression conditionPrincipal =
                new XrmSdk.ConditionExpression();
                // Sets the ConditionExpressions Properties so that the condition
                // is true when the ownerid of the account Equals the principalId
                conditionPrincipal.AttributeName = "name";
                conditionPrincipal.Operator = conditionalOperator;
                conditionPrincipal.Values = new object[1];

                conditionPrincipal.Values[0] = accountName;
                // Create the FilterExpression
                XrmSdk.FilterExpression filterPrincipal =
                new XrmSdk.FilterExpression();
                // Set the FilterExpression's Properties
                filterPrincipal.FilterOperator = XrmSdk.LogicalOperator.And;
                filterPrincipal.Conditions =
                new XrmSdk.ConditionExpression[] { conditionPrincipal };
                // Create the Query Expression
                XrmSdk.QueryExpression queryPrincipal =
                new XrmSdk.QueryExpression();
                // Set the QueryExpression's Properties
                queryPrincipal.EntityName = "account";
```

```
                queryPrincipal.ColumnSet = colsPrincipal;
                queryPrincipal.Criteria = filterPrincipal;
                /// Retrieve the accounts.
                XrmSdk.EntityCollection myAccounts =
                myCrm.RetrieveMultiple(queryPrincipal);
                accounts = new List<ConsoleApplication1.XrmSdk.Entity>();
                foreach (XrmSdk.Entity myEntity in myAccounts.Entities)
                {
                    accounts.Add(myEntity);
                    Console.WriteLine(myEntity.Attributes[1].Value);
                }
                return accounts;
            }
            catch (Exception ex)
            {
                Console.WriteLine("General exception: " + ex.ToString());
                return null;
            }
        }
    }
```

Testing the Account-Matching Method

To test the method in Listing 23.5, you need to pass the organization name to the method parameter. For this, the Main function should be as shown in Listing 23.6.

LISTING 23.6   Function to Pass the Organization Name

```
static void Main(string[] args)
{
    List<XrmSdk.Entity> accounts;
        Console.WriteLine("Accounts that start with the letter A");
        accounts - GetAllAccountsByName("Webfortis", "A%", ConsoleApplication1.
        XrmSdk.ConditionOperator.Like);
        if (accounts == null)
        {
            Console.WriteLine("No accounts found");
        }
        Console.WriteLine("Accounts equal to 'Test Account'");
        accounts = GetAllAccountsByName("Webfortis", "Test Account",
        ConsoleApplication1.XrmSdk.ConditionOperator.Equal);
        if (accounts == null)
        {
            Console.WriteLine("No accounts found");
        }
    Console.ReadKey(); //added for debugging purposes only
}
```

You can run this code by either pressing F5 or by going to the Debug menu and choosing the Start Debugging option. In either case, similar output appears, as shown in Figure 23.10.

FIGURE 23.10   `RetrieveMultiple` method output.

`Delete` **Method**

The `Delete` method deletes an existing instance or record of an entity. This method doesn't return any value and accepts two input parameters. The first parameter is a string containing the entity type, and the second parameter is the GUID of the instance of the entity you will delete.

The example in Listing 23.7 shows how to delete a new account programmatically in Visual Studio 2015 with C#.

LISTING 23.7   Deleting a New Account with C#

```
private static string DeleteAccount(string organizationName,
      Guid accountToDelete)
        {
            using (XrmSdk.OrganizationServiceClient myCrm =
            new XrmSdk.OrganizationServiceClient())
            {
                try
                {
                    myCrm.Endpoint.Address =
                    new System.ServiceModel.EndpointAddress
(GetCrmServiceForOrganization(organizationName));
                    myCrm.ClientCredentials.Windows.ClientCredential =
                System.Net.CredentialCache.DefaultNetworkCredentials;
                    myCrm.Delete("account", accountToDelete);
                    return "Account successfully deleted";
                }
```

```
            catch (Exception ex)
            {
                Console.WriteLine("General exception: " + ex.ToString());
                return "General exception: " + ex.ToString();
            }
        }
    }
```

Testing the Delete Method

To test the `Delete` method, you need to pass the organization name to the method parameter as well as the GUID of the account to be deleted. Because you might not know the GUID of the account but you might know the account name, you can use the `GetAllAccountsByName` method you created previously.

> **NOTE**
>
> Don't forget to replace `Webfortis` with your organization name in all the examples in this chapter.

The `Main` function to delete all the accounts that match with the name `Test Account` should be as shown in Listing 23.8.

LISTING 23.8   Deleting Demo Accounts

```
static void Main(string[] args)
{
        List<XrmSdk.Entity> accounts;
        Console.WriteLine("Accounts equal to 'Test Account'");
        accounts = GetAllAccountsByName("Webfortis", "Test Account",
        ConsoleApplication1.XrmSdk.ConditionOperator.Equal);
        if (accounts == null)
        {
            Console.WriteLine("No accounts found");
        }
        else
        {
            foreach (XrmSdk.Entity myAccount in accounts)
            {
                Console.WriteLine(
                DeleteAccount("Webfortis", new Guid(myAccount.Attributes[0].
                Value.ToString())));
            }
        }
  Console.ReadKey(); //added for debugging purposes only
}
```

You can run this code by either pressing F5 or by going to the Debug menu and choosing the Start Debugging option. In either case, similar output appears, as shown in Figure 23.11.

FIGURE 23.11   Account deletion example.

Execute **Method**

The `Execute` method executes business logic. It returns a `Response` object and accepts a parameter as the input of the `Request` type. You can use this method as a wildcard for all the other methods. This means you can create an account by using this method because the class called `CreateRequest` derives from `Request` and can be used as the input parameter; you receive a `CreateResponse` as the result. The same happens for `UpdateRequest`, `UpdateResponse`, `RetrieveRequest`, and `RetrieveResponse`.

However, this method is usually used for things you cannot do with the other methods, such as closing a CRM case. Although the Case entity can be updated, you cannot update its status by using the `Update` method. To close a case, you need to use the method shown in Listing 23.9.

▶ If you don't remember how to create a case, refer to **CHAPTER 10**, "Working with Service."

LISTING 23.9   Using the `Update` Method to Update Status

```
private static bool CloseCase(string organizationName, Guid caseId)
        {
            using (XrmSdk.OrganizationServiceClient myCrm =
            new XrmSdk.OrganizationServiceClient())
            {
                try
                {
                    myCrm.Endpoint.Address =
                    new System.ServiceModel.EndpointAddress
                    (GetCrmServiceForOrganization(organizationName));
```

```
                myCrm.ClientCredentials.Windows.ClientCredential =
                System.Net.CredentialCache.DefaultNetworkCredentials;
                XrmSdk.Entity myIncidentResolution = new XrmSdk.Entity();
                myIncidentResolution.LogicalName = "incidentresolution";
                XrmSdk.EntityReference incidentId = new XrmSdk.EntityReference();
                incidentId.LogicalName = "incident";
                incidentId.Id = caseId;
                myIncidentResolution.Attributes = new XrmSdk.AttributeCollection();
                myIncidentResolution.Attributes.Add(
                new KeyValuePair<string, object>("incidentid", incidentId));
                XrmSdk.OrganizationRequest closeIncident =
                new XrmSdk.OrganizationRequest();
                closeIncident.RequestName = "CloseIncident";
                closeIncident.Parameters = new XrmSdk.ParameterCollection();
                XrmSdk.OptionSetValue statusValue = new XrmSdk.OptionSetValue();
                statusValue.Value = -1;
                closeIncident.Parameters.Add(new KeyValuePair<string,
                object>("Status", statusValue));
                closeIncident.Parameters.Add(new KeyValuePair<string,
                object>("IncidentResolution", myIncidentResolution));
                myCrm.Execute(closeIncident);
                Console.WriteLine("Case successfully closed ");
                return true;
            }
            catch (Exception ex)
            {
                Console.WriteLine("General exception: " + ex.ToString());
                return false;
            }
        }
    }
}
```

Testing the Execute Method

When you try to test the code in Listing 23.9, you get a serialization error, and the case isn't closed. To avoid any serialization errors, you need to update the reference.cs file associated with the CrmSdk service with the directives on the OrganizationRequest method, as shown in Listing 23.10.

LISTING 23.10   Updating the reference.cs File

```
[System.Runtime.Serialization.KnownTypeAttribute(typeof(OptionSetValue))]
[System.Runtime.Serialization.KnownTypeAttribute(typeof(Entity))]
[System.Runtime.Serialization.KnownTypeAttribute(typeof(EntityReference))]
[System.Diagnostics.DebuggerStepThroughAttribute()]
[System.CodeDom.Compiler.GeneratedCodeAttribute(
 "System.Runtime.Serialization", "4.0.0.0")]
```

```
[System.Runtime.Serialization.DataContractAttribute(
Name="OrganizationRequest",
Namespace="http://schemas.microsoft.com/xrm/2011/Contracts")]
[System.SerializableAttribute()]
public partial class OrganizationRequest : object,
 System.Runtime.Serialization.IExtensibleDataObject,
 System.ComponentModel.INotifyPropertyChanged {
```

The reference.cs file can be found in the Service References folder of the project.

The following code closes the case:

```
static void Main(string[] args)
{
     bool caseresult = CloseCase("Webfortis", new
Guid("752EC4FE-B5C9-E511-80D0-00155DFE0C17"));
    Console.WriteLine("Case result = " + caseresult);
    Console.ReadKey(); //added for debugging purposes only
}
```

NOTE

Be sure to replace `Guid` with your case ID.

Fetch Method

The `Fetch` method executes a query defined by the FetchXML language. In that it uses the `RetrieveMultiple` method, and the FetchXML is passed as a parameter using the `FetchExpression` class.

Here are a few points to remember about the `Fetch` method:

▶ With `Fetch`, you can get results in pages by limiting the number of records returned by page.

▶ With `Fetch`, you can just query the record count or use any aggregation method, such as `Avg`, `Count`, `Max`, `Min`, or `Sum`.

▶ `Fetch` does not support a union join. To view all the tasks for an account by checking all the contacts of a contact, you need to perform separate `Fetch` methods—one on the contact tasks and one on the account contacts—and then merge the results.

▶ The resulting set of records depends on the user privilege.

▶ You can use left outer joins.

▶ There is a 5,000-row limitation on the results of the query per page.

Listing 23.11 shows how to use the `Fetch` method to retrieve all contacts with all their properties.

This is the FetchXML code to use for grabbing the fullname of the contact:

```
<fetch mapping='logical'>
    <entity name='contact'>
          <attribute name='fullname'/>
    </entity>
</fetch>
```

LISTING 23.11   Using the `Fetch` Method to Retrieve Contacts

```
private static void GetAllContacts(string organizationName)
{
    using (XrmSdk.OrganizationServiceClient myCrm =
        new XrmSdk.OrganizationServiceClient())
    {
        try
        {
            myCrm.Endpoint.Address =
            new System.ServiceModel.EndpointAddress(
            GetCrmServiceForOrganization(organizationName));
            myCrm.ClientCredentials.Windows.ClientCredential =
            System.Net.CredentialCache.DefaultNetworkCredentials;
            // Retrieve all Contacts.
            StringBuilder fetchStr = new StringBuilder();
            fetchStr.Append(@"<fetch mapping='logical'>");
            fetchStr.Append(@"<entity name='contact'> <attribute name='fullname'/>");
            fetchStr.Append(@"</entity></fetch>");
            XrmSdk.FetchExpression fetchexp = new XrmSdk.FetchExpression();
            fetchexp.Query = fetchStr.ToString();
            XrmSdk.QueryBase mq = new XrmSdk.QueryBase();

            // Fetch the results.
            XrmSdk.EntityCollection fetchResult = myCrm.RetrieveMultiple(fetchexp);
            Console.WriteLine("\nGetAllContacts found {0} contacts\n"
            , fetchResult.Entities.Count());
            foreach (XrmSdk.Entity entity in fetchResult.Entities)
            {
                Console.WriteLine("Contact fullname = {0}",
                entity.Attributes[0].Value);
            }
        }
        catch (Exception ex)
        {
            Console.WriteLine("General exception: " + ex.ToString());
        }
    }
}
```

NOTE

If you are not familiar with the FetchXML language, you can create a query with the Advanced Find tool in the CRM web user interface and click the button Download Fetch XML to easily get the code you need for a programmatic call.

Update **Method**

The Update method updates data related to an instance of an entity.

This method has only one implementation, and it doesn't return a value. In the same way as the Create method, it accepts one parameter of type Entity. Because all the entities in CRM inherit from the Entity base class, you can pass any Entity class to this input parameter. To use this method, you must set at least the ID property of the entity to be updated (for example, set the accountid property if you want to update an account).

Listing 23.12 shows how to update an existing account programmatically in Visual Studio 2015 with C#.

LISTING 23.12   Updating an Existing Account with C#

```
private static string UpdateAccountName(string organizationName,
            Guid accountId, string newName)
{
    using (XrmSdk.OrganizationServiceClient myCrm =
        new XrmSdk.OrganizationServiceClient())
    {
        try
        {
            myCrm.Endpoint.Address =
            new System.ServiceModel.EndpointAddress(
            GetCrmServiceForOrganization(organizationName));
            myCrm.ClientCredentials.Windows.ClientCredential =
            System.Net.CredentialCache.DefaultNetworkCredentials;
            XrmSdk.Entity myAccount = new XrmSdk.Entity();
            myAccount.LogicalName = "account";
            XrmSdk.AttributeCollection myAttributes =
            new XrmSdk.AttributeCollection();
            myAttributes.Add(new KeyValuePair<string, object>(
            "accountid", accountId));
            myAttributes.Add(new KeyValuePair<string, object>("name",
            newName));
            myAccount.Attributes = myAttributes;
            myCrm.Update(myAccount);
            return "Account successfully updated ";
        }
```

```
    catch (Exception ex)
    {
        Console.WriteLine("General exception: " + ex.ToString());
        return "General exception: " + ex.ToString();
    }
    }
}
```

CAUTION

Note that only the properties you set are updated. This means that in Listing 23.12, only the company name property will be changed; the other properties will keep their values. This happens even though they are not set and they have null values when you send them to the `Update` method.

Early Binding

The examples shown so far in this chapter use late binding. When you use late binding, accessing and using the Organization service is difficult, and you need to explicitly type both the entity name and the attribute name. This makes the code cumbersome to write and sometimes prone to errors.

Instead of using late binding, you can use early binding, which provides IntelliSense support and better code development and use of .NET technologies such as the .NET Framework Language-Integrated Query (LINQ). To use early binding, you must generate the entity classes by using the code generation tool called CrmSvcUtil.exe, a console application that you can find in the SDK\bin folder of the CRM 2016 software development kit (SDK).

NOTE

The default language of the CrmSvcUtil.exe tool is C#, but you can also use it to produce Visual Basic code by adding the `/l:VB` parameter to it.

Here is an example of calling the CrmSvcUtil.exe tool:

```
CrmSvcUtil.exe /url:http://crm2016/Webfortis/XRMServices/2011/Organization.svc
    /out:GeneratedCode.cs /username:bill /password:p@ssword!
```

TIP

You do not need a username and password if you're working with an On-Premises deployment that uses Integrated Windows Authentication.

> **NOTE**
>
> The CrmSvcUtil.exe command shown here takes some time to run because it generates code for everything you need to work with CRM 2016, so be patient.

If you get the GeneratedCode.cs file and include it in your solution, you can work with the Organization service easily. You also need to add references from the following assemblies to your solution (which you can also find in the SDK\bin folder of the CRM 2016 SDK):

▶ microsoft.xrm.sdk.dll

▶ microsoft.crm.sdk.proxy.dll

> **NOTE**
>
> You can also use NuGet to add the assemblies, via the following command:
>
> ```
> Install-Package Microsoft.CrmSdk.CoreAssemblies
> ```

The last assemblies you need to reference are System.Runtime.Serialization and System.ServiceModel, which you can find in the Global Assembly Cache (GAC).

Regular Operations for Early Binding

The following sections cover the following regular operations:

▶ Create

▶ Retrieve

▶ RetrieveMultiple

▶ Delete

▶ Update

However, the following sections also use early binding so that you can see the differences between how you use these methods with late binding and with early binding.

Create Method

To create any instance of an entity such as a new account or contact, instead of using the Create method described earlier in this chapter, use the code in Listing 23.13.

LISTING 23.13   Creating a New Account

```
using Microsoft.Xrm.Sdk.Client;
using System.ServiceModel.Description;

public static string CreateAccount(string organizationName, string accountName)
{
```

```
    ClientCredentials credentials = new ClientCredentials();
    credentials.Windows.ClientCredential =
    System.Net.CredentialCache.DefaultNetworkCredentials;
    OrganizationServiceProxy _serviceProxy =
        new OrganizationServiceProxy(new Uri("http://<<server name>>" +
        organizationName + "/XRMServices/2011/Organization.svc"),
        null, credentials, null);
_serviceProxy.ServiceConfiguration.CurrentServiceEndpoint.Behaviors.Add(
new ProxyTypesBehavior());
    OrganizationServiceContext orgContext =
    new OrganizationServiceContext(_serviceProxy);
    Account account = new Account()
        {
            Name = accountName
        };
    orgContext.AddObject(account);
    orgContext.SaveChanges();
    return account.AccountId.ToString();
}
```

Retrieve **Method**

To retrieve any record of an entity such as an account or a contact, you can use LINQ, using the code in Listing 23.14.

LISTING 23.14 Retrieving an Existing Account Record

```
private static Account RetrieveAccount(string organizationName, Guid accountId)
{
    ClientCredentials credentials = new ClientCredentials();
    credentials.Windows.ClientCredential =
    System.Net.CredentialCache.DefaultNetworkCredentials;
    OrganizationServiceProxy _serviceProxy =
    new OrganizationServiceProxy(new Uri("http://<<server name>>" +
      organizationName + "/XRMServices/2011/Organization.svc"),
        null, credentials, null);

_serviceProxy.ServiceConfiguration.CurrentServiceEndpoint.Behaviors.Add(
new ProxyTypesBehavior());

    OrganizationServiceContext orgContext =
    new OrganizationServiceContext(_serviceProxy);
    Account account = (from a in orgContext.CreateQuery<Account>()
    where a.AccountId == accountId select a).Single();
    return account;
}
```

23

RetrieveMultiple **Method**

You can also use LINQ to retrieve multiple records, as shown in Listing 23.15. When you do this, you don't need to learn how to query and filter attributes in CRM 2016; the LINQ knowledge is enough.

LISTING 23.15   Retrieving Multiple Account Records with LINQ

```
private static void GetAllAccounts(string organizationName)
{
    ClientCredentials credentials - new ClientCredentials();
    credentials.Windows.ClientCredential =
    System.Net.CredentialCache.DefaultNetworkCredentials;
    OrganizationServiceProxy _serviceProxy =
      new OrganizationServiceProxy(new Uri("http://<<server name>>/" +
      organizationName + "/XRMServices/2011/Organization.svc"),
        null, credentials, null);
_serviceProxy.ServiceConfiguration.CurrentServiceEndpoint.Behaviors.Add(
new ProxyTypesBehavior());
    OrganizationServiceContext orgContext =
    new OrganizationServiceContext(_serviceProxy);
    /// Retrieve the accounts.
    var accounts = from a in orgContext.CreateQuery<Account>() select a;
    foreach (Account myAccount in accounts)
    {
        Console.WriteLine(myAccount.Name);
    }
}
```

You can apply any filters you want, as you would do with any other LINQ filter.

Delete **Method**

To delete a record using the organization context, you do it in the following way:

```
Account account = (from a in orgContext.CreateQuery<Account>()
where a.AccountId == accountToDelete select a).Single();
orgContext.DeleteObject(account);
orgContext.SaveChanges();
```

Without using the organization context, you do it as follows:

```
Account account = (from a in orgContext.CreateQuery<Account>()
where a.AccountId == accountToDelete select a).Single();
_serviceProxy.Delete(Account.EntityLogicalName, accountToDelete);
```

Update **Method**

To update a record using the organization context, you do it in the following way:

```
Account account = (from a in orgContext.CreateQuery<Account>()
where a.AccountId == accountToUpdate select a).Single();
account.Name = "demo";
orgContext.UpdateObject(account);
orgContext.SaveChanges();
```

Without using the organization context, you do it as follows:

```
Account account = (from a in orgContext.CreateQuery<Account>()
where a.AccountId == accountToUpdate select a).Single();
account.Name = "demo";
_serviceProxy.Update(account);
```

Metadata

Using the same Organization service described earlier, you can also access all the CRM metadata.

You can also use the Organization service to create, update, or delete entities, as well as to create or delete relationships within entities. You can also use it to programmatically add, delete, or modify attributes to an existing entity.

Using the metadata can be very useful for independent software vendors (ISVs) to look up entities on a setup installer to see whether a solution was already installed or to check whether any conflict exists with the entities of the CRM system on which a customization would be deployed.

By using the Execute method, you can access the submethods necessary to interact with the metadata.

Execute **Method**

The Execute method accepts the following submethods related to the metadata:

- ▶ CreateAttribute
- ▶ CreateEntity
- ▶ CreateManyToMany
- ▶ CreateOneToMany
- ▶ CreateOptionSet
- ▶ DeleteAttribute
- ▶ DeleteEntity
- ▶ DeleteOptionSet
- ▶ DeleteOptionValue

▶ DeleteRelationship

▶ InsertOptionValue

▶ InsertStatusValue

▶ OrderOption

▶ RetrieveAllEntities

▶ RetrieveAllManagedProperties

▶ RetrieveAllOptionSets

▶ RetrieveAttribute

▶ RetrieveEntity

▶ RetrieveMetadataChanges

▶ RetrieveOptionSet

▶ RetrieveRelationship

▶ RetrieveTimestamp

▶ UpdateAttribute

▶ UpdateEntity

▶ UpdateOptionSet

▶ UpdateOptionValue

▶ UpdateRelationship

▶ UpdateStateValue

Each of these submethods is called by using the `OrganizationRequest` and `OrganizationResponse` methods of the organization service.

For example, you might use the `Execute` method to find out whether the custom entity new_MyNewCustomEntity already exists in a CRM implementation.

Listing 23.16 shows how you can add the code for the example, using two parameters: the organization name and the entity name.

LISTING 23.16   Checking for Entity Existence Using Two Parameters

```
private static bool CheckEntity(string organizationName, string entityName)
{
    try
    {
        ClientCredentials credentials = new ClientCredentials();
        credentials.Windows.ClientCredential =
        System.Net.CredentialCache.DefaultNetworkCredentials;
```

```
        OrganizationServiceProxy _serviceProxy =
        new OrganizationServiceProxy(new Uri("http://crmwoifd/" +
        organizationName + "/XRMServices/2011/Organization.svc"),
            null, credentials, null);
_serviceProxy.ServiceConfiguration.CurrentServiceEndpoint.Behaviors.Add(
   new ProxyTypesBehavior());
        Microsoft.Xrm.Sdk.Messages.RetrieveEntityRequest myRequest =
        new Microsoft.Xrm.Sdk.Messages.RetrieveEntityRequest();
        myRequest.LogicalName = entityName.ToLower();
        Microsoft.Xrm.Sdk.Messages.RetrieveEntityResponse myResponse;
        myResponse =
(Microsoft.Xrm.Sdk.Messages.RetrieveEntityResponse)
        _serviceProxy.Execute(myRequest);
        return true;
    }
    catch (Exception ex)
    {
        Console.WriteLine("General exception: " + ex.ToString());
        return false;
    }
}
```

Now if you want to check whether the account or new_MyNewCustomEntity entity exists on the organization with the name demo, you can use the following code:

```
static void Main(string[] args)
{
        Console.WriteLine("Account entity exists = " +
        CheckEntity("demo", "Account"));
        Console.WriteLine("new_ MyNewCustomEntity entity exists = "
        + CheckEntity("demo", "new_ MyNewCustomEntity"));

        Console.ReadKey();
}
```

This code should return true for the Account entity and false for the new_ MyNewCustomEntity entity (assuming that you have not created any custom entity with the name new_MyNewCustomEntity on your CRM system).

Listing 23.17 shows how to programmatically create a custom entity using this web service.

LISTING 23.17   Creating a Custom Entity

```
private static bool CreateCustomEntity(string organizationName,
        string entityName)
{
    try
    {
        ClientCredentials credentials = new ClientCredentials();
        credentials.Windows.ClientCredential =
        System.Net.CredentialCache.DefaultNetworkCredentials;
        OrganizationServiceProxy _serviceProxy =
        new OrganizationServiceProxy(new Uri("http://<<server name>>/" +
        organizationName + "/XRMServices/2011/Organization.svc"),
            null, credentials, null);
_serviceProxy.ServiceConfiguration.CurrentServiceEndpoint.Behaviors.Add(
      new ProxyTypesBehavior());
        // Creates new entity
        Microsoft.Xrm.Sdk.Metadata.EntityMetadata myNewEntity =
        new Microsoft.Xrm.Sdk.Metadata.EntityMetadata();
        myNewEntity.Description = CreateLabel(entityName);
        myNewEntity.DisplayCollectionName = CreateLabel(entityName);
        myNewEntity.DisplayName = CreateLabel(entityName);
        myNewEntity.IsAvailableOffline = true;
        myNewEntity.SchemaName = entityName;
        myNewEntity.LogicalName = entityName;
        myNewEntity.OwnershipType =
Microsoft.Xrm.Sdk.Metadata.OwnershipTypes.UserOwned;
        // Creates primary attribute
        Microsoft.Xrm.Sdk.Metadata.StringAttributeMetadata
 myPrimaryAttr =
new Microsoft.Xrm.Sdk.Metadata.StringAttributeMetadata();
        myPrimaryAttr.DisplayName = CreateLabel("Name");
        myPrimaryAttr.Description = CreateLabel("This is the Name");
        myPrimaryAttr.MaxLength = 100;
        myPrimaryAttr.SchemaName = "new_Name";
        myPrimaryAttr.Format = Microsoft.Xrm.Sdk.Metadata.StringFormat.Text;
        myPrimaryAttr.RequiredLevel =
new Microsoft.Xrm.Sdk.Metadata.AttributeRequiredLevelManagedProperty(
Microsoft.Xrm.Sdk.Metadata.AttributeRequiredLevel.ApplicationRequired);
        myPrimaryAttr.LogicalName = "new_name";
        // Prepare request
        Microsoft.Xrm.Sdk.Messages.CreateEntityRequest myRequest =
        new Microsoft.Xrm.Sdk.Messages.CreateEntityRequest();
        myRequest.Entity = myNewEntity;
        myRequest.HasActivities = true;
        myRequest.HasNotes = true;
        myRequest.PrimaryAttribute = myPrimaryAttr;
        Microsoft.Xrm.Sdk.Messages.CreateEntityResponse myResponse;
```

```
        myResponse = (Microsoft.Xrm.Sdk.Messages.CreateEntityResponse)
        _serviceProxy.Execute(myRequest);
        return true;
    }
    catch (Exception ex)
    {
        Console.WriteLine("General exception: " + ex.ToString());
        return false;
    }
}
```

The code in Listing 23.17 uses the custom method `CreateLabel` to simplify the code used to set up the labels. The labels must be managed in a collection because of the multilanguage feature. This example uses only the English language for the strings, but you can easily customize it to use other languages, like this:

```
private static Microsoft.Xrm.Sdk.Label CreateLabel(string myString)
{
    Microsoft.Xrm.Sdk.Label myLabel = new Microsoft.Xrm.Sdk.Label();
    Microsoft.Xrm.Sdk.LocalizedLabel myLabels =
    new Microsoft.Xrm.Sdk.LocalizedLabel(myString,
    1033);// English code
    myLabel.LocalizedLabels.Add(myLabels);
    return myLabel;
}
```

Now if you want to create a new entity with the name new_MyNewCustomEntity on the organization with the name demo, you can use the following code:

```
static void Main(string[] args)
{
        CreateCustomEntity("demo", "new_MyNewCustomEntity");
        Console.ReadKey();
}
```

NOTE

Be sure the entity name does not already exist in the CRM system; if it does, the `Execute` method will raise an exception. Alternatively, you can use the `CheckEntity` method you created earlier and use the following code:

```
static void Main(string[] args)
{
        if (!CheckEntity("demo", "new_MyNewCustomEntity"))
        {
            CreateCustomEntity("demo", "new_MyNewCustomEntity");
        }
        Console.ReadKey();
}
```

> **NOTE**
>
> You must also set at least the primary attribute on the request, and it must be required. In addition, you can use this web service if you want to show all the options from an Option Set attribute on another application.

As another example, suppose you need to retrieve all possible values for the Shipping Method property for Accounts. Because Shipping Method is an Option Set attribute, you must query the metabase to get the values, as shown in Listing 23.18.

LISTING 23.18   Querying the Metabase to Retrieve Values

```
private static void GetShippingMethod(string organizationName)
{
    ClientCredentials credentials = new ClientCredentials();
    credentials.Windows.ClientCredential =
    System.Net.CredentialCache.DefaultNetworkCredentials;
    OrganizationServiceProxy _serviceProxy =
    new OrganizationServiceProxy(new Uri("http://crmwoifd/" +
    organizationName + "/XRMServices/2011/Organization.svc"),
    null, credentials, null);
_serviceProxy.ServiceConfiguration.CurrentServiceEndpoint.Behaviors.Add(
    new ProxyTypesBehavior());
    Microsoft.Xrm.Sdk.Messages.RetrieveAttributeRequest myRequest =
    new Microsoft.Xrm.Sdk.Messages.RetrieveAttributeRequest();
    myRequest.EntityLogicalName = Account.EntityLogicalName;
    myRequest.LogicalName = "address1_shippingmethodcode";
    Microsoft.Xrm.Sdk.Messages.RetrieveAttributeResponse myResponse;
    myResponse = (Microsoft.Xrm.Sdk.Messages.RetrieveAttributeResponse)
    _serviceProxy.Execute(myRequest);
    foreach (Microsoft.Xrm.Sdk.Metadata.OptionMetadata myOption in
((Microsoft.Xrm.Sdk.Metadata.PicklistAttributeMetadata)
    (myResponse.AttributeMetadata)).OptionSet.Options)
    {
        Console.WriteLine(myOption.Label.LocalizedLabels[0].Label);
    }
}
```

Now if you want to test this method on the organization with the name demo, you can use the following code:

```
static void Main(string[] args)
{
        GetShippingMethod("demo");
        Console.ReadKey();
}
```

Examples of Web Services

Because the WCF web services and REST are platform independent, it is not strictly necessary to access the web services from a .NET assembly or a compiled application. You could access the web services using JavaScript, for example.

> **NOTE**
>
> Check the CRM 2016 SDK for more examples on accessing web services.

JavaScript

This section shows how to get and set the address from an account using JavaScript by querying the CRM OData (REST) service. This automatically sets the contact address when you select an account as the Company Name field (without requiring you to enter it again).

> **NOTE**
>
> To make this example work, you must select an account with the address fields populated with some data. In addition, keep in mind that OData has been deprecated, and Web API should be used moving forward.

> **CAUTION**
>
> The following example works only if you select a company name for a contact and not for a parent contact. However, after you review this example, you can modify it to work with parent contacts if desired.

The purpose of this example is to show how you can consume an OData (REST) service without having to build a .NET application or component to make some of your business customizations.

▶ For more details about working with JavaScript customizations, refer to **CHAPTER 22**, "Customizing Entities."

To create this example, follow these steps:

1. Go to Settings > Customizations > Customize the System and select the Contact entity in Microsoft CRM 2016 (see Figure 23.12).

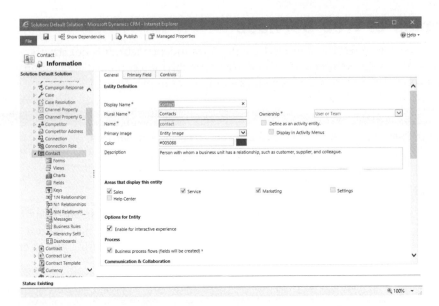

FIGURE 23.12   Contact customization.

2. Expand the Contact entity and click Forms in the left navigation pane (see Figure 23.13).

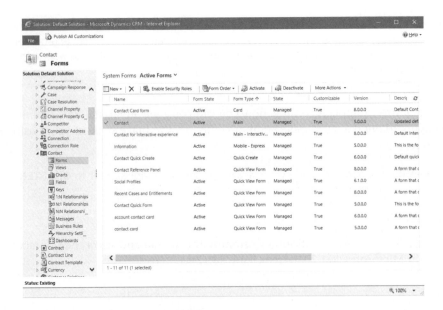

FIGURE 23.13   Forms customization.

3. Double-click the Main form type to open it (see Figure 23.14).

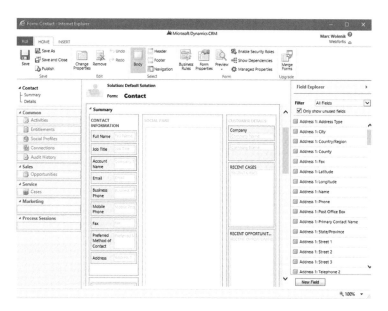

FIGURE 23.14   Main form type customization.

4. Click the Account Name field and click Change Properties. The Field Properties dialog appears (see Figure 23.15).

FIGURE 23.15   Field Properties dialog.

5. Select the Events tab (see Figure 23.16).

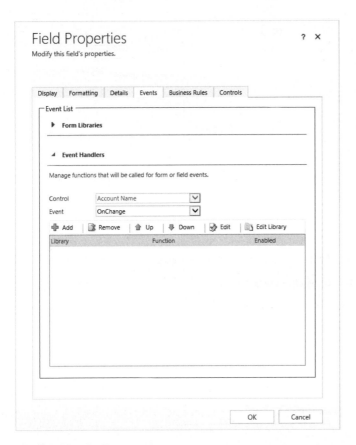

FIGURE 23.16   Events tab.

6. Expand Form Libraries and click Add (see Figure 23.17).

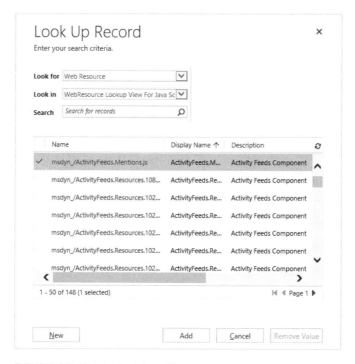

FIGURE 23.17   Adding form libraries.

7. Click New and enter a name, usually with a .js extension (for example, sampleScript. js), enter a display name, and select Script (JScript) from the Type dropdown (see Figure 23.18).

8. Click the Text Editor button and insert the code shown in Listing 23.19 into the text box (see Figure 23.19).

FIGURE 23.18   New web resource.

LISTING 23.19   Consuming an OData (REST) Service

```
function GetAccountAddress() {
    var CustomerID;
    CustomerID =  Xrm.Page.getAttribute("parentcustomerid").getValue();
    // first of all checks if the user has selected a valid parent customer
    // the Xrm.Page.getAttribute("parentcustomerid").getValue() parameter will give
    us a
    // vector with
    // the GUID of the selected customer
    if (CustomerID != null) {
        //Cleans the old address first
        Xrm.Page.getAttribute("address1_postalcode").setValue(null);
        Xrm.Page.getAttribute("address1_line1").setValue(null);
        Xrm.Page.getAttribute("address1_line2").setValue(null);
        Xrm.Page.getAttribute("address1_line3").setValue(null);
        Xrm.Page.getAttribute("address1_city").setValue(null);
        Xrm.Page.getAttribute("address1_stateorprovince").setValue(null);
        Xrm.Page.getAttribute("address1_country").setValue(null);
        RetrieveAccountRecord(CustomerID[0].id);
    }
```

```
    else {
        alert("Select Parent Customer first!");
    }
}


function RetrieveAccountRecord(Id) {
    var context = Xrm.Page.context;
    serverUrl = context.getClientUrl();
    ODataPath = serverUrl + "/XRMServices/2011/OrganizationData.svc";
    var retrieveAccountReq = new XMLHttpRequest();
    retrieveAccountReq.open("GET", ODataPath + "/AccountSet(guid'" + Id + " ')",
    true);
    retrieveAccountReq.setRequestHeader("Accept", "application/json");
    retrieveAccountReq.setRequestHeader("Content-Type","application/json;
    charset=utf-8");
    retrieveAccountReq.onreadystatechange = function () {
    RetrieveAccountReqCallBack(this);
    };
    retrieveAccountReq.send();
}


function RetrieveAccountReqCallBack(retrieveAccountReq) {
if (retrieveAccountReq.readyState == 4 /* complete */) {
if (retrieveAccountReq.status == 200) {
    //Success
    var retrievedAccount = JSON.parse(retrieveAccountReq.responseText).d;
    Xrm.Page.getAttribute("address1_postalcode").setValue(retrievedAccount.
    Address1_PostalCode);
    Xrm.Page.getAttribute("address1_line1").setValue(retrievedAccount.
    Address1_Line1);
    Xrm.Page.getAttribute("address1_line2").setValue(retrievedAccount.
    Address1_Line2);
    Xrm.Page.getAttribute("address1_line3").setValue(retrievedAccount.
    Address1_Line3);
    Xrm.Page.getAttribute("address1_city").setValue(retrievedAccount.Address1_City);
    Xrm.Page.getAttribute("address1_stateorprovince").setValue(retrievedAccount.
    Address1_StateOrProvince);
    Xrm.Page.getAttribute("address1_country").setValue(retrievedAccount.
    Address1_Country);
    }
    }
}
```

23

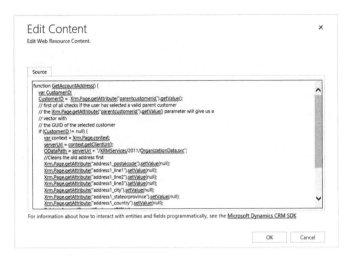

FIGURE 23.19   JavaScript code to call the CRM OData (REST) service.

9. Click OK to close the dialog.

10. Click Save, then Publish, and finally Close to close the Web Resource dialog.

11. Click Add to close the Look Up Web Resource dialog.

12. Under Event Handlers, click Add and enter GetAccountAddress in the Function field (see Figure 23.20).

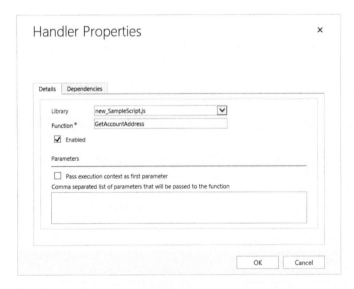

FIGURE 23.20   Handler properties.

13. Click OK to close the Handler Properties dialog.

14. Click OK to close the Field Properties dialog.

15. Click Save, then Publish, and finally Save & Close to close the Entity Contact window.

16. Click the Publish All Customizations button to publish all the customizations.

> **NOTE**
>
> With Dynamics CRM 2016, you don't need to create another web resource for the JSON JavaScript, as you had to do in previous versions of Dynamics CRM. JSON is natively supported in all the modern web browser applications that Dynamics CRM 2016 supports.

To test the solution, follow these steps:

1. Go to Sales > Contacts.

2. Select a contact and double-click it to open it or click +New to create a new Contact. The form shown in Figure 23.21 appears.

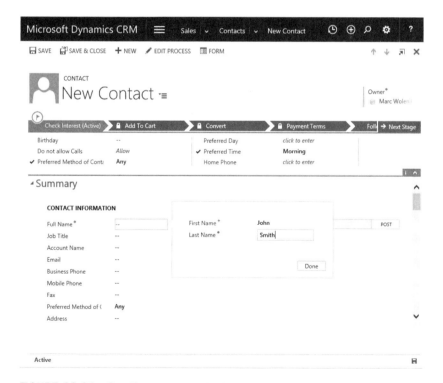

FIGURE 23.21   Creating a new contact.

3. Click the search icon near the Account Name field to select an account (see Figure 23.22).

4. Click OK to close the dialog. You now see the contact address automatically filled in with the selected account address (see Figure 23.23).

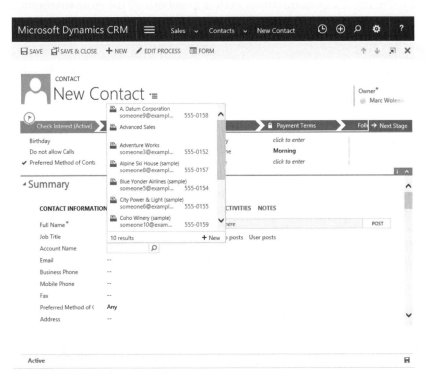

FIGURE 23.22   Selecting a company.

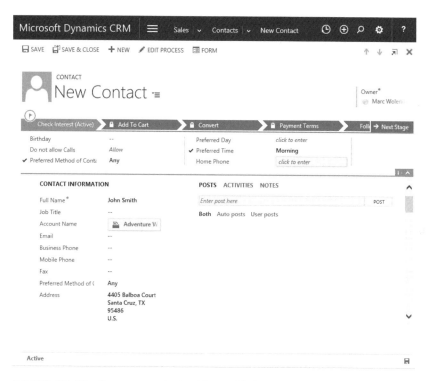

FIGURE 23.23   The new contact address filled automatically with the selected account address.

▶ **SEE** the "Web API" section, later in this chapter, for information on implementing the code shown here with the new Web API code.

If you are not familiar with OData protocol and queries and you want to implement similar customizations, you can use the Silverlight OData Query Designer that is included in the Dynamics XRM Tools managed solution, which you can download from https://dynamicsxrmtools.codeplex.com. You can use this tool to build queries to filter data and select specific columns to be returned to improve the network traffic. While this tool was designed to work with Dynamics CRM 2015, it can still be imported into the 2016 version (see Figure 23.24).

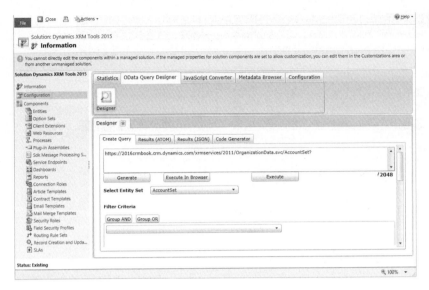

FIGURE 23.24 OData Query Designer in the XRM Tools 2015 managed solution.

Modern SOAP Endpoints

You can use the Organization web service of Dynamics CRM 2016 in JavaScript, using modern SOAP app endpoints. OData can perform CRUD (create, retrieve, update, delete) operations, associate, and disassociate tasks. In addition to all the operations performed by OData, you can also perform the following operations:

▶ Assign records

▶ Retrieve metadata

▶ Execute messages

You can create an XMLHttpRequest object to post requests to the Organization service in JavaScript. The body of the request can be in XML, and you to parse the XML response. You can make both asynchronous and synchronous requests, but the former is preferred. You do not need to write any code for authentication if you are accessing the web service through web resources.

> **NOTE**
>
> Microsoft has provided the SOAPLogger solution in the SDK to create requests in XML format. You can find it at SDK\Sample Code\CS\client\SOAPLogger.

Open the solution in Visual Studio 2015. Go to the Run method in the SOAPLogger.cs file. It provides the SoapLoggerOrganizationService proxy object named slos. You should use it to write your code just as you do with an Organization service proxy.

The following example shows how to assign an account record to some other user. You have the account ID of the Account entity record and the user ID of the user to whom you want to assign the contact record. Listing 23.20 shows how the C# code looks in the SOAPLogger solution.

LISTING 23.20   C# Code for the SOAPLogger Solution

```csharp
public void Run(ServerConnection.Configuration serverConfig)
  {
  try
  {
  // Connect to the Organization service.
  // The using statement assures that the service proxy will be properly disposed.
  using (_serviceProxy = ServerConnection.GetOrganizationProxy(serverConfig))
  {
  // This statement is required to enable early-bound type support.
  _serviceProxy.EnableProxyTypes();
  IOrganizationService service = (IOrganizationService)_serviceProxy;
  using (StreamWriter output = new StreamWriter("output.txt"))
  {
    SoapLoggerOrganizationService slos =
        new SoapLoggerOrganizationService(serverConfig.OrganizationUri, service,
        output);
    //Add the code you want to test here:
    // You must use the SoapLoggerOrganizationService 'slos' proxy
      //rather than the IOrganizationService proxy you would normally use.
    Guid userId = new Guid("8604A92B-264E-E311-B23E-00155D00F819");
    Guid accountId = new Guid("618B1AF2-A161-E311-9AC7-00155D00F819");
    AssignRequest assign = new AssignRequest
    {
        Assignee = new EntityReference(SystemUser.EntityLogicalName, userId),
        Target = new EntityReference(Account.EntityLogicalName, accountId)
    };
    AssignResponse assignResp = (AssignResponse)slos.Execute(assign);
  }
  }
  }
  // Catch any service fault exceptions that Microsoft Dynamics CRM throws.
  catch (FaultException<Microsoft.Xrm.Sdk.OrganizationServiceFault>)
  {
  // You can handle an exception here or pass it back to the calling method.
  throw;
  }
  }
```

> **NOTE**
>
> Be sure to replace Guid in the Listing 23.20 example with your own GUID, or the code will fail.

Build the solution and run the application using F5; the console window then opens. You provide server information and CRM login credentials to execute the code (see Figure 23.25).

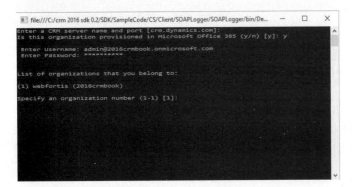

FIGURE 23.25   SOAPLogger console window.

In the bin/debug folder is an output.txt file that will has a POST request and response in XML format. You need to pass this XML request message to XMLHttpRequest and parse the response.

The next example switches to JavaScript code. Listing 23.21 is an example of assigning a record to a user using SOAP messages. You can execute this message using the following:

```
SDK.Sample.AssignRequest(accountid, userid);
```

where accountid is the record GUID of the Account entity record, and userid is the record GUID of the user to whom you want to assign the record.

LISTING 23.21   Assigning a GUID Record

```
(typeof (SDK) == "undefined")
{SDK= {__namespace: true }; }

SDK.Sample = {

    _getClientUrl: function () {

        var ServicePath = "/XRMServices/2011/Organization.svc/web";
        var clientUrl = "";
        if (typeof GetGlobalContext == "function") {
            var context = GetGlobalContext();
```

```
            clientUrl = context.getClientUrl();
        }
        else {
            if (typeof Xrm.Page.context == "object") {
                clientUrl = Xrm.Page.context.getClientUrl();
            }
            else { throw new Error("Unable to access the server URL"); }
        }
        if (clientUrl.match(/\/$/)) {
            clientUrl = clientUrl.substring(0, clientUrl.length - 1);
        }
        return clientUrl + ServicePath;
    },
    AssignRequest: function (accountID, userID) {
        var requestMain = "";
        requestMain += "<s:Envelope xmlns:s=\"http://schemas.xmlsoap.org/soap/
        envelope/\">"
        requestMain += "<s:Body>"
        requestMain += "<Execute xmlns=\"http://schemas.microsoft.com/xrm/2011/
        Contracts/Services\" xmlns:i=\"http://www.w3.org/2001/XMLSchema-instance\">"
        requestMain += "<request xmlns:a=\"http://schemas.microsoft.com/xrm/2011/
        Contracts\">"
        requestMain += "<a:Parameters xmlns:c=\"http://schemas.datacontract.
        org/2004/07/System.Collections.Generic\">"
        requestMain += "<a:KeyValuePairOfstringanyType>"
        requestMain += "<c:key>Target</c:key>"
        requestMain += "<c:value i:type=\"a:EntityReference\">"
        requestMain += "<a:Id>" + accountID + "</a:Id>"
        requestMain += "<a:LogicalName>account</a:LogicalName>"
        requestMain += "<a:Name i:nil=\"true\" />"
        requestMain += "</c:value>"
        requestMain += "</a:KeyValuePairOfstringanyType>"
        requestMain += "<a:KeyValuePairOfstringanyType>"
        requestMain += "<c:key>Assignee</c:key>"
        requestMain += "<c:value i:type=\"a:EntityReference\">"
        requestMain += "<a:Id>" + userID + "</a:Id>"
        requestMain += "<a:LogicalName>systemuser</a:LogicalName>"
        requestMain += "<a:Name i:nil=\"true\" />"
        requestMain += "</c:value>"
        requestMain += "</a:KeyValuePairOfstringanyType>"
        requestMain += "</a:Parameters>"
        requestMain += "<a:RequestId i:nil=\"true\" />"
        requestMain += "<a:RequestName>Assign</a:RequestName>"
        requestMain += "</request>"
        requestMain += "</Execute>"
        requestMain += "</s:Body>"
```

23

```
        requestMain += "</s:Envelope>"
        var req = new XMLHttpRequest();
        req.open("POST", SDK.Sample._getClientUrl(), false)
        req.setRequestHeader("Accept", "application/xml, text/xml, */*");
        req.setRequestHeader("Content-Type", "text/xml; charset=utf-8");
        req.setRequestHeader("SOAPAction", "http://schemas.microsoft.com/xrm/2011/
        Contracts/Services/IOrganizationService/");
        req.send(requestMain);
    },
    __namespace: true
};
```

ExecuteMultipleRequest

All message requests discussed in this chapter up to now (except for `RetrieveMultiple`) work for only one record. If you have to create/update/delete on more than one record, you have to iterate through records and send individual organization message requests for each record, which takes a long time because of Internet latency in the case of Microsoft Dynamics CRM Online. Microsoft introduced a new message named `ExecuteMultipleRequest` in CRM 2011 Update Rollout 12 in December 2012. This message accepts a collection of message requests, which can be a mix of independent `CreateRequest`, `UpdateRequest`, `DeleteRequest`, and other messages.

`ExecuteMultipleRequest` executes each request in the order in which it appears in the collection. Each message request is processed in a separate database transaction. The default batch size is 1,000 for On-Premises installations and also for CRM Online. If the batch size increases to more than 1,000, `ExecuteMultipleRequest` throws a fault before executing the first request. `ExecuteMultipleRequest` cannot invoke another `ExecuteMultipleRequest`. The `Settings` parameter of `ExecuteMultipleSettings` has two members, as follows:

▶ **ContinueOnError**—As the name suggests, if this value is set to `true`, requests keep processing even after a fault has been returned from the last request. If it is set to `false`, remaining requests are not processed in case of any error or fault.

▶ **ReturnResponses**—If the value is set to `true`, it returns responses from each message. If `false`, it does not return responses.

Listing 23.22 creates a console application and uses the `ExecuteMultipleRequest` message to create 1,000 contacts.

NOTE

For any missing references in Listing 23.22, refer to the code sample in the SDK, in the SDK\SampleCode\CS\DataManagement\ExecuteMultiple folder.

LISTING 23.22   Creating a Console Application in C#

```csharp
private static void CreateMultipleRecords(string organizationName)
    {
        ClientCredentials credentials = new ClientCredentials();
        credentials.Windows.ClientCredential = System.Net.CredentialCache.
        DefaultNetworkCredentials;
        OrganizationServiceProxy _serviceProxy = new OrganizationServiceProxy
        (new Uri("http://crmwoifd/" + organizationName + "/XRMServices/2011/
        Organization.svc"), null, credentials, null);
        _serviceProxy.ServiceConfiguration.CurrentServiceEndpoint.Behaviors.
        Add(new ProxyTypesBehavior());
        OrganizationServiceContext orgContext = new OrganizationServiceContext
        (_serviceProxy);
        OrganizationRequestCollection collection = new
        OrganizationRequestCollection();
        for (int i = 0; i < 1000; i++)
        {
            Contact myContact = new Contact();
            myContact.FirstName = "FirstName" + i.ToString();
            myContact.LastName = "LastName" + i.ToString();
            CreateRequest createRequest = new CreateRequest
            {

                Target = myContact
            };

            collection.Add(createRequest);
        }

        ExecuteMultipleRequest exeMulRequest = new ExecuteMultipleRequest
        {
            Requests = collection,
            Settings = new ExecuteMultipleSettings
            {
                ContinueOnError = false,
                ReturnResponses = true
            }
        };
        DateTime startTime = DateTime.Now;
        ExecuteMultipleResponse exeMulResponse = (ExecuteMultipleResponse)
        orgContext.Execute(exeMulRequest);
        DateTime endTime = DateTime.Now;
        Console.WriteLine("Time to create 1000 contacts: {0}", endTime
        - startTime);

        Console.ReadKey();
}
```

Web API

The new Web API interface officially replaces the old OData 2.0 (which is deprecated in Dynamics CRM 2016), with the new version of OData, version 4.0. There are several differences between this new version of OData and the previous version.

The first difference is the authentication that is implemented using OAuth 2.0, as well as the format and the results, are returned. This new version returns data in JSON format, while the previous version returns XML. This makes the new version lighter with regard to web traffic and improves the network performance and avoids the need to convert the XML return to JSON in JavaScript calls, as was required previously.

Because Web API is based on REST, you can use it with HTTP in JavaScript or C# with .NET or any other platform or programming language.

The Web API endpoint looks like this:

```
org-url/api/data/v8.0/
```

where *org-url* is your CRM organization URL, like this:

```
https://2016crmbook.crm.dynamics.com
```

You can always find the right endpoint URL by going to the CRM web interface and navigating to Settings > Customizations > Developer Resources. You can find the Web API endpoint in the Interface Web API section.

If you use the endpoint with JavaScript from the CRM web interface, using web resources, you don't need to authenticate. If you try to use this API from an external application like a Windows Forms Application, in C#, you need to authenticate using the OAuth protocol, explained in the next section.

OAuth

OAuth is a standard protocol for authentication used by most of the popular social networking systems, such as Facebook, Twitter, and LinkedIn. The version currently implemented is 2.0, and for On-Premises implementations it requires IFD.

▶ For more information about IFD, **SEE CHAPTER 28**, "Forms Authentication."

You must authenticate with OAuth if you want to consume the Web API web services from an external client application.

The OAuth endpoints for CRM are https://login.windows.net/common/oauth2/authorize (multi-tenant) and https://login.windows.net/*tenantID*/oauth2/authorize (single tenant) for CRM On-Premises the OAuth endpoint is https://*serverFQDNaddress*/adfs/ls.

When working with OAuth, you need to obtain an authentication token to access the web service. You can use the following code in C# to do that from a CRM Online organization:

```
String resource = "https://webfortis.crm.dynamics.com";
_authenticationContext = new AuthenticationContext(_oauthUrl, false );
```

```
AuthenticationResult result = await _authenticationContext.AcquireTokenAsync(
resource, clientID );
```

The recommendation for OAuth with the CRM Web API is to use the Azure Active Directory Authentication Library (ADAL). With this you can get a client ID that you can pass to the authentication method as follows:

```
// TODO Substitute your correct CRM root service address,
string resource = "https://mydomain.crm.dynamics.com";

// TODO Substitute your app registration values that can be obtained after you
// register the app in Active Directory on the Microsoft Azure portal.
string clientId = "e5cf0024-a66a-4f16-85ce-99ba97a24bb2";
string redirectUrl = "http://localhost/SdkSample";

// Authenticate the registered application with Azure Active Directory.
AuthenticationContext authContext =
    new AuthenticationContext("https://login.windows.net/common", false);
AuthenticationResult result = authContext.AcquireToken(resource, clientId, new
                                                Uri(redirectUrl));
```

Creating Records

To create records of the Account entity, you can use the following code in JavaScript:

```
function CreateAccountRecord() {
    PostOdata({ name: "New Account" });
}
```

You can implement a common JavaScript method called PostData to use on all the examples in this section:

```
function PostOdata( jsonMessage) {
    clientURL = Xrm.Page.context.getClientUrl();
    var req = new XMLHttpRequest()
    req.open("POST", encodeURI(clientURL + "/api/data/v8.0/accounts"), true);
    req.setRequestHeader("Accept", "application/json");
    req.setRequestHeader("Content-Type", "application/json; charset=utf-8");
    req.setRequestHeader("OData-MaxVersion", "4.0");
    req.setRequestHeader("OData-Version", "4.0");
    req.onreadystatechange = function () {
        if (this.readyState == 4 /* complete */) {
            req.onreadystatechange = null;
            if (this.status == 204) {
                var Uriresponse = this.getResponseHeader("OData-EntityId");
                alert(Uriresponse)
            }
```

```
            else {
                var error = JSON.parse(this.response).error;
                alert("error " + error.message);
            }
        }
    };
    req.send(JSON.stringify(jsonMessage));
}
```

You can create more than one entity record on a single OData call. The following example shows how to create one record for the account entity and then create one record for the Contact entity and associate the contact and the account on the same single JSON object:

```
PostOdata(
    {
        name: "New Account",
        "primarycontactid":
        {
            "firstname": "Marc",
            "lastname": "Wolenik"
        }
    });
```

Retrieving Records

To retrieve records, you can use the same sample used for JavaScript in the "Examples of Web Services" section. You saw earlier how to get the address of the Parent Account record in the Contact entity using OData 2.0. You do the same with Web API by replacing the methods `RetrieveAccountRecord` and `RetrieveAccountRecordCallback` as follows:

```
function RetrieveAccountRecord(recordId) {
    var clientUrl = Xrm.Page.context.getClientUrl();
    var webApiUrl = clientUrl + "/api/data/v8.0/accounts(" + recordId.replace
    ("{", "").replace("}", "") + ")";
    var retrieveAccountRequest = new XMLHttpRequest();
    retrieveAccountRequest.open("GET", webApiUrl, true);
    retrieveAccountRequest.setRequestHeader("Accept", "application/json");
    retrieveAccountRequest.setRequestHeader("Content-Type", "application/json;
    charset=utf-8");
    retrieveAccountRequest.setRequestHeader("OData-MaxVersion", "4.0");
    retrieveAccountRequest.setRequestHeader("OData-Version", "4.0");
    retrieveAccountRequest.setRequestHeader("Prefer",
"odata-include-annotations=\"*.*\"");
    retrieveAccountRequest.onreadystatechange = RetrieveAccountRecordCallback;
    retrieveAccountRequest.send(null);
}
```

```
function RetrieveAccountRecordCallback() {
    if (this.readyState === 4 /*Complete*/) {
        if (this.status === 200 /*Success*/) {
            var retrievedRecord = JSON.parse(this.responseText);
            Xrm.Page.getAttribute("address1_postalcode").setValue(retrievedRecord.
            address1_postalcode);
            Xrm.Page.getAttribute("address1_line1").setValue(retrievedRecord.
            address1_line1);
            Xrm.Page.getAttribute("address1_line2").setValue(retrievedRecord.
            address1_line2);
            Xrm.Page.getAttribute("address1_line3").setValue(retrievedRecord.
            address1_line3);
            Xrm.Page.getAttribute("address1_city").setValue(retrievedRecord.
            address1_city);
            Xrm.Page.getAttribute("address1_stateorprovince").setValue
            (retrievedRecord.address1_stateorprovince);
            Xrm.Page.getAttribute("address1_country").setValue(retrievedRecord.
            address1_country);
            var addressText = "";
            if (retrievedRecord.address1_line1 != null) {
                addressText += retrievedRecord.address1_line1 + "\n";
            }
            if (retrievedRecord.address1_line2 != null) {
                addressText += retrievedRecord.address1_line2 + "\n";
            }
            if (retrievedRecord.address1_line3 != null) {
                addressText += retrievedRecord.address1_line3 + "\n";
            }
            if (retrievedRecord.address1_city != null) {
                addressText += retrievedRecord.address1_city + ", ";
            }
            if (retrievedRecord.address1_stateorprovince != null) {
                addressText += retrievedRecord.address1_stateorprovince + " ";
            }
            if (retrievedRecord.address1_postalcode != null) {
                addressText += retrievedRecord.address1_postalcode + "\n";
            }
            if (retrievedRecord.address1_country != null) {
                addressText += retrievedRecord.address1_country;
            }
            Xrm.Page.getAttribute("address1_composite").setValue(addressText);
        }
    }
}
```

23

Updating Records

To update a record with Web API, you need to use the PATCH HTTP command. Here is an example of how to update a record using JavaScript, in which you need to pass the GUID of the account record you want to update:

```
UpdateAccount("00000000-0000-0000-0000-000000000001", { name: "New updated name for
Account" });

function UpdateAccount( accountId, jsonMessage) {
    clientURL = Xrm.Page.context.getClientUrl();
    var req = new XMLHttpRequest()
    req.open("PATCH", encodeURI(clientURL + "/api/data/v8.0/accounts(" + accountId +
    ")"), true);
    req.setRequestHeader("Accept", "application/json");
    req.setRequestHeader("Content-Type", "application/json; charset=utf-8");
    req.setRequestHeader("OData-MaxVersion", "4.0");
    req.setRequestHeader("OData-Version", "4.0");
    req.onreadystatechange = function () {
        if (this.readyState == 4 /* complete */) {
            req.onreadystatechange = null;
            if (this.status == 204) {
                alert("account updated")
            }
            else {
                var error = JSON.parse(this.response).error;
                alert("error " + error.message);
            }
        }
    };
    req.send(JSON.stringify(jsonMessage));
}
```

Deleting Records

To delete a record with Web API, you need to use the DELETE HTTP command. Here is an example of how to delete a record using JavaScript, in which you need to pass the GUID of the account record you want to delete, using a context similar to this:

```
DeleteAccount("00000000-0000-0000-0000-000000000001");

function DeleteAccount( accountId) {
    clientURL = Xrm.Page.context.getClientUrl();
    var req = new XMLHttpRequest()
    req.open("DELETE", encodeURI(clientURL + "/api/data/v8.0/accounts(" + accountId
    + ")"), true);
    req.setRequestHeader("Accept", "application/json");
    req.setRequestHeader("Content-Type", "application/json; charset=utf-8");
```

```
    req.setRequestHeader("OData-MaxVersion", "4.0");
    req.setRequestHeader("OData-Version", "4.0");
    req.onreadystatechange = function () {
        if (this.readyState == 4 /* complete */) {
            req.onreadystatechange = null;
            if (this.status == 204) {

                alert("account deleted")
            }
            else {
                var error = JSON.parse(this.response).error;
                alert("error " + error.message);
            }
        }
    };
    req.send();
}
```

Other Operations

There are many other operations you can do with Web API. Probably one of the most useful operations you can do is an "upsert," which is a combination of an update and an insert in the same call. Basically, an upsert tries first to update a record, but if the record doesn't exist, it inserts the record instead of failing.

> **NOTE**
>
> Refer to the Dynamics CRM 2016 SDK for a complete list of the operations you can do with Web API.

Summary

In this chapter, you have learned about the web services that the Microsoft CRM 2016 system exposes and how to use them to extend CRM's functionality and make customizations.

This chapter discusses the Discovery service that is used to find the right access endpoint for an organization, which is especially useful for multi-tenancy environments. The examples in this chapter show how to use the Organization service to create new records for any entity and how to update, delete, and retrieve existing records. This chapter also looks at the metadata web service that is used to make customizations programmatically (for example, to create a new custom entity or attributes). This chapter also covers how to use the deprecated OData version 2.0 service by using REST on JavaScript code and how you can use `ExecuteMultipleRequests` to do bulk operations and also the new Web API, which uses the version 4.0 of the OData protocol and the OAuth authentication that will need to use to connect to CRM from external client applications using Web API.

Azure Extensions

Microsoft Dynamics CRM 2016 features improved extensibility for cloud computing and Windows Azure.

Introduction to Azure

Azure is Microsoft technology created to build and provide cloud-computing systems and applications. Hosted in the Microsoft data centers, Azure applications give end users about 99.95% uptime, and customers don't need to invest in any infrastructure or IT services for their environment.

Azure services can be grouped into three categories: infrastructure-as-a-service (IaaS), platform-as-a-service (PaaS), and software-as-a-service (SaaS).The concept of cloud computing invites companies to alter their perspective with regard to procuring expensive on-premises equipment and hard-to-manage support and consider moving to a service-oriented service, SaaS, where they pay for the time and resources consumed (similar to what we currently do for electricity or phone services).

Azure is a set of tools and application programming interfaces (APIs) that changes the way a system or an application is designed to support the cloud-computing platform offered by Microsoft. Customers can scale the system as needed by choosing the number of servers they want to have running the same application as usage demands it (and at a low cost per month).

Azure includes the following products, which you can subscribe to separately:

▶ Cloud Services

▶ Data Management

▶ Business Analytics

▶ Identity

▶ Messaging

For a complete list of the Azure products, visit https://azure.microsoft.com/en-us/regions/#services.

> **NOTE**
>
> Windows Azure is not available to purchase worldwide yet (however once purchased and provisioned, any service can be accessed worldwide). At this writing, Azure is available to purchase in 140 countries.

Service Bus Configurations

The Azure Service Bus component enables you to integrate a CRM 2016 deployment with a legacy system. Because the CRM in these scenarios is usually be the Online version, and because you cannot call external web services from plug-ins deployed on the CRM 2016 Online sandbox, you must create a Service Bus application to communicate with the external application through Service Bus.

Microsoft Dynamics CRM 2016 and Microsoft Dynamics CRM Online support integration with Windows Azure. Developers can register plug-ins with Microsoft Dynamics CRM that can pass runtime message data, known as the execution context, to one or more Windows Azure solutions in the cloud. The Windows Azure Service Bus combined with the Windows Azure Access Control Service (ACS) provide a secure communication channel for Microsoft Dynamics CRM runtime data to external line-of-business applications.

This process of using Service Bus to integrate a legacy system or application with Microsoft CRM 2016 involves the following:

▶ Creating a Windows Azure Service Bus account with a subscription

▶ Getting the CRM 2016 Online certificate

▶ Registering a Service Bus endpoint

▶ Creating a listener application

Creating a Windows Azure Service Bus Account with a Subscription

To create an Azure AppFabric Service Bus account, follow these steps:

1. Download Azure PowerShell from http://go.microsoft.com/fwlink/p/?linkid=320376&clcid=0x409 and open a new PowerShell window.

2. Run the command `Add-AzureAccount` to configure PowerShell to talk to the Azure account. In the dialog that appears provide your Azure subscription credentials, as shown in Figure 24.1.

FIGURE 24.1   IFD Login/Verification for Azure authorization.

3. Create a new Azure Service Bus namespace by using this command:

```
New-AzureSBNamespace -Name "WebFortis-Crm2016" -Location "Central US"
➥-CreateACSNamespace $true -NamespaceType Messaging
```

but be sure to change `"WebFortis-Crm2016"` to the name of your organization.
Figure 24.2 shows logged in PowerShell user to the Azure subscription.

FIGURE 24.2   Authenticated PowerShell user.

The output shows `ACSManagementEndPoint`, `ServiceBusEndPoint`, and `DefaultKey`, as shown in Figure 24.3.

FIGURE 24.3   PowerShell output.

TIP

Remember to make a note of the service namespace you enter here; you will need it when you register the Service Bus plug-in.

Getting the CRM 2016 Online Certificate

This book covers how to connect an application with CRM Online, which is the most appropriate scenario for this text. You can, however, connect with CRM On-Premises and in Internet-Facing Deployment (IFD) environments, but to get a certificate, you must complete the following steps, as described in the CRM 2016 software development kit (SDK):

NOTE

You can download the CRM 2016 SDK from http://download.microsoft.com or by searching the Microsoft site for "CRM 2016 SDK."

---

1. Go to CRM Online and download the Windows Azure Service Bus Issuer Certificate by going to Settings > Customizations > Developer Resources (see Figure 24.4).

FIGURE 24.4   CRM 2016 Developer Resources page.

2. Click Download Certificate under Connect This Instance of Dynamics CRM to Azure Service Bus and store the certificate on your local hard disk.

Registering a Service Bus Endpoint

To register the service bus endpoint, you use the Plug-in Registration Tool, which you can find in the CRM SDK in the SDK\Tools\PluginRegistration folder; the file is called PluginRegistration.exe.

▶ To learn more about the Plug-in Registration Tool, which is the same one used to register any other CRM plug-in, **SEE CHAPTER 25**, "Plug-ins."

Run PluginRegistration.exe and follow these steps:

1. Click Create New Connection and select Office 365 for Deployment Type and select the check box Display List of Available Organizations (see Figure 24.5). Click the Login button.

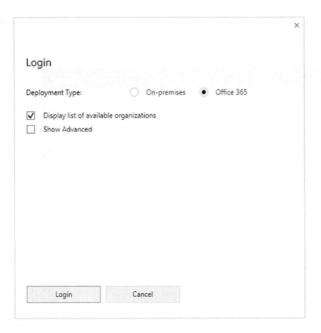

FIGURE 24.5   Plug-in Registration Tool.

2. In the dialog that appears, enter the login information and click the Sign In button (see Figure 24.6). When you're connected, you see a list of plug-ins and custom workflow activities (see Figure 24.7).

FIGURE 24.6   Intranet login dialog.

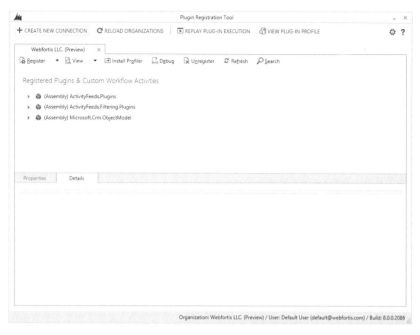

FIGURE 24.7   Plug-in Connection options.

3. Click Register and select Register New Service Endpoint, as shown in Figure 24.8.

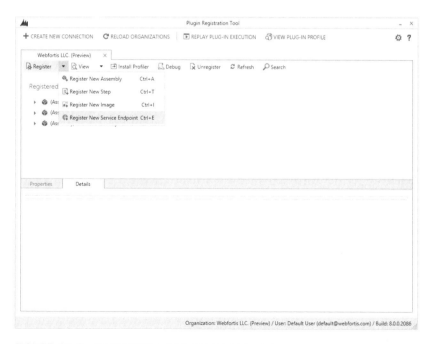

FIGURE 24.8   Registering a new service endpoint.

4. In the Service Endpoint Registration panel that appears (see Figure 24.9), enter a name (any name you want to use to reference your service), a description (optional), the solution namespace from the Windows Azure portal in the Service Bus section (refer to Figure 24.3), and a path (any name that you want to be part of the URL used for the endpoint).

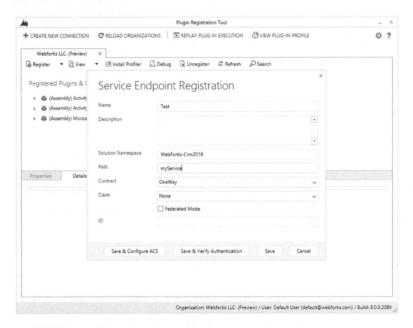

FIGURE 24.9   Service endpoint details.

The Contract drop-down can be any of these types:

▶ **OneWay**—Used to send messages only from CRM 2016 to the service bus. For this type of contract, the listener application must be connected at the time the message is sent; otherwise, the message might be lost. If you don't want to lose messages, you can choose the Queue contract type.

▶ **Queue**—Specifies where the messages will be queued; this is useful for environments that are not fully connected at all times.

▶ **Two Way**—Specifies where the messages can be sent and received from CRM 2016.

▶ **REST**—Creates a REST (representational state transfer) endpoint that works in a two-way fashion.

▶ **Topic**—The same as a queue, but implements the publish/subscribe model.

▶ **Persistent Queue**—Listens for messages in Service Bus and, when available, reads the message, prints the execution context contained in the message to the console, and deletes the message from the queue.

> **NOTE**
>
> To use the Persistent Queue and Topic contracts, the listener applications must be using the Windows Azure SDK version 1.7 or 1.8.

▶ To learn more about the REST protocol, refer to **CHAPTER 23**, "Web Services."

5. Go to https://portal.azure.com/ and log in. After you log in, click Service Bus from the left menu options, as shown in Figure 24.10, and select the namespace and then click the Connection Information button at the bottom of the page.

FIGURE 24.10   Azure Service Bus configuration.

6. In the Access Connection Information dialog that appears, copy the value from the Default Key field to the box under ACS Connection String (see Figure 24.11).

FIGURE 24.11   Azure Access Connection Information.

7. Go back to the Plug-in Registration Tool and click the Save & Configure ACS button. The ACS Configuration dialog that appears, showing the default key you copied earlier under Management Key (see Figure 24.12). Find the certificate file you downloaded from CRM Online and enter its name in the Issuer Name field; it should be crm.dynamics.com for CRM Online if you are in the United States (but if you are in another country, it might be a different localized URL). The certificate file's name will differ for On-Premises deployments.

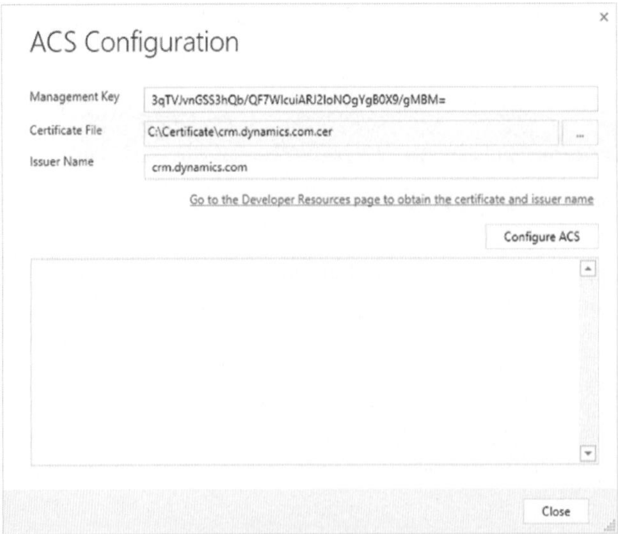

FIGURE 24.12   ACS Configuration.

NOTE

The keys in Figures 24.12–24.14 are for example purposes and you should be sure to use your own keys (and not the ones shown).

8. Click the Configure ACS button, and when a dialog appears warning that the action cannot be undone, click Yes (see Figure 24.13). Next you see detailed process messages with their statuses. After successful configuration, the ACS Configuration dialog should look as shown in Figure 24.14.

Action cannot be undone   [X]

⚠ This action will configure Windows Azure AppFabric ACS to allow
    Microsoft Dynamics CRM to post to the solution and path specified by
    the service endpoint configuration. This action will delete any matching
    component that may already exist and then create the service identity,
    issuer, token policy, scope, relying party, rule groups and rules.

    Do you want to continue?

                              [Yes]   [No]

FIGURE 24.13   ACS configuration confirmation.

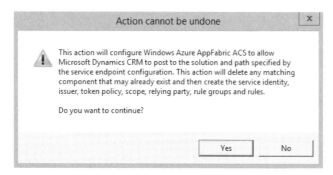

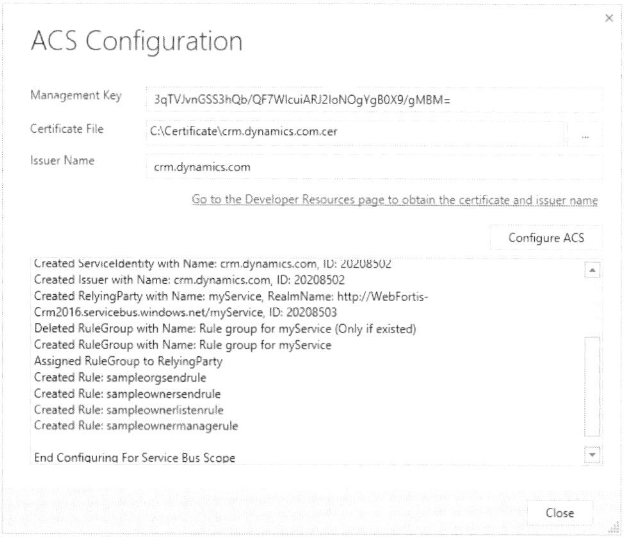

ACS Configuration

Management Key   3qTVJvnGSS3hQb/QF7WIcuiARJ2IoNOgYgB0X9/gMBM=

Certificate File   C:\Certificate\crm.dynamics.com.cer

Issuer Name   crm.dynamics.com

Go to the Developer Resources page to obtain the certificate and issuer name

Configure ACS

Created ServiceIdentity with Name: crm.dynamics.com, ID: 20208502
Created Issuer with Name: crm.dynamics.com, ID: 20208502
Created RelyingParty with Name: myService, RealmName: http://WebFortis-
Crm2016.servicebus.windows.net/myService, ID: 20208503
Deleted RuleGroup with Name: Rule group for myService (Only if existed)
Created RuleGroup with Name: Rule group for myService
Assigned RuleGroup to RelyingParty
Created Rule: sampleorgsendrule
Created Rule: sampleownersendrule
Created Rule: sampleownerlistenrule
Created Rule: sampleownermanagerule

End Configuring For Service Bus Scope

Close

FIGURE 24.14   ACS configuration confirming processing.

9. Click Close to close the ACS Configuration dialog.

24

10. Click Save & Verify Authentication in the Service Endpoint Registration dialog that appears (see Figure 24.15). The verification might take some time to complete. Upon successful verification, you should see a screen similar to Figure 24.16.

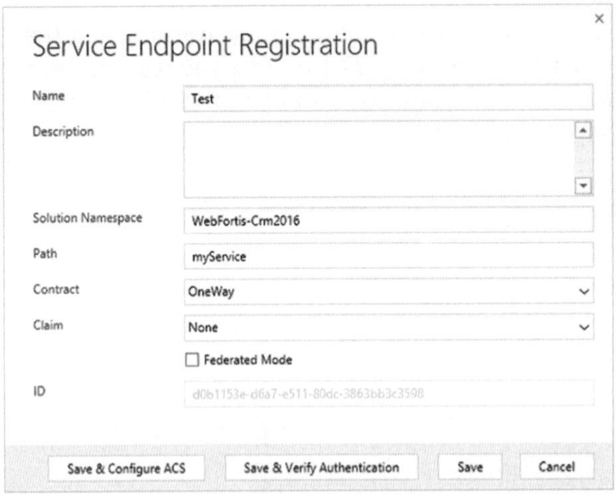

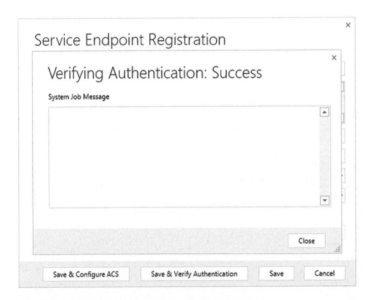

FIGURE 24.15   Service Endpoint Registration dialog.

FIGURE 24.16   ACS verification success.

11. Click Close to close the Verify Authentication dialog.

12. Click Save to close the Service Endpoint Details dialog. You now see the new service endpoint created in the Registered Plug-ins & Custom Workflow Activities list, as shown in Figure 24.17.

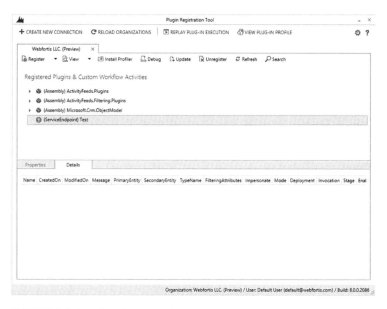

FIGURE 24.17   Service endpoint created.

Now you are ready to configure the CRM events you want to listen to and have sent to Service Bus. To do that, you need to create new steps for the service endpoint you created:

1. Select the service endpoint you created, click Register, and then select Register New Step, as shown in Figure 24.18.

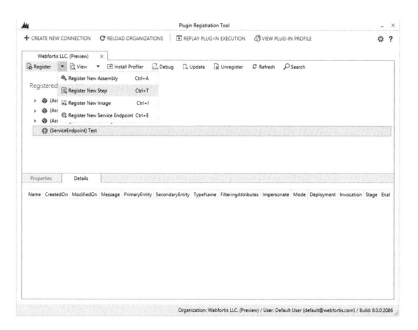

FIGURE 24.18   Registering a new step.

2. Enter Create in the Message field and account in the Primary Entity field, as shown in Figure 24.19.

FIGURE 24.19   Create message for the Account entity.

3. Click Register New Step. You should see the new step created under the ServiceEndpoint node in the Registered Plug-ins & Custom Workflow Activities list, as shown in Figure 24.20.

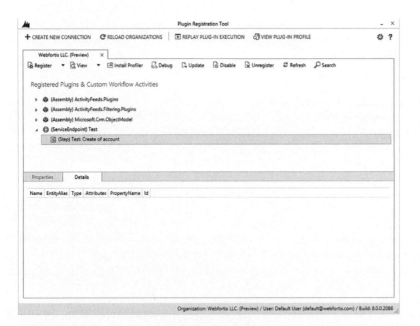

FIGURE 24.20   New step created successfully.

Creating a Listener Application

To start receiving Service Bus messages, you need to create a listener application. To test the listener, you can create a simple console application with Microsoft Visual Studio. This example uses Visual Studio 2015. You need to have the following downloaded and installed in order to follow the example in this section:

▶ WindowsAzure.ServiceBus NuGet package

▶ Microsoft Dynamics CRM 2016 SDK

When you have NuGet and the SDK installed, follow these steps:

1. Right-click References and select Manage NuGet Packages, as shown in Figure 24.21.

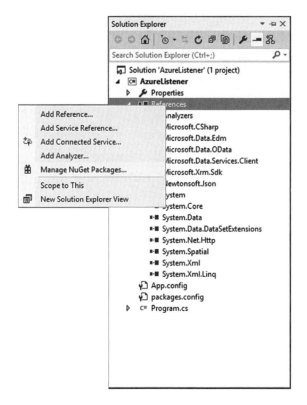

FIGURE 24.21   References > Manage NuGet Packages.

2. Select the Browse tab, type Azure in the search box, select WindowsAzure.ServiceBus version 3.0.9 or higher, and click the Install button (see Figure 24.22).

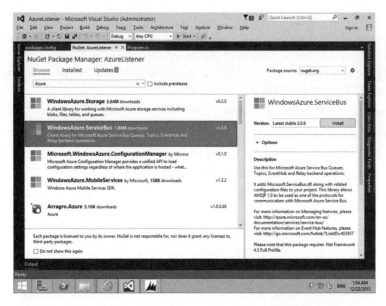

FIGURE 24.22   Selecting the WindowsAzure.ServiceBus option.

References to the Microsoft.ServiceBus.dll, Microsoft.WindowsAzure.Configuration.dll, System.ServiceModel.dll, and System.Runtime.Serialization.dll files are added.

3. Add a reference to the Microsoft.Xrm.Sdk.dll assembly from the CRM 2016 Sdk/bin folder, as shown in Figure 24.23.

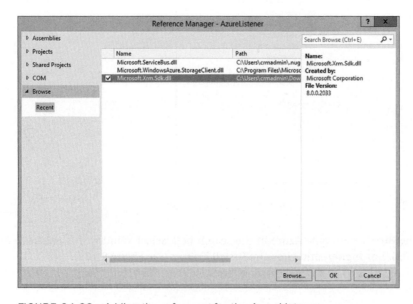

FIGURE 24.23   Adding the reference for the AzureListener.

4. Go to the Solution Explorer, right-click the project name, and select Settings. Ensure that the target framework selected is .NET Framework 4.5.2, as shown in Figure 24.24.

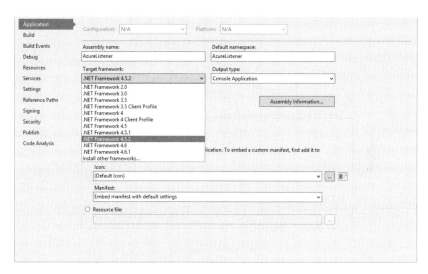

FIGURE 24.24   Selecting the target .NET framework from the drop-down.

After you have added all the necessary references, you are ready to insert the code. To do this, open the program.cs file and enter the following code:

```
using System;
using System.Collections.Generic;
using System.Linq;
using System.Text;
using Microsoft.ServiceBus;
using Microsoft.WindowsAzure;
using System.ServiceModel;
using System.ServiceModel.Description;
using Microsoft.Xrm.Sdk;
namespace AzureListener
{
    class Program
    {
        static void Main(string[] args)
        {
            ServiceBusEnvironment.SystemConnectivity.Mode = ConnectivityMode.Http;
            string serviceNamespace = "webfortis-crm2016";
            string issuerName = "owner";
            string issuerSecret = "321321";//Replace this with Default Key from
Connection Information from Windows Azure Portal
            // Create the service URI based on the service namespace.
            Uri address = ServiceBusEnvironment.CreateServiceUri(Uri.UriSchemeHttps,
```

```
serviceNamespace, "myService");
            Console.WriteLine("Service address: " + address);
            // Create the credentials object for the endpoint.
            TransportClientEndpointBehavior scb = new
TransportClientEndpointBehavior();
            TokenProvider = TokenProvider.
CreateSharedSecretTokenProvider(issuerName, issuerSecret);
            scb.TokenProvider = tokenProvider;
            // Create the binding object.
            WS2007HttpRelayBinding binding = new WS2007HttpRelayBinding();
            binding.Security.Mode = EndToEndSecurityMode.Transport;
            // Create the service host reading the configuration.
            ServiceHost host = new ServiceHost(typeof(RemoteServiceTest));
            host.AddServiceEndpoint(typeof(IServiceEndpointPlugin), binding,
address);
            // Create the ServiceRegistrySettings behavior for the endpoint.
            IEndpointBehavior serviceRegistrySettings = new ServiceRegistrySettings
(DiscoveryType.Public);
            // Add the Service Bus credentials to
            // all endpoints specified in configuration.
            foreach (ServiceEndpoint endpoint in host.Description.Endpoints)
            {
                endpoint.Behaviors.Add(serviceRegistrySettings);
                endpoint.Behaviors.Add(scb);
            }
            try
            {
                // Open the service.
                host.Open();
            }
            catch (TimeoutException timeout)
            {
                Console.WriteLine(timeout.Message);
            }
            Console.ReadLine();
            // Close the service.
            host.Close();
        }
    }
    [ServiceBehavior]
    class RemoteServiceTest : IServiceEndpointPlugin
    {
        public void Execute(RemoteExecutionContext context)
        {
            Entity createdDiag = (Entity)context.InputParameters["Target"];
            Console.WriteLine("Account with name = " + createdDiag.
```

```
Attributes["name"] + "was created");
        }
    }
}
```

The solution presented here works only for a one-way contract. Additional samples in the SDK located in the \sdk\samplecode\cs\azure folder show other contract types.

Let's review this code. For the Service Bus, you need to create a class that will implement IServiceEndpointPlugin, which has a similar interface to the one used for plug-ins (IPlugin).

▶ For more information about plug-ins, **SEE CHAPTER 25**.

This interface forces the implementation of the Execute method. Service Bus calls this method, which sends the context parameter. This parameter contains all the information you need for the entity you registered in the service endpoint. In this case, you registered the Create message for the Account entity, so you should expect to get the Account entity instance when a new account is created.

Updating Variables for the Main Method

You need to update three variables at the beginning of the Main method with your own service information: the serviceNamespace, issuerName (Default Issue), and the issuerSecret (Default Key) variables. You can find the values of these variables in the Windows Azure portal (refer to Figure 24.11).

The Main method starts by creating the service URI (uniform resource identifier) that will connect to your service; you use myService here because that is the path you entered when you registered the service endpoint.

Then you create the credentials object that will need to be passed to the service endpoint. Notice that the credentials are created using the issuer name and the issuer secret keys. You then create the binding object, using the WS2007HttpRelayBinding class. Next, you instantiate the ServiceHost class, which is the object that will be connected to Service Bus.

Then you specify the Service class that implements the IServiceEndpointPlugin interface. Finally, you create and add the Service Bus credentials to all endpoints specified in the configuration and open the host service instance. This sample application will run until a key is pressed, and it is important to close the service host when you are done.

To test the application, press F5, and you see the console application running, as shown in Figure 24.25.

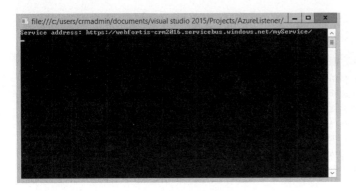

FIGURE 24.25   Testing the Service Bus listener application.

Now go to the CRM web user interface, go to Accounts, and then click + New to create a new account, as shown in Figure 24.26.

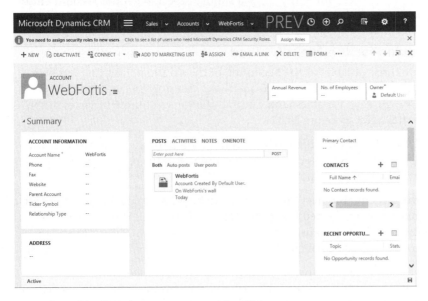

FIGURE 24.26   Creating a new account in CRM.

After you click Save, you see that the message is sent to the custom console application, and you also see the output, as shown in Figure 24.27.

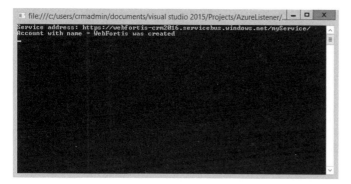

FIGURE 24.27   Account creation event received on the console application.

Azure-Hosted Dynamics CRM

Dynamics CRM hosted on Azure IaaS can leverage a number of cloud-based features. Azure IaaS virtual machines form the core building block of Azure IaaS solution. Virtual machine capabilities are determined by tiers and series. There are two tiers, basic and standard. Basic tier machines are used for test and development workloads where load balancing and auto-scaling are not required. Standard tier virtual machines are used for production environments and are divided into letter-assorted series like A, D, DS, and G.

▶ You can get an Azure trial free from https://azure.microsoft.com/en-us/pricing/free-trial/.

Follow these steps to set up a basic development environment in Azure for Dynamics CRM 2016:

1. Log on to your Azure trial environment and click Virtual Machines on the left menu. Then click Create a Virtual Machine (see Figure 24.28).

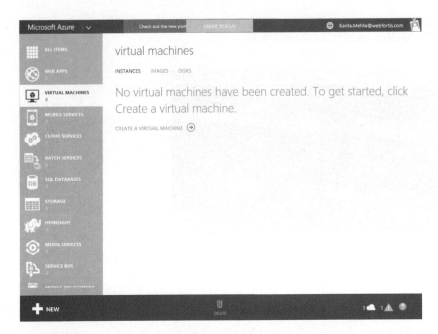

FIGURE 24.28   Creating a new virtual machine

2. Click From Gallery to get an existing image (see Figure 24.29).

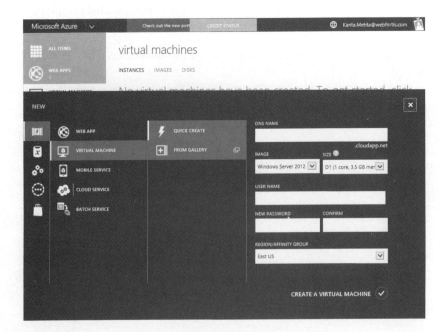

FIGURE 24.29   Selecting an existing image.

3. Select SQL Server 2014 SP1 Enterprise on Windows Server 2012 R2, click the right-arrow button in the bottom-right corner (see Figure 24.30).

FIGURE 24.30   Selecting the Virtual Machine configurations.

4. In the Virtual Machine Configuration dialog that appears (see Figure 24.31), set Tier to Standard and Size to A3 (4 cores,7 GB memory). Provide any other details you'd like to add. Then click the right-arrow button in the bottom-right corner.

FIGURE 24.31   Virtual Machine Configuration dialog.

5. In the new version of the Virtual Machine Configuration dialog that appears, set the Cloud Service DNS Name field and select the region where you want to host the service, as shown in Figure 24.32. Click the right-arrow button in the bottom-right corner. A virtual machine begins to be provisioned as per specifications you've provided.

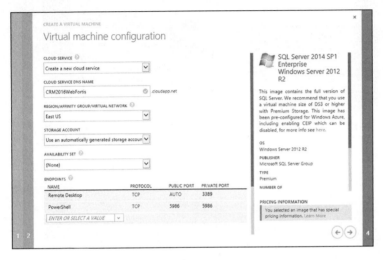

FIGURE 24.32   Virtual Machine Configuration dialog.

6. When the virtual machine status is shown as Running, click Connect at the bottom of the page and provide your login details.

7. After you log in to the virtual machine, open Server Manager and click Add Roles and Features, as shown in Figure 24.33.

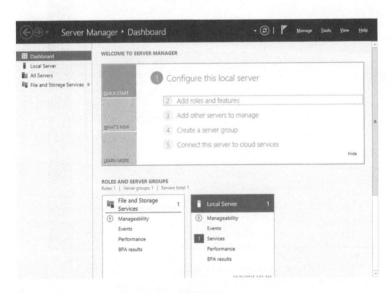

FIGURE 24.33   Adding roles and features.

8. In the Select Installation Type dialog that appears, select Role-Based or Feature-Based Installation and then click Next (see Figure 24.34).

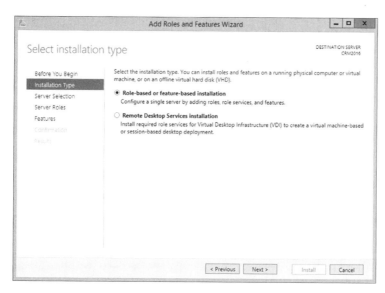

FIGURE 24.34   Select Installation Type dialog.

9. In the Select Destination Server dialog that appears, select Select a Server from the Server Pool and click Next (see Figure 24.35).

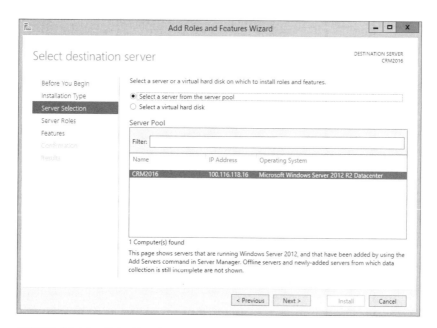

FIGURE 24.35   Selecting the current server.

10. In the Select Server Roles dialog that appears, select Active Directory Domain Services, as shown in Figure 24.36, and then scroll down and select Windows Search Service. Click Next.

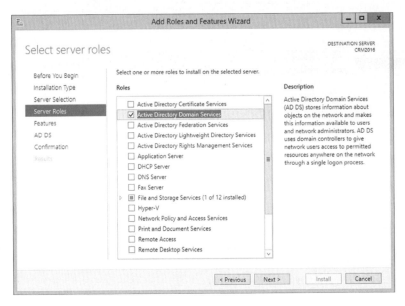

FIGURE 24.36   Select Server Roles dialog.

11. When the requested roles and features are installed (see Figure 24.37), click the Close button.

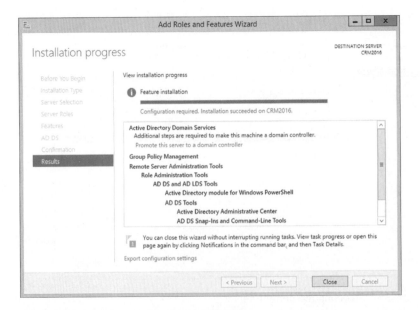

FIGURE 24.37   Completing the installation.

12. After the virtual machine restarts, log in to the virtual machine using the same credentials as in step 6.

13. Open the Server Manager and click Promote This Server to a Domain Controller, as shown in Figure 24.38.

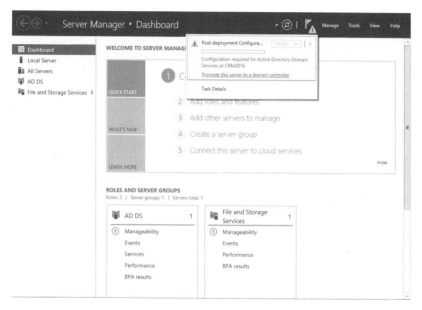

FIGURE 24.38   Promoting the server to a domain controller.

14. In the Active Directory Domain Services Configuration Wizard dialog that appears, select Add a New Forest, specify the root domain as WFLLC.Local, and click Next.

15. Provide the password and confirm password for Directory Services Restore Mode and click Next.

16. Click OK on the DNS server delegation warning that appears. (This setup is for a development environment, so the warning doesn't apply to you.)

17. Verify the NetBIOS domain name and click Next.

18. Leave the default values for the AD DS database, log files, and SYSVOL folders.

19. Review your selections and click Next, as shown in Figure 24.39).

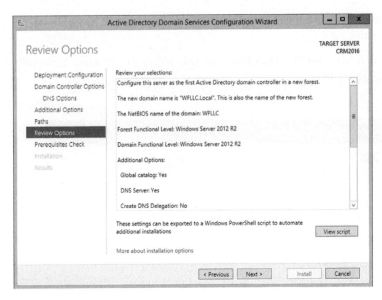

FIGURE 24.39   Reviewing configured options.

20. When the prerequisite checks are passed, click OK and then Install. When the installation is completed, the server restarts automatically.

21. Log in to the virtual machine and open the Server Manager. Click Add Roles and Features.

22. Select Server Roles and then Web Server (IIS) and as well as any other necessary features shown on the next screen (see Figure 24.40).

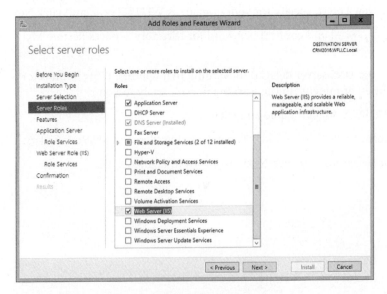

FIGURE 24.40   Selecting the Web Server (IIS) role.

23. Select Role Services on the left, beneath Application Server, and then select HTTP Activation, as shown in Figure 24.41. Make sure .NET Framework 4.5 and Web Server (IIS) Support are also selected.

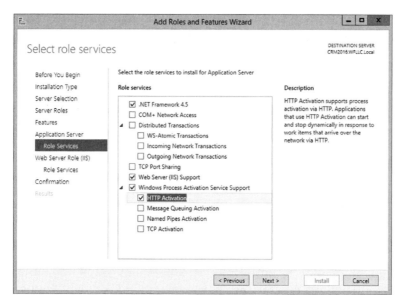

FIGURE 24.41   Selecting HTTP Activation.

24. Select Role Services on the left, beneath Web Server Role (IIS), and then select Management Services. Make sure other check boxes are also selected, as shown in Figure 24.42.

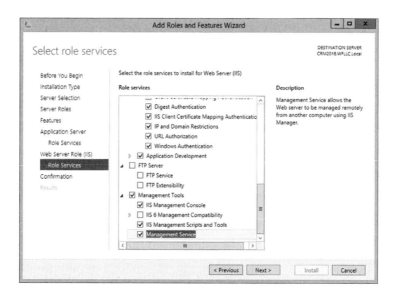

FIGURE 24.42   Selecting Management Service.

25. Select the check box Restart the Destination Server Automatically if Required and click Install.

26. When the installation is complete, click the Close button.

27. In the Server Manager select AD DS on the left and then right-click the server in the middle frame and select Active Directory Administrative Center, as shown in Figure 24.43.

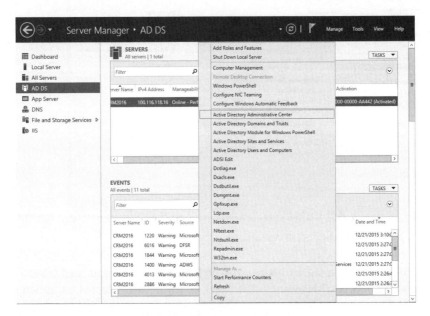

FIGURE 24.43   Selecting Active Directory Administrative Center.

28. Select the domain and then go to the Users folder. Create a new user record in Active Directory that will be used to run Dynamics CRM services (see Figure 24.44).

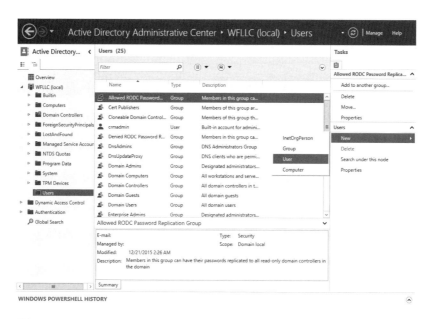

FIGURE 24.44   Creating a new user record.

29. Provide the required details and a password, making sure you select the Password Never Expires check box.

30. Click Member Of on the left side of the screen shown in Figure 24.45. Then click Add and select Performance Log Users and click OK. The user record is then added to Performance Log Users group.

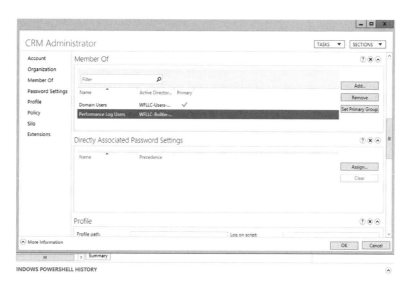

FIGURE 24.45   Adding the user to the Performance Log Users group.

31. Navigate to the domain folder and then create a new organizational unit to install Dynamics CRM, as shown in Figure 24.46.

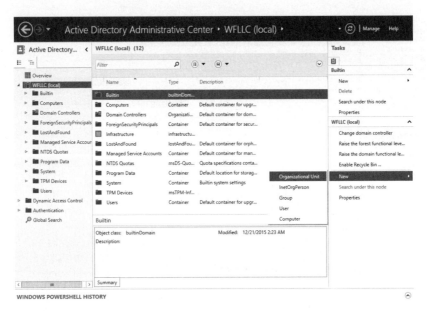

FIGURE 24.46   Creating a new organizational unit.

32. Name the new organizational unit CRM and click OK. Dynamics CRM will then create its AD groups here.

33. Open Reporting Services Configuration Manager and select SQL Server and click Connect.

34. Select Service Account from left menu, set Use Built-in Account to Local System, and click Apply.

35. Select Web Service URL from the left menu and click Apply (see Figure 24.47).

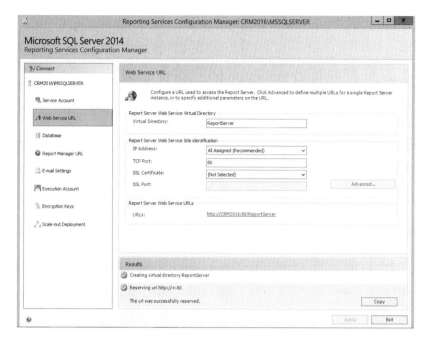

FIGURE 24.47   Configuring SQL Server Reporting Services.

36. In the configuration wizard that appears, select Database on the left side and then select Create a New Report Server Database and click Next.

37. Provide the database server name and set Authentication Type to Current User-Integrated Security (see Figure 24.48).

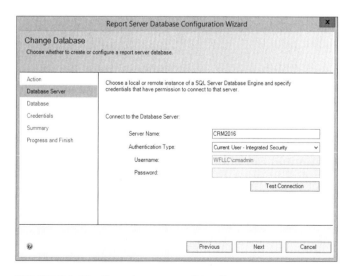

FIGURE 24.48   Report server configuration.

38. Enter the database name and click Next.

39. Keep Authentication Type set to Service Credentials and click Next.

40. The wizard configures the report server database. Click the Finish button to complete the setup.

41. Run Dynamics CRM Server 2016 setup. Select Get Updates for Microsoft Dynamics CRM and click Next.

42. Provide the product key for your Dynamics CRM instance (either the free trial key or from your MSDN subscription) and click Next.

43. Select the check box I Accept This License Agreement and click I Accept.

44. On the next screen, click Install to install any missing required components.

45. Select the installation directory and click Next (see Figure 24.49).

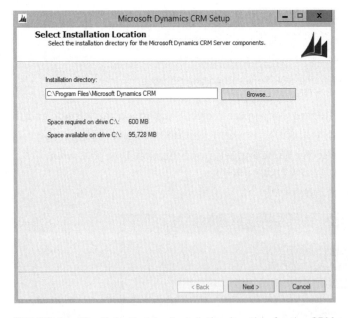

FIGURE 24.49   Selecting the installation location for the CRM server.

46. Select all the server roles, as you are doing an installation of a single server only which by definition has all the roles on the single server, and click Next (see Figure 24.50).

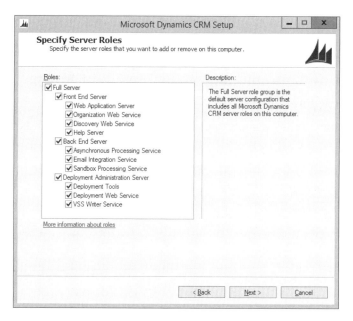

FIGURE 24.50   Selecting server roles for installation.

47. Select the option Create a New Deployment, provide the name of the server running SQL Server, and click Next.

48. Click Browse and select the CRM organization unit created earlier (see Figure 24.51).

FIGURE 24.51   Selecting the CRM organization unit.

49. Provide the credentials of the user account created earlier and click Next.

50. Select Create New Website and provide the port number, in this case 5555. (There might be some other applications running under default port 80 in the future, but because this is a new server, you could use port 80 if desired.) Click Next.

51. Skip the email router settings and just click Next.

52. Provide a display name for the organization and select the base currency and click Next (see Figure 24.52).

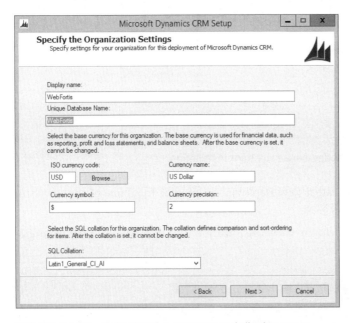

FIGURE 24.52   Selecting the currency and display name.

53. Specify the report server URL. You can copy paste the prepopulated URL for the report server to test (see Figure 24.53). Click Next.

FIGURE 24.53   Configuring the report server.

54. Click the Install button to begin the Dynamics CRM server installation.

55. When the installation is complete, click View the Log File to see if there are any errors. Ensure that the Restart the Computer When the Wizard Closes check box and click Finish to restart the server.

56. Go to Dynamics CRM setup and open the SrsDataConnector folder. Run SetupSrsDataConnector.exe to install Reporting Extensions (see Figure 24.54).

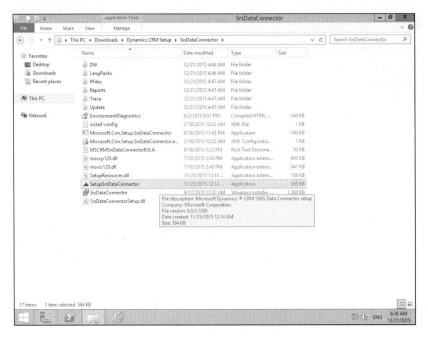

FIGURE 24.54   Navigating to the SrsDataConnector executable.

57. Specify where the configuration database for Dynamics CRM is installed and click Next.

58. Select the SSRS instance name that is used for Dynamics CRM reporting and click Next.

59. Specify the installation directory and click Next.

60. When the verification checks are complete, if there are no errors, click Next.

61. Review your selections and click Install.

62. Click View the Log File to see if there are any errors and then click Finish.

63. Open your browser and go to http://*<server>*:*<portname>*/ to open Dynamics CRM, as shown in Figure 24.55.

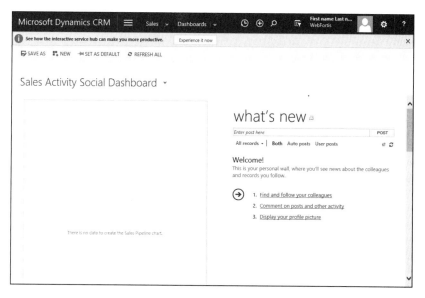

FIGURE 24.55   Dynamics CRM running on port 5555.

Azure ExpressRoute

You can create private connections between infrastructures that are in an On-Premises or Online environment and Azure data centers using by Azure ExpressRoute. ExpressRoute provides more reliability, faster speed, higher throughput, lower latency, and an extra level of protection by not relying on the public Internet to route traffic. With ExpressRoute you get your own private connection to Azure, and Azure acts likes your private cloud.

Azure ExpressRoute is now available for Dynamics CRM online customers.

> **NOTE**
>
> For more information about the ExpressRoute offerings, go to https://azure.microsoft.com/en-us/services/expressroute/.

Summary

In this chapter you have seen how to use the Microsoft Windows Azure platform to interact with Microsoft Dynamics CRM entity events through Service Bus. In addition, you've seen the process required to register a new Service Bus and the sample code and components necessary to listen to these messages.

Finally, this chapter covers hosting Dynamics CRM on an Azure environment and Azure ExpressRoute.

Plug-ins

A plug-in is a .NET assembly that can be used to intercept events generated from the CRM system to perform a variety of actions. An example of event interception is an entity that will be created, updated, or deleted; and an action can be almost anything. Some common plug-in uses include the following:

▶ Performing a complicated update routine on CRM entities/attributes when it might be impractical to use JavaScript or business rules

▶ Grabbing data from another system and updating CRM when an entity instance is being created or updated

▶ Updating another system programmatically from CRM (such as an accounting system)

Plug-ins

By using plug-ins, you can fire a custom action or event on any entity (for example, on the Account entity either before or after it is created, updated, or deleted). In addition, other events can be handled from a plug-in, such as Assign, Merge, and Handle. Refer to the Dynamics CRM software development kit (SDK) for a complete list of supported events. You can download the SDK from the Microsoft website; search for "Dynamics CRM SDK."

> **NOTE**
>
> Not every event works in offline mode of the Microsoft CRM Outlook client. Whereas online mode supports all events, offline clients can manage only half of them. Refer to the CRM 2016 SDK for a complete list of events supported in offline mode, in the file called message-entity support for plug-ins.xlsx, which you can find in the SDK.

Figure 25.1 shows the event execution pipeline order in which the event and the plug-in calls are executed.

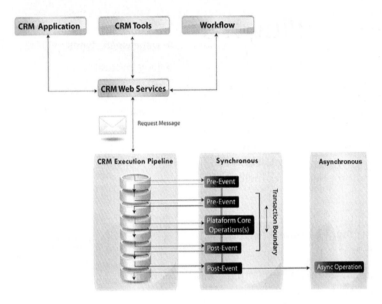

FIGURE 25.1   Event execution pipeline.

TIP

You don't need to restart Internet Information Services (IIS) or any other CRM service when you register or unregister plug-ins.

Isolation

Microsoft Dynamics CRM provides for registering plug-ins either in the sandbox (partial trust) or outside the sandbox (full trust). For Microsoft Dynamics CRM Online, plug-ins must be registered in the sandbox; On-Premises and Internet-Facing Deployment options can be registered in the sandbox or out of sandbox (or using the option none, which is out of the sandbox). CRM hosting providers might not support plug-ins without isolation mode for security reasons. Before you attempt to install a plug-in, check with your hosting provider to determine whether it allows you to use non-sandbox plug-ins. If a plug-in is registered in the sandbox in isolation mode, it will run in partial trust and won't be allowed to access some resources on the server, such as files, the Registry, databases, and so on. This level of isolation, however, allows access to HTTP and HTTPS web resources for external web services communication. The sandbox allows a plug-in to access the CRM services to create, update, or delete any entity on the system.

Developing plug-ins in sandbox mode is the recommended action, because it makes them more secure and supported on all the CRM 2016 deployment types (Online and On-Premises). They are also monitored by the CRM system-generated runtime statistics that can be queried using the `PluginTypeStatistic` entity records. If the sandbox worker process exceeds threshold CPU and memory limits and becomes unresponsive, the system kills it. In this case, currently executing plug-ins fail, but upon the next engagement, the plug-ins execute normally.

Finally, to deploy a plug-in without isolation mode, you need to add it as a deployment administrator, via the CRM Deployment Manager. Failure to do so results in failure to deploy the plug-in.

> **TIP**
>
> Being a deployment administrator is not required for deployment of sandbox plug-ins.

Modes

You can set up plug-ins in synchronous or asynchronous mode. Synchronous mode starts the execution of the plug-in when the event is fired and blocks the CRM application process until the executed method finishes. This option is not recommended if you are performing a process that might take a long time to execute. Regardless of the method used, synchronous or asynchronous, a timeout limit of 2 minutes applies for plug-in executions. If a process needs more time, you should consider using a workflow or another custom background process.

> **TIP**
>
> If you want to prevent another record from being created or updated, synchronous should be the desired mode, in conjunction with the pre-stage (see the next section, "Stages").

Asynchronous mode releases the application process, and the user can continue working while the code is executed. You can check the execution status of asynchronous plug-ins from Settings > System Jobs. These plug-ins are executed by the Microsoft Dynamics CRM Asynchronous Processing Service, which is a Windows service.

> **TIP**
>
> The Microsoft Dynamics CRM Asynchronous Processing Service includes the following services:
>
> ▶ Microsoft Dynamics CRM Asynchronous Processing Service (maintenance)
> ▶ Microsoft Dynamics CRM Sandbox Processing Services

25

Stages

You can set up plug-in steps in the pre-stages (either pre-validation or pre-operation) or post-stages (post-operation):

▶ **Pre-Stage**—This stage is divided into pre-validation and pre-operation and sends control to the plug-in before the real event is executed in the core system. For example, you might attach a plug-in to the Create event of the Account entity; your code would execute before the Account was actually created in the CRM system. With this method, you could prevent the account or the entity record from being created.

▶ **Post-Stage**—This stage is executed after the real event has executed in the core system. So, following the example just described, your code would be executed only after the account record has been created.

Dynamics CRM 2016 allows these stages to participate in SQL transactions as well.

The concept of using transactions now allows the rollback of a plug-in operation. If you have two different plug-ins attached to the same message of an entity and the second plug-in fails, it can now roll back the successful operation performed by the first plug-in. This was not easily done with earlier versions of Dynamics CRM. You can check whether a plug-in is running in a transaction by checking the `IsInTransaction` property of `IPluginExecutionContext`. The stages 20 (pre-operation) and 40 (post-operation) are the ones that guarantee to be part of a transaction, whereas stage 10 (pre-validation) might not be part of it.

Deployment Types

There are three deployment types for plug-ins:

▶ **Server**—The plug-in executes on the server. Execution occurs when users use the web client or the Outlook Online client as well as when any workflow is executed.

▶ **Offline**—The plug-in executes on the client user machine where Outlook is running. This is especially useful when you're running the Outlook client in offline mode.

▶ **Both**—The plug-in executes on the server and in the Outlook client in offline mode. Keep in mind that the plug-in is executed twice: once when Outlook is offline and again when it connects to the server.

> **TIP**
>
> To prevent a plug-in from executing twice because of synchronization, check the `IsOfflinePlayback` property of `IPluginExecutionContext`.

The deployment type you select depends on what you want to do. If you need to grab data from an external system and need to have the user connected to the Internet or the network, you should have the plug-in run only on the server side, and the Outlook client will not have network access in offline mode.

When to Use a Plug-in

You should use a plug-in when you need to integrate Microsoft Dynamics CRM with a legacy system or when you want to extend or customize the original functionality or behaviors of Microsoft Dynamics CRM.

Plug-ins are the best choice for enforcing complex business rules of your business. You could use JavaScript events to add validation on the rules you want to enforce; however, those types of validations work only when CRM is used through the native interfaces (such as the web or Outlook client). If you remember that other applications can be interacting with the CRM system through the web services, service endpoints, and so on, the validations and rules enforcement will work always if you put them on plug-ins or business rules. Plug-ins run on the server side, whereas JavaScript validations run on the client side. It is a good practice to put the validation logic in one place on the server side; that way, you know the hardware and resources you can use. Clients have a lot of different setting configurations on their browsers, and in some cases they might cause your validations to not work properly.

▶ For more information about business rules, refer to **CHAPTER 22** "Customizing the System."

25

TIP

Putting the business rules and validations on plug-ins doesn't mean you do not need to add validations with JavaScript events. In most cases, it is good to have the validations in both places to avoid unnecessary server calls.

NOTE

CRM 2016 has come up with real-time (synchronous) workflows that enable power users to control through workflows business logic that used to be controlled through plug-ins. If you are planning to upgrade from CRM 2013/2015 to CRM 2016, you might want to move your business logic from plug-ins to real-time workflows.

Plug-in Development

To develop a plug-in, you must download the Microsoft Dynamics CRM 2016 SDK from the Microsoft website. You can find it at the Microsoft website by searching for "Dynamics CRM SDK."

Download the MicrosoftDynamicsCRM2016SDK.exe file, save it, and execute it (it is a self-Eetracting cabinet file) by double-clicking the file and entering the directory where you want to extract the files (see Figure 25.2).

FIGURE 25.2   Extracting the SDK files.

To create a plug-in, you must create a new class library project in Visual Studio, using
.NET 4.5.2, by selecting File > New > Project. Then select Visual C# > Windows on the left
and select Class Library in the middle. Enter a name for the project and select a location
and a solution name if they don't auto-populate when you enter the project name
(see Figure 25.3).

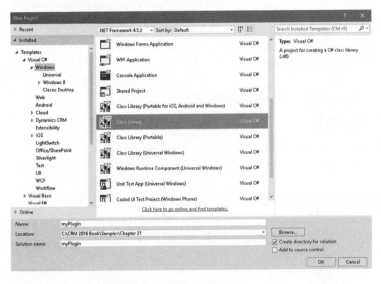

FIGURE 25.3   Creating a new class library project for a plug-in.

This version of Microsoft Dynamics CRM 2016 is based on the .NET Framework 4.5.2, and you can use Visual Studio 2013/2015 to create class libraries. Although you can also create class library projects in a variety of languages, including Visual Basic .NET, the examples in this book use C#.

The project template creates a new public class by default. After you create the project, you must add to your project a reference to the Microsoft.Xrm.Sdk.dll file and a reference to Microsoft.Crm.Sdk.Proxy.dll. These dynamic link library (DLL) files are located inside the SDK\bin subfolder.

Adding References

You can use NuGet to add the assemblies using the following command:

```
Install-Package Microsoft.CrmSdk.CoreAssemblies
```

For more information about NuGet, visit www.nuget.org/packages/Microsoft.CrmSdk .CoreAssemblies/.

To add these references, follow these steps:

1. Go to the Solution Explorer and right-click myPlugin > References (under the root Solution node of the tree). Select Add Reference, as shown in Figure 25.4.

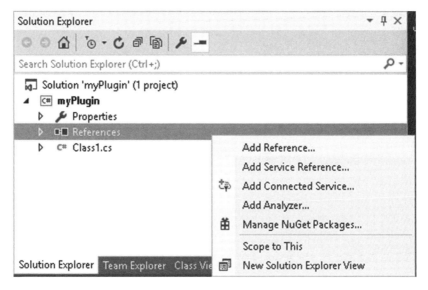

FIGURE 25.4   Adding a reference to a project.

2. Click Browse.

3. Locate the SDK\Bin folder on your local drive and select both the Microsoft.Xrm.
Sdk.dll and Microsoft.Crm.Sdk.Proxy.dll files (see Figure 25.5). (To select more than
one file, hold down the Ctrl key while you click the files you want.)

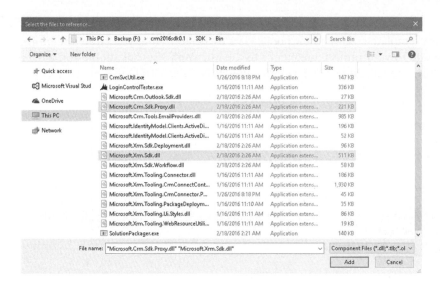

FIGURE 25.5   Selecting the DLLs to reference.

4. Click Add and then click OK to add the references to your project. You can then see
these files inside the References folder of your project in the Solution Explorer
(see Figure 25.6).

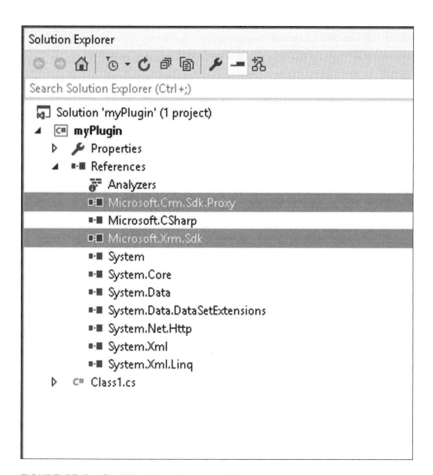

FIGURE 25.6   Checking that the new references were added.

5. Add the `using` sentence to the Microsoft.Xrm.Sdk namespace and implement the `IPlugin` interface, as shown in the following code (where you need to rename `Class1` with the name of your plug-in):

```
using System;
using System.Collections.Generic;
using System.Linq;
using System.Text;
using System.Threading.Tasks;
using Microsoft.Xrm.Sdk;

namespace myPlugIn
{
    public class Class1 : IPlugin
    {

    }
}
```

As with any other interface, you must explicitly implement methods. In the case of the `IPlugin` interface, you must implement the `Execute` method, as shown in the following code:

```
namespace myPlugIn
{
    public class Class1 : IPlugin
    {
     public void Execute(IServiceProvider serviceProvider)
     {
          throw new NotImplementedException();
     }
    }
}
```

The following sections explain the main classes.

IServiceProvider

The `Execute` method of the `IPlugin` interface has only one parameter, named serviceProvider, which is `IServiceProvider` type. From this parameter, you can get the plug-in execution context by entering the following code:

```
IPluginExecutionContext context =
(IPluginExecutionContext)serviceProvider.GetService(typeof(IPluginExecutionContext));
```

This main parameter has a method, `GetService`, that enables you to get other services from the service provider, such as the context of the organization and the context of the tracer service. This enables you to interact with the current CRM trace to add debugging information for the execution of your plug-in. to get an instance of the trace service, use the following code:

```
ITracingService tracingService =
(ITracingService)serviceProvider.GetService(typeof(ITracingService));
```

`IPluginExecutionContext` inherits from `IExecutionContext`, which is a more generic interface that is also implemented by other classes, such as the `RemoteExecutionContext` class used for Windows Azure integrations.

IExecutionContext

From the IExecutionContext object, you can query all the property values associated with the entity and event context where the method is being executed. This class contains the properties described in the following sections.

BusinessUnitId   The BusinessUnitId property returns the GUID (global unique identifier) of the business unit of the user making the request. Notice that this is not the GUID of the entity's record. To return the GUID of the entity's record, you use the new property PrimaryEntityId.

CorrelationId   The CorrelationId property returns the GUID of the plug-in event instance. Every time the event fires, it generates a new GUID that can be read from this property.

You can use this property for tracking and logging purposes, especially when you have more than one plug-in attached to the same event, to see whether the codes execute for the same event pipeline.

Depth   The Depth property returns the depth of the originated event. This property is of integer type and grows as the plug-in execution goes deeper, which can happen if your plug-in calls a web service to update another entity that also fires an event for another plug-in's execution code. You might need to check the value of this property to prevent infinite loops if the web service calls a method that fires the same plug-in execution that might produce a deadlock. The maximum number for the Depth property is set to 8. A system administrator can increase this value by running the PowerShell command Set-CrmSetting on the CRM server by changing the value of the WorkflowSettings .MaxDepth setting.

InitiatingUserId   The InitiatingUserId property returns the GUID of the user who initially invoked the operation.

InputParameters   The InputParameters property is a collection of the request parameters associated with the event. You can use this property to retrieve the entity object for which the event is fired:

```
Entity entity = (Entity)context.InputParameters["Target"];
```

TIP

You may receive the following error when building a solution:

```
'System.Runtime.Serialization.IExtensibleDataObject' is defined in an assembly
that is not referenced.
```

To fix this, add a reference to the assembly System.Runtime.Serialization.

The type of the target input parameter depends on the message. For example, the delete message returns an EntityReference:

```
EntityReference entity = (EntityReference)context.InputParameters["Target"];
```

It is a good practice to verify the type of the target parameter, as follows:

```
if (context.InputParameters.Contains("Target") && context.InputParameters["Target"]
is Entity)
{
    Entity entity = (Entity)context.InputParameters["Target"];
}
```

Also, you must make sure the entity contains the attribute you are looking for. The entity returned in the target parameter will contain only the attributes that were modified or created, and not all the entity fields. For example, the following code attempts to change the name of the Account entity:

```
if (entity.Attributes.Contains("name"))
{
entity.Attributes["name"] = "updated name";
}
else
{
    entity.Attributes.Add("name", " new account name");
}
```

For example, if there is an update operation in the account record where the name was not changed, that field won't be included in the target parameter. If for some reason you always need to know the value of this field, you can register an image for your plug-in. See the "Images" section, later in this chapter.

IsExecutingOffline   The `IsExecutingOffline` property is used only for Outlook clients and returns whether the Outlook client is running in online or offline mode. This property is a Boolean type where `true` = offline mode.

IsInTransaction   The `IsInTransaction` property is used to determine whether the operation is participating in a SQL transaction. This property is a Boolean type where `true` = is in transaction.

IsOfflinePlayback   The `IsOfflinePlayback` property is used only for Outlook clients and returns whether the Outlook client is transitioning from offline to online mode. This property is a Boolean type where `true` = synchronizing with the server.

IsolationMode   The `IsolationMode` property returns the `IsolationMode` mode in which the plug-in is running (none or sandbox). This parameter is an integer type where `0` = none and `2` = sandbox.

MessageName   The `MessageName` property returns the name of the event that invoked the plug-in. It is a string. These are the supported messages for custom entities:

```
Assign
Create
Delete
GrantAccess
```

```
ModifyAccess
Retrieve
RetrieveMultiple
RetrieveSharesPrincipalsAndAccess
RevokeAccess
SetStateDynamicEntity
Update
```

System entities can support other system messages. Refer to the message-entity support for plug-ins.xlsx file in the CRM SDK for a complete list of System entity–supported messages.

`Mode`   The `Mode` property returns the mode in which the plug-in is running. It can be synchronous or asynchronous. This parameter is an integer type where

`0` = synchronous and `1` = asynchronous.

`OperationCreatedOn`   The `OperationCreatedOn` property returns the datetime value of the `SystemJob` created for execution of an asynchronous plug-in. This value is `null` in the case of a synchronous plug-in.

`OperationId`   The `OperationId` property returns the operation GUID when the plug-in is running in asynchronous mode and gives you the ID of the current system job. In synchronous mode, this value is always an empty GUID.

`OrganizationId`   The `OrganizationId` property returns the organization GUID where the plug-in is running. Even though plug-ins are registered by organization ID, having this property helps if you have a generic plug-in that will be installed in different organizations and you need to perform different tasks, depending on the organization the plug-in is running. This way, you maintain only one Visual Studio solution and set of source code.

`OrganizationName`   The `OrganizationName` property returns the name of the organization where the plug-in is running. With this attribute, you do not need to make an API call to get the organization name by giving the organization ID.

`OutputParameters`   `OutputParameters` is the collection of properties returned by an event. A common output parameter is the GUID returned when an entity is created. Be careful when adding parameters on pre-stages because they could be overwritten after the system processes the core event. For example, suppose that you want to return the `accountid` property that is created when a plug-in is attached to the Create event of the Account entity in the post-stage:

```
Guid myAccountID = (Guid)context.OutputParameters["id"];
```

`OwningExtension`   The `OwningExtension` property returns the data associated with the `SdkMessage ProcessingStep` or the service endpoint. This property type is an `EntityReference` class from which you can get, for example, the description of the step that is running where you registered the plug-in.

`ParentContext`   The `ParentContext` property returns the context of the parent pipeline operation, which may happen if the plug-in is registered in the pre- or post-operations.

Sometime the plug-in requires another internal messages to be executed, and this property gives you the context of the parent execution.

PostEntityImages   The PostEntityImages property contains the collection of the images with the properties' names and values after the system executes the core operation.

> **NOTE**
>
> With PostEntityImages, you need to specify the images and what properties you want to have in this collection when you register the plug-in.

PreEntityImages   The PreEntityImages property contains the collection of the images with the properties and values before the system executes the core operation. This is very useful on post-stages to see what values the associated entity had before an update operation, for example.

> **NOTE**
>
> As with PostEntityImages, you need to specify the images and what properties you want to have with this collection when you register the plug-in.

PrimaryEntityId   The PrimaryEntityId property returns the GUID of the entity's record where the operation is performed. If you are working with accounts or contacts, you should use the following code to get the entity record identifier:

```
Guid id = context.PrimaryEntityId;
```

PrimaryEntityName   The PrimaryEntityName property gets the related primary entity name you specified when you registered the plug-in. This property is a type of string and returns the name of the associated entity—for example, Account, Contact, and so on.

RequestId   The RequestId property gets the ID (GUID) of the event execution pipeline. It returns null for synchronous operations.

SecondaryEntityName   The SecondaryEntityName property gets the related secondary entity name if you specified one when registering the plug-in. This entity is commonly used in the Parent Account or Contact of the Account entity. This property is a type of string and returns the string None if no secondary entity name is specified.

SharedVariables   The SharedVariables property is used as a common repository to store properties that plug-ins will share. It is useful when you need to pass a parameter value from one plug-in to another that is being executed in the same event pipeline.

Stage   The Stage property gets the stage at which the synchronous plug-in execution is registered. It can have any of the following values:

▶ 10 = pre-validation

▶ 20 = pre-operation

▶ 40 = post-operation

UserId   The `UserId` property returns the GUID of the user who is executing the operation. Notice that if you impersonate the plug-in's SDK message-processing step, as explained later in this chapter, this returns the user you configure there and not the user who originally initiated the operation, which you find in the `InitiatedUserId` attribute.

IOrganizationServiceFactory

If you need to create an instance of the organization service, you can do it by using the `IOrganizationServiceFactory` instance.

The service instance returned by `IOrganizationServiceFactory` has the method `Create OrganizationService`, which is used get an instance of `IOrganizationService`.

Here is an example of how to use `IOrganizationService` and the `CreateOrganization Service` method:

```
namespace myPlugIn
{
    public class Class1 : IPlugin
    {
        public void Execute(IServiceProvider serviceProvider)
        {

            IPluginExecutionContext context = (IPluginExecutionContext)
serviceProvider.GetService(typeof(IPluginExecutionContext));

            IOrganizationServiceFactory serviceFactory = (IOrganizationServiceFactory)
serviceProvider.GetService(typeof(IOrganizationServiceFactory));

            IOrganizationService service = serviceFactory.CreateOrganizationService
(context.UserId);
        }
    }
}
```

IOrganizationService

To use the CRM services, you need to get an instance of `IOrganizationService`, which provides programmatic access to metadata and data for an organization.

The service instance returned by `IOrganizationService` has the following methods:

▶ **Associate**—Used to create a link between records.

▶ **Create**—Used to create records.

▶ **Delete**—Used to delete records.

▶ **Disassociate**—Used to remove a link between records.

▶ **Execute**—Used, for example, to execute Fetch queries.

▶ **Retrieve**—Used to retrieve a record.

25

▶ `RetrieveMultiple`—Used to retrieve more than one record.

▶ `Update`—Used to update records.

▶ For more information about how to use this service and its methods, refer to **CHAPTER 23**.

`ITracingService`

For debugging purposes, you can use tracing by getting an instance of `ITracingService`. The service instance returned by `IOrganizationService` has the method `Trace`, which is used to add login information that you can then read when profiling a plug-in.

Here is an example of how to use `ITracingService` and the `Trace` method:

```
namespace myPlugIn
{
    public class Class1 : IPlugin
    {
      public void Execute(IServiceProvider serviceProvider)
      {
         ITracingService myTracingService =
           (ITracingService)serviceProvider.GetService(typeof(ITracingService));
         try
         {
             // do your work
             myTracingService.Trace("Plug-in execution starts");
         }
         catch (Exception ex)
         {
             myTracingService.Trace("Plug-in Exception: {0}", ex.ToString());
             throw;
         }
      }
    }
}
```

Plug-in Deployment

Before delving into the details about plug-in development, you should take a look at the deployment options so that you can easily follow the sample code included later in this chapter.

The first step in plug-in deployment involves registering your plug-in and signing the assembly with a strong name key file. A strong name key is necessary for security so that the assembly can be trusted to execute external code, such as when invoking a web service. To sign your assemblies, follow these steps:

1. In the Solution Explorer, right-click your project and select Properties (see Figure 25.7).

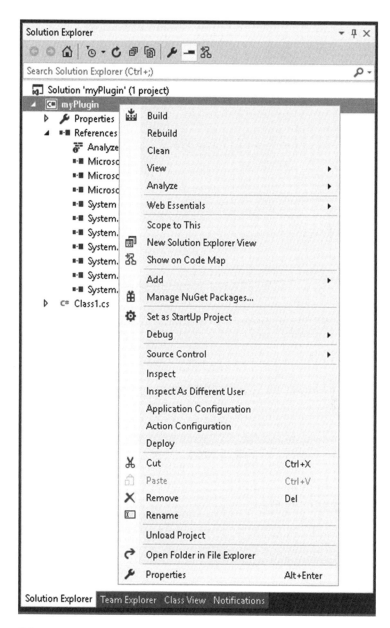

FIGURE 25.7   Properties menu item of the project.

2. Go to the Signing tab and check the Sign the Assembly check box (see Figure 25.8).

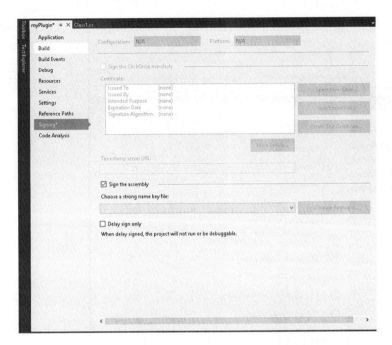

FIGURE 25.8   Signing tab.

3. Create a new strong name key file by selecting New from the drop-down, as shown in Figure 25.9.

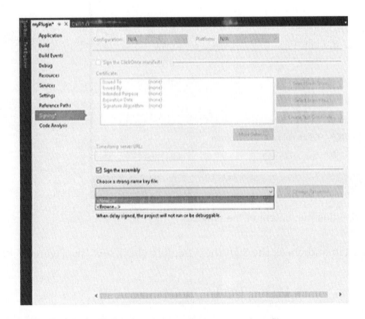

FIGURE 25.9   Selecting a new strong name key file.

4. Enter a name for the key file and, optionally (but recommended), enter a password to protect the strong name key (see Figure 25.10).

FIGURE 25.10   Creating a strong name key.

TIP

Be sure to give the password to any developer who will need to build this plug-in.

---

5. Click OK to close the dialog, and you see the newly created strong name key added to your project in the Solution Explorer (see Figure 25.11).

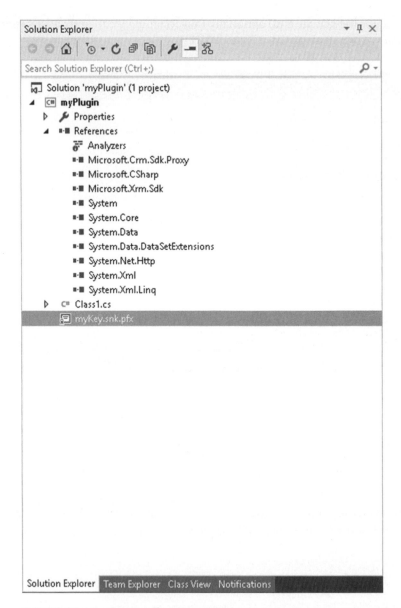

FIGURE 25.11   Solution Explorer with the newly created strong name key.

To deploy your plug-in, you need to register it. You can do this programmatically or using a tool that comes with the CRM SDK called the Plug-in Registration Tool. The Plug-in Registration Tool comes as an application and is located in the SDK\Tools\ PluginRegistration folder.

> **NOTE**
>
> You can also use the Plug-in Registration Tool to register Service Bus endpoints. These types of components are explained in detail in Chapter 24, "Azure Extensions." The Plug-in Registration Tool is also used to register custom workflow activities, which are fully covered in Chapter 26, "Process Development."

Integrating the Plug-in Registration Tool with Visual Studio 2015

You can follow these steps to integrate the Plug-in Registration Tool into Visual Studio 2015 as a recommended option:

1. In Visual Studio 2015, select Tools > External Tools (see Figure 25.12). The External Tools dialog, shown in Figure 25.13, appears.

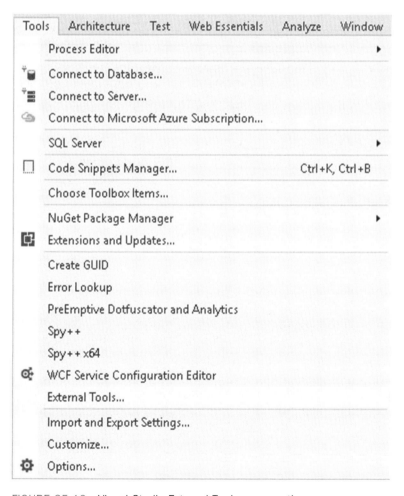

FIGURE 25.12   Visual Studio External Tools menu option.

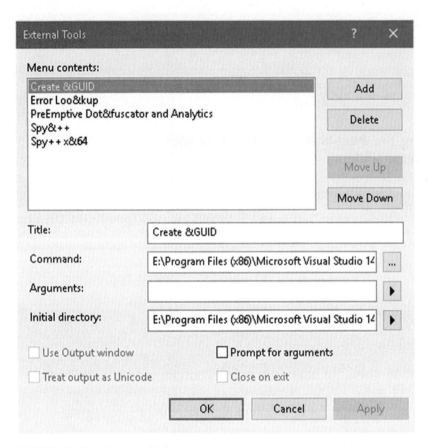

FIGURE 25.13   External Tools dialog.

2. Click the Add button and change the title to CRM Plug-in Registration (see Figure 25.14).

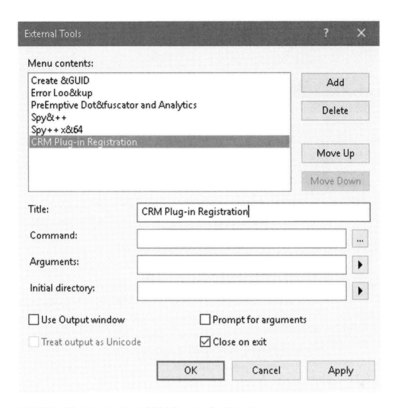

FIGURE 25.14   Adding CRM Plug-in Registration.

3. Click the ellipsis ... button next to the Command field and locate the
PluginRegistration.exe application file, which you should find in the SDK\Tools\
PluginRegistration\ folder (see Figure 25.15).

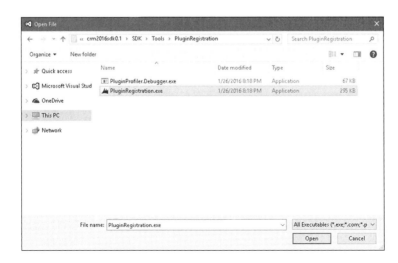

FIGURE 25.15   Locating the PluginRegistration.exe application.

4. Click Open to close the dialog and click OK to close the External Tools dialog. In addition, change the initial directory to the directory where you have the Plug-in Registration Tool.

You can now run the Plug-in Registration Tool from Visual Studio 2015 by selecting Tools > CRM Plug-in Registration (see Figure 25.16).

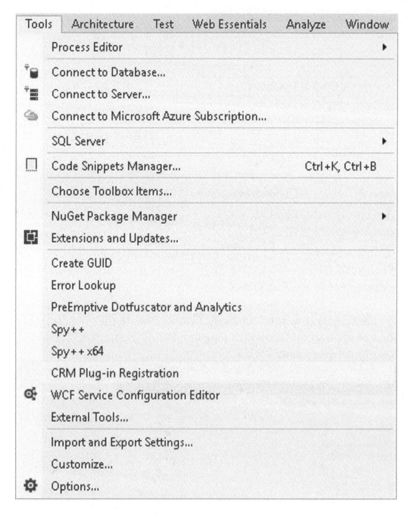

FIGURE 25.16   Accessing the Plug-in Registration Tool from Visual Studio.

Registering a Plug-in

When you run the Plug-in Registration Tool, you must first click Create New Connection and select the deployment type, which can be either On-Premises or Office365 (used for CRM Online deployments). Then you need to enter information for the server name and port (typically 80 for HTTP and 443 for HTTP when using SSL) and the authentication source. You also need to check the Display List of Available Organizations check box, as shown in Figure 25.17.

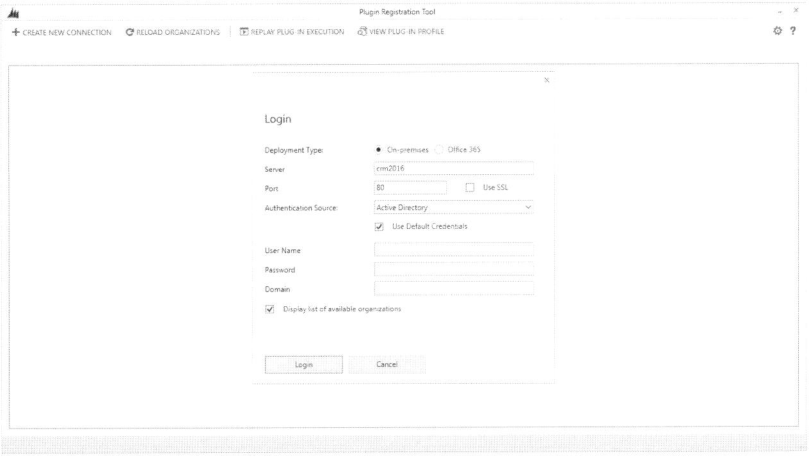

FIGURE 25.17   Registering the plug-in.

The Plug-in Registration Tool has the option to use the credentials of the user you are already logged in as, so you don't have to enter the username and password every time you run the tool. If you want to use a different user credential, you can uncheck the Use Default Credentials check box (refer to Figure 25.17) and enter a valid username, password, and domain.

> **TIP**
>
> The option to use the credentials of the user you are logged in as works only with On-Premises deployments.

The username and password must be valid Windows account credentials and for a valid Microsoft CRM user with administrative roles assigned, as well as deployment administrator rights that can be added through the CRM Deployment Manager. If the plug-in is going to be registered with the isolation mode set to Sandbox, the user doesn't need to be a deployment administrator; in that case, the CRM system administrator role is enough.

After you enter these values, click Login to connect to the organization and then select the organization you want to connect with.

If you need to connect to another organization, you need to click Create New Connection again. Doing so does not disconnect you from the first organization you connected to before but does create another tab with the second organization name you selected (see Figure 25.18).

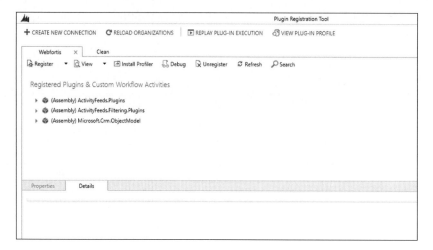

FIGURE 25.18   Connected to more than one organization.

If you are connected successfully to the CRM organization, you see the Registered Plug-ins & Custom Workflow Activities page, as shown in Figure 25.18.

Follow these steps to complete the plug-in registration:

1. Build the Visual Studio solution project so you can register the generated DLL, and make sure to build the assembly signed with a strong key to avoid a build error. Then click the Register button and then click Register New Assembly. The Register New Assembly dialog, shown in Figure 25.19, opens.

FIGURE 25.19   Assembly registration window.

2. Locate your assembly by clicking the ellipsis … button near the top of the Register New Assembly dialog. Select Sandbox under Step 3. (Remember that the sandbox isolation mode is preferred when deploying to a CRM Online environment.) Select Database under Step 4 and be sure to select the class you want to register that appears on the list. Then click the Register Selected Plugins button. When the assembly is registered, a confirmation window appears, as shown in Figure 25.20.

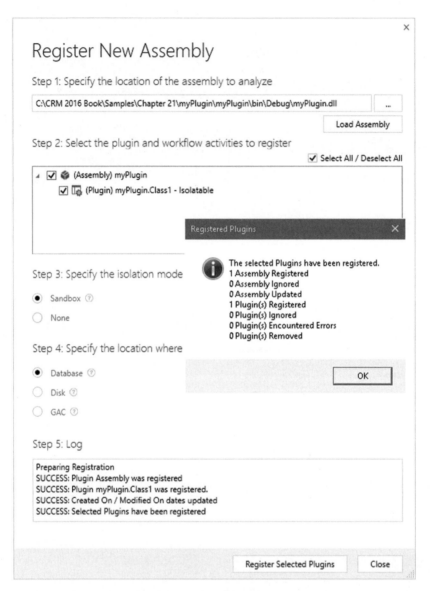

FIGURE 25.20   Registered assembly confirmation.

3. Expand the assembly you registered to make sure your assembly was properly registered (see Figure 25.21).

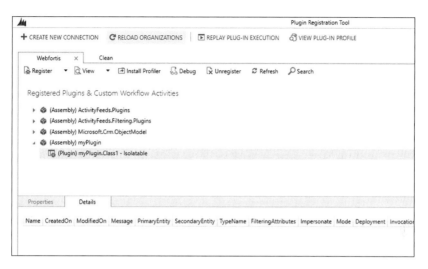

FIGURE 25.21   Reviewing assembly registration.

4. Associate the assembly with an entity and an event by clicking the assembly you registered in the previous steps and selecting Register > Register New Step (see Figure 25.22).

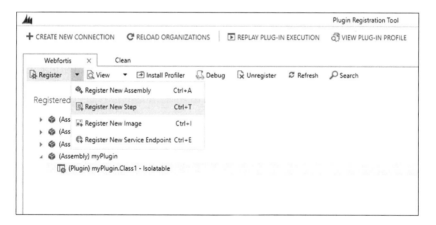

FIGURE 25.22   Register New Step menu option.

5. To register a step (and select the entity and event), enter the message Create in the Message field and account in the Primary Entity field (see Figure 25.23).

NOTE

The Message and Primary Entity text boxes have IntelliSense, so you are presented with a list of values after you enter the first characters.

6. Select the Pre-Operation option from the Event Pipeline Stage of Execution list and leave the other radio buttons set to their default values, as shown in Figure 25.23.

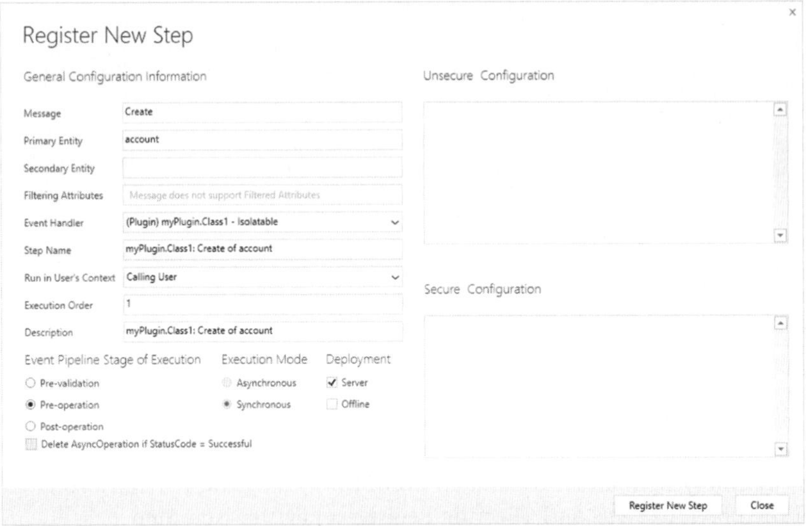

FIGURE 25.23   The Register New Step dialog box.

TIP

You can add impersonation to the plug-in step execution by changing the Run in User's Context field. By default, this value is set to the calling user, which is the user that is executing the operation (Create, Update, or Delete). However, in some cases, you need to do operations in your plug-in where the calling user might not have permissions. In such a case, you can either specify a different user with a higher role and privileges or use the CRM System user (an internal user), which has all the privileges. If you selected a different user, you can find out know who was the original user who fired the message by checking the value of the `InitiatingUserId` field of `IExecutionContext`.

While registering a plug-in, you can store configuration information, using the Secure Configuration and Unsecure Configuration boxes, shown in Figure 25.23. You can store data in any format you want. You can retrieve this information in plug-in code by using a plug-in constructor:

```
public myPlugin()
public myPlugin(string unsecure)
public myPlugin(string unsecure, string secure)
```

The first string parameter contains unsecure information, and the second one contains secure information. Secure configuration is not accessible in plug-ins executing in offline mode. Secure configuration is good for passing sensitive data, such as a connection string that contains a username and password.

7. Click Register New Step to close this dialog box, and you see the new step registered (see Figure 25.24).

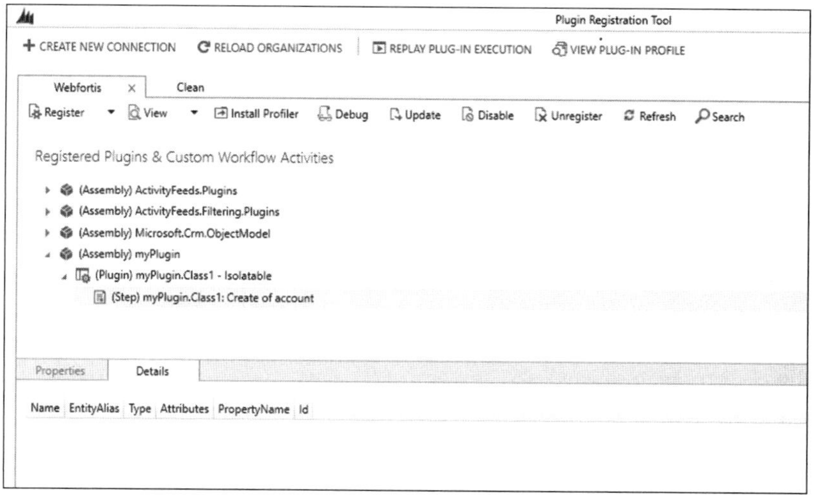

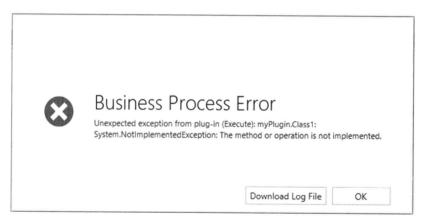

FIGURE 25.24   Step registration review.

As you saw in Figure 25.19, you can deploy an assembly to either the local hard disk or the database server or to the GAC (Global Assembly Cache). The database is the recommended option for production environments that might be deployed on different servers, such as a load-balanced deployment. This way you don't need to deploy the assembly on every server. The local hard disk option is the recommended option for debugging purposes.

Be sure to properly debug and test your plug-in before implementing it to a production environment. If a plug-in has an error, users cannot create accounts if you attached the plug-in to the account Create event and the pre-stage (see Figure 25.25).

Business Process Error

Unexpected exception from plug-in (Execute): myPlugin.Class1:
System.NotImplementedException: The method or operation is not implemented.

Download Log File   OK

FIGURE 25.25   Plug-in errors and exceptions prevent users from creating records on pre-stage.

▶ **SEE** the "Plug-in Debugging" **SECTION**, later in this chapter, for help on debugging.

TIP

With exceptions thrown in plug-ins registered as synchronous, the user gets a dialog about the error. With exceptions thrown in plug-ins registered in asynchronous mode, the exceptions are logged in the system jobs, which you can see by going to the CRM web application and selecting Settings > System Jobs.

Filtering Attributes

When registering a plug-in on the `Update` method, it is a best practice to filter or specify the fields for which you want the plug-in to be fired. For example, you might want the plug-in to be fired only if the Name field of the Account entity changes. If you don't configure the filtering attributes, the plug-in will fire if other fields change, unnecessarily decreasing the performance of the CRM server.

Filter or specifying the fields for which you want the plug-in to be fired is something you can do when you create a new step for the `Update` method (see Figure 25.26).

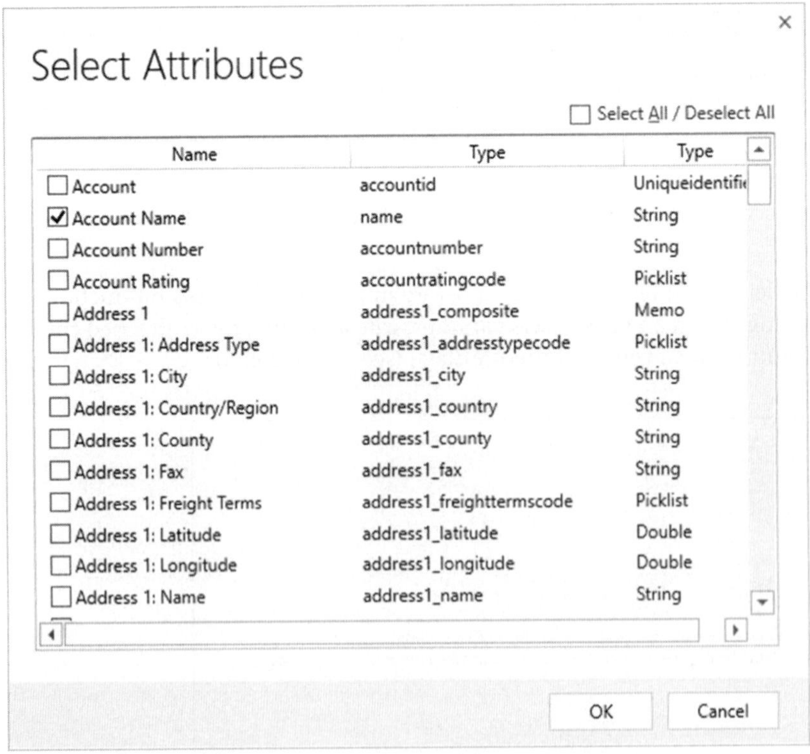

FIGURE 25.26   Filtering attributes for the `Update` method.

Images

Images are useful for update operations; they help you determine the original value of a field before a user fired an update operation.

For example, if you want to compare the value of the Account Name field of the Account entity, instead of getting an instance of the `IOrganizationServiceFactory` to create `IOrganizationService` and perform a `Retrieve` method (which junior CRM developers sometimes do), you can just configure this field on a pre-image and read it directly from there without doing any web service call that will decrease the performance of the server.

You need to create images by using the Plug-in Registration Tool. To to so navigate to Register New Image as shown in Figure 25.27.

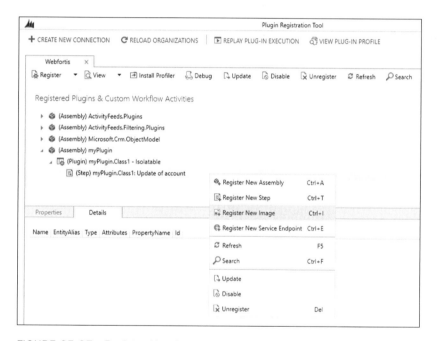

FIGURE 25.27   Register New Image menu option.

In the Register New Image Dialog that appears, set Image Type to be Pre Image or Post Image, enter a name for the image, enter an entity alias, and, in the Parameters field, select the attributes or fields you want the image to contain (see Figure 25.28). Click the Register Image button, and you see the image inside the plug-in (see Figure 25.29).

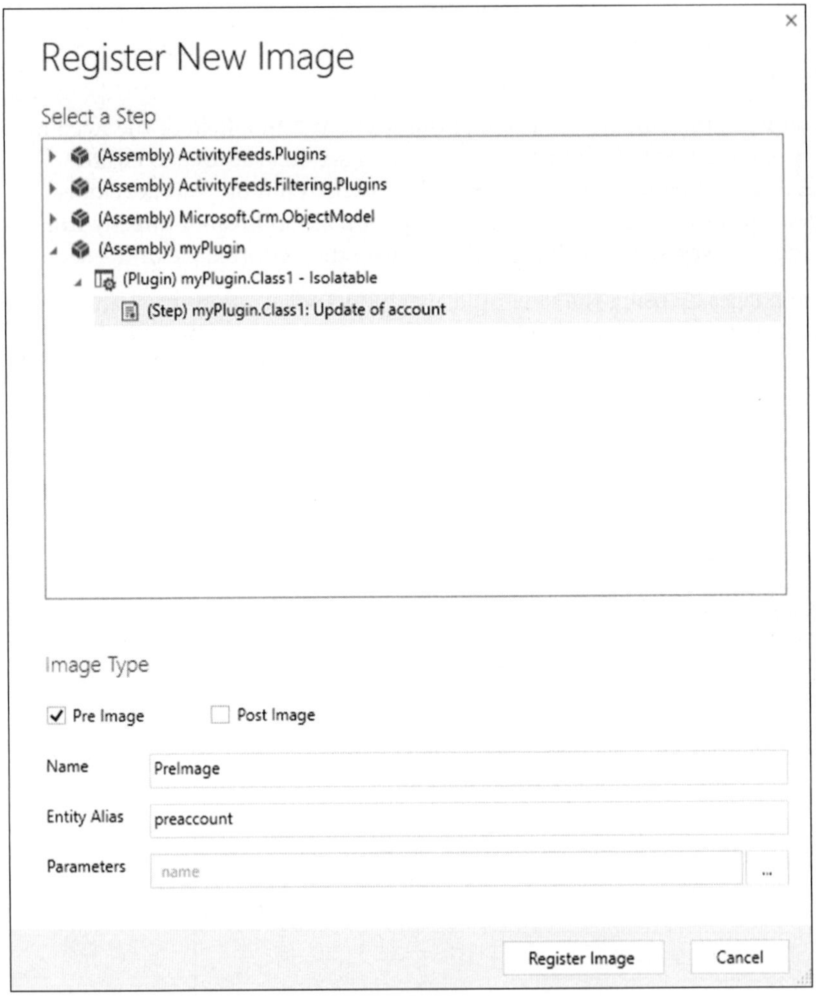

Register New Image

Select a Step

- ▶ 🎁 (Assembly) ActivityFeeds.Plugins
- ▶ 🎁 (Assembly) ActivityFeeds.Filtering.Plugins
- ▶ 🎁 (Assembly) Microsoft.Crm.ObjectModel
- ⊿ 🎁 (Assembly) myPlugin
  - ⊿ 🔲 (Plugin) myPlugin.Class1 - Isolatable
    - 📄 (Step) myPlugin.Class1: Update of account

Image Type

☑ Pre Image   ☐ Post Image

Name	PreImage
Entity Alias	preaccount
Parameters	name ...

Register Image   Cancel

FIGURE 25.28   Register New Image dialog.

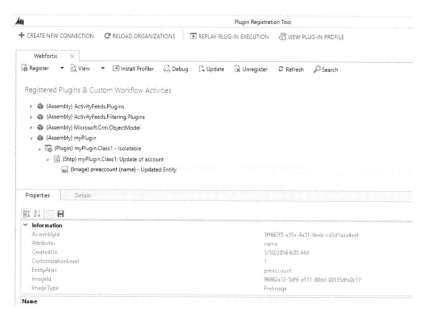

FIGURE 25.29   Image registered.

Unregister a Plug-in

To unregister a plug-in, you select the plug-in you want to delete, the Assembly node, and then click the Unregister button. The confirmation dialog shown in Figure 25.30 appears.

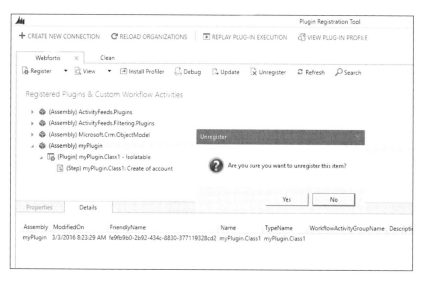

FIGURE 25.30   Plug-in unregistration confirmation dialog.

Click Yes to confirm the operation, and you see a success dialog, as shown in Figure 25.31.

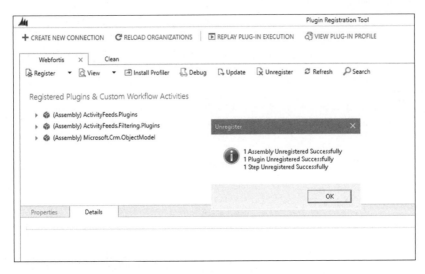

FIGURE 25.31   Successful plug-in unregistration.

Plug-in Debugging

You can debug a plug-in in two ways. The first, as shown in Table 25.1, is by attaching the debugger to the host process. The second is by using Plug-in Profiler. It is recommended that you use either of these methods in a development environment because both methods use Visual Studio and will interrupt all user activity with the server if you attempt to enable debugging in a production environment.

TABLE 25.1   Attaching the Debugger to a Host Process

Plug-in Registration Configuration	Service Process
Online	w3wp.exe
Offline	Microsoft.Crm.Application.Hoster.exe
Asynchronous registered plug-ins (or custom workflow assemblies)	CrmAsyncService.exe
Sandbox (isolation mode)	Microsoft.Crm.Sandbox.WorkerProcess.exe

Before trying either debugging method, you need to build your plug-in with debug mode and put the PDB (project database) file generated by the compiler in the following directory (assuming that you have the CRM server installed on C:\Program Files\Microsoft Dynamics CRM): C:\Program Files\Microsoft Dynamics CRM\Server\bin\assembly. This file is located in the output folder of your Visual Studio project, which is typically located at \debug\bin.

Unfortunately, you must restart the IIS after copying the PDB file. You can do this via the command prompt by running the following command:

```
Iisreset
```

You can also restart the IIS by using a PowerShell command, like this:

```
Restart-Service W3SVC, WAS -force
```

> **TIP**
>
> You must copy the PDB file every time you rebuild the solution in Visual Studio and then restart the IIS.

> **CAUTION**
>
> You must have Visual Studio installed on the server where the CRM server is installed, or you can also install the Visual Studio 2015 Remote Debugger on the server and debug from a development workstation. The example in this section assumes that you have Visual Studio (2015 or later) installed on the same server where the CRM server is installed.

Attaching the Debugger to the Host Process

When you debug by attaching the debugger to the host process, you have to open your plug-in solution in Visual Studio 2015 first and put breakpoints where you want to stop and debug your code. To set a breakpoint, press F9 (see Figure 25.32).

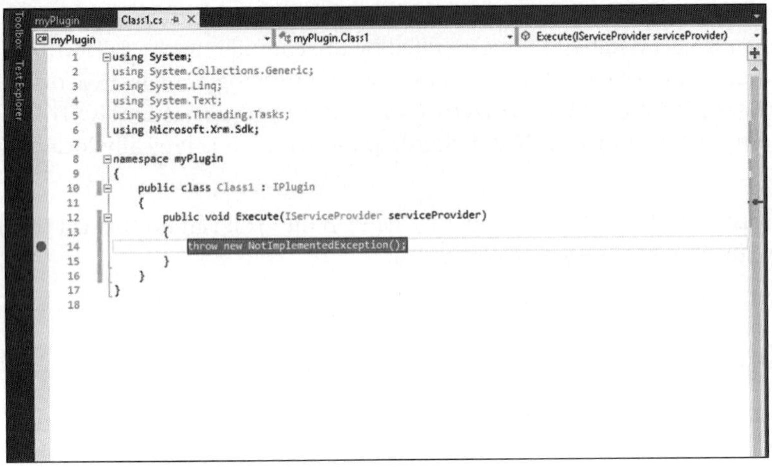

FIGURE 25.32   Setting breakpoints in your code.

You must attach the Visual Studio debugger to the w3wp.exe process, for example, to debug an online plug-in. To do that, select Debug > Attach to Process, as shown in Figure 25.33.

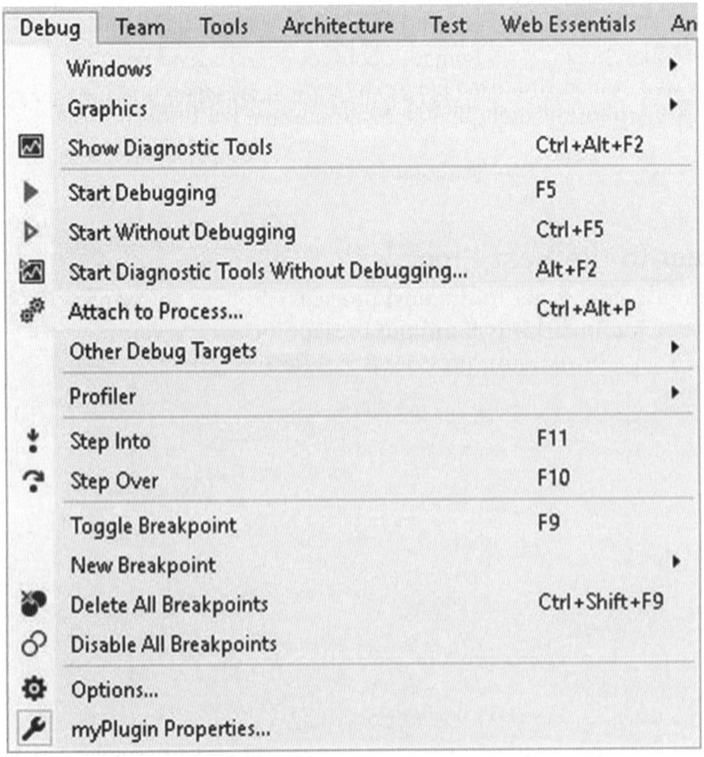

FIGURE 25.33   Attach to Process menu option.

When the Attach to Process dialog appears, check the Show Processes from All Users check box and select the w3wp.exe process, as shown in Figure 25.34.

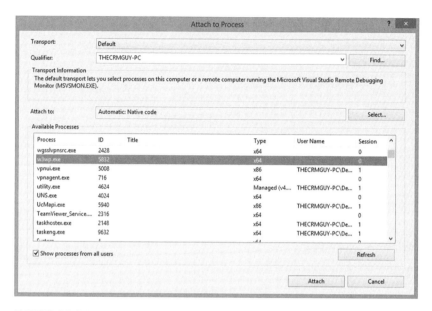

FIGURE 25.34   Attaching the debugger to the w3wp.exe process.

> **NOTE**
>
> If you can't find the w3wp.exe process, it is probably because you need to first open an Internet Explorer window and browse to your CRM organization URL so that IIS will load the application pool represented by w3wp.exe.
>
> You might also find that there is more than one instance of the w3wp.exe process running; this might depend on the number of different websites and application pools running on the same IIS. Because it is hard to say on which one your application is running, we recommend attaching to all the w3wp.exe instances.

If you are using the remote debugger, you must change the qualifier name to the name of the computer where the CRM and the remote debugger are installed.

If the plug-in has been registered with sandbox isolation mode, you must attach to another process instead of the w3wp.exe process. The process that hosts the plug-ins on a sandbox is called Microsoft.Crm.Sandbox.HostService.exe.

Click the Attach button to start debugging the plug-in.

Assuming that you registered the plug-in and associated it to the Account entity on the Create event (as in the earlier example in this chapter), when you go to the CRM web application and try to create a new account, you are automatically switched to the Visual Studio 2015 application (see Figure 25.35) after you click the Save or Save and Close buttons on the Account form.

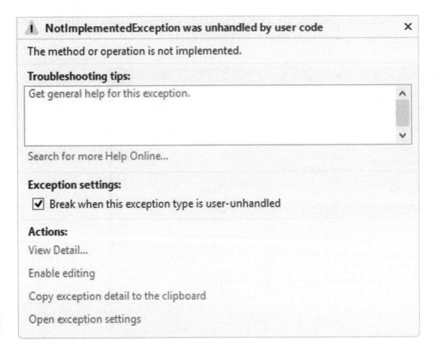

⚠ **NotImplementedException was unhandled by user code**   ✕

The method or operation is not implemented.

Troubleshooting tips:

Get general help for this exception.   ⌃

                                                                            ⌄

Search for more Help Online...

Exception settings:

☑ Break when this exception type is user-unhandled

Actions:

View Detail...

Enable editing

Copy exception detail to the clipboard

Open exception settings

FIGURE 25.35   Debugging the plug-in.

Plug-in Profiler

If you need to debug CRM Online plug-ins or plug-ins in a production environment, you should use Plug-in Profiler. You can install Plug-in Profiler from the Plug-in Registration Tool. To do so, follow these steps:

1. Open the Plug-in Registration Tool, connect to your organization, and click the Install Profiler button (see Figure 25.36).

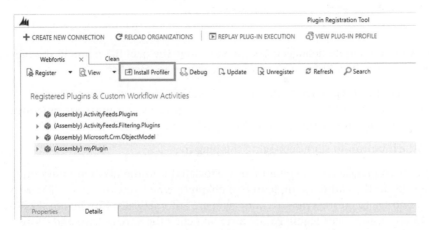

FIGURE 25.36   Installing the Plug-in Profiler.

2. When the Plug-in Profiler is installed successfully, make sure it exists under the assemblies (see Figure 25.37).

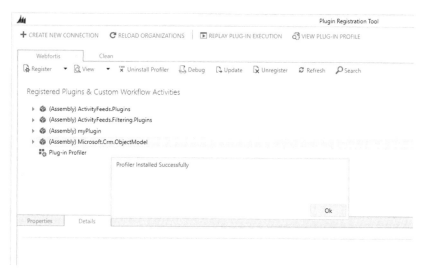

FIGURE 25.37   Plug-in Profiler.

3. Select the plug-in step that you want to debug, and you see the Start Profiling button available in addition to the Debug button (see Figure 25.38).

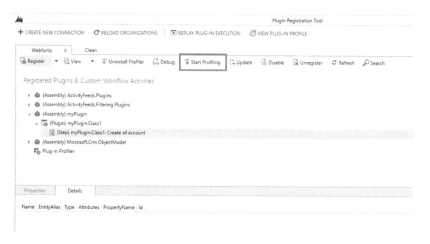

FIGURE 25.38   Start Profiling button.

4. Click the Start Profiling button, and the Profiler Settings dialog appears (see Figure 25.39). These profiling settings are good for most scenarios. Click OK.

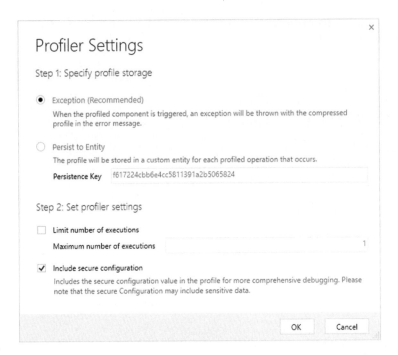

FIGURE 25.39   Profiler Settings dialog box.

5. Perform the steps in CRM so that the plug-in step you are profiling gets executed. The Business Process Error dialog box appears (see Figure 25.40).

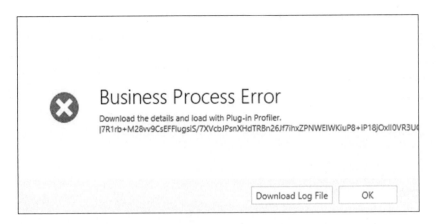

FIGURE 25.40   Business Process Error dialog box.

6. Click the Download Log File button to save the ErrorDetails.txt file on your computer. This log file contains the profile that the Plug-in Profiler will use to play back execution. Open the plug-in solution in Visual Studio and go to Debug > Attach Process and select PluginRegistration.exe (see Figure 25.41). Set a breakpoint in the plug-in code.

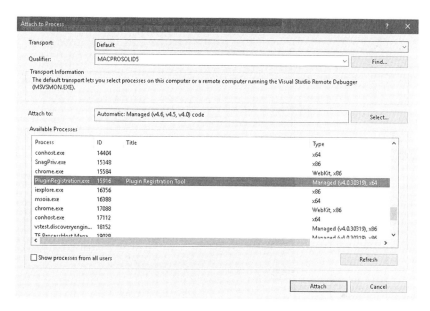

FIGURE 25.41   Attaching the debugger to PluginRegistration.exe.

7. Go back to the Plug-in Registration Tool and click the Reply Plug-in Execution button that is on the command bar or select the step you are profiling and click Debug. Select ErrorDetails.txt for the profile location (Step 1) and select the debug version of the plug-in assembly for the assembly location (Step 2) (see Figure 25.42).

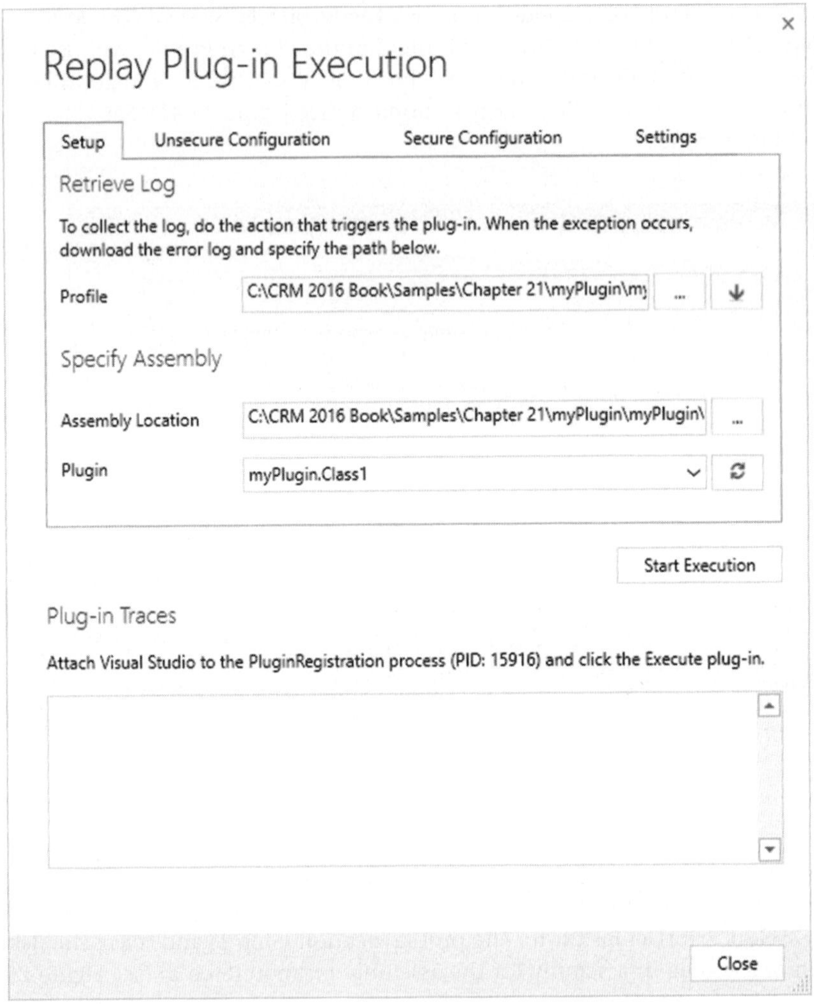

FIGURE 25.42   Debug plug-in.

You can optionally click the down arrow to download the profile execution log from the server (see Figure 25.43). You will have files there if you previously selected Persist to Entity in the profile settings when you started the Plug-in Profiler.

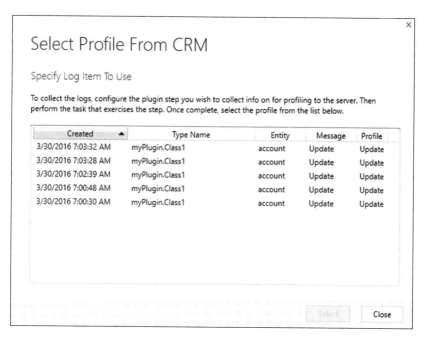

FIGURE 25.43   Selecting a profile from the CRM server.

8. Click Start Execution, and debugging starts in Visual Studio.

Plug-in Samples

The SDK comes with some plug-in samples:

▶ **AccountNumberPlugin**—This sample creates a random account number when an account is created.

▶ **FollowupPlugin**—This sample creates a Task activity when an account is created.

▶ **PreEventPlugin**—This sample demonstrates the use of shared variables to send data through different plug-ins.

▶ **WebClientPlugin**—This sample shows how to access a network resource in a sandboxed plug-in.

▶ **AdvancedPlugin**—This sample shows how to use pre- and post-images, tracing, how to pass secure and unsecure information, and so on.

You can find the code for these samples in C#, within the SDK, in the sdk\samplecode\ cs\plug-ins folder.

You can download the SDK from the Microsoft website; search for "Dynamics CRM SDK."

TIP

Because Microsoft often updates the SDK, it is a good idea to check the download site for updated versions.

Plug-in Distribution

When you develop a plug-in, you register it by using the Plug-in Registration Tool, as explained earlier in this chapter. When you are done with the development and ready to distribute the plug-in, you can do so by creating a solution. Make sure you include the plug-in assembly and the SDK message processing steps in your solution (see Figure 25.44).

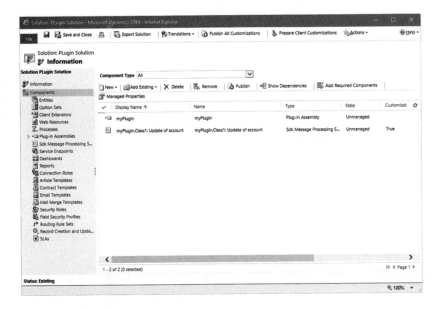

FIGURE 25.44   CRM solution.

▶ To learn more about working with solutions in Dynamics CRM 2016, refer to **CHAPTER 22**, "Customizing the System."

When importing your plug-in solution to another CRM organization, make sure you check the check box Enable Any SDK Message Processing Steps Included in the Solution, or your plug-in won't work (see Figure 25.45).

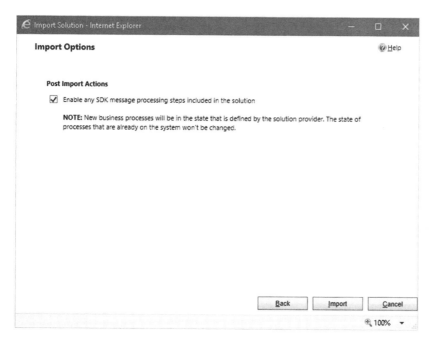

FIGURE 25.45   Enabling Any SDK Message Processing Steps Included in the Solution check box when importing solutions.

CAUTION

Be careful if you change the managed properties of the SDK message processing steps to `false`. If a user who imports your solution unchecks the Any SDK Message Processing Steps Included in the Solution when importing the solution, the only way to enable the steps is by using the Plug-in Registration Tool because the message steps don't show up in the installed solution.

Be careful about using secured configurations in the plug-in SDK message processing steps registration. The secure configuration is encrypted with a specific organization key and might be different from one organization to another. You might need to update this secure configuration manually for each environment where you install your plug-in solution.

Summary

In this chapter, you have learned about plug-ins—what they are and when it is recommended to use them. You have created a basic plug-in and reviewed all the development properties of the `IServiceProvider`, `IExecutionContext`, and `IPluginExecutionContext` interfaces. You have learned how to deploy and register plug-ins by using the Plug-in Registration Tool within the UI. You have also learned how to test and debug plug-ins in two ways: by attaching the debugger to the w3wp.exe process and by using the Plug-in Profiler. Finally, you have learned how to distribute your plug-ins to other Dynamics CRM organizations using solutions.

Process Development

With Microsoft Dynamics CRM 2016, organizations can define and implement business processes. These processes help employees focus on their work rather than do manual steps. Dynamics CRM 2016 has business process flows (BPFs), actions, workflows (asynchronous and synchronous), and dialogs. In addition, tasks flows are a preview feature available in Dynamics CRM 2016 Online only. Business process flows and real-time (synchronous) workflows are processes specifically designed to be used by people who are not developers. However, it is important to understand how and why to use each type of process.

Table 26.1 summarizes the various options available in actions, dialogs, and workflows.

TABLE 26.1   Action, Dialog, and Workflow Options

	Action	Dialog	Workflow
Assign Record	×	×	×
Assign Value	×	×	
Change Status	×	×	×
Check Condition	×	×	×
Conditional Branch	×	×	×
Create Record	×	×	×
Custom Step	×	×	×
Default Action	×	×	×
Link Child Dialog		×	
Page		×	
Parallel Wait Branch			×
Perform Action	×	×	×
Prompt and Response		×	
Query CRM Data		×	
Send Email	×	×	×

(Continued)

TABLE 26.1   *(Continued)*

	Action	Dialog	Workflow
Stage	×	×	×
Start Child Workflow	×	×	×
Stop Workflow/Dialog	×	×	×
Update Record	×	×	×
Wait Condition			*

* Available in asynchronous workflows only.

The steps for creating any of these processes are similar. You start by going to Settings > Processes and clicking the New button. A new pop-up window opens, and in it you select one of the objects from the Category drop-down (see Figure 26.1).

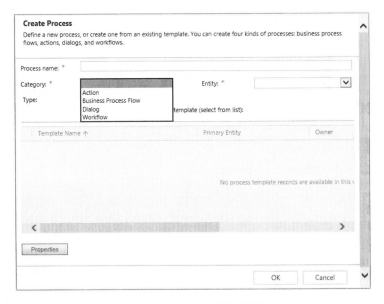

FIGURE 26.1   Processes interface in CRM 2016.

Actions

Actions in Dynamics CRM are used to extend the standard functionality of the system. With actions, business users can implement the business logic, and then developers can hook up those actions to system events. Business users can write business logic the same way as in workflows. If there is a change in business process logic, business users can change the logic in actions without involving any developer. Actions can be tied to specific entities, or they can be global. (To make them global, you select None [global] in the Entity drop-down in the Create Process dialog shown in Figure 26.1.)

You can save actions as a template and then use the template to create new actions. Developers can then invoke the actions via code, using a plug-in, JavaScript, or a custom button on the command bar. Actions can be imported and exported as part of a solution.

Basically, you can think of an action as a wrapper for multiple server-side operations. It boosts performance because instead of sending multiple requests for software development kit (SDK) operations, those calls are bundled into one action, and you need to send only one request to the server. In addition, consider the following:

▶ Actions are called (run as) under security context of calling the user.

▶ Actions are available through organization.svc or organization.svc/web endpoints.

▶ Actions can be invoked using C# code or JavaScript. You cannot invoke actions using OData.

▶ Actions are not supported with offline clients.

▶ Wait and Parallel Wait Branch steps are not available in actions.

▶ Actions support both input and output arguments.

Behind the scenes, the business logic in actions is implemented using a real-time workflow. When you create an action, it is automatically registered as a real-time workflow to execute at stage 30 (core operation) in the execution pipeline.

The following data types are supported for arguments (see Figure 26.2):

▶ Boolean

▶ DateTime

▶ Decimal

▶ Entity

▶ EntityCollection

▶ EntityReference

▶ Float

▶ Integer

▶ Money

▶ Picklist

▶ String

26

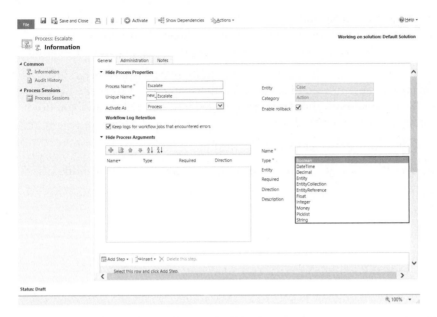

FIGURE 26.2   Supported parameter types for input and output arguments in actions.

You can specify whether an action is part of a database transaction or not. To do so, find the Enable Rollback check box, shown in Figure 26.2. If this is checked, the actions will be part of the main database transaction, and if there is an error, the whole transaction will roll back.

Actions are request and response classes that can be used in the Execute method of the CRM Organization service. You can generate these classes to use in your code by using the CrmSvcUtil.exe utility in the SDK, found under the Bin directory. To include request response classes for activated actions in that organization, you have to pass an additional parameter, /generateActions, at the end, as shown in Listing 26.1.

LISTING 26.1   Request Response Classes

```
CrmSvcUtil.exe /url:http://serverName/organizationName/XRMServices/2011/
Organization.svc
/out:outputFilename.cs /username:username /password:password /
domain:domainName
/namespace:outputNamespace /serviceContextName:serviceContextName
/generateActions
```

NOTE

To download the CRM SDK, search for "CRM 2016 SDK" at www.microsoft.com.

When to Use Actions

You use actions when you want to perform certain steps based on some criteria, such as when a case has been opened for some days and no action has taken place. In this example, a customer calls the customer care support line and would like the case to be escalated. The service representative can escalate the case with one click.

You can implement business logic depending on the number of days the case was open, and then it can be executed from within that case record. You can send email to a senior service manager, change priority, and assign the case to a queue in a single action named Escalate—and all these steps can be performed in a single process. In earlier versions of CRM, you implemented this sort of functionality using workflows.

How to Use Actions

To implement the previous example using actions, you need to create an action on the Case entity, as follows:

1. Go to Settings > Processes and click the New button.

2. In the dialog that appears, enter Escalate as the process name and choose Action as the category and Case as the entity. Then click OK.

3. In the dialog that appears, set the Process Name field and the Unique Name field (used in invoking actions using SDK or JavaScript). Ensure that the Enable Rollback check box is selected. You can save actions as process templates, which you can use to create new actions, and you can keep the check box Keep Logs for Workflow Jobs That Encountered Any Errors checked.

NOTE

For successfully completed action jobs there will be no log.

4. Create an output argument of data type String, named Priority. Also create an argument for a user who is escalating the case. To do this, click the + icon to add a process argument, select EntityReference as the type, and select User as the entity for the EscalatedBy argument. Check the Required check box to make it a required field, as shown in Figure 26.3.

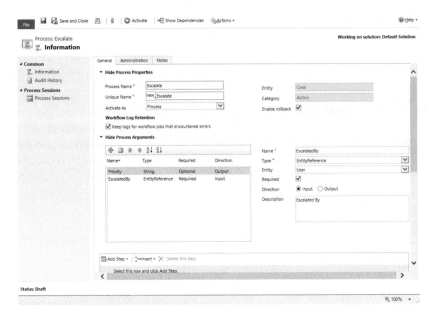

FIGURE 26.3   Input argument.

5. Enter business logic to check whether the case has been created before 30 days from the current date and then send an escalation email to the senior service manager from the user escalating the case. Figure 26.4 shows the escalation email, Figure 26.5 shows the case priority being changed to high, and Figure 26.6 assigns the case to the high-priority queue. Figure 26.7 sets the output variable Set Case Priority = High. Finally, if the case created is less than 15 days from the current date, send an email to the service manager, set the case to medium priority, assign the case to a medium-priority queue, and the set output variable Set Case Priority = Medium (see Figure 26.8).

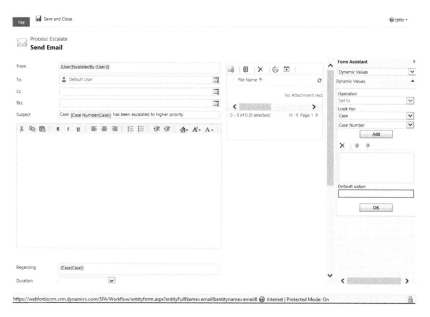

FIGURE 26.4   Escalation email.

FIGURE 26.5   Changing the case priority to High.

FIGURE 26.6   Assigning the case to a high-priority queue.

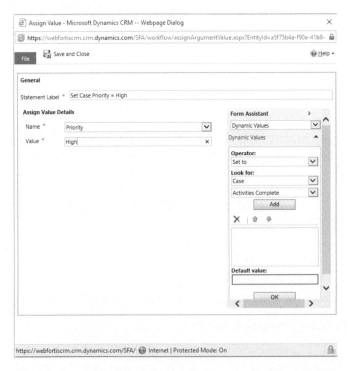

FIGURE 26.7   Assigning the value High to the output argument.

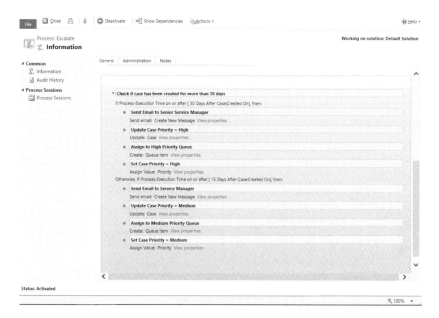

FIGURE 26.8   Business logic in action.

6. Add a custom button named Escalate to the command bar of the Case entity and invoke the `Escalate()` function of the Action.js script when that button is clicked (see Figure 26.9).

26

TIP

To make modifications to the Site Map as explained in step 6 by adding a custom button, download the XrmToolbox from http://xrmtoolbox.codeplex.com. Using the SiteMap Editor included with that tool, you can easily edit the ribbon menu.

To add the custom button to the command in step 6, download Ribbon Workbench from www.develop1.net. You can use Ribbon Workbench to add custom buttons and specify what function to be called on button click.

The `Escalate()` function passes the current case ID and current user ID parameters to the `EscalateRequest` function. This method executes SOAP message to execute the `new_Escalate` actions. The action is executed, and in response, you have the priority value that you have assigned in the action business logic. You can parse the response by using the `ShowResponse()` function of Action.js and use it in an alert message to a customer care representative (see Listing 26.2 and Figure 26.10).

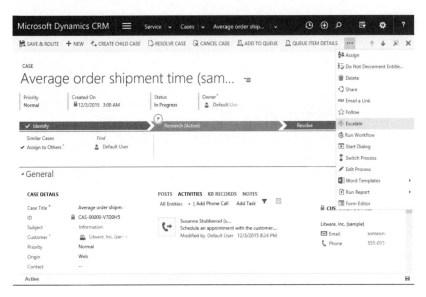

FIGURE 26.9   Custom Escalate button on the case record.

LISTING 26.2   Action.js

```
var requestXML = new XMLHttpRequest();
requestXML.onreadystatechange = ShowResponse;
function Escalate() {//function for the command bar
    var recordId = Xrm.Page.data.entity.getId().replace("{","").replace("}","");
    var userId = Xrm.Page.context.getUserId().replace("{", "").replace("}", "");
        EscalateRequest(userId, recordId);
}
function EscalateRequest(EscalatedById, CaseId) {

    var postUrl = Xrm.Page.context.getClientUrl() + "/XRMServices/2011/Organization
    .svc/web";//WebService Url
    var requestText = "";
    requestText += "<s:Envelope xmlns:s=\"http://schemas.xmlsoap.org/soap/
    envelope/\">";
    requestText += "    <s:Body>";
    requestText += "        <Execute xmlns=\"http://schemas.microsoft.com/xrm/2011/
    Contracts/Services\"
xmlns:i=\"http://www.w3.org/2001/XMLSchema-instance\">";
    requestText += "            <request  xmlns:a=\"http://schemas.microsoft.com/
    xrm/2011/Contracts\">";
    requestText += "                <a:Parameters xmlns:c=\"http://schemas
    .datacontract.org/2004/07/System.Collections.Generic\">";
    requestText += "                    <a:KeyValuePairOfstringanyType>";
    requestText += "                        <c:key>EscalatedBy</c:key>";
```

```
    requestText += "                         <c:value i:type=\"a:EntityReference\">"
    requestText += "                           <a:Id>" + EscalatedById + "</a:Id>"
    requestText += "                           <a:LogicalName>systemuser
</a:LogicalName>"
    requestText += "                           <a:Name i:nil=\"true\" />"
    requestText += "                         </c:value>"
    requestText += "                       </a:KeyValuePairOfstringanyType>"
    requestText += "                       <a:KeyValuePairOfstringanyType>"
    requestText += "                         <c:key>Target</c:key>"
    requestText += "                         <c:value i:type=\"a:EntityReference\">"
    requestText += "                           <a:Id>" + CaseId + "</a:Id>"
    requestText += "                           <a:LogicalName>incident
</a:LogicalName>"
    requestText += "                           <a:Name i:nil=\"true\" />"
    requestText += "                         </c:value>"
    requestText += "                       </a:KeyValuePairOfstringanyType>"
    requestText += "                     </a:Parameters>"
    requestText += "                     <a:RequestId i:nil=\"true\" />"
    requestText += "                     <a:RequestName>new_Escalate</a:RequestName>"
    requestText += "                   </request>"
    requestText += "               </Execute>"
    requestText += "       </s:Body>"
    requestText += "</s:Envelope>"
    requestXML.open("POST", postUrl, true);//true is for async
    requestXML.setRequestHeader("Accept", "application/xml, text/xml, */*");
    requestXML.setRequestHeader("Content-Type", "text/xml; charset=utf-8");
    requestXML.setRequestHeader("SOAPAction", "http://schemas.microsoft.com/
xrm/2011/Contracts/Services/IOrganizationService/Execute");
    requestXML.send(requestText);
}
function ShowResponse() {
    var x = requestXML.responseXML.getElementsByTagName("a:KeyValuePairOfstringany
Type");
    for (i = 0; i < x.length; i++) {
        if (x[i].childNodes[0].textContent == "Priority") {
            alert("The case has been assigned to " + x[i].childNodes[1].textContent
+ " priority queue.");
        }
    }
}
```

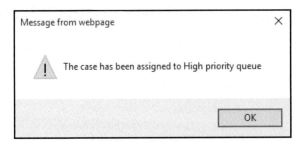

FIGURE 26.10   Alert message with a response from an action.

7. Write plug-ins on pre- and post-stages of the Escalate message (see Listing 26.3). In some scenarios you need to do some data validation before the Escalate message executes, and you can write this business logic in a plug-in and register it on pre-operation of the Escalate message. The plug-in code should validate the business logic and abort the Escalate message if conditions are not met. When you register your plug-in, you see new_Escalate available under Messages.

You have to make sure the action is activated; otherwise, you will get a runtime error. The input parameters of the plug-in context should receive the input arguments defined, and post-operation should have both input and output arguments defined in the actions (see Figure 26.11).

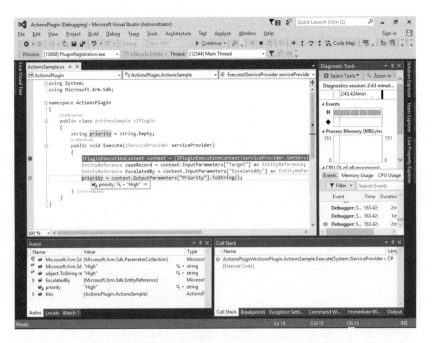

FIGURE 26.11   Post-operation output arguments in the plug-in.

LISTING 26.3   Plug-in Code

```
using System;
using System.Collections.Generic;
using System.Linq;
using System.Text;
using Microsoft.Xrm.Sdk;
namespace ActionsPlugin
{
    public class ActionsSample :IPlugin
    {
        string priority = string.Empty;
        public void Execute(IServiceProvider serviceProvider)
        {
            IPluginExecutionContext context =
(IPluginExecutionContext)serviceProvider.GetService(typeof(IPluginExecution
Context));
            EntityReference caseRecord = context.InputParameters["Target"] as
EntityReference;
            EntityReference EscalatedBy = context.InputParameters["EscalatedBy"] as
EntityReference;
            priority = context.OutputParameters["Priority"].ToString();
        }
    }
}
```

▶ For more information about registering and debugging plug-ins, **SEE CHAPTER 25**.

Business Process Flows

Business process flows (BPFs) provide visual presentations of processes in Microsoft
Dynamics CRM. Business users can create efficient and streamlined business processes that
let end users know where they are and what to do next with current record to reach
a conclusion. Users can the see the BPF control at the top of the entity records.

Enabling an Entity for BPF

You can enable the BPF feature for an entity by allowing it on the form customizations.
To do so, go to Customizations > Customize the System and then select an entity for

which you want to enable business process. Once it is enabled, you cannot reverse it. You get two new fields for the entity: ProcessId and StageId. ProcessId holds the ID of the process associated with the current record, and StageId holds the ID of the current stage of the record in the process. You can have a maximum of 10 active BPFs per entity.

> **TIP**
>
> You can change the maximum number of business flows by updating the Organization entity's `MaximumActiveBusinessProcessFlowsAllowedPerEntity` property.

Enabling Default BPFs

Microsoft provides several ready-to-use business processes for entities. You can enable them from Settings > Data Management > Add Ready-to-Use Business Processes. Go to Settings > Processes, and you see BPFs created and activated for the following entities:

- ▶ Account
- ▶ Contact
- ▶ Campaign
- ▶ Case
- ▶ Marketing List
- ▶ Opportunity

> **TIP**
>
> A BPF must be activated before you can use it. You do this activation by navigating to Settings > Processes and selecting the BPF you want to activate.

The BPF guides users from various stages in sales, service, and other business processes from start to finish. BPFs have predefined stages, and each stage has steps. You can mark steps as required, but even if you do this, you cannot force users to complete that step before moving to the next stage. BPFs can be designed for a single entity, or they can span multiple entities. For example, you can start from a Lead entity and then move on to Opportunity, Account, Quote, Sales Order, Invoice, and then come back to Opportunity to close it as won. You can also have multiple process flows for a single entity. For example, you can have a process flow for low-priority cases and another one for high-priority cases.

> **NOTE**
>
> When returning to the original entity (in the previous example, Opportunity), you are limited in terms of the actions you can perform. For example, you can only close the Opportunity entity, and no other actions are allowed.

Designing a BPF

You can create a BPF by going to Settings > Processes and clicking the New button. You then fill in the name of the BPF and select Business Process Flow from the Category drop-down. BPFs are always associated with an entity, unlike actions, which can be defined as global. Select the entity from the Entity drop-down, which lists the entities for which BPF is enabled (see Figure 26.12).

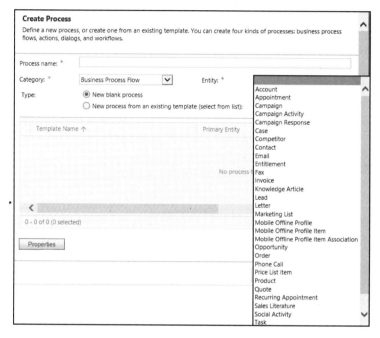

FIGURE 26.12   Creating a new BPF.

Next, the Business Process Flow Designer screen opens. It is divided into three main parts: a command bar at top, a description area, and a process definition area. The process definition area is divided into stages, and each stage has Stage Name and Entity as mandatory fields (see Figure 26.13).

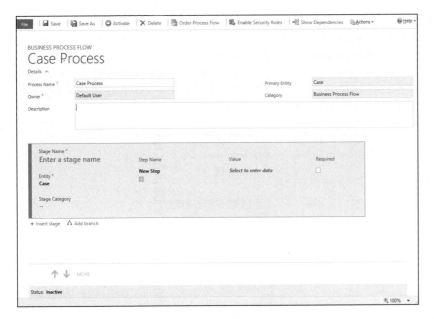

FIGURE 26.13   Business Process Flow Designer screen.

One entity is shown in the Business Process Flow Designer initially, and you cannot change the primary entity (the one selected on the previous screen). You can add other entities to the process in later stages, and the Business Process Flow Designer lists all the entities that have the BPF enabled for. The next step is to click Relationships to select the relationship between the entities; keep in mind that there can be multiple relationships between two entities. This way you can differentiate between them.

When you click the entity name, it is added to the process. You can delete a stage in the process by clicking the X button in the top-right corner of the stage. You can delete any stage in the process, but there is no way to delete the primary entity in the process. A multi-entity process can have a maximum of five entities.

If you have a process flow that moves from case to phone call to task, you might want to update the case record after the task. To do this, you can close the process cycle by selecting the Case entity under Close Process Cycle, and you cannot add any new entities after that.

You can click Insert Stage at the bottom of the Business Process Flow Designer (refer to Figure 26.13) to add a new stage in the process definition. You can select an entity in the process definition and add a stage for that and give them the following properties:

▶ A stage will always be added at the end.

▶ There can be a maximum of 30 stages per entity in a process.

If you have at least three stages, you can move stages up and down by using the arrow keys at the bottom of the Business Process Flow Designer. When you move a stage, all the child steps move along with it. You can select a stage by clicking it; when an X appears on the right side of the selected stage, you can click it to delete the selected stage. When a stage is deleted, its child steps and their labels are also deleted.

When you add a stage, you provide a name to that stage and select the stage category. This stage category is populated from a global option set named Stage Category, which you can customize to your requirements.

To enhance a business process flow with branching, you can create a BPF with multiple branches by using If-Else logic. To add the first branch for a stage, choose Add Branch below the stage and specify the If condition, as shown in Figure 26.14.

FIGURE 26.14   If-Else logic branching.

Click the + button under the branching rule to add another condition to the rule.

To add a second branch for the same stage, choose Add Branch again, below the same stage. The Else clause is displayed. You can choose Else to convert it to Else-If if you have more than two branches from the same stage or if you want to enter a branch only when certain conditions are satisfied.

The branching condition can be formed of multiple logical expressions that use a combination of AND or OR operators. The branch selection is done automatically, in real time, based on rules defined during the process definition. Each branch can be maximum of five levels deep. All peer branches should always merge to a single stage or must end the process.

A stage can have multiple steps, and whenever a new stage is added, a new step is also added. You can add a new step by clicking the + icon. When a step is added, it is added at the end of the selected stage. You can move steps up and down by using same arrow keys that you use for stages. You cannot move a step from one stage to another stage; if you want to do this, you have to delete the step from the stage and then add a new step to the other stage. You can have a maximum of 30 steps for each stage.

You can map a step to an attribute by clicking the text box under the Field column, and you can provide a step label of your own choice, or it will get copied from the selected Fields Display value. If your process requires some steps to complete any mandatory fields before moving to the next stage, you can select the Required column in front of that step. You can have multiple required steps in a stage.

BPFs can also be associated with security roles. Users who have the appropriate security roles can see or use them, and you can have multiple BPFs for an entity. All of them can be associated with a single security role.

In addition, you can set the order of BPFs for each entity. To do so, open a BPF and then click the Order Process Flow button on the command bar. The entity at the top of the dialog that appears will be set as the default (see Figure 26.15).

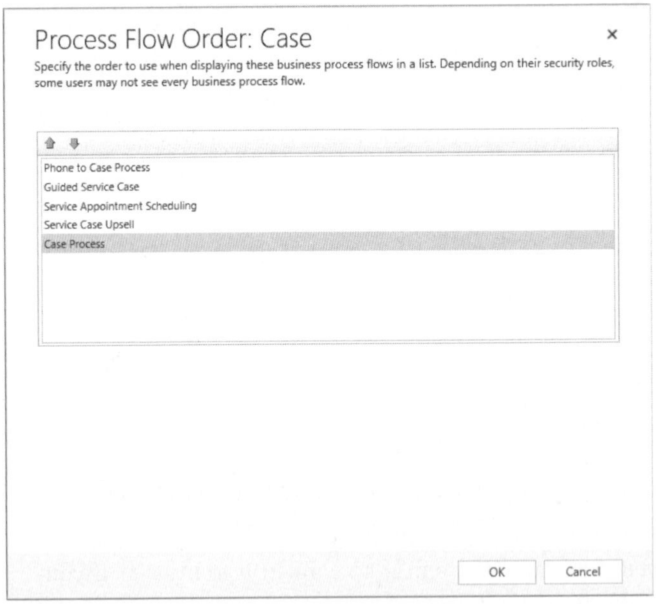

FIGURE 26.15   Setting the order of BPFs.

When a user creates a new record, the list of activated BPFs for that entity is compared with business processes for the security role of that user. The first activated BPF is set by default. Once the record is created, users can switch BPFs via the command bar.

A pop-up window opens after a user selects to switch BPFs from the command bar, with a list of active BPFs for that entity. You can select the process from there, and that process will be activated for that record.

Dialogs

You can use dialogs to have users perform a business process in an order that you want them to follow, such as when a structured flow is required. Dialogs are also good for surveys, such as customer satisfaction surveys where the next question depends on the current answer.

Table 26.2 shows the main differences between dialogs and workflows.

TABLE 26.2   Differences Between Dialogs and Workflows

Dialogs	Workflows
Synchronous	Either synchronous or asynchronous
Interactive (requires user intervention)	Unattended
Starts manually	Start manually or can be triggered by an event (for example, when a record is created, updated, deleted, and so on)

To create a new dialog, follow these steps:

1. From the main interface, navigate to Settings > Processes and then click New.

2. Enter the name Customer Satisfaction Survey for the process. Select Account from the Entity drop-down. Then select Dialog from the Category drop-down (see Figure 26.16).

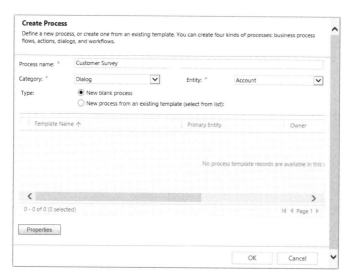

FIGURE 26.16   Creating a process dialog.

3. Click OK, and you see the Dialog Designer (see Figure 26.17).

The following sections explain some of the items in the Dialog Designer.

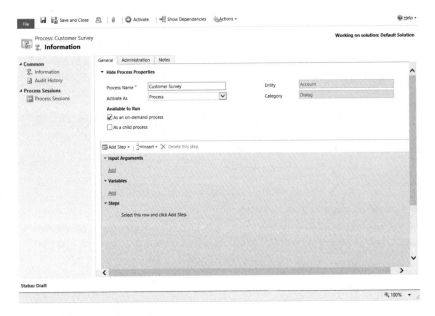

FIGURE 26.17   Dialog Designer.

Input Arguments

Input arguments are used to pass parameters from a parent dialog to a child dialog. The input arguments can be Single Line of Text, Whole Number, Date and Time, Date Only, and Lookup, as shown in Figure 26.18.

When you try to add a new input argument, you are alerted about the need to change the runtime to run as a child process if you didn't do it before.

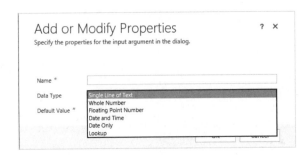

FIGURE 26.18   Input arguments.

Variables

Variables are used to store computed data or strings that need to be concatenated on future pages of the dialog. Like input arguments, they can be set to Single Line of Text, Whole Number, Date and Time, Date Only, or Lookup.

Steps

Steps are similar to workflows, with the exception of the main step, which gives you a Page option. Dialogs contain one or more pages that enable you to interact with users by asking questions the users need to answer. Based on the answer, you can change the flow of the process.

TIP

Think of pages as interfaces or pop-ups that are displayed to the user.

To create a welcome page, follow these steps:

1. Start a new workflow and click Add Step and Select Add Step Page. A red error icon appears.

2. Correct the error (shown with the red X icon) by clicking Add Step and selecting Prompt and Response (see Figure 26.19). After you add the prompt and response on the page, you will see also another red error icon.

NOTE

Of course, you can create the dialog in the order shown (input, variables, and then steps), but for purposes of illustration, you are creating it backward.

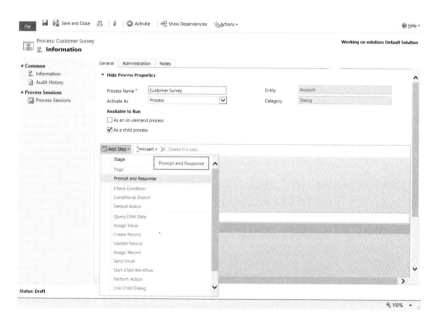

FIGURE 26.19   Adding a prompt and response to the page.

3. As indicated by the error, complete the step by clicking Set Properties. Then you can enter the question, the response type, and the tip for the page.

> **NOTE**
>
> Notice that if the response type is set to None, all the related options at the bottom of the form are disabled.

4. Click Save and Close and add another page with another prompt and response step inside. On this page, set Response Type to Option Set (Radio Buttons), as shown in Figure 26.20. Fill out the other options as shown in Figure 26.20 to ask whether the client is very satisfied, a little satisfied, or not satisfied with your services.

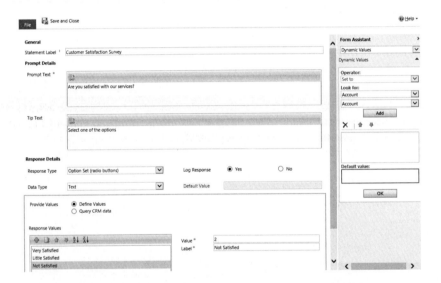

FIGURE 26.20   Customer survey configured.

5. Click Save and Close and add a check condition step, as shown in Figure 26.21.

6. To ask a different question of customers who are not satisfied, click the <Condition> (Click Here to Configure) link to validate the previous page's response. It is recommended to use Response Value instead of Response Label because it is likely that you can change the labels but not the values of the option set.

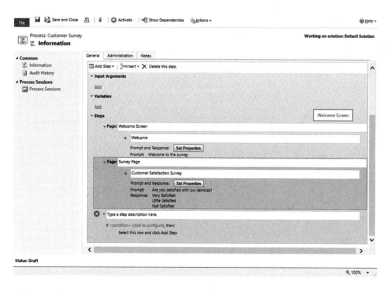

FIGURE 26.21   Adding check conditions.

7. Click Save and Close and add another page with another prompt and response step to ask why the customer is not satisfied. For this question, allow the user to enter a free-text description of the problem. You could add more questions with fixed options on a real process.

8. To record the selections to a field on the entity (even though you can see the user response on the dialog sessions, discussed later in this chapter), select the entire last step, click Add Step, and then click Update Record (see Figure 26.22).

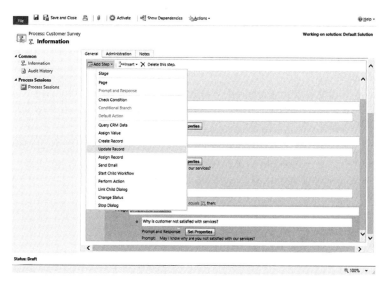

FIGURE 26.22   Adding the Update Record step.

9. Click Set Properties, and in the Description field under the Details section, set a dynamic value from the dissatisfaction response text (see Figure 26.23). You can update any field on the account form with values from the dialog session. This is an important piece to consider when using dialogs and processes: Because you're updating the record, you can easily launch a workflow process on the field values set by the dialogs.

10. Click Save and Close to close the Update Account page, and click Save and Close to close the Dialog Designer.

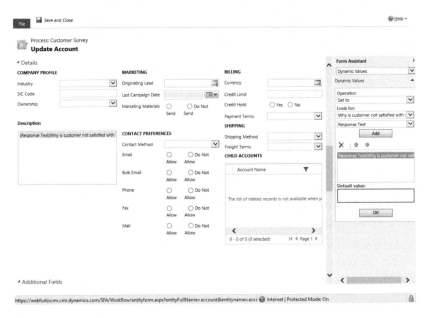

FIGURE 26.23   Updating the Description field, based on the user response text.

Dialog Activation

Before you can use the dialog you just created, you need to activate it by clicking the Activate button. When you click the Activate button, a confirmation window appears.

TIP

You can always deactivate a process by clicking the Deactivate button. If you need to make any change to a process, you must deactivate it first because the capability to edit it is disabled for an activated process.

Testing the Dialog

To test the dialog you made for accounts, you need to go to the accounts. From there, you can select any account record, and you then see a Start Dialog option added to the ... item on the command bar (see Figure 26.24). When you click this button, a new window opens, and from it, you can select the dialog you want to use (see Figure 26.25). Select the Customer Survey dialog and click Add to start the process.

TIP

You need to have the pop-up blocker disabled to use dialogs; otherwise, they won't start.

The first screen shows the welcome text. Even though you didn't add any questions on this page, the user can enter a comment here. You will be able to see the comments and the dialog responses in the Dialog Sessions link that is related to the record you are running in the dialog.

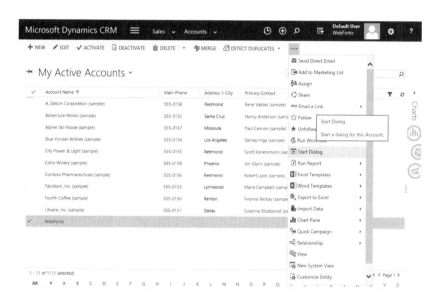

FIGURE 26.24   Start Dialog option.

FIGURE 26.25   Selecting the dialog.

Click Next. You now see the customer survey question you configured; select this option and click Next.

On the next page, you see that the user can answer a question in a free-text form to explain why he or she is dissatisfied.

> **NOTE**
>
> Notice that this field differs from the comment text box that is on the bottom of the dialog because this is specifically related to this question, whereas comments are related to the entire dialog process.

Click Next. The final page asks you for confirmation. If you are okay with all the dialog responses, click Finish. If not, you can move backward and then forward again and click Finish on the last page when you're ready.

> **NOTE**
>
> You can start a dialog by using a direct URL that runs the dialog. (This is helpful for programmatic access such as Interactive Voice Recognition (IVR) software integrations.) You can access a dialog with a URL similar to this for On-Premises:
>
> ```
> http://CRMServerName/OrgName/cs/dialog/rundialog.
> aspx?DialogId=DialogIDHYPERLINK
> "http://crmservername/OrgName/cs/dialog/rundialog.aspx?DialogId=DialogID&
> EntityName=EntityLogicalName&"&HYPERLINK
> ```

```
"http://crmservername/OrgName/cs/dialog/rundialog.aspx?DialogId=DialogID
&EntityName=EntityLogicalName&"EntityName=EntityLogicalNameHYPERLINK
"http://crmservername/OrgName/cs/dialog/rundialog.aspx?DialogId=DialogID
&EntityName=EntityLogicalName&"&ObjectId=EntityObjectId
```

The values for `DialogID`, `EntityName`, and `ObjectID` are found in the URL of the dialog. To grab this URL, you can launch the dialog and press Ctrl+N to get the dialog to open in a new window, where you can see the address bar.

Workflows

A *workflow* is a series of functions or methods, called *steps*, that are performed sequentially. The flow can change the processing direction by using conditionals, referred to as *conditional branches*. Figure 26.26 shows a conditional workflow as it would appear on a flowchart.

A workflow is an excellent tool for managing both data and processes. With workflow rules, you can easily ensure that certain steps are followed and that required business processes are executed.

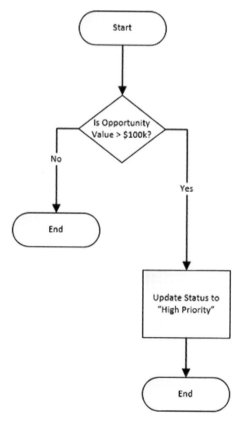

FIGURE 26.26   Workflow flowchart example.

In CRM 2016, workflows are divided into two categories:

▶ Asynchronous workflows

▶ Real-time (synchronous) workflows

Asynchronous Workflows

Asynchronous workflows in Microsoft Dynamics CRM use a Windows service to act as a host application for the workflow engine to work. This Windows service, Microsoft Dynamics CRM Asynchronous Processing Service, must be running on the Windows CRM server (or a designated asynchronous server); otherwise, the workflows won't execute. Figure 26.27 shows the service and its status.

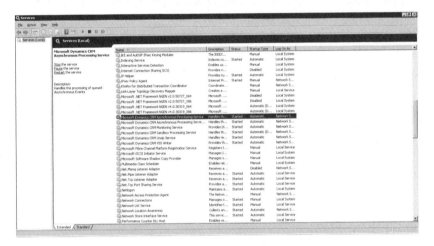

FIGURE 26.27   Checking that the Microsoft Dynamics CRM Asynchronous Processing Service is running.

NOTE

If the Microsoft Dynamics CRM Asynchronous Processing Service is not running, you can't see any of the asynchronous workflows described in this chapter. However, they run as soon as you start this service because the workflows are queued. So it is a good idea to verify that this Windows service is running by going to Start > Control Panel > Administrative Tools > Services and starting the Microsoft Dynamics CRM Asynchronous Processing Service if it is not running.

Another consideration is that asynchronous workflows might not run immediately; depending on the server overhead, they might take some seconds or minutes to complete (or even start). If you need a process to run immediately, you should consider creating real-time workflows, which are executed synchronously, or plug-ins, which can be set to be executed synchronously. Another factor in favor of workflows is that they are treated as entities in CRM, so you can use the Advanced Find tool to look up workflows, and you can also create reports based on them.

▶ Refer to **CHAPTER 25** for detailed instructions about creating and using plug-ins.

By default, any valid CRM user can create processes; however, the permissions to create processes can be configured by roles to prevent users from creating new processes that might burden the system. The security privilege Activate Real-Time Processes is required to activate real-time processes, and Execute Workflow Job is required to start a workflow.

▶ Refer to **CHAPTER 17**, "Settings," for more information about setting permission levels.

Workflows can be started by the particular triggering events and run settings. These are the triggering events:

▶ Record Is Created

▶ Record Status Changes

▶ Record Is Assigned

▶ Record Fields Change

▶ Record Is Deleted

NOTE

The Record Fields Change event enables you to reference any field on the underlying entity. The details of each event are outlined later in this chapter.

These are the run settings:

▶ Run This Workflow in the Background

▶ As an On-Demand Process

▶ As a Child Process

Run This Workflow in the Background

Run This Workflow in the Background is a recommended option, as it determines whether the workflow runs asynchronously or synchronously. When selected, the workflow allows for variables such as wait conditions that are not available for real-time (synchronous) workflows.

TIP

Provided that your workflow doesn't use wait conditions, you can convert your real-time workflows to background workflows and vice versa.

As an On-Demand Process

If the As an On-Demand Process option is specified, the process can be triggered manually by going to the associated entity and clicking ... > Run Workflow, as shown in Figure 26.28. A window appears, allowing you to select which on-demand workflow to run.

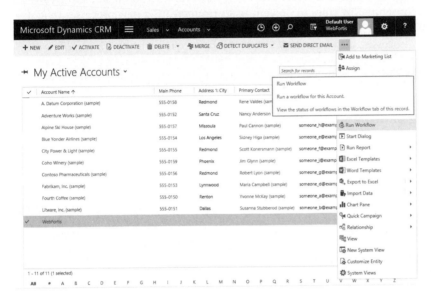

FIGURE 26.28   Running an on-demand workflow for the Account entity.

As a Child Process

Child processes are not executed automatically when the associated events are triggered. Instead, they are executed only when they are called through the Start Child Workflow activity.

If you need to perform a series of steps that are common to other entities or to the organization, using a child workflow makes sense.

> **TIP**
>
> Only the related entities' workflows can be used to call a child workflow. For example, you can't call a child workflow associated with the Invoice entity from a workflow of the Account entity.

A good example of a child workflow is a child workflow created for the Contact entity that could be called from another workflow associated with the Contact entity, which would be fired when an account is created using the Primary Contact relationship. The same child workflow could also be fired from another workflow created for the Phone Call entity that would fire the related Regarding contact.

If neither As On-Demand nor As a Child Process is selected, the workflow still runs automatically if the triggering event is fired.

> **NOTE**
>
> If a workflow calls itself (on the same entity) more than seven times in an hour, the eighth instance fails. This failure happens to prevent a workflow from creating an infinite loop. For example, a birthday workflow (because the loop happens once a year) does not trigger any failure.

To create a new workflow, follow these steps:

To access the Workflow Manager, follow these steps:

1. From the main interface, navigate to Settings > Processes.

2. To create a new process of type Workflow, click New, and the Create Process dialog appears.

> **NOTE**
>
> There are also options to create a blank process or a new process from an existing template. For this example, you're going to create a blank process; however, as explained later in this chapter, when you're working with the process, it can be saved as a regular process or as a process template. If saved as a process template, it can be referenced in this list for additional customization or other options.

> **NOTE**
>
> You can uncheck the Run This Workflow in the Background (Recommended) check box if you want the workflow to be real time, as explained later in this chapter.

3. Enter a name for the new process, select an entity record type, select Workflow from the Category drop-down, select New Blank Process, and then click OK.

> **TIP**
>
> When creating a new workflow, you must associate it with a base entity.

Now you are ready to start adding any of the following steps:

- ▶ Stage
- ▶ Check Condition
- ▶ Wait Condition
- ▶ Create Record

▶ Update Record

▶ Assign Record

▶ Send Email

▶ Start Child Workflow

▶ Perform Action

▶ Change Status

▶ Stop Workflow

These steps are explained as:

▶ **Stage**—Although stages are used for grouping purposes, they are also stored in the database. They enable you to report on the different stages and various stage metrics, such as the number of records affected for each stage. If you have a complex workflow with several steps in it, grouping steps makes the workflow easier to read and understand. You can collapse or expand the stages to fit the screen.

▶ **Check Condition**—A check condition is a Boolean evaluation similar to the If-Then conditional in programming. A check condition can be either true or false.

> **NOTE**
>
> An If-Then conditional indicates how conditions are evaluated—for example if a = b, then c = d.

▶ **Wait Condition**—The wait condition can put a workflow to sleep until a condition changes, such as the property of the associated entity, or after a period of time has elapsed.

▶ **Create Record**—Use this activity to create a new instance of any entity. The user can hard-code the properties or retrieve them from the associated entity.

▶ **Update Record**—This activity updates an existing instance of an entity.

▶ **Assign Record**—This activity assigns the associated entity to a user or a team.

▶ **Send Email**—This activity sends an email by creating a new message or using a template. You can create a new email message or use a predefined template (which is recommended).

▶ For additional information about how to create email templates, refer to **CHAPTER 17**.

▶ **Start Child Workflow**—This activity calls a child workflow. As described earlier, a child workflow needs to be created with the As a Child Workflow setting.

▶ **Perform Action**—This activity calls an action process, as explained earlier in this chapter, in actions. It asks you to select an action from list of available active actions and then select the entity. Then you need to provide values for input parameters, if any.

▶ **Change Status**—This action changes the associated entity status. The status type varies by entity.

▶ **Stop Workflow**—This action stops the execution of the current workflow. You can change the result status of the workflow from Succeed to Canceled. Use this activity step inside a conditional to prevent the workflow from continuing if a property doesn't meet the criteria you expect.

While most of these are self-explanatory, the check condition can be a little tricky.

To add a check condition, follow these steps:

1. Click Add Step and select Check Condition.

2. Enter an optional description in the Type a Step Description Here box. The condition you're going to add says that if the account is equal to some value, perform some action. To add this condition, click the <Condition> (Click to Configure) link (see Figure 26.29).

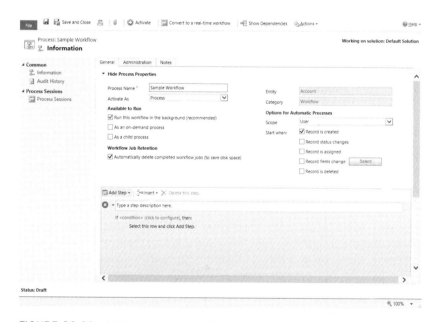

FIGURE 26.29   Using a check condition.

3. Select Account, Account Name, and Equals to enter a fixed-value condition in the Specify Workflow Condition dialog that appears.

▶ For more information about working with the Specify Workflow Condition dialog, refer to **CHAPTER 8**, "Working with Marketing."

4. To set a dynamic value, select an entity from the Entity drop-down and then click the desired field in the list box to set the condition.

5. Click Save and Close to continue.

6. Click Select This Row and then click Add Step. Then click Send Email.

7. Click Set Properties.

8. Enter a subject and body message for the new email (see Figure 26.30).

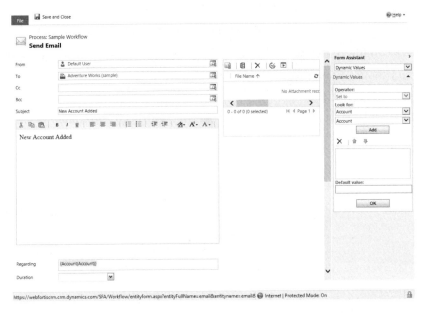

FIGURE 26.30   Configuring the email properties.

9. Click Save and Close.

Workflow Activation   Before you can use a workflow you have created, you need to activate it by selecting the record (in Workflows) and clicking the Activate button. When you click the Activate button, a confirmation window appears.

> **TIP**
>
> You can deactivate a process by clicking the Deactivate button. If you need to make any change to a process, you must deactivate it first because the capability to edit is disabled for an activated process.

> **TIP**
>
> In order to activate or deactivate a workflow, you must be the owner of the workflow.

When a workflow is activated, it is unavailable for further editing. To make additional modifications, you must deactivate the workflow, perform the changes, and reactivate the workflow.

Testing the Workflow   When a new account is created, the process sample is fired, and if the name is the same as the website property, the email is sent. You can see the progress of a process by looking at the status reason. To do that from the CRM web interface menu, click Settings and then System Jobs. In the screen that appears, you can see a column titled Status Reason that lists the various reasons (see Figure 26.31).

> **TIP**
>
> System jobs showing workflow history are available only if the check box Automatically Delete Completed Workflow Jobs to Save Disk Space is not checked.

When working with this screen, you have the option to select from the drop-downs at the top to filter the view. By default, they are set to All System Jobs and All Entities.

Note that the workflow engine is asynchronous and that the workflow might not be immediately triggered when an account is created. When the process finishes, the new email activity is created, and when you go to your activities, you can see the email in the email activities area.

Depending on your email router configurations, the email may be sent directly to the destination, or it may be queued as an activity (see Figure 26.32).

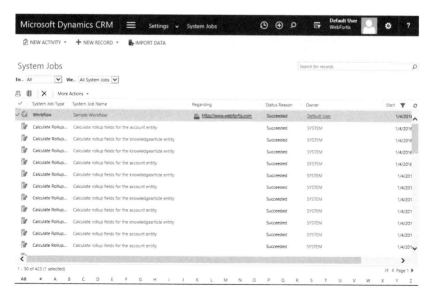

FIGURE 26.31   Monitoring process progress.

FIGURE 26.32   Workflow results with a new email activity created for the new account.

You have to change the drop-down to All Emails to see the email activities because they are not shown by default if your email router is configured to send the emails automatically.

▶ For more details about setting up emails and about using the email router, refer to **CHAPTER 20**, "Email Configuration."

Workflow Events   Workflows can automatically start executing when one or a combination of the following events is triggered:

▶ **Record Is Created**—This event is triggered when a new record of the associated entity is created.

▶ **Record Status Changes**—This event is triggered when a record of the associated entity status changes, such as when a record of an account is activated or deactivated, or when a record of an Opportunity entity's status changes to Won.

▶ **Record Is Assigned**—This event triggers when an instance of the associated entity is assigned to a user.

▶ **Record Fields Change**—This event is very useful because you can use it to trigger a workflow when the selected field of a record from the associated entity changes.

▶ **Record Is Deleted**—This event is triggered when a record of the associated entity is deleted.

Real-Time (Synchronous) Workflows

Real-time workflows, also known as synchronous workflows, are defined by using the Workflow entity record. They execute using the Event Execution Pipeline, much like plug-ins, and they can be executed pre-operation, post-operation, or during the core operation. Also, as with plug-ins, you cannot execute a real-time workflow before the Create operation or after the Delete operation.

Real-time workflows cancel and roll back the core platform operation if they are executing during database transaction and any exception is thrown. Plug-ins and workflows that were triggered by the same event and queued up after execution of the workflow don't execute at all.

All activities and child workflows are part of a single transaction in real-time workflows. On the other hand, asynchronous child workflows are queued and execute in a separate transaction.

> **NOTE**
>
> You cannot use Wait or Parallel Wait Branch conditions in real-time workflows. In addition, these workflows are not queued like asynchronous workflows for execution, and you cannot see the execution logs of real-time workflows that completed successfully.

> **NOTE**
>
> You can convert real-time workflows to asynchronous workflows and back to real-time workflows, if necessary, by selecting the option shown at the top of the workflow configuration page.

In the following steps, you're going to create a real-time workflow with a business requirement that if business users change an opportunity stage, you need to update the probability. Whereas this would have been done using JavaScript in previous versions of CRM, you can do this using a real-time workflow in CRM 2016, as follows:

1. Go to Settings > Processes and click the New button. Select the category Workflow and uncheck the Run This Workflow in the Background (Recommended) check box. (If this check box is checked, the workflow will run as an asynchronous workflow.)

2. In the window that appears, define workflow properties, including the process name, and save the workflow as a template or process. Select whether you want this workflow to run as a child process or on-demand. Finally, opt to retain workflow logs for workflows that encounter any errors (see Figure 26.33).

26

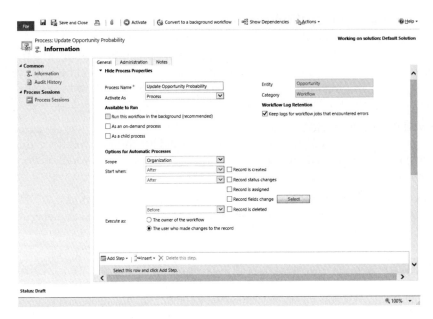

FIGURE 26.33   Real-time workflow properties.

3. In the Options for Automatic Processes section, define the scope of the workflow. You can select at what event this workflow should execute. As indicated previously, you cannot run real-time workflows before record creation or after record deletion; you can select Record Is Created and Record Is Deleted options, but you cannot change the start when the drop-down option is in front of them. For this example, select only Record Fields Change. Click Select Properties and select the Sales Stage option.

Notice that you can also select whether the workflow should run under either owner of workflow or user modifying the record context. In this example, select the user who made the changes to the record.

NOTE

Because of the Execute Context options, there might be security issues to consider relative to what the workflow is doing and why. For example, if the workflow is running under a system administrator (which happens if you select the owner of the workflow context), an error may appear when a user tries to run the workflow. For example, users don't normally have access to data validation across the system due to their security constraints, so such an error might occur with that type of validation.

---

4. Put your business logic in the last section and update the Probability field on the opportunity record when the sales stage changes, as shown in Figure 26.34.

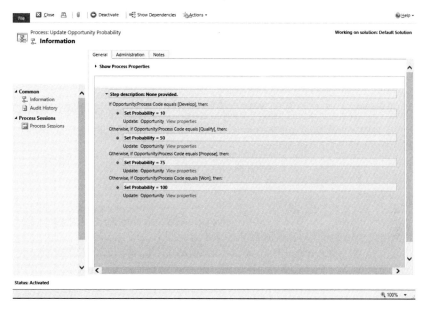

FIGURE 26.34   Business logic in a real-time workflow.

5. Click the Activate button on the command bar to activate this process.

NOTE

You can always covert a real-time workflow to an asynchronous workflow by clicking the Convert to a Background Workflow button in the command bar.

6. To test the workflow, go to an opportunity record, change its process code, and save the record. The real-time workflow executes, and the probability changes according to the business logic defined in the workflow.

Workflow Scope

Workflows created through the Workflow Manager interface can be applied to the following areas:

▶ Users

▶ Business Units

▶ Parent: Child Business Units

▶ Organization

These items are the various scope options that the workflow will apply to across the system. If you select User, the workflow will work for only the user who owns the workflow. If you want the workflow to work on the entire business unit or on the organizational level, you should select the appropriate option for that. Note that only the user who owns the workflow can see the tracking history.

> **NOTE**
>
> If an entity has Ownership Type set to Organization, not User or Team, the scope will always be Organization in the workflow.

Task Flows

Microsoft introduced a preview of a new process called a *task flow* in Dynamics CRM 2016 Online. A task flow is a type of BPF. You use task flows to help users accomplish individual smaller goals, which can help move forward the larger business processes. For example, if someone is working on an opportunity and there are some corresponding tasks for advancing the opportunity to next stage, task flows may be handy.

> **NOTE**
>
> A preview feature is not complete but is made available in a release so customers can get early access and provide feedback. Preview features aren't meant for production use and may have limited or restricted functionality.
>
> Task flows are currently in preview, and they are available for mobile users only. They are not supported for solution import/export.

Task flows operate at the user level. This means if two users are working on the same record and then both launch their task flows, the two users have separate experiences, working on different pages at same time. In a BPF there is only one active flow per record for all users, but in a task flow, different users can work on different task flows for the same record.

Task flows are not enabled by default. You have to enable them by following these steps:

1. Go to Settings > Administration and click System Settings.

2. Click the Preview tab and select the I've Read and Agree to the License Terms check box.

3. Select Yes for Enable Task Flows for Mobile Preview and click OK.

Microsoft provides three task flows out of the box:

► Update Contact

► Make Contact on Opportunity

► After Meeting

You can use them as templates to create your own task flows, or you can create new ones from scratch.

Follow these steps to create a task flow:

1. Go to Settings > Processes and click New.

2. Enter a name for the task flow in the Process Name field.

3. Select Business Process Flow from the Category drop-down.

4. Select Run Process as a Task Flow (Mobile Only).

5. Select the type of entity from the drop-down list and click OK.

6. Click Details to expand the panel and then click Set Image to set an image to use as the task flow's launch icon and background image. In the pop-up window, either upload a picture or select the default image and click OK.

7. In Business Process Flow (Classic), type a name for the page. For each field you want to display on the page, enter a label and select the source and field. Source can be Base Entity and all the lookup fields (N:1) for base entity record.

8. Click Insert Page to add another page to the task flow.

9. To add a branch in the task flow, click Add Branch, set the conditions for when you want the branch to appear, and click the checkmark. Then click Insert Page to add a page in the branch.

10. Set business rules for the task flow by clicking Business Rules and setting the scope to this specific task flow. (You cannot set the scope to be Entity.)

11. When you are done editing the task flow, click Save.

12. Click Activate to make your task flow available for use.

Task Flows on the Mobile App

If you log in to Dynamics CRM mobile and click the leftmost icon in the footer, you see all the available activated task flows. If you have set up the image, you see it as an icon, as shown in Figure 26.35.

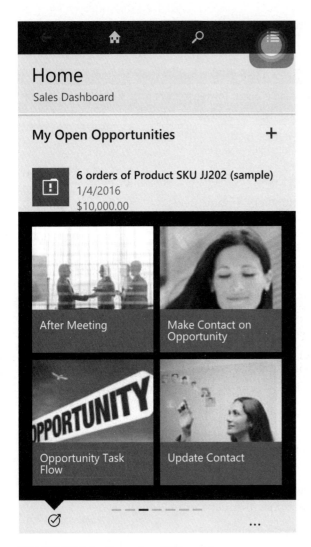

FIGURE 26.35   Dynamics CRM mobile app.

Click that icon, and you see the first page of your task flow (see Figure 26.36).

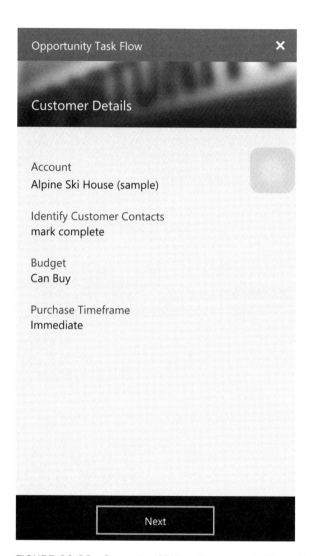

FIGURE 26.36   Dynamics CRM mobile opportunity task flow.

Click the Next button to go to the next page of your task flow. You can update data here and click the Done button to close the task flow or go back by using the Back button.

The task flow is enabled for the Manager, Vice President, CEO-Business Manager, System Administrator, and System Customizer security roles by default.

Exporting and Importing Processes

If you want to be able to export processes, you need to create a solution (Settings > Solutions) and include the processes in that solution. Then you can export the solution and import it to the destination organization. You can also use the SDK to write code in the solution to create solution and package processes.

▶ To learn more about how to create, export, and import solutions, refer to **CHAPTER 22**, "Customizing Entities."

Creating Workflows in Windows Workflow Foundation with Visual Studio

You also create processes by using Windows Workflow Foundation (WWF). WWF project templates are included in the Visual Studio 2013 and 2015 setup.

To start developing workflows with WWF, you must install the following components on a development machine:

▶ .NET Framework 4.5.2

▶ Visual Studio 2013/2015

> **NOTE**
>
> Only Visual Studio 2013 Professional and later will work; the Express version of Visual Studio is not supported. Chapter 22 explains the Microsoft Dynamics CRM 2016 SDK in greater detail.

No-Code Workflows

No-code workflows are XAML (Extensible Application Markup Language) files; they contain workflow markup in XML format.

The advantages of no-code workflows include the following:

▶ Can be deployed without compiling

▶ Easier to develop

▶ Can be deployed on CRM On-Premises servers

▶ Can share WWF activities if you add parallel tasks or Loop-While conditions

Before you can create a no-code workflow, you should first create the workflow with the CRM Workflow Designer interface, as explained earlier in this chapter, and then create a new solution, include the workflow in the solution, and then export it and extract the zip file.

To create a no-code workflow, follow these steps:

1. Open the solution file with Visual Studio 2015 and create a new project based on the Activity Library template (see Figure 26.37).

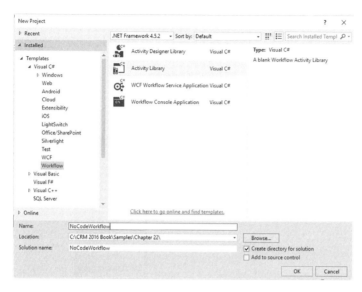

FIGURE 26.37   Creating an Activity Library project in Visual Studio 2015.

2. Add to the project references to Microsoft.Xrm.Sdk.dll and Microsoft.Xrm.Sdk.
   Workflow.dll. These files are located in the SDK\Bin folder.

3. Add to this project the existing XAML file you located in the unzipped solution file
   under the Workflow folder.

4. Add the CRM workflow controls to the toolbox by adding the Microsoft.Xrm.Sdk.
   Workflow.dll file. Right-click the General tab and click Choose Items.
   Then browse and add the file Microsoft.Xrm.Sdk.Workflow.dll, which is located
   in the SDK\Bin folder (see Figure 26.38).

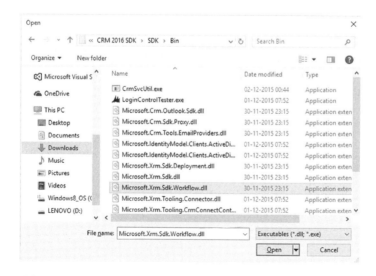

FIGURE 26.38   Adding CRM controls to the toolbox.

After you export the solution, you can unzip the solution file and locate the XAML file, which is included inside the Workflow folder.

When you add the controls to the toolbox, you see a new group of activities that are specially designed to be used with CRM (see Figure 26.39).

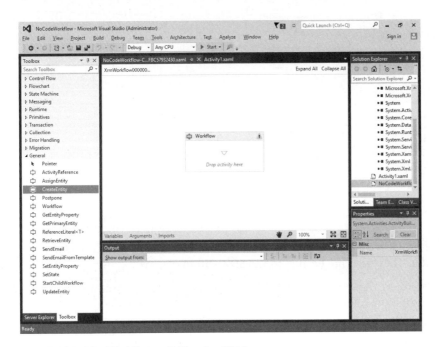

FIGURE 26.39   Workflow activities for CRM.

The following sections describe how to build a workflow that will create a Phone Call activity for every new contact added to CRM.

Development

To start development on the workflow, you need a CRM Workflow activity (located in the General section on the toolbox), which is also included by default when you initially created an empty workflow. Add a CRM CreateEntity activity inside the CRM Workflow activity.

To continue with the workflow development, follow these steps:

1. Add an Assign activity from the Primitives group in the toolbox before the CreateEntity activity.

2. Click the To property and enter CreatedEntities ("CreateStep1_localParameter") (see Figure 26.40).

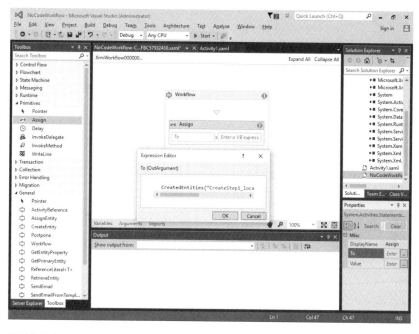

FIGURE 26.40   Assigning to a variable.

3. Click the Value property and enter New Entity ("phonecall").

4. Add a SetEntityProperty activity after the Assign activity (see Figure 26.41).

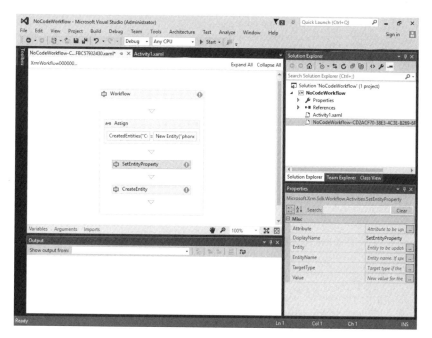

FIGURE 26.41   Adding SetEntityProperty.

5. Enter "subject" in the Attribute property, CreatedEntities ("CreateStep1_localParameter") in the Entity property, "phonecall" in the EntityName property, and "Call this new Contact" in the Value property.

6. Click the last activity you added (the CreateEntity activity) and enter CreatedEntities ("CreateStep1_localParameter") in the Entity property and "phonecall" in the EntityName property.

7. Click Save.

8. Copy the XAML file to the original solution you unzipped.

9. Compress the solution and import it back into the CRM 2016 web interface.

NOTE

Custom XAML workflows are not supported in Dynamics CRM Online.

CAUTION

When working with this type of solution, you may get an error similar to "This workflow cannot be created, updated, or published because it was created outside the Microsoft Dynamics CRM Web application. Your organization does not allow this type of workflow." If this happens, it is because you need to enable declarative workflows on your server. For information on how to do this, see http://msdn.microsoft.com/en-us/library/8da8c71e-84af-441e-b99b-0b59399f10f6#enable_disable.

TIP

Once you manipulate a workflow with Visual Studio, you can no longer edit it with the native CRM Workflow Designer.

Custom Workflow Activities

You can use custom workflow activities to extend the steps available when you create a workflow. By default, you can create steps such as Create, Update, Assign, and Send Email. For example, if you need to add a step that is not on this list, such as for sending an SMS message or calling an external web service, you need to build a custom workflow activity to do so.

Unlike the no-code workflows illustrated previously in this chapter, custom workflow activities are compiled in dynamic link libraries (DLLs), and you can use them from the workflow interface found in either the web or Outlook client applications as new steps.

To create a custom workflow activity, you need to open Visual Studio 2013 or 2015 and create a new project, using the Class Library template that is inside the Visual C# > Windows Project Templates.

After you create the project, you must add the references for Microsoft.Xrm.Sdk.dll and Microsoft.Xrm.Sdk.Workflow.dll. You can find these files in the CRM 2016 SDK\Bin folder.

To use CRM entities' classes in code, you use *early-binding entities*. You need to generate the CRM classes by using the CrmSvcUtil.exe tool (also in the SDK\Bin folder). If you run this utility on the server with the minimum parameters, as follows, you get an output file generated with all the classes needed on GeneratedCode.cs:

```
crmsvcutil.exe /url:http://localhost/Organization1/XRMServices/2011/
Organization.svc /out:GeneratedCode.cs
```

You need to include this file in your solution.

> **NOTE**
>
> The classes generated by the CrmSvcUtil.exe tool are .NET Language-Integrated Query (LINQ) supported.

Next you are going to use sample code to repeat the same example you used for the no-code workflow but this time using a custom activity. You need to delete the Activity1.xaml file created by the Activity Library project template. Then create a new class file named CustomActivityLibrary.cs that contains the code shown in Listing 26.4.

LISTING 26.4   CustomActivityLibrary.cs

```
using System;
using System.Activities;
using Microsoft.Xrm.Sdk;
using Microsoft.Xrm.Sdk.Workflow;
namespace CustomActivityLibrary
{
    public class CustomActityLibrary : CodeActivity
    {
        [Input("My contact")]
        [ReferenceTarget("contact")]
        [Default("{575A8B41-F8D7-4DCE-B2EA-3FFDE936AB1B}", "contact")]
        public InArgument<EntityReference> inContact { get; set; }
        protected override void Execute(CodeActivityContext context)
        {
            // Get the tracing service
            ITracingService tracingService =
              context.GetExtension<ITracingService>();
            // Get the context service.
            IWorkflowContext mycontext =
              context.GetExtension<IWorkflowContext>();
            IOrganizationServiceFactory serviceFactory =
```

```
        context.GetExtension<IOrganizationServiceFactory>();
            // Use the context service to create an instance of CrmService.
            IOrganizationService crmService =
    serviceFactory.CreateOrganizationService(mycontext.UserId);
            // Get the Contact
            Contact myContact = new Contact();
            myContact.ContactId = inContact.Get(context).Id;
            // Creates the Phone Call activity for this contact
            PhoneCall myPhoneCall =
                new PhoneCall();
            myPhoneCall.Subject = "Call this new contact";
            myPhoneCall.RegardingObjectId = new
                    EntityReference(Contact.EntityLogicalName,
                    (Guid) myContact.ContactId);
            crmService.Create(myPhoneCall);
            tracingService.Trace("PhoneCall created.");
        }
    }
}
```

Build the solution in debug mode to create the assembly.

To deploy the custom workflow activities, you need to register the compiled assembly as a plug-in, using the Plug-in Registration Tool, which is explained in Chapter 25 and available in the SDK\Bin folder.

> **NOTE**
>
> If you get a "Public assembly must have public key token" error when registering the plug-in, be sure the assembly is signed. You manage this in the properties of the project in Visual Studio, as explained in Chapter 25.

After deploying the custom workflow activity, you can use it on any workflow. To do this, go to Settings > Processes and click New. Enter a name for the process. In the Entity field, select Contact, and in the Category field, select Workflow. Click OK to move to the next step. Then click Add Step, and you see a new group called Custom Activities Library with the custom activity inside (see Figure 26.42).

Click Add Step, select the custom activity, and click Set Properties.

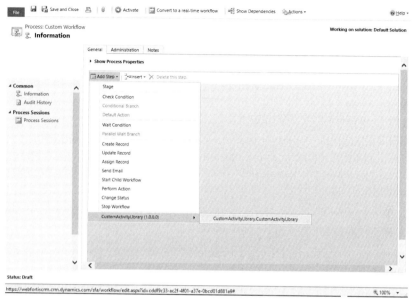

FIGURE 26.42   Using a custom activity on a workflow.

You can set any custom property you added on the code. This example uses the My Contact property used to send the current contact where the workflow will be running.

Click Save and Close to close the Set Custom Step Input Properties and then click Save to save the workflow. Click Activate to test this solution.

> **NOTE**
>
> After you make any change to the code and recompile the solution, you may have to restart the Microsoft CRM Asynchronous Processing Service. In some situations, you might also need to restart the IIS before redeploying the modified assembly. There is no need to start an asynchronous service when working with real-time workflows.

You can install custom workflow activities on CRM Online also—but in sandbox mode only.

> **NOTE**
>
> To learn more about .NET 4.5.2 and WWF development, check http://msdn.microsoft.com.

Summary

This chapter illustrates how to use and work with processes in Microsoft Dynamics CRM 2016. With the use of actions and BPFs, business users have a huge amount of flexibility and a number of options that allow them to implement their specific business logic.
In this chapter, you have learned that dialogs are synchronous and interactive processes, whereas workflows can run both asynchronously and synchronously, and actions can be considered a form of real-time workflows.

Actions can solve some tricky problems by allowing the creation of custom fields (flags) that fire plug-ins from a command bar button. Previously, the only way to fire plug-in code was by creating a custom field that, when updated, would save the record and fire the plug-in attached to a Create or Update event.

In addition, actions allow you to move logic previously managed by JavaScript to plug-ins so that the intellectual property can be protected.

Task flows are the next big thing, allowing business users to create task flows as per their own requirements, with no developer required.

Process development is limitless; in fact, most organizations barely begin to scratch the surface with take process development. It is possible to use it for sales force automation tasks and for alerting of almost anything.

SharePoint

This chapter covers the installation and configuration of CRM 2016 to SharePoint integration, focusing primarily on SharePoint 2013 integration components. This chapter also briefly discusses extending this integration by using C# and the software development kit (SDK).

> **CAUTION**
>
> It is important to realize that when working with SharePoint and Dynamics CRM in an integrated environment, permissions are not transferred, and a restrictive user in CRM could accidentally stumble into the SharePoint document library for every account unless his or her permissions are paired across *both* SharePoint and CRM.

The "Client-to-Server Integration with SharePoint" section of this chapter explains how to install and configure the list component for CRM 2016 and SharePoint 2013, and the "Server-to-Server Integration with SharePoint" section explains how you can integrate CRM Online only with SharePoint On-Premises or Online without installing the list component. Server-to-server integration is recommended over client-to-server due to following reasons:

▶ For client-to-server integration, the user needs to sign in to both Dynamics CRM and SharePoint, whereas for server-to-server integration, the user needs to sign in only to CRM.

▶ The list component must be installed for client-to-server integration, and no software needs to be installed for server-to server integration.

▶ The list component are a SharePoint sandboxed solution and are being deprecated and will no longer be available for both SharePoint On-Premises and Online.

TIP

With all levels of integration, if you are using Outlook, you must run in Online mode to access SharePoint features.

SharePoint and Dynamics CRM 2016

You can use the document management capabilities of SharePoint in Dynamics CRM 2016 just as in CRM 2015. CRM 2016 supports the following SharePoint editions:

▶ Microsoft SharePoint 2013

▶ Microsoft SharePoint 2010

▶ Microsoft SharePoint Online

NOTE

Since Microsoft Dynamics CRM 2011, Microsoft Dynamics CRM has made native SharePoint integration options available out of the box. If however you prefer to use the list component (i.e. leverage the non-native integration), you can do so by installing and configuring the list component. Refer later in this chapter under 'Basic Integration' for more information about this.

The document management integration shows up in two places. First, there is a Documents view on every record in CRM, as shown in Figure 27.1. This integration option allows users to access SharePoint documents by entity across the application.

FIGURE 27.1   Documents option, as shown on the related drop-down for the account record.

Second, there is the Document Management page in System > Settings (see Figure 27.2). This is where administrators set up and configure the SharePoint options that allow the SharePoint documents (refer to Figure 27.1) to be referenced and where they will ultimately reside.

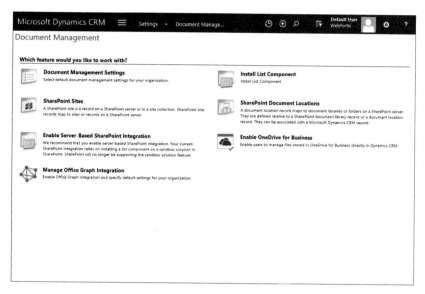

FIGURE 27.2   Document Management console in CRM 2016.

Options available under Document Management include the following:

▶ **Document Management Settings**—This is where you specify which entities will use document management. You can also choose to apply autostructuring around either the account or the contact.

▶ **Install List Component**—The entire purpose of this section is to download the latest version of the list component. At publication time, this included crmlistcomponent.wsp and a PowerShell script to set up a SharePoint site. The list component automatically creates document libraries in SharePoint. The list component includes the following features and benefits:

   ▶ Automatic document library creation in SharePoint, applying a nested organizational structure specified in the Document Management Settings Wizard

   ▶ Automatic site object management in CRM

   ▶ A more secure and user-friendly IFRAME view of SharePoint from within CRM

▶ **SharePoint Sites**—When you run the Document Management Settings Wizard, a site is created here. You can also create sites manually or modify sites that are created automatically.

27

▶ **SharePoint Document Locations**—This is where you view all the document locations that have been created, create new locations, and modify existing locations.

▶ **Enable Server-Based SharePoint Integration**—You can use this option to enable Dynamics CRM SharePoint integration without installing the list component or any other software.

Server-to-Server Integration with SharePoint

Server-to-server integration with SharePoint is supported for Microsoft Dynamics CRM Online in versions since CRM 2015 Update 1 and SharePoint On-Premises or Online. You do not need to install the Microsoft Dynamics CRM list component in SharePoint or any other software to have SharePoint document management functionality within CRM. If you have enabled server-based SharePoint integration, you can't revert to client-based authentication.

Follow these steps to integrate SharePoint 2013 Online and Dynamics CRM 2016 Online:

1. Log on to Dynamics CRM Online as a user having the System Administrator security role and go to Settings > Document Management.

2. Click Enable Server-Based SharePoint Integration to start the wizard for Dynamics CRM Online and SharePoint integration.

3. When the wizard asks you about your SharePoint deployment type, select Online (see Figure 27.3). Click Next.

FIGURE 27.3   SharePoint Deployment Options.

4. When the wizard asks you about the SharePoint site URL, enter it, making sure Dynamics CRM Online and SharePoint Online belong to same Office 365 tenant. The wizard validates the SharePoint site and displays the result there.

5. When the wizard warns you that if you enable server-side integration, you cannot enable or use client-side integration, click Enable.

6. When you see the confirmation message that server-side integration with SharePoint is complete, click the Open Document Management Settings Wizard check box and click Finish (see Figure 27.4).

FIGURE 27.4   Completing the SharePoint setup.

7. In the Document Management Settings dialog, select the check box in front of appropriate entity names and provide the SharePoint site URL. Click Next. The wizard validates the SharePoint site URL.

8. When the wizard asks you how you want to maintain folder structure, select Account or Contact from the drop-down and select the Based on Entity check box (see Figure 27.5). Click Next.

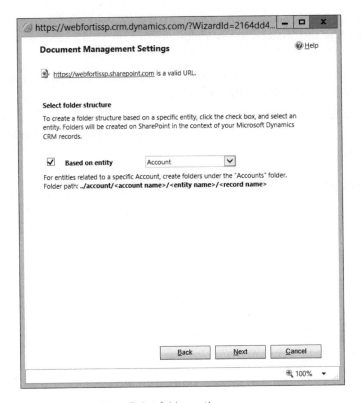

FIGURE 27.5   SharePoint folder options.

9. On the next page, which says that document libraries are being created at the path you specified, click OK.

10. On the next page, which shows the status for all the entities you have selected and shows a failure reason if there was an error for any entity, click Finish. The setup is complete.

If you go to any account record in Dynamics CRM and click Documents, you see a pop-up message about creating a folder in the SharePoint document library (see Figure 27.6). Click Confirm.

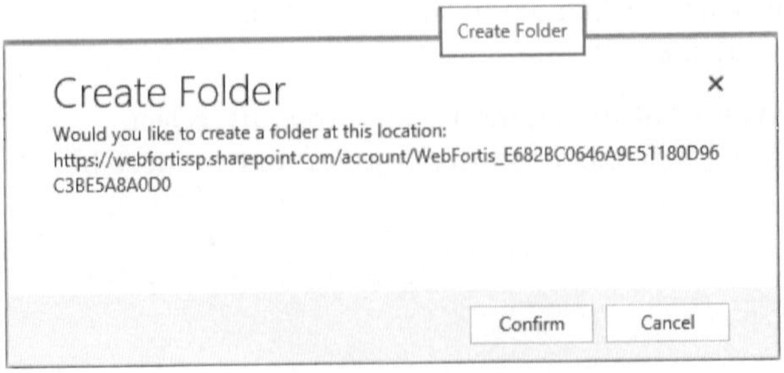

FIGURE 27.6   Creating SharePoint folders.

Once the SharePoint document library is created, you can create new or upload existing documents, and you can also perform SharePoint functions from within the grid interface, such as Check In and Check Out.

Client-to-Server Integration with SharePoint

You have to install the list component in a sandboxed environment of SharePoint to enable SharePoint integration with Dynamics CRM.

> **NOTE**
>
> Follow the instructions for installing the list component in this section if you choose to not use the native integration in your production instance.

This integration is supported for both On-Premises and Online versions of Dynamics CRM and SharePoint. Follow these steps to enable client-to-server integration of Dynamics CRM Online with SharePoint Online:

1. Log on to Dynamics CRM as a user having the System Administrator security role and go to Settings > Document Management.

2. Click Install List Component. In the pop-up window that appears, download the list component for SharePoint 2010 or SharePoint 2013. The SharePoint 2013 extract has three files: crmlistcomponent.wsp (the list component), AllowHtcExtn.ps1 (the PowerShell script), and mscrmsharepointeula.tx (the EULA). HTML components (.htc) files are not enabled on SharePoint 2013 by default. To enable HTC, you have to run AllowHtcExtn.ps1 on the SharePoint server. This step is not required for SharePoint Online. Open PowerShell and navigate to the folder where AllowHtcExtn.ps1 file is extracted. Type the following command and then press Enter:

   ```
   ./AllowHtcExtn.ps1 https://sharepointserver/
   ```

3. Because SharePoint Online does not allow you to install solutions by default, log in to the Office 365 Admin Portal and click Admin > SharePoint in the left navigation pane, as shown in Figure 27.7.

27

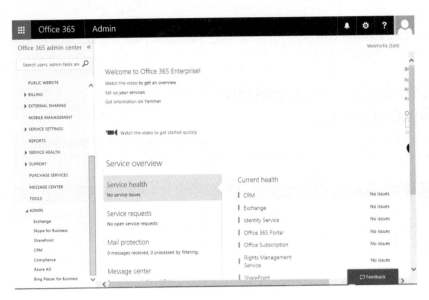

FIGURE 27.7   Office 365 Admin Portal.

4. In the new window that appears, click Settings on the left and then scroll down. Under Custom Script, click Allow Users to Run Custom Script on Self-service Created Sites. Click OK. The changes are made, but it may take up to 24 hours for them to be effective.

5. Log in to SharePoint and click the gear icon and then select Site Settings, as shown in Figure 27.8.

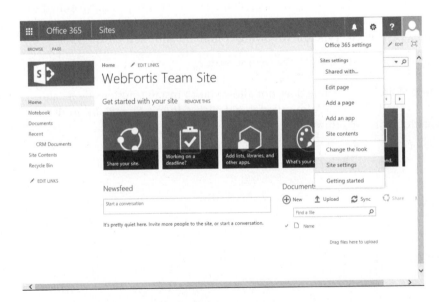

FIGURE 27.8   Selecting Site Settings.

6. Click Solutions under Web Designer Galleries.

7. Click the Upload Solution button.

8. Click the Browse button and select the SharePoint 2013 list component file crmlistcomponent.wsp. Click OK. The Dynamics CRM list component is uploaded to SharePoint.

9. Click the Activate button to activate the solution and click the Close button to complete the installation.

When the solution is activated, the status appears as Activated in the Solution Gallery, as shown in Figure 27.9.

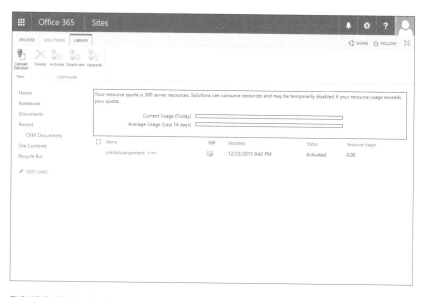

FIGURE 27.9   Activated SharePoint.

10. Go to Settings > Document Management in Dynamics CRM and click Document Management Settings. In the wizard that appears, select the entities for which you want document management to be enabled and provide the URL of the SharePoint site, as shown in Figure 27.10.

11. When the wizard asks you to select the Account or Contact entity for the folder structure, confirm your selection to continue.

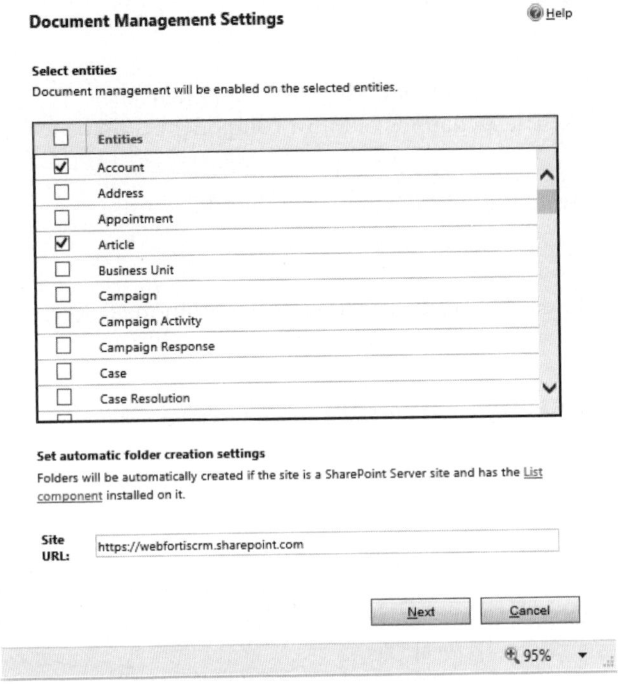

FIGURE 27.10   Specifying the SharePoint URL.

When the document library creation process is complete, the wizard shows the status of the document library for each entity and the failure reason if there was an error.

Integration Features

Once you have installed crmlistcomponent.wsp, creation of document libraries for records is automated. Open a record of your base type or of a type that you set in the wizard to have integration features enabled. Click the Documents section, and CRM detects that a document library for this record needs to be created.

If you click OK, a folder is created for you, and the document locations load the library that was just created.

The options listed in the frame are standard SharePoint options. You can create new folders, upload documents, edit documents, check in, check out, and so on. You can also open the documents directly from CRM without having to first open SharePoint. Any records created as child records to this account (after this step) have their document libraries placed in the Webfortis folder, provided that Account is set as the base type.

If you click Cancel, you have no location created. You can open the Document Locations drop-down and click Add Location to specify where you want this document library to be, or you can link to another document library if it already exists (see Figure 27.11).

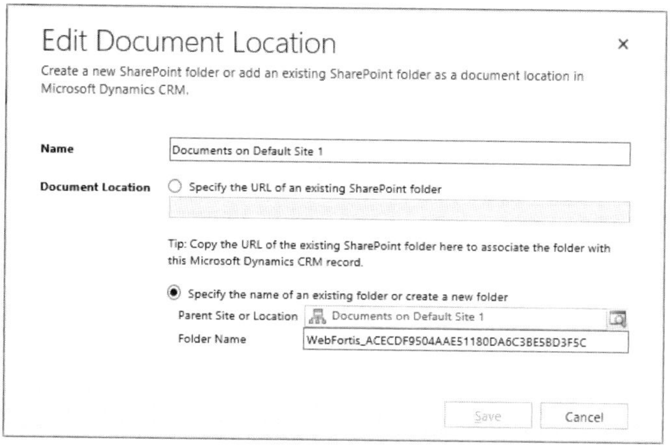

FIGURE 27.11   New or existing library option.

Document Location Option

As you can see in Figure 27.11, you have two options with regard to the document location: You can specify a preexisting SharePoint folder, or you can have CRM create a new folder in a preexisting location.

If you choose to create a new folder, you can specify its name and where it will be created. It can be at the root level, or it can be a subfolder to any preexisting document library. The parent or site location lookup can be either a site or a document location.

If you open the lookup and filter based on document location, you can see all the current locations that will be available as parent folders. When you have finished, click Save, and you can choose between the two locations in the Document Locations drop-down.

You can view your document locations as they are created in Settings > Document Management > Document Locations in CRM.

> **TIP**
>
> Notice that your document locations have automatically generated names. However, you can rename them here.

You can view all of a document location's child locations. Figure 27.12 shows the root Account folder. By navigating to Child Locations, you can see the folder created for Webfortis.

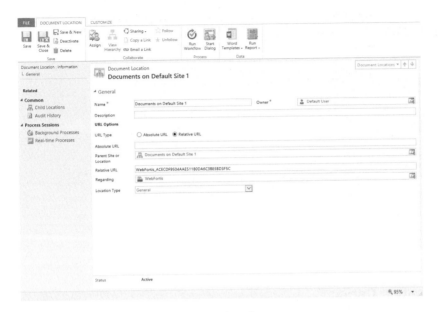

FIGURE 27.12   Renaming a document location.

You can manage the structure of your site and the document libraries manually through the Document Management section as well: Just open a SharePoint site in Document Management, select your site, and click Edit.

Open the child locations and click Add New Document Location. Then fill in the name and relative URL.

> **NOTE**
>
> A relative URL is the document library URL relative to the parent site or location. So, if a default site has the URL https://webfortissp.sharepoint.com/, and the document library has URL https://webfortissp.sharepoint.com/customLocation, customLocation is the relative URL.

> **CAUTION**
>
> Keep in mind that you cannot use this method unless the folder already exists in SharePoint. If it does not exist, you are warned. If you create orphaned document locations, they show up as failures when you validate your site.

Record GUID in Folder Name

When folders are created automatically, the folder name has the record name and record globally unique identifier (GUID) appended to it. You can go to SharePoint and check the folder name (see Figure 27.13). This capability helps in extending integration with Dynamics CRM because the record GUID is easily available in SharePoint.

You can also create document libraries for custom entities. The only requirement is that you enable the Document Management check box (see Figure 27.14).

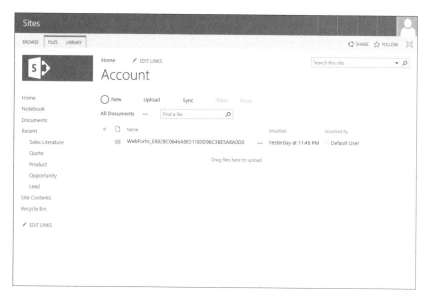

FIGURE 27.13   The folder name with the record name has the record GUID appended.

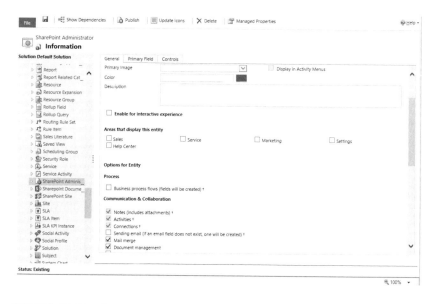

FIGURE 27.14   Document Management selected on the entity.

If you run the wizard again, your custom entity appears in the list.

Extending the Integration

The SDK enables system administrators to extend CRM–SharePoint integration. The following sections cover some of these options.

Entities

The following entities are available for configuration purposes:

▶ **SharePointSite**—This has standard entity metadata, plus attributes that are SharePoint site specific, such as AbsoluteUrl, RelativeUrl, ParentSiteOrLocation (EntityReference), ValidationStatus, and ValidationStatusReason. These are all self-explanatory. The IsDefault property denotes whether the site is your organization's default location.

▶ **SharePointDocumentLocation**—This is basically the same as SharePointSite. The SharePointDocumentLocation entity makes use of RegardingObjectId to associate a location with a specific record.

Configuration Message

The message **RetrieveAbsoluteAndSiteCollectionUrlRequest** is available for configuration purposes. In addition to being a mouthful, this message retrieves AbsoluteUrl and SiteCollectionUrl, and it takes a document location entity reference as the Target parameter. Note that this message works only if the following are true:

▶ crmlistcomponent.wsp was installed.

▶ The location for the parent site exists in CRM.

▶ The SharePointSite.IsGridPresent property was set to true when the parent location record was created.

You can perform all standard create/retrieve/update/delete (CRUD) operations on these new entities. For more information about the CRUD operations, see the SDK.

Operations in SharePoint

Now that you know how to handle the CRM 2016 SharePoint site structure, let's look at the corresponding operations in SharePoint 2013. SharePoint 2013 offers many services that enable you to interact with its contents. This section looks briefly at the following services:

▶ **listsService**—Two useful functions are GetList and AddList. GetList retrieves a list, and AddList creates a list. Listing 27.1 provides a sample function that tries to retrieve a list, and if that list does not exist, the function creates the list.

> **NOTE**
>
> To use `listsService` and `copyService`, be sure to add the following two references:
>
> ▶ **listsService**—http://sharepoint2013/_vti_bin/Lists.asmx
>
> ▶ **copyService**—http://sharepoint2013/_vti_bin/copy.asmx

LISTING 27.1   Retrieving or Creating a List

```
static XmlNode processList(string listname, string listDescr, int libtype)

{
    listsService.Lists listSvc = new listsService.Lists();
    listSvc.UseDefaultCredentials = true;
    XmlNode result = null;
    try
    {

        result = listSvc.GetList(listname);
    }
    catch (System.Web.Services.Protocols.SoapException soExGET)
    {
        if (soExGET.Detail["errorcode"].InnerText == "0x82000006")
        {
            try
            {
                result = listSvc.AddList(listname, listDescr, libtype);
            }
            catch (System.Web.Services.Protocols.SoapException soExADD)
            {

                ErrorLog.handle(soExGET.Detail.InnerText, soExADD.Detail.
                InnerText);
                return null;
            }
        }
        else
        {
            ErrorLog.handle(soExGET.Detail.InnerText);
            return null;
        }
    }
    return result;
}
```

TIP

To create a document library, set `libType` to `101`.

▶ **copyService**—This service contains the `CopyIntoItems` function, which uploads content (as bytes) to a SharePoint library. Listing 27.2 is an example of this function in use.

LISTING 27.2   `CopyIntoItems` Function

```csharp
public uint uploadFile(string fileName, string[] desinationUrl, byte[]
stream)

{
    copyService.Copy copySvc = new copyService.Copy();
    copySvc.UseDefaultCredentials = true;
    uint result = 0;
    bool Throw = false;
    CopyResult[] results = null;
    FieldInformation descInfo = new FieldInformation()
    {
        DisplayName = "Description",
        Type = FieldType.Text,
        Value = "Automatic Upload from CRM"
    };
    FieldInformation[] inf = new FieldInformation[] { descInfo };
    try
    {
        result = copySvc.CopyIntoItems("http://crm2011", desinationUrl, inf,
        stream, out results);
        foreach (CopyResult cr in results)
        {
            if (cr.ErrorCode != CopyErrorCode.Success)
            {
                ErrorLog.handle("Error After File Upload Attempt: " +
                cr.ErrorMessage);
                Throw = true;
            }
        }
    }
    catch (System.Web.Services.Protocols.SoapException soExCopy)
    {
        ErrorLog.handle(soExCopy.Detail.InnerText, result.ToString());
        throw new Exception(soExCopy.Detail.InnerText);
    }
```

```
    if (Throw)
        throw new Exception("The upload file method has failed.");
    return result;
}
```

So, for example, if you want a plug-in to retrieve an attachment as bytes and upload it to SharePoint, you're about 90% of the way there. If you are operating on `ActivityMimeAttachment`, you can use the following to retrieve the attachment as bytes:

```
byte[] filecontent = new UTF8Encoding(true).GetBytes(
(string)_this.Attributes["body"]);
```

Just as with CRM 2016, you can write plug-ins that trigger on the creation, updating, and deletion of SharePointSite, SharePointDocument, and SharePointDocumentLocation entities.

OneNote Integration

Microsoft enabled OneNote integration with Dynamics CRM Online 2015 Update 1. To use the OneNote integration, you must have SharePoint integration with Dynamics CRM Online enabled, as OneNote documents are stored in the SharePoint document library.

Follow these steps to configure OneNote Integration with Dynamics CRM:

1. Log on to Dynamics CRM as a user having the System Administrator security role and go to Settings > Document Management. Click OneNote Integration.

2. When the wizard shows entities that have document management already enabled, select the check box in front of entity name to enable OneNote integration (as shown in Figure 27.15). Alternatively, you can select Customizations > OneNote Integration for that entity. Make sure Document Management is enabled for that entity.

27

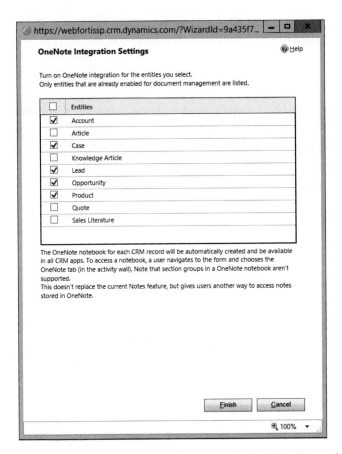

FIGURE 27.15   Selecting entities to enable OneNote integration.

3. Open any record for the entity where OneNote integration is enabled. You can see OneNote tab in the activity wall for that record. The new notebook is created in the default section with the default title Untitled (see Figure 27.16)

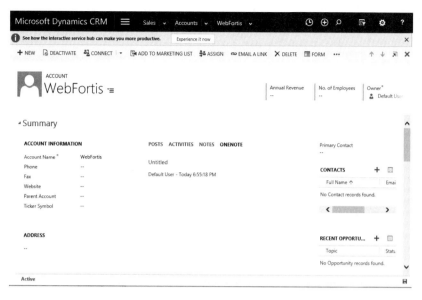

FIGURE 27.16   New OneNote notebook.

4. Click the Untitled link to open notebook in the OneNote app or OneNote Online in your web browser.

5. To view your OneNote records, go to the Documents section of a record, and you can see the OneNote records there.

Summary

This chapter explains how to integrate CRM 2016 with SharePoint 2013 and how to manipulate features to get the data structure you desire. It talks about how to do client-to-server and server-to-server SharePoint integration with Dynamics CRM.

The chapter also briefly covers the additions to the CRM SDK and ways to connect to SharePoint and perform basic custom integrations. It also shows steps to enable OneNote integration with Dynamics CRM.

As mentioned early in the chapter, it is important to realize that when working with SharePoint and Dynamics CRM in an integrated environment, permissions are not transferred, and a restrictive user in CRM could accidentally stumble into the SharePoint document library for every account unless his or her permissions are paired across *both* SharePoint and CRM.

CHAPTER 28

Forms Authentication

This chapter is specifically for On-Premises deployments of Microsoft Dynamics CRM 2016. The information presented in this chapter can be used by organizations that want to expose their CRM to the Internet to provide public access to the CRM organization without having to use virtual private network (VPN) connectivity, or take advantage of other features of Microsoft Dynamics CRM 2016 that require Internet-Facing Deployment (IFD) (such as mobility).

> **NOTE**
>
> While this chapter is geared toward On-Premises deployments of Dynamics CRM 2016, the sections on Active Directory Federation Services (ADFS) are relevant for CRM Online instances where organizations want to integration their Active Directory (AD) for single sign-on (SSO) purposes.

IFD Defined

Internet-Facing Deployment (IFD) is a feature that enables users to log on to Microsoft Dynamics CRM with a type of authentication known as claims-based authentication. Claims-based authentication is a method of authentication that prompts users with a web page interface instead of Integrated Windows Authentication, which is the default installation for Microsoft Dynamics CRM.

The advantage of Integrated Windows Authentication is that it is transparent for users who access the Microsoft Dynamics CRM server from computers that belong to the domain. These users are not required to enter user information such as name and password because they are already authenticated by Active Directory when they initially log on. If you access the Microsoft Dynamics CRM server from a computer that doesn't belong to the domain, you get the Windows Security dialog shown in Figure 28.1.

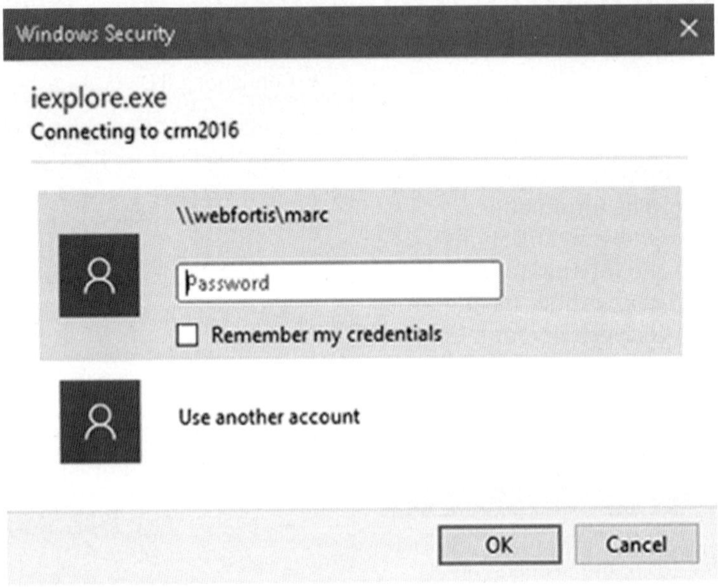

FIGURE 28.1 Windows Security dialog.

The automated login for users who belong to the same domain happens because of a default setting in the Internet Explorer browser. If you want to log in as a different user, change this setting by going to the Tools menu of Internet Explorer and then selecting Internet Options. On the Security tab, click the Local Intranet icon and then click the Custom Level button. Move to the last option and select Prompt for User Name and Password. Click OK to close the dialogs (see Figure 28.2).

If you want to access your CRM server from the Internet or from computers that are outside the network, using claims-based authentication, you must implement the IFD feature.

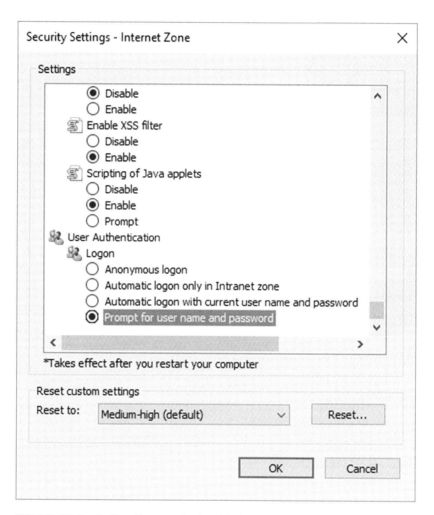

FIGURE 28.2   Setting the security level in Internet Explorer.

If you don't want claims-based authentication, you can leave the configuration set to its default configuration: Windows Authentication. Although IFD is intended to be used by Microsoft Dynamics CRM–hosted service providers to give users a customized login page, you can enable IFD for your own organization with an On-Premises installation, if you want (see Figure 28.3). However, CRM Online uses another type of authentication, based on Office 365 authentication.

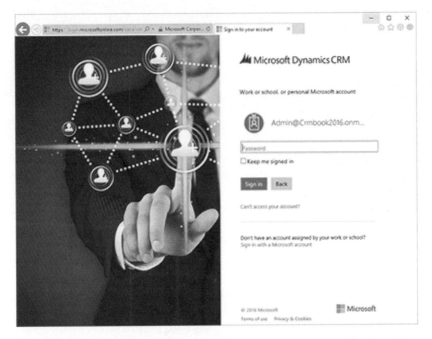

FIGURE 28.3   CRM Online login.

While Microsoft Dynamics CRM is installed using the Setup Wizard, you cannot enable IFD using the Setup Wizard. Instead, you must manually configure IFD as described later in this chapter, in the section "Configuring IFD."

Claims-Based Authentication

With claims-based authentication, the user may enter credentials (username and password) inside a form of a page instead of using the Windows Authentication dialog.

Figure 28.4 shows what happens when you type the Microsoft Dynamics URL for an organization in the browser.

FIGURE 28.4   IFD with forms authentication.

Claims-based authentication requires HTTPS for security reasons, to prevent the username and password from being transmitted over the network in clear text when making a POST method of HTTP, so you must use SSL (Secure Sockets Layer) to protect this sensitive data.

Configuring IFD

After installing Dynamics CRM, to enable IFD, you have to open the Microsoft Dynamics CRM Deployment Manager application that is installed on the server. If you click in the root node, Microsoft Dynamics CRM, you see a screen with the tasks as well as the actions in the right panel containing the tools to configure IFD (see Figure 28.5).

28

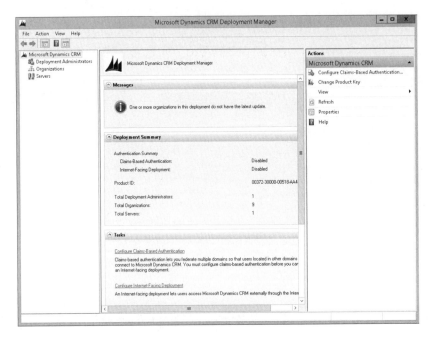

FIGURE 28.5   CRM Deployment Manager.

If you try to click the Configure Internet-Facing Deployment link under Tasks, you get a warning dialog, telling you that you must configure claims-based authentication before you can configure IFD (see Figure 28.6).

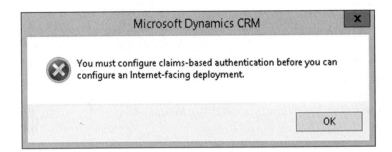

FIGURE 28.6   IFD configuration warning.

Click OK to close the warning dialog and then click the first task: Configure the Claims-Based Authentication. However, when you do this, you get another error (see Figure 28.7).

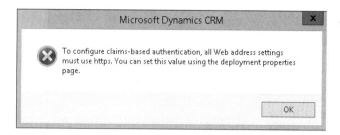

FIGURE 28.7   Configuring claims-based authentication.

After you click OK to close the warning dialog, you need to go to Properties by
right-clicking the top node and selecting the Web Addresses tab. This is where you can
configure HTTPS as the binding type. Figure 28.8 shows the default binding, HTTP,
which needs to be changed to HTTPS with port 443.

Microsoft Dynamics CRM Properties

| General | Web Address | License | Usage Reporting |

Binding Type:

◉ HTTP   ○ HTTPS

Web Application Server:

CRM2016:80

Organization Web Service:

CRM2016:80

Discovery Web Service:

CRM2016:80

Deployment Web Service:

CRM2016:80

When you change the binding type, the website must have the correct
binding already configured. If claims-based authentication is enabled,
HTTPS is required.

Advanced

OK   Cancel   Apply

28

FIGURE 28.8   Configuring HTTPS.

The next sections explain these IFD components.

NOTE

For more information about configuring IFD, download the Microsoft Dynamics CRM Implementation Guide for CRM Online and CRM 2016 (On-Premises) from Microsoft.com. To find it, search for "CRM 2016 IG."

SSL Certificates

Because IFD uses claims-based authentication as its authentication method, resulting in users' credentials being posted to the server, you must encrypt the credentials with an SSL certificate. SSL encrypts information using 1024-bit or 2048-bit encryption, which is the same level of protection used by major banking and financial institutions.

TIP

A certificate of 2048 bits is recommended because it has the more secure level of protection. SSL uses port 443 by default, but you could use any other port. If you're using a firewall, be sure to set the SSL port to allow traffic.

You can obtain SSL certificates from a number of certificate-issuing authorities, including Verisign, GoDaddy, and Thawte. Be sure to get a multiple-domain certificate or an unlimited subdomain (wildcard) certificate because you will need to use the certificate for at least three URL addresses, as explained later in this chapter, in the "DNS Server Configurations" section.

SSL Certification Considerations

If you are not ready to get an SSL certificate and you want to try the IFD feature, you cannot omit the SSL configurations and install the server with HTTP only. However, you can create your own certificates by using the Windows Certification Authority Service (CertSrv).

In that case, you must import the certificate on the Trusted Root Certificate store for your local computer in the Active Directory Federation Services (AD FS) server as well as in the server where you have CRM 2016 installed, as shown in Figure 28.9.

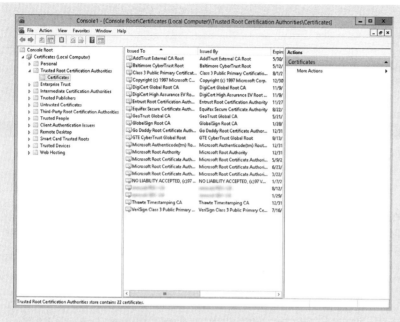

FIGURE 28.9   Trusted root certificate authorities.

You also have to install the same certificate in the Personal\Certificates folder, as shown in Figure 28.10.

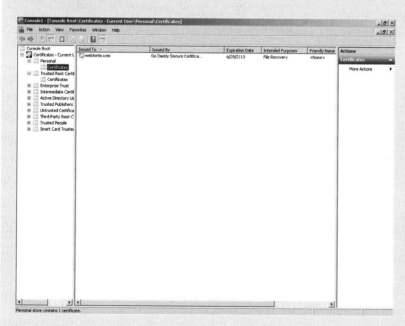

FIGURE 28.10   Personal\Certificates folder.

You need to give read permissions to the user who is running the Microsoft Dynamics CRM application pool (usually a domain user). This can be done by running the Certificates console in the CRM server, right-clicking the certificate, and selecting the Managing Private Keys option. Then you can add the user there and select the Read check box in the Allow column.

TIP

If you are purchasing a certificate, be sure to use a trusted certificate authority so that you do not have to deal with the untrusted certificate stores.

Installing a New Certificate

Complete the following steps to request and install a new certificate through the Internet Information Services (IIS) Manager:

1. Open the IIS Manager application by searching for "IIS."

2. Click the server name on the left and then click the Server Certificates icon.

3. Double-click the Server Certificates icon, click the Create Domain Certificate link under the Actions section on the right, and enter your organization information (see Figure 28.11).

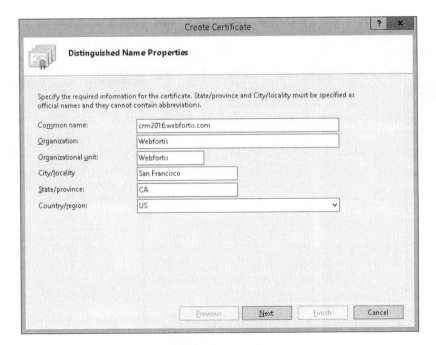

FIGURE 28.11   Creating a certificate.

4. Click Next and select an online certification authority (see Figure 28.12).

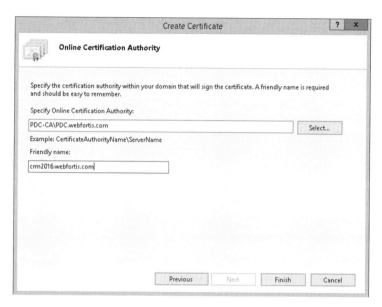

FIGURE 28.12   Online certification authority.

5. Click Finish, and the certificate is created. Notice that if you use a certificate from an online authority, it might take hours to days to get the certificate created.

When this configuration is done, you are almost ready to start working through the Claims-Based Authentication Wizard. If you are running Windows Server 2012 R2, AD FS 3.0 is now included as a built-in server role. However, if you are running anything prior to Windows Server 2012 R2, you need to configure AD FS 2.0. Included here, for your benefit, are discussions about both the AD FS 2.0 and 3.0 configuration options.

AD FS 2.0

If you need to install and configure Active Directory Federation Services 2.0 (AD FS 2.0), you can download it from http://technet.microsoft.com/en-us/evalcenter/ee476597 .aspx (or search Microsoft.com for "AD FS 2.0.")

28

WHERE TO INSTALL AD FS 2.0

An important note is the server where you will install AD FS 2.0 because it installs on the default website created on the IIS. If you try this on the same server where you installed CRM, it won't run because AD FS creates a virtual folder called AD FS inside the default website, which needs the previous .NET Framework, version 2.0.

You can either install AD FS on a separate server with a clean IIS or create another default website on the IIS where CRM is installed so that it won't overlap with the CRM server website. If you use the same server, you have to either configure the new default website to use a port other than the default 443 for HTTPS or use host headers.

Because deploying AD FS on the same server where the CRM lives requires the considerations just mentioned, you should use a separate server for this purpose.

Installing AD FS 2.0

To install AD FS 2.0, you must have .NET Framework 3.5 as well as the web server role/IIS configured. Follow these steps to run the installation:

1. Run the ADFSSetup.exe application that you downloaded from Microsoft. The Setup Wizard appears.

2. Click Next and accept the terms in the license agreement.

3. Click Next and select the Federation Server option.

4. Click Next. The next screen shows you the list of prerequisite software that this component needs in order to be installed.

5. Click Next. The wizard checks the required software and installs any that is missing. When it finishes, it asks you to restart the server.

To configure AD FS, go to the Start menu and open the AD FS 2.0 Management application that is under the Administrative Tools group.

AD FS 3.0

In addition to supporting AD FS 2.0, Microsoft Dynamics CRM supports the latest version of AD FS, version 3.0.

Installing AD FS 3.0

To configure AD FS as a server role on a Windows Server 2012 R2 machine, follow these steps:

1. In the Server Manager select Add Roles and Features (see Figure 28.13).

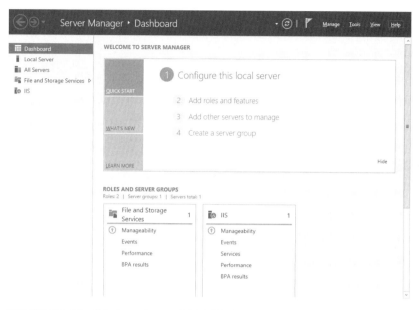

FIGURE 28.13   Windows Server 2012 R2 Server Manager.

2. In the Add Roles and Features Wizard that appears, click Next to continue.

3. Select Role-Based or Feature-Based Installation. Click Next to continue.

4. Select the destination server. Because you're installing on the server that you're currently using, click Next to continue (see Figure 28.14).

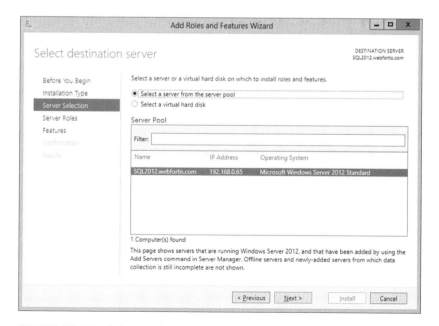

FIGURE 28.14   Selecting the destination server.

5. Select the Active Directory Federation Services option, as shown in Figure 28.15, and click Next to continue.

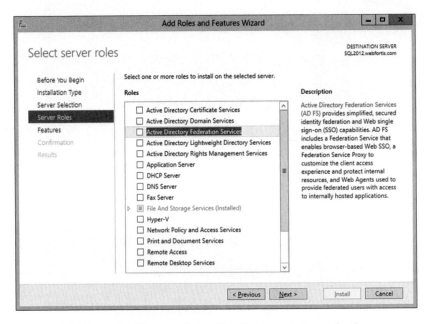

FIGURE 28.15   Active Directory Federation Services option selection.

6. If the system prompts you to install the required features because they aren't already configured, click Add Features. The installer installs the components and returns you to the wizard screen. Notice that AD FS is now listed in the left navigation area. Click Next to continue.

7. In the AD FS configuration that is displayed, click Next.

8. Confirm that Federation Service is checked (see Figure 28.16). Click Next.

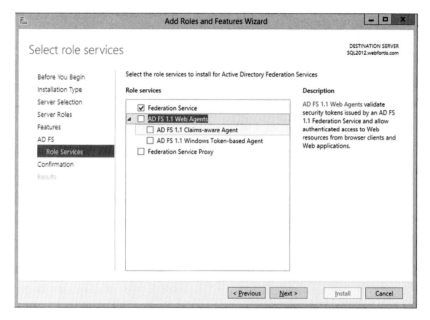

FIGURE 28.16   Federation Service option selected.

9. Review the confirmation for installation selections and click Install.

10. When installation is complete and the installer displays a confirmation, click Close to complete the installation.

11. At the Server Manager interface, notice that the new role is installed and select AD FS from the left-side navigation.

12. In the AD FS configuration interface that appears in the Server Manager (see Figure 28.17), click More in the warning bar displayed near the top of the screen.

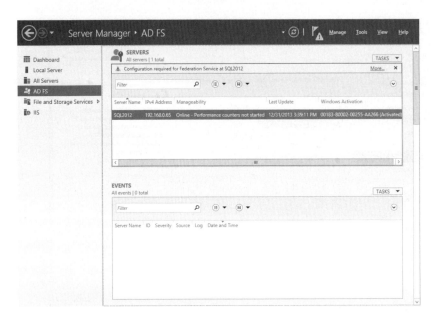

FIGURE 28.17   AD FS configuration.

13. In the All Server Task Details and Notifications dialog that appears, select the Run the AD FS Management Snap-In action (see Figure 28.18).

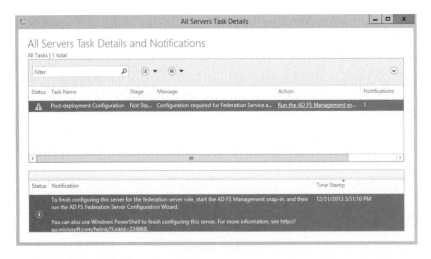

FIGURE 28.18   AD FS task prompt.

The AD FS 3.0 role is now installed on your Windows server, and it now needs to be configured.

Configuring AD FS

Whether you're running AD FS 2.0 or 3.0, the configuration is similar. The screenshots and steps in this section are for the AD FS 2.0 Management application, but they are similar for the AD FS 3.0 interface.

When start the AD FS application, the AD FS Management application present an Overview window as shown in Figure 28.19.

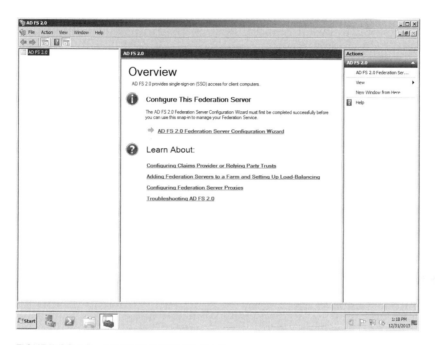

FIGURE 28.19   AD FS 2.0 Management.

To start the configuration, complete the following steps:

1. Click the AD FS 2.0 Federation Server Configuration Wizard link that is under the Configure This Federation Server section on the Overview window.

2. Select the Create a New Federation Service option (assuming that you are installing the first AD FS on the network; if not, select the other option). Click Next.

3. Select Stand-Alone Federation Server and click Next. (In this example, you are creating a standalone federation server, which is recommended for small implementations. Large organizations need to create server farms.)

4. Select a certificate, as shown in Figure 28.20.

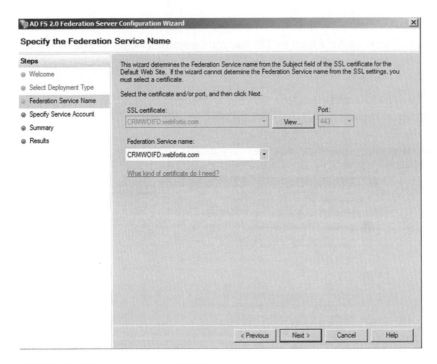

FIGURE 28.20   Selecting a certificate.

5. Specify the service account or create a new domain account and then click Next. When the configurations are done, you see the results of every task with the status.

6. Remedy any failures and rerun the wizard until you get success.

When the wizard finishes, you can find the URL you need to use when configuring the claims-based authentication on CRM. It should look something like this: https://<<*servername*>>.<<*domain name*>>.com/FederationMetadata/2007-06/FederationMetadata.xml.

You can verify that AD FS has been installed properly by checking in the AD FS 2.0 Management application, as shown in Figure 28.21.

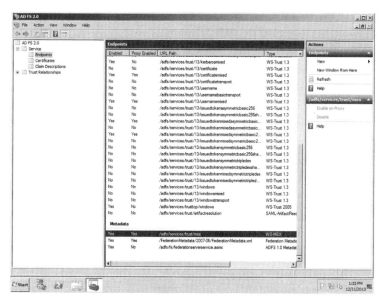

FIGURE 28.21   AD FS service endpoints.

Exporting the AD FS Token Certificate

Now you have to export the AD FS token certificate and import it to the Trusted Certificate Authorities store on the CRM server. To do that, follow these steps:

1. From the AD FS 2.0 Management application, go to the Service\Certificates folder, as shown in Figure 28.22.

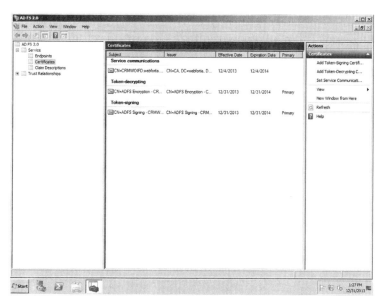

FIGURE 28.22   Viewing the Token-Signing certificate.

2. Right-click the Token-Signing certificate and select View Certificate. The Certificate dialog shown in Figure 28.23 appears.

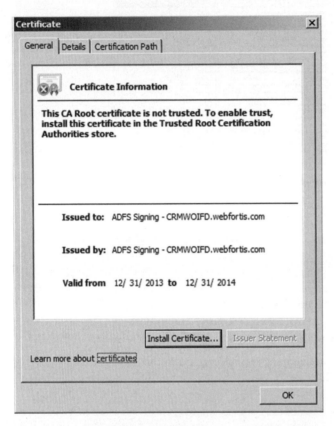

FIGURE 28.23   Viewing the Token-Signing certificate details.

3. On the Details tab of the Certificate dialog, click Copy to File.

4. In the Certificate Export Wizard dialog that appears, click Next.

5. In the Export File Format dialog, select DER Encoded Binary X.509 and click Next (see Figure 28.24).

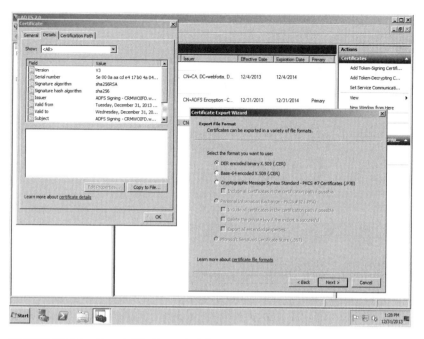

FIGURE 28.24   Export File Format dialog.

6. Enter the filename with the full path where you want to store the certificate file and click Next.

7. Complete the Certificate Export Wizard by clicking Finish.

8. When the message box that says the export was successful appears, click OK.

9. Copy the file you exported to the server where you have CRM 2016 installed and open the Certificates Management snap-in. Go to the Trusted Root Certification Authorities folder, right-click the Certificates folder, and select All Tasks > Import.

10. When the Certificate Import Wizard opens, click Next.

11. In the File to Import dialog that appears, enter the filename with the full path where the certificate file is located and click Next (see Figure 28.25).

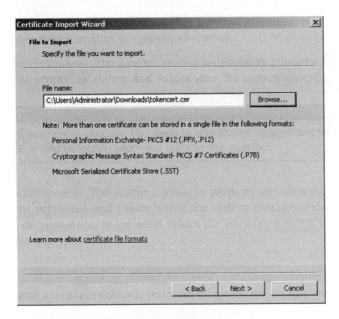

FIGURE 28.25   File to Import dialog.

12. Leave the default Certificate Store setting, which is Trusted Root Certification Authorities, and click Next.

13. Click Finish.

14. When the message box that says the import was successful appears, click OK.

The configuration of the AD FS service should now be complete. At this point, you need to configure the authentication of Microsoft Dynamics CRM to use the AD FS service. The next section shows how to configure claims-based authentication, which is a required step in this process.

Configuring Claims-Based Authentication on CRM

From the CRM Deployment Manager, complete the following steps to configure claims-based authentication:

1. To open the wizard, click the Configure Claims-Based Authentication link in the Tasks pane (see Figure 28.26).

FIGURE 28.26   HTTPS configuration.

2. Enter the Federation URL you got when configuring the AD FS and click Next (see Figure 28.27).

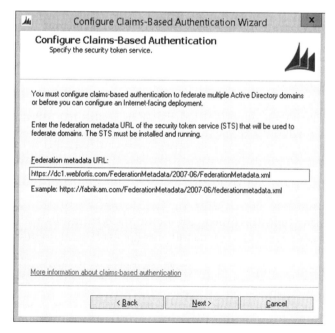

FIGURE 28.27   Configuring federation metadata URL.

3. Select the SSL certificate and click Next (see Figure 28.28). The wizard validates the settings and system requirements and shows any appropriate errors or warnings to the user.

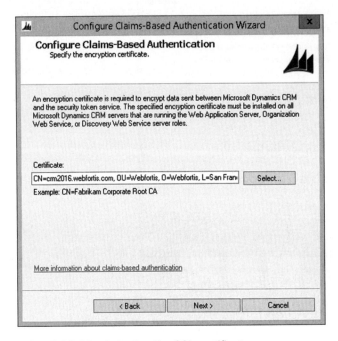

FIGURE 28.28   Selecting the SSL certificate.

4. Click Next to review the configurations.

5. Click Apply to apply the changes.

6. Click Finish to close the dialog.

At this point, the claims-based authentication for CRM should be configured. You have one more step before you can finalize the configuration of IFD, which is to add a relying party trust.

Adding Relying Party Trust on AD FS

After configuring claims-based authentication on CRM, you need to open the AD FS application and add a relying party trust. This is necessary for the AD FS to trust the CRM URLs used by external users. Each organization has a unique URL that the AD FS needs to trust.

> **NOTE**
>
> If you have a multi-tenanted environment, every time you add a new organization, you must manually update the relying party trust from the federation metadata if you want immediate access to your system via IFD because AD FS automatically updates this data only every 24 hours. You can also do this programmatically or through PowerShell.

To add the trust in AD FS, follow these steps:

1. Open AD FS 2.0 by going to Start > Administrative Tools > AD FS Management.

2. Click the Add Relying Party Trust option that is on the Actions panel on the right. The Add Relying Party Trust Wizard appears. You can also get to this wizard by expanding the Trust Relationships folder, right-clicking the Relying Party Trust folder, and then selecting Add Relying Party Trust.

3. Click Start, and in the Select Data Source step, select Import Data About the Relying Party Published Online or on a Local Network, which should be similar to the following: https://fs.webfortis.com/FederationMetadata/2007-06/FederationMetadata .xml. Figure 28.29 shows the data source selection. Click Next.

4. Enter a display name and click Next (see Figure 28.30).

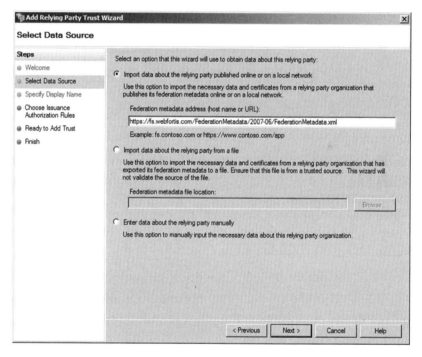

FIGURE 28.29   Selecting the data source.

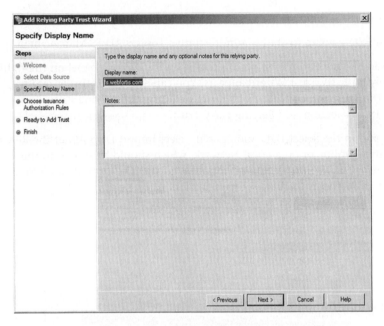

FIGURE 28.30   Specifying a display name.

5. Select the Permit All Users to Access This Relying Party option and click Next.

6. Click Next again to finish. The Edit Claim Rules dialog opens (see Figure 28.31).

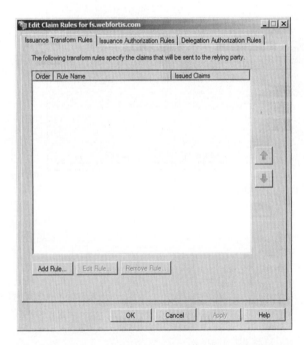

FIGURE 28.31   New Relying Trusted Party Wizard.

Next, you need to complete the following steps to add a rule for the new relying party trust you just created:

1. In the Edit Claim Rules dialog, shown in Figure 28.31, click Add Rule.

2. Select Pass Through or Filter an Incoming Claim from the drop-down and then click Next (see Figure 28.32).

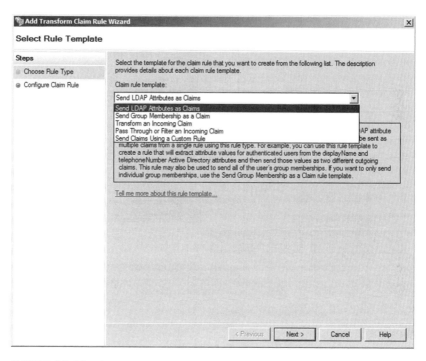

FIGURE 28.32   Selecting the rule template.

3. Enter a descriptive name for the claim rule and select UPN (User Principal Name) as the incoming claim type (see Figure 28.33).

4. Click Finish.

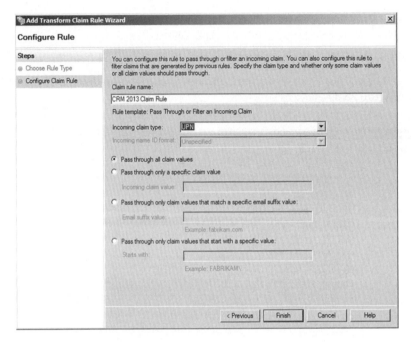

FIGURE 28.33   Configuring the rule for UPN.

5. Create another rule for the primary security identifier definition (SID), repeating steps 1–4 but selecting Primary SID as the Incoming Claim Type (see Figure 28.34).

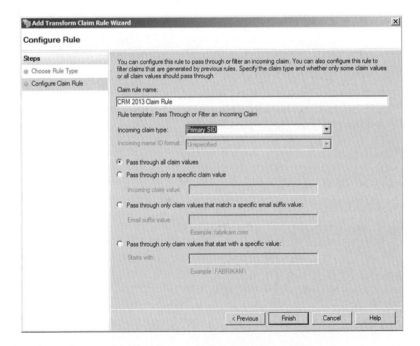

FIGURE 28.34   Configuring the rule for the primary SID.

6. Create another rule for the Windows account name, repeating steps 1–4 but selecting the Windows account name as the incoming type and using the Transform an Incoming Claim rule (instead of the previously selected Pass Through or Filter an Incoming Claim) template (see Figure 28.35).

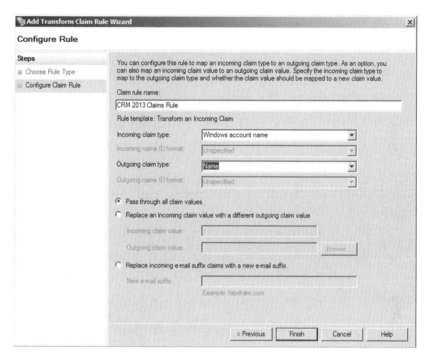

FIGURE 28.35   Configuring the rule for the Windows account name with the Transform an Incoming Claim Rule template.

You should now have three rules created, as shown in Figure 28.36.

28

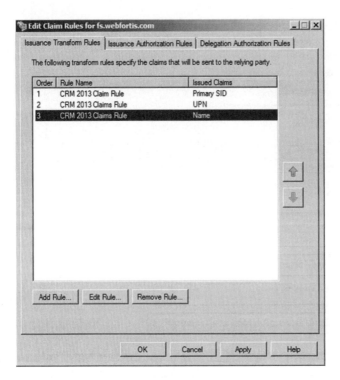

FIGURE 28.36   Three rules created.

7. Click OK to close the Edit Claim Rules dialog.

8. Click the Claims Provider Trusts folder on the left, right-click the Active Directory item in the middle, and click Edit Claim Rules on the right.

9. When the Edit Claim Rules for Active Directory dialog appears, click the Add Rule button (see Figure 28.37).

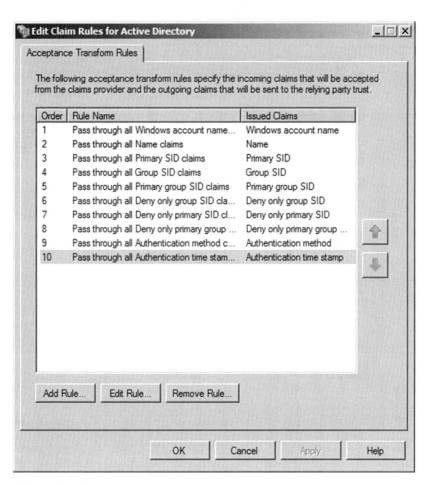

FIGURE 28.37   Adding a new rule.

10. In the Choose Rule Type step, leave the default option Send LDAP Attributes as Claims and click Next (see Figure 28.38).

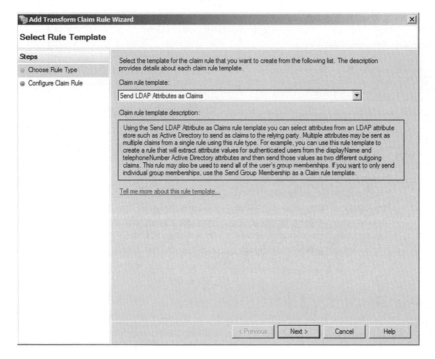

FIGURE 28.38 Adding a new rule.

11. Enter UPN as the claim rule name, select Active Directory as the attribute store, select User-Principal-Name as the LDAP attribute, and select UPN as the outgoing claim type, as shown in Figure 28.39. Click Finish to close this dialog. You should now have 11 rules for the Active Directory claims, as shown in Figure 28.40.

You have now completed the necessary server configurations for forms authentication.

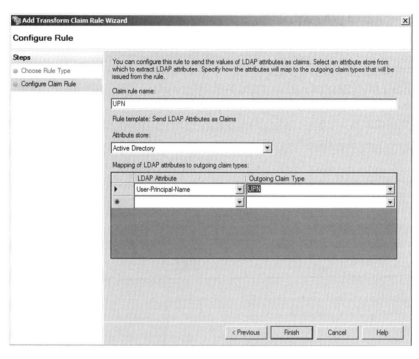

FIGURE 28.39   UPN Active Directory claim rule.

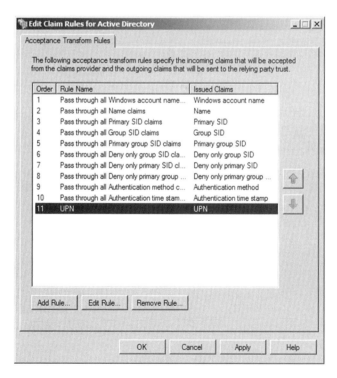

FIGURE 28.40   Eleven rules for Active Directory.

Configuring the CRM Application for Internet-Facing Deployment

This section covers one of the final steps in configuring forms authentication, which is the IFD configuration. To configure this deployment, go to the server where CRM 2016 is installed and open the Microsoft Dynamics CRM Deployment Manager application. Next, complete the following steps to configure IFD:

1. To open the wizard, click the Configure Internet-Facing Deployment link that is in the Actions panel on the right.

2. Click Next and fill in the Web Application Server Domain, Organization Web Service Domain, and Discovery Web Service Domain fields (see Figure 28.41). Click Next.

FIGURE 28.41   Configuring server roles URL addresses.

3. Enter the external domain (for example, auth.webfortis.com), which is the domain address where the AD FS is installed for authentication (see Figure 28.42). Click Next.

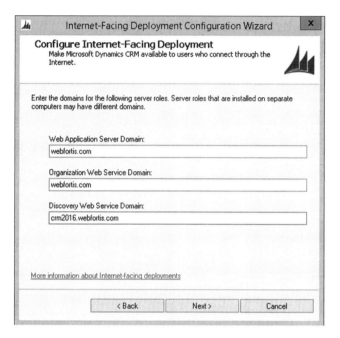

FIGURE 28.42   Configuring the external domain.

4. Verify that the system checks are met, click Next, review the selections, and complete the wizard.

5. Click Apply to start the configurations. When they are done, you see the results.

6. Click Finish to close the dialog.

7. Restart IIS with the `iisreset` command.

If you are configuring AD FS 3.0, you need to take an extra step: In the AD FS Management application, expand AD FS, click the Authentication Policies folder from the left list, and click the Edit Global Primary Authentication link that on the right, under Actions.

Finally, make sure you have Forms Authentication selected in both extranet and intranet lists and click OK, as shown in Figure 28.43.

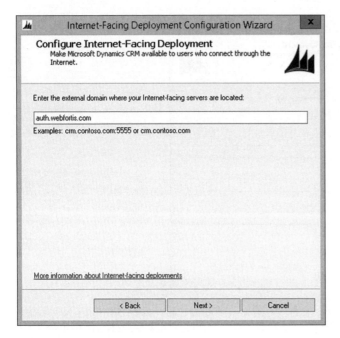

FIGURE 28.43   Forms authentication for a global authentication policy.

Working with IFD and Multiple Organizations

Because multi-tenancy is common, this section covers working with IFD and multiple organizations and how to configure external Domain Name Service (DNS) records to allow for access to the right organization.

DNS Server Configuration

An important consideration when implementing IFD is to configure DNS properly. The installation process doesn't address DNS, and the Forms Authentication page might not work without DNS properly configured.

> **NOTE**
>
> DNS is used to map a domain name to an IP address. Domains are mapped to IP addresses so that, for example, www.*domain-name*.com equals 123.123.12.3. You can also add hosts below the domain, as www, ftp, and so on, and map different IP addresses to them. An example of that might be ftp.*domain-name*.com equals 123.123.12.4.

You must complete some necessary DNS configurations, and the ones you need to complete depend on the DNS server you are using. The example in this section uses the Windows DNS Server Manager.

The DNS configurations described here are required for every organization you set up in Microsoft Dynamics CRM. If you are configuring multi-tenancy, you must create a host entry in your DNS server for each organization unless you use a wildcard host entry. This is because IFD uses a URL in this format: https://*organizationName.domainName*.com.

If your domain name is webfortis.com, your server name is crm2016, and your organization name is Webfortis, the URL to use is https://webfortis.webfortis.com. If you have another organization with the name Test on the same server, it can be accessed using the URL https://test.webfortis.com. You must configure your DNS so that crm2016.webfortis.com, webfortis.webfortis.com, and test.webfortis.com all point to the same IP address.

> **TIP**
>
> To verify the IP address resolved by DNS from a client computer, use the `ping` command from a command prompt window to the IP address. Be sure to run this command internally on the network because most of the firewalls have this protocol blocked.

If you don't specify the organization name in the URL—for example, http://crm2016 .webfortis.com—the Microsoft Dynamics CRM server redirects users to the default organization URL, which in Dynamics CRM 2016 is the first organization that was created during deployment. In this example, this is https://webfortis.webfortis.com/, assuming that Webfortis is configured as the default organization.

Disabling IFD

You can disable IFD by going to the CRM Deployment Manager and selecting Disable Internet-Facing Deployment. When you are asked for a confirmation, click Yes and then click Disable Claims-Based Authentication. When you are asked for confirmation again, click Yes.

Finally, an optional step would be to change the server properties back to HTTP with port 80, instead of HTTPS with port 443.

Summary

This chapter shows how to expose a Dynamics CRM server to the Internet by configuring the IFD feature so that users can authenticate via claims-based authentication over the Internet. This chapter reviews all the required components and configurations necessary to set up this feature, as well as how to enable and disable IFD on a Dynamics CRM 2016 On-Premises installation or deployment.

CHAPTER **29**

On-Premises Deployments

This chapter is largely important for CRM 2016 On-Premises deployments, which differ significantly from Online deployments due to the requirements necessary to install an application on local servers.

However, a couple of things do overlap:

▶ Outlook client configuration options

▶ Setting up your business in Microsoft Dynamics CRM

▶ For more information on Outlook Client configuration options, refer to **CHAPTER 19**, "Outlook Configuration." For more information on setting up your business in Microsoft Dynamics CRM, see the last section in this chapter, "Setting Up Your Business in Microsoft Dynamics CRM 2016."

With these exceptions, if you have a hosted instance of Microsoft Dynamics CRM (that is, Dynamics CRM Online), you can probably skip this chapter, or at least you can skip to the "Microsoft CRM Office Client for Outlook" section of this chapter, because a majority of the material does not apply to you. If, however, you are running your own in-house (that is, On-Premises) version of Microsoft Dynamics CRM, you will want to pay special attention to the requirements in this chapter for configuration, setup, and prerequisites.

The On-Premises version of Microsoft Dynamics CRM is the version that requires the most amount of infrastructure. This is simply because you're dedicating server resources (if not several servers) to host the Microsoft Dynamics CRM application. The other versions (CRM Online and partner-hosted Dynamics CRM) require only Outlook, the email router, and/or a browser and mobile device.

> **NOTE**
>
> *Hosted* Microsoft Dynamics CRM means either hosted from Microsoft or partner hosted. Although with partner hosting you are sometimes given advanced configuration options, it is usually the partner's responsibility to provide the configuration requirements explained in this chapter.

Hardware and Software Considerations

Microsoft Dynamics CRM 2016 is an application that leverages other Microsoft technology. Most businesses deploying an On-Premises version of Dynamics CRM have some of, if not all, the technology required for Microsoft Dynamics CRM 2016, and Microsoft readily admits that if you're not already on the Microsoft platform, the overall price of Microsoft Dynamics CRM On-Premises can be steep because the product requires many core components, such as SQL Server, Internet Information Services (IIS), Active Directory, and so on.

Server

You can deploy Microsoft Dynamics CRM several different ways when considering an On-Premises deployment. These include choosing single-server versus distributed-server deployment and determining which version of Microsoft Dynamics CRM to run.

> ▶ **See** the "Setting Up Your Business in Microsoft Dynamics CRM 2016" section, later in this chapter, for more information about single-server versus distributed-server deployment.

> **CAUTION**
>
> Microsoft Dynamics CRM Server 2016 is supported only on an x64-based architecture computer.

You can install individual server roles in different computers or on the same computer by using the Microsoft Dynamics CRM Server Setup Wizard. In addition, you can add a server role and change or remove installed server roles by navigating to Control Panel > Features > Programs.

Microsoft recommends the following components when considering a single-server deployment:

- ▶ **Processor**—Minimum of x64 or compatible dual-core 1.5GHz (quad-core x64 2GHz or higher recommended)

- ▶ **Memory**—Minimum of 4GB RAM (8GB RAM recommended)

- ▶ **Processor**—Minimum of 10GB of available hard disk space (40GB of available hard disk space recommended)

Windows Server Operating System

The operating system requirements for Microsoft Dynamics CRM Server 2016 are as follows:

▶ Windows Server 2012 R2 Datacenter

▶ Windows Server 2012 R2 Standard

▶ Windows Server 2012 Standard

▶ Windows Server 2012 Datacenter

> **CAUTION**
>
> The following server configurations are not supported for installing and running Microsoft Dynamics CRM Server 2016:
>
> ▶ Windows Server 2012 Foundation and Essentials
>
> ▶ Windows Server 2012 installed by using the Server Core installation option
>
> ▶ Windows Server 2008 family

Active Directory Modes

Active Directory is a Microsoft service that provides authentication and authorization for Windows-based users, computers, and services in a centralized location. It is a necessary component for accessing Microsoft CRM 2016. The advantage of leveraging Active Directory is the single system sign-on process—that is, application access can be granted without requiring multiple sign-ons. When users log on to the Windows network, they are essentially logging on to not only the network but also to all network resources, including printers, file shares, and applications that they have access to. Active Directory works by organizing network objects in a hierarchy.

A forest is the top level of Active Directory. Forests contain domains, and domains contain organizational units (OUs) (see Figure 29.1).

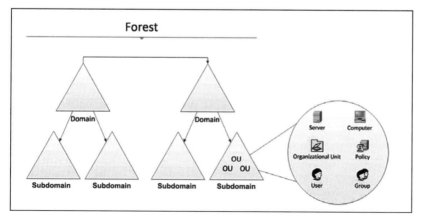

FIGURE 29.1   Graphical display of Active Directory forest, domains, and OUs.

One of the following Active Directory service modes must be running:

- ▶ Windows Server 2008 Interim

- ▶ Windows Server 2008 Native

- ▶ Windows Server 2008 R2

- ▶ Windows Server 2012

- ▶ Windows Server 2012 R2

Other Active Directory requirements include the following:

- ▶ The computer that Microsoft Dynamics CRM is running on shouldn't function as an Active Directory domain controller.

- ▶ When you use the Add Users Wizard, only users from trusted domains in the current forest are displayed. Users from trusted external forests aren't supported and don't appear in the wizard.

- ▶ Installing Microsoft Dynamics CRM Server 2016 in a Lightweight Directory Access Protocol (LDAP) directory that is running in Active Directory Application Mode (ADAM) is not supported.

Active Directory is an integral part of Microsoft Dynamics CRM. Starting with the earliest versions of Microsoft CRM, Active Directory was the centralized location for user management and security for the system. When users first attempt to log on to the network, they are validating who they are against the information in Active Directory. When they are on the network, Microsoft CRM uses another internal security mechanism to determine record access. This division of security is known as authentication and authorization.

Authentication (or who the user is) is the process by which a user is verified by providing credentials. In the case of Active Directory, the credentials consist of a username, password, and Windows domain name. In the Windows and Microsoft CRM model, authentication is determined when a user logs on to the network. When a user attempts to access Microsoft CRM, he is not prompted for credentials because he has already been verified (see Figure 29.2).

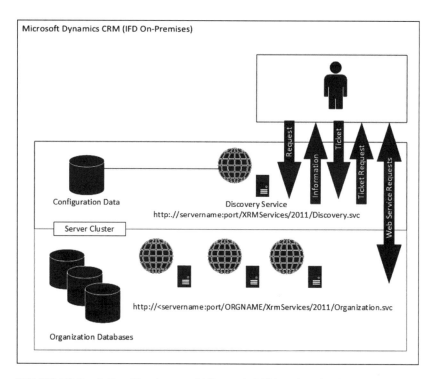

FIGURE 29.2   Active Directory and Microsoft CRM authentication.

Authorization (or what the user can do) is the process by which users are granted the rights to certain resources, based on the security levels and permissions they have. For example, a network administrator might have full access rights to the entire system, whereas a secretary might have very limited access rights.

Further, the previous example is specific to the network rights that users have; however, the Microsoft Dynamics CRM rights they might have are completely independent of their network rights. Therefore, the secretary previously mentioned, who has very limited access rights, might be a full Microsoft CRM administrator and able to do nearly anything in the CRM system, whereas the network administrator might have read-only rights for CRM.

If it sounds confusing, it might be easier to think of it like this:

▶ Users need to be valid network domain users to be given access to Microsoft Dynamics CRM 2016.

▶ After being granted access to Microsoft CRM 2016, users need to be given a security role to determine what level of access they have to work within Microsoft CRM 2016.

▶ No inherent correlation exists between network permissions and Microsoft CRM 2016 permissions.

29

To explain further, just because users can log on to the network does not necessarily mean they have the rights or the capability to log on to Microsoft CRM 2016. The reason for this is that although Active Directory controls network and network resource access, users must also be set up in Microsoft CRM 2016 as valid users. For example, if you have 85 people in your organization, but only the CEO has been set up in Microsoft Dynamics CRM 2016 as a valid user, only the CEO can access CRM; other users who tried to access CRM would encounter the authentication dialog shown in Figure 29.3.

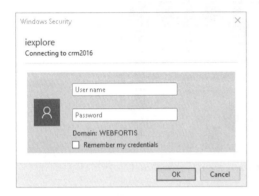

FIGURE 29.3   Login error when trying to access Microsoft CRM.

The number of valid Microsoft CRM 2016 users you can have is established by the version of Microsoft CRM 2016 you purchase, as well as the particular licensing used (see the "Licensing" section, later in this chapter).

Internet Information Services

IIS 8.0 or 8.5 should be installed and running in native mode before you install Microsoft Dynamics CRM Server; however, if it's not, the CRM Setup files install it.

> **TIP**
>
> When you install the Microsoft Dynamics CRM Server web application on a computer that is running IIS, Microsoft Dynamics CRM Server Setup enables HTTP compression by default. Although no modification is necessary, if you use a different method to compress HTTP communications, you might want to disable this feature. To do this, start IIS Manager and then modify the compression options.

Internet-Facing Deployment Requirements

The following items are required for the Internet-Facing Deployment (IFD) feature and are designed for system administrators using Microsoft Windows Server as the claims-based authentication solution:

▶ Dynamics CRM Server 2016 must have access to a Secure Token Services (STS) service, such as the STS called Active Directory Federation Services (AD FS).

▶ Dynamics CRM supports the following versions of AD FS:

   ▶ 2.0

   ▶ 2.1

   ▶ 2.2

   ▶ 3.0

The following must be available after you run Microsoft Dynamics CRM Server Setup and before you configure IFD:

▶ If you are installing Microsoft Dynamics CRM in a single-server configuration, be aware that AD FS 2.0 installs on the default website. Therefore, you must create a new website for Microsoft Dynamics CRM if you're using AD FS 2.0. If you're using AD FS 3.0, there is not a conflict.

▶ When you run the Internet-Facing Deployment Configuration Wizard, Microsoft Dynamics CRM Server 2016 must be running on a website that is configured to use Secure Sockets Layer (SSL). Microsoft Dynamics CRM Server Setup will not configure the website for SSL.

▶ The Require SSL setting enabled in IIS should be set where the CRM web application will be installed.

▶ Multiple IIS bindings, such as a website with an HTTPS and an HTTP binding or two HTTPS or two HTTP bindings, are not supported for running Microsoft Dynamics CRM, and therefore a single binding is strongly recommended.

▶ You access the AD FS federation metadata file from the computer where the Configure Claims-Based Authentication Wizard is run. In addition, the federation metadata endpoint must use the Web Services Trust Model (WS-Trust) 1.3 standard, because previous standards are not supported.

The following encryption certificates are required. You can use the same encryption certificate for both purposes, such as when you use a wildcard certificate:

▶ Claims-based authentication requires identities to provide an encryption certificate for authentication. This certificate should be trusted by the computer where you are installing Microsoft Dynamics CRM Server 2016, so it must be located in the local Personal store where the Configure Claims-Based Authentication Wizard is running.

▶ The certificates for SSL encryption should be valid for hostnames similar to org.*your-domain*.com, auth.*your-domain*.com, and dev.*your-org*.com. To satisfy this requirement, you can use a single wildcard certificate (*.*your-domain*.com), a certificate that supports Subject Alternative Names, or individual certificates for each name. Individual certificates for each hostname are valid only if you use different servers for each web server role.

29

▶ The CRMAppPool account of each Microsoft Dynamics CRM website must have read permission to the private key of the encryption certificate specified when configuring claims-based authentication. You can use the Certificates snap-in to edit permissions for the encryption certificate found in the Personal store of the local computer account.

▶ Refer to **CHAPTER 28**, "Forms Authentication," for more information about IFD configuration.

Database

Microsoft Dynamics CRM supports only one type of database: Microsoft SQL Server. There are several components to Microsoft SQL Server. The following components are covered in the following sections:

▶ SQL Server Editions

▶ SQL Server Reporting Services

SQL Server Editions

Any one of the following Microsoft SQL Server editions is required and must be installed, running, and available for Microsoft Dynamics CRM:

▶ Microsoft SQL Server 2014, Enterprise Edition, x64

▶ Microsoft SQL Server 2014, Business Intelligence, x64

▶ Microsoft SQL Server 2014, Standard, x64

▶ Microsoft SQL Server 2014, Developer, x64 (for non-production environments)

▶ Microsoft SQL Server 2012, Enterprise, 64-bit SP1

▶ Microsoft SQL Server 2012, Business Intelligence, 64-bit SP1

▶ Microsoft SQL Server 2012, Standard, 64-bit SP1

▶ Microsoft SQL Server 2012, Developer, 64-bit SP1 (for non-production environments)

> **NOTE**
>
> No 32-bit versions of SQL Server are supported for Microsoft Dynamics CRM 2016.

SQL Server Reporting Services

The following SQL Server Reporting Services editions are required and must be installed, running, and available for Microsoft Dynamics CRM Server:

▶ Microsoft SQL Server 2014, Enterprise Edition, x64

▶ Microsoft SQL Server 2014, Business Intelligence, x64

▶ Microsoft SQL Server 2014, Standard, x64

▶ Microsoft SQL Server 2014, Developer, x64 (for non-production environments)

▶ Microsoft SQL Server 2012, Enterprise, 64-bit SP1

▶ Microsoft SQL Server 2012, Business Intelligence, 64-bit SP1

▶ Microsoft SQL Server 2012, Standard, 64-bit SP1

▶ Microsoft SQL Server 2012, Developer, 64-bit SP1 (for non-production environments)

NOTE

No 32-bit versions of SQL Server Reporting Services are supported for Microsoft Dynamics CRM 2016.

TIP

Make sure to use the same deployment of SQL Server Reporting Services for each organization in your Microsoft Dynamics CRM deployment. Otherwise, problems might arise.

Microsoft Dynamics CRM Reporting Extensions

The Microsoft Dynamics CRM Reporting Extensions is a component that connects the Microsoft Dynamics CRM computer to the SQL Server Reporting Services computer.

The Microsoft Dynamics CRM Connector for SQL Server Reporting Services has the following general requirements:

▶ You must complete Microsoft Dynamics CRM Server Setup before you run Microsoft Dynamics CRM Connector for SQL Server Reporting Services Setup.

▶ You can install and run only one instance of Microsoft Dynamics CRM Reporting Extensions on a computer that has SQL Server 2012 or 2014 Reporting Services installed.

▶ Separate deployments of Microsoft Dynamics CRM cannot share one SQL Server Reporting Services server. However, a single deployment of Microsoft Dynamics CRM that has multiple organizations can use the same (or more than one) SQL Server Reporting Services server.

▶ Refer to **CHAPTER 16**, "Reporting and Dashboards," for more information about the Microsoft Dynamics CRM Connector for SQL Server Reporting Services.

SharePoint Integration

Microsoft SharePoint is not required to install Microsoft Dynamics CRM 2016, and you can configure the SharePoint server settings after running Microsoft Dynamics CRM Server Setup.

To enable Microsoft SharePoint integration, the following Microsoft SharePoint Server editions are required and must be installed and running, and at least one Microsoft SharePoint site collection must be configured and available for Microsoft Dynamics CRM Server:

▶ Microsoft SharePoint 2010 SP1 (all editions) or SP2

▶ Microsoft SharePoint 2013 or SP1

▶ Microsoft SharePoint Online

To enable SharePoint functionality, go to the Settings area of the Microsoft Dynamics CRM web application and select Document Management. The configuration page shown in Figure 29.4 appears.

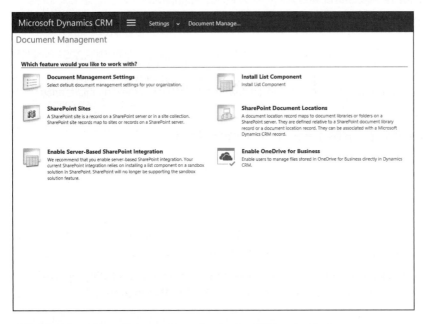

FIGURE 29.4   SharePoint configuration in the CRM web client.

▶ Refer to **CHAPTER 27**, "SharePoint," for more information about this configuration.

Email Router

This section lists the software and application software requirements for Microsoft Dynamics CRM Email Router.

Microsoft Dynamics CRM Email Router Setup consists of two main components: the Microsoft Dynamics CRM Email Router Service and the Rule Deployment Wizard. The CRM Email Router Service installs the Email Router Service and Email Router Configuration Manager. The Email Router Configuration Manager is used to configure the Email Router Service. The Rule Deployment Manager component deploys the rules that enable received email messages to be tracked.

> **NOTE**
>
> When using server-side synchronization, there is no need to use Microsoft Dynamics CRM Email Router.

▶ For more information on how to install and configure Microsoft Dynamics CRM Email Router, **SEE CHAPTER 20**, "Email Configuration."

You can install the Email Router Service and Rule Deployment Manager on any computer that is running one of the following operating systems and has network access to both Microsoft Dynamics CRM and the email server:

▶ Windows 8.1 or Windows 8 (either x64 or 32-bit versions)

▶ Windows 7 (32- or 64-bit version)

▶ Windows Server 2012

> **NOTE**
>
> Download Microsoft Dynamics CRM Email Router www.microsoft.com/en-us/download/details.aspx?id=50373.

Exchange Server

Microsoft Exchange Server is required only if you want to use the email router to connect to an Exchange Server email messaging system. To do this, Email Router can be installed on any of the previously mentioned Windows or Windows Server operating systems that have a connection to Exchange Server. Email Router supports the following versions of Microsoft Exchange Server:

▶ Microsoft Exchange Online

▶ Microsoft Exchange Server 2010 Standard or Enterprise Edition

▶ Microsoft Exchange Server 2013 Standard or Enterprise Edition

> **NOTE**
>
> Although previous versions of Microsoft Exchange Server are not supported with these versions of Microsoft Dynamics CRM Email Router Service and Rule Deployment Manager, there is no reason you couldn't use them with POP3 access and configure the email router to use native POP3 functionality.

If the .NET Framework 4.0 is missing, Email Router Setup installs it on the computer where you install Email Router.

The Rule Deployment Wizard component must be installed on a computer that is running any of the previously mentioned Windows or Windows Server operating systems and has the Microsoft Exchange Server Messaging API (MAPI) client runtime libraries installed.

> **NOTE**
>
> You can download the MAPI client runtime libraries from the Microsoft Download Center, at http://go.microsoft.com/fwlink/?linkid=78805.

POP3/SMTP

POP3-compliant email systems are supported for incoming email message routing. Simple Mail Transfer Protocol (SMTP) and Exchange web services through Exchange Online are the only transport protocols supported for outgoing email message routing.

> **NOTE**
>
> When you use the Forward mailbox option on the User form, the POP3 email server must provide support where an email message can be sent as an attachment to another email message.

If you install Microsoft Dynamics CRM Email Router to connect to a POP3-compliant or SMTP server, the following standards are required:

▶ **POP3**—RFC 1939

▶ **SMTP**—RFC 2821 and 2822

Microsoft CRM Client for Browsers

When using the Microsoft CRM client for browsers, the following browsers are officially supported:

▶ **Internet Explorer (on Windows)**—Version 10 or later

▶ **Firefox (on Windows)**—Latest publicly released version

▶ **Safari (on Mac OS X)**—Latest publicly released version

▶ **Chrome on Windows or Google Nexus 10**—Latest publicly released version

> **NOTE**
>
> Although these are the only officially supported browsers, we've seen alternative configurations work.

The Microsoft CRM web browser client is the recommended option in the following situations:

▶ Remote/offsite access is necessary.

▶ Support staff don't necessarily need Office.

▶ A thin client solution is desired.

To use Microsoft Dynamics CRM Office integration features, such as Export to Excel and Mail Merge, you must have one of the following installed on the computer that is running the Microsoft Dynamics CRM web client:

▶ Microsoft Office 2016

▶ Microsoft Office 2013

▶ Microsoft Office 2010

▶ Microsoft Office 365

> **NOTE**
>
> Microsoft Dynamics CRM 2016 does not work with Microsoft Office 2007 versions.

Microsoft CRM Office Client for Outlook

The Microsoft CRM 2016 client can be installed directly into Outlook and can be accessed by simply navigating to the Microsoft CRM organization name node (see Figure 29.5).

FIGURE 29.5   Microsoft Outlook with Microsoft CRM.

The Microsoft CRM Outlook client comes in two versions, 32-bit and 64-bit. The same client can also run in two modes (online or offline) and can connect to more than one CRM organization and to any Microsoft Dynamics CRM Online organization.

On a standard installation, the offline access is not installed, and although it can be seen by navigating to Outlook > CRM, when you select it for the first time, the system configures itself and installs the offline components. The Offline Access type has the capability to go offline and enables users to work with CRM data while not connected to the Microsoft CRM server. When this is installed and configured, a local version of the data is installed in an installed instance of SQL Server Express Edition 2012 SP1 (installed by the installer).

When users have completed their offline tasks and return to the Microsoft CRM 2016 server, they can click the Go Online button on the ribbon, and a synchronization process checks for updated data on both the Microsoft CRM server and the Microsoft CRM Outlook client.

Finally, note that the Offline Access Client mode does not require installation on a laptop. If you choose to install the Offline Access Client mode on your desktop, it will have the same functionality as the desktop client, but it will install the required components outlined earlier. There are not too many reasons for doing this, however, other than testing and development purposes, because it is unlikely that you'll be taking your desktop offline.

Regardless of which Microsoft CRM client is used, the following operating systems are required for the Microsoft CRM Office client for Outlook:

▶ Windows 10 (both 64-bit and 32-bit versions)

▶ Windows 8 (both 64-bit and 32-bit versions)

▶ Windows 7 (both 64-bit and 32-bit versions)

▶ Windows Server 2012 (when running as RDC applications) and 2012 R2

In addition, the following components must be installed (and running) before you attempt a Microsoft CRM Office client for Outlook installation:

▶ Microsoft Office 2016

▶ Microsoft Office 2013

▶ Microsoft Office 2010

The following components are required. However, the installer automatically downloads and installs them as part of the installation process:

▶ SQL 2012 Express Edition (Offline Access Client mode only)

▶ .NET Framework 4.5.2

▶ Windows Installer (MSI) 4.5.

▶ Microsoft Visual C++ Redistributable

▶ Microsoft Report Viewer Redistributable 2010

▶ Microsoft Application Error Reporting

▶ Windows Identity Framework (WIF)

▶ Windows Azure AppFabric SDK V1.0

▶ Windows Live ID Sign-in Assistant 6.5

▶ Microsoft Online Services Sign-in Assistant 2.1

▶ Microsoft SQL Server Native Client

▶ Microsoft SQL Server Compact 4.0

Licensing

With the different versions now available for Microsoft CRM 2016, customers have greater choice for licensing. There are now four different types of licenses for Dynamics CRM end users:

▶ **Enterprise**—The Enterprise license is designed to deliver full-featured application functionality. No usage limitations apply with this license.

▶ **Professional**—The Professional license is designed to deliver full-featured application functionality. No usage limitations apply with this license.

▶ **Basic**—The Basic license limits some application functionality and is designed for users at entry levels.

▶ **Essential**—The Essential license allows little native functionality but is an excellent option for organizations that need to deploy custom solutions (xRM applications).

29

> **NOTE**
>
> There is also a Workgroup edition of Dynamics CRM On-Premises, which allows a maximum of five users.

For CRM Online, the licenses are referred to as user subscription licenses (USLs), and for On-Premises, as either client access licenses (CALs) or subscriber access licenses (SALs).

> **NOTE**
>
> Regardless of which license the user has, all users who have access to the system have full mobile client access rights.

> **TIP**
>
> The license types and requirements have no inherent enforcement tied to them. Therefore, a user with a Basic or Essential license *can do everything* that a user with a Professional license can do. However, this technically places the organization out of compliance with regard to licensing as far as Microsoft is concerned, and Microsoft will add/incorporate licensing control mechanisms in future releases, so we advise you to adhere to correct usage rights.

> **NOTE**
>
> The license types can be mixed in any given deployment. For example, you could have 15 Professional, 50 Basic, and 25 Essential licenses in one deployment.

Table 29.1 (provided by Microsoft) describes the complexities related to the different versions. Note that Enterprise includes all the rights of Professional, as well as additional products (such as usage rights to Parature and MDM).

TABLE 29.1   Use Rights

Use Right	Professional	Basic	Essential
View announcements	×	×	×
Manage saved views	×	×	×
Use relationships between records	×	×*	×*
Create personal views	×	×	×*
Advanced Find search	×	×	×*
Search	×	×	×*
Use a queue item	×	×*	×*
Export data to Microsoft Excel	×	×	×
Perform mail merge	×	×	×
Start dialog	×	×*	×*

Use Right	Professional	Basic	Essential
Run as an on-demand process	×	×*	×*
Run an automated workflow	×	×*	×*
Read articles	×	×*	×*
Notes	×	×	×
Activity management	×	×	×
Yammer collaboration**	×	×	×
Post activity feeds	×	×	×
Follow activity feeds	×	×	×
Shared calendar	×	×	×
Write custom entity records	×	×	×
Read custom application data	×	×	×
Microsoft Dynamics CRM Mobile Express	×	×	×
Microsoft Dynamics CRM for iPad & Windows 8	×	×	×
Microsoft Dynamics CRM for Outlook	×	×	×
Microsoft Dynamics CRM Web application	×	×	×
Manage user reports, user charts, and user dashboards	×	×	
Run reports	×	×	
Create, update, and customize reports	×	×	
Create and update announcements	×	×	
Read Dynamics CRM application data	×	×	
User dashboards	×	×	
User charts	×	×	
User Interface Integration for Microsoft Dynamics CRM	×	×	
Convert an activity to a case	×	×	
Case management	×	×	
Add or remove a customer relationship for a contact	×	×	
Associate an opportunity with a contact	×	×	
Qualify and convert a lead to a contact	×	×	
Contacts	×	×	
Lead scoring, routing, assignment	×	×	
Lead capture	×	×	
Add or remove a customer relationship for an Account	×	×	
Associate an Opportunity with an Account	×	×	
Qualify and convert a Lead to an Account	×	×	
Accounts	×	×	

(Continued)

TABLE 29.1   (*Continued*)

Use Right	Professional	Basic	Essential
Import data in bulk	×		
Configure auditing	×		
Configure duplicate-detection rules	×		
Define relationships between entities	×		
Define and configure queues	×		
Define and configure dialogs	×		
Define and configure workflows	×		
System reports, system charts, and system dashboards	×		
Customize forms and views	×		
Create Microsoft Dynamics CRM forms, entities, and fields	×		
Administer CRM	×		
Article templates	×		
Create and publish articles	×		
Goal management	×		
Contract templates	×		
Contract management	×		
Territory management	×		
Sales literature	×		
Quote management	×		
Price lists	×		
Product tracking	×		
Order management	×		
Invoice management	×		
Competitor tracking	×		
Qualify and convert a Lead to an Opportunity	×		
Convert an Activity to an Opportunity	×		
Opportunity tracking	×		
Marketing lists	×		
Quick Campaigns	×		
Marketing campaigns	×		
Facility/equipment management	×		
Define and configure business units	×		
Define and configure teams	×		
Define and configure services, resources, and work hours	×		

*Actions can be performed only against records corresponding to entities included in the use rights.

**Requires a Yammer Enterprise license.

TIP

We strongly recommend that you test your system against the use cases described in Table 29.1. As previously noted, there is no mechanism for licensing verification, but Microsoft has committed to rolling out this feature (it is role based), and when it comes, it may render users unable to do their job.

Microsoft CRM 2016 uses named licenses (or user CALs) as well as machine licenses (or device CALs) as its licensing model. Named licenses require that every user who accesses Microsoft CRM 2016 must have a license. If a user leaves the company or no longer needs to use the CRM, the license can be transferred to another individual; however, the previous individual then no longer has access to Microsoft CRM 2016. Machine licenses allow a single computer to be licensed to Microsoft CRM 2016, and multiple users can use the same machine, provided that they aren't accessing it simultaneously. This is a significant improvement with regard to licensing when you consider call centers or similar organizations that operate around the clock. Named and machine CALs can be mixed in a deployment.

In addition to the licensing types previously described, Microsoft also allows you to manage the access mode for Microsoft CRM 2016:

NOTE

The access mode was the licensing model for Microsoft Dynamics CRM 2011.

▶ **Read-Write**—Full system functionality is granted to a user with this type of access. These users have full system access and full permission to modify records, limited only by the security role and privileges set for them.

▶ **Limited-Use**—This CAL is a read-only CAL and comes in two options: administrative and read-only. With this access, users can view all areas and records in Microsoft CRM 2016. However, they cannot make any changes. The administrative version allows users to modify records only in the Settings area.

NOTE

The access differences apply only when Microsoft CRM 2016 is accessed via the web client. To use the Outlook client, you must have the full CAL.

Figure 29.6 shows where on the user record the license type and access mode are set in the Settings > Security > Users section.

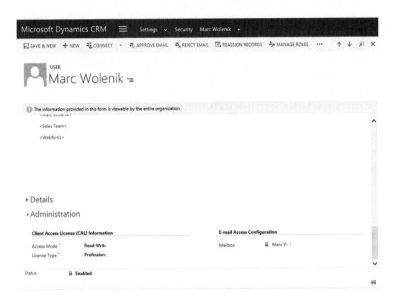

FIGURE 29.6   Microsoft Dynamics CRM CAL information.

To manage licenses in Microsoft CRM 2016, the Deployment Manager is used on the server. From the Deployment Manager, you can view and upgrade licenses by going to the License tab in the Microsoft Dynamics CRM Properties dialog (see Figure 29.7).

Microsoft Dynamics CRM Properties

General	Web Address	License	Usage Reporting

Administrative Users:	0
Enterprise CALs Required:	0
Device Enterprise CALs Required:	0
Professional CALs Required:	11
Device Professional CALs Required:	0
Basic CALs Required:	0
Device Basic CALs Required:	0
Essential CALs Required:	0
Device Essential CALs Required:	0
Server Licenses Required:	1
Product ID:	

Change Product Key

OK	Cancel	Apply

FIGURE 29.7   Microsoft Dynamics CRM Deployment Manager, License tab.

Microsoft has eliminated the need for the External Connector license in Microsoft Dynamics CRM 2016, and users can now access data outside their domain via custom interfaces at no additional charge.

Yammer, Bing, and SharePoint

With the exception of CRM Online for use of Bing Maps (it's allowed), licensing for Yammer, Bing, and SharePoint is separate from the Dynamics CRM 2016 licensing.

Purchasing Licensing

Microsoft makes CRM licensing available in the following:

▶ Retail

▶ Volume

You can purchase retail licensing from any vendor that sells software.

Microsoft makes volume licenses available based on the following criteria:

▶ Size of the purchasing organization

▶ Type of licensing desired

▶ Licensing term desired

▶ Payment options

When purchasing licenses through volume licensing, customers also can add Software Assurance (SA), which enables customers to upgrade their software if Microsoft releases a newer version within a certain time frame. Customers can therefore purchase software and not worry about it being obsolete and/or having to repurchase again when a new version comes out.

Volume licensing is broken down into four methods:

▶ **Open License**—Organizations that Microsoft considers small or midsized (usually with fewer than 250 computers) have the option to purchase licensing and receive benefits such as discounts, SA (mentioned previously), and easy deployment and management. The only restrictions on Open License are that a minimum of five licenses must be purchased at a time, and payment is expected at the time of the transaction. These specific licensing options are available with Open License:

　　▶ Open Value

　　▶ Open Business

　　▶ Open Volume

▶ Each option has different advantages, depending largely on the business needs.

29

> **NOTE**
>
> To learn more about these options, go to www.microsoft.com/licensing/programs/open/overview.mspx.

▶ **Select License**—Organizations have the option to create a payment plan and are given discounts based on the amount of software ordered. Generally, the Select License option is reserved for organizations that have more than 250 computers.

▶ **Enterprise Agreement**—Enterprise Agreement licensing is similar to the Select License option, but there are more significant discounts (usually reserved for larger orders).

▶ **Enterprise Subscription Agreement**—This is a subscription-based model similar to the Enterprise Agreement option. However, because the software is not purchased, it offers discounts at a greater rate. Again, this option is usually reserved for organizations with more than 250 computers.

> **TIP**
>
> Although you can purchase the Microsoft CRM 2016 licenses via retail methods, we recommend purchasing licensing through Microsoft volume licensing rather than retail if possible.

If you are a developer or an independent software vendor (ISV), or if you are interested in enhancing or working with some of the features of Microsoft CRM 2016, you might want to consider acquiring an MSDN subscription license, which includes a copy of CRM for development purposes.

> **NOTE**
>
> You can find more information about the MSDN program at www.microsoft.com/msdn.

Windows Users

Microsoft Windows has separate CAL requirements and, hence, can place restrictions on Microsoft CRM users. Carefully consider this when planning the infrastructure.

Single- Versus Multiple-Server Deployment

You can deploy Microsoft Dynamics CRM across multiple servers or on a single server. Although the method of deployment depends on your system requirements and server availability, some restrictions govern which version you can deploy and how you can do so.

Single-Server Deployment

In a single-server deployment, a single server can perform all these functions:

- ▶ Domain controller
- ▶ Microsoft Dynamics CRM Server
- ▶ SQL Server
- ▶ SQL Server Reporting Services (SSRS)

It is important to consider these functions when planning a deployment because the resource requirements for any one of these functions can be extensive. Therefore, we recommend considering a multiple-server deployment whenever you might be using the server for more than just Microsoft Dynamics CRM.

Microsoft Dynamics CRM 2016 Workgroup Edition is limited to a single computer running Microsoft Dynamics CRM Server, so it is the most common usage of a single-server deployment and is limited to five users.

> **NOTE**
>
> We do not extensively cover the differences between the Workgroup and Professional Server in this book because they are minimal, and most of our readers are deploying and configuring Professional Server.

Multiple-Server Deployments

Microsoft CRM Server can be spread across multiple servers during deployment (and later, if necessary). Having multiple servers offers these benefits:

- ▶ Scalability
- ▶ Performance
- ▶ Server resource allocation and control
- ▶ Shortened disaster recovery time
- ▶ Server roles

Server roles provide the capability to deploy specific services and components to different computers for scaling and performance benefits.

29

You can select three predefined server role groupings when installing Microsoft Dynamics CRM under the custom setup process, as shown in Figure 29.8. By default, all three server role groupings are installed with a typical install:

▶ The Front End Server role provides the Microsoft Dynamics CRM web user interface and services.

▶ The Back End Server role provides asynchronous services, such as the Workflow and Bulk Email services and the Sandbox Processing Service to run code with partial trusts security restrictions.

▶ The Deployment Administration Server role provides the tools and services necessary to manage CRM deployments and organizations.

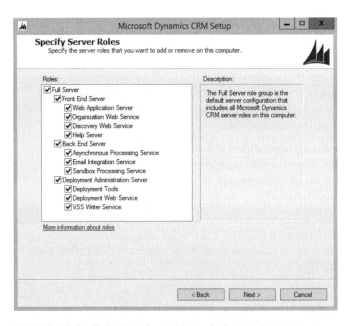

FIGURE 29.8   Role grouping options during custom setup.

The Front End Server role is divided into the following components:

▶ **Web Application Server**—Provides the necessary components and web services needed to run the web application server and to connect the CRM Outlook client that is used to connect users to Microsoft Dynamics CRM data.

▶ **Organization Web Service**—Installs the components needed to run the Microsoft Dynamics CRM external applications that use the methods described in the Microsoft CRM software development kit (SDK).

▶ **Discovery Web Service**—Installs the components required for users to find the organization of which they are members in a multi-tenant deployment.

▶ **Help Server**—Provides the components needed to make Microsoft Dynamics CRM Help available to users.

The Back End Server role is divided into the following components:

▶ **Asynchronous Processing Service**—Processes the queued asynchronous events, including the following:

  ▶ Workflow

  ▶ Data import

  ▶ Bulk email

▶ **Email Integration Service**—Sends and receives email messages when connected to an external email server.

▶ **Sandbox Processing Service**—Provides an isolated partial trust environment to run custom plug-in codes or workflows in a more secure environment.

The Deployment Administration Server role is divided into the following components:

▶ **Deployment Tools**—Installs the Deployment Manager tools and the components required to manage the deployment by using the methods described in the SDK, such as creating an organization or removing a Deployment Administrator role from a user.

▶ **Deployment Web Service**—Provides the service needed to deploy and manage organizations and manage general deployment configuration setting, using the Microsoft SDK automated deployment frameworks.

▶ **VSS Writer Service**—Provides an interface for backup and restore of Microsoft Dynamics CRM data by using Windows Server Volume Shadow Copy Service (VSS) infrastructure.

29

TIP

Keep in mind that no role exists specifically for workflow services. Instead, you must deploy the Asynchronous Processing Service, which handles workflow.

Another consideration related to multiple-server deployments is the Microsoft CRM LAN topology. The topology should include Microsoft Dynamics CRM Server as well as both Active Directory and SQL Server on the same LAN, primarily because of the large amount of network traffic that they create and use. Failure to have a permanent high-speed network connection between any of these computers can seriously affect performance and possibly cause data corruption.

> **NOTE**
>
> Microsoft no longer recommends a team (two-server) topology with Microsoft Dynamics CRM 2016, and the Division topology, which was previously five servers, is now up to six distributed servers.

Microsoft's recommended topology is one of the following:

▶ **Division topology** (six servers, all running Windows Server):

　▶ Computer 1: Domain controller

　▶ Computer 2: Secondary domain controller

　▶ Computer 3: Microsoft Dynamics CRM server

　▶ Computer 4: SQL Server and CRM Reporting Extensions

　▶ Computer 5: Microsoft Exchange Server

　▶ Computer 6: AD FS (typically used for, and required by, CRM IFDs)

> **NOTE**
>
> Microsoft further recommends a separate server for running mobile applications.

▶ **Multiforest and multidomain Active Directory topology**

For very large user bases that span multiple domains and, in some cases, forests, the following configuration is supported:

▶ **Forest X: Domain A: Perimeter subnet**

　▶ Network Load Balanced (NLB) virtual server consisting of the following two nodes:

　　▶ Front End Server: Running Windows Server and Microsoft Dynamics CRM Server with the Front End Server role

　　▶ Front End Server: Another Windows Server running Microsoft Dynamics CRM Server with the Front End Server role

　▶ AD FS Server: Running on Windows Server as the Internet-facing claims-based authentication security token service

▶ **Forest X: Domain A: Intranet**

    ▶ NLB virtual server consisting of the following two nodes:

        ▶ Windows Server, Microsoft SQL Server Reporting Services, and Microsoft Dynamics CRM Reporting Extensions for SQL Server Reporting Services (Server X)

        ▶ Windows Server, Microsoft SQL Server Reporting Services, and Microsoft Dynamics CRM Reporting Extensions for SQL Server Reporting Services (Server Y)

    ▶ NLB virtual server consisting of the following nodes:

        ▶ Front End Server: Running Windows Server and Microsoft Dynamics CRM Server with the Front End Server role

        ▶ Front End Server: Another Windows Server running Microsoft Dynamics CRM Server with the Front End Server role

    ▶ Microsoft SQL Server failover cluster running the following nodes:

        ▶ Windows Server, SQL Server database engine (Server X)

        ▶ Windows Server, SQL Server database engine (Server Y)

        ▶ Windows Server running the Asynchronous Service server role

        ▶ Windows Server running the Sandbox Processing Service server role

        ▶ Windows Server running the AD FS Windows Server role

        ▶ Windows Server running Microsoft SharePoint (required for document management)

▶ **Forest Y: Domain B: Intranet**

    ▶ Exchange Server failover cluster consisting of the following two nodes:

        ▶ Windows Server running Exchange Server (Server X)

        ▶ Windows Server running Exchange Server (Server Y)

Setting Up SQL Server

In order to install Dynamics CRM 2016, you must have SQL Server installed.

Follow these steps to install SQL Server 2014:

  1. Start SQL Server 2014 Setup, and you see SQL Server Installation Center page, shown in Figure 29.9.

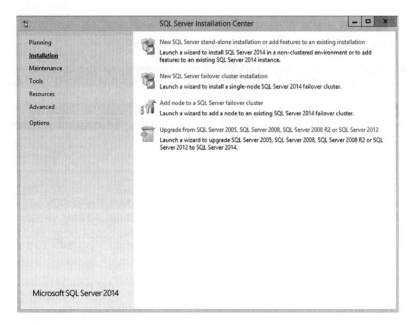

FIGURE 29.9   SQL Server Installation Center page.

2. Select Installation from the left side of the screen and then select the first option on the right, which says New SQL Server Stand-alone Installation or Add Features to an Existing Installation. The Product Key page, shown in Figure 29.10, appears.

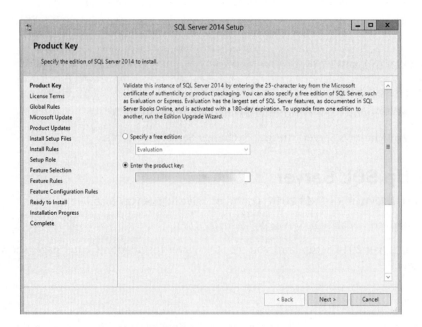

FIGURE 29.10   Product Key page.

3. Enter the product key, if necessary, and click Next. The License Terms page, shown in Figure 29.11, appears.

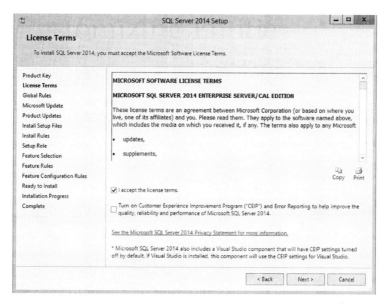

FIGURE 29.11   License Terms page.

4. Accept the license terms and click Next. The Microsoft Update page, shown in Figure 29.12, appears.

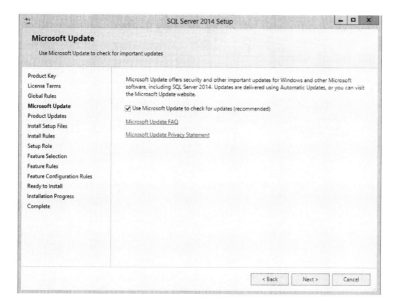

FIGURE 29.12   Microsoft Update page.

5. Select the Use Microsoft Update to Check for Updates (Recommended) check box and click Next. The Install Rules page, shown in Figure 29.13, appears.

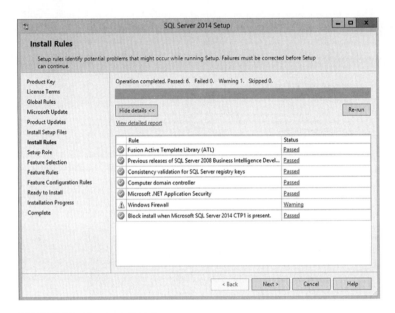

FIGURE 29.13   Install Rules page.

6. When the initial validation completes, click Next. The Setup Role page, shown in Figure 29.14, appears.

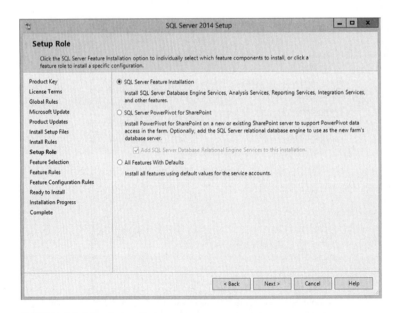

FIGURE 29.14   Setup Role page.

7. Select SQL Server Feature Installation and click Next. The Feature Selection page, shown in Figure 29.15, appears.

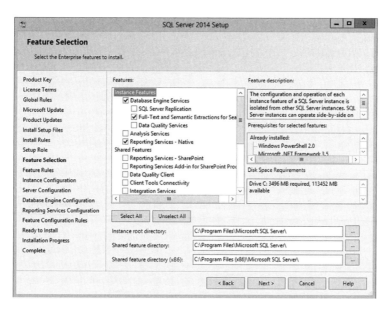

FIGURE 29.15   Feature Selection page.

8. Select Database Engine Services, Full Text and Semantic Extractions for Search, Reporting Service—Native, and Management Tools Basic and then click Next. The Instance Configuration page, shown in Figure 29.16, appears.

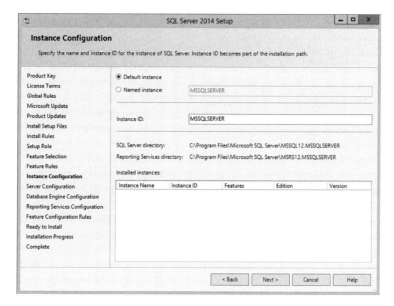

FIGURE 29.16   Instance Configuration page.

9. Leave Default Instance selected and click Next. The Server Configuration page, shown in Figure 29.17, appears.

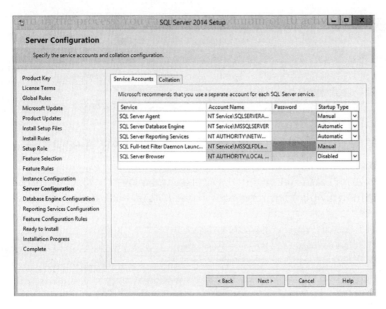

FIGURE 29.17   Server Configuration page.

10. Change the reporting service account to NT Authority\Network Service and click Next. The Database Engine Configuration page, shown in Figure 29.18, appears.

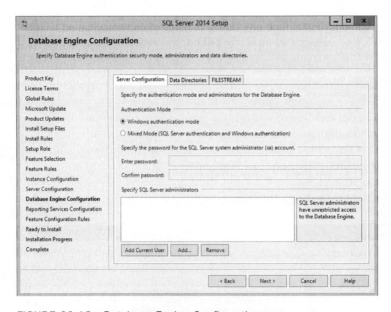

FIGURE 29.18   Database Engine Configuration page.

11. Click Add Current User and then click Next. The Reporting Services Configuration page, shown in Figure 29.19, appears.

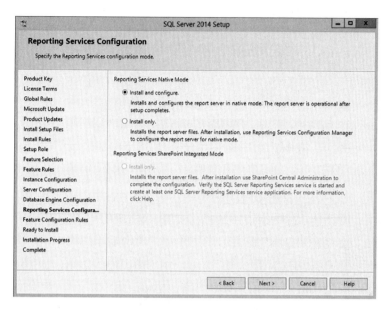

FIGURE 29.19   Reporting Services Configuration page.

12. Select Install and Configure and click Next. The Ready to Install page, shown in Figure 29.20, appears.

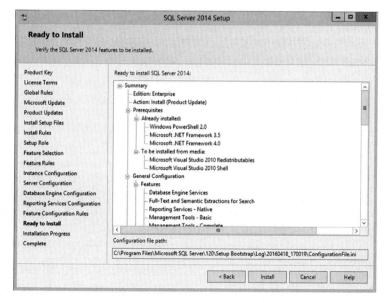

FIGURE 29.20   Ready to Install page.

13. Click Install to continue.

14. When the installation is complete, as shown in Figure 29.21, click Close. Close the SQL Server Installation Center.

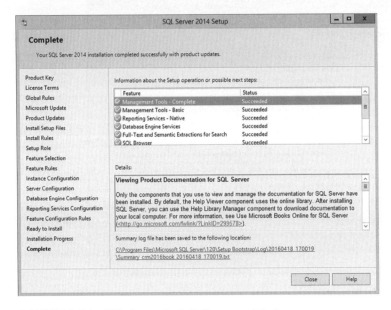

FIGURE 29.21   SQL Server installation completed.

Dynamics CRM Setup Process

When installing Microsoft Dynamics CRM for the first time, it is a good idea to confirm that all the requirements for Microsoft Dynamics CRM listed earlier in this chapter, under "Hardware and Software Considerations," are configured properly, are running, and have the most updated service packs.

In addition, you must have the following as part of the Microsoft CRM Dynamics Server Setup process:

▶ Microsoft CRM license key

▶ Desired Microsoft Dynamics CRM server type (application, platform, or both)

▶ Organization name

▶ An Active Directory OU with either domain admin permissions or full permissions on that OU

▶ Organization friendly name

▶ Desired base currency

▶ Location/port of the Microsoft Dynamics CRM website

▶ Location of Microsoft SQL Server

▶ Location of SQL Server Reporting Services report server

▶ Email router server name (optional)

It is not necessary to have the Microsoft Dynamics CRM server set up to install the Microsoft CRM Dynamics Outlook clients; however, you cannot configure the clients with the Microsoft Dynamics CRM server until the server is set up.

Microsoft Dynamics CRM Server Setup

When setting up Microsoft Dynamics CRM, it is recommended that you set up the server first and then the email router. Although you can install the email router before you install Microsoft Dynamics CRM, it is recommended that you first install Microsoft Dynamics CRM because the service accounts that are necessary to run the Email Router Service are automatically added when you specify the incoming email server during the setup process.

▶ Refer to **CHAPTER 20**, "Email Configuration," for more information about the email router.

Microsoft Dynamics CRM Installation

Follow these steps to complete the Microsoft Dynamics CRM installation:

1. Start the Setup process by launching the Splash.exe file. The Setup screen shown in Figure 29.22 appears.

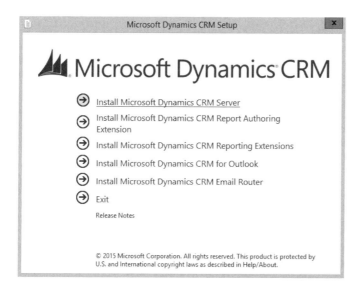

FIGURE 29.22   Microsoft Dynamics CRM Setup screen.

2. Click the first option, Install Microsoft Dynamics CRM Server. The Setup screen shown in Figure 29.23 appears, and you have the option to download updated installation files.

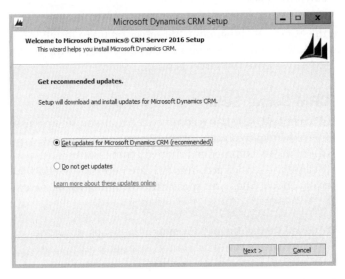

FIGURE 29.23   Microsoft Dynamics CRM setup: getting recommended updates.

TIP

Although you can update Microsoft Dynamics CRM after you've installed it, it is recommended that you get the updates from Microsoft at this point in the Setup process. They are then automatically downloaded to ensure that your installation goes smoothly.

3. Select Get Updates for Microsoft Dynamics CRM (Recommended) and click Next to continue.

4. In the Product Key Information page that appears, enter your license key (see Figure 29.24). When you have finished entering your license key, a message appears with your license status summary; it should match your license agreement from Microsoft. Click Next to continue.

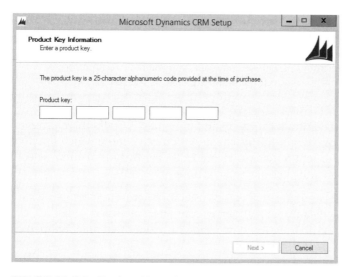

FIGURE 29.24   Product Key Information page.

5. Accept the license agreement and click I Accept to continue. The installer then performs a system check to see whether required components necessary for the installation to continue are installed. If you are not missing any components necessary for the installer to continue, you do not see this screen.

6. If you have missing installer components, as shown in see Figure 29.25, click Install to have them installed. After Setup confirms that all required components are installed, click Next to continue.

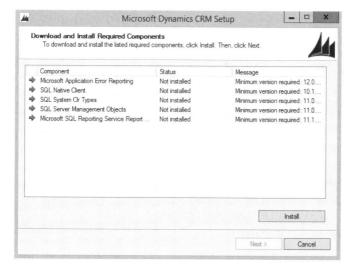

FIGURE 29.25   Microsoft Dynamics CRM installer check for required components.

29

> **NOTE**
>
> This check is for the installer only. If you are missing or have misconfigured required Microsoft Dynamics CRM components, such as SQL Server Reporting Services, you might be able to continue from this screen; however, you will receive an error when the installer performs a system requirements check as the last step.

7. Specify the setup installation location on and optionally install different server roles (as mentioned previously in this chapter). You can choose which (or all) server roles you would like to set up (refer to Figure 29.8). For this installation, select a Full Server installation and click Next to continue.

8. Select the SQL Server computer that will be used for Microsoft Dynamics CRM (see Figure 29.26). By default, no SQL Server computers are listed. However, clicking the Refresh option next to the drop-down shows the ones that are identified on the network.

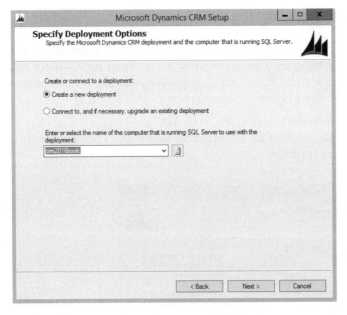

FIGURE 29.26   Microsoft Dynamics CRM SQL Server setup.

In addition, by default, Create a New Deployment is selected. If you already have an existing Microsoft Dynamics CRM deployment, you can select Connect to, and if Necessary, Upgrade an Existing Deployment, and Setup uses that deployment. If you selected a deployment from a previous version of CRM, this option also upgrades the deployment. Click Next to continue.

9. Select the Active Directory OU to be used for Microsoft Dynamics CRM (see Figure 29.27). Clicking Browse connects to Active Directory, which allows you to select the OU. Click Next to continue.

It is recommended to have a dedicated OU for the installation.

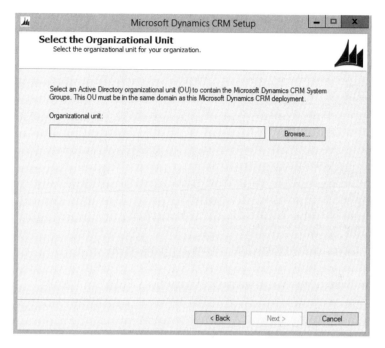

FIGURE 29.27   Microsoft Dynamics CRM select organizational unit setup.

It is important to have domain administrator rights to perform the deployment mentioned in step 9. If full domain administrator rights aren't available, visit this link for the minimum permissions necessary: http://support.microsoft.com/kb/946686. (Although this site is for CRM 4.0, it still applies for CRM 2016.)

10. Select the service accounts to be used for Microsoft Dynamics CRM (see Figure 29.28). Although it is recommended to use different accounts with minimum privileges for each service, you can use the default Network Service account for this quick installation. If you use domain accounts, you need to configure the SPN (service principal name) for each domain account. Click Next to continue.

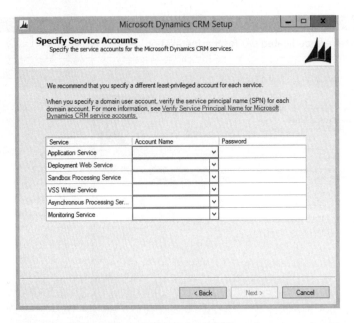

FIGURE 29.28   Microsoft Dynamics CRM service accounts setup.

11. Select the website where you want Microsoft Dynamics CRM to be installed (see Figure 29.29).

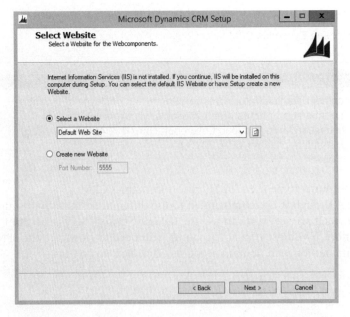

FIGURE 29.29   Microsoft Dynamics CRM website selection for installation.

By default, the application is loaded onto the default website using server bindings (port) 80. However, if Create New Website is selected (see Figure 29.30), the website is created using server bindings on the port you enter in the text box (by default, 5555). The difference is whether you want to dedicate your port 80 for Microsoft Dynamics CRM's exclusive use; other web applications will then not be able to use that port.

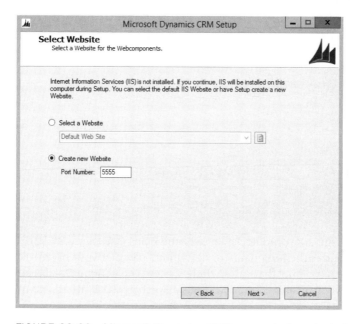

FIGURE 29.30   Microsoft Dynamics CRM new website selected.

CAUTION

Because port 80 is the default port for web traffic, carefully consider your options when selecting this setting. If you're unsure or you have other web-based applications that you are running (or would like to run from this server), we recommend selecting the Create New Website option.

---

12. Click Next to continue.

13. Enter the email router server name (see Figure 29.31) if you're configuring it. (With server-side synchronization, you may not need to use the email router at all.) The email router can be installed on a server with Microsoft Exchange or on a computer that has a connection to an Exchange server. In addition, because Exchange is not required, you can install the email router on any POP3-compliant email server. If you elect to install the email router later, leave the field blank and click Next.

▶ For more information on how the email router works, **SEE CHAPTER 20**.

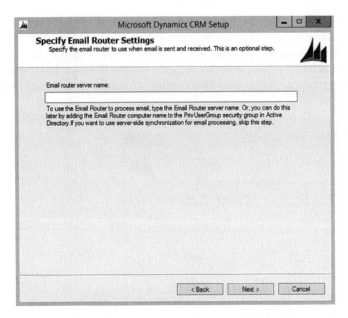

FIGURE 29.31   Microsoft Dynamics CRM email router settings setup.

14. Fill in the Display Name and Unique Database Name fields (see Figure 29.32). The Display Name field is the long name or descriptive name of your organization, and it has a 250-character limit that can include spaces. The Unique Database Name field is the name of your organization, and it has a 30-character limit and cannot include spaces.

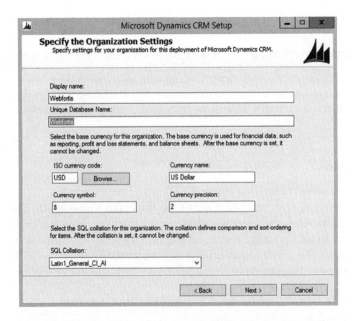

FIGURE 29.32   Microsoft Dynamics CRM organization settings.

Click Browse, and you see the window shown in Figure 29.33 From it select USD. This information is necessary for Microsoft Dynamics CRM to create an organizational database. Click Next to continue.

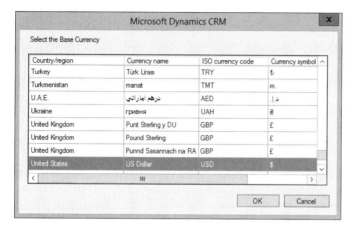

FIGURE 29.33   Microsoft Dynamics CRM ISO currency code selection screen.

15. Enter the Reporting Services server (see Figure 29.34). As indicated, make sure to specify the Report Server URL and not the Report Manager URL. If you're unsure of the difference, you can open a browser window and enter the URL to verify that it is not the Report Manager URL. Click Next to continue.

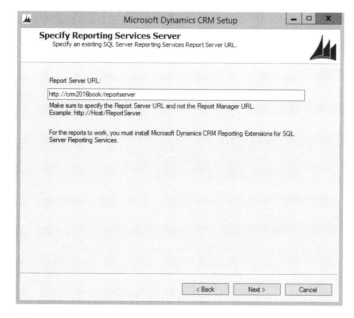

FIGURE 29.34   Microsoft Dynamics CRM Reporting Services server settings.

16. Select whether you want to participate in the Customer Experience Improvement Program (CEIP) and click Next to continue.

17. The last step of the setup involves the system requirements (see Figure 29.35). This is where the proper installation, configuration, and status of each of the following are confirmed:

▶ **Microsoft Windows Operating System**—Version and service pack status. Additional checks include pending restart status.

▶ **Microsoft CRM Server User Input**—License, organization, and ISO specification.

▶ **Internet Information Services (IIS)**—Version and accessibility.

▶ **Microsoft SQL Server**—Version and service pack status.

▶ **Microsoft SQL Server Reporting Services**—Version and service pack status. Also checks the specified URL entered because part of the setup can be resolved to the Report Server.

▶ **Active Directory**—Whether Active Directory is accessible and whether the specified security account has the necessary permissions.

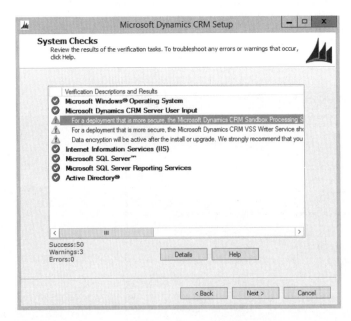

FIGURE 29.35   Microsoft Dynamics CRM system requirements verification.

If any errors arise with these components, you must correct them before continuing with the installation. When everything is resolved, click Next to continue and, if necessary, click Next after you see a prompt to restart the port sharing service.

When you have completed the Microsoft Dynamics CRM setup, you can access the application by opening your browser and navigating to the URL you selected previously. Usually, this is http://localhost or http://localhost:5555, depending on the bindings selected.

When the setup completes, you are prompted to launch the Reporting Extensions for SSRS Setup (see Figure 29.36).

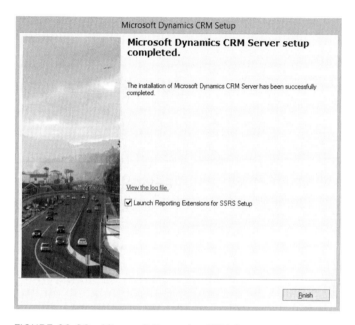

FIGURE 29.36   Microsoft Dynamics CRM Setup completed.

Additional Steps

After the server is set up, there are a few other tasks that either need to be completed for full functionality or are recommended, depending on the type of server installation you've selected.

Reporting Extensions for SSRS Setup

The Reporting Extensions for SSRS Setup is required for Microsoft Dynamics CRM reporting, and by default the Reporting Extensions for SSRS is installed as part of the Microsoft Dynamics CRM installation process. However, unlike with the email router, Microsoft Dynamics CRM Server setup must be completed before you install the Reporting Extensions for SSRS Setup as part of the installation. In addition, installation must be done on the computer that has the Microsoft SSRS that you will use for your installation of Microsoft Dynamics CRM.

To install the Reporting Extensions for SSRS Setup, you can either run the SetupSrsDataConnector.exe file found in the SrSDataConnector directory from the extracted CRM Server setup or by clicking Finish after the CRM Setup completes, provided that you have SSRS on the same server on which you have CRM installed when you checked the option to install this component. Either way, follow these steps:

1. When Reporting Extensions for SSRS Setup Wizard prompts you to download installation files (see Figure 29.37), click the Get Updates for Microsoft Dynamics CRM (Recommended) option and then click Next.

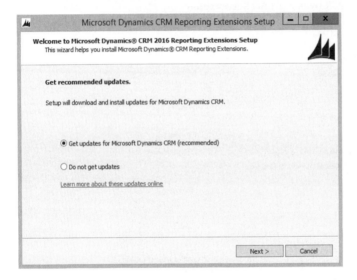

FIGURE 29.37   Getting recommended updates.

2. Accept the Microsoft Dynamics CRM Reporting Extensions license agreement by clicking I Accept.

3. Specify the name of the computer that stores the Microsoft Dynamics CRM SQL Server configuration database (see Figure 29.38). (The configuration database for Microsoft Dynamics CRM is named MSCRM_CONFIG.) Click Next.

FIGURE 29.38   Reporting Extensions for SSRS Setup database server configuration screen.

4. Specify the name of the SSRS instance (see Figure 29.39). The SSRS instance name is where you have the report server database installed. Click Next.

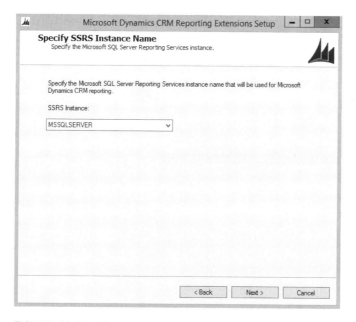

FIGURE 29.39   SSRS instance configuration screen.

29

5. Select the location where you want the files to be installed and click Next (see Figure 29.40).

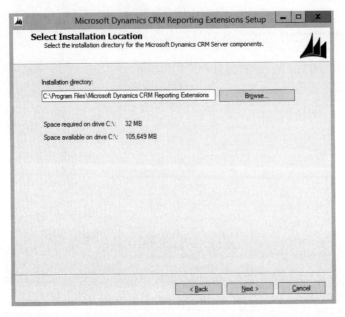

FIGURE 29.40   Reporting Extensions for SSRS Setup installation location.

6. After the system requirements are verified, make any corrections needed and then click Next (see Figure 29.41).

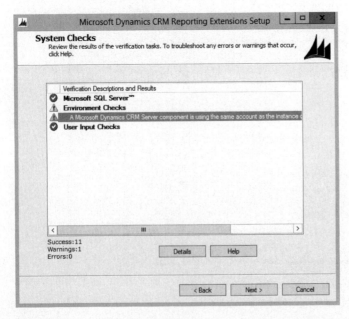

FIGURE 29.41   Reporting Extensions for SSRS Setup System check results.

7. Continue through the rest of the wizard, and when you're finished, the Microsoft Dynamics CRM Data Connector is installed and displays a completion screen. Click Finish. If you encounter any errors here, be sure to update the server with the latest Windows components before re-trying installation.

Deployment Manager

To create new organizations and manage your licenses and database, you need to use the Deployment Manager. You can find the Dynamics CRM Deployment Manager on the CRM server by going to Start, searching for CRM, and selecting Deployment Manager (see Figure 29.42).

FIGURE 29.42   Location of the Deployment Manager.

In order to launch Deployment Manager, you must be a member of the Deployment Administrators group; otherwise, you will receive an error when you try to launch it. By default, the user who performs the installation of Microsoft Dynamics CRM is added to this group.

With the Deployment Manager, you can manage other members of the Deployment Administrators group and set up and manage organizations, your servers, and licenses (see Figure 29.43).

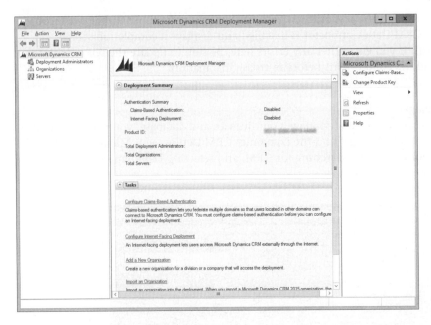

FIGURE 29.43   Deployment Manager.

You add users to the Deployment Administrators group through the Deployment Manager. You add them by right-clicking the Deployment Administrators node and selecting New Deployment Administrator.

Provisioning a New Organization

To provision a new organization, follow these steps:

TIP

You must have a Microsoft Dynamics CRM Server version that supports multiple organizations to add new organizations to your system. (That is, you cannot use the Workgroup edition.)

---

1. Right-click Organizations and select New Organization, as shown in see Figure 29.44.

FIGURE 29.44   Adding a New Organization.

2. Complete the required fields in the New Organization Wizard by entering the display name, unique database name, selecting a base currency via the Browse button, and selecting a currency from the displayed currency options. When you're ready to continue, your form should look similar to the one in Figure 29.45. Click Next to continue. (For more information about these fields, see step 14 in the "Microsoft Dynamics CRM Server Setup" section, earlier in this chapter.)

FIGURE 29.45   New Organization Wizard.

3. Select whether you want to participate in the Customer Experience Improvement Program and then click Next to continue.

4. Enter the location of your SQL Server computer (see Figure 29.46), which by default is the computer specified during the setup where the MSCRM_Config is located. Click Next to continue.

FIGURE 29.46   New Organization Wizard—Select SQL Server page.

5. Enter the URL for your SSRS server (see Figure 29.47) and click Next. The system performs a system requirements check on the organization information, SQL Server, and Reporting Services information entered.

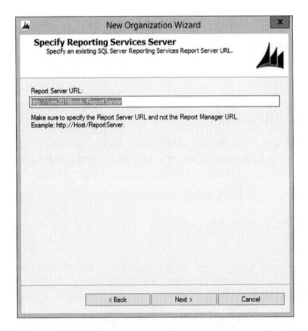

FIGURE 29.47   Entering the SSRS server URL.

6. If there are any problems (such as an incorrect SSRS URL), correct them and then click Next. The entered information is presented for a final review.

7. If any corrections need to be made, you click Back and make them. Click Create to create the organization. The system provisions the new organization (which can take several minutes), and when complete, returns a confirmation that the new organization has been created. It can then be managed in the Deployment Manager.

Within the Organization node, you can also delete, edit, disable, or enable an existing organization. Note that an organization must first be disabled before it can be deleted. In addition, a deleted organization has its organization information deleted only from the configuration database; the organization database remains and must be removed manually via SQL tools.

The Edit options enable you to easily change an organization's display name, the SQL Server, and the SRS Server. This is usually done when a database is moved to a new server.

The Server option displays information about the server, Microsoft Dynamics CRM version, and the role (see Figure 29.48). The License option displays information relevant to the Microsoft Dynamics version and users.

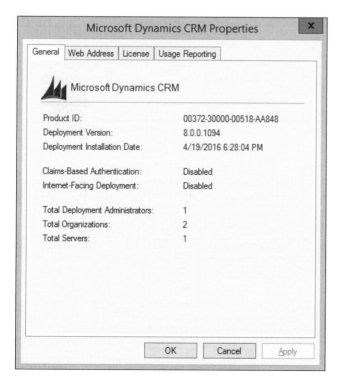

FIGURE 29.48   Deployment Manager displaying licensing information.

If you select the root node that says Microsoft Dynamics CRM and click Properties, you get a summary of the licenses allocated within the License tab (as shown previously, in Figure 29.7).

▶ The Deployment Manager is also used to configure claims-based authentication and IFD. For information about how to perform these configurations, refer to **CHAPTER 28**.

Microsoft Dynamics CRM Clients

With a fully functional web browser interface as well as the Microsoft Dynamics CRM Outlook client, users can choose how they want to work with Microsoft Dynamics CRM.

Regardless of which client you choose to work with, you should add the CRM website as a trusted site on client computers to avoid any security messages or prompts for authentication. To do this, complete the following steps:

1. Go to Start > Control Panel > Internet Options.

2. Select the Security tab.

3. Click Trusted Sites and then click the Sites button.

4. On the Trusted Sites dialog, enter the URL for your CRM website. Be sure to include the http:// or https:// if your server uses a secure (SSL) connection. Uncheck Require Server Verification (https:) for all sites in this zone if you are not running CRM over a secure connection.

5. Click Close and OK to close the Internet Options dialog.

You are now set to install or configure one of the Microsoft CRM clients.

Browser Clients

When accessing Microsoft Dynamics CRM from a browser, users merely have to enter the URL for their Microsoft CRM installation. A default installation URL consists of http://*servername*:5555 or http://*servername*, where *servername* is the name of the CRM server. When users are authenticated on the same network, Microsoft Dynamics CRM loads in the browser automatically. If users are connecting to Microsoft CRM Server via the Internet, by default they receive a Microsoft Windows authentication request consisting of username and password after they request use of the application; however, you can also use forms (IFD) or passport authentication.

▶ Refer to **CHAPTER 28** for more information about how to access the CRM server when IFD is enabled.

Outlook Client

The Outlook client is available in two different modes:

▶ CRM for Outlook

▶ CRM for Outlook with Offline Access

As explained earlier in this chapter, the versions are essentially the same, and only one installation package exists for both.

▶ For more detailed instructions about installing and configuring the CRM Outlook client, refer to **CHAPTER 19**.

Upgrading from Earlier Versions

Microsoft has made the process of upgrading from Dynamics 2015 to 2016 fairly painless. If you are on a version of Dynamics that is earlier than 2015, you will have to upgrade in steps in order to use Dynamics 2016.

CRM for Outlook Client

Microsoft does not require a client upgrade of the CRM for Outlook client for Dynamics 2015 when using Dynamics CRM 2016, but the following conditions apply:

▶ You must be on Microsoft Dynamics CRM 2015 Update Rollup 1 or later.

▶ If you don't upgrade, you will not be able to use the Go Offline feature due to the changes in the database.

When upgrading the client, an in-place cross-architecture upgrade is not supported and requires that you use existing architecture (32-bit or 64-bit) to upgrade or do an uninstall and then a reinstall.

Server

The only supported upgrade to Microsoft CRM 2016 is an upgrade from Microsoft Dynamics CRM 2015. If you're running a version of Microsoft CRM prior to 2015, you must first upgrade to 2015 and then to 2016.

> **NOTE**
>
> Upgrading Microsoft CRM 1.0, 1.2, 3.0, 4.0, or 2011 to Microsoft 2016 is not discussed because that topic is beyond the scope of this book. However, *Microsoft Dynamics CRM 2013 Unleashed* does address this.

Upgrade Options

There are several options to consider when looking at upgrades. However, Microsoft officially recommends one of the following three options:

▶ **Migrate by using a new instance of SQL Server**—We recommend this option for upgrading from Microsoft Dynamics CRM 2015 to Microsoft Dynamics CRM 2016. Although this option requires a different computer for Microsoft Dynamics CRM 2016 and a different instance of SQL Server, it provides the least amount of potential downtime for Microsoft Dynamics CRM users because the Microsoft Dynamics CRM 2015 deployment can remain functioning until the upgrade is completed and verified.

▶ **Migrate by using the same instance of SQL Server**—This option requires a different computer for Microsoft Dynamics CRM Server 2016 but upgrades in-place the configuration and default organization databases, using the same instance of SQL Server. If issues occur during the upgrade, you must roll back to Microsoft Dynamics CRM 2015 to avoid significant downtime.

▶ **In-place upgrade**—Although this option does not require a different computer for Microsoft Dynamics CRM Server 2016 or a different instance of SQL Server, it poses the greatest risk if upgrade issues occur because a rollback and reinstall of Microsoft Dynamics CRM are required to avoid potential downtime.

Considerations When Upgrading

Upgrading is never a one-click operation, and many things need to be considered when developing an upgrade plan. These are a few of the main points that should be considered:

▶ **Attributes**—If you have more than 1,023 attributes (fields) for any entity, you must remove any above that threshold.

▶ **JavaScript**—Run the Custom Code Validation tool (available for download from Microsoft.com) to test where and how your code might need to be refactored.

Although Microsoft Dynamics CRM 2016 supports an in-place upgrade, the following steps are recommended as part of the upgrade process:

1. Back up the existing Microsoft CRM 2015 databases. This includes the SQL Server configuration CRM database and all the organizations' databases for CRM. The database names are formatted as *organizationname*_MSCRM and MSCRM_CONFIG.

2. Back up all reports, including any custom and modified reports from the existing Microsoft Dynamics CRM application. This can be done by performing a backup of the Report Server database.

3. Export and back up all customizations from the Microsoft CRM 2015 application. This needs to be done from the CRM web interface by going to Settings > Customizations > Export Customizations.

When you have completed and verified these steps, follow the steps previously outlined in the "Microsoft Dynamics CRM Server Setup" section of this chapter to upgrade the Microsoft CRM 2015 server to a Microsoft Dynamics CRM 2016 server. After the installer completes its system check and installs any missing components, it automatically recognizes that Microsoft CRM 2015 is installed.

By default, Microsoft CRM 2015 is upgraded with both application and platform server roles as part of the upgrade.

In a multi-tenant environment, when upgrading a Microsoft CRM 2015 Enterprise version with multiple organizations, only the default organization is migrated, and other organizations are disabled, and you have to go to the Deployment Manager and upgrade them one by one.

TIP

If you encounter any issues not mentioned here, check the setup log that is created when the server installation completes.

Setting Up Your Business in Microsoft Dynamics CRM 2016

Regardless of which version and platform of Microsoft Dynamics CRM you're working with, after you finish setting up your system, you need to configure your business. Microsoft Dynamics CRM is extremely flexible and can be made to work with nearly any business. When working with Microsoft Dynamics CRM Online, the wizard walks you through many of the setup steps. However, there are still many things that can be configured, and it is helpful to know about the options if you want to change the configurations. If you're not using Microsoft Dynamics CRM Online, you need to work with these settings. The following are some of the things you need to configure:

▶ **Organizations**—When considering working with your organization, consider the hierarchy of your organization as well as how it is structured. Within Microsoft Dynamics CRM, there are options to break out your organization by business units, territories, and sites. When thinking about how to configure your organization, it is helpful to spend some time preparing how it should be structured within the Microsoft Dynamics CRM 2016 framework—both how it is now and how you believe it will be in six months to two years in the future.

▶ **Business units**—Business units are important and can be used by even the smallest organizations to easily control access and divide records. Although business units can be changed or deleted after they have been created, it is ideal to define what is needed during initial deployment.

CAUTION

Keep in mind that business units must be disabled before they can be deleted. It is a good idea to think about how they will work within your organization.

▶ **Users**—Because Microsoft Dynamics CRM 2016 employs user-based licensing, determining who will need access to the system is important because it will affect not only the cost but also how users in the system will work together. For example, if only customer service people are using the system, it is unlikely that you'll be using the Leads functionality because that is mostly a function of salespeople. Another example is having both customer service representatives and salespeople in the system but not marketing staff; then the Microsoft Dynamics CRM Marketing functionality is likely to be underutilized.

29

TIP

It is a good idea to outline who needs to use the system immediately as well as which users you anticipate being involved later on so that you can plan for both growth and other licensing requirements. We have found that initial estimates of users are usually light because the system is so powerful and easy to use that when users see it, they want to work with it. With the new licensing options for Microsoft Dynamics CRM 2016, having many users isn't as cost-prohibitive as it was with earlier versions.

TIP

Although users are established in the system, they can be deactivated, and other users can use the license.

CAUTION

Note that the practice of letting someone use the license of a deactivated user is not recommended for routine use. This practice should be used only when users leave the company or no longer need access to the Microsoft Dynamics CRM system.

▶ **Customers**—Microsoft Dynamics CRM defines customers in two ways: as Account and Contact entities. These entities can easily be renamed if your organization requires it (for example, Company and Customer instead of Account and Contact). Working with customers is explained fully in Chapter 6, "Working with Customers." However, at this point, it is important to consider the accounts and contacts structure when migrating from other CRM applications because other systems might use a different hierarchy, and data will need to be migrated using this structure. If this is your case, consider referential accounts and contacts where accounts have a parent/child relationship or work with business units instead. (For example, there might be an account called Joe's Auto that has two subaccounts called Joe's Auto–Retail and Joe's Auto–Commercial, and there might be contacts that report directly to either of these, but none to the master parent account of Joe's Auto.)

▶ In addition, although both accounts and contacts are considered customers, you will likely have a mix of records contained within these entities. For example, your Account records might have supplier/vendor records, as well as their contact information.

▶ **Roles**—Microsoft Dynamics CRM 2016 is role based, and every user must have a valid role to work within the system. This is outlined in Chapter 17, "Settings"; however, it is important to recognize the difference in roles that might exist between a user on the network and the same user in Microsoft Dynamics CRM 2016.

▶ The roles that come by default with Microsoft Dynamics CRM 2016 are well defined; however, be sure to review the permissions carefully when utilizing them. The most common cause of users having problems working within their system is permissions issues. In addition, be sure that the role you set for your users has the level of control that you expect.

▶ **Queues and teams**—Using queues and teams is a powerful way of setting up your system to ensure that record loads are leveled and records can be shared when required.

▶ **Email**—When setting up email with Microsoft Dynamics CRM 2016, a number of new options easily extend functionality, regardless of what you're using for your email server.

▶ **Auditing**—Auditing is an extremely powerful feature for managing and reporting data manipulation. This feature is configurable and needs to be enabled because it is disabled by default.

▶ **SharePoint integration**—SharePoint integration requires configuration of the system to a SharePoint server and provides an easy way to manage documents.

▶ For a complete list of all settings and configuration options, as well as more information related to everything in this list, refer to **CHAPTER 17**.

TIP

Be sure to carefully check your settings for email tracking. Occasionally, users set the tracking of emails to All for their mailbox and later find that their personal messages are appearing in Microsoft Dynamics CRM 2016. We generally recommend setting the All option only for dedicated mailboxes, such as support@yourdomain.com or sales@ yourdomain.com.

Summary

This chapter covers how to set up Microsoft Dynamics CRM 2016 On-Premises, with consideration given to both the architecture and the business. As you have learned, extensive planning is recommended, and understanding your options can make a difference between a successful implementation and an unsuccessful one.

NOTE

Microsoft guidance is available in the form of the Implementation Guide (IG), which is available for download from Microsoft.com. Either search for "Dynamics CRM IG" or go to www.microsoft.com/en-us/download/details.aspx?id=50039.

29

How to Get Support for Your System

As a vendor, Microsoft is responsible for providing support for Microsoft Dynamics CRM. It does this in a number of ways, some of which are slightly different for Online users than for On-Premises users:

▶ Service pack updates (On-Premises only)

▶ Hotfixes (On-Premises only)

▶ Hands-on support from Microsoft

▶ Referrals to Microsoft partners

This chapter covers all of these, but it is important to know and recognize that Microsoft offers support for anything on your system, provided that the following are all true:

▶ You have not placed the system in an unsupported state.

▶ The problem is repeatable.

▶ The issue is localized to Dynamics CRM and not related to anything having to do with ancillary products or processes.

In the event that any of these conditions have not been met, you might be out of luck with getting support from Microsoft. Let's look more closely at one of the most common items from the list: unsupported state.

A system is considered to be in an *unsupported state* when modifications have been made outside the software development kit (SDK) recommendations. The most common example that we've seen for this type of issue is an organization using code to do something that you can't do with the configuration user interface provided by Microsoft and not outlined in the SDK framework; it might be as simple as having code show or hide a field or change some of the formatting (for example, the background color) of a form. Although these changes might seem minimal, they require the development and deployment of JavaScript. Even though the code may run perfectly on the current Dynamics CRM implementation, Microsoft might roll out an update that causes the form user interface to differ slightly, thus resulting in an error in the code that users see. Users may be confused by the new error, and if the original developer of the code is no longer available, users may call Microsoft for help with the strange error message. Microsoft will likely review the system and provide feedback that the code as developed is not supported and that it needs to be removed.

> **NOTE**
>
> Microsoft will probably not provide help on how to fix the unsupported code; however, you might get lucky.

Other ways that you can potentially put your system into an unsupported state might include the following:

▶ Modification to the raw files of CRM, such as the .aspx or .html pages that reside on the server (On-Premises only)

▶ Direct SQL interaction (on any level) (On-Premises only)

If either of these problems has happened, you need to restore any of these modifications to their original state if you want to receive official Microsoft support.

Note that it is not illegal to make such modifications (in other words, it doesn't violate the Microsoft use rights), and sometimes circumstances require these types of changes. If the organization is aware of the risks associated with these changes and has anticipated the limitations on the support available (by having enough knowledge about the product or having retained competent partner assistance), Microsoft support is not critical.

> **CAUTION**
>
> Note that unsupported modifications are not recommended for all organizations and should only be made when/if all recommendations for unsupported code usage are heeded.

Online Support

Microsoft provides four different tiers of support for its Online customers:

▶ Basic Subscription

▶ Enhanced

▶ Professional Direct

▶ Premier for (Large Accounts Only)

An organization can select the support model that fits its business and budget when and how it likes.

Basic Subscription Support

Microsoft offers basic support for its online customers at no charge. The support covers most issues with the system (including troubleshooting the Outlook integration piece) and can be used as often as necessary (even on the same issue, if necessary). The specifics are as follows:

▶ **Cost**—Included

▶ **Community forums**—Included

▶ **Service dashboard**—Included

▶ **Access to self-help**—Included

▶ **Web incident submission**—Included

▶ **Unlimited incidents**—Included

▶ **Hours**—Regular business hours

▶ **Response time**—Typically next business day

▶ **Phone support**—Unlimited callback

▶ **Training material**—Self-help materials

Community Forums

You can find the community forums at https://community.dynamics.com/crm/f/117 (see Figure 30.1).

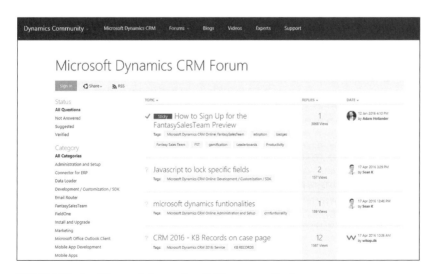

FIGURE 30.1   Microsoft Dynamics CRM community forums.

Technically, the community forums are free to pretty much anyone, and they contain a huge amount of searchable troubleshooting information provided by experts.

> **NOTE**
>
> The forums are usually monitored by a select group of people referred to as Microsoft Most Valuable Professionals (MVPs), who are peers not employed by Microsoft. These MVPs often respond to questions and help users at no cost.

Service Dashboard

The Service Dashboard shows the system's health and provides real-time feedback to users about whether the system is performing as expected (see Figure 30.2).

This information is helpful when you encounter issues related to performance and are trying to determine whether the problem is localized (a bad Internet connection, for instance) or something endemic to the system as a whole.

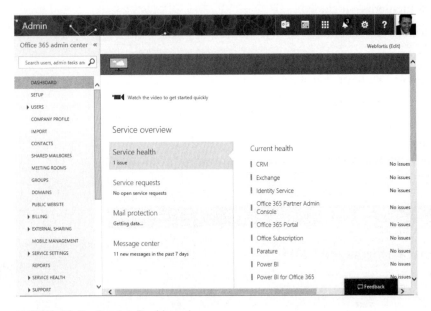

FIGURE 30.2   Service Dashboard.

In-Application Help

Help is available from directly within Dynamics CRM: Just click the question mark (?) on any page. Figure 30.3 shows where to click for Help, and Figure 30.4 shows the Help screen.

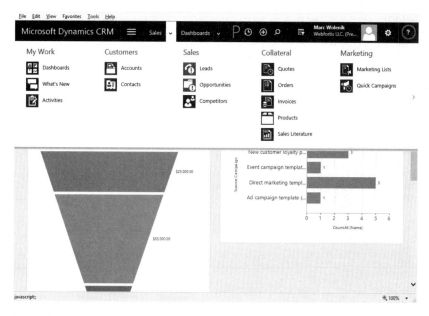

FIGURE 30.3   Help icon.

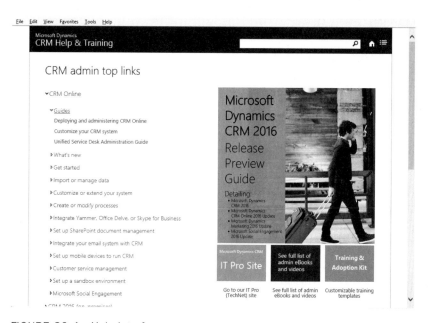

FIGURE 30.4   Help interface.

NOTE

You can customize the Help interface (On-Premises only) to meet specific contextual requirements of your application. This is common in extended (xRM) applications.

Other Support Options

All other support options are via your access to the Office 365 administration interface, as shown in Figure 30.5. Here you can create a web incident and view all incidents.

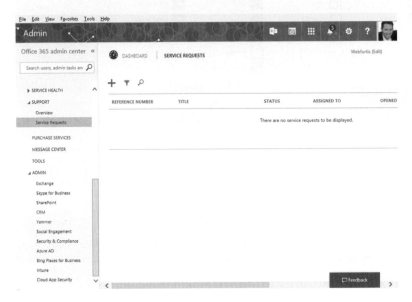

FIGURE 30.5   Accessing assisted support options.

In addition, you can access the dedicated Microsoft support page, at www.microsoft.com/dynamics/customer/en-US/assisted-support.aspx (see Figure 30.6).

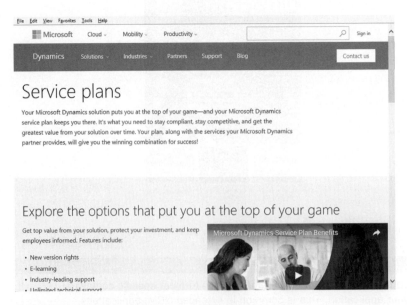

FIGURE 30.6   Microsoft Dynamics CRM support page.

At this site, you can access the following:

▶ Self-support options

▶ Telephone number for direct support

▶ CustomerSource login link

▶ Other support options, including downloads and partner referral resources

Enhanced Support

Enhanced support for CRM Online is a new offering that includes everything included with Basic but with the following added to it:

▶ The price for this level of support is $5 per seat per month.

▶ Response time is increased from next business day to less than 2 hours.

▶ Training materials include additional eLearning options.

This level of support is designed primarily for businesses that require a quicker response time than the basic subscription plan delivers.

Professional Direct Support

Professional includes everything in Basic/Subscription and Enhanced options as well as the following:

▶ The price for this level of support is $9 per seat per month.

▶ There is a minimum purchase of 100 seats.

▶ Response time is decreased to less than 1 hour, with priority routing.

▶ Support time is decreased from local business hours to 24×7.

▶ Training materials can be customized.

▶ The organization receives priority and escalation handling.

▶ Limited advisory support is provided.

▶ A technical account manager (TAM) is assigned to this level of service.

The TAM is a pooled resource, which means your organization will not have a dedicated particular TAM. However, the TAM helps your organization elevate issues quickly and easily.

30

NOTE

The ability to customize the training material is a huge benefit to organizations looking to push out a lot of material quickly and easily, as most of the work has been done by Microsoft, and the materials are frequently updated.

This type of support is reserved for organizations that typically run near-critical applications and want to ensure consistency and priority with regard to support options.

Premier Support (for Large Accounts Only)

With Premier support, organizations obtain the highest level of support from Microsoft. The cost varies depending on the organization and the type of agreement it has with Microsoft and includes all previous options in addition to the following:

▶ Assigned TAM

▶ Full advisory support

▶ Onsite services

▶ Cost (determined by Microsoft)

> **NOTE**
>
> Most large organizations have an enterprise agreement (EA), which is a bundled software pricing mechanism. This type of support is typically part of that EA agreement and includes Premier support.
>
> You can find the Premier support and services page at www.microsoft.com/en-us/microsoftservices/support.aspx.

Finally, partner support (as explained later in this chapter) is always recommended. Here's why: Although Microsoft says it will include support at no cost, it will not provide any level of support for the following:

▶ Configurations

▶ Customizations

▶ Training

▶ Integrations

▶ Other enhancements

Therefore, establishing a partner relationship for any of these concerns will provide the necessary support mechanism for these issues.

> **TIP**
>
> Even if your organization does not need help with configurations, customizations, training, integrations, or other enhancements, we *strongly* recommend that you assign a designated partner (which Microsoft calls a partner of record [POR]) to your account. This way, you have someone to go to if a support issue is outside Microsoft's support model.
>
> Finding a partner is explained in the "Partner Support" section, later in this chapter.

On-Premises Support

On-Premises support differs decidedly from Online support in that it is not free. In fact, when you first purchase CRM On-Premises, you are usually given three support tickets that you can access via the CustomerSource page, as shown in Figure 30.7. To get to this page, from www.microsoft.com/dynamics/customer/en-US/assisted-support.aspx (shown in Figure 30.6), login, and navigate to the support option.

FIGURE 30.7   Microsoft Dynamics CustomerSource.

In CustomerSource, you can create, view, and manage support tickets by selecting Support to get the options shown in Figure 30.8.

If you have exhausted your support tickets, you can purchase them à la carte for approximately $250, or you can buy a bundle.

TIP

Some of the resources, such as access to the forums, can be accessed by On-Premises customers as well, for no charge.

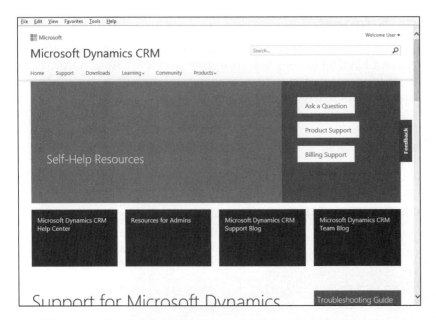

FIGURE 30.8   Microsoft Dynamics CustomerSource support options.

Pros and Cons of Manual Updates

A key difference between Online and On-Premises deployments is the requirement for the organization to manually update their systems with updates and hotfixes from Microsoft. Manual updates present the following pro and con issues for organizations:

▶ Pros:

▶ Organizations can remediate and test updates before applying them.

▶ Organizations are not required to update and can keep a stable version running for years if they prefer.

▶ Organizations can run different versions, depending on their requirements.

▶ Cons:

▶ Updates sometimes cause system instability.

▶ Updates can break customizations by removing deprecated functions.

▶ Updates can be forgotten and not installed, resulting in potential security and/ or functional issues.

▶ Updates require a system administrator.

NOTE

You can access updates from Microsoft at
https://support.microsoft.com/en-us/kb/3036179.

Figure 30.9 shows an example of the manual update page, with a list of available downloads that you can install.

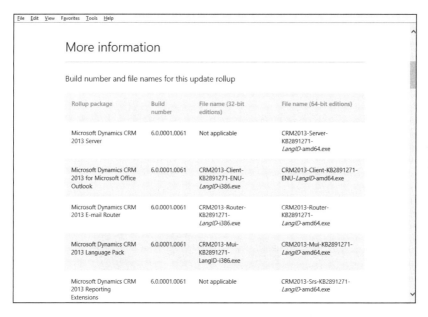

FIGURE 30.9   Microsoft Dynamics updates and hotfixes (Dynamics 2013 shown).

Considerations When Installing Updates

It is extremely important that organizations understand the implication of installing updates. Some updates cumulative, and some require previous versions, and sometimes they update the system and thus result in new functions.

Most On-Premises deployments are complex and involve the following:

▶ SQL Server

▶ Active Directory

▶ Federation Services (optional)

▶ Integration with other applications

Therefore, Microsoft tends to recommend partner support with regard to On-Premises deployments.

Partner Support

Partner support is provided by value-added resellers (VARs) who are well versed in Microsoft Dynamics CRM and have broad experience in managing CRM implementations.

30

To find a partner, follow these steps:

1. Search the Dynamics Marketplace, at https://pinpoint.microsoft.com/en-us/Home/ Dynamics.

2. Enter your location (in this example, the United States), and you see the marketplace specific to your country.

3. Enter keywords if you're looking for a particular product or company. Alternatively, look for the Works with Products category and click Microsoft Dynamics to get to the page shown in Figure 30.10.

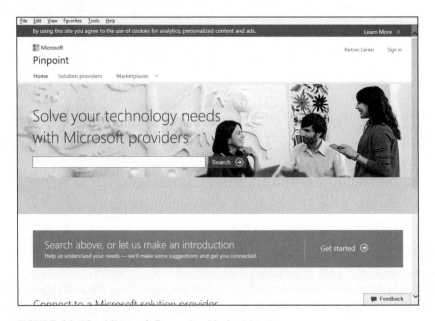

FIGURE 30.10   Microsoft Dynamics Marketplace.

4. Navigate within the application and refine your search based on CRM version, professional services versus companies, and location. Figure 30.11 shows the results for Webfortis.

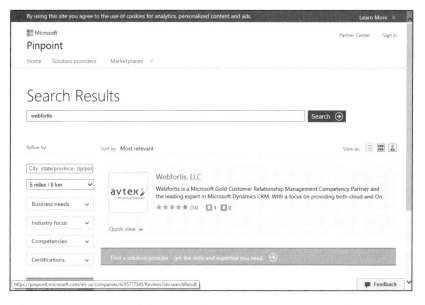

FIGURE 30.11   Microsoft Dynamics Marketplace results for Webfortis.

When selecting a partner, it is highly recommended that you consider the following options:

▶ The partner's CRM competency level (Gold, Silver, or none)

▶ The number of customers the partner supports

▶ The number of certifications the partner has

▶ The number of dedicated Dynamics CRM support staff the partner has

---

NOTE

Because of the way Microsoft ranks partners within the Dynamics families, it is common for providers of Dynamics ERP (with mixed ERP and CRM practices) to have a fairly high ranking in searches for CRM partners. However, it is rarely the case that they have nearly the number of *dedicated* CRM staff that they indicate; they usually just lump all their Dynamics staff together (including their ERP staff) to artificially inflate their numbers, but when queried about CRM staff, it rarely is very high. So be sure to inquire about dedicated CRM staff when selecting a mixed ERP/CRM services company.

The top Microsoft Dynamics CRM partners usually have a direct interaction level with Microsoft support and usually include service tickets as part of their service offerings to customers.

30

> **NOTE**
>
> Visit www.avtex.com/CRMPartner for information and benefits of partnering with Avtex, including special offers for readers of this book: Simply enter the promotion code CRM2016BOOK when prompted.

Summary

Microsoft support varies depending on the implementation, and although some support is free for some implementations (or in the case of forums, free regardless of the type of implementation), we strongly recommend that you form a partner association, no matter what your Dynamics CRM implementation.

Even if you have the help of this book, the complexities and options associated with a Dynamics CRM implementation can quickly and easily overtake a busy network admin, and even companies that have a dedicated support model for Dynamics CRM sometimes find issues that they are unable to resolve. Partners have "been there and done that" countless times and can often provide full-scale support for any organization.

CHAPTER 31

FantasySalesTeam

The market for CRM gamification continues to grow and expand, and Microsoft acquired FantasySalesTeam in August 2015 to further this trend.

The idea is bringing gaming elements into CRM will prompt user interest and create greater user engagement and productivity by tapping into a sense of competition and motivation. Gamification has been shown to result in positive reinforcement and higher system usage. Many kinds of games can be introduced into Dynamics CRM, and they all motivate differently.

The most common type of gamification is individual motivation based on results, typically tied to peer evaluation. An example of this is pitting salespeople against each other in a competition for the most leads brought in or converted or for the amounts calculated for work sold for a period of time. This type of gamification is actually native to the system (via Goals), and with some minor configurations, this information can be shared with the teams for viewing.

FantasySalesTeam takes the concept of gamification to the next level, involving the entire company as either players or fans. FantasySalesTeam helps organizations motivate their employees by creating contests driven by CRM data and involving all the employees.

While FantasySalesTeam was intended to be used and configured by sales managers to motivate sales teams, involving the entire team has an competitive effect in organizations. In addition, it broadly increases CRM usage and adoption.

This chapter explains in the usage and configuration of FantasySalesTeam.

NOTE

There is no additional cost for FantasySalesTeam beyond your CRM Online Professional license. The solution has a web client component that can be accessed by any browser as well as a mobile app that can be installed on Android or IPhone devices.

TIP

You can find FantasySalesTeam by navigating to your Office 365 Admin Portal, selecting your CRM instance, and selecting Solutions > Preferred > FantasySalesTeam.

Installation

FantasySalesTeam is a new solution available for CRM Online subscribers that must be manually installed. To do this, as an Office 365 admin, navigate to the Office 365 Admin Portal by going to https://portal.office.com/ (see Figure 31.1). Then follow these steps:

FIGURE 31.1   Office 365 Admin Portal.

NOTE

FantasySalesTeam runs on a separate web interface that can be integrated with other CRM systems, like salesforce.com, and provides an application programming interface (API) and web services to integrate with any custom solution.

---

1. Click CRM under the Admin group in the left navigation pane to open the CRM Online Administration Center (see Figure 31.2).

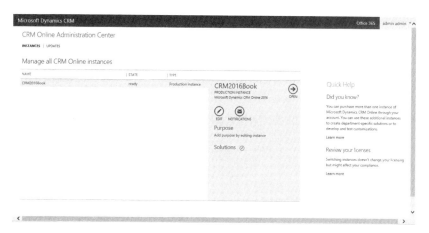

FIGURE 31.2   CRM Online Administration Center.

2. Select the organization for which you want to install FantasySalesTeam and then click the icon to the right of Solutions to access the Solution Explorer.

FIGURE 31.3   CRM Online Solution Explorer.

3. Select FantasySalesTeam and click Install (as shown in Figure 31.3).

4. When the Terms of Service dialog appears, click Install. The installation takes several minutes to complete.

NOTE

At press time, the solution version number was 1.3.3.

5. To verify that the solution is installed, go to CRM and navigate to Settings > Solutions (see Figure 31.4).

FIGURE 31.4   FantasySalesTeam solution installed in CRM.

6. Open the FantasySalesTeam solution and complete the registration form (see Figure 31.5).

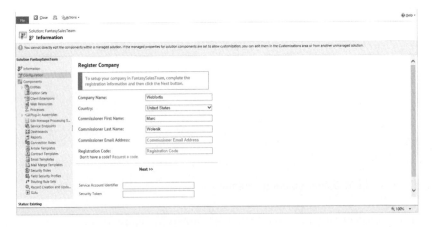

FIGURE 31.5   FantasySalesTeam registration form.

As part of the registration, request a registration code by clicking the Request a Code link to go to www.fantasysalesteam.com/preview (see Figure 31.6). Complete this code-request form, and within 24 hours, you will receive an email.

FIGURE 31.6   FantasySalesTeam code-request form.

7. When you receive the email with the code, go back to the CRM web interface, navigate to the FantasySalesTeam solution, and enter the registration code (refer to Figure 31.5). Then click Next.

8. Enter the service account identifier and the security token, as shown in Figure 31.7, and click Setup.

FIGURE 31.7   Company Registration Successful page.

When the setup is complete, you receive a welcome email with the instructions necessary to set up your first game (see Figure 31.8).

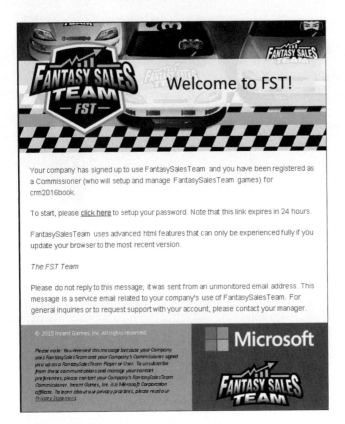

FIGURE 31.8   Welcome email.

9. Click the link in the email that says Click Here.

10. Set up a new password (see Figure 31.9) and click Submit. You are logged in to the FantasySalesTeam portal.

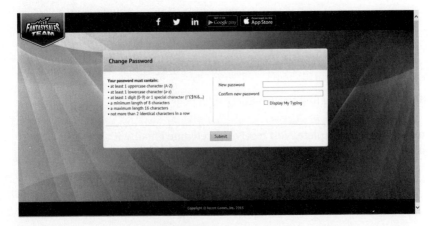

FIGURE 31.9   Changing the password.

10. Optionally upload a photo or select an avatar.

11. Optionally watch any of the 12 videos in the Playbook, which show you how to set up games. If you want to access this page again in the future, you can find it under the Help menu by selecting the Commissioner Help option.

12. A new menu navigation item is added to CRM, as shown in Figure 31.10.

FIGURE 31.10   FantasySalesTeam menu options.

> **TIP**
>
> You can find more information and installation instructions on the FantasySalesTeam website, at www.fantasysalesteam.com/preview.

Configuration

When you have the FantasySalesTeam solution installed, you are ready to configure it. Configuration is required to properly set up who is involved and what the goals are.

Account Types

The first thing you need to do is configure users. Users can have any of the following account types:

▶ Player

▶ Fan

▶ Game Admin

▶ Commissioner

Player

In order to be able to set up a CRM user as a player, that user must have a Professional or Enterprise license for Dynamics CRM.

Fan

In order to be able to set up a CRM user as a fan, that user must have at least a Basic license for Dynamics CRM.

Game Admin

In order to be able to setup a CRM user as a game admin, that user must have at least a Basic license for Dynamics CRM. A game admin user can be the administrator of a single game but does not have administrator rights for the entire system. You can assign game admins by going to the Games menu and selecting Game Admins. Then you can use the Assign or Remove Game Admins from Games tab to assign game admins to games, as shown in Figure 31.11.

FIGURE 31.11   Assigning game admins.

A game admin can log in as any player or fan assigned to the game he or she administers. The game admin can also add or remove players or fans to the game but cannot modify the game settings.

Commissioner

Commissioner is the highest account type, and it has all the privileges needed to manage all the settings in FantasySalesTeam.

Commissioners can also impersonate the other account types, logging in as players or fans, for example, without needing to know their passwords.

Users

Every time you add new users to Dynamics CRM, you are alerted to import those new users in the Commissioners Portal (see Figure 31.12).

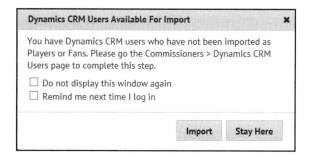

FIGURE 31.12 New CRM users available for import.

You can click Import in this dialog to see the Import Dynamics Users interface (see Figure 31.13). You can also open this interface by clicking Commissioner > Dynamics CRM Users. When importing the users, you can select the account type as explained earlier.

Import Dynamics CRM Users

First Name | Last Name | Search

☐ Show Only Professional and Enterprise   ☐ Hide Imported Users

Last Name Starts With: Any A B C D E F G H I I K L M N O P Q R S T U V W X Y Z

Page Size: 50

Import Selected Users

☐ Import	First Name	Last Name	Email Address	Account Type
☑	user	four	user4@Crmbook2016.onmicrosoft.com	Player
☑	User	one	User1@Crmbook2016.onmicrosoft.com	Player
☑	user	three	user3@Crmbook2016.onmicrosoft.com	Fan
☑	User	two	user2@Crmbook2016.onmicrosoft.com	Game Admin
☑	Marc	Wolenik	Admin@Crmbook2016.onmicrosoft.com	Commissioner Change Role

FIGURE 31.13 Importing Dynamics CRM users.

Select the users you want to import, select the account type, and then click the Import Selected Users button. A confirmation window alerts you that this process might take from seconds to minutes. Click the Import Reviewed button. When the process finishes, you get an email telling you this task has been completed.

Game Setup

You need to set up at least one game to start. To setup a game in FantasySalesTeam, go to Games > Game Setup, as shown in Figure 31.14.

FIGURE 31.14   Game Setup menu option.

The Game wizard helps you create a new game. First you enter basic information about the game. For Game Model, you can select any of the following:

▶ Fantasy Teams

▶ Fixed Teams

▶ No Teams

▶ FST TV

Each model presents different options, but all games share some properties, such as the name of the game and the start and end dates. By default, the start date is set to the next Monday, and the end date is set to the last Sunday of the month, 2 months later. This way, the game can have complete week periods. If you select any day other than Monday for the start day, you will have less than 7 days for the first week period of the game.

Depending on the model you select, you might need to set other attributes. The following sections discuss the four models

Fantasy Teams

Fantasy Teams is the recommended model because it offers most of the features and benefit of FantasySalesTeam.

The Fantasy Teams model allows you to use sport themes, which can be any of the following:

▶ American Football

▶ Baseball

▶ Football (Soccer)

▶ Basketball

▶ Car Racing

31

You need to specify the frequency, which can be any of the following:

▶ Weekly

▶ Monthly

▶ One-Time

You need to select whether you want to enable fans for the game and whether you want to use actuals or targets, as shown in Figure 31.15.

FIGURE 31.15   Fantasy Team model.

Metrics   The Metrics model allows you to measure the way the players can earn points. These can be, for example, *X* number of phone calls made, or *X* number of leads created, or *X* number of deals closed.

The Metrics model allows you to have you to use 20 different metrics. For each metric you must enter a name and the type, which can be any of the following:

▶ Number Of

▶ Revenue or Amount

▶ Percentage or Quota (Default or Linear)

▶ Percentage

Then you set the number of points for which you want the metric set—either every X number of records or a specific number of records reached. (In addition, you can set the roles that each metric will be applied to.)

Player Positions   Depending on the sport theme selected, you will see different positions in the first tab. Figure 31.16 shows the positions available for the Football (Soccer) theme.

FIGURE 31.16   Player positions.

Drag and drop the users in the players list on the right to the positions list on the left.

Awards   You can enter the prizes and awards for up to 10 places per award category. For example, you might offer prizes like a week of time off or an Microsoft Xbox One console.

These award categories are available:

▶ Fantasy Team Awards

▶ Game MVP Awards

▶ Position Awards

▶ Metric Awards

The Metric Awards category shows the number of metrics you created earlier, so you can set different prizes per metric created.

Fixed Teams

The Fixed Teams model is good for setting up a game where people play in teams. Fixed Teams can have a maximum of 100 teams (see Figure 31.17).

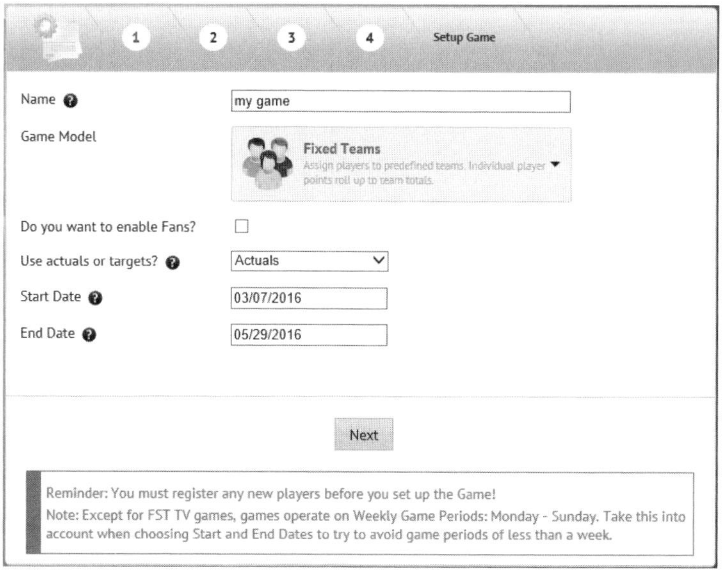

FIGURE 31.17   Fixed Teams model.

Positions   You can configure players after they are assigned to a team. You can change the team names and assign players to teams by dragging and dropping the players available in the players list on the right to the teams on the left.

No Teams

The No Teams model means each player is alone against the others.

Positions   You can select which players will participate in the game.

Awards   For the No Teams model, there are two types of awards: Game MVP award and Metrics award.

FST TV

The FST TV model displays daily, weekly, and monthly sales metrics on TVs around your office (see Figure 31.18). (The other game models can also be displayed on TVs.) With this type of game, there are no winners, so you don't have to specify the awards.

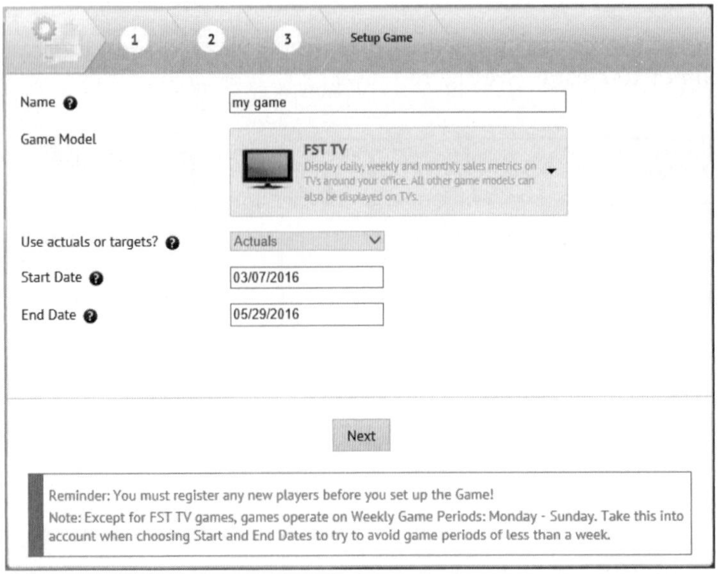

FIGURE 31.18   FST TV model.

Final Configurations

After you set up a game in the Commissioners Portal, you need to activate the team before it will show up in Dynamics CRM.

The last step in configuring a game is binding the metrics you created with Dynamics CRM metrics. Because you enter free text for the metric name in FantasySalesTeam, you need to tell CRM what this mean. Go to Dynamics CRM, navigate to FantasySalesTeam, and then click the Sales metric. You will see all the active metrics, along with the status so you know which ones are already set up and which ones needs to be set up (indicated by Not Setup in the status field).

Open the metric you want to configure and select the type of entity you want to measure for that metric. Figure 31.19 shows the setup for a phone call metric.

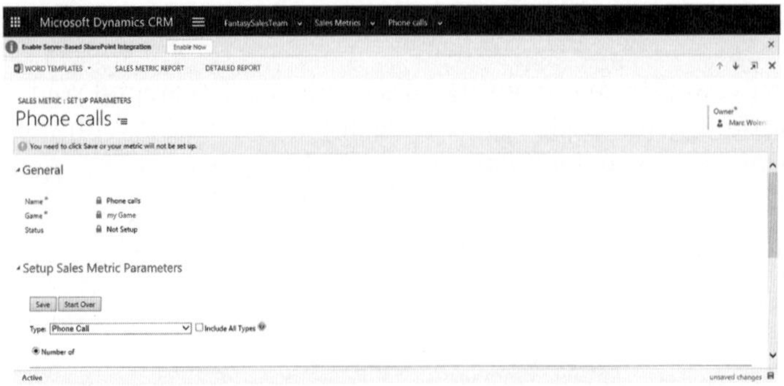

FIGURE 31.19   Phone call metric set up in Dynamics CRM.

Players

Players are the most important users of the FantasySalesTeam system, as the games don't make any sense without players. Figure 31.20 shows the Players Portal.

> **NOTE**
>
> Players must have a CRM Professional or Enterprise license. If someone wants to participate in a game but is not a CRM, consider registering that person as a fan. (See "Fans," later in this chapter.)

FIGURE 31.20   Players.

> **NOTE**
>
> To create a new player, you must first create the user in Office 365 and then import the user into FantasySalesTeam by going to Commissioner > Dynamics CRM Users and setting the account type to Player. The user then shows up in the Players Portal.

In the Players Portal you can configure the following options:

▶ Roles

▶ Handicaps

▶ Player Badges

Roles

It is a good idea to set up roles as you can assign them to game metrics.

You can create roles manually one by one, or if you have a big list of roles, you can upload an Excel file (see Figure 31.21). To do that, you first download the Role template, which has only the Role Name column.

FIGURE 31.21   Add/Edit Roles dialog.

Once you have a few roles created, you can assign them to metrics. Figure 31.22 shows a game metric configuration screen with roles assigned to the metrics.

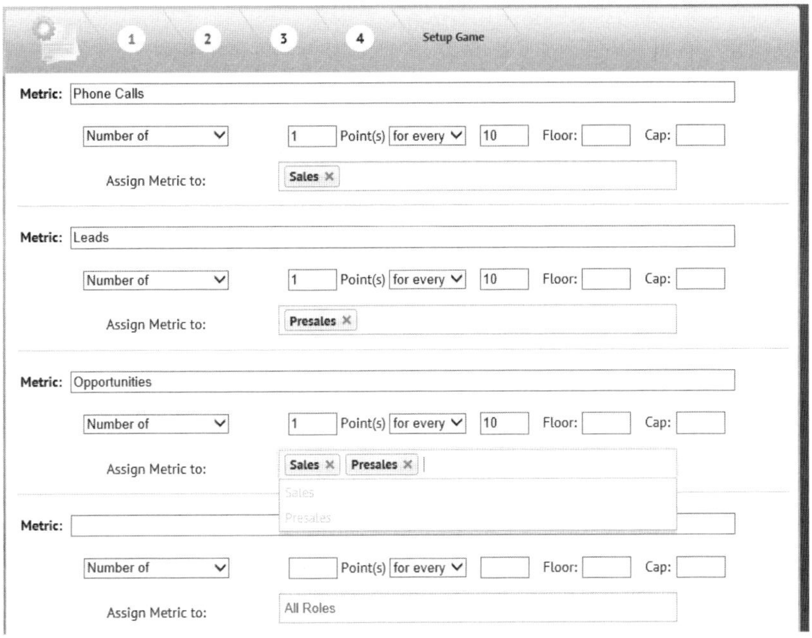

FIGURE 31.22 Roles assigned to metrics.

Handicaps

Handicaps are configured by game, by player, and by metric associated to each game. You must first select a game to see the metrics, and then you can set a percentage number for each metric/player (see Figure 31.23).

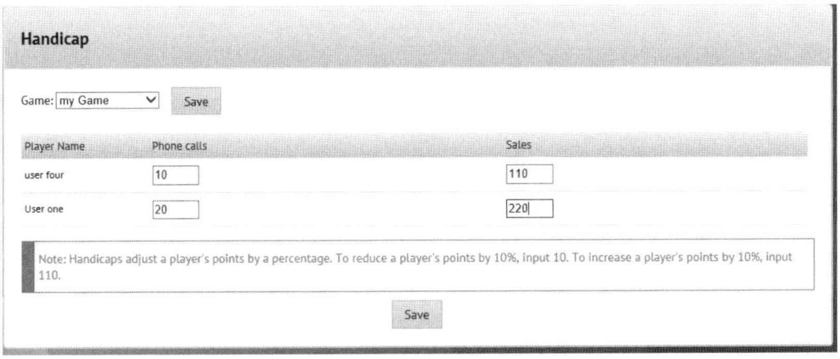

FIGURE 31.23 Handicaps.

This interface allows you to adjust the player points. Entering a value of 10 reduces the points by 10%, and entering a value of 110 increases the points by 10%.

Player Badges

You can see all the badges awarded to the different players as well as manage the badges assigned. As shown in Figure 31.24, you can add, edit, or delete badges.

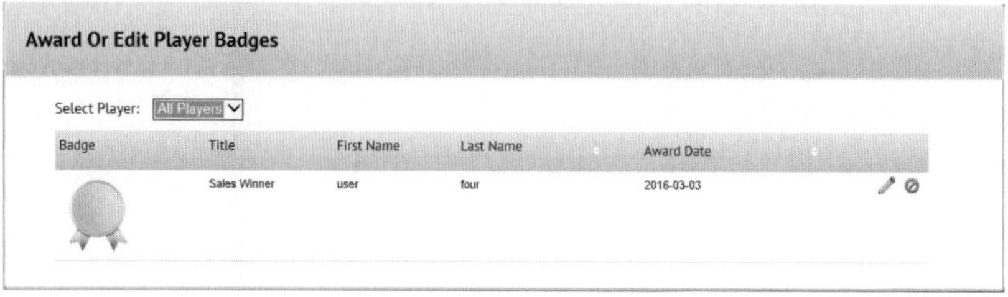

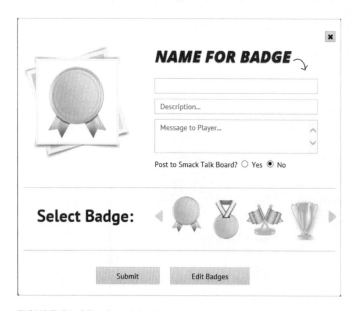

FIGURE 31.24   Player badges.

To manually assign a badge to a player, you must select the player and then click the Award Badge button. A dialog asks you to enter a name of the badge, a description, and a message to the player. You can also select the image of the badge here (see Figure 31.25).

FIGURE 31.25   Award badge.

If you enter a message to the player, an email is sent to the player with the message you entered here, and you receive another email saying that an email was sent to the player.

Players Portal

When a commissioner creates a player, the player receives an email about resetting his or her password, When the player goes to the Players Portal to reset the password, he or she can either upload a photo or select an avatar. Players are also asked to draft the teams for the games they are playing.

Figure 31.26 shows how the interface looks for a Fantasy Team game with the Soccer theme selected when a player must draft the team.

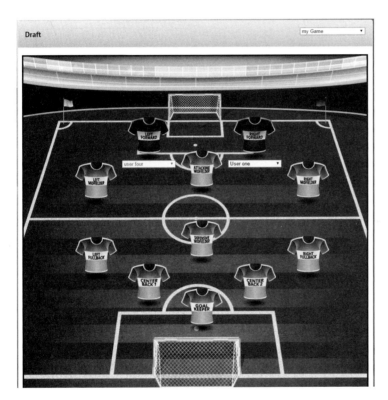

FIGURE 31.26   Soccer game team draft.

A player's profile page (see Figure 31.27) where shows the badges earned and the progress players are making in games in terms of metrics.

FIGURE 31.27   Player profile page.

Fans

Fans are any non-sales employees who want to play games. The Fans Portal allows you to register fans that are not necessarily Dynamics CRM users. You can register one fan at a time by using the registration form shown in Figure 31.28.

FIGURE 31.28   Fan registration form.

To add a large number of fans, you can upload an Excel file. To do that, first download the Excel template FansExcelTemplate.xlsx, which has three columns: FirstName, LastName, and EmailAddress.

Commissioners and game admins can also be fans in the games, but they are not be displayed in the Fans Portal.

> **NOTE**
>
> You cannot delete a fan after you register it, you can instead deactivate it and then you can activate it again if you need it in the future.

When you create a game, you are asked whether you want to let fans play in the game. If you let the game use fans, you need to add the fans to the game manually. You cannot upload an Excel file in this case.

Fans Portal

Fans don't receive an welcome email when you first register them, but the commissioner can set passwords for fans so they can access the Fans Portal, shown in Figure 31.29.

The first time a fan enters the Fans portal, he or she can either upload a photo or select an avatar.

FIGURE 31.29   Fans Portal.

FST TV

FST TV displays the rankings and positions of the players and is helpful in driving participation and competition, as shown in Figure 31.30.

You can configure FST TV to display based on different requirements.

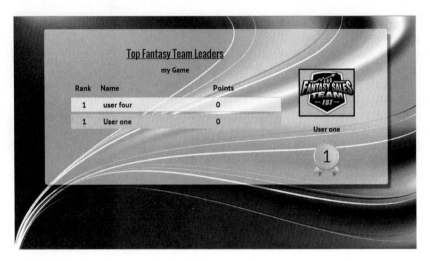

FIGURE 31.30   Stream TV.

Settings

Commissioners can access a number of settings from the Commissioners Portal by going to Commissioner > Settings.

Company Logo

You can upload your company logo, which should be a PNG file, if possible. Figure 31.31 shows an uploaded logo.

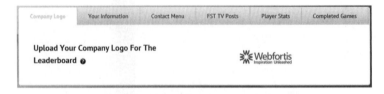

FIGURE 31.31   Company logo.

Contact Menu

You can set a contact menu by entering either an email address or a web page URL, as shown in Figure 31.32.

Company Logo	Your Information	Contact Menu	FST TV Posts	Player Stats	Completed Games

Player/Fan/Game Admin Help Menu > Contact Commissioner

Enter either an email address OR a help page URL:
http://www.webfortis.com

Save

FIGURE 31.32   Contact menu setup.

When you set the contact menu, it is available via Help > Contact Commissioner for players, fans and game admins, in their respective portals. Figure 31.33 shows this menu option in the Fans Portal.

FIGURE 31.33   Contact Commissioner option.

FST TV Posts

You can turn off or on the TV board posts. You can configure the time in seconds of the board post display, the count of post you want to show, and the waiting time. You can configure the same for the other fields, as shown in Figure 31.34.

Company Logo	Your Information	Contact Menu	FST TV Posts	Player Stats	Completed Games

Turn off TV Board Posts	☐
Board Post Display Time (Seconds) ❷	10
Board Post Display Count ❷	1
Display Waiting Time (Seconds) ❷	60
Turn off BAM posts	☐
BAM Post Display Count ❷	1
BAM Display Waiting Time (Seconds) ❷	60

Save

FIGURE 31.34   FST TV Posts.

Player Stats

You can access player stats (see Figure 31.35) from the Commissioners Portal by selecting Player > Home > Player Stats.

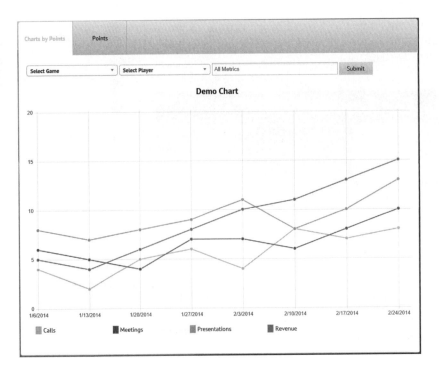

FIGURE 31.35   Player stats.

You can filter the stats by game, by player, or by metric, and you can see the chart by points or a table with the points only. You can export the table to a Microsoft Excel file.

Best Practices

The recommendation is to create one game per month, selecting a Monday for the start date and a Sunday for the end date of the game.

Figure 31.36 shows the overall leaderboard interface for a game that has been setup.

TIP

While the goal is to drive system usage and adoption, it can be fun to put a big TV in a central area, showing the leaderboard, so employees can see the game progress and winners.

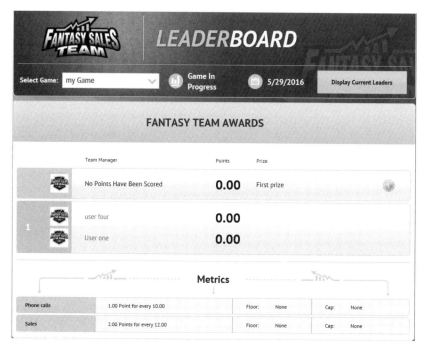

FIGURE 31.36   Leaderboard.

When creating a game and setting up the positions of the players, you should upload from Excel for large number of players. Otherwise, the graphical or table views are recommended.

When working with teams, try to put the most experienced people together in a single team and the most recent employees on another team.

Commissioners can download a kickoff template from the Help menu in the Commissioners Portal. This zip file contains a PowerPoint template presentation that will help you explain the game to the team and employees before launching the games in the company.

Summary

This chapter explains how gamification can drive Dynamics CRM adoption and system usage. By using FantasySalesTeam, your organization can involve the entire organization (not just the sale team). This chapter shows how to install the solution in Dynamics CRM Online and how to configure it.

Organizations can set up several different game types and account types to manage players and fans. Finally, this chapter describes a few best practices for getting maximum benefit out of FantasySalesTeam.

Adxstudio Portals

In September 2015, Microsoft acquired the hugely successful product Adxstudio Portals. Adxstudio Portals provides the ability for organizations running Dynamics CRM to quickly build secure self-service retail portals. Adxstudio Portals extend Microsoft Dynamics CRM to the web, bringing CRM data to life for external users. The Adxstudio Portals solution provides a seamless customer experience with a responsive solution that is optimized for mobile, desktop, and tablet.

> **NOTE**
>
> Since Adxstudio Portals was acquired in September 2015, the product has been roadmapped as a natively integrated product, available as part of the core code set of Microsoft Dynamics CRM, and it was expected to be available sometime in 2016. This chapter was written based on the last standalone Adxstudio Portals product, which many existing customers will have until they are mainstreamed into the new code set when it is released.
>
> Be sure to check for digital updates to this chapter, as it will drastically change once the new product is released.

What Does Adxstudio Portals Do?

Adxstudio Portals connects to Microsoft Dynamics CRM directly and provides the ability for organizations to manage external websites through Dynamics CRM. Since all the data lives in Dynamics CRM, organizations don't need a separate database or content management system.

The external websites can provide an array of functionality, such as lead gathering/management, product sales, customer support, and event registration and payment.

Adxstudio Portals works with all modern web browsers, and the code is standards compliant with HTML5 and CSS3 for polished display options and full accessibility, regardless of the end user's device. (All code is responsive, so no additional effort is necessary for mobile development.)

Adxstudio Portals comes with preconfigured starter solutions that have a variety of product applications, such as forums, blogs, and a product catalog, as shown in Table 32.1. You organization can select the combination of these it wants.

TABLE 32.1   Adxstudio Portals Features

Main Area	Details
Profile Management	Contact Management
	Federated authentication
	User profile management
	Web roles
CRM Web Application	Entity actions
	Entity form
	Entity list
	Entity permissions
	OData feeds
Content Management	Ads
	Files and attachments
	Links
	Redirects
	Rich content editor
	Search
	Sitemap
	Web pages
Customer Service	Help desk
	Account management
	Knowledge base
	Parature integration
Communities	Discussion forums
	Facebook integration
	Ideas
	Issues
	Pools
	Surveys
Channel Management	Customer management
	Opportunity distribution
	Opportunity management
	Entity list
	Entity permissions

Main Area	Details
E-commerce	OData feeds
	E-commerce transactions
	Invoices
	Orders
	Products and catalogs
	Quotes
	Search engine optimization
	Shopping cart
Government Applications	Citizen service requests
	Citizen engagement
	Emergency management
	Permits, licensing, and inspections
Modern Web Standards	Accessibility
	Bootstrap design framework
	HTML5 and CSS3
	Responsive website design
Marketing	Branding and design
	Conference management
	Content management
	Dynamic web templating
	Events
	Lead generation forms

Deployment of Adxstudio Portals

Adxstudio Portals can be deployed in two ways:

▶ Hosted

▶ On-Premises

Hosted requires a monthly subscription fee, and the code lives on Adxstudio Portals servers, which prevents or limits code changes. In addition, there is limited capability to write JavaScript on web forms and entity forms during configuration.

With On-Premises, the code is available for full modification and can be deployed either on an On-Premises server or as a cloud option (that you own).

> **NOTE**
>
> On-Premises in this case is similar to On-Premises Microsoft Dynamics CRM—which is to say that it doesn't need to live on your servers if you don't want it to. You can easily deploy it to a cloud-based environment, just as you can deploy Microsoft Dynamics CRM to a cloud-based (that is, hosted) environment if you wish. However, you are responsible for all updates and hosting infrastructure.

Either deployment option allows for portal design, branding, and the building of custom or dynamic templates.

Adxstudio Portals Installer

The last release of Adxstudio Portals prior to the Microsoft acquisition is version 7.0, and it comes with Adxstudio Portals installer. You can also download the installer from https://community.adxstudio.com/products/adxstudio-portals/releases/adxstudio-portals-7/download/.

The Adxstudio Portals installer allows you to manage Adxstudio Portals components and data in CRM.

When Dynamics CRM Online and hosted Adxstudio Portals are integrated, the Adxstudio Portals installer solution is automatically imported into your Dynamics CRM Online organization. When using Dynamics CRM On-Premises, you need to import the Adxstudio Portals installer solution manually.

To manually install the solution, log in to Dynamics CRM as a user who has the System Administrator security role and navigate to Settings > Solutions. Click Adxstudio Portals Installer at the top of the solutions grid to open up Adxstudio Portals installer solution's configuration page, as shown in Figure 32.1. You can view components that have already been installed, and you can install new components as necessary.

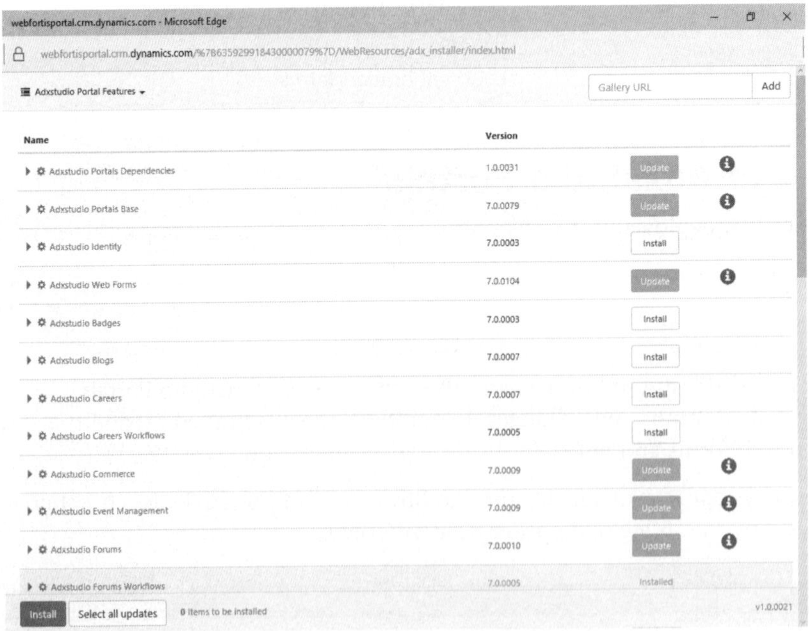

FIGURE 32.1   Adxstudio Portals installer configuration page.

Starter Portals

There are a few starter portals included with Adxstudio Portals that can help you understand Adxstudio Portals. These out-of-the-box options have predefined configurations and components. The following are a few of the starter portals included:

- ▶ Community Portal
- ▶ Retail
- ▶ Partner Pipeline Portal
- ▶ Government Portal
- ▶ Bilingual Company Portal
- ▶ Intranet Portal
- ▶ Conference Portal

You can use these portals as is or you can modify them to better you're your needs. For example, if you are planning to build a portal for an online shopping website, you can start with the Retail portal, which provides basic features like a shopping cart, product reviews, a product catalog, and a store locator. You can then expand and customize it to meet your particular requirements.

Adxstudio Portals Configuration

You can use Adxstudio Portals to display Dynamics CRM data and forms—without writing a single line of code.

In the following sections, you will configure Adxstudio Portals using Dynamics CRM 2016 Online and cloud-hosted Adxstudio Portals, with the Customer Portal installed as a starter portal. You will see how to manage Dynamics CRM data and forms, views, and security, as well as how to do complex multi-step wizard forms using web forms.

Entity Forms

Entity forms in Adxstudio Portals are used to display CRM forms that allow end users to perform create, read, update, and delete (CRUD) operations against CRM entities. Entity forms are created in CRM and then placed into web pages in Adxstudio Portals and can be used in scenarios such as lead generation or profile management. You can use out-of-the-box CRM entity forms or create new forms to use for Adxstudio Portals, and you can show CRM subgrids and notes on the portal web page if desired.

> **NOTE**
>
> In the scenario explained here, there is no coding required to create entity forms with Adxstudio Portals. Rather, you can create point-and-click configurations in Microsoft Dynamics CRM.

Entity forms use the CrmEntityFormView control, which renders the entity form on a web page. This control supports the following features:

▶ CRM field types (except Party List)

▶ CRM field validation rules

▶ Multiple-column layouts

▶ Web resources (HTML and images only)

▶ CRM label language translations

▶ Subgrids (configuration with metadata)

▶ Notes

▶ Lookup-related records filtering

▶ Lookup default view

> **NOTE**
>
> Headers and footer on forms are not currently supported in CRM and Adxstudio Portals. In addition, IFRAMES and CRM form scripting are not supported.

> **NOTE**
>
> If a form contains an IFRAME or any other feature that is currently not supported, this will not prevent the form from rendering in the portal. Rather, those features are simply not present. As a result, you should be sure to thoroughly test your forms for the desired end result.

A common deployment scenario is the creation of a Contact Us form. Users submit their details on the form, and this leads to the creation of a lead record in CRM (either the native Lead entity or a custom entity).

The following example shows a simple example of how to create a form in Adxstudio Portals. Follow these steps to create a Contact Us form:

1. Log on to Dynamics CRM as a user who has the System Administrator security role.

2. Go to Settings > Customization > Customize the System and expand the Lead entity.

▶ For more information about customizing the system, refer to **CHAPTER 22**, "Customizing Entities."

3. Click Forms and create a new main form named Contact Us Web Form, as shown in Figure 32.2. This example shows a few out-of-the-box fields added to the form, such as First Name, Last Name, and Address Fields.

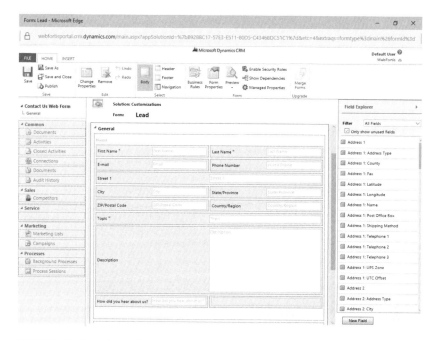

FIGURE 32.2   Adxstudio Portals new Contact Us Web Form in design mode.

4. Save the form and publish all changes.

5. Go to Portals > Entity Forms to create a new entity form.

6. Click New and provide the following details for attributes on the new form (as shown in Figure 32.3):

> **Name**—Contact Us

> **Entity Name**—Lead

> **Form Name**—Contact Us Web Form

> **Mode**—Insert

> **Enable Entity Permissions**—True

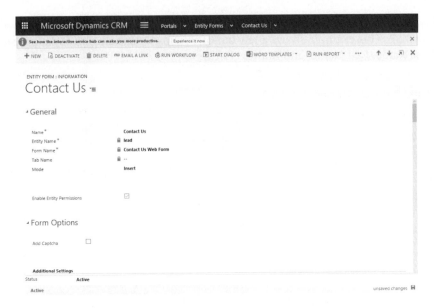

32

FIGURE 32.3   Adxstudio Portals new Contact Us Web Form.

> **NOTE**
>
> Step 6 and Figure 32.3 show a number of attributes and their settings. Here's what you need to know about these attributes:
>
> ▶ **Entity Name**—The name of the entity whose form you want to show on Adxstudio Portals.
>
> ▶ **Form Name**—The name of the form on the entity that is to be rendered.
>
> ▶ **Tab Name**—An optional field. If a form has more than one tab and you want to render just one of them, select the tab. Otherwise, leave this field blank to render the whole form.
>
> ▶ **Mode**—Mode has three options:
>
> ▶ **Insert**—The form should insert a new record upon submission.
>
> ▶ **Edit**—The form should edit an existing record.
>
> ▶ **ReadOnly**—The form should display an existing record's noneditable form.
>
> ▶ **Enable Entity Permissions**—Enable record-level security. (Entity Permissions are explained in detail later on in the chapter.)

7. Navigate to Adxstudio Portals and click the Sign In button in the top-right corner (see Figure 32.4). Log in with the administrator username and password.

NOTE

All starter portals have the following three default contact records created:

▶ **System Administrator**—Username administrator

▶ **Portal Customer**—Username customer

▶ **Portal Contact**—Username partner

The password for all of these is pass@word1.

FIGURE 32.4   Login page for Adxstudio Portals.

8. Once you're logged in, select the Content menu link in the navigation bar.

9. From the floating menu in the top-right corner (see Figure 32.5), click New > Child Page.

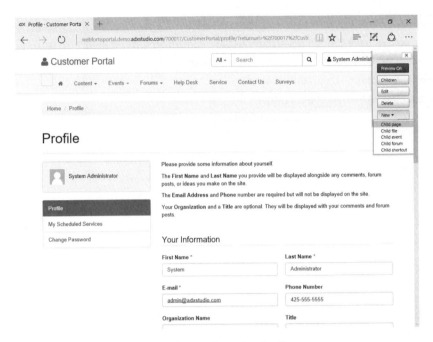

FIGURE 32.5   Select new child page from the floating menu.

10. In the new page that opens, enter Contact Us as the name of the page and select the Contact Us entity form from the Name drop-down (see Figure 32.6). Click Save to continue.

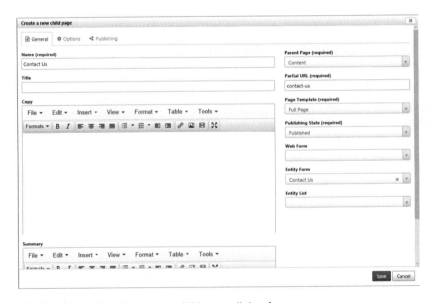

FIGURE 32.6   Creating a new child page dialog form.

11. Once the form is saved, open it. Notice that there are required fields on the page (as shown in Figure 32.7). These are the same fields that are required in Dynamics CRM. Enter the data in the fields and click Submit.

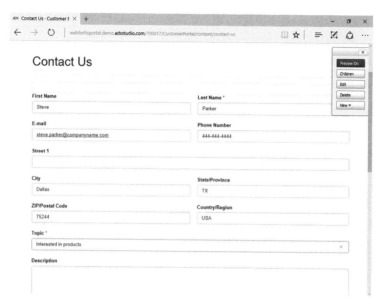

FIGURE 32.7   Previewing the Contact Us page.

12. Navigate back to Dynamics CRM and go to Sales > Leads, and you should see the newly created lead record (see Figure 32.8).

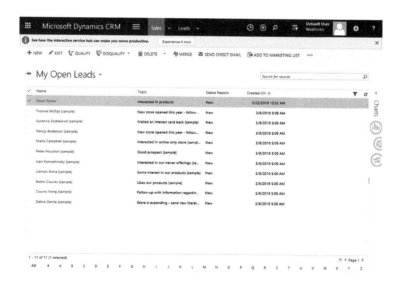

FIGURE 32.8   New portal record created in CRM.

Entity Permissions

Entity permissions are used for record-level security and to secure entity lists, entity forms, and web forms in Adxstudio Portals. You need to select the entity, scope, and privileges (Create, Read, Write, Delete, Append, and Append To) and provide a name to create entity permissions. All of these are the same as for users in Dynamics CRM. In Adxstudio Portals you create entity permissions and add them to web roles.

Consider the following about entity permissions:

▶ Entity permissions can be added to any entity in CRM.

▶ Entity permissions are respected by Search and Liquid templates in Adxstudio Portals.

▶ You can add entity permissions to web roles, which allows you to define roles in your organization that correspond to privileges and record access defined in entity permissions.

▶ You can add one or more entity permissions to a web role, and a contact can have one or more web roles.

Table 32.2 lists the entity permission attributes.

TABLE 32.2   Entity Permission Attributes

Attribute	Description
Name	The name of the entity permission.
Entity Name	Shows all entities in CRM. You need to select the entity for which you want to define entity permissions.
Scope	Can be set to the following: ▶ **Global**—Allows access to all records of the entity specified in the entity permission. ▶ **Contact**—Allows access to only those records that are associated or have relationships with the contact record. ▶ **Account**—Allows access to records owned by the contact as well as those owned by the parent account or contact record in Dynamics CRM. ▶ **Parent**—Allows access to child entity records through the chain of parent permissions. If you have access to the parent record, you can access nominated child records.
Privileges	Select the check box for type of privilege(s) you want to provide. The options are Read, Create, Write, Delete, Append, and Append To.

The next example shows how the user can update his or her contact records. To allow this to happen, the entity permissions need to be adjusted, using these steps:

1. Go to Portal > Entity Permissions in Dynamics CRM and click New.

2. Provide the following details (as shown in Figure 32.9).

   ▶ **Name**—Contact Permissions

   ▶ **Entity Name**—Contact

   ▶ **Scope**—Contact

   ▶ **Contact Relationship**—contact_customer_contacts

   ▶ **Privileges**—Read, Write, Create, Delete, Append, and Append To.
     Click Save.

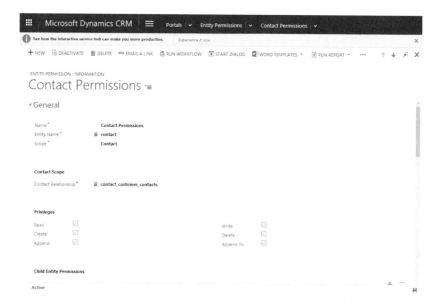

FIGURE 32.9   New Contact Permissions form

3. Scroll down and click the + sign on the Web Roles subgrid. Select the Authenticated Users (as shown in Figure 32.10).

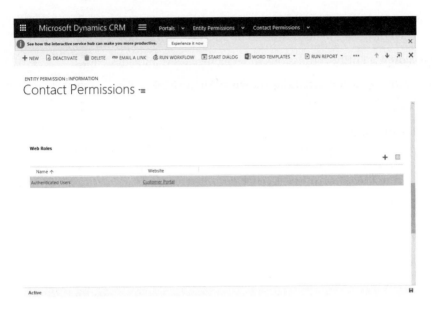

FIGURE 32.10   New Contact Permissions form.

The permissions for the Contact entity have been created and assigned to the Authenticated Users web role. All the contact records that have this role will be able to perform assigned privileges on their related contact records.

To view these permissions, you will create an entity list of contact records. However, prior to doing this, let's dig a little deeper into entity lists.

Entity Lists

Entity lists display the data from Dynamics CRM views on web pages in Adxstudio Portals. Developers do not need to write any code to show CRM data in Adxstudio Portals because they can use a grid and entity lists.

> **NOTE**
>
> Views in Dynamics CRM are stored in the SavedQuery entity, which stores queries in FetchXML format and the formatting of columns in LayoutXML.

> **TIP**
>
> You can configure the entity list to show a search box that looks and performs just like the Quick Search box in Dynamics CRM. Features of the search include:
>
> ▶ The view remains the same and does not change to quick view.
>
> ▶ It supports sorting and pagination features.
>
> ▶ You can specify the page for details view to open an individual record.
>
> ▶ Each record contains a link in first column of the grid to open that record in a model window.

- ▶ You can have multiple views available, and you can select one of them to render data in a grid on a web page.
- ▶ A drop-down similar to those in Dynamics CRM is rendered, and the user can select the view from there.
- ▶ If you enable entity permissions for the entity view, you can add other actions, such as Delete, Download, Create, Run Workflow, and other actions provided by the selected entity.

In the next example, you will work with an entity list that shows the child contact records of the parent record. The user will be able to create, view, update, activate, and deactivate child contacts from the portal. To do this, three forms are necessary—to allow for the creation, viewing, and update operations.

Create the following three entity forms, following the steps shown earlier in this chapter for creating entity forms, only this time use the following configurations:

Contact Create form:

- ▶ **Name**—Contact Create

- ▶ **Entity Name**—Contact

- ▶ **Form Name**—Profile Web Form

- ▶ **Mode**—Insert

- ▶ **Enable Entity Permissions**—True

Figure 32.11 shows the completed form.

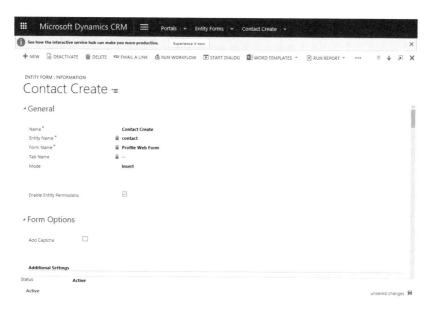

FIGURE 32.11   New Contact Create form.

Contact Edit form:

- ▶ **Name**—Contact Edit
- ▶ **Entity Name**—Contact
- ▶ **Form Name**—Profile Web Form
- ▶ **Mode**—Edit
- ▶ **Record Source Type**—Query String
- ▶ **Record ID Query String Parameter Name**—id
- ▶ **Enable Entity Permissions**—True

Figure 32.12 shows the completed form.

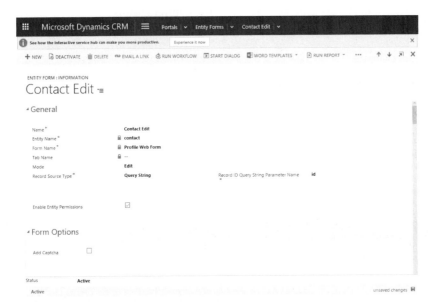

FIGURE 32.12   New Contact Edit form.

Contact Read Only form:

- ▶ **Name**—Contact Read Only
- ▶ **Entity Name**—Contact
- ▶ **Form Name**—Profile Web Form
- ▶ **Mode**—ReadOnly
- ▶ **Record Source Type**—Query String
- ▶ **Record ID Query String Parameter Name**—id
- ▶ **Enable Entity Permissions**—True

Figure 32.13 shows the completed form.

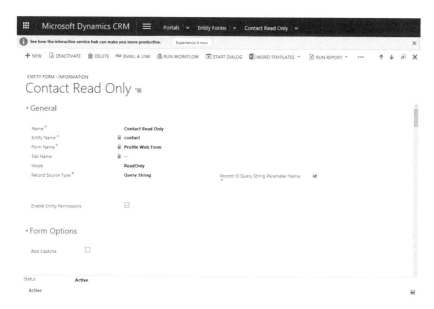

FIGURE 32.13   New Contact Read Only form.

Follow these steps to create an entity list and use the entity forms you just created:

1. Go to Portal > Entity Lists to create a new entity list.

2. Click the New button and provide the following details on the new form:

   ▶ **Name**—Contacts

   ▶ **Entity Name**—contact

3. Click Save, and the View Configuration section is enabled. (If you're unable to save, select a view first.) Click the +View link to add a drop-down that contains the names of all the available system views in the system. Select the view you want to display to Adxstudio Portals users—and note that you can add more than one view. For this example, add the two views Active Contacts and Inactive Contacts.

4. Keep Page Size 10 as the default, but note that you can modify this as necessary.

5. Keep the default value id in the ID Query String Parameter Name field, as shown in Figure 32.14.

FIGURE 32.14   New contacts entity list.

6. Select the check box Enable Entity Permissions.

7. Select the check box Enabled under Search. You can provide Placeholder Text like Search Contacts.

8. Save the record and then go to the Options tab. When entity permissions are enabled, the Configuration section is enabled; however, if entity permissions are not enabled, the configuration section is disabled.

9. In the Configuration section, click the +Download link under Views to enable the Download button to download records from Adxstudio Portals.

10. Click the +Create link to add a drop-down for the entity form that lists all the entity forms for the Contact entity. Select Contact Create from the drop-down list.

11. Click the +Details link in Items and then select Contact Read Only form for entity form from the drop down list, as shown in Figure 32.15.

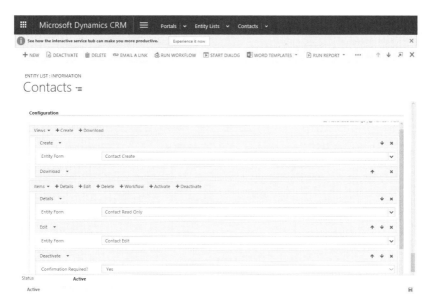

FIGURE 32.15   New contacts configuration.

12. Click the +Edit link in Items and then select the Contact Edit form for the entity form from the drop-down list.

13. Click the +Delete link in Items to add a Delete link under the Actions menu to delete the respective contact record.

14. Click the +Activate and +Deactivate links and select Yes for Confirmation Required? for both. This allows portal users to activate and deactivate contact records.

15. Click the +Column link under Override Column Attributes. This feature allows you to override the column name and width in views. Select the Full Name field from the drop-down, set Display Name to Employee Name, and set Width to 150, as shown in Figure 32.16.

16. Save the entity list record.

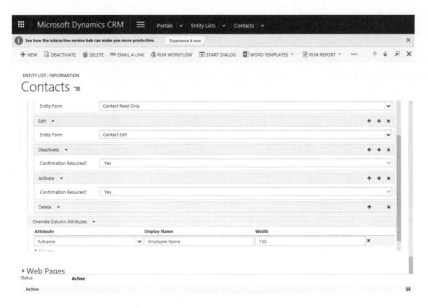

FIGURE 32.16   Entity list options configuration.

Now that the entity list record is configured, navigate to the Adxstudio Portals and select Content Page. Select New Child Page and set Name to Contacts, set Page Template to Full Page, and select Contact from the Entity List drop-down, as shown in Figure 32.17. Click Save.

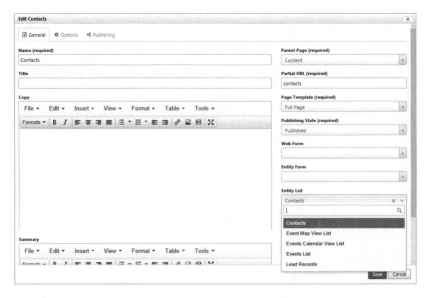

FIGURE 32.17   Adxstudio Portals contacts configuration.

If you view the page, you can see all child contacts that the logged-on user has in Dynamics CRM. If you select the last column icon, you see all actions available, such as Edit, Delete, Activate, and Deactivate, as previously configured in the entity list. In addition, there are options for Create and Download in the top grid, next to the Search text box (see Figure 32.18).

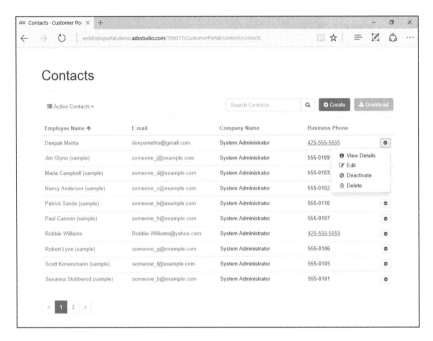

FIGURE 32.18   Adxstudio Portals page for contacts.

Selecting View Details in the contacts form opens a modal pop-up with a read-only view of data, as shown in Figure 32.19.

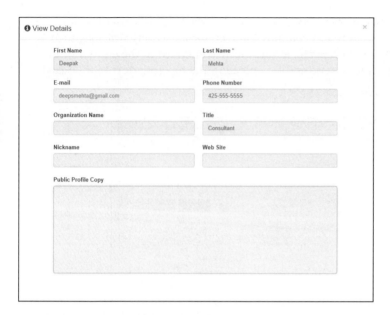

FIGURE 32.19   Adxstudio Portals read-only contacts details.

Selecting Edit in the contacts form opens an editable modal pop-up form, as shown in Figure 32.20.

FIGURE 32.20   Adxstudio Portals editable contacts details.

Entity lists are fairly versatile and can be used to show records in a variety of views, including maps. When using the map view, you need to enable map view and then provide latitude and longitude field mapping from the selected entity. The map view uses Bing Maps to render records as pinpoints on a map, and records that do not have any latitude or longitude values don't show up on the map.

Another popular control is the entity list calendar, which allows rendering of a record as a single event on a calendar. The records that have date fields populated on them are displayed on the calendar. You need to enable calendar view on the entity list record for that entity and provide field mapping for the Start Date field name and End Date field name.

Web Forms

Web forms help in extending the functionality of entity forms by allowing the usage of a single form or multistep wizard with conditional branching logic. Consider the following about web forms:

▶ A web form has one or more steps where you can have entity forms or custom web pages.

▶ You can use web forms in user registrations, surveys, and complex data entry processes.

▶ Web forms that include the CrmEntityFormView ASP.NET control render the CRM form in Adxstudio Portals.

▶ Additional configuration options are available in CRM that provide more flexibility in designing forms and changing attributes, styles, and so on.

When a user interacts with the multistep wizard built using web forms, he or she can move from one form to another by using the Next and Previous buttons. The activity is tracked using web sessions. To enable this, you need to set the Start New Session option to Yes on the Load property on the web form record. Opening the web form record in CRM and going to the related web sessions through the navigation shows those records. If there is any change in web form steps later on, it is recommended that you delete all old web session records.

Each multistep web form has more than one step defined, and each web form step has two main properties—Type and Next Step. In Next Step, you select what would be next web form step record. If your web form step is the last step in the multistep wizard, this field is blank.

For the Type attribute, you have the following options:

▶ **Condition**—This type allows you to evaluate a condition expression. The user inputs some data on web form, and then a condition expression specified in CRM is evaluated. The next web form step to be shown is based on evaluation of the condition expression. For example, in a multistep survey form, you might ask a different set of questions based on the gender of the user. To do this, the Condition type of the web form would have gender=Male as the Condition attribute. Thereafter, you would set the Next Step web form as well as the Next Step if Condition Fails web form. The Next Step web form step is displayed if the condition is true; otherwise, the web form step from the Next Step if Condition Fails attribute is shown.

TIP

Both the Adxstudio Portals and online help provide a wealth of information about how to set and write condition expressions in greater depth.

▶ **Load Form**—This is the option to set which CRM form you want to show on a web form step.

▶ **Load Tab**—You can specify what tab from what form in CRM you want to display.

▶ **Load User Control**—You can create your own custom user controls in .NET and specify the path of the control in your .NET project here.

NOTE

The Load User Control option is applicable only in On-Premises deployments of Adxstudio Portals.

▶ **Redirect**—You can specify some other page in Adxstudio Portals or some external web application or website URL here.

Follow these steps to create a simple three-step survey using web forms:

1. Create an entity named Survey and add three tabs in the form. Add some fields on the form with data types like Multiple Lines of Text, Option Set, and Single Line of Text, as shown in Figure 32.21.

FIGURE 32.21   New survey form.

The first four fields in Figure 32.21 use the same global option set. By using them and the web form metadata, you can create a multiple choice matrix.

2. Go to Portals > Web Forms and click the New button to create a new web form. Provide the following details on the form and save it (as shown in Figure 32.22):

▶ **Name**—Web Survey

▶ **Authentication Required**—Yes

▶ **Start New Session on Load**—No

▶ **Multiple Records Per User Permitted**—Yes

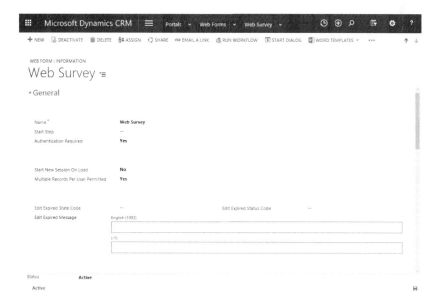

FIGURE 32.22   New Web Survey form.

3. Set Start Step to Lookup and click the +New button to open a new web step form. Provide the following details on the form and save it (as shown in Figure 32.23).

▶ **Name**—Step 1

▶ **Web Form**—Web Survey

▶ **Type**—Load Tab

▶ **Target Entity Logical Name**—wf_Survey

▶ **Mode**—Insert

▶ **Form Name**—Survey Web Form

▶ **Tab Name**—tab_1

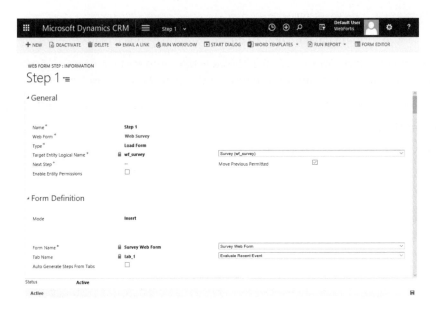

FIGURE 32.23   New Survey Web Form steps.

4. When Step 1 is saved, go to Metadata and create the associated attribute metadata records.

5. Click the +New button for Web Form Metadata and provide the following details (as shown in Figure 32.24):

▶ **Web Form Step**—Step 1

▶ **Type**—Attribute

▶ **Attribute Logical Name**—wf_cost

▶ **Style**—Multiple Choice Matrix

▶ **Group Name**—Rating

Provide similar details for the other three attributes that have the same global option set. Make sure the group name is same for rest of the three attribute metadata records.

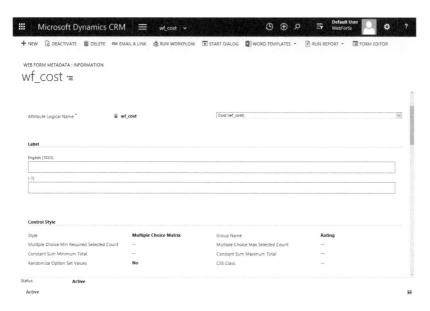

FIGURE 32.24   Web form metadata information.

6. Create attribute metadata for the Location attribute and set the Control Style to Option Set as a Vertical Radio Button List. This changes the options set to radio button vertical list in Adxstudio Portals.

7. Go back to the Step 1 form and select Lookup Next Step and click the +New button to create a new web form step with the following details (as shown in Figure 32.25):

   ▶ **Name**—Step 2

   ▶ **Web Form**—Web Survey

   ▶ **Type**—Load Tab

   ▶ **Target Entity Logical Name**—wf_survey

   ▶ **Move Previous Permitted**—Yes

   ▶ **Mode**—Edit

   ▶ **Form Name**—Survey Web Form

   ▶ **Tab Name**—tab_2

   ▶ **Source Type**—Result from previous step.

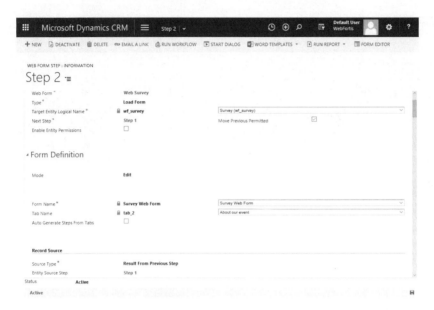

FIGURE 32.25 New survey web form, Step 2.

8. Similarly, create another web form step named Step 3 for the third tab on the form. The Next Step lookup field should be blank here.

9. Log in to Adxstudio Portals with administrator credentials and add a new page. Set Name to Survey, set Page Template to Full Page, and select Web Survey from the Web Forms drop-down, as shown in Figure 32.26. Click the Save button at the bottom.

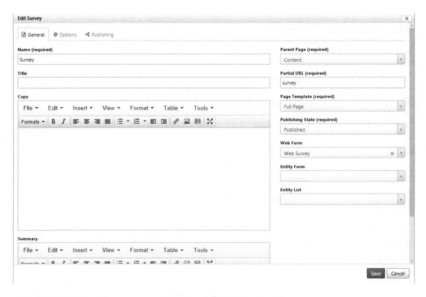

FIGURE 32.26 New survey page in Adxstudio Portals.

When you view the page, you see that the first four attributes have the same option set as a multiple-choice matrix and the Location attribute is shown as a vertical radio button list (see Figure 32.27).

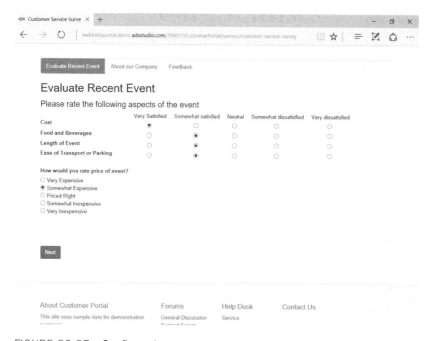

FIGURE 32.27   Configured customer portal.

Test the page by entering some data and clicking the Next button. A new record is created in Dynamics CRM, as the Step 1 mode was configured for Insert. The data submitted in the next two steps is updated (not inserted) on the same record.

Summary

Adxstudio Portals provides a lot of options to display Dynamics CRM forms and views, manage data security, and perform other actions using configuration only. As shown, it is fairly easy for non-developers or functional consultants to configure Adxstudio Portals, and with the coming integration with Dynamics CRM, the expectation is that this easy-to-use configuration will continue to improve.

At press time, Adxstudio Portals had data centers in North America, Europe, and Asia Pacific. It is expected to eventually be available in other data centers where Dynamics CRM Online is hosted.

CHAPTER 33

FieldOne

Field services are typically characterized (or described) as the people providing services out on the road or directly in front of customers or products. The "field" is the resources associated with these services; they can be the employees of the organization and the tools and equipment necessary to complete the services, which can be anything from repairing leased equipment owned by the organization (such as washing machines leased to apartment complexes or servicing parking meters for the city) where there is little or no direct customer interaction, to providing direct interaction with customers (such as providing plumbing services).

Field services also have other metrics of varying importance, including the following:

▶ Tracking employees in the field

▶ Routing employees, based on different conditions, such as these:

　▶ External factors (traffic, for example)

　▶ Priority

　▶ Escalation

　▶ Opportunity

▶ Managing the resources, other than employees, which can include the following:

　▶ The physical equipment they are servicing

　▶ The tools necessary for the servicing

　▶ The vehicles necessary to get to the job

▶ Capturing field notes, time, and costs

▶ Invoicing for the servicing

▶ Scheduling any follow-up activities

▶ Receiving feedback related to the servicing

While there are typically integration components to an ERP system to capture some of this data (for example, the invoicing and related billing/collection), a majority of the other activities are conducted in a CRM system.

In July 2015, Microsoft acquired FieldOne for its field service management strategy and intellectual property and has integrated it into Dynamics CRM.

> **NOTE**
>
> At publication time, Microsoft was still integrating FieldOne into its core product set, and this integration was expected to continue for several new release cycles.

FieldOne Overview

FieldOne Sky is a service management platform that provides service companies with tools to streamline their business processes, manage their resources, and provide better customer service by using real-time mobility, automated routing, and workflow automation that helps reduce costs.

FieldOne Sky is a service cloud–based managed solution that integrates directly into Microsoft Dynamics CRM as a part of the xRM platform. It provides a set of tools that work as part of Dynamics CRM in helping to implement business processes for the installation of products, preventive maintenance, product returns, inventory consumption, and maintenance of service level agreements. FieldOne Sky works along with core Dynamics CRM entities, and it has its own custom entities as well.

FieldOne Sky Installation

The FieldOne Sky solution works with both Dynamics CRM 2016 On-Premises and Online, and it is free for any organization that has a Microsoft Dynamics CRM professional license.

> **NOTE**
>
> Due to the availability of FieldOne Sky integration at publication time, only Microsoft Dynamics Online integration is covered in this chapter.

To install FieldOne Sky, follow these steps:

1. Log on to https://portal.office.com using your Office 365 global administrator credentials and select Admin > CRM on the left, as shown in Figure 33.1. A new window opens, listing all your CRM Online instances (see Figure 33.2).

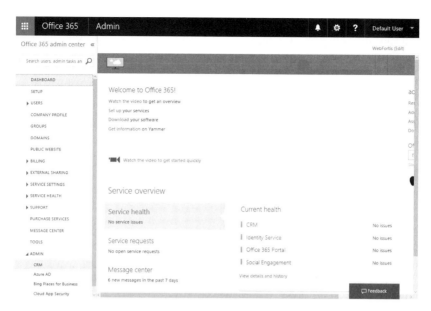

FIGURE 33.1 Office 365 portal interface.

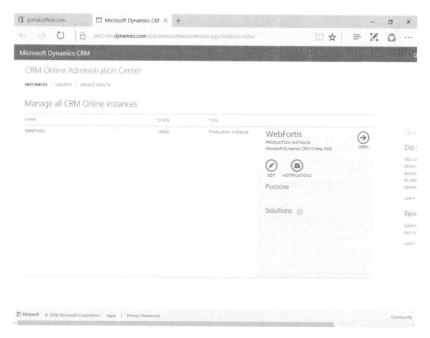

FIGURE 33.2 Microsoft CRM Online instance solutions.

2. Select the CRM Online instance where you want to install FieldOne Sky solution and click the pencil icon to the right of Solutions to manage your solutions for the

selected instance, as shown in Figure 33.2. As shown in Figure 33.3, all the Microsoft preferred solutions are now shown, as along with their status (for example, whether they are installed, whether they have an update available).

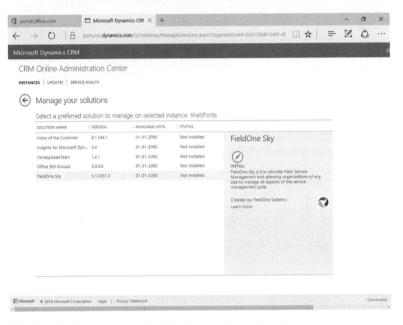

FIGURE 33.3   Microsoft CRM Online Solution Management.

3. Select FieldOne Sky and click Install. The Terms of Service page, shown in Figure 33.4, appears.

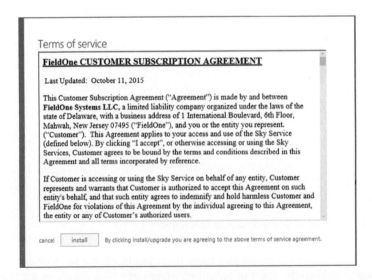

FIGURE 33.4   Microsoft CRM Online FieldOne Terms of Service page.

> **NOTE**
>
> Microsoft has classified the solutions shown in Figure 33.3 as preferred solutions, which means they are the ones offered by or through (in the case of InsideView) Microsoft. No other solutions (either custom or by another solution provider or ISV) will show up here; you have to load them separately through the Solutions Explorer.

▶ Refer to **CHAPTER 22**, "Customizing the System," for more information about solutions management.

4. Click the Install button to accept the FieldOne customer subscription agreement and begin the installation. The FieldOne Sky installation might take some time (in some cases up to an hour or longer). You can leave this page and come back to check the status, which will be shown on the right in yellow, as shown in Figure 33.5.

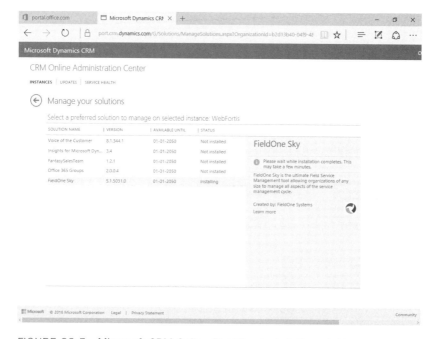

FIGURE 33.5   Microsoft CRM Online FieldOne installation status.

When FieldOne Sky is finished installing, the solution status column display Installed for the status, as shown in Figure 33.6.

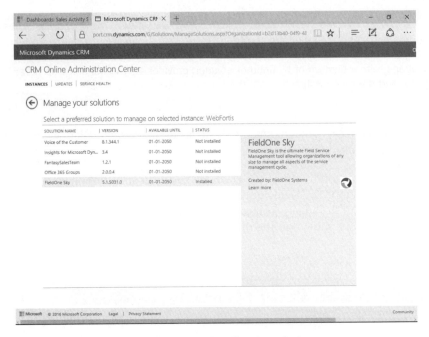

FIGURE 33.6   Microsoft CRM Online FieldOne installed status.

5. Navigate to Dynamics CRM, and you see the new title FieldOne Sky in the navigation bar, as shown in Figure 33.7.

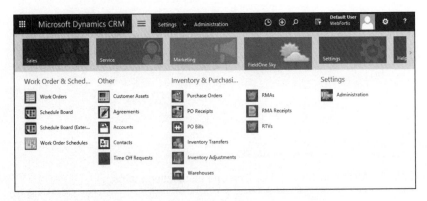

FIGURE 33.7   FieldOne installed in Microsoft Dynamics CRM.

You can now either select FieldOne Sky from the navigation bar or navigate to Settings > Solutions and select the FieldOne Sky solution (see Figure 33.8). On this screen, you can also remove or modify the solution if necessary.

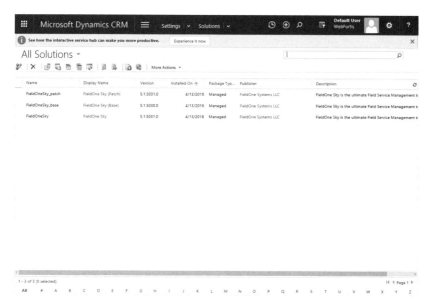

FIGURE 33.8   FieldOne solution in Microsoft Dynamics CRM.

FieldOne Sky Configuration

FieldOne Sky comes with four predefined security roles and field-level security profiles. Because security roles define which entities a user has privileges for and field-level security profiles define which fields a user can see and update, it is important to properly configure them.

If you navigate to Settings > Security > Security Roles in Dynamics CRM, you can configure the FieldOne Sky security roles (see Figure 33.9). If you navigate to Settings > Security > Field Security Profiles in Dynamics CRM, you can configure the FieldOne Sky field security profiles (see Figure 33.10).

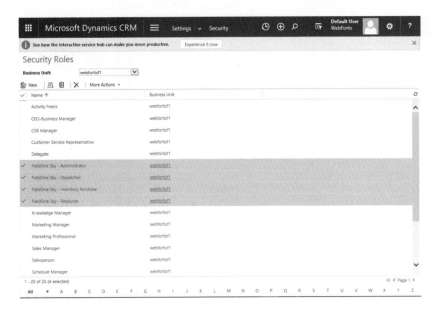

FIGURE 33.9   FieldOne Security Roles page.

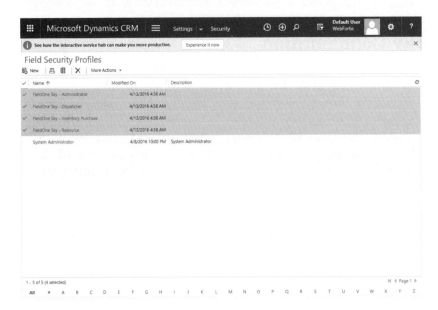

FIGURE 33.10   FieldOne Field Security Profiles page.

The security roles are as follows:

▶ **FieldOne Sky - Administrator**—This role should be assigned to the user who will be responsible for managing the configuration of FieldOne Sky in Dynamics CRM, as it gives the user access to the entire FieldOne Sky Administration area and all FieldOne Sky entities.

▶ **FieldOne Sky - Dispatcher**—This role should be assigned to the user who will be responsible for the following:

   ▶ Managing resources

   ▶ Work orders

   ▶ Scheduling work orders

▶ **FieldOne Sky - Inventory Purchase**—This security role should be assigned to users who will are responsible for the following:

   ▶ Inventory

   ▶ Purchase orders

   ▶ RMA (Return Merchandise Authorization)

   ▶ RTV (Return to Vendor)

▶ **FieldOne Sky - Resource**—Resources are typically the field technicians who access FieldOne Sky using a mobile application.

> **NOTE**
>
> To access FieldOne features, a user must be assigned one or more of the security roles and have a corresponding field security profile. It is recommended that you not make any changes to the existing security roles and field security profiles. Instead, you should copy the existing security role or field-level security profile and make changes with the copied role or profile.

If a user's record is set up as a resource record, the address on the user record is used as the resource's start and end location, and the Latitude and Longitude fields are updated automatically when the user address is updated in Office 365, as shown in Figure 33.11. (If your view doesn't match what's shown in Figure 33.11, be sure to change your form type to Information.)

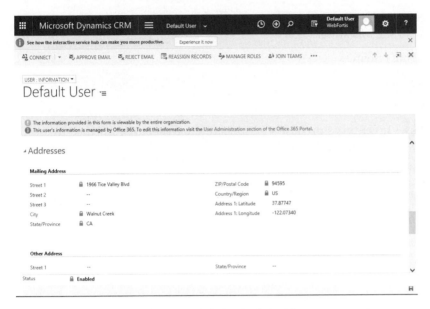

FIGURE 33.11   FieldOne Latitude and Longitude settings.

FieldOne workflows use the email and phone number fields on the user record to send reminders and notifications about work orders to the resource.

FieldOne Administration

You need to configure a number of fields in FieldOne, but only minimally. To do that, navigate to FieldOne Sky > Administration (see Figure 33.12), where you can select and configure the following:

> **NOTE**
>
> The fields explained here are just a subset of the ones that can be configured. Field related to inventory management such as RMA and RTV would be similarly configured for modules that would be deployed and used at your organization.

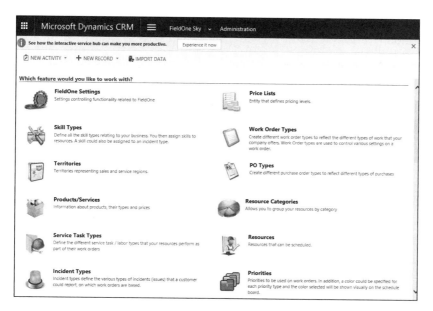

FIGURE 33.12 FieldOne settings.

▶ **FieldOne Settings**—You can configure work order–related configurations here, such as prefix, status, and starting number. Similarly, you can set the prefix and start number for RMA, RTV, Agreement, and other entities.

▶ **Skill Types**—You can add skill types related to your business here. These skill types are assigned to resources and incident types. Having skill types assigned helps in scheduling work orders with proper skilled resources.

▶ **Territories**—Territories are used to define regions where sales and services are provided. Having them defined helps dispatchers in assigning work orders to field agents that are in or close to the territories of the account being serviced.

▶ **Products/Services**—This is the out-of-the-box product entity (that is, native) from Dynamics CRM. You can define the cost and list prices of products and services offered by your business here, and that information will be consumed by FieldOne for servicing purposes.

▶ Refer to **CHAPTER 17**, "Settings," for more information about working with the product catalog.

▶ **Service Task Types**—You can define various service task types and their estimated times to complete. This information is used for creating service tasks for work orders and help in estimating completion times for work orders.

▶ **Incident Types**—Here you can define various types of incidents that customers can report. You can define associated service tasks and products with each incident type. When an incident type is associated with a work order, service tasks, products, and services are prepopulated from the incident type.

▶ **Resource Pay Types**—You can define resource pay types here to help in calculating the resource cost.

▶ **Price Lists**—This is the out-of-the-box Dynamics CRM entity to define different price lists for products and services.

▶ **Work Order Types**—You can define different types of work orders to reflect different types of work the company offers—for example, installation, preventive maintenance, service call, and so on.

▶ **PO Types**—Here you can define purchase order types.

▶ **Resource Categories**—You can define categories to group resources, such as field manager, technician, operator, vehicle, and so on.

▶ **Resources**—Here you can create multiple resources that will be working on work orders. A resource can be a company employee or a company asset.

▶ **Priorities**—You can define work order priorities here. You can assign a different color for each priority that will be used to display on the Schedule Board.

▶ **Work Order Sub-statuses**—You can define various work order sub-statuses for your organization's processes.

▶ **Work Order Schedule Sub-statuses**—You can define work order schedule sub-statuses according to your requirements. A work order can have more than one work order schedule.

▶ **Agreement Sub-statuses**—You can define custom agreement sub-statuses, which can be used to specify current agreement status more precisely.

▶ **Warehouses**—You can create company warehouse records here.

Service Accounts and Billing Accounts

The service account is the place where work orders take place, and when you create a work order and specify a service account, the work order inherits the address of the service account as the location where the field agent needs to go.

> **TIP**
>
> When a work order is created for a sub-account, the parent account is added as the billing account by default. You can change this to a different account, if necessary.

> **NOTE**
>
> Billing accounts are required if an invoice for a work order will be sent to an address other than the service account address. If no billing account is specified, the invoice will be sent to the service account.

You can update the latitude and longitude of an account record by clicking ... > Geo Code, as shown in Figure 33.13.

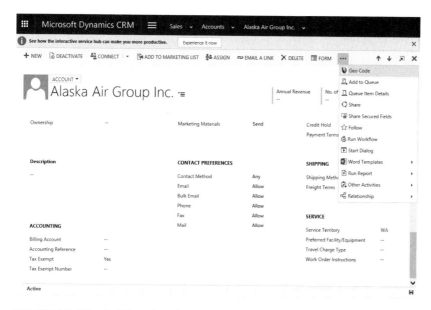

FIGURE 33.13   FieldOne Geo Code settings.

When you select Geo Code, you see a pop-up window with a pin on a Bing map for the address, as shown in Figure 33.14. This helps you calculate travel time for a resource to reach the account location for a work order. In addition, if you change the form type to Information, the form also shows the latitude and longitude fields populated.

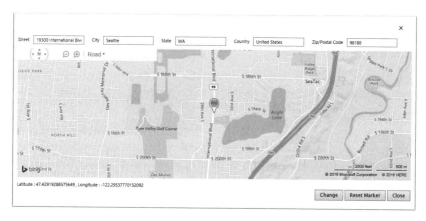

FIGURE 33.14   FieldOne Bing map.

Work Orders

A work order is an order received by an organization from a customer or client, or an order created internally within the organization. It is used to manage and schedule resources and activities. A work order may be for products or services or for different types of work, such as installations, repairs, or maintenance. A work order includes the following information:

▶ Service account

▶ Location where the work needs to be performed

▶ Description of the work

▶ Priority and estimated duration

▶ Skills required

▶ Steps to perform the work

▶ Products and services required

Work Order Process Life Cycle

This section explains the life cycle of a work order, from creation to invoicing. It is important to note that work orders have five main statuses:

▶ Open—Unscheduled

▶ Open—Scheduled

▶ Open—Completed

▶ Closed—Posted

▶ Closed—Cancelled

Open—Unscheduled   When a work order is first created, its status is Open—Unscheduled. There are four ways to create a work order:

▶ **Agreement**—An agreement can be used to automatically trigger the creation of work order for recurring work like preventive maintenance. Agreements can be scheduled to create work orders automatically at a predefined time interval.

▶ **Case**—When there is an inbound call to the support team and the problem could not be resolved remotely, the support engineer on call can create one or more work orders to fix the problem from the case entity record. These are normally break or fix types of work orders.

▶ **Sales Order**—When a sales order is processed and some installation needs to be done at the customer site, a work order can be created from the sales order.

▶ **Ad hoc work orders**—This type of work order is normally created by field agents when they are at customer locations and find that some extra work needs to be performed.

When a work order is created, it can be populated with incidents, products and skills, location, and so on. When a work order has not yet been scheduled, no work order schedule record is created.

Open—Scheduled   When a work order is scheduled to a resource (for example, an individual, equipment, a resource crew), it is in the Open—Scheduled status.

A work order can be scheduled in four ways:

- ▶ A dispatcher can schedule it manually.
- ▶ A field agent can schedule it using the FieldOne Sky mobile application.
- ▶ A dispatcher can schedule using Schedule Assistant.
- ▶ The routing engine can schedule it automatically.

When a work order is scheduled, a work schedule record is created. The work order status is then changed to Open—Scheduled and the work order schedule status is Scheduled.

> **NOTE**
>
> A separate work order schedule record is created for each additional resource.

There are six work order schedule statuses:

- ▶ Scheduled
- ▶ Traveling
- ▶ In Progress
- ▶ On Break
- ▶ Completed
- ▶ Cancelled

> **TIP**
>
> While the schedule status can be updated in a variety of ways, the most common way it is changed is by field agents on the mobile app.

Changing the work order schedule status changes the work order status as shown in Table 33.1.

TABLE 33.1   Work Order Schedule Status Changes on the Work Order Status

Work Order Schedule Status	Work Order Status
Traveling	Open—In Progress
In Progress	Open—In Progress
Completed	Open—Completed
Canceled	Open—Unscheduled

NOTE

When the work order schedule status changes, the work order status changes automatically. The exception is when the status changes to Completed, and there are other incomplete work orders; in that case, those incomplete work orders need to be closed appropriately before the work order status can change.

Open—In Progress   The typical next step after scheduling a work order is dispatching a particular resource. FieldOne Sky provides the options email, text, and Interactive Voice Response (IVR) notification to alert the field agents about work orders scheduled for them.

TIP

The same notification feature can be used to alert customers and vendors, when needed.

NOTE

If notifications are not configured, field agents can log on to the FieldOne Sky mobile application to see their latest schedule.

Field agents review the schedule and then may accept or decline a work order, and the work order status is scheduled. The work order schedule status may be accepted or declined, based on the field agent's action on the work order.

Open—Completed   Field agents update work orders with all necessary information—such as the products used, services performed, duration on tasks, photos for work done, signatures from customers, and mobile payments—by using the FieldOne Sky mobile application. When the work is done, the work order schedule status changes to Open—Complete. The actual time spent on a work order is calculated from the time when the work order schedule status changed from Open—In Progress to Open—Completed.

Review/Approval   A manager reviews a work order once its status is changed to Open—Completed to make sure all details entered in the work order are accurate and to ensure that work was done properly. When the manager is satisfied with the work order details updated by the field agent, he or she changes the status of the work order from Open—Completed to Closed—Posted. When the status changes to Closed—Posted, there is no way to make changes to the work order record.

Invoice   FieldOne Sky automatically creates invoices for products and services used in work orders and makes required inventory adjustments. The system also converts products into customer equipment.

Agreement Process

The Agreement entity in FieldOne Sky is used for preventive maintenance work. It provides a framework for generating work orders and invoices automatically at scheduled time intervals (for example, daily, weekly, monthly) with other details related to the work order, such as products, services, and service tasks.

You can find agreements by navigating to Settings > FieldOne Sky > Agreements, as shown in Figure 33.15.

FIGURE 33.15   FieldOne agreements.

To create a new agreement, click + New icon and provide the following details (see Figure 33.16):

▶ **Service Account**—Select the account record where the work order will be worked.

▶ **Billing Account**—This field is the location where invoices will be sent. It is populated automatically if the selected service account has a separate billing account; you can also select a different billing account.

▶ **Start Date and End Date**—Select the start and end dates for the agreement. The duration is then populated automatically.

▶ **Service Level**—This field is used to categorize agreements, and it can be configured in the Administration section of FieldOne Sky.

▶ **Price List**—Select the price list for products and services that will be used in completing work orders for this agreement.

▶ **Territory**—Select the territory where work orders will take place. This will help the routing engine and Schedule Assistant schedule work orders.

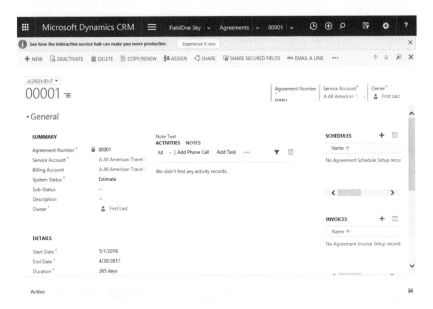

FIGURE 33.16   FieldOne agreement.

Agreement Schedules

When an agreement record is created, you can then create agreement schedules, which define how work orders are generated. To create an agreement schedule, click the +in front of the Schedules subgrid to open a new window and provide the following details (see Figure 33.17):

▶ **Auto Generate WO**—If you want the system to generate work orders automatically, set the value to Yes. To have work orders created manually for each scheduled date, set it to No.

▶ **Generate WO Days in Advance**—If you want work orders to be generated in advance of scheduled dates, provide the number of days. The default value is 7.

▶ **Auto Generate Schedule**—If Auto Generate WO is set to Yes and you want to schedule the work orders automatically as well, set this value to Yes. When a work order is created, the system also schedules it by creating a work order schedule record. The work order schedule is displayed on the Schedule Board.

▶ **Preferred Resource**—If Auto Generate Schedule is set to Yes, then specify the resource for the work order schedule here.

▶ **Preferred Start Time**—Specify the preferred start time for the auto-generated work order schedule.

▶ **Work Order Type**—Select from the options for the types available.

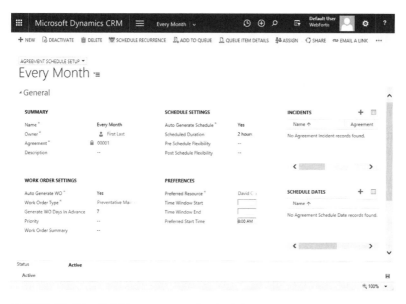

FIGURE 33.17   FieldOne agreement schedule.

You can associate incidents, agreement service tasks, agreement products, and agreement services to the agreement schedule record. When work orders are generated, this information is passed on to those records that help the field agent to complete the work order. The work order summary, work order type and priority will also pass down to work orders generated from agreement schedule record.

Click Schedule Recurrence to specify dates and time intervals for work orders to be generated, as shown in Figure 33.18.

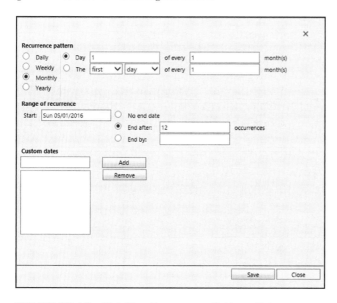

FIGURE 33.18   FieldOne Recurrence Pattern dialog.

> **TIP**
>
> You can create multiple agreement schedules for an agreement—for example, a weekly schedule for the checkup of equipment and a monthly schedule for servicing of equipment. You can always modify work orders to add more products or services, change the price list and work order types, and so on, as needed.

Agreement Invoices

Agreement invoices are different from out-of-the-box Dynamics CRM invoices as they apply specifically to FieldOne configurations. They can be generated in two ways:

▶ **Automatic billing**—The Agreement Invoice entity is used for automatic billing. Customers pay for the product in the system, and it is used for subscriptions, rental fees, and so on. Agreement invoice records are created at a set recurrence interval for a set price and are associated with agreement records.

▶ **Time of service billing**—When a work order is completed and the status is changed to Closed—Posted, clients are invoiced for used services and products for that work order. This does not involve the Agreement Invoice entity but rather the standard work order invoice process.

Schedule Board

FieldOne Sky comes with the Schedule Board, which provides an overview of the scheduled work orders and resources' availability. It also allows you to manually schedule work orders. Navigate to the FieldOne Sky tile in Dynamics CRM Online, and you see two links, Schedule Board and Schedule Board (External), as shown in Figure 33.19. The only difference between these two is that Schedule Board (External) opens in a new window with no Dynamics CRM navigation menu, and the other one opens in the same window.

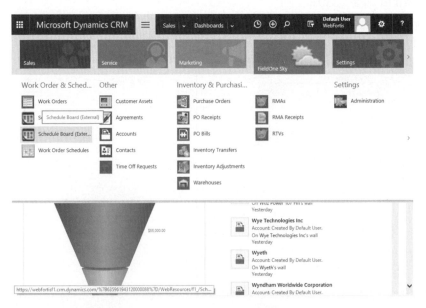

FIGURE 33.19   FieldOne Schedule Board navigation.

When you hover over a work order on the Schedule Board, you see additional information about the work order, such as the work order number, service account name, work order summary, status, territory, and so on (see Figure 33.20). In addition, the color tells you the status of a work order.

FIGURE 33.20   FieldOne Schedule Board with a work order selected.

To configure colors for the Schedule Board, navigate to FieldOne Sky > Administration > Work Order Schedule Sub-Statuses in Dynamics CRM and then make the changes you want to the screen shown in Figure 33.21.

FIGURE 33.21   FieldOne Schedule Board color selection.

The map view displays all the work orders (scheduled and unscheduled), as shown in Figure 33.22.

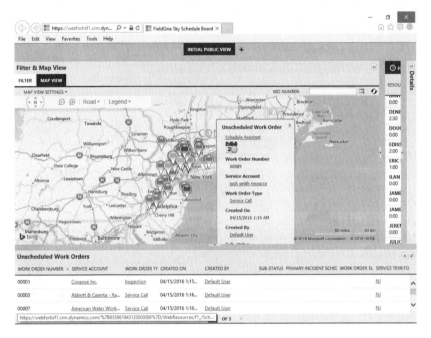

FIGURE 33.22   FieldOne map view.

Gray pins indicate unscheduled work orders. A grid at the bottom of the Schedule Board displays the list of all unscheduled work orders. When you hover over any of the pins, you see details about the corresponding work order.

Manual Scheduling Using the Schedule Board

You can manually schedule an unscheduled work orders in three ways:

▶ You can drag an unscheduled work order from the grid to the Schedule Board, as shown in Figure 33.23.

▶ You can drag an unscheduled work order (gray pin) from map view to the Schedule Board.

▶ You can block a slot in the Schedule Board by first selecting (clicking) and then dragging over the time slot using the mouse and then navigating the Look Up Record dialog that appears (see Figure 33.24). Here you can select a work order from the unscheduled work orders view.

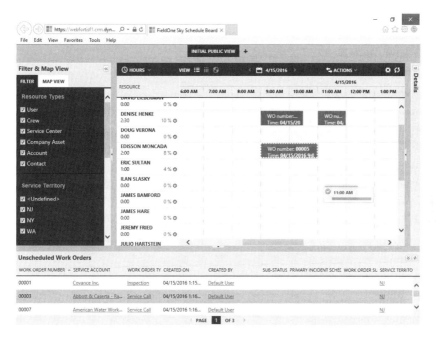

FIGURE 33.23   Dragging from the FieldOne grid to the Schedule Board.

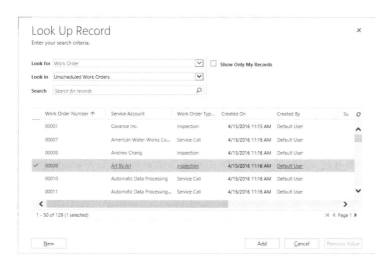

FIGURE 33.24   Looking up unscheduled work orders.

Users can reassign and reschedule previously scheduled work orders by just dragging and dropping them on new time slots. To do this, right-click a scheduled work order to see all the actions you can perform with the work order schedule. You can change its status, get driving directions, and remove it from the Schedule Board. When you remove the work order schedule from the Schedule Board, the work order is displayed again as an unscheduled work order, as shown in Figure 33.25.

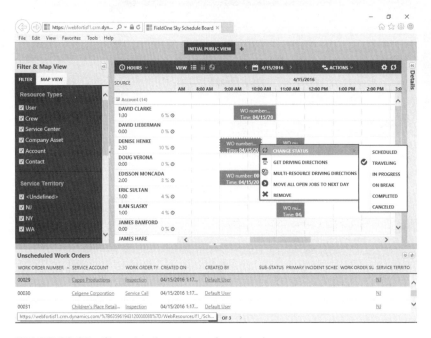

FIGURE 33.25   Changing the status of work orders.

Schedule Assistant

The Schedule Assistant helps in querying available resources and time slot options and then scheduling the work orders with availability. You can launch the Schedule Assistant from the home page grid of work orders or from the entity form of a work order entity by clicking the button Schedule Assistant, as shown in Figure 33.26.

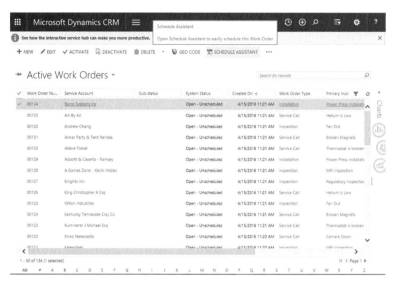

FIGURE 33.26   Launching the Schedule Assistant.

NOTE

You can schedule only one work order at a time by using Schedule Assistant.

Schedule Assistant is an HTML web resource in FieldOne Sky, and it is divided into panes, as shown in Figure 33.27.

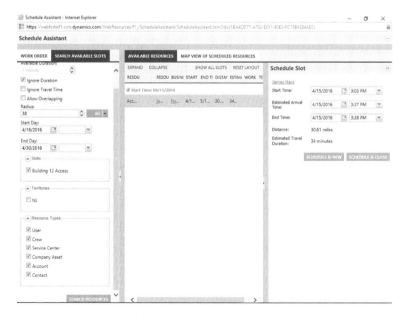

FIGURE 33.27   Schedule Assistant.

The left pane shows the constraints that are used to query the system to find available resources, while the middle pane shows the available resources and the proposed schedule slot.

You use Schedule Assistant to set the following constraints:

▶ **Time Constraint**—This is automatically populated from the Primary Incident Type lookup field on the work order (the Primary Incident Type entity has a Scheduled Duration field). If the associated primary incident type record has that field populated, Available Duration is populated with that value. The default value for Available Duration is 1 minute.

▶ **Radius**—You can specify the radius to considered for resource availability. You can set the units here to miles or kilometers.

▶ **Start and End Day**—You can specify the date range for availability of resources.

▶ **Resources**—If there is a preferred resource assigned for the work order, that resource is listed here. If there is no preferred resource specified for the work order, this constraint is not visible at all.

▶ **Territory**—You can narrow down your search by selecting nearby territories.

▶ **Resource Types**—You can specify what kind of resource types are required for the selected work order. The options available are User, Crew, Service Center, Company Asset, Account, and Contact.

Clicking Search Resources shows all resources available and time slots in the right pane of the Schedule Assistant. In addition, it displays the business unit name, start and end times, distance, and estimated travel time.

Select any time slot from the listed records, and the Schedule Slot pane opens. Here you can click Schedule & Close to create a work schedule record and close the window. Click Schedule & New to schedule multiple resources for the work order. You can click Map View of Scheduled Resources to see all resources on a map, and you can open up the Schedule Board to see scheduled work orders.

> **NOTE**
>
> While not available at publication, FieldOne Sky has a routing engine that allows the system to automatically schedule and reschedule work orders. The advantage of using the routing engine is that it makes optimal use of the company's resources and peoples' time.

FieldOne Sky Mobile App

FieldOne Sky comes with a mobile application that is available on for iOS, Android, and Windows. Field technicians use the mobile app for various activities, including self-assigning work orders, updating work order status, and mobile payments.

You can download the app, connect to your Dynamics CRM instance, and then follow these steps to log on to the FieldOne Sky mobile application:

1. Open the application on your device and then navigate to the Setup menu and click the Connect link next to CRM (see Figure 33.28).

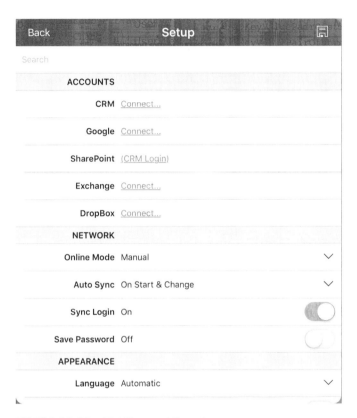

FIGURE 33.28   FieldOne mobile setup.

2. Provide your Dynamics CRM login details and URL and click the refresh icon in the top-right corner (see Figure 33.29). Your device downloads the data and metadata for the app, as shown in Figure 33.30.

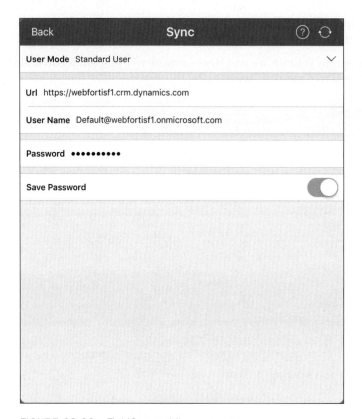

FIGURE 33.29   FieldOne mobile sync setup.

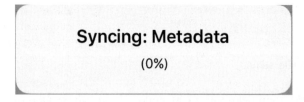

FIGURE 33.30   Synchronizing data from Dynamics CRM to the mobile app.

3. When the configurations, data, and metadata are finished downloading, you see a computer icon in the top-left corner, as shown in Figure 33.31. This indicate whether you are working offline or online. Tap the icon to connect as online.

FIGURE 33.31   FieldOne mobile app.

Scheduling Using the FieldOne Sky Mobile App

The dispatcher is not the only one who that can schedule/reschedule work orders from the Scheduling Board or the Schedule Assistant in Dynamics CRM. By using the FieldOne Sky mobile application, field agents can handle scheduling themselves. Typically a field agent handles scheduling when a work order takes more time than expected and the field agent wants to reschedule the upcoming work order or when an appointment is canceled and the field agent is available to work on some other work orders. In such cases, the field agent does not need to call the dispatcher or someone else to schedule or reschedule work orders.

Field agents can handle work order scheduling from the mobile application in the following three ways:

▶ A field agent can schedule unscheduled work orders by using the list view.

▶ A field agent can schedule unscheduled work orders by using the map view.

▶ A field agent can reschedule a scheduled work order by changing the start date time and the end date time.

The following sections describes the steps involved in each of these methods.

Scheduling Using the List View

Follow these steps to schedule an unscheduled work order by using the list view:

1. In the FieldOne Sky mobile application, click the Work Orders menu and select the work order you would like to schedule.

2. Click the More menu at the lower left and select Resource Schedules, as shown in Figure 33.32. There isn't a record if there hasn't been a resource scheduled for this work order.

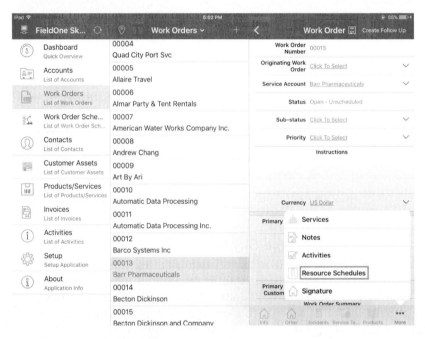

FIGURE 33.32   FieldOne resource schedules.

3. Click the + icon to create a work order schedule for the selected work order.

4. Select Schedule Sub-Status as Accepted and then select the Start Time and End Time. The app calculates and updates the Duration field on the work order schedule.

5. Click Resource to select a resource from the list and assign the work order to that resource.

6. Click the save icon in the top-right corner to save the record. The work order is now scheduled, as shown in Figure 33.33.

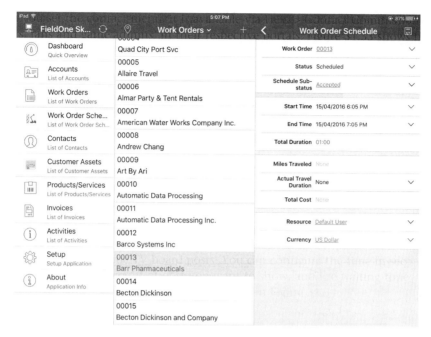

FIGURE 33.33   FieldOne work order scheduled in the right pane.

Scheduling Using the Map View

Follow these steps to schedule an unscheduled work order by using the map view:

1. Go to Work Order Lists in the FieldOne Sky mobile application and click the Map View icon at the top.

2. The app displays all work orders on the map. Zoom into the map to find and choose a work order pin that you'd like to schedule (see Figure 33.34).

3. Click the pin to access the work order information. The app opens the work order record, and you can perform the steps described previously with the list view to schedule the work order.

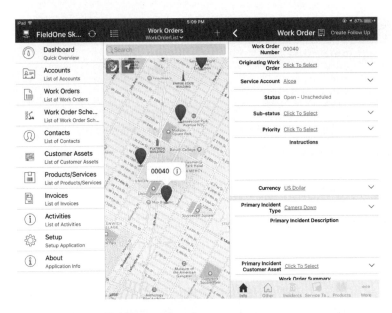

FIGURE 33.34   FieldOne work order map view.

Rescheduling a Scheduled Work Order

Follow these steps to reschedule a scheduled work order:

1. Select a work order schedule from the main menu and click More at the bottom right of the screen.

2. Select Resource Schedules. The app shows resources scheduled (see Figure 33.35).

FIGURE 33.35   FieldOne scheduled resources.

3. Click a record to see the work order information.

4. Change the start date time and end date time and click the save icon.

> **NOTE**
>
> You can also set up notifications sent as text messages to clients when work orders are scheduled or rescheduled by navigating to the Settings > Configuration options.

Customizing the FieldOne Sky Mobile App

The FieldOne Sky mobile application can be customized using the Resco Woodford solution. The Woodford solution allows you to customize the app, manage users and licenses, and manage mobile devices that have the application installed.

There are two ways to use the Woodford solution:

▶ Download the solution and import it into your Dynamics CRM instance. This method is recommended and provides single sign-on.

▶ Download the application on your computer and use it from there. With this method, you have to provide your credentials every time you try to use it.

> **NOTE**
>
> The Woodford solution supports Dynamics CRM online and IFD-enabled Dynamics CRM On-Premises environments.

The Woodford solution allows you to customize the app by adding custom entities and fields, designing views and forms, configuring dashboards, creating different versions of the app for different user roles, and more. You do not need to worry about different device platforms, as any changes made are deployed to all mobile devices, regardless of platform.

> **TIP**
>
> Organizations commonly put their company logo and corporate colors on the application by using the Woodford solution.

To configure the Woodford solution, follow these steps:

> **NOTE**
>
> You must be assigned the system administrator role in order to configure the Woodford solution.

1. Log on to Dynamics CRM where the FieldOne Sky solution is installed by navigating to Settings > Solutions and then opening the FieldOneSkye_base solution.

2. Click Configuration in the left navigation pane and then click the Download Resco Woodford Solution link to save the managed solution file on your computer (see Figure 33.36).

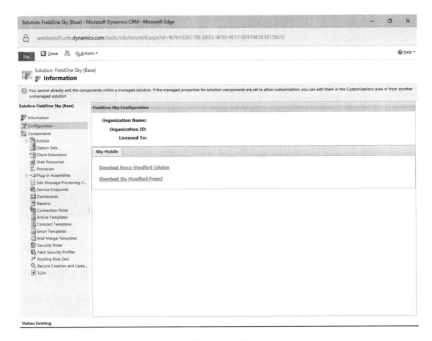

FIGURE 33.36   FieldOne Sky solution configuration page.

3. Close the FieldOneSky_base solution and click the Import button on the solution home page to import the Woodford solution, as shown in Figure 33.37.

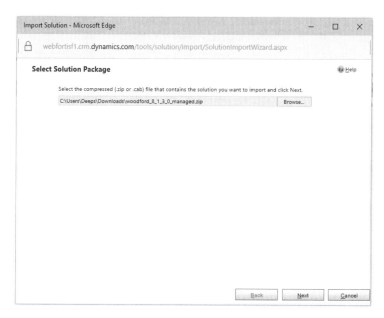

FIGURE 33.37   FieldOne Sky solution import dialog.

4. When the solution is imported successfully, refresh your browser and navigate to Settings. There you should see a Mobile CRM area with a Woodford tile, as shown in Figure 33.38.

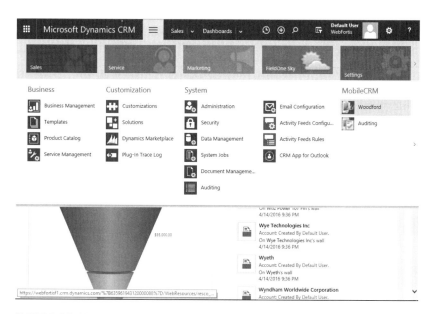

FIGURE 33.38   FieldOne Sky Woodford tile navigation option.

5. Click the Woodford tile, and you see the MobileCRM Woodford link, as shown in Figure 33.39.

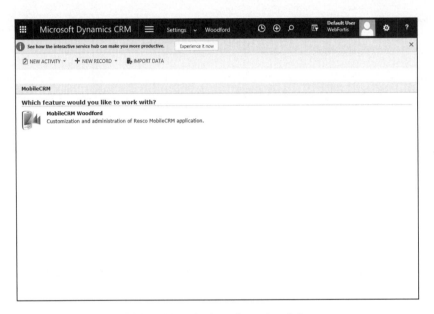

FIGURE 33.39   MobileCRM Woodford configuration link.

6. Select the MobileCRM Woodford configuration link, and you may be prompted to install Silverlight if it is not installed on your computer. Do that if needed. Then provide your details for registration and download the metadata from your Dynamics CRM instance.

7. Configure the app by either starting from scratch or using a template. To download a template from the FieldOneSky_base solution, navigate back to the FieldOne Sky solution and from the configuration page (where you downloaded the Resco Woodford Solution), click Download Sky Woodford Project (see Figure 33.40).

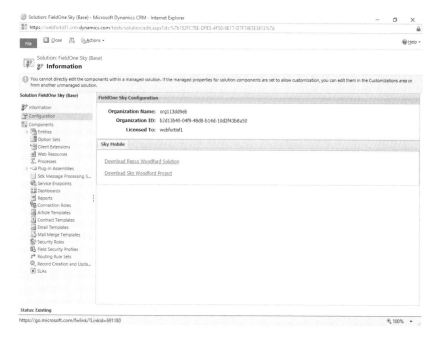

FIGURE 33.40   Sky Woodford project download.

8. After the zip file downloads to your computer, extract the file to a folder, and you see a file with the extension .woodford.

9. Go to back to the Woodford application, click the Import button at the top, and select the .woodford file you just downloaded. As shown in Figure 33.41, the Add Mobile Project dialog opens, and in it you need to provide the following details:

   ▶ **Type**—Standard User

   ▶ **Name**—*YourCompanyName* FieldOne Sky Woodford

   ▶ **Priority**—10

   ▶ **Roles**—Select all FieldOne Sky security roles

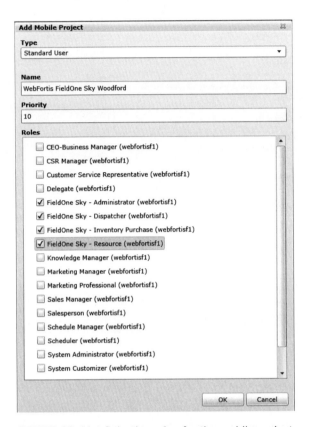

FIGURE 33.41 Selecting roles for the mobile project configuration.

Now, your Woodford solution is ready to configure the FieldOne Sky mobile app. The following sections describe some of the key configuration changes to consider.

Security

If you click Security under Administration in the left navigation pane you can see a list of all devices that are using the FieldOne Sky mobile application connected with your Dynamics CRM instance (see Figure 33.42).

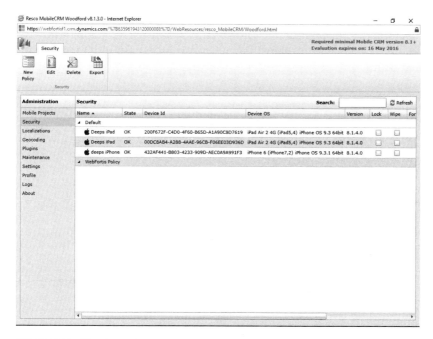

FIGURE 33.42   Security selection for the FieldOne Sky mobile app.

By selecting a device and then clicking Edit at the top, you can perform the following functions (as shown in Figure 33.43):

▶ Lock the application

▶ Wipe the application

▶ Do a full sync on a specific device

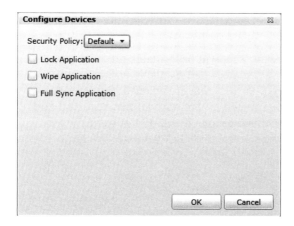

FIGURE 33.43   Configuring devices for use with the FieldOne Sky mobile app.

To define a new security policy, click the New Policy button and then define the session expiration time, when to lock the application, and when to wipe data from application. Select the device and then click Edit to change the policy for the device from the default to the newly created policy.

Customization

If you select Mobile Projects in the left navigation pane, Administration, you can open a project by double-clicking it (as shown in Figure 33.44).

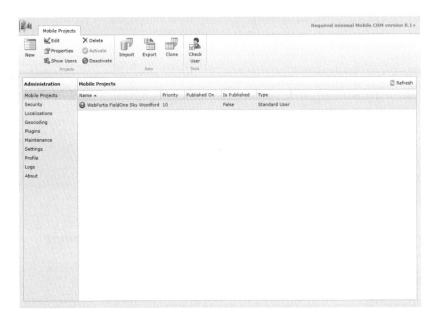

FIGURE 33.44   Selecting mobile projects from the Woodford solution.

The project opens in a new tab, and the left navigation pane provides options for configuring Mobile entities, views, forms, fields, and dashboards.

Select Home to see all entities in the Home pane that will be available on the user's home page in the mobile application. The right pane, titled Available Entities, shows entities that can be added to the home screen. Entities that are enabled for use on the mobile app are displayed in both panes. You can add and remove an by selecting it and then clicking Remove or Add at the top. For this example, if you do not want the Lead entity to be displayed on the mobile app, you select it and click Remove. The Lead entity is then moved to the Available Items list (see Figure 33.45).

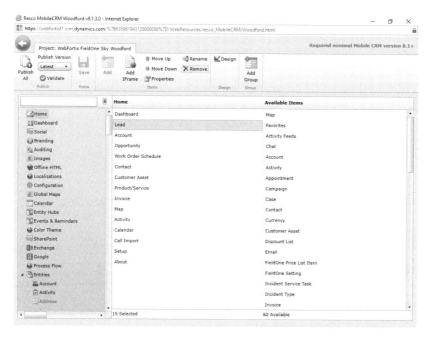

FIGURE 33.45   Selecting available entities to customize.

If you scroll down through the entities in the left navigation pane, you see some entities grayed out. To enable one of these entities, select it and click Enable at top of the form, as shown in Figure 33.46.

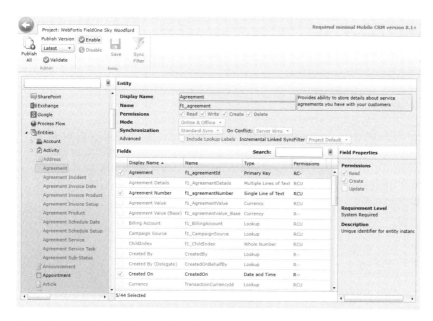

FIGURE 33.46   Enabling entities for the FieldOne Sky mobile app.

The Sync Filter button in the navigation bar defines the information that can be sent to the mobile device from Dynamics CRM. There is already a sync filter defined in the project template for the Account entity, so if you select the Account entity and click the Sync Filter button, you see the conditions defined for Account entity records, as shown in Figure 33.47. You can modify these conditions to meet any specific requirement your organization might have.

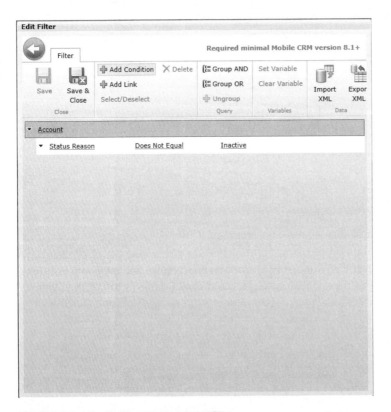

FIGURE 33.47   Configuring the sync filters.

You can define which fields and permissions will be available on the mobile application for specific fields. However, you cannot override any CRM security that might already exist (though you can further restrict, if required). Select the Account entity in the left navigation pane and then expand it. You can see the menu items Forms, Views, Charts, Fields, and Indexes for that entity, as shown in Figure 33.48.

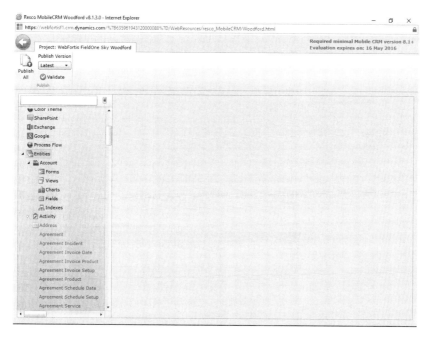

FIGURE 33.48   Entities menu.

Select Fields from the left navigation pane to see all the fields enabled for mobile in the right pane. The fields that are highlighted and for those that have a check box are available in the mobile application. You can select a grayed out field like Account Number and click the check box in front of it, and you can also define the field permissions (Read, Create, Update) in the right pane. After making required changes, click the Save button (see Figure 33.49).

FIGURE 33.49   Editing the available fields.

Selecting Forms under the Account entity in the left navigation pane allows you to edit the available forms. To modify a form, follow these steps:

1. Open the default form of type Edit Form to make modifications to the default form (see Figure 33.50).

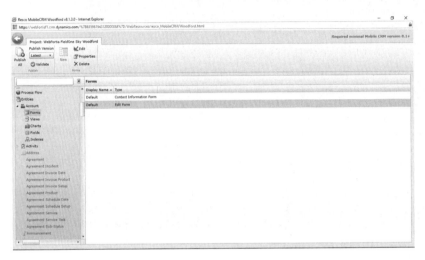

FIGURE 33.50   Working with the available forms for the mobile app.

2. Click the Add Field button and from the list of the available fields, click Account Number to add it to the end of the form (see Figure 33.51). You can drag and drop the field to any position on the form.

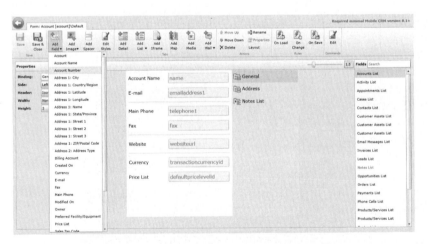

FIGURE 33.51   Adding Account Number to the mobile form.

3. Click Save and Close to save the changes and close the form.

4. Click the Validate button to make sure the changes are valid for the project (see Figure 33.52).

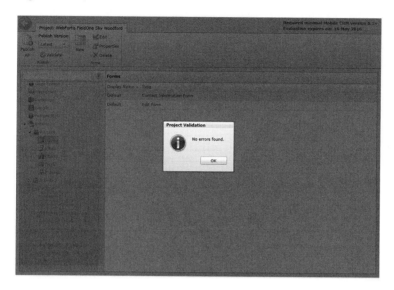

FIGURE 33.52   Validating the changes to the form.

5. Click the Publish All button to push the changes to the mobile devices of users.

6. Log on to the FieldOne Sky mobile application and click the refresh icon to synchronize the configuration, metadata, and data changes. When the app asks you to sync the changes from server, click Sync to get latest updates (see Figure 33.53).

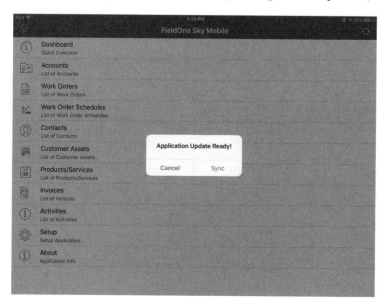

FIGURE 33.53   Syncing data.

7. Navigate to Account, open any account record, and click the Edit icon to open the edit form. You can see that the Account Number field has been added to the Account entity form on the mobile application, as shown in Figure 33.54.

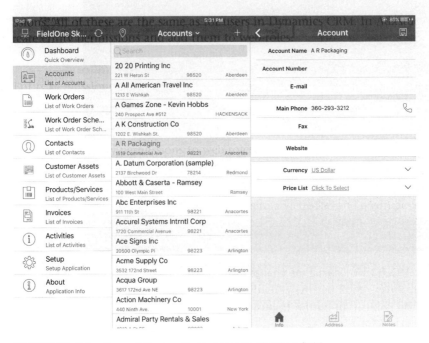

FIGURE 33.54   Account form with an Account Number field.

You can make many more significant customizations by using the Woodford application, including bringing in the Schedule Assistant to the mobile application, creating custom commands, and adding mobile form rules.

Summary

FieldOne Sky is a powerful tool. This chapter covers installation, administration, and configuration of the FieldOne Sky components for Dynamics CRM (including the mobile app). FieldOne has so many applications that this chapter can't list them all. However, this chapter provides a solid start to working with the application and configuring it to work for your organization.

CHAPTER 34

Voice of the Customer

Voice of the Customer is a feature newly introduced to Dynamics CRM that allows users to make surveys. It allows for direct interaction and feedback with customers.

Voice of the Customer allows CRM users to easily create surveys that can be filled out by either anonymous users or named customers. The results obtained can then be analyzed in CRM. This solution uses Azure behind the scenes to allow external users and anonymous users to see and complete surveys.

> **NOTE**
>
> While the Voice of the Customer solution heavily leverages Azure, CRM customers don't need to buy a Windows Azure subscription and pay per use of this service. Dynamics CRM connects to the Windows Azure Service Bus to get the responses by pulling on a configurable interval.

With Voice of the Customer you can using surveys anonymously via Twitter or Facebook, or you can publish results via iFrame on your organization's website. When using specific (or non-anonymous) surveys, Voice of the Customer creates specific links that are tied to the CRM GUID for a contact and can be sent directly to individuals.

> **TIP**
>
> To increase survey response rates, consider the following:
>
> ▶ It should come from a named contact at your organization (ideally one the respondents know).
>
> ▶ Add an image, perhaps even of the contact/user.
>
> ▶ Brand the survey appropriately by including your organization's logo, look and feel, and so on.

Voice of the Customer Deployment

At press time, Voice of the Customer was available only in CRM Online, and it isn't enabled by default. To install it, navigate to the Office 365 portal by logging in to https://portal.office.com and clicking CRM under Admin group in the left navigation panel (see Figure 34.1).

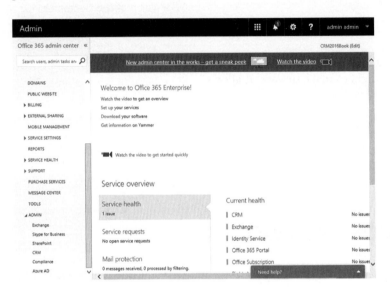

FIGURE 34.1   Office 365 portal interface.

As shown in Figure 34.2, you see a list of the CRM Online instances and a link to see the solutions that are installed. Click the pencil icon next to solutions for the selected instance.

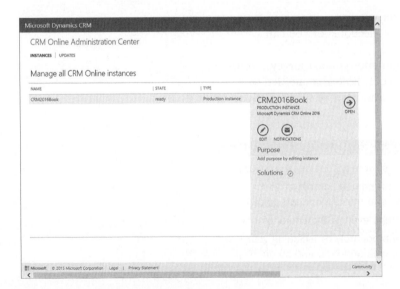

FIGURE 34.2   CRM Online Administration Center window.

Now you see a list of preferred solutions you can install (see Figure 34.3). Depending on the license, you may see different solutions than are shown here. Select Voice of the Customer and click Install.

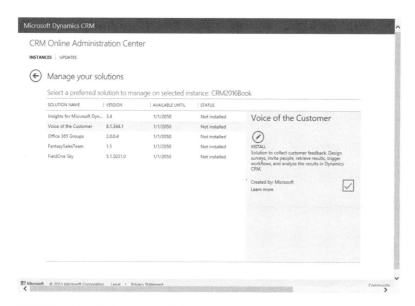

FIGURE 34.3   Selecting the Voice of the Customer solution.

The installation may take some minutes to complete. When the solution is installed, you can see it by going to the Dynamics CRM web interface and selecting Settings > Solutions > Customization, as shown in Figure 34.4.

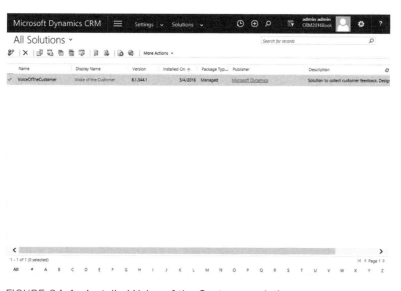

FIGURE 34.4   Installed Voice of the Customer solution.

After the solution is installed, you need agree to the terms and conditions and then click the Enable Voice of the Customer button, as shown in Figure 34.5.

FIGURE 34.5   Enabling the Voice of the Customer solution.

Once the solution is enabled, you see the options Trigger Response Processing and Open Configuration Entity, as shown in Figure 34.6.

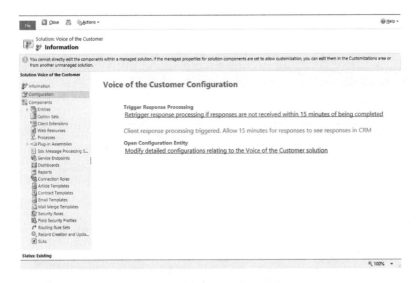

FIGURE 34.6   Voice of the Customer solution options.

You also see a new menu option in the site map, as shown in Figure 34.7.

FIGURE 34.7   Voice of the Customer Main menu.

Voice of the Customer Configuration

You access Voice of the Customer by opening the solution and clicking the Modify Detailed Configurations Relating to the Voice of the Customer Solution link on the configuration page shown in Figure 34.6. Figure 34.8 shows the configuration form that appears.

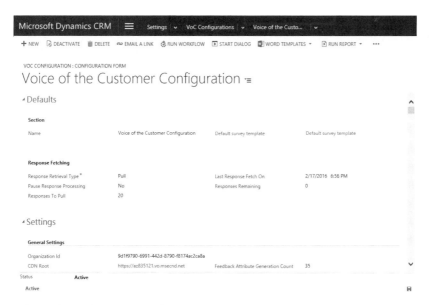

FIGURE 34.8   Voice of the Customer Configuration page.

From here you can make the necessary configuration changes.

Voice of the Customer Customization

Voice of the Customer has several customization options that allow you to tailor the solution to meet a variety of needs.

These three main entities related to the Voice of the Customer solution are the most heavily used:

▶ Survey

▶ Survey Response

▶ Response Outcomes

Survey

To create a new survey, follow these steps:

1. Navigate to Voice of the Customer > Surveys in the navigation bar. You can then see any active surveys you have in the system, as shown in Figure 34.9.

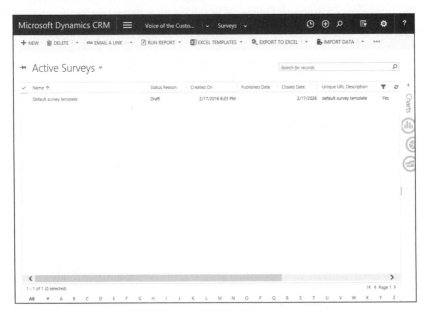

FIGURE 34.9   Surveys view.

2. Click +New to create a new survey. A new blank survey opens, as shown in Figure 34.10.

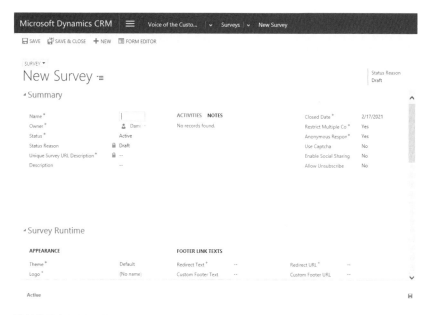

FIGURE 34.10   New Survey page.

3. Enter the name of the survey in the Name field, which is the only required field that's not prepopulated, and then click Save.

The survey entity has three different forms, each with a unique purpose:

▶ Survey

▶ Designer

▶ Dashboard

As shown in Figure 34.11, you can use the form selector to switch to the Survey Designer, which is shown in Figure 34.12.

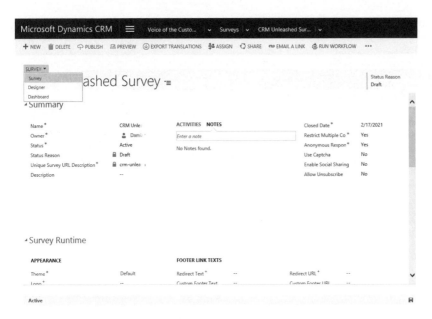

FIGURE 34.11   Form selector.

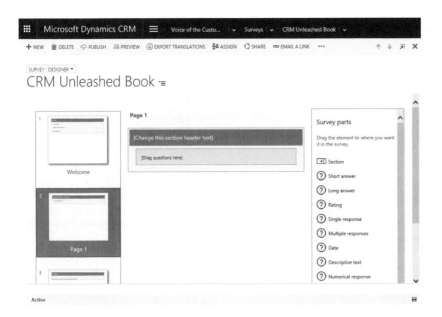

FIGURE 34.12   Survey Designer.

Survey Designer

In the Survey Designer, you can modify a survey's layout and set the survey parts, which can be any of the following:

34

NOTE

The survey designer is actually implemented in Azure as a web role, and the survey is stored to Azure Blob Storage.

▶ **Short answer**—This type of question requires a single line of text for an answer.

▶ **Long answer**—This type of question requires multiple lines of text for an answer.

▶ **Rating**—This type of question requires a rating as an answer. You can change the images to be stars, smiles, or flags. For the star type you can change the number of items from 0 to 12.

▶ **Single response**—This type of question requires a single response from a predefined list of answers.

▶ **Multiple responses**—This type of question requires multiple responses from a predefined list of answers.

▶ **Date**—This type of question requires a date answer, showing a calendar control to the user.

▶ **Descriptive text**—This is a description or instructions rather than a question that requires an answer. It is displayed as fixed text and does not allow user input.

▶ **Numerical response**—This type of question requires a number as an answer. This type of questions blocks the letter keys so users can only enter numbers here. You can allow decimals or whole numbers by setting the Number Type field. You can also set minimum and maximum numbers for validation.

▶ **Ranking**—This type of question requires multiple responses from a predefined list of answers and allows the user to order the selected responses.

▶ **Net Promoter Score**—This type of question asks for scores, such as "How likely is it that you would recommend [us/this product/this service] to a friend or colleague?" and present a slider control with steps from 0 to 10, where 0 means "not at all" and 10 means "extremely." This type of question is good for managing scoring.

▶ **Customer Effort Score**—This type of question asks for scores, such as "How much effort did you personally have to put forth to handle your request?" and present a slider control with steps from 1 to 5, where 1 means "very low" and 5 means "very high." This type of question is good for managing scoring.

▶ **CSAT**—This type of question asks for scores, such as "How would you rate your overall satisfaction with [us/this product/this service]?" and present a slider control with steps from 1 to 5, where 1 means "very dissatisfied" and 5 means "very satisfied." This type of question is good for managing scoring.

▶ **Smiles rating**—This type of question asks for scores, such as "Select the face that best describes your relationship with [Organization/ Product]?" and present images showing different type of emotions, like satisfied, very satisfied, bored, and annoyed. This type of question is good for managing scoring.

▶ **List of rating**—This is a list of questions that require ratings using stars, sad to happy smiles, neutral to happy smiles, or flags (red, yellow, green).

▶ **Single rating in columns**—This type of question requires a matrix of radio buttons to answer questions row by row, with only one option selected per row.

▶ **Multiple ratings in columns**—This type of question requires a matrix of check boxes to answer questions row by row, with the possibility to select one more than one check box per row.

▶ **Fixed sum**—This is a list of questions that require numbers as answers and shows a total of the responses entered. It also provides validation to ensure that the sum of the numbers entered matches the total expected.

▶ **Upload file**—This type of question allows the user to upload/attach a file to the response. It validates the file type allowed as well as the maximum upload file size.

By default, a survey has three pages:

▶ Welcome

▶ Page 1

▶ Complete

While you can add questions to any of these three pages, the submit button is located before the last page, which by default is Page 1, so if you add questions on the last page (Complete), the user won't be able to submit the answers. Also, you cannot remove either the first page (Welcome) or the last page (Complete) as at least two pages are necessary for each survey. You can add new pages between the Welcome page and the Complete page, and you can change the order of the pages—but only the ones that are between the Welcome and Complete pages; you cannot change the placement of the Welcome and Complete pages.

To add a new page, click the page icon on the bottom-left corner, under the page list (see Figure 34.13).

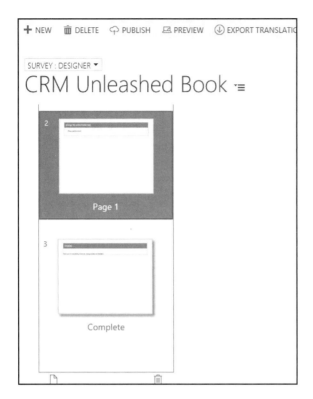

FIGURE 34.13   Page action.

To remove a new page, select the page you want to remove and then click the trash icon at the bottom-right, under the page list. The trash icon is not available for the Welcome and Complete pages.

When you create a new page, you are presented with the New Page form, as shown in Figure 34.14.

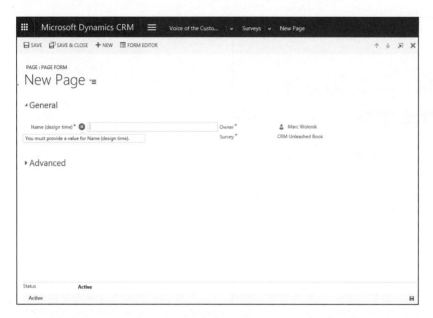

FIGURE 34.14   New Page form.

The Advanced tab is collapsed by default, but you can expand it if you want to change the page type and order (see Figure 34.15). This is useful if you deleted the Welcome or Complete pages by mistake and want to create a replacement for that page.

FIGURE 34.15   New Page form Advanced tab.

After you enter the name of the Page on the New Page form and click Save & Close, you end up in the Survey Designer, as shown in Figure 34.16.

If you want to change the name of the page, you select the page and then mouse over the page title.

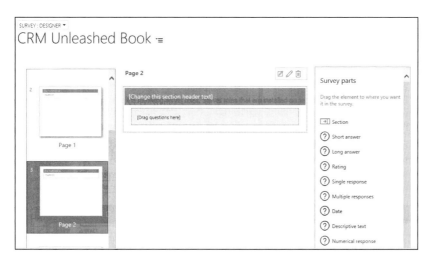

FIGURE 34.16   Changing the page title in the Survey Designer.

CAUTION

Be careful not to click the delete icon here because the Welcome and Complete pages are required for the survey.

There are two ways to edit both pages and questions:

▶ **Quick edit**—Quick edit allows you to make inline changes such as changing the name of the page or the question without leaving the Survey Designer. Figure 34.17 shows the icon for the quick edit option.

▶ **Form edit**—If you want to change a more complicated attribute of the page or the question, you then have to click the default edit icon, which is shown in Figure 34.18.

FIGURE 34.17   Quick edit icon.

FIGURE 34.18   Form edit icon.

If you change the name of the page with quick edit, you see two icons to the left, for saving your changes and for discarding them, as shown in Figure 34.19.

FIGURE 34.19   Changing the page name using quick edit.

The pages have sections. There is one section by default on each page, but you can add more sections if you want. Inside the sections you can add questions.

Questions

The question form has a rich text editor that you cannot use with the quick edit option. With this editor, however, you can use a different font and size than the defaults, as shown in Figure 34.20.

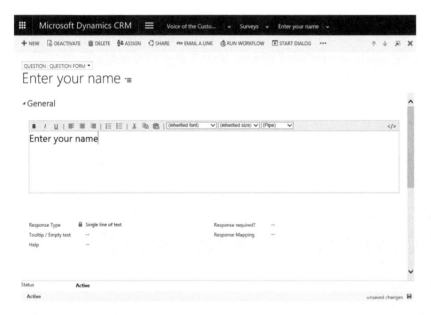

FIGURE 34.20   Question form.

You can also use pipes (User, Product, Service, Customer, Location, Date Time, Other 1, and Other 2), which are found in the rich text control toolbar and are useful when you're sending a survey to a contact using the snippets.

From here you can also set whether you want the question to be required, enter a tooltip, and map the response to a known field like First Name or Last Name (which is useful if you created a lead in the survey options so you know what response should be mapped to the Lead field).

The question form has a Validation tab where you can add validations such as the max length of the text entered or use a regular expression, which is useful if you are asking the user to enter a valid email address or URL (see Figure 34.21).

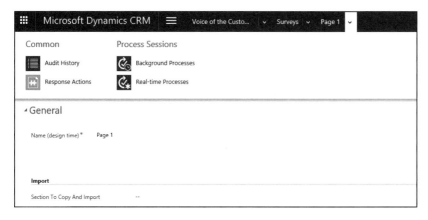

FIGURE 34.21   Validation tab.

Response Actions

You can find the response actions when you edit a page or question by clicking the drop-down arrow at the end of the navigation bar, as shown in Figure 34.22.

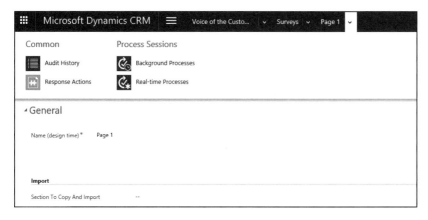

FIGURE 34.22   Response actions menu option.

You can add new or existing response options here. To create a new response action, click Add New Response Action (see Figure 34.23).

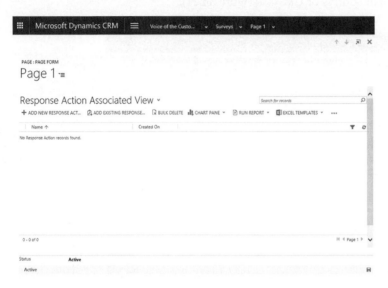

FIGURE 34.23   Response Action Associated View page.

The response actions are intended to be used in conjunction with the response conditions when you use a response routing, as discussed later in this chapter, in the "Response Routing" section.

You need to select one of two scopes, client or server. Depending on the scope, you may have to set different type of fields.

> **NOTE**
>
> After you save a response action, you cannot change the scope.

These actions are available for the client scope:

- ▶ Show
- ▶ Hide
- ▶ Skip To
- ▶ End Survey
- ▶ Chain Survey
- ▶ Toggle Visibility

Depending on the action selected, you will see different fields related to the action that you have to complete. For example, the Show action requires you to set the page and section and, optionally, the grid or question.

For the Server scope, you must select one of the following response outcome types:

- ▶ Complaint
- ▶ Low Score
- ▶ Distress
- ▶ Unsubscribe
- ▶ High Score
- ▶ Contact Request
- ▶ Follow Up
- ▶ NPS Increase
- ▶ NPS Decrease
- ▶ Facial Expression Increase
- ▶ Facial Expression Decrease

Survey Appearance

The Form Designer allows you to design pages, sections, and questions. However, if you want to design the general look and feel of the survey, you need to assign a theme and a logo, which you can do on the Survey Runtime tab of the New Survey page (see Figure 34.24).

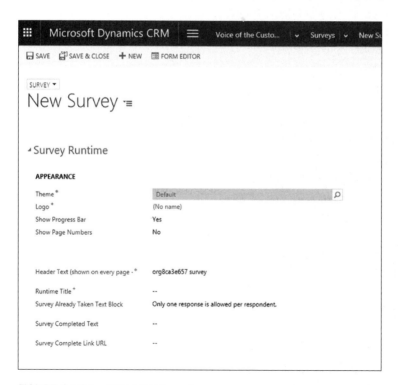

FIGURE 34.24   Appearance section.

It is highly recommended that you change the default Header Text field because it is prepopulated with default text that is visible on every page. It is also recommended that you upload a logo of your company to make the survey look more professional.

To add a logo, click in the Logo field. If you haven't yet uploaded a logo, before New to go to the New Image page (see Figure 34.25).

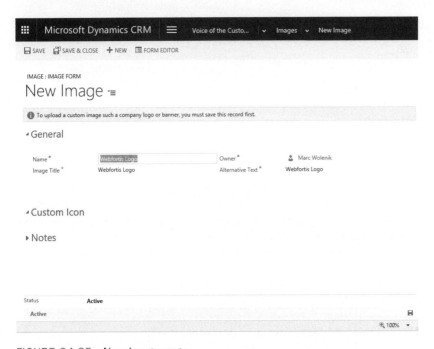

FIGURE 34.25   New Image page.

Enter the name of the logo and click Submit (see Figure 34.26). CRM automatically completes the image title and alternate text with the name you entered before. The custom Icon tab is now expanded, allowing you to upload an image that will be stored in Azure data storage.

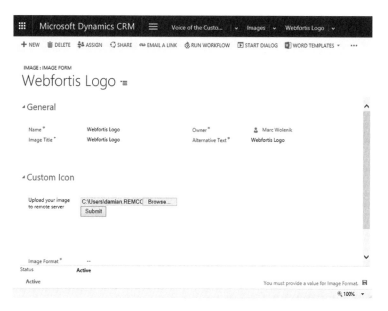

FIGURE 34.26   Uploading an image.

Click Browse, select the file from your local hard drive, and click Submit (see Figure 34.26). After you successfully upload the image, you must set the image format in order to see a preview of the image which in the Preview tab, as shown in Figure 34.27.

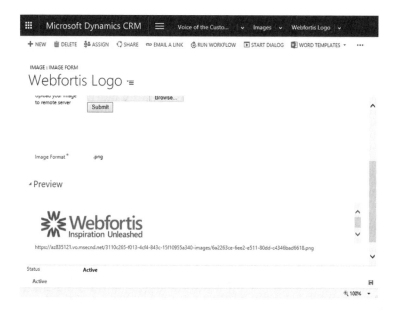

FIGURE 34.27   Image preview.

Once you have set the header title and the logo, the users will see a survey header like the one shown in Figure 34.28.

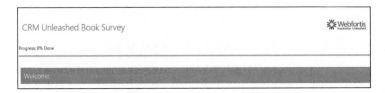

FIGURE 34.28   Survey header.

In addition to changing the header text and logo, there are a few other recommended fields to set:

▶ **Runtime Title**—This sets the page title that is displayed in the browser tab name.

▶ **Redirect Text**—This is the text that shows in the event that the user is redirected to another page.

▶ **Privacy Policy Text**—This text appears in the footer of the survey to the left—but only if you set the Privacy Policy URL field.

▶ **Survey Email Text**—This text appears in the footer near the Privacy Policy Text—but only if you set the Survey Email field.

▶ **Redirect URL**—This is the URL to which the page should be redirected.

▶ **Privacy Policy URL**—This is the URL you want the users to navigate to when they click the privacy policy text you set in the Privacy Policy Text field. If you leave the Privacy Policy Text field blank, you cannot set the Privacy Policy URL field, so make sure you also set that field when setting this field.

▶ **Survey Email**—Enter the email address of the person you want to be contacted. Remember to set the Survey Email Text field as well when you use this field. Leaving the Survey Email Text field blank shows "Contact survey owner" text by default in the email.

You can also change the labels of the Next, Previous, and Submit buttons if you like.

Survey Preview

You can preview a survey before publishing it by clicking the Preview button on the ribbon. (If you don't see it, be sure your pop-up blocker is not enabled because the preview opens in a new window.)

Before letting users fill out the survey, you need to publish it by clicking the Publish button on the ribbon. After the survey is published, you can test it by clicking the Test button.

Using the Surveys

To make filling out your survey quick and easy for users, provide an anonymous link. You can find the Anonymous Link field in the survey form under the Invitations and Actions tab (see 34.29). This link is generated after you publish the survey.

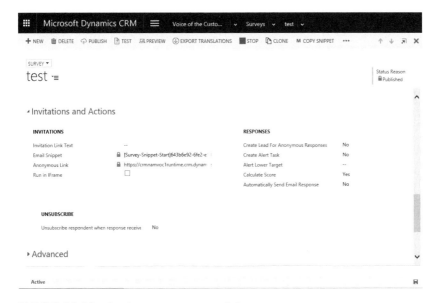

FIGURE 34.29   Setting an anonymous link.

However, to get more details about who responded to a survey, you can use one of the following snippets found on the command bar:

- ▶ Copy Snippet
- ▶ Copy Face Snippet
- ▶ Copy Rating Snippet
- ▶ Copy NPS Snippet

To find these snippets, click the ... in the navigation bar (refer to Figure 34.29). Clicking any of them copies it to the Windows Clipboard, and you can then paste it into an email activity created in Dynamics CRM. This code is then rendered differently for each recipient of the email, with an URL containing information that can later be used to link the response with the contact who completed the survey.

Using Piped Data

You can use piped data to show customer data, such as first name, in the Welcome screen or to prepopulate the answers with customer data. To use piped data in the Welcome page, follow these steps:

1. Create a new survey.

2. Enter a name for the survey and click Save.

3. Switch to the Survey Designer (see Figure 34.30).

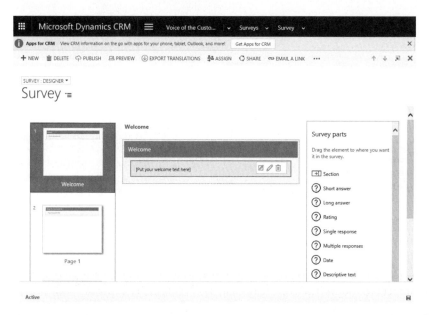

FIGURE 34.30   Survey Designer.

4. Click the edit button on the Welcome section area by clicking on the pencil, to go to the section form and make edits.

5. As shown in Figure 34.31, enter Welcome in the text box under the General section and use the (Pipe) drop-down to select Customer. The text _CUSTOMER_PIPED_DATA_ is appended to Welcome, as shown in Figure 34.32

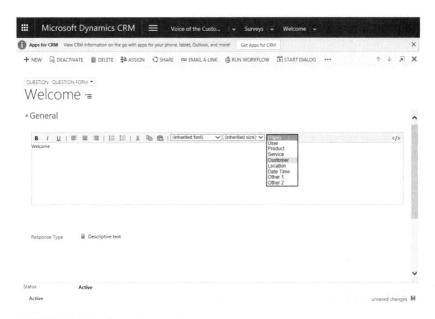

FIGURE 34.31   General question form.

6. Click Save and go back to your survey.

7. Publish the survey by clicking Publish.

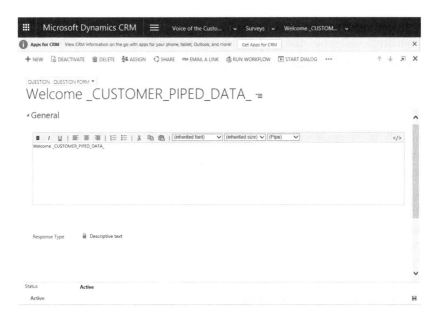

FIGURE 34.32   Welcome Text with Piped data.

When distributing the survey, you need to concatenate the piped data with the code snippet generated from the Copy Snippet actions.

To see the piped data on the Welcome page, after you publish the survey, click Copy Snippet, as shown in Figure 34.33.

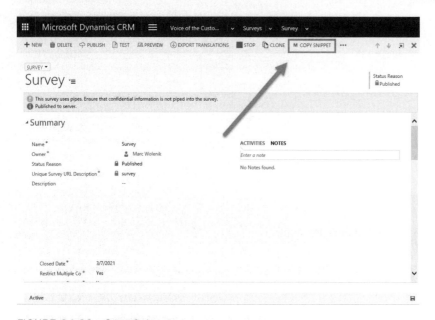

FIGURE 34.33   Copy Snippet.

CRM copies something like the following to the Windows Clipboard:

```
[Survey-Snippet-Start]6f94ea2e-b9e4-e511-80d4-c4346bac03ac[Survey-Snippet-End]
```

NOTE

The GUID changes depending on the survey you have, and it identifies the survey ID.

You need to add the piped data between the end of the GUID and before `[Survey-Snippet-End]`. For example, if you want to send an email to the customer Jim, you need to add the customer parameter with the value `Jim`, as shown here:

```
[Survey-Snippet-Start]6f94ea2e-b9e4-e511-80d4-c4346bac03ac|customer=Jim
➥[Survey-Snippet-End]
```

The easiest way to test this is to go to a contact/lead or an account and send a direct email and copy the snippet into the body of the email, as shown in Figure 34.34.

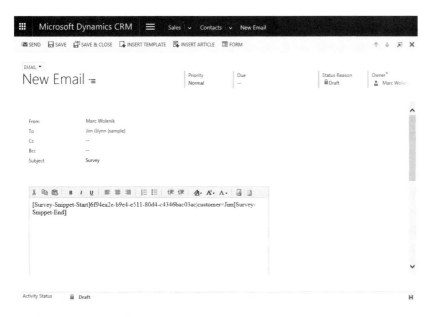

FIGURE 34.34   Email with snippet before save.

You can now click Save to generate the link the user has to click to complete the survey, as shown in Figure 34.35.

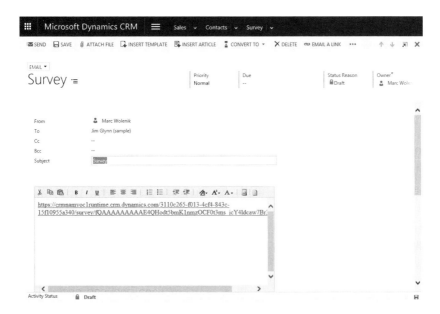

FIGURE 34.35   Email with link generated after save.

When the customer Jim clicks this link, he sees a Welcome page with his name on it, as shown in Figure 34.36.

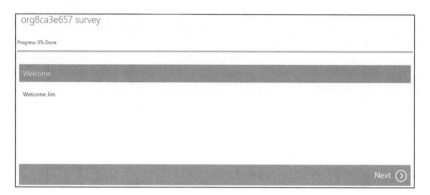

FIGURE 34.36   Welcome page with piped data.

The idea is to create email templates for surveys, so you can make the names dynamic, based on the selected record, when using the code snippet (see Figure 34.37).

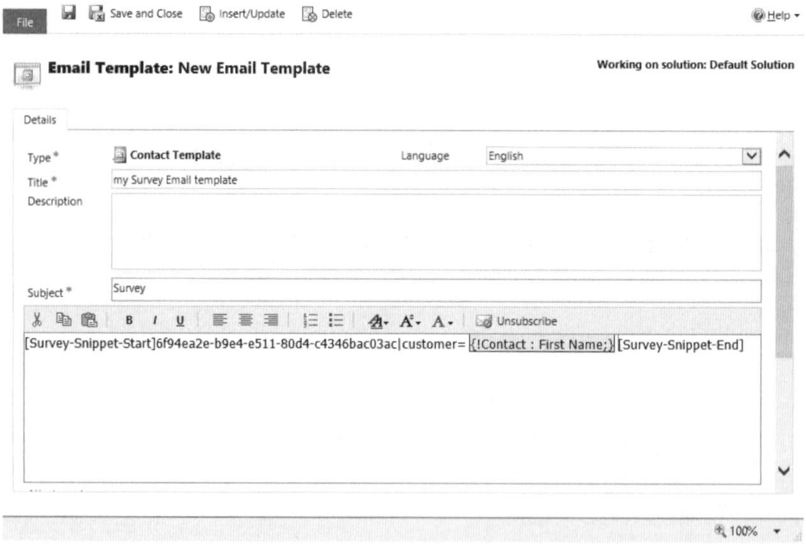

FIGURE 34.37   Using piped data in an email template.

You can then use email templates on workflows or you can go to the contacts list, select the contacts you want to send the survey to, and click Send Direct Email to select the email template.

As mentioned earlier, you can use piped data to prepopulate an answer to a question. This can be useful if you have a question that asks for the customer name but you want to let the customer see his name prepopulated and allow him to change it if he wants. For this configuration, you need to edit the question in the question form and expand the Advanced tab. You can then see the piped option set in the Pre-populate with Pipe field, as shown in Figure 34.38.

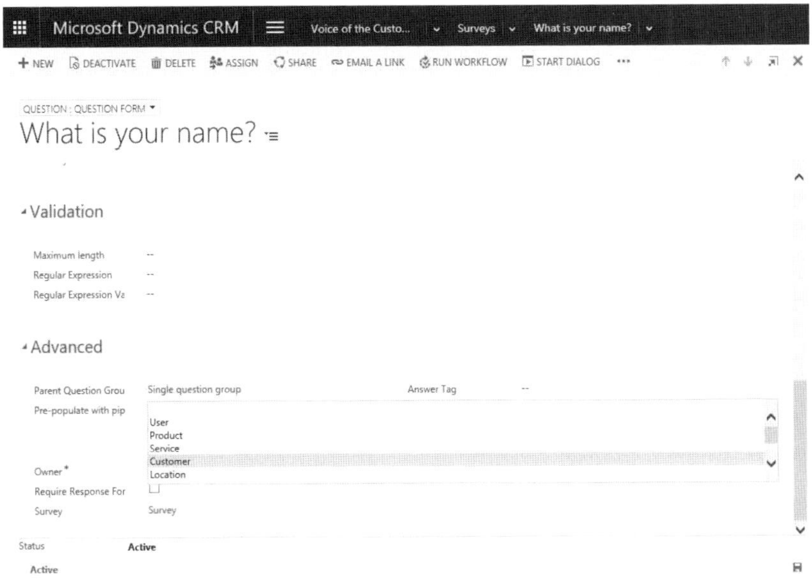

FIGURE 34.38   Pre-populate with Pipe field.

To test this change, make sure you publish the survey and use the same email template. The customer will see the question prepopulated as shown in Figure 34.39.

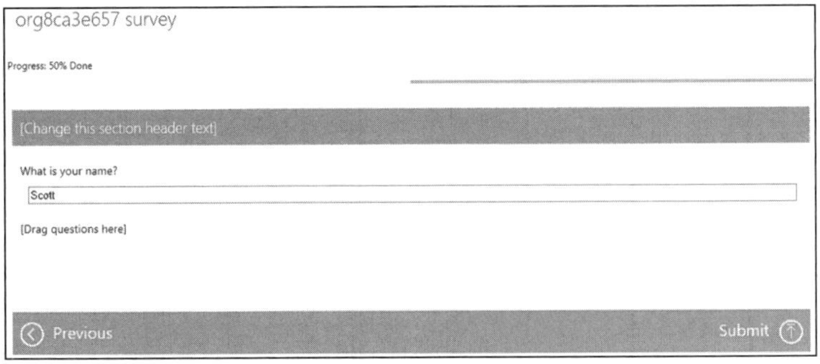

FIGURE 34.39   Prepopulating with a pipe in action.

Table 34.1 shows the piped variables available and how to use them in your email templates.

TABLE 34.1   Piped Variables

Piped Variable	Use in Template
_USER_PIPED_DATA_	user
_PRODUCT_PIPED_DATA_	product
_SERVICE_PIPED_DATA_	service
_CUSTOMER_PIPED_DATA_	customer
_LOCATION_PIPED_DATA_	location
_DATE_TIME_PIPED_DATA_	datetime
_OTHER_1_PIPED_DATA_	other1
_OTHER_2_PIPED_DATA_	other2

Response Routing

Linking response conditions to various response actions via routing is necessary if you want to show or hide a question based on the response to a previous answer. For example, if you have a question with a single response, asking the customer if he is satisfied with your service, depending on the answer, you might want to find out why he is not satisfied. Or if he is satisfied, you might want to learn what he would like even more.

For the example shown in Figure 34.40, there are three questions:

▶ Are you satisfied? (single response, yes/no)

▶ Why are you not satisfied? (long answer)

▶ What do you like most? (long answer)

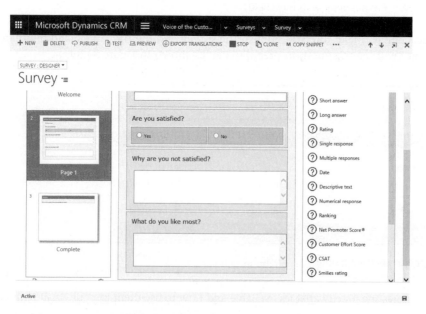

FIGURE 34.40   Questions for a response routing.

Because the last two questions depend on the response to the first question, you need to create a response routing. You can click the drop-down arrow to the right of Survey to access the Response Routings option (see Figure 34.41).

FIGURE 34.41   Response Routings option.

Click the Response Routings option, enter a name for the new response routing, such as satisfied customer, and click Save (see Figure 34.42).

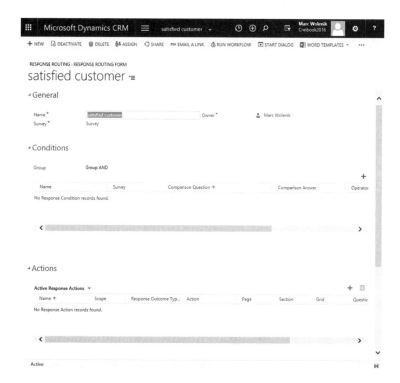

FIGURE 34.42   Satisfied customer response routing.

After you save the new response routing, you can click the + on the Conditions tab to create a new condition. In this case, you select the Are you satisfied? question and the Yes answer; leave Operator set to Selected (see Figure 34.43). Click Save & Close.

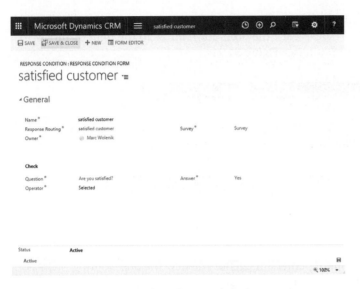

FIGURE 34.43   Condition form for a satisfied customer.

Now in the response routing form you need to create a new action, so click the + on the Actions tab and click on New.

Select Client in the Scope field and enter a name for the response action (such as "show What do you like most? Question"). In the Client tab select the survey you are working on, set Action to Show, set Page to Page 1, and set Section to Page 1. Also set the question you want to show (see Figure 34.44).

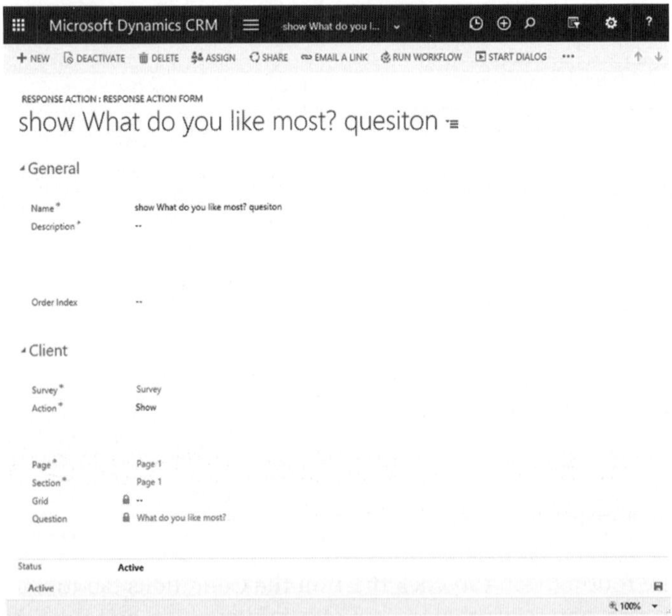

FIGURE 34.44   Response action.

You need to create another response routing for the "not satisfied" condition and response action much the same way you did for the "satisfied" condition.

▶ To see the different types of actions you can take here, refer to the "Response Actions" section, earlier in this chapter.

Survey Dashboard

The Survey Dashboard shows analytic information about a survey, as shown in Figure 34.45. (Be sure to switch the form type in the survey record to Dashboard.)

FIGURE 34.45   Survey Dashboard.

The dashboard shows four charts:

▶ Survey Invites Sent by Survey

▶ Total Response Count by Survey

▶ Average Satisfaction Rating by Survey

▶ Score as Percentage All Routes by Survey

NOTE

The last two charts work best with questions that use ratings or scoring.

Survey Responses

The Active Survey Responses page is where you can see all the completed surveys and the responses to the questions. You can see if the survey was completed by an existing contact or by an anonymous user. Figure 34.46 shows the Active Survey Responses page.

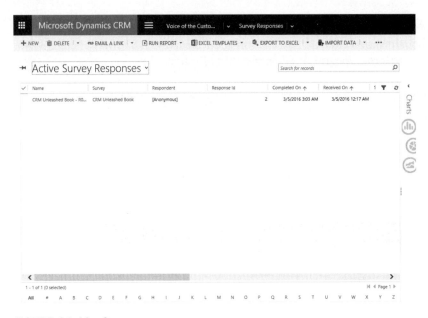

FIGURE 34.46   Survey responses.

> **NOTE**
>
> Answers do not show until the user has completed the survey. They remain in Azure until CRM pulls the completed surveys based on the interval configured in the Voice of the Customer configurations. By default, this interval is three minutes, to get up to 20 responses per request.

Response Outcomes

You can see the response outcomes for your surveys by navigating to Settings > Voice of the Customer > Response Outcomes.

You can run any of these predefined reports:

▶ Net Promoter Score

▶ Question Summary

▶ Survey Export

▶ Survey Summary

The Voice of the Customer solution also come with five custom roles that help users administer or design surveys:

▶ Survey Administrator

▶ Survey Designer

▶ Survey Feedback Publisher

▶ Survey Service

▶ Survey User

Voice of the Customer Troubleshooting

When you need to troubleshoot Voice of the Customer, you can find detailed information under the survey logs, which you find by navigating to Settings > Voice of the Customer > Logs (see Figure 34.47). By looking at the logs, you can find errors not easily discovered during the survey design phase.

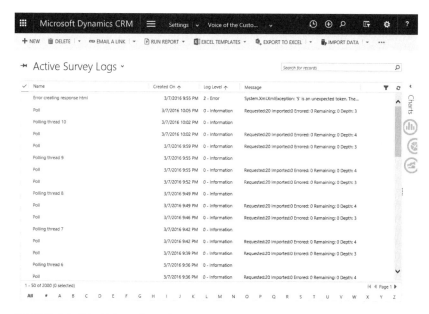

FIGURE 34.47   Voice of the Customer logs.

Responses are processed and retrieved in CRM every 15 minutes. If you don't see them in CRM after that amount of time, you can retrigger the response processing by selecting Settings > Solutions > Voice of the Customer and going to the Configuration section.

Summary

This chapter explains how to install and configure Voice of the Customer, a great survey solution that allows customers to give feedback in a way that integrates with Dynamics CRM. This chapter discusses how to create surveys and change the design basics, how to create response routings to make survey more intelligent, and how to review responses and the analytics provided for the surveys. If you have a CRM Online deployment, Voice of the Customer is a solution you cannot miss.

> **NOTE**
>
> What's happening behind the scenes with Voice of the Customer is that survey definitions are sent to Azure and stored in Azure storage via an Azure SQL database. Responses are temporarily stored in the Azure Service Bus and then sent to Dynamics CRM and then deleted from Azure. The following Azure components are used for Voice of the Customer:
>
> ▶ Azure Cloud Services
>
> ▶ Azure Key Vault
>
> ▶ Azure SQL database
>
> ▶ Azure Blob Storage (survey definitions and partially completed surveys)
>
> ▶ Azure Content Delivery Network (CDN) (images, CSS, etc.)
>
> ▶ Azure AD
>
> ▶ Azure Service Bus

Index

Numerics

C

E

I

IaaS (infrastructure-as-a-service), 1027
  Azure-hosted Dynamics CRM, 1047–1065
    ExpressRoute, 1065
icons, clock icon (ISH navigation bar), 326–327
IExecutionContext class, 1077–1081
IFD (Internet-Facing Deployment), 1187–1190
  AD FS 2.0, 1197–1198
    configuring, 1198
    installing, 1198
    relying party trust, adding, 1210–1219
  AD FS 3.0, 1198–1202
    configuring, 1203–1208
    installing, 1198–1202
    relying party trust, adding, 1210–1219
  claims-based authentication, 1190–1191
  configuring, 1191–1194
  disabling, 1223
  DNS server, configuring, 1222–1223
  SSL certificates, 1194–1197
    installing, 1196–1197
    omitting from IFD configuration, 1194–1196
IFRAMES
  adding/removing, 886–888
  default properties, changing, 888–889
IG (Implementation Guide), 1283
IIS requirements for CRM deployment, 1230–1232
image type option set, 872
images
  registering, 1099–1101
  viewing in Dynamics CRM for Tablets app, 708
Import Data Wizard, 181
importing
  customizations, 920–921

processes, 1157–1158
solutions, 937–943
  with processes or plug-ins, 939–940
incidents, creating, 1290
incoming emails
  Forward mailboxes, 810–811
  tracking, 812–813
incoming profiles
  creating, 802–803
  email router access credentials, 800
increasing survey response rates, 1401
industry standards, Online version certifications, 57–58
infrastructure, comparing Online and On-Premises versions, 6
initial setup and configuration
  MDM
    Double Opt-in for Emails warning, 193
    license/subscription agreement, 191
    role selection, 192
    SMS Marketing Information warning, 193
    Standardized KPIs for SMS warning, 194
    Turn On Full Text warning, 192
  Social Engagement, setting solution defaults, 448–453
input arguments for dialogs, 1134
installing
  AD FS 2.0, 1198
  AD FS 3.0, 1198–1202
  Adxstudio Portals, 1328
  CRM 2016 Report Authoring Extension, 571–573
  Dynamics CRM for Phones app, 713–726
  Dynamics CRM for Tablets app on Windows 10, 682–686
  email router, 793–797
    on multiple computers, 797–799
  FantasySalesTeam, 1300–1305
  FieldOne Sky, 1356–1361

M

N

P

Q

R

S

T

U

W

X